Headquarters Squadron Administr[...]

RHQ Element

Truck, Heavy Utility, Personnel

Truck, Heavy Utility, Computor, With Penthouse

Com[...]

Squadron Headquarters

Humber Scout Car | Truck, Heavy Utility, Personnel | Car, 5-cwt (Jeep) | Car, 5-cwt (Jeep) | Car, 5-cwt (Jeep) | Car, 5-cwt (Jeep) | Car, 5-cwt (Jeep) | Car, 5-cwt (Jeep)

Motorcycle, Solo | Motorcycle, Solo | Motorcycle, Solo | Motorcycle, Solo | Motorcycle, Solo | Motorcycle, Solo | Motorcycle, Solo | Motorcycle, Solo

Headquarters Administrative Echelon

Truck, 15-cwt, GS | Truck, 15-cwt, GS | Truck, 15-cwt, GS | Truck, 15-cwt, Battery Charging With Trailer, 20-cwt, Workshop Servicing | Truck, 15-cwt, Water | Truck, 15-cwt, Water

Lorry, 3-Ton GS | Lorry, 3-Ton GS | Lorry, 3-Ton GS | Lorry, 3-Ton Bulk Petrol | Lorry, 3-Ton Bulk Petrol | Lorry, 3-Ton Bulk Petrol | Lorry, 3-Ton Bulk Petrol

Lorry, 3-Ton GS Ammunition | Lorry, 3-Ton GS Ammunition | Lorry, 3-Ton GS Ammunition | Lorry, 3-Ton GS Ammunition | Lorry, 3-Ton, Mobile Kitchen | Lorry, 3-Ton, 6-Wh, Stores | Lorry, 3-Ton, 6-Wh, Stores

"A" Squadron Administrative Echelon

Car, 5-cwt (Jeep) | Truck, Heavy Utility, Personnel | Truck, 15-cwt, GS | Truck, 15-cwt, GS | Truck, 15-cwt, GS | Lorry, 3-Ton GS Baggage & Sqn Office | Lorry, 3-Ton Bulk Petrol | Lorry, 3-Ton Bulk Petrol | Lorry, 3-Ton Bulk Petrol

Lorry, 3-Ton GS Ammunition | Lorry, 3-Ton GS Ammunition | Lorry, 3-Ton GS Ammunition | Lorry, 3-Ton GS Ammunition | Lorry, 3-Ton GS Ammunition | Lorry, 3-Ton GS Ammunition | Lorry, 3-Ton GS Ammunition | Lorry, 3-Ton Mobile Kitchen With Trailer, 20-cwt, Water | Lorry, 3-Ton, 6-Wh, Stores Motor Mechanics Tools With Trailer, Compressor

"B" Squadron Administrative Echelon

Car, 5-cwt (Jeep) | Truck, Heavy Utility, Personnel | Truck, 15-cwt, GS | Truck, 15-cwt, GS | Truck, 15-cwt, GS | Lorry, 3-Ton GS Baggage & Sqn Office | Lorry, 3-Ton Bulk Petrol | Lorry, 3-Ton Bulk Petrol | Lorry, 3-Ton Bulk Petrol

Lorry, 3-Ton GS Ammunition | Lorry, 3-Ton GS Ammunition | Lorry, 3-Ton GS Ammunition | Lorry, 3-Ton GS Ammunition | Lorry, 3-Ton GS Ammunition | Lorry, 3-Ton GS Ammunition | Lorry, 3-Ton GS Ammunition | Lorry, 3-Ton Mobile Kitchen With Trailer, 20-cwt, Water | Lorry, 3-Ton, 6-Wh, Stores Motor Mechanics Tools With Trailer, Compressor

"C" Squadron Administrative Echelon

Car, 5-cwt (Jeep) | Truck, Heavy Utility, Personnel | Truck, 15-cwt, GS | Truck, 15-cwt, GS | Truck, 15-cwt, GS | Lorry, 3-Ton GS Baggage & Sqn Office | Lorry, 3-Ton Bulk Petrol | Lorry, 3-Ton Bulk Petrol | Lorry, 3-Ton Bulk Petrol

Lorry, 3-Ton GS Ammunition | Lorry, 3-Ton GS Ammunition | Lorry, 3-Ton GS Ammunition | Lorry, 3-Ton GS Ammunition | Lorry, 3-Ton GS Ammunition | Lorry, 3-Ton GS Ammunition | Lorry, 3-Ton GS Ammunition | Lorry, 3-Ton Mobile Kitchen With Trailer, 20-cwt, Water | Lorry, 3-Ton, 6-Wh, Stores Motor Mechanics Tools With Trailer, Compressor

Royal Canadian Signals Corps Detachment - Attached To Regiment

Car, 5-cwt (Jeep) | Truck, 15-cwt, GS | Truck, 15-cwt Wireless | Lorry, 3-Ton Machinery "I" | Lorry, 3-Ton Machinery "Z" Mk II Technical Workshop

42 LAD, Type "C" Armoured - Attached To Regiment

Motorcycle, Solo | Motorcycle, Solo | Truck, 15-cwt, GS | Truck, 15-cwt Machinery "KL" | Truck, 15-cwt Fitted For Wireless | Lorry, 3-Ton GS | Tractor, Breakdown, Medium Diamond T 969b 4-Ton | Tractor, Breakdown, Heavy Mack LMSW 5-Ton

The South Alberta Regiment, November 1944.
This diagram shows the organization and more than 200 tanks and other vehicles of the SAR as they would have appeared at full strength in November 1944.

Under the direct control of Lieutenant-Colonel Wotherspoon was RHQ with his three different command vehicles (scout car, ACV halftrack and Sherman). Although they were part of HQ Squadron, the Recce, AA and Inter-Communication Troops were normally attached to RHQ when the Regiment was in action, and in January 1945 a new RHQ Squadron to control these troops was organized, making this relationship more permanent.

The fighting strength of the Regiment lay in the three squadrons, each with a Squadron HQ Troop of three Shermans and four fighting troops, each with three Sherman Vs and one Sherman Firefly (by the end of the war there were two Firefly tanks in each troop). Reporting to the squadron commander was an armoured halftrack ambulance, a recovery Sherman and a squadron fitters' halftrack, with the job of looking after casualties, human or tank.

The rest of the Regiment served in "the echelons," a somewhat vague term that included all those whose job was to support the fighting elements. Echelon organization was elastic and changeable but generally A-1 Echelon (normally provided by the three fighting squadrons themselves) supplied the fighting squadrons with the means to fight for one day while A-2 Echelon (normally provided by HQ Squadron) resupplied A-1 Echelon and also controlled B Echelon. This latter organization, consisting of such services as the paymaster and dentist, was not always active when the unit was in the field but was set up when the SAR were in garrison.

Finally, two specialized sub-units from other corps, a signals detachment and a light aid detachment, were attached to the Regiment. Signals personnel looked after all communications equipment while the light aid detachment repaired tanks and other vehicles that were beyond the capacity of the squadron fitters.

Drawings by Chris Johnson

SOUTH ALBERTAS

A CANADIAN REGIMENT AT WAR

Overleaf
The Boys from the Bald-Headed Prairie.
The officers and men of HQ Squadron, South Alberta Regiment, pose for their
picture in January 1943. Mobilized from five Alberta militia regiments in June 1940,
the SAR was converted to armour in January 1942 and fought in northwest Europe
as the armoured reconnaissance regiment of 4th Canadian Armoured Division.

SOUTH ALBERTAS

A CANADIAN REGIMENT AT WAR

DONALD E. GRAVES

Forewords by

MAJOR-GENERAL (Retd.) GEORGE KITCHING, CBE, DSO, CD
4th Canadian Armoured Division

and

HONORARY COLONEL STANLEY A. MILNER, AOE, LL.D.
South Alberta Light Horse

with

Additional Research by Douglas Hendry
Maps by Molly Brass
and
Illustrations by George Bradford and Chris Johnson

ROBIN BRASS STUDIO
Toronto

Published 1998 by Robin Brass Studio
10 Blantyre Avenue, Toronto, Ontario M1N 2R4, Canada
Fax: (416) 698-2120 / e-mail: rbrass@total.net

Second printing, August 1998

Printed and bound in Canada by Friesen Printers, Altona, Manitoba

Canadian Cataloguing in Publication Data

Graves, Donald E. (Donald Edward)
South Albertas : a Canadian regiment at war

Includes bibliographical references and index.

ISBN 1-896941-06-0

1. Canada. Canadian Army. South Alberta Regiment – History.
2. World War, 1939-1945 – Regimental histories – Canada.
3. World War, 1939-1945 – Campaigns – Western Front. I. Title.

D768.15.G735 1998   940.54'1271   C98-930757-3

The South Alberta Regiment Veterans Association
wishes to acknowledge the assistance of the
Alberta Historical Resources Foundation
8820 – 112 Street
Edmonton, AB
T6G 2P8

To the Men of

The South Alberta Regiment

(29th Canadian Armoured Reconnaissance Regiment)

Who Served from 1939 to 1945,

And Their Families.

A Soldier

I was that which others did not want to be
I went where others failed to go
And did what others failed to do.
I asked nothing from those who offered nothing
And reluctantly accepted the burden of loneliness.
I have seen the face of terror; felt the stinging cold of fear
And enjoyed the sweet taste of a moment's love.
I have cried, felt pain and sorrow
But most of all …
I have lived times that others would say were best forgotten
After it all, I will be able to say that
I am proud of who I am …
A Soldier.

Anonymous

Contents

Foreword by

MAJOR-GENERAL GEORGE KITCHING, CBE, DSO, CD

GOC, 4TH CANADIAN ARMOURED DIVISION 9

Foreword by

HONORARY COLONEL STANLEY A. MILNER, AOE, LL.D.

SOUTH ALBERTA LIGHT HORSE 11

INTRODUCTION 13

NOTE TO THE READER 15

ACKNOWLEDGEMENTS 16

PROLOGUE

The boys come home. 19

MEDICINE HAT, ALBERTA, MAY 1919

PART I: FORMING

1 "We used to parade every Thursday night." ... 22

CANADA: SEPTEMBER 1939–AUGUST 1940

2 "Look, another dead corporal." 35

CANADA: AUGUST 1940–DECEMBER 1941

PART II: PREPARING

3 "A lovely man who enjoyed the army." 54

CANADA AND BRITAIN: DECEMBER 1941–FEBRUARY 1943

4 "You've got the SARs, they're my pride
and joy." 68

BRITAIN: MARCH–DECEMBER 1943

5 "Say a prayer for me." 82

BRITAIN: JANUARY–JULY 1944

PART III: GRAPPLING

6 "Everything was new and we didn't
know what was going on." 96

FRANCE: 25 JULY–5 AUGUST 1944

7 "The greenest bloody army that ever
went to war." 109

FRANCE: 6 AUGUST–15 AUGUST 1944

PART IV: SLUGGING

8 "It was beginning to look as if a big
show was coming off." 128

FRANCE: 16 AUGUST–18 AUGUST 1944

9 "The situation began to get out of hand." ... 141

FRANCE: 19 AUGUST–20 AUGUST A.M., 1944

10 "The boys from the bald-headed prairie." ... 160

FRANCE: 20 AUGUST P.M.–22 AUGUST A.M., 1944

An SAR Colour Album 177

PART V: ADVANCING

11 "We're off to Berlin!" 186

FRANCE AND BELGIUM: 22 AUGUST–11 SEPTEMBER
1944

12 "Recce at its best." 203

BELGIUM AND HOLLAND: 12 SEPTEMBER–22 OCTOBER
1944

13 "Hell, Bill, let's take the damned place." 218

BELGIUM AND HOLLAND: 23 OCTOBER–7 NOVEMBER
1944

PART VI: PAUSING

14 "The major wasn't dressed to visit
the King." 238
HOLLAND: 7 NOVEMBER 1944–24 JANUARY 1945

15 "If only we had the wisdom
of our generals." 249
HOLLAND: 25 JANUARY–21 FEBRUARY 1945

PART VII: WINNING

16 "Through the mud and the blood." 266
HOLLAND AND GERMANY: 21 FEBRUARY–2 MARCH 1945

17 "To the green fields beyond." 285
GERMANY AND HOLLAND: 2 MARCH–31 MARCH 1945

18 "A ding dong fight in the failing light." 303
GERMANY: 1 APRIL–4 MAY 1945

PART VIII: ENDURING

19 "Trish has a Canadian." 324
GERMANY, HOLLAND AND CANADA: MAY 1945–
JANUARY 1946

20 "I was over and I came back." 336
THE REGIMENT IN THE POSTWAR WORLD:
1946–1995

EPILOGUE

"And not to yield." 345
EDMONTON, ALBERTA: 21–24 SEPTEMBER 1995

APPENDICES

APPENDIX A
Battle Honours, Awards and Decorations 349

APPENDIX B
Roll of Honour, South Alberta Regiment,
1940–1945 351

APPENDIX C
The South Alberta Regiment:
A Working Manual 353

APPENDIX D
Glossary of Military Terms and
Abbreviations 362

APPENDIX E
Nominal Rolls, South Alberta Regiment,
1940–1945 370

NOTES 388

BIBLIOGRAPHY 397

INDEXES 402

MAPS

Map 1   South Alberta stations in Britain, 1942-1944   ... 84

Map 2   The attacks on Tilly-la-Campagne, 1 and
5 August 1944 107

Map 3   Operation TOTALIZE, 7-11 August 1944 111

Map 4   Operation TRACTABLE, 14-15 August 1944   ... 119

Map 5   The trap closes, 25 July-16 August 1944 126

Map 6   The Falaise Pocket, 17-19 August 1944 139

Map 7   The Falaise Pocket, 19-21 August 1944 145

Map 8   The South Albertas' battle, 19-22 August 1944 ... 158

Map 9   The great advance, 22 August-4 September 1944   187

Map 10 The Scheldt battles, September-October 1944 ... 192

Map 11 Moerbrugge, 8-12 September 1944 197

Map 12 The battle for Bergen op Zoom, 25-27 October
1944 220

Map 13 Winter on the Maas, November 1944-
February 1945 239

Map 14 Operation ELEPHANT, 25-31 January 1945 252

Map 15 Operations VERITABLE and BLOCKBUSTER,
February-March 1945 267

Map 16 The Hochwald Gap, 26 February-2 March 1945   273

Map 17 The Hochwald, 4-9 March 1945 286

Map 18 SAR area of operations, March-May 1945 305

Map 19 War in the peat bogs, SAR area of operations,
April-May 1945 316

Foreword

In 1944 during the great battles of Normandy I commanded the 4th Canadian Armoured Division, the main components of which were the 4th Armoured Brigade (Brigadier Leslie Booth) and the 10th Infantry Brigade (Brigadier Jim Jefferson). The only other Canadian armoured brigade in First Canadian Army was the 2nd (Brigadier Bob Wyman).

At approximately 0700 hours on the 8th of August 1944 Wyman was severely wounded by an enemy sniper. At noon that day Major-General Rod Keller, commanding 3rd Canadian Infantry Division, was also wounded. Shortly after these incidents, Lieutenant-General Guy Simonds, the commander of 2nd Canadian Corps, came to my Tactical Headquarters.

General Simonds was very concerned about replacements for senior officers and asked me whom I would like to get to take over from Brigadier Booth in case he became a casualty. We discussed a number of officers in my division, including Lieutenant-Colonel Don Worthington commanding the British Columbia Regiment and Lieutenant-Colonel Gordon "Swatty" Wotherspoon commanding the South Alberta Regiment. Both would be available without delay.

After this meeting I phoned Jim Jefferson and told him that he might lose Swatty Wotherspoon. He pleaded with me to leave Swatty in command of the SAR and not to move him for at least two months. He reminded me that the South Alberta Regiment had only recently been converted into a full armoured regiment and that Swatty Wotherspoon had reorganized his unit to take on new responsibilities and requested that he be left with it. I agreed with him.

To complete the story, Don Worthington was killed on the 9th of August. Leslie Booth was killed on the 14th and his temporary replacement was wounded on the 15th. I only mention this series of tragedies to indicate the pressures that developed for me to take Swatty away from the South Alberta Regiment. I am glad that he was allowed to remain with his Regiment as he helped to make it one of the finest – if not *the finest* – in the Canadian Armoured Corps.

What other factors contributed to make the South Alberta Regiment so effective? Was it the unit's earlier training as infantry? Was it the quality of its officers and NCOs? Perhaps the most important thing was the character of its soldiers – the troopers – who were largely from farms and small communities. I have always felt that, generally, the country man makes a better soldier than the man from the city – unduly deliberate sometimes but self-reliant, used to fixing things himself (instead of hiring someone else to do the job) and always prepared to seize the initiative and do something that gets things going again. Certainly the SAR always "got things going again" and their story is vividly and accurately told in this excellent history.

In 1954 the South Alberta Regiment was merged with other units during a reorganization of the Militia and now has a slightly different name. But for me they will always be the SAR.

"For they are the SAR."

MAJOR-GENERAL (RETD.) GEORGE KITCHING, CBE, DSO, CD

Foreword

ALL OFFENSIVE OPERATIONS CANCELLED FORTHWITH.
CEASE-FIRE 0800 HOURS, 5 MAY 1945. ALL UNITS STAND
FAST UNTIL FURTHER ORDERS.

After years of training and battle, after suffering 316 casualties, the South Alberta Regiment received the above signal at 2350 hours on 4 May 1945 from G4, 4th Canadian Armoured Division Main GO2.

This book is the story of the South Albertas' war. It is a story of hardship, mud, cold, endurance, determination and spirit in which the Regiment achieved its destiny and its men fulfilled their obligations not only to their unit and corps but also to the people of Canada and Europe. To all who read this book, we hope that its record of courage will help you in your daily life.

The South Alberta Regiment is no longer on the order of battle but let me, on behalf of the officers and men of the South Alberta Light Horse (Royal Canadian Armoured Corps), thank our predecessors for the honour of perpetuating their fine unit whose battle honours are emblazoned on our guidon and for compiling the following record of their wartime history.

In closing I will paraphrase the unofficial motto of the armoured corps: "You've been through the mud and the blood and I hope that you reach the green fields beyond." Men of the South Alberta Regiment, your record indicates to me that you deserve nothing less.

COLONEL STANLEY A. MILNER (HON), AOE, LL.D.
SOUTH ALBERTA LIGHT HORSE (RCAC)

A portrait of Canadian armour. A 4th Armoured Division Sherman V at Cormelles, near Caen, on 28 July 1944. The Sherman was the weapon of the South Alberta Regiment in action in 1944-1945 and was a robust, mechanically reliable tank but was outgunned by its opponents.

DND, NEGATIVE ZK-859

Introduction

For Canadians it is one of the most enduring images of the Second World War. Not as recognizable perhaps as the pictures of the US Marines raising the flag on Iwo Jima, Winston Churchill posing with a cigar and a Thompson submachine gun, Spitfires over the white cliffs of Dover, or the blazing wreck of the USS *Arizona* at Pearl Harbor on 7 December 1941 but, still, a photograph almost certain to be reproduced in any book about the wartime Canadian Army. It is not a dramatic image – it depicts soldiers standing in the street of what is, judging from the ruined buildings, a village somewhere in Europe in the 1940s. The importance of this picture is not what it shows but what it represents for it has been described by the Canadian Army's historian as being "as close as we are ever likely to come to a photograph of a man winning the Victoria Cross." That man was Major David Vivian Currie, the ruined village was St. Lambert-sur-Dives in France, and the time was the early afternoon of 19 August 1944.

Dave Currie was an officer in the 29th Canadian Armoured Reconnaissance Regiment (South Alberta Regiment), a unit that is almost forgotten today. This is not surprising considering that it disappeared from the order of battle in 1954 and the only publication about its history was a small pamphlet published in Holland at the end of the war. But it is also unfortunate because the SAR was the only unit in the Canadian Armoured Corps to win the Victoria Cross during the Second World War and Dave Currie was the only Canadian soldier to receive that medal during the Normandy Campaign of 1944. For these reasons, if for no other, their history deserves to be recorded, and this book is an attempt to do so.

The South Alberta Regiment was a unique unit and to fully understand and appreciate it one must grasp two essential facts. First, the SAR was a wartime entity. It did not have a long and illustrious military lineage although it could trace predecessor units back to 1885 (including the magnificent 31st Battalion CEF of 1914-1918) and was itself formed from the best stock of five Alberta militia units. As a wartime creation, and a wartime organization, the South Albertas' object was always to get overseas, get the job done and come home, as quickly as possible. In any case, impressive titles and lengthy lineages can be deceptive because stomping about in red coats and funny fur hats is not what war fighting is about, while as for hoary old traditions, Lieutenant-General Sir Brian Horrocks of the British army perhaps said it best when he remarked that "one good Commanding Officer is worth a ton of tradition with mould on it."

Second, the SAR was a western Canadian unit and western Canadians tend to be practical people with little patience for pretension who possess the too-uncommon virtue of being able to laugh at themselves. Although the original composition of the SAR was watered down by drafts from other parts of Canada, the Regiment never lost its western spirit and managed to convert the new arrivals to their way. Nothing has changed in the fifty-seven years since the unit was formed and the South Albertas still don't take themselves all that seriously. The reader might be amused to know that one of the titles suggested for this book was "Armoured Cowboys: The South Albertas' March on Berlin," a title that actually found merit in some quarters although there were only a few real cowpokes in the Regiment.

The South Albertas did take their soldiering, if not themselves, seriously and at some point their historian has to turn to the sober side of things and discuss the research on which this book is grounded. Regimental history is the most popular form of military history in Commonwealth countries and most such works are based primarily on that frequently cited document, the unit war diary. Unfortunately, most of the war diaries I consulted during my research were full of errors, distortions, exaggerations, irrelevancies and not a few downright falsehoods. This is not surprising as, although it may come as a bitter shock to some researchers, combat units exist for reasons other than to provide them with material and most Canadian units (including the SAR) were more concerned with what was going to happen in the next hour than with providing grist for historical mills to grind decades later.

If the war diaries are problematic, what other evidence is there? There are operation orders, many of which have survived, including written summaries of verbal instructions, but operation orders basically tell what should happen, not what did happen. There are also "sitreps," situation reports submitted to higher formations summarizing events, progress and locations but almost without exception these proved to be exaggerated. This, also, should come as no surprise because, when reporting upstairs, one always tries to put one's best foot forward and this is the reason why villages stated to be secured and start lines affirmed as cleared often turned out to be full of enemy troops – the actual situation was not as good as the reporting unit or formation wanted its superiors to believe it was. The most useful and reliable source turned out to be the wireless (radio) message logs, usually called "operations logs," kept by brigades, divisions and some units. These form a transcript of communications (military "phone conversations" if you will) as they happened and, as care was taken with the information transmitted (otherwise you might call down artillery fire on your own head), actual positions can be accurately translated onto a map. Even these, however, betray signs of editing and to properly study an action you need to examine at least two ops logs (as messages omitted or deleted in one may show up in another), and preferably more.

There are also very useful "after action reports" prepared by wartime army historians. Two such documents, covering the Regiment's actions at the Hochwald in February and March 1945, and in Germany in April and May 1945, have survived. These reports, prepared a few days after the completion of an action, are fairly reliable. At least the SAR seems to have thought so because I was amused to see that the officer tasked with bringing the War Diary for April 1945 up to date (often a punishment for erring officers in the Regiment) simply duplicated the 4th Division historian's after-action report for that period.

An often overlooked source of evidence is the visual record. In this respect I was fortunate because the South Albertas purchased an 8 mm film camera in 1941 and took footage (much of it in excellent colour) of their activities right through to 1945 although shortage of film curtailed lengthy shooting after 1943. This is why I can be so certain about the colour of the fur of the stray dog that joined the Regimental march-past during the district commander's inspection in April 1941 and how I know that small boys with wagons and bicycles greeted the SAR when they arrived in Niagara-on-the-Lake in May 1941. I was also able to procure a copy of the sixty-odd seconds of 16 mm film shot by Sergeant Jack Stollery of No. 1 Canadian Army Film and Photographic Unit at St. Lambert-sur-Dives during the early afternoon of 19 August 1944 and that is why I can be so definite about the effect of the fire of Corporal Pete Woolf's Crusader AA tank on enemy troops hiding in a nearby orchard. There are also five wartime Canadian Army newsreels in the National Film archives that contain useful material on the SAR. Finally, the Regiment possesses a considerable collection of still photographs fleshed out with sketches, drawings, paintings and cartoons, from their own sources and those of other units.

Another overlooked source is the actual battlefields. I have read too many battle studies by authors who have never visited the scenes of the actions they describe – for the serious historian there can be no substitute for "going on the ground" because you cannot describe an action with any degree of accu-

racy unless you examine the positions of *both* opponents on the actual terrain. Many authors neglect this simple truth and try to reconstruct battles by studying maps. It won't work. I should add that "going on the ground" involves more than examining the landforms, vegetation and road networks, particularly when writing about an armoured regiment, because one has to be concerned with the actual soil itself. The best "tank country" is not, as some would have it, "the country with the least enemy anti-tank guns." It is the country over which you can drive an armoured vehicle that, combat loaded, weighs nearly thirty-five tons.

Records, both documentary and visual, maps and the "ground" are all good evidence but, in my opinion, veterans constitute the most important source of information. Some historians complain that they find it impossible to establish properly the time and place of an event described by a veteran whose memory is vague after more than half a century. I must confess that, in the some one hundred and sixty interviews conducted during the course of writing this book, I never encountered that particular problem – perhaps there is something wrong with my methodology. Most South Albertas quite candidly admit they cannot recall exact details of events that took place more than five decades ago. Almost all, however, will recall a day on which someone was killed or wounded and, if you give them a name from the casualty list, a man they knew and remember, it often starts to come back – slowly at first – but it does come back whether they want it to or not. Since casualty records include dates, it is a fairly easy matter to establish a time and place for a veteran's account of an event. In this respect I was very fortunate because Padre Phillips Silcox of the Regiment took the trouble to maintain comprehensive notes on every fatal SAR casualty between August 1944 and May 1945. The Regiment owed much to the good padre during the war – their historian owes much to him after the war.

Information gained through interviews was fleshed out by wartime and postwar correspondence and memoirs. The human instinct to record is an old one – witness the paintings on the walls of cave dwellers – and I was pleased to discover that the South Albertas and their families not only have that instinct in a marked degree but also that they are a very literary group of people. I received three complete sets of wartime correspondence from Bob Clipperton, Arnold Dryer and Don Stewart and I was favoured with many single letters, some private and some official. I will be perpetually grateful to the YMCA for giving every man in the Regiment a small pocket diary at Christmas 1944 because many, among others George Gallimore, Bill Luton, Don Stewart and Joe Strathearn, kept these diaries faithfully to the end of the war in violation of standing orders. In this respect John Neff deserves special mention because he started an interesting and useful daily diary on the day the Regiment first entered action in August 1944 and continued it until May 1945. I was also the beneficiary of dozens of postwar memoirs, ranging in size from two pages to nearly a thousand in length, and many of these are of publishable quality. More than a hundred other veterans wrote letters, sent newspaper and magazine clippings and completed questionnaires about their wartime experiences. Finally, two South Albertas have been the subject of published biographies – the story of Wilf Taylor's interesting life is told in *Beating Around the Bush* by Alan Fry and Wilf Taylor (Harbour Publishing, Madeira Park, B.C., 1989) while the wartime experiences of Trooper Sid Black (and others in AA Troop) are contained in *Soldiers All* by Sherry McNair (Turner-Warwick Publications, North Battleford, Saskatchewan, 1994).

I have used all this evidence to tell the story of a group of young Canadians who went to war. I have tried to tell that story with the humour and plain language favoured by the South Albertas themselves and I have tried to tell it as honestly as possible. At the request of the veterans of the Regiment I have provided information about those men who did not return, so that these fallen comrades, with whom they shared the horror and the humour of the war years, are more than mere statistics. I have also followed the decision of the Regimental History Committee that, with a number of notable exceptions such as

the circumstances surrounding Major David Currie's Victoria Cross, no attempt would be made to link a specific deed described in the text to any medal or decoration that may have resulted. Many of the courageous acts described in the following pages resulted in such awards, but unfortunately many others did not, and it was thought more fair to treat the men of the Regiment as equally as possible. There are parts of the following story that do not make for very comfortable reading but the reader can rest assured that the South Albertas have always triumphed over adversity in war and in peace. Theirs is a splendid record.

Sadly, the South Alberta Regiment is no longer on the Canadian order of battle and when the last veteran musters in the green fields beyond, all that will remain of this proud unit will be a handful of official records, a scattering of memorials and plaques and a Regimental Colour that hangs, with those of other Alberta units, in the Rotunda of the Provincial Legislature in Edmonton. What that Colour represents, and how it got there, is the subject of this book.

DONALD E. GRAVES
Almonte, Ontario
Remembrance Day, 1997

A NOTE TO THE READER

It was my original intention to write the history of the South Alberta Regiment in plain English, avoiding specialized military terminology, so that it would be readily understandable to a general audience. Unfortunately, I found that to be an impossible task because armies do love acronyms and jargon and these literary weeds soon sprouted forth all over my prose. I have therefore included in Appendix D a glossary of the military terminology and abbreviations used in this book.

It was also my plan to keep the discussion of such technical subjects as weapons, tactics and doctrine to a minimum in the main text lest they detract from the narrative but unfortunately some of these topics did slither in. I would therefore advise the reader not versed in such matters to first read Appendix C, "The South Alberta Regiment: A Working Manual," before venturing into the main text so that he or she has the requisite background knowledge.

After some cogitation I decided to retain wartime weights and measures throughout and certain period terminology such as "wireless" instead of the now-common "radio," rather than annoy the reader with yet more editorial intrusions (and there are enough of those) when the older terms appear in quoted material.

To simplify things I have utilized the military twenty-four-hour clock throughout rather than endlessly change times and interpose "AM" or "PM."

The reader should note that the index to the book is in three parts: personal names; other subjects; and illustrations.

Finally, we discovered to our horror that the names of members of the Regiment are inconsistently spelled even in the official records, which presents a challenge to the researcher. If any reader can offer corrections, we would be glad to receive this information.

D.E.G.

When writing a lengthy book such as *South Albertas: A Canadian Regiment at War*, an author amasses debts that he can never fully repay and the most I can do is acknowledge some of what I owe the many people who have helped me over the last four years.

My thanks go first to the South Alberta veterans and their families who patiently answered so many questions and provided me with wartime diaries and correspondence, postwar memoirs and other material.

As the historian of the SAR I owe much to my two predecessors. The late Major (Retd.) Glen McDougall, the Regiment's first chronicler, was very helpful and we spent a pleasant day discussing historical matters on his ranch near Calgary while horses grazed on the front lawn. I must also acknowledge my debt to my late good friend Brigadier-General (Retd.) J.L. "Jack" Summers, MC, CD, who started this history but died in 1994 before it was finished. My work is built on the firm foundations put in place by these two fine soldiers and historians.

When we began this project the SAR Association appointed a committee to steer it through to completion – and they chose its members well. It has been my pleasure to work with five veterans – Major (Retd.) W.J. "Danny" McLeod, MC, Lieutenant (Retd.) Bill Luton, Lieutenant (Retd.) David Marshall, Warrant Officer (Retd.) Vic Childs and Sergeant (Retd.) Tom Milner, DCM – who all helped to lighten my load. I want to particularly acknowledge Bill Luton. He and I started off by getting into an argument over the nature of the officer-enlisted man relationship in the armoured corps but we went on from there to form a great working partnership and a good personal friendship. Bill was an extremely versatile man, successful in business and many other fields, and he was a born historian. Tragically, he died before this book, to which he devoted so much time and energy, was completed. I wish very much that he could have held it in his hands.

Two other SAR veterans played a major part in this project. Lieutenant-Colonel (Retd.) A.F. "Bert" Coffin, DSO, started with the prewar SAR in 1936 and went all the way with the Regiment until the last two weeks of the war. Despite a growing body of evidence that, in the end, was almost incontrovertible, Colonel Coffin denies to this day that he engaged in games of chance between 1940 and 1945. Next there is Lieutenant-Colonel (Retd.) Harry Quarton, President of the SAR Veterans Association, who started as an underage private in the Regiment in 1940 but left it to go on to higher places. While the rest of us argued over who did what to whom, when, where and how, Harry looked after business and kept things on the rails through the exercise of his considerable organizational skills. What goes for Harry has to go doubly for his "executive officer,"

his wife, May, who has devoted much time and energy to ensuring that this project and the Regimental Association functioned smoothly and efficiently. Harry kept us on the rails and May kept Harry on the rails.

I cannot leave the subject of the History Committee without acknowledging the unpaid and, till now, unsung labours of Mary Luton, June Marshall and Sheila McLeod. All three were patient and gracious hostesses during the visits of a monomaniac historian who not only disrupted the tranquillity of their homes but distracted their husbands to the point where they neglected their domestic chores to deal with him.

The South Alberta Regiment has many good friends overseas and first and foremost is Dr. Jean-Pierre Benamou, OBE, director of the *Musée de la Bataille de Normandie* in Bayeux, Normandy. For many decades after the war, Jean-Pierre Benamou kept the memory of the Regiment alive in Europe during a time when it was forgotten in its own country, and when the SAR began to tour the scenes of its old battles he was a gracious host and provided many local introductions. From the outset, he has been unstinting in his support for this project and the Normandy chapters could not have been written without his assistance.

The Regiment owes much to its European friends. In France Mr. Bernard Nourry, the chairman of the Juno Committee, has assisted the SAR during their visits and opened doors for us as have Mr. Bernard Oblin, the mayor of Cormelles, and Mr. Jacques De Diguerre, the mayor of St. Lambert-sur-Dives, a fateful name in South Alberta history.

In Belgium Mr. George Spittael, MSM, and Mr. Jaak de Muynck of Eekloo made sure that we saw everything we should see from Oostcamp to Antwerp. Anyone who has seen *Libera Me*, the great work of George Spittael, knows that he keeps undiminished the memory of the Canadian soldiers who died in his country in 1944.

In the Netherlands Mr. Peter Zevenbergen, the former *burgemeester* of Bergen op Zoom and Mr. Piet van Dijk, his *chef du cabinet*, opened doors for the Regiment which are normally closed while Mr. Wes Besling, who worked selflessly as a member of the Red Cross to assist the wounded of all nations in October 1944, has remained a true friend for more than half a century. Mr. Kees Becht and Mr. Do Meeus and their wives have always assisted SAR veterans on their visits to beautiful Bergen and the Regiment wishes to apologize for drinking so much of Mr. Becht's product during the war (Kees Becht owns a brewery) without paying for it. Special mention must be made of the efforts of the late Jack Rosenboom to gather information about the fighting that took place in and around his factory in Bergen on 27-29 October 1944, which his brother, Leon Rosenboom, turned over to the Regiment. The gratitude and hospitality of the people of Bergen op Zoom shows no signs of diminishing – on a recent visit the present *burgemeester*, Mrs. Ans van den Berg, made great efforts to assist the SAR while Colonel (Retd.) Piet Hoedelmans put at my disposal his own research into the battle for the city. In Nijverdal, Mr. Albert Hartkamp, the chairman of the "Thank You, Canada" committee for more than four decades, was a most knowledgeable guide and Mr. Wim Porterman, local historian and resistance veteran, furnished material from his own research and translations for me. Finally, in Steenbergen, Mr. Johan van Doorn, historian of the 1944 battles in that area, was generous in his assistance.

The South Alberta Regiment is proud to carry the names of all its European friends on its roll as Honorary Members of the Regiment.

Some Albertans come next on my lengthy list. In Edmonton Colonel Stan Milner, Honorary Colonel of the South Alberta Light Horse and President of the SALH Foundation, gave freely of his time and resources to assist us, and his executive assistant, Charmaine Milner, proved to be a great asset in helping to keep this thing going. In Medicine Hat, MWO Jim Ogstan of the South Alberta Light Horse put at my disposal photographs from the SALH archives.

Wartime comrades of the Regiment also came to my aid. Mr. Clem Beauchesne of the Algonquin Regiment gave us *carte blanche* to plunder that unit's fine published history. Dr. Robert Fraser, historian of the Argylls, provided a transcript of the Argylls' interview with Swatty Wotherspoon and searched in their photograph collection for me. Members of the Lincoln and Welland Regiment, in particular Mr. J.A. Dunlop, QC, contributed personal memoirs and other material and we owe a debt of gratitude to 15 Field Regiment, RCA, for permission to reprint material from that fine unit's wartime history. Finally, Lieutenant-Colonel (Retd.) David Wiens of the 4th Armoured Division staff gave me permission to quote from his unpublished memoir, "Intelligence Officer."

I owe much to Doug Hendry, that indefatigable Scotsman, who patiently conducted archival research for me in Ottawa and London, read through the entire Part I and Part II Orders of the Regiment and sifted through countless files at the National Personnel Records Centre to compile the nominal roll in this book.

Major Michael McNorgan, CD, of the Royal Canadian Dragoons and Michael Whitby, both of Ottawa, read and severely criticized early drafts of the manuscript. In McNorgan's case, I ignored some of his advice (at my peril because it was good) as he is a former First Hussar, but nonetheless he caught several embarrassing things before they got loose in print. Lieutenant-Colonel (Retd.) John Marteinson of Toronto, currently writing the history of the RCAC, was also most helpful, as was my old friend *Oberstleutnant* Doctor Winfried Heinemann of the *Militärgeschichtliches Forschungsamt* (there's a handle for you) in Berlin, who assisted with German sources and translations. Major-General (Retd.) Michael Reynolds, CB, of Eastbourne, Sussex, freely put at my disposal German and Polish documentation he gathered for his own book, *Steel Inferno: 1st SS Panzer Korps in Normandy*. Finally, Stuart Sutherland of Toronto inflicted the "death of a thousand cuts" on my writing.

I also owe much to several experts on armour who did their best to enlighten me on technical matters. George Bradford, editor of *AFV News*, executed the fine 1/72 scale drawings which enhance my text. Peter Brown, head of the "Friends of the Tank Museum" at Bovington, gave me material from his extensive collection of British unit histories. In what was a very daring act, David Mountenay, Curator at the Oshawa Military and Industrial Museum, let me play with his working HVSS Sherman for a day and I managed to get out of it without hurting either myself or anyone else. Finally there is Chris Johnson, who is the artist of the unit organizational schemata and Sherman plans and views in this book, illustrations that let the reader quickly grasp matters that I am incapable of putting into words.

It is always a pleasure to work on a project with Robin Brass, who paid no heed to my concerns about the increasing length of the text but did his best to get it all in – and a good job he did. After viewing the mapwork of Robin's daughter, Molly, the reader will agree that professionalism runs deep in the Brass family. The well known Edmonton military artist Ron Volstad contributed the beautiful painting that enhances the colour section of this book. All of Ron's paintings are good but this one is particularly so and I like to think it is because of his special feeling for the Regiment.

Last, but certainly not least, comes my wife, Dianne, who has displayed a valour far beyond the call of any matrimonial duty. She wasn't my wife when I started this book (and, in fact, Dianne might be described as the South Albertas' last war bride) but she was always steadfast in her support, both in Britain and Canada. It was Dianne who drove on the wrong side of the road down twisting country lanes in the Home Counties, avoiding oncoming "juggernauts" (18-wheel trucks) at the last moment, tore her clothing on brambles when we explored abandoned military bases, got chased by submachine-gun-wielding guards off bases that were supposedly abandoned but actually highly classified, and wisely dragged me out of the "Holly Bush" when I was researching "period atmosphere" just before I ordered that third (and critical) pint. Somehow, she survived it all and, along the way, took the many fine photos that grace the pages of this book. Greater love hath no woman.

I can never repay them all but I can at least thank them all.

DONALD E. GRAVES

The boys come home.

MEDICINE HAT, ALBERTA, MAY 1919

There's no such thing as a windless day in southern Alberta. That's what the Albertans say and they should know since many live with the blue line of the Rocky Mountains on the horizon and the breeze can whip down off those peaks at a fair clip. Medicine Hat lies in the southeastern part of the province nearly two hundred miles distant from the Rockies, but according to the local paper there was a chilly wind blowing through that place on 31 May 1919. It fluttered the Union Jacks decorating the two-storey office blocks along the Second Street business section, rippled the red, white and blue bunting adorning the trees and benches of nearby Riverside Park and threatened to steal hats and bonnets from the "massive" crowd gathered on an otherwise fine Saturday morning.

The crowd paid little heed to the wind. There was too much excitement among the men, women and children impatiently waiting, ears cocked for the distant whistle of a Canadian Pacific Railway train, for this was an important day in Medicine Hat's short history. The Great War had come to an end and the Hat's own unit, the 31st Battalion of the Canadian Expeditionary Force, was coming home at last.

The boys come home, Medicine Hat, May 1919. Bands, crowds and small boys greet the 31st Battalion, Canadian Expeditionary Force, as it returns from the Western Front. The war to end all wars was over and a future major conflict was unthinkable. COURTESY, SOUTH ALBERTA LIGHT HORSE.

Known as the Alberta Regiment, they had left the province in May 1915 – almost four years earlier to the day – eleven hundred strong (including one hundred boys from Medicine Hat) anxious to get to grips with "Billy the Kaiser" before it was all over. They needn't have worried as they got their fill. In three years of fighting, the 31st CEF carved a splendid record marked by such distant but meaningful place names as St. Eloi, Ypres, Kemmel, the Somme, Vimy Ridge, Passchendaele, Amiens, Arras and numerous other obscure localities important only for a few days or hours. They also paid an awful price; of the 4,487 men who served with the battalion on the Western Front in 1915-1918, nearly three quarters were killed or wounded.[1]

Now it was all over. As the train approached it was probably some small boy perched in a high place who first spotted it, as there are usually small boys to be found in high places on occasions like these. Belching steam, the train pulled into the station and from "every window heads leant, faces smiled, hands waved" as D Company from the Hat disembarked to a noisy welcome. It was an exciting moment and the local reporter could hardly contain himself:

There were sudden recognitions, exclamations of joy, passionate embraces, kisses, smiles and tears. Years had elapsed since these couples had seen each other – years of horror, bloodshed, darkest anxiety, sometimes of despair. In that time the world had changed … empires had risen and fallen, maps had been redrawn, governments overturned, leading men assassinated, millions of ordinary and extraordinary youths slaughtered.[2]

Resplendent in new uniforms they had been issued only two months before, D Company marched across the tracks and up Second Street. The salute was taken at the town hall, politicians made the obligatory speeches and the procession then moved to Riverside Park where tables had been "laden with pies, cakes, bread and butter, sandwiches, and coffee," and the men "were soon eating and drinking to their hearts content."[3]

The "war to end all wars" was over. The weapons were handed in, the uniforms taken off and carefully put away or thrown in the dustbin, the battalion Colours were laid up in a Calgary church and "Heinie," the captured German pony who had been their mascot, was put out to grass at Banff National Park to spend "the remainder of his days in restful peace."[4] The survivors of the 31st CEF, and the 600,000 other Canadians (one in three of military age in the country) who had served during the conflict, hoped very much that the world would emulate that small horse. Sadly, it was not to be and twenty-one short years later another group of young westerners boarded the green-painted coaches to go off to another overseas war.

This is their story.

PART I

FORMING

Predecessors, 1930s. A squadron of the 15th Alberta Light Horse at Sarcee Camp near Calgary in the 1930s. The horses got paid more than the men but summer camp was always great fun for the western militia as it gave them a chance to look at the prairie from a new perspective.

COURTESY, SOUTH ALBERTA LIGHT HORSE..

CHAPTER ONE

"We used to parade every Thursday night."

CANADA: SEPTEMBER 1939 – AUGUST 1940

Saturday night is the traditional time to relax and have some fun in small-town Canada. In Medicine Hat on Saturday night, 9 September 1939, many were heading out to watch the local baseball heroes, the Tigers, continue their longstanding feud with the Picture Butte Royals while others were bound for the Roxy to see "Suez" with Tyrone Power and Loretta Young or the Monarch to catch David Niven and Ginger Rogers in "Bachelor Mother" – two films and the cartoons for a dime. For those who wanted more liquid entertainment there was the Assiniboine Hotel and other similar establishments while for those who planned to stay at home, Tommy Dorsey, Artie Shaw and Don Turner and their orchestras were on the radio. For the kids, back in school after the summer holidays, the *Medicine Hat Daily News* carried the weekend comics ("Dingle-Hoofer and His Dog," "The Katzenjammer Kids," "Popeye" and "Tim Tyler's Luck"). The weather was good that evening – pleasantly warm but not too hot – and for that everybody was thankful as the summer of 1939 in Alberta had been one of the hottest on record with temperatures surpassing 100° Fahrenheit in late July and staying in the nineties throughout much of August. This heat, coupled with winds of 25-30 miles per hour, had started the farmers cutting early in hopes of salvaging part of what might be a stunted crop.[2]

The weather had been one of the three main topics of conversation in the Hat that summer; the other two were baseball and the situation in Europe. By September the heat wave was over and the crop was turning out better than expected, while the Tigers were holding their own. Matters in Europe had steadily got worse throughout the summer and the *News* had marked the progress of a growing international crisis with ominous headlines: "REPORTED HITLER HAS OFFERED POLAND CESSION OR PARTITION," "ZERO HOUR FOR POLISH REPLY TO HITLER EXPECTED TONIGHT," "DER FUEHRER ANNOUNCES HIS FINAL OF-

Boys, salute the S.A.R.!
Shout 'til the tent poles ring,
Stand and slope your arms once again,
Let every loyal soldier sing;
Drink to all parading hours,
Drink to the camping days,
Drink to the Thirty-First Albertas
The unit of the heart always.

> To the Sigs, to the gunners, to the Vickers and the Hotchkiss men,
> To the guards, to the drill, to the Addjy and all his fussiness;
> Ta-da-dum, ta-da-dum, to the sergeant who never stops callin' us,
> To the work, to the play, to the Colonel who'll love us some day.[1]

FER TO POLAND," and, finally, "NO REPLY FROM GERMANY TO BRITISH ULTIMATUM." On Sunday, 3 September 1939, Britain and France had declared war on Germany and now, six days later, the House of Commons in Ottawa was debating a similar measure. Most people in the Hat knew that this would be the last peacetime Saturday night for a long time.[3]

Medicine Hat had a rather varied military history. The first soldiers to appear on its streets were a colourful bunch known as the Rocky Mountain Rangers. Raised during the 1885 Rebellion to guard the Hat and patrol the international border west to the Rockies, the Rangers were recruited from local ranchers, cowboys and farmers. Although they never saw action, the Rangers were always spoiling for a fight, and they looked it. An eyewitness recorded their tanned "faces almost hidden beneath the brim of huge stetsons strapped on for grim death," their rough, brown, broadcloth uniforms, chaps and their weapons and accoutrements, which included "cross belts pregnant with cartridges, a 'six shooter,' a Winchester slung across the pommel of the saddle, and a lariat coiled at the tree."[4] Mounted "on broncos good for sixty to a hundred miles a day, they soon disappeared in the distance" accompanied by the "loud clinking of bits and jingling of their huge Mexican spurs."

After three months of service the Rocky Mountain Rangers galloped off into history in July 1885. Two decades later, another, more orthodox unit came to town when I Squadron of the Canadian Mounted Rifles, militia cavalry, was raised in the Hat. In 1908, it was expanded into a regiment with the title 21st Alberta Hussars. The Hussars flourished, assisted by the fact that their first commanding officer was a rancher who recruited his own cowboys and their mounts. Good horsemen, the Hussars and the other Alberta cavalry units impressed a British

Predecessors, 1885. Officers of the Rocky Mountain Rangers, Medicine Hat, 1885. Raised from local ranchers and cowboys for service in the Riel Rebellion, the Rangers were a hard-riding and well-armed outfit that never saw action. NAC, C-2872.

officer who saw them in 1913. "The Western Cavalry are fine," he reported in the clipped phrases favoured by inspecting officers, the "physique of the men is just right. They ride daringly and well. They are keen as mustard, and their horses, the broncos of the prairies, show blood and stamina."[5] By 1914, the Hussars numbered four squadrons, two in the Hat and one each in the nearby towns of Taber and Youngstown, with a strength of 334 officers and men and 288 horses.[6]

When war broke out that summer the Hussars were mobilized. Keen to get to Europe, they were disappointed when they were sent to guard bridges, railways and public buildings, but in November 1914 they contributed a sizeable contingent to the 3rd Canadian Mounted Rifle Regiment, an overseas unit organized at Medicine Hat with drafts of militia cavalry from across Alberta. The 3rd CMR went to France in late 1915 but never fought as a unit, being converted to infantry and broken up as reinforcements, and the same fate was suffered by the 113th, 175th and 187th CEF Battalions, which recruited in the Hat and area during the First World War. The greatest number of men from the city served in the famous 31st Battalion.[7]

When the war was over, that magnificent fighting machine, the Canadian Expeditionary Force, was dismantled and Canada's military entered a period of somnolence. A few years later the Alberta militia went through a reorganization which saw many smaller units made part of new and larger entities. The 21st Alberta Hussars became the 1st Regiment of Alberta Mounted Rifles with a squadron each at Redcliff and Brooks while their headquarters and a third squadron were in Medicine Hat. In 1921 they were joined there by the 13th Machine Gun Battalion and the 1st Battalion of the newly-created Alberta Regiment. This latter unit was an infantry battalion, and three years later its title was changed to the South Alberta Regiment.[8]

The 1920s were not good times for the Canadian military. Many wartime veterans had had their fill of soldiering and there was widespread distaste on the part of young men who

refused "to take up military service, even in the modified form adapted to a civilian force" such as the militia.[9] This change in attitudes was not assisted by Prime Minister Mackenzie King's Liberal government, which, convinced war was a thing of the past, began to drastically reduce the defence budget. The militia were particularly hard hit as the funds for training, particularly at the annual summer camps where the officers and men of the small permanent (or regular) force instructed the citizen soldiers, were slashed. No camps were held in Alberta in 1927 and 1928, and the commanding officer of the Alberta Mounted Rifles admitted that the unit was "dormant" during those years. The same was probably the case with the other Hat militia units.[10]

Training funds were increased in 1929, but in October of that year the stock markets crashed and Canada slid into a decade of economic depression. The figures vary but by 1932 between 20% and 30% of Canadians were unemployed and 15.5% of the total population was on relief or welfare. The depression was particularly harsh in western Canada where the economy was based on the export of foodstuffs and raw materials – prices fell and markets dried up. It was also a time of severe droughts and dust storms that devastated eastern Alberta and neighbouring Saskatchewan; over half the people in the latter province and two-thirds of the farm population ended up on relief.[11]

With a varied economic base of ranching, farming, brick and pottery-making plus the steady payroll from the Canadian Pacific Railway, which was the largest employer in the city by 1932, Medicine Hat was spared the worst of the depression's horrors. For small boys the Hat was a good place to grow up in the 1930s as in almost every direction lay that great playground, the open prairie. Danny McLeod, the son of a local road contractor, "never owned a bike" but his dad had "ponies and, on the odd occasion when I would be late for school, I would ride a pony and wrap the reins around a pipe until school let out."[12] Sports were Danny's passion and, like most Canadian boys, his favourite game was hockey. On winter days every skateable piece of ice in the Hat was transformed into a hockey rink as teams of boys, equipped with shin pads made from rolled-up newspapers and shoulder pads cut from rubber tires, recreated the feats of their heroes in the Leafs, Bruins or Canadiens. Summer was reserved for baseball, and other seasons were good for hunting small varmints with .22 calibre rifles and pellet guns.

Most of these aspiring young hockey players paid scant attention to the troubling course of events in Europe. Not that the Canadian government itself, preoccupied with the Depression, seemed all that concerned. The defence budget, low enough in 1931, was slashed nearly in half the following year and maintained at absurdly low levels for the next three. By 1935, in a period of rising international tension, Canada's armed forces, both regular and militia, had reached such a state that the Chief of the General Staff, Major-General Andrew G.L. McNaughton, warned the newly-elected government of Prime Minister Mackenzie King that the nation possessed neither a single modern anti-aircraft gun nor one modern aircraft and that there was only enough artillery ammunition on hand for ninety minutes "fire at normal rates."[13] This had some effect and military spending for all three services was increased over the next four years, the militia budget growing nearly tenfold between 1935 and 1936.[14]

This increase came not a moment too soon, as throughout the decade the world moved steadily toward war. In 1931 a militaristic Japan launched an unprovoked attack on the independent state of Manchuria that broadened into outright war with China in 1937. In 1935 Mussolini's fascist Italy invaded Ethiopia, and attempts by the League of Nations to apply economic sanctions to both aggressors fizzled out because of a lack of resolve on the part of the major European powers. The greatest danger lay in Germany, where Adolf Hitler, at the invitation of the German people, assumed dictatorial powers in 1933 and began a massive programme of re-armament. Three years later he occupied the demilitarized Rhineland and in 1938 he seized Austria. Dark clouds were gathering on the horizon.

Despite government neglect of the armed forces and the prevailing attitude that war was not only unthinkable but not to be thought about, many young westerners joined the militia in the 1920s and 1930s. Some were so eager they could not wait until the mandatory age and enlisted as "boy soldiers" to serve as drummers, trumpeters or general factotums. Dave Currie of Moose Jaw, Saskatchewan, the son of a CPR engineer, enrolled in his home-town unit, the King's Own Rifles, at fourteen in 1927; by 1939 he was a second lieutenant. Young Stan Purdy joined the Calgary Regiment in 1928 and by 1933 had worked himself up to the rank of sergeant. In Battleford, Saskatchewan, young Jack Summers was fascinated with the army and was an avid reader of military history. In the "dirty thirties," when families had little spare cash and children rarely saw new toys, Jack managed to purchase a set of toy soldier moulds from a mail-order catalogue. He scavenged lead from old batteries in the town dump, melted it down, and cast miniature soldiers which he sold to his friends for enough profit to purchase the commercial product. In 1934, as soon as he could, Jack enlisted as a boy in the Battleford Light Infantry.[15]

Other men joined as adults. They were attracted perhaps not so much to military life but by the fact that in many western towns the local militia unit functioned as a social club. Albert "Bert" Coffin, a pharmacist and the son of a rancher from Lethbridge, moved to Medicine Hat in 1935 and joined the South Alberta Regiment the following year. On parade nights after drill in the small Connaught armoury (a converted fire hall) up on the hill, the SAR officers would congregate in their mess and "have a beer or something," pitch horseshoes and "make a social evening of it."[16] Coffin "was barely squeaking by in a very small business" and the militia "was a sacrifice, the uniforms were expensive and then there was the time." He recalled it being "a struggle to scrape up money and nearly everyone had second-hand uniforms, we would get something and have it altered."

By the time Bert Coffin joined the South Alberta Regiment it was the only militia unit in Medicine Hat. The Alberta Mounted Rifles had moved to Vegreville in 1930 and the SAR absorbed the 13th Machine Gun Battalion in 1936. The SAR's headquarters and three companies were in the Hat while D Company was at neighbouring Redcliff, but military activities were minimal as money, weapons and equipment were in short supply. Coffin summarized activity in the unit:

> We used to parade every Thursday night and we never got any pay for that. We used to get a week's summer camp when we got paid and our time at camp was always at Sarcee near Calgary.
>
> Once in a while they would have a TEWT and they would take us off somewhere for a day and we would get a day's pay there. The prewar SAR officers were about half First War veterans and half young fellows like me. For weapons we had old .303 rifles and one Lewis light machine gun which I am sure would not have fired but we would train with it and learn to clear stoppages. On parade night, we would do a little close order drill, parade drill and work on the broken-down Lewis gun.[17]

Things were no better in other western units. Glen McDougall, a lieutenant in the 15th Alberta Light Horse from the Calgary area, recalled that "we learned foot drill, that's about what we used to do in our weekly meetings, we would form up and march about a bit."[18] He remembered "stripping down a Lewis gun but not a hell of a lot more." Private Neil McPherson, who joined the Loyal Edmonton Regiment in early 1939, recalled that a truck "would pick up a bunch of us occasionally and we would go out to the range and fire off some weak World War One .303 ammunition" and then head home.[19] Similar scenes took place across Canada as men came together once a week to go through the motions of military training with obsolete weapons according to outdated tactical manuals.

The high point of the militia year was the annual summer camp. Usually held just before the harvest when men would be needed on the farm, it offered a chance to work with the permanent force at being soldiers "in the field." For farm boys (which is what most of the western militia were) it also provided an opportunity to see the prairie from a new vantage point. Summer camps could be exciting. Bruce Bean, a 15-year-old drummer boy in the SAR, saw one of the tiny RCAF's biplanes crash into the tent lines at Sarcee after catching its undercarriage in a telephone wire while coming in for a landing. No one was hurt. Bruce always remembered the day at Sarcee in 1937 or '38 when the SAR manned its slit trenches against the regular Lord Strathcona's Horse, which, contrary to the accepted tactics even of the First War, made a mounted charge against an infantry position defended by machine guns. Bruce crouched down in his trench when the horses jumped over it, and perhaps more for their spirit than their tactical sense, the umpires ruled that the mounted troops had won the "battle."[20]

The cavalry always seemed to have a good time at camp. According to McDougall of the Light Horse, his regiment would

"go out to Sarcee and go on schemes and wave flags in case we were firing and that sort of thing."[21] Horses were the problem as many of the city squadrons did not have enough and had to rely on mounts brought to camp by the country squadrons. The country men were glad to do so because, as McDougall notes, "a man got $1.25 a day but a horse got $1.50 a day so these country squadrons would come to camp with just barely halter-broke nags." It was difficult enough to ride these animals let alone perform cavalry manoeuvres on them, as a regular officer, Captain Harry Foster of Lord Strathcona's Horse, found out in 1933 when he was sent to a summer camp at Maple Creek, Saskatchewan, to teach riding to a militia infantry unit that had recently been redesignated cavalry. On his arrival, he found three hundred wild mustangs recently corralled from their prairie grazing grounds and a collection of bemused citizen soldiers waiting to watch a permanent force officer literally take a hard fall. It took Foster twenty minutes of very rough riding to break the first horse and a further two weeks of hard work in blazing hot temperatures to turn these prairie flat feet into the Saskatchewan Light Horse.[22]

It was all good fun but in the summer of 1938 training began to have more serious undertones. Most Canadians had not been alarmed when Hitler reoccupied the Rhineland and seized

---

Predecessors, 1933. Major Frank Duval, officer commanding B Company of the prewar South Alberta Regiment, seated with his officers and noncommissioned officers. Note the First World War uniforms, web belts and the two Lewis .303 light machine guns which were stripped and cleaned more than they were fired.

Predecessors, 1930s. The prewar SAR band (right) outside the little armoury in Medicine Hat. In small-town Canada, militia bands were popular organizations and sure to be included in any civic function. (Below) A mortar detachment of the prewar SAR training near Medicine Hat in the late 1930s. The militia did the best they could to train with outdated weapons because there was nothing else available. The junior ranks mess of the SAR at summer camp, probably at Sarcee near Calgary, in the late 1930s. COURTESY, SOUTH ALBERTA LIGHT HORSE.

Their Majesties King George VI and Queen Elizabeth visit Canada in May 1939. The first visit of a reigning monarch to the Dominion, the Royal Visit was the cause of great excitement and a bright moment in 1939 as the world moved toward war.

COURTESY, MARGARET ATKINSON.

Austria because after all the Rhineland was German territory and Austria was a German-speaking nation. But when he began to agitate for the Sudetenland, that part of Czechoslovakia in which there was a sizeable population of Germans, alarm bells began to ring. The Czechs, willing and ready to fight to preserve their freedom, appealed to France and Britain for assistance but western leaders resorted to negotiations which dragged on throughout a long and uneasy summer. On the last day of September 1938, following a shameful act of appeasement on the part of Prime Minister Neville Chamberlain of Britain and Premier Edouard Daladier of France, the Sudetenland was transferred to Germany in return for a promise from Hitler that he had no more territorial demands in Europe. Three days later German troops occupied the Sudetenland; seven months later they marched into the remainder of Czechoslovakia.

Europe was moving toward war. Britain and France, and Canada on a smaller scale, began long-overdue re-armament and the militia began to take its activities more seriously. Glen McDougall thought that "at the time of the Munich Crisis it was just as though a black cloud was hanging over us" but "things picked up mentally over the winter" when he realized that war was inevitable.[23] During the winter of 1938-1939, Bert Coffin of the SAR began to look for a buyer for his drugstore as there "was never a question that I was going into the army" if war came "and I was bored anyway."[24] Across Canada the men of the militia began to prepare mentally for what lay ahead.

For Medicine Hat, 1939 started out as a good year as the city's economy was approaching pre-depression levels. But the storm continued to gather: in March Germany occupied the

Lithuanian city of Memel on the Baltic and began to make threatening noises about the Danzig corridor, the strip of Polish territory that divided East Prussia from the rest of Germany. Through the spring there was a quickening in the moribund Canadian military establishment, and in April members of the regular Princess Patricia's Canadian Light Infantry demonstrated the new Bren light machine gun and Boys anti-tank rifle for the Alberta militia units. Demonstrations were all they got as none of these new weapons were available.[25]

The following month Canadians were briefly cheered when King George VI and his beautiful queen, Elizabeth, toured the country. It was the first time a ruling sovereign had visited the Dominion and they were ecstatically received, as in "the midst of world turmoil this gracious couple embodied a tradition and a continuity that was dear to the hearts of the majority of Canadians."[26] The royal visitors spent only fifteen minutes in the Hat but this short visit, termed the "biggest day" in the city's history, warranted a lengthy spread in the *News*.[27] In Edmonton Captain Bob Bradburn, an officer in the 19th Alberta Dragoons, managed to provide a mounted escort for their Majesties despite the fact that the horse had been struck off the strength of the Dragoons three years before when they were converted to an armoured car regiment. By borrowing mounts from the local thoroughbred association and boots from Lord Strathcona's Horse and purchasing second-hand helmets from a British cavalry regiment, Bradburn managed to put the 19th Dragoons "in the saddle once more."[28]

As the spring of 1939 turned to summer and the heat wave began, the European crisis deepened. At the end of July Hitler announced that he wanted to incorporate the Polish city of Danzig into his Third Reich, and three weeks later Britain and France pledged military assistance to Poland if she was attacked by Germany. Through the long hot days of August, the headlines in the *Medicine Hat News* grew increasingly sombre and an editorial expressed a sentiment widely shared in English Canada: "It is difficult to conceive of any major war in which Britain would be a participant and Canada not" as "Canada can have only one role – that of supporter of the Motherland with all the strength which the Dominion can muster."[29]

In the early hours of 1 September 1939 Hitler attacked Poland. When he made no reply to an ultimatum from Britain and

Captain Arnold Lavoie, South Alberta Regiment, late 1930s. Arnold Lavoie was commissioned in the 13th Machine Gun Battalion and came to the SAR in 1936. By 1939 he was adjutant and he held that appointment in the wartime unit until 1941, when he became a company commander. He subsequently commanded A Squadron when the SAR was converted to armour and led his squadron throughout the campaign in northwest Europe. COURTESY, SOUTH ALBERTA LIGHT HORSE.

France to withdraw, they declared war against Germany two days later. Canada was still nominally at peace but everyone knew what was coming when Prime Minister Mackenzie King called for a debate in the House of Commons on Thursday, 7 September. The next day, H.S. Hamilton, a Liberal backbencher from northern Ontario and a veteran of the First World War, summed up the choice before the nation. Emphasizing that "this war is Canada's war," he concluded:

We are confronted with a philosophy that knows nothing of the individual man but his obligation to obey; that knows nothing of the value of human individuality and human liberty, whose instruments are ruthlessness and unscrupulous force and violence, an utter negation of all the things we have been taught to value, of the philosophy, to which we hold, that has regard for human personality and human liberty, by which philosophy we shall yet achieve the splendid destiny that lies ahead of the Canadian people.[30]

The vote for a declaration of war passed with almost no opposition and the measure was sent to Governor-General John Buchan, Lord Tweedsmuir, for signature.

And so Saturday night came to Medicine Hat. It was a quiet evening punctuated only by the slam of screen doors and shouts as mothers rustled up errant children for bedtime. As the Picture Butte Royals threw the first pitch down at the ball park and the audiences at the Roxy and Monarch settled down to enjoy the cartoons before the main feature, the lights were burning in the little armoury up on the hill. Upon instructions from Ottawa the South Alberta Regiment had mobilized nine days before to provide guards for local bridges and power plants. Now, under Lieutenant-Colonel Gordon Elder, the officers and NCOs prepared to organize a draft for the Calgary Highlanders, one of the Alberta units selected for service overseas. There was a shortage of almost everything, including the proper paperwork, and the newly-appointed regimental adjutant, Captain Arnold Lavoie, struggled to sort out the mess. For this peacetime accountant who had come to the SAR when it had absorbed the 13th Machine Gun Battalion three years earlier, it was a busy evening. By the time Lavoie and those helping him left the armoury late that night, the ball park was quiet, they were mopping the floors at the Assiniboine, and the crowds from the movie houses had long departed for home. Other than the occasional passing car, the only noise to be heard was the chirping of crickets in the dark.

The next day, Sunday, 10 September 1939, Canada declared war on Germany.

Poland resisted the German onslaught bravely but succumbed within a month. By the end of September she had been divided between Germany and the Soviet Union, which in an act of bottomless cynicism had signed a non-aggression pact with Hitler a few days before his army had crossed the frontier. There was not much that Britain and France could do to help valiant Poland as their armed forces were not prepared for war and in any case their leaders lacked the will to fight. Chamberlain and Daladier took comfort in a fantasy that, if they did not attack Germany, Germany would not attack them and contented themselves with dropping propaganda leaflets on German cities. British and French military leaders were confident that this new war would run along the same course as the previous conflict, so throughout the winter of 1939-1940 they built up their forces in France secure in the knowledge that the Maginot Line, the world's greatest permanent trench system, would protect them from sudden attack. It was a strange period and some journalist, making a pun on the newly-coined word "blitzkrieg" (lightning war) used to describe Germany's quick conquest of Poland, dubbed it the "Sitzkrieg." Most people called it the "Phoney War" and everyone sang "We're Going to Hang Out the Washing on the Siegfried Line" (the German equivalent of the Maginot Line) as if such an event would shortly come to pass.

This lull suited Prime Minister Mackenzie King. He had no wish to commit large ground forces to a European war in which casualties might force him to impose conscription. King wanted no repetition of 1917 when an attempt to implement forced military service in Canada had caused riots in Quebec that had nearly torn the nation apart. King and his government knew public opinion demanded that troops be sent to Europe but they hoped to make such a commitment as small as possible.

The mobilization plan for the Canadian Army was based on Defence Scheme

Sergeant Kenny Perrin, 1939. A bank clerk from Medicine Hat, Kenny Perrin served as an NCO in the prewar SAR, was commissioned in the wartime unit and rose to the rank of captain. He was typical of the many young militia officers and NCOs who provided a leavening of expertise for the South Albertas. Kenny Perrin was killed at the Hochwald on 27 February 1945.
COURTESY, SOUTH ALBERTA LIGHT HORSE.

No. 3. Approved in March 1937, it called for the creation of a "Mobile Force" of two infantry divisions that would form the basis of an overseas expeditionary force. These divisions would draw their eighteen battalions from the three infantry regiments of the small permanent force and fifteen selected militia infantry regiments across Canada. In Alberta the Loyal Edmonton Regiment was named for the 1st Division and the Calgary Highlanders for the 2nd Division but it was not planned to place the other militia units in the province on a war footing. They would furnish reinforcement drafts for the two overseas units.[31]

At 1235 hours, 1 September 1939, the Mobile Force was activated and recruiting commenced across the country to bring the chosen units up to their War Establishments, or authorized organization and strength. The South Alberta Regiment contributed officers and men to the Loyal Edmonton Regiment and the Princess Patricia's Canadian Light Infantry of the permanent force (including a future commander of that unit, Major R.A. Lindsay), but the largest draft, two officers and one hundred men, went to the Calgary Highlanders. Hastily organized and equipped as best it could be from the SAR's limited resources, this draft boarded the CPR at Medicine Hat a few days after the declaration of war and set out for Mewata Barracks in Calgary. Among the crowd that sent them off were 17-year-old Danny McLeod and his best friend, Edward "Duffy" Gendron. Never an enthusiastic student, Danny had left high school the previous year to work at a local pottery mill and was up to thirty-five cents an hour by the time war broke out. The crowd cheered the Hat boys heading for Calgary and, caught up in the excitement of the moment, Duffy said to Danny, "You and I should be on the next troop train that leaves this town."[32] They were.

Just when the Mobile Force would go overseas was a matter of some discussion. After much speculation the government announced on 19 September that one division would be sent as soon as possible while the second would be raised and trained in Canada. In the meantime, pending the organization of these two divisions and ancillary units, further recruiting for the Canadian Army Overseas Force was to be cut back. The 1st Canadian Infantry Division, with the Loyal Edmonton Regiment, left for the UK in December 1939 while the 2nd Division, including the

Calgary Highlanders, remained in Canada training at their local camps (Sarcee for the Highlanders). The other Alberta militia units stepped up training in hope that they would be included in any future contingents.[33]

The winter of 1939-1940, the period of the "Phoney War," was a frustrating time for the many young western men who wanted to join the services. Recruiting slowed or closed for most mobilized units in October 1939 and recruiting officers became very discriminating. Sergeant Herbie Watkins from Westlock, Alberta, an eleven-year veteran of the 19th Dragoons, was rejected because, at 32, he was regarded as too old. On the other hand, Jim Gove from Pincher Creek and Ted Palfenier from the Hat were accepted by the Calgary Highlanders, but since both were 18, a year under the minimum age for overseas service, they were held back and spent the winter square drilling at Mewata Barracks. Rejected by the army, some westerners tried the other services but in the first months of the war the standards for the RCN and RCAF were impossibly high. Like many others, Alex McGillivray of Edmonton tried to join the glamour service – the air force – but was turned down on medical grounds and was "mad because the air force turned me down and I was out of a job."[34] A lot of prairie boys were attracted to the navy, which was an exotic service to landlocked westerners. Harry Quarton of Chauvin, Alberta, was too young at seventeen to enlist but screwed up his courage and lied to a RCN recruiter only to be told that there was a six-month waiting list. Prewar militia personnel like Coffin of the SAR and McDougall of the Light Horse put off joining active service army units in the hope that their own regiments would be called out and, in the meantime, said farewell to many comrades who left for the Calgary Highlanders or Loyal Eddies. Beginning to lose patience, Coffin decided to join the field ambulance but Colonel Elder of the SAR told him "to stay out of it, you've got a commission in the SAR but you will never get one in the medical corps."[35] Unable to get into the active service force, many men enlisted in their local militia units in the winter of 1939-1940.[36]

The anxious ones did not have to wait long. On 9 April 1940 the "Phoney War" ended abruptly when German troops attacked Norway. Again, a small but gallant country, assisted this time by an Anglo-French expeditionary force, was helpless in the face of overwhelming German land and air power. His northern flank secure, Hitler now turned west and overran Denmark, Holland and Belgium in early May and then, as an astonished world watched, on 10 May 1940 the German army begin an end run around the Maginot Line through the supposedly impenetrable terrain of the Ardennes into northern France. That same day Winston Churchill replaced Neville Chamberlain as prime minister of Britain, but it was too late – the Allied armies, trained and equipped to fight the previous war, proved incapable of holding the German panzer, or armoured, divisions whose mass employment would come to characterize the Second World War, and German tanks pushed

steadily west. By the end of May the *Wehrmacht* was on the English Channel and the crisis was upon the western Alliance. While the weary men of the British Expeditionary Force waited under German bombing for the Royal Navy to lift them off the beaches at Dunkirk, the Canadian government decided to dispatch the 2nd Division overseas and raise two more active service infantry divisions.[37]

The South Alberta Regiment was chosen to be mobilized for the new 4th Canadian Infantry Division. Actually the name was a misnomer as the new unit would be drawn not just from the prewar SAR but also from four other Alberta militia regiments across the province. On 29 May the commanding officers of these units met at the headquarters of Military District 13 in Calgary to discuss how best to proceed and it was probably at this time that the name "South Alberta Regiment" was chosen, possibly because the prewar SAR was a Medicine Hat unit and Edmonton and Calgary were already represented in the 1st and 2nd Infantry Divisions. The decision was that each of the five units would recruit one company for the active service unit and, according to SAR legend, the commanders then cut cards to choose which company they would contribute. The result was as follows:[38]

HQ Company in Calgary	Calgary Regiment (Tank)
A Company in Medicine Hat	South Alberta Regiment
B Company in Edmonton	19th Alberta Dragoons
C Company in Edmonton	Edmonton Fusiliers
D Company in Calgary	15th Alberta Light Horse

At 0600 hours on 5 June 1940 the active service South Alberta Regiment was mobilized and recruiting commenced at Medicine Hat, Calgary and Edmonton. The cap badge remained that of the prewar SAR, which was the only Alberta unit badge that incorporated the provincial crest of mountains, sky and prairie.[39]

The question of who was to command the Regiment was an important decision and, for once it seems, the authorities made an inspired decision. On the day that recruiting opened, Major James H. Carvosso, a regular force officer from the Princess Patricia's Canadian Light Infantry, received orders to take over the SAR. Carvosso was no amateur; he was a hard-bitten professional with a quarter century of service and an incredible combat record. He had enlisted as a private in the PPCLI in the summer of 1914 at such a young age that he was promptly nicknamed "Pinky" and was wounded twice while serving in the ranks before being commissioned as a lieutenant in 1916. He got his third wound in late 1916 and was out of action for a brief spell before returning in 1917 to be wounded yet again at Vimy Ridge. He managed to rejoin just before the battle of Passchendaele, where he got his fifth wound but remained on duty only to be injured in an accident that incapacitated him until the autumn of 1918, when he got back in time to participate in the final battles of the war. Even for such a hard-fighting unit as the PPCLI, the five-times wounded Carvosso's record was so unusual that the regimental historian allows that "it may be granted that Lieutenant Carvosso had exceptionally bad luck." "Pinky" Carvosso, however, acquired more than wounds in the war; he also received the Military Cross and bar. Opting to remain in the permanent force after the war, he had attained the rank of major by 1940 when he was promoted lieutenant-colonel and given command of the SAR.[40]

The next important appointment was the RSM, the Regimental Sergeant Major, the senior warrant officer responsible for the discipline of the non-commissioned officers and other ranks. The SAR were doubly blessed when Corporal Christopher Seal of the PPCLI was promoted and appointed their RSM in early July 1940. Although he had personality quirks that many disliked, Seal looked every inch a model sergeant major and put a stamp on the enlisted men of the SAR that remains with them to this day. Jimmy Simpson from Wainwright sums up their prevailing sentiment: "I was just a young boy from a farm when I encountered RSM Seal – fifty-six years later I still remember him – my God, we were afraid of him."[41] Such is the effect of a first-class RSM.

The task before these two professionals was to take an enthusiastic but motley collection of civilians and turn them into a trained infantry battalion. They would be assisted by a group of veteran First World War officers, including Lieutenant-Colonel E.A. Pitman, a former commanding officer of the 19th Dragoons, who took a drop in rank to major to become second-in-command of the new unit. In a similar fashion, Lieutenant-Colonels Howard Wright, H.S. Davies, Alf McLean and Harcus Strachan, commanding the 19th Dragoons, Edmonton Fusiliers, Calgary Regiment and 15th Light Horse respectively, also dropped to major to command companies in the new SAR. Strachan in particular was a model for young soldiers because he had won the Victoria Cross at the battle of Moreuil Wood in 1918 and wore the modest ribbon of that medal on his tunic. Captain J.W. Hunter of the Loyal Edmonton Regiment, another First War veteran, assumed the post of

quartermaster while Captain Bert Huffman of the Regina Rifles was appointed paymaster.[42]

A third group of officers was drawn from the junior commissioned ranks of the five militia regiments that formed the SAR. From the prewar SAR came Captain Arnold Lavoie and Lieutenant Bert Coffin. The 15th Light Horse contributed Captain Kenneth Clarke, the medical officer, and Lieutenants Glen McDougall, Rafe Douthwaite and Hugh "Click" Clarke. The Edmonton Fusiliers sent forth Lieutenant Charles Gallimore and the Calgary Regiment Captain James Crichton and Lieutenants Dick Robinson and Stan Purdy but when it came to providing junior officers, the 19th Dragoons from Edmonton were at the top of the list, as Captains G.M. Saul and Bob Bradburn and Lieutenants Thomas "Darby" Nash and Gordon "Gordie" Shell came forward from that unit.[43]

There was no problem getting recruits. So many young and not-so-young men were eager to sign up that the recruiting officers had their pick and a friendly rivalry developed between the five units to turn out the most impressive company. Three weeks after it was mobilized the Regiment had enrolled 941 enlisted men, well over its War Establishment or authorized strength. The grounds for joining the army varied but generally most South Albertas seem to have enlisted for one or more of six basic reasons: there was "a job to be done" in Europe; all their friends were enlisting; they wanted some adventure in their lives; they were personally recruited by a member of the unit; the army was a great improvement on unemployment; and (important for Albertans) the army offered a chance to get off the farm and see the world.[44]

They came from all walks of life. Gerry Adams was a parts man in a garage in Edmonton when he was recruited by Captain Walter Hunter, the quartermaster. Guy Olmstead worked in a dairy in Medicine Hat, Harry Quarton was employed on a newspaper in Chauvin, George Tourond was at a lumber yard in Calgary, Bill Clark had a steady job as a driver for Four X bakeries in Edmonton, and Karl Wickstrom was a barber in the same city. A large majority were farming, either as hired hands like Robert Barr, who was working for $10 a month and board near Blue Ridge, or on their own land, as were Tom Eastwood near Camrose and Robert McCloy at Wainwright. The farmer who employed George White as a hand for $35 a month offered him a $5 raise if he would stay out but George wanted to follow his brother, Dan, serving with the Loyal Eddies. Many of the new recruits were unemployed. Alfred Ball had been laid off from his job in British Columbia so hopped a freight to Calgary and joined up. Adrian Berry and Bill Hinson were high school drop-outs. Bob Clipperton, 16 years old, rode the rails for four days to reach Calgary when he heard that the SAR was opening up and arrived at Mewata Barracks "unwashed" and "looking like a first class tramp."[45] He was accepted despite being three years under the minimum age of nineteen for active service. The five militia regiments contributed some very steady men and future NCOs: Herbie Watkins of the 19th Dragoons got in

The Professional. Lieutenant-Colonel James H. Carvosso, MC and bar, the first commanding officer of the South Albertas. Known to the officers as "Pinky" and to the men as "Old Steelhead," he had enlisted as a private in 1914 and suffered five wounds between 1915 and 1918, but survived to continue as an officer in the interwar regular Canadian army. With the help of RSM Chris Seal, also from the PPCLI, he put in firm place the foundations of the wartime Regiment.

SAR COLLECTION.

SAR officers, Edmonton, July 1940. A mixture of veterans and prewar militia officers drawn from the five Alberta units that formed the wartime regiment (SAR, 15th Alberta Light Horse, Calgary Regiment, Edmonton Fusiliers and 19th Alberta Light Dragoons), some served throughout the war with the SAR, including Stan Purdy from the Calgary Regiment (back row, second from left), Bert Coffin from the prewar SAR (back row, third from left), Glen McDougall from the 15th Light Horse (back row, third from right), Dick Robinson (middle row, fourth from left), Bob Bradburn from the 19th Alberta Dragoons (front row, second from left) and Arnold Lavoie (front row, fourth from right). Also notable in this group are Major Howard Wright (front row, second from right) and Captain Bert Huffman (second row, second from right), two officers who made it their business to identify and commission good soldiers from the enlisted ranks, beginning a longstanding tradition of the Regiment "growing its own." COURTESY, TED TALBOT.

as did Johnnie McRae and Jimmie Smith of the same regiment, while Tom Eastwood and Alex McGillivray came from the Edmonton Fusiliers.

This being the west, not a few of the new recruits were horsemen. Jim Gove was a ranch hand near Pincher Creek while Jack Huntley, aged 17, was at the Sweet Valley Ranch twenty miles out of Claresholm. Being a cowboy "was all right, long days in the saddle," according to Huntley, "but it was not as romantic as people think, mostly milking cows and shovelling manure."[46] A prewar member of the 15th Light Horse, he enlisted as soon as he could. One of the older and more unusual recruits was Soren Thuesen. A Dane who was fascinated with western life, Thuesen had emigrated to Alberta in 1927 to become a cowboy and by June 1940 was working on a ranch near Red Deer. When he heard that the SAR had been mobilized, Thuesen sold his saddle, his string of ponies, and a few head of cattle and joined up in Medicine Hat. Promptly dubbed "Swede," a nickname that took, he thus became, in his words, "a man without a country."[47] "Swede" Thuesen was 38 when he enlisted and he had a personal reason because his family was under German occupation.

In contrast, Danny McLeod was under age by a year when he went with his friend Duffy Gendron to the armoury in Medicine Hat to enlist. Danny had a brief moment of panic when he saw that among the interviewing officers were two men who

certainly knew his age: the doctor who had presided at his birth and one of his former teachers. But Danny got in with Duffy and the other Hat boys like Ev Nieman, whose decision to enlist was almost casual:

I just up and joined. I brought the horses in at noon and started taking the harness off and my dad asked me where I was going. I said, "I am going to join the army." I took the car into town and a good friend of mine, Sid Arrowsmith, came up and said, "What are you doing?" I told him I was joining the army and he got into the car and said, "Let's go." My two younger cousins also joined up.[48]

Some did not find it so easy. Up in Edmonton 18-year-old John Galipeau, having been rejected by the air force, the navy and the army the previous winter, "found myself sitting with a thousand other fellows outside the Prince of Wales Armoury waiting to be called in." As each militia unit "was recruiting for its own company [of the SAR], and each wanted the finest looking soldiers, the best looking men, … they were choosing the tallest, strongest, handsomest fellows first," and "little five foot, six inch, guys like me were passed over." Galipeau waited outside more than a week with the other rejects until finally, late one afternoon, a sergeant emerged and said "All right, you lot, come on in," whereupon they "straggled into the building and

Mess line, Edmonton, August 1940. The regimental offices were in the armoury itself while the personnel were quartered in huts built behind it. Note the incredible variety of clothing, including the sweaters, the despised baggy fatigue pants and the light trousers worn by the two men with their backs to the camera. COURTESY, MARGARET ATKINSON.

signed all the papers attesting that we would serve King and country."[49]

Young or old, short or tall, what the wartime SAR gathered from such willing volunteers was a select group of enthusiastic and healthy young men with a self-reliance and maturity formed early by the "hard knocks" school of the Depression with a common social and geographic background who were inured to physical labour, to being outdoors in extremes of weather, and who possessed mechanical skills and some experience with weapons. In short, they were about as close to the ideal of the raw material for an infantry battalion as Carvosso or any other commanding officer could have wished.

Regimental Headquarters was established at the newly-built Prince of Wales Armoury in Edmonton on 5 June 1940. The first recruits were received the next day and there were almost continuous drafts over the next two weeks. The Medicine Hat contingent mustered daily at the Connaught Armoury for about a week and, according to Ev Nieman, "they started marching us around but we didn't know our right foot from our left."[50] Jack Porter recalled that "someone had a book about the army so we learned about ranks."[51] It was an interesting start to military life and they got to go home every night, but it didn't last long. On 11 June 1940 the group, sixty strong, prepared to board the train for Edmonton, and the Medicine Hat boys, who had known each other for years, marched down to the station in the early evening. They were dressed in their oldest clothes, some with cloth caps, most with their sleeves rolled up as it was a warm evening, and not a few clutching paper bags of sandwiches and other delectables prepared by anxious mothers.[52]

While things were getting organized there was much banter through the windows of the coaches with the crowd on the platform ("Don't worry, ma, I'll be home by Christmas!") and a few sorrowful scenes. "A good part of Medicine Hat was out," Ev Neiman recalls, "and there was the usual cheering and good-byes and tears."[53] None of the boys really minded the tears or, if they did, were not about to admit it as, in Ev's words, "we were on a high, we were going on an adventure." Just before seven, the big coal-burning 2-6-2 engine hauled the three coaches out of the Hat to the accompaniment of cheers and moved slowly down the line as the tall figure of Bert Coffin stood in a doorway and waved goodbye. A brief stop was made at neighbouring Redcliff to pick up the detachment from that town and then, pulling out in the soft light of an early summer evening to the sound of cheers from the "wives, kids and all the town people," the train picked up speed for the journey north.[54]

The process of turning even the most enthusiastic group of civilians into professional soldiers is an old and hallowed one that dates back to the time of Caesar, if not before. Lieutenant-Colonel James Carvosso had been through it as a recruit in 1914 and knew well what had to be done, as did his veteran company commanders. The basic elements of this process involve isolating the recruit from civilian society, instilling habits of discipline, teaching the importance of obedience and instructing him in such basic military skills as drill and marksmanship.

Carvosso wasted no time getting started. On the same day the Medicine Hat and Redcliff boys boarded their train, he commenced recruit training at the Prince of Wales Armoury. Besides men, he did not have much to work with as there was a desperate shortage of just about everything. Bert Coffin remembered how the colonel tackled the problem of uniforms: "Carvosso got in touch with the Great Western Garment company, which had a plant in Edmonton that manufactured overalls" and "got some kind of pattern for military overalls, or he dreamed one up, and he got them to make them and we all wore them."[55] Manufactured of a light brown denim, these overalls, worn with a khaki wedge cap, were the standard dress uniform of the Regiment for the first five months of its existence. They were a workable garment, but after a few washings the colour lightened to yellowish-white and the SAR was soon known in Edmonton as the "Mustard Battalion." The fatigue uniform was even worse. As new Private John Galipeau complained, "Whoever arranged for that fatigue uniform had a real diabolical mind" as it "consisted of khaki work pants, a khaki shirt, and a brown cardigan sweater."[56] "The sweaters were good," but the "pants were all a size 46 waist with a 40-inch leg" and the "crotch hung somewhere between where it should be and your knees." Boots were another problem for the first few weeks but eventually enough black leather army boots arrived for men to discard their disintegrating civilian footwear.[57]

Weapons, particularly modern weapons, remained in short supply for the first year of the Regiment's service. Canada, in response to desperate appeals from Britain for arms to re-equip her army after the disaster of Dunkirk, had shipped most of the available rifles and sixty million rounds of ammunition overseas, and there was little left in the country to equip the newly-mobilized 3rd and 4th Divisions. The SAR did manage to procure enough First War vintage Ross rifles to allow one platoon in each company to practice weapons drill; when that platoon had finished they would turn the weapons over to another platoon. Other modern weapons, equipment and vehicles existed only as terms in official documents or pictures in military manuals.[58]

Nonetheless, Carvosso made a beginning and he made it on that traditional starting place, the parade ground. From 12 June when Bert Coffin and the boys from Medicine Hat and Redcliff reported for duty at 0625 hours, until they left the Prince of Wales Armouries two months later, the daily training syllabus was dominated by one fateful phrase, "M.E.D." (*Manual of Elementary Drill*), which meant, in that descriptive old army term, "square bashing." The soldier's day began with reveille at 0600 and ended at 2230 hours when "Last Post" was sounded by the bugler. Each day was divided into eight training periods, which started at 0830 and ended at 1600 hours, and for the first six weeks "M.E.D." was scheduled for at least four of those periods every day. Day after day, RSM Seal instructed the company sergeant majors who instructed the platoon sergeants who instructed their platoons in close order drill. Hour after hour, throughout the hot months of June, July and early August, the sweating men of the SAR pounded up and down Kingsway Avenue learning the niceties of military evolutions.[59]

For a change from the *Manual of Elementary Drill*, the syllabus alternated lessons from the various *Small Arms Training*

pamphlets – basic weapons handling and maintenance. Most of the recruits were familiar with weapons but the military way of marksmanship presented some problems for one South Alberta who had lived with rifles all his life because "there were things I learned I had not known, or that were different from what I was used to" and "I had to learn a whole new way based on technical details I had never known before."[60] When firing commenced on the miniature range in the armoury on 11 July, the War Diarist recorded that some "very good marksmen were discovered."[61]

The administrative offices were in the armoury itself but the personnel were housed in sixteen huts, sixty men to a hut, erected behind the armoury in the area bounded by the Kingsway and 109th Avenue and 104th and 105th Streets. Some had trouble adjusting to barrack life, but many had lived in bunkhouses, settlers' cabins or logging camps and considered living conditions in the army excellent. Having spent time in all three, John Galipeau thought the barracks were "palatial" with "running water, hot and cold, and rows of wash basins and showers" as well as "flush toilets."[62] Earle Wood was another man who was quite comfortable. Only twenty when he enlisted he "had already been away from home and on my own for five years" and during "that time I had spent about three months in a logging camp so knew something about eating and sleeping with other people, and camp life."[63]

During the first weeks of military life the enlisted personnel were more likely to see RSM Seal than their commanding or any other officer. According to Bert Coffin, Carvosso tended to keep the junior officers away from their men during these early days and left the supervision of basic training to the RSM. This was probably a good idea as Seal was impressive – according to one recruit he "would make his rounds about ten in the morning" and although "you were frightened to death that he might find something you had done wrong or not done properly," the RSM's rounds "also gave you a chance to see this man who was like God to us."[64] Seal "was a sharp looking warrant officer who appeared immaculate, even though he wore the same crummy uniform we did, and he always carried a pace stick with the PPCLI badge which he was forever flipping against the side of his leg." To Private Galipeau, RSM Seal

was the image of how young men want a leader to be. He knew what he was doing, he was competent, he was decisive. He had a voice you could hear for four miles, and eyes like a hawk. He could have the whole regiment lined up in front of him, and he would spot somebody in the back ranks whose dress was not acceptably precise. "Number 5 in Headquarters!" he'd bellow, "You're not a bunch of bloody cowboys. Straighten that bloody belt!"

He drove us until we reached a level of proficiency that was recognized as excellent.[65]

When companies were not drilling, taking small arms training, cleaning their barracks, doing guard duty or any of the

Prince of Wales Armouries, Edmonton, 1940. This armoury served as the first station of the Regiment in 1940. Hour after hour, day after day, the recruits pounded up and down the adjacent streets as they became intimately familiar with elementary drill. COURTESY, MARGARET ATKINSON.

other numerous chores that armies create to keep their men busy, they attended occasional lectures on sex education given by the padre and the medical officer. In a time before the widespread use of antibiotics, venereal disease was regarded by the authorities as a dangerous threat to the soldier's health. The garrison chaplain, C.F.A. Clough, lectured the recruits "about how we were to behave and control ourselves and stay away from the loose women that we were apt to pick up" in downtown Edmonton.[66] The medical officer, Captain Kenneth Clarke, less confident of the essential goodness of human nature, used a more direct approach by showing a collection of films about what might happen if the recruit strayed from the straight and narrow, which he interspersed with enthusiastic and detailed descriptions of the painful methods of treatment that the unfortunate "would suffer in an attempt to arrest the progress of the disease."[67]

Life at the Prince of Wales Armoury was not all drill, work and scare tactics. Volleyball was the main leisure activity in the barrack yard and the men were allowed to use the facilities of the Edmonton YMCA. There were a number of musicians in the ranks, including Corporal Darryl Robertson, a former professional, who formed a dance band with a repertoire that was strong on "The Beer Barrel Polka," a current favourite. Sing-songs were a popular feature at the Sally-Ann (Salvation Army) canteen hut near the armoury and often included "You Are My Sunshine," a big hit in 1940. Evening and weekend passes were generously provided and downtown Edmonton with its movie theatres, parks, beer halls, zoo – and girls – was just a short streetcar ride away. For the boys, the big problem was the awful mustard uniforms; some borrowed proper uniforms from those few fortunates lucky enough to possess them. Jack Porter rented one of these for a dollar to wear to see his fiancée, Audrey, who was a student at Alberta College. After their first pay day, the new soldiers had money to spend on such things; their basic pay was about $40 a month, a magnificent sum to men who had been lucky if they had made half that amount before joining the army, and many had been making no money

at all. Earle Wood summed up the common attitude: "I was getting three squares a day, I could go out on pass most nights and I could have a ball on pay day."[68]

One social activity that began almost at the Regiment's mobilization and continued for six years was dancing. History, in the form of the War Diary, records that the first SAR regimental dance, arranged by the Hostess Club of Edmonton, was held on 1 July 1940 at the Prince of Wales Armouries. Corporal Robertson's dance band provided the music and the "The Beer Barrel Polka" featured prominently. About a month later, an organization was formed to take over social arrangements for the Regiment when the Women's Auxiliary of the SAR was created to "provide a link between members of the units and their wives."[69] Consisting of the wives, fiancées and girlfriends of the officers and men, this sub-unit (which is basically what it was) came under the command of Mrs. Carvosso, who directed it with a will no less iron than that of her husband.

Despite the lack of weapons, uniforms and equipment and the inadequacy of an urban armoury for training an infantry battalion, the SAR made good progress throughout its first eight weeks of service. By mid-July, instruction had reached a point where it was drilling by companies and occasionally the entire battalion would manoeuvre under the eagle eye of RSM Seal. At the end of that month, increased time was given to rifle practice on the miniature range and the first route marches were made. These were short in length, but on 2 August, when the entire Regiment made its first 20-mile hike to the suburban town of Oliver, the War Diarist proudly recorded that "only two men fell out during the trip."[70] The raw recruits were beginning to look and act like soldiers but, before they could become true infantrymen, Carvosso knew they had to go into the field for more advanced training.

His opportunity was not long in coming. On 7 August the Regiment received a warning order to be prepared to move to a new station. Their destination was "the last place God ever made" – Dundurn, Saskatchewan.[71]

CHAPTER TWO

"Look, another dead corporal."

CANADA: AUGUST 1940 – DECEMBER 1941

Dundurn is a small village thirty-five miles south of Saskatoon set in a semi-arid desert of sandhills and short grass. After an overnight train ride from Edmonton, the Regiment marched into their new post at 0630 hours on 15 August 1940 and, as the War Diarist commented, the men got a chance to "look around at much discussed Dundurn."[2] They did not like what they saw as the new camp, the site of an old dump that had been hastily converted, lacked almost everything except sun, sand and flies. Water was available but it was of a milky consistency that did not bode well. It was also in short supply and showers were limited to two minutes: one minute to lather and one minute to rinse as timed by an NCO's watch, but the overworked plumbing system often broke in the middle of this hasty ablution and a shower became even briefer. Dundurn was boiling hot during the day and freezing cold at night – in fact it was the ideal location to toughen up an infantry battalion and nobody in the Regiment had any doubts that "toughening" was what Carvosso had in mind. As Tom Eastwood put it, "You had to tough 'er out or you didn't stay."[3]

On 20 August, five days after the SAR arrived, the route marches began with a twenty-mile return hike under full packs to a terrain feature called The Three Sisters, a name that would appear frequently in the War Diary for the period. The boys marched out under a boiling sun at 0800 and were back in their lines by 1600 hours, tired, thirsty, fly-blown and covered in dust and sweat. They did it again the following day, took a day off for the district commander's inspection, and did it again on each of the two following days. Over the next five weeks, the SAR would make sixteen of these route marches and those men who could not keep up were invalided out of the Regiment as medically unfit.[4]

By the first week of September, Carvosso was satisfied that the physical condition of the men was improving and switched his emphasis to weapons training. The unit had acquired enough full calibre rifles (albeit First World War vintage Ross

Oh, she wears her pink pyjamas, in the summer when it's hot,
She wears her woollen undies in the winter when it's not.
And sometimes in the springtime and sometimes in the fall,
She decides to crawl beneath her sheets with nothing on at all.

Oh, glorious, victorious,
One barrel of beer between the four of us;
And glory be to God there are no more of us,
'Cause the four of us can drink it till it's dry.[1]

rifles) to permit them to carry out marksmanship practice and the men put in a solid week on the ranges. Corporal Neil MacPherson of HQ Company never forgot his platoon's first day at the butts. As he was a former NCO in the prewar Loyal Eddies, "someone decided that I should run the show as I had done range work before the war."[5] Most of the men in his platoon were familiar with weapons but there was "one young lad who said he had never fired a rifle as his folks belonged to a Religion, but he had decided it was his duty to fight for his Country." The rifles "were in terrible shape," Neil recalled, and the "first shot our lad fired from a prone position, despite my efforts to help him, nearly broke his shoulder and pushed him back about a foot." MacPherson suddenly realized that Lieutenant-Colonel Carvosso was standing behind him:

He said to me: "You will just have to be patient with these chaps, as they are from many walks of life." Then he said to our religious lad: "What were you before you joined the Army, private?" To which our boy replied: "I WAS HAPPY, SIR!" The Colonel roared with laughter and walked off swinging his king size swagger stick against his riding breeches.

Carvosso was everywhere. He would appear at the most unexpected moments to observe the progress of the training and intently question officers, NCOs and men. This was particularly true when field craft – elementary tactical exercises at the company and platoon level featuring such elements as movement across country, locating the enemy, advancing to contact, outflanking drills, and night movements – replaced weapons training in the second week of September. Now for the first time the junior officers spent considerable time with their men as they learned the rudiments of the trade alongside them. Each company would go out for the day in the sand hills around the camp to train, eating a lunch of hard tack, cheese and tea

Dundurn Camp, 1940. A miserable place for human beings but heaven for infantry, Dundurn later became the major centre for training reconnaissance units and is still in use today. The water tower was the most visible landmark. COURTESY, MARGARET ATKINSON.

brought out by truck, supplemented by all the cactus berries they could find. "We lived on cactus berries," recorded Private John Galipeau, who particularly disliked one tactical formation where "they used to stretch us out in a single rank as far as the regiment would go and then would pull a left or right turn so that people on the outer end of the wheel would be running at their top speed while the people on the inner end would be slowly walking."[6] In the middle of such an evolution, Carvosso might turn up and transfix a gasping, sweating soldier with the words: "Are you happy in the service, private?" If the man was foolish enough to say "No, Sir," the colonel had a routine response: "Then you are not organized, son, you must get organized!"[7] And off he would stride, laughing and swatting his stick against his riding breeches.

The colonel was harder on the officers, who called him "Pinky" behind his back, than he was on the enlisted men, whose name for him was "Old Steelhead."[8] The ferocious veteran did not have much time for his younger officers who had never seen combat. To Carvosso, recalled Bert Coffin, "the young officers were just a bunch of sods and the enlisted men were heroes, they could do no wrong."[9] "As a sort of example," Coffin went on, "he used to give me hell, say things like 'You're just a goddamned druggist, all you do is sell people things they don't want or need!'" Woe betide any officer who the colonel found not quite up to his high standards in the field. Private Alfred Ball remembered with glee the day his platoon commander brought his men back early from the field and confined them to their tents as a punishment. "The old colonel came along and wanted to know what was going on," so the officer told him that "'I wanted them to go over the top of a hill and they wouldn't, they went around it'" To the platoon's delight, Carvosso replied: "I think they're smarter soldiers than you are. What were you doing up on the skyline if you're fighting the enemy?"[10] The punishment, however, was not lifted.

All through this period, Carvosso, Seal and the company

commanders were evaluating and assessing the men and promoting those who looked like good NCO material. Sometimes the reasons for such promotions seemed rather casual. Lyle Piepgrass was convinced that his first promotion to lance-corporal in 1940 was "because I had a very loud and commanding voice."[11] Danny McLeod was told by his company commander that the reason he was being promoted to the same rank was "not that you deserve it, we just think you will be less trouble that way."[12] However, Danny earned his second stripe at Dundurn when his lieutenant and sergeant were absent one day and he led his platoon on an "advance to contact" exercise. Carvosso, finding out who was in command of the platoon, put him on orders and Danny was "scared to death" but, when he saw Carvosso, the colonel told him "I thought that you handled that point extremely well" and promoted him to corporal.

Carvosso expected NCOs "to know every single thing about the people under your command and to care for them," according to Sergeant James Gove, and when "we were on route marches, we would stop ten minutes in the hour and the colonel would come along and tell some private to take his boot off and if there was a hole in his sock, he would give the sergeant pure hell."[13] Another sergeant recalled being chewed out because he didn't know the first name of one of his lance-corporal's wives. RSM Seal was just as hard on the NCOs and gradually many in the Regiment became aware that the purpose of the two regulars was not an arbitrary display of authority but something quite different. "We learned to stop thinking of ourselves as individuals," concluded Jimmie Gove, "and began to perceive ourselves as a family, a very close knit family."[14]

Recreational facilities at Dundurn were limited. The Sally Ann ran a wet canteen but the sale of beer was restricted to men over 21 years of age, which meant that much of the Regiment could not get served. There was also a dry canteen tent with a ping-pong table where the bouncing ball usually raised a small explosion of the dust that was everywhere along with the ubiquitous flies. An inter-regimental sports league was started but the SAR War Diarist records that the South Albertas lost their first games of soccer and touch football against the 16/22 Saskatchewan Light Horse although they managed to beat the Westminsters at volleyball. This was a humble beginning for a

B Company on the march, Dundurn, 1940. Day after day, week after week, the South Albertas trudged across the prairie to some feature and marched back again. Those who could not keep up the pace were returned to civilian life. COURTESY, TED TALBOT.

sports record that would become legendary. Saturday overnight passes were granted and most men went to nearby Saskatoon, which offered movies, better beer and the chance to look at something other than sand dunes.[15]

A number of special events marked the long, hot, dusty days at Dundurn. The Regiment held march-pasts for the district commander nearly every Sunday and passed his inspection of their tent lines with flying colours. On 23 August one platoon gave an "open air entertainment demonstrating the routine for the day of a normal regiment," but the demonstration had unforeseen results as the "platoon pretending to be asleep in their bunks, actually did go to sleep and were amazed to hear Reveille at 1000 hours in the morning."[16] On 11 September a speaker system set up in camp transmitted a re-broadcast of Winston Churchill's speech to the Commonwealth. The "Blitz" was under way as the *Luftwaffe* pounded London and other cities, and the British prime minister spoke with defiance and courage. On 16 September the SAR sadly suffered its first mortality on active service when 27-year-old Private Henry Moreau died of appendicitis in Saskatoon City Hospital. He was buried in his home town of Therien, Alberta.[17]

Another event took place at Dundurn that is often discussed at reunions with a great deal of retrospective merriment. The official record of this event, as contained in the War Diarist's entry for 26 August 1940, is spare in detail:

1200   A mild epidemic of intestinal influenza has started and several men returned [from a route march to the Three Sisters] as casualties.

1800   Erected a second hospital marquee

2000   Appropriated a third hospital marquee

2100   35 men sick, six ORs running high temperatures sent to camp hospital. Several men slightly ill in their own tents.[18]

The officer who wrote these entries was too modest. It was not a "mild epidemic of intestinal influenza" but a widespread and vicious form of amoebic dysentery caused by bad water or flies (or both) and it broke out in the middle of a twenty-mile route march to the Three Sisters. The results, according to Bob Rasmussen, were dramatic: "We were on our way back from a hike, and the guys were getting all wet because they just couldn't hold themselves because of the dysentery. RSM Seal was shouting, "stay in line, stay in line!" but "the first thing I knew I caught it, fell out of my platoon, took my trousers off and did it right on the side of the column and I wasn't the only one."[19]

By the time the Regiment got back to camp, as the War Diarist noted, the hospital tent started to overflow and more tents had to be taken over. Private Alfred Ball was working in one medical tent where "we had so much dysentery that I didn't have time to write 'dysentery' down on the chart so I just wrote 'the shits' and I later had to do the reports all over again."[20] Although the worst cases were placed in the medical tents, much of the Regiment was afflicted and, as Ball reported, "the latrine was across the ditch and we used to bet whether a man could make it all the way or have to go in the ditch." Carvosso tried to tell the men that it was "mind over matter" and they should be able to control themselves but, late that night, when he himself had to rush through the dark to get to the officers' latrine, he became fouled up in a volley ball net to the great joy of all.[21] For two days, the Regiment was on light duties while the medical personnel tried to cope with the disaster. Some recovered quickly while others had to go to the camp hospital. For the hardier ones, the route marches resumed on 28 August with a stroll of three miles, and thereafter the "Dundurn Trots" were gradually brought under control, although a few men continued to suffer for weeks.[22]

As September 1940 drew to a close rumours were flying around camp that the Regiment would soon be moving to the Pacific Coast. That suited everyone just fine as the boys were tired of Dundurn and its dust, dysentery, sand, flies and more sand in great supply. But those six long weeks under canvas in rural Saskatchewan had made them better individual soldiers and the hard marching, field training, range work and the pressure had melded them together as a unit. Carvosso had taken

Lunchtime at Dundurn, 1940. "We were always happy when the chuck wagon found us" was the original caption of this photo. The ration truck with its bread and cheese sandwiches was a welcome sight in the field at Dundurn whether the boys were route marching, practising field craft or on the range.

COURTESY, TED TALBOT.

A section of No. 16 Platoon, SAR, training at Dundurn in August or September 1940. After three weeks of marches to toughen the Regiment, Carvosso switched to range and field training to teach his officers and men the basics of their trade.

COURTESY, TED TALBOT.

No. 12 Platoon takes a break. Because of a mistake in organization, No. 12 Platoon received the shortest men in their company and was promptly dubbed the "Pee Wee Platoon." The Pee Wees served together throughout the war, becoming No. 4 Troop of A Squadron when the SAR converted to armour in 1942. They proved to be un-holy terrors to the enemy, their long-suffering officers and NCOs, and just about everyone else. Seated in the front row holding his hat in his hands is 30-year-old Corporal Ray Smith from Ed-monton. A prewar 19th Dragoon, Smith was commissioned in 1942; he was killed by a German sniper at Moerbrugge, Belgium, on 10 September 1944.

COURTESY, JOHN GALIPEAU.

Volleyball courts, Dundurn, 1940. Volleyball was always a popular activity. During the dysentery epidemic, "Pinky" Carvosso became fouled in a net while rushing one night to the officers' latrines – a momentous event that is still fondly recalled.

COURTESY, TED TALBOT.

(Right) Ablutions. The facilities at Dundurn were primitive in the extreme and the quality of the water was not good. The result was a mass outbreak of dysentery shortly after the Regiment arrived.
COURTESY, MARGARET ATKINSON.

Company cobblers at work. All that marching was hard on the shoe leather and made much work for the cobblers. Corporal Alf Ball stands at left. Note the variety of uniform. Alf is wearing a battledress jacket and mustard pants while the man on the right wears the fatigue sweater and mustard pants. COURTESY, ALF BALL.

(Right) Officers' lines, Dundurn. The First War-period bell tent was standard issue in the Canadian army until the late 1960s. COURTESY, TED TALBOT.

(Left) Railhead at Dundurn. Thirty miles south of Saskatoon in an arid semi-desert region of sand hills and scrub brush, Dundurn was the ideal place to toughen up a green infantry battalion. No South Alberta who served there remembers it with any great affection.
COURTESY, MARGARET ATKINSON.

(Right) Goodbye to Dundurn, September 1940. After nearly eight weeks of dust, dysentery and flies, the SAR band plays as the trucks are loaded for a change of station.
COURTESY, MARGARET ATKINSON.

Crossing to Vancouver Island, October 1940. Bound for their new camp near Nanaimo, British Columbia, the prairie boys were entranced with what, for many, was their first sight of the ocean. COURTESY, JACK PORTER.

the SAR into the field to make it or break it and the Regiment had passed the test. When they boarded the trains to leave Dundurn on 1 October 1940, 930 strong, one corporal recorded that the South Albertas "were fit, brown as berries and never again in such good shape."[23]

The Regiment was bound for Nanaimo on Vancouver Island. This movement was part of a plan to shift the various units of the 4th Division, which had been training separately across Canada, into locations where they could continue their work through the winter of 1940-1941. The SAR belonged to 10 Infantry Brigade and at Nanaimo they would join the other two battalions of that formation: the Saskatchewan Light Horse and the British Columbia Regiment.

Although most of the Regiment moved by train from Dundurn on 1 October a smaller separate convoy composed of the personal vehicles of the officers and sergeants made the trip by road. There was no Trans-Canada Highway in 1940 and 17-year-old Private Harry Quarton, assigned to drive his captain's car and wife, remembered that "it was quite an experience … all dirt and mud." Even worse was the fact that the family pet, "the biggest bulldog I ever saw," spent the entire journey on the back window ledge noisily passing gas at frequent intervals and thus making the trip seem much longer than the six days it actually took. It was on this journey that Regimental Quartermaster Sergeant Major "Bull of the Woods" MacTavish, who was already becoming a legend in the SAR, came to grief when he used government funds to repair his personal automobile and a subsequent court martial demoted him to sergeant.[24]

The rest of the Regiment made less troublesome progress. After a brief stopover in Edmonton to allow the men a twenty-four-hour leave, it travelled through the mountains and into Vancouver where the South Albertas marched from the station to the docks and boarded a ferry for the Island; for many of these prairie boys it was their "first sight of the sea."[25] Disem-

barking at Nanaimo, the Regiment then marched two miles to Wakesiah Camp on the slopes of Mount Benson. Wakesiah is an Indian word meaning "beautiful place" and the men in the ranks liked what they saw – "everything was green and moist, there were apples on the trees, the water was trustworthy and the people were friendly."[26] After sun-baked Dundurn, Herbie Watkins remarked, "going to Nanaimo was like going from hell to heaven."[27] As they neared the camp, the South Albertas found the "Dukes," the British Columbia Regiment, "lining both sides of the road as a guard of honour to welcome us."[28] It was the beginning of an association between the two regiments marked by intense rivalry that was to last throughout the war.

Wakesiah Camp was still under construction and, until the SAR could move into huts they could see being built, they were quartered in eight-man bell tents and, later, larger marquee tents. The prairie boys did not mind the tents because everyone knew Nanaimo usually enjoyed mild weather and, after all, anything was better than Dundurn. Unfortunately, Nanaimo also enjoys heavy rainfall and the winter of 1940-1941 was to break all records. The War Diarist noted that the first rain fell exactly one week after the Regiment arrived and he faithfully recorded the daily precipitation for the next two weeks, after which point he simply gave up. The first downpour made a feature of the camp's terrain very obvious – the Regiment's area was in a hollow and run-off from Mount Benson ended in their tent lines. According to Bert Coffin, the Dukes "knew that country and they set their camp up on a little rise; ours was down in a little hole and there were soon three feet of water in that hole."[29] The *Short History* records that the officers got the worst of it because their quarters were at the lower end, and it made the enlisted men "very happy when hearing the water running a foot and a half deep through the officers' quarters during a heavy rain."[30] One night, the downpour was so bad that Coffin saw Lieutenant Harold McBain "sitting on a table with a fishing pole with a line dangling into two feet of water in the officers' mess."[31]

The camp lines were a sea of mud and something had to be done. It was, as Bert Coffin reports: "there was an old mine near Mount Benson" that "had been a coal mine and there was a great huge pile of slag there." "By that time," Bert continues, "we had a few trucks and we kept the men busy hauling stuff and down spreading it over the drill area and we kind of made a paved, or semi-paved, area for regimental parades and drills and so on – as soon as the rain stopped enough for that to happen."[32] In a process reminiscent of an ant hill, the "Cinder Chain Gang" went up to the slag heap, crammed the stuff into gunny sacks and loaded it on the Regiment's two trucks, which transported it to another gang who spread it where required. It was a week-long process.

Heating in the tents was provided by coal oil stoves donated by civilians after the Regiment made a public appeal. Harry Quarton in QM stores had the job of picking these stoves up and he describes them as "the dirtiest damned things, if they didn't operate properly, you would find your clothes all covered with black soot."[33] Lieutenant Glen McDougall agreed – many mornings he awoke at Wakesiah "covered all over with black fur."[34] The question in everybody's mind was how long it would take to finish the hutted accommodation which they watched being built beside the tent lines. The civilian workmen constructing the new camp appeared to move in slow motion and the newspapers voiced concern that the men at Wakesiah were forced to live under "deplorable conditions."[35] Private Albert Ball (like many other South Albertas) was convinced that "those buggers were under contract not to drive more than eight nails an hour."[36]

There was another problem about Wakesiah Camp – the food was terrible. It wasn't that the Canadian army was unconcerned about properly feeding its men – "Variety," stated one official manual, "is one of the keynotes of success in catering," and "a wide selection of dishes should be the aim of everyone responsible for maintaining a high standard of messing."[37] The basic ingredients of army food were fine, the problem was the way the cooks mixed them together and presented them at meal times. Take, for example, boiled mutton – that standard Second World War dish which all Canadian veterans will remember. Soon after breakfast at 0800 the regimental cooks assembled 650 lb. of mutton, 30 lb. of carrots, 30 lb. of onions, 5 gallons of Caper sauce and 40 ounces of salt in a series of large vats and boiled the mixture for about three hours before serving it at noon along with potatoes (mashed, boiled or jacketed), and followed it with one of a number of tasty desserts such as lemon curd tarts, date pudding, stewed (boiled into mush) prunes and rice, or stewed apricots and junket.[38]

Rather than face this, some men subsisted on bread alone or, like Private Adrian Berry and his friends, went to the "Lunchbox Cafe" in Nanaimo to "eat salads because we craved

them."[39] Matters came to a head one night in the mess hall at Nanaimo when Ev Nieman and Sid Arrowsmith led a protest over the quality of the food. It started in their platoon but "spread like wildfire through the whole mess hall," recalls John Galipeau, as the men "turned all the serving dishes upside down on the table, started throwing food around, and refused to leave until we were assured that improvements would be made."[40] The food eventually got better but both Nieman and Arrowsmith were warned that "if we had been in [service for] six months, we would have been put in the cells."[41]

As soon as the SAR had finished with the slag heap they resumed training. Much of this had to be done under canvas because of the rain, and the emphasis was on stripping the rifle and Lewis light machine gun. By now the Regiment had almost a full complement of the standard service rifle, the SMLE (Short Magazine Lee Enfield, known as the "Smelly"), but only a few obsolete Lewis guns. Things were looking up, however, as there were a couple of modern Bren light machine guns in camp and, "if you knew the right people and how to go about it, you could have a look at one."[42] The Bren was "regarded as much too complicated to be handled by anyone" but there was no sign of the other weapons and equipment authorized for an infantry battalion, including mortars, submachine guns and wireless sets, although the SAR did receive two 30 cwt. trucks in October.

For variety the training syllabus introduced the horrors of

Heaven, they're in heaven. Wakesiah Camp near Nanaimo, British Columbia. Verdant foliage, good water, mild climate and at least twenty beer joints within striking distance, the South Albertas rejoiced at their first sight of the new station. COURTESY, TED TALBOT.

Rain, rain, rain. Within a week of their arrival, it began to rain at Nanaimo and the downpour was unrelenting for almost three months. Wakesiah became a swamp as the water streamed down nearby Mount Benson and ended in the South Albertas' tent lines.
COURTESY, ALF BALL.

the gas hut, where the men tested the fit of their gas masks and those whose masks failed the test spent long minutes afterwards wheezing, sneezing and coughing a light dose of tear gas out of their respiratory systems. The Regiment also began bayonet practice, at first using the training stick and then graduating to the actual weapon. Hour after hour, they ran at a straw-stuffed sack suspended from a scaffold, made a quick thrust into it followed by another thrust into a second sack placed on the ground "until the procedure was automatic."[43] These were the skills needed for the war their fathers had fought on the Western Front, and this was natural enough because, as Jim Nicholson says, most "of our officers and Senior NCO's were World War I vets and most of our training as infantry followed the methods of the 1914-1918 War – a war they had won."[44] A First War vintage assault course with a trench system was constructed on the slope of Mount Benson and the SAR "went over the top" more than a few times that winter. The Regiment's practice was to make these charges in silence as it was believed that "a line of men with bayonets fixed bearing down on them in silence out of the dawn mists would have a much greater psychological impact on the enemy than screaming and yelling."[45]

Camp life at Wakesiah was usually wet and often miserable but spirits remained high. This was particularly true of Sergeant Jimmy Tennent's band which, being excused fatigues and route marches, attracted an intelligent class of recruit and was full of talented, mischievous young men who often caught the eye of RSM Seal. The buglers of the band were responsible for regulating the camp routine at Wakesiah. Each daily duty or event had its own bugle call, most of which had been handed down from the British army, and along with the music came the little rhymes that British buglers traditionally recited to memorize the calls they had to know by heart. As there were three regiments in camp the buglers of each unit preceded each announcement with a regimental "signature." For the South Albertas, this went "S-A-R, S-A-R, answer this call!" which

alerted the men to listen for the call that followed and the order it communicated. As the bugler sounded the call, he usually recited the ditty in his mind to help him keep the proper rhythm and these little rhymes became engraved in their memories. Bugler Childs can still recite them:

Each day began with "Rouse": "I bought a horse, I bought a cow; I bought a donkey, I sold the horse, I sold the cow, I kept the donkey, and then, the son of a bitch, he died."

Breakfast call next: "Oh come to the cookhouse door, boys, come to the cookhouse door!"

And throughout the day we also allowed sergeants and officers to partake of meals. Sergeants were called by "Green gravel, green gravel, green gravel for breakfast, green gravel, green gravel, green gravel, I say." And officers mess call: "Oh, officers wives eat pudding and pies, and privates' wives eat skilly."

A bit later, sick call: "Sick parade, sick parade, he'll never be sick no more, the poor bugger is dead." …

Later in the morning, there was mail call: "Letter from Lousy Lizzie, letter from Sister Sue."

When a detail such as Guard Duty was sounded, we called: "Come and do a picket, boys, come and do a guard; t'isn't very easy boys, t'isn't very hard."[46]

Although conditions in camp were far from ideal, Nanaimo offered many compensations. The skating rink and bowling alley were popular hang-outs as were the movie theatres. There were also a number of dance halls although those boys who wanted to emulate Fred Astaire were somewhat hampered because they had only their army boots – the cause of much female complaint. For the more adventurous there were, by

A pleasant change in weather. Sometimes, just for a change, it snowed, which was a relief to prairie boys. The Regiment spent the winter of 1940-1941 under canvas waiting for civilian workmen to finish their permanent accommodations but, like most government construction projects, the work progressed with glacial velocity.
COURTESY, ALF BALL.

Regimental consensus, between twenty and twenty-five beer parlours within striking distance of the camp and it became a challenge on pay day to have a beer in each establishment but, as one veteran sadly records, "We never quite made it."[47] If the men were too young to be served in the beer parlours there was always the Eagles Club, which was not so strict, and many an under-age SAR had his first experience with alcohol at the Eagles and paid for it by hanging green-faced out the window of the bus taking him back to camp. The Queen's Hotel in Nanaimo was another place the SAR frequented, and it was there one night that CSM Fergie Fraser of A Company and the newly-demoted Sergeant Bull McTavish started a fight with the Saskatchewan Horse that ultimately engulfed the whole bar and only ended with arrival of the provosts in strength.

The rivalry between the three units in the brigade was carried over into athletics and it was at Nanaimo the Regiment founded its famous sports tradition. The sergeant majors got the ball rolling as men like Fraser, Lawson, Mackenzie, Patterson and, of course, MacTavish began to promote sports activities. CSM Fergie Fraser had run a boxing club in Medicine Hat before the war and a number of his fighters serving in the Regiment formed the nucleus of a regimental boxing team that included Emery "Buster" Ely, "Fergie" Shank, Albert Atkinson, Ev Nieman, Joe Main, "Rocky" Wagner, Sammy Samuels and Gordie Frizzell. In March 1941 the Regimental boxers won the West Coast service championship against an RCN team, and the band and much of the unit was there to greet them when they got off the ferry at Nanaimo late at night proudly clutching their trophy.[48]

But the big sport over the winter of 1940-1941 was hockey, and under the coaching of Quartermaster Captain Walter Hunter the SAR put an excellent team on the ice which included, among others, Alf Ball, Danny McLeod, Kenny Perrin, Bobby Crawford, Archie Naismith, Boney Rathwell and Hal Cook anchored by the stalwart goalkeeping of Eugene "Yudge" Beaudry. The entire battalion paraded to the Nanaimo arena on 24 November to watch the team play their first game and beat Port Alberni 3-1. Thereafter, the War Diarist, having given up on the weather, carefully recorded the team's progress: a 3-1 loss to the Dukes on 4 December, a 10-2 win against Port Alberni on 12 December and a 2-1 win against Nanaimo on 18 December. Then came the fateful game on 8 January 1941 when the War Diarist cryptically notes that not only did the BCR beat the SAR 8-2 but "Cpl. McLeod suffered a fractured leg."[49] Danny McLeod never forgot that night: "I got into a fight at centre ice and I got a lucky punch in and the guy went down but the next thing I know, a whole crowd piled on me and my leg was broken."[50] It was a serious fracture and, after four months in the hospital, "when they finally took all the parts out of my foot, my ankle literally squeaked." Things went downhill after that and in their last game, played on 19 February 1941, the SAR lost 7-1 to Victoria.[51]

Besides rain, Nanaimo holds a place in SAR mythology because of the beauty of its women. As many as twenty members of the Regiment married Nanaimo girls during the seven and a half months the SAR spent on the West Coast, and many engagements were made that resulted in marriage after the unit had left for other stations. It might be thought unusual that a group of young men about to go to war would even contemplate committing matrimony but actually the reverse was quite true. In a time when males were expected to be the breadwinners the economic circumstances of the 1930s had caused many young men to postpone marriage until they had steady employment and that was a rare thing in the Depression. The army provided free bed and board and a regular wage, most of which could be made over to a wife, and it was a financial inducement that many could not resist. The argument in the barracks ran along the line "whether it was better not to get married because your wife might be left a widow, or to get married and then at least you would have had that time together."[52] There was also the consideration that, if the worst happened, the government would provide financial assistance to the widow and any children. Although the future was uncertain, the inducements to marry were better in the army than in civilian life, and the result was that the SAR began a steady parade to the altar.

This trend started early. Stan and Chris Rose of Redcliff tied the knot while the SAR was at Dundurn and Chris, like many of the other young women who married into the Regiment, followed her husband from station to station in Canada. Chris and Stan didn't have much money: "I got $65 a month [wife's allotment] and that's when you learned to make your money go around" and they "allowed us discounts on the trains but we couldn't afford to get berths and we would just sit up."[53] Like their men, the wives had their own unit spirit: "us girls always stuck together and got rooms wherever we could together and had lots of good times, lots of laughs and lots of cries."

On "joining" the SAR, the regimental wives came under command of Mrs. Colonel Carvosso who opened the SAR Women's Auxiliary Hostess House in Nanaimo three weeks after the unit moved to the west coast. According to Chris, "we were a lot of soft kids, mostly, and the colonel's wife ran us like the colonel ran the army. We served coffee, soft drinks and doughnuts."[54] Throughout the winter the Women's Auxiliary organized a number of social events at their club. Colonel Carvosso was usually in attendance and sometimes this could be embarrassing – Chris remembered "some formal do put on in Nanaimo" when the girls "all wore our wedding gowns because they were the only good dresses we had." There was a call that "the next dance was a ladies' choice" and Chris "got up to walk over and get Stan for the dance and who should stop me but Col. Carvosso." She was mortified "because I thought that everyone would think that I asked the colonel to dance with me!"[55]

Old Steelhead, however, proved a true gallant on another occasion involving an SAR bride. Margaret Atkinson of Saskatoon arrived at Nanaimo in January 1941 to be married to her fiancé, Private Albert Atkinson. When the ferry docked, Margaret remembered, "there stood my love, my husband-to-be and five other SAR soldiers – and a sweet, tiny, grey-haired lady – Mrs. Carvosso – who was very British." Mrs. Colonel Carvosso had found the new bride a room in a private home and Margaret, "from a protective railway family," was confident that she "was fully capable to become a wife" as she had "been an excellent cook since age ten, could scrub on a washboard, saw wood, fill coal-oil lamps, etc., knew all a good woman ought to – except the 'personal' side of marriage."

For the three weeks until the wedding, Margaret helped out at the Hostess House in Nanaimo, but one day while the colonel's wife was away "to pack woolen blankets for overseas" a handsome older soldier came in wearing South Alberta badges. Margaret, who knew nothing about military insignia, began to chat with him and in the course of their conversation she confessed her anxiety that because the "colonel is a real tough guy," he might not give Albert a decent marriage leave:

"But I hope we get to have a bit of a honeymoon! Isn't that the decent thing?"

"Yes," he replied, "I do believe it's so! How long would you think?" he asked.

"Oh," I replied, "at least two days … if it's possible only. I'd not make a fuss if we can't, I was thinking maybe that the colonel might be strict – to show them that what he says – goes!"

He started laughing so hard that he wiped his eyes with his handkerchief. "Now, dear, I must go," he said. "I sure hope you get a honeymoon."

On the day of the wedding, Mrs. Carvosso sent a taxi for Margaret and, when they arrived at the church, "patted my veil and wedding bouquet with a gold and black [the SAR colours] bow and all." It was Valentine's Day, 1941 and at the vestibule of the church stood "the older soldier I had talked to at the Hostess House." Margaret was delighted to learn that he was giving her away and "took his arm proudly to walk down the aisle, but when Albert turned around at the altar to look at me, he went white." Private Atkinson had reason to turn pale for the "handsome older soldier" coming down the aisle to give his young bride away was none other than "Old Steelhead" himself. But, as Margaret triumphantly concluded, it all ended well – "Albert got four days leave!"[56]

The Regiment had only suffered six weeks of rain at Nanaimo when training was interrupted by the extensive leave granted for Christmas. On 9 December 1940, 369 men proceeded to their homes on a twenty-day furlough, and when they returned on 27 December, 323 more left, not returning until mid-January. Besides the chance to see their families and loved ones, this holiday furlough provided some relief from the

Private Albert and Margaret Atkinson. Wedding photo, February 1941. COURTESY, MARGARET ATKINSON.

incessant downpour in Nanaimo. Private Bob Clipperton had no regrets about going "back to the prairie where it was deep snow and thirty below because it sure beat the rain."[57] At home, the war news was better than it had been for some time. The *Luftwaffe* was still hitting London and other British cities at night, but in North Africa General Archibald Wavell's tiny army of 35,000 had gone on the offensive in early December against an Italian force six times its size and had rolled Mussolini's soldiers back across North Africa. It was Britain's first successful offensive of the war and everybody was thrilled.

Active training resumed in mid-January 1941 when the second leave contingent returned to Nanaimo. As the rain was still falling, it was much the same work as the previous year but the Regiment now received the Bren guns they had been anticipating for months. According to the newly-promoted Lance Corporal John Galipeau, however, they "did not fire them but practised stripping them wearing blindfolds."[58]

In February and March when the weather improved somewhat, the training emphasis shifted to field craft and the route marches began again to such locations as Shark's Crossing, Cassidy, Baker's Farm and Lantzville. Although he was less prominent at Nanaimo than he had been at Dundurn, possibly because of declining health, Carvosso always knew where every company was and what it was supposed to be doing at any time during the day or night. He was also full of surprises – Sergeant Jim Gove remembered the Regiment coming back into camp late one night, tired after a thirty-six-mile route march, when they "were ordered to slope arms" and "suddenly the band broke loose – Carvosso had brought the band out at 1130 at night and we marched the last mile or two into camp with band blaring." "My god," he recalled, "we were all rejuvenated, arms swinging up and down. That's the sort of thing that made the SAR.[59]

Everybody in the rifle companies had great fun when, as part of a war bond and recruiting demonstration, they carried out an exercise in downtown Nanaimo on 12 February which involved two companies from the SAR and two from the Dukes defending the town while the remaining companies of both regiments attacked it. Every week or ten days, a night exercise was held and on 8 March 1941 the Regiment made a memorable twenty-two-mile march to Lantzville, starting at 0200 in the morning and returning at noon. A new subject on the training syllabus in early 1941 was field engineering as the rifle companies learned to erect and demolish roadblocks, dig trenches and mine roads. In late March and early April, the companies moved, in turn, to Heal's Range to carry out qualifications in the rifle and Bren, usually under downpours of rain. All this training was very intensive but it was largely at the company and not the battalion level. At Nanaimo,

South Alberta track and field team, Nanaimo, 1941. Although it got off to a slow start the South Alberta Regiment carved out a legendary record of athletic success in the wartime Canadian army. The high point was winning the army heavyweight boxing title in 1944 and 1945. COURTESY, MARGARET ATKINSON.

according to Bert Coffin, the "only time you saw the battalion moving as a unit was on a regimental parade, there was no battalion training at this time."[60]

There were also problems in the officers' mess as relations between Carvosso and his junior officers had become strained. Part of a regimental commander's job is to assess and promote those junior officers who are worthy but, in the opinion of Coffin and others, Carvosso "would not promote any officers within the regiment … because he had no respect for or confidence in his junior officers."[61] The old veteran, however, worshipped the enlisted men and would commission officers from the ranks. On 8 March 1941, the SAR for the first time "grew its own" when six young sergeants, Bob Donaldson, Hugh Clarke, Alex McKenzie, Alec Laing, Jay Moreton and Kenny Perrin were commissioned as second lieutenants. According to Jay Moreton the ceremony was pretty perfunctory: "Carvosso called us in, the six of us, one by one, into his office and threw two pips on his desk" and said, "You're now a gentleman and an officer … don't go back to the sergeants' mess unless the sergeants invite you."[62] Growing their own was to become an SAR tradition and all six new lieutenants would see action with the Regiment.

But Carvosso still resisted promoting prewar militia officers who deserved it, preferring instead to rely on the First War veterans who occupied most of the senior positions. Throughout the winter of 1940-1941, relations between the colonel and his lieutenants and captains began to deteriorate. In such a contest, junior officers cannot

win, so they bit their tongues and on one occasion, as Glen McDougall fondly reminisced, they had to do so to keep from laughing. The officers were out on a TEWT on Sunday morning and there "were a lot of seagulls out there and one of them dive bombed Carvosso on his nose to the delight of the officers, who couldn't show it."[63] There were no problems between the junior officers and RSM Seal, who, according to Glen, was "respectful in a vengeful sort of way," which is a nice turn of phrase to sum up the traditional attitude of senior warrant officers to very junior lieutenants.[64]

The tension came to a head in January 1941 when Carvosso removed Captain Arnold Lavoie as adjutant, gave him a bad fitness report, and sent him to the staff of Military District No. 5 in Quebec on the grounds that he could be more useful there. Unfortunately, no one noted that, despite his surname, Lavoie could not speak French and he was soon posted back to the Regiment. This came to the attention of the commander of 10 Infantry Brigade, Brigadier J.B. Stevenson, who overturned Lavoie's adverse report and recommended him for promotion. Stevenson was aware of the "internal troubles" in the SAR and it was his belief that the Regiment suffered from a "lack of patient guidance which has proven so necessary to initiate the citizen soldier into army procedure."[65] He came to the conclusion that Carvosso would have to be replaced.

In late February Major William P. Bristowe arrived at Wakesiah Camp to assume the duties of second-in-command of the Regiment. A few days later he walked into the officers' mess tent wearing his uniform and a pair of Indian moccasins – he was promptly dubbed "Buffalo Bill" and the name stuck. It was clear to everyone that Bristowe was there to take over the

Route march, spring 1941. B Company takes a break and CSM Larry Blain standing in front of the telephone pole keeps an eagle eye on No. 12 Platoon (the Pee Wees), located close to the camera, lest they break loose. They are wearing their fatigue sweaters and mustard trousers. Although the Regiment had received battle dress by this time, it was reserved for more formal occasions. COURTESY, JOHN GALIPEAU.

No. 4 Platoon, HQ Company, Nanaimo, March 1941. This was the carrier platoon of the Regiment but it had not yet received any vehicles. Sergeant Lyle Piepgrass (middle row, third from left) was commissioned in the Regiment in 1943 and badly wounded at Bergen op Zoom in October 1944. Private Neil McPherson (back row, on right) became a Recce Troop crew commander while Private Doug Prenevost (back row, fourth from right) won the French Croix de Guerre as a sergeant in Normandy in August 1944. COURTESY, JACK PORTER.

Regiment and his time came on 21 March when "Pinky" Carvosso left on leave pending a medical discharge from the army. Those who served under the old war horse during the first eight months of the Regiment's existence respect him as a man who did a difficult job the best way he could and his mark remained on the SAR throughout the war.

William Bristowe was a former officer in the British army who had graduated from the Royal Military College at Sandhurst in the fateful year of 1914. After seeing much action on the Western Front, he had reached the rank of acting lieutenant-colonel by 1918. Following the war Bristowe spent two years in the Royal Tank Corps but left the service in 1922 and came to Canada, where he was employed as a mining engineer in the Okanagan Valley. In July 1940 at the age of 44 he joined the Canadian army as a reserve officer and served as an instructor and later as second-in-command of the training centre at Vernon, BC, before coming to the SAR. "Buffalo Bill" was, Glen McDougall reports, a "jovial gentleman and everyone got along with him extremely well."[66]

The same day Carvosso left the Regiment, the South Albertas finally moved into their new hutted quarters after five and a half months under canvas. By now, they were hardened to the weather and were looking smart as the Regiment was beginning to enjoy the first fruits of Canadian war production. Gone were the mustard suits and the awful fatigue uniforms; all ranks now had serge battle dress, wedge caps with their provincial crest badge, regulation pattern web, canvas anklets and, when "walking out," the distinctive black and yellow South Alberta lanyard strung under the left shoulder strap. A sad note at this time was that the Regiment lost its second member on active service when Private Jake Seidler died from peritonitis in Nanaimo General Hospital.[67]

The South Albertas figured they were ready and they were

keen to get overseas because the recent war news had not been good. Following their initial successes in North Africa, the British had been rolled back by the unexpected arrival of a German expeditionary force under the command of a photogenic young general named Erwin Rommel. Still worse, Hitler had come to the aid of the Italians in Greece during the spring and the *Wehrmacht* had overrun that country in a few weeks, despite the efforts of a British expeditionary force which was forced to withdraw to Crete. In May German airborne forces landed on Crete and, after heavy fighting, the Royal Navy evacuated the British forces under heavy air attack.

Many men had left since the unit had been formed in Edmonton. Army standards were so high at this time that any man who did not "cut it" for medical, personal or any other reason was immediately released. Most wanted to stay: Bob Clipperton had enlisted three years under age at 16 but and had hung in through Edmonton, Dundurn and the worst of Nanaimo. "On 1 February 1941," he recorded, "my bubble burst" when RSM Seal "came to the tent and took me in before the colonel" who "advised me that I was being discharged from the army under Routine Order No. 37 – under age." Within hours, Clipperton had turned in his kit, been outfitted with civilian clothes and furnished with a railway ticket to his home in Edmonton.[68] In early May there was a widespread purge of the Regiment and ninety-eight men were posted out, mainly for minor medical reasons such as flat feet, to a new company that was tactfully designated the "disposal company."[69]

By this time the latrines were buzzing with rumours as the unspecified "they" said the SAR would shortly be moving east. For once the rumours were true and an advance party left Wakesiah Camp on 11 May for Niagara-on-the-Lake, Ontario, the Regiment's new station. Everyone was excited about the impending move when two days later the SAR was inspected by the GOC Pacific and looked good on parade despite a stray white dog who tried to join the march past.

On 14 May 1941, preceded by its band and accompanied by small boys on bicycles and the odd rambling mutt, the South Alberta Regiment marched out of Wakesiah Camp for the last time. As the head of the column entered Nanaimo about noon, the town turned out three deep to line the route and cheer a unit it had taken to its hearts. Shortening step to move down the steep street to the ferry docks, the band broke into Vera Lynn's recent hit, "Wish Me Luck as You Wave Me Good Bye," and many did, as the Regiment had acquired wives, sweethearts and friends in this British Columbia town. Under the watchful eye of RSM Seal and the NCOs the men boarded the *Princess Elizabeth* in an orderly fashion and as the South Alberta motion picture camera, a new acquisition, recorded the scene, the *Elizabeth* cast off from the old wooden dock, and Nanaimo's houses and soft mountain backdrop receded in the distance.[70]

At Vancouver, the Regiment boarded two trains and spent a day going through the Rockies. On 16 May, a Friday, one train pulled into Edmonton, the other into Calgary and the men got off to enjoy a forty-eight-hour leave. The Medicine Hat boys "made a very favourable impression" in their home town as, "individually or collectively, they were spick and span, walked with a zip in their eye, and generally boosted the stock of the unit fifty per cent."[71] The men reported back to their

trains on Sunday night and not a single man was late nor was there anyone missing, something that was regarded as "a remarkable feat" in 1941.[72] The trains then proceeded on their way with a small band of recruits they had picked up in Calgary, among them Private Chuck Fearn, who was immediately put to work learning how to strip a rifle. There were sing-songs and stories en route and brief stops in Melville, Saskatchewan, and Winnipeg for quick one-hour route marches to get the "blood moving." Then it was on down through northern Ontario to Niagara-on-the-Lake, where the first train arrived in the morning of 19 May to be met by a crowd, the band of the Dufferin and Haldimand Rifles, and the ubiquitous small boys with bicycles and wagons. The Rifles were in shirt sleeves and shorts, for even in May the Niagara area is humid and the men were sweating as they marched under lush green foliage to their barracks.[73]

Along with the other two regiments of 10 Brigade, the SAR had a job to do in Ontario. They were there to guard thirty-two separate locations among the extensive hydroelectric power installations near Niagara Falls and along the Welland Canal against sabotage. The theory was that one of the three regiments in the brigade would train at Niagara Camp near Niagara-on-the-Lake, while the other two would be on guard, and each month there would be a three-way switch. The Regiment commenced its first shift on guard on 24 May when it moved to Chippawa Barracks. Each rifle company did a nine-day tour of sentry duty followed by three days' leave. At the guard posts the men did either three hours on guard and six off

But the band kept playing. Proudly led by Sergeant Jimmy Tennent's bugle band, the South Albertas march through Nanaimo in April 1941 after being granted the freedom of the city. COURTESY, JACK PORTER.

We Stand on Guard for Thee. Private Albert Atkinson guards the Welland Canal from Nazi saboteurs during the summer of 1941. When they first took over this post, sentries were under orders to fire at suspicious floating objects, an order that was quickly countermanded after bored South Albertas opened up a furious fire on anything they could see. COURTESY, MARGARET ATKINSON.

or four on and four off – Adrian Berry recalls that he "never got enough sleep."[74]

Many of the "vulnerable points" were protected by double apron wire fences with a complicated system of infra-red beams to "assist the vigilant sentry." But, as the *Short History* comments, this new technology still had some bugs in it as "any small object such as waving grass, fog or even skunks would cause them to operate the alarm system" and this "at first caused a good deal of alarm and despondency among the guardians of democracy but later on they were merely referred to as 'them G.D. beams working again.'"[75] Private James Sigouin at Post 37 called out his company under arms one night only to find that a cow had strayed onto his beat. The men were issued live ammunition and were instructed to use it if necessary, and often, particularly in their first few weeks, they did. Skunks were the most unwelcome threat to security and, accordingly, suffered a high casualty rate – Private Lynn Cannady entered regimental legend when, passing the long-deceased body of one of these striped unfortunates, he remarked, "Look, another dead corporal."[76] One officer reports that the canal was a hot spot:

> They thought it quite possible that someone would chuck a bomb in the canal and it would blow up a power station. Our job was to watch the canal and the instructions were to use live ammunition and to fire at any unidentified object floating down the canal. Well, you give a bunch of prairie farmers a rifle and live ammunition and a free hand to use them and it soon sounded like a war was starting. In future, we gave orders that, if the sentry saw anything, he was to call the officer of the guard and he gave the okay to open fire.[77]

While on guard duty, the various platoons were broken down further into sections to man the smaller posts. This provided an opportunity for a section commanded by a corporal "to live on its own, do its own cooking, its own sentry beat," remembered Danny McLeod. It also provided a chance for some fun. Danny was making his rounds one night, fully accoutred and carrying his rifle, when Sid Arrowsmith reached down from a tree with one hand, grabbed one of his web straps and lifted him, startled and kicking, clear off the ground.[78]

The posts around the Falls itself were popular because the men could talk to civilians, particularly young and pretty civilians. The United States was not at war at this time and there were thousands of American tourists wandering through Victoria Park near the Falls, who, with the amiable ignorance that is the hallmark of their nation, would ask the most amazing questions and get even more amazing answers: "Tourist: 'Say, what are you fellows guarding anyway?' SAR sentry: 'We're not guarding anything, we're just here to turn the falls off after everyone goes home'" and so on. Another popular beat was Post 46 near the offices of the Ontario Hydro Corporation, which employed a great number of female clerical staff. As the boys were convinced that Nazi saboteurs would assume clever disguises, they were on the alert and certain to ask any reasonably attractive young stenographer to produce her pass (which contained the important details of name, address and telephone number) before she was allowed to enter the building. It wasn't long before the girls learned to present their identification with thumbs held over the sought-after information.[79]

Although they got tired of pounding their beats (girls and tourists excluded), the SAR remember Niagara as one of their best stations because it offered great off-duty activities. Toronto was only a few hours distant along the newly-constructed Queen Elizabeth Way, Canada's first "super highway," and motorists always picked up hitchhikers who were in uniform. Private Bob Rasmussen was a bit shaken while thumbing back to camp one night when "Colonel Bristowe stopped to pick me up and told me I was out a little late" but said "we'll get you through the gates so nobody will bother you – I thought he was a hell of a good guy."[80] Toronto offered baseball games and just about everything else, but closer to home there was the weekly YMCA dance in Niagara Falls, dances on the dock at Port Dalhousie and the amusement park at Crystal Beach near Fort Erie with rides, games and a dance hall where the band could do a reasonable facsimile of Glenn Miller's new hit, "Chattanooga Choo-Choo." In Niagara Falls there were the Empire and Brock hotels and Ma Prest's famous tea house. Peacetime America was just across the river and the boys could always "shuffle off to Buffalo." So close was the republic that, when the SAR duty bugler sounded "Last Post" at Niagara camp, the American duty bugler at Lewiston on the other side of the Niagara River would respectfully wait for a few seconds after it ended before sounding "Taps," his own end-of-day call.[81] If you didn't have any money, you could pitch horseshoes, play baseball or volleyball in the camp, try to steal fruit from the abundant nearby orchards or go for a swim in Lake Ontario, which never seemed to get warm.

Most of the regimental wives came down to Ontario. Margaret Atkinson rented a room in the household of a large Italian family and, used to western friendliness, she at first found the folks in Ontario "a bit reserved," but she soon warmed them up by "showing pictures of my uncle's ranch and singing cowboy songs with Albert who could yodel like Wilf Carter" and "commenting on their flowers and trees which so amazed me I could never keep quiet." Money was tight so "in the evenings Albert was off duty, we would sit in a corner cafe and nurse a coke." There was a nickel slot machine near their favourite booth and it was not long before Margaret noticed that every third try was usually a winner. She promptly took up gambling: "I would put my nickel in after someone had tried it twice and Albert would take his cap and hold it under and every time I made enough for a show and pop corn."[82]

The Regiment spent seven months on guard duty at Niagara and acquired a bad case of what Lieutenant Glen McDougall called *Canalosis guardomania*. It was all great fun but it wasn't what they had enlisted for and the unit's collective training suffered badly. Between July and December 1941, Bristowe was forced to report that his unit had completed only 10% of its battalion training. Things were better at the company and platoon level as by November he reported that the SAR had accomplished 60% of the former and 75% of the latter. Bad as this sounds, the SAR was no better or worse than any other unit in the British or Canadian armies; even the official historian admits that "apart from the few divisions actually in contact with the enemy, there were in 1941 no troops in the Commonwealth properly trained as training was understood at a later period of the war."[83]

Lieutenant Bert Coffin remembers the Regiment's state of readiness in the summer of 1941:

When we left Nanaimo we were, at the best, at company level; we had no battalion training, we had not reached battalion level by that point. At Niagara we had a job to do guarding the canal and we had one tour of three down at Niagara-on-the-Lake which was supposed to be the training

area but the facilities were limited. But the guard duty was a great thing for *esprit de corps* among the sub-units because they were out there living together, doing their own cooking, running their own show and that was good training that developed the junior NCOs.

We did some useful things down there. All the junior officers had a smartening-up course and some of the senior officers attended staff courses. We also sent a lot of men on mechanical courses for vehicles and carriers. The other ranks got a bit of weapons training at the ranges and we had a carrier school which Dick Lumsden ran but, all in all, Niagara was basically a pretty pleasant sort of thing.[84]

One positive aspect of the Niagara period was that the Regiment at last began to receive modern equipment and weapons. The long-awaited Bren guns, Thompson submachine guns and Boys anti-tank rifles were issued and the transport section boasted twelve assorted trucks and a few motorcycles. The big news was the arrival on 25 June of the first carriers, fully-tracked and lightly-armoured vehicles armed with a Bren gun that provided an infantry battalion with both firepower and mobility. They were tricky vehicles to operate and prone to tipping on steep slopes but the SAR were delighted with them. Soon columns of these little vehicles were raising dust throughout the peninsula as the men of the SAR, BCR and Saskatchewan Light Horse learned how to drive them.

Lieutenant Dick Robinson of the SAR supervised carrier training throughout July and August and it was his claim that "it took at least a week's instruction before anyone could even drive a carrier down the street." This assertion was totally disproved during a regimental "smoker" held in the mess hall on the evening of 9 August when Bandsman Gilbert Johnson and a friend "took a pitcher of beer and went outside as it was warm in the building." One of the new carriers was parked behind the building and the two "decided to sit in it while we drank our beer." What happened next entered South Alberta legend:

I sat down in the driver's seat, my elbow hit the starter button and I said "Hey, it's alive" or something like that. Then I found the switch, started the engine and we tore out of camp

Barracks, Niagara, 1941. This empty canning factory was used as temporary barracks accommodation by the Regiment during the summer and autumn of 1941. Note the ping-pong table in the foreground.

COURTESY, JACK PORTER.

Ready for trouble. Armed and equipped for any eventuality, Private Fred Plahn protects the falls of Niagara, 1941. The United States was not at war at this time and curious American tourists used to ask the South Albertas what they were guarding. The stock reply was that they were not guarding anything; they were simply there to turn the falls off at night. COURTESY FRED PLAHN.

headed for Toronto or some place. A posse ran us down, captured the AFV and crew intact; the regiment's first capture of war booty and PWs. I got 14 days close arrest and an offer from Lieutenant Robinson, the carrier platoon officer, to join his platoon but the band sergeant refused.[85]

There were enough new recruits at Niagara to form a re-inforcement company which was put to learning the basics under the eye of, at first, RSM Seal, and later CSM Fred Bullen. The Reinforcement Company did more route marching that summer than the rest of the Regiment and even picked up a local boy. Reg Maves, a 16-year-old from Niagara Falls, was talked into joining by one of Lance-Corporal Galipeau's buddies, who saw nothing wrong with that because he was only sixteen himself. Reg lied about his age, passed his medical, signed on the dotted line and was taken on strength on 7 July. Galipeau's platoon "took him under our wing, befriending him so that he had someone who knew the ropes to lean on and learn from."[86] Reg joined the Reinforcement Company as they negotiated the niceties of the assault course and the intricacies of close order drill. He was an enthusiastic soldier but it all came to an end "the day he went home on leave proud as heck to be in uniform and told his mother he couldn't get out." Mrs. Maves was having none of it. She made an official complaint that the Regiment had enlisted an under-age boy and a disconsolate Reg was struck off strength.[87]

From May to August 1941 the War Diarist recorded the dreary cycle between the camps at Chippawa, Niagara and Allenburg, the occasional War Bond Parade in Welland or St. Catharines, inspections by senior officers, the recruit company's progress, days on the rifle range, swimming parades, sports events, officers and men posted on courses all around Ontario and, of course, the weather. During one twelve-day period between 28 July and 9 August 1941 the uniform comment on the weather was "hot and sticky" – on most of the other days it was just plain "hot." Like many other westerners, Bert Coffin was not used to the intense humidity of an Ontario summer and recollected that "I've never been so hot in my life, it was stinking hot, and we were doing drill in battledress and gas masks."[88] Going for a swim was a popular off-duty occupation but unfortunately two men lost their lives in swimming-related accidents. On 20 June, Private Frank Mullan from Russylvia, Alberta, drowned in the pond at DeCew's Falls near Allenburg and, ten days later, Private Stanley Milan from St. Paul died after hitting his head when diving in the pool at the Cyanamid plant in Niagara Falls.[89]

The summer of 1941 thus dragged slowly by in a seemingly endless whirl of nine days on, three off, a constant change of posts and perpetual sticky heat. There is one major event that stands out in most veterans' reminiscences of that period and that was the creation of the 10 Brigade composite company to perform at the Canadian National Exhibition in Toronto. Made up of picked men chosen from the SAR, the Dukes and the 16/22nd Horse, this company was issued new uniforms and trained for three intensive days by RSM Chris Seal, the best drillmaster in the brigade, before boarding the ferry at Queenston for Toronto on 18 August. For two weeks it performed a Royal Guard for the governor-general and guards of honour around the city, marched in parades, gave demonstrations at the many recruiting tents set up at the "Ex" and performed twice daily at the grandstand show along with Tommy Dorsey and his orchestra, who, rather unfairly, got higher billing. The SAR band accompanied them and any SAR soldier who was lucky enough to go on this hectic but pleasant duty remembers it with great fondness.[90]

Main guard, Niagara, 1941. For nearly eight months the Regiment rotated through a series of guard posts in the Niagara area. During this time their collective training suffered but their off-duty life improved tremendously. COURTESY, JACK PORTER.

In September the rumour mills began to crank up as the unspecified "they" said the Regiment was going to either Jamaica or Hong Kong. This caused great excitement as the South Albertas were anxious to get overseas and there was little doubt in anyone's mind that they would be chosen – as one veteran says, "We were convinced that we were the best so we would get one or the other."[91] As it turned out the Argyll and Sutherland Highlanders went to Jamaica, the Winnipeg Grenadiers and Royal Rifles of Canada to Hong Kong and the South Albertas went back on guard. It was just as well because the two battalions sent to the East were captured when Hong Kong fell and spent three and a half years in Japanese prison camps. One quarter of them never returned to Canada.[92]

By late autumn the South Albertas were beginning to get restless. The 3rd Division went overseas in November, followed a few weeks later by an entirely new formation, 5th Canadian Armoured Division, which had been speedily formed in the summer of 1941 after a request by Britain for armoured reinforcements. Unfortunately, the quick formation of 5th Division was only made possible by stripping many artillery and technical units from 4th Division, thus further delaying the date when it would be going overseas. The 4th Division was on its way to becoming the "Cinderella" of the Canadian army, and by the autumn of 1941, its own men were bitterly calling it the "non-fighting Fourth."

The war was not going well that autumn. Rommel's Afrika Korps had pushed the desert army out of Libya, brave little Malta was being pounded into rubble by the *Luftwaffe* and U-Boats operating out of French bases were sinking record tonnages and threatening to sever Britain's maritime lifeline. In June, the Commonwealth had gained a powerful new ally when Hitler attacked the Soviet Union but within weeks the fast-moving panzer divisions had driven deep into that vast country and were closing on Moscow. Meanwhile, Japan was making threats in the Far East.

It was a frustrating period for the officers of the Regiment who had to keep their men motivated. The SAR officer ranks, which had gone through some turmoil during the first year of active service, had settled down. Of the forty-one officers serving in November 1941, nine were veterans of the First World War including the commanding officer, the second-in-command and three of the six company commanders. The importance of the peacetime militia was obvious in the make-up of the officers' mess. No fewer than twenty-five SAR officers had held commissions in prewar units of which twenty-one were in Alberta units (eight in the 15th Light Horse, six in the 19th Dragoons and four each in the prewar SAR, Loyal Edmonton Regiment, Calgary Regiment and Edmonton Fusiliers). Nine officers had been commissioned since 1940 and six of these had been enlisted men in the militia.[93]

The veterans were an interesting group. "Buffalo Bill" Bristowe has already been introduced. His second-in-command was Major Howard Wright, who had started in the ranks in the First War before gaining a field commission and had risen to command the peacetime 19th Alberta Dragoons before

What G.P. means to us. "G.P." is "Guard Post" and this Jay Moreton cartoon from the *SAR Christmas Magazine 1941* pretty well sums up the attitude of the boys. Guard Post was boredom, uncertain cooking, the odd moment of terror, tourists and the occasional excitement when an intruder was apprehended.

dropping in rank to go on active service with the Regiment. Wright was stern but fair and his down-to-earth efficiency balanced Bristowe's affability. "He looked the part of a field officer," remembers one SAR veteran and possessed "a quiet, competent, general-like manner."[94] Wright and Captain Bert Huffman, the paymaster, had great influence as "they were the senior statesmen of the Regiment who were thinking three or four years down the road when they would not be there."[95]

"When it came time to assess whether this man would be commissioned or whether this man would be promoted, Huffman and Wright were the key decision makers," recalls Danny McLeod. "If the regiment had been a corporation, Howard Wright would have been the chairman of the board and Bert Huffman would have been the chief executive officer."[96]

The SAR was remarkable in that, among their veterans, four (Captain Bert Huffman, the Paymaster, Captain Walter Hunter the Quartermaster, and Captains R.B.S. Burton and A.F. Watts) had served in either North Russia or Siberia in 1919 and wore the

Company falls in, Niagara, 1941. Occasionally, despite the frequent spells of guard duty, some training was done. Shirtsleeves and shorts were the order of the day through the hot, humid summer of 1941.
COURTESY, JACK PORTER.

ribbons of such exotic medals as the Order of St. Stanislaus and the Order of St. Anne, Second Class. Burton, a Finn who had defended that country against the Russians in 1920, was particularly popular and liked to quote biblical passages in his native tongue to the great consternation of his listeners.[97]

Of the younger generation, Major Arnold Lavoie commanding B Company was regarded as a competent but somewhat unimaginative officer. Captain Bob Bradburn commanding A Company was an obvious contender for higher rank as he "wanted to be a professional soldier and was prepared to pay the price."[98] His men both worshipped and feared him and Bob was at perpetual loggerheads with the adjutant, which is often the sign of a good company commander. Captain Bert Coffin commanding D Company was popular with everyone. A tall, balding man with a quick smile who loved a good joke he "liked people and could see the strengths and weaknesses of any person."[99] And then there were the lieutenants who came in all shapes and sizes. Thomas "Darby" Nash, a prewar stockbroker from Edmonton and a "diamond in the rough," liked to walk with his hands in his pockets; Hugh "Click" Clarke was an avid poker player; Gordie Shell had an academic bent; Fred "Newt" Hughes was regarded as highly intelligent and the best poker player in the Regiment; Stan Purdy tended to be clever but cautious; Kenny Perrin only needed to shave every other day; Glen McDougall had a reputation as a "big strong hairy-legged heiland mon" but wrote poetry in his spare time; Alec Laing played the bagpipes to everyone's discomfort; and Jay Moreton was an amateur artist whose cartoons brightened the pages of the regimental newsletter.[100]

In November the rumours started flying again. This time the "gen" was that the Regiment would be moving to Nova Scotia and this time it was true. At long last the 4th Division was bringing all its scattered children together to train as a complete formation at Debert near Truro. In a letter in the SAR *Christmas Magazine* which appeared that month, Lieutenant-Colonel

Bristowe made it official when he informed the Regiment that it would shortly be "moving to a place" where they would be doing winter training.[101] In the last week of November, the SAR concentrated at Niagara-on-the-Lake and put in three days of route marching to get into shape. They also received the new SMLE No.4, Mk I with its short spike bayonet which, as the War Diarist crowed, "was not yet in general use in the Canadian army."[102]

In the evening of Wednesday, 3 December 1941, preceded by the band of the 16/22nd Saskatchewan Horse, the South Albertas marched through the streets of Niagara-on-the-Lake, which were lined by wives, friends and families, to board their trains. A couple of hard cases were late and almost blotted the Regiment's perfect attendance record during movement but used their initiative to take a taxi to the next town down the line and get on board. That same evening, German reconnaissance elements were fighting in the outskirts of Moscow and a carrier task force from the Imperial Japanese Navy, which had set out from Hitokappu Bay in Japan eight days before, had reached a point approximately five hundred miles west of Pearl Harbor.

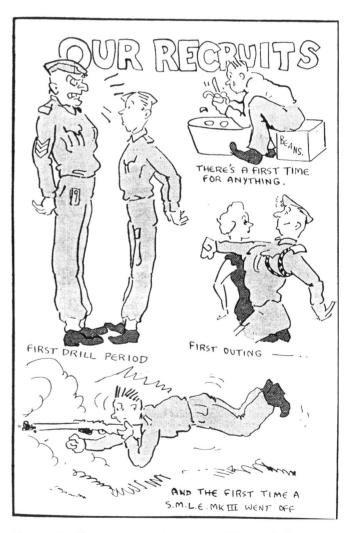

Our recruits. There were enough new men at Niagara to form a recruit company and Jay Moreton looks at the lighter side of recruit life in this cartoon from the *SAR Christmas Magazine 1941*.

PART II

PREPARING

Lieutenant Dave Mallet of Vancouver conducts a class in vehicle
maintenance for his C Squadron troop in April 1943. The tanks were
named with their first letter according to the squadron, thus "Cora"
and "Chloe" for this troop.

DND PHOTO.

CHAPTER THREE

"A lovely man who enjoyed the army."

CANADA AND BRITAIN: DECEMBER 1941–FEBRUARY 1943

It was December 1941 and Bing Crosby had just released "White Christmas." Everyone was singing, humming or whistling that haunting melody as the South Albertas moved east by train to Nova Scotia, but for the Regiment the dream came true when they arrived at Debert in the middle of a snowstorm on the morning of 5 December. Their new camp, constructed to house a full 16,000-man division, sprawled across acres of scrub pine and sand about twelve miles from Truro and was the biggest military station the boys had seen. The trucks dumped them off near their huts but it was still a chore to get through more than two feet of snow with packs, kit bags and weapons. Bristowe gave his men time to settle in and there was no church parade on the dull and foggy morning of Sunday, 7 December 1941, but that afternoon those listening to radios heard of the attack on Pearl Harbor. The news spread like a bush fire and most of the men, as the Regiment's first historian noted, now "felt reasonably safe" about the war's outcome "with the U.S. openly on our side."[2]

The South Albertas had to get familiar with snow because they were at Debert to do winter training. They commenced with an eighteen-mile route march on 11 December, but all real work ceased three days later when most of the Regiment left for

A regiment started out for fame,
　　S-A-R
A regiment started out for fame,
　　S-A-R
A regiment started out for fame
And from the north and south they came,
To join up with the S-A-R!

So fill her up and toast with me,
　　S-A-R
So fill her up and toast with me,
　　S-A-R
So fill her up and toast with me
Here's to the day we cross the sea,
Here's to the good old S-A-R![1]

a Christmas furlough. The unlucky ones who remained were formed into a composite company to do labour details and guard duty until the bulk of the unit returned in the first days of January. "Many of the boys were a little late getting back," the *Short History* records, "and Colonel Bristowe, with the most benevolent smile in the world, was kept quite busy handing out justice" in the "form of four days pay for every day absent which stimulated one and all, to no end."[3]

In January 1942 winter training started again in earnest with day-long route marches of between fifteen and twenty miles with the added innovation that each man cooked his own meal at noon. Ski training commenced on 12 January but it does not appear to have been very effective, nor did many South Albertas enjoy skiing with clumsy army skis strapped to their regulation boots. In any event, it was cancelled a week later when a sudden thaw set in and for the next three weeks the weather alternated between rain, freezing rain and severe snow storms. Beginning in late January and continuing to early March, the individual rifle companies went on overnight bivouacs under Captain Rafe Douthwaite, a former Royal Canadian Mounted Police officer with experience in Arctic conditions. Jim Nicholson recollects that when C Company went out,

We're not sure about this. Thick, clumsy skis strapped on thick clumsy army boots, this section from A Company does its best to learn winter warfare in January 1942. From the left, Bob Fairhurst, Danny McLeod, Mike Nickel, Dave Washburn and Adam Dutka, while, bringing up the rear (but not for long) is "Swede" Thuesen, the Regiment's only Danish cowboy. Mike Nickel from Medicine Hat was killed in Normandy on 11 August 1944; Adam Dutka was killed in Belgium on 12 September 1944. COURTESY, DANNY McLEOD.

"it snowed three feet that night and the roads were closed for four days."[4] The men "rationed out the food and spent a great four days waiting out the action." The bad weather climaxed on Sunday, 8 February 1942, with an icestorm of such severity that the War Diarist recorded "it was practically impossible to move" and that "very rare bugle call, 'No Parades today' was sounded after Church Parade had been cancelled."[5]

The weather was only a minor topic of conversation compared to the persistent rumour that the Regiment was going to be converted to an armoured unit. The gossip mill worked itself into a frenzy after a team from the army personnel section arrived in the last week of January to administer something called the "M Test" to every enlisted man. This aptitude test, a forerunner of those commonly employed today, gauged a man's reasoning capability and his basic mechanical, mathematical and vocabulary skills. Everyone was fairly certain that such testing heralded a change because they knew that the armoured corps would only take men with a high degree of intelligence and good mechanical abilities. The four-day barrage of tests had just begun on 26 January when someone heard on the radio that the division was going to be converted and speculation was rife until the official announcement was made on 2 February that the 4th Infantry Division was to become the 4th Armoured Division and the South Alberta Regiment was now the 29th Canadian Armoured Regiment (South Alberta Regiment).[6] The next day, another CBC report brought the news that Major-General Frank Worthington was to take over command of the division.[7]

Worthy. Major-General F.F. Worthington, General Officer Commanding, 4th Canadian Armoured Division, January 1942 to February 1944. Known as "Fighting Frank" or "Fearless Frank" but most often as "Worthy," he was the father of the Canadian Armoured Corps and a crusty and unconventional general whose troops loved his plain speaking and rough and ready ways. As the armoured reconnaissance regiment of the division, the South Albertas came under Worthy's direct command in January 1943 and the Regiment saw much of the general. SAR COLLECTION.

K nown as "Fighting" or "Fearless" Frank but more often simply as "Worthy," the South Albertas' new general was the father of the Canadian Armoured Corps. Worthington had been born in Scotland in 1890 and moved with his family to California, where, after being orphaned at fourteen, he had worked a spell in the Mexican gold fields before going to sea as a cabin boy. He went around the Horn under sail, survived the San Francisco earthquake and, in between times, fought in the Mexican revolution and various South American conflicts before obtaining his marine engineer papers. When war broke out in 1914, he decided to work his passage back to Scotland to en-

list in the Black Watch, the family regiment, and had got as far as Montreal, where he encountered the Black Watch of Canada, which he promptly joined as a private. Worthy won the Military Medal and bar in the trenches before being commissioned into the Canadian Motor Machine Gun Brigade in 1918 and later the Royal Tank Corps, where he gained experience with a new weapon system.[8]

Tanks, fully tracked armoured fighting vehicles, were the direct outcome of the stalemate on the Western Front imposed by trench warfare. The first tanks saw action in September 1916, and although they were unreliable and vulnerable it was clear that they had great potential. Britain formed a new corps to fight these weapons and its great moment came at the battle of Cambrai in November 1917 when 474 tanks gained most of their objectives despite being denied a complete break-through by determined German resistance. Tanks were now the "word" and every Allied general on the Western Front demanded them for his sector. The Royal Tank Corps made an intensive study of the lessons learned at Cambrai and the result was the Amiens offensive of August 1918 when 600 tanks, including two battalions of the new light tanks, used tactical air support and wireless communication to achieve an outstanding success. By the end of the war the tank had changed the nature of land warfare and the major armies of the world continued to study and experiment with the new weapon.[9]

Unfortunately, Britain lost her early lead and for the next two decades British armoured development suffered from fiscal restraint, the jealousy of the other arms (particularly the artillery) and the indifference of senior officers. Nonetheless, theoretical work in armoured warfare was done by a number of pioneers, both military and civilian, entranced by a "naval concept" of land warfare which saw tanks fighting other tanks on land as warships fought their counterparts at sea. Practical experiments with prototype armoured formations in the 1920s and early 1930s showed these theories to be unworkable and also demonstrated the importance of communications, and the provision of mobility to all arms including infantry, artillery and logistics elements. By 1937 it was decided that four different types of armoured vehicles were required for the British army: a carrier and a light tank for recce work; a cruiser tank for pursuit and exploitation; and an infantry tank for assaulting defensive positions. British armoured doctrine thus called for many different types of armoured fighting vehicles.[10]

This might not have been so serious if two other factors had not intervened. First, British armoured theorists felt that a cruiser tank armed with a large gun would not be mobile enough to be used in the "breakthrough" battle they envisaged. Accordingly they chose the 2-pdr. (40 mm) tank gun as the main weapon of both infantry and cruiser tanks, a weapon capable of penetrating the armour of any known tank in 1939 and easily accommodated in the small tanks of the period. Unfortunately, it was obsolescent within twelve months. The second factor was that Britain had been unable to produce a mechanically reliable tank during the interwar period. Although designs were drawn, there simply weren't the finances or the expertise in British industry to put them into reality. A contributing factor to this problem was the understandable penchant to purchase vast numbers of cheap light tanks equipped with machine guns which were useful for policing India and little else. The result was that by 1939 the greater part of the British tank inventory was obsolescent.[11]

In contrast to the rather patchy British experience, Germany's work with the new weapon system could serve as a model of its kind. Under the terms of the 1919 Versailles Treaty, Germany was not permitted to possess armoured fighting vehicles but, during the 1920s, as part of a rigorous intellectual exercise of analyzing and interpreting the lessons of the First World War, German officers diligently studied the employment, doctrine and equipment of armour. Prototype armoured vehicles, disguised as "agricultural tractors," were constructed and manoeuvres included the use of dummy armoured vehicles mounted on bicycles and cars so that commanders could at least get some idea of the potential of this weapon. Courses in armoured warfare were organized and prototype tanks, self-propelled artillery and infantry personnel carriers were designed. Much energy was spent on developing a sound doctrine for the use of tanks in battle based on the limited field work that could be done, information gleaned from articles in foreign military journals and reports from military attachés. Gradually, the German army evolved a doctrine that stressed the use of tanks in number as offensive weapons utilizing the element of surprise to assault "in waves" to maintain the momentum of the attack. In 1929 theory gave way to practical work when Germany set up a secret armoured training centre at Kazan in the Soviet Union, which, equipped with prototype German vehicles and Russian materiel, trained armoured corps officers, evaluated prototypes of tanks and other vehicles and, more importantly, examined foreign weaponry (particularly British tanks) purchased by the Soviet Union.[12]

Kazan closed in 1933 but by that time the advent of the Nazi regime in Germany brought about a massive programme of rearmament. Because of the preliminary work done in the 1920s, the *Panzerwaffe*, the armoured branch of the new *Wehrmacht*, had a head start. The foremost German armoured theorist was General Heinz Guderian, who created a single versatile armoured formation in which all arms (including support troops) were motorized in an effective combination that could perform a number of roles. In this panzer division, as it was called, movement was geared to the tanks and not the infantry, and it had greater striking power and mobility than the contemporary formations of other nations. The German army formed its first three panzer divisions in 1935 and by 1939 there were six as well as motorized and light divisions. The new *Panzerwaffe* was not used as a separate force during the short Polish campaign – its moment came in May 1940 when it deployed about 2,600 tanks in ten panzer divisions against 3,300 Allied tanks. Although many of the Allied tanks, particularly the later French models, were superior to their German counterparts, the *Wehrmacht* possessed better doctrine, organization and leadership. In six weeks they overran western Europe.

The Canadian experience could not have been more different. Besides the occasional article published by interested officers there was almost no development of armoured vehicles in Canada until 1936 when a training school was established at Camp Borden near Barrie, Ontario. It came under the command of the newly-promoted Lieutenant-Colonel Frank Worthington who had just returned to Canada after sixteen months of service with the Royal Armoured Corps. Worthington's task was to train six militia units that had recently been converted to armour and it was a difficult one as there was a shortage of instructors, money, tools, training devices and, above all, vehicles – most of the school's inventory were obsolescent vehicles or prototypes with little practical value. Things improved slightly when two Mk VI light tanks arrived from England – the first modern AFVs (Armoured Fighting Vehicles) to come to Canada. The type of training carried out and the enthusiastic attitude of the instructors is evident in a *Toronto Star* article published in July 1938. Entitled "Canada's Tank School Trains Men with Rollicking Sweat Boxes and Air Guns at Camp Borden," the journalist quotes Worthington as saying that his ancient vehicles "serve the purpose wonderfully well [as] men who can handle an automobile built in 1914 will surely excel themselves with sleek 1938 models" and that "is the way we feel about our tanks. If we can handle these efficiently, we can handle anything."[13] These were cheerful words to smooth over a bad situation.[14]

Work continued at Borden through the following winter and summer of 1939 as each of the six designated armoured regiments got one week of intensive training. The instruction improved with the arrival of a further fourteen Mk VI tanks from Britain, but Worthy was under no illusions about the nature of the training he could provide with such limited means. As he admitted to a journalist, it might "border on the burlesque" but it "fired further imagination and incentive" as the trainees "got a rare kind of boyish glee from improvising makeshift weapons – excellent training in itself."[15]

When Canada declared war in September 1939, the nation's inventory of armoured fighting vehicles was a pitiful collection of sixteen obsolescent British light tanks, a dozen little machine-gun carriers or tankettes, two prototype armoured cars, six converted civilian cars and an old artillery gun tractor. The attitude of some senior officers toward the new weapon system was evident in November 1939 when one general stated publicly that the "ultimate weapon which wins the war is a bayonet on a rifle carried by an infantryman through the mud" and no one "knows how useful tanks will be" because the "Polish campaign was not a true indication of the power of mechanized armies." For good measure (possibly punctuated with a "harrumph"), this same officer added that the "usefulness of the airplane … also remains to be seen."[16]

Other senior officers were of a different mind and badgered the Minister of National Defence to provide Canadian-built tanks, but, appalled by the high cost, the government dragged its heels. Attitudes changed in May 1940 after the German panzers overran France. "Tanks and more tanks" was now the cry and in June Worthy was asked to draft a plan for the creation of a Canadian armoured corps. He suggested that this new organization be organized on a "corps," not a "regimental" basis, and that the immediate goal should be the complete training of two armoured brigades. His proposals received almost unanimous approval and on 13 August 1940 the Canadian Armoured Corps was officially brought to life under the newly-promoted Colonel F.F. Worthington. It was high time.[17]

But the new Corps had no tanks. To rectify this lack, Worthington was sent to the United States in August to examine and report on the possibility of obtaining American equipment. He was particularly interested in the American-built Renault FT, a 1916 vintage vehicle that had been used by the US until 1935 as a training vehicle. It was not much of a tank, it could move at about 6 mph, had a two-man crew (gunner and driver) and was armed with a machine gun or a 37 mm gun in a turret traversed by the gunner's shoulder. Worthy admitted that the FT "had a great many shortcomings, but in the absence of anything else [it] will be in the nature of a stop-gap."[18] He arranged for the purchase of 250 Renaults as training vehicles and he got them at bargain basement prices – $20 per ton plus 100% making a total of $240 per tank. The US Army generously agreed to improve them to a state where each vehicle could move onto a railway flat car under its own power and the first examples arrived at Borden in October 1940. Here they joined two more modern Valentine tanks just acquired from Britain and were used to train the newly-raised 1st Canadian Army Tank Brigade.[19]

Britain, trying to re-arm after Dunkirk, could spare no more armoured fighting vehicles and Canada was forced to look to her own resources to equip the new corps. A cabinet decision in June 1940 led to an order for 488 Valentine tanks being placed at the CPR Angus shops in Montreal. Worthy questioned the utility of the Valentine, which was verging on obsolescence, and

instead suggested that the government purchase the new American M3 medium tank, then in its initial design stages. Discussions during September 1940 led to a request for 1,157 cruiser tanks of the American M3 type to equip the 1st Tank Brigade and a planned Canadian armoured division. Cabinet approval for this expenditure did not come until January 1941, but in the interim it was decided that these tanks could be manufactured at the Montreal Locomotive Works, the Canadian subsidiary of the American Locomotive Works, one of the prime M3 contractors.

Few Canadian officers versed in armour liked the M3 because its main gun armament was mounted in the hull with only a secondary gun in the turret. At the urging of Worthington and others, a decision was made to manufacture a machine using standard M3 running gear but with a Canadian hull and turret and a British 6-pdr. (57 mm) gun. The Montreal Locomotive Works constructed a mock-up of this new vehicle, christened the Ram, in less than three weeks and American tank experts were impressed by its low profile. Mass production of the Ram I (equipped with a 2-pdr. gun as there were not enough 6-pdr. weapons to go around) began in the summer of 1941.[20]

From its rather uncertain start the Canadian Armoured Corps grew rapidly. One Army Tank Brigade of three regiments was formed in the autumn of 1940 and trained by Worthy during the winter of 1940-1941 and in June 1941 when it was decided to send it overseas, he was promoted brigadier and given command. Further expansion came in the summer of 1941 when the cabinet approved the formation of the 5th Canadian Armoured Division, which concentrated at Borden where it used the rattly old Renaults to good effect before moving to the UK in November. At about that time, Britain requested a second armoured division from Canada and a decision was made to convert the existing 4th Infantry Division to armour. In February 1942 the newly-promoted Major-General Frank Worthington was appointed to its command and one of his first actions was to convince Army Headquarters that a supply of 165 Rams on the docks at Halifax awaiting shipment to 5th Armoured Division in Britain should be diverted to Debert to train his new formation.[21]

The SAR was now an armoured regiment. Reaction to the news varied but the majority were in favour – John Galipeau "liked the idea of not having to walk" into battle and fighting with "nice, thick steel walls around" him once he got there.[22] Like many others, John thought that the technical training in the armoured corps "might lead to something better" in the future, unlike the skills he had acquired in the infantry, which were of little value in the civilian world unless one was interested in a life of crime. Jim Nicholson recollects, however, that "a surprising number said they did not wish to be in a tank" as many regarded it as a claustrophobic existence.[23] Jim

Gove probably summed up the attitude of most of the enlisted men when he comments that "I was 19 years old and had no idea what was going … I was dumb and strong" and "to me it was all an adventure anyway." Glen McDougall's opinion was that the Regiment was "pleased about conversion" particularly as they were going to serve under Worthington, "a lovely man who enjoyed the army and showed it and was as easy with a trooper as he was with a major."[24]

The day after the official announcement, the War Diarist noted that one "can already sense a new spirit of expectancy among officers and men alike as they look forward to intensive training."[25] But the conversion would also mean a drastic reorganization as armoured regiments had four squadrons (HQ, A, B and C) as opposed to the five companies of an infantry battalion. To comply with the new war establishment, A Company (the original Medicine Hat company) of the Regiment was broken up and B, C and D Companies became A, B and C Squadrons respectively, while HQ Company transformed itself into HQ Squadron. The 4th Division was also reorganized: the SAR was now placed with the BCR and the Elgin Regiment in the new 3 Armoured Brigade. Sadly, the changeover meant the loss of many originals from 1940 as the armoured corps had different trades and lower age limits. In all more than a dozen officers and eighty-eight enlisted personnel left, including most of Sergeant Jimmy Tennent's band as armoured regiments did not have such organizations. There were many sad farewells over the next few months as old friends were gradually posted out, including, among others, Majors Grimmet and Davis, Captains Grant Saul and Rafe Douthwaite, that Finnish warhorse Captain R.S. Burton, and Sergeant Majors Lawrence Blain and William Baldwin. On 15 May 1942 there were many dry eyes in the SAR but much respect as the Regiment bid farewell to RSM Chris Seal, a man who can perhaps take more credit than any other for transforming them from raw civilians into soldiers. His replacement was John ("Jock") Mackenzie, a tough ex-miner who had been with the Regiment since June 1940. He would remain RSM for the next four years and, as Sergeant Jack Porter recalled, "kept people like me in line."[26]

The Regiment had a tremendous task before it. The entire unit would have to be retrained in the highly technical armoured trades which, according to the authorized training syllabus, required between four and five months. "Buffalo Bill" Bristowe left for Britain that month leaving Major Howard Wright in command throughout the hectic conversion period and to Wright must go the credit for seeing that the SAR successfully completed this task. As Bert Coffin reports, Wright's tenure in command, "was one of the best things that ever happened to us" and not a great change as "he was commanding officer in fact when Bristowe was there."[27] The first step was reclassification of the enlisted personnel from their infantry trades to the new armoured trades. During a five-day period, the officers interviewed every man and, basing their assessments on his record and his M-Test results, decided whether to

retrain him or post him out. Most of those who left went to non-combat organizations such as the engineers, ordnance or army service corps; those who remained were re-classified into one of the two armoured corps combat trades – gunner-operator or driver-mechanic – or the support trades such as technical storesman, fitter (tank mechanic) and dispatch rider. This preliminary task was completed by 8 February and the Regiment was ready to commence work.[28]

Before that could be done, the Regiment had to have qualified instructors, and sixteen officers and fifty-eight enlisted men were sent to Borden or other places for courses that lasted between six and eight weeks to learn enough to teach the rest of the Regiment. At the same time, a number of trained armoured officers were posted in to assist in the conversion. Many stayed with the South Albertas throughout the war and the SAR picked up some good men this way, such as Lieutenants Hank Carroll, Tom Howard, Jack Roberts and Raynor Woods. Among them was a young former premedical student from McGill, Lieutenant Alec Scrimger, whose father had won the VC as a doctor on the Western Front in the First War, and Lieutenant Leaman Caseley, an older (he was 27) married man from Prince Edward Island. So many familiar faces were disappearing and new ones cropping up that nobody paid much attention when a tall captain with a bashful smile, David Currie from Moose Jaw, Saskatchewan, arrived to take up the duties of transport officer in May 1942. As his wife, Isabel, recalled, Dave had been stationed at the reconnaissance training centre at Dundurn but "he wasn't happy staying as a training officer" and said to her, "every time I send these men off, I think I should be with them."[29] In November 1941, Currie got a transfer to Borden and

The black beret. When the Regiment converted to armour in February 1942 they received the black beret, the trademark of Commonwealth armoured units. The original version of the distinctive headgear was based on a style of hat popular in British girls' schools before the First World War. Here, Troopers R. Perrault (on the left) and Fred Plahn (on the right) proudly display their new headgear at Debert. COURTESY, FRED PLAHN.

was later posted into the Regiment to assist with the conversion process.[30]

Until qualified instructors were available the SAR did what it could with its own resources – studying manuals, attending lectures, watching training films and building plywood mock-ups of tanks. On 28 March 1942 the South Albertas got their first look at their new general when Worthy gave the assembled units of the division "a brief but forceful address" in which his "evident pride and enthusiasm for the Armoured Corps" communicated "itself in no small degree to his listeners."[31]

A few days later the boys exchanged their infantry wedge caps for black berets, the distinctive armoured corps headgear, and the War Diarist recorded that "Weird and wonderful effects are abundant as the men experiment with the 'black bonnets.'"[32] The Royal Tank Corps had originally adopted the beret in 1918 because it was practical to wear in the dirty, oily interiors of the early tanks and by 1942 this comfortable headgear (which was not common in the British and Canadian armies) was regarded as a mark of distinction that set the armoured soldier apart from the "common herd." Worthy was keen on the new headgear because he wanted to promote a general *esprit de corps* in the CAC as opposed to a regimental spirit and explained to the press that he wanted "his men to feel they are members of the division and not of the 'Mudshire Fusiliers.'"[33] The aspiring young tankers would have been perhaps less happy if they had known that the armoured corps' distinctive headgear was originally based on a style of beret "very popular amongst girls' schools in England."[34]

On April Fool's Day 1942 – perhaps not the best of timing – the SAR got its first close look at real tanks when they inspected two Valentines that arrived at Debert. Enough qualified instructors were now on hand to begin teaching the men the three basic armoured skills: driving and maintenance, gunnery and wireless. Each man learned his primary trade and was then cross-trained in a secondary task so that, if necessary, he could take over another crew position. The first courses worked on theory until late April when the division received enough tanks to work with the real thing, and for the next three months consecutive schools were run by the Regiment in two shifts, from 0400 to 1200 and from 1200 to 2000 each day. It was perhaps the most hectic period in the SAR's history, as would-be wireless operators struggled through the intricacies of the No. 19 Wireless Set and the horrors of Morse Code ("the death of a thousand dashes"), prospective gunners stripped, reassembled

Friends and comrades. From the left, Sergeants Bobby Crawford and William "Danny" McLeod with Corporal Edward "Duffy" Gendron at Debert in the spring of 1942. Childhood friends from Medicine Hat, they joined the Regiment in June 1940 and gained rapid promotion. Danny ended the war as a captain with the MC and Bobby as a lieutenant. Duffy Gendron was killed in Normandy on 10 August 1944. Note the black and gold SAR lanyards worn by Danny and Duffy under the left shoulder strap. COURTESY, DANNY McLEOD.

and "dry fired" 2-pdr. and 6-pdr. tank guns and .30 calibre Browning machine guns and aspiring drivers clanked around Debert in Ram tanks with instructors, perched above them on the hatch cover, shouting instructions loud enough to be heard over the noise of the tracks.[35]

Besides the combat trades, courses were also held in tank repair for the fitters and parts supply for the technical storesmen. Almost every man in the Regiment received driving instruction because armoured units were equipped with a great variety of vehicles, from heavy trucks to motorcycles. These motorcycles were not the sedate three-wheeled sidecar combinations the SAR had operated when they were an infantry battalion. The twelve dispatch riders in the new organization rode big powerful Norton or Indian bikes that were a far cry from the sophisticated machines that buzz around modern streets. They were heavy and awkward, took a man's main strength to handle and were also dangerous – two South Albertas were badly injured in motorcycle accidents at Debert. In fact, the statistics demonstrate that, throughout the war, being a dispatch rider was one of the most hazardous occupations in the Regiment. As Adam Wagner puts it:

I started on the motorcycles and I remained on motorcycles because I was crazy enough to stay there. I was with them pretty well all the way through until they took me off because they figured my luck had about run out. It was a pretty dangerous job and, of the twelve original dispatch riders, there were only three left when I left, none of them were killed in action, they were all run over. What the hell, I was young … It's just like children, there's nothing wrong with them, they are just carefree.[36]

Despite the frantic schedule, the Regiment managed to have some fun along the way. A sports programme was started in mid-May, and throughout the late spring and summer of 1942 the baseball team reigned supreme and clinched the divisional championship but the soccer team did less well. There were dances in the messes and even routine duty brought some lighter moments. The camp at Debert, being a large one, included a field security section which regularly tried to snare unwary units by infiltrating security personnel into their area who would try to evade being challenged for identification and steal some piece of equipment or paper that would be reported the following day in a critical report. The South Albertas were caught a few times, the worst occasion being 16 April when the War Diarist lamented that field security had "kidnapped a truck right under our noses – returned that night."[37] More strenuous forms of comic relief were provided by the not-infrequent medical parades for injections and, of course, the gas hut. The gas officer at this time was Lieutenant G.A. Matthewson, an enthusiastic individual, who leaned on a "heavy diffusion" of the wretched stuff to get the right effect. There were many chuckles in the SAR hut lines on St. Patrick's Day 1942 when, as the War Diarist wrote, Matthewson became a victim of his own enthusiasm: "While trying out D.M. Gas in preparation for tomorrow, Lt. Matthewson and two NCOs became quite nauseated" as "the dose was rather strong and resulted in their being laid up for the afternoon."[38]

Most of the Regimental wives travelled to Debert but they did not find Nova Scotia as friendly as Nanaimo or Niagara. According to Isabel Currie it was difficult to find accommodations and the "people in Truro were not very nice as they didn't want so many soldiers around."[39] However, Isabel and her young son, David, did well as they lived at a local family hotel whose owner became a good friend. Many wives and children found accommodation in the village of Belmont about two miles from Debert, and Earle Wood recalled that "we had a nice little SAR family there."[40] For the bachelors, if you couldn't get to Halifax (itself no great delight in wartime), it was better to stay in camp as Truro was a dry town and there wasn't much to do – John Galipeau recalls that on "the weekends, the inhabitants of the largest military camp in Canada roamed the streets of Truro looking for some sort of amusement."[41] There were many wistful memories of Nanaimo and Niagara.

Between April and June 1942 the SAR worked hard at learning its new trade. Officers and men were enthusiastic because it was common knowledge that the division would be moving to Britain as soon as its training had reached a certain level. Colonel Bristowe, Majors Arnold Lavoie and Ted Miles and Lieutenant Glen McDougall were sent ahead to train with armoured units of the British Army. Glen ended up with the British Grenadier Guards on Salisbury Plain and immediately encountered the difference between the British and Canadian armies:

They didn't know what to do with me so they gave me a tank and said "just follow along." I remember one time I had some mechanical trouble so they told me to go back to the camp. It was a beautiful day, sunny weather, and we passed a pub so I said: "Boys, let's go in and get a beer." There was silence and these Guardsmen looked at me strangely because British Guards officers simply don't speak to their men that way. Eventually, I took them in and we had a beer and then away we went. They loved it.[42]

This early group was followed to Britain on 2 May by an advance draft of fifty officers and men. There was universal envy

on the day they left and the film camera was there to record them marching down to the camp railhead to catch the train for Halifax and embarkation.

Three days later, the camera was again on hand to record the proud moment when the SAR received its first tanks. These were 30-ton Ram I machines powered by a 9-cylinder Continental R975 engine fuelled by 90 octane aviation gasoline that produced 400 pp at maximum revs and a top speed of 20 mph. The Regiment immediately began a driving school under the leadership of Lieutenant Darby Nash and the Rams were used for two shifts of driving instruction and one of maintenance instruction each day. They were constantly in motion, and by the time the South Albertas were through with them, Bert Coffin recalls, "there was not much left" and "the transmissions required a mechanical genius to shift gears."[43]

To bring it up to strength the SAR received reinforcements. In early June forty-three enlisted men of the King's Own Rifles from Moose Jaw marched into camp and nine weeks later a group of fifty-five recent graduates from Borden joined the unit. The arrival of these two large drafts ended the largely Albertan composition of the SAR and began a gradual process of dilution that continued throughout the war. The Regiment retained its western spirit, however, and made the newcomers welcome – within weeks they were as proud of belonging to the SAR as the recruits who had joined in Edmonton in 1940.[44]

By June, enough men had mastered their new trades for the Regiment to attempt some advanced training. Late in the month the SAR participated in a brigade exercise, Exercise REPULSE, intended to practise motorized convoy movement, wireless procedure and command skills. For three days, 3 Armoured Brigade exercised near East Mines, Wentworth, Wentworth Centre, Oxford and Pictou, Nova Scotia, as it repulsed an "enemy" landing near Caribou Island. Tanks were not used on this scheme; carriers and troop-carrying vehicles were substituted instead and the Regiment reverted temporarily to its infantry role. A feature of REPULSE was a mock attack by RCAF aircraft, somewhat ironic in view of future events. Both REPULSE and a later one-day scheme, HAWK III, showed that the units of 3 Brigade had much to learn about mobile warfare.[45]

June also brought firing on the tank gunnery range at Spencer's Point on the Minas Basin. The new gunners tried out the 6-pdr. main guns and the secondary machine guns of the Rams firing from stationary and moving positions against floating logs chained together offshore. The SAR retained their infantry marksmanship skills and the War Diarist noted that "some very good tank gunners were turning up."[46] Collective training as crews began in the first week of July. By this time, the SAR had fifteen Rams on strength, about one-third of its war establishment, and after the squadrons had been organized into individual crews, troop training commenced. If they were lucky, a crew trained in an actual tank one or two days a week; otherwise they had to carry out what was euphemistically known as "dismounted drill." As one SAR who had to suffer it explains:

Lengths of 2 x 2 lumber had been fastened together to form a letter H configuration. The troop was paraded to an open space within which we would march from place to place. Each crew was presented with one of the H-shaped structures and told to arrange ourselves in the positions we would occupy in a tank. … We were now imaginary tanks and under the directions and orders of the troop officer, we walked hither and yon over the area forming tank battle formations such as arrowhead, square and line abreast.[47]

"As can be imagined," he continued, "these exercises were accompanied by a chorus of grumbling and muttering, drivers' imitations of running engines and crashing gears, and a goodly amount of laughter."

Nobody really minded, however, as the time was fast approaching when the Regiment would be leaving Canada. On 12 July, instruction came to a standstill when the greater part of the unit went on ten days of embarkation leave and when the men returned on 23 July, the SAR resumed crew training and a further spell on the tank ranges where the practice emphasized "control," not firing. The South Albertas had made a good start but, as Jim Nicholson reports, they never "received a full complement of tanks at Debert" and "further radio and driving training would have to wait until England."[48] On the last day of July Worthy inspected the SAR and, at the same time, the men received their new divisional badge, a square green patch sewn on their shoulders beneath the black and gold regimental "flash" that read "South Alberta Regt. – Canada." Worthy's reputation for bluntness was enhanced when he informed the SAR that "many of you will never see this land again."[49]

By now the drivers were becoming adept at handling the Ram and on 5 August they showed their proficiency when the SAR and the Elgins put on a demonstration of the tank's capabilities. The new tankers' glee was evident as they drove down and over anti-tank ditches, rumbled across barriers of dug-in stumps and crashed through old wooden barns. There was just enough time over the next few days for some more range practice before the quartermaster was ordered to get his stores ready for loading and the Regiment was directed to turn in its tanks and vehicles.[50]

The summer of 1942 was a low point for the Allied cause. Hitler had been rebuffed at the gates of Moscow the previous December but his armies had resumed the offensive in the spring and were deep into the Caucasus and closing on the Don River, while in Africa Rommel's Afrika Korps had advanced into Egypt. In the Far East, Hong Kong, Malaya, the Philippines and the Dutch East Indies had fallen to Japan. A few days before it left Debert, the SAR learned of the 2nd Canadian Division's assault at Dieppe on 19 August and word was already spreading of the high casualties suffered by the units involved in that operation, including their sister Alberta regiment, the Calgary Tanks.

It was now the South Albertas' turn to move closer to the war and on 21 August 1942 the time came for parting. At 1000 hours, the 550 officers and men of the SAR, packs on their backs, kitbags in one hand, rifles in the other and helmets slung over their left shoulder, boarded the CNR train for the journey to the Halifax docks. There was just enough time for a twenty-minute stop in Truro for last-minute goodbyes with families and friends. The boys were not allowed to leave the coaches, so there were hurried embraces through windows with wives and girlfriends while small children were carefully lifted up to kiss Daddy – and then they were gone. At 1600 the Regiment, along with the Dukes and Lake Superiors, boarded His Majesty's Transport *Strathmore*. The ship spent the night moored at the dock and, at 0815 hours on 22 August 1942, moved out into the harbour to take her place in the convoy that was assembling. The SAR was "off at last after two years and three months of waiting."[51]

The voyage lasted only seven days and that was just as well as the *Strathmore* was badly overcrowded. The seas were calm but the food on board was terrible, "fish and sourdough bread for breakfast, lunch and dinner," according to Sergeant Jim Nicholson.[52] It was an uneventful passage except for one evening about 2200 hours when "we heard a heavy metallic banging sound" and "those of us who went up on deck observed a great fiery glow in the sky toward the rear of the

The convoy, Bedford Basin, Halifax, August 1942.
This photograph, a major breach of security regulations, was taken by Ivy Galipeau, wife of Corporal John Galipeau, through the open upper transom of the window of the ladies' washroom on a CNR coach. Ivy stood on the toilet to reach the vantage point while two other SAR wives held her steady. She had been married less than eighteen months when her husband sailed for Britain and she would not see him again for more than three years.

COURTESY, JOHN GALIPEAU.

The most important institution in the life of the British people. The local pub – in this case, the famous "Holly Bush" at Headley in Hampshire, where Sally Stevens (whose only regret was that "while she had played with Canadians in the First World War, in this war she could only mother them") ruled with an iron hand. Run afoul of Sally and you were in deep trouble. The Holly Bush is still going strong and is crowded most evenings with off-duty soldiers from nearby Bordon Camp. PHOTOGRAPH BY DIANNE GRAVES.

convoy." Later they learned that one of the escort destroyers had collided with a tanker but both ships made it back to port.

On the morning of 31 August 1942, HMT *Strathmore* entered the Clyde in Scotland and the South Albertas crowded the rails to catch their first glimpse of Britain. After personal greetings from Worthington and the Canadian High Commissioner, Vincent Massey, who came aboard in the late morning, the transport moved up the Clyde and at 1700 hours anchored at Glasgow. Disembarkation commenced the next morning under a steady fall of rain and by 1200 the Regiment had boarded two trains to begin the journey south. The smaller British railway carriages "with those doors and compartments" were a novelty as were the tiny engines which went "whooo, whooo."[53] With "everyone staring out the windows for their first sight of the Old Country," the SAR set off for their destination south of London. Everything was different – "greener, smaller, wetter."[54] After stops at Edinburgh and York, the first train pulled into Bordon, Hampshire, at six the following morning to be greeted by Lieutenant-Colonel Bristowe, Majors Ted Miles and Arnold Lavoie and the newly-promoted Captain Glen McDougall. Then, as the War Diarist recorded, a "little lonely, tired and bewildered," the South Albertas marched to their new quarters "but after a hot breakfast, with the weather brightening up, everything decidedly improved for the better."[55]

The SAR's new station was in and around the small villages of Lindford, Headley and Headley Down in a scenic part of rural Hampshire. It was split up in squadron billets: RHQ and HQ squadron were at Lindford while the other squadrons were dispersed in the surrounding area, the men sleeping in Nissen huts and the officers in farmhouses. The SAR were not the first Canadian troops to be stationed in this neighbourhood. Nearby Ludshott and Frensham Commons offered open ground for tank training and since 1941 the people of Lindford and Headley had progressively hosted elements of 1 Army Tank Brigade and 5th Armoured Division. They were used to Canadians and it wasn't long before the village children, desperate for sweets because of wartime sugar rationing, greeted the SAR with the traditional salutation "Any gum, Chum?"

When the men explored the area, they soon discovered that greatest of all the many gifts that Britain has bestowed on civilization – the local pub. These friendly and civilized establishments were a far cry from Canadian beer parlours, which were basically alcoholic filling stations "where you had women in one section and men in another, and you just sat there and drank and squabbled."[56] The pub was "just like a home away from home" although, as Bob Wear reminisces, "being Canadian we would drink to get drunk at first, afterwards we learned we could drink and not get drunk, just be civilized and happy."[57] The men soon became familiar with The Fox and Pelican at Grayshott, The Wheatsheaf at Headley and The Rose and Crown near Bordon, which were usually so packed that you had to hold onto your glass; you didn't dare put it down because there was a shortage of glasses and it would disappear. And, of course, there was the famous Holly Bush at Headley, where Sally Stevens held sway – "that 300 lbs. bundle of good humour, whose only regret was that, while she had played with Canadians in the last war, in this war she could only mother them."[58] Run afoul of Sally and you were in trouble because she "could swear and curse and be as raw as any guy we had ever known, and throw out any man who got out of line."[59] Trooper Larry Aspeslet recalled with great satisfaction that he was "billeted just above the Holly Bush and we had to go down to one of the other troop lines for our showers" and "passed three [pubs] on the way and three on the way back so we were always feeling pretty good."[60] Besides the pubs, the Headley area offered a few cafes, the Palace and Empire movie theatres in Bordon and an "interesting house" on Glaysher's Hill which often attracted the attention of the provosts.[61]

As everyone received nine days privilege leave in September 1942 and a similar period every three months or so thereafter the South Albertas soon began to explore the country. On their first leave, most went off to see London or visited relatives, as many had family ties in Britain, but on later leaves they went further afield. Scotland was a favoured destination although most avoided Glasgow, which had a reputation for toughness. Wartime Britain presented daily novelties and not all of them were welcome: black-outs; Nissen huts; Piccadilly Circus and the "Bovril" sign in London; shortages of coal and just about everything else; respirator days when you had to wear your gas mask for half an hour no matter what you were doing; crowded trains; sunken lanes; the smell of wet battle dress; venerable but alert Home Guards and polite but firm police constables; the occasional air raid which usually came at the wrong moment in the hours of darkness; detested "woolly Woodbines" (British cigarettes); bemedalled and brash Americans; the "clomp, clomp, clomp" of hob-nailed boots on cobblestones; friendly but hectic pubs; driving on the wrong side of the road with hooded headlights; mist and fog and rain but flowers in February; ENSA (Entertainment Services Association but known as "Every Night Something Awful") shows which were sometimes good but often terrible; miniature railways and double-decker buses; the German propagandist, "Lord Haw-Haw," on the radio; huge dance halls where two orchestras played on a revolving stage and, above all, the British people, who displayed constant courtesy and whose spirit was never daunted in the face of adversity.

The biggest complaint was the food – if it was good, you didn't get enough; if it was bad you couldn't eat it anyway. Many men rushed straight from the mess hall to the NAAFI (Navy, Army and Air Force Institute) Hut to supplement their diet with a plate of beans on toast made from wartime ration bread, a grey, moist and chewy mass. You always knew when a convoy had come in from Australia because you got mutton (stewed, fried, boiled, roasted or any other way meat can be prepared) for days afterwards. If there was no mutton to mangle, you got concoctions of dehydrated eggs or dehydrated potatoes topped by artificial sausages with a taste similar to grease-laden sawdust. And then there was tea – despite the Canadian predilection for coffee, you got tea (sugar, tea and milk mixed together in advance) because that was what the British army got. Canadian soldiers serving in Britain griped so much about the food that the army launched a full-scale investigation which concluded that, although there was much exaggeration, many of the complaints were legitimate and the poor quality of army messing was due to a combination of severe rationing, difference in British and Canadian dietary preferences, and the poor training of army cooks. Almost every South Alberta would have agreed with the latter conclusion – as one corporal expressed it in late 1943, "the cooks we have here couldn't parboil shit for pigs."[62]

For the single men, the best thing was the British girls. More direct than their Canadian equivalent, they liked to have fun and (at least until 1943 when the Americans began to show up in large numbers) were thrilled by Canadians, who were generally more physically impressive, better uniformed and had more money in their pockets than their British counterparts.

There was also the way the boys talked. The Canadian "accent" is soft to the British ear and even the most socially inept, tongue-tied and bashful trooper from Etzikom or Russylvia at least had the single asset that he sounded like Clark Gable. The result was inevitable – fourteen months after the Regiment arrived in Britain, twenty-seven South Albertas had married British girls, and although there are no reliable data for 1944, indications are that the marriage rate increased in that year. The South Albertas were not unique in this aspect. Jimmy Walker of the Regiment was one of three brothers who served in Britain in different units – three Walkers went overseas, nine came back as each brother returned with a wife and a baby.[63]

Once the South Albertas had settled into their new quarters, attention turned to resuming training. Unfortunately, 4th Canadian Armoured Division, being a newcomer to the United Kingdom, was at the bottom of the list for available weapons and equipment, which went to the 5th Armoured Division, which was but justice as Worthy had hijacked that formation's allotment of tanks in Canada. The result was that there was nothing for the Division and nothing for the SAR – as the War Diarist complained in mid-September, "if we don't get some equipment of some kind we will be forgetting what we do know."[64] The Regiment got no tanks but on 10 September it at least received six tank map cases. The only training that could be done was weapons training at the small-arms range at nearby Longmoor Range, map reading and the inevitable "troop tactics without tanks." The boys were soon walking over Ludshott Common carrying sticks to represent guns and pre-

Carrier training, somewhere in England, 1943. For nearly a year the Regiment was organized in separate tank and carrier troops. The carrier was useful for training but was not a popular vehicle because of its open top, rough ride and tendency to tip. Note the goggles worn by crew members, necessary items because of the dust that tracked vehicles throw up. SAR COLLECTION.

tending to be armoured fighting vehicles while making the appropriate sound effects.

Matters improved slightly in early October when the SAR drew nine carriers and each squadron got three. These little vehicles were not tanks but they were better than walking around in the rain pretending to be tanks. A few weeks later, nine more carriers and seventeen jeeps were received and this at least allowed the troops to practise basic formations and convoy movement. But that was about all they could do as there was also a shortage of No. 19 Wireless Sets, the standard radio, and wireless training, an important aspect of armoured warfare, suffered throughout the autumn. By the end of October, the Regiment had progressed to longer road movements and harbouring schemes. The officers usually made a recce of the route first and the War Diarist complained that "most of these schemes are built around pubs" as the various stopping points inevitably included "the pub in the vicinity."[65]

The carriers were tricky and dangerous vehicles. On 6 November Corporal Harvey McFadden and Trooper Patrick Lynch were practising troop formations on Frensham Common when their carrier tipped going down a small hill. Both men were thrown out and killed when the carrier rolled on top of them, and five days later their troop provided the firing party when they were buried in Brookwood Military Cemetery. Harvey McFadden was a 29-year-old from Red Deer who had been with the SAR since June 1940 while Patrick Lynch, age 21, was a millworker from Medicine Hat who had joined at Nanaimo.[66]

Finally, ten weeks from the day they arrived in England, the SAR received its first tanks, three Ram II models with 6-pdr. guns, which were allocated to the best troop in each squadron. The radios in the new machines had instructions and calibration in Cyrillic script as well as English but Lieutenant Jay Moreton, the signals officer, solemnly assured everyone that, despite the Russian dials, the BBC "still came in English."[67] Tanks and other vehicles continued to trickle in, and by mid-

December the SAR could boast eleven Rams, thirty-six carriers and two scout cars. In the last weeks of the month, they got ten more Rams and, just as important, twenty-nine No. 19 Wireless Sets. They could now start serious wireless training and begin more ambitious schemes involving prolonged movement and harbouring exercises. By the end of 1942 the Regiment had made such progress that it was selected above all the armoured units in the division to provide six tanks to do a demonstration on Frensham Common which was filmed for Fox "Movietone News."[68]

The Canadian Army may have lacked equipment but it did not lack personnel tests and November 1942 saw the appearance of the "Quiz Kids": Lieutenants John Redden and Jack Summers. Nicknamed "Big John" and "Little Joe" respectively, Redden and Summers were reinforcement officers unattached to any unit who had been chosen to administer the M-Test to officer personnel because, as Redden recollects, "we had taken the test and got high marks."[69] They were with the SAR for more than a month; they didn't need this much time to test the forty-three officers, they simply liked the South Albertas and tarried as long as they could. According to Redden, the "Quiz Kids" did "the M-Test routine in several units and, finally, the SAR and we were impressed with the officers and the staff." So they went to see Bristowe, "a hell of a nice old fellow," and "told him we wanted to join the SAR. He promised to do what he could." There were no vacancies at the moment and the two young officers had to wait some months but by the following spring a place was found for them.

Christmas was approaching, the third wartime Christmas for the SAR and their first overseas. Unlike 1941, it would not be a white Christmas as there was no snow in Hampshire until the last day of 1942 and that didn't last long. The first sign of the festive season was the arrival of parcels from Canada marked "do not open until December 25th" but, as the War Diarist pointed out, this exhortation was regarded as "just a means of sealing the packages."[70] The war news was better that

Ludshott Common near Headley/Bordon, Hampshire. This area was near the Regiment's first station in Britain and, since they had no tanks, the boys used to walk across the common pretending to be armoured vehicles while making the appropriate sound effects.

PHOTOGRAPH BY DIANNE GRAVES.

Christmas. Rommel had been turned back at El Alamein and had retreated across the desert to Tunisia only to be caught in a trap following the Anglo-American invasion of northwest Africa in November. In Russia the *Wehrmacht's* summer offensive had ended at Stalingrad where an entire German army, cut off and encircled, was desperately fighting for its life. In the East, the Japanese had been halted by the twin victories at the Coral Sea and Midway and the Allies were on the offensive in New Guinea and at Guadalcanal.

On 23 December the Regiment held a party for two hundred local children. The kids were picked up in trucks and received all the candies, treats and other goodies that the boys could beg, borrow or steal. On Christmas Day, everyone was allowed to sleep in and then received a personal gift from the SAR Women's Auxiliary. The enlisted men

The media discover the SAR. Sergeant George Muehllehner (left) of Calgary poses for the Canadian Army photographer with Troopers Gerald Nelles of Edmonton and Rick Frankson of Camrose in April 1943 in a photo used to illustrate an article on the Regiment by Ross Munro. The vehicle is a Lloyd carrier. Eric Frankson was killed at Moerbrugge, Belgium, on 12 September 1944. DND PHOTO.

proceeded to the mess hall to eat a turkey dinner served by the officers with seasonal cheer "provided by 200 gallons of beer which did not last very long."[71] After a brief visit by Worthy, the men had the rest of the day off and many spent it in their favourite pubs, which "managed to cope with the demand and, apart from a few dust-ups with our friends the Elgins, who were at Headley Down," the day passed peaceably enough.[72]

One topic of conversation that Christmas was the rumour that the 4th Division was about to undergo a major reorganization. This was something all soldiers feared because it might mean their units would be broken up and the personnel redistributed – an appalling prospect to officers and men who had worked hard to build *esprit de corps* and create a "family" in the vast impersonal structure of the army. In October a number of conferences were held at divisional headquarters to discuss matters of organization but these related to more mundane matters such as the number of tanks in each troop. By December, however, there were persistent rumours that some of the units in the division were facing disbandment.

The rumours were true. Both Canadian armoured divisions were about to be reorganized as a result of the Canadian government's wartime manpower policy and changes in the British

army. Mackenzie King's Liberals had entered the war on the promise that there would be no conscription for overseas service, a promise intended to mollify Quebec, which was strongly opposed to such a measure. After the fall of France, the government concluded that conscription was necessary for home defence and in June 1940 passed the National Resources Mobilization Act (NRMA) "to legalize compulsory service at home while still maintaining the position that no Canadian could be compelled to serve abroad."[73] Three infantry divisions of NRMA personnel were created and the Canadian Army thus came to be composed of two kinds of soldiers: the "general" or "active service" volunteer available for combat overseas, and the "zombie" (as he was called by everyone except the government) required to serve in Canada but nowhere else. It was a strange, but typically Canadian, solution to a growing political problem as French Canada grew increasingly resentful of English Canada's demand for overseas conscription. In April 1942 King held a national plebiscite to release the government from its promise not to impose conscription and received enthusiastic approval from every part of the Dominion – except Quebec. The wily King had no real wish to impose overseas conscription and tried to navigate a tricky course under the catchphrase "conscription if necessary but not necessarily conscription." Six months later it became obvious that there would not be enough volunteers to maintain the five divisions and three independent brigades of the fighting Canadian army and some units would have to be broken up.

The second factor was the British decision to reorganize their armoured divisions. In late 1942, Commonwealth armoured divisions were composed of two armoured brigades, each having three armoured and one infantry regiment, as well as artillery, reconnaissance and engineer units. This organization had proved itself to be unwieldy and the War Office decided to reorganize on the basis of an armoured brigade of three regiments and an infantry brigade of three infantry regiments as well as ancillary units. An innovation in the proposed new organization was that reconnaissance, formerly the responsibility of the divisional armoured car regiment, would now be carried out by a new type of unit, the armoured reconnaissance regiment. The Canadian Army decided to follow suit and, on 2 December 1942, General Andrew McNaughton, commanding First Canadian Army in England, informed Worthy of the forthcoming change and suggested he combine his six armoured regiments into three and convert one of his infantry units into the new armoured recce regiment.[74]

Worthington did not agree. He protested that his infantry had no tank or carrier instruction and would have to be completely retrained and he also disliked combining units because it might cause "serious upheaval" and, as both his "Guards regiments have strong affiliations with the British Guards and wear badges closely assimilating the British … I foresee many difficulties."[75] Instead, he proposed disbanding two of his six armoured regiments and converting a third to armoured reconnaissance. Toward that end, he rated the six units under his command. In 4 Armoured Brigade, the general efficiency of the Canadian Grenadier Guards was "good throughout" while that of the Governor General's Foot Guards was "good although not as high as the Grenadiers." The problem was the Sherbrooke Fusilier Regiment which was "not up to standard but progressing." In 3 Armoured Brigade, the Elgin Regiment had "first rate" men but Worthy was "not satisfied with the officers" while the British Columbia and South Alberta Regiments were both rated "good." Concerning the South Albertas, Worthy added that these "men and officers are made up from the Western Provinces and have displayed a good deal of initiative in their earlier training" being "mostly country men" but they had "gone back slightly of late as the Commanding Officer is too old to assimilate the new technique." His suggestion was to include the two Guards regiments and the BCR in the armoured brigade, disband the Elgins and Sherbrookes, and convert the South Albertas into an armoured reconnaissance regiment. McNaughton agreed and on 29 December 1942 Worthy informed the SAR that henceforth they would be known as the "29th Canadian Armoured Reconnaissance Regiment (South Alberta Regiment)."[76]

Old soldiers. Captain Walter Hunter (left) and Lieutenant-Colonel William "Buffalo Bill" Bristowe in England in April 1943. Hunter was the quartermaster of the Regiment at the time while Bristowe commanded the South Albertas from April 1941 to April 1943. "Buffalo Bill" was an affable gentleman and well liked by everyone but appears to have needed some instruction on the correct way to wear a beret. DND PHOTO.

This news caused great rejoicing. The South Albertas now became divisional troops serving directly under Worthy's command and "when the Canadian Army goes into action, the armoured spearhead will be pointed with the 29 Canadian Armoured Recce Regiment."[77] The problem was that no one seemed to know how this new entity should be organized, equipped or trained. The theory was that the armoured recce regiment would give the divisional commander "the means to carry out close reconnaissance of the division's front or flanks, and to supplement information received from outside sources, e.g., on air, intelligence, and armoured cars, so as to enable him to stage his battle."[78] It would therefore require "the resources and armament to fight for their information" if necessary, and that meant tanks. This new role also meant that the South Albertas would have to acquire different skills as the key to good reconnaissance work is the acquisition and timely passage of information back to the commanders and units who need it.

Worthy had some ideas on the subject. He stressed the "necessity of transforming the unit into an intelligence unit" when he visited the Regiment on New Year's Day 1943 to brief the officers on what lay ahead.[79] He also emphasized the "great responsibility" that the South Alberta Regiment would now "have as the spearhead of the Canadian Army" and presented the unit with an experimental .30 calibre Winchester semi-automatic rifle which he wanted tested for its suitability as a tank crew weapon – the first of a number of pieces of prototype equipment or weapons that the South Albertas would test for him over the next six months. On 19 January Worthy elaborated his ideas in a training memorandum which laid down that the Regiment's new role would be "PROTECTION" in "its broadest sense."[80] They would collect information, sift it and pass it back to the divisional commander but they would also be prepared to fight to force the enemy to disclose his positions, brush aside minor resistance, seize and dominate ground, prevent enemy reconnaissance and provide rearguards in a withdrawal. The new organization would consist of a Recce Troop equipped with ten Lynx scout cars, an inter-communication troop with seven of the same vehicles and three fighting squadrons, each with three troops of three Ram tanks and three troops of three carriers. Worthy encouraged the South Albertas to develop "acquisitive alertness" and laid down that the carrier crews must be able to fight as infantry if required.[81]

The Regiment went to it with a will. Throughout January and February 1943 the South Albertas reorganized their three squadrons on the basis of separate tank and carrier troops, attended lectures on the structure and tactics of the German army and also received twelve German uniforms to make training more realistic. On 19 January they held vehicle trials for Worthy and his staff comparing the suitability of the Ram, the carrier, the Lynx scout car and a new Lloyd "baby" tank for reconnaissance work. The Lloyd did well but when it caught fire two days later it was scratched from the list of potential recce vehicles.[82]

In mid-January 1943 the South Albertas changed stations, moving from their billets in and around Headley to new quarters a few miles away in the spiritual home of the British Army, the vast and sprawling complex of permanent buildings at Aldershot. They were assigned to the Talavera Barracks, which had been "built sometime in the last century and had been condemned as unfit after every ensuing war."[83] For the officers, it wasn't too bad as British officers lived in style and their new mess was "a huge room with high ceilings" and a "mahogany table, approximately 50 feet long," which prompted Lieutenant Jay Moreton to suggest placing field telephones every ten feet or so "to aid those requesting food to be passed from a distance."[84] The enlisted men were not so lucky as their quarters had been left in a deplorable condition by the previous tenants and required considerable work to be made habitable but, nonetheless, the men liked Aldershot; being a bigger town used to a large garrison, it had double the number of pubs.

The South Albertas were only at Aldershot for six weeks. On 23 February they moved to the Farnham area, where they were again dispersed in squadron billets dotted around the countryside. February is spring in southern England and, as the *Short History* notes, it was "a most delightful season" as we "were in the heart of the country, with sufficient pubs nearby and RHQ far enough away so that they did not bother the squadrons unduly."[85] This was particularly true of Bert Coffin's C Squadron, whose billets "had been previously occupied by an infantry regiment and boasted an infantry assault and obstacle course." According to Captain Glen McDougall, "Bert looked at me and said 'let's get this thing filled and taken down otherwise someone will get ideas.'" McDougall records that he had never "seen the troops work harder."

February 1943 also marked the Regiment's first try at the Canadian Army boxing championships. Two years before, the SAR had fielded a boxing team in Nanaimo but there had been no opportunity for competition during the winter of 1941-1942. In fact, except for baseball, the unit sports programme had suffered during the hectic months of armoured conversion at Debert. All this changed when the SAR arrived in Britain as the new RSM, Jock Mackenzie, was an avid athlete and a firm believer that victory in sports was the acid test of a regiment's spirit. This belief, coupled with the added attraction that athletes were normally relieved from fatigue duties (particularly the heartily-disliked "pot walloping" or "pearl diving" in the kitchen), resulted in a flowering of South Alberta athletic endeavour. As soon as the Regiment arrived in Britain Mackenzie began by organizing an inter-squadron sports programme including boxing, soccer, football, baseball and volleyball. A major sports day was held in the rain on 10 October which featured all these games plus track and field as well as sack races and a tug-of-war – C Squadron walked off with most of the trophies.[86]

The emphasis on sports soon began to pay off. Over the next six months, the SAR won the 4th Division soccer championship and the divisional cross-country run. Mackenzie, however, reserved his greatest enthusiasm for the "gentlemanly art of self defence" as did "Buffalo Bill" Bristowe, who had once competed for the middleweight title of the British Army. The 1943 boxing team had no trouble winning the divisional championship but the competition was stiffer in the quarter-finals on 13 February although two of the boys, Troopers Joe Main and Rocky Wagner, picked up enough points to get to the Canadian Army Championship finals held a few weeks later. Unfortunately, as the War Diarist sadly recorded, during the finals on 26 February they "put up a good show … but suffered defeat at the hands of more experienced men." Their turn would come.[87]

CHAPTER FOUR

"You've got the SARs, they're my pride and joy."

BRITAIN: MARCH – DECEMBER 1943

The Regiment's training during the winter of 1942-1943 had been hampered by the change of role and the moves to Aldershot and, later, Farnham. The South Albertas managed to carry out a two-day harbouring exercise in late January and during February the emphasis was on TEWTs, both at the squadron and troop level. In March the SAR became the first unit in the Canadian Army to receive a new vehicle, an American White Motor Company halftrack, to test its suitability as a command vehicle. On 4 March, the Regiment conducted Exercise SCOUT III in which troops, squadrons and RHQ practised passing back information by wireless to the commanding officer stationed with two radios in the new halftrack. This exercise proved to be more difficult than planned because of the massive wireless and vehicle traffic generated by First Canadian Army's major scheme, SPARTAN, the largest Canadian exercise held in Britain to that time. On the day following SCOUT III, Worthy came to take a look at the newly-dubbed halftrack ACV (Armoured Command Vehicle), which received good marks although modifications were suggested which he immediately approved. On 8 March the South Albertas were selected to test the Sten submachine gun for its suitability as a personal weapon for tank crews in preference to the Thompson. Opinions on this cheaply and crudely built 9 mm automatic weapon, with its unreliable safety switch, weak magazine spring and other design faults, were mixed but nonetheless it was shortly afterward issued on the basis of one per tank. The Regiment also got its first mortars in March. Normally, armoured regiments did not use these miniature artillery pieces but since the SAR was expected to perform as infantry on occasion, they received 2- and 3-inch mortars for practice.[2]

By the end of March, the modifications to the ACV were finished and Exercise TRACKER was held on 1 April to test it. It passed with flying colours and the Regiment demonstrated its capabilities to senior officers including General McNaughton himself. On 20 April, A and C Squadrons departed for three-

*O*h, here we come! Who? The SAR.
We've travelled near, we've travelled far,
Now it's Hitler's fault, the son of a gun,
We're out to get us a Nazi Hun,
We'll show them who we are.
    And when we get there, there'll be a mess,
    For what we'll do – you'll have to guess.
We will beat the submarine and mine,
    And chase the Hun across the Rhine.
Hi Ho! We're off to war![1]

day schemes and the following day the remainder of the Regiment held Exercise THIRSTY near Petworth. This exercise, as the War Diarist records, was "rightly named as most of the pubs on route were quite dry" and it was followed eight days later by Exercise SUBLIME near Winchester, which was a test of convoy discipline. By now, the SAR had its full establishment of tanks, carriers and vehicles.[3]

These exercises revealed two things. The South Albertas needed a lot more work in the field and, at age 47, "Buffalo Bill" Bristowe was too old for modern armoured warfare, which called for quick thinking and decision-making coupled with a mastery of wireless communications. "Bristowe was too far away from the regimental situation to be a good trainer," comments Captain Glen McDougall, and he "was not that great with armour."[4] McDougall recalls that on "one wireless exercise, Buffalo Bill was sitting there with the control net, and we had just changed the code alphabet and he said: 'move to Lone Tree Heights, I spell in code … I'll be f____d if I spell … move!'" If the South Alberta Regiment was to have a chance against the experienced enemy they were preparing to meet, they would need a younger and quicker commanding officer. The quality of their opponent was clearly spelled out to them by the first South Alberta to see combat in the war, Sergeant Ernie Hill, who spent the first three months of 1943 on attachment to the British 17/21 Lancers in North Africa. Returning to Farnham at the end of April, Hill lectured his comrades on the "simple and tricky" German tactics he had observed and emphasized that the SAR faced an enemy who "attacks at any time, day or night, and is very accurate with all tank weapons and especially his mortars."[5] The Germans were not invincible, he concluded, but they are "very dangerous and very smart."

Worthington was aware of Bristowe's inadequacies and had hinted as much in his letter to McNaughton quoted above. The divisional commander had taken a shine to the SAR and was always appearing in their area. On 8 April he descended on the unit to make a snap inspection. He was quick but thorough, questioning and testing men at random, having at least one man in each troop open his pack (the War Diarist notes that there were many "holey" socks) and making a detailed inspection of their vehicles.[6] Following a Regimental march past, he gave the South Albertas a "pep talk" and it was probably at this time that he made the famous statement that he had chosen them as the divisional reconnaissance regiment because "westerners should have better eyesight, being outdoor men."[7] As usual, he spared no punches and the War Diarist recorded that "he said we were all living on borrowed time and half of us should be six feet under now anyway!" This delighted everyone but Worthy knew that his only-partly-serious prediction might come true if the Regiment did not get a new commander. He had just the officer in mind.

Lieutenant-Colonel Gordon Dorward de Salaberry Wotherspoon of the Governor General's Horse Guards was having a bath when a knock came at the door. It was Friday, 30 April 1943, and Wotherspoon, an instructor at the Royal Armoured Corps Senior Officers' School at Brasenose College, Oxford, was looking forward to a weekend leave in London. He was therefore not happy when he answered the summons to find the adjutant of the school with an order to report immediately to 4th Canadian Armoured Division to take command of the South Alberta Regiment. Never an officer to lack initiative, Wotherspoon immediately got on the phone to a friend on the divisional staff who told him to take his weekend and show up on the following Monday.[8]

Gordon Wotherspoon had a pedigree to match his name. On his father's side, he was descended from the Juchereau-Duchesnay family of New France which had first come to Canada in 1635 while his inheritance from his mother's side was no less impressive. Gordon, known to family and friends as "Swatty," followed his older brother Ian to the Royal Military College at Kingston and finished first in his class for three of four years; in his second year he was runner-up possibly because of some indiscretion over trying to purchase meat pies from a commercial vendor while on exercise. His instructors were impressed by Wotherpoon's "ability … his patience and capacity for hard work" and noted his knack for "grasping and retaining the fundamentals, and pursuing them to their logical conclusion."[9] By his last year, Gordon Wotherspoon was senior cadet under-officer and when he graduated in 1930, he received not only the Sword of Honour for conduct and discipline but almost every other prize or award being offered including the Governor-General's Medal for highest aggregate of marks throughout his four years, setting a record for achievement at RMC that has never been surpassed.[10]

A commission in the permanent force was open but Gordon Wotherspoon saw no future in peacetime soldiering, where the pay was low and the promotion slow. He decided to enter the legal profession, and after graduating from Osgoode Hall Law

Swatty. Lieutenant-Colonel Gordon Dorward de Salaberry Wotherspoon, commanding officer, South Alberta Regiment, 1943-1945. He was "Swatty" to everyone except the South Albertas, to whom he was always "the Colonel" or "Sir." A brilliant soldier and gifted tactician who had the moral courage to refuse a bad order, it was the South Albertas' great good fortune and the Canadian Army's great misfortune that Gordon Wotherspoon never achieved higher rank during the war. COURTESY, WOTHERSPOON FAMILY.

School in Toronto in 1933, he entered a Bay Street law firm. He also joined the Governor General's Body Guard (later Horse Guards), a militia cavalry unit; by 1939 he was a captain, and when his regiment mobilized in 1940, he was adjutant. Wotherspoon went overseas in October 1941 and by the following September, when he was chosen to attend the Royal Armoured Corps' Senior Officers' School at Brasenose, the traditional preparation for higher command in the corps, he was a major and squadron commander. Swatty loved this "great school" run by "very able, brilliant instructors" and the "absolute epitome" of the training that an armoured officer needed to take an armoured "regiment or a brigade into action."[11] His instructors were no less impressed and, after graduating at the top of his course, he was asked to join the directing staff or military faculty of the school. As an acting lieutenant-colonel and the only Canadian officer on the staff, Wotherspoon had "a wonderful learning period," and by the time he was ordered to

SAR officers and NCOs, late 1942 or early 1943. In the back row from left to right: Danny McLeod, Jim Gove, Cyril Bedford, John Knox, Bill Paterson, Wally Jellis, George Penny, Herbie Watkins, Jack Craig, John Monilaws, Roy Campbell, Jim Anderson, Herb Zwick, unidentified, Bob Fairhurst. Second row from the back, left to right: unidentified, Horace Clarke, Alex Laing, J.P. Moreton, Bob Donaldson, Jim Crichton, Gordie Shell, unidentified, H.D. Watson, Kenny Perrin, Ronald L. Hancock and Bob Allsopp. In the third row from the back can be identified Kenny Little (third from left), John Gunn-Fowlie (fifth from left) and Ernie Hill (fourth from right). In the fourth row from the back Bill Swanson is third from the left and Bill Scott is fifth from left. COURTESY, DANNY McLEOD.

take over the South Albertas in May 1943, he was a "pretty skilled tactician."[12] He had also made something of a name for himself in the Canadian Armoured Corps.[13]

On Monday, 3 May 1943, Wotherspoon arrived at 4th Division Headquarters at Aldershot to have an interview with Worthy. The two men knew each other from the early armoured days at Borden in 1940-1941 and Worthy had been watching the younger officer's progress, while Wotherspoon, in turn, thought the crusty general a "superb leader" and a "brilliant tactician."[14] The old warrior was always unconventional – the first thing he did was to hand Swatty a two-page "Appreciation of General Worthington" which "he'd written himself" and say "this is my appreciation, now take it and recognize me." The second thing the new commander received was a brief lecture on the strengths and weaknesses of the Regiment which ended with the words: "you've got the SARs, they're my pride and joy. … You'd better do well with them." Then it was into a waiting vehicle and off to the Regiment.

It was dark by the time Wotherspoon arrived at RHQ in Farnham and nothing could be done that night. The following morning was taken up with discussions with Bristowe and a tour of headquarters and then, accompanied by Lieutenant Bob Allsopp, he set out in the afternoon to visit the squadron areas "to see where they were located and what they were doing in the way of training."[15] Wearing his dress tunic and Sam Browne belt, a snappy forage cap with a prominent Horse Guards badge and carrying a swagger stick, this trim military apparition appeared without warning at each squadron area.

By the time he walked into the officers' mess of Bert Coffin's C Squadron it was evening and Bert and the boys were in the middle of their nightly crap game. Coffin was "the noisiest crap

shooter I ever heard," recalled Lieutenant Gerry Adams and Wotherspoon "didn't raise hell or anything but you could tell he wasn't very happy and I felt sorry for him."[16] Coffin in turn was "not all that impressed" with his new commanding officer.[17] The South Albertas were a down-to-earth outfit with that easygoing but efficient attitude that is the hallmark of the western soldier, while Wotherspoon was an "Upper Canada type of person" and it was Bert's feeling that Wotherspoon's "attitude, the Horse Guards attitude, would not sit all that well with the regiment." Wotherspoon himself was aware of the difference in backgrounds and that night, when his tour was over, he remarked to Allsopp that "he would have to either convert this regiment into guardsmen or become a westerner."[18] Time would tell.

Wotherspoon formally assumed command of the Regiment on 5 May 1943. Despite his initial apprehensions, he was impressed – they "were superb soldiers," he recalled and "highly skilled in their ability to use their tanks. They were very well trained in maintenance, they were well disciplined."[19]

Good discipline or not, Wotherspoon wanted to make his mark. He therefore called RSM Jock Mackenzie into his office and informed him that "you're responsible for the discipline amongst the men, up to the sergeant majors." It was a wise decision because, as he later fondly recalled, Mackenzie was a "tough and a great RSM" and they were all "terrified of him." The new commanding officer knew that the South Albertas had very few bad characters, a quality he attributed to their early training by Carvosso and Seal, but he wanted things tightened up and RSM Mackenzie was just the man to see to that. Five days after he took command, some poor unfortunate from A Squadron received twenty-eight days in the detention barracks for a minor "Absence Without Leave" charge, an unusually heavy punishment for a misdemeanour which, the War Diarist points out, was "very infrequent."[20] To enlisted men like Trooper George Gallimore, the message was clear – the new colonel "was the boss, he made no bones about that and we were scared stiff of him."[21] It did not take long for the SAR to measure up to Wotherspoon's expectations as "they knew I was pretty much of a disciplinarian" and he soon had "difficulty in finding one ungreased nipple in a thousand" during vehicle inspections.[22] He also realized that the "most effective punishment was cutting down on their leaves" and unless the transgressions were serious he usually preferred this penalty to any other.

Wotherspoon's next task was to assess what the Regiment could do – and correct any deficiencies. He began with the officers and over the next few weeks three-hour TEWTs were held in the officers' mess in the evenings (including Saturday night) combined with frequent daytime excursions into the field to test the officers' knowledge. He also assessed each subordinate personally and it was a bad time for the officers, particularly the junior officers, for Wotherspoon was "a hard man to get along with, he demanded excellence where it was sometimes difficult to produce" and young officers used to Bristowe's friendly ways got a rude awakening.[23] "He was very intelligent," recalled Lieutenant Gerry Adams, "but very arrogant and rather cold and I found him a difficult man to work for."[24] Lieutenant Leaman Caseley, somewhat older and a family man, was more measured in his assessment: "Wotherspoon was a pretty good commander but he didn't have much personality and didn't have a knack of talking to junior officers … if he appeared in the mess, he was pretty much by himself and remote."[25] Some of the more perceptive, like Glen McDougall, realized that, under his cold exterior, Wotherspoon "was really rather shy and nobody got that close to him," but "he knew exactly what he was doing and he was the kind of man you wanted to go into battle with."[26] Although the Regiment knew their new commander's nickname it was never used within his earshot – to the South Albertas he was always "Colonel Wotherspoon" or "Sir," but in this book he will be called "Swatty," the name by which he is best known.

The coming of Swatty was a time of trial for the officers but easygoing Bert Coffin managed to miss most of it as he was "nailed for the senior officers' school at Oxford" and "Swatty had put his mark on the regiment by the time I came back."[27] "He had done an awful lot of things," Bert recalled, "he had toughened us up as we were becoming pretty lax under Bristowe." In the end, Coffin's conclusion was the same as every other SAR who served under Gordon Wotherspoon: "He was the right guy at the right place at the right time." The Regiment had its war leader.

Swatty's assessment of his officers lasted through most of May 1943. The Regiment was under control of its NCOs on several days when he took every available officer into the field and the War Diarist dryly noted that "this was no bad thing."[28] Otherwise, large-scale training was limited: C Squadron held a one-day exercise to practice march discipline, while B Squad-

ron went out on an air co-operation scheme but their camouflage was so good the aircraft couldn't find them. Toward the end of the month, C and HQ Squadrons got one-day schemes to practise harbouring and throughout May all squadrons had small-arms and grenade training on the range. The big news in early May was the visit of Canadian war correspondent Ross Munro, who wrote an article about the SAR that appeared in the Canadian Press. Munro described the South Albertas as a "five-in-one regiment" training "hard to spearhead the armoured attacks when the Canadians go to Europe," which was an exaggeration but then one should never believe what one reads in the newspapers.[29] The correspondent did, however, manage to include the names and home towns of an impressive number of officers and men in his small piece.[30]

On 1 June 1943, the War Diarist noted that Corporal Ivan Donkin, who had been with the Regiment since June 1940, was struck off strength to go to OCTU (Officers' Candidate Training Unit). Donkin was another in a succession of young, intelligent NCOs sent to get commissions as the SAR continued the process of "growing its own." Among them was Danny McLeod, who graduated from the Canadian Army OCTU in England in 1943, but Danny was not finished with the business of becoming an officer because he had attracted Swatty's attention and Wotherspoon wanted an SAR officer to graduate from the more prestigious British OCTU at Sandhurst. How it happened is not known – perhaps Swatty pulled strings – but the next thing Danny knew he was "sent up to London to appear before a table full of British generals, admirals, and what have you" and found himself "sitting in a lone chair while they fired questions at me" to assess the former millworker's potential as an officer and gentleman.[31] They must have liked what they saw as 20-year-old Danny McLeod became the first Canadian to attend the RAC course at Sandhurst.

It was quite an experience for a high-school drop out from Medicine Hat to compete against classmates "coming from Eton or Cambridge, Winchester, all the prominent British schools," including "the biggest crop of blue bloods that ever went through the place, lords and barons' sons, the son of the Chief of the Imperial General Staff, the son of the Archbishop of Canterbury, the son of the Lord Mayor of London." The course lasted nearly a year and it was a long twelve months for Danny. He impressed his instructors with his practical knowledge as was demonstrated the day that one of the training tanks had an engine problem and everyone was "in a bit of a panic." Danny "opened the cover, found the problem and fixed it – they just thought that it was incredible for an officer to get his hands dirty." On the other hand, there was the time that he was "one of ten cadets selected from Sandhurst to attend Princess Elizabeth's eighteenth birthday party." Danny was "scared to death because all the guests were from the high aristocracy and I didn't know how to address these people" so he "made himself scarce and spent most of the night hiding behind pillars and palms."[32]

Social graces aside, Danny held his own at Sandhurst, and

Heave, heave! SAR tug-of-war team undoubtedly on its way to victory during a sports day in England, June 1943. In the second photo Trooper Ray Seiferling of Edmonton waits for the pitch; Trooper Sonny Plotsky of Medicine Hat is the catcher. DND PHOTOS.

when he graduated in April 1944, he was awarded the Sword of Honour as the best cadet in his class. General Bernard L. Montgomery presented him with the prize and, while passing it over, remarked: "Well, young man, let's hope that the next time you and I meet, I am pinning a decoration on you on the other side of the Rhine." Montgomery probably said that to every officer cadet he awarded a prize, but in Danny's case he would have cause to remember those words.[33]

This was a great honour but when the newly-minted Lieutenant McLeod returned to his room that day, "at the head of my bed was an officer's shirt, laying in the middle was an officer's tie and laying at the foot of the bed was a pair of brown officer's oxfords." There was a note pinned to the garments: "Sorry I couldn't be here to give you your first salute, Duffy." To Danny, this gift from Duffy Gendron, his boyhood friend from Medicine Hat, was a greater thrill than the prestigious Sword of Honour. "I never did find out how Duffy did it," he recalled decades later, "because he had no business being at Sandhurst with all that brass around." Danny McLeod had blazed a trail that would be followed by many other young Canadian officer candidates, including Ev Nieman of the SAR.[34]

On 3 June 1943 the SAR received a warning order to move to a new station. This move came about as a general shift of 4th Division to the southeast coast of England, terrain familiar to many Canadian troops who had been stationed there for three years. There was a squadron sports day on 5 June and then the Regiment packed up. From 9 June on, the tanks were loaded on "low boy" tank transporters and dispatched in small convoys, the remainder of the Regiment following in vehicles on 12 June. The big transporters always had difficulty negotiating the narrow winding English roads and crowded urban areas, and at the end of each convoy there was usually an officer whose task was writing up the paperwork on civilian damage claims for fences and lamp posts taken out, hedges and walls knocked down and other inanimate objects scraped, dented or squashed flat. The

men in one SAR tank convoy winding through the tight confines of a Sussex village were horrified when "the protruding back-end of one of our low-boys swung out over the sidewalk and flipped over a baby carriage that a young couple were pushing along" and the baby fell out.[35] The war came to a dead stop as a throng of anxious South Albertas crowded around the distraught parents and there were sighs of relief when baby, squalling but otherwise unhurt, was restored to mother's bosom.[36]

The Regiment was delighted with its new station, Preston Park on the outskirts of Brighton, one of the best-known and liveliest coastal resorts in Britain. The men went into billets in the suburbs while the tanks and vehicles were stationed in the park proper, which was so full of young feminine "pulchritude" that, for the first time in the Regiment's recorded history, guard duty became a popular assignment.[37] Brighton offered numerous pubs, pinball arcades, dance halls such as the impressive Dome, and the novelty of an indoor skating rink. The boys took full advantage of these attractions and the War Diarist recorded with great satisfaction that "most everyone" immediately "went into Brighton returning well bent or broke."

Bert Coffin got back from the Senior Officers' school just after the move to Brighton and resumed command of C Squadron. At his first squadron inspection he stopped before Trooper Ralph Whitford, whose face looked as if it had come into contact with a road grader. Ralph "Chief" Whitford from Spedden, Alberta, was one of C Squadron's great characters; he would prove to be a first rate soldier in battle but he was always a terror, particularly with a few drinks under his belt, when he had the nasty habit of picking a fight with the bartender in whatever establishment he happened to be. Bert asked Whitford what had happened to him but the chief would only cryptically state that he "had made an error in judgement." After a lengthy interrogation Bert had the story out of him. It seems the chief had gone into Brighton a few nights before and, as was his wont, had a few drinks in a bar and then took exception to the bartender's face and invited him outside to discuss the matter. The British bartender, a beefy individual, followed the chief outside without hesitation and Whitford was unable to land a single punch before he was knocked unconscious. When he came to, his comrades told him that the bartender was actually the owner of the establishment, his name was

Tommy Farr and he was the former British heavyweight boxing champion and the only man in the history of the ring to go the distance with Joe Louis. Tommy Farr's bar in Brighton became a South Alberta hang-out and Ralph and Tommy became great personal friends but the chief never again misbehaved in Farr's presence.[38]

In the third week of June, the tanks spent two days on the ranges at Beachy Head near Eastbourne in Sussex while the carrier troops fired at the machine-gun ranges at Thunder Barrow Hill, where the tanks later joined them to practise with their hull and co-axial machine guns. Wotherspoon expressed his satisfaction with progress on the range and turned to more advanced training. On 24 June, the Regiment conducted Exercise COUGAR I which pitted A Squadron against B Squadron in an attempt to seize a defended bridge. The exercise was analyzed the following day in an officers' conference which was interrupted by the arrival of Worthy, who inspected the ACV, his "baby," in its final modified form, and toured the tank and vehicle lines. As always he displayed the common touch for which he was famous. Wotherspoon recalled that they encountered a South Alberta working with his head "under a truck and his tools out on the running board."[39] When Worthington put "his foot up on the tools" to talk to the man, the irate SAR, who did not realize who his visitor was, proceeded to berate his commanding general: "Get your g___d f___g foot off my tools, I know where every one of those is, and you've mucked them up." Another general might have taken offence but not Worthy, who simply commented to Swatty, "That's a good man."[40]

COUGAR I was followed by COUGAR II and III in late June and early July 1943 which familiarized the Regiment in screening a divisional advance and providing a rearguard for a withdrawal. There were no manuals on the role of the armoured reconnaissance unit to guide Wotherspoon but by this time he had remedied that lack with a series of typed "Training Bulletins" that circulated in the Regiment. Drafted or revised by Swatty, these bulletins laid down simple, basic procedures ("drills") to be followed by the recce troop, carrier troops and tank troops in the various situations they were likely to encounter in battle. Wotherspoon valued initiative at all levels and stressed that the bulletins were not graven in stone and "*must not be rigid* in their application" but were only "a basis from which to work in order to produce speedy reaction to various situations." The "initiative of the junior leader must *NOT* be cramped or fettered in any way."[41]

Having formulated a basic doctrine for armoured reconnaissance, Swatty now proceeded to more advanced collective

training. An essential skill was the ability to move in unknown territory without getting lost – in short, good map reading. Wotherspoon was convinced that "a successful soldier or commander" had "to be a good map reader."[42] In fact, he was a fanatic on the subject and, according to one SAR officer, Swatty had an advantage because he "could lay a map out and see the depressions and elevations as though they were three-dimensional … it was an art and he was fortunate that he had it."[43] Other SAR officers who did not possess this talent soon attracted the unwelcome attention of their colonel, who commented:

Sunday Dinner Parade, Preston Park near Brighton, England, August 1943. The boys loved their time at Brighton, one of Britain's largest seaside resorts and full of attractions, "both animate and inanimate." SAR COLLECTION.

I taught my fellows map reading pretty well because I made my officers, whenever they were with me, read the map, and you know, there are no signs [in wartime Britain] and I'd give them so long to get me from A to B. Coming back from Wales one time I had one officer, a young officer, with me reading the map, and I told him for every half hour he's late, he loses a day's leave. Well, he got hopelessly lost a couple of times, so I took over, and I said "I'm going to take you again, and you've lost one week of your leave, I'm going to take you out again and you're going to know your map reading by then."[44]

By such gentle methods, Swatty drove the point home and proudly recalled that "by the time we went over to France" they "were all good map readers even down to my sergeants."

In the second week of July, the SAR left its vehicles at Preston Park and went by train west to Minehead in Somerset to undertake an extensive range practice using tanks provided by the 4th Division. The men were billeted in the town, an attractive coastal resort with many pubs, a cinema and dance halls "with a lot of girls for the men to dance with." The ranges were situated on bleak hills facing the Bristol Channel. Shooting began on 8 July and lasted nine days as each tank crew in turn worked through the nine established range exercises, firing the Ram's 6-pdr. main armament at canvas targets on a wooden

Trooper Dexter Colwell cleans his .30 calibre Browning machine gun on a sunny day in April 1943. Colwell was killed sixteen months after this photograph was taken. DND PHOTO.

frame which moved along a miniature railway at the back of the butts. They repeated the process firing at the troop level and finally did the battle practice, which involved firing on the move. In the summer of 1943, the Canadian Armoured Corps was beginning to re-equip with the American-built Sherman tank and the tank crews got an opportunity to fire the larger 75 mm gun of the Sherman. This was the longest period of tank firing the Regiment had undertaken and they noted a problem with the .30 calibre Browning machine guns which were the Ram's secondary armament. The Brownings were "accurate to a degree if fired in short bursts but if the bursts were too long and too often, the barrel would heat up and the rounds would go every which way."[45] Armourer Sergeant Elliot Campbell, who was at Minehead to assist the tank crews in adjusting their weapons, remembered a number of instances when the Brownings became so hot that they would fire prematurely without their triggers being pulled. He scolded the tank gunners to fire in short bursts but too often they "would get excited and stand on the solenoid until the belt was empty and the guns would become so hot that they wouldn't stop firing and just cook off rounds." The problem would continue in action.[46]

Wotherspoon was pleased that the Regiment proved to be "superb shots, brilliant tank shots."[47] Armourer Sergeant Campbell attributed the SAR's shooting ability to the fact that "they were on the range more than any other unit I served with and I served with many."[48] He also remembered that Wotherspoon "did a lot of tank shooting" himself and "was a very good shot." As a cadet Swatty had competed for RMC at the international competitions at Bisley and had won many tro-

phies for his marksmanship – he told the Regiment that he would "take anybody on at one or five pounds per shot" and he rarely lost.[49] The SAR always enjoyed range work and Minehead was a good time for everyone as, after the day's shooting was over, there was plenty to do in the evenings – so much so that when paymaster Captain Bert Huffman arrived with the mid-month pay on 12 July there was great rejoicing as "the multitude of attractions, both animate and inanimate, have imposed a severe strain on slender purses."[50]

July 1943 also marked the first time that Canadian troops went into prolonged action during the war when, after nearly four years of waiting, the 1st Infantry Division participated in the Allied invasion of Sicily. The progress of the Sicilian operation was the topic of the hour when the Regiment returned to Preston Park in the third week of July but for the SAR the prospect of action still lay sometime in the future and it resumed small-arms, grenade and gas training and listening to seemingly endless lectures.

It was now that Trooper Cecil "Blackie" Blackstock ascended to the ranks of the immortals. Blackie was the driver of a water wagon and, before leaving Dorset, he filled his water tank with as much potent West Country cider as he could lay hands on with a view to giving "the boys a treat" when they got back to Sussex. Not long after the return to Preston Park there was much jollity in the vehicle lines during daily maintenance. Sergeant Earle Wood remembered what happened after the orderly officer for the day became "suspicious and discovered that Blackie had a deal going. Consequently I was appointed escort and RQSM McTavish paraded Blackie before Captain Nash" and "there was some very muffled chuckles when the charge of illegally transporting apple cider in a government vehicle came down."[51] Blackie was back in his truck by the time the Regiment changed stations on 7 August 1943, moving from Preston Park to West Worthing in Sussex to be closer to the large tank training area in the South Downs.

By late summer Wotherspoon had decided to make some changes among his officers. Over the previous six months, Majors Arnold Lavoie of A Squadron, Bob Bradburn of B and Bert Coffin of C, as well as some of the more senior captains such as Dave Currie, Darby Nash and Stan Purdy had attended the RAC school at Brasenose College. This gave the colonel a pool of officers qualified for higher command, and between August and October he made a number of personnel changes. Perhaps the most surprising, in view of their uneasy first meeting, was the appointment on 31 August of Bert Coffin, the easygoing commander of C Squadron, to replace Major Howard Wright as second-in-command. Swatty Wotherspoon was nobody's fool and was aware that his somewhat distant nature needed balancing by a man who was friendly, approachable and had a "great relationship with the officers and with the men" but there was more to it.[52] Swatty had discerned that, beneath Bert's affable exterior, the former druggist from Medicine Hat was "a very fine leader" who "picked up tactics twice as fast" as any of his officers and was capable of commanding the Regiment in battle. To replace Bert at C Squadron he promoted Captain Dave Currie, Coffin's former second-in-command, who he had concluded was a fighter who "never backed down from anything" and a "brave and very cool officer" despite his somewhat shy personality and relaxed sense of dress. To balance this scrapper he had the quiet, dependable Arnold Lavoie in A Squadron, who "was the best tactician amongst my officers other than Bert Coffin" and whose strength lay in the set-piece attack. Somewhere in between was Bob Bradburn of B, whose personal manner engendered "fantastic loyalty" in his own squadron but tended to intimidate those not serving directly under him. To offset Bradburn, Wotherspoon appointed Lieutenant Bob Allsopp as adjutant because Bob had known Bradburn in civilian life and was, in his own words, "the only guy in the Regiment who would stand up to him."[53] Finally, Darby Nash was tipped to take over HQ squadron in the near future. The South Albertas now bade farewell to Howard Wright and Bert Huffman, those two stalwarts who had done a marvellous job preparing the Regiment for action, spotting and commissioning deserving young NCOs, and making a considerable contribution to the creation of a fine unit.

The Regiment also gained some good people in August when they received four officers and a number of men from the Saskatchewan Light Horse, their old sparring partners from Nanaimo. The SLH were broken up in the summer of 1943 due to a decision to reduce the number of armoured regiments in the Canadian Army, another result of the government's disastrous manpower policy. The four new officers, Lieutenants Jim Curley, Clive Smith, Ed Reardon and Don Stewart, fitted easily into the SAR because, as Stewart wrote, the "men in the South Albertas are the same type we had in the 'Horses' – good fellows and easy to get along with if you know how to handle them."[54] Stewart himself was actually from New Brunswick and a rarity among South Alberta officers in that he was an RMC graduate, albeit from the shortened wartime course, but Don suspected that Wotherspoon "always thought I flunked out or was expelled, as he never mentioned RMC to me at any time."[55]

The later part of August saw the Regiment undertake a number of squadron schemes on the South Downs in preparation for a series of major exercises scheduled that autumn in Norfolk. A serious incident occurred on 24 August when Trooper Harry Walker of C Squadron was killed during a demonstration the SAR put on for Worthy west of Findon. Walker was a member of a mortar detachment that set up its weapon in front of a tree and began to fire. Unfortunately, they were too close to the tree and the second round hit a branch and exploded, spraying shrapnel among the detachment and killing Walker, a 30-year-old farmer from Grouard, Alberta.[56] Although there was no doubt that the death was accidental, Wotherspoon was worried about Worthy's reaction. He needn't have been:

Worthy was a great fellow. He always called me "my boy" when he liked what I was doing and "colonel" when he didn't like what I was doing. He says "well now, that's very interesting, my boy, – yes, I like that exercise, I think that's great and I'm glad you did it." …

I saw great courts of inquiry coming on and you know, a lot of fuss and fury because they had about a one-inch thick manual on safety precautions, none of which [was useful because] if you followed it, you'd never put an exercise on. But I finally came around to the point. I said, "Well sir, sorry to have to tell you. In the exercise, I killed a man." I used the "I" always when I'm talking about my regiment or what I was doing. And he says, "What's that you say, my boy?" "We killed a man." He said: "My boy, that's what I like, – realism in training. That's a great exercise. I'm going to have you put that exercise on again and I'm going to get all the officers in div[ision] out to see it."

I wasn't sure whether I had to kill a man on the next exercise, but fortunately we didn't.[57]

The Regiment's hard work during the late spring and summer of 1943 had been duplicated by the other units in 4th Division. In September they all prepared to take to the field in a series of large-scale exercises in Norfolk and there was great excitement when the Regiment received orders on 1 September

Maintenance Parade, July 1943. In an armoured regiment, vehicle maintenance never stopped. Note the black denim coveralls, the standard work dress for armoured crews at this time. The tank is a Canadian-built Ram II and the crew is actually from the BCR, not the SAR. DND PHOTO.

to move to West Tofts Camp near Brandon. Lieutenant Hank Carroll was in charge of loading the tracked vehicles onto railway flatcars and his own kindness almost ended in disaster. Learning that there would be a delay, he allowed his drivers to wait it out in a nearby pub for "exactly twenty minutes."[58] Since "not one" of the drivers "would violate the trust our lieutenant had placed in us," they were back in exactly twenty minutes having "ordered as many pints each as we thought we had time for" and having filled all available containers with the best bitter, which they drank on the way back. They returned with "the beer finished, the containers discarded and the tank drivers dead drunk." Carroll was astounded to find the troopers who "had been stone cold sober twenty minutes ago" in this condition but, "having let us go to the pub and being an honourable man, he felt he must make the best of it." As Wilf Taylor reports, that was Lieutenant Carroll's second mistake:

Thomas "Darby" Nash, shown here as a captain in 1943, assumed command of B Squadron in August 1944 and commanded it for the rest of the war. A prewar officer of the Alberta Dragoons, he became the SAR's fourth wartime commander in June 1945.

SAR COLLECTION.

> He picked out the most reliable-looking driver he could see among us and instructed him to drive on the first tank. "Now drive carefully," he emphasized, with a note of hope in his voice, as the driver boarded the tank with what appeared to us to be fairly good form under the circumstances.
>
> *Carefully* would have called for a slow crawl, in low gear and with the least possible throttle, up the ramp and along the cars and over the connecting planks, with great attention to staying dead centre all the way.
>
> Our chosen lead driver put the tank in third gear at full throttle, rattled up the ramp and along the cars and over the connecting planks, not stopping once until he was in perfect position at the end of the last car.
>
> It had been a breathtaking performance. Not one among the rest of us thought it possible to duplicate the feat and it now seemed unlikely we would have the opportunity to try. The train crew foreman was stunned at what he had witnessed and Lieutenant Carroll appeared to be in shock.

The British foreman, concerned about possible damage to his flatcars, offered to arrange the loading with experienced civilians and Lieutenant Carroll and his men then went on their way. The drivers were in Norfolk before Carroll "even cared to acknowledge our existence."[59]

The wheeled vehicles moved north in a convoy which arrived without incident except that Captain Stan Purdy and Lieutenants Alec Laing and Kenny Scott, unable to resist trying to bag some of the wild game which abounded in Norfolk, ran

"into trouble with a local constable for shooting on private property."[60] Most of the men made the journey by train and there was a four-mile hike from the station at Brandon to their quarters at West Tofts Camp, which, as the *Short History* commented, "was not very attractive, being very sparsely settled and having very few pubs or good looking women" but "war is war."[61] On 7 September, the Regiment reassembled with a strength of 660 officers and men and got down to work. Over the next two months they would carry out a series of exercises and schemes that would get progressively larger until the entire 4th Division was pitted against a similar formation.[62]

On 8 September 1943, the SAR left West Tofts for the field to undertake a number of squadron and then regimental schemes to practice its task of providing reconnaissance for the division. During Exercise TAKEX I on 25-26 September Bob Bradburn immortalized himself. "By shouting loudly," the War Diarist recorded, "he managed to convince two platoons" of the Lake Superiors who were acting as "enemy" that "he had a considerable force with him" and they surrendered. The SAR repeated TAKEX on 27 September and then made "a night move involving fording a river and harbouring at 0230 under a torrential fall of rain." Worthy now granted his men a three-day break, which was put to good use by introducing to each other the various units in the division, which had been scattered for much of the preceding year. On 28 September, each squadron of the armoured regiments and each company of the infantry regiments camped in different groups which "contained a mixture of all arms of the Division," as it was Worthy's "intention that two days be spent … visiting other arms, seeing how they worked and inspecting their equipment."[63]

This inter-arms demonstration finished on the first day of October and the Regiment moved back to West Tofts Camp for a short breather. By now, the South Albertas had shaken the softness of the south out of their systems and were getting used to Norfolk, which, the War Diarist commented, "is certainly God's country" but "the men seem to love it, for all its drawbacks, the part of it we are in reminds them very much of the wilds and wastes of Canada."[64] Four days later, the SAR returned to the field to prepare for Exercise GRIZZLY II, a divisional-size scheme that was to get them ready for the even larger BRIDOON at the end of the month, when 4th Canadian Armoured Division would be pitted against 9th British Armoured Division. The SAR always took their intelligence work seriously and the Intelligence Officer, Lieutenant C.S. Ross, was starting to nose around 9th Armoured to find out what he

Recce Troop on exercise, England, summer of 1943. At this time the Troop was equipped with Canadian-built Ford Lynx scout cars capable of 50 mph on paved roads, a feature that led to some wild times in southern England. Lieutenant Jack Summers is on the left and Lieutenant Joel Smith on the right. SAR COLLECTION.

could about the SAR's future opposition, the Royal Gloucestershire Regiment, the armoured recce regiment of that division. On 8 October the Regiment commenced a "runner up" scheme for GRIZZLY II at 0230 hours in which the quiet of the woods was broken as "the sound of No. 19 sets buzzed in the stillness as the time for netting approached." The Regiment crossed its start line at 0650 hours on its way to secure a bridge over the River Thet, an objective they took, and then returned to West Tofts Camp having learned "many valuable lessons ... particularly in regard to a night movement by road." The enlisted men celebrated the next day with a big dance at the camp where music was provided by a "US black jazz band" and the "pulchritude supplied by various British women's units" and "some very charming American Red Cross hostesses," the first North American women many of the boys had talked to in over a year.[65]

The weather was beginning to turn cool and each man was issued an extra blanket as preparations resumed for GRIZZLY II. This was a divisional exercise against a controlled enemy with special emphasis on the role of the SAR as an armoured reconnaissance regiment, the crossing of obstacles and a full-scale attack on a semi-prepared position. On 15 October, Wotherspoon briefed the Regiment on their role and told them that it "affords a chance for us to help 4th Canadian Armoured Division prove itself worthy and enable it to take its place alongside or above the 5th Canadian Armoured Division." There was a sting in these words for the 5th Division, about to ship out for Italy, had not performed particularly well in Exercise SPARTAN the previous spring, and in his closing remarks Swatty emphasized that the South Albertas "must show ourselves to be better than the Governor General's Horse Guards, our counterpart in 5th Canadian Armoured Division." The Horse Guards were not only the colonel's old regiment – they were also commanded by his brother, Ian Cumberland.[66] Swatty's loyalties had undergone a change and around this time he remarked to Bob Allsopp, "I was going to make them Guardsmen but they have made me a westerner."[67]

GRIZZLY II would be a major test and a further week was

devoted to preparations including signals exercises, recce training, night movement and harbouring. The boys got another chance to listen to the black band at a camp dance in which the padre did a "great job in providing feminine company" and then the carrier troops moved to the Stamford battle area on 16 October while the tank troops did last-minute maintenance. By 19 October the entire Regiment assembled in a harbour in the field. Two more days of preparations followed, including one Orders Group held to ascertain "who certain personnel were who had entered a local orchard and pilfered a sack full of apples" and, at the group's conclusion, the "spoils of said pilfering were distributed." The Regiment was ready to go.

GRIZZLY II began at 0830 hours on 22 October 1943 when the Regiment passed its start line on a mission to seize a bridge over the River Thet for 10 Infantry Brigade. The first "enemy," a patrol of the Manitoba Dragoons, were encountered at 1200 hours and the SAR put them to flight. By 1800 hours, 10 Brigade had a bridgehead and the Regiment had "destroyed" thirty-six armoured and scout cars. Conditions were so wet and miserable that night that Wotherspoon authorized an issue of rum – the first time the SAR received this time-honoured British inducement to valour. It came in earthenware jugs marked "SRD" – initials that many have tried to decipher but few have succeeded – the more popular translations being "Service Rum, Demerara," "Service Rum, Diluted" or the cynical "Sergeants' Ration, Double." Actually, as the SAR's quartermaster, Captain Tommy Barford, explains, "SRD simply meant 'Supply and Replenishment Depot'" and the same letters were marked on the large crates of hard tack that would become familiar in the near future.[68] Having downed their tot, the Regiment turned the bridgehead over to the infantry the following day and its lead

Echelons at work, Norfolk, 1943. Sergeant Fred Clark resupplies a Ram tank from his 15 cwt lorry while a DR poses for the camera. Statistically, the twelve DRs had the most hazardous job in the unit. More than half were killed or injured in vehicle accidents. SAR COLLECTION.

New boys and buddies. Troopers Cliff Dobbs (left) and John Neff joined the Regiment in October 1943. Here they pose in front of their Ram II tank in Norfolk. COURTESY, JOHN NEFF.

elements then crossed the river under a drizzling rain to recce the route to Frog Hill, the division's objective. The SAR advanced three squadrons up, passing information back to divisional headquarters, which urged the advance to be "speeded up," but progress was delayed by the umpires, who applied "pressure" to slow the SAR down. The Regiment got on its objective the following day and the exercise finished successfully.[69]

The Regiment got a few days of rest to catch up on repair and maintenance and then began preparations for the "big game" – Exercise BRIDOON – against 9th British Armoured Division. Swatty was happy with the results of GRIZZLY as it was obvious that the SAR could undertake its role but he stressed that the Regiment would have to get information back more quickly, needed more wireless practice, and would have to stop trying to fight for information that could be gained by other methods. One of these methods was demonstrated by Lieutenant Ross, the Intelligence Officer, who issued a detailed briefing on the SAR's forthcoming opponents in 9th British Armoured Division, including names and personalities of senior officers, vehicle markings, tactical methods and recent activities (which included "testing the River Thet for fords"), and concluded that the Glosters were "a very well trained unit that should form a formidable opponent for us."[70] Ross never revealed the sources of this information but then that is the privilege of intelligence officers. Meanwhile the local game stocks continued to decline. On 29 October, the War Diarist noted that fifteen British officers, attached to the SAR as umpires in the forthcoming scheme, "got a rare treat when a game meal was served in the officers' mess, thanks

to the commanding officer whose marksmanship and faithful old shotgun never fails us." No questions were asked.[71]

Exercise BRIDOON commenced on 2 November 1943 at 0700 hours when the Regiment crossed its start line and immediately made contact with the Glosters. The SAR slowly but steadily pressed them back all through the morning and by 1100 hours "our armour dominated" the situation. By afternoon, the SAR was past its day's objectives so it drew back for the night after putting out patrols. This day turned out very badly for the British as they lost half their tanks and, although it was fairly obvious that 4th Division had won hands down, the umpires ruled that the knocked-out British tanks were to be brought back to life. There was little activity on the morning of the second day but the afternoon brought a determined attack by two squadrons of British armour who drove through A Squadron of the SAR straight onto the positions of a Canadian anti-tank regiment, which promptly "brewed" them up for their troubles. For a while, "there was great excitement around RHQ when three enemy [tank] troops surrounded us" but "they were beaten off and withdrew." At 1700 hours, BRIDOON ended, three days before schedule. The reason was simple – 4th Canadian Armoured Division had gone through 9th British Armoured Division like a knife through cheese. This did not sit well with the British, who complained the Canadians had "scored by using Red Indian tactics" and "that their methods were unorthodox and unsporting."[72] The response was short and to the point: "4th Division was training for war, not playing games."[73]

And that war was coming closer to the Regiment in late 1943. In the Far East, the battles for Guadalcanal and New Guinea had been won and Japan was forced onto the defensive as the United States began a campaign of "island hopping" that would bring it ever closer to the Japanese homeland. In Russia, the German forces at Stalingrad had surrendered the previous February and the Red Army had gone over to the offensive during the summer. Despite Soviet appeals for a "second front" in

Norfolk, autumn 1943. Troopers Ryley, Gunn-Fowlie and Nieman pose in front of their Ram II tank. Trooper Holmes is in the turret. COURTESY, WALLY JELLIS.

God's country, Norfolk, 1943. The South Albertas moved to the wilder terrain of Norfolk in the autumn of 1943 for nearly two months of schemes and exercises. They loved it as it was more open and less crowded than southern England. It also contained plentiful stocks of game which they cheerfully depredated, carefully keeping one step ahead of the local game wardens. SAR COLLECTION.

Norfolk, autumn 1943. Gathered around a hastily-constructed fireplace are men from B Squadron HQ, including Trooper John Neff, behind the man lying on ground on the left. It was colder in this part of the country but the boys soon got used to it. COURTESY, JOHN NEFF.

Europe, the western Allies were not able to mount a major invasion of the European mainland in 1943 but did land on Sicily in July and, after a short but bitter campaign, invaded the mainland of Italy in September. For the first time, the Canadian army undertook sustained operations as the 1st Infantry and 5th Armoured Divisions and the 1 Armoured Brigade joined Montgomery's Eighth Army in its tortuous progress up the Italian peninsula. But the big showdown – the cross-Channel invasion – still lay ahead.

On 5 November 1943 the SAR came out of the field into Brandon Camp and were gratified to find that showers had been laid on – they needed them. The following day, they moved south to Sussex, the wheels by road convoy, the tracks by railway. Proud of its success in a major test, it was a happy unit that arrived at Maresfield Camp, its new station in Sussex.[74]

Maresfield was a permanent establishment and a comfortable post with many facilities conveniently close to the tank training ground in Ashdown Forest but, as the War Diarist lamented, far from "the nearest pub."[75] The Regiment took a few days to get settled in and then, on 12 November, the carrier troops commenced training in the forest while the tank troops

did a day's range work at Beachy Head. There had been rumours since October that the SAR would shortly be changing its War Establishment or organization and these rumours were heightened when the Recce Troop was ordered to turn in their Lynx scout cars in exchange for Stuart light tanks. A few weeks later word came that the Regiment's carriers would also be replaced by Stuarts and there were few regrets among the South Albertas when these wretched, crank little machines, so manifestly unsuitable for combat, disappeared from the squadron lines. Although the Regiment had still not received official word of the changes, it nonetheless reorganized its three squadrons on 13 December: each now had five troops and each troop had two Ram medium tanks and two Stuart light tanks. The Stuart (often called the "Honey") was new to the South Albertas and a draft of ninety-five officers and men was immediately sent on a training course to learn about this vehicle. Soon after, the SAR learned that their Rams would be replaced by Shermans and the new vehicles began to trickle into Maresfield. This was exciting news as the Sherman was a far superior vehicle, having a 75 mm gun that could fire not only AP (Armour Piercing) rounds but also HE (High Explosive), which was much more effective against enemy infantry. As the War Diarist recorded on 20 December, the SAR was prepared to handle the changes:

It is expected that soon we shall lose all our Rams and be equipped with two Sherman tanks per troop and two Honeys (M5s) per troop. Although all our Recce Tr[ainin]g has been with Carrier T[roo]ps and Tank Troops, the tactics involved can quite readily be employed with the new light tanks. However troop officers now have much more responsibility and more tactical training will be required before we are ready for battle.[76]

The model of Sherman that came into the Regiment was the type designated by the British as the Sherman V (American M4A4) with five gasoline-fuelled Chrysler engines. The SAR also learned that it would acquire an anti-aircraft troop of six Crusader AA tanks.[77]

The winter of 1943-1944 brought changes in personnel. In late November, the Regiment got a new Medical Officer, Dr. Wilfred Boothroyd. Boothroyd, a 31-year-old medical graduate from Dalhousie University, who had previously served with the Princess Louise Fusiliers, was impressed with the SAR and

Smile for the camera. Captain Bob Allsopp from Edmonton and Major David Currie from Moose Jaw pose for a Canadian Army photographer sometime in 1943. At this time Allsopp was adjutant of the Regiment and Currie was commanding C Squadron. DND PHOTO.

"delighted" to be posted to a unit with "very fine morale." He was the fourth permanent Medical Officer to serve with the Regiment since 1940. The first was K.C. "Casey" Clarke from Alberta, who left in the summer of 1942 to be replaced by Dr. William Mustard, who stayed until March 1943, when he turned over to John "King" Kelly. All three medical officers were somewhat unusual, particularly Mustard and Kelly, as, in Boothroyd's opinion, the SAR "went in for characters in their MOs." His main activity of the day was Sick Parade at 0800 in the morning, when he examined those who came before him and handed out various coloured cards: 10a for full duties, 10b for restricted duties and 10c for no duty at all and confinement to barracks room. Medically, it was undemanding work because his patients were a select group of healthy young men; Boothroyd dealt mainly with "minor things, like colds, traumas of various sorts, fractures and cuts … nothing that a well-trained first aid person could not handle."[78]

Doc Boothroyd became a good friend of another new arrival, Honorary Captain Albert Phillips (usually called Phil) Silcox, a padre who joined the SAR at Maresfield in mid-December 1943. As far as padres went, Silcox was inoffensive, "down to earth" and "not a bible thumping type."[79] Not that anybody took much notice of him. Church Parade was compulsory in the army but, other than that, most of the tough and profane young men who filled the ranks of the SAR were not particularly spiritual in nature and somewhat bemused by the new arrival. However, he seemed okay and their attitude was that he was a nice guy who was "always good for a couple of cigarettes."[80] Few recognized that under the gentle exterior of this "meek and mild fellow" there "was a lot of strength."[81] For the time being, Padre Silcox and Doc Boothroyd, the son of a

missionary, "spent many happy evenings" in their quarters playing "cribbage and discussing theology."[82]

Everyone knew that the cross-Channel invasion would be taking place in 1944 and as the countdown began, older, unfit or incapable officers and men were weeded out of front line units and replaced with younger personnel. There were restrictive age limits in the armoured corps and the rule of thumb was that no man over 35 could serve in combat. The Regiment now lost many older comrades, who were transferred to various training facilities and administrative units. Among the veterans who went were Sergeant Arthur Bellamy of the pay office and Sergeant Louis "Lou" Cramer of the officers' mess, who could make the unusual claim that he had fought in the Spanish-American War of 1898. Herbie Watkins recalled one corporal who left because of the age limit who "cried because he could not go into action with the regiment."[83] Herbie himself was 36 but somehow got around the rules, as did 41-year-old Trooper Emry "Daddy" Vitkovich of B Squadron and that tough Danish cowboy "Swede" Thuesen, who, at 42, was the oldest crew commander in the Regiment. Swede was allowed to stay "because he was in good condition" – in fact he "was in better shape than a lot of the young fellows."[84]

As the older men left they were replaced by young troopers fresh out of the various CACRUs (Canadian Armoured Corps Reinforcement Units). Many got off a truck at Maresfield, heads full of useless knowledge acquired at Dundurn, Borden or Woking to encounter a rude awakening from RSM Mackenzie, a squadron sergeant major or an NCO who immediately informed them that there was "only one way, the right way, the SAR way" of doing everything. Trooper Carson Daly from Nova Scotia recalled that his arrival was "the worst experience of my army life" as he and his fellow recruits "got an awful lecture from a sergeant major" which made them want to get back on their truck.[85] Then "an officer took over and tried to relax us (there were about half a dozen of us)" and "told us that was the duty of a sergeant major." One new man who arrived in 1943 was an old friend. Bob Clipperton had been dismissed from the Regiment in early 1940 for being under age but had re-enlisted as soon as he was legal in December 1941 and had served as an instructor at the impressive new recce training centre at Dundurn before being posted overseas in mid-1943. When he got back to the Regiment, Bob renewed acquaintances with "former buddies from 1940-1941."[86] To his wife, Andy, a corporal in the CWAC at Dundurn, he wrote, "I am really proud to be in this regiment" as the SAR "really have a good name as the crack Regt. in England" and "a smart Colonel." It was no less than the truth.[87]

There were also departures and arrivals in the officers' mess. Captain Harold McBain, an SAR since 1940, went to a training unit while Darby Nash took over HQ Squadron when Major C.H. Punchard left in January 1944. Another SAR who waved goodbye was that stalwart Glen McDougall, who gained a long overdue promotion to major and a temporary posting to the Three Rivers Regiment in Italy to acquire combat experience.

His new unit was nominally francophone and Glen spoke not a word of French but he soon "found that arm waving and bad language, shouted loudly enough, were satisfactory substitutes."[88] A young officer who joined the Regiment at Maresfield was Lieutenant Gordie Irving from Calgary. A former engineering student, he had enlisted in the RCE when the war broke out and risen to become a sergeant-instructor but "got fed up training officers and decided I should be one."[89] Gordie was teaching at the armoured training centre at Woking when he was sent to the SAR to gain some unit experience. Being an Albertan and a poker player he fitted right in and "in no time they were telling me what to do to become an SAR."[90]

Some arrivals were not so welcome. The Regiment had been at Maresfield less than a month when they had a Distinguished Visitor Demonstration on 30 November. This time, the official guests were rather unusual – Emirs Feisal and Halid, the sons of King Ibn Saud of Saudi Arabia – who were promptly dubbed "Feisel and Geezil" by all and sundry.[91] Escorted by Lieutenant-General H.N. Sansom, the commander of 2nd Canadian Corps, the two Arab princes looked out of place as they clambered over a Ram II in their flowing robes but their visit was judged important enough to be immortalized in a Canadian Army newsreel. "Seldom has the Canadian army had two more colourful visitors than these princes," oozed the narrator, "who will tell the folks back home that Canada and the Canadian Army have made no small contribution to final victory."[92] That, of course, remained to be seen but the newsreel is important because it records one of the few times during the Second World War that Swatty Wotherspoon wore a steel helmet. The SAR put on a demonstration attack on the South Downs for the princes featuring "a very elaborate smoke demonstration" which produced clouds of smoke so thick that "nothing could be seen of anything" although "Feisel and Geezil were vastly impressed."[93] The smoke was courtesy of Lieutenant Gerry Adams's carrier troop and Bert Coffin recalls that, after "the exercise and in the mess Swatty said to Gerry, 'Where were you this morning on the exercise? I didn't see you'" and "Gerry, in his typical vocabulary replied, 'Sir, you have cut me to the quick, just call me Smokey.'"[94] From that day Gerry was "Smokey" Adams.

On 14 December the Regiment was warned to prepare for yet another DVD, a warning that came, the War Diarist lamented, while "all the senior officers were on courses, 112 men were on leave and 95 men were on attachment" elsewhere.[95] Christmas was approaching again and the

Feisel and Geezil meet the boys from the bald-headed prairie. Swatty shows the two Arab princes the interior of the Ram II tank in November 1943. This photograph is is concrete evidence that Swatty Wotherspoon wore a steel helmet at least once during the Second World War. He hated the things but insisted that his men wear them and would charge any miscreants he caught. This was not really fair but nobody argued with the colonel about it. DND PHOTO.

SAR was scheduled to spend its second Christmas in Britain at Lydd Ranges on the Channel coast near Hastings. There was just time to hold the traditional local children's party in the gymnasium at Maresfield Camp on 22 December before the Regiment left for Lydd the next day to commence a week of range practice. As always, the SAR enjoyed themselves on the range and Smokey Adams added to his laurels by "scoring three hits on a moving target having only fired two shots."[96] There was much interest in the rate of fire of the new Stuarts and the boys' shooting was so good, according to Corporal Bob Clipperton, that the British personnel at Lydd "hated" to see the South Albertas

coming in to fire on the range cause we make more work for them. When the English tanks fire at the target, they seldom can hit the damn thing. Our outfit has blown them to hell this time & the last time we were here, the tank crews were so good a shot that they knocked the target carriers off the track.[97]

Range work was fun but the barracks at Lydd were dismal affairs with cold, concrete floors and the district offered little in the way of off-duty amusements, being "nothing but rock."[98]

On Christmas Day 1943, the boys got to sleep in until 1000 hours and then were offered a light breakfast of coffee and toast. After a pint of beer to provide some cheer, the enlisted men sat down to a repast of "turkey, potatoes, soup, salad, brussel sprouts, pudding and mince pie" served by the officers and washed up by the sergeants. Each man received fifty cigarettes and a box of chocolates from the Women's Auxiliary and the rest of the day was taken up by two special ENSA shows. There was much seasonal spirit about and the War Diarist noted that when the Regiment went back to the ranges on Boxing Day, not "only the weather was foggy." The first Shermans had started to arrive by this time and on 30 December A Squadron left for Warcop Tank Ranges in Norfolk, where "the living conditions were uncomfortable," to "shoot in" the new tanks. Over the next two weeks they would be followed in turn by the other squadrons until all had four days practice firing the Shermans at Warcop. The remainder of the Regiment returned to Maresfield on the last day of 1943 just in time to celebrate New Year's Eve. It was a cold, clear evening and many men attended a dance in the nearby village – as he made his way back to camp Trooper John Lakes remembered hearing the "church bells ringing in 1944."[99]

CHAPTER FIVE

"Say a prayer for me."

BRITAIN: JANUARY–JULY 1944

Maresfield was a good camp but it did have its problems. It lay between the Channel and London, a route favoured by the *Luftwaffe,* who made nighttime "tip and run" raids throughout the winter of 1943-1944, and there was much air activity during the Regiment's stay. On 22 January 1944, bombs fell close enough to knock the black-outs off the windows and "crack plaster in all corners of the camp," but there were perils in wartime England more dangerous than the *Luftwaffe.*[2]

By 1944, the narrow twisting roads and lanes were crowded with convoys of trucks, tanks, armoured cars and passenger vehicles and there were frequent accidents, particularly at night with a black-out, dimmed headlights and fog. The combination of heavy traffic, wartime conditions and numerous military pedestrians was a deadly one. On 2 January 1944 Trooper Donald McIntyre of the SAR, a 28-year-old native of Lennoxville, Quebec, was killed when he was hit by a truck while walking along a road near Lewes. That same day Trooper Lloyd Ireland was hurt in another accident while Majors Bert Coffin and Bob Bradburn escaped serious injury when they had a collision. Three months later Wotherspoon's driver, Trooper Walter Zwicker, a former merchant seaman who had survived a torpedoing in the North Atlantic, was killed when his jeep collided with a large tanker truck.[3]

The Regiment's twelve Dispatch Riders (DRs) had the most hazardous job and the War Diary is full of references to motor-cycle accidents. The big single-cylinder and twin-cylinder bikes they rode may have been the delight of British schoolboys but they were dangerous, particularly in heavy traffic. The first DR to die was 23-year-old Lance-Corporal Leo Golby from Edmonton who was killed when he collided with a truck near Maresfield on 27 June 1944.[4] Golby was only one of many Canadian soldiers to meet with misfortune on the big machines – so many that William Joyce, the broadcaster of German propaganda known as "Lord Haw-Haw," commented from Berlin on the fact "apparently with some truth, that one ward" of the hos-

*We are the boys of the SAR
You've heard so much about,
We are the finest regiment,
Without a word of doubt.*

*We're not stuck up about
The wonderful things we do,
The colonel says we are the best,
The sergeant major too.*

*As we go marching
And the band begins to play,
You will hear us shouting
The SAR are on their way,*

Hurray, Hurray, Hurray![1]

pital at Bramshott "was filled with Canadian traffic casualties, mostly DRs."[5]

Better things did happen at Maresfield. Over Christmas 1943 the SAR boxing team began preparing for the Canadian Army Championships scheduled for February 1944. The team took the divisional title on 30 December, scoring eleven out of twelve bouts, with heavyweight Joe Main, middleweight Nicky Schan and welterweight Buster Ely doing extremely well. There was much professional interest in Main; Tommy Farr travelled up from Brighton to look at him and expressed a desire to manage him after the war. As a team, the SAR fighters lost to 8 Recce Regiment in the army semi-finals but Main and Ely went as individual contestants to the finals on 19 February 1944. Buster lost his fight in a very close decision but, to the Regiment's great joy, Joe Main won his to become the Canadian Army Heavyweight Champion. He was defeated five days later by a British soldier in the South East Command finals, but Canadian Army champion was achievement enough for a regimental boxing programme that had started three years before in Nanaimo. Over the next few months the Regiment won the divisional football championship, lost by one point to the Argyll and Sutherland Highlanders in the divisional musketry competition but took the 10 Brigade track and field championship. Wotherspoon was ecstatic over his unit's sports triumphs and the "enormous *esprit de corps*" that resulted.[6]

Throughout all this, the Regiment prepared for its role in the forthcoming invasion. When all the squadrons had returned from Warcop, Wotherspoon held an O Group in the first week of January to discuss training plans for the next three months. The Regiment had done well with the Shermans and the Instructor Gunners at Warcop had informed Swatty that the SAR's performance with their new tank was "better than that of other regiments" but more practice was still needed.[7] It was decided that the remainder of January would be devoted to troop level training, February to squadron and March to unit training, interspersed with as much range work as possible. The emphasis, however, was not to be on recce work but on tank-infantry co-operation and behind that change lay a considerable story.[8]

Until 1943, when it gained enough combat experience to formulate its own, the Canadian Armoured Corps followed British armoured doctrine. "Doctrine" is an overworked but important word in the military world because it incorporates the basic principles by which an army fights and as the "way an army fights is a function of its training," doctrine is "the body of corporate knowledge officially approved to be taught."[9] The problem was that British armoured doctrine was faulty and that fault can be traced back to the 1930s when British theorists decided that there should two types of tanks employed by two types of formations: the army tank brigades would man slow, heavily-armoured "infantry" tanks to break through the enemy defences while the armoured brigades would use fast and mobile "cruiser" tanks to exploit that breakthrough.[10]

From 1940 to 1943, Britain's largest military commitment took place in North Africa. In many ways, the terrain suited the British vision of armoured warfare, which envisioned cruiser tanks fighting enemy tanks in a land version of a naval engagement while infantry tanks assisted the foot soldiers to mop up. Unfortunately the Germans refused to play by the rules – the *Wehrmacht* preferred to destroy tanks with anti-tank guns and the German tactic when faced with a British tank attack was simple but devastating: "to lead the advance units of a regiment over his anti-tank guns simply by turning tail."[11] It happened again and again as British armoured units left their infantry and artillery and went off to shoot up German tanks. The German armour would withdraw over an anti-tank gun screen that

would destroy the British armour and when it had been "written down," the German tanks would go in search of the British infantry and artillery. The result was the failure of the mission, heavy casualties, and all three arms very dissatisfied with each other. It was as if the British fought separate battles – infantry, artillery and armoured – while the German army, emphasizing the combined use of all arms, fought only one. What was needed was the realization that all tanks should be prepared to undertake either the infantry support or mobile exploitation role.

Beginning with the battle of El Alamein in October 1942 the nature of the war began to change as the Germans went over to the defensive. During the long retreat to Tunisia, British armoured formations reported difficulties with the efficient German rearguards "well posted on ground of their own choosing" and composed of several lines of defence.[12] British observers concluded that there was "nothing impregnable about this layout" but noted with bitter experience in mind, that "it cannot be attacked frontally by tanks alone" and the answer was a "co-ordinated attack by all arms." As the Allies began to encounter more fixed defensive positions in depth, a new note crept into the reports from the field and emphasis was now put on "the closest co-operation between the arms, both in the planning stage and in the battle."[13] The problem worsened in Sicily and Italy where the terrain consisted of mountainous built-up areas intersected by rivers which offered ideal defensive positions. Ranges came down – the average range at which German tanks

Warming up for the big bout. Boxing was the South Albertas' great passion as Sergeants Besson and Morrison demonstrate at Maresfield. Besson was so anxious to get into the match that he forgot to finish shaving. COURTESY, JOHN NEFF.

A comely corporal. Corporal Emery "Buster" Ely from Gibbons, Alberta, and a young lady identified only as "Molly" at Maresfield, spring 1944. Molly needs some instruction on how to wear the beret correctly but has grasped the essential fact – keep your hand on your weapon at all times. Ely was the Regiment's star welterweight boxer and won his last bout against an American sailor on the ship taking him to Normandy. Buster Ely was granted permission to marry "any time after 19 August 1944" but was killed in action on 21 August 1944.

COURTESY, JOHN NEFF.

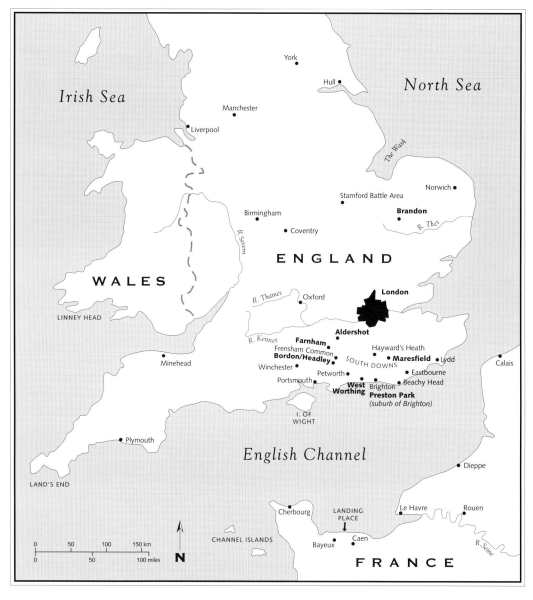

Map 1: South Alberta stations in Britain, 1942-1944. Except for excursions to Minehead and Stamford in 1943, the Regiment spent most of its time in Britain in the area south of London.

of Cromwells and Churchills, both British vehicles, raises another problem with British armour. Between 1940 and 1943 Britain was unable to produce a single battleworthy tank because of bureaucratic mismanagement, limited experience and resources, and a lack of proper engines. The result was poorly-designed, mechanically-unreliable AFVs and in desperation Britain turned to the United States. In 1941, numbers of the American M3 Light Tank were shipped to the desert, where, christened "General Stuart," they performed well although they were no match for their heavier German opponents. The Stuart was followed by the American M3 Medium Tank, known as the General Lee in British service and when the M3 evolved into the improved M4 Medium or Sherman, Britain acquired this tank in 1942. For the first time in the war, the Royal Armoured Corps had a reliable, effective and well-armed (for its time) tank.[16]

The Sherman derived from American thinking on armoured warfare and the American view of tank warfare, like the German, was

were destroyed dropped nearly two hundred yards between North Africa and Italy. German infantry used the terrain to advantage and were able to shoot the infantry off their supporting tanks with automatic weapons while well-concealed German anti-tank gunners held their fire until Allied tanks were almost impossible to miss. Having divided the tanks from the infantry, the Germans defeated each in turn.[14]

Problems with tactics were paralleled by problems in getting effective tanks into service. In May 1943 the Director, Royal Armoured Corps, outlined the general policy for British armour for the remainder of the war. "In general," he began, "our tank policy aims at the compression of U.K. tank production" to a few tried types. The eventual object was to base development of British armour on "the all-purpose tank of the Cromwell/Sherman type, plus a limited number of Churchills."[15] Mention

straightforward and aggressive: "the primary role of the armoured division was to exploit and pursue, not fight enemy armour."[17] American tactical doctrine for the employment of armour and the need to limit the size of tanks because of trans-Atlantic shipping restrictions, led the United States to concentrate on the Sherman. The prototype Sherman was completed in September 1941, full scale production began in July 1942 and it was produced in staggering quantities (one source says close to 50,000) as American industry geared up for the war effort – in 1940, the USA produced only 331 tanks but by 1942 it was producing more tanks than Britain and Germany combined! The Sherman admirably suited the American view of armoured warfare, being an excellent compromise between protection, mobility and hitting power. It was small enough to ease shipping problems and its reliability meant it needed fewer spare parts, which again saved on shipping. By selecting one tank for mass production, the United States was able to crank up its massive automobile industry for large-scale output and by 1943 was turning out enough Shermans for both its own and the Commonwealth armoured divisions. Since the Americans had never intended that the Sherman mix it up with German tanks, they felt no need for it to be of comparable size and hitting power.[18]

At this point in the story, some mention must be made of the opposition. By 1943, it was clear to the *Wehrmacht* that the time of great offensive victories was over and that it would now increasingly fight on the defensive. It possessed the weapons to do so as now the heavy Tiger and medium Panther tanks entered service. The 56-ton Tiger was armed with an 88 mm main gun that could penetrate any Allied tank and possessed armour thick enough to resist almost any Allied tank gun at medium and long ranges. It was not a perfect weapon – the Tiger was heavy, slow, fuel-hungry, mechanically unreliable and possessed a very slow turret traverse – but if it could be brought to the battlefield, it would dominate it. The Panther was a 45-ton vehicle with sloping armour and a high-velocity 75 mm gun superior to any weapon in the Allied inventory and arguably the best medium tank of the war. The *Wehrmacht* also possessed great numbers of self-propelled guns. From 1939 on, the Germans had used obsolete tank chassis to mount artillery and anti-tank weapons to provide close and mobile support for their infantry. These SPGs (self-propelled guns) proved a good thing and the Germans began to mount a whole variety of anti-tank and HE weapons on obsolete running gear to produce a bewildering array of turretless armoured fighting vehicles. The *Wehrmacht* also upgraded its anti-tank guns and by 1943 the standard prewar 37 mm weapon had been replaced by the 75 mm Pak 40. For close-in tank defence, the Germans developed two effective hollow-charge weapons: the *Panzerschreck*, a copy (and an improvement) of an American 2.36-inch bazooka which they had captured from the Russians, and the more common *Panzerfaust*, which was a small, light, disposable one-shot launcher capable of penetrating 200 mm of armour at 30 yards. Finally, as the *Wehrmacht* gradually switched from offence to defence in the mid-war period, the humble land mine began to take on increasing importance and German production figures for mines increased from a modest 150,000 in 1940 to four million in 1943.[19]

To invade the continent the Allied powers would have to overcome such weapons and in the eleven months preceding the Normandy invasion of June 1944 there was a major shift of tactical emphasis in the armoured units of 21 Army Group, the Commonwealth formation tasked with that operation. The provision of Sherman tanks for the armoured brigades and Churchill tanks for the army tank brigades, both equipped with a 75 mm gun capable of firing HE, was beginning to blur the longstanding British distinction between "cruiser" and "infantry" tanks. In December 1943, when Montgomery assumed command of 21 Army Group, things moved swiftly. On 13 January 1944, Montgomery held a conference on the training

of the armoured brigades under his command. Telling his audience to "stop frigging about," he decreed that, in future, there would be only two types of tanks – the "capital" tank and the light reconnaissance tank – and there were to be no more distinctions between army tank brigades and armoured brigades. Henceforth all armoured units could expect to be "employed in any role" and every tank unit must be prepared to work with infantry.[20] A month later, Montgomery expanded on these statements with a printed memorandum circulated throughout 21 Army Group which laid down that "all tank units are expected to be able to operate in close support of infantry in battle" either in the "set piece" attack or in "the exploitation of a disorganized enemy."[21]

These changes percolated down to the Canadian Army. In early 1944, the Canadian formations in the United Kingdom consisted of 2nd and 3rd Infantry Divisions, 4th Armoured Division and 2 Canadian Armoured Brigade. The 3rd Division and 2 Brigade were earmarked for the D-Day assault while 2nd and 4th Divisions were intended as part of the "breakout and pursuit force" after the beachhead had been secured. Although 2nd Canadian Corps issued orders to increase the amount of tank-infantry co-operation work done by the infantry of 3rd Division, this does not seem to have been carried out as these brigades spent only three days training with units of 2 Armoured Brigade in 1944.[22]

The situation was much better with the four armoured regiments in the 4th Canadian Armoured Division. Worthington had interested himself in tank-infantry cooperation and had insured that his infantry and armoured units were familiar with each other's equipment and methods. After the Norfolk exercises Worthington issued 4 CAD Training Bulletin No. 51, which laid out the procedures for tank-infantry co-operation in the division. This directive emphasized proper reconnaissance and warned that tanks "must not enter an area with dug-in infantry unless accompanied by infantry."[23] In November,

Worthy and his boys. Worthy congratulates members of the SAR rifle team which was the runner-up in the divisional competition won by the Argylls on 26 January 1944. Included on the team were RSM Jock Mackenzie and Corporal Swede Thuesen (right). DND PHOTO.

the divisional training instruction emphasized open-range firing as the main training priority but approximately one-third of the lesser priorities involved tank-infantry work. This was in accordance with 2nd Canadian Corps Training Instruction, which emphasized that collective training must be divided into "infantry cum tank and tank cum infantry."[24] Worthington, at least, appears to have been suffering no delusions from a "cavalry mentality" and seems to have set about training his division as best he could for its forthcoming role.[25]

The importance of tank-infantry training for 4th Division was highlighted on 24 December 1943 when the division issued Training Instruction No. 18, which covered the tactical training for armour during the period 1 January-31 March 1944, and directed that tank-infantry co-operation was to be the subject of study in all units. It also directed that 4 Armoured Brigade would train closely with 10 Brigade, the infantry component of the division. This instruction does not appear to have been followed because 10 Brigade did not train with 4 Brigade over the next few months; it trained with the South Alberta Regiment.

Not only doctrine was changing in the first months of 1944. In January Lieutenant-General E.E. Samson was succeeded as the commander of 2nd Canadian Corps by Lieutenant-General Guy Simonds, the "rising star" of the Canadian Army. Simonds, a Montgomery protege, had performed well while commanding the 1st Canadian Infantry Division in Sicily and Italy and had briefly commanded the 5th Armoured Division over the previous winter. He brought with him a group of veteran officers from Italy and, in short order, most of the senior corps staff were replaced while, in the 4th Division, both 4 Armoured and 10 Infantry Brigades were taken over by Simonds's nominees. Worthy was pretty certain that his turn was next.

Worthy was 55 and his age and health (he had been sick late the previous year) were used as the reasons for his replacement. The actual reason was that Guy Simonds did not want him and Guy Simonds moved fast. In early February 1944, he filed an adverse report on the commander of 4th Division which concluded that Worthy did not "understand the technique of higher com[man]d," and had "reached an age where he cannot give useful service in command of an Arm[our]ed Div[ision] in the f[iel]d."[26] Simonds recommended that he be returned to Canada to serve in a training capacity. This criticism might have been justified if Simonds had an extensive background in armour or knew Worthington well but, in fact, Simonds had exactly three months of experience with the 5th Division at a time it was so short of tanks that it could not be put into action as a complete armoured formation and he had been Worthy's superior for exactly three weeks. The old warrior had been expecting the bad news but was distressed that he would never lead into battle the armoured force he had created and trained. As his wife later remarked, however, Worthy "had already fought and won a critical battle in World War II, the Battle for Tanks."[27]

Senior officers. Major-General George Kitching (left) and Lieutenant-General Guy Simonds, spring 1944. Kitching commanded 4th Armoured Division from February to August 1944 and Simonds commanded 2nd Canadian Corps from 1944 to 1945. NAC, PA 132650.

His replacement was Major-General George Kitching. British by birth and a graduate of Sandhurst, Kitching had transferred to the Canadian Army in 1939 and had risen to brigade command in the 5th Armoured Division by late 1943. On 28 February 1944, Worthy took Kitching around and personally introduced him to the men of each regiment. As Kitching remembers, it was an emotional time because Worthy "had commanded the division since its formation and in my remarks I said I was sure that Worthington's departure would leave a gap that would be difficult to fill."[28] The South Albertas had always enjoyed a special relationship with Worthy and were disappointed to learn that their crusty old general was leaving. As one recorded, they weren't quite sure what to make of his replacement, who was "a well dressed, tall, distinguished looking fellow with a British style moustache, British bearing, and British decorum" who "was a graduate of Sandhurst Military College and wore the dress uniform with a Sam Browne belt; all in all, the image of a perfect King's general." "In stark contrast to General Worthington's plain speech and rough and ready fashion," the new commander "spoke to us in proper English manner, complete with proper English accent" and Kitching's "appearance and presentation did little to inspire admiration in the minds of the wild colonial boys of the SAR."[29]

For his part, Kitching knew none of the units in the 4th Division or their commanding officers. "I went around to each unit," he says, "but, basically, the only people I met in my initial visits were officers and senior warrant officers" and "I didn't really get to see or know the men except in speaking to them en masse which doesn't really give you much of a look."[30] Kitching quickly learned, however, about the SAR:

The special thing to me about the SAR was only months before they had been converted to an armoured [recce] regiment and it was incredible to me that they had tucked in.

[Brigadier] Booth [of 4 Armoured Brigade] went down and had a look at them although they weren't part of his brigade and commented to me that "they had a lot of spirit and were damned good." Booth had a better look from a tankman's point of view than I did.

Kitching was concerned about his division's state of training and wanted to undertake more schemes, like those held the previous autumn, but when he proposed this to his superiors, he was told that "there would be no large movement of troops" and "the only exercises we could develop were TEWTs. We could not employ troops on the ground as there was too much movement and, of course, there was."[31] Given the small size of Britain there were only limited facilities for properly training large armoured formations and apparently 4th Canadian Armoured Division was not high enough on the priority list for the use of these facilities. This was unfortunate because, in the opinion of its commander, the division was not yet ready for battle:

Whilst the individual regiments had reached a good standard of training, the essential cooperation between armour, infantry and artillery had not been practised to the extent it should have been. Nor had the brigade and divisional headquarters had enough experience of command and control, on exercises of some duration, that would have taxed their resources and taught them lessons. We rehearsed our communications on Corps map exercises and so improved our battle procedures but it was not possible to create the "fog of war" that engulfs a unit in its first actions.[32]

As it turned out, the Norfolk exercises of late 1943 were the only serious large-scale training the division received before it went into action.

According to Kitching there was another obstacle to training in the spring of 1944: his division's "routines were interrupted almost each week with visits from very important people."[33] This was no idle complaint. The SAR War Diary records DVDs (Distinguished Visitor Demonstrations) on 29 February 1944 for Montgomery, 9 March for King George VI, 17 May for Prime Minister Mackenzie King and 29 May for Eisenhower. Although the men liked to see these famous people at close range and were proud that they showed an interest, a single two-hour visit meant that vital training time was lost in the lengthy preparations required to assemble the 15,000 men of the division in one place, rehearse, parade and feed them.[34]

Changes in command were followed by other changes. In March 1944 the South Albertas went through a reorganization resulting from a decision made that month by Montgomery that all armoured reconnaissance regiments in 21 Army Group were to reorganize on the War Establishment of an armoured regiment although they were to retain their armoured recce titles.[35] As the War Diarist noted with resignation on 13 March

1944, due to "the recent changes in our role and War Establishment from Armd Recce Regt to a dual role of Armd Recce and T[an]k B[attalio]n, another reorganization within squadrons has been necessary."[36] When it was over, the fighting echelon of the South Albertas consisted of a Regimental Headquarters complete with an RHQ Troop of four Shermans, a Recce Troop of eleven Stuarts, an Inter-Communication Troop of nine Humber Scout Cars and an AA Troop of six Crusader AA tanks. Each of the three fighting squadrons, A, B and C, had an HQ Troop of three Shermans and four fighting Troops, each with four Shermans. On paper, the Regiment possessed 78 tanks (61 Shermans, 11 Stuarts and 6 Crusaders) and 9 Humber scout cars. With some minor changes, the SAR would retain this organization until the end of the war.

In late March, the South Albertas received a welcome draft of three officers and seventy-five men from the Royal Montreal Regiment. This unit had mobilized in September 1939 and had been overseas for nearly four and a half years as the recce regiment for First Canadian Army; because of a growing manpower shortage, it was disbanded and its personnel were distributed throughout the CAC as first line reinforcements. Although the new arrivals had no experience with tanks the Regiment was glad to get them and one of the newcomers, Trooper Egbert Taylor, recalls that, although they were joining a unit where "most of the chaps were from the west," they "were given a good welcome" and "settled in and soon made friends."[37]

April brought more changes. On the first day of the month, the SAR lost their status as divisional troops when they were formally placed under command of 10 Brigade, the infantry component of 4th Division. Their job would now be to support the three infantry battalions of that brigade in the coming campaign. Ten Brigade consisted of three Ontario infantry units: the Algonquin Regiment from the northern part of the province, the Argyll and Sutherland Highlanders from Hamilton

Their royal majesties meet the boys from Medicine Hat. Lieutenant Kenny Perrin (on left) and Captain Glen McDougall meet their Majesties King George VI and Queen Elizabeth. The royal couple enjoyed tremendous popularity among English-speaking Canadians during the war. COURTESY, SOUTH ALBERTA LIGHT HORSE.

and the Lincoln and Welland Regiment from the Niagara area. Also attached to the brigade were the New Brunswick Rangers, a support unit which manned heavy mortars and machine guns.

Ten Brigade had been formed in the spring of 1943 and the SAR had worked with it during the Norfolk schemes. In February 1944 it received a new commander, Brigadier Jim Jefferson, a native of Edmonton and a veteran of the Italian campaign who had received the DSO while leading the Loyal Eddies during the bitter winter battle at Ortona. The change in organization "was a great event," wrote the brigade historian, as all the infantry units "had worked with the South Albertas and all had found them most co-operative and superbly trained in infantry cum tank warfare" and the flat feet "were openly pleased at having armour with them, especially S.A.R. armour."[38]

In April, when the spring in Sussex presented a picture of green foliage and cherry blossom, the brigade moved onto the South Downs for some tank-infantry co-operation work with their new armoured comrades. From the outset, each SAR squadron trained with a particular infantry battalion so that the tank and infantry commanders got to know each other and the two arms functioned as a team. For the time, this team approach was an innovation; Kitching was impressed and later thought it paid dividends in action "right up to the German border."[39]

Each squadron went out for an initial day with its battalion and then did progressively longer exercises. Bob Bradburn's B Squadron got the most experience. During April, it was attached to 2nd Infantry Division for four days (2-6 April) for an exercise and then went out with the Algonquin Regiment for a single day's work (10 April) before returning, on 19 April, for a ten-day exercise. Arnold Lavoie's A Squadron had its one-day "familiarization" with the Lincoln and Welland Regiment on 12 April, repeated it on 19 April and then did a four-day exercise on 5-9 May followed by a further four-day period on 12-16 May. Only Dave Currie's C Squadron did not get as much practice with their "flat footed" friends, the Argyll and Sutherland Highlanders, going out for only one day on 10 April but a longer exercise might have been cancelled due to interruptions in the training schedule caused by two DVDs late in the month. By the time the Regiment ceased active training in May when orders came to waterproof its vehicles, A Squadron had ten, B Squadron had fifteen and C Squadron had one day of tank-infantry work. Not much, but it compares well with the three days of tank-infantry training that the D-Day assault brigades in 3rd Division received during the spring of 1944.[40]

The SAR adjusted easily to the new role. It had been a fully-trained infantry unit before being converted to armour and every senior officer in the Regiment, except Wotherspoon and Currie, had been an infantry company commander, while most of the junior officers and NCOs had infantry experience. This was an advantage as, according to Swatty, to be

good tank support for the infantry, you had to be skilled in good infantry tactics, know what they should be doing and how they should do it. If my squadron commander was with the CO of an infantry battalion and thought the infantry battalion was doing something wrong, he had to have sufficient knowledge to be able to say to the infantry battalion commander, "I think that's wrong, sir, I think we can work better together if you do this."

Much more difficult in reverse, because to be a good tank commander, you have to know what the tank can do, what kind of land it can go through, where its fire is best, can be best used. Its ability in close range or in long range to do things. The other way around, it's much easier because you're talking about the man on the ground and you know the limitations of his weapons, and you know, you certainly know the limitation of his feet. ... somebody who doesn't know tanks will commit them into an action across country that looks fine, but if you're a good tank commander, you'll know that you're going to lose half your tanks being bogged down in that area. You have to have an instinct or a training for that and the infantry hasn't got that.[41]

By April 1944 Wotherspoon was satisfied that the South Alberta Regiment was as ready as he could make it, given the restricted training allowed in the last five months. He "had no worries about my regiment; we'd spent the whole [previous] year going through all the five major phases of battle: that's the advance, the attack, the defence, the withdrawal and the river crossing."[42]

Horrors of waterproofing. Just after the Regiment finished waterproofing its tanks in mid-May 1944 it was ordered to the Lydd Ranges, sixty miles from Maresfield. The result was that the entire waterproofing process had to be done over again when they got back. The SAR make their feelings felt about the order in this cartoon by Jay Moreton which was appended to the 10 Brigade War Diary for May 1944.

It was obvious that the invasion would be coming in the next few months. When the Regiment learned on 31 March that all privilege leave would be cancelled at the end of April, they granted leave "fast and furious" throughout that month to give the men a break before the final countdown began.[43] There were other signs that things were getting serious. On 8 April 1944, field censorship went into effect, and an officer or warrant officer would now have to read, approve and initial all outgoing mail to ensure that there were no breaches of security. This was the cause of much complaint – as Corporal Bob Clipperton told his wife, Andy, it was "hard to write a good letter when you know someone is going to read it besides you & worse still when you know the person who reads it."[44] The officers didn't like it any

Work on the tanks continues. Troopers Bill Pachal (on the left) and Ed Ashmore pause from fitting new tracks on their tank, Maresfield, spring 1944. Bill Pachal was killed in the Falaise Gap on 21 August 1944. COURTESY, JOHN NEFF.

Waterproofing begins. Trooper Pat Gregory looks disgusted as he carries out waterproofing at Maresfield in May 1944. The following year he would have a memorable leave in Paris. COURTESY, JOHN NEFF.

better than the men but orders were orders. In AA Troop, some men enlisted the aid of Trooper Bob Blunden to get around the rules. His initials were "R.S.M." so many letters from AA Troop went out with "R.S.M. Blunden" scrawled across the envelope thereby fooling the postal authorities, who would think that the letter had been censored.[45] A few weeks later, an official showed up at Maresfield looking for "RSM Blunden" but got nowhere.

Along with the new restrictions came new equipment, including tank helmets, which no one liked, and camouflage netting for the helmets, which inspired another original Moreton cartoon. By this time, the Regiment had a full complement of Shermans and Stuarts but AA Troop was still waiting for its Crusaders. According to the troop leader, Ed Reardon, they hadn't wasted their time:

The colonel told me in December that I was to command the new AA Troop and that I had better find out about it. For the next four months, we went on constant courses. We went to Lulworth for two weeks for AA training, to Bovington for Crusader training and out to fire at target drogues for two weeks. There was not a course available that we didn't go on including a course at Rolls-Royce in engine work. We were properly trained because Swatty wanted it that way. He was always a jump ahead with the new things.[46]

Danny McLeod fed Swatty's interest in the latest tactics and weapons, and Danny was in a position to know as, following graduation from Sandhurst, he had been posted to the Cana-

dian Armoured Corps operational training squadron at Woking as an acting captain. On his frequent visits to the SAR he had many conversations with the colonel about "all the special equipment: the petards, the Flails, the Fascines, Crocodiles and so on, and the fact that I had incorporated that into the training pleased him no end, especially for future SAR officers coming through the squadron."[47]

On 20 May 1944 the SAR received orders to waterproof its vehicles so that they would be able to drive off landing craft through shallow water onto a beach. The unit had been expecting the order and was familiar with the process; in early February, a "sealing dipper tank" (basically a water-filled trench with in and out ramps) had been constructed at Maresfield and on 6 March the first tank and truck had gone through the test – the tank passed with flying colours but the War Diarist noted that the truck "got a little wet around the edges."[48] That's not how the driver of that vehicle, Trooper George Armstrong, recalls it. He does remember his puzzlement when

they gave me some pails of stuff and some flex tubes and I don't know what all and they didn't know what it was for. We were told to go waterproof my truck and no instructions or nothing so I went and got Sid Arrowsmith and we started out and we were three or four days figuring it out.

One morning, here's a bunch of people and they wanted us to take the truck over and an English senior officer came up and said "You're going to put your vehicle through the dipper tank and go steady." There were American, British and Canadian senior officers there from all over and a tank went first and the driver gunned the engine just as he was coming out of the water and sprayed them with mud.

Then I went and it was an odd thing when the water came up over the cab but none came in.[49]

Waterproofing was a lengthy, painstaking and tedious job. First, the vehicles and their engines had to be spotlessly cleaned, then various sealing compounds, most being asbestos derivatives that stung the hands, with names like *Gripon*, *Boscoprene*, and *Bostik* were used to seal all cracks and cover mechanical and electrical parts. *Bostikote* tape was used for doors and hatches while balloon fabric, sealed and taped, was used on turret rings and gun apertures. The tanks were fitted with metal exhaust extensions and air ducts which would be blown off by an explosive charge detonated from inside the turret when the vehicle reached dry land. It took about seventy hours of work to waterproof a tank properly and about three days to do a truck and it was a job everyone hated. When each crew was finished, they would test the result in the "dipper tank" which was about four feet deep. If their vehicle failed, they started again.[50]

The boys had just begun this task when the Regiment was ordered to stop on 22 May and get ready to move to Lydd for tank firing practice. Wotherspoon protested but the brigade staff were adamant and the best the SAR could do was to express their feelings with a Moreton cartoon. The Regiment went to Lydd on 23 May, fired for one day, and then came back to Maresfield with dirty vehicles and had to start waterproofing all over again. The job took two and a half weeks but, with the exception of Lieutenant Ed Reardon's AA Troop, which had still not received its vehicles, the task was finished by 10 June. The problem was that, once waterproofed, the vehicles could not be moved long distances and the Regiment's transport was now only a few old trucks. This meant that, except for small-arms practice and marching, all effective training ceased.[51]

It was a difficult time. The South Albertas were as prepared for battle as Wotherspoon could make them and he was concerned that they stay fit and alert until their time came. He also set a personal example, as Trooper Bob Wear recalls:

Wotherspoon was wonderful. About two months before D-Day, he began to run with his pack. We were stationed at

The long and the short of it in A Squadron. Lieutenant Gordie Irving, A-1 Troop Leader on the left and Major Arnold Lavoie, squadron commander on the right. Gordie, looking very spiffy, is probably about to make a run into London. COURTESY, GORDIE IRVING.

Maresfield. He would run from the officers' quarters down to headquarters, about half a mile. He would run with his full pack on. His face was red and we all smiled and thought, "The colonel is getting into shape, he will quit that in a few days." He didn't quit. He ran back and forth and pretty soon he got into shape and he was as in shape as anybody in the regiment. Not only that he was the brains of the regiment, too.[52]

For the enlisted men, life at Maresfield became "small arms practice on the ranges firing pistols and the infamous Sten guns, playing team sports, and going out on route marches."[53] For off-duty entertainment, there were baseball, movies, passes to visit the local pubs and dances at the camp. Other than that they waited.

The piano player. Lieutenant Wally Young, Maresfield, early summer 1944. Wally's piano-playing skills made him a popular member of the officers' mess. A former accountant from Edmonton, he was killed by a German sniper at Moerbrugge, 10 September 1944. COURTESY, GORDIE IRVING.

Wotherspoon kept the officers busy with TEWTS that went over the five basic military operations – advance, withdrawal, attack, defence and the river crossing – again and again. The officers' mess was the centre of the commissioned social life, and although he was far from being lively in the mess, Swatty liked to have enough potables on hand to entertain visitors. By the spring of 1944 this was becoming a problem as millions of Allied servicemen were competing for all available alcohol in Britain. According to Gerry Adams, then president of the Mess committee, Wotherspoon hit on the idea of going directly to the source and Gerry "would take a jeep and swan all through southern England and visit the distilleries and try to get our ration of booze increased."[54] "Sometimes," he recalled, "I could talk them into giving us another case or two and that's what I did."

The officers breakfasted as a group, had lunch apart in the field and dined together at night. Swatty tried to make the evening meal a fairly formal affair but this was not popular with the junior officers as, according to Lieutenant Don Stewart, "no one likes the idea except the Colonel, and it's a lot of silliness."[55] On week days the evening meal was followed by a TEWT, but when that was over the fun began. Wotherspoon might stay on but normally he retired to his quarters, where he might "shoot the breeze" over a pot of tea with Captain Bob Allsopp, the adjutant, and Captain Tommy Barford, the quartermaster.[56] Two other officers who usually retired early were Doc Boothroyd and Padre Silcox who, if there were not other pressing matters, would resume discussing theology and playing cribbage. Back in the mess the poker games would be starting up. The regulars included Bert Coffin, Hugh "Click" Clarke, Bob Bradburn, Gordie Irving, Smokey Adams and Frederick "Newt" Hughes. Hughes was such a good player that it was Gerry Adams's belief that he "never drew his pay during the war, he won all his money playing cards."[57] Music was provided by gramophone records or by the officers themselves; Lieutenant Wally Young from Edmonton, an accomplished pianist, might "tickle the ivories" while Major Bill Cromb of the Loyal Eddies, who had been temporarily attached to the SAR in March to teach them infantry tactics, might be prevailed on to render a song in his magnificent tenor.

Saturday night was party night. Adams remembers that "we would send a truck for the nursing sisters at the hospital and take the gals back afterward … it was a pleasant life in that respect."[58] If the boys could not beg, borrow or steal a band, they would dance to records – and 1944 was a great year for dance music with such slow soft tunes as "Stardust," "Begin the Beguine," "I Can't Get Started," "Moonlight Serenade" and "Maria Elena" and the upbeat ones such as the Andrews Sisters' "Boogie Woogie Bugle Boy of Company B" and the immortal "Rum and Coca-Cola." Saturday nights in the officers' mess could get lively – Don Stewart remembered one party when the "pulchritude" included "about a dozen Canadian nurses and a few bewildered little English girls" and commented (to his mother of all people) that Canadian men "are quite a problem to the English gals after the quiet stately Englishmen they were used to" and they must have thought us "an awful collection of knot-heads when the male and the female of the race are both here in their little country."[59] Since nobody knew when the Regiment would be leaving and since the boys wanted to make sure they had a proper send-off before they

Honorary Captain Albert Phillips Silcox. Padre of the SAR from late 1943 until the end of the war, Phillips Silcox was tireless in his efforts to promote the welfare of the men of the Regiment. In garrison, he helped to solve personal and family problems, in action he assisted the Medical Officer in the Regimental Aid Post and buried the dead, often having to scrape the remains of his flock out of incinerated tanks. He wrote the families and loved ones of every South Alberta killed, wounded or missing in action and, as he once remarked, "God alone can measure the tears we shed in silent solitude over these sincere letters to the folks at home." For years after the war he made personal visits and corresponded with the next of kin of the men of the Regiment killed in action. COURTESY, SILCOX FAMILY.

did, sometime in March 1944 they began to dub their Saturday night affairs "farewell parties" and, if they were still there the next Saturday night – well, they had another one.

As the English May passed in all its floral splendour, there were more signs that things were getting serious. Padre Silcox interviewed each man to ascertain the name and address of his next of kin, where his personal effects should be sent in case "something happened," and discuss any problems he might have.[60] Trooper Arnold Dryer had been dating an English girl for some time and, although the couple had made no decisions about the future, when Silcox asked Dryer if he had any "girlfriends or a fiancée," Dryer informed his lady he had given her name "as the latter."[61] The couple would marry the following year. Silcox worked hard at his duties – Jack Porter remembered passing his room in Maresfield many times late at night to hear the sound of typing as the padre worked into the small hours on the onerous task of tending his flock's paperwork.[62]

May turned into June and everyone knew the day must soon come – but when? The moon and tide conditions were right and on both sides of the Channel hundreds of thousands of young, and not so young, soldiers waited. Bob Clipperton wrote his wife, "It's kind of funny, isn't it? We sitting here waiting & about 25 miles away they are doing the same thing."[63] After four years of military service the South Albertas were as well trained as they could be for their part – they were also taut. Corporal Jimmy Simpson recalls that, as "D-Day approached, it was exasperating" because "we really wanted to know when we were going and where we are going" and there "wasn't in my opinion the spirit that there had been previously."[64] Many men in southern England, which had become one large armed camp by the spring of 1944, would have agreed with him. In the first week of June, as the assault formations began to move toward their embarkation ports, the tree-shrouded winding country lanes became crowded with tanks, troops and vehicles while overhead formations of aircraft disturbed the summer skies. It could not be much longer.

Gunfight at the Maresfield Corral. Trooper Wayne Spence (left) of C Squadron and his mates slap leather and cut loose. The boys were just joking around but the .38 calibre Colt and Smith & Wesson revolvers the South Albertas carried at this time were probably accurate at this distance only. COURTESY, WAYNE SPENCE.

In the early hours of 6 June 1944, the SAR were woken by the "extraordinary sound of hundreds of planes going overhead" and "the thunder of guns carried to us from the French coast."[65] That the invasion had started was confirmed at 0700 hours by a German radio broadcast stating that "thousands of ships were approaching the French coast in the area Le Havre-Cherbourg." Although the Regiment did not know it at the time, one "South Alberta" landed in Normandy that day. Reg Maves, the kid who had briefly served with the Regiment at Niagara before his military aspirations were cut short by a protective mother, had enlisted in the RCN as soon as he was legally old enough to be shot at and was serving with the 31st Minesweeping Flotilla off the landing beaches. On 6 June 1944, Reg splashed ashore with a naval landing party and found that the infantry training he had received in the SAR stood him in good stead as the situation on his beach was "somewhat confusing."[66] For the rest of that momentous day all ears were glued to the radio and the official announcements by Eisenhower, Montgomery and General Harry Crerar, the commander of First Canadian Army, were "greeted with cheers in the camp." A large battle map was erected in the officers' mess so that "everyone could follow the beachhead progress hourly" and the War Diarist recorded that "the morale of the regiment has gone up 50% now that they realize that they will soon be getting a crack at Jerry."[67]

But when would they get that crack? According to Captain Jay Moreton the period after D-Day was "a hell of a time because it was a difficult time to keep up the interest of the men." There was also a "different attitude on the part of the men because

Helmets are for the birds. The issue of camouflaged tank helmets to the Regiment in the spring of 1944 draws a response from cartoonist Jay Moreton.

they began to realize that this thing was going to happen … and it was a little scary."[68] The most anxious men in the Regiment were in Lieutenant Ed Reardon's AA Troop as they had still not received their tanks by D-Day. Finally, on 11 June, Ed reports that

they gave us the word to pick up our tanks at the tank delivery regiment. We marched along the rows of Crusaders and eventually came to ours. We were there 20 minutes and I had the six tanks idling and all the stowage was done. Everyone else was still looking at their tanks and there wasn't one troop from the other regiments that knew what they were doing. The captain we were dealing with asked me to give him a hand so we were split up among all the various tank units there and showed them what to do. We waterproofed around the clock in shifts and we finally did it but we just made it.[69]

This task done, the AA Troop joined the Regiment to wait for their turn to cross to France. In the meantime all the SAR and other units of the 4th Armoured Division could do was listen to the progress of the battle in Normandy on the radio and wait. Their spirits were not improved by Lord Haw-Haw, who taunted them as the "gentlemen of the Green Patch, who let the nursing sisters get on the beaches in Normandy before them."[70]

George Kitching was aware of the tension and toured his units giving "pep talks" to reassure them that their turn would come. He arrived at the SAR on 12 June and found it formed up in a hollow square waiting for him under a downfall of rain. He immediately moved the men into the camp gymnasium, had them sit down and told them that "although we are not in the assault forces, we had been chosen for one of the most important jobs" as the division "would likely be fighting against two crack German Panzer Divisions, Adolf Hitler and Hitler Youth Divisions."[71] Kitching assured the SAR, however, "that whatever the Germans put up against us he had complete confidence in our ability as a Division, to overcome these hazards." It was just the right choice of words and the War Diarist commented that everyone "agrees that this is one of the best addresses they have received to date and that neither a more suitable time nor circumstances could have been chosen for it to be given." Kitching's stock went up with the SAR and his prediction about the Regiment's future opponents would turn out to be entirely accurate.

It was back to route marching, range training, baseball and waiting. On 16 June, there was a strange noise overhead and the men looked up to see a German V-1 missile sputtering by on it way to London. The V-1s were a common sight at night and the South Albertas would watch them going over in the darkness with their tail flames marking their path and the tracers from the anti-aircraft guns reaching up for them. During the day, according to Trooper Carson Daley, there were "lots of them" and it "used to be a real sight to see the Spitfires chase them, like dogs chasing a rabbit, to try to turn them round."[72] On 4 July, the little missiles became less funny when one landed in the camp. No one was hurt but the War Diarist, noting that "more injuries occurred by men diving under their tanks, bumping their heads, than by the blast from the bomb," concluded that "a drill is required."[73]

There were V-1s overhead on the Saturday night that Adjutant Bob Allsopp became the first SAR to realize that Padre Phil Silcox was not quite the average army-issue chaplain. The officers were having "their usual Saturday night bash," yet another in that series of farewell parties they had been holding since March. The mess was boisterous and Allsopp was enjoying himself when a steward approached and asked him to come outside. Behind the mess building was a series of slit trenches dug, as per regulation, for shelter during an air raid. The steward wordlessly pointed at one trench and Allsopp went closer to find "Captain Silcox complete with steel helmet firing a pistol at the buzz bombs flying overhead." As they were officially non-combatants, military chaplains were not allowed to carry weapons, but since the padre appeared to be enjoying himself and was not doing any harm (either to the buzz bombs or anything else), Allsopp left him alone and withdrew after reflecting that it was strange behaviour for a man of the cloth. When he came to know Padre Silcox better, he realized that it was but a portent of things to come.[74]

June turned into July. The South Albertas listened to the war on the radio, played baseball, watched the comic character Jane disrobe in the *Daily Mirror* and route marched. Lieutenant "Little Joe" Summers, being of an academic bent, thought that French lessons might keep his B-2 Troop busy and soon the language of Molière was being slaughtered by flat western vowels as his men wrapped their tongues around such useful (and hopeful) phrases as "Tu es belle, ma chérie" and "Voulez-vous coucher avec moi?" The boys were growing tired of waiting and Trooper Arnold Dryer expressed a common sentiment when he wrote his fiancée that "I feel it is getting near the end, but I hope something happens pretty soon as I am sure getting fed up with this."[75] The occasional special entertainment provided a break from the monotony; the Regiment saw the "RCAF Black Out Show" and the "Canadian Army Show" (known as "The Cold Cream Guards") with a cast that included Sergeants Johnny Wayne and Frank Shuster. Everyone was a little tense. Many men wrote and rewrote "last" letters home, "just in case some-

"HELLO BAKER — GRAPEFRUIT NOW — GULP ..."   "OVER"

"Hello Baker." As the time for action drew closer, the South Albertas began to wonder what it would be like when they landed in Europe. Regimental cartoonist Jay Moreton imagines one possibility in a cartoon attached to the June 1944 War Diary.

thing should happen," struggling to translate complex emotions into banal words. To his wife, Andy, Corporal Bob Clipperton expressed what many felt:

> I know I can count on you & I pray that when we have done what our country expects of us, that I will be able to return to you & bring back all the happiness that has been taken away from us through the war. Be bold, sincere, true & above all be happy as much as you can while I am away & when you are thinking of me the most, say a prayer for me, won't you?[76]

On Saturday, 16 July 1944, the officers held their seventeenth consecutive farewell party in the mess and some commissioned heads may have been a little bit thick the following morning when it finally happened. Wotherspoon and the Intelligence Officer "left in a heavily-laden 5-cwt [truck] for ports unknown" to join the divisional advance party for France.[77] The next day, Monday 18 July, the Regiment was ordered to move at midnight and the day passed in a flurry of last-minute activity. At 2230 hours, the quiet of the evening was shattered by the roar of engines as the drivers formed their vehicles in column. There was an hour's wait with "most of the men talking quietly in the grass beside their tanks, with no more excitement than a normal exercise would command."[78] Then the word was given, cigarettes were pinched out, and the men climbed into their tanks and trucks. The first vehicle rolled through the camp gate at precisely 0001, 19 July 1944, and, as the rest followed, the "NAAFI girls stood in the doorway of the canteen with tears in their eyes and waved to every tank and truck that went by."[79]

After a slow and tedious nighttime trip of nearly six hours the Regiment arrived at the assembly area near the East London docks. The remainder of the day was taken up with final waterproofing, paperwork, and replacing the rubber track pads on their tanks' treads with steel ones for active service. By nightfall, the Regiment had no orders to move to the docks and the men prepared to sleep beside or inside their vehicles. London was under constant aerial bombardment by V-1 missiles and the War Diarist records that there were eight air raid alarms and a sky "aglow with a bright orange flash from buzz-bombs landing uncomfortably close by."[80] Several times during the night the men had to head for the slit trenches around the assembly area and, as Trooper Egbert Taylor of A Squadron says, there was nothing else to do so "we bit our nails."[81]

The following day, the South Albertas proceeded to the Victoria Docks. This movement was delayed when a V-1 hit an ammunition truck in the column of a unit ahead of the Regiment, and by the time the SAR got to the scene the truck was "burning nicely."[82] The locals seemed to take it in their stride, Egbert Taylor watched the shopkeepers "sweeping the broken glass from the pavement" as the flaming wreck was "being doused by the firemen."[83] When the Regiment arrived at the docks they found that there was only one specialized LST (Landing Ship Tank) available and that most of their vehicles would be transported in the holds of Liberty ships, the workhorse transport of the Allied navies, which meant that each tank would have to be loaded separately. One by one, the tanks "were picked up by a huge crane and lowered into the holds, four per hold," with each "hold timbered over and the next load set in."[84] It was a time-consuming process that was made worse by constant air raid alarms when the sputtering but deadly little V-1s appeared over the dock area. The task was not completed by nightfall and the Regiment had to spend a second restless night, punctuated by air raid alarms, in the dock area.[85]

Finally, at 1000 hours on 20 July, all the tanks and vehicles were loaded and the South Albertas marched on board four Liberty ships and the LST, which then sailed down the Thames as part of a larger convoy. As the ships passed a Ford Motor Company plant on shore, the workers sent them "a message of good luck over loud speakers." By evening the convoy was off Southend in the Thames estuary, where it anchored in the midst of the masts and funnels of ships sunk earlier in the war.[86]

As there were fierce gales in the Channel, the convoy spent two days sheltering in the estuary. The South Albertas passed the time sunbathing, playing cards, reading and watching film shows. On B Squadron's Liberty ship, the *Matthew T. Goldsboro*, Buster Ely, the Regiment's star welterweight, whipped an American sailor in a boxing match.[87] RHQ Troop and A Squadron did not mind the delay one bit as their tanks were transported in a USN LST and they enjoyed "a cruise ship trip" complete with lovely American rations. When the boys entered the mess hall at the first breakfast call, they stared in amazement at "a big pan of bacon and real scrambled eggs," which was served without limit to each man because "as long as you held your mess kit there the cook would keep shovelling it on."[88] After nearly two years of rationing it was an amazing sight and Trooper Bell reminisces that "I ate like it was Christmas every day."[89] It got even better at dinner time when the boys were served steaks "a foot long, beautiful bloody great steaks which we hadn't seen in three years, so we tucked in."[90] Afterwards John Galipeau and his comrades were resting on deck happily digesting this bounty when a cook emerged from a hatch "with two five gallon pails of leftover steaks and threw them over the side." The Canadians nearly burst into tears at the sight.

The convoy left the estuary in the late evening of 22 July and by midnight was approaching the Channel at Dover. Tracer rounds raced skyward at the V-1s which were heading for London in a seemingly never-ending stream. That was impressive enough but a few minutes later "all hell broke loose" when long-range German coast artillery opened fire and their British counterparts replied. As heavy-calibre shells screamed overhead the South Albertas were ordered to don their life jackets and go below for an hour until the convoy was through the narrows and the firing tailed off. By the late morning of 23 July, the ships were approaching Portsmouth, the assembly area for naval traffic into the Normandy beachhead, which was full of "every kind of ship, boat, carrier and barge imaginable." The convoy spent the night at anchor in Cowes Roads and, at 0630 hours on 24 July 1944, the Regiment sailed for France.[91]

Land was sighted in the late afternoon and, as the South Albertas approached Normandy, it was apparent that a war was in progress. They crowded the decks to watch warships firing at targets inland and a sky full of aircraft flying to bomb targets or returning from such missions. At 1600 hours the convoy dropped anchor off Courseulles-sur-Mer, one of the objectives of 3rd Canadian Division on D-Day, and unloading commenced. Lavoie's A Squadron and RHQ Troop landed directly onto the beach from their LST, but the rest of the Regiment had to wait as their tanks and vehicles were first offloaded onto LCTs or Rhinos, large powered rafts capable of holding several tanks, then taken to the broad beach at the hamlet of Vaux west of Courseulles. After all the labour they had put into waterproofing many South Albertans were disgusted when they traversed about six inches of water to reach dry land. Others were thankful as their landing craft or ferries beached near submerged shell holes. One of them was Corporal John Lardner, who drove off the ramp of his craft into water so deep that it came over the lens of the periscope on the top of his hatch. As he headed toward land, Corporal Art Engel of Recce Troop noted that France appeared to be aflame with bright red flowers. It was only when he came closer to the shore that he realized what they were – the low sand hills surrounding the beach were "awash with poppies."[92]

PART III

GRAPPLING

Evacuating the wounded. A jeep ambulance races through Normandy
sometime in the summer of 1944 with its load of wounded.

CF FILM UNIT, PA 140141.

CHAPTER SIX

"Everything was new and we didn't know what was going on."

FRANCE: 25 JULY– 5 AUGUST 1944

The Allied campaign was not going well when the Regiment landed in Normandy. Two months before D-Day, General Bernard L. Montgomery, the land commander, had outlined the battle he intended to wage once a successful landing had been made. His first priority would be to build up his strength faster than the Germans could bring up their armoured reserves to drive the Allies into the sea and the key was the D-Day objective of Caen, ten miles inland from the coast, and the area between that city and Falaise to the south. Once he had secured these objectives, Montgomery intended to launch the Americans through the German defences into Brittany to capture the ports necessary to supply future Allied advances. The Americans would then wheel on the Caen-Falaise hinge and, moving south then east, drive to the Seine River alongside the British and Canadians, who would advance directly east. Montgomery estimated that his forces would be on the Seine by D+90 (ninety days after the initial landing).[2]

His German counterpart, *Feldmarschall* Erwin Rommel, disrupted these plans. Although hampered by Allied air superiority Rommel managed to bring up two panzer divisions that stymied British and Canadian attempts to reach Caen. On 7 June, the 3rd Canadian Infantry Division encountered strong elements of the 12th SS Panzer Division north of Caen at the little village of Authie. After heavy fighting which cost the North Nova Scotia Regiment more than two hundred casualties while their supporting armour, the Sherbrooke Fusiliers, lost a third of their tank strength, the division's forward movement came to a halt. Three days later, a squadron of the 1st Hussars, supported by a company of the Queen's Own Rifles, were cut to pieces by German armour and infantry at Le Mesnil-Patry. Again, losses were heavy – the Hussars lost thirty-seven Shermans, a third of that unit's total tank loss during the war. Things were no better in the British and American sectors and it soon became evident that Rommel had succeeded in cordoning off the bridgehead.

They used to sing of Lili – Sweet Lili Marlene
Out in the desert at El Alamein,
T'was there the Tommies captured Sweet Lili
Their pride and joy – She'll always be
My Lili of the lamplight, my own Lili Marlene.

When they fought in Europe, Lili was there,
D Day in Normandy – maybe you were there,
This was the song of victory,
They sang to me – its history,
T'was Lili of the lamplight, my own Lili Marlene.[1]

For nearly three weeks there was a deadlock as both sides built up their strength. On 19 June Allied logistics were badly disrupted by a Channel storm that destroyed one of the two Mulberries, the artificial harbours constructed to supply the bridgehead. In the west, General Omar N. Bradley's First American Army managed to take the port of Cherbourg after tough fighting only to find its facilities so heavily damaged that it would require weeks before they would be of any use. Other American attempts to expand their sector were hampered by the nature of the terrain; they were fighting in the bocage country – small fields cut into a checkerboard pattern by thick hedgerows that formed ideal defensive positions. In the eastern, or Commonwealth, sector the ground also favoured the defenders as the Germans were in possession of the ridge south of Caen, from which they could observe all movement. By late June, it was a stalemate.

Determined to get possession of Caen, Montgomery used heavy bombers to flatten the city on the night of 7 July but this had little effect on the Germans. The following day, he launched Operation CHARNWOOD to take the city and gain a bridgehead over the Orne River to the south of it. The 3rd Canadian Division managed to secure a toehold on Carpiquet airfield, which they held in the face of fierce counterattacks. These successes accomplished little, however, as the Germans simply abandoned Caen and took up a strong position to the south. Having spent six weeks trying to get into Caen, the Commonwealth forces now had to break out of it. On 18 July, Montgomery launched GOODWOOD, the most ambitious operation of the campaign to date and the largest British armoured attack in history. Following an air bombardment by more than a thousand aircraft, three British armoured divisions crossed the Orne east of Caen and attacked. The assault went well at first but faltered on the fortified villages along the ridge south of the city and British tank casualties were high – over two hundred vehicles – but, mercifully, most of the crews

Where they came ashore. The beach at Vaux, near Courseulles, where the SAR landed in the last week of July 1944.

PHOTOGRAPH BY DIANNE GRAVES.

escaped unharmed. At the same time, 3rd Canadian Division cleared Caen and the following day the newly-arrived 2nd Canadian Division managed to get a footing on Verrières Ridge, the western extension of the high ground, despite heavy casualties.

Foolishly, Montgomery had led Eisenhower, the supreme Allied commander, to believe that GOODWOOD was a major operation intended to break through to Falaise, when in reality he had intended it only as a holding attack with limited objectives. When GOODWOOD failed, he was not only in trouble with his superiors but faced with the prospect of trying to retain German armoured divisions in the Commonwealth sector to prevent them being shifted west to face Bradley's First American Army, which was finally clear of the difficult bocage and ready to launch a major break-out attack. To keep the pressure on, Montgomery ordered Lieutenant-General Guy Simonds's newly activated 2nd Canadian Corps to take Verrières Ridge.

The Canadian attack, code-named SPRING, went in on 25 July and was a disaster. The German defences were stronger than estimated, Simonds's plan was overly rigid, men were wasted in small piecemeal attacks against well-defended strongpoints and there was poor co-ordination between armour, infantry and artillery. The result was 1,500 casualties – the Canadian army's worst single day's loss since Dieppe. Verrières has been termed "an inordinately bloody classroom in which to learn the harsh lessons of operational soldiering" and it demonstrated that the master in that classroom was the *Wehrmacht*.[3]

The South Alberta Regiment had yet to encounter that grim teacher. Over a three-day period from 25 July to 28 July the Regiment landed at the wide beach west of Courseulles and, as each vehicle came ashore, it drove to a concentration area where the crew removed its waterproofing and waited for their turn to move up to the front. Although they could hear the sound of artillery fire, the reality of their new existence was only made clear for many South Albertas during their first nights in France when they were awakened by the sound of anti-aircraft batteries firing at German bombers raiding under the cover of darkness. Trooper Bob Seccombe of A Squadron realized there was a war on when he saw "rows of Red Cross vehicles heading for the coast."[4] Duncan Ledwidge of B Squadron came to the realization when he and his friends investigated some brewed-up German vehicles not far from their bivouac and discovered the blackened bodies of the drivers still in their compartments. They were shocked but, as Duncan put it, "I was there and I went on my own and I had to make the best of it."[5]

On 29 July 1944 the three fighting squadrons and RHQ moved closer to the front line. Their route took them through Caen in the late morning, and the War Diarist recorded that the "destruction and stench of the city brought home to all ranks that they were nearing a battlefield."[6] It was "the smell of death, a smell that is like no other" that struck Trooper Bert Denning of B Squadron as the Regiment's tanks, preceded by a bulldozer, worked their way through the rubble where the dead, still unburied from the bombing attack of 7 July, "lay everywhere, some scattered about on the ground, in the gutters, on the footpaths, and over the race course at the edge of town."[7] Leaving Caen behind, the Regiment harboured for the night in a grain field just outside the suburb of Vaucelles, where, by 2100 hours, everyone "was dug in, fed and settled down for the night."[8]

The following day 10 Brigade took over a portion of the front between the villages of Bourguébus and Bras on Bourguébus Ridge and during the afternoon the Regiment

I WONDER IF THIS WAS MENTIONED IN THE PAMPHLET ?

The downside of amphibious landings in armoured vehicles. Most of the Regiment splashed ashore in about six inches of water but a few unfortunates drove off the ramps into shell holes, and their fate very nearly became that of the crew in this cartoon by Jay Moreton appended to the July 1944 War Diary.

moved to the little town of Cormelles near Caen ready to support them. As the armoured units of 4th Division came forward that day they encountered a column of 2 Canadian Armoured Brigade moving back for a rest after nearly six weeks of constant fighting. A battle-weary sergeant of the 1st Hussars, watching the Green Patch crews wearing "clean new battle-dress," driving "shiny new tanks" with "crisp" squadron markings and equipment stowed according to regulation, compared them with the filthy, "battle-scarred" and "patched up" Shermans of his own regiment, manned by unshaven crews in "dirty old coveralls" covered with "filth and fighting grime."[9] There was some banter between the two formations but the Hussar felt sorry for the newcomers because he remembered when his regiment "landed, and how we felt so vastly superior to the enemy, until after the first day, and then we realized that we knew nothing at all."

What the Hussars and other Allied armoured units had learned was that the *Wehrmacht* was a skilled and tough opponent whose success in stopping Allied attempts to break out was based on two factors: sound defensive tactics and superior weapons. German defensive doctrine was simple but effective – the object was "to destroy the enemy by fire" and the *Wehrmacht* founded its tactics on firepower deployed in depth.[10] The field of fire

dictated the choice of a defensive position, with easily-concealed locations offering good fields of fire valued above all others. Allied air superiority had forced the Germans to become masters of camouflage, and they went to great lengths to hide their whereabouts – a German tank commander recorded that his crew erased the tracks their vehicle had made in an oat field lest they become a "clear signpost for any fighter-bomber" by laboriously rebending each disturbed blade of grain until it stood upright again.[11] Wherever possible, the *Wehrmacht* tried to deploy in three distinct lines or belts. Advance positions were placed on forward terrain features to deny "the enemy observation and to force him to deploy unnecessarily early."[12] Next came a line of battle outposts "sited to act as a buffer in front of a defended area as well to deceive the enemy as to the site of the main defensive belt." Finally came that main belt or line, defended "primarily by means of the schematically planned fire of all arms," which was strong enough to bring an enemy assault to a halt. Any part of the main defensive line that was evacuated had to be "regained by immediate or deliberate counterattack," but the object was always to destroy an enemy assault by fire before it reached that line.[13]

Even if Allied tanks penetrated the main defensive line, the *Wehrmacht* believed that enemy success was "not guaranteed" if "the defending troops use their weapons to cut off the tanks of the armoured spearhead from the follow-up infantry … since a tank unit by itself cannot hold ground for any length of time."[14] German manuals emphasized that the determination "to hold a position must not be shaken by the appearance of enemy AFVs" as soldiers "caught within the effective range of AFVs

Landing area. Artificial wharf at Courseulles, Normandy. In the distance can be seen ships waiting to unload. SAR COLLECTION.

Allied bombing. The ruins of Caen, destroyed by Allied bombing, July 1944. SAR COLLECTION.

who attempt to run away, will certainly be killed."[15] The Germans would separate enemy infantry from any tanks that approached close to the main defensive line and, once this was done, tank hunters would move in to deal with the tanks with hand-held weapons, mines, grenades and demolition charges.[16]

The task of Allied armour was to assist their infantry penetrate such defences and much thought had been given to the best means of doing so. By the summer of 1944, the established Commonwealth doctrine for an armoured regiment supporting an attack by an infantry brigade was to divide it into three distinct forces: gapping, assault and support. The squadron employed on the "gapping" force was to give "immediate support" to the engineers who made the gaps through the German minefields and wire. The squadron employed as an "assault echelon" passed through these gaps at best speed and moved onto the objective, where its job was to "subdue any opposition on the objective itself and to keep it subdued until the arrival of the infantry." Finally, a third squadron acting as the "support echelon" would "assist the leading infantry components on to their objective by destroying any machine guns, or any other weapons of that nature, which may be holding them up."[17]

In Normandy the terrain and the depth of the German defences combined to restrict the ability of Allied armour to manoeuvre and carry out this procedure. All the carefully worked out doctrine and training for tank-infantry cooperation in the assault, the source of much debate over the previous three years, failed in Normandy. In a memorandum dated 6 July, Montgomery criticized his armour for letting itself be separated from the infantry, so that the infantry was slaughtered by automatic weapons fire and the tanks fell victim to anti-tank

guns and *panzerfausts.*[18] He wanted increased co-operation between the two arms, but for Allied armoured units German defensive positions were only one part of the problem.

The simple fact was that Allied tankers equipped with the Sherman could not do battle on equal terms with their German counterparts. The Sherman was a product of American armoured doctrine which held that tanks did not engage other tanks; their job was to go for the enemy infantry and raise havoc with his communications. This role required a medium tank with a satisfactory gun, a good turn of speed and mechanical reliability – the Sherman had all three and, since it was produced in large numbers and easy to ship, it had become the standard Allied tank. In Normandy, however, the Sherman had to slug it out with superior German AFVs, a role for which it was never intended, and the result was high tank casualties.

To support the infantry, Allied armoured units had to get as close as possible to the enemy but, given its armour thickness, the Sherman could not survive within range of most German tank and anti-tank weapons. Even worse, the Sherman's 75 mm main gun was incapable of knocking out German tanks or SPGs at a decent range – and range was all-important. Almost every weapon in the German anti-tank inventory was capable of penetrating the Sherman's frontal armour at ranges up to 900 and 1000 yards while, at the same range, the Sherman's 75 mm could just penetrate the front of the most lightly-armoured German tank, the Mark IV, with standard AP shot and had no chance against the heavier Tigers and Panthers without using APDS (Armour Piercing Discarding Sabot) ammunition.

Not that the Germans engaged at long range – a postwar American study of 12,000 Allied tank casualties in northwest Europe concluded that, on average, German anti-tank weapons opened fire in that theatre at 804.8 yards.[19] At this distance, every German weapon except the 50 mm anti-tank gun was capable of destroying a Sherman but that tank could not inflict

The end of a Sherman. Destroyed tank of the 1st Hussars, Bray, Normandy, June 1944. This tank was penetrated by at least seven 75 mm AP rounds but did not catch fire. The fact that it did not brew up probably tempted the Germans to continue firing in the belief that it was not yet knocked out. COURTESY, ROY T. LESLIE, 1ST HUSSARS.

equivalent damage on its opponents. In fact it had to hit a German tank several times to destroy it – the same report concluded that while it took a Sherman an average of 4.2 hits to knock out a Tiger, 2.55 hits to knock out a Panther, and 1.2 to knock out a Mark IV, it took the Germans only 1.63 hits to knock out a Sherman.[20] In a tank versus tank or tank versus anti-tank gun duel the Sherman stood a poor chance and in what must be a classic statement of the obvious, the AFV (Technical) Branch of First Canadian Army reported on 2 August 1944 that the "outstanding lesson of the campaign as far as the [armoured] units we have visited are concerned is the fact that the Sherman 75 mm is out-gunned and out-armoured by the Germans."[21]

There were other problems with the Sherman. It burned easily when hit – "Jesus, how they burned!" was how one SAR troop sergeant put it.[22] George Kitching was somewhat disconcerted when, after landing in Normandy, he was introduced to General Miles Dempsey, the commander of Second British Army, and that officer's first words were to ask him whether his tanks were "petrol or diesel?" Kitching replied that they were powered by gasoline and Dempsey "seemed disappointed." Simonds later told him that the British general had lost more than 150 tanks in GOOD-WOOD and since they "were petrol-fuelled Shermans they had caught fire more easily and more rapidly than those fuelled by diesel."[23] British ordnance specialists calculated that four of five Shermans would catch fire when hit, a fact they rightly or wrongly attributed to "stowing extra ammunition inside the turret."[24] Whatever the reason,

the delightfully droll Germans, who had good reason to know, called the Sherman the "Tommy cooker" while Allied tank crews christened it the "Ronson" after the popular brand of cigarette lighter ("Lights first time, every time").

One in four British and Canadian Shermans was the improved "Firefly" model, armed with the larger and more effective 17-pdr. (76.2 mm) gun, which could penetrate the frontal armour of most German tanks, including the Tiger and Panther, at ranges over 1000 yards using APDS (Armour Piercing Discarding Sabot) shot. But the Firefly's armour was no thicker than that of the standard Sherman and, since its long gun barrel easily identified it, the Germans tried to pick it off first. The Firefly was the best Allied tank crews had but it was in short supply (the SAR did not receive any until September), there were problems with its hydraulic recoil system and it was discovered in Normandy that the APDS round it fired was highly inaccurate at ranges over 800 yards.[25]

The German weapon that Allied tank soldiers feared above all others was the notorious 88 mm gun, either in its pure form or mounted on the Tiger tank. There are frequent references in wartime documents to "88 fire," but one American ordnance specialist commented that "to the average US soldier, every heavy-calibre flat-trajectory weapon that fired at him was an '88'."[26] The Commonwealth soldier was no different and a British operational research team noted somewhat smugly that estimates "by fighting soldiers were found to be unreliable since many reported they had been knocked out by 88 mm. when in fact it had been 75 mm. shot, while the reverse mistake had not yet been discovered."[27] It was the smaller German 75 mm gun, in its tank, towed or self-propelled forms, that inflicted most of the AFV casualties. Of forty-five Shermans knocked-out in Normandy that a British research team examined, 82% were destroyed by 75 mm gun fire

More protection is needed. The South Albertas were the first armoured regiment in 4th Division to begin welding tracks on their hulls for extra protection. It was an easy and effective way to upgrade the armour of the Sherman. SAR COLLECTION.

(Right) Lethal killer. The German Pak 40 75 mm anti-tank gun, the standard divisional anti-tank gun of the *Wehrmacht* in 1944. Although Allied tank crews feared the 88 above all else, more Allied tank casualties were caused by this powerful, low-slung and easily-concealed weapon. PHOTOGRAPH BY DIANNE GRAVES.

(Left) The most feared weapon. The German 88 mm dual-purpose anti-aircraft and anti-tank gun. Although Allied tank crews were convinced that every large-calibre enemy AP weapon that fired at them was an 88, post-battle researchers discovered that most Allied tanks fell victim to the humbler 75 mm gun. Their research, however, revealed that when the 88 did go into action, it was "100% effective." COURTESY, W. VAILLANCOURT.

and only 18% by 88 mm gun fire, although the latter was found to be "one hundred percent effective."[28]

As the Germans almost always fought on the defensive in Normandy, Allied tanks were forced to approach well-sited and concealed positions – and take heavy losses. Faced with this prospect, Allied tank crews, not unreasonably, began to ask "when we may expect to have equip[men]t. which is the equal of the German types against which they have to fight."[29] They never got it in Normandy and resorted to welding surplus tank treads on the most vulnerable parts of their vehicles to provide extra armour. This additional weight increased engine wear and fuel consumption but nobody worried too much about that.

In the end the Allied armies were forced to use overwhelming air and artillery strength to grind the *Wehrmacht* down in a campaign of attrition that the enemy could not win. Normandy would see no repetition of the great armoured advances of the early war years – the German soldier was a tenacious and experienced opponent whose weapons effectively balanced the offensive capabilities of the tank. That the Allies' ultimate victory in the summer of 1944 was due to materiel strength should not reflect badly on the fighting qualities of American, British and Canadian soldiers. There is no "elegant formula for the overthrow of a powerful opponent" and, as their "aim was to avoid unnecessary loss of life" the Allies' "vast expenditure of steel and high explosive had this supreme justification."[30]

When the South Albertas moved up to the front on 30 July their route took them near Grentheville, the scene of heavy fighting during Operation GOODWOOD. The results, in the form of dozens of shot-up and burned tanks, were still scattered about and the sight enraged Swatty Wotherspoon as "you

could see one squadron shot up here and another squadron shot up there, and another there, with the Regimental HQ shot up here … they had lost virtually a whole regiment." His feeling was that, if the these tanks had been properly commanded, "there is no way that should have happened."[31] Lieutenant Jack Summers of B Squadron had a more personal (and more understandable) reaction: he "began to question the wisdom" of his "decision to transfer from the engineer to the armoured corps."[32]

The Regiment's new positions revealed worse sights. There were many "dead Germans still lying in the fields … in a very advanced state of decomposition" and Trooper John Lakes of Recce Troop was shocked to see one "wearing a Red Cross arm band."[33] These corpses disturbed Padre Silcox, who felt that, German or not, they should get a decent burial. The good padre did what he could in the immediate area of RHQ and one South Alberta who got caught for one of these unpopular burial details recalled that they dug a hole, placed the German in it, and filled it with their shovels while Silcox intoned, "Well, Jerry, you've had it" but "in such a quiet respectful way that it sounded like a prayer."[34]

On 31 July the Regiment enlarged the trenches in their positions. "All crews have dug large pits and run the tanks over top of them," reported the War Diarist, and the excavated "earth is then used to build banks around the bogies" of the suspension which created "quite a safe and comfortable dug out."[35] Lieutenant Don Stewart wrote to his mother that the chalk soil made "hard digging" but "believe me we *dig* … the first night the fellows tried eighteen inches, but by morning they were down a good four feet."[36] This concern with protection was necessary as the South Albertas were now within range of German artillery and they shortly received their first taste of enemy

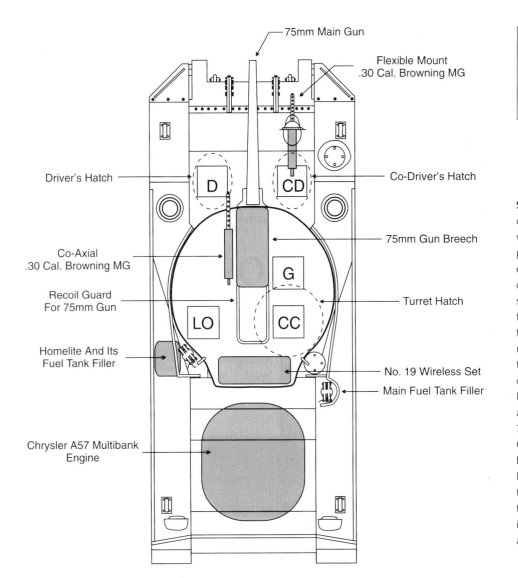

75mm Main Gun

Flexible Mount
.30 Cal. Browning MG

Driver's Hatch

Co-Driver's Hatch

D

CD

75mm Gun Breech

Co-Axial
.30 Cal. Browning MG

G

Recoil Guard
For 75mm Gun

Turret Hatch

LO

CC

Homelite And Its
Fuel Tank Filler

No. 19 Wireless Set
Main Fuel Tank Filler

Chrysler A57 Multibank
Engine

CREW POSITION KEY

CC   Crew Commander
                                    D   Driver
G   Gunner
                                    CD   Co-Driver
LO   Loader-Operator

Sherman V (M4A4). At left, the overhead view of a Sherman V, the workhorse of the Regiment, shows the positions of the crew and the major equipment and weapons. The crew commander (CC) is stationed in the single exit hatch from the turret; in front of him is the gunner (G) while on the other side of the breech of the 75 mm gun is the loader-operator (LO). In the front are the driver (D) and co-driver (CD). The cross-section below has the .30 calibre co-axial Browning and loader's seat removed to show the 75 mm gun breech. Note the size of the Chrysler A57 Multi-bank engine; its bulk necessitated the M4A4 hull being lengthened by eleven inches compared to other variants. The US Army rejected the Sherman V for overseas service but it saw extensive use in Commonwealth armoured formations in 1943-1945.

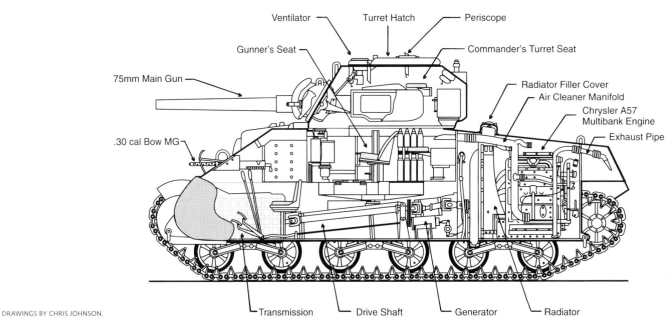

Ventilator   Turret Hatch   Periscope

Gunner's Seat

Commander's Turret Seat

75mm Main Gun

Radiator Filler Cover
Air Cleaner Manifold
Chrysler A57
Multibank Engine
Exhaust Pipe

.30 cal Bow MG

Transmission   Drive Shaft   Generator   Radiator

shelling. Over the next few days, Trooper Tom Clausen recalled, "I was on the ground more than I was on my feet because you hit the ground when anything went off."[37]

Corporal Swede Thuesen remembered that in these early days "everything was new and we didn't know what was going on."[38] This was particularly true of artillery fire – when the first German rounds landed near their positions the boys "thought they were ours and it wasn't until we saw men falling that we realized what was happening." It took time for the South Albertas to learn the crucial difference between the sound of "incoming" or enemy artillery fire and "outgoing" or friendly fire where the shell in flight "was working for George [the Sixth]." A man also had to divine by its noise where incoming was going to land and to recognize the distinct noise made by each kind of enemy weapon: the "moan, hum, whine, wail, shriek, or … whisper" of large-calibre artillery shells and the "abbreviated swishing or buzzing sounds" of mortar bombs.[39] It was the multi-barrelled German *Nebelwerfer* mortar (aptly called "Moaning Minnies" by Allied troops) that everyone feared – it sounded like "the hounds of hell itself might sound, baying and howling with growing intensity as they descend around you." Worse still was the feared German 88 whose shell moved faster than the speed of sound so that you saw the explosion before you heard the heard the noise. Without warning, there would be "a wicked *wham* from a black airburst puff" in the air "followed instantaneously by a metallic screech, a chilling, banshee *yee-ow*!" that resembled "a giant ripping asunder a piece of boilerplate."

After listening to this deadly symphony it became second nature to keep one ear cocked, no matter what you were doing, but until the South Albertas acquired this vital new knowledge, as Corporal Stan Rose says, "the Moaning Minnies would come over and the fellows who had been there awhile would dive for cover but we were a little slower."[40] It didn't take long to catch on – after one day near Bourguébus Ridge Trooper Arnold Dryer of Recce Troop wrote his fiancée that "it gets pretty noisy over here" but, as he wanted "to be a father" at some time in the future, "I did a bit of praying last night."[41]

At this point, just before the South Albertas enter combat, it would be useful to discuss what conditions were like for the men in an SAR tank crew in 1944. Most SAR crews served in the Sherman V (the American Medium Tank Model M4A4), the most numerous tank in the unit (sixty-one of a total of seventy-eight AFVs). Protected by armour that varied in thickness from three inches on the turret front to one inch on the belly plating, the Sherman was a high tank – just under ten feet from the ground to the top of the skull-shaped turret – and long and narrow, being twenty feet from the front fender to the back of the rear deck and nearly nine feet from the outside of one track to the outside of the other. Fully loaded for combat the Sherman V weighed just under 35 tons but its Chrysler A57

power plant (five six-cylinder engines in a multi-bank arrangement hooked to a common shaft with a total displacement of 1253 cubic inches) could move it up to 25 mph for short periods and 20 mph for indefinite periods. The crew consisted of five men, usually divided into the "turret crew" (commander, gunner and loader-operator) and the two drivers, each with specific duties and each part of a highly trained team that was only as good as its weakest member.[42]

The commander was in charge of fighting the tank and, depending on circumstances, might be a corporal, sergeant or lieutenant. His position was on a small folding seat in the right rear of the turret immediately below the large circular hatch with its double half-moon flaps. As the tanks used by the Regiment in Normandy were not fitted with a cupola that would permit all-round vision without rotating the turret, South Alberta commanders usually preferred to command from the open hatch, standing on their seat (which could be raised or lowered) and resting their elbows on the roof of the turret with their head and shoulders exposed. When doing so, they had to be careful of the double hatch doors, which were heavy, awkward spring-loaded affairs and the cause of many injuries. The commander issued his orders over the tank's intercom system – all crew members wore a headset – and with the flick of a switch he could talk with the other tanks in his troop by using either the A or B system on the tank's No. 19 Wireless Set.

The gunner was responsible for firing the Sherman's main armament and his position was on another small seat inside the turret proper below and in front of the crew commander. The gunner's vision was restricted to what he could see through his small periscope, but in action he usually kept his eye glued to the telescopic sight beside the periscope, leaning his forehead against the rubber pad above it. His left hand rested on the small wheel which elevated or depressed the 75 mm gun and its co-axial .30 calibre Browning machine gun while his right was on the handgrip that operated the powerful electric turret motor. By pushing this button, the gunner could traverse the turret through 360° in about fifteen seconds. On the turret floor by his left foot was a small metal box with two solenoid trigger buttons. If he stamped on the left button he fired the co-axial Browning; if he hit the right button, he fired the 75 mm main gun.

Dominating the white-painted interior of the turret was the large breech mechanism of that gun. The loader-operator sat on the side of it opposite the gunner and his tasks were to man the No. 19 Wireless Set fastened to the rear of the turret and supply ammunition to the turret armament. He also had a periscope to view the outside and on the turret walls around him and at his feet were various bins, racks and brackets containing nearly 5,000 rounds of .30 calibre ammo in metal boxes and, officially, about a hundred 75 mm rounds of various types – HE, smoke and APC (Armour Piercing, Capped) – differentiated by their shapes and coloured marking in various combinations of white, red, black, blue and green stripes. Unofficially, crews would take as much ammunition as they could cram into the turret and it was not unusual for the turret floor to be cluttered with an extra thirty to fifty rounds.

The turret crew lived and fought in a very small world. Visualize three grown men perched on stools in the interior of a large four-passenger automobile with the seats removed and an armchair leaning against the dashboard to represent the breech of the main gun and you have some idea of the extent of that world. Now add about one hundred and fifty rounds of 75 mm ammunition (each about two feet long and as thick as a man's arm), the No. 19 Wireless Set which was about as big as a suitcase, the Homelite (an auxiliary generating motor) and the turret motor of almost the same size. That's not all – in the remaining space places must be found for the equipment necessary to fight the tank: 5,000 rounds of .30 calibre ammunition in metal boxes, a signal pistol and cartridges, fire extinguishers, water containers, spare antennae, signal lamps, flashlights, the gunner's quadrant for indirect fire, binoculars, gas masks, hand grenades, at least one Sten gun, rounds for the smoke projector and a first aid kit. That doesn't leave much room free and the crew's personal items – clothing, kit bags, blankets and rations – were strapped on the exterior of the vehicle. In a well-run crew a place was found for everything and everything was in its place.

The driver and co-driver sat in a separate compartment at the bow of the tank. Both had their own hatches with periscopes so that they could see when "buttoned down" and both worried about the position of the main gun because, if it was traversed over their hatches, they could not exit through them. The driver, responsible not only for driving but also the maintenance of the engines, suspension and tracks, was the more senior of the two and sat on the left. In front of him were the two tiller bars by which he steered the tank – if he pulled back on the left bar, it braked the left track and the tank moved in that direction impelled by the still-moving right track. There were no power assists for controls and the driver had to use his main strength to steer the vehicle. On the floor in front of him were two pedals, the clutch on the left and the accelerator on the right, while close to his right hand was the gear lever by which he selected the Sherman's five forward and one reverse speeds. To his left, mounted on the bulkhead of the tank, was a rudimentary instrument panel containing a clock, "idiot lights" for the five engines, a tachometer, speedometer, odometer, ammeter, voltmeter, and gauges for engine temperature and oil pressure.

The co-driver sat to the right of the driver. This lucky crew member had the most spacious compartment in the Sherman V if an area about the size of a steamer trunk can be called spacious. The co-driver assisted the driver in maintaining the vehicle and usually caught any spare jobs going around, including foot patrols out of the tank. His main task in action was to fire the .30 calibre Browning mounted on a pivot in the bow in front of him with a breech that projected back into his stomach. On the floor behind the co-driver's seat was the belly hatch, which he kept well-oiled and which allowed the crew to escape

from the vehicle using the Sherman's sixteen inches of ground clearance.

Riding in a Sherman was not a very comfortable experience. As the crews preferred to keep the hatches open if possible, the drivers were enveloped in clouds of dust thrown up by the tracks while the downdraft from the multi-bank Chrysler power plant, which was sucked in through the main hatch to the air intakes at the lower rear of the turret, ensured that the commander, gunner and loader also received their fair share of dust. The crew felt a gentle rocking motion when the tank moved on paved roads and a stronger rocking motion on dirt roads, but when the Sherman moved cross-country, the ride could be rough – one veteran termed it "rocking and rolling" – and going up or down hill forced the crew to hang on to whatever they could to steady themselves.[43] Nor was it quiet inside the Sherman – the clatter and squeal of the tracks and the roar of the engines were audible even when the hatches were closed, making the intercom a very necessary piece of equipment.

It was worse in action. When the main gun fired, thirty-five tons of dead weight rocked back on the springs and the crew compartments filled with choking fumes of cordite that overpowered the normal interior smells of oil and lubricants. The breech of the 75 mm main gun recoiled a foot back with a crash, the shell casing ejected with a clank, and hit the rubber back stop at the rear of the recoil guard before dropping into a canvas bag below it, and the gun would then return to the firing position, letting the loader-operator shove another shell into the breech. The maximum rate of fire was twenty rounds per minute but only for very short periods as at that rate the hard-working loader would soon tire of hoisting shells, which weighed between seventeen and nineteen pounds depending on type, into the breech. The .30 calibre Brownings, with their frantic mechanical chatter as their cloth belts moved through the breeches at a rate of 500 rounds per minute, were not much quieter.

The tank was the crew's weapon, their mobility and their home, but most armoured personnel had ambivalent feelings about their vehicles. Tanks were attractive targets and the crew's shelter from enemy fire might in a few seconds be transformed into a blazing inferno as a hit from an armour-piercing round ignited the gasoline and ammunition in the interior. Knowing their vehicles' propensity to catch fire when hit and that they had no more than fifteen seconds to escape without injury from a burning tank, Sherman crews practised emergency bail-out procedures until they were automatic. Postwar operational research revealed that, on average, 50.6% of the Sherman crews whose vehicles were hit had a chance of emerging unscathed. These were the odds just to get out of the tank but, since it was common practice on both sides to fire at tank crews who evacuated shot-up vehicles (the infantryman's revenge), the crew's actual chances were much worse.[44]

By the time 4th Armoured Division came into the line south of Caen the Allied campaign was making better progress. On 25 July Bradley's First American Army launched Operation COBRA, the long-delayed breakout from the bridgehead. It was preceded by a carpet bombardment from the US Eighth Air Force that unfortunately killed or wounded more than six hundred American soldiers, including a lieutenant-general, and caused such confusion that the gains on the first day were limited. Bradley pressed on and by 31 July First Army was out of the confining bocage and into the more open terrain at Avranches at the base of the Brittany peninsula. The next day, Lieutenant-General George Patton's Third Army was activated to continue the advance.

Montgomery was keen to keep the pressure on the Germans in the Commonwealth sector to prevent them from shifting their armour to the American front. He issued orders to the commanders of the Second British and the newly-activated First Canadian Army that the enemy was "to be shot up, and attacked, and raided, whenever and wherever possible."[45] On the Canadian front Simonds planned to ease 4th Armoured Division into battle by mounting an attack on the fortified hamlet of Tilly-la-Campagne located on a small rise on Bourguébus Ridge. As George Kitching, the commander of 4th Armoured Division, describes, Tilly was a tough nut to crack, being a hamlet of about eight houses each surrounded by high stone walls which had been turned into small fortresses by the Germans:

> The first thing they did was to strengthen the basements of the houses to withstand heavy pressure from above, then they dynamited the walls so that they collapsed inwards forming a pyramid of stone on top of the basements. These pyramids were sometimes ten feet thick and could withstand the heaviest shelling. Next, they prepared the basements just like a concrete dug-out with weapon slits at ground level for machine guns which were sighted to fire along the narrow gravel roads that ran between the walls enclosing each farm house.[46]

Fortress in Normandy. Tilly-la-Campagne, August 1944. By reinforcing the cellars of the hamlet and demolishing the upper storeys the Germans created a very strong defensive position that required a major assault to take. The German strongpoint had clear fields of fire in all directions. SAR COLLECTION.

The only approaches to Tilly were across flat, open grain fields that provided little cover and it was defended by the elite 1st SS Panzer Division, *Leibstandarte Adolf Hitler*, very determined soldiers.

Two previous attacks against this tough position had failed, and although Rod Keller, the commander of 3rd Division, advised Kitching to leave Tilly alone and "try somewhere else," there was pressure to mount another attack.[47] It came from Montgomery, who telephoned General Harry Crerar of First Canadian Army at 0950 hours on 1 August. The Allied ground commander asked Crerar to keep the enemy "worried" on his front and inquired whether another attack might be made on Tilly that night. The orders then came down the line. Forty minutes after Montgomery's call to Crerar, George Kitching arrived at the headquarters of Brigadier Jim Jefferson's 10 Brigade and informed him that he was to attack Tilly that night. Jefferson selected the Lincoln and Welland Regiment for this task and briefed their commanding officer, Lieutenant-Colonel J.G. McQueen, at 1130 hours. At 1400 hours the South Albertas were warned to support the Links and at 1900 hours Wotherspoon and Major Arnold Lavoie, whose A Squadron got the job, attended Jefferson's O Group at brigade headquarters and then, at 2200 hours, McQueen's O Group at the Links' RHQ. Lavoie then briefed his subordinates, including crew commander Corporal Herbie Watkins, who recalled that it was midnight before his troop was "put on alert." It had taken just over fourteen hours for the word to be transmitted from General Montgomery to Corporal Watkins.[48]

The plan of attack involved a short barrage after which the Links' four rifle companies would move forward. Two companies (A and B) would take up a position between Tilly and the German-held village of La Hogue to prevent any interference from that direction. D Company would then seize Point 63 between Bourguébus and Tilly and establish a "firm base" through which C Company would pass to attack the hamlet itself. Lavoie's A Squadron was to be in a position where, at first light, they could assist C and D Companies to clear the village. There was no information about the strength of the German defenders – Lavoie was told that it was "uncertain."[49] Actually, on the night of 1/2 August 1944, the hamlet was held by nine companies of SS panzer grenadiers with six anti-tank guns in position and twenty tanks and twenty-two artillery pieces in immediate support.[50] This meant that the Links' assault company, with a strength of about 125 officers and men, would be attacking a position held by about five hundred well-entrenched defenders.[51]

It is not surprising that the attack failed. The two companies which were to set up a blocking position ran into heavy enemy fire and withdrew in confusion back to Bourguébus. D Company did get on Point 63 and C Company, the assault company, then moved through them toward the hamlet. They were within two hundred yards of their objective when the Germans "engaged them with MMGs [Medium Machine Guns] from three directions and also with heavy mortar fire."[52] By 0545 hours, the Links had lost 59 casualties and McQueen reported that the attack had failed. As one Lincoln and Welland platoon commander put it: "If we hadn't known there was a war on, we sure as hell knew it after that night – it was just awful."[53]

There wasn't much that A Squadron could do to help the Links. Lavoie deployed two of his troops forward near Point 63 and the other two farther back near a rail embankment. By the time Lieutenant Gordie Campbell of A-3 got his orders it was nearly midnight and he had no time to brief his troop but only told them to follow him and they "would be given their orders as we went along over the wireless set," which caused crew commander Watkins to think "what a way to be going into action."[54] Herbie's tank was in the lead when an infantry officer approached and asked for fire support as his "company was in deep trouble up ahead." Campbell gave Herbie permission to open up and a few minutes later brought the remainder of the troop up to assist. Not that they could see much in the dark but all four Shermans opened an enthusiastic fire with their main weapons and Brownings and, according to Herbie, "it was quite a sight to see & hear all that shooting for the first time." At first light the troop withdrew slightly to the rear but still in a position to support the infantry.

Gordie Irving's A-1 and Jim Curley's A-4 Troops, further back near the railway embankment, were not in a position to fire at all. Corporal John Galipeau remembered that they could observe "the action only by the streaks of tracer and the flash of shell explosions" and, as "I looked at the hell in the village I thought 'why are we doing nothing to help those guys out there'" but, "knew in the dark that there was little we could do."[55] A few seconds later, John's crew encountered the reality of combat:

The Germans were firing airburst and this lad in our tank was up in the hatch and he got hit. We all just froze in the tank. I remember looking up and seeing his shirt open and cuts across the fleshy part of his chest and over his shoulder and then he was out on the deck crying for help and crying in pain. We were all frozen until one of the older men got out on the deck and put bandages and shell dressing on him. And that is when I knew it was war – we all did as those airbursts had been coming over for some time and we had never been concerned.[56]

It never occurred to Gordie Irving to be afraid; he was too concerned about "how do we save our skins and get the job done."[57] He did remember watching a "goddamned sea of fire" as the Links were knocked back that night. When dawn came the two troops remained in their forward position.

The attack on Tilly on the night of 1/2 August 1944 was the Regiment' first action but the South Albertas who participated remember it only as a confusing affair in which their tanks played only a minor role. Swatty was "highly pleased" with A Squadron's efforts and the brigade commander complimented them "for their excellent work."[58] Jefferson was less charitable to the Links and informed them that "insufficient determination had been shown in attacking what should have been a two-company objective."[59] The Canadians had not done with Tilly – over the next three days the hamlet was subjected to an intensive aerial and artillery bombardment. The rocket-firing Typhoons were awe inspiring and Trooper Robert Bruce remembered that when he first saw them roar down with their rockets, "they scared hell out of me."[60]

They had less effect on the defenders of Tilly, who tried to return the Allied fire with interest, and A Squadron, which remained in place north of the village to support the infantry, experienced some heavy shelling. Herbie Watkins was brewing tea on the morning after the Lincoln's failed attack when the "next thing I knew I was flat on my back and could not see but there was lots of excitement" and shouts of "call the ambulance!"[61] Herbie was only temporarily blinded by dirt from the force of the mortar bomb explosion and was soon back in action but his co-driver was seriously wounded. That same day Sergeant James Gove of A-1 was out of his tank to string some wire when he heard incoming and took shelter in some nearby trenches only to find that "the much wiser infantry had booked all the available space."[62] Gove's troop was "not uncomfortable with the persistent shelling as we (erroneously) believed that we were quite safe as long as we stayed inside" because "we never had, up to that time, seen what a direct hit on a tank would do, we were serenely ignorant of the results." The shelling and counter-shelling went on for three days. On 3 August Dave Currie's C Squadron moved up to replace Lavoie's A Squadron, which was withdrawn to have German tank tracks welded to the turrets and hulls of their Shermans for additional armour protection. Apparently, as the War Diarist noted, the Regiment was the first armoured unit in 4th Division "to attempt such a modification and those who have had experience with it can vouch for its usefulness."[63]

On 5 August reports were received that the German fire from the hamlet appeared to be slackening and orders came down for the Argyll and Sutherland Highlanders to mount a probe. The Argylls were sceptical that the Germans had withdrawn because they had observed that "a considerable volume of fire, including mortar fire, was still coming from Tilly."[64] Nonetheless, a thirty-man patrol was sent toward the hamlet at 1700 hours to answer the question: "Is the enemy in occupancy of Tilly and if so in what str[ength]?"[65] The Germans waited until it was within close range and then pinned it down with heavy machine-gun fire and mortars. Lieutenant-Colonel Dave Stewart of the Argylls, observing his men's predicament, requested the FOO of 15th Field Artillery Regiment, who was in his command post with him, to bring down fire to extricate them and this officer twice gave the order for "Fifty rounds rapid!"[66] Fifteenth Field responded magnificently, firing 2400 rounds of 25-pdr. HE, almost their entire ammunition scale, on the hamlet and the patrol managed to get back with the loss of only seven men. The brigade commander now had the answer to his question but Jefferson, feeling that the German response might only be "a strong determined fighting rear guard action in order to gain time for the withdrawal of the main part of his Div[ision]," decided to attack Tilly that night.[67]

At 1900 hours the Argylls were ordered to put in an assault "using not more than two companies" but with tank support from the Regiment.[68] There was little time to prepare and both Stewart and Wotherspoon attended an O Group at brigade headquarters to discuss the operation. Swatty did not like the brigade plan and suggested that an armoured feint should be made west of Tilly to distract the defenders and lay down an observed smoke barrage to cover the main attack. Jefferson was not convinced, but after forty-five minutes of argument

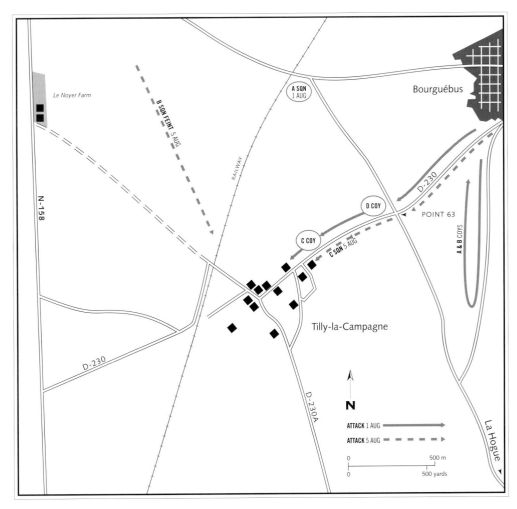

Map 2: The attacks on Tilly-la-Campagne, 1 and 5 August 1944. The solid arrows show the attack on the night of 1 August when A Squadron supported the Lincoln and Welland Regiment. The dotted lines show the assault made by the Argylls and C Squadron from the east and the feint made by B Squadron to distract the defenders.

Swatty had his way and Major Bob Bradburn's B Squadron was alerted to undertake the feint while two troops from C Squadron were assigned to the Argyll assault companies.[69]

Bradburn was only told at 2000 that his squadron had to be in position at 2145 hours. Using Lieutenant Tom Howard's troop to "smoke off" Tilly, he led the other three troops forward. They came under intermittent anti-tank fire that immobilized one tank and then pushed forward although the German fire increased in volume. As it was quite dark by this time Bradburn ordered one of his troops back and then moved ahead with the remaining two, using "fire and movement" tactics. B-3 Troop, under Lieutenant Alec Scrimger, was ordered to go as close to Tilly as possible while Squadron HQ and the remaining troop laid down smoke to confuse the Germans. Scrimger's tanks neared the railway embankment west of the village but reported no enemy and the squadron then withdrew, having accomplished its task of feinting an attack. The squadron had two tanks immobilized but both were recovered. It was Trooper Duncan Campbell's first time in action and he re-

called being "very much afraid" although he remembered that, later on, "you get used to it a little bit but you never really get used to it."[70]

With the hope that B Squadron's efforts had distracted the defenders, the main attack went in at 2300 hours. It had been delayed because, in the darkness, the two troops from Dave Currie's C Squadron had not managed to "marry up" with the Argyll assault companies. In the end Dave dismounted and led his tanks forward to the rendezvous on foot despite heavy enemy mortaring, as by now the Germans had come fully alive – it was only later that he realized he had left his helmet in his Sherman. When the armour and infantry had joined, they moved in towards the objective, the tanks in advance, but intense German anti-tank and machine-gun fire halted this assault just as it had stopped all previous attempts. The Argylls made a determined effort to penetrate the village but, realizing it was hopeless, the two infantry company commanders ordered a withdrawal across grain fields set alight by tracer bullets. The cost was twenty-four casualties.[71]

C Squadron lost four tanks that night but suffered no fatal casualties. To one Argyll the sight of a Canadian Sherman being knocked out came as a great surprise as he realized that "tanks aren't invincible."[72] Ed Hyatt was the driver in a tank that was hit by an AP round that penetrated the turret and wounded all three men in it. Hyatt got the most seriously wounded man out, administered first aid, and injected him with morphine from the disposable syrette pack carried in every tank, and co-driver Nick Ritco carried him to safety. Corporal Swede Thuesen remembers coming up "through the fields, just about dusk" and "there were a lot of German tanks and some German soldiers on the flank."[73] Swede's gunner opened fire but "the tank turned and his m[achine].g[un]. was still firing and he hit my sergeant's tank and the sergeant reported that 'I got a couple of hits but I am okay'." Trooper Ed Davies was the gunner in the tank of his troop commander, Lieutenant Jack Roberts. As they neared Tilly, Ed was having "a great time firing but was a little nervous." He had been told "that there wasn't any heavy armour in there" but "all of a sudden I spotted a big tracer going by" and told Roberts that "there's something heavier in there than machine-gun fire."[74] When the withdrawal began Roberts pulled off the road to cover the infantry but hit a mine, losing a track. Roberts decided "to stay and fight with his tank at all costs to assist the infantry" but Currie ordered him to leave the vehicle and take up a position where his crew could keep it under observation until it could be recovered. They got their tank back successfully the next day.[75]

Thus ended the fourth Canadian attempt to take the German strongpoint. "Congratulations," Montgomery said to Simonds, "you've been kicked out of Tilly again."[76] In Swatty's opinion, the attack was "stupid" as what was required was "a brigade attack, not a reconnaissance in force with less than a battalion."[77] Dave Stewart of the Argylls agreed and was heard to ask during the attack: "What's the matter with those people back there, telling me send those guys in," because it was just "sheer slaughter."[78] Dave Currie was also upset – in fact he "was very 'pissed off' at the whole show," remembered Captain John Redden of C Squadron, but "I think we learned what not to do in the future."[79] The Germans weren't impressed – the commander of a regiment being moved in to replace the SS panzer grenadiers around Tilly informed his men they were facing "Not particularly highly trained Canadian troops."[80]

There was one positive result. For the first time Dave Currie had demonstrated the fighting credo of the South Alberta Regiment – no matter how desperate or dangerous the situation, SAR tanks would render the best support possible to their flat-footed friends and never abandon them. As the Argyll historian noted, the 5 August attack on Tilly was the first time "the Battalion worked in co-operation with the tanks of the 29th Canadian Armoured Reconnaissance Regiment (South Alberta Regiment)" and the "two units were to form a fighting combination which would become famous" as the "men of each unit acquired through experience confidence in the brother regiment, so that later in the war the ordinary Argyll fighting soldier instinctively felt better about any coming operation if he knew the South Albertas were to work with his unit."[81]

There is reason to question the decision of senior Canadian commanders in ordering four separate assaults of battalion size or less on Tilly-la-Campagne, assaults that directly incurred more than three hundred killed, wounded and captured. Brigadier Jim Jefferson was wrong – Tilly was never "a two-company objective" and it should be noted that, when it was finally captured on 7 August during Operation TOTALIZE, it took two British infantry battalions with considerable armour and artillery support nearly a day to do it and they fought against ordinary German infantry, not the redoubtable 1st SS Panzer Division. Reflecting on the matter a half century later, George Kitching thought that, in 1944, First Canadian Army should have brought in the air force heavy bombers and "bombed the place to hell."[82]

Fitters – the tankman's auto mechanics. The boys who kept the tanks going – a picture of a fitters' group. From left to right: Trooper J. Hawthorne, Sergeant Fitzgerald, Sergeant Sinclair, Sergeant-Major Muehllehner, Captain Dick Robinson and Corporal Smith.

SAR COLLECTION.

CHAPTER SEVEN

"The greenest bloody army that ever went to war."

FRANCE: 6 AUGUST–15 AUGUST 1944

On 6 August 1944 the South Alberta Regiment moved with the other units of 4th Canadian Armoured Division back from Bourguébus Ridge to Caen. This move was part of the general realignment of First Canadian Army in preparation for an operation Simonds had been planning. Code-named TOTALIZE, its objective, as laid down by Montgomery, was to "break through the enemy positions to the south and south-east of Caen, and to gain such high ground in the direction of Falaise" that would "cut off the enemy forces … and render their withdrawing eastward difficult – if not impossible."[2] Montgomery's emphasis on cutting off the German retreat reflected the fact that, in the first week of August, Patton's Third Army had ripped wide open the western side of the German front.

As Patton's troops poured through this breach Adolf Hitler sealed the fate of his armies in France. On 3 August, alarmed by Patton's advance, the German dictator ordered Rommel's successor as the German commander in the west, *Feldmarschall* Hans von Kluge, to take all available panzer divisions and counterattack to cut Patton off from his supply lines. In vain, von Kluge protested that any shift of armour from the British and Canadian sector would fatally weaken his defences south of Caen – Hitler was adamant and von Kluge had no choice but to obey. During the night of 6/7 August four German armoured divisions attacked in the Mortain area. At first they made good progress but, forewarned by ULTRA decrypts, the Americans eventually stopped them cold and over a period of two days destroyed much of the enemy armour. Having disposed of this threat, Bradley, who had assumed command of the American armies, ordered Patton to attack to the east in the direction of Argentan. Third Army advanced quickly and by 11 August was behind the German left flank near Le Mans, ninety miles south of Falaise, almost in the rear of the German forces facing the British and Canadians. The German armies in Normandy were in peril of being encircled (see map 5, page 126).

When through the mud, you drag your weary feet,
Under your tunic, your heart may cease to beat.
No matter what becomes of thee,
I'll always smile and think with glee.
That I am LOB, that I am LOB.

When you hear the spatter of Schmeissers in the night,
Then you might wonder, if your cause is right.
No matter how afraid you are,
You'll find me in the nearest bar.
Cause I am LOB, cause I am LOB.[1]

Before that could happen, First Canadian Army had to penetrate the German positions south of Caen. The terrain in this area, a series of gradually rising gentle slopes and open grain fields dotted with walled villages surrounded by small woods and orchards, was good tank country, but what is good tank country is also good anti-tank country and the Germans were expecting an attack. The commander of the 12th SS Panzer Division, *Brigadeführer* Kurt Meyer, recorded that, in the ten days preceding TOTALIZE, all the tank, infantry and artillery units in his division were hard at work constructing the usual "three defence lines."[3] Simonds's problem was to penetrate these lines. He had studied Operation GOODWOOD, which had faltered on the defended villages on Bourguébus Ridge, and had pondered the problems of attacking German defences in depth based on such strongpoints.

Simonds came up with some novel solutions. He decided to attack at night as darkness would provide cover and take away the German advantage in weapons range. To guide the assault formations (as movement in the dark is always a risky business) he planned to employ artificial illumination provided by searchlights bouncing their beams off clouds; light anti-aircraft guns firing tracer rounds on fixed lines to indicate the correct direction; and a navigational guidance system based on signals transmitted over the wireless of the lead vehicles. Simonds also decided to make full use of all available airpower including heavy and medium bombers and fighter aircraft. Finally, he turned to the problem of the infantry, who in previous attacks had been forced to ground by German automatic weapons fire, leaving the tanks, which had gone ahead, vulnerable to anti-tank weapons. To get both arms onto the objective at the same time, Simonds developed an idea that had actually been bruited about for some time – he provided his infantry with their own armoured vehicle.[4] His engineers hastily removed the weapons from seventy-six self-propelled guns and welded metal plates

109

over the apertures to create the first fully-tracked APC (Armoured Personnel Carrier), which could carry an infantry section of ten men in relative safety through mortar and machine-gun fire.

As it finally evolved, TOTALIZE was a complex two-phase operation. The first phase would commence at 2300 hours on 7 August with a heavy artillery barrage on the German defences and carpet bombing by bombers along the flanks of the attack. Then the assault divisions (2nd Canadian and 51st Highland), with their leading infantry brigades in APCs and each supported by an armoured brigade, would break through the German defence lines while their other brigades would follow on foot to mop up strongpoints left by the leading elements. The second phase would begin at 1400 hours on 8 August when, following a heavy air attack by the US Eighth Air Force in front of them, 4th Canadian and 1st Polish Armoured Divisions would advance on either side of Route Nationale 158, the highway that ran straight from Caen to Falaise, to seize the high ground that dominated the latter city. If all went well, First Canadian Army would be in a position to close the northern jaw of a developing trap.

Operation TOTALIZE worried the commanders of the two armoured divisions. The first drafts of the plan had been based on the assumption that the bulk of the German armour, which had frustrated all attempts to advance south of Caen, would be in position when the attack went in, and for this reason Simonds had planned to use only one armoured division in the second phase, keeping the other in reserve. When information reached him early on 6 August that the German armour had been moved west for the ill-fated attack at Mortain, he changed the plan at 1000 hours that day and decided to put in both 4th Canadian and 1st Polish Armoured Divisions together, moving them up to their start lines while the first phase attack was on-going. Each formation would have a limited front in which to operate, about 800-1000 yards wide in the case of 4th Division, and this would restrict the number of tanks that could be deployed. This concerned George Kitching as his division would have "no room to manoeuvre, but also because the enemy commander would quickly appreciate that our attacks were coming on a very narrow front and would then concentrate his smaller forces to deal with them."[5] The commander of 1st Polish Armoured Division, Major-General Stanislaw Maczek, had a similar frontage complicated by the fact that heavily wooded areas (ideal German defensive positions) lay on his front and flank. Maczek thought that the plan forced the armour to "carry out a rigid frontal attack on a narrow front" rather than use their strength of mobility and manoeuvre.[6] Neither general liked the long pause of about eight hours between the two phases, a pause that might result in losing the "momentum of the attack."

On the morning of 7 August Kitching and Maczek expressed their concerns to Simonds but the corps commander proved inflexible. When they asked him to "extend our frontage to give us room for manoeuvre," Simonds refused, as it would mean changing his carefully worked-out plan of attack.[7] The two commanders voiced their apprehension about the long pause and asked Simonds "to call off" the air bombardment scheduled before the beginning of the second phase if the first phase "went so well that we had the enemy on the run."[8] Again, Simonds's reaction was negative – in Kitching's words: "Guy was convinced that we would meet heavy opposition … and would not change his plan" and "there was also some doubt in his mind whether he would be able to call off the bombing mission in time." The die was cast and TOTALIZE would go forward as planned.

All this was, of course, unknown to the South Albertas, who were just happy to be off Bourguébus Ridge. The Regiment's rest area was in a destroyed part of Caen where there happened to be plentiful stocks of alcohol. The South Albertas (in common with most combat soldiers) had an uncanny instinct for locating any kind of alcoholic drink. Not that it ever interfered with their job – consensus in the Regiment was that drinking was a fine thing but not in action as a tank crew depended on each of its members being alert and on the job and no trooper would willingly let his comrades down.

It was a different matter in a rest area, and to their great joy the men of A Squadron discovered a cellar full of champagne and very soon the only man in the squadron "who wasn't full up was Major Lavoie."[9] Other South Albertas had their first encounter with calvados, the fiery liquor distilled from apples that is common in the Normandy region. Like most Canadians of their generation, the boys were not familiar with the more exotic distillations available in Europe, the staples in prewar Alberta being beer and rye whisky, and calvados puzzled them at first. Sergeant Earle Wood remembered that they were unsure whether it was drinkable until Trooper Tip La Foy "poured some on a spoon and lit a match to it – pooff! – it burned" and the boys concluded that it was "good to drink."[10] The stuff was so raw that it would dissolve the plastic liners in the water containers but there was lots of it around – Trooper John Neff of B Squadron had so much that he found it useful "to heat tea water."[11]

Unfortunately, the war intervened. Early on 7 August Swatty Wotherspoon was summoned to an O Group at brigade to learn the Regiment's task in the forthcoming operation. When he returned, he issued orders to prepare for a nighttime move to a concentration area where the South Albertas were to be at 0600 hours. The Regiment's task in the second phase of TOTALIZE would be to support 10 Brigade to take the high ground around the village of Potigny. The Argylls and C Squadron would lead the brigade column and the other two squadrons were to be prepared to support them if necessary. There was much excitement after the squadron commanders passed along this information and the crews got their tanks ready for action.[12]

As the South Albertas prepared to move forward the units in the first phase waited for the aerial bombardment and artillery barrage that would open Operation TOTALIZE. Promptly at 2300 hours the roar of four-engined bombers was heard as RAF Lancasters and Halifaxes droned in to drop their deadly loads on the enemy, raising huge clouds of dust. Before the bombers had finished, 720 artillery pieces brought down a tremendous barrage and the assault columns moved forward under their cover. Despite the searchlights, tracer shells and wireless beams, the dust and the sheer number of vehicles manoeuvring in the dark created confusion and some units strayed off the correct path. Nonetheless, as the eastern sky began to lighten about 0500 hours, most of the objectives had been taken although there were pockets of resistance, notably Tilly-la-Campagne. The first phase was a success, the enemy defences had been ruptured, and there appeared to be nothing between First Canadian Army and Falaise.

That was the opinion of Lieutenant-Colonel Mel Gordon of the Sherbrooke Fusiliers of 2 Canadian Armoured Brigade, whose regiment was on its objective near the hamlet of Crasmesnil at first light. Gordon was certain that the road to Falaise "was wide open" and, wanting to take advantage of the situation, requested permission at 0630 hours to continue the advance down RN 158.[13] His superior, Brigadier Bob Wyman, refused, explaining that his "orders were to form a firm base and that, in

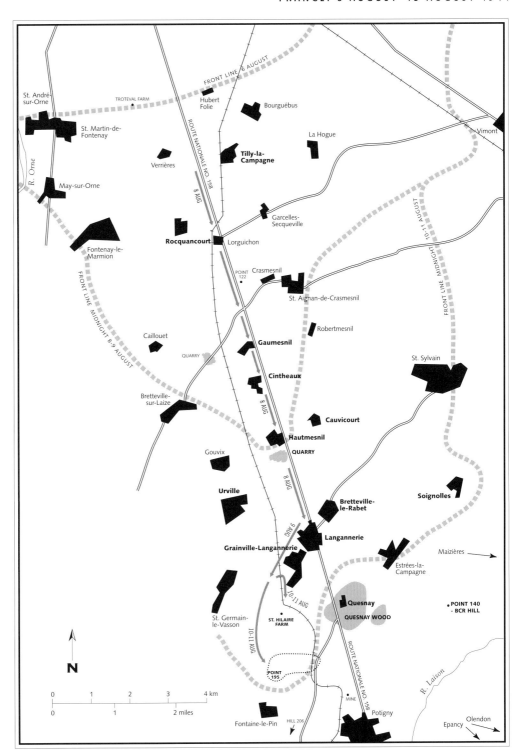

Map 3: Operation TOTALIZE, 7-11 August 1944. The objective was to break through the German defences south of Caen and reach the high ground north of Potigny that dominated the city of Falaise. The Regiment assisted 10 Brigade to clear a series of villages along the RN 158 on 8 and 9 August before supporting the infantry's seizure of Point 195 on 10 August. The Canadian advance was stymied by the stubborn German defence of Quesnay Wood.

any event, the 4th Armoured Division would be passing through us in a few minutes." Wyman's information was incorrect for, as it turned out, it would be nearly eight hours before 4th Armoured arrived at Gordon's position.

As Kitching and Maczek had feared, the long delay was fatal to the success of TOTALIZE. The sheer weight of the initial attack had shaken the German 89th Infantry Division, which bore the brunt of it, but behind the 89th lay the 12th SS Panzer Division and its competent commander, Meyer, was quick to react. When he received only scattered and confusing reports from the forward German positions Meyer drove up RN 158 himself to find out what was happening and encountered soldiers from the 89th Division fleeing in disarray. He rallied these men, turned them back and got them shooting again. He then ordered immediate local counterattacks and followed them up with heavier attacks by elements of his own division, deployed in a number of tank/infantry battle groups. Finally, Meyer created anti-tank gun screens on both sides of the Caen-Falaise highway. Two hours after Gordon had reported the road to Falaise being clear the German front was beginning to stabilize and in the hours that followed the assault formations found themselves involved in fierce fighting. First Canadian Army had lost the momentum and it was up to the two armoured divisions to get it back.

Kitching's plan was to attack on either side of RN 158 with Jefferson's 10 Brigade to the west and Booth's 4 Brigade on the east. It was somewhat ironic that the South Alberta Regiment, a unit which had been trained for just such an operation, was not employed to lead the advance. That job went instead to the Canadian Grenadier Guards, who advanced with one squadron "up" (or leading) commanded by Major Ned Amy. That officer did not receive his orders until 2200 hours on 7 August and had a confusing drive in the dark to the forming up place. At first light Amy's men were in the correct location but they waited in their tanks for nearly four hours until they received orders to move up to the start line and, such was the traffic congestion, it was nearly noon when they got there.[14]

At 1255, nearly five hundred silver B-17s of the US Eighth Air Force roared in and dropped 1,400 tons of bombs. Most aircraft hit their targets, the defended villages on either side of RN 158, but some bombed the Polish and 3rd Divisions in error, inflicting about three hundred casualties. At 1355 Amy slowly and cautiously crossed the start line. He too had seen the burnt-out remnants of the British tanks at Grentheville and his reaction had been similar to that of Wotherspoon: he vowed "never to willingly put my squadron in a position where this might happen."[15] Now, as he advanced down the eastern side of RN 158 there was no sign of the Poles who were supposed to be moving on the left – in fact there was no sign of anyone, friend or foe. "With an open flank and no information on enemy locations," Amy decided that "a bold charge was not an option" and moved carefully. According to Simonds's plan, the advance of the two armoured divisions in the second phase of TOTALIZE was to be supported by hundreds of guns. Unfortunately, the artillery units experienced problems with their communications, suffered from the mistaken bombing, and had difficulty moving into position because of the sheer congestion

of traffic and the fact that many of their positions were subject to German small-arms fire. The result was that Amy had no artillery on call when he moved forward and this only increased his caution.

Before long, he remembered, the "calls started coming in 'to get cracking'" on the wireless and these "calls became more frequent" until another officer was sent forward "to let me know how impatient the various Sunrays [wireless code-name for commanders] were becoming."[16] Amy recalled "telling him what I thought the Sunrays might do," but one of his troop leaders, hearing "the constant proddings" on his set, charged over the brow of a hill and was promptly shot up by waiting German anti-tank guns. A few minutes later Amy's squadron was relieved in the advance by another squadron but progress was no better although the Grenadiers did not report much opposition.

It was not a good day for the two armoured divisions. Kitching went forward late in the afternoon to find out what was holding up 4 Brigade but had great trouble locating Booth as he was not answering his wireless. When Kitching finally found Booth, "he was nearly two miles away from the battle and fast asleep in his tank." Rightfully furious, he gave Booth "a tongue-lashing for five minutes" that reduced that officer to tears but by this time it was too late.[17] Around 1800 hours the commander of the Grenadiers decided to halt and pull his squadrons back into a regimental harbour and 4 Brigade's day was finished. To the east, the Poles fared no better. They were bombed by Allied aircraft, the commander of their liaison unit, a group of British officers who helped them to work with English-speaking formations, was killed, which hampered their communications with 2nd Canadian Corps and, shortly after they crossed their start line at 1355 hours, they reported meeting German Tiger tanks. In the space of ninety minutes the two leading Polish armoured regiments lost forty tanks and informed 2nd Canadian Corps they were regrouping – the Polish day was also done.[18]

Ten Brigade and the SAR had better luck. At 0120 hours on 8 August, the Regiment, with C Squadron leading, tucked in behind the Argyll column and moved forward. "All vehicles moved nose to tail with no lights," recorded the War Diarist, and "the convoy later became long and drawn out, moving by bounds at times speeding up, kicking up dust and making it difficult to see the vehicle ahead and then jerking along with numerous halts."[19] All Trooper Bob Seccombe remembered from that night march was "dust, dust and more dust."[20] The brigade was in its concentration area at about 0330 and, as the sky began to lighten, Corporal John Galipeau of A Squadron emerged from his turret to see a scene of considerable confusion with "trucks with infantry on board … trucks loaded with ammunition ahead of us and, in one case, we saw a kitchen truck come up but it went sailing off."[21]

At 1000 hours the column lurched forward again but progress was slow due to traffic, confusion, dust, shelling and

How far to Paris? Looking more like infantry than armoured corps, Troopers J. L. Gaudet and Gerry Scott of the Regiment pose for a Canadian Army photographer on 8 August 1944 during the second day of Operation TOTALIZE. Six days after this picture was taken Gerry Scott was killed by Allied aircraft. NAC PA-132413.

isolated pockets of German resistance that necessitated long detours. The shelling wounded three South Albertas but there were no fatal casualties on the first day of TOTALIZE. At about the same time the B-17s were dropping their bombs, the Regiment's leading element was just north of Rocquancourt. The Argylls and C Squadron were now ordered to put in an attack on Cintheaux to the south but before they could do that, they had to wait nearly three hours while 2nd Division infantry cleared out a stubborn pocket of German resistance at Gaumesnil, a small village immediately ahead. Finally, in the late afternoon, A and D Companies of the Argylls with two troops from C Squadron moved forward for the attack.[22]

Lieutenant Gerry Adams commanded one of these troops and remembered his experiences that day:

> I was told that I would support this company [A Company], go find the major and he would give me instructions. So I got out of my tank and I found this major [J.A. Farmer] in a shell hole with his officers giving orders and this was late in the day, about 5.30 [1730 hours]. He said "Who the hell are you?" – it really was amateur days. I told him who I was and that I had four tanks. So he said, "Here's your orders, do you want to lead or support?" and I said, "If it's okay with you, I'll support and I'll shoot you in." He said, "Okay, H-Hour is 6 o'clock" and I looked at my watch and it was about quarter to six and that didn't leave much time.
>
> …… So at six o'clock off we went. It was a very tame event, the infantry attacked the town, I didn't fire a shot and the thing was over in fifteen or twenty minutes.[23]

Despite all the training in England it was Gerry's belief that "we were the greenest bloody army that ever went to war."

Cintheaux was taken and the Argylls moved on to the next village, Hautmesnil, and managed to secure it just before dark. Ten Brigade had made the farthest advance in the second phase of TOTALIZE but they were still four miles short of their day's objective, the high ground to the south near Potigny. Satisfied, however, that they had done their job, the Regiment harboured that night just north of Cintheaux.[24]

Disappointed with the results of Kitching's attack, Simonds directed him to continue operations through the night. Kitching ordered Booth to capture the village of Bretteville-le-Rabet east of RN 158 and Point 195. The BCR and Algonquin Regiment got Point 195 as an objective and set out at 0200 on 9 August under the command of Lieutenant-Colonel Don Worthington of the BCR. It was a confusing night march, punctuated by occasional shooting, but at first light Worthington reported by wireless that he was on Point 195. Unfortunately, he had lost direction in the dark and was actually on Point 140, considerably to the east of his true objective, and in the Polish sector. Almost immediately Worthington's force came under heavy German attack for, by accident, they had penetrated to within a mile of the headquarters of the 12th SS Panzer Division and the Germans were ever quick to respond to a serious threat. As the morning passed it became clear to 4th Division Headquarters that Worthington's force was not where it should be, and despite frantic efforts to ascertain their location, they could not be found. Throughout a long and bloody day, the force on Point 140 was gradually whittled down; most of the BCR tanks were shot up and casualties were heavy including both Worthington and Lieutenant-Colonel Art Hay of the Algonquins. In the early evening the Germans overran the last position and, although some men escaped in small groups, most of the survivors were taken prisoner.[25]

For the Regiment, 9 August was a busy day as they assisted their infantry comrades to secure a series of small villages west of RN 158. In the morning C Squadron helped the Argylls clean out the large quarry south of Hautmesnil, a task that was completed by noon. Assigned to the Lincoln and Welland Regiment, Lavoie's A Squadron "married up" with that unit and at 1500 supported the Links' attack on the three connected hamlets of Langannerie, Grainville-Langannerie and Vieille-Langannerie south of the quarry. A Squadron lost two tanks to mines during the approach but the crews escaped without injury. The crew of one of these Shermans, commanded by Sergeant George "Duke" Sands, stayed near their vehicle until it could be recovered, which was done the next morning. The other Sherman, which suffered a broken track, belonged to a troop leader who "ordered the crew to bail out and remain near the tank until assistance arrived while he took over another tank."[26] Corporal Arthur Haddow, the loader-operator, assumed command and led the crew back to the tank under mortar and shell fire. Finding the guns still serviceable, he re-established communications and provided fire support for the attack on the Langannerie villages. After dark Haddow directed the repair of the track and brought the Sherman back to harbour that night.[27]

Resistance in the Langannerie villages was stiff and, during the fighting, Trooper Bob Henning discovered that infantrymen have a different sense of humour. His tank was helping the Links to clear out some farm buildings and "fired AP and HE into the buildings." "When the infantry had finished inside," Bob continued, "they came out and one of them was holding a German helmet with the owner's head still attached." Henning "jumped out of the turret and went down into the ditch and threw up," thinking to himself that "there is no way I can do this" but the next minute the Germans counter-attacked and he was caught outside his tank. "When it was over," Bob Henning "decided that I would have to do what I had to do and that is the way it was for the rest of the war."[28]

By 1800, the Links had cleared Vielle and Grainville-Langannerie while the Argylls, supported by C Squadron, secured Langannerie itself, assisted by "15 or 20 Typhoons complete with rockets and other useful devices."[29] The Argylls' operations were hindered by the fighting for neighbouring Bretteville-le-Rabet, the objective of the Lake Superior Regiment and the Grenadier Guards, which had commenced at 0600 that morning and lasted until 1500 when the village was finally clear. Their work done for the day, RHQ and the squadrons then harboured at 1800 hours in and around Cintheaux.[30]

It was at this moment that the Regiment suffered its first fatal casualty in action. German shelling had increased throughout the day and B Squadron was hit particularly hard as they moved into harbour and lost five men. Trooper MacInnis, hit in the head by shell fragments, was immediately evacuated by ambulance, but died five hours later in hospital having never recovered consciousness. Joe "Pappy Yokum" MacInnis of B Squadron was a 26-year-old truck driver from New Glasgow, Nova Scotia, who had joined the Regiment in Maresfield the previous February.[31]

Most of the defenders of the villages 10 Brigade took on 9 August were from the German 89th Division, which had been badly handled during the opening assault of TOTALIZE. The weight of that assault had surprised senior German commanders, but the 12th SS Panzer Division was still very much alive. Meyer had spent a busy night vigorously shifting all available forces into positions along the high ground north of Falaise. In 4th Division's sector the keystones of the new German defence line were Point 195 and the forested area directly east of RN 158 around the small village of Quesnay. In this latter position, which offered concealment and good fields of fire north, east and west, Meyer placed a battalion of infantry and most of the remaining tanks of his division, a company of the 102 SS Heavy Panzer Battalion with eight Tigers, and a considerable force of anti-tank guns.[32]

Meyer's deployment was to cause problems for the Foot Guards on 9 August. Shortly after 0900, they had been ordered to concentrate at Gaumesnil with the remain-

The Allied tank crew's basic nightmare, no. 1. A 56-ton German Tiger I tank lies abandoned in Normandy. Armed with the magnificent 88 mm gun, it outgunned every Allied tank. Although it was heavy, slow and fuel-hungry, if it could get to the battlefield, it could dominate it. SAR COLLECTION.

The Allied tank crew's basic nightmare, no. 2. The 68-ton Tiger II, an improved model of the Tiger I armed with the 88 mm gun, which entered service in the spring of 1944. Thankfully, there were very few in Normandy although the Regiment encountered them in Germany. AUTHOR'S COLLECTION.

der of the Algonquins to go to Worthington's assistance but the Guards moved very slowly and it was not until mid-afternoon that the combined force went forward. The column left the Route Nationale and were approaching Quesnay Wood when they came under accurate anti-tank fire that knocked out four tanks. The lead squadron then moved with the Algonquin company farther west to a position where they could see the edge of the wood, some fifteen hundred yards away. As the day wore on, it became obvious that the Guards were badly deployed within easy range of the German tank and anti-tank guns in Quesnay Wood. By nightfall, when they pulled back to harbour near Langannerie, they had lost twenty-six tanks.[33]

Despite a day of fairly heavy fighting 4th Division had still not secured Point 195 – and Simonds wanted that ground. When it became clear by the late morning that Worthington's force was not on that feature, orders came down for 10 Brigade to take it in preparation for an armoured thrust further south the next day. Lieutenant-Colonel Dave Stewart of the Argylls learned late in the afternoon that his battalion had to be on Point 195 by first light the following morning. Being an officer "who never went by the book," that being "the Tory personality," Stewart decided to move by stealth and immediately set out with his scout platoon to recce a route.[34] This task accomplished, he returned at 2200 hours and held an O Group at which he informed his officers that in twenty minutes the Argylls were going to move out, on their flat feet, in single file.[35]

Guided by pickets provided by the scout platoon, the Argylls left Langannerie just after midnight and marched through the dark. The gamble paid off and by first light the Highlanders were on Point 195. As they deployed in defensive positions, platoon leaders issued one simple order to their men: "Dig, chum."[36] Within a short time, elements of the Lincoln and Welland Regiment, which had made a similar march, arrived to take up positions on the right of the Argylls facing the village of St. Germaine-le-Vasson, while the remnants of the depleted Algonquin Regiment occupied St. Hilaire Farm a few hundred yards behind Point 195 and abreast of Quesnay Wood.[37]

When they realized what had happened, German reaction was violent. It was fortunate for the two infantry battalions that they had deployed on one spur of 195 (actually a ridge running from southwest to northeast) as, in the dark, they might have run smack into the main German positions located on another spur. Artillery and mortar barrages were brought down on both units in such force that it became difficult and dangerous for men to leave their slit trenches or for casualties to be sent back and food brought forward.

In the late morning, having lost four tanks to anti-tank guns during the approach march, the Grenadier Guards arrived to prepare for a further advance south but, unwisely, positioned themselves on a forward slope while their commanding officer held an O Group. They were hit from three directions by anti-

Watch out. The crews of the Stuart tanks of Recce Troop had one of the most hazardous jobs in the Regiment. This is what happens when a Stuart takes a direct hit from a German 88 mm gun.
SAR COLLECTION.

tank fire and enemy tanks that sniped at them from the edge of Quesnay Wood to their rear and were even attacked by miniature robot tanks. By 1300, when they withdrew to a better position behind the crest of the ridge, the Grenadiers were down to fifteen tanks, a quarter of their strength. Later in the afternoon the Foot Guards came up to relieve the pressure on the Grenadiers, but now German fire in the area was so heavy that it was clear that no advance could be made south of 195 until a full-scale assault was made to clear Quesnay Wood. The units in the vicinity had to content themselves with calling down Typhoons and artillery fire on the suspected enemy positions and armoured vehicles.[38]

The Regiment's task during this day was to support the infantry units which had moved forward during the night. The South Albertas got an early start as, while waiting for the day's taskings, the Regiment took up a position south of Langannerie, with C Squadron in reserve in the village, to add some depth to the defences of the forward units. It was a warm morning with a heavy ground mist. To clarify a confusing situation before he committed the squadrons, Swatty Wotherspoon sent out a number of patrols from Recce Troop. This was the first time that the troop had a chance to undertake its role of probing forward to gain information and three patrols under the command of Corporals Duffy Gendron, Albert Halkyard and Neil McPherson went out that morning.[39]

Corporal Steve Bayko, the gunner in Gendron's tank, remembered that their job was to check out the situation around St. Hilaire farm. The patrol set off in the mist, travelling west from Grainville-Langannerie until at about 0830 hours they came to the rail track that ran south through a cutting to the farm. Rather than move down the cut, which would be a death trap if it was covered by German anti-tank guns, Duffy opted to take a track that paralleled it and utilize the Stuarts' speed to advance to cover. Bayko who was riding, like Duffy, with his

The Farm and the Wood. Pencil sketch by G.L. Cassidy showing a Sherman moving into St. Hilaire Farm with Quesnay Wood in the background. The German blocking position at Quesnay Wood made the Algonquins' location at St. Hilaire farm a hot one and also frustrated all 4th Division's attempts to advance on 10 and 11 August 1944 in the latter stages of Operation TOTALIZE.

REPRODUCED BY PERMISSION OF THE ALGONQUIN REGIMENT FROM *WARPATH: THE STORY OF THE ALGONQUIN REGIMENT, 1939-1945.*

seat elevated and his shoulders and head out of the turret, lowered his seat as the two Stuarts, with Duffy's vehicle in the lead, moved fast down the track. Something bothered Bayko and he was about to traverse the turret when there was a "crash" and a "a flash." He blacked out for a few seconds but when he "came to, I couldn't see for the flames and smoke, right then I knew Duffy must have died as he was sitting half out of the turret." Bayko was "on fire" so he "crawled out, rolled around, pulled off whatever I could and tried to put out the fire." When the lead Stuart was hit, the second tank, commanded by Corporal Arthur McCarty, slewed around and tried to escape but, when Steve looked again, it was stationary, facing back up the track – and burning.[40]

It all happened so fast – in a matter of seconds Duffy was dead, as was the driver of the second Stuart, Trooper Clarence Quinnel, a 27-year-old farmer from Star City, Saskatchewan.[41] The remaining six men escaped, but Bayko was overlooked in the confusion and by this time Steve was in trouble as the "pain was starting to come." Still smouldering, he dived into the adjoining grain field and had just got there when

> the dust started kicking up all around me and I realized it was small arms fire but I couldn't hear it as I was deaf from the blast. I stood up, thinking it was Jerry and I couldn't raise my left arm but it was two Canadian infantrymen who came running up with their Sten guns pointing at me. As my uniform was burnt off they thought they had a Jerry until I pointed to our tanks which were still in sight. They called for a stretcher, sat me down and gave me a cigarette.[42]

Steve ended up at the Algonquin RAP at St. Hilaire Farm, where Captain "Mo" Mackenzie was tending to the wounded

from the forward units. Because of the heavy German shelling Mackenzie worked in a dug-out under a halftrack. As Bayko remembered, he would "pull a stretcher under the half track, and fix you up, pull another one under and work on him." While he waited his turn Steve watched the Grenadier Guards being battered on nearby 195: "There was a whole slug of tanks going over the knoll, getting knocked off, pulling back ... they must have knocked out seven or eight tanks ... it was ridiculous what they were doing, we were trained in hull down positions." Steve Bayko's war was over and three days later he was in England to begin what would be a lengthy stay in hospital.

Halkyard and McPherson had better luck. Halkie winkled his way west behind the Links and very nearly into the Orne Valley before returning. Neil McPherson's crew had been on picket with their tank "King Dog One" the night before and had arrived at RHQ about 0900, "looking forward to a hot meal," but were sent out again to the same area as Gendron's patrol. Approaching the rail cutting Neil opted to move down it and had no problems until he neared St. Hilaire Farm, when he climbed up the side of the cutting to a "turret down" position behind three trees on the embankment to survey the ground ahead. Neil didn't like it but he didn't like where he was so he shouted at his driver "Give 'er shit, Sam!" and King Dog One crossed the embankment and "took off downgrade at great speed, just before about 6 shots removed our trees." McPherson managed to reach a position from which he could spot the German gun flash, reported it by wireless to RHQ, and received the encouraging reply that SWALLOW (tactical air) was available. As he recalled, "Within what seemed seconds, 7 Tiffys [Typhoon fighter bombers] appeared, and let their rockets loose" at what Neil had by now identified as a German AFV positioned in the edge of a tree line, probably Quesnay Wood. The Germans responded by mortaring Neil's position, removing King Dog One's wireless antenna and cutting off his communication.[43]

When the Typhoons had roared away and the smoke had cleared off, King Dog One came under AP fire which passed directly overhead. Looking for the source of this fire, Neil saw what appeared to be a German soldier chinning himself from the barrel of an SPG positioned at the edge of the wood, and it took a few seconds for him to realize that the Typhoons had immobilized the German vehicle and, as its gun was pointing straight at – but over – King Dog One, and as the enemy SPG did not have a turret, the crew were desperately trying to get the barrel depressed to hit him. This realization was confirmed when "we saw another Jerry with a shovel trying to scrape earth out from under the SPG's track."[44]

The message was clear that it was time to go, as a Stuart had no chance against an SPG. King Dog One survived its second crossing of the cutting and McPherson, seeing Halkyard's Stuart returning from its patrol to the west, approached Halkie on foot and passed on the information about the German SPG so that more aircraft could be brought in to deal with it. King Dog One returned to RHQ to repair its wireless set but Neil's crew never got the hot meal they had been hoping for that morning – "just some hardtack and a can of sardines."[45]

Now that the colonel had some information, the squadrons got their tasks. A Squadron went to support the Links on the western end of 195 while B assisted the Algonquins in St. Hilaire Farm and C Squadron remained in reserve at Langannerie. The Links had been having a tough morning as they discovered when daylight came that their positions on "Butcher Hill," as they called it, which they had occupied in the dark, were exposed to German fire from a number of sides. They also had wireless communication problems. Lavoie positioned one of his troops forward to give direct support to the infantry and covered it with his HQ and other three troops somewhat in the rear. The Squadron spent the day shooting at targets of opportunity, and although it came under heavy enemy shelling, there were no casualties.[46]

As the Recce Troop could attest, the road from Langannerie into St. Hilaire Farm was "a perfect killing ground" for German AP weapons. Ordered up to support the Algonquins at the farm, Bradburn opted not to expose all of B Squadron until he himself had a closer look so moved forward with only two troops. The Algonquin commander, Major G.L. Cassidy, was glad to see him; the infantry had been there since 0400 that morning and had been receiving German fire from three directions but particularly from Quesnay Wood which "was quite obviously well held by the enemy." The battalion's 6-pdr. anti-tank guns had been "spotted early in the game" and either knocked out or neutralized.[47] They were therefore delighted when a troop of towed 17-pdrs. arrived at about 1000 hours to help them out and a few minutes later Bradburn rolled up with his two SAR troops. Bradburn assumed command at St. Hilaire

and assisted the troop commander of the 17-pdrs. to place his guns but no sooner were they in position than a Tiger tank opened fire on them from the edge of Quesnay Wood.[48]

Around noon, about the same time the Grenadier Guards were being decimated on the forward slope of 195 a few hundred yards south, the situation worsened. A confusing message was received that a heavy enemy attack was coming in on the Links' positions to the west and "a hail of small-arms fire came over the hill from that direction." "Then, as a final blow," recorded Cassidy, in the early afternoon "Major Bradburn's and his t[an]ks were withdrawn for another task, and we felt very lonely." Mortaring and shelling continued and it was clear to Cassidy that 4th Armoured Division "had run into an efficient example of an anti-tank screen, with not many t[roo]ps but with plenty of 88 mms and tanks." Throughout the day the wood was "periodically cooled off by Typhoon attacks, using red smoke target indicators fired by art[iller]y, but each time the planes disappeared, the shelling and mortaring would recommence." For the Algoons there was no choice but "to sit and take it."[49]

It is not known why B Squadron was withdrawn from St. Hilaire Farm but in any case Swatty decided to replace them with the troop of M-10 self-propelled 17-pdr. guns from 5th Anti-Tank Regiment assigned to the SAR. This unit's heavy anti-tank weapons were normally allotted, on a troop basis, to the other units in 4th Division for defensive purposes, the self-propelled equipment going to the armoured regiments, the towed pieces to the infantry battalions.[50]

By this time the Recce Troop had worked out a safer route to the farm and L Troop of the 5th Regiment was sent that way in the early afternoon guided by their troop leader in a jeep. Unfortunately they made a wrong turn and moved too close to Quesnay Wood – within minutes all four guns were brewed up by AP fire and only one crew escaped. The commander of the last vehicle in action, a Sergeant McAlinden, "was last seen firing his gun while his M-10 was burning" and received a posthumous Mention in Dispatches.[51] The troop leader survived and drove back to Langannerie, where he ran into Captain Jay Moreton of B Squadron. Jay had "heard the firing going on and shortly after a guy turned up and … said his four tanks were gone and he was just a young fellow and he was weeping all over the place."[52] There was nothing that Jay or anyone else could do to comfort the man.

Throughout the day the Regiment suffered from periodic German shell and mortar fire. Occasionally it would taper off and the men would get out of their tanks or trenches but it would start up again without warning. The area was dotted with orchards whose fruit was ripe and, during one of the quiet moments, Trooper Len Thomas of B Squadron convinced his crew commander, Corporal Jim Kroesing, to climb a tree for plums but while Kroesing was up the branches "the Moaning Minnies came down like a hail" and he was not at all happy when he got back in the tank.[53] Thomas comforted him: "You know, corp, the same thing happened to me a couple of hours ago."

In A Squadron mortar fire caught the crew of the tank driven by Corporal Charles Smith outside their vehicle and wounded Trooper Doug Boyes. Smith carried his wounded comrade to shelter and administered first aid and then took him on his shoulder to an infantry RAP, all the while under heavy mortar fire. This was the second time Smith had distinguished himself – the previous day his crew had bailed out of their tank when it was hit in the turret by an AP round – but, in full view of the enemy, Smith went back to the tank, got it moving and managed to save it from being brewed up.[54] Captain Jay Moreton, the Regiment's resident cartoonist, was in his turret when he was hit in the head by fragments from an air burst. When he regained consciousness at a hospital in the rear Jay found himself staring up at John "King" Kelly, a former MO with the SAR and a good friend. "This war must be going pretty badly," remarked Kelly, "if they are starting to shoot my drinking buddies."[55]

RHQ was hit hard. During the day it was in an area of Langannerie that the men called the "Dog Kennels." Trooper Mike Fitzpatrick had just finished digging the nightly shelter trench and had got up on the tank to get something when he heard incoming mortars. He dived for shelter but the mortar bomb "landed four or five feet away" and he was hit. As they put him on a stretcher, Mike heard "the guys saying 'there's another man hit back there but its no use, he's dead.'"[56] The other man was Trooper Kenny Merritt, a scout car driver. Trooper Carson Daley had been talking to Merritt when "the shells started coming over and Ken fell at my feet."[57] A mechanic from Cabri, Saskatchewan, with a wife and three small children, Merritt was 34 when he died.[58] Carson "did not get a scratch" but "was in shock and for nights I didn't sleep."

As 10 August wore on, it became obvious to Guy Simonds that Operation TOTALIZE was grinding to a halt. To the east 1st Polish Division had made some gains but had been stopped by a German defence line anchored on the high ground north of the Laison River, while in the 4th Division's sector the tenacious German defences in Quesnay Wood and south of Point 195 had thwarted all that formation's attempts to advance. The corps commander determined to make one more try to open up RN 158 and late in the afternoon 3rd Division was ordered to put in an assault on Quesnay Wood. It was nearly dark by the time the Queen's Own Rifles and North Shore Regiment advanced under the cover of a heavy artillery barrage, only to be pinned down by fierce artillery, mortar and machine-gun fire. To make matters worse, the Canadian artillery had to cease fire as they were unable to distinguish enemy from friendly troops in the growing darkness. The attack was a total failure and the two battalions suffered heavy casualties.

At 1100 hours on the morning of 11 August, after an advance of about nine miles, TOTALIZE ended when Simonds ordered 3rd Division to take over the two armoured divisions'

positions to allow them to prepare for a new attack. This relief took nearly the entire day to complete and it was not without cost – the Grenadiers lost ten tanks pulling back from the area of 195 while the Foot Guards had to use a heavy smoke screen to avoid similar loss but still lost three tanks.[59]

Until it was relieved at 2000 hours the Regiment carried out the same tasks it had the previous day: A Squadron went back to support the Links and B Squadron, with a new M-10 Troop from 5th Anti-Tank, spent a fairly uneventful day in and around St. Hilaire Farm. Shelling continued to be heavy and A Squadron received the brunt of it. In Gordie Irving's A-1 Troop, Corporal Jim Gove remembered that "Jerry was mortaring us quite heavily" when there was a call from Troop Sergeant Mike Nickel's crew that "Sunray was down." Jim ran over and found that "Mike was quite badly hit." A mortar bomb "had come down and hit his gun and he jumped out to have a look at it to see if it was still in working order and another round hit the tree beside him and a chunk of metal had gone into his back." Jim gave him an injection of morphine and called for the medical halftrack. Padre Silcox was with it and while the two men administered to Nickel, "another round of mortars came down and we both dove underneath the tank."[60]

Mike Nickel, a married CPR worker from Medicine Hat, was 26 when he died that night from his wounds. He had been one of the boys from Medicine Hat who had boarded the train on a warm summer evening more than four years before – he was also the Regiment's last casualty in Operation TOTALIZE.[61]

The South Albertas' "rest area" was a large beet field near the village of Cauvicourt, which everyone called "the Cabbage Patch" after the hamlet in the "L'il Abner" cartoon strip that had replaced the *Daily Mail*'s "Jane" in the affections of the men. Not that anyone got much rest. After they had settled down that night, the boys discovered that there was a medium artillery regiment directly behind them and the 5.5 inch guns fired all night. Jim Nicholson remembered that each time the gunners opened up, "we got a hefty blast which made it difficult to sleep, and by morning we were covered under a thick layer of dust and debris."[62] Worse still, over the next two days a German 150 mm gun, engaged in counter-battery work, tried to hit the mediums and shells often came down on the Cabbage Patch. On the other hand, it was better than St. Hilaire Farm and the South Albertas were grateful for the break. During the next two days, 12 and 13 August, the men were "allowed to clean up and carry out maintenance" on their tanks. The Regiment's auxiliary services truck, provided by the Sally Ann, came up to bring movies, soft drinks, candy and other delectables and the boys enjoyed the luxury of having the cooks provide their meals, as tank crews had to fend for themselves when in action.[63]

The South Albertas also got a visit from the "Chinese Hussars," as the army's Mobile Bath and Laundry units were known, and it was a welcome one as most of the tank crews had been wearing the same clothes for two weeks. The battle dress worn in Normandy was impregnated with a chemical solution that supposedly made it impermeable to gas and less flammable, and most men disliked it because it was heavy, stiff and hot. The Mobile Bath Unit boasted a large boiler which provided hot water to "a dozen or so shower heads out in the open air." In turn, the men "would have a shower and pick up clean underwear and shirts from the great, big pile provided, sorting through until you found something that would fit you," and "handing in your dirty clothes to be washed."[64] Modesty is never a major concern in the army and the bath unit set up two large tents, one containing the showers connected by a duckboard in the open air to a second tent where the men picked up their new clothes. On Sunday, 13 August, the French civilians who lived nearby were going to church along the hillside near the bath unit just as some squeaky-clean South Albertas emerged from the showers. To either their pleasure or dismay, the boys discovered that "all the local young ladies had gathered on the hill to have a good look."[65]

While the South Albertas amused the locals Guy Simonds was planning another major operation, Operation TRACTABLE. The speed of Patton's advance had caused Montgomery to issue new orders to First Canadian and Second British Armies. Monty now changed the overall Allied plan from a "large" envelopment that would trap the Germans against the Seine River to a "short" envelopment which would see the trap sprung farther to the west in the area between Falaise and Argentan. He therefore ordered, in a directive dated 11 August that, while Second British Army was to advance its left flank to Falaise, First Canadian

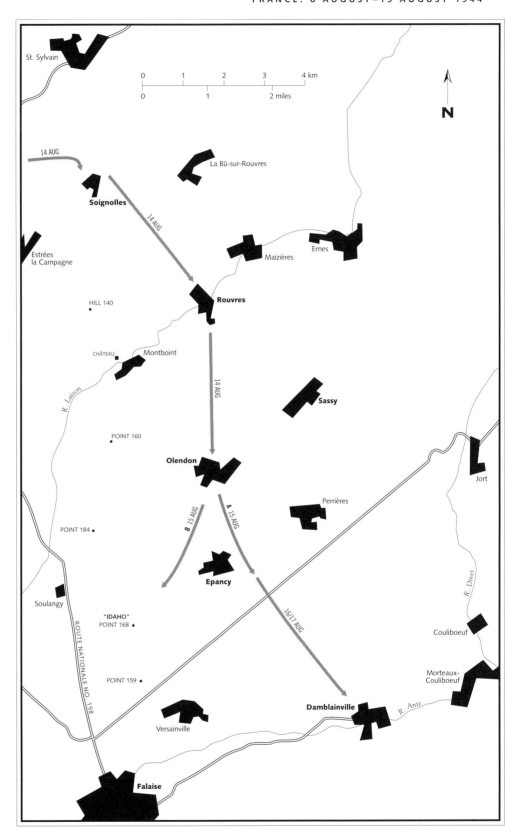

Map 4: Operation TRACTABLE, 14-15 August 1944. Thwarted in his attempt to break through the German defences near the highway from Caen to Falaise, Simonds launched a massive daylight armoured assault on 14 August to seize Points 168 and 159 north of Falaise. Initially successful, the attack bogged down and on 16 August Simonds switched 4th Armoured Division's axis to the southeast toward Damblainville.

Lining up for the mad dash. Operation TRACTABLE, 14 August 1944. Hundreds of tanks and vehicles formed up for the attack, which was a "sort of draw swords and charge affair" one Canadian armoured officer later remembered. All went well until the first units reached the Laison River, which Guy Simonds, the commander of 2 Canadian Corps, had reportedly assured his subordinates was no obstacle. It was. NAC PA-113649.

Army was to "capture Falaise" as its "first priority" and Monty stressed that this "should be done quickly."[66] The Canadians would then "operate with strong armoured and mobile forces to secure Argentan" while at the same time holding a "secure front … between Falaise and the sea." Unfortunately, as some historians have pointed out, although Montgomery had expanded the tasks of First Canadian Army, giving it the major role in closing the trap from the north, he did not see fit to reinforce that army with one or more of the three British armoured divisions available.[67] On receipt of these instructions, the axis of the Canadian attack on Falaise was changed from due south to southwest, avoiding the strong German defences in the Quesnay Wood area along the Caen-Falaise highway. The objective now was to be the high ground (*falaise* is the French word for "cliff") to the east of that highway overlooking Falaise.

TRACTABLE was a straightforward operation – one historian has dubbed it "TOTALIZE in smoke."[68] It was to be a massive armoured thrust that would take place in broad daylight after a short but heavy bombardment by all available artillery and medium and heavy bombers. The attack was to commence at 1200 on 14 August when the six tank regiments from 2 and 4 Armoured Brigades, formed in a massive armoured phalanx and each followed by an infantry brigade in the new APCs, would punch through the German lines under cover of a heavy smoke screen. The job of mopping up isolated pockets of resistance fell to 7 and 10 Infantry Brigades, who would follow behind the assault brigades in trucks. As usual, the SAR's job was to support the three battalions of 10 Brigade onto their objectives.

During TOTALIZE there had been delays in the transmission of orders and Simonds and his staff put considerable effort into ensuring that, for TRACTABLE, every officer knew what he had to do, when he had to do it and where he had to do it.

Throughout 13 August Orders Groups were held at corps, division, brigade and regimental level, to pass out instructions for the forthcoming operation – the three SAR squadron commanders, for example, were shown air photos of the ground over which they would be operating. Two of these conferences had important consequences for the Regiment.[69]

Following his O Group at 1000 hours on 13 August, Simonds spoke to the assembled commanding officers of every armoured regiment in First Canadian Army and expressed his dissatisfaction with their performance during Operation TOTALIZE. In Swatty's words, Simonds "gave us what we used to refer to at RMC as a shit meeting."[70] In his lecture, the corps commander stressed "the necessity for pushing armour to the very limits of its endurance and that any thought of armour requiring inf[antry] protection for harbouring at night or not being able to move at night was to be dismissed immediately." "The tremendous importance of the op[eration] now being undertaken," he continued, "could not be overlooked and although there would probably be cases of the misemp[loyment] of armour this was to be no excuse for non success."[71]

That was how the 4th Division War Diary put it – Swatty Wotherspoon remembered it differently. According to the SAR commander, Simonds "told us we were all rotten, etc., etc." but, the "real thing that got to me" was that he said, "you're all yellow … you're all yellow and henceforth, you will command from your tanks."[72] To Wotherspoon, being ordered "to fight my regiment from my tank" was "one of the stupidest orders I received during the war," as "the last place to command an armoured regiment from is your tank" as it "immobilizes you, and you're so busy trying to be the tank commander and, you might say, the gunner if you have to shoot – at least direct the gun and the tank, that you can't possibly run your regiment." After the meeting was over, Swatty "got back in [my tank] for five minutes, just to see if it was possible I was wrong, but in five minutes I realized I was right." As was clear from this order, Simonds, who had little real experience in the tactical control of armour, simply did not understand how armoured regiments were fought.

George Kitching was appalled by the corps commander's words and told Simonds afterward that

I was sorry he had said what he did in front of my regimental commanders. He accused them of every known sin under the sun including lack of drive, etc., when in point of fact they had only been in action as regiments for a matter of two or three days during which time the concentration of vehicles and material south of Caen was such that it was almost impossible to get a unit moving through it.[73]

Simonds probably paid little heed to Kitching's comments because to Guy Simonds warfare was about plans. There was never anything wrong with Simonds's plans – if they didn't work, it had to be the fault of the units involved. One of his divisional commanders later remarked that, unfortunately, what "looked good to Guy's precise engineering mind on paper seldom worked in practice once the human element was added" but "you couldn't argue with Guy; not and keep your job."[74] For unit commanders like Wotherspoon at the "sharp end" of the business, the damage done by the corps commander's scathing speech was incalculable. When "Simonds called me yellow," he later stated, he "lost me right then and there" and "I never had great respect for the man after that, because neither my regiment nor I were yellow at all."[75]

A second event took place at a 10 Brigade O Group at which Jefferson informed Bob Bradburn that he was assuming command of the Algonquins, whose commander had been badly wounded on Point 140, and Bill Cromb of the Argylls that he was taking over the Lincoln and Welland Regiment, whose commanding officer was being relieved because of poor performance. After the conference Cromb was embarrassed when the Links' outgoing commander complained to him that "his [Lincoln and Welland] officers had let him down" because Cromb knew "that was baloney."[76] These promotions meant that a former SAR now had the Algonquins, and a man who had served with the SAR and the Argylls had the Links, while Stewart of the Argylls had always worked well with the Regiment. The unit commanders in 10 Brigade were men who knew each other and each other's units and who could function as a team. The promotions also meant that the brigade was taking on a distinctly western tone: Jefferson, Bradburn and Cromb were all from Alberta, while Swatty Wotherspoon, that epitome of an eastern blue blood, commanded a regiment whose down-to-earth

approach epitomized the western soldier. As for Dave Stewart of the Argylls, although a Prince Edward Islander, he possessed a tactical brilliance that was positively western in quality.

At 0900 on 14 August, a hot and sunny day, 10 Brigade formed up for TRACTABLE in a flat field near Cauvicourt. There was little confusion because the engineers and provosts had staked out and signed the assembly area and the three infantry battalions, with their men packed tightly into TCVs (Troop Carrying Vehicles or large trucks), formed in blocks seven vehicles wide and ten vehicles deep. Each SAR squadron parked its nineteen Shermans in an extended line in front of its particular battalion (A Squadron with the Links, B with the Algonquins and C with the Argylls), the four tanks of Wotherspoon's RHQ troop, along with attached troops of M-10s and Flail (mine-clearing) tanks, were in front while the Recce Troop in their smaller Stuarts assumed positions on the flanks. In all, the brigade formation consisted of some seventy-nine armoured vehicles and more than two hundred trucks and this was only one brigade – there were six other brigades in the assault, and overall nearly five hundred tanks and fifteen hundred other vehicles were waiting for the order to advance.[77]

It was an amazing thing to see. The author of the *Short History* comments that such "a mass movement of armour and vehicles actually going into the attack has not been seen before or since" as the sight of so many tanks "almost touching each other is more reminiscent of a magazine advertisement for General Motors than warfare as we got to know it later."[78] "I didn't think there were that many tanks in the world" was Trooper Ed Hyatt's opinion.[79] The men had nearly three hours to wait and, during that time, the South Albertas received a hot meal from the echelon cooks.[80]

At 1125 hours the artillery fired red smoke shells on the forward German positions to mark the targets for the heavy and medium bombers that roared in a few minutes later to drop their deadly cargoes. Hundreds of medium and field guns then switched to a combination of smoke and HE to confuse and suppress the enemy. At 1140 the order came, "Move now!" and the armoured brigades in the first wave rumbled straight through the forward German positions, which managed to get off only a few shots before being overwhelmed. The advance was hampered by the smoke and the tremendous clouds of dust created by explosions and hundreds of heavy vehicles that totally obscured all vision and forced drivers to navigate by the sun. Progress was good until the tanks reached the Laison River, some two to three miles south of the start line.

In his briefings on the operation Simonds had reportedly assured his subordinates that the Laison, actually a meandering stream, was "fordable by tanks at all points."[81] In fact, the river's muddy bottom and steep banks formed a major anti-tank obstacle and even an historian who is an outspoken apologist for Guy Simonds's generalship admits that the corps commander's misjudgment in this instance "was an error of major consequence."[82] The advance ground to a halt as hundreds of tanks milled around, under German fire, trying to find a crossing, and it took several hours before the engineers had bulldozed the banks and reinforced the bottom so that they could get across. Confusion reigned at the Laison and, once on the other side, units had to sort themselves out to get going again. By last light, 2 Armoured Brigade was nearly on its first day objectives but 4 Armoured Brigade had done less well. The brigade commander, Booth, had been killed and most of his headquarters vehicles knocked out but Kitching did not learn of this until late in the afternoon when he ordered Lieutenant-Colonel M.J. Scott, the commander of the Foot Guards, to assume command of the brigade. That officer, whose ankle had been broken when his tank ran over a mine, did not get that message for some time, and for nearly six hours there was no effective control of 4 Brigade, whose attack degenerated into three separate regiments fighting three separate battles. At 2000 hours, still three miles short of his objective, Scott ordered the brigade to harbour for the night.[83]

Tactical air support. Ground crew painting white "invasion stripes" on a Spitfire fighter aircraft, spring of 1944. The use of tactical air power in Normandy, in the form of cannon-armed Spitfires and rocket-armed Typhoons, proved to be a mixed blessing. Between 14 August and 18 August the South Albertas were attacked six times by their own aircraft and other units had similar experiences.

CF FILM UNIT, PL 30827

Ten Brigade's day went better. When the order came to move, the mass of vehicles advanced "in straight lines, straight through wheat-fields and hedges, over fences, up and down through potato-fields, bouncing into ditches and on again, surmounting every sort of obstacle."[84] Visibility was poor because of the dust and smoke but the infantry, packed in the large TCVs, thought "this was wonderful" and "were shouting, waving their caps in the air and giving forth Indian war whoops to express their high spirits." After travelling east about half a mile, the brigade made a ninety degree right turn south, the speed increased, and it was not long before the "parade-ground formation was broken, and a careering mass of vehicles headed southwards across country, completely disregarding roads, ditches, fences, or any other obstacles save hedges."[85] In this mad charge, which resembled a chuckwagon race in some colossal version of the Calgary Stampede, the Regiment led the advance and it wasn't hard to follow the trail of the forward units because they left a swathe of tracks in the grain fields. Corporal Bob Clipperton of the Recce Troop remembered that "we felt out of place with our little Stuart tanks darting here and there amongst the Shermans."[86]

As the South Albertas' tanks neared the first village, Soignolles, Allied fighter aircraft strafed the tank troops on the right or western flank of the column. The crews immediately fired off yellow smoke, the authorized recognition signal for friendly troops, but "it was to no avail" and for thirty minutes flight after flight of fighter aircraft swooped in, machine guns and cannon roaring, and the Regiment got "severely strafed."[87] That was not the only mistake the airmen made that day. During the move forward the men could see a towering cloud of smoke and dust in their rear. Later that night the word came that some Allied aircraft (seventy-seven to be exact and most, ironically, from 6 Bomber Group, RCAF) had attacked the Canadian and Polish rear echelons. In desperation, ground units fired off yellow smoke and small artillery spotter planes flew dangerously close to the front of the bomber formations shooting red flares to get them to stop, but the attacking aircraft disregarded all such measures and tragically inflicted more than four hundred casualties on their own ground forces. A subsequent investigation revealed that, while Allied ground forces were using yellow smoke as a signal for friendly troops, Bomber Command was using it as a target indicator. The aircrews responsible were disciplined and "fresh instructions were issued for operations in support of the army."[88]

Some of the bombs fell on the Regiment's A-1 Echelon. The attack caught many of the boys unprepared as they thought the bombers were going to fly over – men actually cheered and waved at the friendly aircraft until they saw the bomb bay doors open and realized what was about to happen. Captain Bob Allsopp, like so many men at this time, was suffering from dysentery brought on by poor diet, inadequate hygiene and the myriads of flies that feasted in Normandy during that long and bloody summer. As Allsopp bluntly put it, "I had the shits and

"B34 has had it." SAR Sherman knocked out in August 1944. SAR COLLECTION

the MO gave me some pills and said 'go back to A-1 Echelon and lie down and get some rest.'"[89] As the bombers roared in – so low that "we could literally see the tail gunners," remembered Corporal Jimmy Simpson[90] – Allsopp huddled under a halftrack but decided "to get the hell out of there" when the ground shook from the explosion of 500 and 1000 lb. bombs.[91] Trooper Gerry Scott of AA Troop was running for shelter along with other members of the troop when he was hit in the head by a bomb fragment. A 22-year-old CPR worker from Montreal, Scott was dead before his body hit the ground.[92]

At Soignolles the 10 Brigade column halted briefly as the leading SAR tank troops became unsure of the correct direction toward the next objective as the tank tracks had degenerated into a tangled mess. Corporal Herbie Watkins of A Squadron remembered that there "was a lot of swearing on the wireless" and Swatty went forward in his scout car (so much for Guy Simonds's orders) to examine the situation at the next village, Rouvres, beside the Laison.[93] He returned just in time to head off A Squadron which was slanting too far to the east. Bouncing across a field in his scout car, his nearly bald head (for Swatty detested wearing

a helmet) clearly visible, he pulled up alongside Arnold Lavoie's tank and told him "that they were to form on me and follow me, and they did" but "I gave them hell at the same time. Probably told them that they had each lost a week's leave" for not reading their maps correctly.[94] The SAR tanks were up to the Laison at Rouvres by 1600 but had trouble getting across the river so the Argylls and Links debussed, moved through the village, where they found German food still warm on the tables, and crossed the stream on foot before pushing on to Olendon, their next objective.[95]

By 1800 A and B Squadrons had got over and moved up to support the infantry, followed by the Algonquins and C Squadron. The South Albertas now began to encounter signs of fighting, Trooper John Neff's crew saw "a carrier brew up with a man trapped in it" screaming "but there was nothing we could do to help him."[96] In A Squadron, Gordie Irving's A-1 Troop was in the lead (a half century later he would complain that "as the first troop of the first squadron they always seem to make us lead") when a Stuart from Recce forged past him toward a ruined farmhouse. "They got him with a panzerfaust," remembered Gordie, and the crew commander, Lieutenant Raynor Woods, was wounded.[97] Irving "didn't know what was going on although I could see the whole thing" but the "next thing I know the Stuart is turned around and comes back and someone is hanging on the side of the turret, maybe it was a crew member who had bailed out and then the tank turns to go off and he grabs on to it." Gordie continues:

At that point we had obviously made contact with the enemy so I snuck my tank up on a hedge, straddled it and I see

Last resting place. Sherman tank graveyard in Normandy photographed in June 1945. After the campaign was over, ordnance detachments towed the many knocked-out Allied tanks to central parks where they were salvaged for spare parts. These tank graveyards were a common sight in Normandy for years after the war. SAR COLLECTION.

Tragic error, 14 August 1944. As they moved forward during the first phase of Operation TRACTABLE, the South Albertas saw a towering column of smoke a few miles to the rear. It marked the scene of a devastating attack by Allied heavy bombers (most from the RCAF) on the rear echelons of 2nd Canadian Corps. COURTESY, GEORGE WHITE.

this damned Jerry that's got a bombthrower [*Panzerfaust*] that hit the Stuart and he's got a radio behind him and he's signalling back home. In the noise he didn't hear us but I can't bring a weapon to bear so I reached down for a hand grenade, pulled the pin, and threw it and that was the end of that guy.

It was now that Danny McLeod entered the battle. Wotherspoon had requested Danny's return from the Operational Training Squadron some months before, but it had taken time before, reverting to his substantive rank of lieutenant, Danny caught up with the Regiment at the Cabbage Patch. Swatty decided that he should get his "battle inoculation" as a crew commander and so sent him to Lieutenant Alec Scrimger's troop in B Squadron. As Danny recalled, after the heady days of having his own squadron, he "came down to earth fast" when his tank, which "had just nicely got under way" hit a mine approaching Olendon.[98] No one was hurt but the suspension was badly damaged and Danny and his men were through for the day.

As the two squadrons assisted the infantry to clear out Olendon, Lieutenant Jack Summers's troop made an interesting haul – nearly a hundred *Wehrmacht*-issue bicycles – which puzzled them. Olendon was cleared by last light and, at 0200 hours on 15 August, two Argyll companies with C Squadron in support moved forward to Perrières, the next village.[99]

That night was a restless one for the Regiment as there was "occasional sniping … and the odd shell" that "fell on our positions but no casualties were sustained."[100] In the late evening the echelons came up to carry out their task of resupplying the squadrons with ammunition and fuel. Corporal Bob Rasmussen, driving a truckload of gasoline forward, remembered that "we got switched by the provost to go around on this hill and when we got to the top it was covered with shot-up tanks and bodies."[101] The hill was Point 140, the scene of the disastrous BCR and Algonquin action five days before, and "it looked like hell" because "there was no one there picking up the bodies." Rasmussen actually recognized one of the corpses and "I just couldn't believe it, I thought 'there's my friend' but I had to drive right by him." Two regimental fitters, Sergeant Wagner and Trooper Brewer, coming forward in their halftrack in the dark, lost their way and were killed when their vehicle was hit by AP fire. Charlie Brewer, age 29, a carpenter from Lethbridge, had joined the SAR in June 1940 and was survived by a wife and son, while Jimmie Wagner, another of the old originals, was a 31-year old American from Portland, Oregon.[102]

The first day of TRACTABLE had been fairly successful and the Canadian attack had decimated the German 85th Infantry Division, which had taken the brunt of the assault. On 15 August, it only remained to press the attack home onto the final objective, code-named IDAHO, the high ridge of ground overlooking Falaise. But the Canadians were now up against 12th SS Panzer, whose intrepid commander, Kurt Meyer, suspecting that a major attack was going to take place in this area, had already surveyed a rearward anti-tank defence line to cover this ridge before TRACTABLE opened and he deployed the remnants of his division there during the night. The fifteenth of August went very badly for 4 Armoured Brigade, who were tasked with taking IDAHO. The temporary brigade commander, Scott, suffering from a broken ankle, failed to exercise good control; the brigade, supposed to move early in the morning, did not set off until 0930; they had to make a long detour around the German-held village of Epancy; and when they finally got on their start line, they had very little artillery and infantry support but did find units from 3rd Division also putting in an attack on the same objective. The result was that, instead of making a concentrated attack, 4 Armoured Brigade probed and prodded the German defences throughout the afternoon, doing little real good. This was unfortunate because the German defence was stretched to the breaking point. At 1200 hours that day Meyer reported that the 12th SS Panzer and 85th Infantry Division had been reduced to small battle groups and he had only fifteen tanks and very few anti-tank guns still in action.[103]

During the day two squadrons of the Regiment supported 10 Brigade. In the morning A Squadron firmed up with the Links in Olendon but had to wait until the Algonquins had cleared Epancy, an onerous and bloody process that took a long time, before they could move forward. Finally, at 1500, the Links with A Squadron attacked and took a wood on a small hill southwest of Epancy. C Squadron spent the day giving fire support to the Argylls in Perrières. The big excitement occurred in mid-afternoon when word came of "an enemy build-up of armour in the woods just south of Perrières." The Argylls and Lincolns had spotted this concentration earlier and requested air reconnaissance – in due time the air force reported one hundred and fifty tanks in the woods preparing for what appeared to be a "full scale armoured counter attack." An air strike was called and thirty-two Typhoons were soon "circling, rocketing and bombing and blasting those woods to shreds and the tanks to smouldering wrecks."[104] In actual fact there were no German tanks in the woods – but everyone was much

Apple blossom time in Normandy. Short hair, moustaches, tans – the hallmarks of the young soldier. South Albertas taking a break on 15 August 1944. Corporal Edon Robinson on the left leaning against tank, Trooper Petrie with arms crossed, a man identified only as "Yorkie," Trooper Reid with tuque and behind him Trooper Stan James. A few minutes after this photograph was taken a German AFV brewed up two nearby tanks and these men were back in their vehicles in short order. COURTESY, JOHN NEFF

happier when the Typhoons winged away because they also attacked 10 Brigade units at Olendon. "Once again the Airforce strafed us," the War Diarist commented, and "Marching Inf[antry] and am[munitio]n trucks on the road were hit and several casualties incurred."

B Squadron had a busy day. In the morning they went out, under the command of Captain Hugh "Click" Clarke, to provide flank protection on the right and moved there only to find units from 2 and 4 Armoured Brigades battling German anti-tank guns near Epancy and itself "pinched" out of battle. "After roaming unproductively around behind 4th Brigade for a few hours," Sergeant Jim Nicholson remembered, we "pulled into a field – not a wise move as Capt. Clark didn't quite have a hold of the handle yet."[105] It was a hot day and the men were glad to get out of their stuffy vehicles, light up (SAR crews did not smoke inside their tanks) and brew tea while Clarke conferred with a FOO whose Ram OP tank accompanied the squadron. John Neff remembered that the field was "on the edge of an orchard near the crest of a hill," and his crew gathered around to watch (and no doubt assist with much advice but no sweat) Corporal Robinson's crew repair a sprocket on their Sherman which had been damaged by AP fire near Epancy.[106]

As usual it happened very fast. The squadron's position provided a covered approach for a German AFV which "sneaked up on our flank and knocked out one of our tanks and the artillery officer's Ram in the space of two minutes," recalled Jim Nicholson.[107] Jim saw the crew "bail out through the flames

which were shooting 6 feet above" the tank but, while "they got out with merely a hair singeing, the B Sqdn crew was not so lucky." Two men, Troopers Tom Brabant and Wilfred Laughton, were seriously wounded and Laughton, a 25-year-old CPR worker from Moose Jaw, died two days later.[108] Hastily mounting up, the squadron popped off smoke and left the area, returning to the Regimental harbour near Olendon at 2200 hours.[109]

B Squadron had discovered that it was a dangerous day to be wandering but, since the situation was fluid, mistakes did happen. Early that morning Dispatch Rider George Gallimore was going forward with a message from RHQ for C Squadron when he approached Epancy. An SAR tank posted outside the village warned George that "it might not be secure" but he decided to go through it rather than make a long detour around.[110] As he rode slowly into Epancy, careful to keep his dust down, there was no one to be seen, except a dead German lying by the well in the village square. "Right then," George recalled, "I knew I was in trouble as his holster was visible" and "in the holster was a Luger pistol" which was "much in demand as a souvenir." Almost at the same time "the shooting started" and George "speeded up as hard as I could and was soon out of range but my dust cloud brought mortar fire down on the road" and he was forced get off his bike and take shelter in a ditch. He was now closer to the German lines and in peril of being taken a prisoner, if not worse. George remembered "lying in that ditch beside my motorcycle and thinking, should I stay put, go on, or turn around?" He decided to go back through the village:

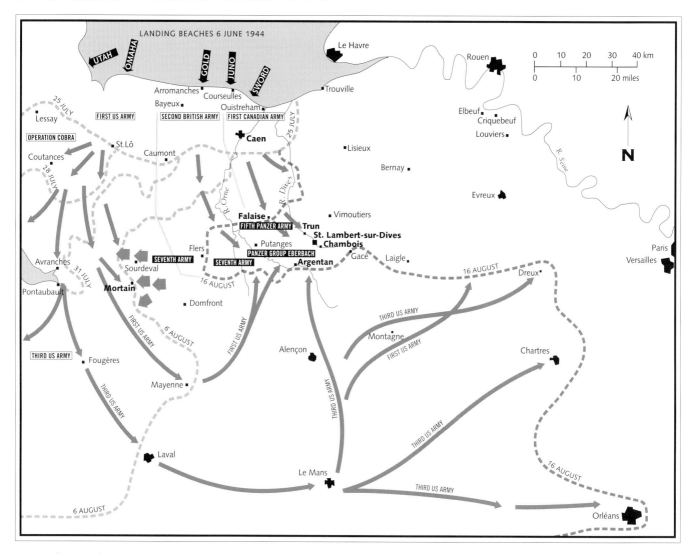

Map 5: The trap closes, 25 July-16 August 1944. On 25 July the First U.S. Army broke through the German line near St. Lô and Patton's Third Army then took over the advance. A major German counterattack was rebuffed at Mortain on 7 August and Patton swung east behind the enemy. By 16 August, when Hitler gave permission to retreat, two German armies were threatened with encirclement and the gap between the Americans and the Canadians was about 25 miles.

Being only twenty years old and still having the courage of a fool, I started the bike and tore off back towards the village. Top speed of the Norton 350 was probably sixty miles an hour and I had the thing wide open in second gear, third was tops, so I was probably doing forty as I approached the village. The smoke puffs appeared again at the windows of the first building on the left and I heard, or perhaps imagined, the snap of the bullets passing overhead. Lying low on the fuel tank I hit the turn in the village, missed the well and turned up the hill to safety.

Unfortunately, Gallimore had to leave the Luger behind.

It was a bitter day for George Kitching. As 4 Armoured Brigade battled its way to the ridge in the late afternoon he was at Jefferson's headquarters. Standing on a jeep the two officers tried to see what was going on ahead and it appeared to them that "the tanks of our armoured regiments were almost on their

objective."[111] The divisional commander then returned to his headquarters and was, in turn, elated when he received news that IDAHO had been taken, and depressed when for the first time he learned that Scott had been injured the previous day and was no longer capable of exercising command of 4 Brigade. At 1800 Kitching left for Simonds's headquarters. The corps commander was "delighted to hear we had captured the ridge dominating Falaise and after he had issued his orders for the next day's operations invited me to stay for dinner." When he returned to his HQ later that evening, Kitching learned the truth of the matter from his staff – 4 Brigade had "not captured the ridge at all but had turned back to wait for additional support." He immediately telephoned the news to Simonds, who did not take it at all well. Kitching assured him that 4th Division was preparing to attack again the next morning but was "ordered to stand down" as there was going to be "a complete change in the Corps plan." Operation TRACTABLE had come to an end.[112]

PART IV

SLUGGING

Moving up, St. Lambert-sur-Dives, 19 August 1944. C Squadron
Sherman moves by SAR tank brewed up in the middle of the
village. Note the tactical sign numbers – this negative has
often been published reversed.

NAC PA-116522.

CHAPTER EIGHT

"It was beginning to look as if a big show was coming off."

FRANCE: 16 AUGUST–18 AUGUST 1944

During the night of 15 August A-1 Echelon came up to supply the squadrons at their forward positions. The term "echelons" has cropped up before and it is time to talk about this important part of the Regiment. In action, the SAR was divided into two parts: the "fighting" component which consisted of RHQ, Recce Troop, AA Troop and the three squadrons, and the "echelons," controlled by HQ Squadron, whose task was to keep the men at the sharp end supplied with whatever they needed to do their job. More than half the officers and men in the Regiment worked in the echelons and their organization and function has been well described by the author of the *Short History*:

> HQ Sq[uadro]n commanded by Maj Shell was divided into A1 Echelon and A2 Echelon and occasionally B Echelon. A1 consisted of the fitters [mechanics] and [tank] recovery group and a small number of petrol and ammo trucks which could be kept well forward, usually in the area of RHQ and was available for immediate requirements. A2 consisted of the LAD [Light Aid Detachment], the balance of the Petrol and ammo, the quartermaster's and the kitchen trucks and the remainder of all the vehicles not immediately needed forward. Their location was usually back out of shell range and their job was to replace at once any requirements which A1 had supplied to the fighting troops, and to ensure that a smooth flow of everything kept coming forward from the RCASC [Royal Canadian Army Service Corps] supply point. B Echelon was occasionally set up and contained the vehicles and personnel who were unlikely to be required forward such as the Paymaster, the Dentist, people who were LOB (left out of battle) etc. The whole arrangement was very elastic and could be altered quite easily if the situation required.[2]

In contrast to the practice in many armoured regiments Wotherspoon did not believe in automatically withdrawing his tanks back to a harbour or laager (a secure position) at night to

*S*luggin' Jerry left and right,
Havin' lots of fun,
'Till one night, we caught him right,
Now he's on the run.

Oh, lay that Luger down, kid,
Lay that Luger down,
Luger-luggin' Ludwig,
Lay that Luger down.

We licked you on the beaches,
Chased you through the towns,
You're not safe if we reach you,
So lay that Luger down.[1]

resupply.[3] The Regiment would harbour if the situation permitted but, if things were tense and the infantry needed support, the South Albertas would stay with them during the night and A-1 Echelon would bring the supplies to the forward positions. Actually, it made more sense as tanks are vulnerable at night and having friendly infantry around was less risky than drawing back to a position where the crews themselves would have to protect their own vehicles in the dark. Most armoured regiments saw the matter differently and disliked exposing their tanks at night, reducing them to "expensive and vulnerable" pill boxes.[4]

Whether the squadrons were in forward positions or in a harbour or laager, A-1 Echelon, using load-carrying vehicles, would come forward and resupply them in the dark. The echelons would pick up gasoline or ammunition at an RCASC supply point or field depot located in the rear and would be guided up to the tanks by "jeep jockeys or motorcycle escort scouts."[5] Sergeant Earle Wood, one of these "jockeys," remembered being "somewhat lonely" as he led "the supply trucks up in the middle of the night."[6] The favoured vehicle was the 60-cwt. or 3-ton truck, which would carry between two hundred and two hundred and fifty four-gallon jerricans – "two rows on the bottom and some on the top," recalled Trooper George Armstrong, "we could get more on but the front end of the truck would become heavy and you couldn't steer it."[7] Some might think that driving an unarmoured vehicle loaded with eight hundred to a thousand gallons of gasoline through unknown country in the dark within enemy artillery range might be a risky business but it never seemed to bother the echelon boys – "I used to smoke with a load of gasoline on the back," comments Corporal Bob Rasmussen.[8]

When the trucks reached the tanks the crews would tell the drivers what they needed and they would dump off the required amount behind each tank. The Sherman possessed a one hundred and forty gallon tank but with five Chrysler engines to fuel it was a thirsty animal and, since no crew wanted to run out of gas, they took every opportunity to top up. Refuelling was a tense time, particularly within range of enemy artillery, and the whole crew pitched in to finish the job as quickly as possible. Jerrican after jerrican was lifted up to the rear deck, up-ended over a large funnel (which was always getting lost or squashed) in one of the two gas tank caps, emptied and thrown aside. It took about twenty minutes to fill a tank, and if they had not already done so the crew would then re-ammunition. One man on the ground opened the wooden boxes, each containing three rounds of 75 mm AP, HE or smoke, and passed the shells to another, who would relay them to a man on the rear deck. Eventually the rounds arrived at the loader-operator inside the turret, whose job it was to stow them in the racks or bins set around the turret basket or place them on the turret floor as "he had to put his hands on them, in daylight or darkness" and had to know exactly where each type could be found.[9] The .30 calibre ammunition for the co-axial and bow Brownings came in metal boxes and these too were stored in their proper place inside the turret. Depending on requirements the trucks might make as many as three trips from the supply point to the squadrons in one night, and the nights were short in Normandy with last light at about 2200 and dawn between 0400 and 0430 hours.

The echelons' vital work is too often overlooked because, if they were doing their job properly, they were not noticed. Wotherspoon thought them "brilliant" and could never recall a time when the squadrons were "short of ammunition and fuel."[10] At "no time during the whole of the campaign in NW Europe did the flow of supplies through our echelons ever fail," wrote the Regiment's first historian; if "the boys in the tanks wanted something, the Ech[elon] saw that they got it."[11]

Rations and mail came up with the echelons. If the Regiment was stationary in a rest area for an extended period, the cooks from B Echelon would provide hot meals but in the field the men in the fighting squadrons normally did their own cooking. Each tank was provided with a small primus stove but these were slow and the crews turned to using a cut-down jerrican filled with a mixture of sand and gasoline to heat their food. That food was normally a Composite Ration Pack that contained fourteen rations (single meals) or, in other terms, breakfast, dinner and supper for a Sherman crew of five for three days (with someone going short a meal on the third day).

The compo pack came in an easily transported wooden crate that, apart from food, also contained cigarettes (usually the detested "woolly Woodbines"), salt, matches and toilet paper (not the softest). Each pack included non-varying food items – tea (already pre-mixed with milk and sugar), biscuit (jaw-breaking hard tack), soup (self-heating), jam (rarely strawberry), vegetables (mostly potatoes), margarine, boiled candy and hard chocolate – and items that did vary according to which one of nine types (A to F, X and Y) of compo ration the crew received. Depending on the kind the boys would get cans of steak and kidney pudding ("snake and kidney"), Irish stew, stewed steak ("stewed snake"), haricot oxtail stew, preserved meat (corned

beef) or M. and V. (meat and vegetable but usually "pork and veg") ration. Secondary meals included sausage, salmon or sardines (sometimes herring but all fish was known as "sewer trout"), baked beans, bacon (more fat than lean, more grease than substance), cheese (so-called) and processed meat (by-products) while the desserts included tinned fruit (all too rare) or a variety of puddings (all too common) such as date, sultana, rice, mixed fruit or treacle. It was a heavy diet (no quiche in 1944) and it was British fare (no account being made of Canadian preferences) worked out carefully by the finest War Office dieticians – or so it was claimed. Necessity being the mother of invention it did not take long for the crews to experiment with the various ingredients to come up with new combinations and most crews became accomplished cooks simply because they had to.[12]

Another thing that came up with the gasoline, ammunition and rations was rum. Quartermaster Tommy Barford notes that rum was "never issued on a standing basis" but he tried to provide enough to keep "a full waterbottle in each tank."[13] Rum was actually a brigade item; if it was felt that it was needed, Barford had to request it from the 10 Brigade QM stores but "since we usually wanted it fast and it took so long" he "managed to keep 40 gallons in my stores." The question of whether to issue the rum seems to have varied from tank to tank, troop to troop and squadron to squadron. Some South Albertas insist they got their rum issue on a daily basis, others remember receiving it only on rare occasions. Despite the standing practice in the squadron or troop, it was, as Barford noted, "the tank commander's choice to use it" but to Tommy's "certain knowledge," the rum was "never mis-used – maybe they had a party when they came out of action but it was never mis-used in action."

The men also regularly received the divisional newsletter, *Green Centre Line* with its cartoon character "Little Joe," and the army newspaper, *The Maple Leaf*, with the popular "Herbie" and beloved "L'il Abner" comic strips, but it was mail that was most eagerly awaited and, when it came, was a great morale booster. The mail service was good – on 11 August Corporal Bob Clipperton wrote his wife that it "is coming over wonderfully well & I get a letter practically every day."[14] The boys also received parcels from Canada with hometown newspapers, cigarettes and Mom's baking being the most popular items. Trooper Art Webster's wife "used to wax oranges and bananas" and send them to him to provide a welcome relief from the heavy and starchy diet provided by compo rations.[15]

The problem came in writing home. You couldn't tell your loved ones the truth, nor did you want to because it would only worry them – as Trooper Arnold Dryer put it to his fiancée in England, "I have seen so much and I wouldn't know how to tell you and they would probably tear it out if I did."[16] The men were forced back on the old standards: the weather, the food and the conjectured date of the end of the war – Dryer tried to put a positive slant on the whole thing by assuring his girl two days after he landed in France and a week before his first action that "I can sure save money over here because there is nothing to buy."[17]

Sometimes, if the opportunity was there, the crews would tune in their No. 19 Wireless Sets to music programmes. It didn't happen that often in Normandy, where the nights were short and tense and the crews often exhausted, unless the Regiment was in a rest area. Swatty Wotherspoon, however, never forgot those special evenings when his scout car or tank crew would run a long lead out to his headset and the "BBC would come in crystal clear, and that lovely girl, it was wonderful to pick it up and listen to her – Vera Lynn – oh, she was great for the troops."[18] The Allied Expeditionary Force and the General Forces Radio stations offered programmes aimed at a Canadian military audience including "Johnny Canuck's Revue" and news or sports round-ups from the Dominion. For everybody (depending on taste) there were: "The Western Five" (Cammie Howard and his Novelty Quintette with Oral Scheer); "Stardust" with Harold Green and his orchestra plus Owen Bradshaw and The All Girl Debonairs; "Nightcap" (informal music with a "lights out" theme); and, of course, the "AEF Ranchhouse," offering an "invitation to climb aboard the old chuckwagon with Corporal Saddlebags of the AFN and various cowboy and hillbilly entertainers."[19]

Although resupply was usually done at night, echelon personnel who were technical storesmen or fitters ("the tank man's auto mechanic") were also busy during the day. Tank drivers paid particular attention to their tracks because they were only good for 1,000 to 1,200 miles and a broken track in a tight situation might spell disaster. Drivers therefore took every opportunity to check tracks, suspension and the fluid levels in their engines. If there were mechanical problems the crew could not handle, or if they needed additional assistance, they called in the fitters, who came under the supervision of the SAR Technical Adjutant, Captain Dick Robinson. Each squadron had a detachment of fitters equipped with a variety of vehicles, including an armoured halftrack, who would come up to the tanks, drawing any parts they might need from the technical storesman's truck.

The engines in the Shermans and Stuarts were fairly robust and easy to maintain. Although they did some tuning, the fitters most often worked on track problems, "changing rollers or bogies, track pads and sprockets," Trooper William Gudwer remembered. He also points out that the Homelite, a small two-cycle engine inside the turret used to charge the batteries when the main engines were shut down, was a constant source of trouble and "a son of a gun to keep running."[20] Using a gas-oil fuel mixture these "chore horses" were vented to the outside of the turret but the fumes "seemed to drift back in a lot." Tank tracks are extremely heavy and the fitters, who used oversized hand tools to work on them, had the reputation of being among the strongest men in the Regiment. One of them was Sid Arrowsmith, who, one night in Normandy, added to his already considerable reputation when he lost patience with a persistent German aircraft that flew over the rear areas in the dark, dropping flares and the occasional bomb, bothering the sleep of the

echelon personnel who very much needed it. Woken up yet again, Arrowsmith ran, half naked, to his halftrack and opened fire on the intruder with the .50 calibre heavy machine gun mounted on the cab. He fired off an entire belt, and although witnesses claim he shot the intruder down, Sid simply said, "That so and so won't bother me any more" and went back to bed.[21]

If the squadron fitters encountered a mechanical problem they could not handle, the tank was sent back to 42 Light Aid Detachment, an RCOC sub-unit with heavier equipment and a mobile workshop, that accompanied the Regiment across Europe. If the job was too big or too difficult for the LAD the tank went back to the divisional ordnance workshops. Tanks that could not move under their own power were towed by one of the ARVs (Armoured Recovery Vehicles) attached to each squadron. The crews of these turretless Shermans equipped with a winch and cables were skilled at getting bogged tanks out of the most unlikely situations and the general rule was that an attempt would be made to salvage every shot-up vehicle. There was one exception – "if a tank had burned, it was left."[22]

Before it was abandoned, however, Padre Silcox sometimes had to do his work. In action the padre, a trained medical person, assisted Doc Boothroyd with the wounded at the RAP, but if there were casualties or known fatalities, he would come up with the medical halftrack and do what had to be done – and that included removing remains from burned tanks and giving them a decent burial. It was Silcox who went with a burial party on 18 August to the area around St. Hilaire Farm to recover Duffy Gendron's dismembered body from his tank and Clarence Quinnel's incinerated body from the second Stuart. Throughout the war, Phil Silcox kept meticulous notes on the circumstances of each SAR fatal casualty, the nature of the wounds and the condition of the body, and the location (including map references and terrain descriptions) of the first field grave that was dug for a fallen comrade. They make for grim reading.[23]

Recovering and burying the Regiment's dead was a terrible but necessary task and in later years Silcox reflected on the work of the battle padres:

We laid each on a blanket, wrapped him in its folds, and lowered him, under the Union Jack where possible, into the earth. Often we even helped to dig the grave and when 'twas all over we tried to beautify the surface; perhaps as grateful civilians heaped floral tributes all around. Then perhaps we might have to take up a brush to inscribe roughly a simple legend which was more eloquent than any casual visitor could understand ….

We offered brief, simple prayers commending them to God's eternal love, sometimes accelerating those prayers to top speed and diving abruptly into any nearby grave ourselves for material protection. And when the fever of battle had passed for a spell, the quiet hours came round, then we sorted out little white sacks of personal stuff, valuables to be

Washing up, August 1944. Sergeant Brown and Troopers Ficht and Pollock get cleaned up by a hedgerow in Normandy There wasn't always spare time to do this and periodically the "Chinese Hussars," the army's Mobile Bath and Laundry Units, would come up to give the boys a good scrub. SAR COLLECTION.

many trips back to the reinforcement holding units in the rear areas and used these trips to scout potential talent for the Regiment's boxing team. It was during one of these journeys that Bert rescued Danny McLeod from a fate (according to Danny) worse than death. When Danny's tank had hit a mine at Olendon on 14 August he had gone back to get another vehicle but had been snagged in the reinforcement organization and found himself sitting in an armoured holding unit as an unattached troop leader. The Fort Garry Horse of 2 Armoured Brigade, which had suffered heavy casualties, had immediate openings for troop leaders and, to his horror, Danny was told he was going to that unit. "As luck would have it," Danny recalled, "who should come down the road at that moment but Bert Coffin" so "I went down on bended knees and said, 'Bert, they're going to send me to the Garries!'"[25] "No bloody way they are," replied Coffin, "you're coming back up to us." Bert went off to see the commander of the holding unit, who just happened to be an old friend, and a grateful Danny was returned to the Regiment.

By the time Operation TRACTABLE ended on 15 August the South Alberta Regiment had been fighting, less a few days in rest areas, for more than two weeks. The first two weeks of action are crucial for new soldiers because, until they experience combat, men do not know how they will react and there is always the danger that fear will rob their self control. If a soldier can survive this period without any unduly traumatic experience and can acquire the basic knowledge necessary for survival in his new and terrifying environment, he gains self-confidence because he has seen the worst (or thinks he has) and is still alive. As one corporal put it, the South Albertas "had our answers now to the questions that had been in the backs of our minds as we approached the front line." They had "seen our tanks hit, men wounded, killed, burned to death, and we found that we were able to handle it. You were always afraid, but you accepted what was happening and you did what you had to do."[26]

As the men gained confidence, so did the unit. "Our outfit is doing better than the rest of them," wrote Bob Clipperton to his wife, "we are called the *Fighting 29th*."[27] There was some truth to this understandable pride. By mid-August, having survived its first two weeks without suffering any of the disasters that had befallen other units, the South Alberta Regiment was beginning to "shake down." It had lost men but its casualties were the lowest of the four armoured regiments in 4th Division. In the first fifteen days of August 1944 seven South Albertas had been killed and forty-six wounded, bad enough but not bad compared to the Grenadiers, who lost thirty-six killed during the same period, the Foot Guards, who lost thirty-four, or the BCR, which suffered fifty-one fatal casualties – forty-three of them on Point 140 on 9 August. The Dukes also lost forty-seven tanks that day while, during the period 1-15 August, the Grenadiers lost sixty-eight tanks (nearly 100% casualties) and the Foot

sent home, usables to his pals. Then we sat down to the toughest task of all and wrote letters to mothers and fathers, wives or sweethearts, to brothers in other regiments, to close friends, and casual acquaintances of whom we knew.

God alone can measure the tears we shed in silent solitude over these sincere letters to the folks at home.[24]

The echelons were not the only South Albertas who did not go into battle. The rule was that a certain number of officers and men were LOB (Left Out of Battle) so that, if a disaster occurred (as had happened to the BCR on Point 140) there would a cadre to rebuild the unit. Major Bert Coffin, second in command of the Regiment, was normally LOB, as were one of the two captains in each squadron and a certain percentage of NCOs and enlisted men. Another man who usually LOB was RSM Jock Mackenzie, who, in contrast to his attitude in England, occupied himself more with echelon work and less with disciplinary matters to everyone's great relief. Being "Left Out of Battle" did not mean that these officers and men did nothing while the squadrons were fighting. The officers had to keep in touch with the situation forward in case a "Sunray" was hit and they had to take over the Regiment, in Bert's case, or go up to a squadron in the case of the captains. In action Swatty usually commanded from his scout car, which was linked by wireless to the ACV manned by the battle adjutant, usually Captain Newt Hughes, and the Intelligence Officer, Captain Hank Carroll. Swatty kept them appraised of the situation and they, in turn, kept Bert up to date. A similar arrangement existed for each squadron whereby one captain acted as wireless "rear link" for the squadron commander who could keep both the ACV and the LOB captain abreast of events. Enlisted personnel who were LOB were sometimes given time off but often worked with the echelons to supply the fighting squadrons. It was a sensible arrangement but a somewhat difficult one for Bert Coffin who was forever waiting to take over command – yet hoping he would not have to.

In the meantime, Bert took much of the administrative burden of the Regiment off Swatty Wotherspoon's shoulders, including ensuring that replacements came up in time. He made

Guards so many that on 15 August they had to reorganize on a two-squadron basis. There are no accurate records for SAR tank casualties during this same time but, calculating on known average squadron strengths, the Regiment probably lost between ten and fifteen tanks in the first two weeks of August.[28]

The reason for the low casualty rate was not that the South Albertas had seen less fighting – the Regiment had been in action on a more consistent basis than any other armoured unit in 4th Division. The low casualty rate was more likely due to good luck and good leadership.

Swatty Wotherspoon had turned out to be an outstanding commander in action. As might be expected from his background, both at RMC and the Senior Officers' school, he had demonstrated a flair for tactics, but it was more than that – Swatty had an innate ability to grasp the essentials of a fluid or confused situation, reduce them to workable simplicity, consider the different courses of action, choose the best one, and render his decision in clear and simple directions to his subordinates in an amazingly short time. He was that rarest of things – a natural commander with an analytical mind who enjoyed solving the problems posed by the "challenge" of war. In Swatty's words: "I loved the fighting and I think my brain worked well on it."[29] As for being an instinctive commander, it was his feeling that

> when you talk about instinct, … what you have got is an extremely well-programmed brain that considers all the factors that it ought to consider in doing it, is able to weigh those factors properly and put the right weight on them and come out with the answer without going through any sort of effort ……
>
> If that's what instinct or intuition is, it is just a brain that brings all these factors in, which you know, sorts them out, puts the right priorities on them and brings out, well, what you should do.

Having made a decision and issued his orders, Wotherspoon did not interfere with his subordinates when they carried them out because he was a firm believer in promoting initiative at all levels. He told his squadron commanders what to do, not how to do it, but he was always available if they encountered unforeseen problems. This was the Wotherspoon style of leadership and it did not change throughout the course of the war.

Swatty also possessed the moral courage to refuse a bad order. It was his firm belief that "if your boss is wrong, you've got to not only stand up to him, but to convince him he's wrong and have the facts to prove that he's wrong."[30] Not that he worried about the consequences: "They couldn't fire me for incompetence and they couldn't fire me for disloyalty. They could fire me for refusing to obey an order but then, if it came up in a court martial, they would look absolute asses." With this attitude (rare in armies) he was fortunate to have the patient Jim Jefferson as a superior and Swatty got along well with the 10

Brigade commander, whom he regarded as a "solid, very solid fellow" who "didn't complain about bad results." For his part, Jefferson realized that, in Wotherspoon of the SAR and Stewart of the Argylls, he had two outstanding subordinates and usually let them have their head. "Basically," Swatty modestly recalled, "I ran the tactics in the brigade" and "Dave Stewart was the number two guy and Dave and I worked very closely together." The excellent relationship between these three officers, plus the ties between all the 10 Brigade unit commanders, contributed to making it a very effective formation.

Unfortunately the same cannot be said of 4 Armoured Brigade. Booth had not performed well in TOTALIZE and, if he hadn't been killed on the first day of TRACTABLE, it is likely he would have been replaced. Prior to Booth's death George Kitching had discussed with Simonds the succession of command in 4 Brigade. If Booth had to be replaced, Kitching's choice was Lieutenant-Colonel Don Worthington of the BCR as "a stop gap for a short period," but Simonds was keen on Lieutenant-Colonel Robert Moncel of his staff.[31] After this conversation, Kitching talked to Jefferson about the possibility of promoting Wotherspoon to 4 Brigade if Booth was incapacitated but Jefferson would not hear of it. Kitching remembered his response as being totally negative:

> That would be fatal to that regiment [the South Albertas]. They've got a good solid base of squadron commanders, they've got good troop commanders. If you upset it, you really upset the whole [of 10] brigade because all the familiarity that has been built up, would go.[32]

"Jeff, we'll leave it," Kitching replied, "and I'll get someone else." When Booth was killed on 14 August the problem became acute but by this time Worthington of the BCR was dead and Scott of the Foot Guards was out of action while Kitching regarded Halpenny of the Grenadiers as "too old." The logical choice was Wotherspoon but since Jefferson had made it clear that if Swatty left his brigade, it would suffer, Kitching had to take the corps commander's choice. In the end it was Moncel, a 26-year-old staff officer with no experience of armour command in combat, who got 4 Brigade. Unfortunately Simonds retained him at corps headquarters until 19 August, leaving the brigade without leadership for five crucial days.

Wednesday, 16 August 1944, dawned "clear and warm" and the South Albertas were up early. The Regiment had been warned that it would move at 0900 hours and there was a "stand to" from 0600 to 0800 hours, but when the move did not occur, the squadrons spent a relatively quiet day and "carried out maintenance."[33] This welcome break resulted from events to the south; while First Canadian Army had been battling its way to the shining goal of Falaise, the Americans had been on the move. On 12 August the lead divisions of Patton's Third

Army were approaching Argentan, which, according to Montgomery's plan for a "short" envelopment of the German armies, was to form the southern hinge of the trap. That evening Patton ordered his troops to take Argentan and push north "slowly" to Falaise to finish the job, but his superior, Bradley, in a move that is still a matter of great controversy, countermanded Patton's order and the Americans came to a halt. The task of sealing off the Germans was now up to First Canadian Army and on 14 August Montgomery ordered Crerar not only to take Falaise but also to drive in a southeast direction to link up with Patton's forces. This meant that the axis of the Canadian attack, which in TRACTABLE had been southwest toward Falaise, would now change once again. Despite giving First Canadian Army a major new responsibility and shifting the direction of their operations, Montgomery still did not see fit to reinforce Crerar with one of the three armoured divisions of Second British Army, which, in the course of events, was in danger of being "pinched out of battle." Crerar translated the field marshal's orders into a direction to Simonds that he was to drive southeast toward Trun as soon as Falaise was taken.[34]

By this time, TRACTABLE had sputtered out on the high ground north of Falaise and early on 16 August Simonds changed the tasks of his divisions. The job of taking Falaise was left to 2nd Canadian Infantry Division and the two armoured divisions were ordered to the southeast: Kitching's 4th Division was to secure a crossing over the Ante River at Damblainville and take Trun (see map 6, page 139), cutting off one of the main German escape routes, while Maczek's Polish Division was to cross the Dives River at Jort and move parallel, establishing another blocking position further to the east. Montgomery was beginning to see that the trap would not be closed between Falaise and Argentan but farther to the east, between Trun and Chambois. During the afternoon of 16 August, while the South Albertas were enjoying a quiet day, he stressed to Crerar the vital importance of capturing Trun. At the same time, he tried to get the Americans moving again and ordered Bradley to push on past Argentan and take Chambois and Trun. If both the American and Canadian armies carried out their tasks, two German armies would be trapped. Unfortunately, because of some confusion caused by a changeover of command in the area, the American attack was delayed for nearly thirty-six hours.[35]

At 1000 hours on 16 August George Kitching issued orders to the 4th Division that reflected the changing situation. The division would have a rest from operations that day but it was to kick off early on the 17th and advance "with the objective Trun and the closure of the gap between the U.S. forces in Argentan and the Brit[ish and Canadian] Forces."[36] Later in the afternoon Kitching amplified these orders by directing Jefferson to secure a bridgehead over the Ante at Damblainville through which 4 Brigade would pass to take Trun. In preparation for this operation, Jefferson ordered 10 Brigade to concentrate in "suitable areas north of Olendon" and warned the South Albertas that they would have a "task" early in the morn-

ing.[37] That night 2nd Canadian Division captured Falaise and the gap between the American and Canadian forces was now eighteen miles wide.

Actually the South Albertas started work during the night of 16/17 August. Dave Currie's C Squadron married up with the Argylls at 2200 hours and moved forward in the dark to the outskirts of Damblainville. For the first time since they had arrived in France, the South Albertas entered an area untouched by war – "grand rolling country all young pine forest & cider apple orchards," Trooper John Neff recorded.[38] As the tanks moved through the orchards the crew commanders had to duck in their turrets to avoid the low branches of apple trees which swept over them and deposited their fruit into the open hatches. It wasn't long before turret floors were thick with a sticky, but fragrant, mess of pulped apples.[39]

By first light C Squadron and the Argylls were in position on a large hill overlooking Damblainville. The town and the valley to the south were shrouded in ground mist but the Argylls' scout platoon had entered Damblainville during the night and reported that it was clear of Germans "with the exception of enemy tanks moving through from time to time."[40] At 0830 the Argylls, supported by Dave Currie's C Squadron and Lavoie's A Squadron, began to clear Damblainville of snipers and, by 1000 hours, the two units had secured their main objective – the stone bridge over the Ante River. B Squadron, meanwhile, had moved out from Olendon at 0400 and by first light had taken up a position on the high ground, where they observed German AFVs in the woods to the south and called down artillery fire on them. Excited B Squadron operators began to hear "our friends to the south" (the Americans) on the No. 19 Sets in their tanks – Trooper John Neff remembered they kept cutting "in on our net."[41]

At noon, the Algonquin Regiment passed through the Argylls' bridgehead and, with A and C Squadrons in support, moved forward to the next objective, a wooded hill 1800 yards south of the town. The infantry and tanks stopped at a railway embankment while the Algoons' scout platoon was sent forward to scope out the ground ahead. This platoon had just crossed a bridge over the tiny Traine River which flowed north of their objective when the entire area was blanketed with enemy mortar, artillery and small-arms fire.[42]

Sitting in "elevated ambush positions south of the Ante" were three Tiger tanks from the 101st SS Heavy Tank Battalion and several SPGs from the *Panzerjaeger* battalion of the 12th SS Panzer Division. As the South Albertas and Algonquins had moved forward to the railway embankment, the commander of one of the SPGs, *Unterscharführer* Alfred Schulz, suddenly "spotted three enemy tanks, just outside a wooded area" and "raced forward" to get in range as he was "planning to get all three of them by myself."[43] Schulz opened fire but "could not observe the result of my fire since the smoke from the discharges lingered a long time ahead of my gun barrel." "The enemy tanks," however, "opened fire on me and I became the prey," Schulz recorded. Minutes later the engine of his vehicle packed up and Schulz and his crew left the battle on foot.

Schulz's target was Don Stewart's C-1 Troop. Currie's C Squadron had moved up to an orchard behind the railway embankment when the Algonquins came and said that they had left a wounded man up on top of the railway tracks to the right of "an underpass and wondered if one of the tanks might volunteer to go out and retrieve this wounded infantry fellow."[44] "Dave Currie came to me," remembered Stewart, "and asked if we might be willing to try it and my men said they were willing." Stewart moved his tank and Corporal Johnny McRae's tank through the underpass, leaving his troop sergeant in the tunnel to provide covering fire. McRae then covered Stewart as he backed his tank up to the embankment where the wounded man lay. "Walter Vandermark, Ben Cunningham and I bailed out of the turret of our tank, ran up the embankment, grabbed the infantry fellow, and brought him down and put him on the back deck of the tank," Don recalled. They "then took off for the underpass" but "to do that we had to pass in front of Johnny McRae, in other words between him and the other side of the field where the enemy were." Just as his tank passed McRae's vehicle, Stewart, who had his head out of his hatch, "felt a heat on my face – I suppose you would describe it as feeling like a hot, wet towel slapping you on the face" and at "that instant Johnny McRae's tank burst into flames; I am sure that was the armour-piercing shell that passed by my face and into Johnny McRae's tank." Three men got out of the vehicle but not McRae, a popular man in the Regiment and a 28-year-old cattle farmer from Westlock, Alberta, who had joined in June 1940. He was killed instantly, as was his driver, 25-year-old Trooper Grant Edwards from Big Valley in the same province.[45]

Don Stewart remembered that Dave Currie immediately came over. The two officers "sat there under an apple tree in this nice orchard, and he was telling me about writing to the next of kin and things like that." "All of a sudden," they heard the Moaning Minnies coming," and "there is six shells coming all at once out of those things." Don and Dave "hit the ground, and these six shells fell in a perfect circle around us in the soft earth of that orchard and nearly buried us but never scratched us at all."[46]

Dave dusted himself off and ranged the guns of his squadron on the woods south of their position and they fired HE into the woods to keep the Germans' heads down while Swatty, whose RHQ was on the hill behind Damblainville, called down artillery. The gunners fired a "16-round salvo" and Dave made corrections from his position. Orders were now received for 10 Brigade to firm up along the railway embankment while 4 Brigade took over the advance. The British Columbia Regiment and Lake Superiors moved up but could make no progress in the face of German fire from well-sited positions.[47]

From the heights behind Damblainville large German vehicle convoys could be seen moving in a northeast direction in the valley south of the town. During the morning of 17 August there was no sign of Allied aircraft but, in the afternoon, they

appeared in great numbers to attack the inviting targets. From its position on the high ground B Squadron had a box seat and Trooper Duncan Cameron and his crew "were on the top of the tank" when they "heard these planes coming in and we thought we were in for a real show."[48] "They dove in," Duncan recalled, "and they circled and came back and then there was dust flying alongside the tank" and one of the boys shouted, "Holy shit those guys are firing at us" and "we all dived for cover." The only casualty was the crew's rum bottle stowed inside the turret but, as Cameron points out, "that's how close those rounds were."

It was now clear to Kitching that the Germans were determined to resist any attempt to move east on Trun from the Damblainville bridgehead and that any advance in that direction would require a major attack. Fortunately, the Algonquins had seized another bridge over the Dives River at the village of Couliboeuf three miles to the east and, when he reported this to Simonds, the corps commander ordered him to "sidestep" his division to the left using secondary country roads, cross the river at Couliboeuf and come into Trun from the back door. The two Guards regiments of 4 Brigade, which had not yet been committed at Damblainville, led this movement, which began at 1600 hours and, since it involved an extraordinary manoeuvre of the division's large number of vehicles in a short time, was only done with difficulty, luck and good traffic control. By early evening the Grenadier Guards were at the outskirts of Trun but, having no infantry with them, their commanding officer "decided to cover the town by fire but not to enter it."[49] Behind 4 Brigade came the 10 Brigade column, which had a slow and wearying nighttime movement through thickly wooded and hilly country. "No sleep again," recorded John Neff of B Squadron that night but there was to be little sleep for the Regiment for the next four nights.[50]

The Algonquins were at the front of the brigade column. Their historian records that "the dust was terrific, the pace tedious, the weariness overwhelming" and "the column would break" frequently "as drivers, during halts, would drift helplessly off to sleep."[51] With their leading company on the decks of B Squadron's tanks and using every vehicle they could muster, including some belonging to the New Brunswick Rangers and 5th Anti-Tank Regiment, the Algoons were in position at first light near the little village of Le Marais la Chapelle, just north of Trun. With fire support from B Squadron the Algonquins had no trouble clearing the hamlet, which turned out to be a wonderful spot as they began "to intercept enemy vehicles, one of which contained a German paymaster and plenty of francs."[52] The South Albertas now encountered civilians in the battlefield area for the first time – "the people were all packed up and ready to evacuate when we came up," Trooper John Neff wrote, "but it was all over in a short time."[53] When "another German truck, loaded with loot, arrived and was scuttled," the Algonquins' historian adds, "the civilians had a field-day sharing in the prize."[54] Neff recalled that "the villagers gave us some powerful green stuff to drink."[55]

The valley of death. The valley of the Dives seen from the ridge to the north. In August 1944 this sleepy little vale became the scene of immense slaughter as it formed the escape route for two trapped German armies. PHOTOGRAPH BY DIANNE GRAVES

The Links, with Lavoie's A Squadron in support, now moved up to Trun but were forced to postpone their attack until Typhoon fighter bombers had finished "working over" the place. When the aircraft had departed in the early afternoon, A Squadron accompanied the Links into the town, which was a mass of flaming wreckage. Enemy vehicles, under the mistaken impression that Trun was in German hands, kept rolling in and the infantry found the pickings very good: "staff cars, reconnaissance cars, armoured halftracks, horse-drawn carts, and a complete ambulance column."[56] It was a red letter day for the Lincoln and Welland Regiment and by nightfall "more than 500 prisoners had been taken and untold quantities of French francs" had swollen the pockets of the unit.[57]

At this point, lest the reader think that Canadians were more interested in getting rich than in preserving democracy, it might be an opportune time to digress briefly and review the "unwritten rules" of war as they were observed by both sides in 1944. When they took prisoners, the first thing Allied troops did was to remove their weapons, ammunition, accoutrements and sometimes helmets and throw them away except for certain weapons such as Luger or Walther P-38 pistols, the Schmeisser submachine guns called "burp guns" by Allied troops, and various ornamental Nazi daggers, which were put aside for safekeeping and eventual sale to rear-echelon troops. The prisoners were then searched and the rule of thumb was that anything found on them belonged to the captor although personal letters and photographs were normally returned. The rest, including money, drink, pens, watches, jewelry, cigarettes, food or whatever the captor desired, was confiscated lest these items assist the German war effort. "Where they were going they didn't

need money and they didn't want to know the time," is how one South Alberta put it.[58] German cigarettes (supposedly manufactured out of old *Wehrmacht* blankets) were disdained but German medals (particularly the flashy Iron and Knights' Crosses), Zeiss binoculars, good quality leather map cases and swastika flags were much sought after as they had excellent resale value. A man had to be careful, however, lest circumstances change and he himself was captured – the Germans did not like to find Lugers and Knights' Crosses in the possession of their prisoners while Allied troops did not like theirs to hand over Zippo lighters and Camel cigarettes. In the looting game, tank crews had an advantage because they had vehicles to haul away their new acquisitions and it was amazing how much could be stowed in a Sherman, or a Panther for that matter.

Currie's C Squadron came up with the Argylls at the tail of the brigade column and, after "having covered approximately 15 miles, on a dark moonless night" by map, by guess and by God, Dave and his troop leaders were "justly proud of our navigation" when at first light they found themselves "within 100 yards of our objective."[59] The squadron took up a position on a height north of Trun and, when the sun rose on 18 August, Currie remembered, "we found that we had a wonderful panoramic view of the Dives Valley."

It was a pretty sight. The valley was demarcated in the north by the ridge on which C Squadron was positioned and in the south by another line of high ground marked by the Forêt de Gouffern. The Dives itself was a small stream with tree-covered banks that meandered northwest from its source near Argentan along what appeared to be, at a distance, a narrow, shallow depression. The open floor of the valley was dotted with small villages readily identified by the spires of their churches. Appearance was deceptive for the bottom of the valley was in reality "a maze of hedgerows, small woods and enclosed fields traversed by sunken country lanes and paths that provided excellent cover."[60] It was an ancient land – the Celts had first settled it, the Romans had come after them and later still came the Normans, who gave it its traditional name of l'Hiesmois after the small town of Exmes where they built a stronghold to dominate the area. In earlier times the valley had been no stranger to the clash of arms and no stranger to English-speaking troops. The graceful keep at Chambois had been constructed by a vassal of Henry II of England and, during the century-long conflict between that country and France that began in the 14th century, l'Hiesmois had changed hands several times as the troops of first one and then another monarch marched along its length. Five centuries of rural somnolence had passed since that time, however, five centuries that ended in the third week of August 1944 when war transformed the tranquil vale of the Dives into a valley of death.[61]

That cruel transformation had commenced when Dave Currie and C Squadron looked down at the Dives on the morning of 18 August. Dave remembered that his men

could see rising clouds of dust, and on closer examination, by field glasses, found that we were witnessing, what we later found out to be the remnants of the German Forces in France trying to escape the pocket. The columns were about three or four miles from our location and seemed to consist of every type and kind of vehicle, gun, tank and horse-drawn equipment that the German Army possessed. The column stretched as far as we could see. It was an awe-inspiring sight, and from the distance, it appeared to be a crushing force. … We deployed into positions facing the enemy and spent most of the day watching the columns inching along in a never-ending stream.[62]

RHQ, which moved behind C Squadron, did not have a good day on 18 August. It had just reached Louvières-en-Auge, north of Trun, when it was attacked by Allied aircraft. As Wotherspoon reported:

One squadron of Spitfires of the RAF started to engage my headquarters shortly after and two flights had bombed and strafed the headquarters and set fire to a vehicle from another formation a few yards away. Yellow recognition smoke was thrown and veh[icles] with Allied recognition markings were in the open with no effect even to the planes diving as low as 200 ft.[63]

Cannon and machine-gun rounds ricocheted off the cobblestone road and hit some of the tanks which "rang like bells," one remembered.[64] Carson Daley was sitting in the back of the medical halftrack "with just my beret on and a bullet came

through the canvas top into a jerrican of water" and the top "caught fire but I put that out with my beret."[65] Daley was out of the halftrack and under a tank in very short order. Captain Bob Allsopp thought the aircraft were "rotten shots and missed us" but, when the yellow smoke was ignored, "we abandoned our vehicles and took cover."[66] Wotherspoon yelled at him to note down the identification markings of the planes but Allsopp found it impossible. Having been attacked at Soignolles three days before, Swatty Wotherspoon was fed up with "friendly air" and ordered the two Crusader AA tanks, which always accompanied his HQ, to open fire. He was dissuaded by Padre Silcox, who

realizing the great danger the force was in and that some means must be adopted to indicate that we were friendly troops ran to his medical vehicle through the centre of the fire – which was the most open spot – and got the Union Jack that he used for burials … and held it down as a strong wind was blowing while another flight was forming up and during the attack of the first plane. The remainder of the flight, on seeing the Jack did not fire although they dove on the position.[67]

The fighters flew off to look for other prey but Carson Daley was "so scared" after that attack that he did not realize that the tank under which he had been sheltering had moved off until someone shook him by the shoulder and yelled, "Get up, they're moving and you are in the middle of the road."[68] Most of RHQ witnessed Silcox's action but the padre was no natural born hero; Corporal Herb Ficht remembered he was "shaking like a leaf" when it was over.[69] That night Swatty wrote Silcox up for an immediate award of the Military Cross.

Farther to the east Maczek's Poles were also watching the German traffic in the valley. They had been switched to the eastern flank of 2nd Canadian Corps and on 15 August had secured a bridge over the Dives at Jort. When Simonds ordered Maczek in the afternoon of 16 August to advance to the southeast, parallel to 4th Division's direction, the Poles poured over the Dives and by the late afternoon of 17 August had taken the village of Neauphe-sur-Dives, a few miles east of Trun and astride the main German escape route, the Falaise-Trun-Vimoutiers highway. Maczek then received orders to "thrust on past Trun to Chambois" and, like 4th Division, the Poles advanced during the night of 17/18 August. Language difficulties, darkness and the confusion caused by German vehicles wandering into their columns, resulted in the division going not to Chambois but to the village of Les Champeaux, six miles to the north. Realizing his mistake, Maczek got on the right road but throughout the day of 18 August his progress was delayed by a battle group of the 21st Panzer Division which had moved into the area to try to keep the northern shoulder of the pocket open. Even worse were Allied aircraft which constantly attacked the Polish columns and inflicted more than two hundred casualties in a three-day period.[70]

A few miles to the south the Americans were closing in on Chambois. The night before, elements of the 90th US Infantry Division had captured part of the high ridge that formed the southern border of the Dives Valley and one of its infantry regiments was only three miles from Chambois. The gap between the Allied armies was now just over six miles wide.

The large numbers of enemy vehicles observed moving northeast during 17 and 18 August indicated that the Germans were trying to escape. The senior German commanders in Normandy, veteran soldiers, had been aware of their peril for some time but were helpless in the face of Hitler's intransigence. The German commander, *Feldmarschall* von Kluge, was under no illusions that, after Operation COBRA on 25 July, his situation could only deteriorate but, when the counterattack at Mortain failed on 9 August, he obeyed Hitler's order to renew it with stronger forces. Before that attack took place, he was forced to use most of the armoured forces he had gathered for it to block Patton's troops moving up from the south. The *Wehrmacht* had now lost the initiative and the two German armies in Normandy, Seventh and Fifth Panzer, were almost encircled. On 13 August, *Generaloberst* Sepp Dietrich, the commander of Fifth Panzer Army, voiced for the first time what other German commanders knew but had been afraid to say: "If every effort is not made to move the forces toward the east and out of the threatened encirclement, the army group will have to write off both armies."[71] That same day, however, Bradley halted Patton and the German divisions facing the Americans were amazed when they stopped their attacks.[72]

Hitler now had a golden opportunity to save his soldiers from an impending disaster but Hitler talked only of advance and never of retreat. On 14 August he ordered von Kluge to make a new attack on the Americans at Argentan but did permit him to withdraw the bulk of his forces slightly to the east to free up troops for this attack. That day, however, First Canadian Army launched Operation TRACTABLE and at 2330 hours von Kluge informed Hitler's headquarters that, if the Americans could not be held in the south and the Canadians in the north, the only alternative was for the Seventh and Fifth German Panzer Armies to withdraw as quickly as possible. The following day, 15 August, von Kluge was out of communication with both his own headquarters and Hitler for more than fourteen hours after his radio car was destroyed by Allied aircraft during a visit to the front line. When he had not shown up by early evening, his chief of staff informed his superiors that it was "five minutes to twelve" and that the only course of action was a withdrawal.[73] Hitler refused to countenance such a move. A few hours later von Kluge re-established contact and, at 0200 hours, 16 August, recommended to Hitler the immediate evacuation of all German troops in the pocket; otherwise, he predicted, in a nice turn of language, there would be "unforeseeable developments."[74]

Hitler did not agree but, at 1245 hours that same day von Kluge again emphasized that the only solution was full-scale evacuation to the east. Three hours later – although he did not have permission from Berlin – the German commander issued orders for a retreat to begin that night and he must have been gratified when some time later permission arrived from Hitler's headquarters for a withdrawal behind the line of the Dives River. This was von Kluge's last service to his fatherland – relieved of command the following day and summoned to Berlin, he committed suicide en route.[75]

By the time von Kluge had ordered a withdrawal the German Seventh and Fifth Panzer Armies were nearly encircled. Some troops, however, had already escaped as, notwithstanding the blindness of their national leader, senior German officers had seen what was coming and had been quietly evacuating troops to the east for some time. Earlier, von Kluge had authorized the withdrawal of "administrative troops and motorized transport," and German commanders stretched the interpretation of this to include complete formations or units.[76] The 12th SS Panzer Division, for example, retained only its headquarters and a battlegroup of five hundred men inside the pocket but sent all its echelon personnel and non-combatworthy troops (gunners without guns, tankers without tanks), a total of nearly 10,000 men, to safety well before permission to retreat was granted and other German formations did the same. The author of one recent study has concluded that 65,000 troops were moved out of the pocket prior to von Kluge's withdrawal order of 16 August.[77]

The authorized German withdrawal began during the night of 16/17 August under the cover of darkness and all major roads and country lanes became crowded with "masses of transport, packed nose to tail."[78] The goal of most of the convoys was Vimoutiers outside the pocket and the best route to that place was the highway that ran there from Falaise via Trun. At first the retreat was orderly, but on the morning of 17 August, the mass of vehicles moving east was spotted by Allied recce aircraft, which summoned the tactical fighters, and soon air force wireless frequencies were buzzing as the excited pilots of Typhoons, Thunderbolts and Spitfires chattered about a "shambles with stuff going in all directions … confused movement … Huge jams and even White flags waved."[79] Allied aircraft flew more than two thousand sorties that day against this heaven-sent target and, for good measure, a few friendly units as well (including the South Albertas). For the retreating Germans, caught on the roads and constricted in huge vehicle convoys, it was a hellish chaos. "There was no end to it," one remembered, "every two or three minutes the spotters shouted 'Jabos [*Jagdbomber* or fighter bombers]' … the planes shrieked down, firing straight along the road" and "every attack was a winner."[80] Another German put it more graphically: "Tank on road – clank, clank, clank; Aircraft approaches – m-m-m-m-m-m-a-a-r-r-r-r-r; SCHRUMPF!! Tank in flames."[81]

Darkness brought an end to the Germans' torment but on

18 August the "Bank Holiday rush" began again at 1030 hours and that day Allied aircraft flew more than three thousand sorties. The situation was changing so rapidly that many of the German columns were unaware that Falaise and Trun had fallen to the Canadians and blundered into these towns only to be put in the bag. Those that took the last open route out of the pocket, the secondary road through Chambois to Vimoutiers, stood a better chance but still suffered from the incessant attention of the fighter bombers. One German officer who escaped that day paused to look back. As he watched the aircraft "swooping down unexpectedly on anything that moved," leaving "mushroom clouds of exploding bombs, burning vehicles" and many of his comrades killed and wounded, it brought to his mind a fragment of a 13th-century Crusader's poem: "Man, horse and truck by the Lord were struck."[82]

Despite the terrible pounding by Allied aircraft, nearly 55,000 Germans, many without their transport, managed to escape from the pocket in the first three days of the withdrawal. Montgomery wanted this exodus stopped and told Crerar at 1445 hours on 17 August that "it was essential" that he "close the gap between First Canadian Army and Third U.S. Army."[83] The following morning at 1100 hours, Simonds summoned the commanders of the four divisions in 2nd Canadian Corps (2nd and 3rd Infantry Divisions, 4th and Polish Armoured Divisions) to an O Group at which he issued new orders. Kitching's division was "to advance S[outh] E[ast] from Trun to Chambois" along the line of the Dives while Maczek's Poles were to advance from the area of Les Champeaux to Chambois "and link up with the US forces in that area thus closing the bag."[84] Kitching was to carry out his part of this operation the next day, 19 August, "as soon as the div[ision] had cleared the enemy from the area north and n[orth] w[est] of Trun." To undertake this clearing job, Simonds ordered that 4 Armoured Brigade and the Algonquin Regiment, which were positioned, after their movements of the previous night, near Trun, were "to deploy in an area about two miles north of it." This entailed, as George Kitching later recalled, changes of orders to the two brigades and, as changes "in plan become more exhausting as they go down the chain of command," his men "must have wondered why I couldn't make up my mind."[85] It also resulted in 4th Division being split: 10 Infantry Brigade was to advance southeast from Trun down the line of the Dives while 4 Brigade with the Algoons was going to move northeast from Trun toward Vimoutiers.

Either Kitching or Jefferson anticipated the move on Chambois because at 1500 hours that day the Regiment with a company of Argylls under command was ordered to move in the direction of that place. Swatty got this order in mid-afternoon and immediately sent for the commander of C Squadron. Dave Currie remembered that Wotherspoon told him that "he had a rather tough assignment." Dave's men were

to "take the village of Saint Lambert-sur-Dives, and from a study of the map, I could see this was placing us squarely in front of the vast array of German forces that we had been watching for most of the day." Dave received "a company of the ASH whose depleted strength was about 55 all ranks" and Swatty also told him "that there was no immediate artillery support, but that later on, there should be some available." Finally, Swatty stressed the importance of the task in relation to the whole campaign and indicated that the German withdrawal had to be stopped."[86] As he left RHQ Currie reflected: "Well, Dave, up to now this has been a pretty good war, but this is it!"

Returning to his squadron Dave rounded up his rear link, Captain John Redden, and his troop leaders and held an O Group to brief them. The squadron then mounted up, picked up Major Ivan Martin's B Company of the Argylls and put them on their rear decks and at 1700 hours moved into Trun, which was to be their starting point. Trun was in flames, Dave thought that "about one-third of the houses in the village seemed to be on fire" and lost Germans were still wandering in to be put in the bag.[87] The squadron had about an hour to wait so the "boys brewed tea, and made last minute preparations for the coming battle."

Shortly before his start time at 1800 hours, Dave lined up C Squadron, fifteen tanks strong, at the edge of the town. At 1800 sharp, the squadron moved out of Trun down a secondary highway, the D 13, for St. Lambert. The lead tank "immediately came under fire from the left" and the troop leader "pulled his tanks back under cover from some buildings." Consulting his map, Currie realized this could only be from the Poles in the Neauphe-sur-Dives area so he headed in that direction and, "sure enough, one of their tank commanders had become a little excited … and had fired first and looked later." The misunderstanding straightened out, the squadron "got under way about twenty minutes late" and proceeded down the dusty D 13, a chalk highway, toward St. Lambert.[88]

St. Lambert-sur-Dives is just over two miles from Trun and it did not take Currie long to reach it. Having decided that his "tanks would lead the attack and, as and when we were able to penetrate the village, the infantry would come up and consolidate," Dave ordered his lead troop to enter St. Lambert.[89] "It was dusk when we went in," Trooper Wayne Spence remembered, "but when all the shooting started and flares went up, it was just like daylight."[90] As the first Sherman, commanded by Sergeant John Slater, nosed into the north end of the village, it was hit by AP fire. The crew bailed out but Slater and Trooper Lloyd LaPrade were wounded.

Currie, whose headquarters troop was immediately behind the lead troop, had just received this report over his wireless when his own tank was strafed by two RAF Spitfires and, when they had gone by, Dave recalled, "the back end of my tank was on fire."[91] A 20 mm tracer round had ignited the bedrolls stowed at the rear of the turret so Dave grabbed a fire extinguisher and started to put the blaze out. Lieutenant Gerry

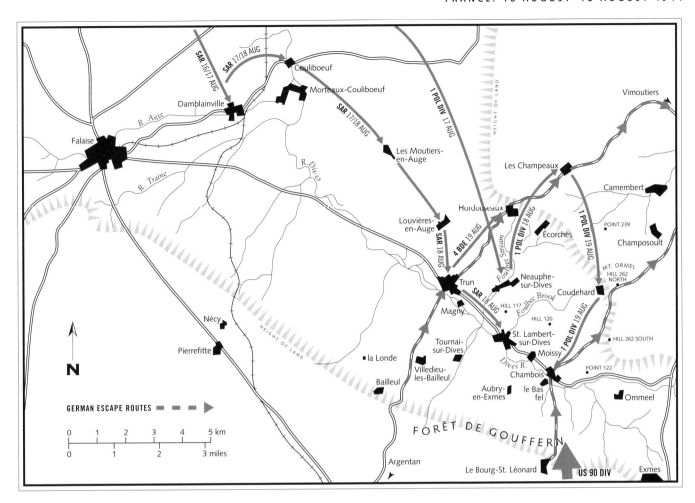

Map 6: The Falaise Pocket, 17-19 August 1944. Thwarted at Damblainville on 17 August, 4th Armoured Division made an "end run" on the night of 17/18 August and seized Trun, cutting off one of the two main German escape routes. At the same time, 1st Polish Division, further east, reached Coudehard, threatening the other escape route. On 18 August Simonds ordered 4th Division to move from Trun to Moissy and 1st Polish Division to move from Coudehard to Moissy via Chambois to seal the pocket. Meanwhile the American 90th Division moved on Chambois from the south and 2nd Canadian Division took Falaise.

Adams remembered an "airplane flying over us, one of our own and … the first thing I know it attacks us." Gerry had "the hatch flaps open and I squatted down in the turret and the shells ricocheted off that flap and came down in the turret." Gerry and his gunner were both wounded and "got out of the turret and on the verge of the road and then it came around a second time."[92]

Frantic crews threw out yellow smoke canisters and pulled open the yellow identification panels which folded like blinds on the back of their tanks. Trooper Jimmy Cooper's crew commander lit a smoke canister and tossed it out of his hatch but dropped the match which set fire to dried leaves on the bottom of the turret and Cooper had to get "down there to stomp out the burning leaves."[93] To Trooper John Hutchinson, the smoke didn't do any good, "they just came whooping down again."[94] Lieutenant Don Stewart agreed; to him it appeared that lighting yellow smoke "was like poking a hornets' nest, they got agitated and came back twice as bad."[95] On the second pass many of the crews were caught out of their tanks and Trooper Jimmy Eastman discovered that he "was small enough to hide in the

bogies" of his Sherman's suspension as the 20 mm rounds kicked up white dust on the chalk surface of the D 13.[96] This time the aircraft knocked out the medical halftrack and wounded the driver. It was all too much for Captain John Redden who "made an effort to get away a shot with my .50 cal[ibre machine gun] but they were too fast."[97] Having done their bit for the Allied cause, the Spitfires departed the scene.

Contacting RHQ, Dave requested two ambulance jeeps to pick up his wounded. After they had arrived, he went forward to the leading troop and, ordering the troop leader to remain in position with his three remaining tanks at the edge of village, walked into St. Lambert alone to see if there was a way to flank the enemy position which appeared to be at the southern end of the village. "By this time it was getting pretty dark," he recalled, and "I could hear the voices of Germans in some of the buildings, but did not run into anybody."[98] Realizing that the Dives, which flowed along the western edge of the village, prevented him from outflanking the German gun, he returned to his squadron and pulled back up the road about two hundred

Where is everybody? Trooper George White's B Squadron crew take a break in Trun, 18 August 1944. Although the armoured corps model steel helmets were unpopular and uncomfortable, the South Albertas wore them during the fighting in the Falaise because of the proximity of German infantry. COURTESY, GEORGE WHITE.

yards in a position to cover the northern edge of the village. Reaching Swatty by wireless, he requested permission "to dismount most of the tank crews and combined with our infantry support, make an attack on the village using the infantry and three tanks." Wotherspoon told him to sit tight until first light so Dave pulled back a little further to a large flat-topped hill and took up a defensive position for the night.

Swatty and RHQ had moved up to an orchard at the outskirts of Trun with B Squadron and Recce Troop. Major Darby Nash, the former commander of Headquarters Squadron, had just taken over B that afternoon and later admitted that "he was not at all happy at the moment."[99] The weather, which had been hot and dry for weeks, was looking threatening, and wireless

Trun, 18 August 1944. From this town the Regiment pushed southeast to cut off the German escape route. COURTESY, W. VAILLANCOURT.

communications began to fail when it started to rain just after last light. Swatty wanted to keep in contact with Currie and left the ACV in the orchard to act as a "relay station" and then took his RHQ Troop of four tanks, Recce Troop, B Squadron and the four M-10s of K Troop of 5th Anti-Tank Regiment down the road to Currie's position at about 2300 hours. The combined force then harboured with C Squadron and the infantry in a large field known to the locals as "les Carrés" on the top of Hill 117 a thousand yards north of St. Lambert.

That same night the armoured recce regiment of 1st Polish Division had reached a point fifteen hundred yards from Chambois, and all indications were that the next day would bring the junction of the Allied armies and the closure of the gap, which was now only three miles wide. "It was beginning to look as if a big show was coming off," recorded the War Diarist and "everybody stood to" during the night "waiting for some movement which would start things flying."[100]

CHAPTER NINE

"The situation began to get out of hand."

FRANCE: 19 AUGUST–20 AUGUST A.M., 1944

The rain, a soft summer drizzle, fell throughout the night but tapered off toward the dawn of Saturday, 19 August 1944. The first few hours of daylight were grey and misty but gradually the sun broke through and the day became "clear and warm." Allied aircraft appeared overhead to take up their work of harassing the Germans and, not surprisingly after the events of the preceding two days, the War Diarist commented that "they were unwelcome by our f[or]w[ar]d troops."[2] At first light, about 0500 hours, Swatty Wotherspoon ordered Dave Currie to attack St. Lambert and, ninety minutes later, reported to 10 Brigade that the attack on ROOSTER (the code-name for St. Lambert) was just starting.[3] While B Squadron covered them, Currie's tanks and Martin's Argylls cautiously entered the village.

St. Lambert-sur-Dives is a long stringbean of a place (see map 8, page 158). About a thousand yards from the north end to the south, it is really four clusters of buildings. At the north, or Currie's end, the Château de Quantité and its attendant *moulin* (mill) on the river bank form one of these clusters; the

> *W*hen you hear the Tigers grinding by your slit,
> Makes you start to wonder, if it's time to quit.
> Just think of me in Gay Paree,
> With some French wench upon my knee.
> For I am LOB, For I am LOB.[1]

other consists of the buildings around the intersection of the D 13 and a country lane running east and west at the foot of Hill 117. The northern end of the village is connected to the southern end by a spaced row of houses bordering the D 13, which, at this point, forms the main street. There are two other clusters in the south end of St. Lambert. One cluster, which includes the *mairie* (town hall), is grouped around the junction of the D 13 and a street leading to the stone bridge over the Dives, while the other consists of the buildings, including the church, grouped around that bridge. The western boundary of the village is formed by the Dives River, at this point about four to five feet deep with banks about six feet high. Bordered by trees and bushes, the Dives cannot be seen from any distance and, in fact, many a South Alberta who fought in the area never saw the Dives – as one put it, "I don't know what they mean by this St. Lambert-on-the-Dives business as I was there for four days and I never saw any water."[4]

Currie deployed his lead troop, now down to three tanks, at the northern edge of St. Lambert. One tank was assigned to move

---

Swatty Wotherspoon's position. View from position of RHQ on Hill 117 north of St. Lambert looking to the south. In the distance can be seen the high ground of the Forêt de Gouffern which American forces reached on 19-20 August, while in the left middle ground is the tower of the keep at Chambois, a landmark visible throughout this part of the valley of the Dives. St. Lambert is just beyond the trees in the right middle ground. Hill 117 was the key to the Regiment's defence of this area and Swatty Wotherspoon held it with determination. PHOTOGRAPH BY DIANNE GRAVES.

141

The little bridge at St. Lambert. Road leading to the bridge over the Dives at St. Lambert. In 1944 there were actually two small bridges over the river, which was divided at this point in its course. There is now only one channel and one bridge. This road and bridge offered the best escape route for the armoured and other vehicles of the two German armies trapped in the Falaise pocket and was the scene of bloody and vicious fighting for three days in August 1944.
PHOTOGRAPH BY DIANNE GRAVES.

down the D 13 with the Argylls, while the remaining two were sent down the long slope to check out the mill and the chateau by the river bank. The Sherman entering the village got about "three hundred yards into it" when it was hit by an AP round. The crew bailed "out in a hurry because we were rather expecting something like that," Trooper Wayne Spence remembered.[5] The turret crew got away safely but the two drivers were wounded by a second AP round, which hit the tank just as they were emerging. This brought the advance to a halt but Currie, who had gone forward on foot with the infantry, had spotted the opposition, "a Mk IV and a Tiger" at the southern end of the village.[6]

Captain John Redden's tank was squadron rear link and positioned some distance back, behind the crest of 117. Losing contact with Dave, he left his own vehicle and ran to Currie's command tank and moved it forward to find his commander. As the Sherman came over the crest of the hill, Redden recalled, "we have a Mk IV Jerry at about 50 yards with his gun pointing away from us. Roy Campbell was the gunner but we had HE in the spout [in the gun] so we just thumped on the [German tank's] sprocket and then laced him with about 6 AP rounds looking for the ammo bin and the engine. He brewed up."[7] This was the Regiment's first confirmed tank kill and Currie's crew got the colonel's prize – a bottle of rum.[8]

At the same time that the first Sherman had gone into the village, Corporal Swede Thuesen and another tank were checking out the buildings along the river bank at the northwest edge of the village. Swede "was looking around" from his hatch but "had my head out as little as possible" when he was hit in the shoulder by a sniper.[9] "I wasn't wounded much," he recalled, "if it had been a little lower, it would have probably hurt the collar bone or the shoulder bone" but "it hardly cut my uniform." As

the wound "didn't bother me," Swede decided to continue on. There were German vehicles and bodies in the vicinity of the mill and château but he could not see any live enemy, so Dave ordered him to come into the main part of the village. Thuesen moved down the D13 and was just coming around the first C Squadron tank that had been hit when his Sherman was brewed up by an AP round. Swede was "shot in the chest and got shrapnel in my face which knocked some teeth out and broke my jaw so I couldn't talk." The tank burned and, as Swede remembered, the crew bailed out quickly:

> For years we had practised how to get out of a tank and, if we hadn't practised that, we would never have gotten out. I guess I was probably knocked down a little on the stand inside the tank. My gunner, he got out before me, he got out over top of me so I must have been pushed down. I felt something lukewarm running down my chest and stomach. I managed to get out and get the earphones off and I got on the ground. The Germans were shooting at us with small - arms fire and we could hear it hitting the tank. We stood behind the tank and none of us got hit but the drivers got burned. The tank brewed.

His troop leader, Lieutenant Jack Roberts, brought his tank down to cover the crew and they managed to get out of the village on foot. Swede, that tough old Danish cowboy, was angry about the whole business – after four years of waiting he had just gotten started and now he was out of the war.

The infantry took over the lead. With Lieutenant Gil Armour's No. 14 Platoon in the advance, the Argylls moved into the village and began clearing out the houses on either side of the D 13. There was little resistance but the Argylls took their time, one section covering while another moved forward and then the two sections reversing their role. As they neared the crossroads at the southern end of St. Lambert there was no sign of the Tiger but Armour spotted a German Panther tank beside a building and called for volunteers to help him destroy it. After a brisk little action involving Armour exchanging blows with the German tank commander, who left the vehicle, and a grenade lobbed in the open hatch, the Argylls "kept watch over the tank until a Piat was brought up to finish it off." This quieted down the opposition at the south end of the village and Dave brought his tanks in to support the infantry.[10]

By mid-morning St. Lambert was cleared and Wotherspoon reported to brigade that the Regiment was "established" in the village.[11] Dave now positioned his force to defend his acquisition. He placed Armour's platoon at the southern crossroad with three tanks in support but withdrew the remainder of his tanks and B Company to the northern end of the village where he established his headquarters. He had about fifty infantry and twelve tanks left and, as the Germans seemed to be coming in from the west, he placed his Shermans in positions that offered good fields of fire in that direction.[12]

While Currie and his men were at work in St. Lambert, Guy Simonds held an important O Group at Kitching's headquarters. Earlier in the day Crerar had ordered Simonds to "seal off the front from Trun to Chambois" and, with the anticipation that the German forces in the pocket would soon be destroyed, Simonds was also "to carry out active reconnaissance to the north-east in the direction of Vimoutiers." During the conference, which began at 1100 hours, Simonds translated these instructions into orders for the commanders of his four divisions (Foulkes of 2nd Infantry Division, Spry of 3rd Division, Kitching of 4th Armoured and Maczek of 1st Polish Division).

The "general outline" of the corps plan was that "when the encirclement of the German forces was complete and they had either been captured or destroyed," 2nd Canadian Corps would "face east and pursue the Boche." Simonds then got down to the details: 2nd Division was to move east from Falaise and "take over the North[ern] portion" of 3rd Division's area "along the line of the river Dives" so that Spry's division "would be thicker on the ground and [able to] close all enemy escape routes." The armoured divisions got the actual job of sealing the pocket. Kitching's 4th Division "was to concentrate their attention" in the area "from inc[lusive] Trun to excl[usive] the town in 3526" while Maczek's Poles were responsible "from incl[usive] town in 3526 to incl[usive] Chambois and Pt 262 in 4242." These orders require some clarification to make them intelligible. The "town in 3526" was the hamlet of Moissy, unnamed on Allied maps, located on the Dives between Chambois and Trun while "Pt 262 4242" was an elevation marked "262" northeast of the hamlet of Coudehard in an area of high ground generally called Mount Ormel in 1944 (see map 7, page 145).[13]

Simonds had ordered Kitching to deploy 4th Armoured Division along the line of the Dives between Trun and Moissy but it appears that these orders were not carried out, nor indeed could they have been without a massive redeployment of the division. It will be recalled that, on the previous day, the corps commander had ordered part of the division (4 Brigade and the Algonquins) to clear the area north of Trun. By the morning of 19 August these units were in positions in and around the village of Hordouseaux astride the Trun-Vimoutiers highway. On the movement forward these troops had encountered several small groups of panic-stricken Germans trying to get to Vimoutiers and there had been a number of small but vicious fire fights. Things began to settle down, however, just as Dave Currie entered St. Lambert, and the Grenadier Guards were told early in the morning of the 19th that 4 Brigade "would be stood down until noon on 21 August."[14] This was welcome news to their ears but, later in the day, Brigadier Robert Moncel (who had finally arrived to take over the brigade after a five-day delay) gave them the bad news that they would be advancing toward Vimoutiers the following day according to orders Moncel had received from Kitching. This meant that the greater part of 4th Armoured Division (the three armoured regiments

of 4 Brigade, the Lake Soups and the Algoons) were going to move northeast *away from the Trun–St. Lambert–Moissy position,* leaving the three remaining units of 10 Brigade (the Links, Argylls and South Albertas) to carry out Simonds's orders for the division to occupy the line of the Dives between Trun and Moissy, a distance of some four and a half miles, to block the German escape.[15]

Such a job required infantry and Jefferson, having lost one of his three battalions to Moncel, was very thin on the ground. He must, therefore, have been happy to learn that he had not been forgotten and that some very good infantry were being sent to assist him. At 1130 hours on 19 August, 9 Brigade of 3rd Infantry Division received orders to relieve Jefferson's overtaxed command. Consisting of three veteran battalions (the Stormont, Dundas and Glengarry Highlanders, Highland Light Infantry and North Nova Scotia Highlanders), this formation had been fighting since 6 June and had an impressive record. It also had an excellent commander, Brigadier John "Rocky" Rockingham, a competent and aggressive officer whose performance on Verrières Ridge during the ill-fated Operation SPRING was one of the few bright spots in an otherwise dismal day for the Canadian army. Before he could help 10 Brigade, however, Rockingham had to wait until his units, in positions around Beumais west of Trun, were in turn relieved by units from the 2nd Division. As this was not expected to take place until that evening he issued warning orders to his three battalions to be prepared to move that night. Otherwise they spent a quiet day.[16]

The 19th of August was not quiet for the South Albertas. Throughout the morning Swatty had relayed the progress of the fighting in St. Lambert back to brigade and division through his ACV, which had moved up again to 117. When the morning mist had cleared, Wotherspoon discovered that Hill 117 offered excellent observation throughout the valley. There was little enemy movement to be seen but the surrounding woods were full of "small parties of Jerries wandering through."[17] For RHQ first contact with the enemy came when "two Ukrainian stragglers wandered into the lines and on being questioned they advised that there were 20 more of them hiding in a farmhouse" near St. Lambert. A detachment went out and rounded them up. As the morning passed Swatty began to deploy the entire fighting echelon of the Regiment in positions around 117. Lavoie's A Squadron and Recce Troop were posted along the D 13 between Trun and RHQ to guard the line of the Dives and to secure communications with Trun. AA Troop, RHQ Troop and K Troop of 5th Anti-Tank Regiment with its four M-10 self-propelled 17-pdrs. were on the hill itself while Dave Currie's C Squadron in St. Lambert guarded the front. For the moment he kept B Squadron in reserve. The problem was that Wotherspoon did not have enough infantry and, as a precaution, with so much enemy infiltration about, he requested that "all available PIATs be brought forward" to 117.[18]

Down in St. Lambert, Dave found that trying to clear the enemy out of the village was like trying to shovel water up hill – there were hundreds of Germans in the surrounding orchards and hedges and they continued to seep into the place. Many wanted to surrender and the sheer number of prisoners soon became a burden; others were trying to get through or around St. Lambert to escape. Dave was walking back up the street after having secured the crossroads when he heard "rapping on the window there and I looked to see two German officers and I waved them out of the building." The Germans came out and surrendered but one "of them had a little pup" which they offered to Currie, who responded, "No, no, you keep it."[19]

The Germans captured that day were not exactly the elite of the Third Reich. Lieutenant Don Stewart thought they were "awful poor troops" who consisted of "pretty scruffy characters in German uniforms a lot of them were wounded and they didn't look like German soldiers, like you picture the SS or like that, many were Mongolians."[20] There were also Armenians, Kazakhis, Turkomen, Ukrainians, Georgians, all volunteers (willing or not) in the German army and many were not combat soldiers but members of communication, construction, garrison, transport, signals and railway units. One group surrendered with about a dozen American GIs who had been captured somewhere to the south and Jimmy Cooper remembered the Yanks "going around different tanks bumming smokes."[21]

There were, however, Germans in the vicinity of the village that were willing to fight and sniping was a constant problem. Lieutenant Jack Roberts was hit by a bullet which creased his head and had to be evacuated back to Doc Boothroyd at the RAP on Hill 117. Captain John Redden was the next to go – as he recalled, about noon, "a convoy of about 25/30 German trucks came into our position. We nailed a few and then out came a white flag with two Jerries." Redden thought he "would be a hero by conning these bastards into giving up" but he was only part way out of the turret when "some ill-informed Jerry" shot him with a rifle.[22] His driver, Corporal John Lardner, was watching out of his periscope and saw what happened: "A German walked toward us with a white flag but another German came around a corner with a Schmeisser and the guy with the flag went down and ducked out of the line of fire."[23] Redden told the crew to take him to the RAP on 117 as Currie "would need another crew commander and rear link."[24] This was an unusual request but, as Lardner comments, there was no choice as "if we had dropped Redden there that would have been the end of him" and "since he weighed about two hundred pounds, we couldn't get him out of the turret anyway."[25] Lardner told the crew to "open up the guns because I am backing out" and took Redden up to 117.

Wotherspoon was furious. He had already chewed out Jack Roberts, who had been hit by a sniper, for not wearing his helmet. Although Swatty rarely wore a helmet himself, that did not prevent him from giving poor Roberts a "severe written reprimand."[26] He was therefore not in a kindly mood when Lardner

pulled up and, as Redden remembered, gave Lardner "shit for not dumping me on the grass."[27] After the medical people had hauled Redden out of the turret with straps, Lardner returned to St. Lambert as fast as possible because dealing with the Germans was preferable to dealing with an enraged Swatty Wotherspoon. Redden remembered the sequel:

So our MO put condition "Poor" on a tag and I am on my way … in a jeep with a stretcher and good old Jack Roberts as a passenger – he had a head wound. The kid driver was scared to death and was hitting shell holes so I told Jack I could not hang on. Anyway he took over the driving and slowed down every time we hit a rough spot. Jack did save me.[28]

At a hospital in the rear, Redden was examined by Doctor John "King" Kelly, an old friend, who "offered me a shot of booze – what a guy."

Swatty cheered up when a "very heavy convoy movement was observed on the Falaise Ridge," actually the Forêt de Gouffern, which formed the south side of the valley.[29] He immediately ordered all tanks within range to open fire and, once started, this firing went on throughout the day as targets presented themselves. A Squadron, facing the Dives, had the best positions and all four troops plus the four M-10s of H Troop of 5th Anti-Tank, which arrived shortly, spent the day firing at the heavy German traffic. Trooper Egbert Taylor recalled 19 August as being "target practice day."[30] Sergeant Jimmy Gove of Gordie Irving's A-1 Troop recalled that the range was far for the 75 mm gun on the Sherman but

We fired a few HE rounds to estimate time of shot and then noted the time the German transport and troops took to arrive at a crossroads. When we had fired several rounds we got quite good at landing our rounds just at the time they got to the crossroads. Afraid we caused one hell of a lot of confusion because the distances were quite extreme and they must of had a lot of trouble figuring out from where we were firing.

While we were engaged in this we suddenly saw, about two thousand yards in front of us, across the [Dives] river, German soldiers running out from behind haystacks and starting to throw bales of hay off the stacks and exposing armoured vehicles. We immediately switched targets and began lobbing AP and HE into the haystacks. It was chaos; soldiers running everywhere and armoured vehicles trying to get free of the hay bales and get into action. …

We kept moving our tank positions to attempt to stop them from getting a fix on us and it seemed to work as none of our tanks got hit at that time.[31]

It was probably one of these German armoured vehicles that hit Corporal Herbie Watkins's tank from A Squadron. Herbie was in a position closer to the river bank and did not have the

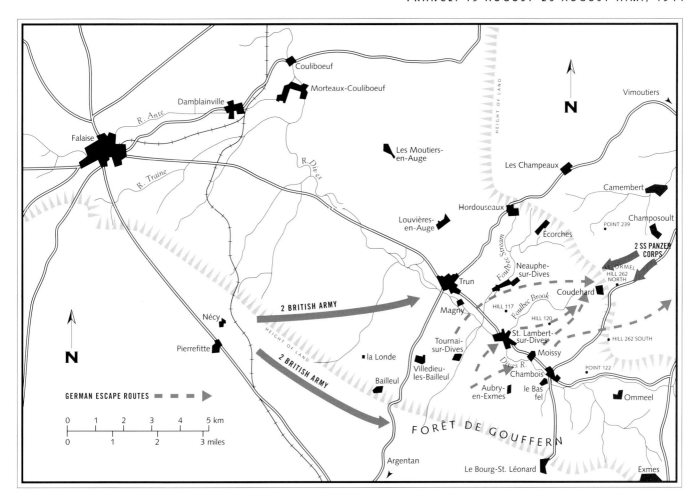

Map 7: The Falaise Pocket, 19-21 August 1944. With Second British Army advancing from the west, First American Army from the south and First Canadian Army from the north, the German armies were encircled in a triangular shaped pocket between Trun, the Forêt de Gouffern and the Dives. The SAR secured St. Lambert and the Poles Chambois on 19 August. At midnight that night the Germans in the pocket began a massive break-out attempt and managed to penetrate both the South Alberta and Polish lines. They were assisted by a "break in" from outside the pocket and, by late afternoon 20 August, had clear routes out of the trap. Far from being able to contain the exodus, both the South Albertas and Poles were soon fighting desperately to maintain their positions.

same good field of fire as Gove. In the early afternoon Watkins asked his troop leader for permission to pull back and "have something to eat" but was told to "remain there and eat behind the tank."[32]After the crew had a hurried meal, Herbie climbed a nearby stack of willow branches to look for targets when "all of a sudden, *whammmm*, and I went flying and a shell went just above me and hit the back of the tank and exploded." Herbie's crew was caught outside their Sherman and the gunner, 21-year-old Trooper Bill Hinson, was killed outright, while a second crew member lost a leg and a third was concussed by the shock of the explosion. The remaining man, Trooper John Sewell, "who had gone behind a barn to do a job," came running up unhurt and asked what had happened only to receive Herbie's honest reply that "it was one time your ass saved your life." Herbie got the tank, which was undamaged, under cover and the two survivors rendered what first aid they could and called for the ambulance which "came up in good time." They then waited for Padre Silcox, who shortly arrived, and the three

of them buried Bill Hinson, an Edmonton boy who had joined the Regiment straight out of high school in 1940, in a corner of the farm yard.[33]

The area around Hill 117 was also dangerous. Trooper Maurice Amyotte was guiding Sergeant Jim Scobie's Crusader to Amyotte's vehicle, which had got stuck on a log, and needed a tow. As they approached the woods, Scobie got out to go forward on foot while Amyotte covered him with a Sten. Scobie "went up one side of a ditch and I went up the other," Amyotte remembered. "We were both hit" by German machine-gun fire and "Scobie took 3 and I took 5 bullets."[34] In response to incidents like these, Wotherspoon established patrols using the Recce Troop's Stuarts and some of Ed Reardon's Crusaders to check out the surrounding woods and bushes, which were full of enemy infantry. Snipers were a constant problem and the Crusaders occasionally cleaned them out by spraying the tree line with 20 mm fire "with devastating results."[35] Trooper John Lakes inspected some of the Germans killed by the Oerlikons and found they "had been ripped apart, with the upper portion facing one way and the lower portion the opposite direction."[36]

Amyotte and Scobie were not the only South Albertas to suffer from Germans infiltrators around Hill 117. A Stuart driven by Trooper Arnold Bateman was hit in the track by a *Panzerfaust* fired from the cover of some bushes. Nine days before, Bateman had escaped from Gendron's tank when it was brewed up near St. Hilaire Farm on 10 August and it was his firm belief, which he expressed numerous times to his new crew, that if a tank gets hit "the best thing you could do was to get out and run like hell."[37] He put this belief into effect on 19 August and was promptly cut down by small-arms fire. The remainder of the crew stayed with the tank, trained the 37 mm and the co-axial .30 calibre on the enemy position and held the Germans off. Seeing their plight Sergeant Doug Prenevost, commanding another Stuart, laid down covering fire so heavy that the crew were able to withdraw safely.[38] Arnold Bateman, age 22, was a farm labourer from Edmonton who had joined the Regiment in 1943. He had married an English girl the previous spring but never saw the son his wife would bear him a few months after his death.[39]

Although they didn't take any casualties on 19 August, the echelon boys had a long and wearying day. As the Regiment was far in advance of the division, they had to travel long distances to the supply points to load up ammo and fuel and bring it down to 117. The problem was to get it to the A and C Squadron crews who were under intermittent enemy fire. A number of attempts were made to take 3-ton trucks loaded with gasoline down to St. Lambert but it was just too dangerous. Corporal Bob Rasmussen actually got to the edge of the village before he was waved off by an Argyll sergeant, who did not want more than a thousand gallons of gasoline anywhere near his position. Finally, Captain Jim Curley and Lieutenant Ed Reardon, commanding AA Troop, devised a shuttle system whereby A-1 Echelon brought the supplies to the hill and they were then transferred to the decks of Reardon's Crusaders in smaller loads and taken to the forward positions. As the D 13 was open to enemy fire, Reardon found a back way into St. Lambert through farm lanes and his crews managed to drop their loads near Currie's headquarters at the north end of the village, where, one by one, each C Squadron tank would pull back and refuel and re-ammunition.

It was hard work and truck drivers, unlike the tank crews, never got a chance to hit back. On his way into Trun to pick up his third load of the day, Bob Rasmussen pulled up for a minute beside Jim Gove's tank north of 117. "How are you, Bobby?" Gove asked and Rasmussen replied, "Jimmy, I am just so goddamned tired."[40] Gove said "I'll show you something that you've never seen before" and handed his binoculars down from the turret. Rasmussen watched as Gove fired HE at a column of German horse-drawn transport over the river and "horses went flying through the air." "Jesus, Jimmy," commented Rasmussen, "how do you get a job like this?"[41]

Around mid-day Swatty began to get messages from Division about the progress of the Poles toward Chambois. At 1255, Division queried whether there had been any contact with "our friends to the left."[42] From Hill 117 Wotherspoon could see the Polish columns moving down the road from Mount Ormel to Chambois, whose ancient Norman keep was clearly visible from his position, and reported five minutes later that the "friends on left," meaning the Poles, were "going straight to COCK [the code-name for Chambois]" and that he was going to make a "left flank attack to cut r[oa]d at COCK."[43] Swatty's intention was to move Darby Nash's B Squadron southwest to an elevation, Point 124, where it would be in a position to either support the Poles at Chambois or interdict the Chambois-Mount Ormel road. B Squadron had not yet got under way when Division informed Jefferson at 1320 that such an attack must be completed "today" and offered to send another infantry company to St. Lambert "if necessary."[44] Apparently Wotherspoon accepted the offer as, within about forty minutes, a scratch company of Links (two platoons from C and one from D Company) under the command of Major R.F. Willson with about fifty-five all ranks) arrived at Hill 117 in TCVs and an APC.[45]

Nash and Willson then went forward to recce the route to Point 124, but within a few minutes Swatty called them back. At 1438, the Poles had reported that they could see the Americans at Chambois and it looked as if they and the Yanks would shortly be wrapping the thing up at that place. At 1500, Jefferson ordered Wotherspoon to "liaise with friends," meaning both the Poles and the Americans, and have them "take care of Cock."[46] The South Albertas and the troops from other units under his command were to go no further but to "Remain firm" at St. Lambert.[47] Swatty decided to retain Willson's company of Links on 117 because he needed infantry, both for defence and to guard the swelling number of prisoners that Dave Currie was sending back from St. Lambert.[48]

Just past noon, things had quieted down in the village and Dave was back in his command post at the intersection at the north end when two jeeps drove up. These vehicles contained No. 1 Canadian Army Film and Photographic Unit, a small seven-man outfit commanded by Lieutenant Don Grant, a former photographer for the *Windsor Star* who had joined the army in 1942. Grant and his men were experienced soldiers who had been recording combat since D-Day and Grant was to receive the Military Cross for rescuing wounded men under fire at Carpiquet in July. They had been in Trun that morning and had taken some good photos when Grant heard a rumour "that we had linked up with the Americans" so the unit "made a run to St. Lambert and found 54 men of B Co[mpan]y, ASH, capturing and controlling the town and taking a terrific number of prisoners."[49] Grant and his men were in the village for about two hours shooting several still shots and some 16 mm film which form a visual record of St. Lambert on a hot Saturday afternoon in August 1944.

Grant recalled that the village and surrounding area were

Brewed up, 19 August 1944. South Alberta Sherman brewed up in the middle of St. Lambert, 19 August 1944, with an Argyll moving forward. This photograph was shot in the early afternoon of 19 August 1944. NAC PA-132192.

full of Germans, and at one point he and his film cameraman, Sergeant Jack Stollery, covered Dave Currie "with handguns" and "backed him up while he went into a building and brought out six Jerry prisoners." The film unit became interested in one Argyll, Private Earl McAllister, who had personally captured one hundred and sixty prisoners by himself. There were plenty of enemy to go around, however and one of Grant's men, Sergeant Milne, shouted that

> there was a whole bunch of Germans running through an orchard. It was a young orchard, we didn't see the top half of them at all, we only saw the bottom half – their legs. The [Argyll] riflemen started to fire, they didn't surrender, they fired back which surprised us. Somebody came up, a tank or something, I couldn't see it, it came up from the other side of the orchard and started to fire but I couldn't see it so I don't know what kind of vehicle it was. They all went away in the direction of the tank.[50]

The vehicle that fired was a Crusader commanded by Corporal Pete Woolf, who had come into the village with a load of gas and ammo on his deck for Currie's squadron. Pete opened up on the orchard with his twin Oerlikons, which, as the *Short History* notes, are "a wicked weapon firing some 450 rounds per minute of 20 mm. HE, with a graze fuse, so that if it touches a twig it will explode and blow a man's arm off."[51] Sergeant Jack Stollery's film camera caught the scene as a rapid series of small explosions scythed through the trees in the orchard, sending leaves, twigs and branches flying. Stollery also recorded the frightened men in the orchard, who appeeared to be Orientals serving in the

Wehrmacht, emerging with their hands up.[52]

A few minutes later, Grant, Stollery, Currie and Woolf were at the northern end of the village when a German truck convoy drove north up the D 13, preceded by a motorcyclist with a sidecar in which was sitting a German officer with a peaked cap and goggles similar to those favoured by Rommel. Again, Stollery recorded the moment on film as the Canadians took cover behind their vehicles and levelled their weapons at the oncoming vehicles – he also caught the enemy officer's eyes which open very wide when he realizes what is happening. The German vehicles were halted without shots being fired and the officer and his driver came forward with their hands up only to be stopped by two Argylls. Grant recalled that the officer "was looking at his map and hoping that what was happening to him, wasn't happening."[53] At that moment, with a 3 1/4 by 4 1/4 Speed Graphic, "a glorified box camera," Don Grant snapped what is probably the most famous Canadian photograph of the Second World War.

Taken from a position in the middle of the intersection at the northern end of St. Lambert, it shows, from the left: Stollery recording the scene in film; a man in shirtsleeves talking to Dave Currie, who is wearing his helmet and holding his revolver (SAR legend holds that the man is showing off a watch he had just acquired from a German prisoner); two Germans walking up from their vehicles; the German officer, who by now has recovered from his surprise and is looking rather arrogant; and two Argylls, identified as CSM George Mitchell and Private John Evans, holding rifles and with a body posture that does not bode well for the supercilious look on the enemy officer's face. This well-known photograph freezes forever in time St. Lambert-sur-Dives in the early afternoon of Saturday, 19 August 1944, but to Don Grant "it was only one day and one picture and there were other days and other good pictures."[54]

A few minutes later, "there was a bit of a shoot-up at the [southern] end of the village" and "although we got pretty close we couldn't see anything without going into open country … and there was no cover."[55] Knowing that he "had some excellent material and a long way to go back," Grant and his men left St. Lambert about 1500.

The "shoot-up" signalled a renewal of the fighting in St.

Somewhere in France, 1944. Perhaps the best known Canadian photograph of the Second World War. Taken by Lieutenant D.I. Grant of lst Canadian Army Film & Photographic Unit, it shows the surrender of a German column at the north end of St. Lambert-sur-Dives at about 1400 hours, 19 August 1944. On the left is Sergeant Jack Stollery of Grant's unit, recording the scene on film. An SAR, wearing a white shirt, is talking to Dave Currie, who is holding a pistol and wearing his steel helmet. In the centre are three surrendering Germans, including an officer with high boots and goggles, identified only as Hauptmann Rauch. Standing with their backs to the camera are two members of the Argyll and Sutherland Highlanders, identified as CSM George Mitchell on the left and Private John Evans on the right. NAC PA-111565.

Somewhere in France, 1997. Shot from the same place as Grant's famous photograph, this scene shows the north end of the village as it appears today. On the left, approximately where the path from a house joins the street, was where Dave Currie stood fifty-three years before. The Regiment has erected a memorial just to the right of the concrete telephone pole across the street from where Dave Currie stood. The D13 is no longer a dusty chalk road but a modern highway. PHOTOGRAPH BY DIANNE GRAVES.

Lambert. By now it was mid-afternoon and the situation began to deteriorate as seemingly hundreds of Germans poured in and small fire fights broke out. There was no logic to the German attacks, they would flare up and just as quickly dissipate. Sometimes the enemy would disappear, other times they would fire a few shots and then surrender. "We were scrambling around a lot" with the tanks, Corporal Bob Fairhurst recalled, "trying to shake the Germans off and get better firing positions."[56] Some of the Shermans, which had not moved for some hours, had run down their batteries and Ed Hyatt was horrified when his Sherman could not be started to get out of the way of German AP fire. "They pulled up an anti-tank gun," he remembered, "and fired one over the top of the turret, one in the ground, and the third one right into the turret."[57] The round did not penetrate and nobody was hurt but the crew bailed out and took cover in a nearby house. They returned after dark, got the vehicle started and removed it to safety. Hundreds, perhaps thousands of Germans, were in and around the village and at one point "late in the afternoon," Dave Currie recorded, "the tanks were running around in circles firing at one another to keep the enemy from climbing on top of them."[58] Just to make matters more lively, St. Lambert now began to come under German artillery fire. As if all this wasn't bad enough, Dave got a call on the wireless from Captain Tommy Barford, the SAR quartermaster. The brigade quartermaster had been pressuring Tommy to account for certain items of issue known as "attractive stores." "Dave, can you give me the number of your binoculars," Tommy asked in an apologetic voice, "brigade wants to know."[59] "Sure, Tommy," was the polite reply, "but I am a little busy now and I will have to call you back."

By this time, however, the Regiment had artillery support. The 4th Division gunners had been left lagging behind during the rapid advances of the last two days, but the field and medium regiments started to come into range midway through the afternoon and the corps artillery not long after. Assisted by Captain Fred Clerkson, the FOO for 15 Field Regiment, Wotherspoon began to call down fire on the many targets he could see across the Dives. Swatty loved calling down fire, which was "great fun," and with Clerkson's help would try to arrange a fire plan "so that they'd be firing on certain roads and concentrate all the Jerries into an area" and then "we would bring down the [heavy] corps artillery and as much additional [artillery] down on that one spot, and the pyrotechnics were wonderful to see."[60] On the south side of the valley, the Americans were also in a position to bring the valley under fire and they joined in the activity. Throughout the day Allied aircraft had been at work – more than 1215 sorties were flown on 19 August as the sightings of enemy vehicles "again exceeded the 2000 mark with more uncountable concentrations and panic, chaos, destruction everywhere visible."[61] Hammered by Allied artillery and air attacks, any German soldiers or vehicles trying to move became immediate targets.

In St. Lambert the situation was so bad by the late afternoon

that Dave Currie requested Swatty to bring down artillery fire close to his positions and then "warned everyone to get under cover."[62] When the rounds came in Currie was horrified – he had been expecting 25-pdr. shells from the field regiments which have "very little effect on tanks." What exploded around the village were shells from heavier 5.5 inch guns that could "easily knock out a tank."[63] Dave complained to Swatty that "mediums are falling all around me" but Wotherspoon replied, "Is it killing more Germans or more of your people?"[64] Dave had to agree that "it's killing a lot more Germans" but, understandably, he didn't much like it. "We were lucky and suffered no casualties," Currie recalled, although "it had a very devastating effect on the Germans and gave us much needed respite, as the tanks were running low on ammunition."[65] One by one the Shermans were pulled in from their positions and brought back to squadron headquarters at the northern end of the village where they were refuelled and re-ammunitioned by Ed Reardon's Crusader shuttle service.

The Poles were now closing on Chambois. To accomplish the objectives given to him that morning Maczek had sent part of his division to occupy Hill 262 and the other part toward Chambois. At 1755, Major H. Zgorelski, the commander of the latter force, reported that he was about to put in an attack on the village. The Poles made good progress and were hampered more by the rubble and destruction caused by air attacks than by the enemy. The lead Polish company was in the middle of the town when they spotted a German force advancing towards them. A machine gun opened up and the enemy threw themselves on the ground, but in a few minutes got up "raised their hands and waved white handkerchiefs."[66] It was only then that Poles realized that these men wore different uniforms and their "tin hats were of a different shape" – then it hit them: "Americans!" Zgorelski went forward to meet Captain Laughlin E. Waters, G Company, 359th United States Infantry Regiment, 90th US Division and in minutes happy Poles and GIs were mixed together and a Polish witness remembered that the Americans patted "them on the back, passing around 'Lucky Strikes' and making a lot of noise."[67] At 1950 hours Zgorelski reported that Chambois was in Allied hands. The two commanders made joint plans for its defence; the Poles turned over 1500 prisoners they had picked up to the Americans and in return began to receive those wonderful American rations. No attempt appears to have been made, according to Simonds's orders, to secure the hamlet of Moissy a mile and a half up the D 13.

Matters in St. Lambert, however, had not improved as a seemingly inexhaustible stream of Germans kept wading across the Dives and entering the village. Between 1800 and 1900 Wotherspoon reported to Jefferson that he "must have relief in form of infantry" as "unless relief comes, Germans will move back in."[68] Infantry were the key to the problem. In the late afternoon Swatty had received C Company of the Argylls but sent them down to St. Lambert along with the scratch company of

Links that had arrived earlier as Currie would need the flat feet during the night. At 1908, Wotherspoon elaborated on the situation to Jefferson:

> 29 Recce now attacked and has been attacked all afternoon by co[mpan]y after co[mpan]y of enemy inf[antry]. Must be fought for few minutes before surrendering. Recce elements reached a point just minus of Cock. One child from LW dispatched to hold Rooster. Can we establish P[risoner of W[ar] cage in area Rooster. Cannot cope with present number of P[risoners of] W[ar].[69]

The increasing number of prisoners was becoming a problem. Most of them surrendered in St. Lambert and Currie sent them back to Hill 117. Swatty estimated that he received two thousand prisoners during 19 August but brigade refused his request that the provosts come forward and set up a prisoner "cage" or compound near his position and he was forced to guard them with his own limited manpower until he could arrange to have them taken back to Trun in any available vehicle.[70] Fortunately, most of the prisoners were very passive and thankful to be out of the war – an Argyll who arrived that afternoon remembered one of them "playing *La Paloma* on a squeeze box. I'll never forget that wistful tune."[71]

When they entered St. Lambert Currie sent Major Gordon Winfield's Argyll C Company south down the D 13. Winfield was to recce the situation south of the village and possibly make contact with the Poles who were supposedly in Moissy, and if not there, in Chambois. The Argylls started down that dusty highway but ran into trouble, as one remembered:

> The road [D 13] was full of wrecked and abandoned vehicles but except for some enemy shells falling into St. Lambert, there was no direct opposition. We had gone as far as Moissy by which time it was quite dark, when we were fired on by small-arms. We couldn't tell where the fire was coming from so hit the ditch. Major Winfield and others were hit by this fire and by enemy grenades thrown at us while we were in the ditch. I ended up on top of an ant hill and the nasty little buggers bit me everywhere![72]

The company evacuated their wounded and then headed back to St. Lambert about midnight. Although they had no way of knowing it at the time, C Company of the Argyll and Sutherland Highlanders of Canada (Princess Louise's) has good claim to being the Allied soldiers who came the closest to actually closing the infamous Falaise Gap.

As the sun began to set, Currie co-ordinated the defence of the village. Armour's platoon of the Argylls' B Company held the intersection by the *mairie* while the remainder of B Company was positioned near the main bridge over the Dives. One Links platoon commanded by Lieutenant J.A. Dunlop held the Château de Quantité and a small knoll near it that bordered the Dives. The remainder of the infantry were positioned midway into the village on either side of the D 13. Three South Alberta tanks were stationed to support Armour, and the remaining vehicles were placed in positions to support the infantry, some midway into the village, some near the Château and the small knoll north of it, and the rest around the northern intersection near Currie's headquarters. A Lincoln and Welland private remembered that in the dark the infantry "had no idea of what the country looked like but we could see the tanks and our job was to protect them."[73]

Wotherspoon also made preparations for the coming night. Early in the evening he sent Darby Nash's B Squadron, which had been in reserve for most of the day, to Point 124. This was a risky move on Swatty's part as Nash's new position was in the middle of orchards and woods that would provide cover for enemy infiltration. From Swatty's point of view, the benefit balanced the risk as Nash would be able to interdict any Germans that moved up the Chambois-Mount Ormel road or got past Currie's blocking position at St. Lambert – in Swatty's opinion, "it was a good place to have part of my force."[74] He was also expecting Rockingham's 9 Brigade to arrive that night and was confident that he would soon be able to provide infantry support for Nash. Possible infiltration around all the Regiment's positions did concern Swatty and he asked for "art[iller]y fire all night."[75] This request was at first refused but later granted.

Around the large, flat field on top of Hill 117 Swatty deployed "4 Shermans, 5 Stuarts, 4 Crusaders, 4 17 pr SPs [M-10] and 3 scout cars, some 80 all ranks" into a defensive perimeter.[76] The tanks and M-10s were placed in firing positions and the spaces in between them were held by "personnel manning ground posts with [.30 calibre] Browning and Brens augmented by patrols." The crews of the M-10s dismounted their larger .50 calibre machine guns and incorporated them in the defence layout. As wireless communications were starting to fade again the ACV was sent back to Trun to act as a relay station. Wotherspoon was anticipating trouble but, since 9 Brigade would be moving in to help out, he was confident. His last message that Saturday, sent at 2345 hours, indicates that his impending relief was on his mind: "Warn people expected tonight to watch out for snipers."[77]

All in all, it had been a good day for the Allied cause. The daily intelligence summary of First Canadian Army issued at 2200 hours stated that, with "the closing of the gap between Chambois … and the Forêt de Gouffern the last escape route is gone."[78] There had been considerable fighting in the areas held by both armoured divisions but it was fairly obvious that the Germans were disorganized and many appeared to want only to surrender. With the trap now sprung it would simply be a matter of locking it shut, mopping up the remnants, and the fighting in Normandy would be brought to a very successful conclusion. The future looked bright and Eisenhower, Bradley and Montgomery already had their gaze fixed on the next phase of the campaign – the advance to the Seine.

The Germans had other ideas. What Allied commanders did not realize was that, on the night of 19 August, the most combatworthy divisions of the two encircled German armies were still west of the Dives River. To Allied intelligence staffs the German escape attempt appeared to be one continuous eastward migration, but there were actually three separate movements out of the pocket. The first had started before the retreat had officially begun on 16 August and it was a clandestine evacuation by some prescient commanders of their echelon and non-combatworthy personnel. The second movement occurred between 16 and 19 August and included two infantry divisions, five panzer divisions and a great mass of rear echelon, service, garrison and other miscellaneous non-combat units. They started in an orderly manner but Allied advances and air power had quickly turned their retreat into a rout. The five panzer divisions, being fully motorized and positioned near the eastern edge of the pocket, had the best luck and managed to save most of their personnel, if not all their equipment. The infantry and the rear echelon troops, dependent on horse transport or miscellaneous vehicles, got caught, lost cohesion and degenerated into a milling mass of small groups either trying to escape, surrender or simply take cover and do nothing – these were the troops that the South Albertas had encountered throughout 19 August. There was a third group of German units still in the pocket, however, who were a much tougher proposition and, as darkness fell on 19 August, they were about to make an organized attempt to break out that would constitute the third and final movement out of the pocket.[79]

German commanders knew what had to be done and how to do it. The *Wehrmacht* had acquired considerable experience on the Russian Front breaking out of encirclements and had developed a simple but effective technique for this most difficult of military operations. The weakest point on the encircling perimeter was selected, it was attacked both from without and from within the pocket and, once a gap had been made, it was held open by strong forces while the encircled troops moved to safety. *Feldmarschall* Walter Model, von Kluge's successor, began to put this technique into effect as soon as he assumed command on 18 August. The 2nd SS Panzer Corps (2nd and 9th SS Panzer Divisions), which had withdrawn to Vimoutiers, was ordered to attack westward from the following day to keep open an escape corridor for the encircled forces, but Allied aircraft, traffic congestion and fuel shortages delayed this attack twenty-four hours. Late on 18 August the German commanders inside the pocket concluded that the trap had been closed (actually it hadn't) but that the encirclement was still loose. The senior German officer inside the pocket, *Generalleutnant* Paul Hausser, decided that his forces would have to make their break-out during the night of 19/20 August in conjunction with 2nd SS Panzer Corps' attack into the pocket the following day – the junction point of the two forces would be the area around Mount Ormel.[80]

At last light on 19 August the German forces in the Falaise Pocket consisted of the remnants of six panzer divisions, seven infantry divisions, one parachute division and some fragments from other fighting units. These were the combat troops but there was also the residue of those Germans who had tried to retreat over the last three days who by now had degenerated into "a mass of stragglers, service elements, and trains."[81] By this time the pocket had shrunk to an irregularly-shaped area of about twenty square miles bordered on the east by the Dives between Trun and Chambois, on the west by a line running from Trun through the villages of la Londe and Bailleul to the Forêt de Gouffern, and on the south by the Forêt itself. Inside this area were perhaps 65,000 to 70,000 men with between one hundred and one hundred and fifty AFVs. For three days they had been under air and artillery bombardment but the combat troops had minimized their losses by staying in camouflaged positions, firing only when fired upon, and moving only after dark unless it was absolutely necessary – it was probably one of these units, hidden behind haystacks, that Gordie Irving's troop had disturbed just west of the Dives during that day. These experienced soldiers stayed under cover as best they could and were quite satisfied to let the "stragglers" from the second movement take the weight of Allied air and artillery attacks. A member of one panzer recce battalion reported that "the horse drawn units around us were breaking up" while his unit "was spending a reasonably peaceful night in a meadow."[82]

Conditions within the pocket, however, were deteriorating – supplies, particularly gasoline, were almost non-existent and wireless communication had broken down. The concentration of troops was an advantage, however, as command could be exercised on a very immediate level. One German officer recalled that by 19 August his division's staff had been reduced to two men – the divisional commander and himself – who sat on one side of a farmhouse kitchen table while the corps commander and his sole remaining staff officer sat on the other side. This being the case, it did not take long for Hausser to inform his subordinates early on the morning of 19 August that the break-out would take place that night.[83]

At 0700 that morning, while Dave Currie and C Squadron were starting to clear St. Lambert, Hausser appeared at the slit trench which was the headquarters of *Generalleutnant* Eugen Meindl's 2nd Parachute Corps. Meindl, a veteran of fighting in Norway, Russia, Italy and France took one look at Hausser's face and said "the lid's shut tight now! Which means, I suppose that we'll have to try and shove it up again?"[84] "That's just what I have come to talk to you about," replied Hausser and the two officers then drew up plans for a break-out attempt to begin at midnight.

Meindl's paratroops, about 2000 strong, would lead the attempt. After crossing the Dives on foot under cover of darkness, they would move toward Mount Ormel, where at first light they would open a breach through the Allied encirclement and meet up with the 2nd SS Panzer Corps attacking from the east to support them. Similarly the 353rd Infantry Division would cross the Dives and take and hold Hill 262 South. This vanguard would be followed by the remaining panzer units, who would cross the river either at St. Lambert or Chambois and, using farm roads and lanes, escape through the breaches already opened. Last would come the infantry divisions, who would bring up the rear and follow the established routes to safety. All troops would travel light and only a few anti-tank guns were to be taken along. All other artillery pieces would be destroyed after they fired their remaining rounds during the day of 19 August and then the gunners would join the breakout. This is the reason German artillery fire landed on Dave Currie's force during the afternoon of 19 August.[85]

St. Lambert was vital to the success of the German plan. There were only three bridges across the Dives (at Trun/Magny, St. Lambert and Chambois) capable of bearing tanks. Hausser knew that Trun was in Allied hands although, because of confusion inside the pocket, he apparently did not know that Chambois had fallen during the evening of 19 August. The bridge at St. Lambert was the best bet for his motorized forces and, throughout the afternoon and early evening of 19 August, while Currie's men were fighting in the village, German recce troops had cautiously investigated the Dives around St. Lambert, being careful not to draw fire. Darkness had fallen and Meindl's paratroops were assembling in small groups in the woods west of the Dives when the commander of the reconnaissance battalion of 1st SS Panzer Division sent a wireless message describing the available escape routes back to his divisional headquarters. It ended with the sentence: "Our crossing stands or falls at St. Lambert."[86]

St. Lambert, 19 August 1944. Photograph by Lieutenant D.I. Grant taken from about midway in the village looking north up the D 13. The wreckage of a German convoy is strewn about and the damage caused by artillery fire is evident. This was only the first day – things would get much worse in St. Lambert. The inset, an enlargement of the centre of the photo, shows a column of German prisoners under guard by Argylls being marched to the temporary SAR PW cage on Hill 117. NAC PA-152373.

Their War Diarist records that, for the South Albertas, the night of 19 August 1944 "was rather hectic with considerable infiltration by enemy infantry."[87] The author of these words could not know it at the time but this was a masterpiece of understatement for during that "hectic" night Meindl's men crossed through the Regiment's positions. The paratroops had moved close to the Dives at 2230 hours and small scouting patrols were sent on ahead followed by the main body of four regiments, broken down into smaller groups. Meindl accompanied a detachment that moved immediately behind the forward elements but his party had only moved a few yards when they came under fire from tanks "patrolling the D 13" and "well placed fire with 2 cm. cannon."[88] Progress was slow as the Germans frequently had to take cover. "Luckily," Meindl recorded, "the enemy was letting off illuminant shells" and this "enabled us to find the spots not being fired over and creep through." Just past midnight, Meindl reached the Dives, where he encountered the advance guard, "who had found a shallow spot south of the mill [of St. Lambert]," and although "it was a nasty job getting the whole crowd across the stream without lights, noiselessly," it was done. Almost immediately the paratroops encountered "three tanks standing on a little knoll" and detoured south around them only to encounter a fourth tank which "opened fire at a distance of thirty metres." The Germans hit the ground and, "alerted by the sound of running footsteps," the "enemy tanks all opened fire." Fortunately for the Germans it "was too high and went over our heads."

The paratroops were pinned but at that moment "there was a mad shooting match on the part of the enemy infantry in St. Lambert" which distracted the tanks and so, "centimetre by centimetre," the group crawled around the tanks so close that they could hear "the crews talking to one another." Then, "all of a sudden other tanks opened fire" which "must have been positioned along the edge of the heights to the rear … on Hill 117" but, again, luckily for Meindl and his men, "their fire was directed towards St. Lambert." The paratroops, sizing up the positions of the tanks, then turned northeast, moving along the bushes and hedges that bordered the Dives until they came to the junction of that river and the Foulbec stream. They followed the stream-bed north of Hill 117, but, at a point where a lane leading from the hill to Neauphe-sur-Dives crossed the Foulbec, they were pinned by fire from another tank, which "fired tracer trajectory." It was now almost 0400 hours and, as it would soon be growing light, the German general began to get worried. The group made another detour around the tank and continued northeast along the stream, their movement aided by confused firing that broke out in St. Lambert and Neauphe-sur-Dives, and by a morning ground mist created by the hot, humid weather. Toward dawn, Meindl recorded, a "soft, light rain began to fall and enveloped us in its folds," and this "was very welcome." By 0530 he was in the Polish sector near Coudehard but his party was trapped for nearly two hours by three Polish tanks positioned at the end of the ditch in which they lay.

Around 0730, violent shooting broke out in the vicinity of Mount Ormel and the Polish tanks withdrew. Meindl could recognize the characteristic sound of the German MG 42 machine gun, called the "Spandau" by Allied troops, which had a rate of fire so fast that it sounded like a zipper being pulled. He also noted that "the style of shooting" in short bursts was characteristic of "my paratroopers." Next came the "wham, yee-ow!" sound of 88 mm air burst and it was clear to him that heavy fighting was taking place in and around Hill 262 North. At 1130 he made contact with Hausser, who had followed him out with another small party, and as Allied artillery fire was now coming down, the two crouched in a shell crater to plan the next move. Hausser agreed with the paratroop general's plan to circle around the Polish position and attack it from the north and Meindl immediately undertook this task. His four regiments had become scattered in the night – some men had broken out in small groups, others had been pinned down west of the Dives – but he gathered up all the combat troops he encountered, put them under any available officers, and set them to work encircling the Polish position. By late morning this task was well in hand.

Giving credit where it is due, Meindl's penetration of the South Albertas' positions during the night of 19/20 August was a first-class piece of infantry fieldcraft that succeeded from a combination of luck and skill. Meindl was fortunate enough to ford the Dives at the St. Lambert Mill, the junction of A and C Squadron's positions. He wisely avoided the heavily-defended Hill 117, working around it using the cover and direction provided by the Foulbec stream to make his way into the Polish sector. Given the amount of ground the Regiment had to cover – the four Shermans of Gordie Irving's A-1 Troop alone had a frontage of 300 yards[89] – it was not difficult for the Germans to move through them. Meindl's men were also aided by the dark, mist and rain, and distractions caused by firing in St. Lambert and other places. Not all of his paratroops got through with him; many were stopped and even those that did make it out were so scattered and disorganized that it took him hours to organize an attack.

The biggest single factor working in the paratroopers' favour was that there were no Canadian infantry in position because, contrary to Wotherspoon's expectation, 9 Brigade did not relieve the South Albertas that night. Vision from a tank is bad enough in daylight – it is worse at night, which makes armoured vehicles vulnerable to a stealthy approach by a determined enemy. As one SAR put it, "I could imagine a *Panzer-faust* in the hands of a determined German creeping up on us."[90] Conversely, if a tank crew opened fire on enemy infantry infiltrating their positions, that enemy would quickly realize from the nature and position of the weapons used, that they were facing armour unsupported by infantry. The South Albertas were aware that there was enemy infiltration on the night of 19/20 August but, without the support of infantry, little could be done to stop it except expose their vulnerability by opening fire. Most chose to open fire.

153

In St. Lambert, Dave Currie remembered that, during the night, "there was considerable firing and no one got much sleep."[91] C Company of the Argylls returned from their patrol to Moissy just after midnight and joined their comrades and the Links holding the main street. Not possessing the strength to hold the entire village, Currie had no way to prevent German armour and vehicles from entering St. Lambert under cover of darkness, and it was now that the problem of trying to fight tanks in built-up areas became apparent. Corporal Walter Fengler's Sherman was in the best position near the *mairie* at the intersection of the D 13 and the street to the bridge, but the other two tanks in this part of St. Lambert did not have good fields of fire. A member of Fengler's crew, Jim Cooper, never forgot that night:

Things were quiet at first, we had the radio on and were just shooting the breeze. It got on towards night and we were taking turns on radio watch while the rest of just dozed. About two or three in the morning we heard all this goddamned noise outside our tank. Walt Fengler, our crew commander, looked out and he got back in quickly and says, "Hey, there are Jerries out there … what are we going to do?" We replied that the best thing we could do was do what we were supposed to do – start shooting. Fengler says: "What are we going to use?" We said, "That's up to you, you're the crew commander."

We swung the turret around and fired a couple of shots at vehicles moving behind us, swung around again and opened up with the machine guns and then we shot 75 AP down the road, figuring there might be a tank among those vehicles which we could hear but not see. We were firing AP and then HE and it sure scared the living hell out of the guys in the other [South Alberta] tanks [near Fengler's Sherman]. We set a truck on fire and it must have been full of mortar bombs, Moaning Minnies, and that stuff started going off and you should have heard it.

Fengler says, "Pass me the Sten," and we gave it to him and he started firing out of the turret but it jammed. So he passed it to Young and got another one and was shooting out there. Young went to clear the goddamned thing and it fired and the bullet went right through my leg, between the knee and the ankle. I said to Young: "Jesus, you shot me" and he says, "I'm sorry." It sure hurt some.

We stayed until daybreak and I don't know how much shooting we did because our tank was the only one that could do any shooting because of the way we were positioned. Everything quieted down at daybreak but our radio went dead and we were told to abandon our tank and we did and went in with the infantry. I was evacuated by jeep ambulance in the morning.[92]

This commotion is probably the firing that Meindl saw coming from the direction of St. Lambert just as his group was trying to circumvent Hill 117.

Having got through A Squadron's positions, the German infiltration surged around B Squadron near Point 124. B Squadron, isolated in wooded country with no infantry, had the worst position in the Regiment. The squadron had posted a strong guard but, in "the early morning hours," Sergeant Jim Nicholson recalled, "we became aware of the enemy moving past us."[93] Trooper John Neff became aware sooner than most as, at about 0200 hours, "things had quieted down and I left the tank to do a job that we should all do once a day."[94] (Actually, because of rampant dysentery, many South Albertas were doing that job several times a day.) Neff continues:

I went to a ditch 50 yards from the tank. As I sat there with my pants down I heard a low whistle and a rustle near by. Just then someone fired a flare and there in the ditch not 15 feet away from me was the biggest Jerry I ever saw. … I beat him to the draw, for I had laid my pistol all loaded for bear, on the ground in front of me. I went back to the tank without finishing my job.

Soon afterward the squadron heard tanks moving near them which did not bode well at all.

At 0500, Sunday, 20 August, Wotherspoon informed Jefferson that "friends have not yet arrived" and that there had been much "enemy filtration incl[uding] some tanks which they [SAR] are unable to stop as they are too thin on the ground."[95] At this point, the SAR commander had no idea just how much damage had been done by this "filtration" but it is clear from his next message sent at 0700 that he was optimistic that he would shortly be able to link up with the Poles, supposed to be at Moissy:

Pos[ition]n still roughly same. Isolated fighting by small bodies. HQ under fire by snipers during night. Child [C Company of the Argylls] which came under command last night unable to obtain his objective [Moissy] between Rooster [St. Lambert] and Cock [Chambois]. 29 Recce able to get to their objective and people under command [infantry] will probably do so at first light. Whole front filled with bodies of enemy t[roo]ps. No recce parties from friends [9 Brigade] arrived yet.[96]

During the first few daylight hours the South Albertas' situation was worrisome but not out of hand. Just as Wotherspoon sent the message quoted above, however, the greater part of the German units involved in the break-out (armour and infantry) started to approach the Dives from the west, their movement assisted by rain and mist, woods, sunken lanes, orchards, and the wreckage from the previous days' air and artillery attacks. Between 0700 and 0800 the rain stopped but the sky remained overcast with cloud cover so low that few Allied aircraft would be overhead on this day. As visibility improved the South Albertas began to observe considerable enemy movement across the river. Wotherspoon wanted to call down artillery fire, but at 0745 division informed him that there was to be no "shooting SW of [Dives] River unless definitely recognized enemy" as "12 Br[itish] Corps moving from wood to river."[97] At long last the British Second Army, which had disappeared from the Canadian situation maps for the past five days, was about to re-enter the battle. The prohibition on artillery fire did not sit well with the SAR commander as it was becoming increasingly obvious something big and bad was happening across the Dives. At some time after 0745 he stressed for the third time in four hours that 9 Brigade had not yet arrived and emphasized that he must "have all art[iller]y support possible to hold firm today" – and suggested that "ammunition columns to guns be given highest traffic priority."[98]

It was too late. Over the next forty-five minutes masses of German infantry with some armour attacked the entire line of the Dives between Trun and Chambois with the greatest numbers heading for St. Lambert. The Germans hit the South Albertas between 0800 and 0830 when "waves of German inf[antr]y began moving against [our] positions" although it "could hardly be called an attack as there was no fire plan, simply a mass movement of riflemen."[99] Nonetheless the pressure was serious and the Regiment was hard put to hold them off. At 0845 Swatty informed brigade that, unless "support arrives may be pushed out of pos[ition]s" as a strong "counter attack coming in."[100]

There was little warning in St. Lambert. Lieutenant Don Stewart was shaving behind his tank when someone yelled that the Germans were attacking. Stewart's troop, which was down to two tanks, was positioned to support the two infantry platoons (an Argyll platoon and a Links platoon commanded by Lieutenant J.A. Dunlop) holding the area around the Château de Quantité in the northwest corner of the village beside the Dives. Stewart jumped into his tank, leaving his battledress blouse and personal diary behind as the infantry opened a brisk fire. A German paratrooper, *Gefreiter* Johann Bohnert, who had failed to break out the night before participated in this attack. He recalled rushing forward shouting "Sieg Heil!" and men falling "in droves" but "we used their bodies for cover and also as parapets over which to fire."[101] The two infantry platoons, totalling only thirty men, could not hold and withdrew under the cover of smoke fired by Stewart's Shermans. As the two tanks pulled out, the German infantry pushed forward and Stewart was in trouble:

> As we backed up we backed into sort of a sunken roadway, which meant that our tanks were down so low in this roadway that we couldn't fire the guns. The embankments on both sides prevented us from firing. The German infantry came right up along the edge of this embankment and they were shooting at our heads.[102]

Stewart, like many crew commanders, had given away the .50 calibre machine gun mounted on the turret hatch to the infantry because it interfered with movement in and out of the

tank. The only weapon he could bring to bear was his pistol and he "actually got one of the Germans aiming at him but another got him in the head." The bullet penetrated the front of Stewart's helmet but was deflected by the rubber headband inside and, after creasing his scalp, it emerged from the back of his tin pot. Don was struck unconscious and when he came to, he was near the northern intersection where Currie had his headquarters and where the infantry platoons had firmed up after their withdrawal.

Things were also bad at the south end of the village. A Tiger rolled over the bridge toward the D 13 and "began firing armour-piercing and high explosive 88-millimetre shot into the house used by No. 10 Platoon [of the Argylls] as their headquarters," recorded the regimental historian.[103] The Argylls asked one of the South Alberta tanks stationed in the middle of the village to do something about this Tiger and it pulled from behind a building to get a clear shot. The Tiger fired first and the Sherman brewed up. The crew bailed out but the driver, Corporal George Tourond, was trapped in his compartment until rescued by two Argylls who braved enemy small-arms fire to get the badly burned man free. Unfortunately, Tourond, a 25-year-old lumber worker from Pincher Creek, Alberta, died of his wounds a few days later.[104]

One of the other Shermans at the south end, commanded by Corporal Mickey Ottenbreit, was also hit. Ottenbreit's crew bailed out and worked their way back to the north end of the village under enemy small-arms fire where, on his own initiative, Mickey took over another tank whose commander had been wounded and continued the fight. This tank had been hit

Close call for Don Stewart. On 20 August, Lieutenant Don Stewart's troop was forced back from their position by a massive German attack. As his Sherman withdrew along a sunken road Stewart came under fire from German infantry running along the banks, which were level with his turret. He actually managed to get one German with his .38 revolver but another shot him with a rifle. When Don regained consciousness he discovered that the bullet had penetrated his helmet but had been deflected by the rubber headband and had exited without causing him serious injury. He talked the quartermaster into giving him the helmet as a souvenir. COURTESY, DON STEWART.

the day before and its 75 mm was not in good operating order. It jammed after a few rounds but when Mickey's gunner reached for the clearance tool necessary to fix the weapon, he discovered that it was missing. Although there were German infantry in close proximity, Mickey leapt out and ran to a neighbouring Sherman, borrowed the necessary implement and ran back to his own vehicle. The gunner cleared the 75 and Mickey returned the tool, again under fire, to its owners. A few rounds later his gun jammed again and he repeated the process and in fact was forced to make this harrowing journey several times throughout the day.[105]

As the morning wore on, Dave Currie was forced back from the southern and central parts of St. Lambert and concentrated his infantry and remaining tanks at the north end of the village. There were so many enemy in view that "at one stage," Dave Currie remembered, "I was firing at snipers who were pinging bullets off the top of the tank and I had spotted them so I used a rifle I carried in the tank."[106] His small force was only saved by the fact that the Germans did not want the north end of the village; they simply wanted to cross over the Dives and move east. Currie met any enemy attempts to move up the D 13 with heavy fire and called down heavy artillery concentrations on the area of the bridges – and that was about all he could do.

A Squadron had it a bit better. They were in good cover in positions that had fine fields of fire while the Germans had little protection once they left the tree-lined course of the Dives. As the lines of enemy infantry emerged into the open, A Squadron opened with everything, as Sergeant James Gove recorded:

Immediately in front of us there was a small rise (about 300 yards) and it was over this rise that the first attack came, about a company strength of camouflaged Germans led by an Officer who strode out in front encouraging his men on. We tank commanders opened fire with our .5 inch Brownings (each tank commander had one mounted on his turret) while our gunners opened fire with the 75 mm and the co-driver's .30 Browning. They took to the ground right away and returned small arms fire which while not too accurate did knock out Gordie Irving's .50 Browning. This exchange of fire went on for 15-20 minutes then suddenly stopped. While we were trying to figure out what they were going to do next suddenly we saw several Germans rise from positions to our flanks with rocket launchers (panzerfausts). We immediately engaged them and put them to ground but not before they had hit one of our tanks (my C[or]p[ora]ls) which forced me to break cover and race over to assist them in getting out of there.[107]

The .30 calibre Brownings were the most effective weapon against this type of attack but, as Trooper Bob Seccombe, a gunner in Sergeant Duke Sands's Sherman, pointed out, "We fired so much with the machine gun that the co-driver started laughing because the bullets were dropping down in front of us."[108] The rifling on the barrel of Seccombe's co-axial .30 calibre "was completely gone" so he "changed barrels" and started up again. The German attack was broken up but the enemy started to work their way along the bushes that bordered the Foulbec stream in the middle of the squadron's position.

By 0930, the War Diary recorded, "the situation began to get out of hand as there was just too many infantry."[109] Wotherspoon reported to brigade: "Enemy broken through and heading north" of St. Lambert.[110] Fifteen minutes later, Swatty requested help: "General attack is reported by 29 Recce and are asking for assistance." To beat the Germans off, Wotherspoon moved RHQ Troop's four tanks into positions on the west slope of 117 and they "began to mow down the advancing Infantry."[111] It was not enough so Wotherspoon ordered A Squadron to attack straight down the D 13 to the area of Hill 117. John Galipeau's A-4 Troop participated in that attack:

The Germans had cut off the road between "A" Squadron and Headquarters, and they were attacking. We were to throw them back. Our troop crossed an open field of forty or fifty acres on which grain had been cut with a binder and stooked, took up a defensive position, and launched a counterattack. The Germans came across the field ducking from stook to stook, and the four tanks picked them off with the machine guns. It was just a slaughter.[112]

It was now that Corporal Herb Roulston, a crew commander and one of A Squadron's stalwarts, added to an already great reputation for coolness. Galipeau witnessed the event:

I was loading the machine gun in my tank. All the crew commanders were keeping their heads down as far as possible, with only their eyes above the rims of their hatches – all except Herb Roulston. I looked over through the periscope and saw him out of the turret on top of his tank, sitting with his feet across the opening of the hatch, having a turkey shoot with a captured German rifle, sniping at the Germans running from stook to stook. I said to the troop officer, "Take a look at Roulston."

He took a look, then picked up the microphone and said over the radio, "Roulston, get down out of there. You're going to get shot."

Roulston picked up his own microphone and replied, "Haven't you heard? There's a war on," and stayed right where he was.[113]

Lavoie's men had ended the threat to RHQ, but all along the Dives, the damage had been done. Thousands of Germans were now in and behind the Regiment's positions and the South Albertas were in danger of being cut off. A prisoner revealed that "the idea behind the attack was a mass recce to find any holes in our lines to enable the large force trapped in the pocket to find a way through" and the enemy had found those holes.[114] At 1012, 10 Brigade reported that the enemy was "breaking through" and ordered the Links to get "across as many roads NE of Trun as possible to take care of enemy drifting through."[115] At 1030 heavy fighting was reported in Trun and later messages make it clear that, after Currie had been forced away from the southern end of St. Lambert, the Germans poured across the Dives and into the maze of sunken lanes and tracks that crisscrossed the area between St. Lambert and Mount Ormel.

Canadian and American artillery units shelled this area the entire day without cease. Hundreds of guns were engaged on this work and targets were so plentiful that it "was not uncommon," reported 13th Field Regiment, "to see the regiment engaging targets in one direction, with medium artillery nearby firing in the opposite direction."[116] "The carnage was unbelievable," records the gunners' historian, "as the regiments fired one Mike target after another into the diminished pocket."[117] A "Mike" target was a target engaged by all the guns in a regiment – the 15th Field, for example, recorded firing "three minutes intense" from its twenty-four 25-pdr. guns and then repeating it "thus sending over seven hundred rounds crashing onto a pinpoint target in a little over five minutes."[118] German casualties were heavy and many prisoners "expressed a greater dread of the artillery's massed fire than of fighter-bomber attacks – shells seemed horribly personal and the fires lasted longer than those resulting from dive bombing and strafing."[119]

The enemy escape route from St. Lambert to Mount Ormel ran near B Squadron's positions and Sunday, 20 August 1944, was a bad day for Darby Nash and his men. They had heard movement, including vehicles, during the night and, at first light, Sergeant Jim Nicholson recalled, they discovered that the enemy "were in uncomfortably close proximity to us, advancing along two sides of the field" in which the squadron was positioned "and up the sunken road which ran along to our left."[120] The mist, rain and nearby bushes and hedges made visibility poor but as it grew light the squadron spotted German armoured vehicles and immediately opened fire. Lieutenant "Peachy" Howard's tank of B-1 Troop brewed up a Panther which had stopped on the other side of a hedge – a "single survivor got out … with all his clothing burnt off."[121] Corporal Eden Robinson then knocked out an SPG that "had stopped right beside him."[122] The German armour moved away but there were great numbers of enemy infantry moving around the squadron's positions – so close that, at one point Darby Nash was "scouting on foot around the road hedge" when he "encountered 4 or 5 enemy soldiers running by in front of him not farther than 3 feet."[123] Nash "flopped down" and gave Nicholson's "tank a signal to fire over his head, an action I promptly took."

Many of the Germans were willing to give up and by midmorning Nash had to send B-1 and B-2 Troops to Hill 117 to escort about a hundred prisoners, including a considerable number of wounded, to the Regiment's makeshift "cage." As he moved back with his rear deck full of German prisoners Lieu-

tenant Jack Summers was hailed by Polish infantry heading in the opposite direction. The Poles were not known for being kind to prisoners, particularly if they examined a German's paybook and discovered that he had fought against their country in 1939. The infantry wanted to know why Jack was wasting time transporting prisoners and offered to take them off his hands. The offer was tempting and Jack was cogitating on it when a German sergeant standing directly on the deck behind his hatch said quietly in perfect English, "I beg of you, do not give us to the Poles."[124] Somewhat startled, Jack declined the offer and went on his way. Closer to 117 the two B Squadron troops "nailed another Panther," and, on the return trip, "ran into a whole convoy of Jerry halftracks and trucks" which they shot up and left burning.[125]

While this was going on, B-4 Troop, down to two tanks commanded by the troop leader and the troop sergeant, had moved farther to the east to be in a better position to fire on a sunken road packed with enemy troops. The troop's permanent leader, Lieutenant Dave Mallet, was sick with jaundice at this time and it was under the command of a replacement officer. Corporal Stan Rose was in the troop leader's tank and remembered that "the battery went dead on us and we couldn't traverse the turret … and we couldn't get the engine started."[126] This was always a danger when crews were using the electric motors that elevated the main gun and rotated the turret but not using the main engines enough to keep a good charge in the battery. "A Polish scout car came up," Stan continued, "and a Polish officer spoke to our officer and told us that the Jerries were making a breakthrough." To the crew's amazement, the troop leader then "got out of our tank and into the Polish scout car and left us taking the troop sergeant's tank with him" thus abandoning his crew, already one man short, to their fate in a dead tank with numerous enemy in the immediate vicinity. As if that wasn't bad enough, he later reported the three men "missing, presumed dead" but Stan and his companions made a liar out of the man. "We buttoned down the hatches," Stan recalled, "got the Homelite battery charger going and it was smoking and it looked like we had been burned out so the Germans ignored us and kept moving by our tank." The crew had to forgo easy shots on passing German tanks but, finally, got their engines started, backed cautiously away and returned to the main squadron position. They never saw the officer again, someone dropped by to pick up his belongings, and B-4 rejoiced when Dave Mallett returned to them a short while later.

By late morning, the Germans had infiltrated all along the Dives and secured two crossing places – the bridge at St. Lambert and the ford at Moissy – but, after heavy fighting, had been rebuffed in attempts to take the bridges at Trun and Chambois. Word that the Dives had been forced spread quickly among the encircled forces and a stampede took place as hundreds of motor vehicles and horsed transport, intermingled with armoured vehicles, headed for St. Lambert and Moissy. Wotherspoon

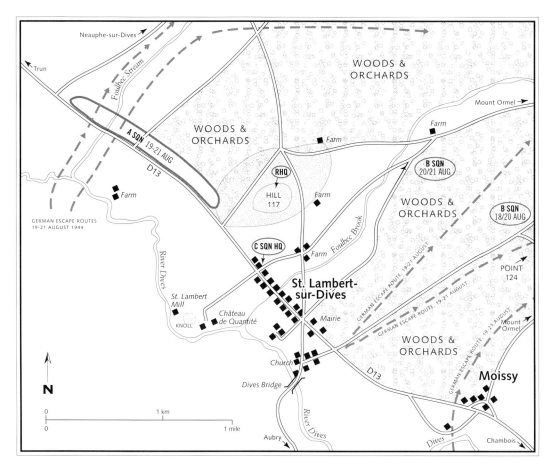

Map 8: The South Albertas' battle, 19-22 August 1944. The Regiment took up positions around St. Lambert on 18 and 19 August. During the night of 19/20 August a large force of German paratroopers penetrated the Regiment's thinly-held lines and were able to break through the Polish positions to the east. In the early morning of 20 August a massive German assault hit the entire area between Trun and Chambois and the Regiment was fighting for its life. B Squadron, isolated to the east, withdrew to a new position but, when no infantry support arrived, was overrun by German infantry on the night of 21 August.

The Poles were in serious trouble. *Generalmajor* Mahlmann, the commander of the 353rd Infantry Division, had managed to cross the Dives at Moissy early in the morning and reached Hill 262 South although he lost almost all his tanks and vehicles doing so. The Poles had not occupied that feature and, early in the afternoon of 20 August, Mahlmann opened up the first clear escape route out of the pocket. It was closed a few hours later by Polish recce units, which forced him to withdraw to the east, but by then Meindl had opened a better route around Hill 262 North. That energetic officer had spent the day assembling small assault groups from the German troops (including the odd tank or SPG) who reached his position near the Mount Ormel area and throwing them against the Polish positions. Many wanted no part of this fight and the paratroop general became disgusted with this "pack of rascals" who "had no thought in mind other

reported "Fighting confused, cannot give number of t[an]ks, Art[illery] fire has been brought down on them."[127] A German artillery officer caught up in the rush remembered that many of the shells burst in the trees where the columns were trying to take shelter and wooden splinters "created dreadful wounds, men rolling, screaming, with torn stomachs" and all "order was gone."[128] *Generalmajor* Heinrich von Lüttwitz, commanding the remnant of the 2nd Panzer Division which was trying to get to St. Lambert that morning, witnessed the resulting panic that broke out as "numerous trains of vehicles ran into direct enemy fire of every description, turned back, and in some cases drove around in a circle until they were shot up and blocked the road." It was chaos as towering "pillars of smoke rose incessantly, from petrol tanks as they were hit, ammunition exploded, riderless horses stampeded, some of them badly wounded. Organized direction was no longer possible."[129] Some German tanks did get through the village and Wotherspoon reported in a few minutes that he was bringing down artillery on enemy tanks northeast of St. Lambert.[130]

than the dash forward with their hands stuck above their heads" whom he could recognize by their "shuffling gait" along the "ditches at the side of the road, ready to throw themselves flat on their faces if a grenade exploded 500 meters away from them."[131] He contrasted them with his paratroopers who were "in tatters … in many cases wounded … dead beat and starving … but despite all still carrying their weapons, very often two or three, still on the job." Enough men were willing to fight for Meindl to put steadily increasing pressure on Maczek's division which now become separated into two groups, at Chambois and Hill 262 North, both fighting hard.[132]

Maczek was also under attack from outside the pocket and at 1055 was forced to report that the armour had broken through his front north of Hill 262 North.[133] Late in the afternoon of 20 August, Meindl succeeded in linking up with the German forces outside the pocket and opening up a clear escape route – over the Dives at St. Lambert or Moissy then by back roads and tracks to the high ground at Mount Ormel and on to Vimoutiers. Both the Poles and the South Albertas were battling desperately but did not have sufficient force to prevent the Germans from breaking out and, in fact, they needed help just to hold their own positions. That help would have to come from 3rd and 4th Divisions and the question is, what were those formations doing?[134]

Under the date of 20 August 1944, the words "confusion", "obscure" and "uncertain" appear frequently in the war diaries, operations logs and other records of the units and staffs of 3rd Canadian Infantry and 4th Canadian Armoured Divisions. The massive German attack that hit the line of the Dives at 0800 resulted in considerable enemy infiltration east and northeast of Trun, which distracted the attention of Kitching and Jefferson from the more serious situation to the south around St. Lambert. At 1012 Jefferson, whose 10 Brigade headquarters were at Trun, ordered the two units in the vicinity (the Links and that part of the Argylls not at St. Lambert) "to get astride as many r[oa]ds out of Trun as possible to take care of enemy drifting through."[135] The two battalions could not immediately comply with this order as they were pinned by further enemy attacks so the job had to be put off until they were relieved by Rockingham's long-anticipated 9 Brigade.

Rockingham had not moved forward the previous night as, by the time he was relieved by units of the 2nd Division, it was dark and he decided to wait until morning. "Many confusing reports [were] received during the night," recorded the 9 Brigade war diary and things didn't improve the following day.[136] The brigade was formed up on the road ready to go at 0800 hours when the first information came in of the German attack and that resulted in a "slight change of plan." Nine Brigade had still not moved at 0945 when Wotherspoon's appeal for help ("Gen[era]l attack is reported by 29 CARR and are asking for assistance") was passed to them by 4th Division.[137]

This did spur things on and, led by the Stormont, Dundas and Glengarry Highlanders, the brigade column finally moved off. The Glens were in Trun by 1118 when they reported that the enemy had broken through "all along the main road … which we are to occupy" and the situation was "very unclear."[138] By prior arrangement between Jefferson and Rockingham, the Glens now passed under command of 10 Brigade and went into defensive positions at Trun relieving the Links. The next 9 Brigade battalion, the North Nova Scotia Highlanders, took up the lead and were just approaching Trun when a report was received that the Germans had broken through to the northeast. At this point 9 Brigade halted while Rockingham went ahead to make an appreciation, which appears to have taken about an hour, and it was not until after 1200 hours that the advance resumed – the last infantry battalion in the column, the Highland Light Infantry, only reported that they were through Trun at 1415. Rockingham was now less than two miles from Hill 117.[139]

By this time, early afternoon, the D 13 from Trun to St. Lambert was infiltrated by German infantry around the area of the Foulbec stream. George Kitching became aware of this problem after he assured Simonds that morning that the road to St. Lambert was clear and the corps commander proceeded down the D 13 "in his scout car," only to be "fired at, fairly decisively, by a lot of German infantry who were on the other side of the river." Simonds returned to Kitching and said, "That was a bloody stupid briefing you gave me about St. Lambert." The corps commander was angry, Kitching recalled, "because Guy Simonds didn't like being shot at."[140]

The German infiltration between Trun and St. Lambert may have been the reason behind Rockingham's decision not to move down the D 13 but instead to turn off in the direction of Neauphe-sur-Dives, twelve hundred yards to the northeast of Hill 117. Whatever the reason, Rockingham did not come forward to Wotherspoon's relief during the afternoon of 20 August but chose instead to take up a position behind the South Albertas that was too far away for his brigade to render them any support. By 1500 the North Nova Scotia Highlanders were in Neauphe-sur-Dives while the Highland Light Infantry stopped in an orchard midway between that place and Trun. The two battalions then did nothing for the remainder of the afternoon, although they encountered small groups of Germans who had crossed the Dives and were making for Mount Ormel. At 1700, to ease the complicated command structure in the area, Rockingham's units were placed under command of Jefferson's 10 Brigade. For the time being, however, the Regiment would get no assistance from 9 Brigade.[141]

Nor would they get any assistance from their own division. After being relieved at Trun, the Links and the Argylls (less the companies with the SAR) were not sent to St. Lambert but ordered to a position northeast of Trun. That still, however, left the greater part of the division (4 Armoured Brigade, the Lake Soups and the Algonquins) in positions around Hordouseaux to the north. The previous day Moncel had warned them that they would be advancing toward Vimoutiers and the Foot Guards led off at first light on 20 August. They had moved as far as Les Champeaux. which the Poles had captured three days previously, when their orders were cancelled and the five units were told to return to their previous positions because "information had been received that a large enemy armoured column was attempting to break through."[142] The "highway was filled with a confused congestion of vehicles as the entire brigade turned around and rushed back to its original position" which was three and a half miles north of Hill 117. The "balance of the day," recorded the Foot Guards historian, "was passed in tense expectation of orders and in observing the awful destruction in the plain [valley] below."[143]

The South Albertas and the troops with them were on their own.

"The boys from the bald-headed prairie."

FRANCE: 20 AUGUST P.M. – 22 AUGUST A.M., 1944

During the afternoon of 20 August things were somewhat quieter around Hill 117. Wotherspoon continued to call down fire from every artillery unit that would respond on the German columns that he could see from his excellent position and was sure he could hold until 9 Brigade finally arrived. He kept the Recce Troop's Stuarts and some of AA Troop's Crusaders busy on continuous roving patrols to the north and east to prevent the Germans from getting through while the remainder of the Crusaders kept up their supply shuttle to St. Lambert. Any movement near St. Lambert was dangerous – on one occasion Pete Woolf was bringing a load of gas and ammo down to C Squadron on his deck when he was surrounded by enemy infantry and had to fight them off before he could go on his way. The echelon trucks continued to bring the supplies forward to Hill 117, but they had to avoid the D 13 and take a circuitous route by way of Neauphe-sur-Dives and then through back lanes onto the hill. Once unloaded, the trucks were filled with German prisoners and sent back the same way.[2]

Prisoners were a constant headache. Throughout the afternoon increasing numbers started to come in, many of them badly wounded, and the commander of the South Albertas had to use a proportion of his limited strength to disarm, search, guard and eventually transport them. Many Germans were anxious to surrender; others were not and would open fire on their own comrades if they attempted to give themselves up. A Waffen SS officer who attacked across the Dives that day admitted under interrogation that, when the men of the group he was with streamed back in the face of overwhelming Allied firepower, he "took up a position at the rear to hold up the retreat and I shot the first one to come along."[3] "Then someone at the rear started to wave a white flag on a stick," he continued.

Some folks come from the peaks and passes,
We're from the land of the waving grasses.
Now, while you fill up your glasses,
We'll continue bumping asses.
For we are the S-A-R!
For we are the S-A-R!

We're the boys from the bald-headed prairie,
We can ride anything that's hairy.
Ride them with, or without, a saddle,
Anything with hair on, we will straddle.
For we are the S-A-R!
For we are the S-A-R!

Fifty years from now, my ladies
When we do this dance in Hades.
We will put the Devil in classes,
We will teach him bumping asses.
For we are the S-A-R!
For we are the S-A-R![1]

"We shot him at a distance of 100 m." After a "second attempt with a white flag had also proved unsuccessful," he got the group moving forward but, in a few minutes, "another white flag appeared, and again we fired at the troops surrendering." A few minutes later, this officer was captured, having killed more of his fellow countrymen than many Canadian soldiers.

This attitude on the part of some Germans made the business of accepting the surrender of large numbers of the enemy a very tricky business. During the afternoon, Lieutenant Robert Burns went down from Hill 151 to bring in a group of Germans who were observed waving a white flag near the Dives. Doc Spaner of Recce Troop, whose tank had been knocked out the previous day, was one of two troopers who accompanied him on this job and he never forgot what happened:

We reached the top of a rise. About 100 yards in front of us, a group of about 30 Germans were gathered around a soldier waving a white flag. The lieutenant stopped us and waved them to come in. There was a disturbance among the men around the flag; an officer (more than a lieutenant) among them was haranguing them in a voice that carried to us, but we could understand nothing. He stepped out from the group and waved our lieutenant to come closer, he obeyed and advanced 10 to 15 yards, we two troopers following. He [Burns] stopped and waved again for the Germans to advance. We were now quite close. The German officer screamed again at his men, pulled a pistol from his holster and aimed. Now we understood that he was ordering the white flag to be lowered. Immediately our lieutenant pulled his gun.

I dropped to my knees, aimed my Sten gun, pulled the trigger and the gun jammed. I heard a round of gunfire, the lieu-

St. Lambert-sur-Dives. View looking west from the D 13 to the Château de Quantité and the knoll which commanded the western flank of Dave Currie's defence of St. Lambert. On the morning of 20 August 1944 a mass German attack forced the Links and Argyll infantry defenders of this area and Don Stewart's SAR troop to withdraw back towards Hill 117. PHOTOGRAPH BY DIANNE GRAVES.

tenant about 100 feet off on my left spun and fell. The rest of the Germans broke into line, the white flag came down and some raised their guns. I could do nothing but throw my gun down and run back to the top of the hill moving in a zig-zag path hoping to escape the bullets coming in my direction. Luckily I escaped ... I never can, nor ever will forget the scene of the Canadian and German officers aiming their pistols at each other on the slopes of a hill in that field in France.[4]

Robert Burns, a married 29-year-old insurance underwriter from Montreal, had served with the Royal Montreal Regiment before coming to the South Albertas in the spring of 1944.[5]

A Squadron was busy throughout the afternoon trying to fight off attacks from Germans who were using cover provided by the bushes along the Foulbec stream to get past their positions. "Several times," Jim Gove remembered, "I took a couple of my crew and with No. 36 grenades attempted to clear out the dried creek bed nearest our position," but "for our trouble we picked up 4 or 5 prisoners and got a few scares from bursts of Schmeisser fire."[6] The problem, Jim continued, was that the squadron "did not have any Infantry with us so it became very difficult to carry out operations among all the trees, bushes, etc." As Guy Simonds had discovered earlier, the presence of Germans in the area made it difficult to get down the D 13. When Don Stewart was evacuated in a jeep ambulance later in the afternoon, the journey through this area was a harrowing experience:

They put us on a stretcher jeep, and George Tourond was on one of the stretchers, and there was a badly wounded German NCO on the other stretcher beside him. There was a wounded German sitting underneath them, and a couple of Canadians, including myself, sitting in the jeep. As our driver took us out, the road back from headquarters to the hospital area was completely cut off by the German attack

and we had to drive right through their lines. There were some of them that were such rough-looking characters that you wondered if they even knew what the Red Cross stood for. Some would raise their rifles as though they were going to have a shot at us. I think the fact that we had wounded Germans riding with us was what saved our necks and allowed us to get through there.[7]

In turn the South Albertas respected the Red Cross and did not fire on German vehicles carrying the international insignia of a non-combatant but there were so many German vehicles with Red Crosses that they began to wonder. Herbie Watkins finally decided that he had enough of all these German medical vehicles going by, and Herbie was feeling somewhat scratchy on 20 August as he had received no replacements for the three men of his crew he had lost the previous day but had been told to stay in his position and fight his Sherman. Herbie did what he could, using his 75 and co-axial .30 calibre on the enemy infantry he could see across the Dives, but avoided firing at Red Cross vehicles. After a while, he decided there "were too many" so he put a round of HE into a German ambulance, which disintegrated all over the landscape in an impressive explosion. His troop leader, Gordie Campbell, was furious because he had issued repeated orders not to fire on ambulances, but Gordie cooled down after a subsequent examination revealed that the vehicle had been used as an ammunition transport.[8]

B Squadron's day, which had started off poorly, did not improve in the afternoon. They had already sent one load of prisoners back to RHQ but shortly after mid-day they had collected hundreds more. Without consulting Wotherspoon Major Darby Nash decided to withdraw the squadron north about a thousand yards to a crossroads of two farm lanes. Swatty Wotherspoon was not happy when he learned of this change although he realized that the B Squadron commander was "perhaps right because there were Germans just swarming around them."[9] Swatty would have preferred that Nash stayed at Point 124 and "called the artillery down on top of his tanks" to deal with the German infantry, but relying on the judgement of his subordinate, he accepted the decision and reported the move to Jefferson.[10] Nash and B Squadron were still isolated but everyone expected that 9 Brigade infantry, which now were in Neauphe-sur-Dives, two thousand yards away, would soon be moving up. Sergeant Jim Nicholson was anxious to see the flat feet come up and kept an ear cocked by "netting into the infantry frequency" with his A set.[11] Soon after moving, Nicholson's crew engaged a Tiger at 3000 yards but didn't "even annoy him." It soon became obvious that B Squadron had moved from pan to fire as the new position "was thickly treed on all sides, and the field of fire was severely limited." The squadron spent the afternoon shooting up columns of "light vehicles" they could seen moving northeast out of St. Lambert and the crews were intrigued by the chatter they could hear on the wireless from the Americans, a few miles to the south. Darby Nash felt "like cutting in and yelling 'How are you coming over there, Yanks?'" but he had to maintain wireless silence.[12]

Church at St. Lambert. Located in the southern end of the village near the bridge, this church was used as a rallying and control point by the Germans who were able to move across the Dives bridge at St. Lambert after they forced Dave Currie back from the southern end of the village on the morning of 20 August 1944.

PHOTOGRAPH BY DIANNE GRAVES.

German traffic continued to move through St. Lambert throughout the afternoon. *Generalmajors* von Lüttwitz of the 2nd Panzer Division and Harmel of the 9th SS Panzer Division used the church as a command post to rally panic-stricken troops and co-ordinate movement across the village which was one big traffic jam. Allied artillery fire made crossing the two small Dives bridges "a particularly ghastly affair." "Men, horses, vehicles and other equipment that had been shot up while making the crossing," wrote von Lüttwitz, "crashed from the bridge into the deep ravine of the Dives and lay there jumbled together in gruesome heaps."[13] "Full speed ahead and across," was how another German soldier put it who traversed the bridge that day, "the river below almost brimming with the bodies of men and horses, and the ruin of vehicles."[14] The Germans were keenly aware of the presence of Currie's force at the other end of the village and, as they moved through St. Lambert, "the panzers concentrated the fire of their heavy guns on the enemy-held houses, which he had turned into fortresses." As targets presented themselves, the South Albertas fired back and they fought so effectively that von Lüttwitz was convinced that he

was under constant attack. "Throughout the whole afternoon," he commented, "enemy tanks tried to break through again into St. Lambert from Trun, while other tanks kept the road leading northeast from St. Lambert under constant fire."[15]

In actual fact Dave Currie was just barely hanging on. He had positioned his five remaining Shermans and his infantry, amounting to about 120 men under the command of Major Ivan Martin of the Argylls, to defend the houses grouped around his headquarters. "This day," Dave later recalled, "was hard on officers," and by the early afternoon he had lost all four of his troop leaders and only five infantry officers were still on their feet: Martin and Lieutenants Dalphe and Whitehead of the Argylls and Captain Dickie and Lieutenant Dunlop of the Links. Dave spent most of his time with the infantry and Dickie remembered that after one of Currie's frequent "visits to our weapon pits, my men felt that nothing would force them off the pos[itio]n."[16] Currie gave the infantry "the feeling of being a part of a team that could accomplish anything" but he "never showed the strain under which he must have been working."[17]

Dave tried to visit his crews at every opportunity. His gunner, Lance-Sergeant Reg Campbell, remembered that "he kept us in the picture at all times."[18] Currie's command style was low key. Dave did not believe in exhortations or dramatics – he

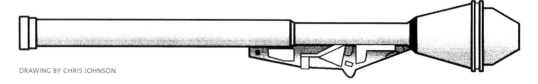

DRAWING BY CHRIS JOHNSON.

Tank killer – the Panzerfaust. Introduced in early 1944, the German *Panzerfaust* (correctly *Faustpatronen*) was a one-shot, disposable infantry anti-tank weapon and the grandfather of all such modern weapons. About three feet long, the first models could penetrate the armour of a Sherman at ranges less than eighty yards. Improved models were constantly introduced throughout the war and the weapon's range and penetration capability increased. The *Panzerfaust* was the nemesis of Allied armoured forces and the Allies never matched it for effectiveness.

would simply show up "very peaceful," tell the men what was happening and go on to the next tank. Trooper Ed Davies remembered that "he would come over, very calm, and say hello to us and ask how it was going."[19] By this time the South Alberta crews stayed in their tanks "pretty well all the time," recalled Davies, and "we didn't move far, only to different firing positions – take position, fire a couple of rounds, change position." "It was pretty scary by that time," and some had trouble coping with their fear. Corporal John Lardner's driver, a heavyweight on the South Alberta boxing team, refused to leave the shelter of his tank for any reason whatsoever and John had to feed him and look after his needs. It takes one kind of courage to step into a ring, and the man had that in spades; it takes another to sit in what could be your coffin and stare death in the face. "We didn't think we were going to live," recalled Trooper Ron Virtue and, this being the feeling, the crews appreciated a visit and a few words from Dave.[20]

What kind of a man was this apparently fearless squadron commander? Swatty Wotherspoon summed Dave Currie up as an officer: "He wasn't a brilliant tactician, but he was very stubborn, and if you gave him an order to do something that was within his capabilities, he would do it, period."[21] Swatty knew that, having told Currie "to stay at St. Lambert, that's all I had to say" and "having said that, he'd stay there." One of Dave's troop leaders, who came to know him very well, summed up Dave Currie, the man and the soldier:

He was a former mechanic from Moose Jaw, Saskatchewan, who never looked for a place in the sun but was content to be just what he was. If I was to describe him, I would say that he was somewhere between Gary Cooper and Jean Beliveau in appearance and stature. He was a quiet and undemonstrative man and a small grin from Dave meant the same as hilarious laughter from another person. Dave was always a very private individual but he was also easy-going and very matter of fact. He gave his orders clearly and distinctly and had confidence in his abilities. Everybody in the Regiment held him in high regard.[22]

Sergeant John Gunderson, who took over command of a troop at St. Lambert after all C Squadron's officers had been wounded, remembered that

just to go up and talk to him was enough to give us confidence. I still don't know how Major Currie did what he did – but without his example I do not believe we could have held out. He didn't give a damn how close the Jerries were, and he always had the same every-day expression, just as if we were on a scheme. He was wonderful.[23]

Dave's example was followed by the men of C Squadron, particularly Corporal Ottenbreit. When Mickey's second tank was knocked out, he and his crew used their personal weapons to continue fighting as infantry.[24]

Throughout that long afternoon Dave's men fired down the length of the village at the Germans, the Links and Argylls trying to hit the German soft-skinned vehicles and infantry, the SAR tanks trying to hit the German tanks and SPGs. Allied artillery fire continued to fall in the area, including a few short rounds that landed on Currie's positions. The streets and lanes at the southern end of St. Lambert became congested with burning vehicles intermixed with dead men and horses. The Germans returned the fire but made no attempt to attack – their goal was to get through the bottleneck of St. Lambert and move northeast as news that an escape route had been opened had quickly spread among the trapped units.

German SPG knocked out in Normandy. The *Wehrmacht* mounted a variety of powerful weapons on the hulls of obsolete tanks to create numerous types of SPGs. Low-slung, well-armoured and well armed, they were dangerous opponents, particularly if in concealed positions. Someone got this *Sturmgeschütz III* in Normandy. SAR COLLECTION.

Occasionally German tanks or vehicles took a wrong turn and drove toward Currie's positions. Red Cross vehicles were usually permitted to proceed – Trooper John Hutchinson remembered a "halftrack that came barrelling across in front of us with … a bunch of guys in there with white flags and bandages on their head. They drove down across the field and out and I guess they were headed back home."[25] In mid-afternoon one German MO requested assistance for his wounded and Currie and Martin, using Lieutenant Al Dalphe of the Argylls as a translator, discussed arrangements with him. In the middle of the conference Dave was called to a nearby tank to speak with RHQ and, while he was inside the vehicle, Martin and Dalphe were killed by an artillery shell that landed almost at their feet.[26]

Dave was now down to three infantry officers and it is probable that at this time he asked Swatty for permission to

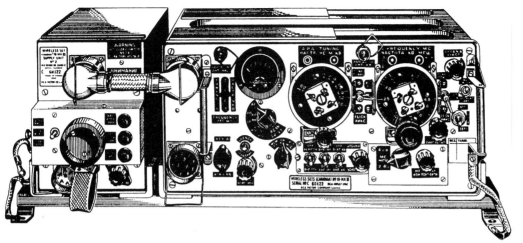

The nervous system. Good communications were essential to armoured units and Commonwealth crews relied on the No. 19 Wireless mounted in their tanks. Manufactured in Canada by Northern Electric, Canadian Marconi and RCA Victor, it was a massive affair with three parts: a High Frequency A Set for long-range communication up to a range of 10 miles; a VHF B Set supposedly good for 1000 yards but more likely 300 yards; and an Intercom for internal communication by the crew.
COURTESY, SERVICE PUBLICATIONS.

Troop and did not come back. Then the J Troop commander went to see what he could see and did not return – it later turned out he was captured by the Germans. There was now only one officer remaining in 103rd Battery, Lieutenant J.R. Flowers commanding L Troop, and Flowers decided to continue on to St. Lambert.[31]

The two troops, eight Ram towers and eight 17-pdr. guns, moved down the D 13 and were near the Foulbec stream at 1400 when they came under heavy German machine-gun fire which wounded the J Troop sergeant and the men in two jeeps driving behind the gunners' column. These jeeps belonged to Don Grant's No. 1 Film and Photographic unit who had decided that "the pictures [from 19 August] were so damn good, we were willing to try for some more" and were on the way back to St. Lambert.[32] The unit's jeeps had followed the Rams down the dusty chalk highway but the tracked vehicles made so much noise that Grant didn't hear the German machine gun that

opened up on us from behind and got my driver in the head and hit all three men in the jeep behind. It blew out the windscreen, spare tire and the glove box on my jeep. I couldn't get my driver's foot off the accelerator and we crashed into a ditch. Stollery in the jeep behind managed to keep going up to a cut in the road up farther. Stollery and I got within hailing distance and we found out that everyone was alive but I was the only unwounded man. I stayed with my driver until an armoured ambulance came up and took him away while the New Brunswick Rangers sent down a couple of bren gun carriers and got the other men away. I then crawled six hundred yards to the other jeep and I had German riflemen periodically sniping at me. I crawled by some Germans in a ditch, one guy with his guts hanging in his lap said "wasser, Englishman" but he still had his rifle so I kept an eye on him. I finally got to the other jeep which was still operable and one of your [South Alberta] tanks was there and the crew commander said "I could see your trouble but I couldn't see who was shooting at you." I started up, tore up a slope and down a slope and then I was out of there. It was a hairy afternoon.

At about 1430 hours, J and L Troops arrived at the northern edge of St. Lambert where, as Flowers later reported,

withdraw from St. Lambert. Wotherspoon told him to stay but it must have been a hard decision for Swatty to make as he knew that Currie would not have made such a request unless the situation was truly desperate.[27] Dave broke the news to his men – John Lardner remembered him telling his crew that "we were staying right here" while Trooper Jimmy Eastman recalled Currie coming "up to the side of our tank and saying 'dig out everything you've got, all the shells – everything you've got, this is it.'"[28] Reg Campbell remembered that "we knew it would be a fight to the finish, but he was so cool about it, it was impossible for us to get excited."[29] Those crews he couldn't talk to in person, Dave reached by wireless – as he later reported, "I called the boys up on the air and told them what to expect and I told them that they were to sit pat because we weren't going anywhere."[30] The "usual answer" came back: "Okay, boss."

It was at this low moment, between 1400 and 1500 hours, Sunday, 20 August 1944, that help finally arrived. Ironically, it did not come from 9 Brigade, which was at this time sitting a few thousand yards to the north, but from the 103rd Battery, 6th Anti-Tank Regiment. This was a corps unit and the gunners' arrival was purely accidental – 103rd Battery had been assigned to Rockingham and had moved at the tail of the 9 Brigade column that morning, but in the confusion of the situation around Trun it lost contact not only with the infantry but also with one of its three troops. The battery commander, a major, did not realize that Rockingham had turned off to Neauphe-sur-Dives and, after waiting in vain for the missing troop (K Troop) to show up, ordered his second-in-command to take the remaining two troops (J and L) to their original destination, St. Lambert, while he tried to locate 9 Brigade headquarters and find out what was going on. Instead of doing that, the second-in-command, a captain, wandered off to locate the missing K

fighting was going on ahead of us. We stopped to get information and found that this was one of our f[or]w[ar]d positions. The HLI & NSR [North Novies] had not yet occupied their areas. Positions which according to our information had been cleared and occupied were still in enemy hands. Our orders were to deploy in these areas and only the action in St. Lambert kept us from moving directly into enemy areas.

Only a small group of houses in the [north] west end of St. Lambert were occupied by our troops. There were one company of Argylls and five Sherman tanks of the Alberta Regiment.

Flowers decided to join the party and his gun detachments "immediately deployed for crash action." He positioned seven of his weapons facing south and the remaining one aiming back up the D 13 toward Trun and began to open fire at all available targets. "As soon as the guns were in action," recalled Sergeant Firlotte of L Troop, "we left two men on each gun and deployed the rest in all-around protection as infantry working in cooperation with the Argylls." The gunners provided a much-needed boost for Currie's beleaguered force and their factual and terse after-action reports provide a clear picture of the hell of St. Lambert that hot Sunday afternoon in August:

Report of Lt J.R. Flowers, L T[roo]p
Enemy troops were in houses at a cross roads about 500 yards from L1 [gun]. They were firing from these houses and from a disabled armoured car which they used as a pillbox. Sgt Gates fired AP and a round of HE into this corner. The car was hit and burned and fire from this point stopped for a while.

Enemy infantry in large numbers were passing through an orchard south west of the town. At the request of the platoon commanders in this area, we deployed two Browning guns to get cross fire on this orchard. These guns caused heavy casualties, estimated at 200 by the infantry platoon commander.

… An SP gun had been dug in and camouflaged south west of the town. This gun had not fired but men were working on it and an ammunition lorry was beside it. Sgt Stenner on L4 fired two rounds at this target. Both gun and lorry burned and exploded.

Men from L1, L2 and L4 engaged enemy infantry with rifle, Bren and Browning fire. This fire was effective and casualties were caused.

Report of Sgt Firlotte, L T[roo]p
As soon as L1 gun went into action, he engaged a house with a machine gun nest in it, afterwards it was also found to contain an ammo dump, this quietened the house down and set it on fire, later it blew up. (2 rounds APC [Armoured Piercing, Capped], 1 round HE).

L4 was the next gun to open fire. They fired at the request of the squadron com[man]der of the SAR; the target was believed to be an SP [gun]. The first round set it on fire, the second blew it up. Both rounds were APC. L4 engaged a target believed to be a MG nest in an armoured car. It was hid but discovered by the sun reflecting on its wind shield. 1 round APC blew it up. Range 500x [yards].

L1 next engaged a Tiger at a range of 800x [yards] right down the road [D 13] and scored a direct hit with an APC. The tank stopped and then he fired a round of HE hitting the same hole enlarging it to about two feet in diameter. You could see right through the tank.

In the meantime the men employed as infantry were doing magnificent work, accounting for approximately 200 enemy with rifles, Brens and Brownings (30 [calibre]).

Dave remembered that things started to die down in the late afternoon and the shooting became "spasmodic and in the lulls, increasing numbers of prisoners were coming in."[33] Many were badly wounded, so he

established a first aid post in one of the houses near Squadron Headquarters. We used two Germans who spoke fluent English, as interpreters to issue instructions to the prisoners. As they came in, we lined them up, took all weapons, including knives; we also took blankets and any first aid supplies they might be carrying. The blankets and first aid supplies were turned over to the German doctor who ran the medical post.

Currie sent the prisoners back to Hill 117 in shifts:

As soon as we had from thirty to fifty prisoners, we picked an officer or NCO and put him in charge of the group. They were then instructed to march down the road, where they would be met and conducted to a PW area. I was not able to spare escorts for these prisoners, so we had one of the tanks on top of the hill just outside St. Lambert placed so that it could watch the prisoners from the time they left St. Lambert until they were picked up by our people in the rear. The location and purpose of this "Watch Dog" tank was explained to the prisoners and of the more than 2500 that marched down the road in the next 48 hours, only one tried to escape. He took off through the fields but did not get very far.[34]

It had been a hard day for the South Albertas. By late afternoon Wotherspoon thought his men were becoming tired and, again, "asked if relief could be sent, infantry particularly being needed." At 1700 Wotherspoon reported to Jefferson that the situation was "generally OK" and that his three squadrons were busy engaging "targets of opportunity." There was little change over the next two hours and, at 1900, Swatty again described things as "quiet" except for some shelling in St. Lambert and "some mopping up to do."[35]

Elsewhere, the afternoon had seen ferocious fighting around the Polish position at Hill 262 North. Throughout the day Maczek had been asking for assistance for his division, which was under attack "by the whole force of the German army in retreat."[36] As he recalled, his "cries of alarm were received with a certain disbelief by the Canadian staff [of 2nd Corps]" who "obstinately insisted that St. Lambert-sur-Dives, occupied by the 4th Canadian Armoured Division, sufficiently protected the Polish Division."[37] Maczek was also running low on ammunition and other supplies as his echelons were having trouble getting through the enemy to reach him. According to the Polish commander it was only when Simonds arrived at his headquarters late in the afternoon and saw his situation at first hand that the attitude of the staff began to change – and it changed fast. At 2000 hours Simonds ordered Kitching to have 4 Armoured Brigade "attack S[outh] E[ast] from the Hordouseaux-Les Champeaux area with the objective the area Champosoult-Coudehard" to aid the Poles.[38] Kitching lost his temper:

As far as I was concerned this did not make sense and I said to General Simonds words to this effect: "To hell with them [the Poles]. They have run out of food and ammunition because of the inefficiency of their organization; our people have been fighting just as hard but we have managed to keep up our supply system." That was about as far as I got because he peremptorily ordered 4th Armoured Brigade to rescue the Poles immediately.[39]

Simonds then turned his attention to cutting off the German escape route from St. Lambert to Mount Ormel. He wanted to do it that night as, according to the 4th Division War Diary, there was a "rumour" that the headquarters of the German "7th Army carried in some sixty Panzer t[an]ks would attempt to break out between Trun-St. Lambert during the night and the Corps Comm[an]d[er]r wished every possible precaution taken to ensure that all escape routes were sealed."[40] (In fact the commander of the German Seventh Army, Hausser, and his staff had broken out of the pocket that afternoon on foot). This task was given to the Highland Light Infantry of 9 Brigade who were to be supported by the 1st Hussars of 2 Armoured Brigade. Jefferson, who now had 9 Brigade under command, ordered the two units "to seize the gen[eral] area [around] Pt 124" which would interdict the various tracks and country lanes along which the Germans moved.[41] As Jefferson was also concerned that the "Hun would attempt to break out tonight with a force reported to be 100 t[an]ks," he organized an anti-tank gun screen across the front of 4th Division under the command of Lieutenant-Colonel Douglas Harkness, commanding officer of the 5th Anti-Tank Regiment and future Minister of National Defence.[42] Harkness began to assemble anti-tank units, and the two troops of 17-pdrs. from 103rd Battery, who had fought so well in St. Lambert that afternoon, except for one damaged gun, were taken out of the village at 2000 hours

that evening. By this time, however, the North Novies were supposedly on their way in to beef up the South Albertas' positions.

The problem was that the Nova Scotia unit moved incredibly slowly and did not even begin arriving in the SAR area until late in the evening. The Novies' commanding officer then "made a reconnaissance into St. Lambert and found it an awful spot with death and destruction rampant."[43] Between 2100 and 2300 hours, the Novies began to deploy in and around Hill 117 but their colonel refused to take Wotherspoon's advice about where to position his companies. Having been on the hill for forty-eight hours, Swatty knew the danger spots in the vicinity and cautioned the Novies' commander about placing a company in a farm southeast of the hill. As he recalled:

The damn fool, he thought he knew better, and so he says, "We're going to put a company out there." And I said, "Don't, put them with my HQ tanks." "No, I'm going to put them out there, that's where they should be." I said, "Well, pretty heavy fighting down there." "Yeah, yeah," [he replied]. He didn't listen to me at all.[44]

The North Novies deployed one company in Neauphe-sur-Dives, one company on 117, one company in St. Lambert and their last company in the farm east of the village.[45]

If anything, the Highland Light Infantry were even slower. They had reached a position midway between Trun and Neauphe-sur-Dives at 1439 hours and stayed there almost the entire day. At 2000 there was an O Group at the battalion headquarters when the commanding officers of the HLI and 1st Hussars made plans to move forward to the area round Point 124. The battalion moved off at 2120 and two hours later, having covered one thousand yards, was in the centre of Neauphe-sur-Dives, where it married up with the 1st Hussars. The Hussars were not in the best form that night, and their regimental history admits that the morale of the unit was low after serious losses during TRACTABLE. Having met, the two commanding officers made a recce of the area over which they were to advance, a task that occupied them until 2300 hours.[46]

While this was going on, German columns continued to move over the bridge at St. Lambert or across the ford at Moissy and make their way out of the pocket. There were armoured vehicles among this exodus – at 2030 Wotherspoon reported:

Large numbers of t[an]ks about 100 seen moving NE some distance south of Rooster [St. Lambert]. Seem to be missing our pos[itio]n but might threaten left flank. Cannot tell yet where they are going to strike. Poles to be inf[or]m[e]d.[47]

An hour later, von Lüttwitz, having spent nine hours coordinating movement through the village under artillery fire, left St. Lambert. Just as he was leaving, the remnants of the 116th Panzer Division – a few tanks, fifty vehicles and five guns – which had spent the day under camouflage west of the Dives –

arrived at the bridges. It took them nearly two hours to negotiate their way through the little village because of streets full of destroyed vehicles, confusion, stragglers and Allied artillery fire but they were finally free of the jam and reformed on the other side.[48]

Wotherspoon continued to call in sighting reports. At 2100 he reported "t[an]k f[or]m[ation]s moving NE across left flank. Just moving on." As this might be the major German break-out expected that night, Jefferson asked for further details but Swatty had nothing more to add for the moment and, at 2130, replied that he would "try and get info to you as soon as possible." Thinking that the HLI and 1st Hussars might encounter this force when they moved forward, Jefferson warned them at 2200 that "29 Recce report enemy t[an]k formations moving across left flank." Apparently he got no reply as, at 2300, he repeated the warning to Rockingham of "enemy t[an]k f[or]m[atio]ns moving across left flank," and asked for "location of children [9 Brigade units]." This brought the HLI alive and almost immediately they informed the two brigade commanders that the unit was "now in position. Held up by recce but everything okay."[49]

Everything was not okay. Both the HLI and Hussars were still in Neauphe-sur-Dives and the Hussars' commanding officer had decided that, despite orders, he was not going to move that night. Captain Gerry Stoner of the Hussars' C Squadron remembered linking up with an HLI company and making slow progress but that "sometime after midnight" the column "came to a stop." Stoner got out of his tank several times to talk to his squadron commander, Major Dudley Brooks, and ask "what the hell is going on?" only to receive the reply, "I'm buggered if I know, Gerry" but "I think the CO has decided we have to stay here because we can't go forward in the dark."[50] It was true – as the Hussars' historian puts it:

Since the tanks arrived late in the evening, their juncture with the HLI was not completed until after dark. It was still a considerable distance to the objective with one sunken road the only route. Everything was confusion, yet all ranks knew that their handful of armour and one under-strength battalion of infantry were expected to prevent the enemy from escaping from the pocket in the centre … The road through the dense woods which the tanks were to use was cluttered with burnt-out German vehicles and on the dark rainy night the crews could see nothing ahead.

Although it was plainly evident that the enemy was pulling out in great haste and utter disorganization, it was deemed impossible to follow him by night.[51]

Apparently neither Jefferson of 10 Brigade nor Rockingham of 9 Brigade were informed of this decision and the two brigadiers thought all was well. At 2309, Jefferson reported to 4th Division that the "situation seems well in hand along Trun-St. Lambert road."[52]

And then it began to rain.

Dave Currie thought the night of 20/21 August "passed relatively quietly."[53] At 2300 a company of North Novies finally arrived in St. Lambert and, for the first time in forty-three hours, Dave felt secure enough to leave his men and go back to RHQ at about 0100 to let "the Colonel know that everything was under control." Earlier Wotherspoon had made a trip to the rear to attend an O Group at 9 Brigade, a journey he did not want to undertake as "we were in there, fighting like mad, and I got a message that I was put under command of Rockingham … because they were taking over our area."[54] Swatty tried to wriggle out of it but Rockingham was adamant so Wotherspoon got into his scout car and drove up the D 13 to Trun. He had "to shoo off a few Germans on the way, to get out of my way" and arrived an hour late to find the O Group finished and Rockingham out of contact. On his way back, he stopped at Jefferson's headquarters and got the order placing the Regiment under 9 Brigade rescinded but had another "little private war" with the Germans on his way back to RHQ.

The crews of A Squadron were fully aware of the infestation in that area as there were enemy all around their Shermans. One remembered that night as being "quite harrowing" as

although it was dark, there was just enough light from the skyline that I could occasionally see columns of men going by. I knew they were Germans, but I never opened fire. I just mentioned it to the troop officer, who was sitting in the operator's seat, that I could see them going by. If the machine-gun company on the ground [No. 10 MG Company or The New Brunswick Rangers] had started shooting we would have supported them, but we were very vulnerable in the dark, and it made more sense to let them go. The guys in some of the tanks told me later about suddenly becoming aware of Germans right down beside their tanks. They would hear them feel the tank and whisper "Panzer! Panzer!" then skittle off into the darkness.[55]

B Squadron was even more vulnerable. Major Darby Nash and the crews of his eight remaining tanks were the men most anxious for the arrival of the Hussars and Highland Light Infantry. The squadron had been told to stay in their isolated position "until relieved" and they expected that relief at any moment. Throughout the day Jim Nicholson had kept his A set netted to the infantry frequency hoping to hear that they were moving up. His B set suffered from what sounded like German jamming and, in any case, as the aerial had been shot off, it was almost useless. Nicholson did not like the squadrons's position one bit as the visibility "from a tank commander's view atop the tank was extremely poor – less than 100 feet into the field of fire" and he was strongly tempted "to dismount a man or two to ground level where things were somewhat better" but Nash's orders were "to man your tanks at all times."[56] Nicholson recalled that it "was an evening of relative quiet" and the men were tired, having had almost no "sleep for two days." In the rear link tank, commanded by Captain Wilf Gallimore, the operator, Trooper Guy Olmstead, kept his earphones on as he leaned against the breach of the 75 mm main gun and closed his eyes a few minutes. "So it finally got dark," Trooper John Neff recorded, "and with darkness came rain."[57]

Stan Rose's three-man crew had managed to get back to the squadron after their misadventure of the morning. A man from another tank, Trooper George McDonald from High River, came to pay a visit, but as he was climbing in through the hatch he dislodged a Sten gun lying ready for use and it fell through the open hatch, hit the bottom of the turret basket and went off, killing McDonald instantly. There was no time to do anything except wrap the body in a groundsheet and lay the 33-year-old former meat plant worker on the ground.[58]

Olmstead and some of the other squadron operators intercepted Wotherspoon's reports about the large formation of German tanks moving northeast of St. Lambert but apparently Nash did not receive these reports until much later. In the event, it was not German tanks that were the problem that night; it was German infantry.

Nicholson recalled that he made periodic attempts to raise the troops coming to their relief "but to no avail."[59] By 0100 hours, 21 August, it was too late – the Germans "were all around us," John Neff recorded, and though the B Squadron crews "kept up a random fire and kept throwing hand grenades into the hedges and ditches in an effort to drive them off," there were just too many enemy.[60] Neff "was standing on the back deck of our tank with Sten gun" when he heard movement about Corporal George Evans's tank about twenty feet away. "It seemed to me," he recalled, that the Germans "were pouring petrol about his tank and then one of them threw a grenade and the tank went up in a sheet of flame." Three of the crew bailed out but two men, Troopers Ouelette and Walton, were trapped in the blazing vehicle and burned to death. It was decided after a subsequent examination of their Sherman that the Germans had used some sort of phosphorus incendiary device. Denis Ouelette, age 23, was a store clerk from Bonnyville, Alberta, while Harvey Walton was a 20-year-old milkman from Toronto. Both had joined the Regiment in 1943.[61]

Nash was out of his tank conferring with Sergeant Al Holmes when Evans's Sherman burst into flames and "realizing that we were being infiltrated by the enemy (unseen in the darkness and dense bush) … made the decision to retreat."[62] Sending out an order "every tank for himself" over his B set, Nash then waited on the ground until all the tanks had got out before mounting Holmes's vehicle and taking up rear position in the column.

Nicholson's B set was useless and he only realized that the squadron was pulling out when he

saw a tank (one of ours) approach the crossroad, striking back toward R.H.Q. Another followed, then another and another, each visible for a few seconds in the glow of the fire

[from the burning Sherman], then vanishing in ghostly procession into the darkness to our rear. All we could hear during this strange spectacle was the sound of ammo exploding from the burning tank. My operator John Neff and I watched until what we considered to be the entire B Squadron had passed by, and only then did I get on the intercom to my crew. "The Squadron has pulled out," I said, "let's get the hell out of here."[63]

His Sherman had only three of its engines working and, after "an agonizing 5 minutes revving up the motors, my driver Stan James headed slowly past the burning tank" and into the dark. To Neff the withdrawal was

the wildest ride ever made by a group of tanks. It was blacker than the ace of spades with a constant rain falling, but yet the night was lit with burning tanks and houses and the vivid streaks of tracer & gun flashes and the weird light of flares. Our tanks bumped over fields and ditches. The Germans fired small-arms tracer and wherever there was a ricochet they would slap in an 88.[64]

Nicholson only became aware that he had caught up with the squadron when he "bumped into the rear tank."[65]

Captain Wilf Gallimore's crew was also late withdrawing from the position. Gallimore's operator, Guy Olmstead, had been trying to transmit the message about the German tank formation to Nash over his B set but "there was bushes and trees about" which interfered with transmission as the range of the B Set was quite short.[66] Olmstead finally got through to Nash on the regimental frequency but by now the squadron had withdrawn, so Nash said "it's a hell of a time to tell me, you're surrounded and get the hell out of there!" Gallimore told his driver, Trooper Bill Pachal, to pull out, but in the darkness, Pachal drove the tank into the bed of Foulbec brook and it bogged. He tried desperately to get it moving again but it was no use and Gallimore ordered the crew to bail out. They "had not got 100 feet," Guy Olmstead remembered, "when we were challenged in German and then they opened fire." Pachal and the gunner, Trooper Dexter Colwell, were killed instantly. Dexter Colwell, age 21, a former CNR worker from Winnipeg had been with the Regiment for two years while Bill Pachal, a 35-year-old truck driver from Edmonton, was one of the old originals from June 1940. He was survived by a wife and a daughter.[67]

Gallimore and Olmstead were taken prisoner, separated and questioned. Guy Olmstead was brought before a German officer who

asked me, "are you with the tanks?" so I said "yes." Then he said, "Where are the Poles?" and I said "I don't know." He said, "You must know and if you don't tell me, I take your life." I was tired but I wasn't afraid and I said, "You're a soldier like me and you know I cannot tell you."

They marched us off, still in the dark, and we had no contact with each other until the early morning hours when Gallimore told me that Pachal and Colwell were dead. The Germans I was with had the palms of their hands marked with luminous paint and they would open their hands to show the soldiers following where to go – I was quite amazed by how professional they were.

We came to a meeting place and it seemed to be a farm yard and there was an officer there in charge who was mad, he just screamed in German, he was violently mad because they were late getting there or something, or maybe because they hadn't shot us.

We walked all night. There was occasional strafing but I don't remember being strafed in our area. We may have been shelled, I don't remember, but there was plenty of evidence of it, dead horses and bodies and blood on the road.

Our next stop was Bernay on the same day after we walked all night. They took us into a restaurant in Bernay and gave us a really good meal.[68]

Guy Olmstead eventually wound up in a camp near Mosburg, north of Munich, and was liberated the following May.

The surviving tanks of B Squadron made their way in the direction of Hill 117 but they moved cautiously – as Nicholson remarked, it was essential that RHQ "be alerted to our approach as, with enemy all around, we might be easily mistaken for advancing Germans" and "we did not wish to be on the receiving end of the powerful M-10s protecting RHQ."[69] Nash was unable to get through by wireless, as most of the vehicles on 117 were only turning their wireless equipment on every half hour or so to conserve batteries. Nash called his crew commanders together for an O Group but it was interrupted by German machine-gun fire followed by an AP round that hit the engine compartment of Lieutenant Peachy Howard's Sherman and "clipped the lower part of his fan [so that] when he started up it sounded like 25 thrashing machines."[70] The squadron kept moving west until they hit the D 13 at which point Nash made contact with RHQ and requested that a burst of 20 mm tracer from the Crusaders be fired straight up into the air so that he could pinpoint RHQ's location. It turned out that they were only a quarter of a mile away and Darby Nash soon returned the very tired and somewhat battered survivors of B Squadron to the fold. John Neff was horrified when he overheard his squadron commander assuring Swatty Wotherspoon that he "would take the remnants of our squadron, 5 of our 19 tanks back to the crossroads if he wanted us to go." "I felt like punching the Maj[or]. on the nose," Neff recorded. "I couldn't see much point in going back there and besides we had only 3 rounds of HE, about 4 [rounds of] AP and box and a half of Browning [.30 calibre] and our gas gauge showed empty."

One of the B Squadron tanks got out a different way. Dave Currie remembered that, about 0300, "we heard a tank coming down the road" from "the direction of our own lines."[71] Unsure whether it was friend or foe, his men held their fire until the vehicle "came between us and a burning building" when they identified it as a German AFV and knocked it out with a round in the engine compartment. A few minutes later, another tank "wandered into the rear of our area" and "almost ran over one of the infantry defensive positions." Again, Currie's men held their fire until they could identify the vehicle. "The tank stopped and the motor was turned off," he recalled, and then he heard a voice saying "I wonder where the hell we are" and everybody relaxed. It turned out to be the B Squadron crew who "had been wandering most of the night lost."

Darby Nash's men had been overrun because they had no infantry support. They had been expecting the Highland Light Infantry to move forward to be in a position at first light "to seize the gen[eral] area [around] Pt 124" and cut off the German escape route.[72] The HLI did not move forward as ordered because the 1st Hussars did not move forward. The commanding officer of the Hussars must have thought his decision a wise one when, at 0215, Wotherspoon reported to Jefferson that a German attack "north of Pt 124 forced our child back across the river [the Foulbec stream]."[73] Word of B Squadron's problems quickly reached the 1st Hussars – Captain Gerry Stoner remembered that his squadron commander told him that "someone had just come out from the SAR and that they were in a hell of a mess."[74] The Hussars' historian records that the unit received the news by means of a "dispatch rider who had been with the SAR's tanks in the wooded area between the Hussars and Pt. 124" who "came through RHQ in a highly excited state" and "reported that the SAR had been overrun in the dark by German infantry with bazookas."[75] If the Hussars were a bit nervous before, this news really shook them. As their historian quite honestly admits:

On that dark night with the infantry so thin on the ground the words "overrun" and "bazookas" were sufficient to make everyone fearful. All ranks remained on guard the rest of that eerie night while houses burned behind the tanks and woods re-echoed with machine-gun fire. … The CO pondered the situation when he returned and decided that moving in the black night would be an "out of the frying pan into the fire" venture. A hectic and miserable night was spent with machine-gun fire, solid shot and mortar fragments flying through the harbour of the infantry and tankmen in all directions.[76]

The HLI had less to fear from German infantry in the woods but, as the wireless logs for the night of 20/21 August 1944 reveal, they proved no more aggressive. In fact the message traffic between the HLI, Rockingham of 9 Brigade and Jefferson of 10 Brigade verges on the comic. At 0210, the HLI reported that they were "moving off now" but the unit seems to have been distracted by a fire fight that broke out in the position of the North Novies' D Company, which, contrary to Wotherspoon's advice, had been deployed in a farm house east of St. Lambert.[77] One platoon of that company was overrun while the other two pulled back to Neauphe-sur-Dives. Ten minutes after stating they were "moving off now," the HLI informed Rockingham they were going to the assistance of their fellow infantrymen. "We are going to give the enemy in the farms in front of NNS a short blast," they reported, "to help the NNS out."[78] This seems to taken the battalion about an hour because at 0310 they informed the 9 Brigade commander that they were now in the rear of the North Nova Scotia area and asked: "Should we dig in or move?"[79] Nearly fifty minutes later, at 0400, they had still not moved and the HLI commander elaborated on the situation as he saw it:

We are now in rear of NNS pos[itio]n. We have not yet gone ahead because t[an]ks cannot go ahead of us in the dark. The heavy friends in front [B Squadron of the SAR] have withdrawn and we would have to go in only with friends as we have not made a proper recce. We will have to go in on our flat feet and a compass bearing.

We have two alternatives. First, to wait here where we are and form a strong pos[itio]n. Second, to go ahead alone and on our own flat feet and fight for it all the way in the dark without support of our heavy friends and not get dug in properly before daylight. Will you give a reading please. Please hurry with answer.[80]

Unfortunately it took almost an hour for Rockingham to reply but when he did at 0500, he did not mince his words:

HLI will carry out intention laid down last night. They will start immediately. It is vital track be cut at first light and that certain weapons that they have be on the ground at that time. They will be supported by friends from the rear [1st Hussars] or to the flank [SAR] and they will move as soon as possible. Every ten minutes of progress until first light will be reported to me.[81]

The phrase "certain weapons that they will have on the ground" is a reference to the 103rd Battery's 17-pdrs., which were to protect the HLI once they got into position at Point 124.

If Rockingham thought this strong message was going to light a fire under the HLI he was in for a disappointment as, by first light, nothing had happened. At 0530 he requested the HLI to give him a "sitrep [situation report] on your heavy friends [1st Hussars]" and "every 10 minutes as to progress."[82] No progress reports came in. At 0600, well after first light, Jefferson began to grow impatient and queried Rockingham whether the HLI had "started to move yet?" and had they "carried out liaison with friends [the Poles] to the left?"[83] At 0615, seventy-five minutes after he had been ordered to pull his finger out and get going in no uncertain terms, the HLI commander reported that

he had "not moved as yet."[84] Rockingham responded in less than a minute that it was "vital" for him to "move immediately without support. You will get s[up]p[ort]. later."[85] At 0620 the reply came back: "HLI preparing to move off to attack high ground NW of Chambois now."[86] The HLI may have been light infantry but they were certainly not fleet of foot because it wasn't until 0720 that the unit reported they were, finally, "Moving off now."[87] By this time Jefferson had lost patience and asked Rockingham for "an explanation as to why we were not informed of delay in HLI advance."[88] No reply is recorded.

What was holding the Highland Light Infantry and the Hussars up in the first hours of daylight on Monday, 21 August, was hundreds of Germans who wished to surrender. "At first light," recalled Gerry Stoner, "these people came out of the woods with or without their rifles."[89] He was impressed by the sheer number of enemy wanting to give up and asked his squadron commander "what the hell are we going do with all these bloody people?" The HLI began to round them up but, as fast as they got one batch together, more came out of the woods. By this time the Hussars' commanding officer "was anxious to get going" – Stoner remembered him "cursing and swearing" that "if we have to, we will run over them" but it took the HLI and Hussars nearly two hours to get underway. There was little opposition, one German tank was brewed up, and at 0943 the two units reported that they were "on the objective" at Point 124.[90]

It was the same in the South Albertas' positions and it became quite clear as the morning advanced that most of those Germans who had not already escaped were starting to give up. "You could feel the change in the situation," Dave Currie later wrote, and "we could tell the end was in sight."[91] At 0730, he reported that the enemy around St. Lambert had "had about enough." "With this, the Jerries on our whole front," noted the War Diary, "were ordered to surrender or suffer the consequences" – and they certainly did.[92] Trooper Harvey Bergquist of A Squadron remembered them coming up to his tank "by the hundreds" saying "hello, hello."[93] John Galipeau recalled "Germans by thousands in columns of regimental strength," coming in "led by men carrying white bedsheets tied between poles to signal surrender."[94] Trooper John Lakes of Recce Troop attributed the change in enemy attitude to the rain which continued to fall: "The Germans were cut off from mail, hot meals and shelter, and now had to endure the rain. As a result we were swamped with Germans surrendering."[95] On this, the third day of the battle, Allied artillery fire tapered off as the pocket had become so small that "no shelling" restrictions had to be put into place to prevent friendly troops being shelled.[96]

The South Albertas spent the day rounding up prisoners. The problem was that some Germans were still willing to fight and the boys never knew what would happen when a large enemy group emerged from cover. About 1000 Lieutenant

James Reed and Sergeant Alvin Bell of C Squadron were out of their tanks doing a foot recce of the area west of the Dives when they were killed by enemy fire. Alvin Bell was a 32-year-old farmer from Halfway Lake, Alberta, who had been with the Regiment since it was formed and had married an English girl just before crossing to France. James Reed, age 21, was a former history student at the University of Toronto who had come to the SAR in 1943.[97]

Sadly, Bell and Reed weren't the Regiment's only losses on this day of "mopping up." Corporal Buster Ely of B Squadron, the Regiment's star welterweight, was active in rounding up prisoners using an abandoned German halftrack vehicle that he had found. He was last seen heading into the bush accompanied by Trooper James Carragher to bring in another batch of enemy. Their bodies were later found and the nature of the wounds revealed that both men had been cut down by machine-gun fire. Emery Ely, 25, a farmer from Gibbons, Alberta, had been with the Regiment since the beginning while Carragher, a 26-year-old logger from Sturgis, Saskatchewan, was a former member of the 16/22 Saskatchewan Horse who came to the South Albertas when that unit was broken up in 1943.[98]

Many of the prisoners were wounded and required medical treatment. Dave Currie recalled that, in mid-morning,

a convoy of ambulance vehicles came in and demanded that we let them through in the name of mercy. I took a look in the ambulances and the wounded were piled in like cordwood. I told the German doctor that if he were really interested in saving lives, he had better go to our lines and to our hospital. He didn't have enough gas in the ambulance to go anywhere else. He finally decided that we were right and took off for our hospital.[99]

Dave was being generous when he used the term "our hospital" because that "hospital" was actually Doc Boothroyd's RAP on Hill 117. Since the previous Friday, three days before, Boothroyd and his small staff, including Padre Silcox, had been trying to cope with the overwhelming numbers of enemy wounded. Boothroyd was assisted by German medical personnel and "there was no distinction made in the uniform the wounded person wore" as he "triaged" or divided the wounded into categories.[100] Those whose condition was hopeless were made as comfortable as possible and put aside, "those who needed urgent medical treatment who could be saved … were evacuated, those who weren't urgent, were treated with bandages and morphine and evacuated later." At this point, the evacuation procedure "was going hell for leather to the field ambulances and rear hospitals," Boothroyd recalled, and for him the days on Hill 117 became a never-ending stream of "shell dressings, bandages, splints and morphine syrettes." In the midst of this horror, Boothroyd looked up to see a German officer

in immaculate uniform and I still remember his boots as being shiny, standing there leaning against the fence post in the middle of the bodies and blood and general mayhem. I recognized his rank, he was a major, and the fact that he was a doctor and I went over and spoke to him rather abruptly and asked him "what the hell he thought he was doing there and couldn't he help in some way," and he said, "yes, he probably could as he had been the head of surgery in a general hospital" but "I am not going to take orders from you, I only take orders from senior officers." So I went to Swatty and I won't tell you his exact words as they are unrepeatable but he said, "have you got a gun?" I said, "Yes, to defend myself." Swatty said "Take that and tell that bastard if he doesn't go to work, you'll shoot him." So I went back and told the German officer exactly that and he saluted me because I was bringing an order from a colonel and then he got down on his hands and knees and got to work.

The recalcitrant German doctor turned out to be "very skilful" and got "gratifyingly bloody." Boothroyd found that not all Germans were like this officer, "the epitome of German character, right by the rules." He remembered giving a "bag full of morphine syrettes" to a medical sergeant from a panzer unit who "practically wept because he could now go and administer to his worst patients."

Many of the prisoners spoke good English. Ed Hyatt had a disconcerting experience when he "came across this German captain who saw by my flashes that I was from Alberta and asked me 'what part?'"[101] Hyatt told him and it turned out that the German had lived in Hyatt's home town "before the war and knew me as a boy and that he and my dad had both worked for the same farmer." "He told me exactly where our house was in the village," Hyatt recalled, "but when I asked him why he had gone back to Germany, he replied that he had no choice because he was a reserve captain and it 'would be my family or else but I am glad that I am out it.'" The prisoners were searched and several South Albertas became quite wealthy – or at least thought they were wealthy. John Galipeau remembered the prisoners had "loads of French money and … it wasn't going to do them any good where they were going."[102] John's crew would "keep nothing under a 100 franc note" but still accumulated a "duffel bag full of French money [that] lay on the back of our tank for months and months." The crew estimated that they had about $50,000 worth but, "since it was German occupation money, we couldn't really spend it" and, eventually, "the duffel bag got thrown out in the ditch."

There is really no accurate count of the number of prisoners taken in the battle of the Falaise gap. Allied estimates tended to be highly inaccurate because, as each batch of prisoners was passed along, the receiving formation added them to their total, with the result that some Germans were counted several times. At one point Montgomery claimed that as many as 133,000 prisoners had been captured but this figure was revised downward – the consensus is that about 50,000 Germans were captured by all three Allied armies. Swatty Wotherspoon, who had an unbending competitive attitude in everything he did, never forgave 10 Brigade for not having a "forward enough prisoner cage" with the result that he had to send "most of our [South Alberta] prisoners over to another div[ision – 3rd Division] who got all the credit for taking those prisoners, and we didn't get any credit for them."[103]

Unfortunately, more Germans escaped than were taken prisoner or killed. Major Heinz Guderian of the 116th Panzer Division, son of the famous panzer general, recorded that, after the remnant of his division got through the bottleneck at St. Lambert the previous midnight, it drove all night through the maze of tracks and lanes between St. Lambert and Mount Ormel and at first light was outside the pocket – and this was only one of a number of organized groups that broke out on the night of 20/21 August. Most of the German AFVs that made it across the Dives at St. Lambert were lost due to bogging, mechanical breakdown or simply running out of fuel. The 116th Panzer Division, for example, had five tanks when it set out but had lost them all by the time it got to St. Lambert. They picked up two SPGs from another formation but one of these was lost when it took a wrong turn and went north up the main street of the village, where it was knocked out (this was possibly the enemy AFV that Currie remembers being shot up during the night). Still the 116th Panzer Division managed to get fifty vehicles and one SPG out of the trap. Meindl held the breach open throughout the morning of 21 August but by then there were fewer and fewer troops coming out. The last organized group to emerge was a battlegroup from the 10th SS Panzer Division, who came by his command post at 1100 hours and assured him that there was nobody behind them. At 1600 hours, having kept the escape route open for nearly twenty-four hours – an impressive piece of soldiering – Meindl withdrew toward the east.[104]

Early in the morning 4 Armoured Brigade set out to rescue Maczek's Poles on Hill 262 North. They became involved in some heavy fighting but by now the *Wehrmacht* was pulling out, and by late morning the Grenadier Guards broke through to the embattled Poles, who were almost out of food and ammunition. "Almost the first question the Poles asked," recorded the Grenadier historian, was "Have you a cigarette?"[105]

Several supply convoys were dispatched to the Poles that day – 10 Brigade organized one for the Polish units at Chambois and tasked the SAR with the job of delivering it. Major Bert Coffin recalled being "up at RHQ instead of back LOB where I was supposed to be," and "Swatty volunteered my services to take it [the convoy] to the Poles."[106] Bert picked up "four or five bren gun carriers loaded with the needed supplies" and set out. Nobody really knew where the Poles were but he eventually ran into the HLI on Point 124 and they contacted the Poles and asked them to come and get the goods. Bert's route took him right through the lanes and carts east of St. Lambert which formed the German escape route but,

In the whole trip, which took most of a day, we were not shot at nor did we see a live German. There were lots of dead ones, but I don't know what happened to them. They might have been killed by the Poles, by artillery fire or by air attacks. I doubt it was the Poles because they had not been searched. Tommy [Thompson, Bert's driver] checked over the first ones we saw and found out that they all had a good supply of assorted money. We were able to take back a fair addition to the Regimental funds so it was not a total loss.

While it could have been, and I was expecting it to be, a rather sticky task, as it turned out, it was pretty routine. The crews of the Bren gun carriers all had weapons and I had a Thompson gun but no one saw a thing to shoot at.

Throughout the morning of 21 August the North Novies gradually moved into St. Lambert and, in the early afternoon, relieved Currie and C Squadron. Dave, who had had almost no sleep for three or more days, was so tired that Sergeant John Gunderson "actually saw him fall asleep on his feet while he was talking to one of the relieving officers" but "one of the boys caught him before he could fall to the ground."[107] Captain R.F. Dickie's company of Links was formally relieved at 1400 hours and marched up the dusty D 13 to join their regiment, conscious they had done a good job. As they moved into the village the North Novies experienced trouble with numerous small groups of Germans who were not sure whether they were going to fight or surrender. They asked the Regiment for help and the War Diary records that, in the afternoon, the South Albertas were "ready to pull out of our positions but the infantry had not got fully in and we were ordered to remain until they did."[108] The two weak companies of Argylls, who had lost all but one of their officers and a third of their men over the past two days, were also asked to remain but this was too much for Swatty, who by now had become totally exasperated with 9 Brigade. At 1604 he complained to Jefferson that "the 2 coys [companies] of ASH [Argylls] who have done magnificent job should be relieved by friends who arrived during night [North Nova Scotia Highlanders]."[109] This seems to have had effect and the Argylls marched up the D 13 that evening. Unfortunately for the Regiment, 9 Brigade still did not feel in control of the situation at last light so the South Albertas "prepared to stay again in the same area" until morning.[110] That night Dave Currie "slept like the dead for about eight hours" and, when he woke up, the "birds were singing and all shell fire had ceased; it was so peaceful."[111]

By the morning of 22 August the Regiment was anxious to get out of the area of St. Lambert because it stank. In the past three days thousands of men and horses had been killed within a radius of three miles from Hill 117, and St. Lambert, in particular, was an affront to the eyes and the nose. "When we had come to St. Lambert," Dave Currie remembered, "it was a

After the battle, no. 1. In the southern end of St. Lambert a calcined German corpse lies in the foreground while the Panther in the background may be the same one taken out by the Argylls on the morning of 19 August. The village was partly ruined by the fighting.

neat, small, quiet French village" but when "we left, it was a fantastic mess" as the "clutter of equipment, dead horses, wounded, dying and dead Germans, had turned it into a hellhole."[112] One Panther tank was still on the Dives bridge where it had been hit, while another had been pushed off the bridge into the ditch. There were two knocked-out Panthers near the *mairie* and a Tiger with its turret blown off on the main street and another at the southern crossroads hit by the 103rd Battery gunners. Across the river in the orchards and farm fields there were more than a dozen knocked-out German tanks or SPGs and three more were found in the north end of the village. Burned out trucks, halftracks and armoured cars littered the streets and lanes of St. Lambert and the area around it.[113]

The worst thing was the number of dead – Trooper Carson

Daley visited the village shortly after the fighting stopped and "never witnessed such a sight in my life" as

> it was nothing but dead Germans piled one on top of each other all along the hedgerows. It is something that I shall never forget. There were bulldozers working and I believe they dug three large trenches and the German prisoners rolled the bodies in and there were people there searching the bodies, there were tanks going up the road and there were bodies being crushed under them.[114]

The most reliable estimate is that ten thousand German soldiers were killed in the fighting in the valley, and most of them lay within a few miles of Hill 117. The entire water system of the

173

After the battle, no. 2. The wreckage of a German horse-drawn column litters the sunken lane leading from the ford across the Dives at Moissy. Thousands of horses were killed during six days of unceasing aerial and artillery bombardment and their carcasses, which decomposed rapidly in the hot August weather, presented a major health problem in the area for months afterwards. The South Albertas called routes like this "Dead Horse Gulch." BY KIND PERMISSION OF THE TRUSTEES, IMPERIAL WAR MUSEUM, LONDON, B9668.

valley was poisoned by the corpses, which decomposed quickly in the hot weather, and there was a great fear of an epidemic, forcing Allied authorities to truck in water to the civilian population for months afterwards. The Falaise pocket after the battle was such a terrible sight that even a hardened soldier like Montgomery was impressed. He told his personal aides, among them Swatty's brother-in-law, Major Trumbull Warren, that "if you young men want to see what war is like, you go down [to the pocket area] and take a look." "We went down there," Warren recalled, "and it was just unreal, the only way they could bury the dead was by bulldozers."[115]

The South Albertas had grown inured to man's inhumanity to man but they did not enjoy witnessing man's inhumanity to animals. Thousands of horses were killed or injured during the fighting and as Trooper Wilf Taylor commented, "They had not declared a war, they had just got caught up in it."[116] Many of the poor beasts, injured and crazed, had taken shelter in the Dives river bed near St. Lambert and the sound of their shrieks so disturbed one of Dave's men that he got permission to go down and put them out of their misery – it was a heartbreaking but necessary task that required hundreds of rounds. A British operational research unit that later spent weeks investigating the results of the fighting in the pocket refused to examine the horse transport that was destroyed because "the stench of dead horses was so overpowering that where there was any number of horse-drawn vehicles that area had to be passed with all speed."[117]

The main roads in the valley were made impassable by clusters of burned-out and abandoned tanks, as well as other armoured fighting vehicles, trucks, cars, carts and just about every other kind of transport imaginable. Allied investigators later toted up the results. In the area around the city of Falaise they counted 121 tanks or SPGs, 56 other armoured vehicles, 659 trucks, 352 cars, 22 motorcycles and 60 artillery pieces. In an area starting about two miles west of the Dives and stretching east to Vimoutiers they found 187 German tanks or SPGs, 157 other armoured vehicles, 1778 trucks, 669 cars and 252 artillery pieces, with most of these located around St. Lambert. The investigators concluded that aircraft and artillery had been effective against soft-skinned vehicles but considerably less so against armoured vehicles as the great majority of the German armoured vehicles (80%) had been destroyed or abandoned by their own crews.[118]

It was all very impressive but the fact remains that much of the German Fifth Panzer and Seventh Armies escaped from the trap, even if they lost most of their vehicles. German records are understandably very imprecise for this period and there has been considerable debate over the number who evaded encirclement. The most recent study has concluded that a total of 165,000 enemy soldiers escaped from the pocket either before the retreat began on 16 August or during the period 16 to 21 August. This same study calculates that 44,800 Germans broke out from midnight on 19 August until Meindl closed the escape route at about 1600 hours on 21 August. There is reason to suspect that this estimate is too high but the fact of the matter remains that more Germans escaped than were killed or captured in the battle of the Falaise Gap. The Allied trap had failed.[119]

"Someone had to pay for the broken pots," commented Maczek and George Kitching got the bill.[120] At 1100 hours on 21 August he was called to Simonds's headquarters and relieved of command of 4th Armoured Division. Kitching was "naturally very shocked and emotionally upset" but made a number of points in his own defence: the five-day delay before Moncel took over 4 Armoured Brigade which left that formation leaderless during a crucial period; the confusion caused by constant changes of orders; and the heavy casualties the division had sustained in its first three weeks of action.[121] Simonds had no good answer for any of these points and the two men, close personal friends, parted. Later that afternoon Brigadier Harry Foster, the same officer who ten years or more before had tried to teach a bunch of prairie flat feet to become cavalry, arrived at Kitching's headquarters to assume command of 4th Division. "It was an awkward moment," Foster recalled and both men were uncomfortable.[122] "In spite of errors," Foster continued, Kitching "had turned the division into a formidable fighting force and [he] felt that if Simonds had given him a few weeks longer he could have straightened things out to everyone's sat-

Major-General Harry Foster. A prewar officer of Lord Strathcona's Horse, Harry Foster assumed command of 4th Canadian Armoured Division on 21 August 1944 and led it until November 1944. NAC, PA 131220.

isfaction." "We had a drink," Harry remembered, "I wished him godspeed" and then George Kitching was gone.

Kitching paid the price but no senior commander on the Allied side is without blame in the failure to trap the German armies in Normandy. Bradley ordered Patton to halt his advance to the north on 13 August, and when the Americans resumed that advance on 16 August, command confusion delayed their attack for thirty-six crucial hours. Montgomery put pressure on both Crerar and Simonds to take Falaise, but when First Canadian Army experienced troubles breaking through the German defences south of Caen, he did not see fit to reinforce the Canadians with additional armour. The Second British Army also has some responsibility in the matter because it did not appear to be the most aggressive of formations. By 18 August, its advance elements had reached Necy, about four miles from St. Lambert, but it took the British nearly forty-eight hours to make contact with First Canadian Army at Trun. Their slow progress did not result from determined enemy resistance because they allowed every German infantry division on their front to disengage on 20 August and make its way to the east.[123]

It is 2nd Canadian Corps, however, that has to answer for much of the failure because that formation was tasked with advancing to Chambois to complete the encirclement. Simonds had issued the orders to complete that objective at 1000 hours on 18 August. Kitching's 4th Division was to advance from Trun to a point exclusive of Moissy while Maczek's 1st Polish

The Allied tank crew's basic nightmare, no. 3. The Panther was the standard medium tank of the *Wehrmacht* in the last years of the war. A 45-ton vehicle with well-sloped armour and a powerful long 75 mm gun, it was a dangerous opponent. This example has been caught and tamed by an Allied armoured crew whose commander poses proudly in the turret. NAC, PA 169094

sion commanders and Jefferson of 10 Brigade. None of these officers seems to have realized just how thin the Canadian line was during that period. As has been described above, attempts to thicken that line by bringing in Rockingham's 9 Brigade failed because of that formation's hesitant and confusing movements – it had been expected to relieve the Regiment during the night of 19 August, but did not fully get into position until 22 August. For nearly three days the South Albertas and the troops that fought with them were forced to battle against superior numbers with little real assistance from either 3rd or 4th Canadian Divisions other than artillery support. The only thing that really saved Wotherspoon and his men was the fact that the Germans did not want to overrun them but simply get around them. Certainly there was no possibility of stemming the German exodus – as Lieutenant Jack Summers of B Squadron summed it up: "It was like trying to stop a buffalo stampede, they went around us, they went over us and they went under us."[124]

Division was to make an "end run" through the high ground at Mount Ormel, take Chambois and Moissy and link up with 4th Division. These orders were never properly carried out. Maczek took Chambois but his units, caught up in heavy fighting around Mount Ormel, did not link up with 4th Division at Moissy. In fact the line of the Dives between Chambois and Moissy was never in the possession of Allied troops during the period 19-21 August. As for the 4th Division, most of its strength (three of four armoured regiments, two of four infantry battalions) was sent not to Chambois but to Hordouseaux in the northeast and was not actively engaged between 18 and 21 August in preventing the German breakout. Of the remainder of the division, the greater part of the Lincoln and Welland Regiment and the Argyll and Sutherland Highlanders never got further south than Trun. It was therefore left to the South Alberta Regiment, two companies of Argylls, one company of Links, 10 Machine Gun Company (New Brunswick Rangers) and two troops of self-propelled M-10s from 5th Anti-Tank Regiment to hold the line of the Dives between Trun and St. Lambert against the major German breakout attempt which began on the night of 19 August. This force, amounting to about 600 to 800 men with about 70 AFVs of all types had to cover a front approximately three miles in length against an estimated 60,000 to 70,000 Germans with as many as 100 armoured vehicles. It was an impossible mission and it failed.

The so-called Falaise Gap was never properly sealed. During the period 18-20 August, Allied troops never occupied the Dives between St. Lambert and Chambois and responsibility for that failure must lie with Simonds, his two armoured divi-

One thing was clear. The South Albertas had fought a hell of a battle – they knew it and so did the other fighting men of the Canadian army. It was this action, Bob Clipperton concluded, "that proved to the rest ... just how tough and determined the South Alberta Regiment was" and wherever "we went after that battle, whether in action or on leave ... people would look at our flashes and you would hear a comment: 'There's one of the SARs, they fought at St. Lambert.'"[125] That reputation had not been won without cost – the Regiment lost thirteen killed and thirty-six wounded between 18 and 21 August.

For Dave Currie, the main result of the battle was a personal one. There "is much to fear in war," he commented later, "but to me, the greatest fear was the possibility that I might not measure up to that which was asked of me. St. Lambert proved to me that I could measure up, and left me with the certain conviction that we would be equal to the task ahead of us – the defeat of Germany."[126] Any South Alberta who served with Dave Currie at St. Lambert would doubt very much if the man knew the meaning of fear, as he had displayed outstanding leadership and quiet courage under the most trying of circumstances, and Wotherspoon, who knew better than most what Dave had been through, immediately applied for an award of the DSO to the commander of C Squadron.

Swatty Wotherspoon himself regarded the three-day fight around St. Lambert as "a thrilling experience."[127] Just before RHQ finally left Hill 117 at 0900 hours on 22 August, he could not resist the temptation to let the world know how he felt by firing several "V for Victory" bursts (three short, one long) from the Bren gun on his scout car.

An SAR Colour Album

Uniforms of the South Albertas. The oil painting by Edmonton artist Ron Volstad depicts (from left) a
sergeant in summer drill and wedge cap armed with a Lee-Enfield, 1941; a lieutenant in battledress, 1943;
and a trooper in tank suit armed with a Sten gun, 1945. The tank is a Sherman V (American M4A4).

SOUTH ALBERTA REGIMENT VETERANS ASSOCIATION.

Predecessors, 1939. In 1938 the 19th Alberta Dragoons were mechanized but, in honour of the Royal Visit of May 1939, Captain Bob Bradburn of the Dragoons formed a mounted troop to escort Their Majesties. Borrowing horses and kit and purchasing second-hand helmets from a British cavalry regiment, he managed to put the 19th in the saddle again. Bradburn commanded either a company or a squadron in the Regiment until August 1944 when he took over the Algonquin Regiment.

COURTESY, HARRY QUARTON.

The immortal Sherman. A study of a 4th Canadian Armoured Division Sherman V at Cormelles outside Caen on 28 July 1944. This is possibly a tank of the British Columbia Regiment. The straw is an attempt to provide some camouflage. At this point the armoured regiments of the division had not yet welded extra track links onto their hulls for extra protection – they would be doing so very shortly.

DND, NEGATIVE ZK-859

"Clanky" and its crew. From left to right, Trooper Gordon Holstrom, Corporal John Lardner and Trooper Dick Mitchell, members of Major Dave Currie's tank crew, relax on "Clanky," the C Squadron command tank, 28 July 1944. These men survived the war but "Clanky" came to a bad end at Bergen op Zoom on 28 October 1944 when it was destroyed by a direct hit from a Canadian 5.5 gun. "Clanky" and crew made the cover of *Liberty* magazine, 16 December 1944, but by this time "Clanky" was no more. DND, NEGATIVE ZK 869-1.

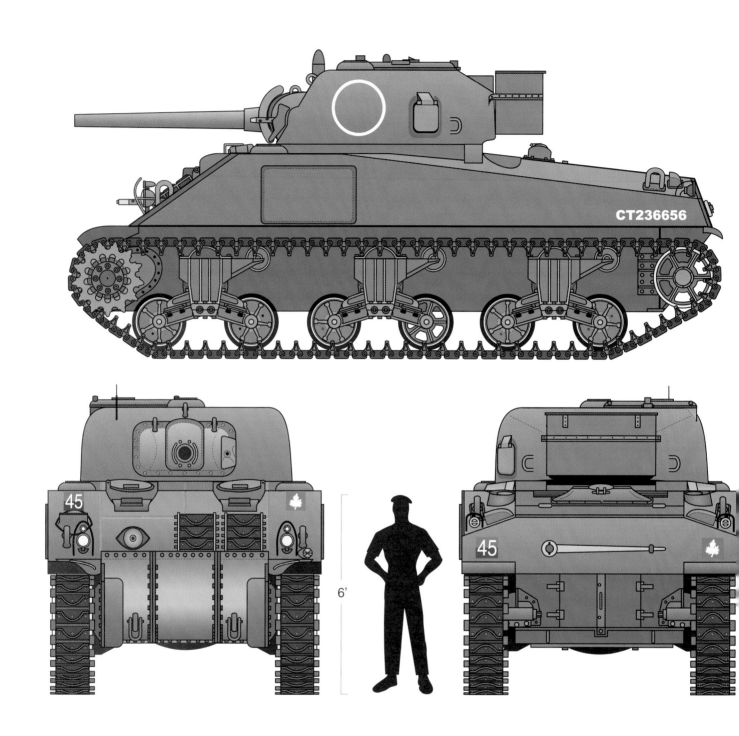

Armoured Reconnaissance
Regiment Unit Serial and
Arm of Service Sign

4th Canadian Armoured
Division Formation Sign

Sherman V (M4A4), Normandy, 1944. In Normandy the Sherman V with its 75 mm gun was
the most numerous tank in the Regiment. This example is marked with the Tactical signs of
C Squadron, SAR, and bears the unit's "45" serial and 4th Division formation sign.

1:35 scale illustration by Chris Johnson.

Currie, VC. Major David Vivian Currie, VC, officer commanding
C Squadron, South Alberta Regiment, photographed in early
December 1944. He wears the ribbon of the Victoria Cross, the only
such award to the Canadian Armoured Corps during the war and
the only such award won by the Canadian Army in Normandy.

DND, NEGATIVE ZK-938.

Brewed-up. Oil sketch of a brewed-up South Alberta Firefly near Veen, 6 March 1945, by Private F.T.V. Savard of the Argyll and Sutherland Highlanders.

REPRODUCED BY KIND PERMISSION OF THE ARGYLL AND SUTHERLAND HIGHLANDERS OF CANADA.

Mountains, sky and prairie. The badge of the South Alberta Regiment was the provincial crest. It was originally adopted as the badge of the Alberta Regiment in 1921.

AUTHOR'S COLLECTION.

Regimental flash. Wartime wool SAR regimental "flash" or shoulder title in the unit's colours of black and gold.

COURTESY, DAVID MARSHALL.

(Above) The Colour. Regimental Colour of The South Alberta Regiment carrying the battle honours of the 31st Battalion, CEF, (The Alberta Regiment) won in 1915-1918 and the battle honours of the Regiment won in 1944-1945. This Colour is displayed today in the rotunda of the Alberta Legislature.

COURTESY, DANNY MCLEOD.

(Left) The Regiment remembers St. Lambert. South Alberta memorial at St. Lambert-sur-Dives erected by the Regiment on land deeded in perpetuity by the people of the village. It is located on the D 13 highway directly opposite the spot where Dave Currie and Pete Woolf stood in the famous photo taken on 19 August 1944.

COURTESY, DANNY MCLEOD.

And not to yield. Edmonton, 1995. Vic Henderson escorts
C.R. "Speedy" Fast as he drapes the Colour of The South Alberta
Regiment over the piled drums of The Loyal Edmonton Regiment so
that they may be consecrated by a military chaplain. Fast joined the
Regiment in 1941 and Henderson in 1945.

PART V

ADVANCING

Liberators. Having advanced from Normandy through Belgium to Holland, a B Squadron troop carries out maintenance on a street in Bergen op Zoom watched by the usual bevy of fascinated small boys. Note the frying pan hanging from the back of B20.

NAC, PA 140896.

CHAPTER ELEVEN

"We're off to Berlin!"

FRANCE AND BELGIUM: 22 AUGUST–11 SEPTEMBER 1944

Rockingham's 9 Brigade finally relieved the Regiment at 0900 hours, 22 August 1944, and the South Albertas pulled out of their positions around Hill 117. During the morning the Regiment concentrated at Trun prior to moving to a small orchard to harbour, where Wotherspoon gave the boys the good news that "rest was of primary importance" as they would not be wanted for some time.[2] On the following morning, however, as the squadrons were carrying out a much-needed "maintenance and clean up," word came down that the unit would move that day with 10 Brigade although it was unlikely that it "would be called upon to do a fighting role."[3] Not that the Regiment was capable of much fighting at this point because tank casualties over the last week had been extremely heavy – the SAR had completely written off a lot of tanks since 15 August and there were dozens of others, less badly damaged and repairable, scattered among various workshops.

When the order to move came at midday, Corporal Walter Vandermark of C-1 Troop shouted, "we're off to Berlin!" into his intercom as he did every time his Sherman started out.[4] The Regiment fell in at the end of the brigade column and, after a trip of twelve miles, harboured that night near the village of Le Sap. The following day, 24 August, the SAR did thirty miles, ending up in the outskirts of Bernay (see map 5, page 126) and, on 25 August, it continued on to Vraiville. The South Albertas now experienced the joys of being liberators as they entered towns and villages unmarked by war whose inhabitants greeted them with splendid enthusiasm. Corporal John Galipeau remembered that the people "crowded the sidewalks and spilled out into the road; our drivers had to just creep through the mobs" as the boys "were showered with flowers and fruit, bottles of cognac and cider, and there were girls all over the tanks and trucks."[5] The crew of John Lakes's Stuart enjoyed the "exuberance of the villagers, and the wine bottles that were produced were most tempting but we could not linger because there was another village down the road waiting for its liberation."[6] There were pretty girls everywhere and Trooper Gerry

> *W*e'll push you 'cross the river
> And through the field of grain,
> You'll wish you had never heard
> Of the Normandy campaign.
>
> Lay that Luger down, kid,
> You haven't got a chance.
> Luger-luggin' Ludwig,
> You're all washed up in France.[1]

Bird, driving one of the large B Echelon kitchen trucks, became so distracted by the smiling beauty of one *jeune fille* that he took his eyes off the road for a moment and promptly ran into the back of the truck in front of him.[7]

It was a good time to be an Allied soldier. As the American and Commonwealth armies moved toward the Seine, they encountered little German resistance and there was general optimism that the war would soon come to a victorious end. Danny McLeod recalled thinking at this time "that we've broken the backs of these people and this thing may be over sooner than we thought."[8] Bob Clipperton echoed these sentiments when he wrote to his wife, Andy, on 23 August that it was "only a matter of time now & if I am not sent to Japan I should be home this year."[9] There were Germans around, however, and you had to be careful entering newly-liberated villages because the enemy were sometimes just pulling out the other side. Doc Boothroyd had a close call at one such nameless hamlet in France – he had just gotten out of his jeep when "a bullet went right through the back of the seat." As he remarked, "I guess Padre Silcox and I discussed mortality that night."[10]

The speed of the German retreat caught Allied commanders off guard. Montgomery had planned to reach the Seine by D+90 but the first Allied units actually reached that river on 18 August, or D+73. The question of logistics now began to dominate Allied councils as the farther the two army groups (British 21 Army Group and the American 12 Army Group) advanced, the longer their supply lines became. Montgomery urged that a single massive thrust, using forty divisions, be made in his sector to cross the Rhine and seize the Ruhr, the industrial heartland of Germany. As he put it, "we haven't the resources to maintain both Army Groups at full pressure" and the "only policy is to halt the right and strike with the left, or halt the left and strike with the right." "If we split," he warned, "and advance on a broad front, we shall be so weak everywhere that we will have no chance of success."[11] Eisenhower saw the logic in this but Eisenhower was also receptive to the urging of General Omar Bradley that his American 12 Army Group take a princi-

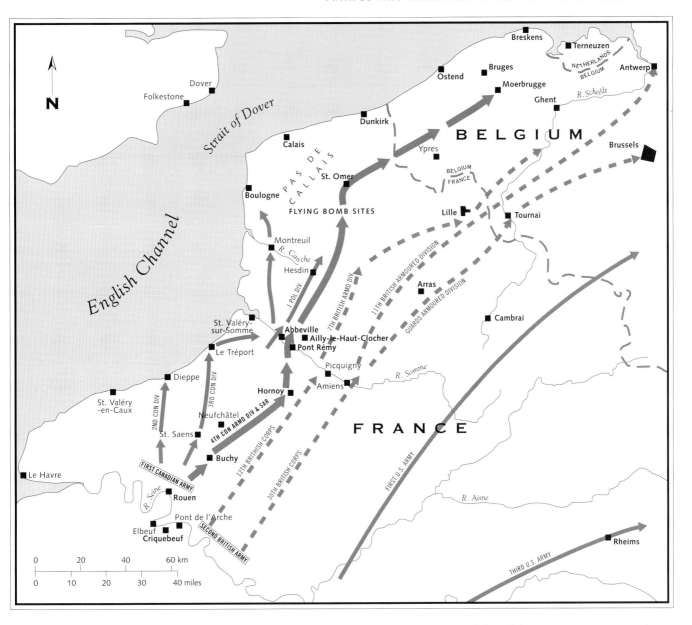

Map 9: The great advance, 22 August-4 September 1944. For nearly two weeks the Allied armies followed the retreating Germans as they withdrew from France. The war looked to be over after both Paris and Antwerp fell.

pal part in any forthcoming operations. Unfortunately the question became one of nationalities – whether the Allied armies should advance on a broad front, which would see the Americans play a major role, or on a narrow front, which would see the Commonwealth forces play a major role. A dangerous gap was beginning to emerge in Allied strategical thinking, but for the time being the future looked bright – on 25 August Paris was liberated and the following day SHAEF (Supreme Headquarters Allied Expeditionary Force) stated that the victory in Normandy had "brought the end of the war in Europe within sight, almost within reach."[12]

That prediction turned out to be inaccurate. The *Wehrmacht* had suffered a serious defeat but managed to escape from the consequences because of a major Allied error. Having failed to

trap the German armies in the Falaise pocket, Allied commanders compounded this fault by not using their air superiority to prevent the Germans from crossing the Seine River. The weather, which was variable from 20-23 August, played some part in this failure but the surprising decision taken on 21 August to switch the targets of medium bombers from the Seine bridges to German supply depots on the eastern bank was disastrous. Several bridges were left intact and the Germans took full advantage of this heaven-sent opportunity to use these crossing points, plus temporary bridges and rafts, to get 240,000 men, between 25,000 and 30,000 vehicles, and over one hundred AFVs to safety. Having done this, they then destroyed these bridges to deny them to the Allies.[13]

On Saturday, 26 August, the South Alberta Regiment

Over the Seine. Ten Brigade's crossing point of the Seine River near Criquebeuf, France, August 1944. Note the airbursts in the sky. COURTESY, M. AMYOTTE.

reached Tostes, just south of the Seine. The previous day Simonds had ordered Harry Foster's 4th Armoured Division to seize "by coup-de-main" a bridgehead in the area of Criquebeuf. During the evening of 25 August the Lincoln and Welland Regiment, which was leading the 10 Brigade column, arrived at La Haye Malherbe, a few miles south of the river and, at 2000 hours, the Links's scout platoon accompanied by Lieutenant Wally Young's troop from A Squadron and five Stuarts from Recce Troop moved forward to find a route to the Seine. It was too dark to do much that night but the next morning Young's troop and the Recce tanks accompanied the Links as they occupied Criquebeuf-sur-Seine without fighting. The Germans, however, occupied a strong position on high ground on the north bank of the river and, as the engineers began to construct a bridge to a low-lying island in the Seine, they came under heavy shelling. A Links platoon managed to cross the river in a boat they had discovered, and when they reported no enemy defences in the immediate area of the far bank, Bill Cromb decided to send one company across and they were established near the hamlet of Freneuse by last light on 26 August.[14]

Foster now had a bridgehead but attempts to enlarge it ran into determined German resistance. By 27 August all of the infantry of 10 Brigade had crossed over, and as they moved up to positions on the far bank they were supported from the south bank by the Regiment, which "shelled the top of the hill [on

the north bank] continuously to keep the enemy's heads down."[15] The Links and the Argylls tried to take the two commanding hills, Points 88 and 95, but heavy German fire drove them back, and the Argylls suffered a severe loss when much of their headquarters element was captured after it took a wrong turn and drove into the German positions. The following morning, 28 August, the first SAR tanks began to cross on two rafts but, since the "rate of crossing was only 4-5 vehicles" an hour, it took nearly the whole day to get all of the Fighting Echelon over.[16] By 1900 hours, all the South Alberta tanks were on the north side and RHQ set up shop in Freneuse.[17]

Throughout the day the tank troops who arrived on the north bank provided fire support for the Argylls and Links as they struggled to secure Points 88 and 95. Ten Brigade finally took the high ground at the cost of heavy casualties but Foster had already decided that Criqueboeuf was too vulnerable to German artillery and, during the previous night, the divisional engineers had constructed a bridge at the neighbouring town of Elbeuf. Moncel's 4 Brigade poured over this bridge on 28 August and the Germans, having delayed the division for two days and gained valuable time, withdrew to the north.[18]

The division was over the Seine and the advance resumed on 30 August. By now it had been in action without pause for more

Crossing the Seine. Where the Regiment crossed the Seine with 10 Brigade, the north channel viewed from the island in the middle. PHOTOGRAPH BY DIANNE GRAVES.

than two weeks and was badly in need of a rest period. Simonds had promised Foster that his men would get that rest when they reached Buchy and, spurred on by that reward, 4 Armoured Brigade led the division as it drove steadily north under a downpour of rain. Buchy was taken on the last day of August and the division heard the welcome news that the Polish Division would take over the lead while it would go into corps reserve for four days "during which time we would regroup and refit."[19] This order was received at 1830 hours, but two hours later the South Albertas got another message which "cancelled previous orders" and told them to be prepared to continue the march that night.

Just after midnight, the Regiment fell in at the tail of the 10 Brigade column and resumed the march under a steady drizzle. It was a long and tedious movement and drivers frequently fell asleep during the halts and delayed progress. To prevent this happening, a member of A Squadron recalled that, when the South Albertas stopped, "the co-driver would get out and lean on the tank ahead so that if the column started moving, he would wake up and go back and get his own tank going."[20]

Swatty was caught off guard by the unexpected change of plans on 31 August as he had accepted an invitation to dine with a French count and countess who resided in a castle near the Regimental harbour. Swatty always kept "a suit of civvies" in his kit so, properly attired, he attended at the castle, the aristocratic French couple "dug up their best wines" and the colonel enjoyed "a beautiful dinner." "About 10 o'clock at night," he sadly recalled, "we were just getting into the fine 40-year-old cognac" when word came that he was needed as the Regiment was resuming the advance. With reluctance, Swatty got into his scout car "and we went about 20 miles" that night. When morning came, there was a lengthy halt while 10 Brigade waited for 4 Brigade to take over the lead so he "stopped in a farm house to have some breakfast" and read the London papers which had just come up with the mail. These papers contained the citations for the first British Victoria Crosses awarded in Normandy and Swatty was studying them when Harry Foster drove up. Since the divisional commander "looked tired and sort of upset," Wotherspoon invited him to have a bite to eat and Foster gratefully accepted. Swatty takes up the story:

> I said to the general, "Have you seen yesterday's papers, sir?" No, he hadn't seen them. I said, "Look at this, look at the VCs. He said, "Yeah, that's fantastic." I said, "I want to tell you about one of my officers, Dave Currie." I said, "I recommended him for a DSO, but he's done far better work than any one of these VC's. He said, "Well, get that [DSO] recommendation back. I hope it hasn't gone beyond your brigade, and put him in for a VC."[21]

It was done. The paperwork for the DSO, awarded for an act of "meritorious or distinguished service" by an officer, which Swatty had begun immediately after the fight at St. Lambert

was withdrawn and a new application submitted for the Victoria Cross. Instituted during the Crimean War the VC was the highest tribute to heroism that a soldier in the Commonwealth could receive during the Second World War and was only granted (often posthumously) for exceptional gallantry in the face of the enemy. Wotherspoon, more than anyone, knew what Dave had been through at St. Lambert and what he had accomplished and, although Swatty was not averse to helping out the process, he always remained firm in the belief that "if there was any man who deserved the VC, Dave Currie did."[22]

During the afternoon of 1 September the advance continued and the Regiment harboured that night near Arraines. The following day they passed through Hellencourt and moved up to the Somme, crossing that river the next day and concentrating in and about the town of Ailly-le-Haut-Clocher near Abbeville, where they were informed that they would get two days for rest and maintenance.[23]

Advancing. A South Alberta Sherman rolls down a tree-shaded country road in France, late August 1944. COURTESY, R.H. ALLSOPP.

The quick Allied approach to the Somme upset German plans. Hitler and his commander in the west, *Feldmarschall* Walter Model, had planned to make a stand on that river but these intentions were overtaken by events. Patton's Third Army outflanked the intended German position to the south, while the British 30 Corps "bounced" Abbeville after a daring advance during the night of 29 August and captured the commander of the German Seventh Army in his pyjamas. The Somme line was now breached and Montgomery urged his armoured division commanders "to push boldly ahead" into Belgium "creating alarm and despondency in enemy rear areas."[24] The two formations obeyed with alacrity – on 3 September the Guards Armoured Division took Brussels and on the following day the British 11th Armoured Division captured Antwerp, the second largest port in Europe. The Allies were now eighty miles from the Rhine.

To the recently-promoted Field Marshal Montgomery, the Rhine and the vulnerable Ruhr beyond were the objectives that mattered above all else. On the same day that Antwerp fell, he urged Eisenhower to make "one powerful and full-blooded thrust towards Berlin." Eisenhower, who had assumed supreme command of the Allied forces in the field, replied that, although Montgomery's planned operations in the north would have priority in terms of supplies, they would not be undertaken at

Bob and the Doc. Captain Bob Allsopp (left) and Captain Wilfred "Doc" Boothroyd relax on the steps of the château at Ailly-le-Haut-Clocher. COURTESY, R.H. ALLSOPP.

the expense of other operations. He therefore issued a directive on 4 September not only ordering Montgomery to secure Antwerp and seize the Ruhr but also ordering Bradley's 12 Army Group to seize Frankfurt on the Rhine. Bradley interpreted this order to mean that Patton's Third Army, which had been halted for lack of supplies, could now continue its forward movement. Despite paying lip service to the primacy of the northern "single thrust," Eisenhower had given tacit approval to the "broad front" policy favoured by Bradley and Patton. Patton's advance, however, bogged down at Metz after Model rushed his few mobile reserves into the area. Allied momentum was beginning to slow but Montgomery was convinced that he had a plan that would get it back again – on 10 September he received Eisenhower's approval for a bold operation that would take Second British Army from Belgium to the Rhine. Code-named MARKET GARDEN, it called for the paratroop divisions of First Allied Airborne Army to seize three crossing points over the Maas, Waal and Rhine rivers, clearing the way for Second British Army to outflank the Siegfried Line and be in a position to move across the north German plain.[25]

All this, of course, was unknown to the South Albertas – they were just happy to have a break at Ailly. "After a good night's sleep," recorded the War Diarist on 3 September, "the Sq[uadro]ns started in on the greatly needed maintenance drive."[26] Swatty decided it was time to celebrate by

holding a formal dinner but the South Albertas' billets at Ailly did not have a space that would hold all his officers and their guests. He called in his second-in-command and said, "Bert, I think we should have a mess dinner and this room isn't big enough." Coffin replied, "Leave it to me, sir." Within "twelve hours," Swatty recalled with pride, "a whole wall had been taken out, the house had been shored up, and we had a lovely mess with things very well done."[27] All through 4 September, "RHQ went slightly wild with the preparations for the dinner" and "Scout cars and jeeps were much in demand all day for hunting up the required beverages and the long forgotten delicacies."[28] Wally Young scored a great coup when he "found a liquor store in Abbeville and conveniently produced fourteen bottles of champagne."

Swatty invited the commanding officers of every unit who had fought alongside the Regiment in Normandy and the menu for that occasion, dated "Somewhere in France 4 Sep 44," has survived.[29] It contains an interesting assortment of exotic dishes: "*Le potage du canon* (cannon soup), *salade de cartouche* (cartridge salad), *la mitrailleuse poulet* (machine-gun chicken), *boeuf à la cavalrie* (cavalry beef), *la pomme de terre à la tranchée* (trench potatoes), *la carrotte à la Coffin* (Coffin's carrots), *le haricot du poilu* (soldiers' beans), *la fraise au Clan Stewart* (Stewart strawberries) and *la poire chef du brigade* (brigadier's pears). As Quartermaster Tommy Barford complained, the beef was well named because it had the texture of old horse and "was the toughest piece of meat I ever tasted."[30] Nonetheless a good time was had by all. A band was scared up from one of the infantry regiments and "played throughout dinner, although at times it could

Even the RSM has to unwind sometime. Sergeant Doug Prenevost (left) and RSM Jock Mackenzie relax at Ailly-le-Haut-Clocher, France, September 1944. COURTESY, R.H. ALLSOPP.

The regimental brains trust. From the left, Captain "Newt" Hughes, the battle adjutant, Lieutenant Hank Carroll, the intelligence officer, and Captain Bob Allsopp, the adjutant, relax at Ailly, early September 1944. These three officers provided Swatty Wotherspoon with the information he needed to command the Regiment in battle. COURTESY, R.H. ALLSOPP.

scarcely be heard through the din."[31] Not to be outdone, Wally Young tickled the ivories and, from "the noise of the piano and the strength of the vocal cords," recorded the War Diarist, the resulting racket "resembled a typical South Alberta Regt party."

While it rested at Ailly the Regiment received a number of reinforcements. One of the new arrivals, Trooper Ian MacPherson, recalls that he had been given the choice of any of the four armoured regiments in the division but chose the South Albertas because "I didn't want anything to do with the rest."[32] MacPherson came up in a truck with other reinforcements and was assigned to A Squadron, where Corporal Herbie Watkins "sort of took us under his wing and gave us information about how to survive, how to make a bivouac, cook meals, etc." Ian thought the SARs "were the wildest looking bunch of buggers I had ever seen, playing poker with stacks of French money and hung all over with German revolvers and binoculars." One of the newcomers was a reluctant arrival. Trooper David Marshall had been languishing in the holding unit for 4th Armoured Division and he and three friends had gone off on an illegal expedition from their camp the day the unit assignments were made. When they returned they discovered that, in their absence, their fate had been decided:

All our plans to join some well known glorious regiment like the 1st Hussars or The Fort Garry Horse … or the Foot Guards or the Horse Guards or the Grenadier Guards had gone up in smoke. We found that during our absence we had become members of the South Alberta Regiment. *The What?*

We were a sorry foursome, feeling that the world had played us another dirty trick. How wrong we were. We found later that the SARs had a unique method of fighting that resulted in many fewer casualties and an operational success rate second to none. Also, due to the lower turnover of men, a supportive family atmosphere prevailed. Men who had been with the regiment since mobilization were still there, which lent a degree of stability and a feeling of belonging that can only come with men who know each other well. That unauthorized stroll was probably the most fortuitous walk I ever took.[33]

Marshall remembered the morale in the Regiment as "very high" when he joined it because the South Albertas "had seen much hard fighting and knew that they had done a good job." But it was still difficult being the new boy:

It felt great to be with such a positive group but I was very much alone. I knew that I was here because one of their friends had become a casualty and I was taking his place. … There was no resentment shown to me, on the contrary they made me very welcome but I was the outsider. I could not join in any of the conversation as it was about people I did not know, places I had not seen and battles I had only read about. It takes a long time to become one of the boys and in war we are not always given that time.[34]

While Allied soldiers were enjoying the role of liberators, Adolf Hitler was desperately trying to build up the defences of the Siegfried Line. This defensive belt along the western border of Germany had been constructed in the 1930s as the counterpart to the French Maginot Line but over the last five years it had been allowed to run down – its armament had been removed, its fortifications were antiquated by 1944 standards and it had no garrison. In early September the new German commander in the west, *Feldmarschall* Gerd von Rundstedt, estimated that he needed six weeks to place the Siegfried Line in a proper state of defence and to gain that time the Allied juggernaut would have to be stopped.[35]

This would require manpower but German manpower was at a premium in the early autumn of 1944. The *Wehrmacht* had suffered catastrophic losses of personnel and equipment on both the eastern and western fronts during the summer, and the few mobile reserves available were put into battle against Patton's Third Army. The panzer and paratroop formations that had escaped from the Falaise Pocket were sent back to Germany to be refitted and there were no troops or reinforcements available for the northern part of the German front facing Montgomery's 21 Army Group. Worse still, the British capture of Antwerp had cut off and trapped the German Fifteenth Army along the Channel coast. Even *Feldmarschall* Walter Model, the commander of Army Group B which faced Montgomery's 21 Army Group, did not know the real gravity of the German manpower situation – on the same day that Antwerp fell, he requested twenty-five fresh infantry divisions and six panzer divisions to be sent to the west. As one historian commented, he "might as well have asked for the moon."[36]

Taking a break. Men of the AA Troop enjoy a welcome and deserved break during the advance from France. Seated on the Crusader tank is Trooper H. Kerr. Standing from left to right are Troopers Dan Larkin, H. Clark and J. Miller. In the front are Troopers Anderson, Blunden and Fitzgerald. COURTESY, M. AMYOTTE.

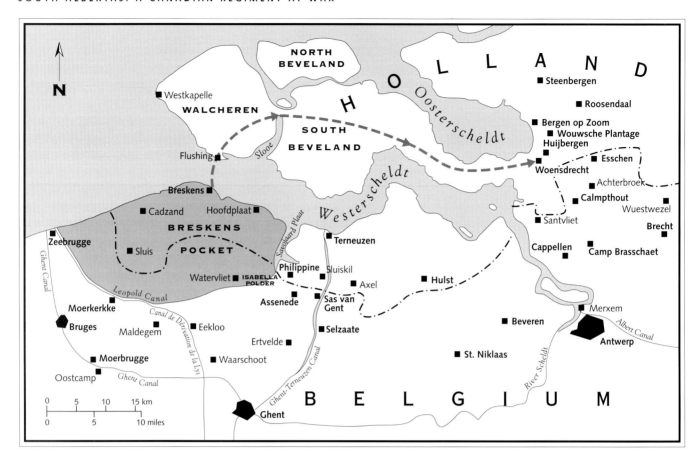

Map 10: The Scheldt battles, September-October 1944. British armour took Antwerp on 4 September, trapping the German Fifteenth Army in the Breskens area, but when the British failed to cut off the South Beveland Peninsula, that army escaped using the route marked by the dotted line. First Canadian Army now got the job of taking the approaches to Antwerp but, since the infantry divisions were clearing the Channel ports, 4th Canadian and 1st Polish Armoured Divisions had to continue the advance. On 8 September 10 Brigade got a bridgehead over the Ghent Canal at Moerbrugge but an attempt to break into the German defences of the Breskens Pocket was rebuffed at Moerkerkke. In all it would take the Canadians nearly three bloody months to open the port of Antwerp.

To get men, Hitler resorted to improvisation. Garrison and fortress units, training schools, officer cadet schools, depot staffs, men on leave or convalescents, police, anti-aircraft, naval and labour personnel were hastily converted into combat troops and formed into temporary units which were sent to the west. By these expedients, he came up with 135,000 men, most of which were not first-class troops but still able to fight from defensive positions. *Reichsmarschall* Hermann Goering now came to his leader's rescue. Under the German system Goering's *Luftwaffe* controlled all airborne units and Goering offered 30,000 men drawn from paratroop units either training or refitting, trained paratroopers in convalescent depots, and *Luftwaffe* pilots and ground crew converted to infantry. Most of these men were paratroops in name only but since they were "young, ardent and loyal," they "could be relied upon to fight for Hitler to the end."[37] Goering's offering was hastily formed into the First Parachute Army and sent to Belgium and Holland under the command of General Kurt Student, the architect of the airborne invasion of Crete in 1941. This was a helpful addition but it would still take time to organize these new troops

into units and position them at the front – and Hitler was also running out of time.

Unfortunately Allied leaders handed the German dictator exactly what he needed. The 11th British Armoured Division's capture of Antwerp intact on 4 September was a great feat but Antwerp lies fifty miles from the sea and the Germans controlled the Scheldt estuary, the inland waterway to the port. Antwerp was useless until these approaches were secured but the commander of the 11th Armoured Division, Major General P.B. Roberts, received no orders to advance beyond Antwerp and did not see fit to do so on his own initiative. It was not that Allied generals were ignorant of geography – they were distracted by the shimmering gleam of the Rhine and beyond in early September. Not only did Antwerp remained closed to Allied supply ships but the Germans also retained possession of the South Beveland peninsula, which permitted Hitler to evacuate by water the eight trapped divisions of the Fifteenth Army from the mainland, draw them through that peninsula and ultimately reposition them on a new defence line which ran along the length of the Albert Canal east of Antwerp.[38]

On 6 September, Hitler ordered the commander of the Fifteenth Army, *General* Gustav von Zangen, to hold a bridgehead south of the Scheldt to permit his troops to be evacuated. The evacuation from the small port of Breskens across to Flushing began the day Antwerp fell and continued for seventeen days during which 86,100 infantry and 616 artillery pieces were rescued to fight again without any interference from the Allied forces. Von Zangen established his bridgehead in what was to be called "the Breskens pocket," an area along the Belgian coast from Zeebrugge to Terneuzen and roughly bounded by the Leopold Canal. Hitler immediately designated this position as *Fortress Scheldt Sud* meaning that the garrison was expected to fight to the last man. To gain time to build up his defences, von Zangen also established an advance position along the Ghent Canal west of Breskens and ordered the commanders of the 64th and 245th Infantry Divisions, tasked with holding that position "to make a stand." If that was not clear enough, *Reichsführer* Heinrich Himmler promulgated an order on 10 September proclaiming that any German soldier who surrendered would be regarded as a deserter and not only would "every deserter ... find his just punishment" but "his ignominious behaviour will entail the most severe consequences for his family" who, upon "examination of the circumstances ... will be shot."[39] The German retreat was over.[40]

The Regiment's rest came to an end on 6 September 1944 when First Canadian Army resumed its advance. The 2nd and 3rd Divisions now turned off to the Channel coast to clear the ports of Boulogne, Calais and Dunkirk and 4th Armoured Division took over the lead. The SAR covered sixty miles on 6 September, the longest single day's advance it ever made and harboured that night close to St. Omer. For David Marshall that day was memorable because he discovered that there are perils in war besides enemy action. Like many earnest and impressionable young Canadians, Marshall had signed the *National Pledge* ("My Resolution as an Aid to our National Effort and for the sake of others I purpose to abstain from the use of all alcoholic liquor as a beverage for the duration of the war and the period of demobilization"). He had held true to his word for three years but, on 6 September 1944, under the stress of active service, David Marshall fell from grace. It all started

when we made a short halt and stopped beside a house built right next to the road. We sat on top of the tank waiting for orders to move when a man opened the second floor window right beside me. He asked something that I interpreted to mean "how many?" to that I replied "cinq" at which he produced six small glasses and lined them up on the window sill. He poured a clear liquid into them, which I really did not think was water, offered each of us a glass and proposed a toast. We could hardly refuse.[41]

This was bad enough but when the column halted again down the road, the tanks were surrounded by the usual crowds of cheering civilians, including "a priest dressed in the old traditional garb, long black robe and flat hat, who upon seeing me reached into his cassock, pulled out a bottle of wine and shoved it up at me." Marshall could only think of Paul's admonition to Timothy, "Stop drinking nothing but water, take a little wine for your digestion, for your frequent ailments." "These two lapses," he sadly recorded, "started me on the downward path." [42]

There was more alcohol available the next day, 7 September. This was the day that Sergeant Frank Freer of B Squadron acquired the nickname of "Fast Brew" for his ability to consume an amazing amount of drink during a short halt.[43] Late in the afternoon, the South Albertas' lead elements crossed the border into Belgium near Dixmude and the boys immediately noticed that

Belgium was very different from France. Everything was so much cleaner. The French hadn't been fussy about their streets, which had been quite dirty. The Belgian streets were meticulous. As we drove by ... the women would be out scrubbing the sidewalks in front of their houses. Belgium seemed to have a great many pretty girls who smiled at us as we passed by and we found them very attractive.[44]

Lieutenant Don Stewart thought that going "from France into Belgium was just like going from night into day, Belgium is so neat and clean and rich after the dirt and squalor of France."[45]

The following day, 8 September, the division pushed on. Moncel's 4 Brigade was directed towards Bruges while 10 Brigade, temporarily under the command of Dave Stewart of the Argylls in the absence of an ill Jim Jefferson, was ordered to secure a crossing of the Ghent Canal south of that city. The Argylls and C Squadron were leading the brigade column with Lieutenant Jack Roberts's C-2 Troop in the van. Shortly after midday Roberts's four tanks entered the small Belgian town of Oostcamp, a few miles from the canal, and received a tumultuous reception. The local head of the Resistance, Baron Thierry Peers de Nieuwburgh, donned his Belgian army uniform for the occasion and climbed aboard Roberts's tank to warn him that the bridge over the canal in the neighbouring village of Moerbrugge was wired for demolition. Perhaps the happiest man in Oostcamp that day was Sergeant Jack White of the US Army Air Corps, who had been hiding in the town after bailing out of his damaged aircraft some weeks before. He greeted the South Albertas with the words: "Am I glad to see you guys!" It took Roberts's troop some time to get through the crowded streets and it was not until mid-afternoon that he was able to push on to Moerbrugge, which was actually a continuation of Oostcamp.[46]

Moving down Stationstraat, Roberts's troop sergeant's tank cautiously approached the canal bridge. David Marshall, the loader-operator in that tank, remembered what happened next:

Liberation, 8 September 1944. Joyful Belgians enthusiastically greet Lieutenant Jack Roberts's troop from B Squadron as it enters Oostcamp near Moerbrugge on 8 September 1944. These photos and a number of others in this chapter are reproduced from *De Slag om Moerbrugge: 8-12 September 1944* by Dr. C.H. Vlaemynck.

Belgians meet the boys from B. Standing in front of one of the first SAR tanks to enter Oostcamp on 8 September 1944 are, from the left: Sergeant Jack White of the US Army Air Corps, who had been hiding since his bomber was shot down; Maurits Reynaert; Baron Thierry de Nieuwburgh, head of the local resistance (in uniform); and the town's police chief.

DE SLAG OM MOERBRUGGE

We moved along a narrow street parallel to the canal and separated from it by a row of buildings that provided us with some cover. The enemy were a few yards away on the other side of the canal listening to our progress. We found the bridge intact. The sergeant edged his tank, with me tucked inside, towards the bridge and out in the open away from the protection of the buildings while discussing the situation with Lieutenant Roberts who was somewhat behind us and now out of sight. Roberts gave his troop the order to cross and with our driver rapidly increasing speed as we headed toward it and with only a few yards to go, a deafening explosion hit us as the German engineers blew up the bridge. We were sitting out in the open with pieces of bridge falling all over and around us when the enemy started firing with a barrage of anti-tank and small arms fire. The Argylls, who were walking beside us, ran for cover and we started backing up hoping that the tank behind us would get the same idea, no time for a fender bender, and simultaneously we opened fire with our 75 mm gun and our two machine guns.[47]

As the rest of C Squadron and the remaining Argyll companies came up they took positions along the canal bank. They were followed by the other two squadrons. When B Squadron passed through Oostcamp, the men in Trooper Tony Devreker's Sherman were amazed when he suddenly jumped down from his tank and enthusiastically embraced a little old grey-haired lady at the edge of the crowd. In response to their puzzled questions, Tony told the boys that the woman was his grandmother, whom he had not seen since he had emigrated to Canada with his parents in 1927. The story sounded entirely plausible but, since Tony was a well known joker, nobody was sure whether it was the truth or not.[48]

Meanwhile, at divisional headquarters, Harry Foster weighed the pros and cons of "trying to rush the crossing without proper planning or artillery support" and decided to go ahead as he "anticipated the same sort of short sharp fight we had experienced at earlier river crossings, followed by a general enemy withdrawal."[49] The order came down in the late afternoon for the Argylls to establish a bridgehead over the Ghent Canal at Moerbrugge (see map 11, page 197). Major William Stockloser, commanding the battalion, passed on the news to his company commanders and, one of them, Major Bob Paterson

inquired about the assault boats and was told there weren't any assault boats: they were forty, fifty or one hundred miles back and couldn't be brought up in time. And I asked the obvious question: "Well, how do you expect us to cross the Canal?" I was told it would be a "crossing of opportunity," and I thought, "Well, opportunity for whom: the Germans or us?"[50]

The Argylls "scrounged around and found a couple of old rowboats which were quite heavy and quite leaky." While A Company, supported by Darby Nash's B Squadron, moved to a position north of the crossing site and opened a furious fire to create a diversion, the men of D Company launched their fragile craft into the canal near the destroyed bridge. The Ghent Canal at this point is about sixty to eighty feet wide but it must have seemed like a mile to the four men who made the first crossing. The company commander, Major Pete MacKenzie, remembered that

> we sent across the first boat: I think [it] had four in it. And they took the rope across. We figured it would be faster to pull the thing across than try and row it. … When the second or third group crossed … the boat sank. We lost two men, so weighed down with their equipment that they just sank straight to the bottom. [We] Pulled the boat back as quickly as we could, emptied [bailed] it, and got the rest of the Company across.[51]

With such a vessel it took the Argylls more than seven hours to get three companies over the canal. They were fortunate that their chosen crossing point, Moerbrugge, lay exactly on the boundary of two German divisions holding the Ghent Canal line and each German divisional commander assumed the other was responsible for defending the village. For this reason, enemy reaction was slow but when the Germans got themselves sorted out, they immediately "began to direct mortar and 88 mm fire on the crossing" inflicting heavy casualties and in two hours the Argyll's C Company lost a third of its men.[52]

The infantry worked their way into Moerbrugge, which is basically a T-junction formed by the intersection of Kerkstraat, the street leading down from the canal, and the Legeweg or highway to Bruges. Major Bob Paterson's C Company took the left or north side of Kerkstraat while Major Pete MacKenzie's D Company took the right with B Company on their right at the Legeweg. The Argylls didn't get too far because the Germans began to infiltrate in behind their positions trying to cut them

off from the crossing point. Logistical problems limited the amount of artillery ammunition available and 15 Field was unable to bring down effective fire on this enemy movement. The Germans had no such limitations and directed heavy artillery, mortar, 88 and 20 mm AA fire at the bridgehead and at the west bank where the sappers of 8 Field Squadron were trying to set up their bridging equipment. By first light on 9 September, the sappers' historian recorded, "machine-gun and 20 mm fire was brought to bear directly on the [bridging] site from three separate directions and it became impossible even to walk across it."[53]

That day was a long one for 10 Brigade, but its units worked together like the first-class fighting team they had become. The South Albertas had withdrawn the previous night to a harbour near Oostcamp but B Squadron moved back to the canal at first light. During the night, three companies of Links had crossed over in the one remaining boat and established themselves with the Argyll's D Company in the southern part of Moerbrugge. The German 64th Infantry Division mounted several major attacks to eliminate the bridgehead but, with direct fire support from B Squadron's Shermans and the heavy machine guns and mortars of the New Brunswick Rangers, the Links were able to drive the enemy back from the canal bank and stop their infiltration. Sergeant Pete Woolf, who had perfected the use of the 20 mm Oerlikons against ground targets at St. Lambert, prowled the dyke on the west side of the canal pouring fire into the German-held buildings on the opposite side. At one point German vehicles worked themselves into a position where they "were bringing down a very heavy concentration of observed HE fire."[54] Lieutenant Jack Summers of B-2 went forward along the canal dyke on foot to locate these enemy spotters and then brought his troop up to drive them off. With this, enemy shelling became less accurate and the sappers recommenced work on the bridge while FOOs from 15 Field crossed the canal and directed artillery fire on the German counterattacks.[55]

Moerbrugge "was ablaze" the entire day with "small arms fire, grenades and piats" and the "air was a frenzy of automatic fire and the shouts and groans of wounded Germans."[56] The infantry beat off attack after attack but the crisis came at 1900 hours when

The canal at Moerbrugge. This modern view looking north shows where the canal has been widened to create a harbour. In 1944 it was the width shown in the background. PHOTOGRAPH BY DIANNE GRAVES.

the enemy teed up what was to be his last attempt at dislodging us. Counter attacks on both left and right flanks came in after a severe mortaring. One platoon on the right was overrun by sheer weight of numbers and the platoon commander was killed. But the company on the left [C Company of the Argylls] held, and those on the right forced the enemy back with great slaughter. They made three attempts to rush the defences, each time they formed an extended line some three to 400 yards away in open field. They came on in ragged lines, their grey greatcoats flapping at their ankles. Each time the God given Bren guns cut enormous swathes in their ranks. More ammunition had been secured for the artillery and with DF tasks called, and with the New Brunswick Vickers, and South Alberta Brownings sealing off the flanks, the enemy was held.[57]

It had been a near thing but the Argylls and Links grimly held on to their positions through the night as the sappers frantically tried to complete a bridge so that the South Albertas could cross over.

The enemy artillery at Moerbrugge was very heavy and John Neff of B Squadron thought that 9 September "was the worst shelling of the war bar none."[58] Trooper Carson Daley was Darby Nash's operator that day and Nash established his B Squadron HQ inside a bakery on the west bank of the canal. Daley remembered "the smell of bread" but then "they were putting the mortars to us and all of a sudden one came through the roof and the place filled with dust."[59] When the dust settled, Carson discovered he was wounded and was evacuated to England a few days later. Trooper Erle Foster from B was eating a meal with his crew when a mortar "stonk" came down. Foster flung himself under his Sherman and was trying to crawl through the open belly hatch when he was killed by a shell fragment that bounced off the tank track beside him. Erle Foster was a 22-year-old CNR worker from Wainwright, Alberta, who had joined the SAR in June 1941.[60] Troopers Boney Rathwell and Vern Storvik were badly wounded in similar incidents and both later died of their wounds although Rathwell survived long enough to see the end of the war. Vern Storvik was a 21-year-old farmer from Bawlf, Alberta, who had come to the SAR in October 1943 while Boney Rathwell was a 23-year-old CPR worker from Medicine Hat who joined the unit at Nanaimo in November 1940 and had been one of the stars of the 1940-1941 hockey team.[61]

Perhaps the most tragic death was that of Trooper Lloyd Woods. Woods was the co-driver in one of the halftrack ambulances and was moving through Oostcamp on 9 September when German shells started hitting the town. "Seeing through the [vision] slot, [that some] civilians were in danger, he opened the door 3 to 4 inches to see if they needed assistance" but just "at that moment a shell burst against buildings overhead and a fragment came through that narrow opening piercing his abdomen."[62] Woods, age 20, a labourer from Winnipeg

who had joined the SAR in 1943, died of his wounds a few hours later.[63]

During the night the sappers finally got a Bailey bridge over the canal and, at first light on 10 September, B Squadron prepared to cross into Moerbrugge. A section of sappers went over first to check the Kerkstraat for mines and, while they waited, the lead troop gunned their multi-bank Chryslers to get them warm. The men of Bob Paterson's beleaguered Argyll C Company, by now reduced to thirty-six men, heard "the engines start up" and "knew they were coming … Jesus, what a glorious moment, I'll tell you."[64] At 0700 B Squadron crossed the bridge and went "rumbling up the tile, brick and glass littered" Kerkstraat and the Argylls "could hardly see the Shermans for the tears of relief flooding their eyes."[65] Some men actually kissed the rough steel hulls and the tanks' presence in the village had an immediate effect as "things were rather tight before they came and one could hardly stick his finger above the ground without having it blown off but 15 min. after the tanks went through us we were walking around."[66]

The plan for 10 September called for B Squadron to firm up with the Argylls in Moerbrugge while A Squadron, with the Links, expanded the bridgehead in the direction of Lekkerhoek, a small village about a mile and a half to the east. C Squadron would remain in reserve on the west bank of the canal. The Germans had been forced back from Moerbrugge but they continued to offer ferocious resistance and the terrain favoured the defender. "The country here was flat," recalled David Marshall, "the roads running straight with trees and deep ditches along each side, not good tank country."[67] It was ground where "a well spotted anti-tank gun could keep you off that road and force you to use the fields and ditches" but "here other problems could develop, such as getting bogged down … or getting stuck in a ditch that was deeper than it should have been." The roads leading out of Moerbrugge were mined but you "couldn't get off the road because the ground was too soft," remembered John Galipeau, and the trees that lined the roads "had been pruned [only] to the height of about eight feet" from the ground which meant that a crew commander "could see nothing but trees."[68]

B Squadron found out quickly that the Germans were prepared to fight and fight hard when it took up positions at the edge of town and immediately came under fire from all types of weapons. The squadron replied by setting fire to the farm houses and hay stacks that dotted the flat fields to the east of Moerbrugge. B-1 Troop, which was about a mile north of the village, suffered from heavy AP and *Panzerfaust* attack. Sergeant Jim Kroesing's Sherman was brewed up but the crew, although burned, bailed out and began to run back through the ditches that bordered the road, pursued by German infantry. Corporal Cliff Strathdee, was seriously wounded and fell behind but Tony Devreker picked him up and carried him to safety. Tony

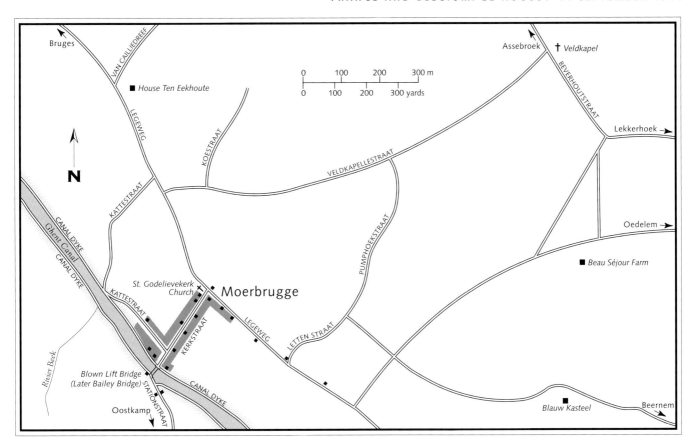

Map 11: Moerbrugge, 8-12 September 1944. The Argylls crossed the Ghent Canal and took Moerbrugge on 8 September but ferocious German resistance hampered the efforts of the engineers to get a bridge over the canal. The situation eased when SAR tanks crossed on 10 September but efforts to advance east from Moerbrugge to Lekkerhoek and Oedelem met with heavy fighting. Having delayed the Canadians, the Germans withdrew to a new defensive position in the Breskens Pocket on 12 September.

himself had facial burns but he had energy enough not only to carry Strathdee but also to shoot two Germans with his .38 revolver when they tried to block his escape – no mean feat. As if that wasn't enough, he also picked up three prisoners and brought them back with him. Another member of Kroesing's crew, Trooper Rick Frankson, was hit in the chest and, although he managed to do another sixty yards, collapsed and died. Eric Frankson was a 23-year-old farmer from Ohaton, Alberta, who had joined the Regiment in 1941. Before the day was through, B Squadron had lost four tanks.[69]

In mid-morning, Lavoie's A Squadron, which was down to three fighting troops, married up with the Links and prepared to move out to Lekkerhoek. Gordie Irving was in a good mood that day. It had been his continual complaint since landing in France that his A-1 Troop, because it came first on the order of battle, inevitably ended up leading either the squadron or the Regiment, but on 10 September Lavoie informed Irving that his troop would be the last in the squadron column and Gordie rejoiced: "The kid is in reserve."[70] A Squadron hadn't even started when their forming-up position came under artillery fire. Lieutenant Wally Young's troop then led the way out of Moerbrugge toward the Lekkerhoek road – and immediately ran into trouble.

The ditches, farmhouses and haystacks east of Moerbrugge were thick with German infantry, whose automatic weapons forced the Links to ground. Wally had just got on the Lekkerhoek road when two of his tanks were knocked out by *Panzerfausts* at close range. Minutes later, Wally was hit in the head by a sniper and killed instantly. The 31-year-old accountant from Edmonton, whose piano playing had made him a popular member of the officers' mess, had enlisted in the Edmonton Fusiliers in 1942 before being commissioned the following year and joining the SAR. His crew brought the tank back to Moerbrugge and Gordie helped them take Wally's body out of the turret. In the meantime Lieutenant Ray Smith's A-4 Troop, only two tanks strong, took over the lead and moved forward, some distance apart, to try to spot the enemy positions. A few minutes later, John Galipeau, the loader-operator in Sergeant Mackenzie's tank, heard Smith's operator say on the wireless: "Sunray shot dead by sniper, am pulling back to take him out."[71] Ray was conscious when the crew got him to the ambulance but he died on the way to the RAP. A married 26-year-old former clerk with International Harvester in Edmonton and a prewar member of the 19th Dragoons, Ray Smith was one of the old originals who had enlisted as a private in the Regiment

Picadilly Commando. Armoured bulldozer of 8 or 9 Field Squadron, Royal Canadian Engineers, at Moerbrugge. Throughout the campaign in northwest Europe, the sappers played an important, if unsung, role in every major action. *DE SLAG OM MOERBRUGGE*

South Alberta tank casualty at Moerbrugge. The Regiment paid heavily in the fighting of 10-11 September 1944. This Sherman V has lost both its tracks, but its bow .30 calibre Browning is missing, indicating that the crew may have removed it for ground action. *DE SLAG OM MOERBRUGGE*

Trying to make it run again. South Albertas working on their Sherman V after the battle at Moerbrugge. *DE SLAG OM MOERBRUGGE*

The Allied tank crew's basic nightmare, no. 4. A German Pak 40 75 mm anti-tank gun abandoned by its detachment near Moerbrugge. The standard anti-tank gun of the *Wehrmacht* in the last years of the war, this powerful and easily-concealed weapon destroyed more Allied tanks than the dreaded 88 mm. *DE SLAG OM MOERBRUGGE*

in June 1940 and had been commissioned in late 1941.[72]

Mackenzie now took over the lead and began to fire into a farmhouse that he suspected was a German strongpoint. Suddenly, John Galipeau remembered,

> twenty or thirty Germans came out of the building with their hands up in surrender. I had been firing the Browning … and I lowered my aim so it would just cover them. And the Browning "cooked off" [and] hit a prisoner in the middle of the group. I thought Mac was going to have a breakdown. I felt bad, too, because it was totally unintentional, and the poor guy had thought he was out of the war for good.[73]

Mackenzie's crew got the prisoners sorted out and then resumed the advance up the Lekkerhoek road. His Sherman had only moved a short distance, Galipeau reports, when "we hit a mine that blew off a track and disabled the tank, and immediately afterwards heard the crack of an anti-tank gun and an AP round hit the front of the tank, so we bailed out."[74] The crew crawled back to safety along one of the deep ditches that lined the road. In the space of thirty minutes the two leading troops of A Squadron had lost their officers and three of the six tanks they put into action.

When Mackenzie reported back to squadron headquarters with his crew, he was told to take command of a tank whose commander had been wounded and back he went up the Lekkerhoek road. In less than a hour he returned, on foot, with a sad story to report. As he approached the hulk of his previous tank, Mackenzie had "made a side trip in an attempt to take out the anti-tank gun" that had hit him but "received a hit from a gun firing from a different position."[75] Mackenzie "barely had time for a smoke before he was ordered to take command of another tank" whose commander had been killed and "he was once again off to battle."

Mackenzie joined up with Gordie Irving because it was now

After the fighting was over. Local folk pose in front of knocked-out SAR Sherman. The haystacks in the background provided excellent cover for both German machine guns and *Panzerfaust* teams and the South Albertas learned to ignite them as a matter of standard procedure. *DE SLAG OM MOERBRUGGE*

Civilians pose on the wreckage. After the battle was over at Moerbrugge there were knocked-out South Alberta Shermans scattered across the landscape. This one has suffered damage to its running gear and there is massive perforation in its bow caused by some very powerful projectile or explosive. *DE SLAG OM MOERBRUGGE*

Belgian beauty and the beast from Alberta. The South Albertas took seriously the business of providing extra protection for their tanks but all that spare track did not help this Sherman V knocked out at Moerbrugge. *DE SLAG OM MOERBRUGGE*

Bootless and dead. This member of a German MG 42 crew, still draped with his ammunition belts, lies dead at Moerbrugge after the battle. Some Belgian has already taken his boots but has left his own worn pair of clogs in exchange at the corpse's feet. *DE SLAG OM MOERBRUGGE*

Gordie's turn – as he put it, "in no time at all I'm No. 1 again."[76] Gordie gathered up what was left of the three troops – a total of four tanks – and resumed the advance. Having seen what had happened to Young and Smith, Irving was determined that the snipers were not "going to get me and down went the hatch – it was the only time in the whole war that I closed my turret hatch." On the way up Gordie lost one tank, commanded by Corporal D.B. McCaig, to a *Panzerfaust*. Trooper Robert Barr was in that Sherman and remembered that they "got hit by a bazooka" and "got out all right but my leg was banged up below the knee." Shortly after the crew were out, "they blew the turret right off it."[77]

Gordie placed his surviving tanks in good cover behind farmhouses and then "just opened up every gun and fired at everything that moved."[78] The shooting went on for nearly thirty minutes and Gordie concluded that we "overpowered them with firepower and pretty soon they pulled out." This being done, he decided to "make a dash" for Lekkerhoek and, backed up by the Links, reached the hamlet which the infantry se-

cured. When the Links were firmly in position Gordie pulled the remnants of the squadron back to Veldkappel, a crossroads midway between Lekkerhoek and Moerbrugge, and firmed up there for the night. It had been a costly day for A Squadron – David Marshall of B Squadron remembered watching from the canal bank "the tell tale plume of smoke rising hundreds of yards into the air indicating the burning of another A Squadron tank."[79]

On the following morning, 11 September, C Squadron advanced with the Links out of Lekkerhoek in the direction of Oedelem. Jack Roberts's troop had the lead and, having seen the casualties caused by mines on the roads, Roberts opted to move through the fields despite the danger of bogging in the thick, wet soil. The infantry moved along the ditches at the side of the road while the four Shermans of Roberts's troop made slow but steady progress through two fields. Then it happened

199

Pee Wees at Putte. A-4 Troop at Putte, Belgium, in early September 1944. The original "Pee Wee Platoon" from Edmonton days, A-4 retained its high-spirited approach to discipline throughout the war. Here the sappers have created a ramp allowing the troop to take advantage of the protection offered by a stone wall to form a strong position. NAC, PA-132019.

– an AP round hit the turret of the troop sergeant's tank. David Marshall, the loader-operator, recalled that the Homelite exploded "filling the tank with burning gasoline and smoke." The crew bailed out fast:

> The gunner shared the hatch with the sergeant's legs and I shared it with the gunner's. Before I could get that far I had to disconnect the recoil shield of the gun, swing it out of the way, and then squeeze behind the gun and out. One thing I had forgotten to do was to remove my earphones and as I was going over the side the cord got stuck, stopping my headlong dive to the earth, flipping me on my feet which were already in motion, and heading for the comparative safety of the ditch.[80]

Marshall suffered burns to his face and was evacuated to a hospital in the rear. He had been with the Regiment exactly eight days.

Roberts continued but his tank had just "stuck its nose through a hedgerow" when "boom, a bazooka [*Panzerfaust*] got us in the turret," remembered gunner, Ed Davies.[81] Davies was knocked unconscious but

> Jim Ferguson, the wireless operator, kept kicking at me and telling me to get out and I guess it was just a reaction but I crawled out. We were in a ditch along the hedgerow and I had a bad wound in the leg. I could feel the blood pumping

out as I crawled. I said to the others to go back and I'll stay here and they went. I lay in the ditch and I could hear some guys talking so I crawled up and they were Germans. I crawled back and kept quiet. About twenty minutes later the ambulance came up and took me back. I was out of the war.

Roberts's co-driver, Trooper Cliff Glaude, remembered that

> We all hit the ground except for Roberts ... and I was left with two wounded and Roberts was still in the tank with his head in the turret. I went back to get him but when I looked at him ... I just dropped him. One guy had a great big hole in his stomach so I put a patch on him and the wireless operator had both hands burnt, the flesh was just hanging. Him and I took the ditch to the right and we finally made it back.[82]

Jack Roberts was a 27-year-old engineering student at the University of Alberta who had joined the SAR in April 1942. He had been previously wounded at St. Lambert and had only been back with the Regiment for a few days when he was killed.[83]

C Squadron could make no headway in the face of the German anti-tank guns covering the fields and mines on the road, which accounted for two more Shermans whose hulks blocked the route. The Links were pinned by heavy machine-gun and 20 mm AA fire. A Squadron swung over to help but had no better luck than the previous day. Sergeant Gerald Hussey's Sherman had the lead but, as Trooper Egbert Taylor recalled, Hussey tried to cover some prisoners from the hatch with his pistol and "was hit in the side of the head." He "slumped to the floor" of the tank, Taylor continues,

> and we had to back the tank up and unload him half way back to the Canal. We used ammunition belts to lift him out of the turret. I was on top hauling and the gunner was lifting him from below. Once out, several of the infantry helped lower him to the ground.
>
> We had put a shell dressing around his wound but from the nature of the wound, the size of half a crown, he was a goner and I think he was dead by the time we lowered him to the ground.[84]

Hussey, age 23, was a truck driver from Montreal who had enlisted in the Royal Montreal Regiment in 1939 and had joined the Regiment in March 1944. He was engaged to an English girl at the time of his death.[85]

Gordie Irving took over command again and the advance was led by Sergeant Ted Palfenier, who was commanding one of the first 17-pdr. Sherman Fireflies to reach the Regiment. Palfenier got as far as a field near a crossroads some distance east of Lekkerhoek when his brand-new tank was knocked out by an anti-tank gun. The crew bailed out and ran for safety but German machine-gun fire killed Troopers Adam Dutka and Gerry Hamm. Dutka, age 24, was a miner from East Coulee, Alberta, who had been with the Regiment since Edmonton in June 1940, while Gerry Hamm was a 31-year-old fisherman from Sydney, Nova Scotia, who liked to entertain his crew with stories of his adventures as a rum-runner during the Prohibition years.[86]

Ted Palfenier made it back safely and came over to Gordie's Sherman to try to help him pinpoint the location of the German gun. As they were talking, an AP round took the left front sprocket off the tank and Gordie told Palfenier to clear out to some safer place. Ted took shelter behind a stone farmhouse being used as a casualty collecting point but ten minutes later was cut in half by an AP round that went through both ends of the house and damaged one of the halftrack ambulances. Ted Palfenier was a 24-year-old nurseryman from Medicine Hat who had joined the Regiment in June 1940.[87]

By this time A Squadron was down to between two and four tanks and C Squadron had also lost heavily. The infantry could make no headway without tank support but the South Albertas could not continue taking the heavy casualties in men and vehicles they had suffered for the last two days. The flat fields between Moerbrugge and Lekkerhoek were littered with more than a dozen knocked-out or brewed-up Shermans. It appeared to be a stand-off but the Germans had had enough and late in the afternoon A Squadron saw the enemy "falling back and opened fire on them."[88] There was no possibility, however, of mounting a pursuit that day.

The fighting of 10-11 September cost the South Alberta Regiment eleven men killed, including three officers, and twenty-seven wounded. The Regiment had to completely write off seven tanks and dozens of others would spend time in the workshops to be battleworthy again.[89] Losses had also been heavy among the Argylls and Links, and the 10 Brigade historian summed up Moerbrugge as a "costly, grim, and bloody action" that served notice "that the great breakout run, the days of quick, joyous liberation, had ended."[90] Harry Foster agreed and he took responsibility for the high casualties. He believed that the swift advance from Normandy had lulled him into "a dangerous sense of invincibility" and that Moerbrugge was his "first serious tactical mistake of the war."[91]

Moerbrugge was the opening round in what would become known as the Battle of the Scheldt. The full story of that battle has been ably told elsewhere.[92] Here we are concerned only with the operations of the Regiment and its parent formations, 10 Brigade and 4th Armoured Division, but to place those operations in proper context, it is necessary to briefly discuss the broader strategical background (see map 10, page 192).

Although Antwerp was captured on 4 September, its facilities were useless because the Germans dominated the approaches to the port. There were three major German positions in the Scheldt: the Breskens Pocket on the south shore of the estuary; the heavily-fortified island of Walcheren at the mouth of the estuary; and the South Beveland peninsula which connected that island with the mainland north of Antwerp. On 8 September, 4th Armoured Division had gained a bridgehead at Moerbrugge over the Ghent Canal, the covering position for the Breskens Pocket, but the reduction of the pocket itself was a job for infantry and the infantry formations of First Canadian Army were miles back in France. Five days before, Montgomery had ordered Crerar to capture the Channel ports of Le Havre, Calais, Boulogne and Dunkirk and three days later had emphasized that he needed "Boulogne badly" to further his advance to the Rhine. Crerar therefore informed his subordinates on 9 September that a "speedy and victorious conclusion to the war" depended "upon the capture of the Channel Ports."[93]

The priorities changed in mid-September. On the 10th and 12th of the month Montgomery had discussions with Eisenhower during which he argued his concept of a "narrow front" strategy versus the American concept of a "broad front." The field marshal did not win the debate but did get Ike's permission to carry out MARKET GARDEN, his plan to take Second British Army to the Rhine. In granting Montgomery this concession, however, Eisenhower stressed the importance of opening Antwerp as soon as possible. The Allied armies badly needed that port's capacity to unload 40,000 tons of supplies daily, for by mid-September they were experiencing major logistical difficulties. The problem was not supplies themselves; the problem was transporting them. The supply line of the British and Canadian 21 Army Group stretched three hundred miles to the Channel near Bayeux and that of the American 12

Army Group a hundred miles farther to Cherbourg. Bombing had seriously disrupted the French railway network and the Allies depended on road transport to get cargo forward to the front. Whole divisions were grounded and their trucks impressed into the supply service, tank transporter vehicles were hastily converted into massive cargo carriers, one-way express highways were created which operated twenty-four hours a day, and use was made of transport aircraft and the limited capacities of those Channel ports that had been taken. By all these means the Allied logistical services managed to deliver enough supplies to sustain the two army groups but not enough to support two major offensive operations.[94]

The solution to the problem was Antwerp. On 12 September Montgomery informed Crerar that the "early opening of Antwerp is daily becoming of increasing importance and this cannot repeat cannot take place until Walcheren has been captured and the mouth of the river is open for navigation."[95] He asked for Crerar's "views as to when you think you can tackle this problem." Crerar hesitated, as well he might, for the fact was that First Canadian Army was the "Cinderella" of the Allied forces in northwest Europe. It had received the unglamorous task of clearing the Channel ports while the other Allied armies had made the headline-grabbing advances, and its priorities in matters of supply had suffered accordingly. In mid-September 1944 First Canadian Army was scattered from Le Havre to Antwerp, a distance of nearly two hundred miles. Two of its infantry divisions were "grounded" for lack of transport, two more were busy with the Channel ports, and only the 4th Armoured and 1st Polish Divisions were available for immediate operations. Nonetheless, when Montgomery raised the possibility of tackling Antwerp in a letter to Crerar on 13 September, the Canadian commander took it as an order. This was unfortunate as, in the words of the Canadian army's historian, Montgomery had set Crerar "a task far beyond the limited resources of his Army."[96]

This fact seems to have eluded Montgomery because his eyes, and those of his subordinate British commanders, were fixed firmly on the Rhine, which they hoped to reach by means of MARKET GARDEN. So entrancing was this objective that Montgomery ordered Second British Army to move east from Antwerp rather than to drive north and cut the South Beveland Peninsula, the escape route for von Zangen's Fifteenth Army. Throughout September von Zangen was able to evacuate his divisions from the Breskens area and bring them back into defensive positions east of Antwerp. The Allied commanders had given Hitler the time he needed and, three weeks after the fall of Paris, the *Wehrmacht* had recovered its balance, established a cohesive defence line in the west and continued to deny the Allies the use of Antwerp.

Operation MARKET GARDEN, the largest airborne assault in history, commenced on Sunday, 17 September. When it ended nine days later, the Allies had driven a sixty-mile salient into the German front in Holland but it was a salient that led

nowhere because they had failed to take the Rhine bridge at Arnhem – the infamous "bridge too far." Thwarted, Montgomery continued to argue his "narrow thrust" into Germany but the strategical question was settled at a conference of Allied senior officers on 22 September when it was decided that the Allied Expeditionary Force would advance on a "broad front." This same conference also established that opening Antwerp was now "a matter of urgency" but it still took five days for Montgomery to issue new directives to his army group making the port the priority for First Canadian Army but the Ruhr a priority for Second British Army. These orders effectively split the two armies, which would be moving *away from each other*.[97]

Crerar did his best to carry out Montgomery's wishes but he simply did not have the resources to clear the Channel ports and open Antwerp at the same time. Nor did he receive much help. Montgomery had hinted that airborne forces might be available but their participation was later refused. There was a shortage of landing craft, which restricted amphibious operations, and the Canadians could not expect the enthusiastic support of the RAF's Bomber Command, which growing tired of being chained to land operations, was anxious to resume what it considered to be its primary task – the destruction of German industry. Canadian requests for heavy bomber attacks to flood the defences of Walcheren Island were met by intransigence on the part of senior British air force officers and one, Air Chief Marshal Sir Charles Portal, actually went to the extent of stating that "the constant application of the heavy bombers to the land battle, when it is not essential and its only purpose is to save casualties, must inevitably lead to demoralization of the army."[98] These were amazing and unfortunate words for the head of a supposedly Allied service, and in the end it took the intervention of Montgomery to get RAF assistance. The result was that the opening of Antwerp took longer and cost more lives – many of them Canadian.[99]

On the night of 11 September 1944 the problems of their senior commanders were far from the minds of John Galipeau's crew. They had been sent back to the ordnance park to pick up a new tank and, having some free time, decided to go out and get drunk "to celebrate being alive." The boys found a bar "with a good supply of cognac and an old wind-up gramophone with plenty of music on record" and settled themselves in. "By closing hour," John recalled, "we were having a wonderful time drinking with the owner and dancing with his wife and daughter" but "decided we had better get some sleep, not that we really cared, and so said goodbye." "You coming tomorrow?" asked the owner who "had no objection to our practice of doubling and tripling the price of a bottle of cognac." "Oh yeah, we'll be back tomorrow," the boys replied but the next day they went back to the front in their new tank.[100]

It was clear to this A Squadron crew and everyone else in the Regiment that the war was far from over.

CHAPTER TWELVE

"Recce at its best."

BELGIUM AND HOLLAND: 12 SEPTEMBER–22 OCTOBER 1944

The battle of the Scheldt forms the backdrop for the South Alberta Regiment's operations during the autumn of 1944. While his infantry divisions dealt with the Channel ports General Harry Crerar of First Canadian Army wanted to maintain "constant pressure" on the Germans but did not want to commit "important forces," meaning his armoured divisions, "to offensive action."[2] On 12 September 1st Polish Division was ordered to clear the area between the Ghent-Terneuzen Canal, which bisects northwestern Belgium, east to Antwerp while Foster's 4th Armoured Division was to clear the area west of that canal. The 4th Division went to work on 12 September and the South Alberta Regiment, scouting ahead of 10 Brigade, "had a grand day" as it "was back to its old role and worked as a Recce Regt."[3] Splitting up into small elements the three fighting squadrons, AA and Recce Troops spent the day investigating the many small bridges in the area between the Ghent and Leopold Canals before returning to harbour at Donk.

During the advance from France, reconnaissance work for the division had been handled by the Manitoba Dragoons, an armoured car regiment. Now, the SAR Recce Troop resumed its role of scouting ahead of the Regiment and guarding its flanks. "This was Recce at its best," recalled one troop member, "out in front of everyone probing and searching out the enemy."[4] The forty-four men in the Recce Troop had interesting but highly dangerous work as they manned Stuart tanks with armour so thin that, as one South Alberta remarked, "a well-oiled German could pee through them at a thousand yards."[5] To survive in the Recce Troop required

> When you hear the Minnies moaning loud and clear,
> Shaking up your insides and landing mighty near.
> Then is the time I have no fear,
> As I drink your EFI beer.
> When I am LOB, when I am LOB.
>
> When you meet the Wehrmacht, over the next canal,
> I'll drink a toast and wish you luck, old pal.
> When you go into the attack,
> Just think of me, I'm ten miles back.
> Cause I am LOB, cause I am LOB.[1]

initiative, self-reliance and aggression tempered by a dash of caution – it also helped to be slightly crazy. "They were so good with those anti-tank guns," one member of the troop commented, "they could hit you no matter what you did."[6] It wasn't everyone's cup of tea – Bob Clipperton noted that "we had a hard time to get reinforcements to come into Recce Troop because it was a sort of suicide squad as you weren't supposed to fight back, you were supposed to find the enemy not fight him."[7] Jack Cheney summed up the troop's role:

> We worked together in twos, we were very seldom with the Regiment and they would send us out and we were probing the side roads and flanks. If we ran into heavy fire we would just withdraw and the squadrons would move in and handle it. They liked us because we saved them from a lot of trouble.[8]

Recce Troop personnel tended to have independent natures – one of the foremost practitioners of the art in the Regiment, Sergeant Albert Halkyard, summed it up: "I did the colonel's job for him but I did it my way."[9]

And it certainly was the "colonel's job" because Swatty Wotherspoon was a fanatic about gathering accurate and timely information. He had a standing policy to have as many vehicles as he could muster from the Recce, AA and Inter-Communication Troops out at all times. Not all were involved in recce work; Swatty was also a firm believer in good liaison with neighbouring units and formations and it was a policy that paid off:

Gordie greets the mayor. Lieutenant Gordie Irving, A-1 Troop, and the Burgomaster of Maldegem, 12 September 1944. The joy of the Belgians on being liberated is evident. Gordie Irving, at 6 feet 6 inches tall, was a German sniper's dream. COURTESY, DANNY McLEOD.

Rolling, rolling, rolling. SAR Sherman V in Belgium or Holland, September 1944. This tank is in amazingly clean condition and the absence of spare tracks welded on the hull for extra protection indicates that it is probably a replacement vehicle for the heavy losses suffered at Moerbrugge. SAR COLLECTION.

We knew more at my RHQ than the divisional commander because I had a recce patrol over with the neighbouring brigades, whether they were in our division or not. We sort of covered the front, and widely too. As a result, we got the first information because the division didn't have that.[10]

South Alberta liaison officers ended up in some strange places. When MARKET GARDEN commenced on 17 September Swatty sent Danny McLeod to the headquarters of the British 30th Corps, tasked with the landward part of the operation. As a lowly regimental commander from an entirely different army, Swatty had absolutely no right to do this but, as Danny McLeod commented, it was typical Wotherspoon:

In my case I was sent there to sort of eavesdrop as to what was happening. You told them why you were there and that you would appreciate any information they could give you. Swatty always had extra officers around and he used them for whatever tasks he had: liaison, looking for good harbours, or whatever. Swatty was a fellow who dealt with the present but was always projecting into the future and he liked to have "hands on" information constantly.[11]

Liaison and recce work was good training for junior officers, who learned quickly that their colonel always thought in terms of "what, who, where, when, how – and you had better think in those terms if he visited you or you had to report to him."[12]

So the South Albertas spread out on 12 September to feed information back to the colonel, the brigade and the division. To Danny McLeod, back with the Regiment after his misadventure at Olendon, the next few days were

an interesting time because we were given Typhoon support and that was nice but we were so thin on the ground that we could not occupy a position. We would go up, do a scorched earth policy by day, and then pull back by night into a safe harbour. At this stage of the game we had ex-pilots with VHF sets and they were superb and could talk their language, describe the target in their terms and even make suggestions at a way to come at it.[13]

As Sergeant Jim Nicholson's B Squadron crew learned on 12 September air support could be a tricky thing. It turned out to be a very bad day for Jim. First of all, his regular troop leader was absent and he got stuck with a new lieutenant who was going into action for the first time. Things got off to a poor start in the morning when the officer managed to get the troop lost, thus confirming the old army saying that "the most dangerous thing in the world is a second lieutenant with a map." They did not improve when Nicholson was informed that there was an "88" ahead and was asked to "act as a decoy (I remember the word vividly) and draw the fire of this gun."[14] This would require him to take his Sherman along an elevated dyke road with no cover and with Typhoons hovering about. Having seen the dubious benefits of tactical air support in Normandy, Jim was reluctant to expose his tank but, for insurance, "quickly spread out the [yellow] recognition strip over the back." It was well that he did as the aircraft immediately "dived diagonally across my tank" at treetop level, "released their rockets and climbed away." His loader-operator, Trooper John Neff, remembered that the rockets "were fired when the planes were right over our heads and the sound they made was enough to scare a man to death."[15] Unfortunately the Typhoons' targets were two Foot Guards tanks "working their way up on a highway about 400 yards to our right" and the Guards lost two men killed and two Shermans "rocketed out of this world."[16]

Jim's troop was so delayed by these and other incidents that when they finally got to their objective, a small bridge, the Germans blew it in front of their eyes. It was getting on toward evening and time to withdraw to the squadron harbour but the green troop leader ordered Jim to send his co-driver to check out a building deep in a neighbouring wood before they pulled back. Jim was reluctant to do this as the co-driver, Trooper Jack Frankson, had lost his brother Rick at Moerbrugge two days before and he knew the man was still feeling that loss. He therefore "offered to go through the house myself but the Lieutenant rejected my offer" so Nicholson shot up the house with his main gun and Brownings and – after a suitable pause – reported it clear. All in all, it had been a long day for Jim and on the way back to harbour he expressed his frustration with the new troop leader to his crew over the intercom. In no uncertain terms, Nicholson debated the limited extent of the officer's intelligence, expressed serious doubts about the legitimacy of his birth and suggested that he go and perform certain anatomically impossible acts. Unfortunately Jim had forgotten to flick over his mike from the B Set to the intercom and the entire troop, including the troop leader, heard the blue language. The officer said nothing (perhaps he was learning) but there was unrepressed laughter from the other crews.[17]

New officers could be tricky. Swatty Wotherspoon always liked to have five or six extra lieutenants on strength and when one joined the Regiment, he had an unvarying routine. The first step was a personal interview at which Swatty would size up the new arrival, ask a few pertinent questions about his background and lecture him about the role and purpose of the Regiment. This lecture always ended with a clear expression of Wotherspoon's personal philosophy that an officer's first and foremost responsibility was to the men under his command. That being said, he would lean closer to the newcomer and quietly but firmly say, "If you let your men down I will shoot you myself," before dismissing him.[18] These preliminaries over, new lieutenants joined RHQ for a few days, where the colonel could keep an eye on them and "to let them know what the sound of shot and shell was like before they had to command a troop."[19] This, Swatty believed, "helped no end, and you could train them while they were doing it." The newcomers might then be sent out on liaison jobs and if they did well at that they would go into action for a few days as a crew member in an experienced troop leader's tank. Then, and only then, would they receive command of a troop.

Some green lieutenants had trouble making it past RHQ. Adjutant Bob Allsopp recalled one young officer who was assigned a liaison job in a scout car and received permission to visit a friend in one of the squadrons. The driver brought him back to the RHQ area at 2200 hours that night, stinking drunk, and had to carry him into his billet. Allsopp immediately put him on charge and Wotherspoon gave the miscreant two choices: "Return to England with an adverse fitness report or stay with the Regiment and get every dirty job I can think up." The lieutenant decided to stay and for two months carried a heavy load until Swatty finally let him off the hook. He turned out to be a very good officer.[20]

Wotherspoon took the trouble to screen new officers because being a troop leader was not only the best but the most demanding job in the armoured corps. Junior armoured officers were much closer to their men than, for example, artillery or infantry officers because they were also members of a tank crew, a team whose members depended on each other's skills. It was a tight little world and, in such close confines and in the tension of battle, crew members quickly got to know each other's strengths and weaknesses. Tank crews had to be commanded in a way that was different from command in the infantry or artillery. As one armoured officer commented, "the use of naked authority" was not "the best way to control a tank crew" because no "shield of rank or education was of any avail behind which to hide any faults."[21]

Despite the screening process, bad apples occasionally did get command of a troop. When this happened, they either smartened up quickly or their crews got rid of them. Trooper Ron Virtue of C Squadron remembered an officer who briefly assumed command of Don Stewart's troop after Stewart was wounded at St. Lambert:

> This fellow came over from England and of course we hadn't shaved and were wearing German pistols and he told us to get cleaned up. He wanted to go over skylines and we told him that we wouldn't last long that way and one day [Corporal Walter] Vandermark just pointed a pistol at him and told him to get down the road and that was that and we never saw him again. I spoke to Dave Currie about this after the war and he told me that, if the man's crew didn't want him, Dave didn't want him either.[22]

Crews could make life miserable for an officer they did not want. One officer "became such an irritant" that his crew "would only obey orders and nothing more." When the tank had to move, "the belongings of everyone else were packed and stowed but his were left for him and he was also left a tin of spam to warm up while the others ate" their meals in common.[23]

It wasn't all one way, as Gordie Irving demonstrated during the night of 12 September. Gordie's troop had a good time that day and got as far as the town of Maldegem, where,

> as we went in, the Germans were going out the other side. The town went wild and, in few minutes, the crews were out of their tanks and partying with the crowds. The burgomaster came up and shook hands with me and presented me with the key to the town and then I got a call on the wireless and they said: "Get back here, you are way ahead of the bomb line" and I said "you can't do that, we're celebrating." But we had to pack it all up and go back five miles or what-

Chow time in AA. Trooper Bill Kennedy (left) and Sergeant Pete Woolf sort out the compo rations, Belgium, September 1944. In the field, tanks crews had to do their own cooking and of necessity the South Albertas became accomplished chefs. COURTESY, W. VAILLANCOURT.

ever it was. On the way back, I saw guys with yellow recognition markers on their decks.[24]

That night there was a "stand to or alert" for the entire Regiment. In Gordie's troop, however, "the boys were pretty thin on the ground and it certainly was not one hundred per cent" because some of his troop had decided to absent themselves without leave to return to Maldegem and continue the party. Early in the morning one of his men woke Gordie to complain that he had not been relieved on guard so Gordie "went on duty and took the next guard shift." A little while later, he heard the black sheep "coming back from town and they were all stoned so I put them all under close arrest." "It was part of my job," he commented, "to scare the hell out of them because you just cannot do that in war."[25]

For one reason or another, troop leaders usually did not last long. Continuity of leadership was provided by the troop sergeant and the two corporals who commanded the other three tanks in the troop and their role was very important. John Galipeau, himself a troop sergeant, summed it up this way:

> The troop officer was the general administrator, but the sergeant was the one who saw that the decisions the troop commander made were carried out. The troop officer directed the troop and was the one who knew the tactics and objectives for the day, but the sergeant was the one who really knew the men who would be carrying out the orders, and often had more battle experience. It seemed as though new troop officers who came to us directly from Officer Training School without NCO experience in battle became early casualties. Troop officers who were not killed were promoted and moved to more senior positions with the squadron or Regimental Headquarters but the sergeant was there day after day. The officers relied a lot on the sergeants.[26]

Bert Coffin agreed and, reflecting on the matter years later, thought that the Regiment "had probably some of the strongest efforts from the corporal crew commanders because a lot of those guys were more experienced and did a better job than the troop commanders."[27] The balance between officer, NCO and man was a fine one but it was a foolish young lieutenant who ignored his veteran crew commanders' advice.

Bad time for the Algonquins. The Algonquin Regiment's crossing point at Moerkerkke, showing the double canals and the embankment in the centre. On 13 September 1944 the Algoons lost heavily trying to gain a bridgehead in the strongly-held Breskens Pocket. PHOTOGRAPH BY DIANNE GRAVES.

The advance from the Moerbrugge bridgehead brought 4th Division up against the Leopold Canal, the boundary of the German stronghold in the Breskens Pocket. The enemy did not appear to be in great strength and Harry Foster decided to try to seize a bridgehead from which the armoured units of the division would "fan out in both directions to clear the North bank of the canal Leopold."[28] The job fell to Bob Bradburn's Algonquins and, throughout 13 September, preparations were made for the attack. Foster had learned his lesson at Moerbrugge and by evening more than sixty assault boats, reconnaissance boats and civilian craft had been assembled and "the entire divisional artillery and all mortars and machine guns in the brigade were made available in support of the operation."[29] The point selected for the crossing was a blown bridge site on the road north from Moerkerkke. At this place, unfortunately, the Leopold Canal and the Canal de Dérivation de la Lys run parallel, each ninety feet wide, with a dyke of the same width between them. The attack was to go in under cover of darkness at 2200 hours and involved the four rifle companies of the Algonquins with an eighty-man detachment from the Links to act as a ferry party.[30]

The terrain in this area did not permit the Regiment to provide direct fire support for the crossing. In the evening of 13 September all three squadrons moved up near Moerkerkke and "did a little indirect shooting from a map" but that was all they could do as there was no good location for a FOO to correct their fire.[31] The Algonquins crossed at 2330 hours and had considerable trouble getting the heavy boats over three dykes and two canals but by morning all four companies were established on the German side. Enemy reaction was violent – *Generalmajor* Sanders, the commander of the 245th Infantry Division defending the area, received orders "that the bridge-head must at all costs be eliminated" and he counterattacked with all available forces.[32] At first light on 14 September heavy German attacks started coming in and fire was brought to bear on the engineers who were trying to build a bridge. Sanders also moved troops onto the middle dyke between the two canals and their fire sank many boats and threatened to cut off the Algonquins, who were starting to run low on ammunition.

By 1200 hours the situation was so bad that Harry Foster decided that the "only sensible alternative was to withdraw before any more good men were killed."[33] Every available useful weapon within range, including every 75 mm in the Regiment, opened up to provide covering fire and a smoke screen to cover the withdrawal. The Regiment alone fired a total of 1600 rounds and Sanders, who was on the receiving end, thought it was "the most incredible barrage" he had ever seen and was astounded when "at the conclusion of this prodigious effort," the Canadians retired instead of attacking further.[34] Most of the Algoons had to swim both canals to get to safety and one major was surprised when, soaking wet and almost naked, the returning men were greeted by a sapper sergeant who "had a large bunch of Dutch cigars, taken from a shelled-out store window" and "was calmly handing one to each survivor, while the shells still whistled overhead and crumped into the buildings."[35] The Algonquins paid a bitter price for Moerkerkke, losing 153 officers and men killed, wounded or missing, and Harry Foster took full responsibility. "Once again, without double-checking on German strengths in the area," he admitted, "I made the mistake of believing the intelligence experts."[36]

Until the infantry divisions could begin clearing the Breskens Pocket, the 4th Division would have to hold the line. Simonds ordered Foster to secure the Leopold and "maintain contact, and exert some pressure" on the enemy.[37] This was not an easy task as the terrain in this area of Belgium and Holland is polder land, or land reclaimed from the sea, and it is not good ground for tanks – in fact you couldn't pick worse ground for tanks. Polders are large fields, crisscrossed by canals and dykes. The canals function both as drainage and transportation systems while the dykes, which vary between fifteen and thirty feet in height above the fields serve to control the water levels in the canals and drainage ditches. The polders were soft and soggy at the best of times and the Germans partially flooded them, creating inundated areas that restricted vehicle movement to the roads on top of the dykes. The Germans established strongpoints at the intersections of the dykes (and thus the roads) and covered all approaches with well-sited infantry and anti-tank weapons, creating "killing grounds" through which the Canadians had to move. The enemy also used the dykes themselves as defence works, digging into the reverse slopes, creating positions "almost immune to artillery and mortar fire." It was ideal ground to defend and a nightmare to attack.[38]

During the ten days that followed the abortive attack at Moerkerkke the Regiment helped to clear the Germans out of the area between the Leopold and Ghent-Terneuzen Canals. On 16 September Wotherspoon was given command of a battle-group that included the Algonquins (less one company), two troops of M-10s and attached engineer and artillery units and ordered to secure the area east of Eekloo. Swatty concentrated at Eekloo and moved east at 1400 hours. All available tanks from the Recce and AA Troops were sent ahead in two-vehicle patrols to establish the condition of the bridges in the area.[39]

Lieutenant Ed Reardon's Crusader was just approaching a small bridge when his driver

> skidded to a halt and ... I hollered "What's going on?" I looked over the side of the tank and there was a sign in English saying "Fresh eggs". So we sent the co-driver over and we covered him very closely and everything seemed fine and he came back with a big basket of eggs and was just handing it in when "powww!" the bridge went up from end to end. If we hadn't stopped for eggs, we would have been in the middle of that bridge.[40]

Seeing bridges blown in front of their eyes was not an uncommon experience for the South Albertas. Trooper Arnold Dryer wrote his fiancée that his crew "came to a town that a canal runs through and just before we got there Jerry blew the bridge." The people in the other side of the town "saw the people in the one

"**Some dame and myself in Belgium.**" That was Trooper John Neff's original caption on this photo taken at Sleydinge on 16 September 1944. COURTESY, JOHN NEFF.

half giving us flowers so they sent three girls swimming with flowers for us."[41] Due to the destruction of the bridges, progress was slow although there was little German resistance. At 1900 hours, the Regiment harboured for the night with B Squadron at Zwaantje and the remainder at Daasdonck.[42]

On Sunday, 17 September, Swatty employed C Squadron and Recce Troop on a "mass recce" east of Waarschoot while the remainder of the Regiment stayed in reserve. This took until 1530 hours when it was reported that all bridges were blown and the enemy had pulled out some time before. That morning the sky was full of a seemingly unending stream of aircraft as three airborne divisions flew over Holland to commence Operation MARKET GARDEN. On the following day the South Albertas were ordered to move north and "mop up" the area from Oost Eekloo to Phillipine and Sluiskil near the Breskens Pocket.[43]

During the afternoon of 18 September Albert Halkyard was leading a patrol of two Stuarts north of Assenede. Halkyard reported a German AFV to RHQ and Swatty asked him, "What the blazes are you doing up there?"[44] "That wasn't where I was supposed to be," Halkyard remembered, but the colonel continued, "If you're that good, see if you can make the Dutch border." Halkie and his two-tank patrol crossed the border and became the first Canadian troops to enter Holland. Jack Cheney, Halkyard's gunner, remembered that "we had gone up this road and picked up some light fire and Halkyard said 'we are going to pull back out of this'" so "we went up this other road and he said 'guess what, according to the map, we are in Holland.'"[45] Corporal Bob Clipperton, who drove the second Stuart, re-

called that about a mile into Holland the Germans "opened up on us."[46] The two tanks were moving on a road beside a railway and they suddenly spotted "a bloody big gun on the tracks."[47] Halkyard sent a wireless message to RHQ that entered SAR legend: "Have crossed the Dutch border and sighted railway gun. Am engaging same."[48] He then advanced on the German artillery piece and Cheney remembered that "the Jerry crew was there, they were right around the gun but we went in there guns blazing and a couple of them jumped into the canal."[49] The Germans disposed of, Halkyard's crews were now the proud new owners of a 315 mm railway gun.[50]

There was no sign of the Germans and since it had been a long morning, Halkie decided that it was time to get something to eat. Just as they got out of their vehicles, enemy artillery rounds came in – Halkyard was about twenty feet from his tank when a "105 mm shell hit it. Nobody got killed because it dropped right through the open hatch and exploded inside the tank and everybody was out of it." The other Stuart towed the vehicle back until an ARV could come up for it and, having earned their pay that day, Halkyard's patrol returned to the Regimental harbour.[51]

As the South Albertas approached the main German positions on the Leopold Canal, enemy resistance grew stronger. Extensive flooding limited off-road movement but mines and obstacles restricted movement on the roads. In the early evening, near the hamlet of Nieuwberg, Darby Nash's B Squadron ran into a German anti-tank gun that hit Sergeant Alan Holmes's tank killing Trooper Walter Andrew, a 31-year-old former aircraft worker

Over the border. Halkie's crossing point from Belgium to Holland on 18 September 1944 when his patrol became the first Canadian soldiers on Dutch soil. The original Dutch customs post is the building in the middle ground. The figure standing on the left is Swatty Wotherspoon, the son of the wartime commander of the SAR.
PHOTOGRAPH BY DIANNE GRAVES.

Halkie. Sergeant Albert E. Halkyard, MM, Recce Troop. From August 1944 to May 1945, Albert Halkyard led the advance of the South Alberta Regiment in a thinly-armoured Stuart light tank and survived the war without getting a scratch. "Halkie" was the first Canadian soldier to enter Holland from the west in September 1944 and the first Canadian soldier to enter it from the east in April 1945. COURTESY, ALBERT HALKYARD.

from Maymont, Saskatchewan, who had joined the Regiment in 1943.[52] Holmes pulled back and Jim Nicholson's crew took the lead. Nicholson remembered that encounter:

We were in a wooded area, with a meadow before us containing haystacks, from which Sgt. Holmes had just pulled back, having had one of his crew killed. With the infantry supporting us, I led B-1 Troop into the gathering dark down the narrow road to the meadow, a road which we afterwards referred to as "Bazooka Alley." During the half-hour fire fight that ensued, I could see our own infantry hunkered down in the ditches one either side each time my 75 mm flashed its fire. ...

Suddenly the tracers were bouncing off my main gun, creating glowing spirals to left and right. Our gun was literally red hot. ... When I replenished the Browning ammo that night I threw out 12 empty boxes. This was the most firing we had ever done in such a short period of time.[53]

B Squadron lost three tanks in this action after the Algonquins were pulled away for another job, and the Regiment had no infantry protection that night when the "enemy began to infiltrate ... knocking out two tanks with bazookas and making it necessary for the Sq[uadro]ns, particularly B Sqn to defend their t[an]ks from ground pos[itio]ns."[54]

On 19 September the South Albertas continued to drive north. C Squadron was approaching the hamlet of de Katte near Sas van Gent when they encountered mined roads and came under heavy German anti-tank gun fire. Don Stewart, who had returned to his troop after recovering from his head wound at St. Lambert, was leading that day:

We had been advancing up a road and had been sniped quite severely from a group of buildings and some haystacks on one side of the road. We engaged that and burnt the haystacks. The infantry officer at the time was sniped and killed right beside our tank. At that moment we had an order to pull back off the road because some other vehicles were coming up – don't know what the vehicles were or why [they were coming up]. Anyway we pulled off onto a little sideroad: I pulled in first and Sgt. (Charles) Smith "or Smitty", pulled

in behind me with his tank. The corporal's tank pulled in on another road. After we were told to advance again, of course Sgt. Smith's tank came out first and I followed him. He proceeded up the road and I came along to pass him. Just as I was about to pass him and go ahead, an 88 mm around the bend of the road ahead opened up and knocked out his tank.[55]

Trooper John Hutchinson was in Smith's tank:

I don't know if I had a premonition or what. We were always told to wear our tunic in the tank because of fire. I didn't have my tunic on but I had my gloves off so I pulled them on before we took the lead. I don't know why I did it, I just did it. We hadn't gone a hundred yards and that was it. It went through the driver's hatch, it got me and it got Smitty the crew commander. Oakley had his arm bashed up. I got out of the tank and it was burning. I got burnt and my leg got shortened up. Smitty and I were thrown on to a halftrack with a tarp over it. I was in hospital about twenty-nine months, skin grafts, bone grafts, etc. I was still in hospital when I was discharged from the army.[56]

The AP round killed Trooper Ross McKee. A married man with two children, McKee was

First field grave, Belgium, September 1944. When fatal casualties occurred, it was Padre Silcox's task to give the remains a decent burial and erect a marker to make easier the task of the Commonwealth War Graves Commission. This is the grave of Trooper Walter H. Andrew from Maymont, Saskatchewan, killed in his tank at Oost Eekloo by a direct hit from a German anti-tank gun. The flowers have been added by Belgian civilians.
COURTESY, JACK PORTER.

a 31-year-old farmer from Porcupine Plains, Saskatchewan, and a
former member of the 16/22nd
Saskatchewan Horse who had
joined the SAR in September
1943.[57]

Stewart's driver, Trooper Ron
Virtue, remembered that his gunner, Corporal Walter Vandermark,
opened fire on the German anti-
tank gun and "knocked it out on
the first shot, and the German crew
came towards us down the ditch
past our tank."[58] But Don Stewart's
troubles weren't over. As he moved
past the destroyed anti-tank gun "a
shell struck my tank and a bogey
wheel was ripped off it."[59] This
round came from a tank in another
SAR squadron and Stewart "found
out later that a new reinforcement
officer there had got all excited
when he saw me and thought I was
a German and proceeded to shoot."
"We bailed out," Don commented,
"and that was the end of the activi-
ties for the day." C Squadron had lost five Shermans, four of
which were later recovered. B Squadron also had problems with
mines and obstacles but joined the remainder of the Regiment
at a harbour just south of Sas van Gant during the late
evening.[60]

The advance continued on the following day but progress
was limited due to fallen trees laid across the roads by the Germans to create obstacles. The leading troop of B Squadron was
nearly hit by an artillery concentration called down by the
Grenadier Guards, who were working in the area, and had to
wait until the shooting was over before they could proceed.
Lavoie's A Squadron suffered heavily this day from mines and
mortars and were approaching Valk north of Assenede when
they came under anti-tank gun fire that brewed up one of their
tanks, killing Trooper Wilfred Homer. The remainder of the
crew bailed out but a second round killed Trooper George
McCaffrey just as he was jumping from the turret. Wilfred
Homer was a 23-year-old truck driver from Dryden, Ontario,
who had joined the SAR in August 1943 and was survived by his
wife and one son. George McCaffrey was a 37-year-old miner
from East Coulee, Alberta, and an old original who had enlisted
in June 1940. That night RHQ moved into Assenede, where the
squadrons joined them in the late evening.[61]

On 21 September, while A remained in reserve, B and C
Squadrons moved north again but progress was no better than
the previous day because of mines, barriers and obstacles on
the roads and flooding. At one point B Squadron passed

Direct hit. Sergeant Smith's tank, Staak, Holland,
after a direct hit by a German anti-tank gun in
the driver's compartment. The driver, Trooper F.R.
McKee from Porcupine Plains, Saskatchewan,
was killed instantly. COURTESY, J.L. SUMMERS.

through the little town of Posthorn where
"one side of the street is Belgian and the
other side Dutch, both sides trying to
outdo each other in their welcome."[62]
They had got as far as Sluiskil by late afternoon, when they were called back to
Assenede because the Regiment had received a new task. Lavoie's A Squadron
was to support the Algonquins in a second attack into the Breskens Pocket at the
Isabella Polder, a land bridge about three
hundred yards wide formed by a dyke at
the east end of the Pocket area. Lavoie's
squadron and three patrols of six tanks
from Recce Troop moved up to the
Algonquins at 1200 hours but, the War
Diarist noted, the "enemy had prepared
this location and was evidently determined to hold it in reasonably great
strength as it is the only spot from which
an attack could be launched, the remainder being bounded by water."[63] As the
Algonquins' historian describes, any operations around the Isabella Polder
"would be extremely sticky" because the
countryside was

inundated, forcing us to make any large effort right up a dike
road, or in the words of the C.O. [Bob Bradburn] "Up a
bloody funnel." The enemy was dug in solidly in concrete
bunkers beneath the dikes. This area, the boundary between
Holland and Belgium, naturally had many fixed defences,
and these the Germans were improving and putting to good
use. Further, the quality of the troops against us was demon-
strably high. They were skilled in the use of their weapons,
and the defensive belts of fire that they had woven were almost impossible to traverse, even at night. The machine-gun
fire, for instance, was laid on so that it would sweep the dike
tops at about eight inches height. One could not even crawl
under this.[64]

The Algonquins managed to get a platoon across the polder
but it was pinned down by heavy and accurate German fire.
There was little A Squadron could do to help their flat-footed
friends as "it was impossible to bring fire down from the flanks"
because of the flooded terrain and the tanks could barely show
their turrets "over the dyke without coming under heavy enemy
fire."[65] Another platoon managed to get across the polder late in
the afternoon and was followed by a third, but strong counterattacks overran the leading platoon and forced the others to
withdraw. That night one troop from A Squadron stayed in the
forward positions while the remainder of the squadron pulled
back to a harbour in the rear.[66]

Lavoie's men spent two more days supporting the Algoons at the Polder. Unable to survive on the dyke road because of German anti-tank guns, they tried to manoeuvre into positions where they could bring fire down on the German positions. During the afternoon of 24 September a troop of M-10s from 5th Anti-Tank Regiment joined the squadron to assist them "in knocking out some likely enemy pillbox positions" but the Germans retaliated and "things became a little warm when the enemy started opening up with a few rounds of AP and HE in retaliation for the pillbox shoot."[67] Each night at least two A Squadron troops stayed with the infantry and the darkness hours were uneasy ones as the German 64th Infantry Division, which opposed the Canadians, proved to be very aggressive patrollers. On 25 September Darby Nash's B Squadron came up to relieve Lavoie only to be greeted by a German loudspeaker that urged the Canadians to give themselves up. This caused much amusement because, as John Neff remarked: "Jerry wants us to surrender?"[68]

That same day the South Albertas received a new job. While the bulk of the division held the line of the Leopold Canal, the Regiment was to take over the south coast of the Scheldt from Antwerp to the line of the Ghent-Terneuzen Canal, a distance of some fifteen miles. B Squadron continued at the Isabella Polder, A Squadron moved to Axel and the remainder of the Regiment, two companies of Argylls and two troops of M-10s were stationed in the Dutch town of Hulst, ten miles west of Antwerp. Daily patrols would be mounted along the coastline, but as to "do this task with t[an]ks would put too much mileage on the t[an]ks, therefore, they are to be kept in central reserve in case they are needed to flush out any Jerries in conjunction with the infantry."[69] These patrols were carried out with Stuarts and a special jeep troop formed under the command of Captain Jim Curley. The Regiment moved from Assenede to its new area on 27 September and commenced its new task by carrying out a

mass recce of all bridges and roads. This preliminary work was finished on 28 September and from then until the South Albertas left Hulst, three standing patrols of the coast were made each day, beginning at 0600 hours. The Regiment was assisted in this task by members of the Belgian and Dutch underground organizations, who reported any undue activity to Swatty, who would dispatch a patrol to check it out. The two troops of M-10s positioned two vehicles in a position to fire at any German shipping that appeared, relieving them in turn.[70]

All in all, except at the polder, it was a fairly quiet period. In fact, it was so quiet the journalists showed up in "Albertania," *their* new name for Hulst. The result, "South Alberta Regiment First Canadian Formation [sic] in Holland" written by Alan Randall hit the wire services soon after:

Any resemblance in this dateline to Canada's foothills province is strictly according to fact. The foothills are far off but the men of Alberta are right here. …

Their headquarters is in Hulst with everything nice and convenient. Hot and cold water. Electric lights. A pub right on the premises. Even a pool table. And the townspeople to cook their meals.

From here the Alberta Regiment under a lieutenant-colonel from Toronto, fan out over the countryside day and night in jeeps, armoured cars and light reconnaissance tanks. All across the area is the network of the white army working with the Canadians.

"Ours is a sort of holding, or garrison job for the present," explained Capt. Bob Allsopp of Edmonton ….[71]

And so on.

Assenede, Belgium. The Regiment was stationed here for several days in September 1944. COURTESY, J.L. SUMMERS.

The polder. Polder land, Belgium – flat, soggy, boggy, watered by numerous canals and ditches, it was easy to defend and a nightmare to attack across. PHOTOGRAPH BY DIANNE GRAVES.

The South Albertas spent nearly two weeks at Hulst and it was a pleasant time. Except for the occasional shell, there was little German activity and much of the recce work was undertaken by the resistance groups. As Swatty recalled, communications were very good:

We took over the local telephone exchange and I could talk from my halftrack. I could talk to Paris, I could talk to London and I could talk to Berlin. I could also talk to the Dutch resistance just across the Scheldt river. So we used to have regular contact with the resistance by telephone and find out where the Germans were, and then we could take them on by indirect fire and have a great time.[72]

B Echelon moved up to Hulst and for the first time since leaving England the bulk of the Regiment was concentrated in one place and garrison life was re-established. Unfortunately, the revival of garrison routine also led to RSM Mackenzie re-asserting himself. While the South Albertas were in action, the RSM usually turned a blind eye to minor infractions of discipline and eccentricity of dress among the tank crews. Now he cracked down and the War Diarist lamented on 28 September that discipline,

which for the past two months had slackened off, has now changed. Guards, pickets and all personnel on duty are now properly dressed and smartness in saluting and carriage is once again being stressed. A big change was noticed in this respect during the day and undoubtedly the civilians have been impressed.[73]

Nonetheless, the sojourn at Hulst was a good time. Arrangements were made for films to be shown in the town cinema, sporting events were organized and six per cent of the men at a time received day passes to Ghent. The boys got along very well with the local Dutch civilians and the War Diarist took note of the various social activities. On 1 October Swatty invited the townspeople to watch a movie furnished by the Regiment's

Special Services Officer. This broke the ice and, when a dance for the enlisted personnel was held three days later, "the building was crowded not so much with the men as with the civilians of the area who had not had a dance in four years."[74] Swatty received a pair of wooden shoes from the Dutch and proudly wore them on stage. On 7 October the Regiment arranged a field hockey match, providing a team "composed of 6 of the local lovelies with 6 of our men against a Hulst team of similar composition."[75] The match was followed by a band concert from the Argylls' pipe band, to which the locals responded enthusiastically, if not to the bagpipes, at least to the Highland dress of the pipers. The following day saw a soccer match between the South Albertas and the local team, which was attended by a "large civilian crowd" and "an equal number of the men," who came "to observe the more interesting gender of the civilians and of course to cheer our team on to victory."[76]

One event took place at Hulst that was not so pleasant. In early October the entire Regiment was paraded to witness three men, who had been charged and convicted of the rape of a Belgian woman, drummed out of the unit. Over the years so many tales have grown up around this affair that the truth of the matter is almost impossible to establish. The incident took place at Assenede during the evening of 23 September. Following a complaint by the husband of the woman concerned, an identification parade was held the next day at which the couple, accompanied by Padre Silcox, walked past the ranks of every soldier in the Regiment who had been in the town the previous night and picked out four men.[77]

Two of them were from Don Stewart's troop but Don was not permitted to see them or give evidence at their court martial a few days later. He knew them both well: one was a perennial troublemaker but a good man in action; the other was a quiet boy who had never been a problem. As he recalled, "The impression I got from the rest of the boys in the troop was that the two men had been doing some drinking and that the lady was quite willing till her husband showed up unexpectedly and the fat was in the fire."[78] That there was some doubt that a rape had actually taken place was evident at the court martial when two of the five officers sitting in judgement found the men "guilty" while two others found them "not guilty."[79] The deciding vote for "guilty" was cast by the senior officer, who later admitted that he "had been under instructions from corps to make an example of the men." Wotherspoon decided to do just that and ordered three of the men to be formally drummed out of the Regiment – a most unusual punishment. As the adjutant, Captain Bob Allsopp, recalled, the parade was held "to discipline the Regiment more than anything" and "to impress on the other boys the seriousness of the situation and to make everyone realize that you just didn't get away with things like that."[80]

The ceremony of drumming a soldier out is a British military tradition that dates back at least to the 17th century. It has been used only rarely in the Canadian Army and only then for the most serious of offences – usually cowardice in the face of the enemy. It is a public spectacle of humiliation and the South Albertas called on parade that day had no idea what they were about to witness – as Corporal Bob Rasmussen remembered, "we didn't know what it was about but there had been rumours floating around."[81] Those who were present never forgot it – particularly Trooper George Gallimore, who was a member of the prisoner escort:

We marched on, – guard, prisoner, guard, prisoner, four guards in all. The charge and the sentence was read and then RSM Mackenzie came over, knocked off the prisoners' berets and slashed off their shoulder straps, regimental flashes, etc., with a straight razor. All the time he was talking and not under his breath: "You son of a bitch, what you've done to this regiment, whatever it gets you, you deserve." He was a tough little bugger, Mackenzie, he was a Scots miner, tougher than hell.

I was so scared stiff, my knees were going and I wasn't one of the ones who were guilty. After he was finished, and it only took a couple of minutes, we had to march all the way round the regiment, every foot of the way, and these damned drums were beating, I don't know where they got the drums.[82]

The drummers were borrowed from the Argylls and they beat a slow, solemn pace as they led the wretched little group, consisting of the hatless prisoners and their escort, past the men of the Regiment. "They marched them right in front us," Jack Cheney recalled, "and it was a pretty ghastly experience."[83] When the prisoners had passed the last man, the escort delivered them to the provosts waiting to transport them to the "glass house" or military prison in Britain to serve terms of between two and five years "penal servitude to be followed by discharge with ignominy from His Majesty's service."

Wotherspoon had intended to impress and he succeeded. To George Gallimore the ceremony "was like capital punishment and I don't believe in capital punishment and I didn't believe in making a terrible spectacle of those guys, no matter what they did, but that was the British way of doing it and so – at least we didn't shoot them."[84] John Lakes thought that "no man on that parade would ever want to participate in a drumming out ceremony again" as, although "there was no sympathy for the culprits, it was a very unpleasant experience."[85] When it was over, Don Stewart remembered, Wotherspoon "called all the officers forward in a group around him and gave us a tongue lashing about discipline and things like that" and "I suppose that was aimed at me as much as anybody else."[86] One thing is certain – during the remainder of the war no soldier of the South Alberta Regiment was ever convicted of a serious crime.

A couple of adjutants. Captain Bob Allsopp, the adjutant (left), and Captain "Newt" Hughes, the battle adjutant, pose with the ACV, September 1944. The ACV or Armoured Command Vehicle, with its elaborate communications equipment, allowed Swatty Wotherspoon to command the SAR while at a distance from RHQ. This vehicle was a rare White Motor Company model not normally supplied to the Commonwealth armies. Note Hughes's leather jerkin – the weather is starting to get cooler. COURTESY, R.H. ALLSOPP.

Three men in a boat. Lieutenant Tom "Peachie" Howard, Trooper G. Mandryk and a Dutch civilian identified only as Johann, in the latter's boat near Philippine, October 1944. The Regiment's stay at Hulst provided a chance for the South Albertas to form good relations with the local population. COURTESY, JOHN NEFF.

While the Regiment was at Hulst the two infantry divisions of First Canadian Army finished clearing the Channel Ports and moved north to the Scheldt area. Third Division started reducing the Breskens Pocket on 6 October but, in the face of determined German resistance (stiffened by the order that the families of soldiers who surrendered would "be looked upon as enemies of the German people" and treated accordingly), it took them until 2 November to clear the south bank of the Scheldt.[87] Meanwhile, 2nd Division drove north from Antwerp to cut off the South Beveland Peninsula and isolate the German garrisons on the north bank of the Scheldt. The division advanced on 2 October but almost immediately encountered the German "fire brigade" in Holland – the 6th Parachute Regiment – a tough and experienced unit that was able to resist all Canadian attempts to take the vital town of Woensdrecht. In the fighting in and around this town 2nd Division suffered heavy casualties and could make no headway and since that formation's rear and flank were wide open, they required protection.[88]

The Regiment got the job. On 9 October the South Albertas, with one company of Algoons under command, was assigned to the 2nd Division, and moved immediately to the area of Brasschaet north of Antwerp. Don Stewart's troop was leading when the column got to Antwerp and Don was troubled when he was directed to a long tunnel under the Scheldt River. He had his doubts about that tunnel:

> They told us the engineers had swept it thoroughly for mines and there was no danger whatsoever – but they would like to have a troop of tanks go through and make sure the engineers had done their job. How we would prove that except by drowning, I don't know. Anyway we took the first tank troop through the tunnel and it was kind of a hair-raising experience.[89]

The rest of the column followed and there were many pursed lips as the South Alberta tanks and other vehicles moved through the seemingly endless underground passage. Safely back in the open air the Regiment moved north and deployed: RHQ and B Squadron at Brasschaet, A Squadron on the right at Brecht and C Squadron on the left at Calmpthout. The Regiment was now covering a front of some eight miles.[90]

Advance parties had been sent to all the squadron areas and the shift to the new positions went smoothly. During the next ten days, Swatty sent out daily patrols, usually in the strength of a troop or two troops of tanks supported by a platoon or two of infantry. These patrols probed the German defences, engaged in speculative shooting, took prisoners for their intelligence value, and deliberately drew German fire so that the locations of enemy guns could be marked down for the attention of friendly artillery and aircraft. It was classic recce work and, as most of the actions were very small in scale, good training for the troop leaders.[91]

It was also a busy time. On 10 October A Squadron brewed up an enemy armoured car and the next day B-3 and B-4 Troops got into a hot little action at a German roadblock and called in the Typhoons who managed to drop "a few short." On 12 October, twenty-four Spitfires made two separate attacks in the afternoon to bomb and strafe enemy artillery positions located by SAR patrols. On 15 October a mixed patrol from RHQ Troop and Recce had another hot firefight at a German roadblock and brought back some prisoners. Night patrols were now mounted, assisted by 125 men of the Belgian resistance who had been assigned to work with the Regiment, and there were several encounters with German infiltrators attempting to mine the roads and tracks in the area. On 17 October an echelon ammo lorry hit one of these mines and disintegrated, although the driver and co-driver escaped with only minor wounds. The Regiment took forty prisoners over a period of ten days but the Germans facing them did not seem to be a very aggressive lot – the War Diarist commented that the prisoners "didn't seem to have much interest in fighting and were glad the war was over for them." Nor did they appear to be well equipped, having "been more or less thrown into the battle and dished out on our front without any bigger weapons than a MG, last war rifles and a few mortars."[92]

One amusing incident occurred during this period. On 15 October Brigadier T. J. Rutherford, the commander of the Canadian Armoured Corps Reinforcement Unit at Woking, arrived at RHQ to pay a visit to Swatty, who was an old friend. Rutherford, a veteran of the First World War, "claimed to have been something of an expert on Patrols" and, as Bert Coffin recalls, "nothing would do but that he wanted to go out on one of our patrols." Bert describes what happened:

> Swatty tried to talk him out of it but he wouldn't budge so Swatty called [Lieutenant] Stu Lindop in and told him to take the old boy out as his gunner. They were to do a little

tour outside the camp and let the old boy shoot a couple of rounds at a bush or something and come back. In no way were they to get anywhere near the Germans.

Some hours later they came back and the old Brig was just bubbling over. That idiot Lindop had taken him way up into enemy territory and the Brig had seen and shot at a German, so he claimed. When the big push came a few days later it took a whole week for the division to get that far. Swatty was just fit to be tied but there was little he could do but grin and bear it.[93]

Arnold Lavoie's position at Brecht was very close to the enemy. A Squadron "was on one road with a row of houses along it, and a quarter of a mile over from our position was another road lined with houses … held by the Germans," John Galipeau remembered.[94] The Germans "made the occasional sortie over to our side of the village, but after a few bursts of Browning they all ran back to where they were supposed to be." On the morning of 15 October, Lavoie decided to mount an "exploitation attack" to clear the Germans out of those houses and "to ascertain in what str[ength] the enemy were on our front, to capture prisoners and to make him feel we have a fair amount of str[ength] here at Brecht as his patrols have been very aggressive the past few nights."[95] The attack was made by one troop from A Squadron supported by a platoon of Algonquins with additional covering fire from another troop on the flank. At 1030 hours the A Squadron force moved forward to the enemy-held houses and the tanks took up positions to support the Algoons who began to clear them. They were immediately hit by enemy artillery and mortar fire and the Germans defenders knocked out Corporal Herb Roulston's Sherman with a *Panzerfaust*. Herb evacuated his crew and was arranging for the recovery of his vehicle when a second Sherman was hit. Two crew members bailed out unharmed but the driver, Trooper Norman Craig, a 21-year-old truck driver from Rouge Valley, Quebec, who had joined the SAR in 1943, was killed, while Corporal Russell White and Trooper Rod Debay were wounded and pinned inside their vehicle by German small-arms fire.[96] Roulston and another trooper volunteered to go back and get the two men out. Braving mortar and small-arms fire, they made it to the tank, made some minor repairs, got it running and drove it back to safety. By this time the Germans were thoroughly stirred up and the shelling increased so, after the Algonquins had finished their work and taken fourteen prisoners, the A Squadron troop withdrew at 1300 hours.[97]

At Brasschaet B Squadron's position was at a Belgian military camp about four miles north of the town. A military airstrip lay at the northern edge of that camp – the Germans were on one end of the strip, the SAR were on the other, and it was a fine field of fire for both parties. For four days the squadron patrolled their side with the Fusiliers Mont Royal, but whenever the tanks appeared, they drew heavy mortar fire. It didn't damage them but often destroyed the crew's personal gear and

Morning brew-up. Somewhere in Holland or Belgium, late September or early October 1944, the South Albertas have morning tea before setting out on their work for the day. The weather is turning cooler and they are starting to add warm clothing. SAR COLLECTION

cooking utensils strapped to the back of the turrets. A few days later B Squadron discovered a British Mustang fighter in almost perfect condition in one of the hangars at the airfield. There were other aerial novelties about at this time. On 18 October the South Albertas saw their first V-2 missiles, which had been aimed at Antwerp but dropped short in their area. One of these new German weapons hit a Mobile Bath Unit creating "a crater 80 feet across" and leaving "bits of men and clothing hanging from trees all around."[98]

In contrast C Squadron had a fairly quiet time at Calmpthout. Danny McLeod remembered that "we did not want to attract too much attention" so "we did the odd little sortie, we skirmished out with the Fusiliers Mont Royal but, other than the odd patrol to identify the enemy and some counter-battery work, it was pretty quiet for us."[99] Their worst problem was sniping and the squadron had one man wounded by artillery fire. For Danny the biggest scare came the night that the Dutch woman who owned the house he was billeted in "said that she had daughter in the cellar who was about to give birth and asked for the assistance of an army doctor."[100] The squadron didn't have a doctor but it did have two medical orderlies and Danny told them to go assist the woman. The orderlies rightfully protested that "they never had any training in obstetrics but I told them to get down there and they went to the cellar with their medical kit." It all came right in the end and the healthy newborn boy received the Christian names of the orderlies.

It was at Calmpthout that Corporal Frank Moan of C Squadron immortalized himself. Frankie Moan, like Herb Roulston of A Squadron, Tony Devreker and Daddy Vitkovich of B and Sid Arrowsmith of the fitters, and others, was one of those natural leaders admired by their comrades. Danny regarded him as "the heart and soul of my troop, he was the mature guy, the leading athlete and the all round handy man – Frankie could do anything."[101] Danny never forgot the day at Calmpthout when he wanted to hold a small O Group for my troop but no one could find Moan, who was one of my crew commanders. I went storming out to find him and, for some unknown reason, I opened the door of a shed between two buildings and there was Frank, wearing a top hat of all things, and about to butcher a dead pig suspended from the ceiling of the shed. This was about the time that our corps commander, Guy Simonds, had issued strict order regarding the looting of civilian food supplies, including livestock. I said: "What!" but before I could continue, Frankie broke in: "Boss, let me tell you. That poor little pig was walking down the street and a shell dropped and split him ear to ear. You wouldn't waste it, would you? It's pork chops, tonight, Boss!" That was Frankie Moan.

When trying to procure food from the civilians, language could be a problem, as one of Don Stewart's men discovered when he went to a farm to get some eggs. Unable to communicate with the Belgian farmwife, he began to flap his "wings" and go "cluck, cluck, cluck" to get the message across to the good lady, who promptly "thought he was after her and ran away."[102]

During the Regiment's time in the Brasschaet area German shelling was constant, if not heavy. Anytime they saw a shell fall, crews made a "shell report" giving the time, direction and location of the burst, and these "shell-reps" give some idea of conditions in the area. On 13 October, for example, one hundred and eleven artillery rounds, ranging from 81 mm mortar to 88 HE, fell in the South Alberta area between Brecht and Calmpthout.[103] Whether the incoming landed close or far, the boys always respected enemy artillery fire; the saying in the Regiment was that "it isn't the shell with your name on it that worries you, it's the one marked *to whom it may concern*."[104] "The mortars never bothered us much," Jack Cheney commented, "except that the bombs would slam onto the side of the tank and they didn't do us any harm but it was like being inside a drum with somebody beating on it."[105] George Gallimore, being a DR on an unarmoured motorcycle, held a much different opinion. After he had been mortared off his bike for the second time in a few months, George felt he needed a less stressful lifestyle and wangled a transfer to Recce Troop.[106]

The worst casualties from the shelling occurred at 0730 hours on 11 October when a German mortar "stonk" hit a

Eekloo, Belgium, 4 October 1944. The issue of heavy tank suits ("zoot suits" the boys called them after the nattily-dressed social phenomenon back home) was welcomed in October as the weather turned cooler. In this cartoon attached to the 4th Armoured Division War Diary for October 1944, the artist portrays the difficulties of identifying LOs (Liaison Officers) from the various units wearing these suits at divisional headquarters. His tank suit, map board, Browning and Humber scout car were the trade marks of the LO.

house serving as a billet. One mortar bomb came through a window and burst in the middle of a room where six South Albertas were getting dressed. Five men, Troopers Harold Freer, Samuel George, Gordon Holmstrom, Harold Rae and Phillip Rodd, were badly wounded while a sixth, Trooper Lloyd Corner, was injured so severely that he died later from his wounds. Corner, a 27-year-old former member of the Royal Montreal Regiment who had joined the SAR in March 1944, was survived by a wife and three children.[107]

The weather, which had been variable in September, turned cold, wet and surly in October. Wartime tanks were not heated and, since the hatches were normally open, they were very uncomfortable in cold or wet weather. Lieutenant Jack Summers of B-2 thought an umbrella might solve the problem of keeping dry while commanding in the rain and rigged one up over his turret hatch. Unfortunately, the first time the driver started up, the downdraft into the turret caused by the five Chrysler engines was strong enough to collapse it over his head. Jack sadly tossed the wretched thing overboard and carried on being wet.[108]

A partial solution to the problem arrived in mid-October when the crews received new tank suits or coveralls, which, as Don Stewart described in a letter to his mother, were complicated but efficient wearing apparel:

We have just been issued with tank "zoot-suits" which are the best things the Canadian army has ever issued. Just like the flying suits of the airforce with plenty of zippers, thick lining, a parka hood and about a hundred pockets. By manipulating the zippers a bit the suit can be made into a pair of coveralls, a trench coat, or a sleeping bag. Pretty zooty, eh?[109]

Everybody had their own way of wearing the new gear. Some men, like Lieutenant Johnnie Guyot of B-1 Troop, affected a swashbuckling appearance by leaving the lower lengths of the zippers on the trousers undone so that they looked like bell-bottoms.[110]

The Recce Troop was doubly blessed – not only did they get the new clothes, they also drew new tanks. Their Mark V Stuarts, powered by Wright aircraft engines that would provide forty miles per hour, were replaced in late October by the Mark VI model, "with twin Cadillac motors and automatic transmissions" which made the Recce drivers "the envy of all the other tank drivers" in the Regiment.[111] The new machines, Bob Clipperton enthused, "were very efficient, the firepower was the same but, man, could those tanks travel – up to 55 mph."[112] Since speed often meant survival to the Recce crews, they were a happy bunch of young men in October 1944.

Throughout that month there was growing concern over the delay in opening Antwerp. Clearly, the Canadians needed assistance but Montgomery, still hoping to get to the Rhine, refused to make Antwerp the main objective in his Army Group and some Allied senior commanders were becoming exasperated with him. On 3 October Admiral Bertram Ramsay of the Royal Navy publicly castigated the British field-marshal during a meeting "for not having made Antwerp the immediate objective of highest priority."[113] This did not budge Montgomery from his fixation on the Rhine, and even when he decided four days later that the logistical situation would not permit him to reach that river before the onset of winter, he still dawdled over Antwerp. On 9 October he issued a new directive that re-affirmed Antwerp as the goal of First Canadian Army but he gave it no additional forces for the task.[114]

In the end, it required the direct intervention of Eisenhower to get Montgomery to move. The supreme Allied commander informed the British field-marshal in no uncertain terms on 10 October that the immediate "possession of the approaches to Antwerp" was "an objective of vital importance."[115] Incredibly, it still took Montgomery nearly a week to give the necessary orders and it was only on 16 October, forty-two days after the port had been first captured, that he issued a directive stating that Antwerp was "vital to the Allied cause" and the "whole of the available offensive power of the Second [British] Army will now be brought to bear" to assist the Canadians to clear its approaches.[116] This directive was the genesis of Operation SUITCASE, which launched 4th Armoured Division on a northward drive to the Maas River.

The division began to concentrate in the rear of the Regiment's position at Camp Brasschaet on 17 October 1944. The purpose of SUITCASE was to prevent the Germans interfering with 2nd Division as it tried to capture the South Beveland peninsula and it involved four divisions from four different Allied nations (1st Polish, 4th Canadian, 49th British and 104th American) under the command of British 1st Corps. The first objective of Foster's 4th Armoured was the town of Esschen, an important rail centre about five miles north of Camp Brasschaet, and Harry planned to attack with his two brigades moving on parallel centre lines along the two main roads that led to Esschen, 4 Brigade on the left and 10 Brigade on the right. As usual, the terrain favoured the Germans, being "typically lowland, a criss cross of water filled ditches, verges and fields that would not hold tanks or carriers, narrow cobbled roads, new brick, tile and glass houses, and considerable forest land of

young evergreens."[117] The South Alberta Regiment would not be playing a major part in the opening stages of the operation. Their job was to establish a "firm base" at Camp Brasschaet and to provide right flank protection. Nonetheless, Swatty participated in the planning for the attack and was able to hand Jim Jefferson a "complete order of battle of the enemy forces in the area," which the Regiment had compiled over the previous ten days.[118]

On 19 October, the day before SUITCASE began, a neat little action occurred at the airfield at Camp Brasschaet. Two troops from B Squadron went out with Major Jim Swayze's company of the Lincoln and Welland Regiment to capture prisoners and assess enemy strength. The operation "was a classic," Swayze recalled. "We put the infantry on the left … and the tanks over on the right and the infantry would go until they were fired on." The infantry would go to ground and then the tanks would open up, "giving covering fire and moving in as though they were going to rush through them." "We had one platoon rush in, pick out 14 prisoners and put them on the back of the tanks and get them out. … We didn't lose a man."[119]

Operation SUITCASE commenced at 0730 hours on the grey and wet morning of 20 October 1944. For 10 Brigade the first day went smoothly, the Argylls took the village of Kapellenbosch while the Algonquins, supported by A Squadron, took Achterbroek. The advance continued on 21 October, the Germans "giving ground slowly and stubbornly," but the Links were able to gain the first objective, the Rosendaal Canal, and by last light the brigade was four miles from Esschen. Jefferson ordered his three infantry battalions to make a night march and be in a position to put in an attack on that place at first light on 22 October.[120]

Under cover of darkness and supported by 15 Field, which fired on all known enemy positions, the three battalions moved forward. By morning, in the words of the brigade historian, they had advanced "some four miles through and behind the German defences," an advance that "was perhaps the best illustration of the proper use of one of the major principles of war – 'surprise.'"[121] Bob Bradburn and the RSM of the Algonquins "bumped into an awakening enemy group, and a pistol fight ensued, plus some hand-to-hand battling" before the Germans surrendered.[122] Esschen taken, the first phase of SUITCASE had gone well and there was a pause for a day as preparations were made for the next move.

The Regiment saw relatively little action during the opening stages of the operation. A Squadron helped the Algonquins to take Achterbroek and both A and B Squadrons supported that regiment on the second day of the attack. At 1000 hours on 21 October, however, the Regiment was given responsibility for the division's left flank and that afternoon RHQ and B and C Squadrons moved west to the village of Kolonie Kinderwelzyn, where they were joined two days later by A Squadron. The South Albertas were about to start up the road to glory – a road they would remember in later years as "Hulk Alley."[123]

CHAPTER THIRTEEN

"Hell, Bill, let's take the damned place."

BELGIUM AND HOLLAND: 23 OCTOBER – 7 NOVEMBER 1944

You had to feel sorry for the senior staff of 4th Canadian Armoured Division. For more than a month, they had been stationed in a comfortable location "on the carefully tended lawns of a fashionable chateau" near Eekloo and their worst problem had been the rain which flooded the parking lot. Life at Eekloo was good until 16 October when the staff had to up stakes and move to another château near Schilde, north of Antwerp, in preparation for Operation SUITCASE. Everybody was sad to leave their cosy billet but many perked up on 18 October when they learned of vacancies "on a Sanitary and Water duties course to be held in the UK" in November "and, since cleanliness "is next to godliness and godliness is next to home," not a few decided to apply. Two days later, SUITCASE commenced and the staff switched locations yet again, this time to a chateau near Oudegracht, but at least the move took them "from chateau to chateau, and the new one seems as pleasant as the last."[2]

The senior staff of the division had every reason to be confident that better billets lay ahead. The successful advance of Jefferson's 10 Brigade during the opening days of Operation SUITCASE had broken the defence line of Von Zangen's Fifteenth Army north of Antwerp wide open and there was hope "that a trap may be sprung" that would eliminate that army south of the Maas River. Von Zangen and, more particularly, the commander of the German 67th Corps which was facing the Allied advance, *Generalleutnant* Otto Sponheimer, had made repeated requests for permission to retire behind the Maas but had received the usual orders to hold every foot of ground to the last man. In early October the two German generals decided "to act independently" and began a clandestine evacuation of all non-essential personnel who were south of the Maas and commenced construction of new positions north of the river. The essential thing was to gain time by holding Allied "forces as long as possible" until everything was ready and

In Bergen op Zoom, op Zoom, op Zoom
I got me a room, a room, a room.
I went to my doom, my doom, my doom,
In Bergen op Zoom, op Zoom, op Zoom.
The babes they were fair, were fair, were fair,
Their forms were so rare, so rare, so rare.
I was glad I was there, I was there
Up in Bergen, Bergen op Zoom.

Oh I didn't say much, lest I get in Dutch,
Up in Bergen, with a virgin.
Oh they banished my gloom, in my nice hotel room,
Up in Bergen, Bergen, Bergen op Zoom.[1]

67th Corps was successful in this objective until 10 Brigade seized Esschen. According to the corps' chief of staff, this meant that an "enemy break-through had practically succeeded" and a "critical situation of the first water had arisen." The main German evacuation route over the Maas was the Moerdijk bridges north of Bergen op Zoom and it was therefore essential to establish a temporary new defensive line, hinged on Bergen, that would gain time for a safe withdrawal. As the two divisions facing the Canadians, 245th and 346th Infantry Divisions, were "near the end of their strength in officers and men," that line would have to be held with better troops.[3]

Better troops were made available. The 6th German Parachute Regiment, an oversized unit of four battalions, had been fighting hard against 2nd Canadian Division in the Hoogerheide-Woensdrecht area for the last two weeks to prevent the South Beveland Peninsula falling into Allied hands. When 2nd Division cut off the peninsula on 16 October, this unit was redeployed against 4th Armoured Division. Composed of a cadre of "long-experienced, battle-tried, active parachutists," fleshed out with "very good replacements," it was shifted into position south of Bergen op Zoom on 23 October.[4] At the same time, elements of *Kampfgruppe* Dreyer, an ad hoc but well-armed formation built around good quality parachute and *Luftwaffe* troops, was shifted into position on 6th Parachute Regiment's left. The new German defence line centred on the extensive pine forests of the Wouwsche Plantage, a large plantation southeast of Bergen, and was anchored on the east by a strong position in the village of the same name (see map 12, page 220). Harry Foster's division was now up against the best in the German Fifteenth Army.

That fact became apparent when the Foot Guards and Lake Soups of 4 Armoured Brigade tried to attack from Esschen northwest to the village of Wouwsche Plantage on 23 October.

The German defenders, drawn from *Kampfgruppe* Dreyer and largely composed of men of the Hermann Goering Regiment, fought hard and the anti-tank fire was "so heavy," recorded the 10 Brigade historian, that "almost a squadron of [Foot Guard] tanks were left simmering" when the two units withdrew.[5] That night the Argylls, under 4 Brigade command, went in with two troops from the Grenadier Guards. Six of the Guards' tanks bogged in the soft ground. The remaining two advanced but the infantry coming behind saw the second vehicle knocked out with a *Panzerfaust*, blocking the escape route of the lead

That wretched parking lot. The senior staff of 4th Division Headquarters liked life in their chateau at Eekloo except for the parking lot which often flooded, the subject of this cartoon attached to the October War Diary of the 4th Division. They looked forward to future accommodations of a better sort.

Sherman, "which was captured and driven off" by the triumphant Germans.[6] The following night the Germans used this tank against another attack on the village by two companies of the Links (under 4 Brigade command at this point) and that unit's historian noted that the "surprise effect" on the Canadians "was considerable."[7] While 4 Armoured Brigade was banging its head against Wouwsche village, however, the South Albertas had managed to open up "the whole German defence line" south of Bergen op Zoom.[8]

It came about this way. The Regiment, less A Squadron, had concentrated southwest of Huijbergen in the morning of Monday, 23 October 1944, ready to protect the division's left flank. Recce and AA Troops, backed up by B and C Squadrons, checked out the immediate area that day. It was quiet with the exception of the occasional enemy mortar or artillery shell, and civilians reported that the Germans had pulled out for the north. There were still some enemy lurking in the vicinity, however, and Sergeant Charles Browning of Recce Troop had an exciting time when he captured forty-two prisoners.[9]

That night the Regiment formed a defensive laager near a woods west of Huijbergen. "Throughout the night," the War Diarist recorded, "there was intermittent mortar and shell fire around RHQ and at 2300 hours the alarm was sounded on hearing a few bursts of MG fire in the area."[10] It was a restless night with German artillery and mortar fire falling in the area of the harbour. When there was a general stand-to at dawn, Albert Halkyard's crew were unable to wake their driver, Vern Easton, and discovered that he had been killed by a shell fragment that had struck him while was asleep. They buried Vern

close to the spot and George Gallimore, who had had enough of being a DR, came into Halkyard's crew to replace him. Easton, a 24-year-old blacksmith from Islay, Alberta, had been wounded when Duffy Gendron's patrol had been knocked out in August and had only returned to the troop the day before.[11]

On the morning of 24 October Swatty Wotherspoon ordered the Regiment to advance towards Huijbergen. Dave Currie had the lead and called down a medium artillery concentration on the woods east of the village, prior to advancing through them. This concentration caught Darby Nash, whose B Squadron was coming up behind, unprepared and Darby had to rush "around madly in his scout car to get out of the danger zone of our own medium art[iller]y."[12] Swatty was expecting to have to fight for Huijbergen but, at 1345 hours Dave Currie reported it clear of the enemy. Just north of the town his lead troop, commanded by Danny McLeod, seized an intersection from which two roads branched off: one was a cobblestoned road that ran due north to the village of Wouwsche Plantage, the other was a narrow dirt track, called the Huijbergsche Baan, that led northwest to Bergen op Zoom. As the reports came in to RHQ, Swatty began to form a picture in his mind of the situation in his front and it became clear to him that the Germans had withdrawn to a new defence line which must run somewhere from a point south of Bergen east to Wouwsche village where, it appeared, judging by the stubborn defence of that place, the enemy had his main strength. Having secured Huijbergen, any advance up the two roads leading north from there – either against the flank of the strong German position at Wouwsche village or, better still, up the Huijbergsche Baan directly to Bergen op Zoom – would be very advantageous. Excited about the possibilities, Swatty rushed off to Jefferson's HQ

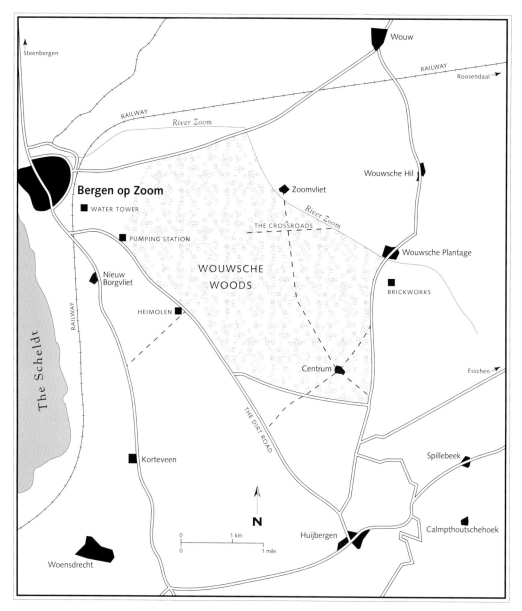

Map 12: The battle for Bergen op Zoom, 25-27 October 1944. While the remainder of 4th Division moved on Bergen from the southeast, the Regiment got the job of providing flank protection. Arriving at Huijbergen on 24 October, they discovered that there was a back way into the city via the Huijbergsche Baan or "The Dirt Road" but Wotherspoon's efforts to convince his superiors to advance along this route were to no avail and 10 Brigade became involved in heavy fighting in the Wouwsche Plantage-Centrum-Zoomvliet area. Finally, on 27 October, after the Germans had withdrawn north of the Zoom, SAR tank patrols entered Bergen in the late afternoon.

ber and advance, not northwest to Bergen, but due north towards Wouwsche village. Swatty was disappointed as he regarded Bergen as the more important objective, but that night he deployed with his main strength on the right so as to be able to support the brigade in the morning. A Squadron, which had come back under command in the afternoon, was positioned in the hamlet of Spillebeek, directly south of Wouwsche Plantage, while B Squadron was behind them at Calmpthoutschehoek, where Swatty established his RHQ. Between that place and Huijbergen a miscellaneous collection of units – a squadron of the Manitoba Dragoons, AA Troop, tanks from the 4th Division HQ troop, and two sections of the Algonquin carrier platoon – covered the front. Only Dave Currie's C Squadron remained on the left at Huijbergen with Danny McLeod's troop in an advanced position near the junction of the two roads leading north.[15]

In the evening of 24 October Swatty learned that B Squadron was to support Bob Bradburn's Algonquins the following morning and at 2100 hours Darby Nash attended Bradburn's O Group at the Algonquin RHQ, which was located at Wolfsheuvel

in the afternoon of 24 October "to obtain the B[riga]de picture and explain our pos[itio]n in the hope that this [advance to Bergen] may be done."[13]

He sold the idea to Jeff, who took it to Harry Foster. Although Foster's staff acknowledged that "active patrolling" by the Regiment "had resulted in a slight enemy withdrawal," Harry's attention was fixed on Wouwsche village.[14] He intended to take that place and advance north to cut the main east-west highway out of Bergen op Zoom. He therefore ordered Jefferson to concentrate his brigade in the Huijbergen area on 25 Octo-

Farm, southwest of Esschen. The meeting was "held in the top loft of a large barn" which, because no lights could be shown, required Nash and the other officers to clamber up "a dizzy succession of ladders" feeling their way "through haybales, and skirting openings in the loft floor" until they "finally came to a tight little cubicle, lit by a pressure lamp, and containing about twenty-five officers in various stages of suffocation."[16] From Huijbergen Bradburn planned to drive directly north along the cobblestoned road toward the village of Wouwsche Plantage, skirting the large pine woods of the same name. When Darby returned to the Regiment, Swatty held his own conference to make plans for the morning. Darby asked for protection on his left flank and Danny McLeod's troop got this job with orders to advance along the Huijbergsche Baan. Danny would be followed up that road by the remainder of C Squadron, which was ordered to "carry out a recce" in the direction of Bergen op Zoom.[17] Arnold Lavoie's A Squadron meanwhile would move north from Spillebeek to provide right flank protection for Nash.[18]

Darby Nash wasn't the only member of B Squadron moving around in the dark that night. During the day the men in Lieutenant Johnny Guyot's B-1 Troop had "noticed a sizeable herd of cattle" in the vicinity and, as they "warmed up their M & V rations, someone mentioned the cattle." Strict orders had been issued prohibiting the taking of food from civilians but the men were tormented by the thought of "steaks and roast" until "with one accord," remembered John Neff, "we all said – why not?" A patrol went out, led by Sergeant Jim Kroesing, and it returned a few hours later with a white cow, "the only one they could find in the dark." In a western regiment there is never any shortage of men who know butchering and in a few minutes the cow had been dispatched and hoisted up on the barrel of the troop's 17-pdr. tank ready for skinning. "The big problem," Neff remembered, "was the lack of light, however, we did manage to get it quartered" and distributed to the four crews in the troop, who turned in that night with visions of fresh beef dancing in their heads.[19]

A t 0700 hours, 25 October, the Algonquins moved in TCVs to Huijbergen where they debussed and married up with Nash's B Squadron. This took some time to arrange and that was unfortunate because a local farmer complained to the colonel that "his one and only white cow was missing." Swatty ordered Sergeant Joe Walmsley, the Regimental police sergeant, to make a search for the animal and this caused some consternation among a certain troop in B Squadron. The boys of B-1 decided that the best thing to do was to share their largesse with another troop and hastily divided "the four quarters into eighths, more easy to conceal." The problem was what to do with the telltale hide, head and entrails but Jim Kroesing "was never one to be stumped by such problems and quickly dug a trench about six feet long and two feet wide, burying the damning evidence, neatly mounded it over and placed a stake at one end complete with a German helmet." Both troops passed the inspection and shortly afterward left to support the Algonquins. As John Neff's tank pulled out, he glanced back and was horrified to see "a dog struggling to pull a long cow's tail from what appeared to be a German grave."[20]

The Algonquins moved up the road to Wouwsche village and immediately encountered mines and booby traps. Bradburn took his time as he did not like the situation on his left flank, where the thick pine woods provided excellent German defensive positions, and throughout the morning sent out "scouting sections, supported by a tank troop" to nose "out possible enemy locations."[21] There was very little enemy activity except for some shell fire which wounded Lieutenant Stu Lindop. On Bradburn's right, Lavoie's A Squadron tried to keep pace with him as they worked forward slowly over open, wet fields.[22]

By mid-day Bradburn was approaching Wouwsche village but, still concerned about his left, he halted while he sent the Algonquin carrier platoon to probe the Wouwsche woods. The carriers moved cautiously down one of the many bush tracks through the pine trees and reached the small village of Centrum in the middle of the woods, from which five roads radiated in all directions like the spokes of a wheel. The platoon found no enemy in the village and Bradburn deployed two of his companies to hold Centrum while he moved with the remaining two against Wouwsche village. As the Algoon infantry and South Alberta tanks approached in the late afternoon, they encountered a strong enemy position in a brickworks at the south end, while at the same time German mortar and artillery fire increased in tempo. By this time A Squadron had reached a point directly east of Wouwsche village but came under such heavy German automatic weapons and *Panzerfaust* fire that they were forced to pull back slightly.[23]

It was clear to Bradburn that a major effort would be necessary to take the brickworks. As the light was failing, Jefferson ordered him to firm up for the night and wait until morning when the Argylls would be up to support him. Nash's four B Squadron troops and two from A Squadron stayed with the Algonquins that night while the remainder of Lavoie's squadron shifted to the Regiment's left flank to support Dave Currie's C Squadron, which had spent the day moving up the Huijbergsche Baan, the dirt road toward Bergen op Zoom.[24]

Dave was short of tanks and the squadron was only running three troops that day commanded by Lieutenants Harold Kreewin, Danny McLeod and Don Stewart. Danny, whose task was to provide flank protection for B Squadron, was first up the dirt road. This route, which skirted the west side of the main Wouwsche woods, was lined on both sides with deep ditches but the trees had been cut back on the verges to a distance of about twenty-five feet on either side. Danny was not expecting any trouble "and we just took it slow with the troop's turret guns traversed to cover all fronts."[25] Then he spotted "a knocked out Staghound" armoured car of the Manitoba Dragoons and "this put me on the alert." He continued to move up cautiously and soon "spotted trip wires in the woods on either side of us." He continued to advance slowly and by noon had reached a point nearly west of Centrum.

Swatty now asked Danny if he could get some prisoners to aid in identifying the enemy in front. A few minutes later Danny picked up two Germans, who shouted for their comrades to give up, and as they rose from their trenches Danny realized to his horror that the troop "had driven right into the German position without realizing it, so well were they camouflaged." Twenty-six Germans in all gave themselves up and were identified as soldiers from the 6th Parachute and Hermann

Goering Regiment. Danny pushed on until he was close to the hamlet of Heimolen which consisted of a road junction with some buildings clustered around it. He ordered Frank Moan to take his tank down and "dust off" another group of buildings to the left while he took the troop through the intersection. At that moment, some Germans ran across the road and the troop opened fire, wounding two of them. As they moved up through the intersection Moan asked for permission to dismount and put a shell dressing on one German who was in a bad way but Danny told him to stay in his tank, A few minutes later, he turned around in his turret, just in time to see Moan "scampering back into his tank with a Luger pistol shoved into his back pocket."[26]

Moan then moved to the farm buildings on the left but, as Danny recalled,

> instead of "dusting them" with HE and machine-gun fire, he dismounted and entered the buildings alone and armed with a Sten gun. He returned with seven prisoners from the Hermann Goering Division. In the meantime, I had called his tank but had gotten no reply and I finally shouted, "if there is anyone in that bloody tank, answer me right now!" This brought someone on to say that "Moan was in the house taking some prisoners." When he got back, I went over to him and said, "Fire that Sten gun" and he said, "What do you mean?" I said, "Fire it into the ditch!" It was covered with dust and rust and it wouldn't fire. "Well, Boss, imagine that," Moan said, "I might have had to whip each of them, one at a time."[27]

Some distance behind were Don Stewart's and Harold Kreewin's troops. Don did not like the look of that road and was convinced that the Germans were hiding in the pine forest and, after his head wound at St. Lambert, Don was "very sensitive about sticking my head out of the turret of the tank and getting sniped again." As his troop moved slowly up the Huijbergsche Baan he "kept very low in the turret, just barely peeking over the rim of it when I could manage to do that."[28] As they moved along, "someone took a shot at me" and the "bullet hit the raised rim of the turret hatch I was peeking over; it spattered on the rim and wiped the camouflage net right off my helmet" and "after that I was even lower in the turret."

By late afternoon, Danny was approaching the outskirts of Bergen op Zoom when he "encountered a very substantial German position and got into a heavy fire fight."[29] When he reported his location and asked for assistance, there was consternation because he was much closer to Bergen than anyone had intended he should go. He was told "to make his way out of there as best you can" and that Stewart's troop would be up to cover him. Danny pulled slowly back down the road but was then told to stay where he was as there was trouble behind him. What had happened, it transpired, was that the Germans had let the tanks "penetrate their first line" and then "opened up on

them from the rear."[30] Stewart's tanks came under "direct close range bazooka fire" from the tree line and his four Shermans were soon furiously firing into the woods to keep the German infantry from getting any closer. Kreewin was ordered to cover Don and lost two tanks doing so.[31]

Neither troop was thus in any position to help Danny, whose four tanks were some distance ahead, "lined up on the road, one behind each other, one tank with its gun to the left, one with the gun to the right, one facing back down the road and one covering the rear."[32] Danny remembered that he was almost out of ammunition:

> Moan called me up on the wireless, his tank was right behind mine, and said, "Do you have any ammunition?" I replied, "I don't have a round, not a round, do you have any?" He said, "I have one round of smoke." I told him to "blast the son of a bitch into the woods, they don't know we don't have any ammo." So he did.
>
> Everything was quiet. It's hard to judge time on an occasion like that, I don't know whether it was fifteen minutes or an hour that we were halted there. Then there was a tremendous explosion on the side of Moan's tank and I turned around and saw four of the crew get out, but not Frankie.

Corporal Frank Moan, a 31-year-old stockbuyer from Villeneuve, Alberta, was dead.[33]

"All hell broke loose," Danny remembered, as the Germans "put on an impressive display of fire and attacked."[34] It was time to go and Danny pulled back down the road to where Dave Currie had his headquarters, about two miles north of Huijbergen. Once there, he consolidated with the survivors of the other two troops.

It had been a frustrating day for Swatty as C Squadron had come very close to Bergen op Zoom, but with only three tank troops and no infantry he could not clear out the German positions along the Huijbergsche Baan. As the War Diarist noted, "if the higher command had been quick enough to exploit this initial breakthrough made by C Sqn there would have been little difficulty in dislodging the enemy completely from this area and pushing on to Bergen op Zoom."[35] Now the Regiment would have to go back up that road the following morning and a forewarned enemy would put up a stiff fight which might have been avoided if Foster and Jefferson had opted to throw the weight of the division along that route rather than direct it on Wouwsche village.

What made it doubly unfortunate is that no less a person than Montgomery had just made Bergen the primary objective of 4th Armoured Division. There had been a great stir among the senior staff when the field-marshal arrived at divisional headquarters at Château Oudegracht at 1030 hours that morning, and they were pleased to see Monty was wearing "his usual costume" of "slacks, flying jacket and beret."[36] Foster was less pleased when Montgomery told him that he expected 4th Division to capture Bergen-op-Zoom" by "the day after tomorrow." "I'll try," was Harry's honest reply.[37]

The senior staff had "hardly recovered from the flurry of excitement – not to mention the cleaning up," caused by Monty's visit when orders came to move the headquarters to Huijbergen. The officer commanding the headquarters squadron, Major Clarence Campbell, brother of Lieutenant Gordie Campbell of the SAR and a future power in the National Hockey League, immediately set out to recce a new location. The site he chose was not up to the staff's usual high standard, being a muddy field so close to the front that "it was well in advance of [10] bde HQ." It also appeared to be dangerous as, on his recce, Campbell actually "saw mines lifted" and "a recce veh[icle] blown up." Headquarters reluctantly moved up to this mud patch and spent "a rather uneasy night" disturbed by the noise of small-arms, machine-gun, mortar and artillery fire. This was hard service indeed but everyone was comforted by the assurances of Lieutenant Colonel Fred Wigle, the divisional GSO I and Swatty Wotherspoon's brother-in-law, that "warmer and quieter days are ahead" as their next HQ location would "be the best hotel in Bergen op Zoom."[38]

Before anyone got a soft bed in Bergen, the division had to get there. On the morning of 26 October Jefferson decided that the best thing would be to clean out the pine woods between Wouwsche village and the dirt road. A Squadron was ordered to help the Argylls clear out the woods immediately east of the dirt road while B Squadron helped the Algonquins do a similar job on their right. Meanwhile C Squadron with a company of Links was to move up the Huijbergsche Baan toward Bergen. On this day the Regiment would have the assistance of flail tanks from the 22nd Dragoons and Crocodile flame-thrower tanks from the Fife and Forfar Yeomanry, units of the 79th British Armoured Division. While 10 Brigade was engaged on this work, 4 Brigade would protect their flank.[39]

It all looked good in theory but Thursday, 26 October 1944, turned out to be a terrible day. Don Stewart had a bad feeling that morning, "so bad that before setting out, he solemnly shook hands with a brother officer in C Squadron as if they would not be seeing each other again."[40] That done he led his troop up the dirt road behind Danny McLeod. Danny got up past Heimolen and was making good progress when a *Panzerfaust* round went across the bow of his tank. It shouldn't have missed "but the Germans were firing from concrete bunkers and the apertures had limited fields of fire."[41] He requested Crocodiles to come up and eventually was told that they were on their way. Danny's three tanks were deployed on either side of the road, when

> two Crocodiles came up between us. They didn't net in their wireless but just came up between us and continued straight up the road. I waved and shouted at them: "Start your flame, start your flame!" They ignored me or perhaps they thought

I was just cheering them on, or perhaps they didn't see me. The lead Crocodile hadn't gone more than fifty yards when he was hit by a *panzerfaust* and went into the ditch on the right. The next one didn't have to be told, he lit up and just blasted the hell out of the bunkers on both sides of the road.

The bunkers taken care of, Danny pushed on but he asked for infantry support because it was very obvious that the Germans were in greater strength than the previous day. Major Jim Swayze's company of Links joined him and Swayze remembered the situation on the road: "We had great difficulty and then we had to leapfrog forward about 50 yards at a time ...... We didn't go into the woods very far I can tell you, with all the mines. I don't think we went 25 yards off the road."[42]

The combined force pushed forward and by late morning had reached Frank Moan's tank. Danny wanted to recover Frank's body but when he asked for volunteers from his troop, nobody came forward because they had all been Frank's friends. With the assistance of Sergeant Fred Clarke from echelon, Danny did the job himself:

> Keep in mind that I was just a punk kid at the time. We got onto the tank and looked inside the turret. Frankie's body was fairly stiff and he was slumped over what was the crew commander's seat. He had been standing when he was hit and fragments from a *Panzerfaust* had just laced the whole of his back and he had collapsed onto the seat. We got a rope around him and we pulled him up to the hatch but I had to reach down and twist his head in order to get it out through the turret.
>
> It was fortunate for me that Padre Silcox was standing on the ground outside, waiting. We laid Frankie on the side of the road and the padre sat down beside him as if he was still alive and made his notes. He assured me that I had no more concerns or worries about Frank and he would take care of things from that point on.
>
> I don't think I ate for two days after that.[43]

Don Stewart was behind Danny. The problem with the Huijbergsche Baan was that, after one troop had gone by and dampened the ardour of the Germans in the woods with HE and .30 calibre fire, the enemy would filter back and hit the next troop. The result was that a number of small separate battles were fought along the length of that road during 26 October and each troop was convinced that they alone were carrying the weight of the fight. Don's task was to protect the second Crocodile, which he had called in to help with a particularly troublesome German position. As the Crocodile splashed the German trench with liquid flame, an enemy paratrooper popped up and knocked the vehicle out with a *Panzerfaust*. Stewart admired

the way the crew of the flame thrower tank bailed out. They were a British crew and they did everything just exactly by the numbers according to the rule book. The first fellow jumped out; he had a Bren gun and he set it up as covering fire. The next fellow came out behind him and covered him. Two more came out and they leapfrogged back exactly as though they were in a practice drill of some sort. All four or five of them got away scot free.[44]

Danny, meanwhile, pushed on to "get back to where we had been the day before" as the "theory was that the Germans had put on a big show that day and that generally indicated that they were pulling out."[45] He didn't encounter the same resistance he had met the previous day but late in the afternoon Dave ordered him to pull back and firm up with the infantry at a point just north of the intersection near Heimolen. Danny and his attached infantry company set up a position out in the open as the woods were full of mines and the infantry took casualties when they ventured too far into them. At about last light, Dave told him to come back for an O Group at squadron headquarters, which was about a quarter of a mile down the road. It was only when he walked back down the road that Danny realized the extent of the fighting that had been going on behind him:

All I could see were burning tanks. As I approached one, I saw what appeared to be somebody trying to shove open the driver's hatch which was blocked by the main gun barrel. Thinking it was a driver trying to get out of the hatch I de-

cided to play the hero and go over and get him out. The cold hard fact was that the man inside had been dead for hours because that tank had brewed up earlier in the day. Every so often, however, a round of ammunition inside the tank would explode and push the hatch up against the gun barrel. I couldn't see the condition of the tank clearly in the dark but every time I tried to get near it, there would be another explosion and I would have to move back. I finally left it and moved down the road.[46]

When he found Dave, Danny's first question was "What the hell happened?" and Dave told him.

B Squadron had moved out that morning to support the Algonquins who were to take the brickworks south of Wouwsche village and exploit north from Centrum to the hamlet of Zoomvliet. Leaman Caseley's B-4 Troop, which had spent the night with the lead Algonquin company, got the job of assisting the move on Zoomvliet while Johnny Guyot's cattle rustlers from B-1 drew the job of supporting A and C Companies at the brickworks. The remaining two troops were positioned to give fire support.[47]

The attack on the brickworks went well. The Links had taken most of the village the previous day and, with the help of the Crocodiles, the two Algonquin companies cleared out the German position. As 4 Brigade units were now moving into Wouwsche village, they then shifted to Centrum.

The attack against Zoomvliet ran into trouble from the outset. During the previous night the Germans had infiltrated the road behind the lead Algonquin company, laying mines and setting up anti-tank positions in the ditches that lined it. The CSM of the Algonquin B Company, which was the forward company, was captured while driving back from Centrum that night, and in the morning, when D Company of the Algonquins attempted to move up with B-3 troop, they ran into trouble when a *Panzerfaust* took out one tank while Sergeant Al Holmes's tank was immobilized by a mine. Caseley's B-4 Troop and the Algonquins' B Company were cut off at a crossroads a mile and a half north of Centrum.[48]

Trooper Duncan Ledwidge of B-4 remembered that "it was pretty rough up at the crossroads."[49]

Wouwsche Woods. The Wouwsche Plantage woods south of Bergen op Zoom. This extensive pine tree plantation which was heavily mined by the Germans proved to be a very difficult area for 10 Brigade to move through in October 1944. Here the New Brunswick Rangers have taken over a German position to emplace their 4.2 mortars. COURTESY, LEON ROSENBOOM.

About an hour after first light the position came under heavy and accurate German artillery and mortar fire that caught them unprepared. Ledwidge and his loader-operator were behind their tank shaving "when they started hitting us" and "all of a sudden the loader/operator jumped and said 'Jesus, I got hit.'" Duncan pulled a piece of shrapnel out of the man's rear end and put a shell dressing on the wound. Leaman was also hit: "I got a shrapnel wound in my forehead and it started to bleed pretty bad but it wasn't that serious so they put a shell dressing on it and we all got out of the tank and went over to the infantry."[50] The commander of the Algonquin B Company was seriously wounded but when his men tried to evacuate him on a carrier, it ran over a German mine that blew it "end-over-end for thirty yards."[51]

Under cover of their artillery bombardment, the Germans pushed an anti-tank gun around the corner of a building a few hundred yards west of the crossroads and began to take potshots at Leaman's tanks. Corporal Chuck Fearn saw the enemy weapon being manhandled into position and drew it to the attention of his gunner who was a new replacement. The man had left the safety on his weapon and by the time he was ready to fire, Fearn's tank was knocked out.[52] Then, one after another, the remaining three tanks in the troop were put out of action either by shell or anti-tank fire. Much of the damage was minor, Ledwidge's tank lost its turret motor and the crew could not traverse the turret and had to "jockey the tank around to get our machine guns where we wanted to fire them."[53] Leaman contacted Darby Nash to tell him that "I can't fight my tanks."[54]

Aware of the troop's plight, Darby called down heavy artillery fire from 15 Field. The artillery response was quick and accurate because a FOO from 15 Field, Captain Jack Forbes, was also at the crossroads and his wireless served as the beleaguered force's communications link. At 15 Field's RHQ and battery command posts, "small groups gathered around the earphones to hear how the battle progressed" and "the gunners sweated with a will as target after target was engaged."[55] Trooper David Marshall, who had returned to the Regiment after recovering from the wound he had received at Moerbrugge, was the loader-operator in Darby's tank that day:

I was passing messages on to the squadron commander wherever he might be, and back to the CO and who knows where he was. My new job was nervewracking because, having done some fighting, I could understand the situation that these fellows were in when they called for help. I could hear the shells through the radio and see those columns of black oily smoke but felt helpless and a bit of a slacker sitting in comparative safety when all the others were having such a bad time.[56]

In the early afternoon, Darby and Bob Bradburn decided that they would try to evacuate Caseley and the Algonquins. Nash ordered Lieutenant Johnny Guyot's troop up to a position where they could give covering fire. Johnny was down to three tanks, his own and those of Jim Nicholson and Jim Kroesing. Nicholson's tank had an electrical problem and the fitters were working on it when the order came so Guyot told Jim to get it fixed as fast as possible and follow him up the road and moved out with his other tank and some sections of Algonquin infantry.[57]

Guyot was in the lead as the two tanks came up to Holmes's disabled Sherman knocked out by a mine that morning. As Johnny manoeuvred to get around the obstacle, the woods were suddenly full of Germans who opened a heavy fire with automatic weapons that drove the infantry back. Guyot's tank was hit by a *Panzerfaust* – it burst into flames and the crew bailed out. Kroesing was now in a very bad position, surrounded by enemy infantry who were stalking him with *Panzerfausts*. Fortunately for him, Jim Nicholson came up at that moment and the two Shermans "began mowing down the trees" lining the road with HE and the Germans backed off. But nobody was going any farther up that route.[58]

Guyot's crew were all wounded. The loader-operator, Trooper Walter Kenyon, was able to crawl back through a ditch to safety under heavy enemy fire and the two drivers, Troopers John White and John Porter, also managed to get away. Johnny Guyot and his gunner, Trooper Melvin Danielson, were both badly wounded and taken prisoner by the Germans, who removed them to one of their dug-outs and attempted to administer first-aid. It was too late for Guyot, who died from loss of blood, but when the firing had died down, the Germans permitted Danielson to be evacuated under a flag of truce to a

Leaman's lost troop. Pencil sketch by G.L. Cassidy showing the crossroads northwest of Centrum where Leaman Caseley's troop and a company of the Algonquins were cut off for nearly a day during the battle for Bergen op Zoom.

Canadian ambulance. Unfortunately he died following an operation to amputate his leg. Melvin Danielson was a 19-year-old farmer from Stockholm, Saskatchewan, who had been with the Regiment for only eight days, while Johnny Guyot was a 28-year-old salesman from Verdun, Quebec, who had been with the South Albertas a month. "Too bad he didn't last longer," wrote John Neff about his troop leader that night, "as he was a fine chap."[59]

Back at the crossroads Leaman was doing his best to encourage his men. Trooper Duncan Ledwidge remembered him "moving from tank to tank with a bandage on his eye and head" trying "to keep everyone's morale up."[60] There were enemy infantry in the nearby woods but the infantry and tanks were able to put down enough small-arms fire to keep them at a distance and they were assisted by the heavy artillery fire that fell on the

into a German minefield that brought progress to a halt. The woods of the Wouwsche Plantage were "a sticky place to take" as

> The defences were elaborate and well-concealed. Tank movement was limited, particularly in fire effect. The enemy possessed, (and, since he planned an eventual retirement, was prone to use) large stores of shells and mortars bombs dumped here for just such a stand. The presence of many anti-personnel mines, wire, and other obstacles concealed in the underbrush made infantry infiltration difficult, particularly at night.[62]

To make matters worse the area had been the home of a German mine and demolitions training school and the instructors, specialists in their trade, had supervised the layout of the mine defences.[63]

The Germans are a technically minded people and, during the war, devised some ingenious booby traps and demolitions. The types feared most by the infantry were the *S-Mine* and *Schü* (shoe) mines. If set off, the former bounced a few feet into the air before detonating and spraying its contents of over three hundred steel balls and metal bits out to a distance of sixty feet at waist height. The *Schü* mine was a small plywood box, which made it hard to detect, containing seven ounces of explosive, just enough to blow off a man's foot. The *Wehrmacht* also had forty different anti-tank mines in their inventory but the most common were the *Teller* mines, plate-shaped contrivances which could be set to detonate when weights between 175 and 400 lb. passed over them and which contained enough explosive to knock the track off a tank or damage its suspension. In the woods of the Wouwsche Plantage both the infantry and anti-tank mines were fitted with anti-lifting devices that would detonate them in a sapper's face if he was not very careful when he tried to disarm them.[64]

The *Wehrmacht* threw in a new twist south of Bergen. They planted large demolition charges on the dirt road with long-delay igniters which could be set at any time from ten minutes to twenty-one days. Vehicles and troops passed over these charges for some time in complete safety, but ultimately they would explode. When the Fife and Forfar recovery Churchill tried to drag one of the knocked-out Crocodiles away, it trig-

The lost troop. The crossroads north of Centrum and south of Zoomvliet where Leaman Caseley's troop was cut off on 26 October 1944 with a company of Algonquins and only extricated under the cover of a tremendous artillery bombardment and smoke screen. PHOTOGRAPH BY DIANNE GRAVES.

German positions. By late afternoon Nash and Bradburn were ready to make the rescue attempt. Under cover of a tremendous smokescreen laid down by 15 Field and every other available artillery unit in range, the Algonquin carrier platoon dashed forward to the crossroads and managed to evacuate the men of the Algonquin B Company and B-4 Troop without casualties. Leaman had to leave his four tanks behind although two of them were later recovered.[61]

While Nash's B Squadron was having bad trouble north of Centrum, Arnold Lavoie was having no better luck to the west. He had jumped off with the Argylls in the morning with the job of clearing the Wouwsche woods. The plan was that one Argyll company, accompanied by a troop of South Alberta tanks, would move up the dirt road while two more companies, each with a troop of A Squadron tanks, moved through the woods. As the Argylls were delayed getting into position, the advance did not begin until noon, and almost immediately the force ran

gered one of these charges and the resulting explosion turned the derelict vehicle on its side and blew its turret clear across to the other side of the road. Trooper Bob Seccombe of A Squadron saw the incident and remembered seeing the Crocodile "on its side and I looked up into the turret and I could see nothing but blood and bits of uniform."[65] It was an impressive thing to see the mangled remains of a 35-ton tank scattered around the vicinity and is clearly remembered by every man who passed it on the Huijbergsche Baan.[66]

A Squadron had a wretched day because of mines and lost four tanks in the process. The driver of one of these vehicles, Trooper James Foster, was trapped when his tank brewed up after hitting a mine on the dirt road and died in the fire. A 21-year-old farmer from One Four, Alberta, Foster had been with the South Albertas since Nanaimo.[67] This was the tank that Danny McLeod saw, still on fire, when he walked back down the dirt road that night. Corporal Charles Smith lost his tank to another mine but got out and began clearing mines with his co-driver. He wasn't the only South Alberta to become a temporary sapper – Trooper C.R. "Speedy" Fast remembered that, after his tank hit a mine and lost its track, his sergeant and he "got out and checked it out and saw all these wires around so we tied a piece of string to the wire, got behind the tank and pulled it and it blew up."[68] Lavoie called for flails to come up to clear the woods but they got bogged in the wet ground. The Argylls and

A Squadron could make no progress and pulled back to the dirt road south of C Squadron's position late in the afternoon. By this time the road was littered with knocked-out tanks and other vehicles which gave it the name by which it is best remembered: "Hulk Alley."[69]

At 1930 hours the infantry and South Alberta tanks firmed up in their positions for the night. It had been a bad day for the Regiment, which had lost a dozen tanks, three men killed and ten wounded, including two troop leaders. It had also been a hard day for the brigade and the advance on Bergen op Zoom, noted the Algonquins' historian, "had slowed to a snail's pace and with the exception of the South Albertas on the far left flank of the [Wouwsche] wood, the entire 4 Div. advance had almost ground to a halt."[70]

Things went better on the following day, Friday, 27 October 1944. Harry Foster's plan was to renew the drive on Bergen with 10 Brigade pushing from the south while 4 Brigade, which had advanced as far as the village of Wouwsche Hil the previous day, would move in from the east. Harry was under pressure – Montgomery had told him to take the city that day and correspondents were flocking around divisional headquarters because Bergen, which had already been "liberated" several times by the BBC, would be the first large Dutch city captured by First

Hulk Alley. The Huijbergsche Baan, the dirt road that was the back way into Bergen op Zoom, was the scene of heavy fighting on 25 and 26 October 1944. The results are seen in this picture. Judging by the damage to its suspension and running gear, the SAR Sherman in the foreground appears to have run over a heavy demolition charge. COURTESY, LEON ROSENBOOM.

(Right) The Huijbergsche Baan today. Much of the Wouwsche Plantage is now a conservation area and the trees have grown back close to the border of the road, which is now paved. PHOTOGRAPH BY DIANNE GRAVES.

227

Canadian Army. On 10 Brigade's front the main thrust would be made by the South Alberta Regiment supported by the Links who were under Wotherspoon's command. Swatty planned to use A and C Squadrons, each accompanied by a company of Links, to advance while Recce Troop would provide forward patrols. B Squadron, which had suffered heavily on 26 October, was given a badly-needed day of rest to refit and reorganize.[71]

At 0800 Wotherspoon established his tactical headquarters on the dirt road just south of Heimolen. The South Albertas expected the worst but when the two squadrons slowly advanced during the morning, "only slight opposition was met," and by noon Lavoie's A Squadron had pushed through the Wouwsche woods nearly to Zoomvliet while C Squadron moved past Heimolen up the dirt road. The local people told the forward troops that the Germans had withdrawn to Bergen and Wotherspoon pushed C Squadron ahead. By 1345 hours, Danny McLeod's troop with a company of Links was at a pumping station a mile and a half from the centre of the city. It began to look as if the way into Bergen was clear and Swatty brought A Squadron and its attached infantry company over from the right and ordered them to take up a position at the village of Nieuw Bergvliet, a mile or so south of Bergen, which Recce Troop had reached that morning. Numerous civilian reports that the Germans had withdrawn from the city continued to come in, as did a report that there were enemy armoured vehicles just north of it. Wotherspoon called down a divisional artillery concentration on their reported location and then pondered his options. The last thing he wanted was to get involved in street fighting in a medieval town but the persistent reports that the Germans had withdrawn could not be ignored. Finally, about 1500 hours, he decided to send two SAR tank patrols into Bergen op Zoom.[72]

Danny McLeod of C Squadron and Albert Halkyard of Recce Troop got the job. By mid-afternoon they had pushed with a company of Links as far as the water tower near the railway tracks which skirted Bergen to the east. Dave Currie gave Danny the orders "you're to dismount your infantry and make an excursion into the city with your troop and see if it is occupied." Danny left his infantry behind and set out with his three tanks on the shortest route into the centre of the city while at the same time Halkyard took a more roundabout route with his

An unsung hero. Ad de Munck, the Dutch Resistance fighter who guided Danny McLeod's tank into Bergen op Zoom in the afternoon of 27 October 1944. If the Germans had moved back into Bergen, his fate would have been very uncertain.

COURTESY, PIET HOEDELMANS.

two Stuarts. Dave had told Danny that someone from the underground would show him the way and in a few minutes a Dutch resistance fighter, Ad de Munck, appeared and took up a position on the fender of Danny's tank as they proceeded across the railway tracks and into the city.[73]

The people of Bergen op Zoom had been anxiously awaiting their liberators for nearly two weeks. The city was packed with refugees from the heavy fighting at Woensdrecht and Hoogerheide to the south and for the last twenty-four hours the occasional artillery round had fallen on the city, driving the population to their cellars. During the morning of 27 October it was obvious that the Germans were pulling out because their demolition parties destroyed most of the church towers in the city to prevent them being used as OP points as well as the bridges over the Zoom, which bisected the city. The Germans had disappeared about an hour before Danny and Halkyard set out and the people were in a high state of anticipation when the first South Alberta tank appeared at the outskirts of the city. Bergen, remembered Danny, went "absolutely bananas," with the "old girls with their grey hair waving towels and orange flags and crying" and "we just got hemmed in by people crowding around the tanks and could only make very slow progress."[74] Finally, at about 1615 hours, the troop entered the *Grote Markt* or main square, where they were surrounded by hundreds of frantically cheering men, women and children "offering flowers" as "our boys were handing out cigarettes and chocolate."[75] A few minutes later Halkie pulled into another side of the square with his two tanks and Danny went over to speak to him. At that moment there was a "burst of machine-gun fire" and Danny spun around to see "the crowd had scattered" and "a body lying in front of my tank."[76]

A tragedy had occurred. A Dutch civilian perched on Danny's tank had pulled the barrel of the co-driver's .30 calibre Browning knocking the gun's trigger against the driver's leg and causing the gun to fire. A burst went into the crowd at the front of the tank wounding a young boy and killing two teenage girls, Coba Coppens and Gemma Huygens. Coba Coppens was struck in the chest and died instantly – that was the body Danny had seen – but Gemma Huygens managed to drag herself around a corner before collapsing on the street. Trooper Joe Strathern had his head out of the hatch of his tank "because all these people were cheering and yelling but as soon as the gun went off, everyone dropped like a dead log."[77] Danny and his men were hardened soldiers but the accidental death of these two innocents at a moment of triumph nearly made them distraught. Danny didn't know what to do but he was saved by a local civilian:

Down below. For weeks before Danny McLeod and Albert Halkyard's tanks entered the city in the afternoon of 27 October the people of Bergen had been sheltering in their cellars. When they emerged to find that they were liberated, the town went wild.

COURTESY, PIET HOEDELMANS.

Out came Wes Besling, the little guy who was the head of the Red Cross in Bergen, and he said, "I will be right with you" and the next thing I knew, he was back with a bucket of sand and he put sand over the blood and covered the girl with a blanket. An ambulance arrived and they loaded the girl onto it. I have thought a thousand times since that moment that, if Wes Besling was not there, I would have had to back my tank up, pull around, leave that girl and keep on going but Wes Besling took care of it. Then we discovered this other girl and we went round to attend to her but she had died.[78]

The people of Bergen confirmed that the Germans had withdrawn north of the Zoom and Danny and Halkyard reported the southern part of the city clear of the enemy. At the RHQ, Swatty had a decision to make – whether to move into Bergen now or wait until the next day. He discussed the matter with Bill Cromb and finally made his decision, according to the *Globe and Mail*'s Ralph Allen, with the famous words: "Hell, Bill, let's take the damned place."[79] At about 1800 hours, the remainder of C Squadron was ordered to mount the Links' forward companies on their decks and move into the city, followed by A Squadron and Swatty and Bill. The "two tired, cold and anonymous lieutenant-colonels" and their men, wrote Allen, "now owned the city of 22,000 almost undamaged and in the mood and condition to give them the noisiest and most effervescent welcome Canadian troops have yet received anywhere in Holland."[80] By 2030 hours, a combined South Alberta and Lincoln and Welland headquarters had been set up in a hotel on the *Grote Markt* and Harry Foster could report to Montgomery that Bergen op Zoom was in Allied hands.

The Hotel de Draak (Dragon Hotel) had been in business for 547 years when Swatty Wotherspoon and Bill Cromb walked through the front door during the evening of Friday, 27 October 1944. One of the oldest hostelries in Europe, it had survived fires, floods and the eight previous sieges of Bergen. During the Renaissance, it had been a favourite watering hole of the German artist Albrecht Dürer, who had immortalized the proprietress and waitress of his time in two drawings (possibly done to pay his bill). According to Bob Allsopp, Bill Cromb immediately grabbed the best room and Swatty got the next best, which overlooked the square where the South Albertas parked their vehicles.[81]

Having taken the city, Swatty was determined to hold it. The Germans had withdrawn behind the Zoom, which ran along the north end of the city. According to the information Swatty and Cromb had, this former river turned into a canal was supposed to be shallow enough to be crossed on foot. It was actually a formidable obstacle about one hundred feet wide with steep banks nearly fifty feet deep and a stream, six feet in depth at the bottom, bordered with concrete "dragon's teeth" that rendered it impassable to tanks. The Germans had blown two of the bridges across the Zoom and had erected a concrete barrier three feet thick at the north end of the third and main bridge. It was clear that the enemy had given up most of Bergen only to withdraw behind this barrier.

After leaving the tragic scene in the *Grote Markt* that afternoon Danny McLeod had been ordered to ascertain whether the Zoom was defended. He left the main square and guided his troop down the narrow winding streets in the direction of the main bridge. Deploying his tanks on either side of a broad boulevard that led to the bridge he ordered them to move forward but to spray the approaches with .30 calibre and be ready to fire HE at anything in the vicinity. The troop "moved out and went closer and closer to the bridge" and then:

All of a sudden: "Bang!" An AP shot creased one of the tanks. The Germans shouldn't have missed and, looking back, I can only conclude that the obstacle over the Zoom obscured their vision. And then all hell broke loose, down went the smoke and we started to back out and returned to an intersection.[82]

Danny deployed in a defensive position around the intersection – his troop would stay there for several days.

There being no doubt that the Germans were going to defend the Zoom, Swatty deployed A and C Squadrons in positions to cover the canal and called for artillery fire on the northern edge of the city. The Germans responded with artillery and mortar fire. One of their favourite targets was the tower of *Sint Gertruidniskerk* overlooking the *Grote Markt* – convinced that it was being used as an OP, they hourly fired an AP round which rang its bell. The exchange of artillery fire forced the people of Bergen back into their cellars and their situation was made no

happier when patrols from the German 6th Parachute Regiment infiltrated across the Zoom and told them the *Wehrmacht* was coming back in the near future. Both the civilians and the Canadians spent a restless Friday night punctuated by small-arms and artillery fire.[83]

Gordie Irving never forgot that night. "The kid" had been assigned a position on the eastern end of the Zoom and "it looked pretty relaxed." Gordie told his men "let's sleep indoors" so "we took our bedrolls into some house, fixed blankets up over the windows, and bogged down for the night."[84] Gordie had a wireless lead out to his tank and, just after he had settled in, Arnold Lavoie came on to tell him, "You've got to get out, they're putting a 25-pdr. deal [bombardment] on" and the shells would be landing in his area. "It was too late," Gordie recalls,

No mean obstacle. A good view of the Zoom as it was during the war. Allied intelligence had predicted that it would not be an obstacle to further advance – it was. In the afternoon of 27 October the Germans gave up the main part of the city and withdrew behind this massive anti-tank ditch after blowing the bridges. COURTESY, PIET HOEDELMANS.

Deutsche Technik. The Germans left one bridge over the Zoom intact but blocked it by this massive concrete barrier. It took three days of heavy fighting for 10 Brigade to gain a toehold north of the Zoom – at which point the paratroopers withdrew to new defensive positions to the north. COURTESY, PIET HOEDELMANS.

(Below) The Zoom today. On the left of the stream can be seen the concrete tank obstacles ("Dragon's Teeth") emplaced by the Germans to defend the stream.
PHOTOGRAPH BY DIANNE GRAVES.

> they were already in the air. So we didn't have time to pack up our tanks again so I am out on the ground directing the tanks at night backwards to get the hell onto the road and get the hell out of there. And we did but those shells were landing all around us. We went back and I guess they were trying a low trajectory shoot to get the houses on the other side of the canal. The problem is that whatever they were doing back at the Hotel de Draak, they didn't get the signal out to us soon enough.

Irving was furious and complained to Arnold Lavoie the next morning. "I was really upset about what a hell of a night we had to put in there," he commented, "and lo and behold they say they think I am getting a little too upset and I better have a rest so they sent me down to Antwerp for a couple of days of recreation and fun." It was the first leave he had received since landing in France three months before.[85]

German fire could be just as dangerous. Don Stewart's crew felt "they would like to have a hot meal, so they fired up the cook stove" in a house and put on "some eggs they had

Ringing the bell. AA Troop Crusader crews carry out maintenance in the *Grote Markt*. In the background can be seen the tower of Sint Gertruidnis church. The Germans fired an AP round through the tower on an hourly basis, ringing the bell. COURTESY, WES BESLING.

scrounged."[86] Unfortunately, the enemy "across the canal spotted the smoke coming out of the chimney" and "thought it would be nice to put an armour-piercing shell through the house" on speculation. The round went into the front wall of the house, through the stove which Don happened be standing beside (which "sort of disappeared") and continued "out through the back door and knocked down the privy that was behind." There would be no home-cooked food for Don's crew that night.

Darby Nash's B Squadron moved into town on the morning of 28 October to bolster the line along the Zoom. At 1000 hours, the burgomaster hoisted the flag of the Netherlands at the city hall next to the Hotel de Draak and presented Swatty and Bill Cromb with a very thoughtful gift "of wines and spirits, which was all that was left by our oppressors, as a token of our gratitude."[87] Less welcome were the hordes of "civil affairs personnel and visiting officers from almost every formation mentionable and newspaper correspondents" who "streamed into RHQ throughout the day."[88] Among them was Clarence Campbell from divisional headquarters come to claim the de Draak for the senior staff but Swatty proved as determined to hold onto his comfortable billet as he was the rest of the city. He cagily "observed to Maj Campbell that the arrival of Div HQ would interfere with his conducting of the battle" and, as an "increasing amount of art[iller]y and mortar fire" was falling on the city, Campbell became convinced "that at this stage of the battle Main Div HQ was better off in its present location."[89]

One has to feel some sympathy for the headquarters personnel forced to remain in that muddy field near Huijbergen but on the other hand war is hell – even for staff officers.

The artillery exchange went on throughout that Saturday. The gunners of 15 Field, firing from their own muddy field south of Bergen, were shooting at targets only nine hundred yards away, "the closest range at which a target was ever engaged, and in order to clear the crests of buildings and trees some troops had to use Charge I [the minimum powder charge]."[90] The divisional medium guns chimed in during the afternoon and the Germans responded as best they could. The enemy mortars were the worst; their "primary charges could be heard as a ripple of dull sound, and fifteen seconds later they would be exploding in their dozens in the midst of the littered streets and tileless buildings."[91] It was the opinion of the 10 Brigade historian that "the mortaring and shelling withstood here ranked in intensity with any action of the brigade to date. It was a hail of bombs throughout." Lieutenant Lyle Piepgrass, one of the old originals from 1940 who had risen from the rank of private in the Regiment, was badly wounded by one shell, a wound that eventually cost him a leg.

The Argylls began to filter into Bergen on 28 October and two companies moved up to the sidestreets near the Zoom. The plan was that they would put in a daylight attack across the river and in preparation the artillery stepped up its fire, but the shells from one medium regiment kept falling short and landing in the friendly area of the city. Outside C Squadron headquarters in the

The tragedy, 28 October 1944. C Squadron tanks parked along the Steenbergsestraat. In the afternoon of 28 October a 5.5 shell from a Canadian medium regiment that had been firing short for some time landed on the deck of one of these tanks and killed seven South Albertas, as well as men from the Argylls and 15 Field, and wounded scores more. COURTESY, DANNY McLEOD.

The scene today. The shell landed on the rear deck of Dave Currie's command tank, "Clanky," which was parked in front of the three-storey white building on the right-hand side of the street. PHOTOGRAPH BY DIANNE GRAVES.

municipal tax building on Steenbergsestraat, Dave Currie was talking to two officers, Captain Bob Donaldson of his squadron and Captain Alec Scrimger. "Scrimmy" Scrimger was a popular officer – John Neff regarded him "as one, if not the best, troop leader B Squadron ever had" and he was also Dave's personal friend.[92] He had just returned to the Regiment after being absent for several months and was technically LOB that day but had volunteered to go into the city to sign up men for the current war bond drive. He took the opportunity to visit Dave, and as he was talking to him and Donaldson, several soldiers were lined up in front of the municipal tax building – South Albertas waiting to purchase bonds at the squadron office and Argylls waiting to move up to the Zoom.[93]

The shell – a 5.5 shell from the medium regiment which had been firing short for some time – landed on the rear deck of Dave's tank, "Clanky." Dave, Donaldson and Scrimger heard it coming and hit the street, but the men outside the office didn't stand a chance and were cut down by a spray of fragments which went through the front of the tax building at the height of a man's head. The three officers got to their feet and then Scrimger collapsed – a small splinter had hit him in the chest, piercing his heart and he died within seconds. The same short round also killed a number of Argyll infantry and the FOO from 15 Field attached to C Squadron, Captain Harold Mogie,

whose office was in the tax building, and six South Alberta enlisted men: Corporal Robert Goodyer and Troopers Dennis Hoare, Tip Lafoy, John McDonell, George Mungall and John Stone. Hoare, a 19-year-old printer's apprentice from Springhill, Nova Scotia, was a particularly tragic case because he had only joined the Regiment nine days before. Danny McLeod, up at the Zoom, knew something had gone dreadfully wrong because he "had no wireless communications with squadron headquarters for a long time" and repeated calls only brought the response, "Wait out."[94] It was a terrible incident and Dave Currie was so upset over the loss of Scrimger, a close personal friend, that Swatty sent him back to Antwerp for a 48-hour leave.[95]

The Argylls had problems at the Zoom that afternoon. One company attempted to cross but was driven back by a hail of small-arms fire and it was decided to wait until dark and make a two-company attack across the western end of the canal while the Links provided a diversionary attack at the east end. The Argyll attack was beaten back but the Links managed to get thirteen men over who entered a factory complex on the north side only to spend the night chasing German paratroopers "up one alley and [then] they chased down the other alley."[96] At one point the opponents were only separated by a high wall and there was much shouting back and forth. The Germans taunted the Links calling them "Canadian pigs, Canadian swine" and other such dreadful and fear-inducing Teutonic insults so the Links responded with unprintable Anglo-Saxon witticisms and taunted the paratroopers in turn: "We're in here. Come and get us. We've got knives. Come in and see what our knives are like." As one Link recorded, "They didn't come."[97] While these pleasantries were being exchanged, the Argylls managed to get a company across at the western extremity of the Zoom and in the early morning both toeholds on the north side were firmed up as more Links and Argyll companies crossed.[98]

Throughout 29 October there was fierce fighting on the north side of the Zoom. In mid-afternoon the Algonquins crossed over and moved through the Argylls but the Germans still obstinately defended every building. While this was going on, C Squadron and Recce Troop prowled the south side of the Zoom pouring fire into the German-held buildings, while the engineers worked desperately to demolish the concrete obstacle on the bridge so tanks could cross. AVRE tanks fired 215 mm Petard shells into it – they bounced off but the sappers were able to rig explosives and at 1445 hours the obstacle was blown and a troop of BCR tanks crossed over, followed by more infantry. The tanks were just as quickly forced back to the south side by vicious German anti-tank fire and the infantry continued to fight on alone. The battle was finally decided by events outside the city – on the morning of 30 October 4 Armoured Brigade advanced north of Bergen and, threatened with encirclement, the tough German defenders of the Zoom, the 6th Parachute Regiment, pulled out for the Maas.[99]

Taking direction. Troopers E.O. Sutley and S. Warner tactfully let Jenette Bakx of Bergen teach them how to cook. By this time, after three months in the field, the boys were excellent cooks but it is always best to be modest and polite in front of strangers (particularly young and pretty strangers). Other South Albertas hover in the background, probably hoping Jenette has some girlfriends. Note the white-painted end of the 17-pdr. gun on the Firefly, an attempt to disguise its length (and thus its identity) from German anti-tank gunners, who always fired at the 17-pdr. tanks first. NAC, PA 176887.

Only C Squadron and Recce Troop participated in the fighting along the Zoom on 28-29 October. A and B Squadrons remained inactive throughout 29 October and the next day the entire Regiment was "given permission to close down their wireless comm[unicatio]n" although a "listening watch" was to be maintained at RHQ.[100] This was the result of a reluctant decision by Harry Foster, made at the urging of his senior medical officer, to give his division a forty-eight hour rest period in Bergen. The division, particularly the infantry battalions of 10 Brigade, which had born the brunt of the fighting since Normandy, was exhausted. It was welcome news to the Regiment and the boys have many fond memories of their time in Bergen op Zoom.[101]

"As it was the first time that the regiment had halted in a large town that had received very little war damage," David Marshall remembered, "the ambience of the whole situation was new and exciting."[102] The various tank troops were billeted in private homes but did their maintenance and cooking on the streets, providing entertainment for the citizens of Bergen, particularly the small boys who, like small boys everywhere, were fascinated with soldiers and their various gadgets. The South Albertas patiently put up with the Dutch kids' endless questions, fed them chocolate and candy, and let them handle the equipment in the hopes that it might bring an introduction to an older sister. There were plenty of pretty girls around but you had to be careful, as Troopers Earl Aucoin and Bobby Blunden of AA troop found out their first day in the city:

We got cleaned up a bit and were around the streets and met two young ladies. We started to talk and walk and, all of a sudden, we were surrounded by a bunch of armed Dutch underground. They told us the girls were collaborators and they were taking them into custody. We decided to let them go and later we saw them being paraded through the streets and they had shaved their heads.[103]

The Dutch had many scores to settle. When German prisoners were put to work in a local park digging graves for the casualties incurred in the fighting, "it afforded the Dutch a chance to let the German soldiers know what they thought of them." "The provosts kept everyone well away," Marshall recalled, "but that did not stop a lot of justifiable verbal abuse being heaped on the luckless enemy."[104] Some of the Dutch had more on their

Resting place. First field graves of the Canadian soldiers killed liberating Bergen op Zoom. The Dutch immediately covered them with flowers and, when the war was over, asked that the Commonwealth War Graves establish a cemetery in the city so that their Canadian liberators would always remain close by.
COURTESY, LEON ROSENBOOM.

minds than verbal abuse – Doc Spaner of Recce Troop spent a lot of time in Bergen repairing old hunting rifles given to him by the Dutch resistance, who wanted to use them against the Germans.[105]

One thing Bergen had in quantity was alcohol – "plenty of good stuff to drink and some not so good," recorded John Neff.[106] "Fortunately, or unfortunately," wrote the Algonquins' historian, "depending how one looks at it, the civilians chose this moment to wreak their vengeance on a collaborators' distillery."[107] The Dutch invited the Canadians to fill their boots, and they did, and just about very other container that would hold liquid. When word of this bonanza spread there were traffic jams around the building until it was drained dry. That livened up things so much that the civil authorities were forced to post a notice in the city on 30 October forbidding the civilians to give "strong drink to the troops."[108] There were many thick heads and some minor accidents but no real harm came to anyone although there is a persistent rumour that two Algonquins died after being overcome by fumes when they tried to go swimming in one of the huge pot stills in the distillery.[109]

The Hotel de Draak was the centre of much activity. Its bedrooms, hallways, cellars and bathtubs were crowded with sleeping South Albertas and Links, who soon added their graffiti to that of the Germans who had previously occupied it. Trooper Charlie Farquhar of B Squadron remembered that the cattle rustlers took their ill-gotten gains from Huijbergen and "dug a

hole in the patio of the hotel and roasted this steer."[110] If the Dutch had thought the Canadians were rather wild before this, the sight of a group of tankers roasting a haunch of beef on a spit over an open fire must have given them pause. It was at the de Draak on Halloween night that the brigade officers held a party during which Bill Cromb gave the first public performance of the well-known "Bergen op Zoom" song quoted at the beginning of this chapter (the words of which vary according to the audience).

Quartermasters took the opportunity to issue winter clothing and the Chinese Hussars came up to give everyone a much-needed bath. The Auxiliary Services put on a welcome meal for the whole brigade, with food provided by the army and cooking done by the women of the town. The Services also arranged to take over a local cinema on the *Grote Markt* and screen movies three times a day. There was a bit of flap the first night when a member of a Recce Troop accidentally hit the trigger of his Stuart's 37 mm main gun which – unknown to him – was loaded and put an AP round into the cinema, but nobody was hurt.[111]

Everybody enjoyed themselves at Bergen and, to George Gallimore, the memory that comes back after more than fifty years is sitting in that crowded cinema with everybody singing along as the bouncing ball on screen highlighted the words: "I'm walkin' my baby back home, I'm walkin' my baby back home."[112]

On 2 November 1944 the South Albertas pulled out of beautiful Bergen and headed north. The division's objective was now Steenbergen, a few miles below the Maas and the Moerdyjk bridges, the German escape route over the river. The enemy withdrew in phases towards these bridges, putting up obstinate rearguard actions whenever they felt that the division's advance was moving too quickly. During this closing phase of Operation SUITCASE, the Regiment's job was to provide left flank protection for the advance, and it accomplished this task without having to do much fighting. A few days later the German Fifteenth Army made good its escape over the

(Right) Where Bill and Swatty stayed. The Hotel de Draak on the *Grote Markt* had been in business for 547 years when Swatty Wotherspoon and Bill Cromb walked through the front door in the evening of 27 October 1944 and grabbed the best rooms. Swatty obstinately defended his possession of the de Draak against a determined takeover bid from the senior staff of 4th Armoured Division. It was here at a Halloween party held by the officers of 10 Brigade that Bill Cromb gave the first public performance of his famous composition, "In Bergen op Zoom, op Zoom, op Zoom." The AFV is a Ram OP tank from 15 Field Regiment. COURTESY, PIET HOEDELMANS.

(Below) There's always room for one more Stuart. Being first into the city, the SAR secured the best billets and areas in Bergen. Here Recce Troop and RHQ Troop vehicles are seen in the *Grote Markt* or town square. NAC, PA 142088.

Maas and took up new positions along the north bank, blowing the Moerdyjk bridges behind them. SUITCASE had ended and it was perfectly clear to everyone that this war would not be over by Christmas. The South Albertas were at Steenbergen on 6 November when they were told "to stand down" and that they would have no operational role for the immediate future. Two days later, the last German bastion in the Scheldt, Walcheren Island, was taken by amphibious assault (see map 10, page 192).[113]

That same day Harry Foster lunched in Antwerp with the senior officers and staff of First Canadian Army. The battle to clear the Scheldt – that crucial, neglected and hard-fought operation was over – at a cost of 13,000 casualties, half of them Canadian, and the approaches to the great port were open, although it would take another three weeks to sweep the mines from the estuary. The staff were in a self-congratulatory mood and Foster recorded in his diary that night that lunch was a "veritable sea of red tabs" with many "red faces by the end of the meal."[114] The commander of 4th Division was not as happy with the outcome – as he noted, "it has taken over 60,000 Canadian and British troops with a full armoured division to beat an already retreating and battle-weary enemy infantry [force] desperately short on armour, ammunition, food and transport." "By God the Hun knows how to put up a fight!" was his conclusion. For the time being, however, as Allied leaders planned the offensives that would take them into the heart of the Third Reich, First Canadian Army could look forward to a static period guarding the line of the lower Maas River.

Deutschland kaput. The hull of an SAR Sherman provides a handy place for this visual arts display by three young Dutch men from Bergen. The Dutch, having suffered more than four years of occupation by the hated *moffen*, their word for the Germans, were thirsty for revenge. COURTESY, DANNY McLEOD.

The blonde from Bergen. Whoever she was, this young lady certainly captured the attention of Sergeant Frank Freer's B Squadron crew. From left to right, Frank Freer, and Troopers S.E. Jacobsen, A.G. McGillivray, W.F. Austen and P.J. Viennau pay rapt attention and the likely question on their minds is whether she has any girlfriends who might like to meet their liberators. The censor has whited out the boys' shoulder flashes. NAC, PA 140429.

PART VI

PAUSING

Media attention at Kapelsche Veer. Trooper Cliff Allen (left) and Corporal Jake Wiebe (right) look out of their hatches while an Argyll Bren section is stationed nearby. This photo, shot by a *Toronto Star* reporter who interviewed Allen and Wiebe the day the shooting ended on the Veer, was widely published. The turret crew, who were buttoned down and did not know the press were about, later became annoyed at Allen and Wiebe for not informing them of the photo opportunity. The extra track lengths welded all over the hull were common but their weight compounded the problem of moving on the glutinous surface of the Veer – on the other hand, no SAR was going to give them up.

COURTESY, JAKE WIEBE.

CHAPTER FOURTEEN

"The major wasn't dressed
to visit the King."

HOLLAND: 7 NOVEMBER 1944–24 JANUARY 1945

On 10 November the South Albertas took over their stretch of the Maas between Raamsdonk and Waspik. Not that the boys saw much of the river; at this point in its course, it was contained between steep dykes on both banks and any daylight movement along the top of these dykes drew German fire. Two squadrons maintained the line while the third was in reserve and there were frequent shuffles to give everyone a rest. About this time the Regiment received its first allotment of 48-hour leaves to Brussels, which was untouched by war, and the boys gratefully took advantage of all that city had to offer. Captain Don Stewart wrote to his mother:

> *I* think about you often,
> And I write you every day,
> But there's so very little
> That seems worthwhile to say.
> It either rains or doesn't,
> It's either hot or cold;
> The news is all uninteresting,
> Or else it's all been told.
>
> The only thing that matters
> Is the fact that you are there,
> And I am here without you,
> And its lonesome everywhere.
> I think about the way you smile,
> And I recall your touch –
> And distance lends enchantment,
> And – I miss you very much.[1]

There is no more war in Brussels than there is in Toronto, and I think the people are better dressed and the stores better stocked there than any place in England or Canada. ... we all had beautiful hotel rooms with baths, much better than the Royal York [Hotel in Toronto]. The rooms and meals for two days cost us thirty francs each which is literally nothing.[2]

Other than light shelling which caused no casualties the war ground to a halt for the SAR. The Regiment mounted night patrols of their side of the Maas and enforced a strict curfew for local Dutch civilians. The Germans had stripped this part of Holland with their usual efficiency and the Dutch had little food and no fuel – the winter of 1944-1945 is known in Holland as the "Hunger Winter." The South Albertas went back on rations.

The first Regimental parade in months was held on 16 November to decorate Albert Halkyard of the Recce Troop and Tony Devreker of B Squadron with the Military Medal for their part in the recent fighting. Wotherspoon took the opportunity to make a brief speech in which he emphasized that "since August, we have averaged better than 100 Germans a day."[3] He also made a particular point of singling out the troop sergeants for

praise because "the gains made by and the success of the regiment to this point have depended mostly on the sergeants."[4] The next day the Regiment turned in their trusty but inaccurate old Colt and Smith and Wesson .38 calibre revolvers and received new 9 mm Browning automatics in return.[5]

That day the German V-2 rockets were seen rising from their firing positions just across from the Maas and they were

a spectacular sight. In the day we could hear them as the rocket motors gathered force and then see them rise into the air, slowly, majestically, a marvel of modern science. At night we could see the trail of flame as they rose into the air and out of sight on their way to London. It may have been beautiful to watch but we could not help but think of the destruction it would create when it landed.[6]

The Regiment moved to the town of Vught south of 's-Hertogenbosch and well back from the Maas on 25 November. The local Dutch "had their own pronunciation of Vught which included a sound almost like clearing the throat" – one way that strangers (including spies) could readily be identified.[7] The SAR's new quarters were in the buildings of a religious order which had also been used as a barracks by the Dutch SS, and the previous occupants had left "elaborate black and white drawings of chivalrous Panzer troopers rescuing women and children in a smoking village" and some other not so chivalrous illustrations that would have shocked the original owners of the property. The buildings had been damaged by Typhoons but the Regiment soon got them in order as, although "there is a great deal of work to do, everyone seems to be looking forward to a period where we will be out of the line and also static."[8] The day after they moved in, the enlisted men opened the "Albertania Club" with a reading room, billiards room and bar.

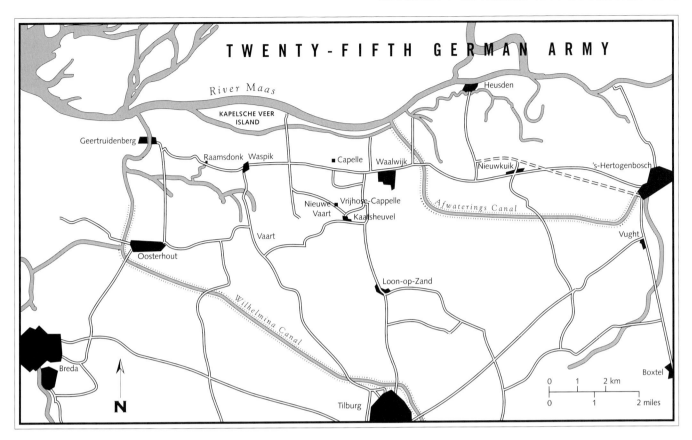

Map 13: Winter on the Maas, November 1944-February 1945. The South Albertas' area of operations during the winter of 1944-1945. Note the location of the Kapelsche Veer.

If any man in the Regiment doubted the nature of the regime he was fighting, those doubts were dispelled at Vught. Near the town was a German concentration camp where slave labourers had repaired damaged aircraft and it was a ghastly place. Harry Foster was shaken by the sight of strangling posts where prisoners had been executed and the banks of ovens used for the disposal of corpses. In his diary that night he asked himself, "What sort of people do such things to their fellow humans?"[9] The Canadian Provost Corps was made of sterner stuff and in a display of the sensitivity for which they were famous, promptly converted part of this grisly establishment into No. 1 Canadian Field Punishment Camp and Detention Barracks, the military prison for the Canadian Army in northwest Europe.

Although the war had quietened down, November 1944 was a big month for the South Alberta Regiment. Rumours had been circulating for some time that a major decoration was pending for Dave Currie. There had been no official confirmation but suspicions were heightened on 12 November when army photographers arrived to take pictures of Dave, who was only told that this attention was part of special publicity feature. Looking terribly embarrassed, he rolled past in a scout car (not his own) and dutifully shook hands with Bert Coffin and Darby Nash for the cameras.[10]

On the day the Regiment moved to Vught Swatty called Dave to RHQ in the late afternoon and told him that he was now

"Major Currie, VC," that he was going back to Canada and that his fighting days were at an end.[11] Dave was "staggered, sat down, had a cigarette and thought it over" and then went back to C Squadron.[12] His two captains, Don Stewart and Bob Donaldson, had been with him when he received the call to RHQ and Don Stewart remembered that they were curious:

He came back a short while later, came in, sat down and continued our normal small talk. Finally, Bulgy [Donaldson] asked him what HQ wanted him for. "Well," he said, "you know my last two initials. They are going to give me that." (His name as you know was David Vivian Currie, initials D.V.C.). He sat there calm and collected, while Bulgy and I and I think the SSM all shouted and celebrated for him. Then he announced that he couldn't fight with us any more, had to go back to Canada, had a date with King George in England, and wanted me to drive him to Ostend the next day.[13]

There was great rejoicing among the South Albertas when the official announcement was made. Dave's Victoria Cross was the only such medal won by the Canadian army in Normandy and would be the only VC won by the Canadian Armoured Corps during the war. It let the world know something that every South Alberta already knew – the Regiment was the best

Zoot suits. C Squadron crews pose in their new tank suits at Vught, Christmas 1944. They were a practical, warm and much-liked garment. COURTESY, CLIFF ALLEN.

in the business but for Don Stewart and many others it brought sadness as it meant that Dave would be leaving. On 26 November Don drove him into Ostend:

> A jeep ride, a salute, a wave goodbye, and he was gone in his tank suit to meet the King. Modest, quiet, calm, unruffled, unflappable, reasonable and considerate. He was probably as frightened as any of us were most of the time, but gave the impression of being completely fearless, cool as ice in action.[14]

The award was confirmed the next day at a regimental parade by Bert Coffin, who was commanding as Swatty had been called to take over the brigade in Jeff Jefferson's absence. Bert had some other news: the SAR were going to get a new general, their fourth in nine months.[15]

The new commander of 4th Armoured Division was Major General Chris Vokes. This appointment was not a promotion – Vokes had been commanding the 1st Infantry Division in Italy – but a straight switch of commands with Harry Foster. Neither general was happy about the move and it really made no sense as Vokes was an infantry commander while Harry Foster was a cavalryman who had demonstrated in the previous three months that he had learned to fight armour. The official reason for this curious transfer has never come to light but there is a strong probability that it resulted from a simple mistake.[16] Whatever the reason it was an unhappy and truculent general who arrived in November 1944. Regarding himself as a seasoned veteran, Vokes had little time for his new formation's reputation. A few weeks after taking over, he became "heartily sick" of hearing his staff speak of "nothing but the exploits of this great division" and straightaway informed them that

I will be obliged if you will henceforth refrain from telling me how many shells have been fired out of the mouths of your tanks at Buggeroff Zoom, Sphitzen-on-the-Floor and other places. I know a little bit about fighting and about tanks and about what they can and cannot do.[17]

That, however, remained to be seen.

Another more famous general briefly entered the Regiment's life at this time. On 26 November the SAR was informed that they had been selected to provide the guard of honour for the forthcoming visit of Dwight D. Eisenhower, Supreme Allied Commander. Although it may have had more to do with the fact that the Regiment was in reserve, the South Albertas were certain that they had been chosen for this prestigious duty because they were the best regiment in the army. Captain Kenny Perrin of A Squadron was tasked as the guard commander, assisted by Lieutenants Smith "Tiger" Bowick and Ed Reardon, and spent two days drilling his hundred-strong unit for the event and making arrangements with a Dutch civilian in Vught to clean and press the guard's uniforms. The SAR looked their best on 29 November when Eisenhower, accompanied by a proud but nervous Captain Perrin, inspected the spotless ranks. All went well but it got better after the parade was finished and there "was an issue of rum for all ranks of the guard."[18] Trooper

The general from Italy. Major-General Chris Vokes, commander of 4th Canadian Armoured Division from December 1944 to the end of the war. His lateral transfer from command of lst Infantry Division in Italy proved to be an unpopular move for all concerned. NAC, PA 140573.

Guard of Honour. Looking a little nervous, Captain Kenny Perrin accompanies General Dwight D. Eisenhower, Supreme Allied Commander, as he inspects the South Alberta Guard of Honour at Best in November 1944. Generals Harry Crerar, Commander of First Canadian Army, and Guy Simonds follow. Things got better for the Guard when they received a special issue of rum that night.

John Neff recorded with satisfaction in his diary that the guard "all got rather high in the evening."[19]

Vught was a quiet time for the Regiment but armies can never let well enough alone and it was not long before Wotherspoon started three training courses – an officers' tactical school, an NCOs' training school and a basic trades course for new reinforcements – to be run over the next few months. This instruction was required as the Regiment had received many new officers and men and they needed to be properly prepared for action. Among the new arrivals were four "homegrown" lieutenants who had been SAR NCOs: Bobby Crawford, Ivan Donkin, Ernie Hill and Ev Nieman. By the first week of December, when Swatty returned after a ten-day period in command of the brigade, training and retraining were in full stride. On 2 December the colonel held another Regimental parade and stressed that the South Albertas must continue to show "Esprit de Corps, cunningness and all-out effort."[20] The following day the Regiment's rest period came to an end when it received an order to move back to the Maas.

In Canada the big news that sixth wartime winter was young Maurice ("the Rocket") Richard of the Montreal Canadiens. With support from veteran Habs captain Toe Blake and forward Elmer Lach, the Rocket was breaking all records for goals scored in the National Hockey League and had catapulted the Canadiens over the ailing Leafs into first place in the standings. It is not likely that Prime Minister Mackenzie King followed ice hockey and in any case he had more pressing concerns; his government was in a crisis because King's too-clever manpower policy had finally come home to haunt him. In September the Canadian public had learned there was a desperate shortage of trained infantrymen in Europe after a wounded officer, Major Conn Smythe, spilled it to the press. In response, Minister of Defence J.L. Ralston made a lightning tour of the fighting fronts and spoke to senior officers to find out about the problem. He did not like what he heard. On 8 October, Ralston interviewed Harry Foster, at that time commanding 4th Armoured Division, and Harry talked plain to the man. "Politicians can't seem to get it through their heads that in war there are casualties that must be replaced," he recorded in his diary, and "We need live bodies, not wishful thinking."[21]

It was clear that the government would have to either impose conscription for overseas service or disband some of the combat formations in Europe because there were simply not enough infantry to replace the casualties of the recent fighting. The first alternative was not acceptable to Quebec while the second was not acceptable to the rest of Canada and King was caught on the horns of a dilemma that was very much of his own making. Throughout the autumn of 1944 he twisted and turned trying to outmanoeuvre the pro-conscription forces in his cabinet and prevent the country dividing over the issue. The morality of the situation – that more than 60,000 NRMA soldiers were perfectly safe in Canada while the active service units in Europe were being bled white – never seems to have bothered him because it was all a matter of politics and politics were everything to Mackenzie King. Grasping at straws, he accepted the assurances of Lieutenant-General Andrew McNaughton that enough trained infantry could be obtained by a determined effort to get NRMA personnel to volunteer for overseas service, although this advice was contrary to the beliefs of both Ralston and the senior military staff. King therefore decided that McNaughton should replace Ralston and in a tricky manoeuvre during a cabinet meeting on 1 November he forced the defence minister's resignation.[22]

McNaughton imediately began a vigorous three-week campaign to get the zombies to volunteer for active service. It failed miserably and on 22 November the chief of the general staff, Lieutenant-General J.C. Murchie, advised McNaughton that voluntary methods would simply not make up for the shortfall in infantry. The cabinet was now in a crisis and six ministers were prepared to resign if King did not bring in conscription, but their putative revolt was stymied by the about-face made by the prime minister on 23 November when he announced that conscription would be imposed for overseas service and that 16,000 NRMA troops would shortly be ordered to Europe. There was a widespread outcry in Quebec, fights between active service and NRMA soldiers, and near-mutinies by some home defence units, including an incident at Terrace, BC, where for two days the regiments of 15 Brigade refused to do duty and surrounded their barrack lines with an armed guard. The unrest settled down but uncertainty over the future of the government remained in Ottawa until 8 December when the Liberals survived what amounted to a non-confidence vote in the Commons on conscription – 143 to 70 in their favour with thirty-four Liberal members from Quebec voting against their own party. As the House then prorogued itself until 31 January 1945, King could relax and he celebrated by staying in bed until noon on the morning following the debate, convinced that he, and only he, had preserved the nation.[23]

There was no love lost between the active service soldiers and the despised zombies. In November 1944 Vic Childs, a former SAR who had left the Regiment when it converted to armour in 1942, returned to Canada after being wounded while serving with the RCASC in Europe. He went to Niagara Falls to visit his fiancée and there encountered Benny Bennett, another wounded former SAR, who had won the MC while serving as a Can Loan officer with the British Army in Normandy. One day the two vets arranged to meet their ladies after the ladies had finished work and, having nothing better to do, decided to pass the time in Niagara Falls, NY, where they "spent a fine afternoon, in many bars, regaling all those ignorant Americans about the battles fought by Canadians across the pond."[24] Eventually, as the appointed time for meeting their better halves approached, the two men wended their way back to Canada across the bridge spanning the Niagara River. They were feeling no pain and looked quite a sight for Vic "was wearing dark glasses and walking with a cane and Benny looked like a Hollywood hero with his left foot in a walking cast and also a cane." As they "stumbled back into Queen Street," the two heroes noticed "literally hundreds of poor benighted zombies bumbling about looking, I supposed, for someone to guide them to the fleshpots of Niagara Falls." Benny Bennett had an inspiration:

"Vic," he said, "look at all those lost souls wandering about without any purpose; perhaps we should have a parade." So away we went, Benny in his officer's uniform, cast and all, and me a Private in my uniform with overseas patches and ribbons, complete with upside-down good-conduct stripe and wound stripe. To the zombies' unknowing eyes, we must have looked like a General Staff.

We proceeded to organize them, I cried out for them all to fall in for a special parade and inspection and we lined them up in threes at the open order, right at a four-cornered intersection in rush hour. We had about one hundred lined up and traffic was backed up in four directions for many blocks.

At this time, our two beloved ladies happened to pass by and after one horrified look, they hurried on, completely ignoring us, as well they should. Finally, several police cars arrived on the scene, and happily, they were led by an elderly sergeant who wore First War ribbons and who saw immediately what we were doing. Swallowing a smile he saluted Benny sharply and said, "Sir, would you kindly dismiss your parade and let us get the hell out of here."

Benny returned the salute, dismissed the parade, and we staggered off only to spend a long, long evening explaining to our beloved ones that you must not allow a rabble of soldiers to gather without supervision.[25]

The feelings of active service soldiers (and most Canadians) about King's wartime manpower policy were reflected in a piece of doggerel that made the rounds in late 1944:

Seventy thousand zombies, isn't it a farce?
Seventy thousand zombies, sitting on their arse.
Eating up the rations, morning, noon and night,
Squatting here in Canada, while others go to fight.

Seventy thousand zombies, hear the buzzards sing,
Here's our thanks to you, Quebec, and old Mackenzie King.
Never mind our comrades, let them be the goats,
As long as politicians protect their slimy votes.

Seventy thousand zombies refuse to play the game,
God, our fair Dominion must hang its head in shame.
Recruits are badly needed, you hear the urgent shout,
But seventy thousand zombies reply "We're staying out!"[26]

One soldier who most certainly had not stayed out was on his way home at this time. As the film cameras whirred and the flashbulbs popped, Harry Crerar personally congratulated Dave Currie at the headquarters of First Canadian Army before dispatching him to Buckingham Palace to receive his Victoria Cross from the hand of King George VI. There was a screw-up along the way and Dave had to be rushed across the Channel in a motor torpedo boat but managed to arrive on time at the Palace wearing the oil-stained tank suit he had lived in for weeks. The press made much of it:

The major wasn't dressed to visit the King. He dashed up to the front door of Buckingham Palace with a tankman's greasy coveralls over his battle dress. …. He doffed the coveralls in a palace anteroom, quaffed a drink of water proffered by a court attendant and walked along the carpeted dais to face his ruler.

The major bowed to the King when the Lord Chamberlain announced his name and the award. He stood stiff as a ramrod while the morning-coated Lord Chamberlain read the citation of his gallantry then stepped forward.

The quiet warrior. Major Dave Currie, SAR, November 1944. Essentially a shy man, this former mechanic from Moose Jaw, Saskatchewan, set an example of leadership and courage at St. Lambert-sur-Dives in August 1944 that has rarely been equalled in the Canadian Army. COURTESY, SOUTH ALBERTA LIGHT HORSE.

Old comrades. After receiving his Victoria Cross at Buckingham Palace, Dave Currie took the time to visit all the wounded of the Regiment he could find in English hospitals. Here he poses with a South Alberta who lost a leg in the fighting in Europe.
COURTESY, DANNY McLEOD.

The King picked up the Cross from a velvet cushion held by a brigadier and pinned it on Currie's battledress tunic. His Majesty, dressed in naval uniform as admiral of the fleet, smiled and chatted with the Canadian major for a minute or so and shook his hand in congratulations as the khaki-clad orchestra struck up "God Save the King."

The investiture over, Currie donned his coveralls and stepped out in the rain of the palace courtyard to face a photographic barrage.[27]

For Dave Currie, it sure was a long way from Moose Jaw, Saskatchewan. Over the next few days, seemingly endless "photo opportunities," questions and interviews followed until Dave was put on a plane for Canada along with fellow VC winner Major Jock Mahoney. Before he left England, however, Dave

somehow found time to visit many wounded South Albertas in hospital and Trooper Robert Barr recalled with delight that he showed them his medal and let them hold it.[28]

Dave's wife, Isabel, and their 9-year-old son, David Junior, were living with her parents in Owen Sound, Ontario. They knew nothing about the award but had received a message that Dave was coming home on Friday, 15 December. Isabel was recovering from an appendicitis operation and was resting one morning when there

was a knock at the door and there were some army people. In those days we lived from day to day and feared anyone coming to the door. However, they didn't scare me much because I had got a message that Davie was coming home.

There were two officers and they said that they wanted to

243

speak to me. One said he was a major from the personnel section and asked me when I had last heard from my husband and I said "awhile." He went on and on, asking me whether I had heard anything. He didn't seem to know too much about what he was talking about. Finally he said, "I've got some news for you." And I said, "I hope it's good."

Then he told me that Davie had won the VC. I was sitting in a chair and I didn't jump up and down which I was expected to do. I said "That's very nice, but how is he?" He said, "He's won the VC! Aren't you excited about this?" And he started pacing the floor. I said, "Why? You have to remember that Davie was the kind of person who would say, 'I didn't do this by myself, it was my men,'" and I was very pleased and even more happy that he was fine. They couldn't understand that.[29]

Isabel knew her man well. A BBC tape of one of the many interviews that Dave gave at this time has survived and, when asked the inevitable question, "Tell us what it is like to be a VC winner," Dave Currie put the whole thing in perspective:

Sure, I'll tell you about it. I think it's the highest honour that can be paid on the field of battle but the honour belongs to the regiment: to the colonel for the very able direction and support he gave; to the other squadrons for the flank protection they gave during the job and particularly to my own boys and the boys of the Argylls who were with me on the spot. I also think that, if either of the other two fighting squadrons had been given the job, it would have been done just as well.[30]

He never varied that opinion to the day he died.

In Owen Sound, young David came home from school for lunch while the two officers were talking to Isabel and she recalled that when

he saw the army car in front of the door he thought his dad was home. When he came in, he saw that he wasn't. My younger brother was only five years older and the two boys were like brothers. They had to be told what was going on. I said, "Okay, boys, just remember one thing, you are no different than when you walked in this door." I also told them not to say anything as we were told not to say anything until Sunday night [10 December 1944].

Isabel was putting the children to bed "about 8 PM when the doorbell rang and it was the newspaper reporters" as "it turned out that, after he left me, the army major had gone straight to the newspapers and told them everything." So much for security. "By Sunday night," she recalled, "they were coming up, the paper people, from Toronto, they were coming from everywhere."

She was badgered by the media the entire week before Dave got home. He flew into Montreal on Friday, 15 December, and then caught a train for Toronto, where Isabel planned to meet him that day. Her doctor only allowed her to go on the condition that he accompany her on the journey and there was some question on Friday morning about whether the trip was possible as a record 22-inch snowfall the previous night had covered much of southern Ontario. But Isabel was determined, and although the train was late, it made it through. For all of the long and slow trip she was annoyed by a persistent man and woman team from the *Toronto Star* who wanted an "exclusive story on the return of Dave Currie, war hero" and was thankful when she finally disembarked at Union Station in Toronto in late afternoon. Isabel tried to spot the husband she had not seen for twenty-seven months in the bustling crowd but couldn't find him. Then she heard her name called and there he was – tired but happy and, best of all, in one piece. They dodged the reporters and went across the street to the Royal York Hotel, where a suite had been reserved.

If the Curries thought they were going to get some time together, they were mistaken. They had hardly got into their rooms when the phone began to ring and visitors started knocking at the door. Mostly it was people anxious for news of husbands, brothers, sons and friends overseas either in the SAR or other units and there were so many that it wasn't long before the couple established a procedure. Isabel would usher a visitor into one room of the suite or hold an inquirer on the phone while Dave would talk to another visitor in the other room. When he was finished, he would either take the phone call or invite the next visitor into his room for a brief chat. It went on for four hours until the district commander, Major-General A.E. Potts, arrived to take the couple to dinner at his home. When Potts brought them back the phone messages had stacked up and to give the couple some peace he ordered the hotel to stop taking messages and letting visitors through to the Curries' suite. While Isabel finished unpacking, Dave did his best to respond to the last round of messages, and when she went in to see how he was making out she found him stretched out on a couch, sound asleep. Dave Currie, the quiet warrior, was home.

In Holland meanwhile the South Albertas had pulled out of their comfortable quarters at Vught on 4 December to reassume their old position along the river near Capelle (see map 13, page 239). They were there only four days and then moved back from the river to Dongen, where they spent nearly two weeks taken up with unit schools, maintenance and the occasional squadron dance. On 9 December a Regimental parade was held in the morning in preparation for an inspection by Vokes in the afternoon and the SAR got their first look at their new general.[31]

Even during this relatively tranquil time there were dangers about. On 16 December four men of the SAR driving in a jeep struck a mine on a little-travelled road just south of the Maas. Two men, Sergeant Thomas Donald and Trooper Kendal Rowe, were killed outright and, although the site of the incident was under German observation from across the river, an ambulance managed to evacuate the two wounded men to a hospital where one, Sergeant Earl Fortin, died the next day of his wounds. It was regarded as too hazardous to send the ambulance back a second time so volunteers from the Recce Troop went into the mine-infested area on foot and brought out the two dead men on stretchers. Thomas Donald was a 37-year-old native of Lachine, Quebec, who left behind a wife and daughter, as did Kendal Rowe, a 23-year-old machinist from Wainwright, Alberta. Earl Fortin was a 22-year-old mechanic from Montreal who was survived by a wife and four children.[32]

Not all casualties during this period were caused by the Germans. On 19 November, Trooper David Low, a 21-year-old DR from Minburn, Alberta, died in Britain from injuries he sustained in September when his motorcycle was sideswiped by a scout car near Eekloo.[33] Another DR and an old original from 1940, Trooper Alexander Robertson, was killed on 17 December in a head-on collision with a truck at a street intersection.[34] A particularly tragic death was that of 22-year-old Armourer Sergeant Raymond Coté from Montreal on 5 February 1945. One of Coté's assistants was working on a .30 calibre machine gun when the weapon accidentally fired and hit him in the chest. Corporal Bob Rasmussen was there when

> Ray Coté fell into my arms. … He was working here and he started to move and I was at the front of the truck talking to the driver and I heard this bang and I turned around and all I could see was his face turning ashen. We carried him to the RAP, bandaged him up and took him down the line. But it was a tracer round, he got phosphorus in his heart and he died a few hours later.[35]

The war came alive again on 16 December 1944 when the *Wehrmacht* launched a major offensive in the Ardennes area of Belgium, eighty miles south of 1st Canadian Army's positions along the Maas, with the intention of driving straight through the Allied forces to capture the vital port of Antwerp. Hitler had rebuilt the panzer divisions decimated in Normandy but had held them back from the western front so that they could undertake this massive blow upon which he pinned his hopes of staving off defeat in the west.

It was a desperate measure but the German attack caught the American Ninth Army unprepared and they fell back under the weight of the onslaught. Assisted by overcast skies which prevented Allied airpower from playing an active role, the *Wehrmacht* made good progress for the first week but the stubborn American defence of Bastogne and St. Vith slowed the momentum of the German attack and, thereafter, the arrival of reinforcements and overwhelming air support gradually turned the tide. One panzer division came within seventy miles of Antwerp but stalled at the Meuse River, out of gasoline. Fighting continued in the Ardennes for another month but the

crisis period had passed by New Year's Day, 1945. The Ardennes offensive cost the *Wehrmacht* about 100,000 casualties, 800 tanks and 1000 aircraft and did not accomplish a single one of its objectives. It did, however, lengthen the war as Allied leaders were forced to postpone their own offensive measures until the enemy threat had been eliminated.

As a precaution against enemy infiltration, Vokes initiated a vigorous programme of patrolling along the Maas and occasionally across the river. On the night of 16 December the day the German offensive began in the Ardennes, A Squadron was ordered to put a patrol over the canal separating the south bank of the Maas from the island of Kapelsche Veer to capture a prisoner. Gordie Irving recalled that the troop leaders drew cards,

Tragic accident. Armourer Sergeant Ray Coté, who was killed in a tragic accident in February 1945 when a loaded .30 calibre machine gun the armourers were working on discharged accidentally. He was 22 years old. COURTESY, JACK PORTER.

high card losing, to see who would take the patrol over. Gordie "drew a Queen and was just sick but fortunately someone got a King."[36] The loser was Lieutenant Earle Johnston, who went over that night in a boat with two members of the Dutch Resistance and four men from Recce Troop. The patrol made contact with the Germans, shots were exchanged, confusion reigned and the men were split up and had to find their own ways back to the boat. Johnston arrived late at the anchorage only to find that the boat was gone and he had to swim back to friendly territory. He went back to the rear "for a few days rest."[37]

Two days later, the SAR were moved to the Capelle area but on 20 December were ordered back to Vught. They returned to the former convent they had cleaned up the previous month to find it in a "deplorable condition."[38] Christmas was now approaching and Quartermaster Captain Tommy Barford had prepared a special meal for the boys, but all his plans went awry when orders were received early in the morning of 25

December that the Regiment had to be ready to move at 1300 hours and that one troop from each squadron had to be on stand-to at all times. This order was later cancelled but the Regiment was directed to remain at a "30 minutes warning" status to move.[39] As a result of the confusion "dinner was a little late" but it "consisted of a pint of beer, canned turkey, mashed potatoes, creamed carrots and peas, with peaches and mince tart for dessert." Each man received an orange, an issue of cigarettes, a small parcel from the Women's Auxiliary and a pocket diary from the YMCA.

Like many others Trooper John Neff was disappointed and regarded Christmas 1944 as "the worst on record" because the men did not get any time off.[40] Trooper Arnold Dryer's crew ran "an extension up from the radios in the tank" and listened to "the AEF [radio] all day, playing cards and doing nothing."[41] Dryer counted his blessings as there were "a lot of the boys who are not with us this Christmas so I think I am pretty lucky." Despite all this Christmas-spoiling commotion, which had been occasioned by events in the Ardennes, the Regiment remained at Vught over the New Year. Although German aircraft were rarely seen John Neff recorded "buzz bombs and V-2s by the dozen going over" in his diary.[42] The Regiment "managed to get in a certain amount of jubilification" on New Year's Eve and the next morning was "Sunday routine" with a late breakfast.[43] Trooper Neff was still disgruntled and recorded that day: "What a way to start the new year, nothing to do but count the Buzz-bombs and play bridge & chess."[44]

On 1 January 1945 the Regiment went through a minor reorganization when RHQ Squadron (not be confused with HQ Squadron) was formed under Captain Kenny Perrin to control the Recce, AA, Inter-Communication and RHQ Troops. This new entity may have derived from an attempt by Wotherspoon to have an "assault squadron" of infantry in halftracks attached to the Regiment on a permanent basis.[45] This was turned down by division and army, but Swatty wanted to streamline the structure of the Regiment to make it more efficient in the field and created RHQ Squadron to control all the miscellaneous and independent combat elements of the SAR that did not come under the fighting squadrons.[46]

Throughout the winter the squadrons held occasional dances to which they invited the local beauties. Trooper Arnold Dryer thought his squadron's dance in early January was "one of the best we have ever had" although it was "not easy getting an orchestra that's four years behind on the music and a hall that's been hit a few times, no lights and make something out of it," but "we even got a good lunch from our rations and checked coats, hats, pistols and rifles."[47] These functions were popular with the Dutch girls although some men suspected that the food was a bigger attraction than the South Albertas. John Lakes comments that at one dance, "when it came to the sandwiches, the determined rush by the fair ladies was rather like a sale in a New York department store" and "our massive pile disappeared before any of us got a bite."[48]

On 4 January the SAR moved to Etten, where they remained four days. Along with the rest of 4 Division they were now providing a "counter attack" force to repel any enemy attempt to cross the Maas. The division was divided into three battlegroups and the SAR, with the Lake Superior Regiment (less one company) under command, formed one of these *ad hoc* groups. It was apparently a confusing time at divisional headquarters as on 7 January the Regiment was told that in future it would function as divisional reserve, support for 10 Brigade on the Maas, left flank protection and liaison with the 1st Polish Division. To properly accomplish any one of these roles would have taken much of the strength of the Regiment, and Bert Coffin, in command during Swatty's temporary absence as director of the divisional officers' school, quite properly protested, to no avail. Meanwhile the buzz-bombs continued to come over; Trooper Neff noted on 6 January that "we can see part of the Antwerp AA barrage" firing at a distance in the dark.[49] He and his comrades in B Squadron had "lots of fun stopping cars at night" while on guard duty and he gleefully recorded the time that he and Jim Nicholson "stopped a Limey Brig[adier]. and laid down the law to him for driving with his lights on."

There was much recce work by all squadrons to map out possible routes in the surrounding area for troop movements to meet a German attack. The Regiment continued wandering around until 10 January when it received orders to move to Kaatsheuvel near the Maas. The SAR was now on the left flank of 4th Division and their position adjoined that of 1st Polish Division. Great care was taken to maintain proper liaison with the Poles, who had a habit of shooting first and asking questions later. Albert Halkyard of Recce Troop recalls how it was done:

We would go up to a little old farmhouse not too far from the river, and we would go over to the Poles and try to establish the divide line for the night. But you had to find someone who could talk English. There was a famous old tree and the tree was usually the divide line: "Come this side and we shoot and if we go to that side you shoot."[50]

At Kaatsheuvel the individual crews were billeted in private homes, and although the Catholic population of the village was at first somewhat suspicious of the largely Protestant SAR, the two groups eventually warmed to each other. Many lasting friendships and not a few marriages resulted from the Regiment's stay in the small towns and villages along the Maas during the winter of 1944-1945. For the Dutch, although having soldiers billeted in their homes was often an inconvenience, the boys brought their rations and fuel allowance with them and this permitted families who had endured four years of occupation under the *moffen* – their term for the hated Germans – a semblance of normal life. For the South Albertas billeting was a welcome change from camp and barrack life; it provided them with the chance to get a home-cooked meal and, perhaps most important of all, it gave them a respite from the impersonal army life in the warmth of a family environment. Not that many appreciated it at the time because most were young soldiers interested in what young soldiers are usually interested in, and that was a far cry from family life – unless there was a comely daughter in the house. Reflecting on the matter in later years, however, many South Albertas realized that the winter on the Maas was a blessing because it softened a soldier's life and a soldier's life in wartime is a continual test of hardness.

The South Albertas have many fond memories of their Dutch hosts during that last winter of the war. Trooper Fred Jefferson from Montreal, a recent reinforcement, was billeted with a family in Capelle. The husband, a doctor, had been taken as a forced labourer to Germany but his wife and children adopted the young trooper and quickly taught him to speak Dutch. Christmas was approaching and in the Dutch version of Christmas Sint Niklaus (the original Santa Claus) is assisted by *Swarte Piet* (Black Peter), who puts coal in your stocking if you

Looking good. From left, Sergeants J. Kroesing and E. Beaudry and an unidentified South Alberta about to embark on leave, Holland, 1944. SAR COLLECTION.

are bad and a toy if you are good. Fred, a black man, immediately acquired a following of village children anxious to learn what their fate would be on Christmas Eve.[51]

Arnold Dryer's crew was billeted with a family ruled by the mother who, like most Dutch housewives, was a fanatic about keeping a clean and tidy house. She would fly into a temper and shout "Canadees no good" when the boys tracked "in a bunch of mud or blew the lids off the stove starting it with petrol," but "a few minutes later, after she cleans it up, there is nobody like Canadians."[52] When Dryer's crew had to join the Kapelsche Veer battle in late January, they told their landlady "we were going on leave and she started giving us the old line about being careful and not [to] drink too much." When they returned a

couple of days later, in the small hours of the morning, this maternal soul was there "counting us as we came in the door" and "was happy when she found all her crew had come back." For Dryer's crew and the rest of the Regiment, life on the Maas was a curious blend of violence and domestic tranquillity and the warmth of their Dutch hosts is perhaps summarized by a phrase many heard that winter: "*Kom, zit by de kachel, en drink een kopje koffie* (come, sit by the stove and drink a cup of coffee)."

The war began to heat up again in the two weeks that followed the move to Kaatsheuvel as the SAR got to do some shooting over the Maas. Beginning on 11 January each squadron undertook to fire at pre-registered targets to practise the crews in the techniques of indirect fire, but the problem was that, owing to the dykes on both banks of the river, it was difficult to observe the fall of shell. The targets were varied but, more and more, one began to predominate – the island of Kapelsche Veer on the Maas near Capelle. During the night of 13 January B Squadron fired in support of a Royal Marine attack on this island. The attack failed but the War Diary noted that the "enemy seem to be very touchy concerning" any attempt to fire on Kapelsche Veer and would return fire.[53] On 15 January, one German shell hit "an ammo lorry to the south of the town and for 15 mins we were regaled with a beautiful display of pyrotechnics."[54] The SAR tanks continued to fire on the morning of 16 January and the turret gunners "enjoyed being able to pop off as many rounds as they wished."[55] That afternoon RAF Spitfires and Typhoons "attacked, bombed and strafed enemy pos[itio]ns on the island." The individual squadrons continued their shooting over the river for another nine days, assisted by two instructor teams from the Royal Canadian Artillery. It was not unpleasant work; the individual troops would drive up to the river in the morning, shell the Germans, take a break for lunch, shell the Germans some more and drive back to their billets in the late afternoon.[56]

Occasionally, individual tank troops were called upon to provide direct fire for the infantry. Lieutenant Ivan Donkin of B Squadron specialized in this work and became greatly beloved by the Algonquin Regiment, who christened him "Mighty Donkin." According to the Algoons,

Donkin suffered from mild pyromania – he loved to burn down buildings, preferably with Germans sleeping inside.

Daily for a week he would zig-zag up to the dike, poke the gun snout over, and blast away until he had several satisfactory blazes going. One day he selected as his target a house which was suspected to be a concreted pill-box in disguise. After firing at it all afternoon from various angles, and finally running out of ammunition, he was packing up to go home. While he and his crew were taking a last look at the place, the sound of a buzz-bomb came down from the north-east. As it neared the river, the jets stuttered, then cut out. The bomb spiralled down, swung towards the far shore, hit and exploded. When the dust cleared, Donkin's target was no more. It was the only time he was known to comment on a waste of ammunition.[57]

January 1945 was not all shooting. On the 19th the SAR boxing team, which had been coached over the last few months by four professional Dutch boxers from 's-Hertogenbosch, won the 10 Brigade championship and everyone knew that this was only a warm-up for bigger things. On the same day news came through that Padre Phil Silcox had been made a Member of the British Empire for his personal efforts to ward off a friendly air attack in Normandy the previous August. Wotherspoon had originally cited Silcox for the Military Cross but had been informed by higher authority that padres were not eligible for this medal. Their fighting man of the cloth was by now a popular figure in the Regiment and the boys were "very pleased" about the MBE as "it was extremely well deserved."[58] Three days later, the new RHQ Squadron held a memorable dance at which there were "girls for all and the fact that the dance hall adjoined a beer tavern was well appreciated."[59]

By the last week of the month, however, it was clear that something was afoot along the Maas. On 24 January Trooper Joe Strathern of C Squadron noted in his diary that "Big Guns" were "moving up with lots of alligators [amphibious tracked vehicles]."[60] The next day the War Diarist commented that "much equip[ment] had been brought into the area," including artillery "of all sorts and size" which "crammed the roads," while "a pioneer outfit from army moved into Kaatsheuvel and the BCR and white painted Buffalos passed through Sprang."[61] It didn't take a genius to figure out that the reason for all this commotion had to be the Regiment's main target of the last two weeks – the Kapelsche Veer. The time had come to go back to the sharp end.

The Hunger Winter. The winter of 1944-1945 was known as the "hunger winter" in Holland. The Germans had stripped the country of foodstuff and there was widespread starvation, especially in the areas still occupied by the Germans. Nothing edible went to waste: here Dutch civilians, desperate for food, cut up cattle killed in the fighting around Bergen op Zoom. NAC

CHAPTER FIFTEEN

"If only we had the wisdom of our generals."

HOLLAND: 25 JANUARY – 21 FEBRUARY 1945

The Kapelsche Veer is a low, flat, treeless island in the lower reaches of the Maas. Formed by the division of that river into two channels, a wide northern branch called the Bergsche Maas and a narrow, southern branch known as the Oude Maasje, the Veer is a boggy spit of land, five miles long and one mile wide at its broadest point, narrowing to about a thousand yards at its eastern extremity where it becomes a double dyke. These dykes, about twenty feet high and thirty feet wide, with steep sides that slope at a forty-five-degree angle, protect the south bank of the river from the current, which is very strong in this area. On the northern side of the island is the small ferry harbour that gives it its name, for "veer" is Dutch for "harbour" and, thus, Kapelsche Veer means "the harbour of Capelle," a nearby village.

When the *Wehrmacht* withdrew north of the Maas in November 1944, Allied troops did not occupy the Veer. It was felt that it could be easily dominated by fire and the units responsible for the sector contented themselves with occasional patrols.

When this bloody war is over,
Oh, how happy I will be,
When I get my civvy clothes on,
No more soldiering for me.

No more church parades on Sunday,
No more begging for a pass,
I will tell the Sergeant-Major,
To stuff his passes up his ass.[1]

This insignificant piece of boggy ground only became important in December 1944 when Allied intelligence anticipated that, in conjunction with the offensive in the Ardennes to the south, the Germans would attempt an assault across the Maas. Such an attack was planned but it is unclear whether the enemy intention was serious or simply a ploy to distract Allied intelligence. In any case the projected German attack was cancelled, much to the relief of *General* Eugen-Felix Schwalbe, whose corps had been tasked with carrying it out. Schwalbe had been disturbed to learn that, in the face of not only Allied air and artillery superiority but the massed firepower of two armoured divisions, his troops were expected to cross the river in rubber assault rafts and civilian ferries armed with 37 mm guns. In fact, he was so disturbed that "he awoke the day after he had been told of the plan" to ask himself, "Are we really going to cross the Maas or did I merely dream it all?"[2]

There was one outcome from this stillborn operation. In mid-December 1944 the Germans established an outpost on

The Veer today. Looking peaceful in the sun, the island of Kapelsche Veer as seen from the south bank of the Maas. In January 1945 it was a barren place with no trees and an ideal defensive position. PHOTOGRAPH BY DIANNE GRAVES.

249

the Veer and retained it as a forward position to give "battle in-oculation" to green troops who were regularly rotated onto the Island from the north bank of the Maas.[3] It wasn't long before the existence of this post became known to the South Albertas, whose area at that time encompassed the island. On or about 17 December Corporal Alfred Engel of Recce Troop led a patrol onto the Veer and moved along the dykes but "got shot at and had to get out of there in a hurry."[4] Engel was sure that the Germans were tunnelling into the dykes but, as he recalled, "they wouldn't believe it." He went over twice more in the following nights but nobody would credit his claim that the Germans had a permanent post on the Veer. The Regiment left the area soon after and the Kapelsche Veer became a Polish responsibility.

The Poles quickly discovered the presence of the Germans. During the night of 29 December a Polish patrol exchanged shots with the enemy and confirmed that they were entrenched in the area of the ferry harbour. Maczek disliked having a Ger-man OP on his side of the Maas and, on New Year's Eve 1944, he mounted an attack against the German position with three companies of infantry, supported by tanks firing from the south bank. The Germans beat it off easily at the cost of 49 Polish casualties. This failure revealed that the Germans had constructed "a system of interlocking positions, linked by tun-nels in the dykes and commanding every approach," which had supporting fire from artillery and mortars on the north bank of the river.[5] Maczek spent a week preparing for his next attack, code-named Operation MOUSE, which went in on the night of 6/7 January 1945. This time the Polish commander threw ele-ments of two infantry battalions, supported by tank and artil-lery fire, against the Veer, but again he was rebuffed at a cost of 133 killed and wounded.[6]

Lieutenant General John Crocker, the commander of British 1st Corps, which at this time controlled 1st Polish and 4th Ca-nadian Armoured Divisions, wanted the Germans off the Kapelsche Veer but, before issuing orders for a new assault, he apparently investigated other possibilities. All "efforts to have the area drenched with heavy bombers and set alight with the new Napalm bombs developed by the U.S. were unavailing," however, and he therefore turned to the Royal Marines, am-phibious light infantry.[7] On 13 January, 47 Royal Marine Com-mando mounted Operation HORSE, a nighttime assault plen-tifully supported by artillery. The Marines too were beaten back with a loss of 49 casualties.[8]

Crocker ordered another attack on the Veer. As a staff officer with 4th Division, Major Hubert Fairlie Wood, later wrote, there were reasons for this order. The enemy position "was a thorn in the side of the troops guarding the Maas" as the Ger-mans "could observe movement, direct fire and mount patrols to harry our forward localities." Second, "a determined assault" might convince the Germans that the direction of 21 Army Group's "forthcoming offensive" would be in Holland rather than to the south in the Rhineland where it was actually sched-uled to take place. The third reason, and most "dangerous of

all" according to Wood, was the matter of "Allied prestige," as to allow the Germans to remain south of the Maas would have "engendered in the troops of 1st British Corps a belief in the superiority of the German soldier." Prestige is about the worst possible reason to mount a military operation but, as Wood concludes, after "the first unsuccessful attempts to drive them out, the liquidation of this sore spot became unavoidable." On the morning after the failure of Operation HORSE, Crocker gave Chris Vokes the job of taking the Kapelsche Veer.[9]

This was not good news for 4th Canadian Armoured Divi-sion. "The div[ision] is proud, of course, to have the dis-tinction of being a pinch hitter," their war diarist wrote, "but the pleasure, if NOT the distinction is a dubious one."[10] The as-signment was no more welcome at 10 Brigade Headquarters when Vokes passed it along on 16 January with a detailed plan for the attack. This plan, drawn up by corps and divisional staff, utilized much of the considerable resources available to an Al-lied commander in the last months of the war. Code-named Operation ELEPHANT (the size of the code-names escalating, it appears, in direct proportion to the size of the operations), the assault would be supported by no fewer than three hundred artillery pieces ranging from the 75 mm tank guns of the South Alberta and British Columbia Regiments to the 5.5 inch guns of the medium artillery regiments – the "heaviest concentration of artillery ever allotted to the Brigade, or perhaps to any simi-lar formation, for a single action."[11] No one expected artillery alone to bring victory and the operation orders contained the comforting statement that, when "considering the bombard-ment of the bridgehead position it should be borne in mind that the extraordinarily good f[iel]dworks of the German g[ar]r[iso]n are practically impervious to neutralization or de-struction."[12] This was a cheerful thought but if all that artillery wasn't expected to have much effect, what was going to work?

Despite the fact that three previous attacks on the island had failed and the Germans were alert for another, the planners of Operation ELEPHANT thought that the element of surprise might just bring success. They called for a daylight assault by three infantry companies under cover of a heavy smoke screen but with no preliminary bombardment; two companies would attack from the right and move west against the German posi-tion at the harbour while the third would attack from the left and move east against the same objective. To get the Germans out of their "extraordinarily good fieldworks," the planners in-troduced flamethrowers. Crocodiles would have been ideal for this job but since the ground on the island was "only thinly fro-zen and churned up very quickly into seas of mud," the employ-ment of tanks was not considered.[13] Instead, six Wasps (flame-thrower carriers) were allotted to the assault companies, which were also issued with twenty-four portable flame units. The most amazing part of the scheme was the provision of fifteen canoes for a third force that was to seal off the harbour from the north. Setting out from the eastern tip of the island, this waterborne force would paddle under cover of smoke down the north or main channel of the Maas and land on both sides of the ferry harbour to prevent the Germans from being reinforced from the north bank.[14]

The canoe party was Chris Vokes's personal contribution. The commander of 4th Division was not happy about his orders to take the Kapelsche Veer – as far as he was concerned, "the Germans could have stayed there for the rest of the war" as "they were doing no harm."[15] Although he thought that the operation would be "a great waste of young lives," Vokes felt he "had to do it – you just can't say no when an order comes down" – but only took the job "if two weeks were granted to him to conduct special training and rehearsals for one of his battalions, plus adequate supplies." Crocker gave Vokes everything he wanted, including canoes, but in a postwar interview Vokes implied that his unusual request was a ploy to get the operation cancelled:

When the action was first suggested to me, I said I would take it on, very reluctantly, if they could provide me with twenty-eight Peterborough canoes, because I had visions of sending the troops down the river in those silent craft under the cover of darkness. For a while I thought that by asking for the canoes, I might have turned the whole thing off. Well, it wasn't. The canoes were provided – flown in specially from Canada – and I had to go ahead.[16]

If Vokes was that unsure about the prospect of success, he should have perhaps tried harder to call off the operation. His reluctance to do so, despite his qualms about the assault, may have been due to the fact that Operation ELEPHANT would be the first time he commanded 4th Division in battle and as the new boy he did not want to make waves.

Unfortunately, the command situation at the top was mirrored at the lower levels. The veteran commanders of the South Albertas, the Argylls and the Lincoln and Welland Regiment, the three units that would play an important role in the forthcoming operation, were absent when the plans for ELEPHANT were made. Swatty was supervising the divisional battle school and Bert Coffin had the South Albertas. Vokes had removed Dave Stewart from command of the Argylls after Dave had protested the unnecessary casualties Vokes's winter patrol programme was costing his battalion and the Argylls were now led by Major R.D. McKenzie, the second-in-command. Finally, the Links, who had been chosen to make the initial assault, had lost that magnificent warrior Bill Cromb, gone home on leave after five years overseas, and were commanded temporarily by Major Jim Swayze. When it comes to protesting orders or getting them changed, new or acting commanders don't have the influence that veterans do – as Swayze later remarked, "You only demand so much … you only do what you're told."[17] He recalled that the plan for Operation ELEPHANT was "laid out" and it was simply a case of "take this" and do it.

The Links got one week to prepare and the assault companies, wearing newly-issued white snowsuits, practised on dykes similar to those on the Veer. Vokes showed up one day to watch Major Ed Brady's company going through its paces using smoke and flamethrowers. At the end of the drill, he commented that "I think you've got things pretty well in hand here" and strode off but had an afterthought a few minutes later and returned to tell Brady that he should order his men to fix their bayonets when they actually landed on the island.[18]

The sappers of 9 Field Squadron, RCE, were more helpful. While the Links practised their assault tactics, the engineers built a bridge over to the eastern end of the Veer using the footings of a previously-demolished structure as a foundation. The bridging site was only five hundred yards from the German positions and, although it was under the cover of a dyke, the enemy could bring down fire on all the approaches. The sappers therefore had to work at night and, lest the noise of heavy trucks draw fire, they brought all their materials in by water on man-propelled rafts, or by land on a two and a half ton trailer, also man-propelled, down the icy dyke roads. The bridge, completed the day before the attack, was such a twisted, cobbled-together, unsteady-looking structure that someone dubbed it the "Mad Whore's Dream" and that was the name that 9 Field Squadron neatly lettered on the sign they erected beside it.[19]

All this activity did not go unnoticed by the garrison of the Veer, which consisted of the reinforced No. 10 Company of the 17th German Parachute Regiment. This unit had been formed, along with its parent formation, 6th Parachute Division, in October 1944 from comb-outs from the *Luftwaffe*, stiffened by veterans, and was commanded by *Generalleutnant* Hermann Plocher, a veteran who had first seen combat in Spain in 1936. Plocher wanted to evacuate the Veer but all his requests to withdraw were met with flat refusals by his superior, *Generalleutnant* Kurt Student, who told him bluntly to hold the island "at all costs."[20] Orders being orders, Plocher stationed No. 10 Company, about one hundred and fifty strong, on the Veer and they constructed elaborate underground positions in the dykes around the harbour with emplacements for more than a dozen machine guns, whose fire covered all available approaches. They also sent out aggressive patrols in the week before the attack and there were a number of small firefights in the dark when they encountered similar Canadian patrols. This German activity concerned the 10 Brigade War Diarist, who noted that the enemy's "persistent patrolling" in the area where the attack was to take place was "rather disquieting."[21]

Operation ELEPHANT commenced at 0715 hours on Friday, 26 January 1945. Ninety minutes before, the first smoke rounds came down as the artillery started to build up a diversionary smoke screen to confuse the defenders. The main smoke screen was laid just before the attack went in and it was thickened by artificial smoke generators dispersed around the

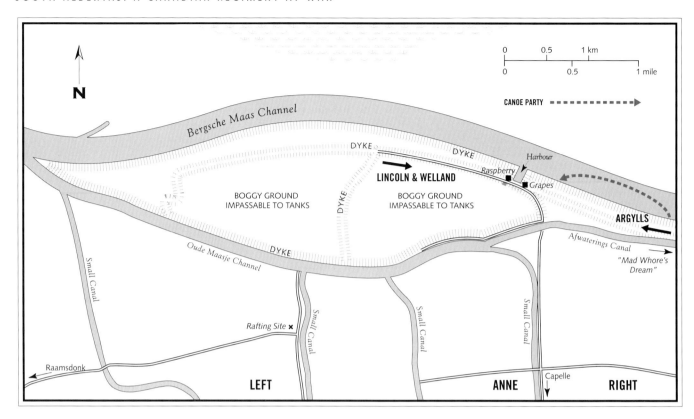

Map 14: Operation ELEPHANT, 26-31 January 1945. Following a series of unsuccessful attacks on the German position at Kapelsche Veer, 10 Brigade launched a major attack on 26 January which saw the Links attack from both the left and right with the addition of a canoe party in the main channel of the Maas. When this was totally rebuffed, the Links and the Argylls spent five bloody days trying to take RASPBERRY and GRAPES from opposite directions. SAR tanks assisted both units, crossing to the Veer either over the "Mad Whore's Dream" or on rafts from the rafting site south of the island.

island. The engineers held their breath as the first vehicle, "a half track loaded with smoke containers," crossed the "Mad Whore's Dream." It "hit the steep ramp at about 30 MPH and came down with a tremendous crash," but as "nothing gave way" the relieved sappers exhaled and declared their rickety span to be structurally "sound."[22]

The right-hand attack went in first. At 0725 hours Major Jim Dandy's C Company of the Links moved over the "Dream" with four Wasp carriers to prepare to move along the dyke to link up with Major Owen Lambert's A Company, which crossed in amphibious Buffalo tractors about a mile and a half to the east. Dandy immediately discovered that his Wasps couldn't climb the dyke because of the weight of their flamethrower equipment. He reckoned that, if he could get one carrier up, he could tow the rest up and tried to blow the flame fuel tank off a carrier by lodging a hand grenade under it – "it just dented the metal."[23]

Lambert's company lost one of their Wasps reaching the island and the other one couldn't get on the dyke. Lambert decided to press on and his men, choking in the harsh acrid fumes of the chemical smoke, moved east along the dyke toward the centre of the German position, which was formed by two houses which some fructally-minded planner had code-named GRAPES and RASPBERRY.[24]

The sixty-man canoe party also reached the island by the bridge. When they attempted to launch their craft into the main river channel, they discovered that there was an inch of ice on the river – a fact that had been reported at 0500 that morning by the Algonquins, who were monitoring river conditions, – and the party was forced to haul their canoes over the ice to reach open water. By the time they moved downstream both the men and their weapons were thoroughly soaked by the freezing water but their troubles were just beginning. The ice along the river bank forced them out farther into the main channel of the Maas where the smoke was less thick, and as they paddled furiously toward the harbour they came under fire from the north bank of the river. Matters were not helped when the wind began to shift, thinning out their smoke cover even more. Several of the fragile craft were sunk and the party was forced to land on the Veer near where Lambert's A Company had reached the island. They were now halfway to their objective but only about fifteen were still on their feet. As soon as they were on top of the dyke they came under heavy fire from German machine guns firing on fixed lines through the smoke along the dyke top, but when they tried to return this fire they discovered that their weapons, which had been soaked in the canoes, were frozen solid and would not work. The survivors withdrew to the mainland.[25]

Lambert pressed toward the centre of the German position. His company was within thirty yards of GRAPES when the Germans opened up with every weapon they could bring to bear through the smoke, and the volume of fire brought the Links to a standstill, five of the six officers in the company were killed or wounded, and Lambert was last seen "walking up the dyke all by himself," swearing and cursing "until he disappeared in the smoke." He did not come back.[26] Attempts to flush out the defenders with the portable "life-buoy" flamethrowers proved useless as most of the men carrying them were cut down. One Links officer commented on the difficulties of these weapons:

I had lifebuoy flamethrowers. I think I had ten. Lost every goddamn man; every one of them was killed. You can imagine what it was like. I think they weighed about 60 pounds. He's got army boots on with metal cleats on the heels filled with snow. He's walking on an angle … carrying the goddamned thing; trying to manoeuvre is almost impossible. And the minute they shot any flame … they were a target and every one of them got it. I always felt really badly about that [because] we asked for volunteers. I didn't want to take them in the first place, but they felt that's what we had to have so we took them. And I never used them again.[27]

By 0945 A Company's advance had been brought to a halt and the survivors began to dig in along the dyke, a few hundred yards short of their objective. At that moment the Germans brought down a heavy and accurate mortar barrage from the north bank of the river and then counter-attacked, driving the remnants of A Company back on the positions of Dandy's C Company behind them. Dandy tried to advance but this movement became confused when he and all the other company officers became casualties. At 1130 the attack on the right was over and the remnants of Dandy and Lambert's men were withdrawn from the Veer.[28]

Progress on the left, or western side, was initially good. Major Ed Brady's B Company crossed to the island in Buffaloes and then moved along the dyke toward RASPBERRY, the westernmost of the two houses. Then they ran into trouble, as one corporal remembered: "You couldn't see in front of you and the phosphorus [smoke] got into your lungs … Their slit trenches were all covered with snow" and "you couldn't tell where their fire was coming from … And talk about cold."[29] Brady kept advancing but, as he recalled, "they opened up on us both with mortars and machine guns" and I "started losing men hand over fist."[30] His men "were just going down like ten pins" and, realizing that he "would just lose more and more men," Brady decided to pull back and dig in at the junction of the main dyke and a smaller dyke that ran north from his crossing spot. The Germans immediately began to infiltrate around his position using the dykes as cover, snipers became active, and Brady's situation was very shaky.[31]

By noon it was obvious that the assault on the Kapelsche Veer was a total failure. So much for the element of surprise.

The South Albertas had taken little part in the morning's battle. Lieutenant Tiger Bowick's A-3 Troop had provided indirect fire on immediate call for the Links and some echelon personnel had been detailed to help with the smoke generators. Among them was Trooper George Armstrong, who remembered that he and Jack Spillet "went up after dark [on 25 January] and here was some 10 Brigade people and they were going to make a kayak [canoe] attack in there and that's what these smudge pots [smoke generators] were for." The two men "put them where they wanted and it was so damn cold that Jack and I were using socks for mitts." Just before first light, "we lit these smudge pots and they were pleased with the smoke cover they gave." "Later," George continued, "they brought up a kitchen truck and Jack and I were getting something to eat when we heard that all of those kayak fellows were lost … They said that there was no smoke as apparently the wind blew it down the wrong way. I mind that we never finished our meal, we were just sick."[32]

During the morning a large audience gathered in RHQ at Kaatsheuvel to follow the course of the fighting on the wireless but the "news coming in was very meagre."[33] A few minutes later the crowd thinned out after a German artillery shell demolished "a building across the street" and "a large piece of shrapnel rocketed through the orderly room bringing dust and plaster down on the heads of the assembled multitude." At 1500 an order came down from brigade to send officers out to recce tank routes to the Kapelsche Veer.[34]

It was clear to Brigadier Jim Jefferson that taking the island was going to require a set-piece operation, slow and deliberate, and it was going to be a thoroughly nasty business. The revised plan was to push on the central German position from both sides – the Links from the left and the Argylls from the right – with SAR tanks supporting both units. Getting armoured vehicles onto the Veer was not going to be easy. The "Mad Whore's Dream" might be capable of supporting tanks but, as the Germans held the centre of the island, a raft would be needed to get them on the west end. An alert went out to 9 Field Squadron of the RCE and they began to assemble materials to build a Class 40 raft on the bank of a subsidiary canal about 450 feet directly south of the Oude Maasje channel.[35]

The first South Alberta tanks, two Stuarts commanded by Sergeant Vaughan Stevenson and Corporal Matthew McSherry, crossed the "Dream" at 1900 hours that evening. They had no problems but as soon as they climbed onto the dyke and moved forward they found that "there was not one good road to work on" and the slippery surface of the dyke was so narrow they could not turn around but "had to proceed in reverse all the way when we moved back."[36] Stevenson consolidated with the Argylls, who were under heavy mortar fire from the opposite bank of the Maas. For the next two days, until relieved by other crews, he and McSherry provided direct fire support, evacuated wounded and brought up ammunition and supplies to the forward positions.

A fine field of fire. View from the German position on the Kapelsche Veer looking east along the dyke over which the Argylls had to advance. The dyke tops offered the only firm footing for the Canadians but they provided excellent fields of fire for the defending German paratroopers. The Veer is now occupied by cows and they are welcome to it. PHOTOGRAPH BY DIANNE GRAVES.

The wireless code-name for the Royal Canadian Engineers is HOLDFAST. It is a good handle for these practical soldiers and at no other time did the sappers live up to it than on the night of 26/27 January when they constructed the raft at the Veer. They began to unload the heavy components – pontoons, piers, stringers and flooring – about midnight and then spent eight terrible hours assembling them:

The trap doors on the pontoons were all frozen tight and had to be chopped and prised open with picks. When this was accomplished it was found that the drain plug-holes were frozen solid with ice and mud. Most of the ice was chopped away with a bayonet, and that in the threads thawed out by inserting fingers in the hole. The next job was getting the piers joined. Since the canal was full of cracked ice from 2" to 5" thick it was extremely difficult to keep the square ends clear to hook them up. Incidentally the square ends were not square, as they were covered with lumps of ice and frozen mud, as were the connecting hooks. To add to the unpleasantness of the situation a German patrol sallied forth from the VEER and shot the site up for awhile before being driven back by the Lincoln and Welland Regt. Then a severe snow storm came along to impair even further the miserable working conditions. In spite of this by 0830 hours next morning [27 January] the raft was ready and a ramp constructed by a section of 3 Troop 9 Field [Squadron].[37]

What the author of this account does not say is that it was impossible to build that raft without some of the sappers standing waist deep in water just at the freezing point.

Waiting for the engineers to complete this onerous job was Lieutenant Kenny Little from A Squadron with three Shermans of his troop. At 0830 on 27 January the sappers waved him forward and Little's driver gently nosed down the ramp but:

Unfortunately, the tide had gone down and the approaches to the raft were impossible. Rubble, wood, anything was thrown down to allow the t[an]k to get on the raft. The feat was accomplished but in doing so, the raft buckled in the centre and settled on the bottom of the river. So with some difficulty, the Sherman was backed off and had to wait until the raft could be strengthened and the tide was higher.[38]

The sappers looked at the thing, scratched their heads, and reported that there would a long delay.

The Kapelsche Veer was not a good place to be that Saturday. Neither the Argylls nor the Links had much luck in closing in on the German position, which could only be approached along the dyke, the width of which restricted the number of men that could be used for an attack to platoon size – about twenty to twenty-five men – and German automatic weapons fire soon sent them to ground. What it amounted to was attacking over open ground in platoon strength against an entrenched and reinforced German company generously supplied with machine guns and with plentiful mortar fire on call from the north bank. All the weight of artillery and tactical air (when it was available) was useless; what was needed to get into the German position were flamethrowers or direct fire from tanks at close range. But all the Wasps had bogged down and, knowing the fate of the men who used them on the first day, nobody wanted to carry the heavy life-buoy flamethrowers. Tanks it would have to be but, as will be seen, the Kapelsche Veer was probably the worst ground in Europe on which to operate armoured vehicles.

The Links made three attempts to take RASPBERRY that

morning but the closest they could get was three hundred yards and their position was in danger of being cut off by Germans infiltrating along the north side of the dyke and coming in behind them. On the right the Argylls had farther to go but managed with the help of the Brownings of Stevenson and McSherry's Stuarts to get within a thousand yards of GRAPES before they too were pinned down. Unable to move in any direction the infantry huddled in shallow water-logged slit trenches they hastily scraped in the ground, cold, wet and hungry because it was difficult to get food up to them. It also proved almost impossible to recover the dead, and the corpses, clad in their white snow suits, lay scattered where they had fallen. The only succour for the men on that island was the occasional issue of SRD rum, which one remembered as "a very good stimulant for morale and health in this type of weather and operation."[39] Gordie Irving, who was on liaison duties with the Poles during Operation ELEPHANT, later asked an infantry officer what it was like on the Veer and never forgot the man's reply: "My men came to me and said they were cold and I gave them clothes, they said they were hungry and I tried to give them food, they told me they were scared and I told them we were all scared."[40]

The infantry suffered constant casualties from heavy and accurate German mortar fire. Frustrated, they called down artillery "stonks" using the FOOs from 15 Field who shared their forward positions with them. Tiger Bowick's A-3 Troop fired on the Veer throughout the day, at one point shooting HE for thirty minutes at the request of the Links. The Germans replied by mortaring Bowick's position and the crews were forced to close their hatches. By mid-afternoon three of Bowick's own crew were overcome by carbon monoxide fumes from the Homelite, which they had to keep running to keep their batteries charged, while all of his crews, having spent more than twenty-four hours in their unheated vehicles, were suffering from exposure. At 1700 hours, they were relieved in their tanks by Lieutenant Earle Johnston's A-4 Troop. The German mortaring never let up through the day and the gunners had a busy time as they attempted to locate and neutralize the German positions and break up persistent enemy attempts to cross the Maas and reinforce the garrison at the harbour. Towards evening, one FOO detachment on the Veer decided "that they had earned the bottle of rum" they had thoughtfully brought with them and someone was just reaching for it when a mortar bomb burst on the edge of their trench.[41] After "digging the dirt out of their eyes," the gunners discovered "that not only had the shell cut off the aerial [of their wireless], but it had neatly decapitated the bottle, which was now quite empty." Curses rang out.[42]

Conditions were no better for the Germans, who had to suffer heavier shelling and the attentions of a squadron of Spitfires which strafed the harbour area during the day. Canadian artillery frustrated numerous tries at reinforcing the garrison but some specialists from the engineer and anti-tank platoons of the 17th Parachute Regiment did succeed in crossing the Maas.

Their job was to assist the garrison against tank attack, because the Germans fully expected that the Canadians would use armour, and at 1430 hours the paratroopers on the Veer were warned to "check their anti-tank weapons."[43]

The tired sappers of 8 and 9 Field Squadrons, RCE, worked the entire day to repair the raft and improve the ramp to the launching site. They were hampered by the fact that the river level was low (the Maas is tidal at this point) and the weather so cold that ice kept forming on the bank. Four LVT (Landing Vehicle, Tracked) Buffaloes had to be kept in constant motion nearby to prevent it freezing solid as the sappers dragged the damaged end of the raft onto land, jacked it up and began mending the damage caused by Little's tank.[44] This chore was done by mid-day but work in the afternoon was interrupted by heavy mortar fire that kept driving the sappers to shelter. Nearby, the crews of Little's three Shermans waited patiently for the sappers to finish their hammering, including Trooper Bob Broberg, who dove for shelter under his tank when the mortar bombs began to land. Unfortunately, as he recalled, "my foot was sticking out and it got hit by shrapnel."[45] Bob's war was over.

Until the raft was finished, Ken Little was going nowhere. Concern over the need to get Shermans, with their 75 mm HE weapons, onto the Veer led to Lieutenant Wilf Kennedy being ordered at 1500 to take over two tanks from his A-2 Troop. Wilf was a good choice for this assignment because, unlike most South Albertas, he was no stranger to water, boats and islands, having served briefly as an officer in the RCN before becoming a diesel engineer on an ocean tug working out of Vancouver. Kennedy and his second tank, commanded by Corporal Sidney "Rizzy" Risdale, headed for the "Mad Whore's Dream." The "Dream" was nominally a Class 18 bridge (a structure able to support eighteen long tons of weight or 40,320 lb.) while, fully loaded for combat, a Sherman weighed nearly thirty-five short tons (70,000 lb.). Even worse, as Wilf's tank approached the "Dream," the engineers realized to their horror that the extra tracks welded on every available surface for additional protection increased its weight by several tons. On paper it was impossible for a Sherman to cross the "Dream" and onlookers probably closed their eyes as Wilf's driver, with his seatbelts unfastened for a quick exit, eased the tank onto the bridge, which went down under its weight – but held – and then slowly, very slowly, guided the tank across the narrow, icy span until it reached the other side. Risdale also got over without mishap and there were now Shermans on the Kapelsche Veer. "Their arrival," one Argyll officer remembered, "a considerable achievement in itself, gave the riflemen new heart."[46]

It took Kennedy some time to move along the treacherous dyke to the forward infantry position, where he picked up Lieutenant Alan Earp and a small detachment from the Argyll pioneer platoon. Wilf's job was to protect Earp and three of his men while they cleared the dyke of mines so that the infantry could advance the next morning. It was 2230 and quite dark when the combined group moved east and they immediately came under fire. Kennedy's tanks were unable to reply because his Sherman, which was in the lead, could not use its weapons for fear of hitting the mine-clearing party, while Risdale behind him could not bring any guns to bear. Earp and one of his men did their best "to cover the two [up ahead] with [the mine] detectors, with small-arms."[47] "Seeing this," he remembered, Kennedy let him fire "his .50 calibre [turret] Browning machine gun, which as a former recce officer, I knew how to use" and "we blazed away with this and were able to test a fair amount of track before having to withdraw … quite pleased with what we were able to accomplish."

The two tanks backed up slowly to the forward Argyll position, followed by Earp's men. When it appeared they were out of harm's way, Wilf "raised his hatch," Earp recalled, "thanked us for our help and made us a present of the Browning."[48] Unfortunately, as "he was standing in the turret taking down our names, he himself was hit and the tank withdrew." For Earp and his men, the "exhilaration of what had seemed a successful skirmish was quickly dissipated" but they "proudly bore the Browning on our jeep for the duration of the war." Wilf Kennedy, a 31-year-old native of Strawberry Hill, British Columbia, had been shot through the head but the wound was so clean that his crew were "at first doubtful as whether he was actually hit" or had simply fainted.[49] He was evacuated with great difficulty but died sixteen hours later.[50]

At about the same time that Earp and Kennedy were clearing the dyke on the right, the engineers managed to raft Ken Little's three tanks across on the left or western end of the Veer. Ken went first and his journey by raft in the dark under a fall of snow up a small canal and then into the Oude Maasje and across to the island, was an epic:

The weather was very cold and the ice flows began to freeze together, there being a solid mass across the water at the time. After a long struggle with the shifting tide and the monstrous ramp the tank was loaded. The far side of the canal [actually the Oude Maasje] 450' away could not be seen for the falling snow. The four petters [raft engines] roared at full throttle and the raft moved slowly away from the shore with an acre of ice pack frozen to it. All the crew chopped, pushed and pulled at the thick blocks of ice jammed between the frail pontoons and piling up around the propellers. Each time a L.V.T. passed it was hailed to come and circle the raft thus loosening up the pack. About 10 to 15 feet was gained each time. Then perhaps the tide would shift and loosen the pack and a few more feet would be gained, all the while the 4 petters roaring at top speed and the crew fighting the ice with boathooks and oars. Then an L.V.T ran into the raft in the darkness and snow and shifted one pontoon 3 feet under the raft and tank. Miraculously it held together though everyone had reconciled themselves to an icy grave. By turning the propellers alternately to the left and right a few more feet were gained against the ice now piling up

against the far bank. No one thought it even remotely possible to reach the far bank [the Kapelsche Veer] and unload the tank, it was just a matter of time before a pontoon would give in to the relentless pressure of the ice and sink the whole issue. Three hours from the far shore the raft was close enough so that a passing L.V.T could be hooked on, on the shore and the raft pulled up so the tank could be disembarked through 3 feet of packed ice. It wasn't possible, the crew nearly fainted. For once seeing was not believing.[51]

Having got Ken over, the sappers then took the raft back and brought over his other two tanks. With Shermans available on both flanks there was now hope that the business could be finished on the following day.[52]

At about 0900 hours, Sunday, 28 January 1945, the Argylls and the Links renewed the attack. On the left, Kenny Little led his three tanks east along the dyke but the temperature had risen and, instead of ice, thick glutinous mud now became the major obstacle to movement. When Little's second tank bogged badly, blocking the third vehicle behind it, Ken ordered them to remain where they were and support him with fire as he moved forward with the infantry against RASPBERRY. On the right, Lieutenant Ernie Hill, who had come up to replace Wilf Kennedy, advanced with his two Shermans and two Stuarts. As they inched their way forward along the treacherous dyke tops Little and Hill laid down heavy "speculative" fire on possible enemy positions. By 0940, Hill was almost at GRAPES but heavy automatic weapons fire and mortaring had driven the Argylls to ground behind him and he had no infantry support. As his ammunition was running low, he reluctantly backed up to where the infantry were taking cover, intending to resupply and start forward again. Ken Little had a similar experience; he came close to RASPBERRY but the infantry, which had been forced by German fire to take cover behind him, became disorganized when their officers were killed or wounded. Despite the heavy artillery fire brought down on the north bank of the river, German mortar bombs continued to fall thick and heavy along the dyke top. At this point the infantry's communications failed on both flanks and operations came to a halt in the late morning until the flat feet could get themselves organized.[53]

That done they started back up the dykes at about 1400 hours. On the right, the Argylls got a Wasp on top of the dyke and it moved forward but "there must have been some misunderstanding for instead of stopping at the inf[antry] pos[itio]n the driver speeded up and made for the objective at GRAPES."[54] Ernie Hill had been having trouble communicating with his other crews and the infantry by wireless and had left his tank to work on foot. Without hesitation his gunner, Trooper Albert Broadbent, assumed command of Hill's vehicles and immediately moved them up the dyke to provide covering fire for this brave but unplanned assault by the Wasp crew. The Wasp got stuck in the mud just short of GRAPES but managed to get off a few shots with its flamethrower – one onlooker reported with awe that "he had seen four Germans flamed in a slit trench," who, "after they had beaten out the flames, … continued to fight until they were killed."[55] A very stalwart bunch, these paratroopers, but the advancing Argylls managed to grab some prisoners and by late afternoon were in possession of GRAPES.[56]

Trooper Broadbent of A Squadron made this success possible and this was a surprise as nobody in his crew thought Albert capable of commanding a tank, let alone an *ad hoc* troop of four tanks engaged in one of the worst battles the Regiment had yet experienced. John Galipeau, a member of Broadbent's troop, knew the man as well as anybody:

> He was one of those people who never seem to be concerned about his appearance. He always looked rumpled even in a uniform which he appeared to have pressed with a waffle iron. He was quiet and was quite happy to remain in the background. Whereas some of the glamour boys would be surrounded with friends, Albert had only one or two that he palled around with. He was friends with everybody in the troop but not that talkative. He would voice an opinion in a group discussion but he was never argumentative. He carried out orders without complaint and did his job well but he never showed any signs of being a leader.[57]

Albert Broadbent became a leader on the Kapelsche Veer when he took over command of the tanks on the right after Ernie Hill was evacuated with frostbitten feet. There were more senior men in the troop but Broadbent's tank was in the lead and had the only working wireless.

Broadbent manoeuvred his tank into "position in a small bend in the dyke from where it could depress its guns sufficiently to rake the north slope of the dyke with m.g. fire."[58] That sector was held by a platoon of 17th German Parachute Regiment, about twenty-five strong, under the command of *Stabsfeldwebel* Heinrich Fischer. Fischer, a veteran of combat in Russia and Italy and "an old soldier who described himself as a fox," warned his men not to move or expose themselves.[59] Unfortunately, most of his paratroopers were "betrayed by their own carelessness" and attempted to shift some point during the day only to be "picked off one by one" by what Fischer described as "sniper accuracy." Broadbent was no stranger to this kind of shooting – it was the same as potting gophers with a .22 calibre rifle near his hometown of Leedale, Alberta – and hunting was in his blood for Albert Broadbent was a warrior of the Cree people. Albert did the spotting from his turret but most of the shooting was done by Trooper Slim Tillsley, another gunner and an artistic man who liked to decorate the white interior of his tank with cartoons when he had a spare moment.[60] At one point Fischer caught "a fleeting glimpse" of Broadbent "searching the ground with binoculars but the slightest attempt to leave a slit trench brought down an immediate burst of m.g.

fire."[61] The German estimated that Broadbent and Tilsley killed seventeen of his men and wounded five. Despite these losses, Fischer was so filled with "a soldier's admiration of a good job well done" that, at his prisoner of war interrogation, he felt compelled to single out for praise the unknown (to him) Canadian tank commander who had wiped out his platoon. This deadly fire kept the Germans down and permitted the Argylls to move along the dyke and get possession of GRAPES.

Ken Little had it harder on the left as he had only his own Sherman to support the Links' attack on RASPBERRY. He could see the tanks on the right working west along the dyke and it looked like this thing would shortly be over. With his help the Links had secured RASPBERRY by mid-afternoon but not very securely because the Germans kept popping up in the rear of the infantry from positions they had constructed in the dyke. This caused such confusion that, at 1600, the infantry fell back a few hundred yards to regroup, leaving Little by himself. He remained in his position, trying to support the Argylls whom he could see fighting around GRAPES but after an hour was forced to back down the dyke to re-ammunition. As his driver's vision to the rear was extremely limited, Ken opened his hatch to guide the man through this tricky manoeuvre and was killed instantly when a German sniper shot him in the head. Kenny Little, a 35-year-old bank clerk from Brooks, Alberta, had been one of the young men who had boarded the CPR train at Medicine Hat that warm evening in June 1940.[62]

By the late afternoon of 28 January the situation appeared to be good, if somewhat uncertain. The Argylls had GRAPES, although they were still having trouble clearing the area around the house, which was a rabbit warren of trenches and tunnels. On the left the Links had secured RASPBERRY but were having problems with German infiltration into their rear. They also had no tank support as, when Ken Little's crew had brought his body back to where the other tanks in the troop were stationed, they bogged in the mud blocking the dyke on the left to vehicle traffic.[63]

Major General Chris Vokes was anxious to finish the business. The three days of heavy fighting at the Kapelsche Veer, coming at a quiet time in the war after the German offensive in the Ardennes had ended but the Allied offensive against Germany had not yet begun, had attracted considerable media attention. When the name of the island began to crop up in the nightly *Wehrmacht* high command communiqués broadcast from Berlin as a shining example of the obstinacy of the German soldier defending his *Vaterland*, journalists rushed to 4th Division headquarters like crows flapping down on road kill. This attention was not welcomed by Vokes as he was involved in a slugging match over which he really had no control and there was little he could do except to urge subordinates to greater efforts.[64]

Vokes's tension became apparent when Lieutenant David Wiens, an intelligence officer with 4th Division, was called forward because the general wanted him to interrogate the prisoners captured that afternoon. When Wiens got up to the front, he found four Germans in the yard of a tavern where Vokes "had ordered them stripped to their shorts and had the guard pour pails of ice-cold water over them, apparently in an attempt to soften them up."[65] Wiens, an experienced interrogator, "could have told him, that procedure had proved counter-productive" when dealing with prisoners from elite units and, although the paratroopers "were near collapse, teeth chattering and bodies turning blue," they "were not talking."

Wiens decided to try a more subtle approach:

I don't know what Vokes expected of me but, against his objections, I had one of the prisoners brought inside, gave him a blanket and a shot of schnapps to warm him up and only then attempted to get him to talk. Some interrogation – with the General shouting questions and hurling curses at the man. Vokes was really in a rage at his attack being stalled for so long, and his impatience did not make my job any easier. It may have been the alcohol or my promise that the sooner he talked the sooner would his pals outside be allowed to get warm that broke his silence. Eventually I was able to get enough details on the strengths and locations of the German defences to satisfy the General. The prisoners were then given back their uniforms and taken back to the PW cage.[66]

Wiens was disgusted with Vokes's behaviour, not so much with his treatment of the prisoners because war is a tough business, but because of the man's lack of self-control.

That night the 17th German Parachute Regiment gave everyone an object lesson in toughness. Although the Links and the Argylls were on GRAPES and RASPBERRY, the Germans were still present in strength, hiding in their extensive network of tunnels. They waited until dark when the South Alberta tanks would be unable to provide accurate fire support and then, at 2200 hours, emerged, beside and behind the Canadian positions, to launch a vicious surprise counter-attack forcing the two units to withdraw a few hundred yards back down the dyke on their respective sides of the harbour. The hard-won gains of the day were lost and the paratroopers still owned the Veer.[67]

On the Veer. Sketch of the Kapelsche Veer, January 1945. This sketch by an officer of 15 Field shows the forward position of the Argylls and looks west toward RASPBERRY and GRAPES, the German strongpoints whose location is marked by a pile of rubble with smoke rising from it. In the background can be seen the little village of Capelle south of the Maas. Note the casualties scattered about and the tank (lower left corner) positioned well forward to support the infantry.

REPRODUCED FROM SPENCER'S *FIFTEEN CANADIAN FIELD REGIMENT* BY PERMISSION OF THE 15 FIELD, RCA.

During the bitterly cold night of 28 January, fresh crews from C Squadron relieved the A Squadron boys who had been fighting for the last forty-eight hours. Lieutenant Orlando Bodley replaced Lieutenant Earle Johnston's men at the direct fire support position, code-named ANNE, Lieutenant Ken Wigg's crews from C-4 Troop took over from Albert Broadbent's crews on the right, and Sergeant Duke Sands and fresh men took over the vehicles on the left. The two Stuart crews from Recce Troop were relieved at the same time. A similar process took place with the infantry companies and artillery FOOs on the island – it was impossible to keep men in the waterlogged, shallow trenches, exposed to constant shelling and sniping for more than twenty-four hours and, as it was, many had to be evacuated with frostbite.[68]

Corporal Jake Wiebe recalled how replacements were found for the crews on the island:

We were all sitting around and we heard that there were some tanks on the island. The sergeant-major came around and said: "We want four volunteers for a tank." I asked my crew but none of them were foolish enough to volunteer and I certainly didn't volunteer. The sergeant-major could have said, "You, you and you" but he did the right thing and said, "Boys, draw straws." I was unlucky and I drew a short straw and two of my crew drew short and, of course, this tank needed five men so they got two from another crew.[69]

Trooper Art Baker, one of Broadbent's men, was sent back along the dyke to guide the relief crews up to the tanks. Art was "half asleep and doddling along and they were yelling and hollering at me to get down and, all of a sudden, 'shewww, shewww' – there were sniper rounds going by my head and I got down fast."[70] When Wiebe got into the Sherman he was to take over, "there were four inches of ice inside it." His comment: "What a place to die."[71]

Trooper Ed Hyatt was in one of the crews that relieved Johnston's men at ANNE. A few minutes after they took over, Ed got a funny feeling:

We were standing at the back of the tank and we had the Homelite going to keep the batteries charged up and suddenly I said to the fellows "Duck" and we jumped into the canal and a mortar shell hit right where we had been standing. I don't know why I said "duck". Fortunately for us it was so cold that the canal was frozen and we didn't get wet.[72]

Dawn on 29 January revealed an island strewn with the "bodies of German and our own dead, wrecked vehicles, etc.," and to Ken Wigg it "looked like a 1914-1918 battlefield."[73] Trooper Joe Strathearn, a gunner in one of Duke Sands's crews had a similar reaction: "The thing I remember most were the bodies. We even ran over German and Canadian bodies, what can you do?"[74] At first light, German mortar fire from the north bank, which had been intermittent through the night, began to pick up in tempo. The Canadian artillery responded and the daily duel between the two banks of the Maas got under way again. The FOOs of 15 Field, who shared the wretched conditions on the dykes with the infantry, directed the fire and, conscious "of the desperate conditions in the forward areas," the 25-pdr. detachments, struggling in wet, muddy gun pits, "worked their hearts out striving to get accurate fire away at top speed."[75] Before the operation was over, 15 Field would fire 14,000 rounds, twice its original planned allotment; the other field and medium regiments, the 4.2 inch mortars and the

tank guns, of not only the South Albertas but also the British Columbia Regiment, expended a similar rate of ammunition.

It didn't seem to have had any effect when the attack on GRAPES and RASPBERRY was resumed at 0700 hours. German mortar fire and machine-gun fire was as heavy and accurate as ever and the infantry were soon forced to ground. By this time, the snow on the Veer had disappeared, churned and melted by the constant explosions, and the infantry realized that their white snow suits, far from providing camouflage, made them obvious targets against the grey-brown earth of the dyke tops. The attack got nowhere because on both flanks the South Albertas had trouble with the viscous mud. Duke Sands's tank, the only mobile Sherman of the three on the left, bogged as it moved forward and the Lincoln and Welland Regiment had no tank support. On the right, one of the Stuarts got badly stuck in a position that blocked all vehicle traffic behind Wigg's two Shermans. Ken tried five times without luck to push it and even fired HE at it to try and dislodge it – that Stuart would not budge. Orders went out for the sappers to bring a bulldozer over the "Dream" and construct a diversion around it, a difficult job that took them nearly eighteen hours to complete.[76]

In the late morning the attack on the right got going again. By 1245 the Argylls and Wigg's two tanks had taken GRAPES but were unable to move west to secure RASPBERRY due to the perpetual problem of German fire pinning the infantry down. The Links were unable to approach from the left because none of Sands's tanks were moving and the best he could do was to render long-range fire support. The good news was that a prisoner reported that there were only seventy paratroopers still

Recce Troop on the Veer. SAR Recce Troop Stuart tanks on the Kapelsche Veer. The vehicle in the background bogged badly and blocked the dyke top. It resisted all attempts to either move it or blow it up and, finally, the sappers were forced to spend eighteen hours to construct a diversion around it.
COURTESY, ARGYLL AND SUTHERLAND HIGHLANDERS.

alive and twenty of these were wounded. Not much happened during the rest of the day because the bogged tanks hampered operations on both flanks. By last light on 29 January the German-controlled part of the island had been compressed to the few hundred square yards around the wreckage of the house at RASPBERRY and the west side of the harbour. But the paratroopers were still obstinately resisting despite the fact that Bodley's four tanks had fired airburst directly over their heads all afternoon while two Crusaders, which had come up under the command of Jack Summers, had laced their positions with 20 mm Oerlikon fire. This was in addition to the fire from Wigg and Sands's tanks, the weapons of the infantry and such heavier artillery as could be brought down without hitting friendly troops. So ferocious and close was the volume of fire poured onto the German trenches that the Links complained their forward positions were being hit and hastily deployed recognition panels.[77]

That night was a busy one. On the right the engineers managed to finish the diversion around the Stuart while on the left a fourth Sherman under Sergeant William McKie was rafted over to join Sands. McKie was supposed to go forward and support a mine-clearing operation by the Links on the dyke but was unable to reach the island in time so Sands, who had managed to get his tank unstuck after hours of labour, went forward in his place. He had only moved a few feet when he again fell victim to the mud and, despite every effort, was unable to move. The Germans were also active and boats were seen crossing the Maas, either reinforcing or withdrawing the garrison on the island, which brought calls for artillery fire to prevent the movement. On the right Wigg's two crews made foot patrols from GRAPES towards RASPBERRY to recce the route they planned to use in the morning.[78]

At first light on 30 January Ken Wigg's two Shermans at GRAPES opened fire on the ruins of the house at RASPBERRY. A problem immediately became apparent – the Brownings of these tanks, which Wilf Kennedy had originally brought over to the island three days before, had fired so much that their barrels were worn smooth and they had neither range nor accuracy. Operations were delayed until new guns could be rushed over and it was not until 1115 that the Argylls began to move west along the one hundred yards of dyke that separated GRAPES from RASPBERRY, supported closely by Wigg's tanks and every weapon that could be brought to bear. Despite the terrific covering fire, the infantry were again forced to ground by German automatic weapons and, once they were stationary, mortared from the north bank of the river. The Argylls pulled back but gave it another try at 1500 – again they were beaten back and this time they had to leave some of their wounded. The paratroopers may have been tough soldiers but they fought a fair war – at 1530 they held their fire while stretcher parties went out under the Red Cross flag to pick up the men on the dyke. That done, everyone opened up again.[79]

In the late afternoon the Argylls made their third attempt to cross those one hundred terrible yards. By this time Bert Coffin had moved his scout car onto the island and was controlling the tank battle from the Argylls' command post on the Veer. Jake Wiebe remembered Bert coming up to his tank and saying, "Let's get this damn show over, take this place" and "then he buggered off – I would have done the same in his place."[80] Coffin reinforced Ken Wigg with two more Shermans, which made it over the shaky "Dream" and around the perilous diversion by the bogged Stuart and Ken had four tanks in column when the Argylls pushed west at 1630 hours. Progress was measured almost in inches and the German fire was heavy but Wigg's Shermans blanketed the entire area with HE and .30 calibre until the paratroopers called down smoke from the north bank which obscured the crews' vision. The Argylls got into RASPBERRY, which was "a mass of rubble," and "started to dig into the ruins for the tunnel that was known to be there."[81] They couldn't find it but threw demolition charges into every hole they could see.[82]

Now all that remained was to move along a short stretch of dyke to the west and join up with the Links' position. That battalion had been unable to take a direct part in the fighting of the day because three of Sands's four Shermans on their side of the island were stuck in the mud and the fourth could not get around them. As the infantry knew well by now, any attempt to move along the dyke without close tank support was doomed to failure so the final push would have to be made by the Argylls moving west from RASPBERRY. Sands's four tanks did what they could to support the Argylls with fire. Joe Strathern remembered

shooting off a lot of HE with our guns as low as they could go. … We couldn't get our guns low enough. There was no enemy artillery but the odd bazooka and lots of rifle fire. [Corporal] Walter [Fengler, the crew commander] couldn't stick his head out, he had the two flaps [of the turret hatch] open and there were bullets zinging off them.[83]

An Argyll platoon started out and immediately came under heavy mortar and machine-gun fire from the north bank of the Maas. Wigg opened fire across the river but "it was impossible to pinpoint the German positions."[84] The Argylls fell back to RASPBERRY and there was a delay while the tanks re-ammunitioned from a supply brought forward by the one mobile Stuart. At about 1800, just as the light was beginning to fail, another attempt was made with Corporal Nichol's Sherman going in front of the infantry while the other tanks covered him from their positions. Nichol stopped in front a large crater on the dyke and at that moment was hit by a *Panzerfaust*. The War Diarist recorded the fate of the crew:

This t[an]k was the only one in the Regt that was fitted with the new all-round vision cupola and because of this the turret cupola flaps were down [i.e. the turret was "buttoned up"]. When the projectile hit it wounded the co-driver Tpr LaPrade, L, M45749, and set his compartment on fire. The driver Tpr Noble G.W., M45582, was quick to grab an extinguisher and put the fire out. He leapt out of his driver's hatch to find that the [turret] crew were unable to lift [open] their hatch. He pulled it open allowing the boys to bail out and upon returning to the front of the t[an]k, found Tpr LaPrade struggling to get out of his compartment. He jumped up on the hull and started to pull LaPrade out when a burst of MG fire cut LaPrade's head off. Noble was also hit in the head, staggered and fell on the NORTH side of the dyke.[85]

Lloyd LaPrade was a 25-year-old labourer from Thorhild, Alberta, who had joined the South Albertas in Nanaimo in February 1941 and had previously been wounded at St. Lambert. George Noble was a 24-year-old farmer from Fallis, Alberta, who had joined the Regiment in June 1940.[86] "No further attempts," noted the War Diarist, "were made to go forward until the following day."[87]

Things were quieter that night. There was some concern that the Germans might use the knocked-out tank as a pillbox so Sergeant George Penney on the left, who had managed to get himself unstuck, moved his Sherman within sixty yards of it and stayed there, without infantry protection, throughout the hours of darkness, using his Brownings to beat off a couple of German attempts to enter the vehicle. The crews on the Veer remained on alert throughout the night, shivering in the unheated interiors of their tanks. In Cliff Allen's Sherman, conditions were made worse by the fact that for twenty-four hours all the crew "had to eat was boiled eggs and hard tack and this made quite an odour in the tank and everybody blamed everybody else."[88]

At first light on Wednesday, 31 January 1945, Lieutenant Bobby Crawford, who had brought up fresh crews to replace Ken Wigg's men, supported the Argylls as they moved the last few hundred yards and joined up with the Lincoln and Welland Regiment at 0800. There was no sign of the Germans except a few dazed prisoners and the occasional mortar bomb sent over from the north bank. Most of the garrison had been evacuated during the hours of darkness.[89]

Everybody realized it was over for sure when reporters were escorted onto the Veer to talk to real front-line soldiers. As the South Albertas knew, you had to be careful with the press because they were prone to sensationalize things. The best way to handle them was to be as reticent as possible – but to make sure they got your name and hometown right – lest they exaggerate some chance remark into a heroic feat that your buddies would never let you forget. Lieutenant Alan Earp was startled when he read the account of his mine-clearing operation with Wilf Kennedy which was published in the *Toronto Star*: "Earp was with three pioneers when the Germans opened fire. He reached

for his Sten but it jammed, so he pulled out a revolver. When it jammed also, he climbed into the nearest tank, got a machine gun and fired 1,000 rounds which finally dispersed the enemy."[90]

Troopers Cliff Allen and Elmer Stewart of the South Albertas got it just right. When a reporter questioned them about the fight, with "the tankmen boldly going on top of the dyke, silhouetted against the sky," to get possession of GRAPES they let an infantry sergeant do the initial running.[91] "A Jerry with a bazooka could have nailed them, but they came up here," the flat foot enthused, "they've been wonderful those guys in the tanks." By the time the reporter got around to Cliff, he didn't have to add much but only modestly ventured: "We sort of gave them a little help, I guess." Not that the boys didn't like some press attention. Jake Wiebe and his co-driver had their hatches open when a reporter approached them and talked to them for a few minutes. The turret crew, who had their hatch closed, were unaware of what was going on and when the drivers' picture later appeared in the papers, they were annoyed with Jake for not alerting them to the photo opportunity.[92]

The remainder of the day was spent, the War Diarist recorded, "in removing the dead from the positions" and adding, somewhat sardonically, that, although the "cold and exposure had very bad effects upon the infantry," the "freezing of the dead was beneficial in the removal of them."[93] It was a grim business; Private Donald Stark of the Argylls remembered "stacking the fellows – the dead – in the panel truck, like they were pieces of wood ...... you looked at it and you just walked away."[94] George Noble's body was recovered from the base of the dyke where he had fallen and taken back and buried with the other SAR fatal casualties after a service conducted by Padre Silcox.

Casualties had been heavy on both sides. When brigade asked for a German body count, "the estimated figure submitted by all units concerned was some 150" but this was later revised downward to 64 paratroopers killed and wounded, and 34 taken prisoner, although some of the German wounded had been earlier evacuated.[95] Plocher, the commander of the 6th Parachute Division, later estimated that "to hold this isolated bridge-head" from mid-December to 31 January "cost him between 300 to 400 serious casualties, while another 100 men suffered severely from second-degree frost bite."[96] On the Canadian side, the Lincoln and Welland Regiment lost 39 officers and men killed and 35 wounded; the Argylls lost 15 dead and 35 wounded and the Regiment 4 dead and 5 wounded for a brigade total of 133 casualties. When this figure is added to the 231 casualties incurred by the Poles and Royal Marines in previous attempts to take the Veer, the total cost to get possession of what the Canadian Army historian, waxing lyrical, called "a little patch of ground that hath in it no profit but the name," came to 364 killed or wounded.[97]

General Harry Crerar, the commander of First Canadian Army, complimented "all ranks on a difficult task well done" but nobody was in the mood for cheering.[98] Jim Jefferson submitted a post-battle report which stated that the initial assault had no chance of taking the Germans by surprise, the extravagant use of smoke was almost useless, and the operation should have been "conducted at a very slow pace" with tank support from the outset.[99] Vokes was forced to agree with these criticisms of his own plan but defended the use of the ill-fated waterborne force, which he felt would have succeeded if the wind had not shifted the smoke screen, a full moon had not made the preparations visible to the Germans, and there had not been "severe icing conditions."[100] Since all of these factors were observable and thus predictable before the initial assault went in, the Lincoln and Welland historian has the matter entirely right when he concludes that

> the tactics of the first day were the result of some very serious misconceptions which developed from an increasingly urgent need to capture a stubborn German stronghold of questionable military value. The results were tragic: the initial tactics employed were inappropriately based on surprise and speed, rather the less spectacular, though tested principles which eventually led to the island's capture after five long days.[101]

The Links took a long time to recover from the Veer. As Major Jim Swayze, their commanding officer at the time, commented, "It was a turning point in that we had so many casualties. It was a different Regiment afterwards."[102]

Vokes's handling of the operation caused bad feelings in 4th Armoured Division. His quartermaster, Lieutenant Colonel John Proctor, who had faithfully served three previous commanders, was so disgusted that he went to Simonds and asked for a transfer to get away from Vokes, saying "I have backed him up but I can't serve him any more."[103] Proctor was transferred and promoted. Jim Jefferson was also very upset – Swatty Wotherspoon remembered that after the Veer the brigade commander always tried to keep his headquarters as far away from Vokes as possible and often pitched tents beside Swatty's own RHQ, which "was a bloody nuisance, I can tell you."[104]

At the lower levels, the reasons for Operation ELEPHANT remained a mystery. Gordie Irving recalled that the "way we understood it is that someone said that we want everything clear to the other side of the Maas River and those guys are on this side

and we want them out."[105] "Tactically," he concluded, "it didn't mean a thing to spend all that manpower." Like most of 10 Brigade, the South Albertas were puzzled as to why so many had to die for such a useless piece of real estate. "If only we had the wisdom of our generals," Jake Wiebe remembers the boys saying at that time, "if only we had the wisdom of our generals."[106]

When the fighting was finished, Captain Dick Robinson had a problem. As Technical Adjutant of the Regiment, he was responsible for removing the tanks on the Veer, which, as the War Diarist noted, included "a total of 8 Shermans and 2 Stuarts of which 3 Shermans on the left are badly bogged, on the right 1 Sherman bazookaed, 3 Shermans unable to use the road back for fear of bogging and 1 Stuart stuck."[107] It took Robinson three days, using all available ARVs and fitters, to get the lighter Stuarts clear, freeing the way for the three mobile Shermans on the right to return to the mainland but he had absolutely no luck with the four Shermans on the left and the knocked-out vehicle at RASPBERRY which appeared likely to become permanent war memorials. At this point Dick had an inspiration and asked for permission to write off the five vehicles to 1st Polish Division, who now had responsibility for the Veer. Much to his relief and that of his tired fitters, it was received and the bogged tanks became a Polish problem. Nobody knows how long it took them to get those Shermans off the island but they were not there when a party from the Regiment passed that way six months later.

The next three weeks after the Veer were relatively quiet. The Regiment moved back to the Kaatsheuvel area and resumed shooting across the Maas and the crews involved in this work received special training from the gunners on ways of including meteorological calculations in their target calculations. The Germans responded with V-1 buzz bombs, many buzz bombs, which flew overhead on their way to Antwerp – on one day alone in February Trooper Joe Strathern counted fourteen coming across the Maas. All in all, things were pretty low key, so low key that the boys in B Squadron got bored and began to fish in the local waterways with hand grenades. It was just as well perhaps that the Regiment received a shipment of track extenders, gadgets which widened the area of the tank tracks giving them better grip in muddy con-

The face of the Kapelsche Veer. "I was that which others did not want to be, I went where others failed to go, and did what others failed to do ...... I am a soldier." Private Carl Montage, C Company, Argyll & Sutherland Highlanders of Canada (Princess Louise's), on 31 January 1945, the day it ended. COURTESY, ARGYLL AND SUTHERLAND HIGHLANDERS.

ditions. These were difficult items to fit and the work kept the crews out of mischief for a few days. When it came to new equipment, however, the Poles did better as they received an entire complement of new Shermans equipped with the high-velocity 76 mm gun. On 15 February Trooper John Neff went over to Dongen with some friends from B Squadron to look at these new vehicles and complained in his diary that the SAR had to "do all its work with old tanks."[108]

Sports were a big item in February 1945. C Squadron set up a handball court in Sprang, an activity "that the local inhabitants found curious," and the Regimental hockey team began to clean up. As always, the Regiment's main athletic endeavour centred on the boxing ring (and the wagering that accompanied it) – in fact it might fairly be said that, to the South Albertas, winning the war was really secondary to winning the Canadian Army boxing championships. Bert Coffin had taken care during his frequent trips back to the reinforcement holding units to recruit any good fighting talent he could find, while over the winter RSM Jock Mackenzie had engaged professional Dutch boxers to coach the SAR fighters. These efforts paid off – the Regiment had no problem winning the 10 Brigade Championship on 19 January, and at the divisional finals, held on 21 February, South Alberta fighters won no fewer than four of the five classes in which they competed. Corporal Johnnie Knox secured the lightweight title, Corporal Sammy Samuels won the welterweight and, for the second year in a row, Trooper Joe Main left the ring with the heavyweight title. There were smiles and fat wallets all round the Regiment when the last bout finished that night.[109]

It was good to have a bulging wallet in February 1945 because the SAR began to receive its allotment of leaves to Paris. On 17 February Major Arnold Lavoie took a large party to the "city of lights" for a seven-day leave, which because of transportation problems, ended up being fourteen days. John Neff was one of the lucky ones and his diary contains only the brief comment: "Paris and how???"[110] Lieutenants Tiger Bowick and Bill Luton got a forty-eight to Brussels but ran afoul of a mixture of Dutch Kummel liqueur

and cheap Belgian champagne that resulted in Bill making intimate contact with the "avocado-green carpet" on the stairs of the Atlanta Hotel, the Canadian officers' leave centre in Brussels.[111] Many senior officers were absent on less onerous tasks: Swatty was still commanding the divisional battle school and Darby Nash was instructing in England while Captains Stewart, Summers and Mackenzie were also there taking courses. One old familiar face showed up at this time. Glen McDougall, now a major, managed in October 1944 to shake himself free from the Three Rivers Regiment of the Italian "Spaghetti League" and get to northwest Europe. Bert Coffin rescued him from the reinforcement machinery and brought him back to the Regiment but there were no positions for squadron leaders available so Glen "hung around and around and, eventually, got ordered to sit on a court martial board" that occupied him until February when he took over A Squadron in Lavoie's absence.[112]

Dances were always a popular activity and on 7 February C Squadron held a frolic that entered Regimental legend. It was organized by Lieutenants Bill Luton and Pete Burger who were charged with this duty because, in the SAR as in any good military unit, junior officers were given a multitude of diverse tasks – actually more tasks than they could properly handle – to

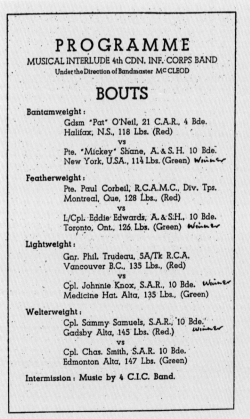
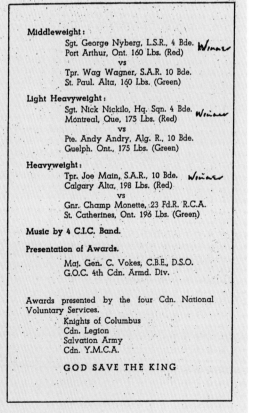

Programme from 4th Armoured Division Boxing Championships, 21 February 1945. Five days before they went into the Hochwald battle, the SAR boxing team triumphed at the divisional championships. Of the fourteen fighters on the programme, five are from the South Alberta Regiment and the boys won four of their fights, including the heavyweight title. To the South Albertas, winning the Canadian Army boxing championships was an objective almost as important as winning the war.

teach them responsibility, make them more flexible, keep them out of mischief, and because no officer more senior wanted these jobs. Burger and Luton, being young and keen, tackled the organization of the squadron dance with enthusiasm. The first problem was to find musicians but Bill rounded up a Dutch band called "The Hawaiians" and although "a hula in wooden shoes seemed improbable … there they were."[113] He was proud of this accomplishment until the boys in C Squadron complained that they "did not want to spend the whole evening listening to the strumming of guitars" so he "set out on another search for music, and located a band who claimed they could swing like Benny Goodman." Bill now had "two bands, and only enough cigarettes to pay for one" so he decided to "unhook" the "Hawaiians" despite the fact that this almost caused an "international incident."

For his part, Pete Burger found a suitable hall in Kaatsheuvel and then the two officers worked on their major problem – rounding up female "talent" to dance with the boys. They decided to enlist the help of a local matron who agreed to invite young Dutch lovelies to the affair on one condition: that "only girls of *good character* would be allowed and she would be the arbiter."[114] Being innocents in such matters both officers agreed to what appeared an eminently sensible arrangement and all seemed well until the night of the dance when Bill and Pete "posted ourselves at the door with our hostess to see that only *approved* girls were admitted." "Right off the bat," Bill remembered, they had problems because some of the men brought dates who "did not meet the standards of our judge" and there were "loud protests" from the other boys who claimed "that the girls who were being admitted were all 'Sunday School' types and no fun at all." Thankfully, the author of this history does not have to expound on the difference between a "fun" girl and a "Sunday School type" as the South Albertas appear to have had their own methods of ascertaining what seems to have been a crucial distinction. In any case, as Bill related, the problem

In spring a young man's fancy. Just after the Veer battle, the SAR received its first allotment of leaves to Paris. Here Troopers John Neff (left) and George Povey relax at a sidewalk cafe after a busy day spent, no doubt, diligently touring the city's cultural attractions. In his diary for the period covering his leave in the "city of lights," Neff wrote simply: "Paris and how???" COURTESY, JOHN NEFF.

was got around "with the help of Dutch beer from the pub and cognac brought in from Belgium" and "a good time was had by all."

Well, not quite all because, midway into the evening, Chief Whitford cut loose. What happened that night has grown in the telling over the years and there are some who claim that the chief actually ascended to a balcony, drew his 9 mm Browning, and shot out the rotating reflecting ball on the ceiling of the hall, sending Dutch girls of both types screaming for the exits. Bill Luton's memory of the incident is more modest; he only states that Whitford "got into an argument with the Dutch bar tender and proceeded to get in behind the bar and bust things up."[115] The two lieutenants "asked a couple of men to take care of the Chief" as, if officers got officially involved, "it could become serious, and, moreover, Kaatsheuvel was home to R.H.Q." and any commotion would be sure to cause trouble in high places. To the relief of Luton and Burger, "Johnny Hughes, a tough little scrapper, went in and brought the much bigger Whitford out quietly."

It was perhaps just as well that the Regiment soon went back into action as these quiet periods could be stressful. As usual the Poles, who seemed to have some special intelligence source, were the first to know. On 18 February the War Diarist noted that there were many rumours "about us moving" which "seem to have been started by the Poles" who came into SAR's area "looking for good billets."[116] Nobody believed these rumours because it was felt that the Polish Division would go into action first as it was "equipped with new Shermans while we still have many of our old originals." Guess again – the next day orders came down to prepare for a move and on 19 February the Regiment said goodbye to the Maas and concentrated at Best. Here, the crews spent two days "thoroughly checking their vehicles and armament" and getting ready for a "big show." At a 10 Brigade O Group held on 21 February Bert Coffin found out what that show was about – it seems there was a job to be done in Germany at some place called the Hochwald.

PART VII

WINNING

Setting out. Photographed near Louisendorf on the morning of 26 February 1945, the South Albertas, with the Algonquins on their decks, move up to their start line for the attack on the Hochwald Gap.

NAC, PA113907.

CHAPTER SIXTEEN

"Through the mud
and the blood."

HOLLAND AND GERMANY: 21 FEBRUARY–2 MARCH 1945

The Hochwald was part of the last German defensive position before the Rhine. In early December 1944 Montgomery's 21 Army Group had been given the task of destroying the enemy defences between that river and the Maas preparatory to an assault against central Germany. Montgomery had assigned the job to Crerar's First Canadian Army and Dempsey's Second British Army, which immediately began to plan for the attack, but Hitler's offensive in the Ardennes threw the Allied timetable off and it was not until late January that preparations were resumed. To clear the west bank of the Rhine, Montgomery wanted two separate but converging attacks: First Canadian Army, with two British corps under command, would launch Operation VERITABLE and drive southeast to the German city of Xanten on the Rhine, while Ninth American Army would carry out Operation GRENADE and drive northeast to the same objective. The planning for VERITABLE was based on the assumption that the ground would be frozen and passable for vehicles and tanks, but unfortunately the weather warmed up in early February and the ground in the low-lying area over which First Canadian Army had to operate became a sea of mud which was quickly rendered almost impassable by the thousands of vehicles. Worse still, the Germans, who had three months to get ready, had prepared three fortified belts – the last of these was the Hochwald "Layback" or reserve position, sited on high ground a few miles west of the Rhine.[2]

The strength of the German defences became apparent when Crerar launched VERITABLE on 8 February 1945. The initial assault was made by the British 30 Corps and it went in after the heaviest preliminary bombardment of the war. Four hundred aircraft from Bomber Command hit the German cities of Goch and Cleve in the first stage and then, over a five-hour period, more than one thousand artillery pieces, ranging from 40 mm Bofors guns to 8-inch howitzers, dumped 160,000 shells on the German positions. This weight of fire flattened the enemy defences, dazed the defenders and turned the ground, already soft and muddy, into pudding. Progress was good at

> *A* casual drive through the Hochwald,
> A shoot by the light of the moon,
> Watching for 88 airburst, hearing those mortars croon.
> This is a lovely way to spend an evening,
> Can't think of anything I'd rather not do.[1]

first but German resistance gradually stiffened and it took two weeks of tough fighting to clear the first two defensive belts of a stubbornly-resisting enemy. The Canadian and British troops driving from the north did not get any help from the Americans to the south as the flooding of the Roer Valley had forced Ninth US Army to postpone GRENADE. By 21 February 1945, however, First Canadian Army was closing on the Hochwald Layback, and it was decided that a new operation was necessary to break through to the Rhine.

Code-named BLOCKBUSTER, it was to be carried out by Guy Simonds's 2nd Canadian Corps. Simonds would have five divisions (2nd and 3rd Canadian Infantry, 4th Canadian Armoured, 11th British Armoured and 43rd British Infantry) under command. His plan called for an initial attack by his infantry divisions to seize the high ground west of the Hochwald around the German towns of Calcar and Uedem to serve as a launching pad for the next phase of the operation – the breakthrough of the Hochwald position itself – to be carried out by the two armoured divisions. BLOCKBUSTER was scheduled to begin on 26 February 1945.[3]

Bert Coffin learned some details about the business at a 10 Brigade O Group on 21 February. In the middle of the discussion, the brigade major returned from divisional headquarters with information on the approach march that would have to made from Best into Germany – he commented that "it was quite the worst [march] we had ever been asked to do, and that … nobody knew where we would eventually concentrate" – a statement that turned out to be entirely accurate.[4]

At 0015 hours on 22 February 1945, "a beautiful night, with a moon bright enough to allow us to drive without lights," the Regiment moved out of Best in a long convoy headed for who-knows-where but somewhere in Germany.[5] At Nijmegen the wheels and tracks separated, the wheels taking a corduroy road of logs laid by the sappers and the tracks a winding route over steep hills and low valleys "with mud almost two inches deep,

266

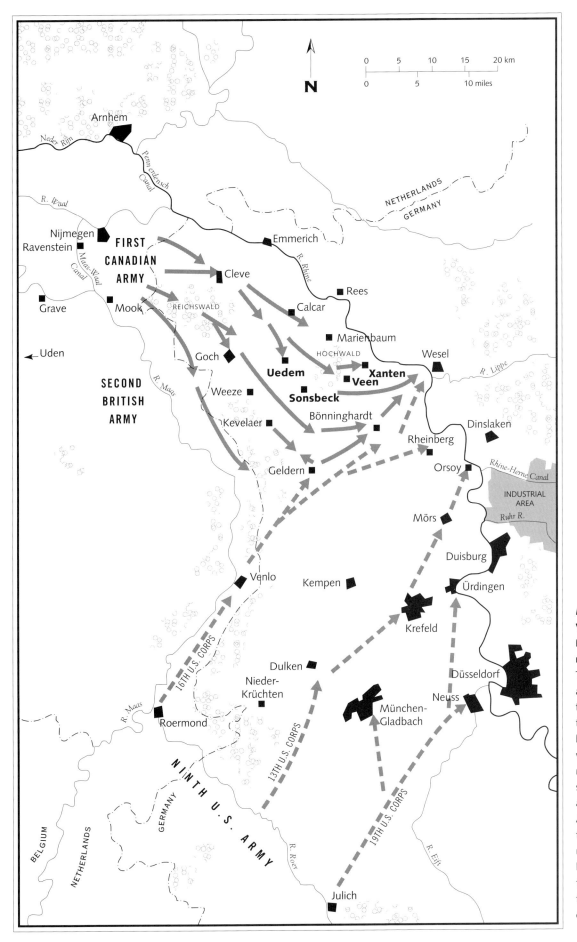

N

0   5   10   15   20 km

0   5   10 miles

Arnhem

Neder Rijn

Pannerdensch Canal

R. Waal

NETHERLANDS

GERMANY

Nijmegen

Ravenstein

FIRST CANADIAN ARMY

Emmerich

R. Rhine

Cleve

Rees

Grave

Maas-Waal Canal

Mook

REICHSWALD

Calcar

Marienbaum

HOCHWALD

Wesel

R. Lippe

Uden

SECOND BRITISH ARMY

R. Maas

Goch

Uedem

Xanten

Veen

Sonsbeck

Weeze

Bönninghardt

Dinslaken

Kevelaer

Rheinberg

Orsoy

Rhine-Herne Canal

Geldern

INDUSTRIAL AREA

Mörs

Ruhr R.

Duisburg

Venlo

Kempen

Ürdingen

16TH U.S. CORPS

Krefeld

Dulken

Düsseldorf

Nieder-Krüchten

Neuss

13TH U.S. CORPS

R. Maas

Roermond

München-Gladbach

NINTH U.S. ARMY

BELGIUM

NETHERLANDS

GERMANY

R. Roer

19TH U.S. CORPS

R. Erft

Julich

Map 15: Operations VERITABLE and BLOCKBUSTER, February-March 1945. Three Allied armies attempted to clear the last German positions on the west bank of the Rhine – while Ninth US Army moved from the south, First Canadian and Second British Armies attacked from the north. It took nearly five weeks of heavy and bloody fighting to break through the German defences.

with lots of loose rocks in it that cracked and jarred around the tracks and bogies."[6] Part of the tracks' route lay along a railway and the rough ride knocked off many of the new track extenders. During the night the Regiment crossed the German border and one trooper remembered feeling a "strange sense of unease" as the South Albertas were no longer "liberators, we had become the conquerors, a very different role, physically and psychologically."[7] This unease was not helped by a sign at the border which read: "STOP SMILING. YOU ARE NOW ENTERING GERMANY." The journey was long and tedious with many delays occasioned by heavy traffic and wrong turns and it was a thankful Regiment that finally arrived at a harbour in a muddy field near the hamlet of Hau, close to Cleve, late in the morning of 22 February. The area was "crammed with t[roo]ps, t[an]ks and guns," noted the War Diarist. "Many friends were near us and we really felt like we were feuding again."[8]

When the crews had finished maintenance they began to explore the area and it quickly became apparent, as the *Short History* commented, "One thing that was available was meat on the hoof."[9] In contrast to Holland this rural part of the enemy's country seemed to have no shortage of food whatsoever and the boys quickly began to round up the livestock. "This is not according to the rules," commented the War Diarist,

but in some cases it was a question of whether we or someone else had them. RHQ T[roo]p has a herd of 3 cows which they milk faithfully. The fitters have a couple of hens tied by the legs to a bail of straw. Obviously we are back to the country life again. All this is very well but Maj Coffin did object to the carcasses of many a beef hanging from the 17 Pr's. Besides b[riga]de called up to ask who was in a Sc[out] C[ar] that had a pig on the back of it and who had driven into our RHQ. It was revealed that the culprit was the RSM with our dinner.[10]

This new diet proved too rich and the MO, Captain Jock Maloney, had to treat so much dysentery that he noted in his medical report that "while it is admitted that in terms of tons of explosives dropped on German soil during this month the RAF holds the record" it was "the firm belief of this unit that in tons of 'other material' the SAR came second to none."[11]

The German farmhouses also contained other things, including top hats, part of the farmer's formal wear for weddings and funerals. By and large Canadians are not an outwardly demonstrative people (when you live next door to the Yanks, modesty becomes a positive virtue) and lack a readily apparent national characteristic except one – Canadians have a fatal weakness for outlandish headgear. It was not long before top hats appeared in the Regiment and Glen McDougall insists to this day that he saw a South Alberta crew commander "courteously tipping his top hat to General Crerar or somebody like that as he drove past in his tank."[12] Hats, livestock and any other

useful, or potentially useful, items were stowed away on the tanks and the South Alberta Regiment on the march began to resemble nothing so much as a gypsy clan using rather large and clumsy transport. Newsreel footage from February 1945 shows a tank from the Regiment driving by with every available space on its hull, deck and turret covered with a fantastic variety of items including what appears to be a rocking chair tied to the rear deck. The weapons, however, were always kept clear of impediments.[13]

The day that the South Albertas arrived at Hau, Bert Coffin attended another O Group at brigade to get the final details for the Regiment's role in the forthcoming operation. He didn't like what he heard. Simonds's plan (which was never committed to paper) called for 4 Armoured Brigade with the Links and Argylls under command to seize the ridge from Calcar in the north to Uedem in the south on 26 February while at the same time 3rd Division would take Uedem and 2nd Division the northern part of the Hochwald Ridge. The following day, 11th British Armoured Division would attack the southernmost extension of that ridge while 10 Brigade (actually the Regiment and Algonquins with attached troops of flails, M-10s, Avres and Crocodiles) would seize the Hochwald Gap.

This feature has been described by a South Alberta officer who was to take a prominent part in the coming battle:

Beyond the Calcar-Uedem ridge lay a wide valley, on the far side of which rose another line of hills, even higher. On these heights were two substantial woods, the Hochwald (literally "high forest") and the Balbergerwald, separated by a narrow opening about three hundred yards wide and a mile long – the famous "Hochwald Gap." Approaching from the west, the open country rising from the valley was funnelled into this gap by the two forests. About a third of the way along was Point 72.6 [metres], a hill that marked the height of land and which had the code name "Albatross." From it the land sloped down toward the eastern end of the gap, roughly defined by a dirt track, which was a small section of a long road code-named "Mack"[14]

To get to that objective, LION Force (the SAR and Algonquins) would have to cross a boggy, flooded valley and fight their way through successive German defence lines in a nighttime dash. On their left front would be the line of the German-held Hochwald Forest while on their right flank would be a raised railway embankment, also German-held, which offered ideal defensive positions. The good news was that the attack would go in at night to provide cover. The bad news was almost overwhelming: the "going" maps distributed showed the valley floor marked as "impassable to tanks," searchlights would provide "artificial moonlight," AA guns would fire tracer on fixed lines to indicate direction and there would be a short but intensive artillery barrage. As one SAR officer summed it up, the Regiment would have to advance across impassable ground with an "artillery barrage to alert the enemy when we were setting out, tracer shells to show where we were going, and light to expose us on the move. Why the hell didn't they drop announcements to the Germans and sell tickets?"[15]

The most controversial part of the plan, itself controversial enough, was a proposed "right hook" by A Squadron and the Algonquin carrier platoon. While the main attack went in on the Gap they were to move south, skirt Uedem and cross the railway at a point where it emerged from a cutting to become an embankment. They would then advance and seize the southern end of the gap

A hard nut to crack. Uedem in the Hochwald area. This town, well fortified and defended by paratroopers, proved to be a very tough nut for 3rd Infantry Division on 26 February 1945. The defenders were still holding out when the SAR began their advance against the Hochwald the following day. SAR COLLECTION.

while the main force took the northern end. Neither Bert Coffin nor Bob Bradburn of the Algonquins liked the sound of this "right hook" at all – it was entirely too risky, the forces committed were too weak and success would depend on a number of variables that were beyond the control of the Regiment. They formally protested to Jefferson that it be dropped but were told to carry it out.[16]

The really bad news, which was not known to the South Albertas at the time, was what was waiting for them. They were about to run into some old acquaintances. Overall responsibility for the defence of the Hochwald was vested in General Heinrich von Lüttwitz's 47 Panzer Corps with the 6th Parachute and 116th Panzer Divisions under command. Lüttwitz was an experienced commander who had caused trouble for the SAR at St. Lambert and his two divisions could be expected to put up a tough fight, as 116th Panzer was a veteran formation while 6th Parachute Division had proved ferocious opponents at the Kapelsche Veer. Three weeks of hard fighting had ground the 116th Panzer Division's strength down but it still possessed between fifteen and thirty battleworthy tanks, which were fleshed out by about fifteen SPGs of the 655th Heavy Anti-Tank Battalion and the static weapons of a fortress anti-tank battalion. As if that was not bad enough, the German defences also included fifty 88 mm guns which had been stripped from local AA defences and, just to add additional complications, the defenders were supported by plentiful artillery – 717 mortars, 1,054 guns and 54 *Nebelwerfer* projectors according to First Canadian Army intelligence sources. The Germans were expecting the Canadian attack. Plocher of the 6th Parachute "could always estimate, exactly when the [Allied assault] would

begin and when it would end" because "once an attack had been halted he would be given at least three days rest to bring in his reserves and new weapons."[17] Hitler had ordered his commanders on the west bank of the Rhine to fight for every foot of ground as he was desperate to keep the Allies away from the river, not only because it was his last and best natural defence in the west but because, with the Allied air forces' destruction of the German rail system, it provided the only method of moving coal and steel out of the industrial Ruhr.[18]

Nobody liked this thing. A small force of one infantry battalion and one armoured regiment was to attack without surprise across bad ground for tanks against veteran German units with considerable tank and artillery support, positioned on three sides of the route of the advance and determined to defend their homeland. It all sounded like a prescription for disaster and there was a feeling of unease in the Regiment when the details became available because everyone realized that this one would not be easy. In the three days before the operation, Bert Coffin and Bob Bradburn of the Algonquins made every possible preparation, including the construction of a sand table model by the intelligence officers of both regiments. This was used to brief everyone down to the level of the crew commanders at a large O Group held in the late afternoon of 25 February.[19]

When Lieutenant Bobby Crawford of A Squadron returned to his troop after that O Group, Trooper Ed Thorn scanned his face carefully when he asked the question, "What's it look like, Bob."[20] Crawford replied, "I think maybe we're okay, the map indicates a railway track … and we should be able to get down that and get around to where we want to go." But, for the first time, Thorn "felt something bad." Lieutenant Bill Luton

269

Anti-tank ditches in the Uedem area. These obstacles further limited the movement of the Regiment's tanks when it tried to take the Hochwald Gap. NAC, PA 145740.

on its start line in time and by 2230 hours reported it had secured the high ground north of Uedem in the face of stubborn German resistance. Third Division's attack against Uedem was delayed until their supporting armour had finished other tasks and their attack against that town did not go in until 2100 hours. Uedem was defended by paratroopers who put up a stiff fight that lasted all night but by morning 3rd Division reported that only snipers were left in the town. The way was now clear for the third phase of the operation – the attack on the Gap by the SAR and Algonquins, and the ridge to the south by 11th British Armoured Division.[24]

With the Algonquins on their back decks, the South Albertas had moved out of Hau at 0800 hours on 26 February to be ready to put in the attack scheduled for that night. Recce parties had marked the route but progress became difficult as the tanks and wheeled vehicles tried to get through thick mud with the consistency of prairie gumbo and a depth of three feet churned up by the traffic of three divisions. The Regiment spent nearly the entire day trying to move a distance of less than five miles and one South Alberta officer remembered that march as

remembered that each squadron was ordered to leave one troop out of battle, which, to him, was a "sobering thought" as it "seemed like someone in the command chain smelled a possible wipe out."[21] There was concern that so many of the veteran officers in the Regiment were absent: Swatty was still at the divisional battle school, Arnold Lavoie of A was on leave, Darby Nash of B was instructing on a course, while Dave Currie had left C Squadron and his replacement, Major Stan Purdy, would be taking it into action for the first time. Even the perpetually cheerful War Diarist expressed concern about doing a "night attack over such bad ground that a day show would be bound to fail."[22] BLOCKBUSTER looked so bad that darkness appeared to be about the only thing the Regiment had going for it. The War Diarist added, a trifle more optimistically, that, despite attacking across ground that "seems to have been chosen for its poor tank going," the South Albertas could probably get onto the objective, "provided it is done at night."[23]

a jumbled confusion of stops and starts, of moving ever closer to the sound of battle, and of an overriding sense of foreboding. All soldiers know that waiting beforehand is worse than fighting itself, but this day was unusually so for me, perhaps because the wait was so long, more likely because the battle going on could so clearly be heard, and sometimes even seen. I had an eerie feeling that we were slowly, but inevitably, moving towards doomsday.[25]

BLOCKBUSTER kicked off at 0430 hours, 26 February 1945. On the left the 2nd Infantry Division fought off a German armoured counterattack before attacking and securing the northern end of the Hochwald ridge. At midday 3rd and 4th Divisions moved to take Uedem and the high ground between Goch and Calcar. TIGER Force, the 4th Armoured Division's component of this attack, had spent nearly eight hours trying to get forward through the thick, heavy mud of the area, which was made worse by a steady drizzle of rain. Nonetheless it got

Wherever they were going it took the whole day to get there through the mud and heavy vehicle traffic. The new track extenders turned out to be a blessing for those tanks equipped with them, but by early afternoon twelve Shermans, all the Stuarts and many of the wheeled vehicles had become hopelessly bogged and the ARVs were hard at work trying to get them clear. Finally, at 1945 hours, after nearly twelve hours of this hellish odyssey, Coffin and Bradburn decided to concentrate in an area near the village of Keppeln, preparatory to making the final move to the start line for the attack. By this time, night had set in, "dark and rainy," and every road in the area was blocked with "a perfect welter of vehicles, nose to tail, inching their way by fits and starts towards the shell-illuminated horizon to the south-east."[26] This pause allowed the ARV crews to catch up and most of the tanks left behind were able to come up with the column.[27]

But there was still nearly a mile to go to reach the start line near Kirsel. The operation was already eight hours behind and, based on their experiences getting this far, both Bert Coffin and Bob Bradburn realized that there was little hope of starting the attack before daylight. They also had reports that the start line was not clear of the enemy and that 3rd Division was having trouble clearing Uedem. All in all, it appeared that the best thing would be to delay so that the attack could go in under definite cover of darkness the following night. Jim Jefferson agreed and passed the request up to Vokes. While they were waiting for a reply, the two commanders sent a scout car out to recce a new route forward to their start line. It returned around midnight with information about a possible route, at about the same time that orders were received from division through brigade "to push on through," despite the "possible confusing situation," cross the valley by first light and "secure the objective by that time."[28] The right hook was also ordered to proceed.

"It was midnight," the Algonquins' historian recorded:

Outside the farmhouse serving as a headquarters, the vehicles were now jumbled into practically a solid block, so that those who had unwisely double-banked were unable to get back into the column. Drowsed with inaction and fatigue, drivers were everywhere dropping off to sleep, and were difficult to awaken. It must have been easily the Colonel's [Bob Bradburn] most dismal hour.[29]

Orders were orders and the attack had to go in as directed.

Following an O Group to disseminate information on the new route, the South Albertas, with A Squadron leading and Bob Bradburn's Algonquins on their decks, moved out at 0130 hours, 27 February 1945. It was another terrible journey. The column soon encountered a vehicle stuck in the road belonging to a brigadier from 2nd Division who peremptorily ordered them to divert around it and stay off the road. The lead tank tried this and became bogged. The problem was reported to Jefferson by wireless and the reply came back "that ruthless measures must be used to ensure that the adv[ance] carried on down the road," meaning the brigadier had better stand back and stay out of the way.[30] Words were exchanged but a compromise was reached – a bulldozer was brought up to clear a path around the vehicle which was left unharmed. So treacherous was the going, however, that all the light Stuart tanks became stuck attempting to pass this obstacle. Things got worse a few hundred feet down the road where a huge mud hole prevented the wheeled scout cars going any farther. Bradburn and Coffin transferred to two tanks from RHQ troop and the advance continued but the "mud was now so bad that it became an

Off they go. The South Albertas, with the Algonquins on their decks, setting out near Louisendorf on the morning of 26 February to move up to their start line for the attack on the Gap. At this point the ground is fairly firm; it shortly got worse and the two units took nearly twenty-four hours to get through mud that was nearly three feet deep. NAC, PA 113672.

individual effort to get [for]w[ar]d" as tanks "got stuck, were pulled out and got stuck again."[31] Finally, it was every vehicle for itself and "each t[an]k found its own way to the FUP" at Kirsel, a small hamlet northeast of Uedem from which the attack would be launched but only about half the tanks and, thus, half the infantry reached this point.[32] One of the four Algonquin companies had been stranded when the Stuarts had got stuck and another was only thirty men strong. Coffin and Bradburn would have to attack the Hochwald Gap with only three weak infantry companies supported by B Squadron. At the same time A Squadron was dispatched to undertake the "right hook" and C Squadron was sent to the high ground north of Uedem to render fire support. It was about thirty minutes until first light.[33]

The attack went in at 0600 hours just as dawn was breaking. It was a dramatic scene, "more dramatic," one South Alberta thought,

The going gets worse. Trooper Joe McEachern looks slightly embarrassed (or annoyed) as a Canadian Army photographer records him hooking up his bogged tank to a towing cable in preparation for being pulled out of the mud. Note the extenders on the tracks, which rendered the tanks more mobile. These had been fitted weeks before but, unfortunately, most were broken off during the long march from Holland into Germany. NAC, PA167115.

Into the valley of mud. A B Squadron Sherman with Trooper Alan Forbes perched on its rear deck tries to plough through nearly three feet of mud to reach the start line for the attack on the Gap while other South Albertas observe and no doubt offer helpful advice. The mud is so deep that the Sherman is dragging its belly, leaving a smooth mark on the surface. NAC, PA 179024.

than anything from Wagner: flashes from German guns lit up the horizon ahead, and our own artillery made the one behind even brighter, houses and barns were flaming fiercely along the way and sending sparks way up into the darkness – obviously the battle here had been very recent. The distinctive acrid odour of a burning house (not at all like a camp fire) would stay with me always.[34]

The initial assault consisted of two Algonquin companies, A Company on the right, supported by Lieutenant Ed Reardon's B-2 Troop and B Company on the left backed up by Lieutenant Jimmy Orr's B-1 Troop. Their job was to seize the first German defensive trench, code-name PELICAN, and establish a firm

position through which the Algonquin C Company and B-3 Troop would move to assault the next line, codename CHICKADEE.[35]

Assisted by the dim light, rain and mist, the assault force moved down off the ridge into the shallow valley in front of them. There was surprisingly little resistance and the biggest problem turned out to be the mud as the valley floor was one big bog watered by numerous drainage ditches. By the time the leading elements were approaching PELICAN, only four tanks (half the number that had started), three on the left and one on the right, were still moving. Nonetheless, the first trench line was taken at about 0700 hours.[36]

The Germans now began to wake up and within minutes the lead elements and the ridge behind came under fire from three different directions. The ridge was such an unhealthy place that C Squadron, which was stationed there, was forced to pull back behind the crest to avoid being hit. When he had moved up that morning Lieutenant Bill Luton had been shocked to find that a Grenadier Guards tank knocked out the previous day had been commanded by a high-school classmate whose incinerated body had not been removed from the vehicle. Now he and his crew watched as the German anti-tank gunners fired at the derelict. As he noted, "from the comfort of a (temporarily) safe position it was a thrilling – and chilling – demonstration of shooting and the following comments were heard:"[37]

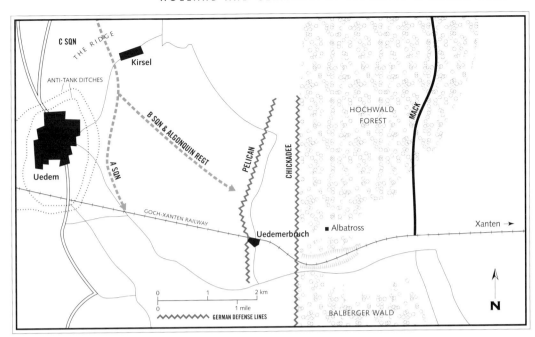

Map 16: The Hochwald Gap, 26 February–2 March 1945. While 3rd Division took Uedem, 11th British Armoured Division was to take the Balbergerwald, 2nd Division to move down from the north to clear the Hochwald Forest, and 4th Division to seize the Hochwald Gap. Simonds had hoped to be able to use the railway embankment of the Goch-Xanten railway as his main route but it proved impracticable. Delayed for nearly half a day by muddy ground, the SAR and Algonquins attacked on 27 February. B and C Squadrons helped the infantry take the Gap but A Squadron was wiped out trying to secure the railway embankment. The fighting continued for another three days but all attempts to move east from the Gap were stymied by fierce German resistance.

The nightmare march. Pencil sketch by Major G.L. Cassidy showing Algonquin infantry and SAR tanks trying to get forward during the night of 26/27 February 1945 to launch an attack on the Hochwald Gap through deep, clinging mud. By now the two units had been on the march for more than twelve hours and, because of the terrible going, had covered about five miles.

Onward they ploughed. Looking terribly embarrassed about the whole thing, Trooper Ed Demars guides his Firefly (a Ic Hybrid model) through two to three feet of mud. Generals Vokes and Simonds committed their armoured regiments across ground like this – but very few tanks made it. Note the worn white camouflage on the barrel of the 17-pdr. gun intended to conceal its length. Also note the amazing variety of equipment, containers and other useful things fastened all over the vehicle. Not visible in this picture is a kitchen sink tied behind the turret. NAC, PA 113675.

"Did you see those A.P shells go in one side of the turret and out the other?"

"Sure did, didn't even seem to slow down."

"And those pieces of hot metal spurting out the side of the turret?"

"Yeah ... makes a fellow think."

"No, you can't do that."

The amount of fire coming down on the ridge actually forced the Algonquins' C Company to move forward with B-3 on the heels of the two assault companies. Trooper David Marshall, the loader-operator in Sergeant Fred Freeman's tank, remembered that

when we approached the edge of the valley, Fred told the driver to move the tank as fast as he ever made one move. We raced down the side of the valley following the tracks of the tanks that had gone before. I have no idea how long it took us to get to the bottom, it seemed like hours. We passed abandoned tanks and carriers, destroyed by enemy fire.

We were now in the open in broad daylight, in sight of the enemy's guns. He opened up on us, we could see shells drop-

ping all around and I never prayed so fervently in my life. This was the only time in the war that I thought I would not make it. I couldn't see how we could ever get out of this alive. We were sitting ducks. The good Lord did see us through and as a "bonus" gave us the day off. Just after crossing the first ditch we came under direct anti-tank fire and found ourselves pinned behind some houses. Every time we moved the German anti-tank guns who had our range fired on us, so we stayed, in the rain, in the mud, unable to go forward or to go back.[38]

Artillery was called down on the Hochwald ridge and it had some effect. Otto Diels, an anti-tank gunner with the 116th Panzer Division, remembered B-3 Troop's approach:

The Canadian tanks were ploughing through deep mud and seemed unable to maintain their usual speed, some could be seen sliding and looked difficult to control. We laid our gun on the leading tank but by the time we were ready to fire, it had already been hit and we swung our gun to another, but that too, stopped with smoke pouring from it. The third tank at which we aimed fired first and a shell burst only yards in front of us, the fragments clanging off our gun's shield. Quickly we re-aligned our gun but once again a shell burst close by, this time fragments injuring one of our loaders. Then the tanks seemed to falter and we fired, our shot glancing off a Sherman tank. All the while the Canadian gunners were firing tracer as markers for their tanks and shells were whizzing around us.[39]

Actually, none of B-3 Troop's tanks were knocked out but they had to continually shift position as the German gunners ranged on them.

It was too much for the troop leader. Telling his crew that "he had a headache and was going to get an aspirin," he got out of his tank and didn't bother to inform his troop sergeant, Fred Freeman, that he was leaving the battle.[40] "The next thing we knew," Fred remembered, "there was no answer on the radio and we got kind of disorganized." When he realized what had

happened, Fred assumed command of B-3 and straightened things out. On his way to the rear the officer passed Leaman Caseley's B-4 Troop, waiting in reserve on the Kirsel ridge, and paused long enough to warn Leaman: "Be careful – an 88 is over there."[41] Caseley shot back, "Shouldn't you be doing something about that?" but the man hurried on. Arriving at the rear he was cool enough to have lunch with Stan Rose's crew, although he did not tell them why he was not fighting, and then went to the RAP and had himself tagged and evacuated as a "battle exhaustion" casualty. He never returned to the Regiment. It was the officers who felt most strongly about the matter and they never forgave him. Six months later, two SAR lieutenants on leave in Britain were having a drink in a mess when this "battle exhaustion" casualty, still wearing regimental flashes, came up and greeted them. They coldly turned their backs and refused to acknowledge his existence.[42]

With B-3 Troop pinned, the two surviving tanks of B-1

It looked easy on the map. The photo and pencil sketch show the approach to the Hochwald Gap (the ridge in the background in the photo) as seen from the high ground at Kirsel, the SAR's start line on 27 February 1945. The shallow valley between proved to be one vast bog that quickly rendered the Regiment almost immobile. The objective was ALBATROSS, the small knoll or pimple on the ridge in the background (in the sketch) located in the gap between the Hochwald Forest on the left and the Balbergerwald on the right. To get there, "Lion Force" had to cross the shallow valley below the gap, which turned out to be a bog watered by irrigation ditches and enfiladed by fire from the railway embankment which can be seen on the right in the sketch as it enters the Balbergerwald, where its course is a cutting through the trees.

moved forward with the Algonquin C Company when they attacked CHICKADEE at 0800 hours. This position was taken despite heavy enemy artillery fire which forced the two tanks some two hundred and fifty yards to the west where there was a sheltered firing position near some buildings. So far, so good, but a few minutes later Coffin received bad news about the fate of the "right hook."[43]

G len McDougall's A Squadron and the Algonquins' carrier platoon had started out at about 0600 hours and quickly encountered problems with the going. Lieutenant Tiger Bowick's tank bogged and Bobby Crawford took the lead but, in the dark, failed to see one of the large anti-tank ditches which encircled Uedem and slid into it. Crawford then took over Corporal Rizzy Risdale's tank but the advance was halted until a way was found around the maze of ditches and trenches surrounding Uedem. It was nearly 0900 and broad daylight when McDougall's force began to skirt the town and move south to reach the railway where they would begin their attack. The entire area was a maze of farm lanes, trenches and ditches and the column reached the railway several hundred yards west of and closer to Uedem than their intended crossing point. This would not have been a problem if Uedem had been completely secured by 3rd Division but it quickly became apparent that determined pockets of Germans were holding out in that battered town.[44]

Due to problems with the mud the combined force was now down to ten tanks and four carriers. McDougall left two Shermans, commanded by Sergeant Duke Sands and Corporal John Galipeau, to guard his rear and pushed on for the railway with his eight remaining vehicles and the carriers. Crawford had the lead, Glen was the fourth tank in the column with his rear link, Kenny Perrin, immediately behind him, and Corporal Joe McGivern was the tail end. As the small column wove its way past the burning ruins of Uedem, Glen looked back in his

Tank ditch at Uedem. Forced to skirt around obstacles like these, A Squadron's right hook movement came to grief when it entered a heavily-defended area. SAR COLLECTION.

turret to see "a panzerfaust grenade lobbing in from behind me from the basement of a house."[45] It missed and McDougall ordered the last two tanks in the column to "put some HE into the house and there was no more response from the Germans." By now the head of the column had crossed the railway and was about one hundred yards beyond.

Their approach was spotted by the Germans. The area south of Uedem was supposed to have been cleared by the 11th British Armoured Division that morning on their way to seize their objective, the Balbergerwald on the ridge. But, as their historian records, the leading British elements had "run into trouble from bazooka-parties and more self-propelled guns" which had halted their advance.[46] Liaison between 11th British and 4th Canadian Armoured seems to have been faulty on this particular fact and there were German anti-tank guns in position south of Uedem and a number of dug-in Tiger tanks. Trooper Ed Thorn, the gunner in Crawford's lead tank,

saw this Tiger tank straight ahead about five or six hundred yards. I hollered at the guys "Tiger ahead!" and I had an HE round up the spout so I just triggered it off and let it go, I hollered at Maxie Gilbert, the loader, "APs, Maxie!" and I zeroed in on this Tiger and I hit him where I was told to hit him right where the turret joins the hull and the round ricocheted off to the right. I lowered my sights a little bit and I hit him again and I got him bang on. Just as I was doing this there was a "wheeesh" overhead. Over to the right about half a mile they had dug these Tigers in and I said to Bob Crawford, "I hope Watkins gets those guys." Herb Watkins had the 17-pdr. and I don't know what happened but the next one caught us.[47]

Glen McDougall heard Crawford report the Tiger but he also saw fire coming in "from an anti-tank gun on the right" which he immediately engaged.[48] John Galipeau listened on his A Set as McDougall

came on the air and reported he was receiving fire. Immediately afterwards, I heard him directing his gunner: "Gunner, traverse right." And again, "Gunner, traverse right." I realized that the squadron commander had forgotten to switch to the intercom and was broadcasting his order over the air, which meant that the gunner couldn't hear him. I flipped my microphone switch and said, "You're on the A Set."[49]

Glen kept firing at the anti-tank gun and thinks he might "have hit his ammunition because there was a hell of a burst of flame from one of my shots."[50]

But the Germans now had the range and within a matter of minutes had knocked out the first three Shermans in the column. Ed Thorn's tank was hit "right in front of me because I had the power traverse in my hand and I looked down and it was just like someone hit me on the shoulder with a sledge hammer."[51] The tank caught fire but, as Ed recalls, "I am not so sure we caught fire on the first shell or the second shell. I think maybe we got hit twice." The turret crew bailed out and the loader got some assistance from Ed: "Our loader, Maxie Gilbert, was a boy from Edmonton and he was quite a bit older than us and he wasn't very agile getting out of the tank. I got him under my arms and just shoved him out of the hatch." The turret traverse was jammed and the turret continued to swing crazily around in a complete circle, hampering the efforts of the two drivers, Troopers Albert Boyer and Hammy Hamilton, to exit the furiously burning vehicle through their hatches. They coolly waited until the gun had gone by, jumped out and were about twenty feet away when the Sherman blew up. Boyer dived into a ditch for cover only to discover that it was full of human excrement, forcing him to quickly tear off his tank suit.[52]

The tail-end tank, commanded by Corporal Joe McGivern, and the one in front, commanded by Corporal Herbie Watkins, were also hit. Trooper Art Baker, the driver in McGivern's tank, "was out cold" but McGivern went around to the front and pulled Art out waking him up.[53] The turret crew in Herbie Watkins's tank got clear "headphones and all" although Trooper Ian MacPherson was still wearing his when he "hit the ground and the resulting wrench injured my neck."[54] The driver, Trooper Harvey Amey, remained in the burning tank so Herbie "ran around to the front of the tank, got up and lifted his hatch and then dropped it."[55] Amey, a married 34-year-old factory foreman from London, Ontario, who had joined the Regiment the previous October, was quite dead.[56]

With the tanks at both the head and tail of the column knocked out, the ones in the middle were trapped. Kenny Perrin tried to extricate his tank and bring it alongside Glen McDougall but it was hit in the turret ring by an AP shot that cut through the gunner's leg and killed the loader-operator, Sergeant Harold "Jake" Jacobsen. Perrin and the gunner, Trooper John Bell, exited through the turret hatch but Kenny apparently returned to the tank to see if he could help Jacobsen. Bell's leg was hanging by a thread of muscle and skin and Glen, seeing him emerge, grabbed his morphine syrettes and jumped down from his turret to help. Bell recalled that "I crawled back through a hedge but my leg got caught in the hedge and I turned around and brought it through."[57] By the time McDougall caught up with him, Bell's leg had dropped off and Glen was amazed that "there was no blood" because "the shot seared the stump."[58] He gave Bell an injection and offered him another one but Bell said, "No, I just want to get out."[59] A big Algonquin sergeant heaved him onto a carrier and Glen watched it drive away with Bell "waving one leg in the air and hoping for better things."[60]

The crews of the remaining tanks trapped in the centre of the column fired off as much ammunition as they could and then bailed out in anticipation that their vehicles would shortly be hit. There were now about forty South Albertas on the ground under German artillery and small-arms fire but fortu-nately one of the brewed-up Algonquin carriers was a Wasp and its burning tank full of flammable mixture provided a heavy smoke screen for the survivors. Some made it out on the re-maining carriers, others moved back to safety through the elaborate trench system around Uedem, and some were cap-tured by the enemy.[61]

Trooper Bob Seccombe, the gunner in Herb Watkins's tank, thought he would have to fight on the ground so went back to his tank to recover the Brownings but when he returned, every-one had disappeared. Seccombe moved back through the trenches with some other survivors until they "could hear what sounded like a bunch of bees coming down the road, it was some machine-gun outfit and they were firing down that road and they were firing at everybody who moved."[62] He managed to calm the machine gunners down and got to safety on their carriers. There was friendly and unfriendly artillery fire falling everywhere and a mortar bomb killed Trooper Fred Belsey, a 24-year-old truck driver from Oyami, British Columbia, who had joined the Regiment in September 1944.[63] Glen McDougall led one party to safety through the trenches but Bobby Crawford, heading another group, was pinned down by Ger-man machine-gun fire and finally forced to surrender. Crawford's party was immediately surrounded by "these young SS troopers, 16 or 17 years old and hard as nails."[64]

Joe McGivern, whose tank was "popping like a popcorn ma-chine" from the force of its exploding ammunition, guided three or four men into a nearby house that was hit by a Cana-dian artillery barrage called down on the suspected German positions.[65] Art Baker remembers that they were "blown from room to room" and at one point a tracer round came through the building, depositing burning phosphorus on Joe Arkles's head, but his comrades managed to brush it off before it could do him injury. "One shell," Arkles recalled, "went right through the room we were standing in and when I walked into the next room I didn't know whether I was entering heaven or hell."[66] There were Germans in this house but the Canadians were so covered with dust and plaster that they "went by and did not notice us," recalled Baker, but "when they did there were so many around us with guns pointed at us that they saved our lives as a mortar bomb landed and many of them were killed or wounded."[67] Arkles never forgot one strange thing – "at the back of the house, there was a tethered goat and that poor little bugger was bleating all the time we were being shelled in there."[68]

The prisoners were herded back to the German lines under guard. On the way, Joe Arkles recalls, they passed two Tiger tanks "pulled up side by side and the crew commanders were shaking hands" – Joe thought to himself: "You sons of guns, celebrating your victory and here we are."[69] When they reached a German headquarters they found Crawford's group waiting and one of A Squadron's Shermans with a German officer perched in the co-driver's hatch. Art Baker found the sight so funny that he "burst out laughing and the guard behind bumbled me one in the back of the head with his rifle butt. I thought he was going to shoot me, he was so mad."[70] Nonetheless, Arkles remembers that Baker had the presence of mind to talk the Germans into letting him get into the tank where he "turned the power traverse on and told them it was air conditioning" causing "the battery to run down in about five minutes."[71]

Next came a field interrogation conducted by a friendly German sergeant speaking perfect English, who began by assuring the South Albertas that his countrymen "had lost this war but we will win the next."[72] The Germans didn't often get Canadian armoured crews alive and they were fascinated by the boys' tank suits which were immediately confiscated to assist the German war effort as were their cigarettes. "They really respected the Canadians," Art recalled, and "told us that they call the English 'Tommies' and the Canadians 'the Tommy SS' but said they reckoned that the Canadians would not take prisoners, they'd shoot them."[73] The South Albertas hastily assured their captors that these nasty rumours were untrue and, when the interrogation was finished, the group was sent back to Wesel on the Rhine for transportation to a prisoner of war camp. Art Baker remembered that journey:

We marched with one *feldwebel* and a private. Lt. Crawford was in the lead. We came to Wesel, just after the Typhoons had finished with it and there were piles of rubble everywhere and people everywhere with two-wheeled carts, horse and man drawn, loading parts of bodies on them. When they saw us, they came at us to do us in. The two guards we had backed us out of there, saying they would shoot anyone who tried to harm us. We got to the railway station and the Hitler Youth there gave Lt. Crawford a hard time showing off for the civilians.[74]

For Bobby Crawford and his fellow prisoners the shooting war was over.

Herbie Watkins was one of the last to return from the debacle. After he had discovered that his driver was dead Herbie couldn't find his crew but rounded up Trooper Art Pagee from another tank and five Algoons and led them through the trench system. Pagee "was kind of shocked and he said my back is pretty sore," Watkins recorded. "I looked at him and he had five pieces of shrapnel in him." Herb "pulled out a flask I always carried and gave him a drink of whisky and put some in each wound and dressed them and the boys finished the rest of the whisky." The group pressed on until the Algonquins could see some of their men and left to join them. Herbie and Art now went up on the road and "who should be coming along but General Guy Simonds in his Staghound." "He was smoking," Herb continued, "and I asked him if he had a spare cigarette because I lost my pipe and everything in the tank" so "he threw us down a pack of cigarettes and told us where the Casualty Clearing Station was, a couple of miles down the road." Simonds didn't offer a lift and Herb took Art there on foot and,

after he had ensured that Pagee was looked after, hitched a ride in a jeep back to RHQ where he arrived about 1600 hours.

He walked in, "pretty well shook up and pretty well played out," smoking one of the corps commander's cigarettes only to encounter fellow pipe-smoker Glen McDougall, who demanded "what the hell are you doing smoking a cigarette?" Herbie explained the circumstances. Glen said "I'll fix you up and pulled out a pipe with a tooth hole through the mouthpiece and gave it to me." He also gave Herbie a very large drink and told him to lie on a nearby cot and, as Herbie remembered, "in a few minutes, I was sound asleep until they woke me up at 3 PM the next day and asked me if I was going to stay there for the rest of the war."[75]

Bert Coffin learned of the disastrous fate of A Squadron's "right hook," a "fate he had unfortunately predicted," late in the morning.[76] With the exception of Amey and Belsey, who were known to be dead, there was hope at first that the rest of the men had escaped and would eventually work their way back to safety, particularly Kenny Perrin, a popular man in the Regiment, who had been seen alive outside his tank by three witnesses. When the fighting in the area died down a few days later Padre Silcox examined the wreckage and discovered Amey's incinerated body in his Sherman but the fire in Perrin's tank had been so ferocious that all he could find were ashes and the remains of a watch and a 9 mm Browning automatic. The weapon was identified as Perrin's, the watch could have belonged to either Kenny or Jacobsen, and the Regiment continued to hope that both men had been taken prisoner. When they were not on the list of South Albertas reported to be in German custody, it was gradually realized that they had died in the burning tank. Both had been with the Regiment since the beginning in June 1940 and were sorely missed. Harold Jacobsen was a 29-year-old dairy worker from Edmonton who was survived by a wife and daughter, while Kenny Perrin, "the best person I ever met," according to his gunner, John Bell, was a 25-year-old bank clerk from Medicine Hat who had risen from private to captain since 1940.[77]

By mid-morning it was obvious to both Bert and Bob Bradburn that the attack was in danger of grinding to a halt in the face of ferocious German artillery fire. The South Albertas had been under heavy bombardment in Normandy and at Moerbrugge but this was the worst they had experienced. It didn't help that Bert had a frustrating morning, switching his command post from tank to tank as each got stuck in the thick mud, and since no wheeled vehicle could move in the stuff, he was concerned about getting supplies to the forward positions and evacuating casualties. He requested Ram ammunition carriers from brigade but in the meantime had to use the Regiment's ARVs, which were better occupied in unsticking tanks, to bring supplies up to the front. He could get no information on the wireless from the leading troops except the frustrating message, "Wait out, wait out," and finally decided to go forward and take a look for himself.[78]

Bert wallowed "through mud up to my knees" to a farmyard at the foot of the ridge and was talking to two infantry officers when the "Moaning Minnies wound up on us." "We were in between two tanks," he recalled, "one of ours and an artillery OP tank and these Moaning Minnies got too hot and the tanks didn't like it much so they cranked up and moved away and left us standing there." The infantry officers ran for the cover of a barn but Bert "rolled over into this tank track which was quite safe except kind of lonesome" so he "started to run for the barn myself but just as I got there the Minnies came over again and I saw this concrete thing about two feet high and I dived into it as I thought that would make a great shelter and it was a pig pen and it was wet." When he emerged, dripping with pig shit, "everyone was killing themselves laughing" and, commanding officer or not, when Bert asked for a ride back to his RHQ on a tank, the crew refused "and told me I could walk."[79]

The problem with the forward squadron proved to be the infantry's concern that every time the tanks used their wireless, it brought down a fresh German barrage. The enemy artillery was getting steadily worse and by noon, as the Algonquins' historian records, the troops on PELICAN and CHICKADEE were in serious trouble because

the enemy had tumbled to the magnitude and extent of the advance and was now concentrating the full force of his considerable artillery and mortars on the floor of the valley. From a vast ring, which virtually encircled our thrust, he was able to bring down fire from hundreds of guns, and many, many mortars, some of them of the fifteen barrel variety. From across the Rhine, far to the north, his heavier calibre artillery could also deliver a deadly weight of metal.[80]

The Regiment's attached FOO was unable to function because his OP tank had bogged and all artillery fire had to be called down from the FOO attached to the Algonquins, which was a laborious procedure. Although the forward positions reported that there seemed to be "no opposition from ALBATROSS," the ultimate objective in the mouth of the gap, the South Albertas and

Algonquins could not go forward because of heavy fire coming from the railway embankment in the vicinity of the hamlet of Uedemerbruch.[81]

Coffin ordered Lieutenant Pete Burger's C-3 Troop down from the ridge to "quell any counterattack from this direction." As Trooper Sam Hunter, the loader-operator in the troop's 17-pdr. tank, recalled, Burger immediately ran into trouble:

We went down the hill on a road; we were not the first tank – I could see others ahead of me through my periscope. The ground on the right side of the road was above the level of the tank. I'm sure there were Jerry troops up there – I thought I heard grenades thrown from above exploding on the side of the tank. We came to the bottom of the hill and turned right through a wide open farm field which sloped uphill to our right. We got part way across when the tank second or third behind me got hit by a German 88 firing up the hill to our right, but did not brew up. There were some houses and barns ahead, grouped together, but not a village; we turned right and hid behind them.[82]

The tank that was hit was that of Corporal Walter Fengler. A few minutes later Burger's tank got bogged in an anti-tank ditch and the troop, now down to two vehicles, was more or less trapped. Late in the day a smoke screen was laid down to get them out.[83]

As the afternoon began to wane it was clear that the attack could not be pressed home and Coffin and Bradburn decided to wait for darkness to make their next move. At last light, all the remaining tanks of B Squadron, including the Squadron

Knocked out in the Hochwald. Pencil sketch by Major G.L. Cassidy showing SAR tanks knocked out at a farm near the Hochwald Gap in February 1945.

The high ground, February 1945. Canadian artillery pounds German positions in front of the Hochwald Ridge. Taken from the high ground where C Squadron was positioned to support the South Alberta and Algonquin attack, this photo shows the infamous Hochwald Gap in the background with the Hochwald on the left and the Balbergerwald on the right. NAC, PA113681.

HQ Troop and Leaman Caseley's B-4 Troop, together with four AVRE tanks, two ARVs and one Ram ammo carrier, rushed as best they could into the valley, their decks crammed with supplies and ammunition for the infantry. B Squadron replenished at PELICAN under constant mortar fire and the infantry casualties were evacuated. What was perhaps the South Alberta Regiment's longest day was finally at an end.[84]

During the last hours of 27 February the plan of attack was revised. The Argylls, now back under the command of 10 Brigade, were coming to join the battle. Throughout the afternoon their companies had been filtering into the valley and the plan was that they would push forward through the Algonquins and, with the support of C Squadron, take ALBATROSS, the pimple in the middle of the gap. Meanwhile, B Squadron would firm up with the infantry at PELICAN and CHICKADEE. Major Stan Purdy of C Squadron did not learn of his task until past midnight and it was 0100 hours, 28 February, before the squadron began to wind down off the Calcar ridge onto the valley floor. There was a two-hour delay while the Argylls and the supporting artillery got themselves sorted out and Bill Luton and his crew were amused when music programs from the BBC, whose broadcast wave length was close to their assigned wireless frequency, kept coming in over their headsets. Bill Luton passed the time composing new words (which have been quoted above) to a popular tune of the day, "Can't think of anything I'd rather do." At 0330 hours the order came to advance but the going "became bad, then worse, then terrible: soft mud, deep ruts, water-filled holes." Luton's C-1 Troop laboured on "getting stuck, backing up, trying again, using the winch," until they finally made it to slightly higher, and drier, ground. Unfor-

tunately, of the thirteen tanks in the squadron only the four vehicles of C-1 made it onto the Hochwald Ridge – the remaining nine had bogged in the marshy area which the going maps had "classed as impassable for tanks."[85]

It was decided that Leaman Caseley's B-4 Troop, which had come forward to PELICAN, would support the Argylls in the attack. Between 0300 and 0400 Leaman moved forward with his four tanks to shoot the Argylls onto their objective, ALBATROSS and the dirt road code-named MACK in the middle of the Gap. Surprisingly, opposition was light and the objectives were seized without trouble, except heavy mortaring. At the same time Luton was ordered to take his four tanks to support the Argylls right flank company in a position near the railway. Bill opted to move through the woods, which was difficult, and lost his 17-pdr. tank when its long barrel became entangled in a tree. He disposed his remaining three vehicles in a small strip of woods (actually part of the Balbergerwald) between the Gap proper and the railway. This was in the British sector, but as there was no sign of 11th Armoured Division, he claimed "squatter's rights."[86]

By first light, 28 February 1945, Leaman's tanks were on the ridge line below ALBATROSS supporting the Argylls whose four companies were strung out along the width of the Gap and preparing to move through it, Lieutenant Ed Reardon had the two tanks of his B-2 Troop somewhat to Leaman's right while the remainder of B Squadron (nine Shermans) was at CHICKADEE. Luton's C-1 Troop with three tanks was in the gap at the far right while the other nine tanks of C Squadron were scattered over the valley floor trying to get themselves unstuck. The situation was looking good as dawn broke – 10 Brigade had the middle of the gap, 2nd Infantry Division was expected to drive south through the Hochwald Forest on the left to link up with them while it was hoped that 11th British Armoured Division would take their objective – the Balbergerwald on the right of the Gap.

The situation looked good but that was deceptive. What had happened was that the Germans had withdrawn from the gap itself because it was a professional habit of the *Wehrmacht* not to waste men trying to hold ground that was better defended by firepower. The Germans put up stubborn resistance in the two flanking forests (the Hochwald and the Balbergerwald) but decided to defend the gap from reverse slope positions on the eastern side of the ridge. Any attempt to advance over and through the gap to the divisional objective of Xanten immediately ran into a storm of fire. It was also a characteristic of the *Wehrmacht* that, if important ground was lost, a vicious counterattack was launched before the enemy had time to consolidate his position. The German commander, von Lüttwitz, judged that the Hochwald Forest on the left of the Gap was important enough to warrant a counterattack and, at dawn, he sent forward a battalion of the 24th Parachute Regiment and an armoured battle group from 116th Panzer Division.[87]

The German attack did not come in until about 0900 hours and it was preceded by one of the heaviest bombardments the Regiment had ever suffered. One South Alberta remembered that "the noise was indescribable" and "we could see through the periscopes, trees shattering all around us and could feel the tank rock with the explosions."[88] Luton recorded that the veterans in his troop stated that they "had never been exposed to the like of what Jerry threw at us: field and medium artillery shells, mortars of all sizes, 88 A.P. and airburst, 'Moaning Minnies,' and even artillery shells coming from *behind* us, the latter – a freak result of the curvature of the Rhine – were particularly dangerous since we were conditioned to ignore any whistle from that direction."[89] One mortar bomb damaged Ed Reardon's tank and wounded Ed, so that Sergeant Frank Freer's vehicle became the last survivor of B-2. When the shelling stopped, the German tanks and infantry moved forward toward the left side of the Gap.

That morning had started badly for Leaman Caseley. At first light he too had lost his 17-pdr. Firefly when it lodged its barrel in some trees and was knocked out either by a *Panzerfaust* or an anti-tank gun. Another German gun had glanced an AP round off Leaman's turret onto the rear of his tank "where it knocked out three engines and set fire to the bed rolls fastened to the rear deck."[90] Leaman was giving a situation report to RHQ on the wireless but "excused himself, climbed out of the turret, put the fire out, climbed back into the turret and continued with his conversation."[91] Deciding that his position was not a healthy one, he threw some smoke grenades and backed up, his two working engines screaming, into the cover of some trees where he could still provide fire support for the Argylls up ahead. At about that moment, a sniper's bullet hit a phosphorus smoke grenade lying on the top of the turret and it exploded shooting flaming phosphorus all over the tank. Leaman swept it off with his gloves. In his new position, however, he was out of touch with the other two tanks in his troop, which were some distance to his right under the command of Sergeant Freer.[92]

The German armour and infantry approached the Argyll B Company in the most advanced position near the MACK road. This company took heavy casualties (it would have only seventeen unwounded men by nightfall) but fought off all enemy attempts to overrun its position, killing more than a hundred

paratroopers and knocking out one tank with a PIAT at close range. The enemy came so close that the company commander personally "shot and killed the commander of a German tank who had told the company to lay down their arms and surrender."[93] The German armour, estimated to be a mixed collection of ten to fifteen Panthers, Mk IVs, SPGs and Tigers, milled around B Company and approached the top of the Gap.

Waiting for them about two hundred yards below the crest line were four Sherman 75s of B Squadron. Leaman was on the left; on the right were Sergeant Lawrence Freeman of B-3 Troop with another tank from the same troop commanded by Trooper Pat Gregory and the last remaining tank of B-2 commanded by Sergeant Frank Freer. It was the perfect ambush position and David Marshall, the loader in Freeman's tank, remembered what happened:

> Over the rise in front of us came the snouts of two tanks, a Tiger and a Panther, heading our way. When our gunners had them in their sights, and before the German tanks could level out to bring their 88's down onto us, our three tanks opened fire with all guns blazing and stopped the attack, destroying the Panther and forcing the Tiger to retreat.[94]

Both Freer and Freeman bounced 75 mm AP rounds off the front turret of the Tiger which, if they didn't destroy it, at least scared the crew who backed out of this hornet's nest. For his part, Leaman only claims to have fired at an SPG but later investigation of the ground revealed that he had brewed up a Mk IV and that three other German AFVs had been knocked out. The enemy assault withered away and then the shelling started up again.[95]

As calls for assistance came in from the infantry up on the Gap, Bert Coffin decided to call in an air strike. This was the first day that the weather was good enough for aircraft to participate in BLOCKBUSTER and arrangements were made for the supporting artillery to "lay down a smoke screen across our front and anything past it was fair game."[96] At his position on the right side of the gap near the railway Bill Luton was thrilled: "Jerry was about to get it, but good." One trooper remembered those big Typhoons, with their deadly armament of eight rockets, each about five times as effective as the explosive charge of a Sherman HE round, as they came roaring in:

> Talk about beauty in action – it had to be those planes. We would hear them first and then see them come swooping in to have a look at the situation, then up and around again. When they had the target lined up they would dive down towards it and, at the last second, release their rockets which swooshed out from under their wings. Seconds later we heard tremendous explosions and saw smoke and debris in the air as evidence of the rockets hitting the target. Oh it was wonderful.[97]

It wasn't so wonderful to Bill Luton and his men. As the smoke came down to mark the forward positions for the aircraft, Bill realized to his great distress that it "landed in the gap *behind* us," meaning his three tanks were now in the target area.[98] He frantically tried to contact someone on the wireless but the No. 19 set in his tank, C11, was giving trouble that day and, as his operator frantically twisted the dials, "a sound was heard overhead, unlike any ever before experienced in battle, something like the noise of a high-speed train passing through a tunnel." Bill "paused in wonderment, and then heard an explosion, sharper and louder than a shell, just in front of C11. A rocket! I looked up to see the

The Allied tank crew's basic nightmare, no. 5. A German *Jagdpanther*, a combination of the 88 mm gun and the hull and suspension of the medium Panther tank with heavy and well-sloped armour. The Germans deployed some of these AFVs against the SAR at the Hochwald. CANADIAN ARMY PHOTOGRAPH.

Tiffy flaring away." His crew desperately threw out yellow smoke grenades, the marker for friendly troops, and "smoke blossomed gloriously on both sides of the tank, and just in time." The crew of C11 breathed a sigh of relief: "But no: he kept coming and dove directly at C11." Bill saw a

> great puff of smoke and instinctively ducked inside [the turret], a futile gesture against a rocket. Again came the sound of the express train in a tunnel – and again the explosion. We were still alive to hear it! The Tiffy had missed again. Simply incredible: two tries at a sitting target, at short range, in good visibility, with calm air, and no anti-aircraft fire!

The aircraft missed Luton's crew but they appeared to have scared off the remaining German armour because, although there were constant reports throughout the day of enemy AFVs in the Gap, none ventured close enough to attack.

Things got worse. At noon the Argylls tried to make another push through the Gap but were forced back by ferocious enemy fire that made it impossible for any tank to support them. It was clear, noted the War Diarist, "that more infantry would have to be committed to bring the situation under control."[99] The Links now came up and tried to cross over the high ground on the left with the support of the remaining runners from B Squadron but were quickly stopped by heavy German artillery fire. Another air strike was called and the shelling continued without pause on both sides. At last light, word came that 4 Armoured Brigade would be moving through the Regiment

that night to carry the attack through the Gap while 2nd Division, which had been slowly but steadily clearing the Hochwald Forest from north to south, was now approaching the Gap itself. By this time, "the plight of the infantry," noted the War Diarist, "was bad" as they "needed arms and hot food." Bert Coffin, realizing something had to be done, "ordered up the RAP and 2 cooks. Arrangements were also made to create a small arms dump of PIATS, Brens, Rifles and SA a[mmuni]-tion" at a forward position.[100]

Bert Coffin's voice, after two days of talking without rest, had given out and Captain Gordie Irving came forward to relieve him at the tactical headquarters, which was set up in a farm building at PELICAN. The problems of supplying the forward troops and evacuating the wounded had not grown any better but at least the Ram ammunition carriers requested the day before had finally appeared. This "gave some relief to the Stuarts and the ARVs" and "at last the fitters could concentrate wholeheartedly upon the job of debogging and recovery instead of petrol and ammunition replenishment."[101] The echelons did their best but wheeled traffic simply could not descend into the valley and even the roads leading up to it were treacherous quagmires. To the truck drivers, like Bob Rasmussen, it was the same old story: "Back and forth, back and forth. That was what it amounted to. [RQSM] McTavish would give me rum when he thought I needed it. The mud, the mud. Back and forth."[102] At a secure location, the trucks offloaded onto any tracked vehicle that could get through the mud including Crusaders, Stuarts, Ram ammo carriers (Wallabies), Crocodiles, Flails and

AVRE tanks, OP tanks and halftracks. In his diary for 27-28 February 1945 Trooper George Gallimore of Recce Troop described what it was like for the men engaged on this work:

Desperately muddy. We were used as carriers of ammunition. We left at first light for about five hours, the odd shell coming in. … We are in a field with RHQ and are being shelled constantly. Went up to TAC HQ with a load of ammo. The Shermans were up in this field muddier than hell, and most of them were stuck. Went up all night and stayed all night with B Squadron. Stayed all night and mortared and snipers. Pulled out in the morning. Kept bringing up ammo, snipers pretty busy, settled in a barn.[103]

Their efforts were much appreciated by the infantry and the 10 Brigade historian commented that the South Albertas not only showed "their great fighting spirit" but "had held on with the infantry, feeding them and running supplies until they were so fatigued that many crews were sick in their tanks from exhaustion."[104]

Getting supplies forward was one thing, getting the wounded back was just as bad. In the morning of 28 February the RAP moved to PELICAN to be closer to the forward positions. Doc Boothroyd had left the Regiment in October and the MO was now Captain Jock Maloney. At the RAP Maloney and Padre Silcox, his medically-trained assistant, "triaged" the wounded as they were brought in by the medical halftracks which were connected by wireless to RHQ, the RAP and all the squadron headquarters, or if the halftracks were not available, by any other vehicle that could make it through the mud. Failing that, they were carried by stretcher parties.

Driving the medical halftracks was a risky business that required a certain kind of man. Trooper Eric Nichols had been a member of a tank crew in B Squadron but in December 1944 switched over to driving the squadron ambulance vehicle "because I was alone and if anybody made a mistake, it would be me."[105] Nichols summed the job up:

They never ordered me to go out, they asked me to go out. If a tank got knocked out they would just give me a map coordinate and I would go in. They would come over and tell me. The crew would usually be gone when I got there but I would often take someone with me. We had these morphine syrettes and you just pushed it in the arm, whether they needed it or not – if they were hurting, they didn't mind at all. We had a stretcher in the back but we didn't go out often, just if things were bad and, if things were bad, we were very busy.

Things were bad at the Hochwald. Nichols and his fellow driver, Trooper Vincent Chaney, made many trips under enemy fire to bring out wounded men – at one point they picked up more than twenty-four wounded that the infantry had been

forced to abandon after they had been driven back from a position. The Germans held their fire. Nichols lost one of his helpers on 27 February when fragments from a German mortar bomb which landed near his halftrack killed Trooper John Bartlett, who was riding with him. This was a particularly tragic loss because Bartlett, a farm labourer from Edmonton, was, at 47 years of age, too old for combat and had only been retained in the Regiment because he served as a batman to the officers and a waiter in their mess. John Bartlett had nothing else to do that day so he volunteered to go out in the ambulance.[106]

Fourth Armoured Brigade, in the form of the Grenadier Guards, made their attack during the early hours of 1 March. Bill Luton had been warned to expect some activity from "friends" but was surprised when no one showed up from the Guards to make a foot patrol over the ground which by this time he was coming to know very well. Nor was any attempt made by the Grenadiers to net in on his wireless frequency to achieve additional direct fire support from his three Shermans, which were in good positions. The noise of tanks moving up behind him was the first notice Bill had that the attack was actually going in and then

the darkness erupted in sound, light and fury unleashed, as three Sherman tanks charged over the crest at full speed and firing all guns: 75's, turret Brownings, forward Brownings, in a spectacular display of armoured might. How awe inspiring it was, and unfortunately, how stupid …

Suddenly the dark valley in front showed a flash of flame from two locations (there may have been more, but my view to the right was restricted by trees). The German gunners had a perfect aiming point: the line of machine-gun tracers coming from each Sherman. It was all over in seconds – one tank brewed up, two others were knocked out.[107]

This was not the only attack the Grenadiers attempted and the unit lost a total of ten tanks that night.

They were therefore not in a position during the morning of 1 March to assist the Lincoln and Welland Regiment, which was ordered to put in an attack on the left side of the Gap. B Squadron went forward instead with a total of about eight tanks in four troops commanded by Lieutenant Jimmy Orr and Sergeants Freer, Freeman and Kroesing. They encountered German armour and, as the War Diarist noted, it was a hot fight:

The A[nti] T[an]k gun, mortar and m.g. fire seemed to intensify. Sgt Freer aided in the destruction of one AFV. Sgt Freeman also helped out but had been having quite a tough time himself. Shots were landing rather close. One gouged a large hunk of metal off the back of his turret, cracking the inside, and another ripped the stowage and shovels off the back deck.[108]

David Marshall was in Freeman's tank and remembered that action:

Talk about tense. To be hit with a projectile from an 88 mm usually means the end of the Sherman. The speed at which it travels and its size will make it penetrate our armour and destroy everything inside, including the crew. This time there was a Hand that protected us. The first 88mm gouged a hunk of metal off the back of the turret cracking the inside but causing no other damage. The second one ripped some stowage and shovels off the back deck. We rushed out of that spot.[109]

It was a short-range, tank versus tank duel, made confusing by the woods and the smoke. Jim Kroesing's crew had it the worst as they "were suffering very badly from the effects of exposure and gas poisoning [almost certainly from the Homelite]" and "were repeatedly sick in the tank making it thoroughly nauseating and yet they fought determinedly throughout the day until relief came later in the night."[110] Subsequent examination of the ground revealed that B Squadron had knocked out four Mk IV tanks and an 88 mm anti-tank gun in this hard fought action. The Links, however, were not able to get on their objective and had to pull back.

Up in the Gap Luton's C-1 Troop had a busy day on 1 March. Bill had been reinforced during the night by two tanks from C-2 Troop, one of them a 17-pdr. Firefly commanded by Sergeant Tom Milner. Milner had spent the previous night mired in the valley but had got unstuck during the day and was ordered during the dark to reinforce C-1 at the forward position. He led the two tanks forward on foot and had a difficult time locating anyone until the words, "'Oh, shit!' from about four feet away really startled me."[111] It turned out to be two signallers who put him on the right path. Luton's force, now up to five tanks, had no problems beating off a weak German infantry attack early in the morning and Bill remembered "one brave German officer [who] died within a few feet of the edge of the gap near C11, having continued a charge after his men had taken flight."[112]

That being done, Bill's first task of the day was to undertake a recce on foot to locate the German guns that had knocked out the Grenadier Guards the previous night. He went forward with Sergeant Bob Fairhurst and they managed to pinpoint an SPG positioned in a ruined farm building but almost immediately the two men were pinned down by heavy and accurate MG 42 fire. Every time they tried to move, tracers flew overhead, and their positions in the mud as deep as they could go finally became so ludicrous that both burst out laughing. It took them a long time to wiggle back to safety assisted by a mutual exchange of fire between the unknown German and an Argyll Bren gunner. When he arrived back at C11, Bill found that his wireless problems were over – during his absence two crew members, Troopers Wilf Utke and Lloyd Braithwaite, had salvaged a working No. 19 set from one of the knocked-out Guards tanks, a tricky job as it had to be done under German observation.[113]

The German artillery continued without pause and the Regiment lost several casualties. Sergeant Frederick "Beans" Clark of HQ Troop, C Squadron, a prewar member of the Edmonton Fusiliers who had been with the South Albertas since the beginning, was killed when he was caught by shell fragments outside his tank. He was survived by a wife and a son. Trooper Arnold Allen a 22-year-old machinist from Bayfield, New Brunswick, who had been with the Regiment since the previous August, was also killed by an artillery round.[114]

By now most of the South Albertas had gone without sleep for days and some were reaching the breaking point. Among them was Bill Luton, who during the late afternoon, suddenly spotted a Tiger tank moving up the "gap directly in front of our position" and screamed at his gunner, Wilf Utke, to open fire. When "no A.P. shell cracked forth," he "turned sharply to find Wilf, not looking through his telescope, but at me – strangely."[115] Luton glanced at the Tiger again and "it very slowly dissolved, much in the manner seen in the 'Star Trek' movies when someone is 'beamed.'" Bill was

struck speechless; this hallucination was the result of four continuous days without sleep – or was it? Was I going mad? Was I cracking up under the strain? Not being able to trust your senses is one of the most frightening sensations possible. I remembered my first night on Kapelsche Veer when an infantry lieutenant kept firing at an imaginary enemy. "Battle fatigue" I had said to myself rather smugly – smugly because for sure I would never go "nuts" like that.

Within the next hour or so hallucinations would happen again. I would be talking to someone – and in the middle of a sentence he would slowly fade out and the real world would fade in. One positive was the *realization* all was not right. My actions became tentative, because I looked at things and asked myself, "Is this real or not?" What the others thought of me, I do not know, but at least Fairhurst [his troop sergeant] did not call back to squadron to suggest that the boss should be taken out.

The hallucinations disappeared that night and Bill was never troubled by them again but it would be another thirty hours before he got any sleep.

For the South Albertas the battle for the Gap ended in the afternoon of 2 March when the Regiment was relieved by units of the 2nd Canadian Infantry Division. "For shelling and misery," wrote the 10 Brigade historian, the battle "had been unparalleled" because once "the first thrust failed to breakout, the game was up and the succeeding days of ceaseless battering were agonies of hopelessness."[116] The unofficial motto of the armoured corps is "through the mud and the blood to the green fields beyond." By 2 March 1945, most South Albertas reckoned they had been through the first part and it was high time for the second.

CHAPTER SEVENTEEN

"To the green fields beyond."

GERMANY AND HOLLAND: 2 MARCH – 31 MARCH 1945

B̲ert Coffin was anxious to get the Regiment "ship-shape again." Three days of hard fighting and hard going had taken a heavy toll on men and vehicles and nobody at RHQ was happy during the evening of 2 March when an inquiry came down from "our higher formation" regarding the SAR's tank strength because such interest was an indication that something wicked was coming the Regiment's way. That night Lieutenants Pete Burger and Ken Wigg took their troops up to relieve Bill Luton on the ridge – Bill's men had done a good job and RHQ "made sure that a hot meal was ready for them on their return." Burger and Wigg would spend the next four days at that isolated position.[2]

During the morning of 3 March the Regiment received a warning order for a move. Nothing happened that day, however, except that some visitors showed up at RHQ. One of them was Swatty Wotherspoon, who had finally managed to extricate himself from the divisional battle school only to be ordered to take over 4 Armoured Brigade, whose commander was ill. The colonel had now been away from the Regiment since mid-January and many South Albertas wanted to see him back – foremost among them Bert Coffin. Swatty stopped off to see the boys on his way to 4 Brigade because "I knew I'd get more information out of them than I would out of the brigade."[3] "They were great," he remembered, "they had cattle hanging, quarters of beef hanging from their guns." Having got himself in the picture, Swatty departed and the next visitor was a German civilian who "had the temerity to enter" RHQ "and ask for some of his belongings." The man "was, of course, the owner of the farm [serving as RHQ] and appeared to believe he had a perfect right to go into his own house and make off with [his own] valuables." "Well," concluded the War Diarist, "he did not stay long."[4]

More welcome was the news that the American Ninth Army, which had launched Operation GRENADE on 25 February, was

> *W*e kept pushing forward, moving all the time,
> Fought through France and Belgium, to Holland
>   and the Rhine.
> Onward to Berlin we did go,
> We fought the foe – ran into Joe.
> And we kept singing Lili, my own Lili Marlene.
>
> When you think of the fighting in France and Italy.
> You think again of Lili – she's part of history.
> Now she'll live on in history,
> For she will be, our Sweet Lili.
> Our Lili of the lamplight, our own Lili Marlene.[1]

moving on the Rhine from the southwest. The American advance, coupled with the pressure exerted by First Canadian Army, rendered the German position on the west bank of the river untenable, but it also increased the determination of *Generaloberst* Alfred Schlemm, the commander of First Parachute Army, to hang on to his shrinking bridgehead to gain time to evacuate his troops to the far bank. Hitler had refused all Schlemm's previous requests for permission to withdraw with the statement that "not a fit man must cross the Rhine" but Schlemm stressed to his superiors that, if he did not get his eleven divisions to safety, there would be no forces available to defend the east bank of the river against the inevitable Allied assault. Confident that permission would eventually be granted, Schlemm pulled back from the Hochwald on 4 March to a new position nearer the Rhine. It was anchored in the south by the fortified hamlets of Veen and Winnenthal, which guarded the last lateral road to the Rhine bridges at Wesel. As their retention was key to Schlemm's plans for a withdrawal, he garrisoned them with his defensive specialists – paratroopers.[5]

At 1130 hours on 4 March Bert Coffin learned that Veen would be the South Albertas' next objective. The Regiment would come under the command of Lieutenant-Colonel Fred Wigle of the Argylls and the plan was that the two units would "form a fast moving group" with the infantry carried in Kangaroo APCs and drive straight for Veen.[6] The advance element would consist of B Squadron and B Company of the Argylls, who would establish a firm base at the hamlet of Labbeck, on the other side of the Gap, and then exploit forward to a group of farm buildings marked on the map as Haneshof. Under Captain Click Clarke, the advance element pulled out at 1330 hours and had no problems getting to Labbeck, where they captured two Italians busily employed laying mines on the road. By mid-afternoon Labbeck had been secured and a troop and a platoon went to Haneshof, where they cleared the buildings and shot

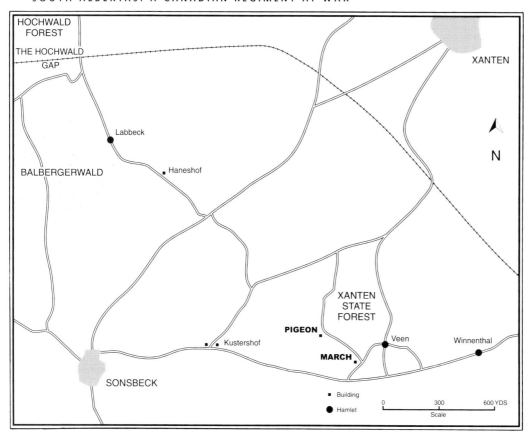

Map 17: The Hochwald, 4-9 March 1945. The Germans began to evacuate to the east bank of the Rhine but set up defensive positions at Veen and Winnenthal to cover the last bridges over the river. Ordered to secure Veen, the SAR sent B Squadron by way of Labbeck, where it fought a vicious little action at Haneshof, while the other two squadrons moved south through the Balbergerwald to Sonsbeck. Delayed by mines and anti-tank guns, the SAR supported the Algonquins' attack on Veen, which was rebuffed, and the village was not taken until 9 March. MAP BY CHRIS JOHNSON.

got a third. This brought to life a German machine-gunner who had also evaded capture and he opened up at the Argylls clustered around the tanks on the road.[9]

Trooper Bert Denning, the co-driver in one of the tanks hit by the *Panzerschreck*, was knocked unconscious. He remembers "coming to" but being "unable to open my hatch as the barrel of the 75 was directly over it."[10] Fortunately for Bert, the "driver managed to get out and I was able to crawl over and out through his hatch. As I crawled to the rear of our tank I saw our gunner, Jim Case, lying on the ground, bleeding badly from a leg wounds." Jim Cooper was the gunner in the tank brewed up by the anti-tank gun:

We turned into a ball of fire inside and the crew commander didn't move as fast as me and we both got stuck in the hatch and I had to drop back in. We all got out on the right hand side of the tank. I didn't know

them up before pulling back to Labbeck for the night. From this time until the end of the war it became standard operating procedure to "light up the landscape" each night by firing HE into any structure that might provide cover for the enemy during the hours of darkness.[7]

Jim Jefferson wanted Haneshof occupied so at first light on 5 March Sergeant Fred Freeman took B-3 Troop back up to the hamlet with a platoon of Argylls. The Germans had moved back in during the night and, as the Canadians approached the first building, which was flying a white flag, one troop member recalled that "we received an unexpected greeting. We were blanketed with heavy machine-gun and bazooka fire. The Argylls jumped off and got into a fight that progressed satisfactorily" as B-3 "poured shot and shell into the buildings from both sides" and "raked them with machine-gun fire."[8] The infantry cleared the buildings, rousting thirty-five prisoners and things were looking good when a German *Panzerschreck* crew (an 88 mm anti-tank rocket launcher served by two men), who had evaded capture, fired from the door of a house from which a white flag was clearly flying. They knocked out two SAR tanks and seconds later an anti-tank gun firing from a nearby wood

what direction we were going, so we followed them and we had to go over a hedge and behind some buildings to get out of there. That's when Neff the loader-operator was killed. He was just new to the crew and he didn't know what was coming off, I guess. I got shrapnel and face burns. I clambered over the hedge. They were shooting right past the building and you had to time yourself before you got going because they kept plunking these two tanks. It was a couple of young German kids having real good fun, I think.

Just past the building, I looked behind me and I saw this guy coming with something sticking out of his face. I said, "Come on, come on."[11]

The man "with something sticking out of his face" was Denning. The hollow-charge of the *Panzerschreck* round had caused the interior face of the armour on his tank to splinter and a piece of metal nearly eight inches long and three inches wide had been driven through Bert's face below his left cheekbone. Someone grabbed Bert, pumped a morphine syrette into his arm and threw him on the deck of the one surviving tank.

The Argyll platoon commander was so angered by the firing

from a house with a white flag that he lost his temper and marched up to the front door with his pistol drawn. The German machine-gunner cut him down, but when the Argylls moved back into the house, the enemy surrendered. David Marshall remembered that it was a very sad B-3 Troop that returned, with the infantry and prisoners, to Labbeck:

> Of the four tanks we started with ours was the only one left. Of the fourteen men in the destroyed tanks, two were dead, … and eight wounded. As this was obviously no longer a healthy spot we returned to Labbeck. Before doing so, we silenced the enemy machine guns and loaded all the remaining Argylls and our own men onto our tank, a total load of 24 passengers. They sat and lay on the deck, clung to the sides and sat over the front. As hot machine guns can sometimes discharge, or a trigger happy gunner may see a likely target, I unloaded them. Anyhow with so many clinging all over the tank we were no longer a fighting vehicle but had become a transport.[12]

After they had laid the wounded out on the road for the ambulance to pick them up, "a QM sergeant passed around a bottle of very thick rum." "Never," recalled Marshall, "has anything tasted so good and had so little effect" for B-3 was severely shaken – of the nineteen members of the troop who had gone into action on 27 February, only eight were still alive and unwounded.

As for Bert Denning it was only when he woke up in a field hospital that he became aware how serious his injuries were – "my head and face were covered in bandages and my left arm had been shattered and was in a cast."[13] Bert was flown to Britain with the metal shard still in his face and in a very tricky bit of surgery the doctors were able to remove it. He would be in hospital for a long time to come.

The vicious little action at Haneshof on 5 March cost the lives of Troopers Allen Gee and Howard Neff. Neff, a 20-year-old shipyard worker from Kingston, Ontario, had been with the Regiment for just eight days. Allen Gee, usually called "Big Gee," a 23-year-old farm labourer from Corlea, Saskatchewan, had been with the South Albertas since the previous September. "It wasn't a great feeling," remembered Jim Nicholson, "pulling my tank over to bypass Big Gee's tank with him still lying there in the road." Ironically, just after the survivors had returned to Labbeck, "the ration truck came up with the mail which included an authorization for Gee to proceed on leave to the U.K."[14]

On 5 March, while B Squadron was pushing on to Veen down the road from Labbeck, the greater part of the Regiment and the Argylls moved through the Balbergerwald toward Sonsbeck. Recce Troop had scouted this route the previous night but had not been able to get far as the Germans had blown a large crater in the road, and when the column got up to this obstacle it was clear that the engineers would have to construct a bridge over it. The sappers got to work in the late afternoon but since 3rd Division had not yet cleared Sonsbeck, it was only at 0800 hours on 6 March that the column moved again out on the so-called "mad dash to Veen," which "was to be pushed on ruthlessly and any opp[osition] to be bypassed if possible."[15] Progress was good until the lead tanks emerged from the Balbergerwald (where the South Albertas caught their first glimpse of the country across the Rhine) and began to descend to Sonsbeck. The road was cratered, and while working around these obstacles, three tanks in quick succession hit mines and several others bogged; although they were out of the Hochwald, they weren't yet out of the mud. The Flail mine-clearing tanks, which were not at the head of the column, had a difficult time getting forward to begin their work and immediately bogged. Eventually the column got moving and made

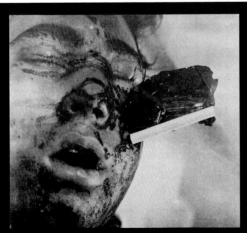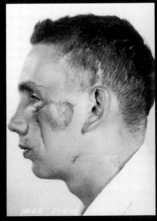

Haneshof, 5 March 1945. Albert Denning with the jagged fragment of metal embedded in his face by the same anti-tank round that knocked out his B Squadron tank. The second photo shows him six weeks later after the doctors had removed the fragment. Then, the fragment itself, eight inches long. AP rounds impacted at such a high velocity that fragments and bits of metal from the interior face of the tank were often broken off and converted into deadly missiles. In all, Denning was sixteen months in hospital. COURTESY, ALBERT DENNING.

Don't splash them, they're Lincoln and Welland! SAR Sherman passes Lincoln and Welland infantry near Sonsbeck, 7 March 1945. The South Albertas felt sorry for the flat feet because they had to walk and had no armour protection; the flat feet felt sorry for the boys because they were penned up in their mobile coffins. There was something to be said for both points of view. NAC, PA 115578.

good progress until they approached the hamlet of Kustershof, on the Sonsbeck road west of Veen, where they encountered yet another large crater, this one seventy feet wide, with mines planted around its edges. There was another delay while a bulldozer and a bulldozer tank picked their way forward, moving slowly and carefully when they passed vehicles because the shoulders of the road were mined. Up to this point there had been no sign of the Germans but mortar bombs started coming in and Lieutenant Frank "Peachy" Howard was evacuated after being hit in the head by shell splinters.[16]

By 1600 hours the crater was filled and the column got under way. The feeling was that the Germans had withdrawn leaving only mines, roadblocks and a thin screen behind them. The advance element, C-3 Troop and 15 Platoon of the Argylls' C Company in Kangaroo APCs, were just approaching a crossroads not more than a thousand yards west of Veen when an anti-tank gun brewed up the lead tank commanded by Corporal Walt Fengler. Fengler's gunner, Trooper Joe Strathern, had not been happy that morning when his crew had been designated lead tank ("you guys will be the clay pigeon for today" he recalled) and that night he had something to tell his diary:

We left our lines to go down this open road alone. There were flooded fields each side and down this road where it comes to a T crossing there was a nice-looking, red-brick, two-story house that appeared to be undamaged. All was

fairly quiet until we got right along side of the building. Then we take a hit. Walt gives us orders to bail out. He never had to give the order twice. We all managed to hit the top of the road safely.

At the same time, three German soldiers came running out of the house with their hands up, we drew our pistols. No one thought of grabbing the sten gun when we bailed out. At this instance, a machine gun opens up from a hedgerow on our left. Bill empties his pistol in its direction and then we all hit the left hand ditch which was full of water. The three Germans hit the right hand ditch. We never saw them again.

Being at least two miles from our lines, our only thought was getting back. Each time we came to a culvert and had to go up and over, the machine gun missed us by only inches. When we got back to our lines, the infantry was in a terrible state. The Germans had this road zeroed in and presighted. We had to lay there, flattened out for some time before we could crawl back towards Squadron HQ. There were many dead and wounded Canadians on the road and in the ditches.[17]

The second AP round hit one of the APCs, taking off the Kangaroo commander's head. The two knocked-out vehicles blocked the narrow road so Glen McDougall, who had taken over C Squadron after Stan Purdy had been evacuated with a knee injury, deployed his three troops (C-1 was LOB) in and around the farm buildings in the area. It looked as if the Germans were going to fight for Veen and prisoners picked up that day informed the intelligence officers that "all [German] troops this side of the Rhine were ordered not to retreat one step" but "to fight to the last round, retreat would mean death."[18]

Nevertheless the Argylls were ordered to put in a two-company attack that night. They would have no tank support as the South Albertas could not get past the two derelict vehicles blocking the road into Veen from Sonsbeck. From a distance Veen looked like an inviting little hamlet – in reality the paratroopers, with their usual industry, had turned the "innocent-looking brick farmhouses" into "true fortresses, buttressed within by concrete and extra-thick brick walls" with every window "a gun position" and "cellars, tunnels and obstacles of all sorts" which "allowed the defenders good comfort, safety and secure communications."[19] Veen was defended by picked troops from the German Parachute Army Assault Battalion and they threw the Argylls back with heavy casualties and the loss of thirty-two prisoners.[20]

That night two crews from A Squadron tried to move the vehicles blocking the road. In the process one of their own tanks got bogged in the mud and the engineers had to be called in, and even then it was not until 1100 hours on 7 March that the road was finally clear. By this time B Squadron had worked its way slowly down from Labbeck, its progress hampered by mines, to a position around a crossroads northwest of Veen where they could bring it under fire. In the late morning Vokes and Jefferson arrived at RHQ headquarters and planning went forward for a two-battalion attack on Veen. The Regiment was detailed to support the Algonquins, who would attack north of the Sonsbeck-Veen road while the BCR would support the Links attacking south of that road. The assault was timed for 1600 hours. Lavoie's A Squadron would provide the Algonquins with close support while the other two squadrons would provide fire support.[21]

The ground around Veen was terrible. Flat and muddy, it offered little natural cover and was bad going for man and

Veen, Germany, March 1945. Defended by the German Parachute Army Assault Battalion and heavily fortified, this little hamlet defied the efforts of 10 Brigade, the Regiment and the BCR to capture it in March 1945. NAC, 145751.

Approaches to Veen, March 1945. The roads were narrow and mined, the fields were soggy and almost impassable, the solidly-built farmhouses were enemy strongpoints and the flat terrain offered an ideal field of fire for anti-tank guns. SAR COLLECTION.

If yer knows of a good 'ole, get in it! Sergeant George Penney, Lieutenant T.F. Howard and Corporal A.G. Tuff in a nice 'ole, the cellar of a German farmhouse, near Veen on 7 March 1945. The original caption reads, "Plenty of German mortars dropping around this house at this time." DND PHOTO. NEGATIVE 47463

machine. The Algonquin's A Company wallowed forward at 1600 hours but met such a hail of mortar and automatic weapons fire that only twenty-five all ranks were still on their feet when, with the help of Lieutenant McKechnie's A-2 Troop, they managed to get one house of their objective – a group of buildings scattered around a crossroads code-named MARCH west of Veen. That was as far as they got. On his way up, McKechnie ran over a mine which blew in his belly hatch and wrecked his wireless, and his Sherman was then hit twice by an anti-tank gun firing from a woods to the north. He managed to get behind the cover of a building but shortly discovered that "he could not move his tank a foot either way without being fired on by" the anti-tank gun and, "being a prudent man, he stayed where he was and engaged what targets he could see from his boxed-in position."[22] Finally a third hit forced the crew to bail out but the gunner, Trooper James Forbes, stayed in the tank and fired off all his ammunition before leaving.[23]

The rest of A-2 fared no better. The second tank was knocked out and the third, commanded by Corporal Carl Wicke, then moved up laying down smoke and firing into the buildings at the crossroads to assist the infantry. Wicke was immediately hit twice by that well-served German anti-tank gun, the second AP round killing the loader-operator, Trooper Douglas Harper, a 22-year-old machinist from Whitby, Ontario. Wicke remembers seeing

the other tanks ahead of me fire smoke and bail out. We were around this house and I said in the mike, "driver reverse,"

and they hit us and it burned right away. I was wounded but I didn't realize it until I hit the ground and they got me in the leg. They took me into this barn. That was the third tank I lost during the war.[24]

McKechnie took his crews and the Brownings from his tanks into the infantry position to reinforce their tenuous hold on the one house they had captured at the crossroads. There were many wounded but Carl Wicke refused both evacuation and morphine until more seriously wounded men had been looked after – McKechnie finally had to order him to go to the rear. Just before last light McKechnie was joined by two tanks from A-1 Troop, a third having bogged on the way up.[25]

It was no better on the left. A-3 Troop lost one tank to bogging but the remaining two helped the Algonquin B Company attack their objectives – three clusters of farm buildings code-named PIGEON. The company lost half its men but got two of the clusters and was trying to secure the third when Bradburn ordered them to abandon the attack and firm up where they were. The tanks were sniped at by that persistent German anti-tank gun from the woods to the east, and nothing, not even major artillery concentrations, seemed able to neutralize it. Just before last light two tanks, all that remained of A-4 Troop, came up to reinforce the position and a third Algonquin company tried to push through to Veen but was decisively stopped by mortar and machine-gun fire. The Links and the BCR meanwhile had no luck south of the village and when darkness brought an end to the shelling and small-arms fire, Veen remained securely in German hands. For the survivors of the Algonquin infantry companies and the A Squadron tanks that stayed with them, "the only thing was to sweat out the long, dark night, and to be soaked by the rain that began to fall with the darkness."[26]

The dawn of 8 March brought clear weather and at both positions the infantry and tanks co-ordinated plans to renew the attack. Their luck wasn't much better this day. An attempt to link up MARCH and PIGEON was stopped by fire from a pill box located between the two places while at MARCH an attempt to seize the remaining buildings in the crossroads cost the Algonquins' A Company half their remaining men in two hours of fighting. Trooper James Forbes led two of his crew in this attack, but when it was beaten off he went back to manning his Browning in a defensive role. The infantry at MARCH were particularly bothered by a well-sited German machine gun that raked their position and "various men tried various angles of fire in order to silence this Jerry weapon" including Lieutenant Jack Fraser, MC, of the Algonquins, who

was almost reckless with daring in his sallies from the shelter of the house, through the orchard to try his hand at knocking out the machine gun which harassed them from the window of the neighbouring house. But at last he tried once too often and the boys watching from the little house

Rolling, rolling, rolling – keep those Shermans rolling. South Alberta Sherman and Stuart advance against Veen with the support of a Holstein cow, 7 March 1945. The future of the cow, as soon as the Canadian Army photographer departed the scene, was uncertain – but probably short. DND PHOTO.

saw him fall. 'Twas then that Lyle Evans [of the SAR] rushed out to the rescue, picked up Mr. Fraser and carried him back to the house; but just as they reached the kitchen a mortar or shell exploded in the orchard and a fragment zipped through the window opening, penetrated Evans' skull and stilled his brain forever. Then it was discovered that this sacrifice had been in vain for Jack Fraser himself was beyond recall.[27]

Lyle Evans was a 23-year-old farm boy from Brussels, Ontario, who had served with the Regiment for a year and had been wounded at St. Lambert. He would never realize his great ambition – to become a member of the Royal Canadian Mounted Police.[28]

At PIGEON a try at the third cluster of buildings was beaten back by a hail of grenades. As John Galipeau of A-4 remembered, "it was useless" to attack as the "houses had been built back in about the 1400s, and they were built to last with stone walls three feet thick."[29] Galipeau and Sergeant Duke Sands

held our position for two days, waiting for orders to attack or withdraw. There were snipers everywhere, and we didn't get out of the tanks during the day the whole time. Sergeant Sands and his crew were on the side opposite the enemy po-

sitions, and so were safe to dismount and move around to heat up some food. My tank faced the enemy positions. We ate hard tack and bully beef and drank cold water from our water bottles. With us was a small group of infantry, an officer and ten or a dozen men. Two or three were lost to snipers, and one when he went down into the basement of the house and lay down on a bed. It was booby trapped and blew up.

The tanks at both places could render little support during the daylight hours as they were stalked by anti-tank guns both in Veen and the surrounding woods, but they provided additional strength for the infantry at night. By the time darkness fell on 8 March the average strength of a rifle company in the Algonquin Regiment was thirty-three officers and men as opposed to their full strength of about one hundred and twenty-five. Lavoie's A Squadron in position with them had a total strength of eight tanks.[30]

Major General Chris Vokes was much in evidence at RHQ on 8 March; "the rest of the time he spent in the B[riga]de Op[eration]s room next door."[31] The commander of 4th Armoured Division was getting impatient – he had been joking in the senior staff mess that he would be knighted when Veen fell and would in future be known as "Vokes of Veen."[32] It wasn't quite so funny to the men in the forward positions but, despite all the brass around, Captain Dick Robinson, the South Alberta Technical Adjutant, scored a great coup when he "whipped an Opel away from under B[riga]de HQ noses" and the War Diarist hoped it would "be in good condition soon."[33] It didn't matter what you were driving around Veen, however, because the place was lousy with mines. Over a period of three days Padre Silcox witnessed the destruction of a Sherman, a carrier and three jeeps by mines including a "provost jeep loaded with "GREEN ROUTE UP" signs" that "detoured skyward and landed a crumpled heap in the field."[34] He supervised the removal of six bodies and, after sweeps by Flails and man-portable mine detectors failed to find anything, the sappers probed a two hundred yard stretch of road with their bayonets and discovered several large wooden mines that had been missed in their previous excursions.[35]

The fighting began to cool off on 9 March 1945. There was an appreciable weakening of German fire and the Algonquins managed to consolidate their positions at both MARCH and PIGEON while the South Albertas escorted a Crocodile forward which burned out the pill box between the two places. At 2100 hours that evening it was decided to mount a major assault the next morning with C Squadron supporting the Argylls. The squadron commander, Glen McDougall, was only informed of this decision at 2300, which did not leave him much time to prepare but then

Time out. On their way to attack Veen, Corporal Lyle "Blackie" Levers's Firefly was disabled by a mine. Three members of the crew, showing the strain of the recent heavy fighting, pose in front of their vehicle – from left to right: Trooper Elmer Stewart, Trooper Cliff Allen (holding that night's dinner) and Corporal Blackie Levers. COURTESY, CLIFF ALLEN.

A picture they never showed mother. Blackie Levers's crew pose in front of their knocked-out Firefly. From left to right: Elmer Stewart, Blackie Levers, Cliff Allen and Dave Clendenning (holding a German Schmeisser MP 40 submachine gun). It was the custom in this crew, as it was in many SAR crews, for each man to have his own binoculars as four pairs of eyes were reckoned to be better than one. Their faces reveal a mixture of stress, fatigue, relief ... and dirt. COURTESY, CLIFF ALLEN.

Glen was a fairly unflappable type. One of his troop leaders remembered seeing him at the Hochwald, when everyone had "taken shelter from a barrage of shells, … sitting calmly in the open smoking his pipe, attending to a call of nature – and taking his own sweet time about it, too."[36]

That night, having made their point as it were, the German Parachute Army Assault Battalion pulled out of Veen. Schlemm had received permission to withdraw across the Rhine on 6 March and, during the intervening four days, while his rearguards held off First Canadian Army, he had carried out a

Out of action. The goose did not long survive having its picture taken and now lies on the tank with its neck wrung – however, Cliff Allen remembers that that it gave the crew the trots. Note the chicken wire netting around the 17-pdr. to camouflage its length and the German 98K Mauser rifle leaning against the tank – just in case. COURTESY, CLIFF ALLEN.

Cleaned up and ready to go again. Looking spruce and fit after the Hochwald, Corporal Blackie Levers's crew pose proudly with the new Firefly which replaced the one they lost on the way into Veen. From the left, Dave Clendenning, Elmer Stewart and Cliff Allen. Elmer has moved his Browning holster to his left hip for a quick "cross draw" with his right hand while Cliff proudly displays the crew's Schmeisser MP 40. COURTESY, CLIFF ALLEN.

massive evacuation of the west bank of the river and, for the fourth time since August 1944, Allied airpower proved incapable of preventing the escape of a major German army.[37] Corporal John Galipeau at PIGEON became aware that the Germans were leaving during the night because he "woke up at about three in the morning to hear what I had come to recognize as the signal the Germans gave when they were pulling out: three quick bursts with a Schmeisser machine gun."[38] The Argyll assault, which went in at 0530 hours on 10 March, turned out to be a "non event." Only a few snipers were encountered and it quickly became obvious that the paratroopers had gone and for that everyone was truly thankful. The Regiment's job in the Hochwald was now over and that afternoon it was stood down for a rest.[39]

But Padre Silcox still had work to do. He went forward that day to the crossroads at MARCH as he "had been told I would find a good many bodies awaiting some padre and his party."[40] In the field before the crossroads, two "Argyles and a Nazi lay" but the "Sherman at the intersection was 'all clear' – all the crew had escaped." Silcox continued to "a brewed up Sherman in the middle of the field" where there "was evidence that one lad, Douglas Harper of Whitby, hadn't made it, but a third Sherman ditched beside the nearby house, was 'all clear.'" After finding another dead infantryman in the orchard the padre entered a barn where, in one of the pig pens,

lay a heap of Algonquin dead. I crawled over the partition and rolled over the top man who lay face down – 'twas Jack Fraser. I shall never forget the queer feeling that came over me as I caught sight of his M.C. ribbon, its white and royal blue as clean and lovely as the day of presentation …. "The paths of glory lead but to … a bloody heap in a pig-sty."

From this pig-sty I moved on into the human quarters which were strewn with broken furniture, dishes, rubble, hundreds of spent Browning cartridges, and miscellaneous equipment. Across the heap of cartridges on the kitchen floor lay the body of one man for whom I was especially looking – Lyle Evans, a trooper of the South Albertas from Brussels, Ontario, – and in the living-room beyond (how ironical that term now!) lay another 'Goon.'

The burial parties, the sorting of the little white sacks of personal possessions ("valuables to be sent home, usables to his pals") and the paperwork – records, letters and more letters – would follow. It was work that Phil Silcox took seriously and he was still writing letters and making visits to next of kin for years after the war ended.

By this time, usually, the telegrams, those awful wartime telegrams, had been sent to homes across Canada. "The Minister of National Defence," they read, "sincerely regrets to inform you that" lieutenant, sergeant, corporal, trooper, son, husband, father or brother has been killed, wounded or reported missing in action. The families of the South Albertas posted missing at the Hochwald faced a long and agonizing wait before they learned whether their loved ones were alive. Mary Funnell, the wife of 25-year-old Trooper Fred Funnell of A Squadron, was only informed on 11 March that her husband had "been officially reported missing in action" on 27 February.[41] Two weeks later she received a letter from the Department of National Defence to confirm that he was missing but "that does not necessarily mean that he has been killed."[42]

Like all the loved ones of South Alberta casualties Mary Funnell eventually heard from Padre Silcox. He wrote on 21 April 1945, apologizing for the delay, because the six intervening weeks "must have been wretched ones for you at home" but pleading the press of "innumerable duties."[43] "As to the prospects" of her husband and the other men captured in the "right hook" on 27 February still being alive, the padre continued,

we are hopeful! We are always cautious about allowing our feelings to run away with us, for the grim realities are always sober reminders that anything can happen. But relatively speaking the circumstances suggested to us that these men were all right. And there has been no reason to change that opinion.

What happened is that on that morning, 27th Feb., his squadron ran into a mess of trouble as they set out to attack enemy positions on the edge of Udem. So far as we know the casualties were fairly light. We have definitely identified the four known dead, and we know of certain others who were evacuated to hospital wounded. The crews were not seen afterwards – and the fact that they were CREWS, and not just so many men, suggested to us that they were likely taken captive altogether.

Mary Funnell was still waiting to learn whether or not her husband was alive in the middle of May when she got another telegram telling her that the Department of National Defence was "pleased to inform you that A 107236 Trooper Frederick Arthur Funnell previously reported missing in action is now officially reported safe in United Kingdom stop."[44] Sometimes the mills of government can grind very slowly – on the same day that Art Baker's mother received a telegram reporting him missing in the Hochwald, Art recalls, "she got a summons to go to court because I hadn't answered my enlistment call, my draft call."[45]

The fighting was over and the recriminations now began. On 12 March the officers of the South Alberta Regiment were ordered, along with every other officer in 4th Armoured Division, to attend a lecture by Chris Vokes. The divisional commander "complimented us on a job well done," recorded the War Diarist, but "stressed that during the next two weeks of rest we must all strain to correct certain weaknesses."[46] For "tank men" this was to be the "ability to endure long periods of mental strain and physical restraint." The War Diarist was being tactful as usual – Lieutenant Bill Luton of C Squadron, who was present that day, has left a much different version of Vokes's address:

The scene is etched in memory: an overcast sky, an open field, and more officers than I had ever seen gathered together in one place. Once all were assembled, we were submitted to abuse the like of which I have never heard in the army. Vokes blamed the failures of BLOCKBUSTER on the officers in the field and the men they led. Our faults ranged all the way from cowardice to incompetence to lack of physical fitness – he did not miss any bases – and he gave all kinds of advice on what we should do to make ourselves over to his mould.

In doing this Vokes exemplified at its worst a fault, unfortunately all too common among the senior commanders of the Canadian Army: blaming the men at the sharp end for a lousy plan. Nothing could have been more stupid than the strategy that Vokes himself implemented in sending 4th Division through the Hochwald Gap. He should have been apologizing to us instead of shouting the disgraceful comments he made. I was not close enough to the front of the group to note whether or not he was sober; I do know that on one other occasion he was unmistakably drunk on a formal inspection parade.[47]

These are strong words but there is much truth in them. Operation BLOCKBUSTER reflected badly on the generalship of both Simonds and Vokes – the original direction was laid down by Crerar but the detailed planning and execution of the attack were their responsibility. Simonds never committed a plan for BLOCKBUSTER to paper; in a postwar interview he stated that his major concern was to secure "a route through which the momentum of the advance could be fully maintained to its conclusion" – the city of Xanten on the Rhine. There were three possible routes: the Calcar-Xanten road, the Goch-Xanten railway and the Goch-Sonsbeck road. Of these, the first was considered "too cratered" and "deployment on either side would be limited due to floods," while the third was a "good road" but "the approaches were too narrow and unfit for traffic" and it was in the British sector. This left the railway, which was "reported to be a well-founded embankment and free of mines and, so far as Air Recce would show, free of demolition." Simonds was apparently aware that the terrain in the gap area was not good going for tanks – "his greatest worry was the low

Knocked out. Trooper M.E. Lang poses on a German Mk IV knocked out near the Rhine in March 1945. NAC, PA-114964.

armour; BLOCKBUSTER demonstrated he had learned nothing in the intervening six months. Vokes was worse. He divided his division into "sort of penny packets" which he then scattered across the landscape – mostly stuck in the mud – thus fulfilling the old military adage, "use 'em two at a time, lose 'em two at a time." Reflecting on the battle in later years Swatty Wotherspoon concluded that Chris Vokes simply "knew nothing about armour, absolutely nothing" and "was a disaster as an armoured division commander."[50] "Crafty Chris," as he became known in 4th Division, also had a distinct command style – he was a first-class bully who be-

ground immediately west of the strong Hochwald position towards which movement of armour and reinforcements would normally be slow and difficult." This was a masterpiece of understatement but, to get around this problem, Simonds planned "to push the development of the chosen maintenance route along the railway line to ensure a speedy build up of the situation." Thus, the infamous railway embankment was chosen as the route of the advance and, thus, the Hochwald Gap became 4th Armoured Division's objective.[48]

Vokes translated these intentions into orders for the attack. In verbal instructions to the senior officers of the division issued on 22 February he stressed that "the long term weather forecast is that we shall have fine weather for the next two or three days and the ground in the conc[entratio]n area and the cross country route … should be fair going for t[an]ks."[49] He also emphasized that "the great danger" was "the heavily def[ended] town of Udem on the right flank."

As it turned out, the 4th Armoured Division ran straight into a mud hole, Uedem was not cleared in time, the railway embankment was unusable because nobody could live on top of it and the seizure of the Gap itself, due more to a display of grit on the part of the Algonquins and South Albertas than anything else, proved to be an illusory success because the Germans simply withdrew to the reverse slope of the Hochwald Ridge and blocked any and all Canadian attempts to move east to the Rhine.

When it came to the actual handling of the battle both generals proved uncommonly clumsy. By 28 February Simonds had managed to pile elements of five brigades from three different divisions into a bog about three miles square. Simonds had shown in Normandy that he did not understand how to employ

lieved that threats were the best incentive. When Lieutenant-Colonel Ned Amy of the Grenadier Guards refused to use the railway embankment death trap to attack into the Gap, Vokes reputedly threatened to put not only Amy but his entire regiment under arrest.[51]

Bad generalship, good troops – but what of the cost. One commentator has described the 1945 Rhineland battles as being the "charge of the Light Brigade" for Commonwealth armoured units and the statistics bear that out – particularly for the South Albertas. Between 8 February and 10 March, the seven armoured brigades (four British, two Canadian and one Polish) which fought in the Rhineland lost a total of 385 tanks. The heaviest losses incurred by a single brigade were those of 4 Canadian Armoured Brigade of 4th Canadian Division, which lost 98 tanks between 25 February and 10 March, a testimony to the viciousness of the fighting in BLOCKBUSTER. Not included in 4 Brigade's total are the losses of the South Albertas and they were bad – very bad. During that same period the Regiment lost 61 tanks, a casualty rate that was about one hundred per cent of its tank strength and nearly sixteen per cent *of the total tank loss* incurred in both Operations VERITABLE and BLOCKBUSTER. By this time in the war there were lots of tanks available to make up for losses; the problem was replacing trained soldiers, and 10 Brigade's casualties in BLOCKBUSTER were heavy – 858 killed, wounded and prisoner – the heaviest losses suffered by the brigade during a single operation. The Regiment's portion of this total was ten killed and seventy-three wounded or taken prisoner.[52]

Bert Coffin and the other senior officers of the Regiment tried to get the message upstairs that the operation had been a shambles. They used the unlikely medium of a report prepared by the divisional historical section with the title "Record of Operation 'BLOCKBUSTER' – Prepared by 29 Cdn Armd Recce Regt." that was a detailed, comprehensive and nearly unreadable account of the Regiment's role in the recent fighting. As it was to be "vetted" by the senior staff, Bert and the squadron commanders had to be careful about what they said. In the "Comments and Lessons" sections, however, they managed to get in a few oblique statements that Vokes and his planners might read with profit before their next attempt at a major operation. Concerning the enemy defences, the South Albertas noted that, "When the enemy has many prepared pos[itio]ns covered by A[nti] T[an]k guns, the answer is to pass through his screen *under cover of darkness*."[53] They pointed out the old truism: "That which has always been considered *good t[an]k country is also excellent A[nti] T[an]k country*." They noted the problems with the mud: "As it was impossible for wheels to go f[or]w[ar]d, track veh[icles] had to be used for supplies." When all else failed, "we found a length of rubber hose invaluable for syphoning petrol out of more or less static" tanks and vehicles, which is a fairly sad comment on the rather harebrained logistical arrangements for the attack. Most importantly, they emphasized that "*Information coming from a higher level was very scarce*, hard to get, late and inaccurate." There is no evidence that Vokes ever saw this document which, reading between its lines (and you have to, so carefully is it worded), is a damning indictment of his generalship.

Bert and Bob. Bert Coffin (left) commanded a company or squadron in the SAR from 1941 to 1943 when he became second-in-command, an appointment he retained to the last two weeks of the war. Bob Allsopp was adjutant of the Regiment from 1943 to 1945.
COURTESY, R.H. ALLSOPP

Taking all this into consideration, Bill Luton's resentment of that speech made on an open field near the Rhine, a resentment shared by the majority of the officers and men in the 4th Canadian Armoured Division, is not only understandable – it is justified. The men of that formation had done their best under impossible conditions against a skilled and tenacious opponent and they deserved praise, not the condemnation they received from their superiors.

The good news was that the shooting had stopped for a while and the Regiment was going back to friendly Holland for rest and recuperation. The warning order came on 12 March and the Regiment moved out that night at the tail end of the 4th Division column. Part of the march lay over Guy Simonds's beloved railway embankment, where the sappers had

finally finished their work – a week after the division had seized more useful roads. As the War Diarist noted, it was a nightmare for an armoured unit: "Many tanks drove off the road, and some turned over on the bad embankment."[54] Late on the morning of 13 March the South Albertas reached their new harbour, "an exceedingly cold and hard concrete floored factory" in Tilburg but the men were "happy to be billeted again in bedsheets and clothes!"[55] The Regiment was now given a week to lick its wounds.

A nearby park provided a convenient locale not only to meet Dutch girls but also to dispose of the loot from the Hochwald. What resulted, according to one South Alberta, was "a monster garage sale … with all the goodies we had accumulated offered at the best bargaining prices we could get."[56] The Dutch, whose country had been stripped by the Germans, now got a chance to get some of their possessions back – at a price. All "kinds of junk, from motorcycles to linen" were presented but the most saleable items were bicycles and foodstuffs – one part of the park soon resembled Smithfield Market in London "what with all the beef and poultry and pork being displayed."[57] The only fly in the ointment was that prices in Tilburg had become depressed after a Scots division stationed in the area "had done some fancy underselling."[58] Nonetheless, most everything was disposed of and the tanks began to resemble armoured fighting vehicles instead of overcrowded moving vans. Most South Albertas never gave a second thought to the acquisition of what, after all, was private property – the feeling was that if they didn't get it, somebody else would. Padre Silcox did have qualms, however, and at the church parade on Sunday, 18 March, he announced that he had thought about taking as the text of his sermon the scripture, "Let him that stole steal no more," but "figured he'd let it go for the time being."[59]

Now that the Regiment was static for a period the journalists showed up. To be fair, wartime reporters were a far cry from the motor-mouthed, pretty-faced "talking heads" that infest modern television screens. They saw enough, and knew enough, to guess what was really going on, but you still couldn't tell them the truth and, even if you did, they couldn't report it because of censorship. Ross Munro wrote it this way: "Commanded by Maj. A.F. Coffin of Medicine Hat, Alta., and Calgary, the tanks rolled down the slope and through the valley to help an Ontario infantry regiment break through the lines of trenches which screened the forest itself."[60] "The mud," he continued, "was terrible but, although many tanks were bogged, the SAR got through and with their guns helped put the infantry over this obstacle." In ten short paragraphs Munro skilfully managed to include the names of no less than eleven South Albertas (and their home towns) including "Frank Freer, Dawson Creek, B.C., nicknamed 'First Brew' for the amazing speed with which he can brew up a can of tea in a bivouac." Someone must have put a "spin" on that one because the nickname was "Fast Brew" and Frank Freer didn't get it because of his predilection for tea. Bert Coffin made the obligatory (and banal) summation of the recent action: "Our greatest obstacles in the Hochwald battle were mud, mines and anti-tank obstacles, all well covered by enemy fire, [which was, if you think of it, quite a lot] but the regiment was first into the Hochwald and last out. We did a lot of cleaning up on the southern part with the infantry." So much for the folks back home.

As usual, the term "rest period" was deceptive. Squadron parades were held, the RSM and squadron sergeant-majors began to pay attention to the minutiae of dress and deportment, and training schools were started to instruct the many new reinforcements, both officers and men, who had come up to replace the men lost in the Hochwald. Spring, however, had finally arrived so RSM Jock Mackenzie got the football team out on the ground and for the fourth year in a row they won the division championship, but, sadly, were knocked out in the Canadian Army semi-finals by a team from army headquarters. These "HQ boys played good football," commented the War Diarist, but then, being headquarters personnel, they had more time to practice so it really wasn't fair.[61] The echelons and administrative sections were busier than ever and it was somewhat ironic that as a result some of the men who had fought so hard in the Hochwald got more work. It was the custom in the South Alberta Regiment, and a good custom, that every effort was made to rest crews who had seen long and hard action by removing them from the fighting troops for a period and giving them jobs in the squadron headquarters. Unfortunately, during a quiet period, these headquarters were busy with "administrative details" and that often meant a lot of activity for men sent back "for a rest." On the other hand, there is an old army saying: "If you can't take a joke, you shouldn't have joined up."

Considerable time was spent on maintenance, either repairing damage sustained in the Hochwald or getting newly-delivered replacement tanks (and there were many) ready for battle. Walt Fengler's crew were puzzled by their new vehicle, a reconditioned D-Day Sherman with the name "Clumsy" – who would give a tank such a name?[62] In an armoured regiment maintenance never ends and the drivers went over their engines and suspension, the gunners checked weapons and checked them again, the loader-operators worked on the wireless sets and the crew commanders made sure that everyone did their jobs and furnished anything needed. The squadron fitters assisted with any major mechanical problems the crews could not handle while the armourers did the same for the weaponry. The

South Albertas prided themselves on putting the maximum number of tanks and vehicles on the road. Swatty Wotherspoon thought his men "were brilliant in keeping their equipment up" and sometimes, as he noted, the South Albertas also kept up the equipment of other units:

> If there was a tank abandoned on the roadside [with] somebody else's battle numbers [tac signs] on it, our fellows coming along would have our number on it in nothing flat, and tow the tank to where they could strip it or make it go again. We were the only regiment, I think, … that went in with six [Crusader] anti-aircraft guns and came out with the same six anti-aircraft guns. My command vehicle halftrack [the ACV], it went right through training in England and right through to Germany because of the very high competence of the mechanics.[63]

Actually it was better than Swatty knew – the Regiment went into Normandy with six Crusader AA tanks but came out with seven as they "recruited" one abandoned by a British formation and ran it for the duration.[64] As for the ACV, not only did it make to Germany; it served in the postwar Canadian army before ending up in Sarcee Camp, near Calgary, as a display vehicle. They cranked it up a few years back and it was still running well.[65]

On 15 March an incident occurred that reminded everybody that, although they were out of action, there are always hazards in war. A Squadron was working on its vehicles in the Tilburg park watched by the usual bevy of fascinated Dutch kids. Sergeant Herb Roulston of A-4 Troop was standing in the turret of his Sherman while a brand new reinforcement was priming No. 36 grenades on a tarp spread over the back deck of the tank. The new man suddenly said, "Sarge, this grenade is smoking" and Roulston, looking down, realized to his distress that the man "in error, had picked up and pulled the pin on one of the grenades that was already primed, and it was about to explode."[66] At that moment, "the kid dropped it, and rolled it down by the tarpaulin." For Herb, it was a bad moment:

> Herb scrambled to undo the tarp strings so he could get it. Finally he had the grenade in his hand, and he had to decide what to do with it. He didn't know whether to drop it in the tank or on the street or to throw it. If he were to throw it, he couldn't see where it was going to land, and there were children all over the place. Before he could make a decision the grenade exploded, and that was the end of the war for Herb.

Herb Roulston lost his hand and the irony was that his Military Medal, awarded for an incident the previous October when he had rescued two wounded men under fire, came through the following day. Captain Gordie Campbell of A Squadron presented it to him in hospital.[67]

On 14 March, after nearly two months absence, Swatty

Wotherspoon returned to the South Albertas. During his time away, the Regiment had carried out two very tough jobs – the Kapelsche Veer and the Hochwald – and Bert Coffin had done a fine job under the worst possible circumstances and it was no reflection on Bert that everyone was glad when Swatty came back. To the men the colonel was always a distant figure but, like him or not, they wanted him around when they went into action because they respected his abilities and his independent attitude toward senior officers. Lieutenant Ev Nieman remembered that the first question the men in his troop would ask him when he returned from an O Group concerning a forthcoming "show" was not "where are we going or what are we doing?" It was "where's the colonel?"[68] If Ev said that Swatty "is with us," they would reply "fine" but if he said "the colonel is not with us, he has been posted to brigade," his men would become shirty and say "the hell with it, we are not going!" "Of course they would," Ev concluded, "but they would bitch a lot."

Wotherspoon had now been commanding the South Albertas for nearly two years. This was something of a record in 4th Division, where the average duration of command of an armoured or infantry unit was between six and eight months, and Swatty himself was getting concerned about his chances for promotion. On several occasions he had taken command of either 4 or 10 Brigades for long periods when their brigadiers were absent and he was somewhat annoyed that his brother, Ian, now had command of 5 Armoured Brigade. The problem was not that Vokes disliked him – these two very different men actually "got along extremely well" although Swatty "used to argue with him and tell him that I didn't think he was doing the right thing that way or the other way."[69] In Wotherspoon's opinion Vokes "didn't know anything about armour, and you can't fight armour if you don't really know what they can do." It appears that two factors worked against Swatty's promotion: the first was the great number of officers of his rank and the relatively small number of brigade commands (four armoured and twelve infantry) available in the fighting Canadian Army – the second was the personal enmity of Guy Simonds. Late in the war Swatty got up the nerve (never a hard thing for him) to ask Vokes about his promotion and Vokes told him that he had "recommended him three times and all had been turned down." Wotherspoon "didn't see how it could be anybody else but the corps commander."[70]

Swatty was a well known epicure and the officers had a pleasant surprise for him – during his absence they had engaged a real French chef for their mess. The War Diarist noted that the man "comes to us with a great name in culinary circles," having previously worked for First Canadian Army Headquarters and a Base Reinforcement Unit, two organizations where officers had the time to take their dining seriously.[71] This initiative, so unlike the South Albertas who were, as their adjutant once remarked, "a very plebeian regiment," probably resulted from the intervention of Glen McDougall and Gordie Irving, who were now directing the affairs of the mess.[72] Being relative

sophisticates, Glen and Gordie set about improving the officers' life style. The purchase of "30 bottles of 4 Star Cognac at 125 francs each" was one of their first acquisitions and the French chef a natural second.[73] They tried him out on steak fried in onions, and when he passed this test with flying colours, he was allowed to prepare the meal for a formal mess dinner held on 16 March and attended by Brigadier Jefferson and the battalion commanders of 10 Brigade. Oysters were procured for this occasion but there was "almost a mutiny in the kitchen" when the new chef was told to fry them instead of doing them according to the approved *cordon bleu* method, which is to gently sautée them in their own juice and a light white wine.[74] The Frenchman shouldn't have complained so much; at least the boys hadn't asked him to prepare "prairie oysters," that fine old western Canadian delicacy. Nor did they ask him to join in the "War Dance," the SAR officers' late night ritual which, unfortunately, because of modesty and modern sensitivity, cannot be described in detail.

The enlisted men, always better informed than the officers when it came to locating and acquiring stocks of alcohol, would have laughed if they had known of the latter's purchase of cognac at 125 francs the bottle. They had found larger supplies of better product at cheaper prices. Trooper John Neff of B Squadron recorded that "we had more than enough to drink" at Tilburg while John Galipeau, who replaced Herb Roulston as the troop sergeant of A-4, noted with satisfaction that, along with a lot of new responsibilities, rank did have its privileges – he was now entitled to "purchase a 40 ounce bottle of liquor once a month."[75] Inevitably, Chief Whitford of C Squadron got into trouble. As his troop leader later recalled, the chief was always a handful:

A big man, the Chief, and the descendant of a long line of warriors. A better gunner in action there never was, one of the few men who really *enjoyed* fighting. He could get carried away, too. Once when some Jerries were surrendering he shouted: "Shoot every one except the man with the white flag!" But out of action, trouble was his middle name. I could not help smiling over the recollection of how he had so amazed a group of Dutch civilians at Tilburg when he jumped out of a second story window to escape regimental incarceration. … Normally, when we went back to fighting, 1 Troop got him back, he was just too good a guy in action to waste locked up somewhere.[76]

Most of the men didn't get up to mischief but passed their spare time writing to their wives, girlfriends and families, watching movies put on by the Auxiliary Services, and trying to relax. Those who did cannot be blamed – when your life expectancy is measured in days, not decades, you try to pack in as much as you can.

And Europe, old and wicked, was an exciting place for young men coming from a considerably less sophisticated nation, which is exactly what Canada was in 1945. Take Trooper David Marshall of B Squadron, that former paragon of his church's youth organization, whose decline had begun the previous September when he had broken the National Pledge. David slid further down the slippery slope in March 1945. His rest period started off quietly enough – on 16 March he recalled trying to find the Chinese Hussars with Trooper Emry "Daddy" Vitkovich, the steady older man and convinced socialist who kept an eye on the younger lads in B-3 Troop. David and Daddy never found the Hussars that day but did come across a British NAAFI, where they lunched on sandwiches and beer. Marshall then went on telephone watch at Squadron HQ and was there when Sergeant Fred Freeman walked in "with two 48 hour passes for Paris looking for someone to take them off his hands" – oh lucky day.[77]

The next morning Troopers Marshall and Pat Gregory left for the city of lights. They got there without any problems and at the Canadian Leave Centre were given "the biggest hotel room I had ever seen" equipped with "two beds, a bathroom with a bath tub with *hot and cold* water, and a funny bathroom fixture that shot water straight up but you wouldn't use it to do a job nor did it look like any urinal I'd ever seen."[78] Uncertain about the intricacies of Gallic plumbing, the two South Albertas wisely left the thing alone and "spent the next two days looking over the town and looking over the girls." Paris was thrilling because the "best looking and the best dressed bevy of females to be found on earth seemed to be parading up and down the streets just for our benefit." To their credit, however, Marshall and Gregory were anxious to broaden their horizons and tried to get tickets to the one cultural event known to every red-blooded Canadian boy – the *Folies Bergères* – but unfortunately there were no seats available. Instead, the helpful lady at the Legion Auxiliary Services Centre offered them tickets to the *Club Mayol*, a less well known attraction. Having no choice, Marshall and Gregory "took them with considerable scepticism and disappointment" but their attitude changed when they got to the club and were conducted to a box seat right next to an elevated runway.

"What a spot," Marshall remembered with enthusiasm:

We could look down on the audience and all the red tabs of the very high priced help and all the other officers and here we were, two lowly troopers, with the best seats in the house. We didn't know how good they were until the show got under way.

It was somewhat of a musical show with comedians, in English, jugglers and dancing girls. Then these dancing girls started to take their clothes off. And then they walked right around the walkway directly in front of us, first with only some of their clothes off and then with all of them off, except for some fancy hats. They may have had a fan or two, I don't remember. We could have reached out and touched them, if we hadn't been frozen with embarrassment.

On Saint Patrick's Day 1945 the beast began to stir again. The South Alberta Regiment received a warning order that it would shortly be moving to the divisional training area and the move was made two days later to "a scrubby pine forest" in a patch of sandy soil near Loon op Zand. Here the Regiment went into tents, the officers' mess sporting a large new one borrowed from 10 Brigade, which they furnished with tables and chairs on loan from a priest at Tilburg and couches acquired in Germany. For social visits the mess also had its Opel passenger car, which Dick Robinson had managed not only to get running but to smuggle back to Holland from the Hochwald. Much to Bert Coffin's disgust, he was riding in it the day "it blew a tyre" and Bert went gunning "for Public Enemy No. 1, our poor Tech[nical] Adj[u]tant." It was obvious that something big was about to come off as Holland was filling up with Canadians, including 1st Canadian Corps from Italy. The "Spaghetti League" had now wound up and for the first time in the war the two armoured divisions, three infantry divisions and two independent armoured brigades of the fighting Canadian Army would be going into battle together.[79]

Meanwhile, everyone was listening to the exciting news. In the east the Soviet army, which had started a massive offensive in January that had taken them into East Prussia by the end of February, were now threatening Vienna and poised on the Oder, ready for the final assault on Berlin. In the west, Montgomery's 21 Army Group was preparing to cross the Rhine north of Wesel while Bradley's 12 Army Group was ready to break out of its bridgehead at Remagen and make a second assault over the river near Mainz and Karlsruhe. Allied aircraft had reduced most German cities to rubble and a desperate Hitler began to part from reality as he changed senior commanders, planned grandiose counteroffensives by moving pins on maps and drafted children and old men into *ad hoc* units. On 20 March 1945 he stepped briefly outside his bunker to make his last public appearance – decorating some Hitler Youth who had rendered distinguished service. The youngest was a 12-year-old boy who "had arrested a spy, and when Hitler asked him how he had discovered the man," the child proudly answered, "He wore his corporal's stripe on the wrong arm, my Führer."[80] The Second World War was moving toward its inevitable end but nobody expected the fighting to be over much before summer because, between the Allies and final victory, was the *Wehrmacht*. Battered and bleeding, it was still the toughest and most professional fighting force of modern times.

The Regiment spent five days camped under the pines at Loon op Zand doing "an indoctrination in the art of tank warfare as practised by 4th Armoured Division: troop manoeuvring, target shooting and TEWTs."[81] This was intended to be a "finishing school" for all the new reinforcement officers and men but, as Bill Luton remarked about his own instruction, "all these skills were merely the tools of the trade: combat with the enemy was where the rubber met the road, and almost nothing in all those many courses taught much about that. I had learned

Rhine Shoot, March 1945. Piles of 75 mm HE are stacked behind their tanks as the South Albertas wait for the order to open fire. The crews lived in dug-outs under the vehicles. SAR COLLECTION.

more in two weeks of BLOCKBUSTER about *fighting* than in the previous two years of training."[82] Luton noted, however, that,

> For the veterans (one of which I now considered myself), the training was pleasantly routine. Having been through a similar initiation period in November, I realized the ones approaching their first action did not view the exercises with the same detachment, and the urge to "pull the leg" of the newcomers was almost irresistible. When I had encountered this good-natured hazing, the big talk had been about St. Lambert, Moerbrugge, Bergen op Zoom; now it was of Kapelsche Veer, the Hochwald Gap, Veen and here I could stretch things as well as the next man. After all, some chatter about 88's and Moaning Minnies provided a touch of realism.

Newly-promoted Sergeant John Galipeau of A-4 found he had a problem. Just after he got his tanks to the training area and his men settled in under canvas, he was issued with a brand new troop leader and a crew of four very green reinforcements who had no experience whatsoever. John didn't say "too much to the troop officer" who stood by and listened "while I talked to the crew. I explained to them what they were getting into, told them what to be prepared for, passed on the kinds of things

you learn through experience."[83] "We can always replace tanks," John advised them, "but men are harder to replace" and he "tried to point out the small errors that, in battle, can cost you your life." He hoped they got the message but somehow he doubted it because, "during their short military life," sergeants and corporals "had always been smartly dressed with everything shining and clean and their rank badges very much in evidence, the very picture of military authority." What were they to make of this "grubby little man in a torn and filthy tank suit, wearing boots that had not seen a decent polish in weeks, his beret shoved to the back of his head and not a rank badge in sight," who acted "like he had some authority."

On 22 March Swatty learned about the forthcoming show at a 10 Brigade O Group. Second British Army would cross the Rhine the following evening but 9 Brigade and the 1st Canadian Parachute Battalion would be the only Canadian troops to take an active part in the initial amphibious assault, codenamed Operation PLUNDER, or the airborne landing, codename VARSITY. Canadian artillery units would support the British attack and, to add weight to their fire, it had been decided to repeat an artillery tactic used in the Rhineland battles and stage a series of PEPPERPOTS, or bombardments by all available barrels including those of the four armoured regiments of 4th Division. This was a new one for the South Albertas – they had fought as infantry and armour; now they would become gunners. Over the next two days preparations were put in hand for a move to the firing position on the west bank of the river; the 17-pdr. tanks, which would not be used in the artillery role, were removed from their troops and temporarily formed into a separate squadron; and plans were made to use the Recce and AA Troops as ammo carriers.[84]

The new job was not popular. As the best armoured regiment in 4th Division, if not the Canadian Army, if not the world, the South Albertas had rightly expected that they would have a leading role in the forthcoming operation. On second thought, maybe not the leading role but at least employment as armour. Wotherspoon sensed the mood and, a few hours before Operation PLUNDER commenced on the evening of 23 March, held a Regimental parade. Trying to foster some unit pride among the many reinforcements, he told them "how highly we were regarded by our fellow units and that this show could make them regard us more highly than ever" and stressed his watchwords: "Co-operation, cunningness and all-out effort."[85] It was a good try and probably impressed the new boys but Bill Luton remembered that the colonel "was less convincing" when he outlined "the importance of the indirect firing role in the next few days."[86] As Luton put it: "If indirect firing had been our cup of tea, we would have signed up for the artillery in the first place."

On 25 March the Regiment moved to their firing position on the bank of the Rhine just south of Cleve. Many South Albertas recall that Cleve, heavily bombed and shelled during the battles of February, presented a scene of devastation worse than anything they had seen since Caen. At the firing area, the 75 mm Shermans were positioned, pits dug to shelter the crew, ammunition was stacked by the hundreds of rounds and an attempt made to camouflage because German counter shelling was expected. It was a good idea but in the flat open area of the river bank "it would have taken a blind German not to see us" as, despite the tree branches covering the tanks, "what was sitting there looked like Sherman tanks, not Sherwood Forest."[87] Guns laid, ammunition ready, wireless netted in, target information recorded, the Regiment waited for the order to open fire – and waited, and waited. Three days passed, the monotony broken only by the occasional volleyball game, movies and a thunderstorm which produced a panic because, as Bill Luton wrote to his fiancée, there "was a great crash, and half of the troop were on the point of going under the tank when suddenly it was realized it was a clap of thunder."[88]

At 1445 hours on 28 March 1945 the order finally came. For the next fifty-one hours, with some pauses, the South Alberta Regiment bombarded targets across the Rhine in and around Emmerich. Nobody ever saw what they were shooting at; target information was received by wireless and the corrections made. Transport details drawn from the echelons, Recce and AA Troops moved the ammunition from the ordnance dumps and dropped it behind each tank, where the crews "spent time in the turret firing the gun or loading it while the rest of the crew on the ground unloaded truckloads of ammunition and unpacked boxes of shells." It was hot, heavy and, for the most part, boring work that served to give the South Albertas an insight into why gunners are such strange people – it also gave many of them

permanent hearing problems and not a few draw pensions today as a result.[89]

By the beginning of the second day the guns were beginning to show signs of stress. Problems were encountered with the recoil systems, which, not being designed for such sustained periods of firing, began to overheat. The hydraulic buffer oil became hot enough to expand and had to be "bled off," which was all right as long as the crews remembered to top up the system when the weapon cooled. Overheating caused frequent jamming in the breech mechanisms, which made for irregular firing, and this was made worse by the fact the drivers were helping out with the guns and, being inexperienced with the main guns, did not know how to clear them. On and on it went – fire, shell ejects, load shell, gun ready, fire, shell ejects – round after round, hour after hour, day after day.[90]

The men in the 17-pdr. tanks either helped with the firing or "carried out maintenance." Trooper Wilf Taylor was not involved with the "Rhine shoot" and, fed up with going over his tracks, suspension and fluid levels for the umpteenth time, decided to go hunting. A man from another troop had told him that there was a herd of deer in a nearby thicket and Wilf got a rifle and went into the wood. He "brought down a young buck in fair condition, then dressed him out" after apologizing to the animal for taking his life, as he had been taught by old Thomas Pedro, the Stony Indian who had instructed him in the ways of the hunter in the foothills of the Rockies years before. It was a small animal, Wilf remembered, "compared to our Alberta bred mule deer but there was enough of this buck to provide everyone with fresh deer steaks after I packed the meat back to our bivouac." It was a welcome change from compo rations and, for Wilf Taylor, a refreshing act of normality in the midst of war.[91]

By the morning of the third day of firing, tempers were beginning to wear thin. When Bill Luton gave an order to one of his crews the loader responded "F___ you!" This was "a serious offence at any time in the army, but especially so in the face of the enemy" but, as the man was known to Bill as "a good soldier – one of the best actually – just over tired," he wisely "let it go and had no further trouble."[92] Accidents also occurred. Troopers P. J. Viennau, B.G. Bankey and J.R. Dervin suffered injuries when they did not get clear of the recoil in time but the worst incident took place on the afternoon of 28 March and it involved Corporal Tony Devreker of B Squadron.

One of the best known and best liked men in the Regiment, big, bluff, brave Tony was always quick with a laugh and always quick to help a pal. He had been hit at Moerbrugge the previous September in the same action where he got the Military Medal for helping to rescue wounded comrades under enemy fire. They sent him back from the hospital early because, being of Belgian descent with a reason to hate Germans, he had made trouble at a nearby prisoner of war camp "by going around with a pole and knocking the prisoners' tents down."[93]

Tony was loading that afternoon in Corporal Stan Rose's tank and the gun was so hot that he had trouble ramming a shell home in the breech. The procedure in such a case was for the loader to

swing back the deflector guard, pick up a spent round and, using the round as a battering ram, drive the shell home. In the middle of the base of the shell is the firing pin which one does not hit, and to avoid that critical point the open end of a spent case is used to hit the stuck round, thus totally missing the pin. As soon as the round was fully home the firing mechanism would immediately slam shut and the gun would be ready to fire.[94]

Tony was a driver but, knowing this procedure, picked up a spent shell casing to ram the round home but unfortunately he "swung it like a bat, struck the pin and exploded the shell in the breech."[95]

David Marshall was standing behind the tank when he "heard the explosion and saw the flames shoot out of the turret."[96] Stan Rose was inside that turret but in the gunner's seat on the other side of the breech when the shell exploded and remembers that Tony "got the worst of it."[97] David shouted for someone to call the "meat wagon" and then got on the deck with another man to see what they could do. By this time Stan had staggered out of the turret with burns and perforated eardrums but there was no sign of Tony so, while the other man held him by the waist, David leaned down into the hatch "trying to get a grip on Tony whom we could hear but not see" in the smoke-filled interior. Marshall finally got hold of Tony's clothing and, with the assistance of some others, pulled him free of the turret.[98]

"Tony was about the worst mess I had seen," recorded Marshall. He "had his right hand blown off at the wrist, his left thumb and part of the flesh of the hand, shrapnel wounds in his face and arms, as well as being burnt."[99] Tony's eyes were also gone but he was conscious and talking when Trooper Eric Nichols and Padre Silcox arrived shortly afterward with the halftrack ambulance. Eric Nichols remembers clearly that Tony, a Catholic, said to Silcox, "You're a good little soldier, padre, but you're the wrong denomination."[100] They took him away and Padre Silcox made the final entry: "Lived for two days, conscious and courageous, but died in hospital."[101] Tony was 21 years old.

David Marshall was shaken. He had tried to comfort his friend when they got him on the ground, "holding him and reassuring him that everything will be all right." Tony's death made Marshall "feel very mortal" and being mortal, he uttered the soldier's prayer: "Thank God, it's not me."[102]

At 1800 hours on Good Friday, 30 March 1945, having fired 38,325 rounds onto the east bank of the Rhine, the Regiment stood down from its guns. In the meantime, the war had gone on – the British assault had been successful and 3rd Division had gone over to expand the bridgehead. To the east the Soviets had forced the Oder River and were almost within artillery range of Berlin, while to the south the Americans were across the Rhine in great strength and had nearly encircled one hundred thousand German troops in the Ruhr. It was ironic that, although they had been fighting this war longer than either the United States or the Soviet Union, the Commonwealth armies of 21 Army Group were not allowed to take the final objective, Berlin, but were directed across the north German plain to secure the great ports on the North Sea and the Baltic – a reflection of the changing balance of world power. First Canadian Army, back in its traditional place on the left flank, was given the job of clearing northern Holland and then moving in concert with British Second Army. The South Albertas joked that with any luck the war would be over before they got into it but everybody knew that the beast was waiting.[103]

In the meantime the clan began to gather. Swatty was back, as was steady, quiet Arnold Lavoie of A Squadron, while Darby Nash was dragged (no doubt protesting) out of his instructor's job in Britain to resume command of B and Stan Purdy came back from the hospital to take over C Squadron from Glen McDougall. Stan had ended up in the same ward as Ed Reardon and the two of them, more bored than hurt, escaped from their beds one morning "and did the town."[104] Whey they got back, Ed remembered, "five or six guys who were recuperating told us that they had spent all day covering up for you buggers." The medical staff were not amused and, labelling Purdy and Reardon as "uncooperative," discharged them so they "hitch-hiked up to the Regiment and were back in action in 48 hours." A gaggle of junior officers also returned. Leaman Caseley and Ivan Donkin of B pulled in, Danny McLeod (who had been wounded at Bergen) came back to take over a troop in C Squadron and Captains McKenzie, Stewart and "Little Joe" Summers, who had been in England taking courses, also showed up. Poor Jack got snagged in the reinforcement machinery and was glumly contemplating life in some lesser outfit when Bert Coffin bailed him out and got him home again. In a similar fashion, veteran sergeants, corporals and troopers, recovered from wounds or fresh off courses, returned to a warm welcome from their comrades. Everyone wanted to be in for the final act because, after nearly five years, the South Albertas were a long way from the group of enthusiastic but green young recruits who had first laid eyes on "Pinky" Carvosso and Chris Seal. They were now members of the most professional outfit in the business and they were impatient to get over that river, finish the job and go home.[105]

The orders came soon enough. Just after breakfast on 31 March Swatty Wotherspoon held a squadron commanders' O Group and gave them the news that the Regiment would cross the Rhine that night. When he returned to C Squadron, Major Stan Purdy opened his own O Group with a favourite phrase: "We're going feuding."[106]

CHAPTER EIGHTEEN

"A ding dong fight in the failing light."

GERMANY: 1 APRIL – 4 MAY 1945

Most of the day was spent getting ready. The tanks were fuelled, ammunition loaded, rations stored and last minute repairs and adjustments completed. At 1330 hours on 31 March the loader-operators began to net their 19 Sets to the proper frequency, a complicated task made necessary by the technology of wartime wireless that was always done several hours before a move or operation because it was taken for granted that the Germans were listening. In each squadron, the operator in the commander's tank broadcast the code for the day on the assigned frequency and soon the harbour resonated with the "Able, Able, Able," or whatever the code was, and high pitched whistles as the loader-operators in each tank tuned their own wireless sets to the correct frequency. "All stations

> South of the Kusten, down Echelon way,
> That's where the TO, and the Quartermasters stay.
> A quiet night told me, it's better to stay,
> South of the Kusten, down Echelon way.
>
> You may seek, you may search, you won't find him,
> He is there where the SS can't shell him.
> No ammunition, or rations, or petrol
> Will come while bullets may spray.
>
> Friesoythe is peaceful, it's back of the line,
> The provosts are nailing up, the "Out of Bounds" signs.
> But the odd 88 says, it's better to stay,
> South of the Kusten, down Echelon way.[1]

Able One, report my signals … all stations, over …. Hello Able One, Hello Able One, Okay, over … Hello, Able One, only getting strength 3, over …" and so on until the job was finished and the communications system was working at optimum level.[2] By 1700 the Regiment was formed with the crews standing by their vehicles, smoking, talking or joking, but as usual it was a case of "hurry up to wait" for the order to move did not arrive until nearly midnight.[3]

Next came the Rhine. The South Albertas had the dubious honour to be the first armoured unit of 4th Division to use a new pontoon bridge over to Emmerich on the east bank. It had only been completed that day and it was no easy job for the Royal Canadian Engineers as the river is about fourteen hundred feet wide at this point and the current is strong. The

---

A bridge too long. During the night of 31 March/1 April 1945 the South Albertas became the first armoured unit in 4th Division to cross the Rhine. They moved across this pontoon bridge in the dark and it was an experience that few wanted to repeat. NAC, PA 130060.

The face of Germany, 1945. The ruins of Emmerich, destroyed by Allied artillery and aerial bombardment. It resembled most German cities in the last months of the war. SAR COLLECTION.

bridge floated on pontoons spaced about twenty feet apart and each fitted with a powerful outboard motor, tended by a sapper, run at full speed to keep the structure straight against the current. The engineers brightly assured anyone who would listen that the flimsy-looking thing would bear the weight of tanks but it was perhaps just as well that visibility was obscured by darkness and rain at thirty minutes past midnight, Easter Sunday, 1 April 1945, when the first South Alberta tank gingerly felt its way down the ramp and eased onto the bridge.[4]

As that vehicle disappeared into the blackness the rest of the fighting echelon followed, well spaced out and moving at the steady, very steady, speed of three miles per hour. Danny McLeod hated that bridge: "I thought we were going to go straight into the drink because there was so much slack, but all of a sudden it tightened up and the nose lifted."[5] Driver Jimmy Eastman remembered that the "pontoons went down, down, down and it seemed like I had to give a lot of gas to get power and all the way over it was like I was driving up hill."[6] Bill Luton was oblivious to it all. Being of an intellectual bent, he reflected somewhere in the middle of the river on that dark and rainy night illuminated by "the occasional gun flash," that the Rhine "was the barrier that marked the limits of the Roman Empire for four centuries," and "how many of us would re-cross it?"[7] Only Luton would be thinking about the Roman Empire at a time like this but then Bill was from Ontario, which might explain it. To most of the South Albertas it was a terrifying experience to drive over that swaying, undulating and clearly impermanent construction with its pontoons bouncing up and down and the river roaring by a few feet away.

They all made it safely and were in harbour at some obscure locality called Bienen by 0400 hours when Swatty returned

from brigade with their orders. The word was that the British 43rd Division had cleared the immediate east bank of the Rhine and were pushing to the next defensive obstacle, the Twente Canal in Holland, about thirty miles to the north. The 4th Division was ordered to take over that area and try to get over the canal. Ten Brigade would go first followed by 4 Brigade and the Regiment's job was to lead the division's advance, move fast and, hopefully, seize a bridge over the Twente in the vicinity of Lochem. At 0700 hours Albert Halkyard got on the road to recce the route to the north and over the next hour every man and tank in Recce Troop followed, spreading out across the country to get Swatty the information he wanted on routes, bridges, the enemy and the general situation. It was a sunny day in Germany, the boys were over the Rhine and the South Alberta Regiment was open for business again.[8]

The British promptly shut it down. Halkie reported that the route reserved for 4th Division's advance was filled with vehicles from the British 43rd Division which had "sprawled across

No fraternizing! Signs such as these greeted the boys every time they entered Germany. There is no official record of a member of the South Alberta Regiment ever violating this direction. SAR COLLECTION.

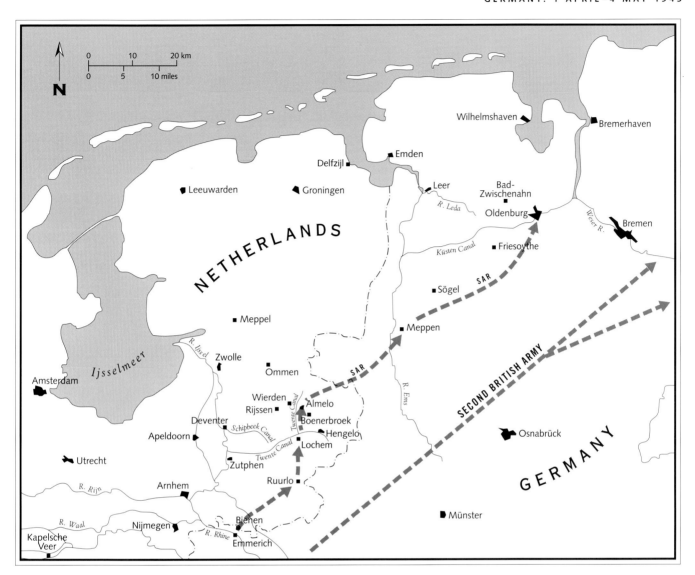

Map 18: SAR area of operations, March-May 1945. After participating in an artillery bombardment of the east bank, the SAR crossed the Rhine at Emmerich and moved to the Twente Canal, where they spent a week guarding the flank of 4th Division which was moving on Meppen. In mid-April they were sent to the east to provide right-flank protection for the division as it moved on Oldenburg.

it" because their own road was obstructed by blown bridges. Strictly speaking, this was against the rules because 4th Division had priority but shouting about priorities made little difference in the middle of a traffic jam that extended for miles. The Regiment's advance was delayed and Swatty was furious – the War Diary tactfully noted that the "CO was very annoyed at not being allowed to go ahead and keep hot on the heels of the enemy" but there wasn't anything that could be done although the colonel went forward himself late in the afternoon, possibly looking for someone to shoot. By this time, most of the Recce patrols had been either swallowed up in traffic or co-opted to serve as auxiliary provosts and the mess was so bad that the order to move did not come until 1830 hours, about eight hours behind schedule and nearly at last light. The Regiment made slow and laborious progress and there was much muttering about the Limeys, a strange people known to drive on the

wrong side of the road. The only bright point of the day was provided by Halkyard, who managed to pick his way through the traffic, and by late afternoon his patrol had become the "furthest north Canadian fighting unit on the continent of Europe." Just to drive the point home, Halkie crossed into Holland and thus became not only the first Canadian soldier to enter that country from Belgium but also the first to enter it from Germany.[9]

Daylight on 2 April found the Regiment strung out, scattered in four or five vehicle groups at the orders of the provosts, somewhere on the road to Ruurhlo, which was on the road to Lochem, their objective. The Recce patrols had better luck this day, however, and early in the morning two Stuarts led by Sergeant Tom Paterson were approaching an unblown bridge when they spotted what looked like mines on the road. They dismounted and started to clear the mines when they were interrupted by an enemy motorcyclist but, as "both sides were

The Twente Canal near Almelo, Holland. The Regiment spent several days along this waterway in April 1945 exchanging insults and the occasional round with the German paratroopers who held the other side. PHOTOGRAPH BY DIANNE GRAVES.

Paterson evacuated the wounded and kept the bridge under observation. By this time the Regiment had managed to concentrate and when Swatty learned the news of an intact bridge over the Twente he dispatched Bill Luton's C-1 Troop forward to back up Paterson with C-3 to follow after they picked up some infantry. Luton remembered that the order "produced a momentary feeling of exhilaration" as "this could be a small version of the capture of the Remagen Bridge over the Rhine by the Americans," but when he got up to the bridge, he changed his mind.[13] The Twente, like most European canals, was contained between dykes and the dyke on the north side offered excellent cover for German tanks. Even worse the only approach was a narrow paved road, and since the shoulders were reported as being mined, his troop would have to proceed in single file. Luton contemplated waiting for the infantry to come up but there was no time. He decided to move his tank forward until it was in turret down position and, if that did not draw fire, move to a hull down position and, if the Germans still didn't react, cross the bridge. He had just started to move when "a tremendous explosion shook the ground and a spectacular mass of debris shot far up into the air."

The bridge was blown and it would now require an assault to get over the Twente Canal. As nobody knew when or where that would take place, Swatty decided to concentrate the Regiment in Lochem in a central position to move out in any direction. By the time the South Albertas got there, they found the 43rd Division gone and the town held by Albert Halkyard and his two Stuarts, who were glad to see them because the British had lost two Shermans to a Tiger tank in the vicinity and even Halkyard wasn't going to take on a Tiger with Stuarts. The squadrons didn't see any German tanks but snipers were active, and that night Lieutenant George Johnston of A Squadron, a 28-year-old clerk from Toronto who had only been with the Regiment since January, was shot and killed while observing the canal from his turret. Swatty ordered the squadrons to position themselves for all-around defence but to let as many men sleep as possible as the boys had been on the move for most of the past two nights.[14]

Other than some sniping it was a quiet night and in fact the next few days were quiet. On 3 April the Lincoln and Welland Regiment made an assault across the Twente at Delden, twenty

surprised," the German "managed to get away unhurt."[10] After clearing the mines the patrol crossed the bridge and kept going to the Twente Canal with Corporal Jimmy Simpson's tank in the lead. As they came around the bend in the road Simpson saw the canal and, more importantly, an unblown bridge over it – at that moment his Stuart was hit by a German anti-tank gun. Trooper John Lakes, Simpson's gunner, remembered that there "was a flash and a bang in the turret" and then someone yelled "Bail out! We are hit! Bail out!"[11] Lakes checked the position of the 37 mm gun to ensure that the forward hatches were clear for the two drivers and only then saw that his left foot was

> turned completely backwards, with the heel to the front, and the toes to the back. My left leg had been shattered and was just hanging by some sinews. Furthermore, I was bleeding profusely.
>
> I hoisted myself up on to the top of the turret. It was a long fall to the road below. But there was a lot of shooting going on, and I was not at all in a good position there. I decided to do a belly flop, keeping my chin back to avoid being knocked out on the landing. This did work. I crawled over to a shallow depression beside the road.

Jimmy Simpson wrapped a tourniquet around Lakes's leg (it was later amputated) and the next thing John knew, "somehow I was put on the back of the hull of the Paterson tank" with Jimmy "still applying the tourniquet. Then we started off on a hasty retreat." Before Paterson could get under cover, however, his gunner, Trooper Clarence Lorensen, a 28-year-old railway worker from Macdowall, Saskatchewan, was hit in the head and killed instantly by German small-arms fire.[12]

miles east of Lochem and, for a change, 4 Armoured Brigade got the bit between its teeth and began to storm north. Over the next few days the armoured brigade's advance took them further and further away from Lochem and, by 5 April, their spearheads had entered the German town of Meppen, fifty miles northeast. The Regiment and the rest of 10 Brigade tailed behind this movement; the South Albertas left Lochem on 3 April, slept overnight by the roadside, and by the evening of 4 April were at Boenerbroek, which was south of Almelo and, as one trooper noted, "east of Rectum."[15] As the division was now advancing in a northeast direction it became essential to provide some kind of left flank protection and the Twente Canal provided a convenient barrier. On 5 April at 1200 hours the Regiment was ordered to the Almelo area to take up this job and the next day A and C Squadrons and Recce Troop took up positions along the Twente south of Almelo. B Squadron went into reserve ready to support the Algonquins, who were ordered to clear that town and Wierden, its neighbour to the west.[16]

The Regiment spent three days along the canal. Individual tanks from Recce Troop established OPs and two troops from A and C Squadron were usually in the forward positions while the others stayed in reserve. There wasn't much to see as the dykes prevented direct fire over the canal, which was about eighty feet wide, and nobody who liked life went on the top of those dykes. On the other side were elements of 6th Parachute Division and the Hermann Goering Regiment, old acquaintances. They had come up with a new trick – using *Panzerfausts* like mortars to lob rounds over both banks in an attempt to hit the tanks. Not to be outdone, Trooper Jim Hambling decided to reply with the Commonwealth equivalent – the PIAT or Projectile, Infantry, Anti-Tank – a spring-loaded affair that had both proponents and detractors but was essentially a weapon which required a good sense of humour to operate properly. Hambling cranked the thing up and disintegrated a German with his first shot scattering "various parts of his anatomy … all over the surrounding scenery."[17] As Hambling was a member of 42 LAD this had to be beginner's luck but the War Diarist was filled with admiration for this "remarkable feat" and Hambling shortly afterward received a promotion to lance-corporal.[18] Exchanging fire across the Twente became such good sport that the boys from echelon came up to try their hand at the game and "anybody who could spare the time was going down there to take a pot shot at Jerry."[19] This brought down enemy mortar and machine-gun fire, so the South Albertas replied with 75 mm HE observed and corrected by Recce Troop tanks who worked themselves as high as they dared on the slopes of the dyke.

Leaman Caseley now commanded Recce and he and Corporal Art Engel were dissatisfied with their observation position, which was not high enough. They climbed a nearby spruce tree with a long wireless lead but came down in a hurry when a German MG 42 started to prune it about their ears. Leaman and Art couldn't figure out where this fire was coming from but they worked out that there had to be a German OP somewhere

in the forward slope of the far dyke which called it down. It was then that Art Engel, a farmer's son from Castor, Alberta, noticed the cows on the German side of the canal. The most unobjectionable of animals, the cow is a passively curious creature and these beasts had stopped grazing to stare at a section of the far dyke. Art knew cows so he searched that area carefully with his binoculars until "just below the bank I saw about three inches of face, this was the German observation post."[20] Very slowly he moved his Stuart up until he could train the gun "where I saw this head and about a half an hour later when the cows stopped eating and started looking there again I fired an AP round and I saw a cloud of dust and a helmet going about 60 feet into the air." Enemy fire in the area became much less accurate after that, and when Art crossed the canal a few days later, he "found a dead body laying on the road, most of the head was missing and no helmet." Never underestimate a farm boy; they make good soldiers.

Corporal Dan White of A Squadron had a similar problem. His troop was supporting some infantry in an area where a road ran close to the canal but nobody could get by because of a particularly nasty but elusive German machine-gunner. Dan remembered "a couple of Limeys in a truck who passed us and went right on down" to the canal.[21] "Pretty soon," he continued, "we saw them bailing out and they came back and said, 'Why didn't you tell us?'" The reply was, "You didn't bother to ask." That German machine-gunner disturbed Dan's peace of mind:

We sat there all bloody day and this guy would fire from this point and later on from that point but we couldn't pick up where he was until it was late in the afternoon when I just happened to see the heat waves coming off his barrel. We immediately turned the turret and got a bead on the position. But then he moved and fired from another position which we couldn't spot so we waited and, sure enough, he moved back to the first position and started firing from there. We had AP in the gun and, as soon as the gunner saw the heat waves coming off the barrel, he thumped on the firing button and you could see that machine gun going up in the air.

As two sergeants from echelon found out, you had to be careful moving near the Twente. Jack Porter and Earle Wood were returning from a trip to the rear in a 60 cwt. truck when they encountered a young Dutchman pushing a motorcycle with Lake Superior Regiment markings. They promptly "commandeered" the bike, intending no doubt to return it to the Lake Soups, and threw it in the back of the truck.[22] As they were driving away the Dutch boy began to shout and wave his arms in the air but, thinking "he was upset over our cavalier attitude," Porter and Wood ignored him. It was only when they got down the road that "we realized he had been warning us against going the route we were taking." At the same moment, the MG 42s opened up and then, as Earle recalls,

Liberation, April 1945. Joyful Dutch civilians greet 10 Brigade Infantry mounted on a South Alberta tank in some town in Holland. Scenes likes these were common throughout the last few months of the war. COURTESY WIM PORTERMAN.

we came upon a blown-out culvert (approximately a three-foot gap). I didn't want to stop because I wasn't sure where the gunfire was coming from so I gave the truck full gas and we managed to jump the gap. Fortunately, we usually drove in four-wheel drive and I guess the front wheels grabbed as soon as they landed and pulled the rest across.

By this time we realized we were on a dyke paralleling the Twente Canal and that our enemy was likely across the canal to the west. Shells were pounding into the back of the truck and one came through the door and clipped the shoulder strap of Porter's uniform. All at once we spotted several trucks piled up on a bridge ahead of us, which meant we definitely had to stop. A bullet had hit the gas pedal and I could no longer give it gas.

It was time to leave and Wood and Porter jumped into a ditch. They then crawled to a nearby farmhouse where "to our great relief there were two young Dutch girls who welcomed us as liberators and took us to where their mother made us a big feed of eggs and potatoes, so we felt pretty good." The next day Earle took four troopers back to the scene of the crime and recovered not only his own truck with the motorcycle inside but, being a good echelon man, an extra 60 cwt. from another unit in perfect running order.

The Algonquins cleared Almelo without problems but

Wierden proved to be a hornet's nest. When B Squadron moved in to help them on 7 April, David Marshall remembered that they made "liberal use of machine-gun ammo by spraying all the bushes and any likely spot where the enemy might be hiding" and "saw one Algonquin shoot a German soldier as he stepped around a corner and aimed his bazooka at us. Thank you, Private Algonquin, whoever you may be."[23] Getting fed up, the Algoons called in the Typhoons "to rocket and bomb the enemy gun positions which still kept our tanks at bay."[24] One aircraft was hit by ground fire and the South Albertas watched the pilot bail out and come down "between the lines, but fortunately just on our side of the canal in a nice wet bog to cushion the fall. He needed the cushion too; his chute opened frighteningly close to the ground." The boys found the man "soaking wet and a bit shaken up, but otherwise unharmed," so they "brought out some army issue dark rum and the British pilot was one happy fellow when he was taken back to headquarters."[25]

For several days the forward positions in and around Wierden were so close to each other that there was considerable confusion about who owned what. On 8 April Trooper Karl Wickstrom was driving Trooper Hugh Christian to his tank at the south edge of the town and unfortunately took a wrong turn with his jeep and ran straight into German territory. Machine-gun fire killed Wickstrom but Christian managed to get clear of the vehicle and was taken prisoner. Karl Wickstrom, a 34-year-old barber from Breton, Alberta, and one of the originals from 1940, was survived by a wife and a son. That day another South Alberta died in hospital. Trooper Marvin Bergquist, a 28-year-old farmer's son from Hardisty, Alberta, had joined the Regiment at Nanaimo in the spring of 1941. He had fought well in Normandy but had been diagnosed with tuberculosis and evacuated to England in January.[26]

B-1 Troop did not participate with the rest of the squadron in the fight for Wierden. On 4 April they were sent back to the rear area because someone had decided that A-2 Echelon needed protection and that suited Jim Nicholson just fine because it gave him time to work on a secret weapon he had designed. The troop had a glorious time watching the fitters at work and one day an amazed John Neff saw Sid Arrowsmith pick up a piece of Sherman suspension weighing 675 lb., casually carry it a few feet away and put it down again. The high point was when a Staghound pulled into the courtyard of the troop's billet and got stuck in the mud. It was Guy Simonds's personal vehicle and Nicholson's crew were given the job of getting the corps commander unstuck – "Imagine a General this far forward," Neff confided to his diary that night.[27]

Back at the Twente the German fire began to slacken and there was a growing suspicion that the enemy had pulled out. Bill Luton came to this conclusion as early as the morning of 7 April but squadron headquarters told him "it was important to establish that for *certain*," so Bill decided to go for a stroll. Just before dawn he and Trooper Lloyd Braithwaite moved up to the dyke bank, where Braithwaite "hoisted his beret on the barrel of his Sten," but the Germans did not fall for that old trick. By now it was light and, deciding that "there was only one way to know for sure," Bill jumped up on the dyke in plain view and proceeded to walk along the top. Braithwaite joined him but nothing happened. Bill went back to his tank and, "feeling a little pleased" with himself, reported that "the enemy had pulled out for sure." A few minutes later he received a call from brigade telling him "to send a patrol across the canal to recce the area." Luton was furious: "No sleep, a night under fire, a tense morning patrol, no breakfast, and why in hell did some bastard sipping his coffee in comfort twenty miles back need more confirmation than I had risked two lives to get?" Thoroughly disgruntled, he jumped down from his tank to encounter Trooper John Barnett, the gunner in his troop sergeant's tank who was just lighting a cigarette. "Get your Sten gun," Luton told him. "We're going across the canal." Barnett's reaction was understandable: "Holy Jesus Christ!" and "the cigarette dropped out of his mouth onto the ground."[28]

Trooper E.K. Perry volunteered to accompany them and the three men walked along the friendly side of the Twente for some distance looking for something to use as a raft – "a barn door, an outhouse, a dock – with real luck, a boat" but could find nothing. Finally Luton got fed up, stripped off his tank suit, emptied his pockets and "dropped off into the canal." It was not a long swim "but those big triple-soled tank boots did not help, nor did trying to keep a Sten gun more-or-less dry." Arriving on the other side he walked back down the bank to a point opposite his troop, being careful to warn them: "Don't shoot. It's me – your Boss!" Communications were established and it was clear that in this area, the Germans had pulled out. Returning to the Canadian side, Bill made his report and ate some breakfast and, since there were no Germans to worry about, the troop spent the day lazing around in the warm April sunshine. For the rest of his life Bill Luton was known to the South Albertas as "the man who swam the Twente Canal" but, as he noted, "it was the swimming that seemed to have caught the fancy" of the Regiment because "in the Thirties not much swimming was done on the bald-headed prairie whence came so many recruits of the South Alberta Regiment." Never underestimate a boy from Ontario; they also make good soldiers.[29]

Luton had established that the Germans had pulled back from the Twente but it took some time for all to this to percolate through RHQ and upwards. On 8 March Lieutenant Ken Wigg crossed over in a boat that he had found and confirmed that the enemy had gone. As the day progressed it became clear that 6th Parachute Division was still hanging firmly onto Wierden but had "rolled up" its positions to the south along the canal. The next day Dutch civilians began to traverse the Twente to let everyone know that the Germans were now gone

from the area so Swatty decided to send out a patrol which would work as far west from Wierden "as possible."[30] To lead this expedition Swatty chose Sergeant Herbie Watkins of A Squadron and gave him two tasks: he was to report on enemy dispositions west of Wierden and, second, he was to keep his eye out for a Mercedes-Benz staff car as Swatty wanted a personal automobile that was grander than the Opel the officers had acquired in the Hochwald. Preparations for this patrol were interrupted by a warning order from brigade for the Regiment to make ready for a long move.[31]

It is a sign of Swatty's confidence in Herbie that he gave him his own personal scout car and driver to carry out his mission while at the same time cheerfully volunteering Arnold Lavoie's vehicle. Herbie selected Corporal Dan White to accompany him and they set out at 0600 hours on 9 April. Dan recalls that everybody expected trouble and Trooper Herb Wolgien, Lavoie's driver, who was nervous because of his German descent, told him, "If we're taken prisoner, you try and get back,

A good day's bag. Near Rijssen, Holland. Trooper Vic Henderson of Recce Troop (with goggles) ponders how to get more German PWs on the deck of his Stuart. COURTESY, VIC HENDERSON.

because they won't take me alive."[32] The two cars had no problems getting across the canal but they were captured by the Poles who were beginning to move into the area, and, with language difficulties, "had quite a time trying to explain to them who we were and what we wanted to do."[33] The Polish commander insisted that there were Germans west of his position, and would not let them continue but finally Herbie had him call Swatty and the Pole let them go while "wishing them good luck." They continued west of Wierden and began to pick up prisoners, and then encountered a member of the Dutch underground who said that he would guide them to Rijssen, the next major centre. As they drove through a wooded area they

Buzz bombs. One of the reasons that the Germans resisted so obstinately in the Nijverdal-Wierden area in April 1945 was to protect the last V-1 launching sites within range of Antwerp. Here a South Alberta examines a launching rail in June 1945. SAR COLLECTION.

heard an explosion and it later turned out that there were indeed Germans around and they had just blown up a V-1 site. The direct route to Rijssen was blocked by booby-trapped trees so their Dutch guide took them a long, roundabout way and when the two scout cars finally got there late in the morning a tremendous crowd, forewarned by the civilian telephone system, erupted in a joyful frenzy.

It was Herbie Watkins's moment of triumph. Exactly eight months and nine days before, he had gone into his first action at Tilly-la-Campagne in Normandy, and since that day he had taken part in every major battle fought by the South Alberta Regiment and been shot out of more than a dozen tanks (the last one at the Hochwald) but remained essentially the same old (he was 38) unflappable, soft-spoken, pipe-smoking Herbie who had come to the Regiment from the 19th Dragoons in June 1940. A good man in battle and a good friend to the younger men out of battle, Herbie Watkins was a rock to the South Albertas. The crowd waved their orange flags and cheered, the boys cheered back – even the German prisoners cheered – as Sergeant Watkins was greeted by the burgomaster, signed the town guest book as "Liberator," and accepted a glass of milk as a toast while the pretty young Dutch girls sang "Oh my darling, Clementine." It was glorious.[34]

When the patrol got back that afternoon the Regiment had already moved out, for Germany. RHQ later estimated that on 9 April Herbie and his men had liberated two towns, six villages and ten thousand people but unfortunately they never found the Mercedes that Swatty hankered after.[35]

Delayed by traffic and mud, the Regiment had a long and tedious march from the Twente to Meppen, where they harboured on 11 April. Their future role was uncertain but for the time being they were given a few days of rest in pleasant and undamaged Meppen. The crews stayed in civilian houses and made themselves comfortable, so comfortable that Bill Luton almost felt sorry for the German woman who owned the home that was his crew's billet:

> Imagine a Sherman tank in the middle of your lawn, big muddy tank boots on your living room carpet, a couple of guys in greasy clothing sitting on your velvet sofa, a Coleman stove cooking bacon on the walnut dining room table, careless young men making use of your best Dresden china – you get the picture. Then you can sympathize with the German *Hausfrau*, who returned to the home from which she had been evicted. … she put her head in her hands and sobbed, not a loud wailing cry, just the heart-broken cry of a woman seeing her treasured possessions defiled. Then she turned and ran.[36]

On the other hand this was the homeland of the enemy and a cruel enemy as Danny McLeod's crew discovered when they

> started nosing around the damned house and we see this SS officer's pictures and some of these photographs were of this guy at a hanging and another one showed him with prisoners down on the ground – they had been served a meal and he had knocked the food over and they are down on their hands and knees picking it up. Then we opened up the cupboards and they were full of Red Cross parcels. I got his particulars and sent them back but Swatty told me later that the man "was killed in action and he is never going to be held accountable."[37]

It was better to stay on your guard.

By this time, mid-April 1945, the war seemed to have passed the South Albertas by. The Soviets were forty-five miles from Berlin while the American 12 Army Group had surrounded more than one hundred thousand German troops in the Ruhr and were about to drive east into Czechoslovakia. Second British Army in the north was advancing towards Bremen, while to its left 1st Canadian Corps were busy clearing northwest Holland of the enemy. As for 4th Canadian Armoured Division, 4 and 10 Brigades had already advanced north of Meppen and were closing on Friesoythe, two-thirds of the way to the divisional objective, the city of Oldenburg. Since crossing the Rhine the Regiment had not seen any really hard fighting and they were thankful for that but at the same time disliked the "sarcastic remarks being passed by other people to the effect that we should put up the L of C [Lines of Communication] troops patch."[38] Such insults were hard to swallow and it was a happy Lieutenant-Colonel Wotherspoon who came back from an O

Group at division in the morning of 13 April with orders for the Regiment "to move forward to Garrel and then swing north to Friesoythe" to occupy the enemy and prevent them from concentrating at that place.[39] This was armoured reconnaissance, the South Albertas' favourite job, and, just to make it official, the Regiment was removed from 10 Brigade and brought directly under Vokes's command as divisional troops.

The South Albertas were on the road very fast. Swatty had suspected that the call to divisional headquarters meant that something was up so he ordered the squadrons to be ready to move before he left and, while still at headquarters, directed the squadron commanders to meet him at Vrees for an O Group. They were there at 1030 hours when he arrived in his scout car. Swatty's O Groups were always brief and to the point and he probably worked it all out in his head during the drive back to Vrees. He later summarized his method:

Cross this one off. A German SPG (in this case a *Panzerjaeger* IV) knocked out near Meppen in April 1945. The entire upper hull and gun have been blown away from the lower hull and running gear, probably the result of the detonation of the ammunition stored in the vehicle. SAR COLLECTION.

When you're issuing orders, you really ought to have all the facts that will affect your decision in making those orders and if you get any of them wrong then you are lessening your chances for success. …

When I was at the senior officers' school and while I was training my regiment for a year, I put together a book with an appreciation of the situation for each of the five basic types of action. I put in a draft order for each and when later formulating orders, I would, and I could do it in a few minutes, skim this book …… when there was something like a river crossing, I would go and read my appreciation and draft order for that to make sure I had thought of all the things there should be in my orders, and then I checked them against those in my book.

I was always trying to make sure that I hadn't missed anything, that I had thought of all the factors that I ought to and that I had asked myself all the necessary questions that I ought to have asked. … I don't think that's "going by the book," I think that's taking experience and saying experience is something that you should listen to. It's like people saying "but that's old history" – well I think old history is one of the greatest learning places.[40]

This job looked interesting. To carry it out the Regiment would need infantry and engineers because there were a number of small towns and rivers that had to be cleared or crossed. The division had no infantry to spare but the Regiment did get three troops of the British 1st Special Air Service Regiment, tough, quiet men equipped with armoured

jeeps, and a troop from 9 Field Squadron, RCE. The ground was low, flat and wet with numerous small rivers (Canadian creeks) and irrigation ditches. The number of water obstacles worried Swatty and, twirling a lock of his thinning hair around a finger as he always did when cogitating on a problem, he directed that a bridge-laying tank be requested from division. The O Group took no more than thirty minutes and by 1130 C Squadron was on its way north to carry out a fighting reconnaissance of the nearest water barrier, the Marka River (see map 19, page 316).[41]

How far to Berlin? B Squadron crews questioning a liberated Polish forced labourer. By this late time in the war the roads were crowded with the displaced population of Europe trying to get to their own homes. COURTESY, DAVID MARSHALL.

Some fun in the sun. At Friesoythe, Germany, 16 April 1945, Troopers L.A. Schmidt and H.N. Smith display their musical virtuosity on a captured accordion. Note the heavily loaded Stuart tank behind them – by this time late in the war the South Albertas had become so adept at living on the move that their tanks began to resemble gypsy caravans. NAC, PA 167244.

Patrols from Recce Troop had already gone out and had reported that all the crossings over the Marka had been blown by the Germans. Bill Luton's C-1 Troop in the lead had the job of finding a place for the sappers to build a new bridge and, having chosen one, the engineers came up to supervise its construction. "A troop from B Squadron came up to haul material: some logs from Jerry road blocks, some timbers and planking from a shed, push them together with the tanks, and *voila!* – a bridge."[42] The problem was that "it was more like a gigantic beaver dam" and a "design defect" soon became apparent – "not enough space had been left between the logs for the water to flow through, and so it promptly began to back up and flow around the end." C Squadron made it over the Marka but the vehicles following did not and reluctantly Swatty ordered the engineers to abandon it and build a new structure on the main road from Vrees. Meanwhile, the Regiment's request for a bridge-laying tank was refused by division "after some four hours of heckling" by RHQ.[43]

On the next day, 14 April, the Germans began to come alive. Arnold Lavoie's A Squadron was over the new bridge at 0530 hours and they pushed on to the hamlet of Denome, where he

encountered some enemy infantry but, by 1100, had cleared that place and moved on to the next river, the boggy Soeste, a few miles to the north. Here Lavoie dismounted some of his crews, who waded to the opposite side and established a bridgehead. Meanwhile, Darby Nash's B Squadron followed and with help from the SAS, who seemed to appear and disappear as they pleased, secured a second crossing over the Soeste near Gronheim. Stan Purdy's C Squadron pushed north from their position, crossing the Soeste on a bridge belonging to the Lincoln and Welland Regiment working to the left, but had a vicious little firefight with enemy infantry at the village of Augustendorf. Recce Troop ranged all over the Regiment's front looking for crossing points and Albert Halkyard's patrol was working with a C Squadron troop which came under fire near Augustendorf. Trooper George Gallimore, Halkyard's co-driver, had been checking out a farmhouse which was empty although there was "warm food still on the table," and had just got back into his tank, which he was driving that day, when a German SPG knocked out a Firefly belonging to the C Squadron troop.[44] Gallimore "backed up right beside him and I remember I pushed over a telephone pole because I couldn't see and we lifted those guys off onto the back of our tank."[45]

That day two things came down from divisional headquarters. The first was a Valentine bridge-laying tank, which was rather surprising given the attitude of the previous day, and the second was a change of orders. The Argylls had taken Friesoythe and the Regiment's task was now to recce a route to Oldenburg, the divisional objective, from the southwest.[46]

Friesoythe had been a bad action for the Argylls as it had cost them their commanding officer, Lieutenant-Colonel Fred Wigle, Swatty Wotherspoon's brother-in-law. There was great concern at this time about attacks from German resistance groups, the so-called "Werewolves," and when a rumour spread among the Highlanders that Wigle had been shot by a German civilian they burned a large part of Friesoythe to the ground in retaliation. Actually Wigle had been killed in a counterattack by regular enemy soldiers but what was done was done and nobody lost any sleep over it. By this time in the war, the Canadians were not messing about and the standard procedure was to set on fire any structure that might conceal enemy troops. "I think we are all latent arsonists," one South Alberta noted, "we did not leave a haystack or barn unburnt, and if a house did not have a white flag, then it went too. These were favourite hiding spots for enemy tanks and guns. Did you ever see a haystack move? Once is enough."[47]

The next day, 15 April 1945, was a memorable one in the history of the Regiment. During the previous night the hard-working sappers began to construct a new bridge over the Soeste in B Squadron's area. They were finished by 1000 hours in the morning and A Squadron crossed the river to help B expand the bridgehead. There were German infantry about and the two squadrons were soon firing HE and Browning into buildings and woods to keep them at a distance as they tried to push through to the next village, Varrelbusch. Sergeant John Galipeau of A-4 had been having trouble with his new troop leader and the man's green crew since the Regiment had crossed the Rhine. They "didn't seem to have an ounce of survival instinct," he recalled and he caught them one time crossing an open field "sailing along like they were on a Sunday drive in Camp Borden."[48] The drivers "had opened their hatches and raised their seats and were enjoying the ride – and making perfect targets for any snipers in the area." Another time, the troop was taking a quick meal break and Galipeau found the new crew had completely unloaded their tank. "They had laid out their bedrolls and taken off their pistols and hung them on the tank, and they were busy washing and shaving," while the officer "had hauled a chair out of the house and was sitting in the sun with his tunic off." Galipeau was furious and tried to tell the officer that this was "no weekend camping trip" but that he "was in Germany and those guys out there in those funny uniforms are out to blow our heads off." He got them packed up but began "to wish that we would run into a real fire fight that would scare some sense into these guys."[49]

He got his wish at Varrelbusch. Galipeau was covering the troop leader's advance with his Firefly when the man came on the wireless to say, "I've just been fired at. There was an explosion and a little while later another explosion. What could it be?" Galipeau wasn't sure but told him to stay where he was while he moved his tank forward to where the officer's tank "was sitting on the roadway just outside the front yard of a house." Suddenly, John recalled,

the house started to smoke, and I realized what had happened. Whoever was in the house had got hold of a *Panzerfaust* and fired the bazooka at the officer's tank. Instead of destroying the tank, the shell had hit the hedge and exploded. In the meantime, the flame from the bazooka had set the house on fire.

Just then I noticed some German infantry creeping through the low bushes on the edge of the village. Since the officer was ahead of me, I said, "I've spotted enemy infantry on the edge of the village. Can you open fire?"

He said, "My gun's jammed."

Galipeau gave up in disgust and went after the Germans himself but by the time he got there they had disappeared. At that moment, up popped "some of the wild and crazy British S.A.S. troops" with "their armoured jeeps with machine guns mounted through the armour plate where the windshield should be." He told them about the Germans and the SAS began to enthusiastically deal with them while John "went back and got the troop officer going again." He explained what had happened with the *Panzerfaust* and had his gunner, Slim Tillsley, give the officer's gunner a quick lesson on clearing a jammed 75 mm, something he should have been taught before being sent to the Regiment.[50]

This crew was lucky that day, another veteran crew was not. Trooper Luke Iltchuck, who had been shot out of a tank at Labbeck on 6 March, was the driver in Corporal Harold "Snookie" McGillivray's tank in B Squadron. Luke remembered that they were moving up on 15 April when he thought to himself "watch this lump of ground" they were approaching.[51] "There was a German behind the lump," he concluded, "and he shot us up with a *Panzerfaust*." The crew bailed out but Luke and Snookie were wounded – it was Iltchuck's second time and he worried that, if he went back into action, it might be "three tanks and out." That same day Jim Nicholson of B-1 got a chance to try out his "secret weapon" – two .30 calibre Brownings he had rigged on a mount in front of his hatch, spaced one foot apart and set to cross-fire at 150 yards to provide some firepower that he could use without exposing himself from the turret. John Neff exulted that the tracer from the two weapons set the bush on fire.[52]

Stan Purdy's C Squadron also had a difficult morning. The previous day they had got into the middle of a tree plantation, *Forst Cloppenburg*, which was not at all inviting, and they now had to move through this wooded area to come in on Varrelbusch from the east. As they approached the trees they came under small-arms and *Panzerfaust* fire and replied with Browning and HE before proceeding in short rushes, lead tanks moving forward while following tanks covered before moving forward in turn. Tom Milner's tank had just completed one of these rushes when Milner turned around and saw a sight that froze him – he was staring at the "business end" of a *Panzerfaust* held by a German who had let him go by and then risen out of the ditch to fire into his rear – and there was absolutely nothing he could do. It was that German's unlucky day because, in his eagerness to get Milner and in the noise of the firefight going on around him, he failed to hear Bob Fairhurst's tank coming up the road *behind* him. Fairhurst never forgot the incident: "He couldn't hear my tank. I stopped and he turned around in horror and the boys put the Browning on him and down he went into the ditch. Then he stood with his hands up but the Browning cooked off by itself and killed him."[53] C Squadron finally cleared the *Forst Cloppenburg* and were about a mile west and northwest of Garrel in the mid-afternoon when RHQ called them back with orders to circle around the other squadrons and secure a hamlet with the interesting name of Amerika. Their advance would take them over the ground of a small *Luftwaffe* airfield northeast of the village of Varrelbusch.[54]

Halkyard had been out that way in the morning with his tank and a Sherman troop. Halkie was in the lead and "it was a beautiful morning," George Gallimore recalled, when suddenly, "right out of the ground ahead of us a couple of hundred yards, right out of the ground from a ditch or dug out," like some primeval behemoth, lumbered their worst nightmare – a German Tiger II tank.[55] Called the King, or Royal Tiger, this 68-ton

This thing will spoil your day. What Halkyard's crew saw rising up out of the ground at Varrelbusch airfield on the morning of 15 April 1945 – a 68-ton Tiger II with its huge 88 mm gun pointing straight at their tiny Stuart. They got away and, later that day, Danny McLeod's troop took it out after a hard-fought little action. CANADIAN ARMY PHOTO.

instructed his gunner, Carson Daley, to put the first rounds in their tracks to immobilize them. This worked and Milner recalled that Carson then "went back to the first tank, and put one amidships and then he went to the second tank and put one amidships – at that the whole damned thing went sky high about five hundred feet."[57] Carson remembered that the first tank "just blew up and the one behind caught fire and we had the two of them."[58] The explosion, the troop figured out later, was because one of the tanks was towing 500 lb. aerial bombs which the German were using as mines and they detonated.[59]

RHQ was anxious for Danny "to press on." Having heard of a Tiger in the vicinity he was not about to take chances so decided to make a foot recce forward and dismounted from his tank. Years later he thought to himself, "You dumb bastard, they could have had snipers in those woods" but he arrived at the tree line, where in the fading light he could make out an armoured vehicle some eight hundred to a thousand yards ahead behind a blown bridge over a small creek.[60] As he recalled, "I put the binoculars up to my eyes and I swear that the muzzle of this thing was sitting at the edge of my binoculars, it was so huge." Danny was looking at the same King Tiger Halkyard had encountered that morning.

Returning to his troop, he discussed the situation with Tom Milner and they decided to move the troop's two 17-pdr. tanks forward clear of the trees and open fire. This was done, and they immediately came under fire from the Tiger but just as quickly returned it. Carson Daley recalled that he fired "three shots and they ricocheted into the air off the Tiger and my knees were knocking something terrible."[61] Tom Milner recalls firing eight rounds of 17-pdr. AP and that "either the first or the second did something to the gun in the turret, and the barrel was left pointing cockamamy."[62] Danny remembers watching the 17-pdr. rounds go "whewww" and they just glanced off."[63] Matters were not helped by RHQ, which prodded Danny by asking "how are you making out, we've got to move."[64] Danny pointed out to them that, even if he got the Tiger, they would still need a bridge to get across the creek ahead. A few thousand yards away, the other troops in the squadron were monitoring the fight on their wireless and Bill Luton remembered "it was fascinating to sit there and listen to Danny McLeod masterminding the battle over the air and hear the firing, which was not far away. The pyrotechnics were not bad either."[65]

Danny now brought his two 75 mm Shermans up to add

monster from the Henschel factory at Cassel, with face-hardened armour plate up to four inches thick and an 88 mm gun almost longer than their Stuart, represented the ultimate in *Wehrmacht* tank design. "Get in reverse, back up!" Halkyard shouted at his driver, Sonny Plotsky, just as the first 88 round hit nearby and the "dust rose, the tank was just full of dust." Plotsky threw the automatic transmission into reverse but the tank nearly stalled because his foot was on the gas pedal and there were some anxious seconds until the Stuart jerked backwards.[56] Another round came in, and then another – that "bugger fired three shots at us and missed," remembered Gallimore, which allowed Halkyard to take cover behind a building where the four Shermans of their supporting troop were waiting. The South Albertas only had one weapon that could even damage a Tiger and that was a 17-pdr. so the supporting troop's Firefly moved up to fire and was just as promptly knocked out.

Contact with the German tank was broken until C Squadron pushed toward the airfield in the early evening. Luton's C-1 Troop was on the left, Danny McLeod's C-2 and Ken Wigg's C-4 were on the right. It was close on twilight when Danny began to take AP fire from a wooded area ahead. The source was identified as a German Hetzer SPG with a 75mm gun but the troop was able to knock it out without much trouble. He then moved into the wood and spotted two other German tanks moving across the nearby airfield, one towing a trailer. Sergeant Tom Milner manoeuvred his Firefly forward to the tree line and opened fire at a range of about twelve hundred yards, having weight to his fire. "We fired everything," he remembered, and "to this day, I cannot tell you what happened, whether an HE hit the muzzle brake and bent it back or it was a 17-pdr round that hit, but it was bent back about six inches."[66] At this point the Tiger commander decided that perhaps discretion was the better part of valour and began to back away, but "backed a little more broadside to us" and Danny "thinks it was an HE round that set the engine compartment on fire." The Tiger began to brew. When it was over, Milner recalled, "a Tiger tank lay all shattered and in pieces, a barn had burned to the ground, and a house had been blown to bits."[67] By now it was dark and Danny was ordered to pull back and laager for the night. As they did so, Tom Milner remembers that a British SAS jeep pulled up beside his tank and the driver shouted, "Thanks, chaps, we weren't too sure how we were going to get around that corner" and then drove off into the darkness. Danny moved his troop back some distance and they "lit up the landscape" pouring HE into every flammable structure they could see. That done, they settled down for the night, having fought one of the most successful single-troop actions in the history of the South Alberta Regiment. It had been, the War Diarist concluded, "a ding dong fight in the failing light."[68]

There was not as much action on 16 April. Swatty shoved out Recce patrols on either flank and then pushed A and B Squadrons on to Garrel while C Squadron was directed to circle around the town to the east and try to secure crossings over the Aue River, the next water barrier. The squadron was on the road early but had a difficult time with boggy ground, mines and a huge crater blown in the best road by the enemy. Bill Luton's troop was moving up to the Aue in the early afternoon when he saw "some tree branches lying across the way ahead," and thought to himself that was "strange" as "no winds have been blowing lately to bring these down."[69] He had gone about a hundred yards farther when his tank "was rocked by a tremendous explosion, which seemed to lift the left side in the air." Nobody was hurt by the mine but it became clear as the day progressed that the Germans had a major defensive line on the far side of the Aue and there was no way the Regiment was going to be able to "bounce" it as they had the two previous river lines.[70]

The entire area was thick with mines and *Panzerfaust* teams. Recce Troop lost three Stuarts, including the troop commander's tank, and two men were killed. Trooper Bill Carr was the driver of one tank that hit a mine at a road junction near Varrelbusch and the blast tore a great hole in the bottom of the light tank killing him instantly. Carr, a 33-year-old electrician from Halifax, had been with the Regiment for a year. Trooper Eldon Owen was badly wounded by small-arms fire after bailing out of his tank which had been hit by a *Panzerfaust*. Owen, a 25-year-old former mechanic from Toronto, was evacuated but died in the Casualty Clearing Sta-

tion. Mines, either the conventional type or large aerial bombs rigged with pressure sensitive detonators, were the biggest problem. In the four-day period from 15 April to 19 April, the Regiment lost five Shermans, four Stuarts and an ambulance halftrack.[71]

A and B Squadrons pushed into Garrel and encountered little resistance although one tank was knocked out by a *Panzerfaust*. At 1100 the burgomaster offered to surrender and Swatty accepted the surrender "if it were made forthwith; but that should any t[a]nks be fired upon, shot up by bazookas or blown up by mines, the Regt would withdraw and resume the attack."[72] Furthermore he ordered that every building that did not "show a white flag would be fired on." The town proved to be such a tangle of obstructions, demolitions, obstacles and mines and there being enemy skirmishers in the outskirts, Wotherspoon thought it safer to withdraw the squadrons in the afternoon to their previous night's harbours. A few days later Swatty decided that Garrel would be an excellent place to put A-2 Echelon and sent an officer with an interpreter to demand that the burgomaster "organize the civilian population and get them to clear out all the mines in the area, to fill in cratered roads, to move the road blocks and to ensure the safety of our troops." The reply came back that "it was not possible" so Swatty forthwith summoned the burgomaster to RHQ and told him that, "if a hair on the head of one of our men was touched, five houses at the scene of the crime would be burned to the ground" and "in the meantime he would do as we say." "In no time flat," recorded the War Diarist, "the civvies were working in the streets" and by the end of the day, Garrel was cleaned up.[73]

Swatty was not interested in Garrel; what he wanted was Oldenburg. If he could push across the Aue, he would be on one of the main roads to that city and the Regiment would be the first into Oldenburg, the objective of 2nd Infantry Division moving on the right. During the afternoon he ordered the Valentine bridge-laying tank to move up to the Aue from Varrelbusch but it hit a mine on its way in the area of the airfield. Swatty later described this as his "greatest disappointment of the war," as he

felt it reasonably certain that had he been able to put his sq[uadro]ns across the [Aue] river he might well have entered the City of Oldenburg the following morning. The regt had broken through all the inf[antry] on its front and the only real opposition that remained was the enemy gun line immediately across the [Aue] river.[74]

Now he would have to fight for it.

At this point, 16 April, Swatty decided that, since the division appeared to have forgotten the Regiment existed, it would have to look to its own resources. The South Albertas were now beyond the range of all but medium artillery so Swatty directed that each day one squadron would act in the indirect fire role to

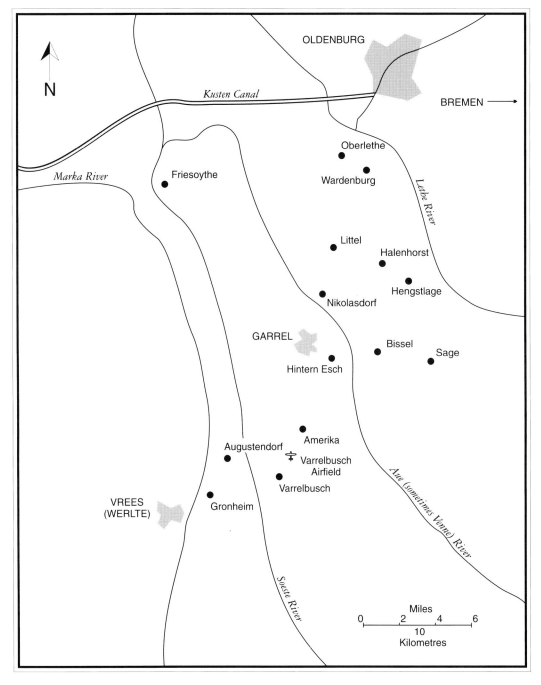

Map 19: War in the peat bogs, SAR area of operations, April-May 1945. In the last weeks of the war the SAR fought its own campaign trying to seize Oldenburg while providing right flank protection to 4th Division to the west and maintaining contact with 2nd Division to the east. They nearly got Oldenburg before the rest of 4th Division but were stymied by a lack of bridging equipment and fierce German resistance. MAP BY CHRIS JOHNSON.

South Albertas so Swatty managed to get some old friends, a company from the Lincoln and Welland Regiment. He also procured a squadron of Staghound armoured cars from the Manitoba Dragoons and a troop of M-10s to increase his strength.[75]

The South Albertas had fought as armour, infantry and artillery and it now appeared they would become sappers. The job of organizing and commanding the new Regimental engineers fell to Captain Jack Summers and Jack wasn't too happy when he got the news. A few days before, Swatty had sent him back to B Echelon for a break, telling him he had done enough and that there were plenty of other young officers around. "Little Joe" Summers was just enjoying his first night of good sleep in weeks when a DR thundered up with an order for him to report to RHQ. When he got there, Swatty asked Jack if he remembered the mines and demolitions course he had taken in 1943 and Jack, with a sinking heart, replied he did – all the young officers had taken this course as it was held near London and weekends were free. It turned out that Jack was now the only officer qualified in demolition work who could be spared and that he was therefore in command of the South Alberta Sappers.[76]

Jack took over the Valentine bridge-laying tank (which had been repaired), a bulldozer and thirty men from A Echelon known as "Wally's Commandos" after their NCO, Sergeant Wally Jellis. The "commandos" had been formed because Major Gordie Shell, commanding HQ Squadron, believed that the Germans would infiltrate the echelon positions during the night and he wanted his own infantry protection. Wally's men patrolled at night but never found any enemy because, as one

provide artillery support on call. The single troop of engineers had proved insufficient to clear the numerous mines, obstacles and demolitions and build bridges so Swatty decided to organize another troop from within the Regiment. His biggest need was infantry to clear built-up areas and protect the tanks in wooded areas. The SAS were great fighters and clearly enjoyed their work but they did not seem to be in the same war as the

wag said, they made so much noise on patrol that they could be heard for miles around. The commandos proved to be better engineers and over the next two weeks constructed twelve bridges, filled in twenty large craters (some more than fifty feet across) and cleared hundreds of mines. They had no Flails so, if the real engineers were not around to do the job, the SAR sappers just pushed abandoned German transport in front of their armoured bulldozer and, if the vehicle hit a mine, they scraped it aside and got another old truck or car. "As we got better at the job," Wally remembered,

> Joe Walmsley, provost sergeant, painted a couple of signs naming the bridges. The best one was "Summers Bridge", then one was named "Wally"s Bridge." One time we tried a scissors bridge. Once the Regiment was over the bridge and it was lifted we found that one end had been sitting on a 500 lb. bomb which later proved to be dud. When we started a job, we stayed with it until it was finished, sometimes lasting two days.[77]

Having got properly organized, Swatty continued the advance on 17 April. The Regiment would have to cover a twelve-mile front and his intention was to demonstrate as though he was going to approach Oldenburg from the southwest but he actually intended to get into the city from the southeast. A and B Squadrons and Recce Troop spent the day checking out the routes to the east while the engineers filled in craters and bridged obstacles. In the evening the bridge-laying tank was brought up to the Aue and a bridge laid over which C Squadron passed. This was a sad day for the Regiment because it lost Bert Coffin who departed to take over command of the Argylls. Nobody could picture Bert in a kilt but everyone "was sorry to see him go as the smiling face and shining pate of 'Bert' were known to all ranks."[78] The steady and quiet Arnold Lavoie now became second-in-command of the Regiment while Glen McDougall replaced Arnold at A Squadron.

The Regiment got over the Aue on 17 April and pressed on to the next barrier, the Lethe, with B Squadron leading. Maurice Amyotte of Recce Troop remembered that day as his crew had "just passed a sign saying it was 13 km to Oldenburg and that's when we hit the mine."[79] The Stuart caught fire and Amyotte had a difficult time getting the wounded driver out because the barrel was over his hatch. In the end, the crew evacuated but they all suffered burns. On 18 April B Squadron was at the Lethe and the Links company splashed over to establish a bridgehead while the sappers came up to construct a bridge. The bridge over the Lethe was finished on 19 April and B Squadron passed over to seize a small airfield on the other side. A and C Squadrons, which had secured the hamlets of Sage and Bissel on the near side, then passed over.[80]

By this time it was beginning to look as if the thing would soon be over. The Russians had almost completely encircled Berlin and their artillery was shelling the streets above Hitler's

Defence by demolition. Typical road in Lower Saxony over which the Regiment advanced in the final push on Oldenburg. Off-road movement was treacherous due to the soft ground while the Germans planted mines and demolitions on the road. Needing considerable engineer support, the Regiment formed its own unit of sappers and here they have built a small bridge over a gap in the road caused by German demolitions. The white tape was used to mark areas clear of mines. COURTESY, W. VAILLANCOURT.

bunker, bringing dust down on the maps he was using to feverishly plot grandiose counter-offensives with troops who no longer existed. The Americans had taken Nuremberg and were over the Danube, Vienna was under siege and the British were close to Hamburg. Nobody in the Regiment wanted to be the last man to die in a war that was winding down. There were still new reinforcements coming up, including a couple of the despised zombies, but Swatty wisely made a point of concealing their identity and nobody knew who they were, and in the end they did their duty just as well as the volunteers. Some of the new boys wanted to get into action while they still had the chance. Carson Daley remembered going back to echelon for some reason and meeting a fellow he had trained with who was anxious to see some fighting because "it's pretty well over and I can't go back and tell my family I didn't kill a German." Carson wisely told him to "stay right where you are."[81] On 19 April this man, Trooper Lyle Craig, was killed when the Sherman he was driving was struck by an anti-tank gun. Craig was a 21-year-old farmer from Ernfold, Saskatchewan, who had only joined the Regiment four days before it crossed the Rhine.[82]

On 20 April, A and B Squadrons got as far as the village of Littel, C Squadron providing indirect fire support from the rear. As Hitler's empire went through its death throes there were all kinds of funny people wandering around the landscape. The Régiment de Maisonneuve from 2nd Division was on the immediate right and they strayed into the South Albertas area displaying that light-hearted and independent attitude towards war and discipline which is the hallmark of the

French-Canadian soldier. German civilians, many of them males of military age, clogged the roads as did liberated prisoners of war and displaced persons. B-1 Troop got a good laugh when a French officer who had escaped from his prisoner of war camp greeted Lieutenant Jimmy Orr by kissing him on both cheeks to Orr's mortal embarrassment.[83]

That same day Bill Luton encountered a problem with the official non-fraternization policy. He was working forward with Ken Wigg's troop, the two officers having only four tanks between them, and was checking out a group of intact farm buildings when "an attractive young fraulein came running out full tilt to meet us" who "was not only good looking, but also had lots of nerve, since she headed directly toward the guns and the soldiers whose evil treatment of women had been broadcast widely by German propaganda."[84] She volunteered to show Bill and Ken Wigg "who had moved up as soon as he spotted our fraulein" just where the German positions were and "her long blond hair and big blue eyes did not hurt her case, either." Luton was studying his map to digest this information when Ken Wigg,

A bad one. One of the worst South Alberta tank casualties of the war. Corporal E.P. "Yudge" Beaudry's Sherman was hit by an 88 mm gun near Halenhorst, Germany, on 19 April. Trooper Lyle Craig was killed but the rest of the crew escaped safely. The ammunition inside the tank later detonated and blew the turret off. SAR COLLECTION.

being a little older than I and being from Montreal and all, was quick to size up the real opportunity. A man of prompt action, he jumped out of the turret carrying his map and took Ilse inside the house. I was a bit taken aback, but 1 Troop could not let 4 Troop down in the face of danger, and so I followed. Ken was at the large kitchen table with the topo map spread out so Ilse could point out *exactly* where the German troops were

The padre takes a look. Padre Silcox examines the burned-out interior of Beaudry's tank. It was the padre's unenviable job to remove the remains of South Alberta fatal casualties from their shot-up vehicles and give them a decent burial. COURTESY, W. VAILLANCOURT.

lying in ambush – which seemed to be a time consuming operation. When he finally turned around, I complained "Ken, did you have to get so damn close just to show her the map? And put your arm around her to help with the pencil? What about no fraternizing?" Such biting remarks did not jar Ken one little bit. I think he was about to suggest the 1 Troop tanks should go check out the Jerry positions while he worked here on strategy, when an older couple came climbing up from the cellar where they had been hiding. That kind of broke up the little tete a tete.

Sadly, the two young officers went back to work.

That day A and B Squadrons, with C Squadron providing fire support, had moved as far as Littel, six miles from Oldenburg. The ground in this area was one gigantic peat bog and the tanks could not move far off the roads for fear of bogging, and the roads themselves soon became useless after a squadron of tanks had passed over them and their hard crust was broken. One C Squadron tank broke through the surface and mired one of its tracks. Efforts to pull it out resulted in both tracks going in, further efforts left the hull submerged and the black muck was starting to reach the rear deck when the crew decided that it was time to remove their personal possessions and abandon the thing. It may still be there. Glen McDougall remembers his squadron halted on one of these roads when a motorcycle went by and "shook the ground so much that the tank moved."[85] B-1 Troop managed to get all four of its tanks hopelessly bogged on 20 April and, just to complete their disagreeables, a Spitfire flew over and bombed them. It missed.[86]

The ground made for slow going. The tanks dared not move far off the roads and, of course, the Germans mined the roads, blew craters in them or put up obstacles and then covered these barriers with anti-tank guns. On 21 April, A and B Squadrons got into the hamlet of Nicolasdorf but increasingly strong enemy resistance prompted Swatty to order them back to their harbours of the previous night. The next day C Squadron moved forward with the company of Links and B Squadron went out with a company of the Régiment de Maisonneuve and were as far as the hamlet of Hengstlage by 1550 hours. By 1700 hours all the squadrons were on the line of the Kusten Canal, a few miles from Oldenburg, but again were withdrawn for the night. The Regiment lost Stan Purdy this day when he suffered a broken ankle after running over a mine in his scout car, but Stan was not too unhappy about it, saying "the war is over for me."[87] Danny McLeod's troop was nearby and Danny "went to the rum bottle and gave him a few shots" and Stan was feeling no pain when they put him in the ambulance. A little while later Swatty called up to complain "that it is one thing if you have a casualty to give him a drink, it's another thing to send him back to the MO pissed out of his mind." Click Clarke now received his majority and took over C Squadron.[88]

German resistance was increasing, not slackening, as the Regiment got closer to Oldenburg. Up to now the prisoners (over two hundred) had been a mixed bag from various units, including paratroopers, infantry, service units and even a few marines. Now the Regiment began to take prisoners from the 8th Parachute Regiment, a more professional outfit, and the boys began to stay alert. It was well that they did so because the same day that Stan went up on a mine the Germans infiltrated C Squadron's nighttime position near Halenhorst with "bazooka parties" and launched an attack. Bill Luton, sleeping with his crew in a dug-out underneath their tank, was "startled awake by an explosion so sharp that it sounded almost in my ear" and "came instantly awake, sure that trouble had come, and sat up so quickly my head hit the bottom of the tank." In a minute, his crews were in their vehicles, "the tank engines roared into life, the turrets were traversing toward the ruckus, and the wireless was operating."[89]

Corporal Jake Wiebe of C-4 only woke up when one his fellow crew members "crawled over to me on his knees" and said

"Jake, your tank's burning." I thought to myself, "what the hell is he doing down on his knees" and then I heard this whistling coming through the building – they were gunning

it. I said, "Let the s.o.b. burn." After all, we had lost a lot of men and by that time we were as hard as nails.

Anyway we get up there and I looked at the situation and I knew the infantry was around but they hadn't stopped them. They probably figured they weren't going to do anything. So I got out there with my driver and my loader-operator and we sneak up to the tank and put the fire out with an extinguisher and then I thought we should strafe the damned area but I didn't think we should do it from the tank because the m.g. was on the top but from the ground and then they would think it was infantry. So we got the ground mount for the Browning and fired one box from one side and another box from the other side. We ran out of ammo and went to another tank to get some more but the gunner thought we were Germans and lobbed a grenade at us and it landed between me and Click. So then we gave it up and went back into the house and Ken Wigg the officer was there and I brought the rum from the tank and we drank it because we were all slightly wounded. Ken Wigg said, "You'll get a medal for it."[90]

They never did but the firing died down a few minutes later. It turned out later that the German patrol had come down the road from Halenhorst directly through the position of the Links. "The Links had a slit trench covering it," one South Alberta officer remembered, "saw the patrol loom up out of the darkness nearby, aimed a Bren gun at point blank range – but the gun jammed."[91]

It had been a close call. The following day, 23 April, B Squadron moved forward to secure the hamlet of Hengstlage while C Squadron took Halenhorst. B Squadron worked forward with a company from the Régiment de Maisonneuve and ran into fierce enemy resistance near Hengstlage; first they were shelled by German artillery and then came under anti-tank fire. Trooper David Marshall was commanding the Firefly in his troop that afternoon:

It was about 3.00 pm when we came under this AP fire. Each crew commander was trying to locate it when it got our range and we took an AP to the turret about a foot down from where I was standing. Except possibly in built-up areas where there may be danger from snipers, we always fought standing with our head out of the turret. As visibility is very poor when you view the scene through the periscope, the only way of doing it properly is to stand up and look.

The shell gouged out a hunk of the tank, showering me with fragments and blinding my right eye with blood. I figured that was quite enough and ordered the crew out. The enemy gun was concentrating on my tank and it was hit again as we bailed out. It then turned its fire onto the other three tanks who right smartly headed for the shelter of the trees, as we could not spot the gun(s).[92]

David's war was over. That night the interrogation of prisoners, "much better bred than what we had picked up previously," revealed the Regiment was facing a German force of about two brigades made up of elements of the *Grossdeutschland* Panzer Division and the 61st Parachute Regiment.[93]

The following day C Squadron fought a battle against enemy infantry dug in around the hamlet of Hintern Esch. Sergeant Tom Milner's tank was approaching some farm buildings "which seemed quiet" until "a sniper surfaced and was killed with the .30 calibre." Assuming that where there was one German, there were probably more, Tom spotted a slit trench which "had a lot of enemy in it." The problem was how to get them out without going too close. He "got an empty shell casing, filled it full of gasoline from the tank, poured it in the slit

The boys from B. Trooper David Marshall's Firefly with (left to right) Troopers Smith, Rose and Emry "Daddy" Vitkovich lounging on top. Daddy Vitkovich, a steady, older man, kept an eye on some of the wilder youthful elements in B Squadron. COURTESY, DAVID MARSHALL.

trench and let fly with a round from the verey pistol." The resulting blaze decided the Germans "to come out and they did." They were paratroopers and they "weren't happy about being taken prisoner," remembered Tom, "and with at least two of them, I thought it was going to be a shoot-out on the spot but they finally put down their arms and that was that." Encouraged, he "got prowling around again and found another slit trench" and "just let fly with a verey pistol down the hole and, again, another nine or so came out, four of those did not want to be taken prisoner." It was, he recalls, "a bit awkward for me because the only weapon I had on hand was a 9 mm Browning but I finally chased them down and we had about nine more prisoners." A 17-pdr. round through the upper corner of a shed convinced two more prisoners to exit it quickly with hands raised, increasing Milner's total bag for the day to twenty.[94]

Fortunately (or unfortunately depending on how you look at it), 24 April 1945 was the Regiment's last day of heavy fighting in the war. On that day Swatty lost the company from the Links and the squadron of the Manitoba Dragoons and, as the SAS had been removed previously and 2nd Division had no infantry to spare, there wasn't much he could do to get through the German force in front of him. He went to see Vokes to complain but 4th Division, which had been engaged for ten days in heavy fighting to secure a bridgehead across the Küsten Canal west of Oldenburg, had none to spare. As "it was impossible for the regt to proceed without inf[antry], its role was now changed to that of maintaining contact" and that meant "when the Germans pulled out, the Regt advanced against a mass of mines, booby-traps, and craters."[95] Swatty had tried hard but his South Albertas would not be the first troops into Oldenburg and, realizing that, he took a 48-hour leave to Holland leaving the Regiment in the capable hands of Arnold Lavoie.[96]

For the next ten days the squadrons moved up during the day, made contact with the enemy, shot them up and dropped back to secure harbours at night. Everybody knew it was coming to an end and it became a case of "one hand for George [the Sixth] and one hand for me" as no one wanted to be the Regiment's last fatal casualty. German response was variable; sometimes they would fight hard, sometimes not. "The war has been going well," Bill Luton wrote to his parents on 25 April, "we are sort of half expecting to receive news of a link up with the Russians in a day or two" but "the Jerries continue to fight" and, although the prisoners "are all convinced the war is lost ... they are still ordered to keep it up."[97]

Everyone was getting tired and, as the fighting began to wind down, each troop was relieved in turn and given twenty-four to forty-eight hours to rest. C-2 Troop got their break on the night of 26 April, broke out their rum bottles and had a party – the big topics of discussion were when would it all be over and what they were going to do when they got home. Danny remembered that Trooper Vic Carpenter of his crew was a source of much amusement because he entertained them with tales of his young son who had been born just before Vic had enlisted in 1943. The next day word came down that it had all been changed and the troop was now on call to advance to contact. Danny moved out and almost immediately ran into a mined road so he called for the engineers to come up and clear it. While they waited for the sappers to get to work, Carpenter asked if he could visit a nearby farmhouse to find a frying pan to replace one that some discourteous German had put a hole

Waiting to go in. A and B Squadrons lined up along a road somewhere in Germany in the last days of the war. The contrivance above the main gun is a smoke projector, which allowed the tanks to provide their own smoke screens. As one SAR officer remarked, "When I got into trouble, my standard procedure was to poof off smoke, pull all triggers and screw off in the surrounding confusion." COURTESY, GEORGE WHITE.

through a few days before. Danny told him to sit tight and was talking to the sapper officer when out of the corner of his eye he saw Vic walking across the field. He was about halfway to the farmhouse when a sniper shot him in the stomach. The troop did what they could but Carpenter died on his way back to the RAP and when they packed up his kit that night they found an unfinished letter to his wife, asking her "not to spoil my child before I get home."[98] Victor Lloyd Carpenter, a 21-year-old foundry worker from Fort Frances, Ontario, had joined the Regiment the previous November and was the last South Alberta killed in the Second World War.[99]

Three days later, on 30 April, Danny's number came up. He was waiting for the engineers to put a scissors bridge across a creek but he "didn't know what we were going to get into when we got across so decided to do a recce, going up the next ridge where you could see for some distance."[100] He got across the bridge "no problem" and moved out into a field "where the grain was high but we could not see any disturbance," meaning that it was likely clear of mines. His tank had only gone about three hundred yards when it hit two rigged demolition charges. Danny had his head out of the turret, both his eardrums were burst and one of his ears was split in two. He had to pull back and as he passed Bill Luton's tank, Danny called out, "Bill, the

wind is whistling through my ears."[101] The incident made quite an impression in C Squadron as Danny had gone between the two charges – exactly between them. If he had gone over one or the other, it might have been the end of Danny and his crew. "Talk about the luck of the Irish," Bill commented, "what about the luck of the Scottish McLeods!" Danny's war was over.

That same day Adolf Hitler committed suicide in Berlin. By now the German armies were collapsing on all fronts, the Americans had linked up with the Russians on the Elbe and the British were on the Baltic. The Regiment suffered its last casualty on 2 May when RHQ was caught in an enemy artillery bombardment. Trooper Bob Seccombe waited until it was finished and then got out of his tank "but one of the German gunners had a shell left and it hit the ration box of the tank behind me and I was wounded by a flying can of bully beef."[102] By this time the South Albertas had reached Oberlethe and Wardenburg, four miles from Oldenburg. That place capitulated on 3 May and the War Diarist noted that "our objective had been taken, and it will only be a matter of hours before we return to our formation."[103] The Regiment had been on its own "roving commission" for nearly three weeks and, as the 10 Brigade historian noted, the South Albertas had written "an Odyssey of their own." He summarized their accomplishments:

Here comes the sun. By late April 1945 it was beginning to wind down and Swatty relieved each troop in turn for 24-48 hours to give them a rest. Here a Firefly crew relax on a sunny day while doing maintenance somewhere in Germany. On average, an SAR tank crew carried out between one and two hours of maintenance on their vehicles every day. SAR COLLECTION.

They had been given the task of working north toward Oldenburg on the left of the 2nd Division, but not in contact with it. Their front was 20 kilometres. They had one company of Lincolns, and some wild British SAS with them for a while, but their magnificent effort was mostly their own – just one regiment of tanks, and no artillery support except what they could wangle from their blue patch [2nd Division] to the east. The roads were terribly cratered. They did their own filling. There were many small bridges blown and a large one across the Lethe River. They built their own. There were hostile populated towns such as Garrel. They did their own negotiating and held the peace. There were infantry rearguards. They captured and killed scores. There was a well defended airport, they captured it and knocked out two SP's and a Tiger tank in the doing. They lost over 40 tanks, and but few men. Had it not been for the broad Kusten Canal and a lack of heavy bridging material, they might well have been in Oldenburg before the 2nd Division. They did a job unparalleled for initiative, and did it in true Albertan style – well.[104]

On the evening of 3 May 1945, Swatty, who was temporarily commanding 10 Brigade, visited the Regiment and told the officers that in his opinion the South Albertas had "fought their last battle."[105] The next day the order came to move through Oldenburg and concentrate at the large airfield on the outskirts of the city. Everyone was looking forward to seeing Oldenburg, which had been their objective for so long, and a "handsome place it was, too" with impressive buildings that "lined clean streets, the houses were solid, green lawns and flower beds abounded, and a strange air of normalcy pervaded" as "civilians were out on the sidewalks going about their business, women rode by on bicycles, children played about."[106] As the column moved through the city, however, they got a grim reminder of why some German soldiers fought so hard to the end – the bodies of deserters were still hanging from the trees and lampposts where they had been strung up as an example.[107] The Regiment concentrated at the airfield under a downpour of rain and waited for the next move.

Around 2000 hours Bill Luton "noted that the rain was easing off" and, being a lover of nature, watched as a low, evening sun created a double rainbow, "the colours of the secondary, outer rainbow being reversed and less intense, but still magnificent."[108] Bill had never seen such a phenomenon and "was struck dumb with wonder; the rainbow lingered for several minutes and I stood motionless gazing skyward at this unusual sight." Just at that moment Ken Wigg came running up, very excited.

"Bill," he shouted, "the war is over!"

PART VIII

ENDURING

Back to Bergen. Remembrance Day, November 1945. Brigadier Swatty
Wotherspoon (wearing peaked hat) and, to his left, Lieutenant-Colonel
Bert Coffin of the Argylls (tall figure in Balmoral beside civilian in top hat)
attend ceremonies at Bergen op Zoom.

COURTESY, PIET HOEDELMANS.

CHAPTER NINETEEN

"Trish has a Canadian."

GERMANY, HOLLAND AND CANADA: MAY 1945 – JANUARY 1946

It was true. The German forces on the front of 21 Army Group had surrendered unconditionally and the whole wretched business was finished. The official ceasefire was to take place the next morning but, when the news flash interrupted a Glenn Miller tune at 2030 hours on 4 May 1945, the War Diarist recorded that "nobody could believe his ears, and then realizing what they had heard, everybody started leaping around and cheering."[2] Lavoie immediately authorized a double issue of rum and "in a limited manner everyone had a good time."

According to Bob Clipperton the Recce Troop's reaction was far from limited. "We were in our tanks and we had our foot on the siren button and we were just making a hell of a racket. Pretty soon someone came up and banged me on the head and said: 'Cut out the racket, the adjutant's got a headache.' We didn't pay any attention to that, we just kept blowing the sirens."[3] Over at C Squadron Captain Don Stewart had "the squadron net turned off and the BBC on instead," when "the news flash came through about the surrender." Nobody got "very excited, just sort of shook hands" and said, "Well, we made it."[4]

Sergeant Earle Wood found peace more dangerous than war. He recalled that a French-Canadian infantry unit on the other side of the airfield "started going crazy and shooting everything in sight and we had quite a few ricochets that were more dangerous than anything I had been through in the whole war."[5] One South Alberta took it all in his stride. Glen McDougall had got himself "a nice billet with a feather mattress and quilt" for the night and was "ready for a long sleep when all of a sudden a DR arrived with orders for an O Group. So I cursed and swore and went over to RHQ where everybody was drunk and they invited me in for a drink. I said 'Is that all, I'm going back to bed.'" And he did.[6]

The next morning, commented the War Diarist, the Regimental area "was quiet" as most "people had a bad headache" and "kept pretty well to themselves."[7] At 0800 hours, the official order came through to "cease hostilities" and in his diary Don

Trees heeft een Canadees,
Same in een jeep en dan vol gas.
Laat ie fyn zyn, laat ie fyn zyn,
O, wat is het meisje in haar sas!

Trish has a Canadian,
Full speed together in his jeep.
Let it be good, let it be good,
That girl is sure in fine humour![1]

Stewart recorded a common reaction: "I'll be damned – hard to believe."[8] Late in the morning Arnold Lavoie attended an O Group at 10 Brigade and, on his return, gave the squadron commanders the welcome news that 4th Armoured Division would not "have any permanent policing duties" in Germany but would form a mobile reserve.[9]

The following day, 6 May 1945, brought confirmation that the Germans were actually surrendering and the War Diarist lamented that it was now back to "spit and polish soldiering."[10] That afternoon Padre Silcox held a voluntary church service in one of the ruined hangers at Oldenburg and, to everyone's amazement, almost every man in the Regiment attended and more transport had to be procured to get them across the airfield. It was a day to be thankful and thoughtful and Bill Luton took the time to write a letter to his fiancée, Mary, that he had "been looking forward to writing for a very long time." Bill was "still very bewildered by the turn of events" and it all "did not seem real" – but, he concluded, "Let us then thank God for His mercy and be humble before the sake of those who have not our good fortune."[11]

It was a popular sentiment.

Now that the shooting has finished, it is time to assess the South Alberta Regiment as a military unit. Every Canadian soldier who fought in the Second World War thinks his regiment was the best – all you have to do is ask him. The regimental tradition is firmly embedded in the armies of the Commonwealth, and although wartime British, Canadian, Australian or New Zealand soldiers paid lip service to such motives as "King and Country," "the national effort" or "ridding the world of evil," this was for public consumption. In combat they fought for their comrades and for "the Regiment," that elusive but all-important concept that for more than three centuries has "sought out the hearts of its soldiers" and "raised those men to deeds they did not know they were capable of."[12] In May 1945 the South Albertas had more reason than many to be proud of their achievements. At St. Lambert, Moerbrugge, Bergen op Zoom, the Hochwald, in the last few miles to Oldenburg – and many places in between – they had carved out a reputation that was second to none among Canada's fighting soldiers. Historians, however, are a contentious breed at best and can never take anybody at their word – it is not enough to write that the SAR was a very good military unit; evidence must be marshalled to prove it so.

Perhaps the best place to start is with the casualty figures. There is an old saying that there are "lies, damned lies, and statistics" and it is a good piece of advice but sometimes statistics can be revealing. Consider the South Alberta Regiment. Between 1 August 1944 and 4 May 1945 the Regiment lost a total of 82 men killed, 339 wounded and 15 taken prisoner. Padre Silcox kept careful records of the fatal casualties and at the end of the war classified them according to the cause of death[13]:

Killed by artillery fire (HE or AP) out of tank	20
Killed by artillery fire (HE or AP) in tank (including *Panzerfausts*)	10
Killed by small-arms fire out of tank	16
Killed by small-arms fire in tank	6
Killed by mines	5
Killed by mortars (in or out of tank)	4
Killed by burns	3
Killed in various accidents	6
Weapons mishaps	3
Motorcycle accidents	2
Killed by Allied aircraft	1
Total killed in accidents	6

An ironic note to these figures is that eight South Albertas were killed by so-called "friendly fire" – one by Allied aircraft in Normandy and seven by Canadian artillery at Bergen.

Special mention must be made of the officer casualties. South Alberta officers had a habit of leading from the front and they paid the price. Of the fifty-seven lieutenants known to have held troop commands in the Regiment between 1 August 1944 and 4 May 1945, nine were killed, twenty-eight were wounded (Danny McLeod three times and Leaman Caseley twice), one taken prisoner and one evacuated as a battle exhaustion casualty – a loss rate of almost seventy per cent. The leading cause of death was small-arms fire – no fewer than five officers were sniped in their turrets. Two other troop leaders, Kenny Perrin and Alec Scrimger, were killed after they had been promoted to captain.[14]

The Regiment's tank casualties are more difficult to calculate because the records are imprecise and tanks classified as "knocked out" one day might be back in action again the following day. For example, the official First Canadian Army figure for the SAR tank losses in the Hochwald, 27 February–10 March 1945, is 61 while Regimental records show a total of 47.

Oldenburg airfield, May 1945. It all ended during the evening of 4 May when the Regiment was ordered to cease hostilities. By this time they were at a much-battered *Luftwaffe* airfield near Oldenburg. Here five men from C Squadron pose against the tail of a Messerschmitt 109 fighter aircraft. COURTESY, CLIFF ALLEN.

The discrepancy is due to the fact that the higher figure represents the total number of tanks reported by the Regiment as being out of action during that period while the lower is probably the number of tanks put out of action indefinitely as some vehicles were knocked out, repaired and hit again over a two-week period. It was not uncommon for a crew to lose several tanks – Sergeant Herbie Watkins had no fewer than thirteen Shermans shot out from under him and most South Albertas lost two or more tanks to various causes during the war.[15]

There is a set of records that provide rough but fairly accurate overall figures for the Regiment's tank losses. This is the War Diary of D Squadron of the Elgin Regiment, the armoured delivery unit for 4th Division, which was tasked with the job of bringing new vehicles forward from the ordnance parks and getting them ready for issue to the fighting units as they were required. D Squadron also picked up refurbished or repaired tanks from the divisional workshops and "recycled" them to the front line units. The system was that if knocked-out tanks could be repaired by regimental resources they stayed with their units but, if they were sent back to the divisional workshops, they went after repair to D Squadron for delivery to any of the four armoured regiments in the formation. The delivery squadron kept records for the tanks (either new or refurbished) it issued, but it should be noted that these figures include not just battle casualty replacements but also new tanks such as the Stuart

Mk VI vehicles supplied to all the armoured regiments in the division in October 1944. It should also be noted that these figures do not include tanks put out of action but repaired within the Regiment. Although not exact, the squadron's records, however, are perhaps the most reliable source on which to calculate the Regiment's general figures for tank losses and replacements and, according to this evidence, the South Alberta Regiment received 204 AFVs of all types between 1 August 1944 and 4 May 1945 – a replacement rate of 283% of its War Establishment or authorized strength.[16]

When we compare the South Albertas' personnel and tank replacement figures with those of the other armoured regiments in 4th Division, an interesting anomaly appears.

The figures for personnel casualties are as follows[17]:

Unit	Officers Killed (% of Unit Total)	Other Ranks	Total
Foot Guards	12 (10.08%)	107	119
Grenadier Guards	15 (14.15%)	91	106
British Columbia Regiment	12 (11.1%)	95	107
South Alberta Regiment	11 (13.92%)	71	82

The figures for tank replacements, as based on the delivery records of D Squadron, are as follows:[18]

	Total Number	Percentage of War Establishment Replaced
Foot Guards	226	313.9%
Grenadier Guards	185	256.9%
British Columbia Regiment	171	237.5%
South Alberta Regiment	204	283.3%

Of the four armoured regiments in the division, the South Albertas had the lowest fatal casualties (although the proportion of officers to other ranks killed was the second highest) – between 20 and 25% lower than the other armoured units – yet, in terms of tank replacements, the South Albertas' figures were the second highest in the division. The conclusion is inescapable – the Regiment saw more than its share of hard fighting yet suffered a relatively low casualty rate. The question is why?

To properly answer that question is a lengthy process and it must start with an examination of the background of the South Alberta Regiment. The unit was raised from excellent raw material, a group of young men inured to physical labour, handy with machinery, and products of the "hard knocks" school of the Depression (and, in western Canada, the Depression was indeed a hard school) whose common geographical and social background promoted group cohesiveness. Although nominally the "South Alberta Regiment," it drew on the personnel of four other Alberta militia units and it might better have been called (as was reflected by its cap badge) the "Alberta Regiment." The two regulars who moulded the wartime SAR, Lieu-

tenant Colonel James Carvosso and RSM Chris Seal, had the advantage of working with first-class personnel and had few problems turning this mixture of veterans, prewar militia and raw recruits into a well-disciplined infantry battalion with a family atmosphere that looked after its own – the hallmark of a good unit.

The fine work done by Carvosso and Seal served the South Albertas well in the long years between 1940 and 1944. Their efforts were amplified by the veterans of the First War, notably Major Howard Wright and Captain Bert Huffman, who took the trouble to spot, encourage and commission young soldiers who would take the Regiment into battle. In this respect, the SAR's record of "growing its own" was impressive – thirteen officers who fought with it in 1944-1945 began their military careers as privates in the Regiment.

The foundations were sound but there is also the question of spirit. Although its original composition gradually changed as it received men from other parts of Canada, the SAR never lost its western outlook. Western Canadians tend to be practical, plain talking people who like to "get on with the job." This can sometimes make for a certain light-hearted attitude and it sometimes seemed that the only thing the South Albertas took seriously was athletics, particularly boxing. The South Albertas may have generally displayed a fairly relaxed manner to the whole thing but when the time came to do their work, they did it and they did it well.

And it didn't matter what the job was. When they were infantry, the South Albertas were good infantry; when they became armour, they tried to be the best armour; when they were made armoured reconnaissance, they trained hard for that new role; when they were attached to 10 Brigade they worked at becoming the best infantry support unit possible; and, finally, when they reverted to armoured recce in the last weeks of the war, they slipped back into it as though they had been doing it all along. The South Albertas fought as armour, infantry, artillery and some, for their sins, even ended up as sappers – it made absolutely no difference – and if, by some awful chance, they had been converted into a Mobile Bath and Laundry Unit, they would have complained endlessly and produced the hottest water and the cleanest soldiers in the Canadian Army.

All these factors are important but still do not fully explain the unit's record. The SAR was not the only regiment in the fighting Canadian army to enjoy good human material, training by veteran officers, promotion from within, a family atmosphere and a relaxed attitude to life if not war – the British Columbia Regiment, for example, possessed many of these same characteristics. Where the South Albertas differed from other regiments, particularly other armoured regiments, was in two things.

The first was good and consistent leadership from top to bottom. The marriage of Lieutenant Colonel Gordon Dorward de Salaberry Wotherspoon, that personification of the eastern military establishment, with the South Albertas, the embodi-

The boys of Recce. The survivors of Recce Troop, Holland, June 1945. From August 1944 to May 1945 this troop suffered fifty percent casualties. Kneeling at bottom, left to right: Tpr. Golden, Lt. Mills, Sgt. D. Prenevost, Tpr. Toporowski, Tpr. Maynard, Tpr. Deneau, Tpr. Barclay. Standing, left to right: Tpr. La Fleur, Capt. Don Stewart; Cpl. Forster, Sgt. Albert Halkyard, Tpr. Ramsey, Tpr. Haun, Cpl. Art Engel. Tpr. McGee, Tpr. Roberts, Tpr. Spaner, Tpr. Gallimore, Tpr. Gilboe, Cpl. "Daisy May: Row. Sitting on left tank, left to right: Tpr. Buchan, Tpr. Henderson, Cpl. Bob "Homer" Clipperton, Tpr. Ford, Tpr. McGovern, Cpl. Jimmy Simpson and Tpr Plotsky. On right tank, sitting left to right, Cpl. McSherry, Tpr. Layton, Tpr. Owczar, Tpr. Forsyth, Tpr. Relkov, Cpl. Samuels, Tpr. McKenzie, Tpr. Folland. COURTESY, BOB CLIPPERTON.

ment of a western regiment, was so extraordinary a connection that only a second-rate novelist would attempt it in fiction. It was the Regiment's great good fortune to be not only trained but led in combat by Swatty, and they had him for the unusually long period of twenty-six months from April 1943 to June 1945. During that same length of time the Foot Guards and Grenadier Guards each had three commanding officers while the British Columbia Regiment went through four.

Tactically brilliant, possessing the moral courage to argue with his superiors, supremely confident in his own abilities, Swatty Wotherspoon was the ideal man to take the Regiment into battle. His influence within both 10 Brigade and 4th Division became stronger as time went on because a competent officer always gains in reputation the longer he stays at one level. Wotherspoon's advice could not be ignored and he had no reservations about airing his opinions, because, unlike many of his superiors, he had no intention of making a career in the postwar army and therefore did not hesitate to "rock the boat." Swatty's objective was to win the war as soon as possible and he became impatient with anything or anyone that prevented him from reaching that objective.

Things were just as good at the middle level. Swatty picked and groomed his officers in 1943 and the Regiment had their services for long periods. Bert Coffin served as second-in-command from August 1943 to the last weeks of the war and fought the Regiment in two of its hardest actions: the Kapelsche Veer and the Hochwald. Arnold Lavoie commanded A Squadron throughout the combat period to the last weeks of the war when Glen McDougall took it over, while Darby Nash had B Squadron from mid-August 1944 until the end of the war. Only C Squadron experienced a major change in commanders but even that was not unduly traumatic – Dave Currie led it from Normandy to Bergen op Zoom and Stan Purdy then had it almost to the end of the war when Hugh Clarke took over. It should be noted that, with the exception of Dave Currie who joined the Regiment in 1942, all of these officers had started with the South Albertas as lieutenants or captains in 1940. They knew their men and the men knew and trusted them.

Finally, the Regiment had good leadership at the lower ranks. As the casualty figures for troop leaders attest, there was no lack of junior leadership in the Regiment although the inevitable result was a fairly constant turnover of lieutenants.

She's finished! A happy group of South Albertas pose with war trophies at Oldenburg airfield in May 1945. On the day the war ended, Padre Silcox held a voluntary church service in a ruined hangar – to everyone's amazement almost the whole Regiment showed up to pay their respects both to their fallen comrades and to their fighting padre. COURTESY, CLIFF ALLEN.

No officer commanding a troop in August 1944 was still commanding one in May 1945 – they had been killed, wounded, promoted, replaced or transferred. The continuous rotation of lieutenants at the troop level was offset by the sergeants and corporal crew commanders, many of whom served with their troops through nine months of combat and provided consistency of leadership. The Regiment seems to have been blessed with a number of highly competent NCOs who were a steadying influence and whose experience, due to the relatively low casualty rate, increased as time went on.

From colonel to corporal, the South Albertas were thus fortunate to have good leadership but there was a second factor that worked in their favour – their tactical role. By the time the Regiment entered battle in 1944 the nature of armoured warfare had changed – there was no repetition in northwest Europe of the great armoured breakthroughs that had characterized the early period of the war; the Allies only managed such penetrations at the very end of the Normandy campaign (and, even then, failed to trap the Germans) and during the last few weeks of the conflict. The *Wehrmacht's* sound defensive doctrine, coupled with high-velocity anti-tank guns, *Panzerfausts* and mines, ensured that any attempt to penetrate a German defensive line in 1944-1945, despite overwhelming air and artillery superiority, was going to be a slow, grinding process.

Such processes are always hardest on the infantry and it is the infantry who are the key because only the infantry can take *and hold* ground. Tanks are mobile gun platforms; they can take ground but cannot hold it, as the South Albertas' experience in the Falaise and south of Oldenburg attests, while the artillery as

an arm can neither take nor hold ground, only support the other arms to do so. Infantry were the key and there was never enough infantry in 1944-1945, particularly in the Commonwealth armoured division, which consisted of four armoured regiments (or battalions to give them their tactical size) and four infantry battalions, a ratio of one to one. The *Wehrmacht*, with more experience in mobile warfare, instituted an armour to infantry ratio in its panzer divisions of one tank battalion to every two or three infantry battalions – in contrast, the Commonwealth organization was top heavy in armour. The theory was that the infantry brigade of three battalions would make the "break in" while the armoured brigade of three tank regiments would make the "break through." It never quite worked that way in 1944-1945 and too often the armoured brigades waited for a situation that never came while the infantry brigades not only started battles – they finished them.

This was the case in 4th Canadian Armoured Division where 10 Infantry Brigade, not 4 Armoured Brigade, was the "cutting edge" of that formation. It was 10 Brigade that led the battles from Normandy to the Rhine and Jefferson's brigade, by accident or design, was a balanced formation of all arms, capable of carrying out a variety of operations over a variety of terrain. Its main strength lay in its three infantry battalions but it was augmented by its integral artillery and specialist units and, above all, by its own armoured component provided by the South Alberta Regiment. The brigade had a tank-to-infantry ratio of one-to-three (or four Shermans for every company of infantry), which, as it turned out, was a good balance. Jefferson's wartime brigade was a forerunner of the tactical arrangements favoured by modern armies which are based on an "all arms" concept and it proved, from August 1944 to May 1945, to be the most effective component of 4th Division. As part of this balanced all-arms team the South Albertas worked more closely for longer periods with the infantry than did any other armoured unit in the division and the wise decision always to have, if possible, the same SAR squadron working with the same infantry battalion resulted in the creation of effective tank-infantry teams in 10 Brigade. Finally, it should be emphasized that the South Albertas were an infantry regiment before being converted to armour, and most of the senior officers and

NCOs in the Regiment knew the infantryman's job well and understood the infantryman's needs. In the end, the South Albertas always protected their infantry and their flat-footed friends always protected them and for the Regiment the dividend was lower casualties despite heavy fighting.

Put it all together and what you have is a very good armoured regiment. The last word on the matter, however, should not come from the South Albertas (or their historian); it should come from the men of 10 Canadian Infantry Brigade because they are the ones who really know. Lieutenant Douglas Beale, C Company, Argyll and Sutherland Highlanders of Canada (Princess Louise's), puts it this way:

The SAR – South Alberta Regiment – were to us the best tank regiment that ever fought. I won't downgrade some of the others that we were associated with from to time in fighting, but the SARs, you could depend on them – and they weren't sitting away back shooting to help you, they were right up with you. And you just felt they truly supported the infantry.[19]

T he war in Europe officially came to an end on 8 May 1945 and there were celebrations, particularly in London where the streets became the scene of one great day-long party. In Oldenburg, meanwhile, the Regiment listened on the wireless to the news of the celebrations and the speeches of the King, Churchill and other leaders but the War Diarist noted that "the feeling was not of elation, but rather 'I wish the hell we were out of this mud hole and in London – but much better Canada at home.'"[20]

It would be some time before the boys would see home again. On the day the fighting ceased there were 281,000 Canadian soldiers on the European continent and they faced a long wait for repatriation as there was competition from Britain and the United States for the limited shipping space available. The authorities had foreseen this problem and, since no one wanted a repetition of 1919 when Canadian troops waiting for months for transport home had rioted, plans had been made to keep the men busy. As soon as hostilities ended a comprehensive programme was started to accomplish these objectives.

The official repatriation policy followed a "first in, first out" basis. For each month of war service in Canada a man got two points while for each month overseas he received three. Men who had been wounded in action, married men with wives and dependents in Canada, single men with dependents in Canada and married men without dependants got a bonus increase. As soon as the official policy was announced much frantic arithmetic took place as men toted up their point scores – that total had a direct effect on how much time they would have to wait to go home. As the 4th Armoured Division had been the last major formation of the Canadian Army to go overseas, many in the Regiment knew they faced a long wait.

There was one way to shortcut the process and that was to volunteer for the Canadian Pacific Force, a division-sized formation of 25,000 being organized to serve in the Far East. A man who volunteered for the Pacific force got the highest priority for repatriation and thirty days "clear leave" in Canada before he had to report. This inducement was so great that many volunteered to get both a quick trip home and a good leave even if it meant eventually ending in some malaria-infested jungle fighting the Imperial Japanese Army, who by all accounts were thoroughly nasty people.

For those with low point scores, including many of the zombies who had been conscripted for overseas service the previous winter, and for those who wanted to stay in Europe, there was the Canadian Army Occupation Force, a 10,000-man organization formed for police duties in Germany. It was ironic that Major General Chris Vokes was drafted for this duty. He read of his appointment in the *Maple Leaf* and was very unhappy as he reckoned he had "been away from home for at least 2001 days."[21] His reaction: "the bastards!"

As soon as the shooting stopped the Regiment began to look for a better home than the battered and semi-ruined buildings of Oldenburg airfield. RHQ discovered a mental hospital at nearby Offen and the Regiment moved in on 9 May, leaving their tanks at the airfield. For the first time since Vught, the previous December, the SAR was together under one roof, and in short order they had the building cleaned up, repaired, the lights working and the water running, which made "a wonderful change from pumps and gutted candles."[22] There were still inmates in part of the building and they would "make faces" at the boys from behind the bars of their windows so the boys made faces back.[23]

The South Albertas also began to clean themselves up in preparation for two major inspections. Tommy Barford issued all his stocks of new battledress and the boys got busy sewing on their badges. Sergeant Jake Wiebe went into Oldenburg and found three German tailors happy to work for cigarettes and installed them in a room at Offen where they cleaned, pressed and altered the men's uniforms. Jake brought in Swatty's uniform for a touch-up and one of the German tailors, noting the ribbons and the pip and crown rank of a lieutenant-colonel, asked who it belonged to. When Jake replied that it was the uniform of the *Befehlshaber* (commander) of the Regiment he was amazed to see the German spring to attention, click his heels and salute the colonel's battledress before carefully applying an iron to it.[24]

Those first weeks of peace were a strange time. Sergeant Pete Woolf survived the war only to be injured when a scout car skidded in the mud and collapsed his tent. A group of officers went off to visit "Colonel Sandy McCoffin" of the Argylls and brought back souvenir German pistols from a large pile on permanent display in front of the Argylls' RHQ. Beer was in short supply; nobody could find any film for the regimental film camera; and the weather varied from downpour to incredible

Just a little refreshment for the lads. It was decided that the most efficient way of dispensing the liquid refreshment at the Regimental Picnic was to dump it into one vat and ladle it out – so they did. It helped that, shortly before the war ended, Quartermaster Tommy Barford had captured the alcohol stocks of a German division. COURTESY, W. VAILLANCOURT.

them around his jeep and briefed them on demobilization plans and after he had driven off the Regiment paraded behind the officers' mess where every man got two bottles of much appreciated cold beer. For most SARs the major event of those first weeks of peace was the party held in the late afternoon of 18 May when the Regiment "rolled out the barrel." The War Diarist recorded the "abundance of beer and assorted wines also some rum, champagne and punch" on hand – part of Quartermaster Tommy Barford's largesse from German stocks captured just before the fighting

heat. Much against his will, Gordie Irving got tapped to run the brigade officers' club and was the first of a succession of officers and men who would pack up over the next five months. RSM Jock Mackenzie re-asserted himself and laid on a compulsory one-hour drill parade every morning for all junior officers, warrant officers and sergeants. Two lost American officers drove up to ask the way to their Zone of Occupation; the boys invited them into the mess for a drink and they were still there the next day, having decided that the SAR was a better place to be than the United States Army. Questionnaires were distributed to those who wanted to join the Pacific Force and sixty-nine men volunteered – including Padre Phil Silcox.[25]

On 14 May Vokes came to inspect the Regiment which was formed at 1400 hours ready to receive him. The divisional commander was three hours late, and when he did show up it was pretty obvious he had been celebrating – that night Don Stewart noted in his diary: "Old boy corned."[26] Three days later Simonds arrived to find 10 Brigade drawn up in a hollow square in weather so hot that several men fainted. The corps commander gathered

stopped – and the officers and sergeants "dished out" hot dogs and hamburgers to the men.[27] As Trooper Ian MacPherson remembered, it was a grand time: "We were out in the middle of the bush, and they poured all this alcohol into one big tub and of course you had your army mug and you scooped out and went back, ate a hot dog, and had a drink. We were the drunkest regiment in the Canadian army at that time."[28]

In the last weeks of May the Regiment began to prepare for a move to Holland. From this time on the composition of the

Hold that camera steady, man! Festivities are well under way at the Regimental Picnic and the photographer is beginning to feel the effects. SAR COLLECTION.

SAR would begin to change as the Pacific volunteers and high point men left to be replaced by new faces. It was army policy that men be demobilized in units recruited from their home provinces so many Albertans who had fought with other units were shifted into the Regiment to await their turn at repatriation while SAR men recruited in other parts of Canada were drafted to Ontario or Maritime units. Others were sent to the Occupation Force including a very reluctant Leaman Caseley, who was in England when the war ended and discovered that the "only way to get back to the continent was to volunteer for the occupation army."[29] Caseley did but managed to hide out in the Regiment until the paperwork caught up with him and off he went in a jeep. He would not get home until March 1946.

On 26 May the Regiment returned to friendly Holland. Their new quarters were in the area of Raalte-Zwolle and RHQ was lodged in the magnificent surroundings of

To the victors, the spoils. The castle at Raalte which was the Regimental Officers' Mess when the SAR returned to friendly Holland in June 1945. SAR COLLECTION.

a castle, the ancestral home of Baron De Palthe. The first high-point men went home on 31 May and new men were posted in to take their places, beginning a process that would continue over the next six months. Swatty Wotherspoon, who had returned from commanding 10 Brigade, wanted steps taken to preserve the Regiment's wartime record before the veterans left. In early June, he dispatched an officers' party headed by Arnold Lavoie to photograph the scenes of the last ten months' fighting. Wotherspoon also wanted every man in the unit to have a brief wartime history of the SAR and Major Glen McDougall got that job. According to Glen, the colonel "called me into his office and, pointing a bony finger straight at me so that there was no mistake," pronounced sentence: "You will write the Regimental history."[30] It was a job that Glen did not need as he had also been tasked as Education Officer, responsible for the many training and rehabilitation programmes that would shortly be getting under way. Orders were orders, however, and using the scarce documentation that was available, fleshed out by personal memories, he managed to write and print an 87-page booklet entitled *A Short History of the 29 Cdn Armd Recce Regt (South Alberta Regiment)* and it was a very creditable piece of work under the circumstances.[31]

That month the Regiment gradually began to turn in its tanks. Most men were relieved at being freed from the daily

chore of maintenance but there was some sadness at watching the faithful vehicles, cleaned and "shining like new," being driven off to the ordnance park, for it meant that the South Albertas were no longer fighting soldiers. On 28 June the last Sherman clanked off to its fate and the SAR became an armoured regiment in name only. Few South Albertas ever became emotional over their wartime steeds but it took some time to get used to the sight of squadron areas without the usual bustle around the tank lines. It was another indication that the thing was winding down.[32]

On 9 July 1945 Lieutenant-Colonel Gordon Dorward de Salaberry Wotherspoon, DSO, was struck off strength from the SAR to take over 4 Armoured Brigade as an acting brigadier. There were many in the Regiment who did not like Wotherspoon but there were none who did not respect him both as a commander and as a soldier. The South Albertas had seen at first hand the results of poor leadership in other units, both in garrison and in action, and knew it their great good fortune to have had the same commanding officer for such a long period. His replacement and the Regiment's fourth commander was Darby Nash of B Squadron. A Calgary native, Darby had enlisted in the 19th Alberta Dragoons as a trooper in October 1939, was commissioned as a second lieutenant the following winter and had joined the SAR at Edmonton in July 1940. He was a likeable, relaxed, down-to-earth man and the perfect choice for the difficult task of commanding the Regiment during the final phase.[33]

The exodus now began. Three days after Swatty left, the Regiment said goodbye to that steady old warhorse Arnold Lavoie, who had commanded either a company or a squadron in the Regiment for five years. Quartermaster Tommy Barford also left at this time as did Captain Gordie Campbell and Lieutenants Ev Nieman and Ivan Donkin, all 1940 veterans. New officers and men, strange to the Regiment but all Albertans, were posted in to await their turn for repatriation and the collective face of the SAR began to change.

One former SAR who often visited was Bert Coffin of the Argylls. Bert has good claim to being the only South Alberta to make it all the way to Berlin as he commanded the composite Canadian battalion that performed ceremonial duties in the ruined capital of the Third Reich during July 1945. When Bert had finished this task and Glen McDougall had finished writing the history they made a trip to the French Riviera, travelling in the regal splendour of the magnificent Horch limousine that was the official conveyance of Lieutenant-Colonel Sandy McCoffin of the Argyll and Sutherland Highlanders.[34]

For those South Albertas who had low point totals the Canadian Army proved to be very inventive when it came to finding things for them to do while they awaited repatriation. Training programmes were organized and many men made up educational deficiencies or acquired new skills or trades during this period. Leaves were frequent and "truck tours" to Amsterdam, Antwerp and Paris were instituted as were boat tours and "walking" (hitchhiking) tours in the Netherlands. The emphasis was on keeping the men busy to keep them out of trouble for there was temptation aplenty in postwar Holland.

The basic problem was the country was dirt poor. Its economy had been systematically undermined by the Germans for five years and its currency was nearly worthless. The medium of exchange was the cigarette and if there was one thing Canadian soldiers had in plenty it was cigarettes. Since they

The crew of Contributor pose after it was all over. From the left, Sergeant Jim Nicholson and Troopers J. Johnson, John Neff and J. Frankson. This crew served from Normandy to Oldenburg with very few changes. Neff kept a diary throughout the war and Nicholson later wrote an extensive memoir of his experiences. On the turret can be seen Nicholson's secret weapon. COURTESY, JOHN NEFF.

could acquire 1000 smokes for about $3.00 and could sell them for 1000 guilders or $400 at the official rate of exchange of forty cents to the guilder, it is not surprising that a tremendous black market in tobacco products developed. This rendered futile Dutch attempts to restore their economy but all efforts to stop the practice proved to be useless and the authorities more or less turned a blind eye to the trade. The Canadian soldiers

awaiting repatriation in Holland were thus wealthy young men who wanted to have some fun and they had a lot of fun in that wild, crazy summer of 1945, which the Dutch still remember as the "summer of the Canadians."[35]

Dances and parties were one of the most popular activities. On 16 June the SAR officers held a dance at Raalte Castle, which they had taken pains to decorate. It was "a great success," the War Diarist noted, "though, as usual, the band seemed to disintegrate as the evening went on."[36] The Regiment did not neglect the enlisted men. An SAR dance hall was opened over the "Harmonie Cafe" in Zwolle and dances were held on three evenings a week – Canadians paid one guilder (about forty cents) admission while ladies were admitted free. This establishment was organized by the Regiment but, as David Marshall remembered, the "army kept up a barrage of orders concerning our conduct and putting off limits certain civilian 'houses.' You can be sure that anything that looked good was 'off limits' or 'out of bounds' or for 'Officers Only.'"[37] It didn't matter as with money (or cigarettes) to burn, the boys found other places to have fun.

They also found Dutch girls to have fun with them. As the summer of 1945 wore on there was concern in the Netherlands, at that time a very conservative society, about the effect thousands of wealthy and healthy young Canadian men were having on their country and its womenfolk. The Dutch particularly disliked the sight of military vehicles full of laughing soldiers and local girls driving at high speed through their towns and there were more than a few mutterings among Dutch males that in some ways Canadian military occupation was almost as bad as German. A popular song in Holland that summer was "Trees heeft een Canadees" (Trish has a Canadian), a ballad about a Dutch girl who took up with a Canadian only to have her heart broken when he returned home. As might be expected, there were two results from all this frantic social activity: the illegitimacy rate in the Netherlands trebled in 1945-1946 and great numbers of Canadian soldiers requested permission to marry Dutch women. In the SAR the first three such applications were submitted on 10 August 1945 and more followed. Jim Nicholson, Peter Konvitsko and a number of other SARs brought wives back from Holland, and they were not alone – in all the Canadian government would provide passage to Canada for 1886 official Dutch war brides and 428 children.[38]

It was a wild time but it was also a difficult time for men who just plain wanted to go home. In early July British newspapers criticized the behaviour of the Canadian Army after men in an uncomfortable transit camp at Aldershot rioted and caused considerable property damage. In a letter to his fiancée, Trooper

Arnold Dryer of the SAR expressed the feelings of many about the incident:

> Most of those boys have been over for five years and they only volunteered to fight. They bring them back to the hole of Aldershot and tell them the shipping was cut down from what the US and the British promised. They were quite willing to let the Canadians go in at Dieppe, block the Hitler and Gothic lines in Italy and take all the heavy defences along the coast of France, Belgium and Holland and now, as one woman put it in the paper, they would be better off if they had the Gestapo. I say they forget easy.[39]

Dryer himself was waiting for permission to marry his British sweetheart, but when it finally came he did his best to conceal it from his comrades as he was sure they would engage in the traditional practical jokes played on military bridegrooms. He was right:

> I came in late one night and found my bed upside down and everything loose tied to something, then another night they went out and got a goat and tucked it in my bed. I just put it out in the hall and about three in the morning three of the pups started running it up and down the hall. The goat had a piece of chain around its neck – it woke everyone up.[40]

For the Regiment as a whole perhaps the most important activity that summer was sports, and the SAR continued to add to their laurels. Ed Reardon took over as coach of the SAR track and field activities and formed three teams from Medicine Hat, Calgary and Edmonton. On 3 June 1945 the SAR Edmonton team won the brigade sports meet while the losing teams consoled themselves with an issue keg of beer. The Edmonton boys were hot – they took the divisional championship next, went on to the army championship and won that but met defeat in the final Canadian interservice competition. It was an amazing record for a single team from one small unit.[41]

But boxing was always the South Albertas' greatest passion and over the past eighteen months they had twice demonstrated that their fighters were the best in the Canadian Army. There was a big match between the boxing teams of the 4th and 5th Canadian Armoured Divisions scheduled for 17 August in Utrecht and, a month before, the War Diarist noted that the regimental boxers were in intensive training. Just before the event Swatty Wotherspoon spent a weekend with his brother, Ian Cumberland, then commanding 5 Armoured Brigade in 5th Division. The two brothers had always been rivals and Swatty figured there might be a chance to make some money as, according to Swatty, Cumberland thought 5th Division "had a pretty good team of boxers but he didn't really know his ass from a hole in the ground."[42] Over a dram or two in the brigade mess Swatty began to take bets – 5th Division's fighters against 4th Division's fighters, who were mostly from the SAR. The bets came in fast and furious and Swatty got "a little scared" about the amounts being tossed around so, calling a momentary halt, excused himself and put in a phone call to the South Albertas to ask if the boys could cover the action. The reply was "give us an hour, sir," and one hour later the Regiment phoned back to say "we've got so much money, you can take everything." Swatty resumed matching bets and by the end of the day the wager was up to 22,000 guilders, at which point the 5 Brigade officers "got frightened" and the book was closed. So confident were the SAR about the outcome that the War Diarist noted that the amount "was quickly covered, in fact twice that amount could have been had," but only "first come were the lucky ones." Two hundred men from the Regiment were present in the theatre at Utrecht next day when the 4th Division boxers won the bout, 18 to 13, but, as the War Diarist sadly noted, "5 Div couldn't or wouldn't cover their original wager of 22,000 guilders but only 7,000 guilders."[43] Still, that was $2800 Canadian (about $30,000 in 1995 dollars) and Swatty's share alone "paid for an awful lot of leaves from then on."[44]

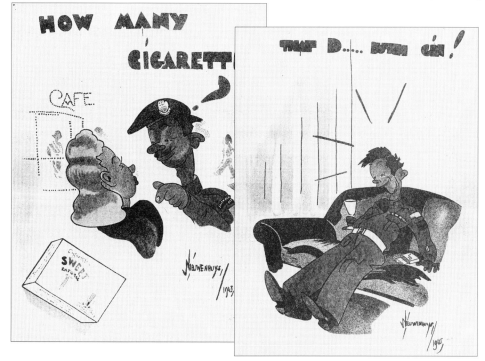

The "Summer of the Canadians," 1945. Two cartoons by Dutch artist Jan Niewenhuys from the *Maple Leaf* show the perils (or pleasures) of life in Holland in the summer that followed the end of the war. SAR COLLECTION.

Row, row, rowing their boat. Members of the Echelon row their boat on the Ijssel River near Zwolle in June 1945. From the left: Larry Hyttenbrauch, Jim Gudwer, "Chad" Chadwick, "C.J." La Franier, Pat MacDonald and "Icky" La Pointe. More than half the men in the Regiment worked in the Echelons keeping the crews supplied with everything they needed – in the opinion of their colonel, they "were brilliant." COURTESY, W. J. GUDWER.

prisoners contracted dysentery. Joe Arkles went from 160 to 120 lb. in two months of captivity. Ed Thorn had been wounded in the right arm at the Hochwald; the Germans gave him some basic medical treatment but he kept the arm in a sling until the day a Scottish soldier presented him with a pail of rocks and told him to "carry this wherever you go, night and day." This practical physiotherapy prevented Ed's arm from deteriorating. To get out of the camp Art Baker volunteered to drive a Red Cross truck to deliver food parcels and was strafed several times by Allied aircraft despite the prominent markings on the white-painted vehicle. He was in Lübeck the day a British armoured unit liberated the city and saw a sight he would never forget. As the first Stuart entered the main square "a young Hitler Youth threw a grenade at it and then he ran but the Stuart followed him up the steps of a big public building and ran right over him."[47] After the SAR prisoners were liberated they were flown to Britain to convalesce for a month and, figuring he would get home faster, Art volunteered for the Pacific Force "but they kicked us out."[48]

Those who were accepted for the Pacific got a swift return to Canada. Among them was the newly-promoted Captain Danny McLeod, who did not return to the Regiment after his release from hospital but went straight to British Columbia to train with the armoured regiment being organized for the Pacific Force. Knowing that Pinky Carvosso, the Regiment's first wartime commander, had retired on Vancouver Island, Danny telephoned him one day and the old war horse was delighted and insisted that they meet at the Empress Hotel in Victoria. Carvosso had followed the Regiment's doings through the newspapers and army friends and was full of questions about the unit. So they sat for a pleasant hour or so – the grizzled old veteran who had enlisted as a private in 1914 and ended up as a captain with the Military Cross in 1918 and the young veteran who had enlisted as a private in 1940 and ended up as a captain with the Military Cross in 1945 – and talked about the Regiment that Carvosso had formed and the splendid name it had made for itself.[49]

Some South Albertas managed to get home early. Among them were the seriously wounded, who were returned to Canada as soon as they were fit to travel. Steve Bayko, who had been badly burned in Normandy, made it back to Canada in June 1945 after an extensive series of skin graft operations. He was discharged with a 20% pension for "gunshot wounds from an exploding pistol" – actually his burns were from flare cartridges which ignited when his Stuart was hit and covered him with burning phosphorus.[45] Over a three-month period Bert Denning had a series of operations to reconstruct his face at Basingstoke hospital in England before coming back on a hospital ship in September. In all Bert was to spend sixteen months in hospitals in Britain and Canada. Other wounded SARs had similar experiences and some never recovered their health – Boney Rathwell, one of the Regiment's best hockey players, died in 1959 from wounds sustained at Moerbrugge in 1944.[46]

Another group that deserve special mention are the fifteen South Albertas who were taken prisoner of war. They were held in various German PW camps but the majority of those captured at the Hochwald ended up at Stalag XIB near Schwerin. The train journey to that camp was particularly bad as the men were packed so tight into cattle cars that half would stand and half would sit in shifts. For rations on the four-day journey they received four-fifths of a loaf of bread and a piece of sausage an inch and a half long. The rations in the camp were worse – turnip soup with a few potato skins was a staple – and most of the

Those members of the Pacific Force who were gambling that the war in the East would be over before they got into it were delighted on 17 August 1945 when Japan agreed to surrender unconditionally. One of them was Corporal George White, who recalls getting "drunker than a skunk" that day.[50] According to Cliff Allen, who was home on leave in Sudbury, "there was no lack of drink" and the civilians "hoisted us on their shoulders."[51]

By the autumn of 1945 most of the veterans and married men had been repatriated but the Regiment itself remained in Holland. It moved to new quarters at Blaricum-Laren in September 1945 and continued the official programme of educational and rehabilitation activities and the unofficial programme of having as much fun as possible. There was a tea shop and a tavern in the local village and arrangements were made for a twice-weekly dance for the enlisted men. Unit strength continued to dwindle as men left for home when their point scores came up, and there was concern that too many senior NCOs were leaving. The SAR was becoming a shell – in October the three fighting squadrons were disbanded and the Regiment was reformed into two squadrons: HQ and F Squadron. By now the South Albertas were on notice that they would be leaving for Canada and on 18 October they learned that they would be shipped to the UK at the end of December. Events, however, moved faster and a champagne party was held in the officers' mess on 17 November when the departure date was moved forward to early December. There was still time for some good deeds and Bill Luton organized Christmas events for the local children. On 1 December F Squadron entertained 300 kids while HQ hosted more than 500 with films, candy and presents. On Sint Niklaus Day itself, 6 December, the entire unit hosted 750 children and the next day Luton distributed hundreds of toys, chocolate and biscuits to the children's wards of nearby hospitals and a local TB sanatorium. When Bill returned from this pleasant duty that evening he helped the other officers and sergeants serve the enlisted men the last SAR Christmas meal. Four days later, on 11 December 1945, the South Alberta Regiment left Holland.[52]

They paused at a transit camp in Ostend, then crossed the Channel to Dover by ferry on 14 December before ending up in another transit camp at Whitley in Surrey. Everyone received ten days leave for Christmas but were back at Whitley in early January when they had a surprise visit from "Buffalo Bill" Bristowe, their commander in 1941-1943, who was now a Civil Affairs officer in Britain. On 9 January 1946 the South Alberta Regiment sailed from Southampton on the *Queen Elizabeth,* which, after more than six years of service as a trans-Atlantic troopship, was not as splendid as she had once been but was still a far cry from HMT *Strathmore* which had brought them over to Britain in 1942. The passage was swift (the SAR always seems to have had luck with their waterborne travel) and the ship sighted land at 1515 hours on 14 January and docked at New York that evening.[53]

It was a breathtaking moment; after "the blackouts and dimouts of Europe, the panorama of lights from the skyscrapers of New York was a mighty welcome sight."[54] If the boys wanted to see more of the big city they were disappointed because when they disembarked the next day they were transported to the Hoboken Train Station and found lines of grim-faced American MPs stationed to make sure they got on the waiting CPR train – and off they went on the long journey to Alberta. Toronto was the first Canadian stop and the bands played, the Red Cross served coffee and doughnuts, and the Ontario boys like Bill Luton left for their homes in that province. Then it was on again through the rocks and trees of northern Ontario to Fort William (Thunder Bay), where they had another brief stop and then on again to Winnipeg, where they arrived in the early evening of 17 January. There was just enough time to have a dance (the last of their many wartime dances) before they got back in their coaches for the journey across the snow-covered prairies to Medicine Hat. At Winnipeg a major from the Second (or Reserve) Battalion of the Regiment, which had continued as a militia unit in the Hat throughout the war, boarded the train to make final arrangements for the homecoming.[55]

They were at Regina in the early morning of 18 January and a number of the Saskatchewan boys, including George Armstrong, Jack Spillet and Jack Summers, jumped off to disperse to their homes in that province.[56] Finally, at 1300 hours the Regiment pulled into Medicine Hat – almost five and a half years to the day that Lieutenant Bert Coffin, wearing his second-hand uniform, and a rag-tag bunch of sixty young recruits, dressed in their oldest clothes, had boarded the CPR coaches for Edmonton on a summer's evening in June 1940. Six of those young men were buried overseas.[57]

Swatty Wotherspoon was waiting to greet them. He himself had arrived from Europe only a few days before and had gone straight out west to meet the Regiment when it returned home. His son Richard (young Swatty), who had not seen his father for five and a half years, remembered receiving only a quick hug during the brief stop his dad made in Toronto.[58] After Darby Nash had formed the unit, Swatty took the salute while the onlookers cheered, including many school children who had been given a half day's holiday and issued with Union Jacks and Red Ensigns which they "waved lustily."[59] Factory sirens wailed, car horns blared and church bells rang as the boys marched through the Hat to the little armoury up on the hill. Here the mayor of the Hat and a brace of federal and provincial politicians made the obligatory speeches and then the men broke ranks to hug wives, children and friends, including many comrades who had returned on earlier drafts. Coffee and doughnuts were served but the *Medicine Hat News* reporter noted that most of the South Albertas, having been forced to imbibe the inferior European product for years, preferred the "good old Alberta beer" which had been thoughtfully provided by the Second Battalion.[60] The party lasted for two hours and then the Calgary and Edmonton detachments marched to the station and boarded the train again, anxious to get to their own homes.

Now, it really was over.

CHAPTER TWENTY

"I was over and I came back."

THE REGIMENT IN THE POSTWAR WORLD: 1946–1995

And so they came home. The story of the South Albertas for the next half century as they moved from their warrior youth through their middle years to old age is part of the story of Canada itself during that time. Most seem to have prospered in the buoyant economy of the 1950s and 1960s, although some did not. Many took advantage of government programmes for overseas veterans to acquire education, housing and civil service positions. Jack Summers and Bill Luton did graduate work at university, Alan Forbes from Trinidad acquired a Bachelor of Commerce degree and there are many similar stories. Quite a few used the experience with heavy equipment they had gained to get a start in the trucking and construction business. Other SAR veterans became barbers, businessmen, teachers, doctors, policemen, stockbrokers, corporate executives, machinists, salesmen, store owners, jewellers, hotel owners, civil servants, firemen, industrial workers – the variety is endless – and not a few went straight back to the farm and stayed there.

Some of their peacetime occupations were unusual and, in the case of Vic Henderson of the Recce Troop, highly dangerous. Vic joined the Toronto Police Department in 1948 and spent twenty-five years on the bomb squad during which time he saved many lives and had a number of close shaves.[2] Wilfred Boothroyd, a former MO, became interested in psychiatry and, after further study in that field, joined the staff of the Sunnybrook Veterans' Hospital in Toronto and spent twenty years as the head of the psychiatry unit of that institution. That fighting man of the cloth, Padre Silcox, decided that his time with the South Albertas had ruined him for regular parish work

We used to ride on horses, or march on weary feet,
Before we were the 19th, and mechanized complete.
We blazed a trail through history
As cavalry and infantry,
But now we are the 19th – the armoured 19th.

Cavalry they called them, very smart Dragoons,
Fusiliers were proudly, numbered by platoons.
Served in the First War, in the line,
While Currie led, they crossed the Rhine,
And now we are the 19th – the armoured 19th.

Service again in Nineteen Thirty-Nine,
Infantry and armour, soldiers of the line.
Then at the end of the campaign
They changed the name, and we became
Troopers of the 19th – the armoured 19th.

Both our parent units were considered great,
We're proud of their records, and we're here to state,
We'll hold their traditions, keep them bright,
Always trained for the fight
Because we are the 19th – the armoured 19th.[1]

and so joined the Ontario Correctional Service (a similar flock he was once heard to remark) and did much good work in his quiet persistent manner. A strict teetotaller, the good padre admitted to a fellow South Alberta years after the war that, although he didn't hold with drinking alcohol, his service with the Regiment had shown him that there were certain occasions when it was permissible – if not downright necessary.[3]

In the five months between his return home in December 1944 and the end of the war in May 1945 the newly-promoted Lieutenant-Colonel David Currie, VC, made seventy public appearances exhorting Canadians to step up war production or buy bonds and endured endless official receptions, interviews and "photo opportunities." It was a torment for this essentially shy man but Dave stuck it out for the good of the service. By June 1945, however, he had had enough and, resigning his commission, gathered up Isabel and young David and took the summer off. He then accepted a job in the paper industry at Baie-Comeau, Quebec, and the Curries spent the next fifteen years in that province, where, always mechanically minded, Dave designed and patented new equipment for the logging industry. They were in Montreal in 1960 when they got a call from recently-elected Prime Minister John Diefenbaker asking if Dave would take the position of Sergeant-at-Arms of the House of Commons. After much soul-searching Dave accepted, served for eighteen years, and is fondly remembered by all staff who were on Parliament Hill during his time and by the elected members as a fair and "compassionate man with a sense of humour that, because of his discretion, was often revealed only by his wry smile."[4]

Swatty Wotherspoon went back to his law practice in 1946 and became a King's Counsel in 1952. Much of his firm's work was for their biggest client, the Eaton department store chain, and Swatty became increasingly involved with that retail giant until he joined it as chairman in 1965 and served in that capacity until his retirement in 1981. Although he had been a distant figure as a commanding officer, he delighted in talking about the war with his old soldiers, preferably over a convivial glass or two, and when he purchased a 500-acre working farm near Uxbridge, Ontario, he always had time for SAR veterans, regardless of rank. There is a story (which may be apocryphal but certainly is typical) that, while inspecting a new Eaton store in Alberta in the 1970s, Swatty and a group of senior corporate executives on a tight schedule were touring the sub-levels of the structure when one of his old troopers emerged unexpectedly from an access hatch where he had been checking the wiring. The two South Albertas recognized each other and Swatty held up his quietly fuming subordinates while he spent twenty minutes talking over old times. Rank, be it military or corporate, does have its privileges.

There were other South Albertas who could not leave well enough alone and joined up again. Gerry Bird fought in Korea with the Royal Canadian Artillery, Speedy Fast and Jim Gove served with the Royal Canadian Ordnance Corps, Peter Konvitsko went to the Royal Canadian Army Service Corps and Wayne Spence ended up, of all places, in the RCAF. Many SAR veterans served with Lord Strathcona's Horse, the regular armoured regiment in western Canada, among them Vic Childs, Bob Thoresen and Fred Jefferson. Fred, an accomplished pianist, and Vic, an enthusiastic singer, used to take over the piano in the Lord Straths' sergeants' mess in the 1950s and entertain a somewhat impatient group of postwar NCOs with old South Alberta songs.[5]

That natural soldier Danny McLeod stayed in the army when the war ended. He served as a squadron commander with the Strathconas, did a tour as an International Control Commission observer in Southeast Asia during the first Viet Nam war and spent time on attachment with the American 1st Armored and 82nd Airborne Divisions. Danny was at Wainwright in the late summer of 1946 when he was ordered to report to Calgary in dress uniform. No one could tell him why so Danny got into his best tunic, buckled on his Sam Browne belt and went to Calgary fully expecting (he must have had a guilty

Coming home. Margaret and Albert Atkinson (wearing his "first civilian suit"), 1945. They met while Albert was stationed with the SAR at Dundurn, married in Nanaimo, and lived at Niagara and Debert before the Regiment went overseas in the summer of 1942. Now they had a lifetime to spend together.
COURTESY, MARGARET ATKINSON.

mind) to face a court martial. He was relieved to find out that Field-Marshal Montgomery, then on a cross-Canada tour, was planning to stop at Calgary airport and wished to present him with the Military Cross he had earned during the action at the airfield at Varrelbusch in April 1945. In making the award the field-marshal may have recalled the words he had spoken the last time the two had met at Sandhurst in the spring of 1944. For the next fifteen years Danny was a fixture in the Royal Canadian Armoured Corps as he imparted to successive generations of young troop leaders the lessons he had learned in places like the dirt road into Bergen op Zoom. His last ten years in the service were on the Directing Staff of the Royal Military College at Kingston, Ontario, and no better officer could have been chosen to serve as an example to young cadets. Danny retired in 1971 and remained in Kingston, where he is still very active today.[6]

The Regiment also left its mark on the postwar Alberta militia. Bob Bradburn commanded the Loyal Edmonton Regiment from 1954 until 1958 when he was promoted brigadier-general and given command of the 23 Militia Group before retiring in 1963. One of his predecessors as commanding officer of the Loyal Eddies was Bill Cromb, who had commanded the Links during the war. Darby Nash took over the 19th Alberta Dragoons in 1946 and stayed with them until 1948 when he moved to the west coast, where he commanded the BCR until 1951 before ending his military career as an acting brigadier-general in command of 22 Militia Group in 1956. Arnold Lavoie had the 19th Dragoons from 1950 to 1954 and was followed in command by Newt Hughes, one of the Regiment's wartime adjutants and its best-known poker player. The Dragoons were full of old SARs. Ernie Hill, who had enlisted in the Regiment in 1940 and been commissioned in 1944, served as a squadron commander with them before being promoted lieutenant-colonel and given command of the Edmonton service battalion, while another SAR, Dick Hicks, also served as a squadron commander with the Dragoons before going on to command the Edmonton Provost Corps. Bob Rasmussen was the RSM of the Dragoons by the time he retired from the militia in 1969. Harry Quarton joined the Dragoons in 1946, was commissioned in 1952, took over 7 Ordnance Company in 1965 and ended up commanding the Loyal Edmonton Regiment. During his military career, which spanned forty-six years and ended in 1986, Harry served as the senior aide-de-camp to five lieutenant-governors of Alberta. In southern Alberta Glen McDougall served with the militia staff in the early 1950s while Stan Purdy went into the Royal Canadian Army Service Corps and commanded 7 Column at Calgary from 1959 to 1961.

Outside Alberta, Jack Summers re-entered the militia after completing postgraduate studies in pharmacy in the United States and joining the faculty of the College of Pharmacy of the University of Saskatchewan. Jack created and commanded the first militia pharmaceutical unit in the west and then

Coming home, Lieutenant Lyle Piepgrass, 1943 and 1945. He enlisted in the Regiment as a private in 1940 and was wounded by artillery fire at Bergen op Zoom in October 1944. COURTESY, LYLE PIEPGRASS.

went on to take over the Saskatoon Light Infantry before ending his military career in 1972 as a brigadier-general in command of Prairie District. He retained a lifelong fascination with military uniforms and history, wrote two books on these subjects, was active in surveying and preserving the battlefield sites of the 1885 Rebellion in Saskatchewan and was also regularly called upon to serve as an outside examiner of postgraduate theses in military history presented at the University of Saskatchewan. During a military career that spanned nearly four decades Jack once reckoned he had worn every uniform issued to Canadian soldiers from 1906 to 1980.[7]

Swatty Wotherspoon assumed command of the Governor General's Horse Guards in May 1946 and retained it until 1949 when he received a long overdue promotion to brigadier and command of 19 Armoured Brigade (Reserve) in southern Ontario. Due to the press of his business activities Swatty retired from the army in 1954 but when Worthy died in 1967, leaving vacant the post of colonel-commandant of the Royal Canadian Armoured Corps, Swatty was the choice of the "black hats" to succeed the father of the corps in that position. He served for a five-year term from 1968-1973 and his record as a wartime leader was further recognized with the rare award of a Doctorate in Military Science from RMC.

The years passed, and then the decades, and the South Albertas prospered, or did not as the case may be, in the postwar world. They were successful in at least

Duffy never came home. Duffy Gendron's grave at Cintheaux Commonwealth War Graves Cemetery. He was one of the South Albertas who did not return from overseas. PHOTOGRAPH BY DIANNE GRAVES.

one thing – having children – and how they had children. In the three decades after 1945 Canada's population doubled as the wartime generation, making up for lost time, contributed to a demographic phenomenon called the "Baby Boom." By 1967 half the country was under the age of twenty-five and this first postwar generation, with its long hair, short skirts and loud music, proved impatient with Dad's stories of the dirty Thirties, the Dundurn trots, route marching, buzz-bombs and Moaning Minnies. It all comes round, however, and now the Baby Boomers have to cope with a second postwar generation which is no more respectful to them than they were to their parents. Let's leave it at that.

How do the South Albertas feel about it all now? Some, like Robert Broberg, simply reply "I was over and I came back," but, very generally, most are positive about the experience – with certain important qualifications.[8] Bob Seccombe thinks it "was the best education I ever had but I wouldn't wish it on anybody."[9] Jimmie Walker agrees: "For people like me who came back, it was the best time I ever had and I couldn't have paid for it" as "I got off the farm and swore I would never go back and I never did."[10] Jimmie Bell also thinks that it "was the best part of my life, it made a man out of me."[11] Len Angus feels that his army life "was as good as university. You got to see the world and in a way it benefited me. I doubt I could do it all over again but I think I would try."[12] On repeating the experience Ron Virtue disagrees: "No, I would not do it all over again – I couldn't be that lucky again."[13] For David Marshall the important thing about his army experience was the human factor because it "gave me an understanding of how people react under duress and it gave me firsthand knowledge of the importance of personal relationships and reliance on others."[14]

Other SAR veterans are less positive.

Reward for a job well done. In the summer of 1947 Viscount Alexander, the Governor-General, awards Sergeant (Retd.) Tom Milner of C Squadron the Distinguished Conduct Medal for his 1945 action at Hintern Esch in Germany.
COURTESY, TOM MILNER.

Meniere's disease. I figure the explosion [in his tank at the Hochwald] was the cause of it. I applied for recognition to the pension board. I got a reply that there was no record of the explosion, that really shook me.

You know when we went on that trip to Europe, it made me feel good to see all the people honour us & treat us with respect. I felt my life hadn't been wasted all together. How many veterans are there that think like me? The lucky ones are in those cemeteries over there.[17]

Jimmy Cooper expresses one view: "I think it set back your life time. Discipline I learned but nothing else and you come back home and you're three years older. After the war I had a half dozen jobs before I finally settled down."[15] Some, like J. White, never did talk about the war and don't want to now:

I came home and never said anything about what I had done. It was behind me and I just sort of let it go. I hear too much talking and yakking about it. We just bought a bar, my son and I, and you should hear some of those veterans even today – lie like hell, they do.[16]

For many the tension did not end in 1945. The widow of one distinguished veteran recalled the many times her husband would come down in the morning "looking pale and tired" and say "I had a bad war last night." There are some who have been permanently marked such as the veteran who admits that "I never recovered" as "I still don't like noises and I don't like crowds, don't even like going to church." Another has a similar reaction: "I still can't go into a crowd and I haven't been able to work as hard as I should." One ex-trooper, captured at the Hochwald, is understandably bitter:

My nerves are shot. Through the years I became an entertainer for people who thought it was fun to see me jump. I struggled through life, going from job to job. I had to leave my trade, take jobs where I was away from people, finally ended up on disability, then retirement. When I applied for an army [medical] pension, [I] got 25%. I thought now I should be okay then I developed

Regardless of their personal feelings about the war, most SAR veterans enjoy attending Regimental reunions. The first such event was held in Edmonton in February 1946, shortly after the Regiment returned from Europe, when four hundred South Albertas and their wives sat down to dinner in the Macdonald Hotel while the band of the Loyal Eddies played the Regiment's unofficial march, "Colonel Bogey." Darby Nash presided and Swatty, who had delayed his return to the east after welcoming the SAR home in Medicine Hat, attended with his wife as did Bob Bradburn and Jim Jefferson. It was a splendid affair and the dining, as the *Edmonton Journal* reporter remarked, was "a far cry from the dust-covered iron rations on which the unit made its first meals in Normandy."[18] Warrant Officer Harry Quarton, who had left the Regiment in 1942, arrived in Edmonton that evening from Europe and, hearing that there was a SAR "do" at the Macdonald, went right over to the hotel to find out what was going on. A kindly desk clerk stowed his kit and the boys invited Harry to join the party.[19]

Since then there has been a reunion either every year or every second year. Some of the early gatherings tended to get a bit lively, but as the boys settled down with wives, families and jobs, they became more staid. The reunions are usually held in the west as that is where the greater part of the SAR settled. The favoured sites for the first two postwar decades were Edmonton and Calgary but in 1965 the SAR returned to Medicine Hat for a memorable and well-attended meeting. Around this time they raised the funds for a memorial stained glass window to their war dead which was installed in a Calgary church. Informal reunions also took place from time to time and the veterans of the Recce Troop, in particular, meet at regular intervals. By the 1980s the Recce boys liked to camp out together once a year in

Montgomery meets McLeod for the second time. Field-Marshal Bernard L. Montgomery pauses in a cross-Canada tour to award Captain Danny McLeod the Military Cross for the action at Varrelbusch airfield on 15 April 1945. Danny McLeod enlisted in the SAR as a private in 1940, was wounded three times and finished the war as a captain. COURTESY, DANNY McLEOD.

Talking over the "good" old days. Lieutenant-Colonel Dave Currie, VC, visits the 19th Alberta Dragoons in Edmonton sometime in the 1950s and meets some former comrades. From the left: Lieutenant-Colonel Harry Quarton (on floor) and, behind Harry, Lieutenant-Colonel Ernie Hill, commissioned in the SAR during the war. On the couch, from the left, Lieutenant-Colonel Arnold Lavoie, Lieutenant-Colonel Dave Currie, Lieutenant-Colonel Ken Clarke, Brigadier-General Bob Bradburn and RQMS Grant Flaws. Bradburn, Currie and Lavoie were the Regiment's three squadron commanders when it landed in Normandy in July 1944. COURTESY, HARRY QUARTON.

had a big job to talk the wife into going. We found out when it was and we sent in our money ahead of time. Everybody in the regiment knew me but most had not seen me for years so when we walked in at Medicine Hat and picked up these two tags marked "Halkyard," they were all over me.

Dave Currie was another who stayed clear of SAR gatherings although he maintained contact with the other military units in which he had served. "The SAR brought back too many painful memories for Davie," says Isabel Currie, because they "reminded him too much of the many friends he had lost."[22] Any South Alberta, however, who travelled to Ottawa and took the time to go and see Dave Currie would always receive a friendly welcome. Dave never liked to talk about his wartime experiences and it was only after a number of appeals from the Army Historical Section that he agreed to write a personal account of the action at St. Lambert for a French historian researching a book on the Falaise battle. Dave was no writer and struggled for weeks with the thing until finally it was done, typed up and sent off to the Frenchman, who promised to send a copy of his book in return. He never did but Dave's account pops up from time to time in European military history magazines.[23]

their motor homes and talk about old times. As Andy Clipperton, the wife of Corporal Bob Clipperton, commented, "Things come out that they have never told their wives about and we've learned so much more of what they endured" as "it is good for them to finally speak of unspeakable things."[20]

In 1987 the SAR held its first regimental tour to Europe when a large group of veterans and their wives (plus two Argylls who tagged along for the trip) flew to London. In England the SAR visited their old stations at Brighton, Maresfield and Bordon-Headley, where they had a pint for old time's sake in the "Holly Bush" and then telephoned 93-year-old Sally Stevens, who not only remembered them but scolded them for their wartime behaviour. Then it was off to the continent and all the old familiar places: Caen, St. Lambert, Moerbrugge, Bergen op Zoom, Kapelsche Veer and the rest. Stops were made at each of the beautiful Commonwealth War Graves Cemeteries where men of the Regiment have their final resting place.

Some SAR veterans have avoided such Regimental functions because they wanted to put their past behind them. One of them was Sergeant Albert Halkyard, MM, who did "a lot of crazy things after the war" but eventually settled down as a farmer. Halkyard didn't say "a word about the war for forty years, I just tried to hide and keep out of the way."[21] By 1987 he felt he had put enough distance between himself and the war years and so decided to attend the annual reunion scheduled at Medicine Hat. Halkyard recalls that he

The South Albertas respect the feelings of those members of the Regiment who have decided to close and not re-open a part of their lives. For the others their spirit is still strong enough for them to maintain their affiliations for more than half a century despite the fact that the South Alberta Regiment itself ceased to exist in 1954.

Its demise came as a result of a massive reorganization of the militia in that year. It was decided by Army Headquarters that the SAR of Medicine Hat would be replaced by elements of a new unit to be formed from an amalgamation with two Calgary artillery regiments. Mayor Harry Viner of the Hat and concerned local citizens were upset, not only because the SAR would disappear from the order of battle but also because the headquarters of its successor would move from the Hat to Calgary. Through the summer of 1954 they waged a fierce battle against the changes which, at one point, grew so heated that the GOC Western Command, Chris Vokes, recommended that the SAR be left alone. This did not please the Chief of the General Staff, Guy Simonds, who was adamant that not only would the SAR be amalgamated but it would adopt the name South Alberta Light Horse. This title, partly derived from the 15th Alberta Light Horse, a prewar militia regiment from the Calgary area, found little favour in Medicine Hat. In the end the matter was officially closed on 28 September 1954 when the Minister of Defence, Brooke Claxton, signed the order bringing the South Alberta Light Horse into existence. On that day, the South Alberta Regiment was struck off the order of battle, its honours and those of the 31st Battalion CEF were transferred to the SALH, and its unique badge with the Alberta provincial crest was no longer seen on military headgear.

It is hard not to feel sympathy for the supporters of the South Alberta Regiment, who struggled hard to save the unit but made a major tactical error – they were adamant that the title of the new regiment be "South Alberta Regiment (29 Armoured Regiment)" and nothing less. If they had compromised on the subtitle (29 Armoured Regiment), the result might have been a name that would have more fully preserved the flavour of their traditions such as "South Alberta Regiment (15th Light Horse)" or "South Alberta Regiment (Light Horse)." Unfortunately, in trying to defend everything, the defenders of the SAR lost almost everything. The struggle over the name was only one part of the controversy, however; there was also much opposition to the move of the headquarters of the new regiment to Calgary and the fact that these headquarters were returned to Medicine Hat in 1960 is an indication of the senselessness of the 1954 decision.

Of course the boys paid no attention and carried on because, although the SAR may have disappeared from the order of battle, the Regimental Association continues to represent the South Albertas and will do so until the last veteran has gone to his reward and, who knows, their children and grandchildren may keep it going. The spirit of the South Albertas is indomitable and never was that more apparent than in the years following the Vancouver reunion of 1989 when Major General George Kitching was the featured speaker. The last time Kitching had addressed the boys was in a gymnasium at Maresfield on a rainy day in June 1944, but if the South Albertas assumed their former divisional commander was going to recall the glory days, they got a rude awakening. Calling them an "idle bloody shower," Kitching castigated the SAR for never revisiting their European battlefields and erecting plaques at the scenes of their most important actions, never procuring their Regimental Colour and never publishing a more extensive record of their wartime history. He challenged them to make up for these deficiencies and the Regiment rose to the challenge. The Association immediately began a fund-raising campaign to accomplish these goals.[24]

Three years later, the Regiment undertook a major European tour to erect and dedicate a number of memorials – the first result of their fund-raising. One South Alberta who was very active in promoting both this tour and the Regiment's other goals was Fred Bullen, an old 1940 original who had been commissioned in another regiment. Shortly before the tour departed Fred was taken mortally ill and, when Danny McLeod went to visit him, he handed Danny a cheque for $10,000 and asked that some of it be given to those veterans who might not have enough money to accompany the tour to Europe. Danny did exactly that.[25]

Danny McLeod was active in the preparations for the 1992 tour and as the Regiment planned to visit the *Musée de la Bataille de Normandie* in Bayeux he phoned the director, Dr. Jean-Pierre Benamou, to arrange the timing. Upon learning who he was, Benamou asked "Where have you been?" and then explained that the people of France had heard nothing of the Regiment since August 1944 yet the unit was the focal point of the largest display in his museum – a diorama of the battle at St. Lambert.[26] The genial director, who has since been awarded the OBE by the British government for his efforts to preserve the role of the Commonwealth forces in Normandy, arranged a splendid reception in Bayeux. By this time, the Association had raised funds to erect plaques at Cormelles, where the Regiment concentrated before first going into battle. There is also a plaque on a Sherman tank with South Alberta markings at Eekloo in Belgium, and in the Honour Room of the city hall in Bergen op Zoom, and the Regiment plans to install plaques at Moerbrugge and Uedem in the near future.

Some places overseas had changed, some hadn't, but they are all full of memories for the South Albertas, particularly the Commonwealth War Graves Cemeteries at Brookwood in England, Bény-sur-Mer, Bretteville, Bayeux and Cintheaux in France, Adegem in Belgium, and Bergen, Groesbeek and Holten in Holland, where men of the Regiment are buried. Cemetery visits can be a difficult thing for the South Albertas as the names on those uniform white headstones and the number of those headstones evoke "many emotions: anger at the waste of young lives, sadness at the loss of friends, wonder as to why they were taken and we were not, and some guilt at feeling thankful we were spared bullets that would have ended our lives."[27] There were many cemetery visits on the 1992 tour and, during a wreath-laying ceremony at Holten near Nijverdal, a very touching scene occurred. A large crowd of local citizens had gathered to respectfully watch the South Albertas, 116 strong, parade to honour their dead. Shortly before the ceremony ended, a torrential downpour of rain occurred but within a few minutes every veteran was sheltered by an umbrella held by a willing and grateful onlooker.[28]

It was well that the Regiment undertook these activities when it did because the tide was beginning to ebb. Dave Currie died in June 1986, just twelve days after he and the other surviving Canadian VC winners had been honoured at a Legion convention in Edmonton. Following his retirement from the Commons in 1978 Dave had devoted much of his spare time to

Grown older but not bolder. Veteran SAR officers relax during the 1992 Regimental Tour of Europe. From the left, Lieutenant-Colonel Bert Coffin, DSO, Major Danny McLeod, MC, and Captain Leaman Caseley, MC. Bert Coffin was the second-in-command of the Regiment from 1943 to 1945 while McLeod and Caseley won the Military Cross while serving as troop leaders with the unit. Coffin came through the war unscathed but Caseley was wounded twice and McLeod three times. COURTESY, DANNY McLEOD.

painting and the Curries' Ottawa home is full of his beautifully-rendered natural scenes. Although the VC changed his life Dave maintained to the end the same consistent attitude to the decoration – that it was not his personal award but that he wore it for the men who fought alongside him at St. Lambert. "It is an honour," he remarked six weeks before his death, but "you carry it for a lot of people who aren't here any more."[29]

Two years later Brigadier-General Gordon Wotherspoon died at the age of eighty. Universally respected as a soldier and business leader, Swatty's funeral service on 3 December 1988 at St. James' Anglican Cathedral in Toronto, a church designed by his great-grandfather, was attended by the lieutenant-governor of Ontario, hundreds of friends, associates, comrades and as many South Albertas as could get there. By now the recessional was in full flow: Arnold Lavoie had died in 1979, followed by Bob Bradburn, Padre Silcox, Darby Nash, Jock Mackenzie, Newt Hughes and many others. Each Association newsletter added new names to a lengthening list of old comrades who had mustered in the green fields beyond.

By the end of 1992 the Regiment had met two of George Kitching's challenges – they had erected memorials in Europe and dedicated them on the ground. Plans were now made to meet the third challenge and publish an extensive history to

Brigadier-General J.L. Summers, MC, CD (1920-1994). A native of Battleford, Saskatchewan, Jack Summers began his military career in 1934 as a boy soldier with the Battleford Light Infantry. He came to the Regiment as a lieutenant in 1943 and commanded a troop in B Squadron at St. Lambert before taking over the South Alberta sappers in April 1945. Jack Summers once reckoned that during his military career he had worn every uniform issued to the Canadian army between 1906 and 1980. COURTESY, IMAGERY PHOTOGRAPHY, SASKATOON.

expand the small booklet Glen McDougall had produced under great pressure in 1945. The natural choice of author was the SAR's own historian, Jack Summers, and on his return from the tour in 1992 Jack began in his organized way to gather the documentation and conduct interviews. Unfortunately illness intervened and he died in January 1994, whereupon the task came to the present author.

In 1995 there was a tremendous celebration in the Netherlands as more than 12,000 veterans, their families and friends, from Canada, Britain, the United States and Poland came to the country at the invitation of the Dutch people for festivities to mark the fiftieth anniversary of the end of the war. A number of SAR veterans attended this anniversary, John Galipeau, Vic Henderson, David Marshall, Ed Reardon and Art Webster among others – and they received a splendid reception as the Dutch people have never forgotten the sacrifice the Canadian Army made to free their country. In the five decades that have passed since the wild, crazy 1945 "summer of the Canadians" feelings have softened and it is now remembered fondly in the Netherlands as a golden bygone time and has even been made the subject of a television series. In fact so fondly is that time recalled that the organizers of the 1995 event singled out Trees (Trish), the heroine of the 1945 song "Trees heeft een Canadees," as part of the festivities.

The SAR veterans who returned to Holland were simply overwhelmed by the reception. Although they are very appreciative of the efforts made on their behalf, the veterans of the Regiment (and other Canadian veterans) are sometimes puzzled by the unflagging gratitude shown by the citizens of the countries they liberated, particularly as their own nation seems to have forgotten their wartime sacrifices. The attitude of the Europeans was well summarized by Albert Hartkamp, the chairman of the 1995 "Thank You Canada" committee in Nijverdal, during a brief address given at the Commonwealth War Graves Cemetery at Holten:

Sometimes your people ask us: "Why do you Dutchmen do so much for us as Canadians?" When you look around you, you have the answer. Those soldiers which are buried here, and those Canadian soldiers like you, gave us back our freedom. Many of your young men gave their life for our liberation. That brings out emotions but it affirms our special feelings for you as Canadians. …

The period from 1940 to 1945 was a black period for my country. We remember it but we can't stand still, we have to go further. We must try and

Bergen marks its liberation. A half century to the day after his tank first entered the *Grote Markt* at Bergen op Zoom, Danny McLeod recreates the event on 27 October 1994 to the enthusiastic applause of the townspeople, as seen in this clipping from the local newspaper. COURTESY, WEST BRABANT BN.

prevent a new war. You can ask us "Is it meaningful to remember all those who died nearly 52 years ago?" We think it is and that we must not forget those who sacrificed their lives for our freedom. Let it be a warning for the future. Our children and grandchildren must know what happened. They must know what war is and they must try to prevent another war.[30]

Back in Canada in 1995 the South Albertas were planning their own celebration to mark the fact that, fifty-five years after it was first authorized, the Regiment had finally procured its Colour or flag. Regimental Colours at one time marked a unit's presence on the field of battle, and they now identify it on parade – they are embroidered with the names of a unit's important battles and are its most treasured possession. In the case of the SAR the battle honours on its Colour included not only those won by the Regiment during the Second World War but also those gained by the 31st Battalion in 1915-1918. Under the stewardship of a committee consisting of Jay Moreton, Danny McLeod, Alan Graham, Honorary Colonel of the South Alberta Light Horse, and Stan Milner, Honorary Lieutenant-Colonel of the SALH, it had taken the SAR nearly five years to raise the funds, establish the design, have it approved by the proper heraldic authorities and pay for the manufacture of the Colour. They had now met the fourth and final challenge posed by George Kitching, and the Association planned to mark the event with a number of special ceremonies during the reunion scheduled in Edmonton that September. The most important was to take place on the grounds of the Alberta Legislature when Lieutenant-Governor Gordon Towers would formally present the Colour to the Regiment, after which it would be

consecrated by a military chaplain and laid up for permanent display in the rotunda of the provincial legislature building. Detailed planning for these ceremonies had occupied the Association executive for much of the preceding twelve months as they tried to co-ordinate the timing of the various military and civil organizations invited to participate.

Any reader who has followed the South Albertas' story this far will know that they have often run afoul of established authority and in this respect their luck hasn't changed since the shooting stopped. Just when the executive thought that their arrangements had been finalized, a functionary in the Department of National Defence issued a fiat stating that, because the South Alberta Regiment had been removed from the order of battle in 1954, it had no *official* status as a military unit and therefore its Colour had no status and therefore units of the Canadian Forces could not participate in the planned consecration of that Colour nor pay proper military respects to it, and, by the way, the Colour could not be referred to as a Colour because it wasn't, officially, a Colour. This fatuous edict threatened to disrupt all the Association's carefully-made plans for the Edmonton reunion.

It also made the Regiment angry because they rightfully regarded such bureaucratic hogwash as an insult. It is always a mistake to rile the South Albertas and their reaction was predictable – the executive immediately called in the considerable number of markers it had with the higher ranks (particularly the higher armoured ranks) of the Canadian Forces as well as enlisting the aid of anyone who might possibly be able to assist their cause.[31] In the end it was absolutely no contest and the functionary retreated under the smokescreen of a face-saving (for him) compromise. In a letter to the Association dated 13

South Alberta memorial at Eekloo, Belgium. To remember their liberators the towns in the area procured an ex-Belgian army Sherman and reconditioned it to serve as a memorial. It bears SAR markings and is in better condition than many of the Regiment's wartime vehicles. PHOTOGRAPH BY DIANNE GRAVES.

Old reliable. The South Albertas' ACV as a static display at Sarcee, near Calgary, in the 1980s. The Regiment was the first armoured unit to receive this type of vehicle and they got the White Motor Company model which was rarely seen in the Commonwealth forces. They kept it running from April 1943 to May 1945 and, a few years ago, they brought it to a reunion and cranked it up. It ran smoothly. COURTESY, GEORGE GALLIMORE.

What happened to all those tanks? Monument at Moerbrugge constructed out of the wreckage of the many South Alberta tanks lost there in September 1944.

PHOTOGRAPH BY DIANNE GRAVES.

April 1995 he informed the SAR that, although they could not officially possess a Colour, they could possess a "replica of the approved design for commemorative purposes as a permanent memorial" but they could not "consecrate" this memorial, they could only "dedicate" it because only official Colours could be "consecrated."[32] His unkindest cut was that units of the Canadian Forces could "come to attention for, but not present arms to, the replica Colour, since it is not consecrated and not an active Colour in the full sense." Having covered his own posterior, this gentleman then departed the scene, never to be heard from again.

It was all rather silly, but there is a more serious side to this matter for it calls into question the nation Canada has become since the Second World War – and what kind of a nation permits a minor bureaucrat to treat a group of distinguished veterans in such a shabby manner? The South Albertas know more than most that the Canada of the 1990s is not the Canada of the 1940s and they are saddened by the changes – as one remarked: "I think we failed, as the country I fought for isn't the country we have now."[33] Others feel that these changes were necessary but what concerns all of them is that Canada's record during the Second World War is no longer being taught in the schools and what little the postwar generations know of the conflict is largely influenced by foreign films and television. That record is outstanding – of a population of just under eleven million people, more than one million men and women served in the three armed services – and must never be forgotten.

To the South Albertas and other Canadian veterans this neglect or distortion of our nation's wartime effort is not a detached argument about how best to interpret history in the educational system. They have a personal stake in the matter because they have seen at first hand the sacrifices made to preserve freedom between 1939 and 1945 and are concerned that, if Canadians do not remember those sacrifices, they may have to learn the same bitter lessons again.

"And not to yield."

EDMONTON, ALBERTA: 21–24 SEPTEMBER 1995

The South Albertas began to trickle into the Edmonton Westin Hotel during the afternoon of Thursday, 21 September 1995. The boys had met many times since the end of the war but this was a special occasion as the Regiment had finally procured its Colour and planned to consecrate this important military symbol that weekend. The 1995 reunion therefore attracted veterans who had not been at such functions for years and there were many joyful encounters as old comrades from across North America recognized each other in the hotel lobby.

Three busy days lay ahead. The reunion schedule contained an impressive list of briefings, business meetings, a church parade, receptions and formal meals. To most, however, the event that counted was the ceremony scheduled for the following Saturday when the lieutenant-governor of Alberta would present the SAR with its Colour during a parade on the grounds of the provincial legislature building. The Regimental Colour (and it was called exactly that throughout the reunion) was on prominent display and it was an impressive sight. Centred on a dark blue field with a black and gold fringe was the Alberta provincial crest with its mountains and wheat fields encircled by maple leaves. An outer wreath of laurels was adorned with the battle honours won by the 31st Battalion in 1914-1918 and the South Albertas in 1944-1945 – honours that included such fateful names as

> *Tho' much is taken, much abides; and tho'*
> *We are now not that strength which in old days*
> *Moved earth and heaven, that which we are, we are,*
> *One equal temper of heroic hearts,*
> *Made weak by time and fate, but strong in will*
> *To strive, to seek, to find, and not to yield.*
>
> TENNYSON, "ULYSSES"

Passchendaele, Vimy Ridge, the Somme ... St. Lambert, Bergen op Zoom, Kapelsche Veer, the Hochwald. It was an attractive object and it excited much admiration.

By the end of the first day, in true SAR fashion, the boys had taken over the hotel. The Regimental badge adorned the lobby and knots of older men could be seen holding forth in the restaurant and taking up all available seats in the bar. Not only SAR veterans were present on this early autumn weekend in Alberta's capital – a number of visitors from Europe had travelled a long way to present the SAR with medallions for their role in liberating Normandy and Bergen op Zoom including Dr. Jean-Pierre Benamou from the museum in Bayeux. There were many

Guard of Honour. The troopers of the South Alberta Light Horse, the successor to the South Alberta Regiment, mount a Guard of Honour on the steps of the Alberta Legislature as the SAR enter the building to lay up their Colour in September 1995. COURTESY, SOUTH ALBERTA LIGHT HORSE.

In Holland, they never forget. Every Christmas Eve the schoolchildren of Nijverdal place a lit candle before every grave in nearby Holten Commonwealth War Graves Cemetery. This ceremony began as an initiative of Wim Porterman and Albert Hartkamp of Nijverdal, who are shown standing among the candle-lit graves. COURTESY, WIM PORTERMAN.

a few laughs as men forgot drill that had once been second nature and feet slipped on dew-laden grass. Laughter or not, they were a distinguished looking group, the youngest seventy and the oldest eighty-seven years of age, and well turned out in black berets, regimental ties, blue blazers, grey slacks and white gloves.

Over the next hour other units gradually began to arrive. The band of the Loyal Edmonton Regiment, resplendent in scarlet tunics and white Wolseley helmets, showed up first and began to play a medley of traditional military favourites and the South Albertas were soon marching to the stirring sounds of "Soldiers of the Queen" and their own "A Southerly Wind and a Cloudy Sky." Next to arrive was a gaggle of young people from the 19th Alberta Dragoons, now a cadet unit, in dark green uniforms. Finally, the South Alberta Light Horse marched on, their full dress sand tunics making a pleasant contrast with the dark blue and grey of the SAR. Watching from the sidelines were a dozen or so South Albertas (promptly dubbed "Recce Troop" by a wag) confined through age or infirmity to wheelchairs, some proudly bearing the "45" Tac sign.

family members as, early in the Regiment's postwar history, it became a tradition to invite wives and children to reunions. Thus, Isabel Currie attended with her son and grandchildren, as did Swatty's Wotherspoon's son and daughter-in-law and many others, including Trooper Ian MacPherson's family, who paraded no less than four generations – the youngest of whom, Keith Sauve, was heard to remark to his mother, "This place is full of grandpas!"

On Saturday morning at 0830 hours sharp the South Albertas boarded the buses for the trip to the grounds of the provincial legislature. The ceremony was not to start until 1100, but as it was an elaborate business, it required some practice for men who had not done any "square bashing" for half a century. There was an undercurrent of excitement during the brief drive through downtown Edmonton, so changed from the small western city where the SAR had mobilized in 1940, but there was also sadness, a sadness reflected in a common refrain: "If only Swatty … or the Padre … or Jack … or Tom" – or so many others who had gone on before – "were here to see this."

At the legislature, Fred Jefferson formed the unit. He had come to the Regiment at Bergen in October 1944 as a young replacement and had ended his military career, twenty-six years later, as a sergeant-major in Lord Strathcona's Horse. Now he patiently but firmly walked the South Albertas, ninety strong, through the various stages of the ceremony, interrupted by not

It was warm and it was sunny and, amazingly, it was a windless day. Near the appointed hour the parade was formed waiting for Lieutenant-Governor Gordon Towers, who arrived promptly at 1100 and came forward with Bert Coffin to where the new Colour had been unfurled on the piled drums of the Loyal Eddies. It was then consecrated by the Reverend Doctor David Carter, former Speaker of the Alberta Legislative Assembly and son of the last padre of the postwar South Alberta Regiment. A veteran himself, Towers had lost a good friend with the SAR and, noting that this ceremony was "long overdue" and that it was a great pleasure "on behalf of all Albertans and the Canadian people to correct this oversight," he presented the Regiment with the Colour they "so justly deserve."[1] Danny McLeod received it for the SAR and it was a proud moment for the veterans and an emotional one for those bystanders privileged to see it.

On a day such as this, the Regiment could not forget its war dead and Harry Quarton read the Roll of Honour – that list of the men who had died on active service. To most spectators that sunny morning they were just names; to the South Albertas they were comrades still alive in their minds as young men with whom they had shared the dangers, joys and hardships of the war years.

The first name on that list was Captain K.E. Perrin – Kenny Perrin, a 25-year-old bank clerk from Medicine Hat who joined the prewar SAR in 1937 and died in the disastrous "right hook" at the Hochwald on 27 February 1945. The list continued: Captain A.C. Scrimger … Lieutenants Johnston, Roberts, Smith, Young – that was Wally Young whose piano playing was the mainstay of entertainment in the officers' mess until a sniper got him at Moerbrugge … Sergeant Alvin Bell, killed at St. Lambert on 21 August 1944 … Sergeants Clark … Wagner, Corporal E.E. Gendron – "Duffy" Gendron from Medicine Hat, who died near the Quesnay Wood on 10 August 1944 … Corporal J.G. McRae … Corporal F.B. Moan – Frankie Moan, killed on the dirt road into Bergen on 25 October 1944 … Lance Corporal L.J. Golby – Leo Golby, from Castor, Alberta, killed when his motorcycle collided with a truck in June 1944 … Troopers W.H. Andrew … J.F. Bartlett … L.L. Craig … A. Gee … R.H. Goodyer.

That was Bob Goodyer. Killed by the fatal short round at Bergen on 28 October 1944, he was a 22-year-old clerk from Montreal who joined the Regiment the previous summer and was survived by a wife. The list contained the names of six other men who died in the same incident, including Trooper Tip Lafoy, a 34-year-old farmer from Notikwin, Alberta, who joined the SAR in June 1940 and left behind a wife and daughter; Trooper John McDonell, a 26-year-old mechanic from Carlyle, Saskatchewan, who joined in 1943; Trooper George Mungall, a 33-year-old hotel clerk from Edmonton and one of the old originals, who also left a wife and daughter; and Trooper John Stone, a 31-year-old hotel clerk from Trochu, Alberta, who joined the Regiment in October 1941 and married a British girl the same year he was killed.[2]

Harry Quarton continued … Troopers Walton, Woods, and so on through to Trooper Karl Wickstrom who took a wrong turn at Wierden in April 1945 and ran into a German machine gun. Two minutes silence were observed and then a bugler sounded "Last Post" just as it had been sounded at Queenston in the summer of 1941 so many years before.

These respects paid, their new Colour was trooped, or formally displayed to the South Albertas. Next, in a moving ceremony, the South Alberta Regiment and the South Alberta Light Horse joined ranks in formal acknowledgement of their joint military heritage. Raised from the same small towns that had produced so many of the wartime South Albertas, not a few of the "Sallies" were the grandsons (and granddaughters, for the army has changed) of the men of the SAR.

By this time the Regiment had been on parade nearly three hours, a long time to ask of soldiers in general and longer still for men of their vintage. One veteran took faint and had to be helped to the sidelines – among the first to go to his assistance were Dave Currie's granddaughters, both medical professionals. A few minutes later, the SAR's part in the ceremony came to an end and they left the parade ground to the stirring accompaniment of "The Green Hills of Tyrol" played by the Edmonton Police Pipe Band.

Their heads were as high and their backs as straight as the boys could make them. It was their moment and they had earned it, these veterans raised during the Depression and come of age in conflict, these fighting men from an older Canada, a less sophisticated, but in many ways a better Canada. It's doubtful we'll see their like again. Not that there won't be wars in the future – there will always be wars – but they will be fought by regular soldiers and it is unlikely that this country will again send forth the best of its youth in large numbers to fight in foreign lands. Twice in this century it has happened and if Canadian politicians and diplomats have a seat at the international table today, it is not so much because of any efforts on their part but because of the sacrifices made in two wars by men like these dignified old soldiers parading on a sunny day in September. Remember them well.

There was a ripple of applause from the audience as a proud Danny McLeod took their salute at the edge of the field – and then the South Alberta Regiment marched off.

APPENDIX A

BATTLE HONOURS, AWARDS AND DECORATIONS

BATTLE HONOURS OF THE 31ST BATTALION, CEF
(THE ALBERTA REGIMENT)
1914–1918

Mount Sorrel	Somme, 1916	Flers-Courcelette
Thiepval	Ancre Heights	Arras, 1917, 1918
Vimy, 1917	Arleux	Scarpe, 1917, 1918
Hill 70	Ypres, 1917	Passchendaele
Amiens	Drocourt-Quéant	Hindenburg Line
Canal du Nord	Cambrai, 1918	Pursuit to Mons

France and Flanders, 1915–1918

BATTLE HONOURS OF THE 29TH CANADIAN ARMOURED RECONNAISSANCE REGIMENT
(THE SOUTH ALBERTA REGIMENT)
1940–1945

Falaise	Falaise Road	The Laison
St. Lambert-sur-Dives	Moerbrugge	The Scheldt
The Lower Maas	Kapelsche Veer	The Rhineland
The Hochwald	Veen	Twente Canal
Bad Zwischenahn	Woensdrecht	

North-West Europe, 1944–1945

AWARDS AND DECORATIONS OF THE
SOUTH ALBERTA REGIMENT, 1940-1945

Victoria Cross
Currie, Major David Vivian

Distinguished Service Order
Coffin, Lieutenant-Colonel Albert Frank*
Nash, Major Thomas Boyd
Wotherspoon, Lieutenant-Colonel Gordon Dorward de
    Salaberry

Military Cross
Bowick, Lieutenant Smith Freemont
Caseley, Lieutenant Leaman
McLeod, Lieutenant William John
Summers, Captain John Leslie

Distinguished Conduct Medal
Broadbent, Trooper Albert G.
Milner, Sergeant Thomas Edward

Military Medal
Devreker, Trooper Albert (Tony) (Died of Wounds)
Forbes, Trooper James F.
Freeman, Sergeant Lawrence Frederick
Freer, Sergeant Frank Elsworth
Haddow, Corporal Arthur
Halkyard, Sergeant Albert Edward
Kroesing, Sergeant James E.
Ottenbreit, Corporal Michael
Roulston, Sergeant Herbert
Woolf, Sergeant Garth Leavitt

Member of the British Empire
Silcox, Honorary Captain Albert Phillips
Doherty, SQSM Walter Joseph***

Croix de Guerre with Silver Star (France)
Irving, Captain Gordon Ernest

Croix de Guerre with Bronze Star (France)
Prenevost, Sergeant Douglas Sylvester

Bronze Cross (Netherlands)
Penney, Sergeant Wilfred George

Bronze Star (United States)
Hughes, Captain Frederick Newton

Mentioned in Dispatches**
Bergquist, Trooper Marvin A.
Bowick, Lieutenant Smith Fremont
Bundy, Squadron Sergeant-Major Edgar Foster
Irving, Captain Gordon Ernest
Nichols, Trooper Eric Price
Prenevost, Sergeant Douglas Sylvester
Quarton, TQMS John Henry***
Rose, Corporal Stanley Thomas

Commander-in-Chief's Certificate**
Gove, Sergeant James Kenneth
Mackenzie, Regimental Sergeant-Major John
Porter, Sergeant John A.
Roberts, Lieutenant James Milne (Killed in Action)
Robinson, Major Richard
Rollinson, Sergeant J.E.
Smith, Sergeant Jame Charles
Webb, Sergeant George William

---

*   Although Lieutenant-Colonel Coffin received his DSO while serving with the Argyll and Sutherland Highlanders, it was awarded for his actions while commanding the South Alberta Regiment during the battles of February-March 1945.

**   The paperwork for the award of Mentions in Dispatches and Commander-in-Chief's Certificates was not complete when the Regiment stopped keeping records in December 1945. As a result the names of some South Albertas who received these awards may not be listed.

*** Awarded for service outside the Regiment.

ROLL OF HONOUR, SOUTH ALBERTA REGIMENT, 1940–1945

The following South Albertas did not return from the war. This list also includes one man who died after the war as a direct result of his wounds. The Regiment's casualties are listed alphabetically by rank and those officers who had served as other ranks in the SAR are denoted thus *.

NUMBER	RANK	LAST NAME	FIRST NAME	MIDDLE NAME	BORN	AGE	DATE	CAUSE OF DEATH
	CAPTAIN*	PERRIN	KENNETH	ELIAS	AB	25	1945/02/27	KILLED IN ACTION
	CAPTAIN	SCRIMGER	ALEXANDER	CARRON	PQ	22	1944/10/28	KILLED IN ACTION
	LIEUT	BURNS	ROBERT	CHARLES	PQ	29	1944/08/20	KILLED IN ACTION
	LIEUT	GUYOT	JEAN	MARC	PQ	28	1944/10/26	KILLED IN ACTION
	LIEUT	JOHNSTON	GEORGE	McDONALD	ON	27	1945/04/02	KILLED IN ACTION
	LIEUT	KENNEDY	WILFRID		BC	31	1945/01/28	DIED OF WOUNDS
	LIEUT*	LITTLE	KENNETH	WAYNE	US	35	1945/01/28	KILLED IN ACTION
	LIEUT	REED	IRWIN	JAMES	ON	21	1944/09/01	DIED OF WOUNDS
	LIEUT	ROBERTS	JOHN	MILNE	AB	27	1944/09/12	KILLED IN ACTION
	LIEUT*	SMITH	RAY	CLARKE	AB	26	1944/09/10	DIED OF WOUNDS
	LIEUT*	YOUNG	WALLACE	HAY	AB	31	1944/09/10	KILLED IN ACTION
M/45527	SGT	BELL	ALVIN		MB	32	1944/08/21	KILLED IN ACTION
M/45361	SGT	CLARK	FRED	WATSON	AB	35	1945/03/01	KILLED IN ACTION
D/23278	ARM/SGT	COTE (RCEME att)	RAYMOND	RICHARD	ON	22	1945/02/05	DIED OF WOUNDS
D/76550	SGT	DONALD	THOMAS		SCOTLAND	37	1944/12/16	KILLED IN ACTION
D/77190	SGT	FORTIN	EARL	WINSON	ON	22	1944/12/18	DIED OF WOUNDS
M/44872	SGT	WAGNER	JAMES	SHOUP	US	31	1944/08/14	KILLED IN ACTION
D/76412	L/SGT	HUSSEY	GERALD	JOHN HERBERT	PQ	23	1944/09/11	KILLED IN ACTION
M/45309	L/SGT	JACOBSON	HAROLD	BRANDT	DENMARK	29	1945/02/27	KILLED IN ACTION
M/45221	L/SGT	NICKEL	MICHAEL	JOSEPH	AB	26	1944/08/11	DIED OF WOUNDS
M/10657	L/SGT	PALFENIER	THEODORE	EMERY	SK	23	1944/09/12	KILLED IN ACTION
M/44866	CPL	ELY	EMERY	ERNEST	AB	25	1944/08/21	KILLED IN ACTION
M/44963	CPL	GENDRON	EDWARD	ERNEST	SK	24	1944/08/10	KILLED IN ACTION
M/45567	CPL	McFADDEN	HARVEY	DONALD	SK	29	1942/11/06	KILLED IN CARRIER UPSET
M/44838	CPL	McRAE	JOHN	GEORGE	AB	28	1944/08/17	KILLED IN ACTION
M/45353	CPL	MOAN	FRANCIS	BERNARD	SCOTLAND	31	1944/10/25	KILLED IN ACTION
M/45296	CPL	TOUROND	GEORGE	WILLIAM	AB	25	1944/08/31	DIED OF WOUNDS
M/45620	L/CPL	GOLBY	LEO	JAMES	AB	23	1944/06/24	DIED OF INJURY
D/116325	L/CPL	GOODYER	ROBERT	HENRY	PQ	25	1944/10/28	KILLED IN ACTION
G/4546	TPR	ALLEN	ARNOLD	REILSTON	NB	22	1945/03/01	KILLED IN ACTION
A/108854	TPR	AMEY	HARVEY	HERBERT	ON	34	1945/02/27	KILLED IN ACTION
A/117327	TPR	ANDREW	WALTER	HAROLD	SK	31	1944/09/18	KILLED IN ACTION
M/44899	TPR	BARTLETT	JOHN	FREDERICK	NF	47	1945/02/27	KILLED IN ACTION
L/53789	TPR	BATEMAN	ARNOLD	EDWARD	AB	22	1944/08/19	KILLED IN ACTION
K/50705	TPR	BELSEY	FREDERICK	CHARLES	BC	25	1945/02/27	KILLED IN ACTION
M/28832	TPR	BERGQUIST	MARVIN	EDWARD	AB	28	1945/04/08	DIED
M/45023	TPR	BREWER	CHARLES	EDWARD	AB	29	1944/08/15	DIED OF WOUNDS
H/10276	TPR	CARPENTER	VICTOR	LLOYD	MB	22	1945/04/27	KILLED IN ACTION
F/52639	TPR	CARR	WILLIAM	BORDEN	NS	33	1945/04/16	KILLED IN ACTION
L/36349	TPR	CARRAGHER	JAMES	CHARLIE	SK	26	1944/08/21	KILLED IN ACTION
H/95371	TPR	COLWELL	DEXTER		MB	21	1944/08/21	KILLED IN ACTION
D/77099	TPR	CORNER	LLOYD	ATKINSON	PQ	27	1944/10/12	DIED OF WOUNDS
B/107016	TPR	CRAIG	LYLE	LEWIS	SK	21	1945/04/19	KILLED IN ACTION
D/142356	TPR	CRAIG	NORMAN	ROY	PQ	21	1944/10/15	KILLED IN ACTION
L/105448	TPR	DANIELSON	MELVIN	ALEXANDER	SK	19	1944/10/27	DIED OF WOUNDS
A/105460	TPR	DEVREKER (MM)	ANTHONY		BELGIUM	21	1945/03/30	DIED OF WOUNDS
M/45257	TPR	DUTKA	ADAM		AB	24	1944/09/12	KILLED IN ACTION
M/45667	TPR	EASTON	EDGAR	VERNON	SK	24	1944/10/23	KILLED IN ACTION
M/45301	TPR	EDWARDS	EDWIN	GRANT	AB	25	1944/08/17	KILLED IN ACTION

NUMBER	RANK	LAST NAME	FIRST NAME	MIDDLE NAME	BORN	AGE	DATE	CAUSE OF DEATH
A/105434	TPR	EVANS	LYLE	ALEXANDER	ON	23	1945/03/07	KILLED IN ACTION
M/45791	TPR	FOSTER	JAMES	MARTIN	MB	27	1944/10/26	KILLED IN ACTION
M/35657	TPR	FOSTER	ERLE	MILTON	AB	22	1944/09/09	KILLED IN ACTION
M/28839	TPR	FRANKSON	ERIC	OSCAR	SK	23	1944/09/11	KILLED IN ACTION
L/41462	TPR	GEE	ALLAN	JOHN	SK	23	1945/03/05	KILLED IN ACTION
F/31964	TPR	HAMM	GERALD	FRANCIS	NS	31	1944/09/12	KILLED IN ACTION
B/116229	TPR	HARPER	DOUGLAS	EDWARD	ON	22	1945/03/10	KILLED IN ACTION
M/45068	TPR	HINSON	WILLIAM	LESLIE	AB	22	1944/08/19	KILLED IN ACTION
F/44046	TPR	HOARE	DENNIS		NS	19	1944/10/28	KILLED IN ACTION
H/45765	TPR	HOMER	WILFRED	NEWTON	ON	23	1944/09/20	KILLED IN ACTION
M/45651	TPR	LAFOY	TIP	ORLANDO	SK	34	1944/10/28	KILLED IN ACTION
M/45749	TPR	LAPRADE	LLOYD		AB	25	1945/01/30	KILLED IN ACTION
L/84518	TPR	LAUGHTON	WILFRED		SK	25	1944/08/17	DIED OF WOUNDS
L/100368	TPR	LORENSEN	CLARENCE	WARREN	SK	28	1945/04/02	DIED OF WOUNDS
M/50588	TPR	LOW	DAVID	ALEXANDER	AB	21	1944/11/19	DIED OF WOUNDS
M/45737	TPR	LYNCH	PATRICK	JOSEPH	AB	21	1942/11/06	KILLED IN CARRIER UPSET
F/2870	TPR	MacINNIS	JOSEPH	AMBROSE	NS	26	1944/08/09	DIED OF WOUNDS
M/45247	TPR	McCAFFREY	GEORGE		ON	37	1944/09/20	KILLED IN ACTION
M/12348	TPR	McDONALD	GEORGE	ALEXANDER	ENGLAND	33	1944/08/20	KILLED IN ACTION
L/53251	TPR	McDONELL	JOHN	ALEXANDER	SK	26	1944/10/28	KILLED IN ACTION
D/26765	TPR	McINTYRE	DONALD	STEVENSON CAMPBELL	PQ	28	1944/01/02	DIED
L/36329	TPR	McKEE	FERNS	ROSS	SK	27	1944/09/19	KILLED IN ACTION
L/36757	TPR	MERRITT	KENNETH	FRANKLIN	MB	34	1944/08/10	DIED OF WOUNDS
M/45764	PTE	MILAN	STANLEY		POLAND	19	1941/07/01	DROWNED
M/45480	PTE	MOREAU	HENRY		AB	27	1940/09/18	DIED
M/44856	PTE	MULLAN	FRANK	JOSEPH	N. IRELAND	31	1941/06/20	DIED
M/45142	TPR	MUNGALL	GEORGE	WILLIAM	ENGLAND	33	1944/10/28	KILLED IN ACTION
C/121748	TPR	NEFF	HOWARD	WILSON	ON	20	1945/03/05	KILLED IN ACTION
M/45582	TPR	NOBLE	GEORGE	WILLIAM	AB	24	1945/01/30	KILLED IN ACTION
M/105696	TPR	OUELLETTE	DENIS		AB	23	1944/08/21	KILLED IN ACTION
B/111305	TPR	OWEN	ELDON	MARTIN	ON	24	1945/04/16	DIED OF WOUNDS
M/44942	TPR	PACHAL	WILLIAM	FREDERICK	SK	35	1944/08/21	KILLED IN ACTION
L/54869	TPR	QUINNEL	CLARENCE	LEONARD	SK	27	1944/08/10	KILLED IN ACTION
M/31539	TPR	RATHWELL	JOHN		AB	23	1959/07/09	DIED OF WOUNDS RECEIVED 1944/09/09
K/42899	TPR	ROBERTSON	ALEXANDER	JAMES	MB	23	1944/12/17	DIED
M/45090	TPR	ROWE	KENDAL		AB	23	1944/12/16	KILLED IN ACTION
D/137049	TPR	SCOTT	GERALD	ARCHIBALD	PQ	22	1944/08/14	KILLED IN ACTION
M/45484	PTE	SEIDLER	JAKE	VALTON	SK	21	1941/03/30	DIED
M/41761	TPR	STONE	JOHN	CHARLES	MB	31	1944/10/28	KILLED IN ACTION
M/105698	TPR	STORVIK	VERNON	ELSWORTH	AB	21	1944/09/10	DIED OF WOUNDS
M/45169	TPR	WALKER	HARRY	GEORGE	US	31	1943/08/24	KILLED ON DUTY
C/38287	TPR	WALTON	HARVEY	WILFRED	QB	20	1944/08/21	KILLED IN ACTION
M/44863	TPR	WICKSTROM	KARL	JOHN CLIFFORD	SWEDEN	34	1945/04/08	KILLED IN ACTION
H/8567	TPR	WOODS	LLOYD	ALFRED	MB	20	1944/09/09	DIED OF WOUNDS
F/51693	TPR	ZWICKER	WALTER	St CLAIR			1944/04/06	DIED OF INJURIES

THE SOUTH ALBERTA REGIMENT:
A WORKING MANUAL

The Organization of the South Alberta Regiment in Battle
In action the SAR was divided into a number of components whose organization and vehicles are illustrated on the front endpaper of this book.

RHQ (Regimental Headquarters), under the direct command of Lieutenant-Colonel Wotherspoon, consisted of the necessary vehicles and personnel for the execution of command. RHQ normally comprised the RHQ Troop of four Sherman tanks, all or part of the Recce Troop with eleven Stuart tanks, all or part of Anti-Aircraft Troop with seven Crusader AA tanks and all or part of Intercommunication Troop with nine Humber scout cars. The RAP (Regimental Aid Post or unit medical section) usually accompanied RHQ.

The "sharp end" of the SAR was formed by the three fighting squadrons (A, B and C) each commanded by a major. At full strength (and they were rarely at full strength) each squadron consisted of a Squadron HQ Troop of three Sherman tanks and four fighting troops, each commanded by a lieutenant troop leader, with four Sherman tanks. Also attached to each squadron were echelon personnel who manned the ARV (Armoured Recovery Vehicle – the tanker's "tow truck") and undertook first-line maintenance.

The number and types of AFVs (Armoured Fighting Vehicles) in the Regiment was sixty-one Shermans, eleven Stuart light tanks, and seven (including one unauthorized) Crusader AA tanks. The nine Humber scout cars of the Intercommunication Troop were not fighting vehicles as such and were normally parcelled out to the squadron commanders and utilized for liaison work. The main fighting power of the Regiment lay in the forty-eight Shermans of the twelve fighting troops.

Not be confused with RHQ was Headquarters Squadron which consisted of the necessary vehicles and personnel for the administration of the whole Regiment. When all or part of the Recce, AA and Intercommunication Troops were not attached to RHQ, they came under control of HQ Squadron. Also attached to HQ Squadron was the commander of 42 LAD (Light Aid Detachment) and the signals officer from the RCCS (Royal Canadian Corps of Signals) detachment.

Armoured Fighting Vehicles
The major fighting vehicles of the SAR are illustrated in the accompanying 1/72 scale line drawings.

In 1942, following its conversion to armour the South Alberta Regiment was equipped first with Ram I tanks and later with Ram II tanks. The Ram was based on the chassis and running gear of the American M3 Medium tank (the Grant tank) with a Canadian-designed hull and turret. The Ram I model was armed with a 2-pdr. gun (40 mm) and the Ram II with a 6-pdr. gun (57 mm); neither weapon was capable of firing HE (High Explosive) projectiles.

Following its conversion to armoured reconnaissance in early 1943 the South Alberta Regiment was organized in mixed tank and carrier troops, either combined together in a single troop or, late in 1943, organized in separate carrier troops and tank troops within the same squadron. The main armoured fighting vehicle in 1943 was the Ram II tank while the Recce and Intercommunication Troops were equipped with Canadian-built Ford Lynx I or II scout cars.

In early 1944 the SAR was converted to the war establishment of an armoured regiment as described above. The major tank at this time was the Sherman V (American Medium Tank M4A4) armed with a 75 mm gun capable of firing HE projectiles. The Recce Troop was re-equipped with Stuart V light tanks armed with a 37 mm gun, the Intercommunication Troop was re-equipped with Humber I scout cars, and the newly-formed AA Troop was issued Crusader III AA tanks armed with twin 20 mm Oerlikon guns in a powered turret. With these vehicles the Regiment entered battle in August 1944.

Beginning in September 1944 the Regiment began to receive Sherman VC Firefly tanks (the Sherman V armed with a 17-pdr. or 76.2 mm gun) and, later, Sherman IC Hybrid Fireflies. By the spring of 1945 there were enough of these AFVs to provide each troop with two 17-pdr. gun tanks. In October 1944 the Recce Troop was completely re-equipped with the improved Stuart VI light tank.

In March 1945 the Regiment received three Ram ammunition carriers (called Wallabies), which were a turretless Ram tank. A similar vehicle dubbed the Kangaroo was used as an APC (Armoured Personnel Carrier) by the Canadian Army.

In April 1945 the Regiment became the only armoured unit in 4th Canadian Armoured Division to receive a Valentine bridge-laying tank, which proved very useful in the last weeks of the war.

Range and Penetration: The Statistics and the Reality
The problems that Allied armour crews faced in northwest Europe in 1944-1945 are illustrated in the table on page 356, "Penetration Chart: Tank Gun Comparisons." The column on the left lists five major German AFVs and three Canadian AFVs with their maximum armour thickness in brackets. The columns on the right show the penetration capability of their armament.

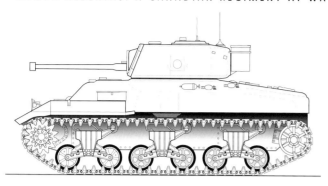

Cruiser, Ram II

Manufacturer: Montreal Locomotive Works
Weight: 32.5 tons fully loaded
Height: 8 feet, 9 inches
Width: 9 feet, 1 inch
Length: 19 feet
Crew: Five
Armament: Main: 6-pdr. (57 mm) gun
　　　　　　 Auxiliary: Two .30 calibre Browning machine guns
Wireless: No. 19 Wireless Set
Armour thickness: Max.: 3.0 inches
　　　　　　　　　 Min.: 0.5 inch (belly plate)
Engine: Continental 9-cylinder radial, 400 hp at 2400 rpm
Top speed on paved road: 25 mph
Fuel capacity: 150 US gallons
Fuel consumption: 1 mile per gallon
Fording depth: 36 inches
Used in the SAR: 1942-1944

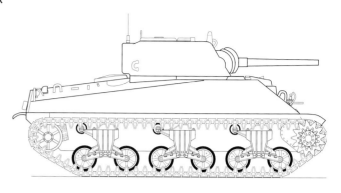

Sherman V

American Nomenclature: Medium Tank M4A4
Manufacturer: Detroit Tank Arsenal (Chrysler)
Weight: 35 tons, combat loaded
Height: 8 feet, 11.5 inches
Width: 8 feet, 7 inches
Length: 19 feet, 10.5 inches
Crew: Five
Armament: Main: 75 mm gun
　　　　　　 Auxiliary: Two .30 calibre Browning machine guns
Wireless: No. 19 Wireless Set
Armour Thickness: Max.: 3 inches
　　　　　　　　　 Min.: 1 inch (belly plate)
Engine: Chrysler A-57 Multi-bank, 450 hp at 2400 rpm
Top speed on paved road: 25 mph
Fuel capacity: 130 US gallons
Fuel consumption: 1 mile per gallon
Fording depth: 40 inches
Used in the SAR: January 1944-May 1945

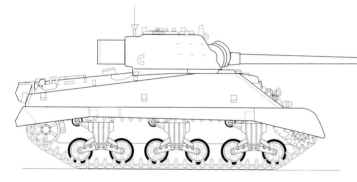

Sherman Vc Firefly

American Nomenclature: No designation
Manufacturer: Detroit Tank Arsenal (Chrysler)
Weight: 36 tons, combat loaded
Height: 8 feet, 11.5 inches
Width: 8 feet, 7 inches
Length: 19 feet, 10.5 inches
Crew: Four
Armament: Main: 17 pdr (76.2 mm) gun
　　　　　　 Auxiliary: One .30 calibre Browning machine gun
Wireless: No. 19 Wireless Set
Armour thickness: Max.: 3 inches
　　　　　　　　　 Min.: 1 inch (belly plate)
Engine: Chrysler A-57 Multi-bank gasoline, 450 hp at 2400 rpm
Top speed on paved road: 25 mph
Fuel capacity: 130 US gallons
Fuel consumption: 1 mile per gallon
Fording depth: 40 inches
Used in the SAR: September 1944-May 1945

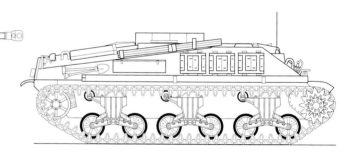

Sherman ARV I

Manufacturer: Detroit Tank Arsenal (Chrysler)
Weight: 30 tons, loaded
Height: 6 feet, 10 inches
Width: 8 feet, 7 inches
Length: 19 feet, 10.5 inches
Crew: Two
Armament: .30 calibre Browning machine gun
Wireless: No. 19 Wireless Set
Armour Thickness: Max.: 3 inches
　　　　　　　　　 Min.: 1 inch (belly plate)
Engine: Chrysler A-57 Multi-bank, 450 hp at 2400 rpm
Top speed on paved road: 29 mph
Fuel capacity: 130 US gallons
Fording depth: 40 inches
Used in the SAR: 1944-1945

1/72 scale illustrations by George Bradford

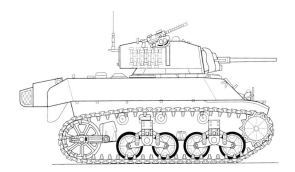

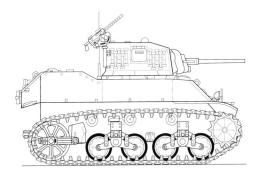

Stuart V

American Nomenclature: Light Tank M3A3

Manufacturer: American Car and Foundry (US)

Weight: 15.5 tons combat loaded

Height: 8 feet, 6 inches

Width: 8 feet, 5 inches

Length: 16 feet, 6 inches

Crew: Four

Armament: Main: One 37 mm gun

            Main: Two .30 calibre Browning machine guns

Wireless: No. 19 Wireless Set

Armour Thickness: Max.: 2 inches

                  Min.: 0.5 inch (belly plate)

Engine: Continental, gas, 7-cylinder radial producing 262 hp at 2400 rpm.

Top speed on paved road: 36 mph

Fuel capacity: 110 US gallons

Fuel consumption: 2 miles per gallon

Fording depth: 36 inches

Used in the SAR: January-October 1944

Stuart VI

American Nomenclature: Light Tank M5A1

Manufacturer: Cadillac and others

Weight: 16.75 tons

Height: 8 feet, 5 inches

Width: 7 feet, 6 inches

Length: 15 feet, 10 inches

Crew: Four

Armament: Main: One 37 mm gun

            Auxiliary: Two .30 calibre Browning machine guns

Wireless: No. 19 Wireless Set

Armour Thickness: Max.: 2 inches

                  Min.: 0.5 inch (belly plate)

Engine: Twin Cadillac V-8, Series 42

Top speed on paved road: 36 mph

Fuel capacity: 89 US gallons

Fuel consumption: 2 miles per gallon

Fording depth: 36 inches

Used in the SAR: October 1944-May 1945

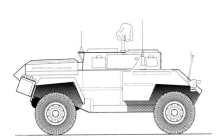

Crusader III, AA Mk. II

Manufacturer: Nuffields and others

Weight: 22 tons

Height: 7 feet, 4 inches

Width: 8 feet, 8 inches

Length: 19 feet, 8 inches

Crew: Four

Armament: Twin 20 mm Oerlikon guns in power turret

Wireless: No. 19 Wireless Set

Armour Thickness: Max.: 51 mm

                  Min.: 7 mm

Engine: Nuffield Liberty V-12

Top speed on paved road: 27 mph

Range: 100 miles

Fording depth: 39 inches

Used in the SAR: June 1944-May 1945

Car, Scout, Humber Mark I

Manufacturer: Humber Ltd. (UK)

Weight: 3.39 tons

Height: 6 feet, 4 inches

Width: 6 feet, 1 inch

Length: 12 feet, 7 inches

Crew: Two or Three

Armament: 1 Bren .303 light machine gun

Armament: 1 Thompson .45 submachine gun

Wireless: No. 19 Wireless Set

Armour Thickness: Max.: 14 mm

                  Min.: 4 mm

Engine: Rootes 6-cylinder in line, 79 hp at 3300 rpm

Top speed on paved road: 60 mph

Fuel capacity: 24 US gallons

Fuel consumption: 10 miles per gallon

Fording depth: 36 inches

Used in the SAR: January 1944-May 1945

1/72 scale illustrations by George Bradford

Type (Max. armour)	Calibre	Projectile	Projectile Weight (lb)	Muzzle Velocity (fps)	Penetration of Homogeneous Armour Plate at 30° Angle (in millimetres) at:							
					100 yds	250 yds	500 yds	914 yds	1000 yds	1500 yds	2000 yds	2500 yds
Panzer IV (80 mm)	75mm KwK 40	APCBC	15.0	2460	99	–	–	–	88.5	–	70	61.5
Panther (110 mm)	75mm KwK 42	APCBC	14.99	3060	–	–	131	–	127	104	90	79
Jagdpanther (80 mm)	88mm KwK 43	APCBC	22.36	3280	–	–	179	–	164	–	136	123
Tiger I (100 mm)	88mm KwK 36	APCBC	20.75	2675	120	–	112	–	102	–	88	–
Tiger II (180 mm)	88mm KwK 43	APCBC	22.49	3280	–	–	150	–	140	–	121	–
	AP40		16.1	3379	–	–	207	–	164	–	113	–
Ram II (76 mm)	6 pdr.	AP	6.25	2693	–	–	–	42	42	–	–	–
		APCBC	7.0	2775	93	–	87	–	80	–	67	–
		APCR	3.97	3528	–	–	–	–	–	–	–	–
		APDS	3.25	4050	143	–	131	–	117	–	90	–
Sherman V M4A4 (76 mm)	75mm M3	APCBC	14.9	2030	74	–	68	–	60	–	47	–
		APDS	8.4	2850	143	–	131	–	117	–	90	–
Sherman Firefly (76 mm)	17 pdr. Mk. IV	AP	17.0	2900	–	–	–	109	–	–	–	–
		APCBC	17.0	1900	149	–	140	–	130	–	111	–
		APDS	7.6	3950	221	–	208	–	192	–	161	–

Key to Ammunition Types

AP — Armour Piercing

APCR — Armour Piercing Composite, Rigid

APDS — Armour Piercing Discarding Sabot

APCBC — Armour Piercing Capped, Ballistic Capped

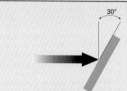

The arrow indicates the path of a projectile impacting a plate of armour that is 30° from the vertical.

Calibre: The diameter of the inside of the gun's bore, defined as the diameter of a cylinder that fits inside the lands of the rifling. It is also used as a measurement of the gun's length. Therefore, an 88mm 71-calibre gun is 71 x 88 = 6248 mm long. The longer the gun, the more powerful it is likely to be. Calibre length is generally indicated by the notation "L/..." and was used by the Germans in their gun nomenclature. The 88mm KwK L/71 would therefore be 71 calibres in length, or, as in the equation above, 6.25 metres long.

Sources: First Canadian Army Intelligence Summaries: 20 (16 Jul 44), 108 (16 Oct 44, 214 (30 Jan 45).

Penetration Chart: Tank Gun Comparisons. This chart compares the penetration of homogeneous armour plate in millimetres at an angle of 30 degrees. Note the superiority of the German KwK 42 75 mm gun mounted on the Panther and the 88 mm gun mounted on the *Jagdpanther* and Tiger tanks. The equivalent Allied weapon was the 17 pdr. (76.2 mm) gun mounted on the Sherman Firefly but the Firefly was no better armoured than other Shermans. Most so-called AP shot used in 1944-1945 was actually APCBC (Armour Piercing, Capped, Ballistic Capped). Both the Allies and the Germans had an APDS (Armour Piercing, Discarding Sabot) round.

Note that the five main German tank guns were capable of penetrating the 3-inch (76 mm) armour of the Sherman V at 1000 yards range while, at the same range, the Sherman 75 mm could just penetrate the 80 mm of armour on the German Mk IV or *Jagdpanther* but had little chance of penetrating the heavier armour on the Panther and Tiger tanks without using APDS ammunition. The Sherman Firefly, with its 17-pdr. (76.2 mm) gun was capable of penetrating any German tank except the Tiger II at 1000 yards range and, using APDS shot, the most heavily-armoured German tank at 2000 yards. The problem was that the Firefly was no better armoured than the normal Sherman and its long gun barrel betrayed its identity. Talk of long ranges is really meaningless, however, because postwar research revealed that the normal range at which German tanks and anti-tank guns opened fire in 1944-1945 was 800 yards, a distance that ensured penetration of every tank in the Allied inventory. The German tactic was to hold their fire as long as possible and their first targets were the easily-identified Fireflies.

The range and penetration of tank guns were only part of the problem. The SAR encountered German armour in Normandy but it became very scarce in the autumn of 1944 and was only met again in large numbers in the Hochwald in February 1945 and during the final push across the Rhine in April and May 1945. This does not mean that things were better if German armour was not present; German anti-tank guns had the same hitting power as their tank guns and there were also those two overlooked but very effective weapons: the *Panzerfaust* and the humble mine. Postwar research revealed that, from January 1945 to the end of the war, these two weapons accounted for almost 25% of all Canadian tank casualties.

What is a Tank?

A tank is a mobile gun platform and its role is to establish firepower on the battlefield in the area where it can be used most effectively to win the battle. Armoured firepower must be concentrated, yet flexible enough to be switched from one part of the battlefield to another and armoured regiments have to possess the ability to adjust rapidly to meet changes in the tactical situation.

Although they are imposing in appearance, tanks have certain limitations which must be understood if they are to be used properly. They possess restricted visibility and are vulnerable to enemy infantry in wooded or built-up areas. They present attractive targets, indeed primary targets, for the enemy, and they draw fire. They are susceptible to mechanical failure and can easily bog or break down when traversing unsuitable terrain, which includes soft or wet ground. Finally, they carry only a limited amount of fuel and ammunition and in action must resupply at frequent intervals.

Tactical Role Number One: Armoured Reconnaissance

The SAR was trained as an armoured reconnaissance regiment with the role of probing and pressing the enemy to gain information for the armoured division commander. There were four basic rules of reconnaissance work: watch and report enemy movements; examine and report on all ground; draw the enemy's fire, if ordered; and obtain identifications by capturing prisoners or examining enemy dead.

The armoured recce regiment had two main tasks – recce and protection – plus the subsidiary role of observation. Recce involved absolute freedom of movement while protection meant conforming to friendly or enemy movements, and the two were not compatible. As timely warning of the enemy was essential, protection also meant offering active opposition to the enemy to prevent his interfering with friendly forces and was usually undertaken during a withdrawal. Observation was a form of static recce done during daylight. The rule was: recce or observation or protection but not at the same time.

The SAR's own Recce Troop gave Colonel Wotherspoon close, intimate and detailed reconnaissance on his own front and flanks. The amount of use made of the troop in its reconnaissance role varied with the type of operation. It was not usually used in set-piece attacks but it came into its own in fluid situations. Recce patrols (always two tanks) were spread across the front of the Regiment on as many axes as possible; this was particularly important in pursuit where the main axis on a line of advance would in all probability be blocked by demolitions or obstacles. Colonel Wotherspoon, by the extensive use of his Recce Troop, had every opportunity of discovering alternative ways around such obstacles.

Tactical Role Number Two: Infantry Support

Although it was a specialized armoured reconnaissance regiment, the SAR fought most of its battles providing tank support for the three infantry battalions of 10 Canadian Infantry Brigade. Its three squadrons were usually allotted to the infantry battalions of the brigade as shown in the organizational diagram on the back endpaper. The SAR performed well in this role for a number of reasons including the fact that, having been an infantry regiment, it was familiar with the infantryman's strengths and weaknesses. It also helped that many SAR squadron commanders had previously commanded infantry companies.

The South Albertas' usual form of assistance was direct fire support against targets that were holding up the infantry. The theory was that the tanks would neutralize enemy machine guns while the artillery and infantry would neutralize the anti-tank guns and *panzerfausts* (hand-held, hollow-charge, throwaway anti-tank missile launchers and very nasty) that were dangerous to the tanks. It sometimes didn't work out that way and the South Albertas were often faced with the problem of carrying out their role of infantry support while defending themselves against anti-tank weapons.

The infantry support role required the very closest co-operation and liaison between armour and infantry – and this had to be based on an understanding of each arm's potentials and restrictions. SAR commanders found that their main problem was to get the infantry to realize the limitations of the tank, as infantry officers often had unrealistic beliefs about its capabilities. Nonetheless, it was the responsibility of the SAR commanders (at the regimental, squadron or troop level) to ensure that his flat-footed friends got all the support they needed, and if they were unable to carry out an infantry officer's wish, they would usually suggest an alternate method that they could carry out and which would accomplish the same object. From the outset, in the spring of 1944, the same SAR squadron always worked, whenever possible, with the same infantry battalion in the brigade (A Squadron with the Lincoln and Welland Regiment, B with the Algonquin Regiment and C with the Argylls) and this paid enormous dividends as the squadron/battalion attachments soon evolved into highly effective tank/infantry teams. The problem was that the high casualties suffered by the infantry resulted in a constant turnover of officers in the infantry battalions and the SAR had to constantly "break in" new partners.

There were no hard and fast rules on how to conduct infantry support. The ground over which the battle was to be fought (the state of the going and the cover available), the extent of enemy opposition and the tactical situation determined the method to be used and the degree of detailed co-operation necessary between the two arms. Command varied – sometimes the armoured corps officer led the tank/infantry team and sometimes the infantry officer, but since the infantry commander was the major partner, the armoured commander would always, if possible, adjust his plan to the infantry plan of action. The amount of time spent on joint planning and reconnaissance varied according to the size of the operation, but since time was usually short, it was another dividend of the permanent squadron/battalion groupings that the respective commanders knew each other and this simplified liaison. This was also an important consideration because, until the spring of 1945, the Regiment's tanks were not equipped with outside telephones by which the infantry could communicate with the crews. Communication therefore had to go through the cumbersome medium of the wireless net or, as most often happened, by personal contact and shouts.

An important consideration was how the infantry would

enter battle – on their feet, in APCs (Armoured Personnel Carriers), in TCVs (Troop Carrying Vehicles or large trucks) or on the tanks. The transport of infantry on the tanks represented the highest degree of integration as the infantry and the tanks they were supporting moved as a single party. The SAR could carry an entire infantry battalion on its decks (and did so at the Hochwald in February 1944) and the respective commanders could move in the same vehicles with their communications. The disadvantages, however, were considerable, in that in shell-swept areas considerable casualties to the infantry might occur and the tank was of course not free to fight when encumbered in this manner. It was a rule that the infantry were not carried on the tanks of the leading troop or troops of the Regiment, which were left free to manoeuvre and fight as the situation required.

Having captured an objective, the infantry normally dug in and organized its defence. Since they were vulnerable to shell-fire and counterattack until their supporting weapons come up, it was sometimes necessary to keep tanks in the forward positions rather than withdraw them to the rear to resupply. The SAR, in contrast to most armoured regiments, would stay with their infantry in the forward positions if they were needed and would resupply in these forward positions.

Command and Control
The command and control of the South Alberta Regiment was based on wireless (radio to the modern reader). The commander issued his plans and orders at the beginning of an operation but thereafter only exercised general control over his units; the actual tactical handling of his squadrons or troops was left to the commander on the spot, variations to the original plan being arranged over the wireless. Wireless was the nervous system of an armoured regiment and good communications were of paramount importance.

Efficient wireless communications demanded the highest standards of procedure, operation and maintenance and these could only be obtained by constant practice. The Regiment and its sub-units were connected on a wireless "net" (shown on the back endpaper of the book). The advantages of this system are apparent; everybody was in the picture all the time, as they could hear what was happening along the whole front of the Regiment. Commanders could speak to their subordinates directly, and subordinates could consult their superiors when in doubt. A Regimental net was not always necessary so squadron nets were often used instead.

Wireless had limitations. It disclosed the presence of troops to the enemy who might be listening so that codes had to be used and the use of map reference codes and place name codes was standard.

The No. 19 Wireless Set in each tank had three parts and functions:

The A set (sender/receiver – long range)
Provided communication between the regimental commander, recce troop, echelon commanders, HQ sqn, sqn leaders and troop leaders. Also provided rear link to next higher formation. The 19 A set had a range of ten miles.

The B set (sender/receiver – short range)
Provided communications between the tanks of a troop and between regimental and squadron headquarters. This communication was possible on the A Set as well. and, in fact, the SAR seemed to have preferred the A to the B Set as the latter set was found to be very problematic. The official range of the B Set was one mile but it was actually be much less in wooded or built-up areas.

The Intercommunications ("intercom") system gave communication between the members of each tank crew, via the wireless harness and the wireless set.

The "brain" of the Regiment was RHQ. Normally, the following officers were stationed at RHQ in action: the commanding officer, battle adjutant, intelligence officer, signals officer and the RHQ Troop leader. Colonel Wotherspoon sometimes commanded the Regiment from his scout car and if this was the case he was in constant contact with RHQ through the battle adjutant and intelligence officer in the ACV (Armoured Command Vehicle, sometimes Alternate Command Vehicle) who acted as his links and also his "rear link" to 10 Brigade, passing information or orders to and from the brigade to the commanding officer or second-in-command. A parallel set-up existed at the squadron level where the commanding major commanded either from a tank or his scout car, with his "rear link," or battle captain, providing communication back to RHQ.

Orders prior to an operation were usually transmitted at a meeting, briefing or conference called an "Orders Group" or "O Group." Before a major operation, it might be necessary for a regimental commander to give out his plan personally to all troop leaders and tank commanders but he would not go into details as this was the province of the squadron commanders. Following a Regimental O Group or other briefing by the commander, squadron commanders would then hold their own O Groups based on the same principles and, subsequently, troop commanders would, if there was time, give their orders to their crews. Only too often there wasn't time and the South Alberta troop leader's O Group would consist of the shout "follow me" as he got into his tank.

Armoured Tactics: The Fundamentals
The basis of all SAR tank tactics was *fire and movement*. Reduced to its ultimate simplicity, this meant that moving tanks were always covered by stationary tanks. While fire and movement formed the basis of tactics for most arms during the war, it was particularly applicable to armoured warfare, where the gun in a stationary tank was said to have an advantage of five to one over the gun on a moving tank.

To use fire and movement properly, *the armoured commander had to be able to use ground properly* as ground was of the greatest importance in achieving surprise and obtaining cover. Ground, and the cover to be gained from it, varies from the desert to the jungle. Cover, in itself, has two meanings: cover from view and cover from fire. By using the former one hopes to attain surprise; by the latter one hopes to attain protection.

The Tank Troop and its Tactics

Quite truthfully, it can be said that the history of the South Alberta Regiment at war in 1944-1945 was the history of a collection of individual tank troops. The troop of four tanks was the largest sub-unit that could conveniently be controlled by one officer, it was the most useful size for the task of infantry support, and since it was also the smallest self-supporting fire unit, troops were rarely split and allotted two different tasks.

It was essential that the whole troop work as a "team" and that the three subordinate tanks be able to operate in action with minimum orders. Much therefore depended on the initiative of the individual crew commanders and their acting in accordance with the intention of the troop leader without waiting for specific detailed orders. Battle drills, well practised, enabled an unexpected situation to be met by almost instinctive action on the part of crew commanders, with each tank operating as part of a team which understood the methods employed by its other members.

When a squadron or a troop was working alone or in conjunction with troops of other arms, the sub-unit commander had much greater freedom of initiative and was likely to be operating over a wider area. In battle the disposition of his troop was the responsibility of the SAR troop leader. The formation chosen depended on the nature of the country and the dispositions of the enemy and, unless specially ordered to adopt a specific formation, it was the troop leader's job to dispose his tanks in the most effective manner. As the troop was the basis of all armoured regiment tactics, the principles of its employment apply equally to the squadron or regiment and, as noted above, armoured tactics were based on fire and movement combined with an appreciation of the ground.

In using ground, there were two normal positions for a tank: "hull down" and "turret down." Hull down positions exposed the turret of a tank and only the hull was protected by the ground. It was the normal direct fire position. Turret down positions were those in which the whole of the tank was protected by the ground and only the crew commander's head or periscope appeared over the skyline. It was the preliminary fire position and enabled the commander to observe and from it he could creep forward into a hull-down position. It was also possible, depending on the ground, to use semi-indirect methods of fire from a turret-down position.

Troop formations were very simple. The four basic formations were "line ahead," where the four tanks moved in a single file one behind each other; "line," where the four tanks stationed themselves abreast of each other; "one up," where one tank moved in advance while the remaining three moved in line; and "two up," where two tanks moved in line followed at some distance by the remaining two tanks in line.

The principle of fire and movement in the troop of four tanks was as follows. Over most types of country, the troop was able to move in square or box formation with two tanks "up." The troop normally moved from one firing position to the next; the two rear tanks covering the leading ones forward until they were established on the next fire position, when the rear tanks themselves moved up under their cover to join them. If possible, a moving tank was always supported by a stationary one.

A troop normally moved in "line ahead" formation when running parallel to and covered by a crest or sky line, and when there was a clear view on the opposite flank. When forced to cross a crest line a quick dismounted reconnaissance was made if possible but, if time or circumstances did not permit this, the crest was crossed in "line" so that all guns could be brought to bear without delay against any enemy who opened fire.

Positioning supporting tanks so that they could give immediate and effective cover was the constant preoccupation of the commander. If there was danger of an unexpected attack on either flank, the troop formations of "two" and "three up" were adopted as these formations permitted the fire of half or three-quarters of the troop to bear and permitted rapid manoeuvre in any direction. When the troop moved in line ahead, the leading tank was responsible for the front, the second for right flank protection, the third tank for left flank and fourth tank for protection to the rear.

The position of the troop leader varied in accordance with the circumstances. For example, in enclosed country, it was obviously undesirable for him to lead and a "point" tank was usually sent ahead. In the SAR, it seems to have been the custom for the troop leader to go first because usually he had not been given enough time to brief his troop and it was easier to say "follow me" and lead the way. Unfortunately the result was a very high casualty rate for troop leaders.

Special mention must be made of smoke. The object of smoke was to impede the enemy's firepower and observation and every tank possessed the means of firing smoke projectiles at close range (either from their smoke projectors or by using smoke grenades). The amount of smoke that could be produced by tanks was not great but it was sufficient to prove a valuable asset if it should be necessary to turn and make a temporary "getaway" before renewing the fight. As one South Alberta troop leader put it: "If I got into trouble my procedure was to poof off smoke, pull all triggers and screw off in the ensuing confusion."

SHELLDRAKE, HOLDFAST and SWALLOW

These terms were the wireless code names for, respectively, the artillery, the engineers and tactical air support.

The amount of artillery available to the Regiment varied considerably between static and mobile operations. In the former, the control of fire was normally centralized and the amount available was, therefore, considerable. At the Falaise Gap and the Kapelsche Veer the Regiment was eventually able to call on the support of hundreds of artillery pieces. In the pursuit, armoured regiments often moved beyond their artillery, something the Germans were careful to plan their delaying positions around, and, at Moerbrugge for example, the Regiment had only minimal artillery support.

Artillery fire was normally called down by FOOs (Forward Observation Officers) from the RCA who accompanied the SAR into battle. They were equipped with a more powerful wireless set, the No. 22, than the armour and infantry and generally the gunners' communications net was excellent and was often used by commanders to get messages back and forward. FOOs with armoured units worked from Ram II OP (Observation Post) tanks which, with their armament removed, were able to accommodate the FOO and a small staff. FOOs with the accompanying infantry worked on the ground. The FOOs were brave men and, because they were not often rotated out of the job, suffered a high casualty rate. They also became very experienced combat leaders, by watching others at work, and south of Bergen in October 1944 an artillery FOO took over an Algonquin/South Alberta detachment after the armour and infantry officers became casualties.

Artillery OPs manned by FOOs were invariably deployed as far forward with the leading element as possible. Early in the battle it was probable that the guns fired from their pre-battle positions, in which case there were a number of previously registered targets in the area of operations. The FOOs were able to call for the fire of all the divisional resources plus such army medium and heavy artillery that was capable of firing on the front and flanks of the Regiment. Under the system used by Commonwealth artillery units, a FOO could, within a matter of a few minutes, bring in the fire of the twenty-four guns of a field regiment (Mike Target), the guns of all the artillery in 4th Armoured Division (Uncle Target) or the guns of every artillery unit in range (Victor Target).

The South Alberta Regiment was also skilled in calling down artillery and Colonel Wotherspoon had such a high opinion of his troop and crew commanders' ability in this respect that he felt that the Regiment "didn't need the artillery officers with us, as long as we had one at my HQ that could conduct artillery," but on the other hand, "he always liked to have them because you'd get the support faster." One of the reasons the support came in faster through a FOO was that the artillery wireless net, a marvellous piece of technical ingenuity, was far superior to the armoured or infantry wireless nets. On many occasions, notably at the Kapelsche Veer in January 1945, the other arms used it to conduct the battle.

One element of the Royal Canadian Artillery that is often overlooked but deserves special mention was its anti-tank units. In 4th Armoured Division this was 5th Canadian Anti-Tank Regiment, which was equipped with powerful 17-pdr. anti-tank guns, either in the towed version or mounted on the M-10 Motor Gun Carriage, an SPG (self-propelled gun) based on the Sherman chassis and possessing a turret. The towed weapons were allotted, usually on the basis of one troop of four guns to each battalion, to the infantry while the self-propelled weapons worked with the armoured units. The SAR usually had one troop and sometimes two of M-10s working with them and they provided a powerful increment to the Regiment's firepower particularly in the time before the South Albertas had the Firefly 17-pdr. tank.

HOLDFAST, engineer support, was provided by the sappers of 8 or 9 Field Squadrons, RCE (Royal Canadian Engineers). These practical and too-often-unsung soldiers did any job going – among the tasks they performed for the South Albertas were building bridges, rafting, clearing mines and demolitions, destroying enemy fortifications, constructing quick field fortifications, improving and repairing roads and building new roads. The sappers' contribution to battle is often ignored and nowhere was this more true than at Moerbrugge in September 1944 and the Kapelsche Veer in January 1945 – in the final analysis, if the sappers had not done a magnificent job in these actions, these battles could not have been fought, let alone won.

And then there was SWALLOW, tactical air support provided by the Royal Air Force and Royal Canadian Air Force. In Normandy, the system of tactical air control was slow, clumsy and inefficient and the results were extremely variable – when it worked well, it worked very well, but often it did not work. It could also be very dangerous as fighter-bomber pilots tend to be an aggressive lot at best, and on several occasions during the war the SAR were attacked by their own tactical aircraft despite the fact that they showed friendly troop recognition panels and fired off the yellow smoke marking friendly troops. That does not include mistakes made by the heavy bombers of the RCAF who attacked the echelons on 14 August, killing one trooper and wounding many others. When fighting a tough battle the last thing an SAR crew commander needed was a trigger-happy fighter pilot, with a hazy knowledge of AFV recognition, hovering over his head in a Typhoon armed with eight 5-inch rockets and four 20 mm cannon. The Allied air forces never seemed to grasp the simple fact that an aircraft is basically a piloted artillery shell and needs to be subject to the same rigid control as friendly artillery lest it hit the wrong target.

Things improved as the campaign went on. By the early autumn of 1944, the South Alberta Regiment was able from time to time to call on the assistance of the air force (without heading for cover) to provide support by air-to-ground attack with bomb, rocket or bullet. Direct air support was arranged through the Air Support Signals Unit TENTACLE, which was normally allotted to 10 Brigade HQ, or occasionally to RHQ. This TENTACLE was equipped with powerful wireless for direct communication with the higher tactical air HQ which controlled the air effort, and with aircraft in flight. The TENTACLE could brief these aircraft, which might already be overhead in a "cab rank," waiting to be called in to attack. In this case, support could be arranged without delay and it could be very effective.

Maintenance, Repair and Replacement

The primary responsibility for maintenance and minor repairs rested on the tank crews themselves. Maintenance was carried out daily according to the parade maintenance system, which laid down specified tasks that had to be completed to ensure that the tank's engines, running gear, auxiliary power systems, armament and wireless were kept in good operating condition. Each crew member had certain jobs that had to be done at the first parade of the day, during halts on a march, at the last parade and during lulls in firing. Under normal circumstances, parade maintenance required forty-five minutes in the morning and two hours in the evening. If the tactical situation permitted, one day was set aside each week for advance maintenance to do lengthier tasks that could not easily be accomplished during the daily sessions.

Typical daily duties for the crew of a Sherman V under the "parade maintenance" system were as follows:

Crew commander: Check internal and external stowage, turret intercom, fire extinguishers, order other tests as required and complete all relevant paperwork.

Driver: Check fluid levels with engines running and off, check gauges, check lights, check periscope, engine and transmission compartments, clutch, air cleaners, throttle controls, fuel filter, inspect suspension at regular intervals, lubricate anything requiring it.

Co-Driver: Assist driver as required, check and oil bow .30 calibre Browning, test intercom, check periscope, clean compartment thoroughly.

Gunner: Clean and test main gun and co-axial .30 calibre, test turret traverse by hand and power, check periscope and telescopic sight, align sights as required, assist in checking suspension, oil weapons, check recoil and stabilizer systems, fill or bleed as required.

Loader-Operator: Check all electrical systems, carry out wireless netting drills, check periscope, assist driver with checking oil levels in engine, maintain Homelite, replenish drinking water, check all hatches, ports, etc., in turret and oil if necessary, check interior lights, check turret chamber and floor for any oil leaks from equipment.

More advanced maintenance and repair was carried out by the fitters. Each squadron had one fitter's halftrack and an ARV which worked under the Regimental Technical Officer. The tank crews did the small jobs, the squadron fitters did the bigger or more complicated jobs and anything they couldn't handle went to 42 LAD (Light Aid Detachment) the specialized mechanical sub-unit attached to the Regiment and, eventually, to the divisional RCOC (Royal Canadian Ordnance Corps) workshops. If a tank went to the workshops, however, it rarely came back to the Regiment as, after being fixed or refurbished, it was sent to the delivery squadron for issue on a "first come, first served basis" to any of the four armoured regiments in the 4th Canadian Armoured Division.

Vehicle casualties were reported daily and crews usually remained with a broken down vehicle and were responsible for defensive action to guard it. Replacement tanks and new models were held in D Squadron of the Elgin Regiment, the delivery unit for 4th Division and requested as casualties occurred. Similarly, first line personnel reinforcements were held in D Squadron and called up as needed. Each SAR squadron also tried to keep a certain number of crews spare.

Casualty Treatment and Evacuation

The casualty evacuation system was based on a number of stages. If a tank crew member was wounded, his crew would render immediate first-aid, which usually consisted of a field dressing, tourniquet and probably an injection of morphine from the disposable syrettes carried by each crew commander. Sometimes the crew would evacuate the casualty using their own vehicle; more often he was evacuated by either one of the medical halftrack ambulances attached to the Regiment (known rather graphically as the "meat wagon") or, if enemy fire was not heavy, by a jeep ambulance.

The first step in the evacuation process was to the RAP (Regimental Aid Post), where the SAR Medical Officer, assisted by a trained staff including Padre Silcox, would render further aid and "triage" the casualties. Those who needed immediate and advanced treatment to save their lives were evacuated first, those who were only lightly wounded were evacuated second and those whose condition was hopeless were made as comfortable as possible and evacuated last. Evacuation was done by unit transport from the scene of the wound to the RAP and by field ambulance units (either jeeps or trucks) from the RAP to an ADS (Advanced Dressing Station) and then to a CCS (Casualty Collection Station). Further treatment and "triaging" was done at these points and the casualty was then evacuated, depending on the seriousness of his wound, to a field hospital, a convalescent depot or, for the most serious cases, by air or sea to a hospital in Britain.

Sources

This appendix is drawn from a number of official and private sources, and interviews with SAR veterans.

Official publications consulted include: *Memorandum on the Use of Smoke.* 1942; *The Use of Wireless in Armoured Formations.* 1942; *Tank Country.* 1943; *The Tactical Employment of Armoured Car and Reconnaissance Regiments. Part 1. General Principles regarding the Tactical Employment of Reconnaissance Regiments, 1943; The Tactical Handling of the Armoured Division and its Components. The Armoured Regiment 1943; Anti-Tank Tactics, 1943; The Employment of Reconnaissance Regiments. 1944; Message Writing and RT. 1944; Vehicle Data Book. Canadian Army Overseas, 1944; Netting Drill for Wireless Set No. 22. 1944; Data Book. Canadian Manufactured Tank Type Vehicles; Signal Training (All Arms) Pamphlet No. 10. Signal Tactics Part IV. The Armoured Regiment and the Armoured Car Regiment; Royal Armoured Corps Training. Volume I – Tactics. Pamphlet No. 1. The Armoured Regiment, 1948; The Tank Troop Leader's Manual, 1951; Crew Duty Card. Parade Maintenance, Sherman V, 1944;* TM 30-410, *Handbook on the British Army,* Washington, 1942; *Data Book. Canadian Manufactured Tank Type Vehicles.* Ottawa: Department of Munitions and Supply, February 1945; *Vehicle Data Book. Canadian Army Overseas.* London: Canadian Military Headquarters, 1944.

Secondary sources include: F.M von Senger und Etterlin, *German Tanks of World War II* (New York, 1969); *M4A4 (75mm) Sherman,* Reprint of 1942 manual by Allied Command Publications, Ottawa, 1996; Alvin Coox and L. Van Loan Marshall, *Survey of Allied Tank Casualties in World War II* (Washington, 1951); David Fletcher, *Sherman VC. M4A4 Firefly,* (Darlington, 1997); R.P. Hunnicutt, *Sherman. A History of the American Medium Tank* (San Rafael, 1976); Peter Chamberlain and Chris Ellis, *British and American Tanks of World War Two* (New York, 1969) and *Ram and Sexton* (Windsor, Berkshire, n.d.); and B.T. White, *Armoured Cars – Guy, Daimler, Humber, AEC,* (Windsor, Berkshire, 1970).

Interviews with the following South Alberta Regiment personnel: A.F. Coffin, 27 August 1995; J. Cooper, 19 August 1996; Danny McLeod, 24 August 1995, 21 January 1996; T. E. Milner, 26 November 1995; W.C. Luton, 12 December 1996; A. Halkyard, 10 November 1995.

GLOSSARY OF MILITARY TERMS
AND ABBREVIATIONS

AA Troop Anti-Aircraft Troop. In the SAR this consisted of six legal Crusader AA tanks plus an extra illegal vehicle they aquired on the way.

A net See "wireless."

A-1, B-2 Troop, etc. See "troop."

A-1 Echelon See "echelon."

A-2 Echelon See "echelon."

active service See "Canadian Army."

ACV Armoured Command Vehicle (sometimes Alternate Command Vehicle), the radio-equipped halftrack at RHQ which functioned as a mobile command post in action.

adjutant An officer, usually a captain, responsible for seeing that the orders of the commander of the regiment are carried out and who assumes the burden of all regimental staff, paper and administrative work.

AEF Allied Expeditionary Force. The official title of the Allied armies which landed in France in 1944.

AFN Allied Forces Network (radio).

AFV Armoured Fighting Vehicle, a general term that includes both wheeled and tracked vehicles.

AHQ Army Headquarters in Ottawa .

air burst When a shell explodes in the air rather than on the ground, can also be used for ranging.

air chief marshal A rank in the RAF and RCAF equivalent to general in the army.

Algoon(s) A member (members) of the Algonquin Regiment.

AP Armour-Piercing, solid shot intended to penetrate steel and concrete. Obsolescent by 1944.

APC Armoured Personnel Carrier.

APC Armoured Piercing, Capped shot. An AP shot with cap to concentrate the force of the round. Obsolescent by 1944.

APCBC Armoured Piercing, Capped, Ballistic Capped. An APC round with a second, ballistically streamlined cap. Most so-called AP shot in 1944-1945 was actually APCBC.

APDS Armoured Piercing, Discarding Sabot shot. An AP shot with a sabot or sheath of the bore calibre of the firing weapon which fell away in flight to leave a smaller tungsten core which, impelled with great velocity, was capable of both greater range and penetration .

appointment A role that, in theory, could be filled by a person of any rank, e.g. squadron commander, this could be a major, captain or even a lieutenant, see also"rank" .

armourer A specialist soldier who repairs weapons.

artillery Generally, all weapons, including tank weapons, other than small arms, can be classified as artillery. In this book the term is used to describe weapons over 40 mm calibre manned by troops of the artillery arm and excludes those manned by the infantry, i.e. mortars.

ARV Armoured Recovery Vehicle. Each squadron in the SAR had one of these useful vehicles which were basically armoured "tow trucks" utilizing either Ram or Sherman chassis.

ASH See "Argylls."

Ashcans See "Argylls."

Argylls The Argyll and Sutherland Highlanders of Canada (Princess Louise's), one of the three infantry regiments in 10 Brigade.

automatic weapons Small-arms (under 20 mm in calibre) that fire repeatedly at one pull of the trigger. This category includes the smallest AA guns, machineguns, light machine guns and submachine guns.

auxiliary services Organizations such as the YMCA, Knights of Columbus and Salvation Army which provided films, candy, mail services, etc. to the fighting troops.

AVRE tank Armoured Vehicle, Royal Engineers. A specialized tank used by the sappers that could undertake a number of tasks.

AWL Absent Without Leave (not "AWOL").

B net See "wireless."

B Echelon See "echelon."

Bailey bridge A portable bridge made out of prefabricated components which, once assembled, was capable of bearing 75 short tons over a 120-foot span.

barrage A line of artillery fire placed in front of advancing troops for the purpose of neutralizing the enemy defenders. There were different types, (e.g. box, rolling and creeping). The term is often misused for any kind of artillery bombardment.

battalion The basic infantry tactical manoeuvre and administrative unit. A Canadian infantry battalion in 1944-1945 consisted of just over 800 men organized in an HQ company, four rifle companies, a carrier platoon, scout platoon and support company. See also "terminology, American."

battle dress The working uniform of the Canadian soldier in the Second World War, consisting of a blouse or jacket and trousers, manufactured from tough khaki serge.

bazooka Name originally given to the 2.6-inch anti-tank rocket launcher developed by the Americans in 1942. Canadian soldiers often called German *Panzerfausts* or *Panzerschreck* weapons (see those terms) "bazookas."

BBC British Broadcasting Corporation.

BCR The British Columbia Regiment.

billet When a soldier slept indoors, his sleeping place was called a billet.

bivouac When a soldier slept outdoors, his sleeping place was called a bivouac.

Blue Patch 2nd Canadian Infantry Division, after its shoulder patch.

Bomber Command That part of the Commonwealth air forces devoted to the strategic bombing of Germany.

boss In the SAR it was the custom for subordinates to address all commanding officers up to the rank of major as "boss." Swatty Wotherspoon was always addressed as "Colonel" or "Sir."

Boys anti-tank rifle An oversized .50 calibre rifle issued to Commonwealth troops in 1939-1941 as an anti-tank weapon. It was almost useless.

Bren gun The standard light machine gun of the Commonwealth armies in the Second World War. Derived from a Czech design, the Bren (Brno-Enfield) was a .303 calibre, magazine fed weapon with a cyclic rate of 450 rpm. The Bren was highly accurate and probably the best light machine gun ever designed.

brew up A tank that was hit and set on fire. Can also mean preparing tea.

brigade Formation of two or more units, nominally of the same type commanded by a brigadier. Canadian infantry brigades in 1944-1945 consisted of three infantry battalions and a support (heavy weapons) company. Canadian armoured brigades consisted of three armoured regiments (battalions). See also "terminology, American."

Brigadeführer A rank in the Waffen SS (see "SS") somewhat higher than brigadier but lower than major-general in the Canadian Army.

brigadier An officer who commanded a brigade. He was higher in rank than a colonel and lower than a major-general. The American equivalent was a brigadier-general.

Browning pistol A 9 mm automatic with a 13-round magazine, the Browning was issued to the SAR as a personal sidearm from November 1944 onward. It was an excellent weapon and is still in service.

Browning .30 calibre Standard belt-fed, air-cooled machine gun with a cyclic rate of 550 rpm which was used as the auxiliary weapon in both the Sherman and Stuart tanks.

Browning, .50 calibre Heavy anti-aircraft machine gun, belt-fed, and air-cooled. Shermans issued to the SAR were equipped with one on the turret roof but most crew commanders gave them away to the infantry.

Buffalo See "LVT."

CAB Canadian Armoured Brigade.

CAC Canadian Armoured Corps. In 1945 it became the Royal Canadian Armoured Corps.

CACRU Canadian Armoured Corps Reinforcement Unit.

CAD Canadian Armoured Division.

calibre Most armies used the measurement of the internal diameter of a gun barrel as a means of classifying weapons, thus a 20 mm or 76 mm calibre weapon. The Commonwealth armies also had an older British system of using the weight of shell the weapon fired. Commonwealth troops manned 2-pdr. (40 mm), 6-pdr. (57 mm) and 17-pdr. (76.2 mm) anti-tank weapons and the 25-pdr. (85 mm) gun/howitzer. Weapons with calibres less than one inch were usually designated by a decimal point, thus the .50 calibre (half inch) and .303 calibre (nearly a third of an inch) weapons.

Can Loan A system whereby junior Canadian infantry officers were loaned to the British Army for a period because of a severe shortage of junior officers in that service. Most of them never returned to the Canadian army.

Canadian army In 1939, the Canadian army consisted of the Permanent Active Militia and the Non-Permanent Active Militia. The first was the regular army, usually referred to as the "Permanent Force," which had an authorized strength of 4,268 officers and men and 354 horses in 1939 but was short of its establishment. The Non-Permanent Active Militia (NPAM) was the civilian volunteer force and the equivalent of the Territorial Army in Britain or the National Guard in the United States. Called the "militia," its numbers fluctuated but, in 1939, about 46,000 officers and men were trained out of an authorized strength of 86,308 officers and men.

The declaration of war brought the organization of the Canadian Active Service Force mobilized from the regular and militia establishments and this was deployed in Europe. By 1945 it had a strength of just over 400,000 men formed in three infantry divisions, two armoured divisions, two independent armoured brigades, additional corps and army troops as well as headquarters and support echelons. Canadians who joined the Active Service force were known as "active service" or "general service" personnel and, until January 1945, all Canadian soldiers who went overseas were volunteers.

A manpower shortage led the Canadian government to pass the National Resources Mobilization Act in 1940 which imposed conscription for males. Soldiers compulsorily enlisted under this act were required to serve only in Canada and not overseas until December 1944 when the government, faced with replacing heavy casualties in Europe, changed the act to require NRMA personnel to serve in Europe. At this time there were just over 63,000 soldiers enlisted under the NRMA who were called "zombies" by everyone but the government.

Canadian army, ranks Generally, the army was divided into commissioned officers and enlisted men. Commissioned officers held the Sovereign's Commission, were saluted by the enlisted men and ranged in rank from lieutenants up to general. The enlisted ranks were divided into three categories: warrant officers, non-commissioned officers and private soldiers. Warrant officers were promoted from the ranks and held the Sovereign's Warrant but were not saluted. There were two categories: class I included regimental sergeant-majors, class II included all other warrant officers. Between the warrant officers and the private soldiers were the non-commissioned officers who were not saluted, their ranks were sergeant and corporals. Private soldiers, depending on their arm of service and unit, were called private, trooper, gunner, sapper, signalman, fusilier, guardsman or rifleman.

Canadian Expeditionary Force The Canadian army that fought in France in 1915-1918.

canteen The enlisted man's social institution. A wet canteen was one that served beer, a dry canteen also sold personal items such as razor blades and chocolate bars.

carrier A small, lightly-armoured, fully tracked vehicle used to carry the mortars and machine guns of an infantry battalion and for a multitude of other purposes. There were different types but the average weight was about four tons and the average speed was 30 mph on roads and 20 mph off road.

Casualty Clearing Station A stage in the casualty evacuation system after the RAP (see that term).

CCS See "Casualty Clearing Station."

centre line The axis of a formation or unit's advance, usually a major road .

CEF See "Canadian Expeditionary Force."

child Code for a sub-unit (see that term). A "child" of an armoured regiment was a squadron, of an infantry battalion, a company.

Chinese Hussars Mobile Bath and Laundry Unit.

Class 30, Class 40, etc. Weight designations for structures or vessels constructed by the engineers. A Class 30 structure would bear 30 long tons (see that term) of weight.

co-axial machine gun Machine gun mounted beside the tank's main gun which traversed or elevated as that gun traversed or elevated.

co-driver Junior member in a tank crew who assisted the driver with driving and maintenance tasks, manned the bow .30 calibre Browning in action and caught every other miscellaneous job going around.

Colour(s) The "flags" of a regiment, once they marked its place in the line of battle, now they are highly important ceremonial devices that bear the regiment's battle honours.

Colt revolver A .38 calibre (see that term) six-shot revolver issued to the SAR in 1942-1943 as a personal sidearm.

commission See "Canadian army, ranks."

company The basic sub-unit and tactical element of an infantry battalion, consisting of 125 officers and men at full strength and organized in an HQ platoon and three rifle platoons. See also "terminology, American."

Composite Ration Pack (compo pack) The basic ration of the armoured crew consisting of fourteen meals with nine different menus according to type.

concentration (area) Area in which units come together preparatory to mounting an operation or commencing a march .

concentration (artillery) Artillery fire into a limited target area done as quickly as possible.

corps In the general sense, the term means the units and soldiers of a single arm (infantry, armour, artillery, engineers, etc.). In the specific sense the term means a formation of two or more divisions (see that term) with additional artillery and support units, commanded by a lieutenant-general.

counter-battery Artillery fire intended to neutralize enemy artillery.

coveralls The tank suit issued to Canadian armoured crews in late 1944, sometimes called "overalls." Prior to this they were issued with one-piece garments of black denim which were also called overalls or coveralls.

crew commander Senior member of a tank crew. Depending on circumstances this was either a lieutenant, sergeant or corporal.

Crocodile tank Churchill tank equipped with a flamethrower.

Crusader AA tank A British manufactured tank converted to an AA vehicle by the addition of a powered turret armed with two 20 mm Oerlikon guns.

CSM Company Sergeant-Major.

cupola Raised area around the turret hatch with apertures that provided all-around vision for the crew commander.

cyclic rate The number of rounds an automatic weapon fires per minute whether or not it has the ammunition to do so.

CWAC Canadian Women's Army Corps.

cwt. Abbreviation for hundredweight, a British unit of weight of 112 pounds.

DCM Distinguished Conduct Medal. Awarded to enlisted personnel who have performed service of a distinctly gallant and distinguished nature in action in the field.

debus Get out of a truck or other vehicle.

detention barracks Where badly behaved soldiers go and if they don't become better soldiers after a spell in the detention barracks, they might end up in the "glass house" or military prison.

direct fire (DF) Artillery fire in which the target is in view of the firing gun. All anti-tank gun fire is usually direct fire, as is small-arms fire.

dispatch rider There were twelve DRs in the SAR who rode motorcycles and it was an exciting and very dangerous job.

division The major operational and fighting formation which consisted of troops of all arms and was commanded by a major-general.

division, armoured The Commonwealth armoured division in 1944 consisted of an armoured brigade of three armoured regiments, an infantry brigade of three infantry battalions, a motor battalion (armoured infantry), an armoured recce regiment and artillery, engineer and service components. Total strength was about 15,000 all ranks and nearly 300 AFVs.

division, infantry The Commonwealth infantry division in 1944 consisted of three infantry brigades, each with three infantry battalions, a recce regiment (armoured car) and artillery, engineer and service components. Total strength was about 18,200 all ranks.

DR See "dispatch rider."

dragon's teeth Concrete tank obstacles.

driver Tank crew member responsible for driving the vehicle and performing first line maintenance on the engine, tracks and suspension.

driver-mechanic The armoured corps trade to which the drivers and co-drivers of a tank crew belonged.

drumming out A traditional British army practice dating back at least to the 17th century. When a soldier was found to be so worthless that the army was better off without him (and in the 17th to 19th centuries you had to be a pretty bad soldier to be found worthless) he would be "drummed out" of his regiment after being stripped of all regimental and rank insignia. As he was paraded before the ranks, the drummers and fifers played the "Rogue's March," which had the words "Fifty I got for selling my coat, fifty for selling my blanket, if ever I enlist for a soldier again, the Devil shall be my sergeant."

DSO Distinguished Service Order. Awarded to officers for individual instances of meritorious or distinguished service in war in combat or in conditions equivalent to combat.

Dukes Nickname for the British Columbia Regiment or Duke of Connaught's Own.

DVD Distinguished Visitor Demonstration.

echelon(s) Service component of a unit. In the SAR, more than half of the personnel belonged to the echelon whose task was to provide everything that the fighting echelon required. The echelon was normally divided into A-1 Echelon which supplied the fighting squadrons with all supplies required for a single day's operations; A-2 Echelon which replenished the stores of A-1 Echelon; and B Echelon which was set up occasionally and consisted of such essential but non-combat services such as the paymaster, dentist, etc. Maintenance personnel also served in the echelons.

EFI Expeditionary Force Institute, the NAAFI (see that term) outside Britain.

ENSA Entertainment Services Association, the British equivalent of the USO and known as "Every Night, Something Awful."

Fähnrich German rank equivalent to officer cadet.

Fascine tank An AVRE (see that term) equipped with fascines, bundles of material that bridged holes and gaps.

Feldmarschall German rank equivalent to Commonwealth rank of field-marshal.

field artillery Artillery integral to division-size formations and armed with weapons of between 75 mm and 105 mm calibre. In the Commonwealth armies, the standard weapon was the 25-pdr. (85 mm) gun/howitzer, in the American and German armies, the standard weapon was the 105 mm howitzer.

field regiment Artillery unit equipped with twenty-four 25 pdr. gun/howitzers organized in three batteries each with two troops of four weapons. See also "terminology, American."

field-service cap See "wedge cap."

Firefly Sherman tank armed with a 17-pdr. (76.2 mm) gun.

fitter A tank mechanic.

fixed lines When a weapon has been fixed (usually with stakes or other devices) to fire through a limited traverse, it is said to be firing on fixed lines. A useful arrangement to concentrate fire and save ammunition.

Flail tank A tank equipped with a powered, rotating drum, fixed ahead of the hull. As the drum rotated it "flailed" the ground under the drum with chains thus exploding any mines.

flash Regimental title worn on the upper shoulders of the battle dress blouse or jacket.

FOO Forward Observation Officer. Artillery officers equipped with wireless who accompanied combat units to call down artillery fire.

Foot Pads Nickname for the Governor General's Foot Guards.

forage cap A fancy name for a wedge cap, see that term.

formation A military organization consisting of two or more units (see that term) which could be of different arms of service (artillery, infantry, armour). The smallest formation was a brigade but divisions, corps, armies and army groups were also formations.

forming up place (FUP) An area where a unit or formation formed before undertaking an operation, usually an advance or attack.

gallon, Imperial A unit of liquid measurement consisting of five quarts.

gallon, US A unit of liquid measurement consisting of four quarts .

Gefreiter German rank equivalent to lance-corporal.

General German rank equivalent to Commonwealth rank of lieutenant-general.

Generalleutnant German rank equivalent to Commonwealth rank of major-general.

Generalmajor German rank equivalent to Commonwealth rank somewhere above brigadier but below major-general .

Generaloberst German rank equivalent to Commonwealth rank of full general.

general service See "Canadian army."

George His Majesty King George VI of the United Kingdom, King of Canada and Emperor of India.

GFN General Forces Network (radio).

glass house Slang term for military prison.

GOC General Officer Commanding.

Goo Goo Foo Goos Nickname for the Governor General's Foot Guards.

Goons See "Algoons."

Grannies Nickname for the Canadian Grenadier Guards.

Green Patch 4th Canadian Armoured Division, after its shoulder patch.

ground burst When an artillery shell explodes on the ground.

GSO General Staff Officer.

gun Artillery piece which usually fires at angles of 45 degrees or less, has a high muzzle velocity and a long range.

gunner Lowest enlisted rank in the Royal Canadian Artillery and the generic term for all soldiers of the artillery arm.

gunner-operator The armoured corps trade to which the gunners and loader-operators of a tank crew belonged.

halftrack A lightly-armoured truck with its rear wheels replaced by tracks.

harbour A place where armoured units pulled back to re-supply, usually a secure area near a village or wood.

HE High explosive.

Hetzer SPG A German SPG (see that term) with a 75 mm gun protected by well-sloped armour and mounted on the chassis of the obsolescent 38t tank.

HLI Highland Light Infantry Regiment.

HMT His Majesty's Transport.

HOLDFAST Wireless code for Royal Canadian Engineers.

hollow charge Sometimes called a "shaped charge," this projectile relied for its effect on the detonating force it contained. When it struck, a fuse detonated explosive at the end remote from the shaped cavity at the front of the round and an explosive wave, passing forward, created a jet of molten metal that would penetrate armour plate and spray a mass of flame and melted metal fragments into the interior of a tank. Hollow charge projectiles were ideal for low-velocity, hand-held anti-tank weapons and the American bazooka, British PIAT and German *Panzerfaust* and *Panzerschreck* weapons utilized them.

Homelite A small two-stroke engine inside the turret of a Sherman which was used to keep a charge in the batteries when the main engines were not being used and which generally gassed everybody inside the vehicle.

howitzer An artillery piece capable of firing at angles greater than 45 degrees and which, compared to a gun, has lower muzzle velocity, a shorter range but a heavier shell.

HQ Headquarters.

HQ Squadron Headquarters Squadron. The sub-unit in an armoured regiment that controlled the echelons (see that term). Not to be confused with RHQ .

indirect fire (IF) Fire in which the target is not in view of the firing weapon.

intercom See "wireless."

Intercommunication Troop The SAR had nine Humber scout cars which were manned by the men of this troop. They were used to do liaison work, some recce tasks and as alternate command vehicles.

Iron Cross The German system of medals was very simple compared to the Allied system. The order of the Iron Cross was promulgated in 1813 and had several degrees. The lowest was the Iron Cross, Second Class, and the order rose through the Iron Cross, First Class, to the Knight's Cross which had several grades: Knight's Cross with Swords, with Oakleaves, with Diamonds. The Knight's Cross was a flashy medal, a Maltese Cross worn at the neck and, since German soldiers tended to wear their medals in action, it had prime souvenir value and was usually removed from PWs (see that term) lest it promote the German war effort.

jabo *Jagdbomber,* German soldier's slang for fighter-bomber.

Jagdpanzer Literally "hunting tank," German term for one type of SPG (see that term) whose primary tactical role was to engage enemy AFVs.

"Jane" of the Daily Mail Comic strip character famous for getting into situations where she ended up disrobed.

jerrican or jerrycan German-designed steel container designed to hold four gallons of petrol, water or other liquids.

Jerry British and Canadian soldiers' slang for German soldiers.

Kangaroo See Ram tank.

King Tiger See Tiger tank.

Knight's Cross See "Iron Cross."

Kubelwagen The military equivalent of the Volkswagen and the German answer to the jeep.

Lake Soups The Lake Superior Regiment.

LAA Light Anti-Aircraft.

laager, or leaguer Sometimes used interchangeably with harbour, a laager was a position to which armoured regiments pulled back to re-supply but was not as secure as a harbour. They therefore "circled the wagons" in a defensive position .

LAD Light Aid Detachment. The RCOC sub-unit (see that term) attached to the SAR which undertook second line repair and maintenance on the tanks.

lanyard The cord worn under the left shoulder strap by all officers and men of a regiment when in their best dress. It was braided of the regimental colours and served as an additional emblem to distinguish the men of the unit. The SAR lanyard was black and yellow.

LCT Landing Craft, Tank.

Lee-Enfield rifle A .303 calibre, clip-fed, bolt action rifle which was the standard service rifle of the Commonwealth armies in two world wars and Korea.

Lewis gun A .303 calibre, drum-fed, light machine gun on a bipod mount which was the standard l.m.g. in Commonwealth Armies to 1939.

Life buoy Life preserver. Term used to describe the portable flamethrowers used by Commonwealth troops because of their shape.

Limey Canadian slang for the British. The term originates in the 18th century when the Royal Navy issued lime-juice to its sailors to prevent scurvy.

Links (Links and Winks) Members of the Lincoln and Welland Regiment.

loader-operator The tank crew member responsible for loading the turret armament and operating the wireless.

LOB Left out of Battle.

LOC Lines of Communication.

long ton The British ton, 2,240 lb.

Lord Haw-Haw William Joyce, a renegade Briton who broadcast daily on German radio programmes intended for a British audience. He got his nickname from his raucous laugh. At war's end Joyce was convicted of treason and hanged so the last laugh was on him.

lorry British term for truck. Actually, the British army differentiated between "lorries" which had a load-carrying capacity greater than one long ton and "trucks" which had a load-carrying capacity of one long ton or less (see "long ton").

Loyal Eddies The Loyal Edmonton Regiment.

LST Landing Ship, Tank.

Luftwaffe The German air force.

Luger automatic pistol A German 9 mm pistol with an 8-round magazine which was a very prized souvenir.

LVT Landing Vehicle, Tracked. An amphibious, lightly-armoured, fully tracked vehicle sometimes called a "Buffalo."

LW Lincoln and Welland Regiment.

M-10 A self-propelled gun armed with a 17-pdr. in an open turret based on the Sherman chassis and suspension.

M-Test A Canadian army aptitude test that measured basic mechanical and reasoning skills.

M and V Meat and Vegetables, one of the basic meals provided in the "Composite Ration Pack" (see that term).

MBE Member of the British Empire. The lowest of the five classes of the Order of the British Empire and awarded for services in the field or before the enemy or for services to the Commonwealth.

MC Military Cross. Awarded to officers of captain's rank or lower, including warrant officers, for gallant and distinguished service in action.

MM Military Medal, awarded to enlisted personnel for individual acts of bravery and devotion under fire.

maintenance A never ending task in an armoured regiment. The checking, servicing and repair of a tank's engines, running gear, weapons and other equipment.

marquee A large tent capable of sleeping 30-40 men.

medium artillery Artillery integral to division-sized formations and equipped with guns between 105 and 155 mm in calibre. In the

Commonwealth armies, each division had a medium regiment with sixteen 4.5 or 5.5 inch guns.

medium regiment Medium artillery regiment, see "medium artillery."

mess Generally, the term means the army's dining hall. More specifically, in terms of officers, it means their dining and social area and, by derivation, came to mean the officers in a unit as a group.

MG Machine gun.

MG 42 *Maschinengewehr* 42, a belt-fed 7.92 mm machine gun with a cyclic rate of 1000 rpm and the standard machine gun of the Wehrmacht in the last years of the war. Sometimes called the "Spandau" by Allied troops.

Mike target A target engaged by all the guns in an artillery regiment.

militia See "Canadian army."

Mk IV tank The standard German tank during the Second World War. It was a 30-ton vehicle armed with a 75 mm gun and there was usually one battalion of Mk IVs in a panzer division.

Moaning Minnie Allied soldiers' term for the German multi-barreled *Nebelwerfer* (see that term) mortar.

mortar Smooth-bore artillery piece which is fired only at angles greater than 45 degrees. Canadian infantry battalions had integral 2-inch and 3-inch mortars. The heavier 4.2-inch mortars were manned by support battalions and companies.

mortar bomb The projectile fired by a mortar. American soldiers called them mortar rounds.

MO Medical Officer – the "Doc."

MP(s) Military Police(men). The American equivalent of the provost corps.

Mulberries Artificial harbours, constructed in parts in Britain and towed to Normandy.

NAAFI Navy, Army and Air Force Institute. Organization which provided canteens for Commonwealth troops.

napalm Jellied petroleum used as a very effective anti-personnel weapon.

Nebelwerfer German term for multi-barreled smoke mortar. What originated as a useful artillery piece to lay down smoke screens fast evolved into a weapon feared by Allied troops. German *Nebelwerfers* came in a number of calibres, ranging from 75 to 300 mm. The classic weapon was the six-barreled 150 mm variety which could be loaded and fired every ninety seconds.

net See "wireless."

netting, netting drill See "wireless."

NCO Non-Commissioned Officer.

NNSH North Nova Scotia Highlanders.

No. 19 Wireless Set See "wireless."

No. 36 grenade Standard British/Canadian anti-personnel grenade.

non-commissioned officer See "Canadian army, rank structure."

North Novies Nickname for North Nova Scotia Highlanders.

NRMA National Resources Mobilization Act, see "Canadian army."

NSR See "NNSH."

O Group Orders group (see that term).

Oberfeldwebel German rank approximately equivalent to company sergeant-major.

OCTU Officer Candidate Training Unit.

OP Observation Post.

Orders Group A meeting at which orders were given for a forthcoming operation or movement.

P-38 See "Walther P-38."

pace stick The badge of office of a warrant officer in the Commonwealth armies, this was a highly-polished wooden measuring device one pace (2.5 feet) long with a hinge that allows it to be expanded to double pace length (5 feet). If you saw somebody coming your way carrying one of these, it was best to disappear.

Panther tank Standard German medium tank in the late war period. It was a 45-ton vehicle with well-sloped armour that carried a long 75 mm gun. Each panzer division usually had one battalion of Panthers .

Panzer German word meaning "armour" which came to mean "tank" or "armoured."

Panzerfaust A hand-held, disposable anti-tank weapon that fired a hollow-charge round capable of penetrating the armour of any Allied tank. Allied soldiers called them "bazookas."

Panzerjaeger German term meaning "anti-tank."

Panzerschreck Anti-tank rocket launcher crewed by two men firing a hollow-charge round of 88 mm calibre. A development and improvement on the American bazooka and called the "stove pipe" by German troops. A nasty weapon.

PEPPERPOT A Commonwealth artillery tactic developed in 1945 which brought every weapon over 20 mm calibre that could fire some kind of explosive round into use in a preliminary bombardment.

permanent force See "Canadian army."

petard A large mortar bomb of 215 mm calibre fired from special AVRE tanks and used to demolish bunkers and obstacles.

petrol Gasoline.

phase line Arbitrary lines chosen as "reporting" features so that when a unit passed a phase line, it reported doing so to higher command.

PIAT Projectile, Infantry, Anti-Tank. A spring-loaded hollow-charge anti-tank weapon that was, surprisingly, very effective.

pioneer Another term for sapper (see that term). Pioneers were engineers integral within an infantry battalion.

platoon A sub-unit of an infantry company commanded by a lieutenant and consisting, at full strength, of about 35 men.

point (terrain) A terrain elevation usually measured in height above sea level, thus Point 145 was 145 yards or metres above sea level.

point (tactical) The leading man or tank in an advancing unit.

provost(s) The Provost Corps was the army's police force.

PW Prisoner of War. It is not "POW;" that is an Americanism.

QM Quartermaster.

Ram tank A medium tank manufactured in Canada with a Canadian designed hull and turret and an American chassis and suspension taken from the M3 Medium tank. The Ram I was armed with a 2-pdr. (40 mm) gun, the Ram II with a 6-pdr. (57 mm) gun and was used by the CAC to train in 1942-1943, after which it was replaced by the Sherman. The Ram then served as a base for a number of specialized vehicles: ARVs (see that term); Ram OP tanks for the FOO (see that term) attached to armoured regiments; turretless vehicles were used as gun towers, APCs (see that term) called Kangaroos, and ammunition carriers called Wallabies.

Ram OP tank See "Ram tank."

RAC Royal Armoured Corps.

RAF Royal Air Force. The subject of much envy because they slept between sheets, this service was also known as the "Brylcream Boys."

rank The level in the army hierarchy that determined a soldier's level of authority and pay. Not to be confused with "appointment," which was the job he did.

RAP Regimental Aid Post.

RCAF Royal Canadian Air Force; the comments on the RAF also apply.

RCASC Royal Canadian Army Service Corps. Responsible for storage and transport of supplies, including the vehicles assigned for that purpose.

RCCS Royal Canadian Corps of Signals. Responsible for army communications down to unit level.

RCE Royal Canadian Engineers.

RCEME Royal Canadian Electrical and Mechanical Engineers. Responsible for the repair of electrical devices and vehicles.

RCOC Royal Canadian Ordnance Corps. Responsible for the procurement and issue of ordnance stores comprising armament and ammunition, fighting vehicles, unit transport, radios, electrical equipment and general stores such as buckets and mops.

RCN Royal Canadian Navy, see comments under "RN."

recognition panels, smoke Yellow panels (on the deck of a tank) or smoke was the Allied ground forces' signal for friendly troops.

red tabs Officers of the rank of brigadier and above and colonels on the general staff wore scarlet hat bands and tabs, or gorget patches on their collars – "the high-priced help."

rear link The first captain in an armoured squadron who maintained a wireless link with RHQ and was prepared to take over should the squadron commander be killed or wounded.

recce Reconnaissance. Also used as a verb as in, "Let's go recce that pub."

Recce Troop In the SAR, the Recce Troop consisted of 11 Stuart light tanks which were usually sent out in five two-tank "packages" or patrols.

regiment A very tricky word as it is used differently in Commonwealth armies than in other armies. In most armies (the German and American for example) a regiment is a military unit with two or more battalions – the Commonwealth equivalent is a "brigade." In the Commonwealth the term "regiment" has a traditional meaning dating back to the 17th century and is used in the titles of units that are actually of only battalion strength. Thus a Commonwealth infantry regiment is actually a battalion as are armoured regiments. The reader unfamiliar with this terminology should simply translate "battalion" every time the word "regiment" is used in the Commonwealth context and "regiment" every time "brigade" is used. See also "terminology, American."

regiment, armoured An armoured unit with approximately 70-80 armoured vehicles. See also "terminology, American."

regular See "Canadian army."

Reichsmarschall Marshal of the Reich. A special rank created by Hitler for Hermann Goering, the commander of the *Luftwaffe*. His men called him *der dicke Hermann*, "Hermann the fat boy."

Renault FT tank A small obsolescent American two-man tank based on a French design from the First World War and purchased by Canada in 1940 to train the infant CAC.

Rhino ferry or raft A large powered raft used to ferry tanks and heavy vehicles from ships to the landing beaches.

RHQ Regimental Headquarters.

RMC Royal Military College. The Commonwealth equivalent of West Point, there is one at Sandhurst in England and Kingston in Canada.

RMR Royal Montreal Regiment.

RN Royal Navy, the "senior service" but liked better by soldiers than the RAF or RCAF.

Ronson Nickname for Sherman tank after the popular lighter which lit "first time, every time."

Ross rifle A .303 calibre, clip-fed, bolt-action rifle which was the standard Canadian service rifle in 1914 but later replaced by the Lee-Enfield. Used for training during the Second World War and by snipers as it was highly accurate.

Royal Tiger See Tiger tank.

RQMS Regimental Quartermaster Sergeant-Major.

RSM Regimental Sergeant-Major, arguably the most important person in existence.

SALH South Alberta Light Horse.

Sally-Ann Salvation Army.

salvo Artillery tactic where all guns fire at the same moment for maximum shock and morale effect on the enemy.

Sam Browne belt A brown leather harness worn by commissioned and warrant officers consisting of a waist belt and a shoulder belt over the right shoulder. Named after the one-armed British general who designed it.

sapper Lowest enlisted rank in the Royal Canadian Engineers and the generic term for all engineers. The term derives from the specialized troops who used to construct "saps" or approach trenches to enemy fortresses in the 18th century.

SAR The South Alberta Regiment.

SAS Special Air Service Regiment, an elite British commando unit that has little do with the air force despite its title.

scheme Training exercise .

Schmeisser submachine gun 9 mm automatic weapon with a 25-round magazine, the Schmeisser MP 40, called the "burp gun" by Allied soldiers, was taken into Canadian service by some SAR tank crews to replace the wretched Sten (see that term).

scout car Lightly armoured four-wheeled vehicle equipped with a bren gun and usually manned by two men. Humber scout cars were used by senior SAR officers as a personal vehicle and alternate command vehicle.

section The lowest infantry sub-unit consisting of ten men at full strength commanded by a corporal.

SHAEF Supreme Headquarters, Allied Expeditionary Force. Eisenhower's headquarters.

shell A hollow artillery projectile which contains HE (see that term) or some other payload such as smoke.

shell dressing A thick bandage carried by every soldier and used for immediate first aid for the wounded.

SHELLDRAKE Wireless code-name for artillery.

Sherman tank Standard tank of the CAC from 1943 onward, it was an American-designed vehicle of 29 tons armed with either a 75 mm or 17 pdr. gun and very robust mechanically.

shot Artillery projectile which is solid and used to penetrate armour or concrete.

short ton The American ton (2,000 lb.).

SHQ Squadron Headquarters.

slit, slit trench The proverbial "fox hole" .

small-arms Direct fire (see that term) weapons integral to infantry units which include pistols, rifles, submachine guns and machine guns.

Smith and Wesson revolver .38 calibre (see that term) six-shot revolver issued to the SAR in 1942-1944 as a personal sidearm.

SMLE Short Magazine, Lee-Enfield, see "Lee-Enfield rifle."

solenoid trigger An electrical trigger operated by a button.

SP Self-propelled.

Spandau machine gun See MG 42.

SPG Self-propelled gun. Used in this book to refer to tracked German AFVs without turrets. The *Wehrmacht* had many different types ranging from standard artillery pieces with unarmoured hulls; assault guns (heavily armoured bodies with high velocity

HE or AP weapons) and *Jagdpanzers* (very heavily armoured bodies with large calibre high velocity anti-tank weapons).

squadron The sub-unit of an armoured regiment consisting of an SHQ troop of 3 tanks and four fighting troops, each of 4 tanks. See also "terminology, American."

SQMS Squadron Quartermaster Sergeant.

SRD Service and Replenishment Depot. Letters marked on cases of hardtack and flasks of rum issued to the troops.

SS *Schützstaffel* The SS were the security arm of the Nazi party and gradually became the most powerful organization in the Third Reich responsible for all police and intelligence services (including the Gestapo), concentration and extermination camps, weapons manufacture and many other functions. The military branch, the *Waffen SS* (armed SS), expanded throughout the war and consisted of nearly thirty divisions by 1945. They had a reputation as very good but very fanatical soldiers.

SSM Squadron Sergeant-Major.

Stabsfeldwebel German rank equivalent to company sergeant-major in the Canadian Army.

Staghound Heavy armoured car armed with a 37 mm gun.

stand to Basically, an alert. When a unit "stands to" at dawn (as most did) it meant that the unit was alerted and prepared for a possible enemy attack.

Start line Arbitrary line, usually based on a prominent terrain feature, chosen to indicate the start of an operation. Once, beyond the start line, a unit would expect to make contact with the enemy, often they made contact while moving to the start line.

Sten submachine gun 9 mm submachine gun hastily designed and manufactured with a bad reputation for jamming. Crude but effective (when it worked) it was known as the "Plumber's delight" and took its name from the names of its designers (Shepperd and Turpin) and its place of manufacture (Enfield).

stonk Originally, this term meant the "Standard Regimental Concentration" of a field artillery regiment's guns onto a limited target area (see "concentration, artillery"); it later came to mean any quick, heavy bombardment by guns, howitzers or mortars on a target area.

Stuart tank A light tank armed with a 37 mm gun used for recce tasks in Commonwealth armoured regiments.

submachine gun Hand-held automatic weapon.

sub-unit A component of a unit (see that term). A squadron was a sub-unit of an armoured regiment, a company was a sub-unit of an infantry battalion.

SUNRAY Wireless code for commander.

swagger stick An implement carried by commissioned officers in Commonwealth armies, it was a leather-covered stick about eighteen inches long and used for drawing tactical evolutions in the dirt, swatting against the leg and disarranging carefully folded items during a barracks inspection. It was also handy for propping up a loose sash window.

SWALLOW Wireless code for tactical air (see that term).

syrette Disposable needle for injections.

tactical air Aircraft devoted to the ground battle.

tank suits Garments similar to aircrew's flying suits issued to Canadian tank crews in the autumn of 1944.

TCV Troop Carrying Vehicle. A large truck.

technical storesman Armoured corps trade for those working in the supply echelons providing spare parts.

terminology, American American equivalents for Commonwealth unit and formation terminology are as follows:

Commonwealth	American
army	army
corps	corps
division	division
brigade	reinforced regiment
regiment (infantry)	infantry battalion
regiment (armour)	tank battalion
regiment (artillery)	artillery regiment
company (infantry)	company
squadron (armour)	tank company
squadron (engineer)	engineer company
battery (artillery)	artillery battalion
troop (armour)	tank platoon
troop (artillery)	artillery battery
platoon (infantry)	platoon
section (infantry)	squad
crew commander	commander
loader-operator	loader
co-driver	assistant driver or bow gunner

TEWT Tactical Exercise Without Troops, a term that encompasses the whole spectrum from map exercises, wireless exercises, study sessions and "war games."

Thompson submachine gun .45 calibre weapon utilizing either a 50-round drum magazine or a 25-round box magazine. Heavy but reliable it was used by Commonwealth troops in the early and middle war years and some preferred it to the Sten gun which replaced it.

Tiger tank The standard German heavy tank of the late war period. Armed with an 88 mm gun, the Tiger I weighed 56 tons, the Tiger II (also known as the King or Royal Tiger) weighed 68 tons. A feared opponent.

Tommi, Tommis German soldier's slang for British soldiers.

Tommi SS German soldier's slang for Canadian soldiers.

Tommy Cooker German soldier's slang for the Sherman tank.

tracer Projectile containing phosphorus which left a mark or "trace" in its trajectory and was used to correct aim.

traverse To align in the horizontal plane.

troop The basic tactical sub-unit of armoured regiments, four tanks commanded by a lieutenant. In the SAR they were often designated C-1 (1st Troop in C Squadron), B-3 (3rd Troop in B Squadron) and so on. See also "terminology, American."

trooper Lowest enlisted rank in the armoured corps.

turret crew Term for the crew commander, gunner and loader-operator who fought in the turret of the Sherman.

ULTRA Top secret intelligence source based on the Allied ability to read German coding machines.

Uncle target A target engaged by all the guns in the divisional artillery.

unit Basic tactical military organization of one arm (artillery, infantry, or armour). In the infantry the normal unit was the battalion (see that term), in the armour and artillery, the unit was normally a regiment. See "terminology, American."

Unterscharführer Rank in the Waffen SS equivalent to corporal.

VC Victoria Cross. The highest decoration in the Commonwealth awarded to officers or other ranks who demonstrate outstanding valour or devotion to their country in the face of the enemy. By custom, the VC ranks above all other orders and decorations.

verey pistol Large calibre, smooth bore pistol used to fire flare cartridges.

Victor target A target engaged by all artillery within range.

Waffen SS See "SS."

Wallaby See "Ram tank."

Walther P-38 pistol The other standard German sidearm, it was an automatic with an 8-round magazine.

War Establishment Authorized wartime strength and organization of a unit.

warrant See "Canadian army, ranks."

warrant officer See "Canadian army, ranks."

Wasp A carrier (see that term) armed with a flame-thrower.

wedge cap A folding cap worn in the early and middle war years by all ranks and officially called the "field-service cap."

Wehrmacht Nominally, this term means all three German fighting services; in this book it is used to denote those German soldiers who fought on land and which included elements of the *Heer* (army), *Luftwaffe* (air force), *Waffen* SS and, toward the end, the *Kriegsmarine* (navy).

wet canteen A canteen (see that term) where beer is served.

wheels Wheeled vehicles in an armoured regiment.

wireless The modern term is radio. The wireless system or "net" was the means by which the South Alberta Regiment was commanded and was based on the No. 19 Wireless Set in each fighting vehicle. The No. 19 Set had three components: the "A Set", a long range sender-receiver with a range of ten miles; the "B Set" with a range of one mile (but actually less); and the inter-com which allowed the crew members to talk to each other. At the flick of a switch, the No. 19 Wireless could be switched to one of these three components. For a more detailed explanation of wireless system see Appendix C.

Prior to commencing an operation the wireless operators would carry out netting or netting drill at either the regimental or squadron level to ensure that all the No. 19 Sets were tuned to the same frequency.

Wolseley helmet Type of white sun helmet still worn by some Canadian regiments as part of their ceremonial full dress uniforms.

Woodbines A too-common brand of British cigarettes detested by Canadian soldiers.

zombie Useful and expressive term for a man conscripted under the National Resources Mobilization Act of 1940. Zombies were required to serve in Canada only and could not be sent overseas unless they volunteered for "general" or "active service." See "Canadian Army."

Naturally there was no love lost between the zombies and general service volunteers and, when serving together, the latter could often promote a good brawl by singing "The Zombie Song" to the tune of "Oh My Darling Clementine":.

I'm a zombie, I'm a zombie
I'm a zombie, Yes I am,
I'd much rather be a zombie
Than an active service man.

Now, come listen, all you zombies
You drink our wine, you drink our beer
But you won't turn active service,
You're a handcuffed volunteer.

NOMINAL ROLLS, SOUTH ALBERTA REGIMENT, 1940–1945

PART I

OFFICERS WHO SERVED WITH THE SOUTH ALBERTA REGIMENT, JUNE 1940–MAY 1945

These officers served with, or were attached to, the Regiment. Awards shown are those received at the time of joining the Regiment. For awards or decorations earned while serving with the Regiment, see Appendix A. The ranks are, as can best be established, the highest achieved during service with the SAR.

LAST NAME	FIRST NAME	MIDDLE NAME	RANK	REMARKS
ADAMS	GERALD	CHARLES DESMOND	LIEUTENANT	
ALLSOPP	ROBERT	HENRY	CAPTAIN	
BAKER	D	F	LIEUTENANT	ATTACHED
BARFORD	CUTHBERT	ALLEN LYNCH	CAPTAIN	QM
BODLEY	ORLANDO	A	LIEUTENANT	
BOOTHROYD	WILFRED	ERNEST	CAPTAIN	RCAMC
BOWICK	SMITH	FREMONT	LIEUTENANT	
BOYD	W	S	LIEUTENANT	ATTACHED
BRADBURN	ROBERT	ARCHIBALD	MAJOR	
BRISTOWE	W	P	LIEUTENANT-COLONEL	
BURGER	PETER	M	LIEUTENANT	
BURNS	ROBERT	CHARLES	LIEUTENANT	
BURTON	RICHARD	B. S.	CAPTAIN	
CALLAGHAN	L	E	CAPTAIN	
CAMPBELL	GORDON	ALEXANDER	CAPTAIN	
CARROLL	HENRY	LEONARD	CAPTAIN	
CARVOSSO (MC)	J	H	LIEUTENANT-COLONEL	
CASELEY	SAMUEL	L	LIEUTENANT	
CHANDLER	R	J	CAPTAIN	RCAPC
CLARKE	HUGH	HARDING	MAJOR	
CLARKE	KENNETH	ANDREW CONNAL	CAPTAIN	RCAMC
COFFIN	ALBERT	FRANK	MAJOR	
COPPING	WILLIAM	T	LIEUTENANT	
COTTER	JOHN	LESLIE	2/LIEUTENANT	
COX	E	C	CAPTAIN	RCOC
CRANSTON	ROBERT	BROOKS	LIEUTENANT	
CRAWFORD	ROBERT	E	LIEUTENANT	
CRICHTON	JAMES	H	CAPTAIN	
CURLEY	JAMES	PHILIP	CAPTAIN	
CURRIE	DAVID	VIVIAN	MAJOR	
DAVIES	HERBERT	SAMUEL	MAJOR	
DAWSON	E	G	CAPTAIN	
DEANE	J	A	LIEUTENANT	ATTACHED
DICK	J	S	LIEUTENANT	
DONALDSON	ROBERT	HECTOR	CAPTAIN	
DONKIN	F	I	LIEUTENANT	
DOUTHWAITE	C	R. R.	CAPTAIN	
DUNN	R	H	LIEUTENANT	ATTACHED
ELLERY	W	A	LIEUTENANT	
ERSKINE	R	W	LIEUTENANT	
FARRELL	H	S	CAPTAIN	RCAMC
FENTON	J	W	LIEUTENANT	
FULLER	W	S	LIEUTENANT	
GALLIMORE	CHARLES	WILFRID	CAPTAIN	
GAMMON	C	E	LIEUTENANT	
GEORGE	JOHN	KENNETH	CAPTAIN	RCAPC
GARARD	W		CAPTAIN	CDC
GILBERT	D	I	LIEUTENANT	

LAST NAME	FIRST NAME	MIDDLE NAME	RANK	REMARKS
GOODALL	JACK	DAL	LIEUTENANT	
GRIMMETT (MC)	A	M	CAPTAIN (MAJOR)	
GUNN-FOWLIE	JOHN	ALEXANDER	LIEUTENANT	
GUYOT	JEAN	MARC	LIEUTENANT	
HANCOCK	RONALD	LAWRENCE	LIEUTENANT	
HARVEY	D	F	LIEUTENANT	ATTACHED
HILL	ERNEST	F	LIEUTENANT	
HOLTON	LUTHER	JANNA	LIEUTENANT	
HOWARD	PHILIP	B	LIEUTENANT	
HOWARD	THOMAS	FRANCIS	A/CAPTAIN	
HUFFMAN	M	B	CAPTAIN	RCAPC
HUGHES	FREDERICK	NEWTON	CAPTAIN	
HUNTER (MM)	J	WALTER	CAPTAIN	
IRVING	GORDON	ERNEST	A/CAPTAIN	
JEWETT	C	F	LIEUTENANT	
JOHNSTON	EARLE	E	LIEUTENANT	
JOHNSTON	GEORGE	MCDONALD	LIEUTENANT	
KELLY	JOHN	K	CAPTAIN	RCAMC
KENNEDY	D	S	CAPTAIN	
KENNEDY	WILFRID		LIEUTENANT	
KREEWIN	HAROLD		LIEUTENANT	
KULYK	N		LIEUTENANT	
LAING	ALEXANDER	GEORGE	CAPTAIN	
LARKE	A	E	H/CAPTAIN	CHAPLAIN SVCS
LAVOIE	ARNOLD	JAMES	MAJOR	
LINDOP	STUART	H. W.	LIEUTENANT	
LINDSAY	K	M	LIEUTENANT	RCEME (42 LAD)
LITTLE	KENNETH	WAYNE	LIEUTENANT	
LOWREY	R	E	H/CAPTAIN	CHAPLAIN SVCS
LUTON	W	C	LIEUTENANT	
MacDONALD	J	J	H/CAPTAIN	CHAPLAIN SVCS
MALONEY	J	H	CAPTAIN	RCAMC
MALLETT	DAVID	JOHN	LIEUTENANT	
MARTIN	KENNETH	FAIRWEATHER	LIEUTENANT	
MARTIN	C	A	LIEUTENANT	
MATTHEWSON	G	A	LIEUTENANT	
McARTHUR	H	T	LIEUTENANT	ATTACHED
McBAIN	HAROLD	ERNEST	CAPTAIN	
McDOUGALL	GLENHOLME	LLOYD	MAJOR	
McGREGOR	G	J	CAPTAIN	RCAMC
McKECHNIE	W	H	LIEUTENANT	
McKENZIE	ALEXANDER	DAVID	CAPTAIN	
McLEAN	JOSEPH	A	MAJOR	
McLEOD	WILLIAM	JOHN	LIEUTENANT	
MERRYWEATHER	ROY	CORNEY	LIEUTENANT	
MILES	EDWARD	ANDREW WILLLIAMS	MAJOR	
MILLS	D	W	LIEUTENANT	
MILLYARD	D	M	LIEUTENANT	RCCS
MORETON	JOHN	PORTER	CAPTAIN	
MUSTARD	WILLIAM	T	CAPTAIN	RCAMC

LAST NAME	FIRST NAME	MIDDLE NAME	RANK	REMARKS
NASH	THOMAS	BOYD	LIEUTENANT-COLONEL	
NIEMAN	E		LIEUTENANT	
ORR	J	A	CAPTAIN	
ORR	JAMES	I	LIEUTENANT	
PATERSON	JOHN		LIEUTENANT	
PATTERSON	C	W	LIEUTENANT	
PEAT	W	S	LIEUTENANT	
PERRIN	KENNETH	ELIAS	CAPTAIN	
PERRY	F		LIEUTENANT	
PERRY	J	G	LIEUTENANT	
PIEPGRASS	LYLE	BOYSON	LIEUTENANT	
PITTMAN	E	A	MAJOR (COLONEL)	
PUNCHARD	C	H	MAJOR	
PURDY	STANLEY	ROBERT	MAJOR	
RANCE	P		CAPTAIN	RCAMC
REARDON	EDWARD	HENRY	CAPTAIN	
REDDEN	JOHN	HENRY	CAPTAIN	
REED	IRWIN	JAMES	LIEUTENANT	
RHODES	R	S	CAPTAIN	
RIDDELL	S	R	LIEUTENANT	
ROBERTS	JOHN	MILNE	LIEUTENANT	
ROBINSON	RICHARD		MAJOR	
ROSE	A	H	LIEUTENANT	ATTACHED
ROSS	C	S	A/CAPTAIN	
ROSS	D	W	LIEUTENANT	
SAUL	G	M	CAPTAIN	
SCARRETT	LESLIE	RYDER	LIEUTENANT	
SCHOLTEN	DICK	AREND	LIEUTENANT	
SCRIMGER	ALEXANDER	CARRON	A/CAPTAIN	
SHELL	GORDON	LAWRENCE	A/MAJOR	
SHUTE	D	M	LIEUTENANT	
SILCOX	ALBERT	PHILLIPS	H/CAPTAIN	CHAPLAIN SVCS

LAST NAME	FIRST NAME	MIDDLE NAME	RANK	REMARKS
SMITH	CLIVE	ALBERT	LIEUTENANT	
SMITH	JOEL	KITCHEN	CAPTAIN	
SMITH	RAY	CLARKE	LIEUTENANT	
STEWART	DONALD	EDWIN	CAPTAIN	
STRACHAN (VC)	HARCUS		MAJOR	
SUMMERS	JOHN	LESLIE	CAPTAIN	
TALBOT	EDWARD	CRYDERMAN	LIEUTENANT	
TAYLOR	R	M	LIEUTENANT	
THURBURN	HECTOR	MCLAIN	LIEUTENANT	
TRICKEY	A	G	LIEUTENANT	
VAN CAMP	H		LIEUTENANT	
WATSON	ALEXANDER	WILLIAM	LIEUTENANT	
WATSON	H	D	LIEUTENANT	
WATTS	A	F	CAPTAIN	
WEIR	E	A	CAPTAIN	RCEME (42 LAD)
WHITE	R	T	LIEUTENANT	
WHITE	ROBERT	ARTHUR	LIEUTENANT	
WICKS	S	G	A/CAPTAIN	RCCS
WIGG	K	R	LIEUTENANT	
WILEY	G	M	LIEUTENANT	
WILLIAMS	ARTHUR	LEONARD	CAPTAIN	CDC
WILLIAMS	A	R	LIEUTENANT	
WILMOTT	D	M	LIEUTENANT	
WILSON	V	B	CAPTAIN	CDC
WOOD	S	W	LIEUTENANT	ATTACHED
WOODS	GEORGE	RAYNOR	LIEUTENANT	
WOTHERSPOON	GORDON	DORWARD DE SALABERRY	LIEUTENANT-COLONEL	
WRIGHT	MARSTON	HOWARD	MAJOR	
WYATT	J	L	MAJOR	
YOUNG	WALLACE	HAY	LIEUTENANT	
ZACHARUK	A	H	LIEUTENANT	

PART II

ENLISTED MEN OF THE SOUTH ALBERTA REGIMENT, JUNE 1940–MAY 1945.

This roll has been compiled from a variety of sources and is as complete as the existing records allow. There may be omissions or inaccuracies, particularly in the spelling of names, where sometimes two or even three alternatives existed. The list includes men who were attached to the Regiment and the notes column specifies from which corps they were attached. Some men started out serving with the Regiment but were transferred to or attached from other arms as required. Reorganization caused much change in an attached soldier's parent unit, hence some soldiers have three different designations in the notes column. Ranks have not been included in this nominal roll, nor have soldiers who were attached from other units for temporary purposes (such as troops in transit or training).

Explanation of Notes

1. Soldier served with the regiment in Northwest Europe during hostilities.
2. Soldier was later commissioned and served with the regiment as an officer.
3. Soldier was attached to unit from Royal Canadian Ordnance Corps.
4. Soldier served in 42 Light Aid Detachment, RCOC (later RCEME).
5. Soldier was killed in action, died of wounds or died while in service.
6. Soldier was serving with unit but belonged to the Royal Canadian Army Service Corps.
7. Soldier was attached to unit from Royal Canadian Corps of Signals.
8. Soldier was attached from or belonged to the Royal Canadian Electrical and Mechanical Engineers.

NUMBER	LAST NAME	FIRST NAME	MIDDLE NAME	JOIN SAR	NOTES
M/45385	ABEL	GEORGE	THOMAS	1940/06/10	
H/8475	ABERDEEN	A	R	1943/10/04	1
F/57303	ABOUD	C	G	1944/12/17	1
M/45317	ABOUSSAFY	MICHAEL		1940/06/14	1
M/44867	ADAMS	BRUCE	JOSEPH	1940/06/07	
M/45383	ADAMS	GERALD	CHARLES DESMOND	1940/06/21	2
M/45255	ADAMS	JOHN	WILLIAM	1940/06/14	1
M/45273	ADAMS	SAMUEL	LEWIS	1940/06/11	
B/149704	ADAMS	WILLIAM	R	1944/11/04	1
L/84683	AICHELE	A		1942/05/30	
M/45715	AIRHART	HUGH		1940/11/22	1, 6

NUMBER	LAST NAME	FIRST NAME	MIDDLE NAME	JOIN SAR	NOTES
A/107349	AITKEN	W	R	1944/10/14	1
B/135359	ALDRIDGE	T	L	1944/10/19	1
G/4546	ALLEN	ARNOLD	REILSTON	1944/10/08	1, 5
B/132381	ALLEN	CLIFF	E	1944/11/04	1
L/108201	ALLEN	G	A. D.	1945/03/25	1
A/58206	ALLEN	G	E	1943/01/01	3, 4
C/38236	ALLEN	J	R	1943/12/23	
M/45338	ALLEN	JOSEPH	WILLIAM	1940/06/18	1
B/31905	ALLEN	L	G	BY 1944/05	7
M/44776	ALLEN	MAURICE	REGINALD	1940/06/06	
B/135951	ALLEYNE	S	ST. A	BY 1944/05	6
G/51420	ALLISON	H	E	1944/09/16	1

NUMBER	LAST NAME	FIRST NAME	MIDDLE NAME	JOIN SAR	NOTES
L/84646	ALTICE	F		1942/05/30	
M/45329	AMBLIE	ARNE	RIEDER	1940/06/19	
M/45199	AMBURY	CHARLES	GARNER	1940/06/13	
A/108854	AMEY	HARVEY	HERBERT	1944/10/19	1, 5
D/139605	AMYOTTE	MAURICE	W	1943/10/04	1
M/45565	AMYOTTE	MOISE		1940/06/26	1
H/20674	ANDERSON	A	J	1943/01/08	1, 3, 4, 8
M/45792	ANDERSON	ALBERT		1941/02/19	
M/45621	ANDERSON	ANTHONY	JOSEPH	1940/06/26	
M/45604	ANDERSON	ARTHUR		1940/06/24	1
M/28835	ANDERSON	CHARLES	R	1941/03/25	1
L/51382	ANDERSON	D	E	1943/10/04	1
M/7809	ANDERSON	D	F	1945/03/25	1
M/44864	ANDERSON	EDWIN		1940/06/08	
M/45519	ANDERSON	GLEN	LEWIS	1940/06/22	
M/106494	ANDERSON	H	L	1944/10/11	1
M/49010	ANDERSON	JAMES		1940/06/27	1
M/45705	ANDERSON	JAMES	GORDON	1940/11/22	1, 6
M/45160	ANDERSON	JOHN	DONALD	1940/06/11	1
M/28367	ANDERSON	L		1941/11/02	
M/45662	ANDERSON	ROBERT		1940/07/08	
M/45403	ANDERSON	SAMUEL	WILLIAM	1940/06/19	
A/117327	ANDREW	WALTER	HAROLD	1943/12/23	1, 5
A/87268	ANDREWS	G	E	1944/10/05	1
M/65666	ANDREWS	P	E	1941/08/16	
B/142281	ANGLESTAD	E	T	1943/12/23	1
H/77609	ANGUS	L	L	1943/07/16	1
K/49828	ANNAND	A	J	1943/10/04	1
M/45617	ANONSON	GEORGE		1940/06/27	
B/114888	ARDAGH	R	B	1944/02/04	3, 4
M/65840	ARENDS	J	B	1941/08/16	
L/106486	ARKLES	JOSEPH	WHITE	1944/10/19	1
M/45314	ARMITSTEAD	RICHARD	LAWRENCE	1940/06/12	
M/44775	ARMOUR	CHARLES	REDVERSE	1940/06/06	
M/104447	ARMSTRONG	E	L	1943/08/20	
M/44993	ARMSTRONG	GEORGE	JOHN	1940/06/11	1
L/64275	ARMSTRONG	GEORGE	McLEAN	1942/07/26	1
B/134665	ARMSTRONG	J	T	1943/10/04	
M/45630	ARMSTRONG	JAMES		1940/06/28	1
M/45556	ARMSTRONG	JAMES	EDWARD	1940/06/24	
M/44887	ARMSTRONG	JOHN	DUNCAN	1940/06/08	
M/45077	ARMSTRONG	KENNETH	GEORGE	1940/06/08	1
M/45451	ARNAULT	JOSEPH	THEOTPHILE	1940/06/21	1
M/45377	ARNELL	THOMAS		1940/06/18	
M/66024	ARNOLD	A	D	1941/08/16	
M/45064	ARROWSMITH	SIDNEY		1940/06/11	1
D/36102	ARSENAULT	E	A	1945/02/07	1, 6
G/27834	ARSNEAULT	J	R. L.	1944/11/22	1, 6
M/57012	ARTINDALE	KARL	ZENAS	1942/07/26	1
L/74306	ASHBACHER	R	H	1943/10/04	1
M/45375	ASHMORE	EDWARD	BRIAN	1940/06/10	1
M/45038	ASHMORE	FELIX		1940/06/10	
M/45756	ASPESLET	ANTON	OSCAR	1941/02/19	
M/45343	ASPESLET	LAWRENCE	EDWIN	1940/06/17	1
B/80733	ASTLE	G	W	1945/03/24	1
A/109098	ATKINS	E	W	1944/11/16	1
M/44891	ATKINSON	ALBERT	JOSEPH	1940/06/10	1
M/45048	ATKINSON	FRANK	EDWIN	1940/06/11	1
F/40867	ATWOOD	G	W	1945/03/25	1
F/33101	AUCOIN	EARL	J	1943/10/04	1
F/35279	AUSTIN	W	F	1943/10/04	1
L/36427	AXTELL	B		1943/09/24	1
M/8730	AYLWIN	L	N	1945/03/24	1
M/45080	AYRES	RAYMOND	WILLIAM RODNEY	1940/06/10	1
M/45628	BABIUK	HARRY	EMANUEL	1940/06/13	
K/15901	BAGG	DOUGLAS		1944/12/08	1
M/44979	BAHTOON	LEOPOLD		1940/06/10	

NUMBER	LAST NAME	FIRST NAME	MIDDLE NAME	JOIN SAR	NOTES
—	BAILEY	J	O	—	
D/47028	BAILY	W	C	1943/10/03	1, 6
B/63152	BAIRD	H	G	1943/07/02	1
B/119018	BAKER	ARTHUR	ERNEST	1944/11/04	1
M/45312	BAKER	EDMUND	CHARLES	1940/06/07	
M/51128	BAKKEN	A	E	1943/10/04	1
M/44810	BALDRY	JAMES	STANLEY	1940/06/06	
M/45318	BALDWIN	WILLIAM	SEPTIMUS	1940/06/14	
M/45723	BALFOUR	MELVILLE	DURIE	1940/11/22	1
M/45280	BALL	ALFRED	CHARLES WILLIAM	1940/06/14	
L/64148	BALL	FREDERICK	WALTER	1942/07/26	
M/45189	BALL	SEPTIMUS	TELFORD	1940/06/13	
D/131710	BALLARD	R	E	1943/10/04	1
C/121170	BANKEY	B	G	1944/09/16	1
M/45110	BANNERMAN	COLIN	ALEXANDER	1940/06/10	
A/22618	BANNISTER	K	R	1942/12/11	3, 4
M/28828	BARBER	C		1941/03/25	
C/94981	BARBER	W	M	1944/02/04	3, 4
M/45619	BARBER	WILLIAM	CLINTON	1940/06/26	1
M/45288	BARBY	OTTO	ALEXANDER	1940/06/11	
M/7512	BARCLAY	J		1944/10/05	1
D/131301	BARIL	B		1943/10/04	1
F/86635	BARKHOUSE	L	K	1944/05/06	1
M/44844	BARLOW	TOM		1940/06/08	
M/45366	BARNES	ALFRED	GEORGE	1940/06/19	
M/45503	BARNES	HAROLD		1940/06/24	
M/101151	BARNETT	HOWARD	E	1942/06/02	1
L/84607	BARNETT	JOHN	J	1942/05/30	1
L/84556	BARNETT	P	A	1942/05/30	
B/95326	BARR	H	R	1942/05/14	3, 4
M/45469	BARR	ROBERT		1940/06/19	1
B/137436	BARRE	M	C	1943/10/04	
L/36242	BARROWMAN	WILLIAM	LONGMUIR B.	1943/09/24	1
M/44899	BARTLETT	JOHN	FREDERICK	1940/06/08	1, 5
M/45098	BARTOLO	HENRY		1940/06/12	1
M/44945	BASARABA	NICHOLAS	WILLIAM	1940/06/08	
M/45315	BASKERVILLE	JOHN		1940/06/12	
L/53789	BATEMAN	ARNOLD	EDWARD	1943/07/16	1, 5
D/76574	BATTY	H	L	1944/03/19	1
M/45254	BAUM	RUDOLPH		1940/06/14	
K/76871	BAWDEN	JAMES	W	1943/07/02	1
D/76386	BAXTER	G	C	1944/03/19	
D/142714	BAXTER	J	A	1944/09/13	1
D/109827	BAXTER	W		1944/03/19	
H/63985	BAYKO	STEVE		1943/10/04	1
M/45538	BAYNHAM	WESLEY		1940/06/25	
M/45512	BEACON	ELMER	CHARLES	1940/06/12	
M/44795	BEAN	BRUCE	ELTON	1940/06/06	1
M/44982	BEATON	JOHN	EDWARD	1940/06/10	
M/45244	BEATON	WILLIAM	ALBERT	1940/06/10	
M/45362	BEATTIE	JOHN		1940/06/17	
M/40829	BEATTY	G	J	1940/07/17	3
M/45122	BEAUDET	LOUIS	ARTHUR	1940/06/10	
M/44769	BEAUDRY	EUGENE	LOUIS JOSEPH	1940/06/05	1
K/69039	BEAUPRE	W	A	1943/10/04	1
C/38407	BEAVER	J	T	1944/12/21	1, 4, 8
M/44976	BEDFORD	CYRIL	HERBERT	1940/06/10	
M/44811	BEGG	DUGALD	ALEXANDER	1940/06/07	
D/139356	BEIGLEMAN	D		1943/10/04	
M/45741	BELCOURT	MIKE		1941/02/19	
M/63666	BELCOURT	W		1944/03/19	1
M/66040	BELL	A	A	1941/08/16	1
B/115400	BELL	A	D	1945/01/18	1
M/45527	BELL	ALVIN		1940/06/19	1, 5
D/132682	BELL	F	C. R.	1943/10/04	1
M/45435	BELL	GORDON	WILBUR	1940/06/13	
B/136079	BELL	JOHN	A	1943/10/04	1

NUMBER	LAST NAME	FIRST NAME	MIDDLE NAME	JOIN SAR	NOTES	NUMBER	LAST NAME	FIRST NAME	MIDDLE NAME	JOIN SAR	NOTES
M/45355	BELL	OLIVER	JAMES	1940/06/13	1	M/44937	BOTTINEAU	ARCHIE	PETER	1940/06/07	
M/44778	BELLAMY	ARTHUR	JAMES	1940/06/06		M/45578	BOULAY	HECTOR		1940/06/26	
M/29242	BELLAMY	L	G	1941/10/04		M/45412	BOULTON	GEORGE	FRASER	1940/06/17	
M/45747	BELLINGHAM	HORACE	GEORGE	1941/02/19		B/159601	BOURNE	T	R. N.	1945/04/25	1
K/50705	BELSEY	FREDERICK	CHARLES	1944/09/16	1, 5	D/137537	BOUTHILLIER	H	P	1943/12/03	1, 6
M/45065	BELSHAM	DONALD	EDMUND	1940/06/12		A/65857	BOWDEN	W	J	1945/03/25	1
K/74386	BENNETT	A	W	1945/03/09	1, 8	M/45596	BOWDITCH	GEORGE		1940/06/25	
M/44773	BENNETT	CECIL	ALEXANDER	1940/06/06		B/157520	BOWEN	D	P	1945/04/25	1
M/45809	BENNETT	DOUGLAS	E	1941/05/21	1	M/45114	BOWIE	JOHN		1940/06/10	
M/45795	BENNETT	GEORGE	LOUIS	1941/02/19	1	L/84679	BOWLIN	J		1942/05/30	
M/12454	BENNETT	K	R	1941/10/04		K/40563	BOWMAN	E	G	1945/03/25	1
M/45794	BENNETT	L	T	1941/03/26		D/77144	BOYCE	GEORGE	R	1944/03/19	1
D/131489	BENNETT	M	R	1943/10/04	1	D/77277	BOYCE	HARRY	R	1944/03/19	1
L/58777	BENNETT	THOMAS	FRANCIS	1942/07/26	1	M/45165	BOYCE	NORMAN	JAMES	1940/06/10	
—	BENSON	H	J	—		F/43708	BOYD	H	G	1945/03/02	1
M/45187	BENTLEY	GEORGE	RYERSON	1940/06/12		H/14101	BOYER	ALBERT	EDWARD	1944/12/08	1
D/76358	BENTLEY	J		1944/03/19		B/133561	BOYES	DOUGLAS	W	1943/10/04	1
M/45784	BEREZAN	MICHAEL		1941/02/19		M/45726	BOYLE	GORDON	RUSSELL	1940/11/22	
M/45398	BERGE	OLE	BERNSTON	1940/06/18	1	M/45250	BRABANT	THOMAS	NOEL	1940/06/13	1
M/44960	BERGET	WILLIAM	OLIVER	1940/06/08		K/12092	BRADBURN	W	E	1940/09/18	
L/84560	BERGIN	L	C. J.	1942/05/30		M/45095	BRADBURY	EDMUND	ERSKINE	1940/06/12	
M/103468	BERGQUIST	HARVEY	LEE ROY	1943/07/02	1	A/86765	BRADLEY	J	K	1944/05/06	1
M/28832	BERGQUIST	MARVIN	EDWARD	1941/03/25	1, 5	M/45450	BRADSHAW	GORDON		1940/06/21	1
B/19744	BERLINQUETTE	WILLIAM	JOSEPH	1941/10/27		K/50145	BRAITHWAITE	LLOYD	S	1944/07/08	1
M/45190	BERNARD	NOE	JOSEPH	1940/06/13	6	M/66032	BRANCHFLOWER	R	A	1941/08/16	1
M/50571	BERNAS	F	J	1941/08/16		M/45269	BRAUNBERGER	FLOYD	LLOYD	1940/06/14	1
L/36428	BERNNIER	R	A	1943/09/24	1	M/44959	BRAY	GUY	LEE	1940/06/08	
M/44757	BERRY	ADRIAN	DOUGLAS	1940/06/05		M/45426	BRAY	JOHN	ROBERT	1940/06/19	
M/3646	BERTIE	J	L	1943/10/04		D/76330	BRAYTON	W	J	1944/03/19	1
B/62941	BERTON	E	J	1945/03/25	1	L/84709	BREADNER	A	W	1942/05/30	
D/76561	BERTRAND	RAYMOND	H	1944/03/19	1	M/45806	BRESSLER	ALBERT		1941/05/21	1
M/44849	BESSON	HOWARD	JOSEPH	1940/06/08	1	M/45023	BREWER	CHARLES	EDWARD	1940/06/08	1, 5
L/84585	BETTCHER	A	L	1942/05/30	1	D/122733	BRIAND	H		1942/12/18	3, 4
M/45473	BEVAN	PHILIP	GORDON	1940/06/11	1	M/45113	BRIARD	FREDERICK	EDWARD	1940/06/11	
M/45516	BEVINGTON	ALLAN	SYLVESTER	1940/06/22		M/45605	BRINK	ALBERT	ALLAN	1940/06/24	
M/44868	BICKLE	LEX	EDWARD	1940/06/07		A/116546	BRINKMAN	E	W. L.	1945/02/28	1
M/45242	BILINSKY	STANLEY		1940/06/10		M/104610	BROADBENT	A	G	1943/08/20	1
D/117060	BILODEAU	J		1942/04/01	3	M/102541	BROADBENT	H	P	1943/03/05	1
D/22896	BIRCHARD	N	E	1943/03/20	1, 3, 4, 8	L/84555	BROBERG	ROBERT	ENOCH	1942/05/30	1
L/100420	BIRD	GERALD	E	1943/10/04	1	M/44765	BRODERICK	ARTHUR	WARD	1940/06/05	
M/45289	BIRKENSTOCK	ALFRED	THEODORE	1940/06/14		D/76300	BRODERICK	J	J	1944/09/10	1
M/28818	BISHOP	K	C	1941/03/25		L/64077	BROOK	CHARLES	ERNEST	1942/07/26	1
L/84639	BJOLVERUD	K	O	1942/05/30		D/76038	BROUSSEAU	JOSEPH	FERNAND	1944/10/14	1
M/102328	BLACK	SIDNEY	J	1943/10/04	1	M/45700	BROWN	ELSDON		1940/11/22	
F/56479	BLACKBURN	R	E	1944/10/05	1	M/45638	BROWN	HUGH	ALEXANDER	1940/06/28	1
M/45798	BLACKLOCK	ROBERT	HENRY	1941/02/19		M/45212	BROWN	LEWIS		1940/06/15	
M/45139	BLACKSTOCK	CECIL	PITT	1940/06/13	1	D/16301	BROWN	R	E	1943/04/21	1
M/44994	BLAIN	LAWRENCE	BONHEUR	1940/06/10		M/45590	BROWN	ROBERT	WILLIAM	1940/06/25	1
L/84614	BLAMPIED	H	G	1942/05/30		M/45041	BROWN	THOMAS	HERON	1940/06/10	
D/76549	BLANCHETTE	G	M	1944/03/19		D/77829	BROWN	V	A	1944/03/19	1
M/49005	BLOMGREEN	EDWIN	BERNARD	1940/06/26		M/44840	BROWNING	CHARLES	BAIN	1940/06/08	1
B/133562	BLOW	E	E	1943/10/04	1	M/45200	BROWNLEE	BENJAMIN	CLYDE	1940/06/12	
F/32869	BLUNDEN	ROBERT	M	1943/10/04	1	L/64284	BRUCE	ROBERT	ALEXANDER	1942/07/26	1
A/86601	BOAKES	ARTHUR	W	1944/09/16	1	M/44884	BRUNTON	DAVID	RAMSAY	1940/06/08	
M/45781	BOBROSKE	EMIL		1941/02/19	1	B/32724	BRYARS	J	T	BY 1944/05	7
M/45117	BOHN	HELMUT	JAMES	1940/06/10		M/105404	BRYDGES	F	H	1943/11/19	
M/45302	BOHNE	LORIL	REDFORD	1940/06/12		M/45739	BRYDGES	GEORGE	CLINTON	1941/02/19	1
M/45121	BOLES	ALLAN	LLOYD	1940/06/10		M/45743	BRYGADYR	MICHAEL	HARRY	1941/02/19	
A/107611	BOLTON	H	D	1944/10/05	1	H/8779	BUCHAN	G	E	1944/05/06	1
M/45046	BOND	M	EDWARD	1940/06/11		M/45393	BUCHANAN	HUGH		1940/06/19	1, 6
A/116445	BONDY	F	J	1943/10/04		M/44796	BUCHANAN	TERENCE		1940/06/06	
D/122707	BONIN	M		1942/04/01	3, 4	A/57904	BUCHANAN	W	D	1943/09/10	1
B/69965	BONNELL	EDGAR	J	1944/08/11	1	K/66122	BUCKBERRY	R	C	1943/09/24	
M/36462	BOOTH	R	E	1940/10/17		M/44797	BUCKHOLZ	EMIL	EDWARD	1940/06/06	
D/142453	BOOTHMAN	R		1944/09/12	1	M/45535	BUDD	ALBERT	VICTOR	1940/06/24	
H/14285	BORGER	E	A	1945/02/26	1	B/50035	BUDREAU	C	H	1943/08/20	1
M/45376	BOROSKAE	MIKE		1940/06/14		M/41081	BULLEN	FREDERICK	CYRIL	1940/06/05	
M/45125	BORTON	FREDERICK		1940/06/11	1	M/107824	BULLEY	W	A	1944/12/17	1

NUMBER	LAST NAME	FIRST NAME	MIDDLE NAME	JOIN SAR	NOTES
M/45081	BULLYMORE	GORDON	WILLIAM FREDERICK	1940/06/10	1
M/45339	BULMER	THOMAS	MORDY	1940/06/17	
M/45704	BUNDY	EDGAR	FOSTER	1940/11/22	1
L/64603	BURGESS	GLENN	DEWEY	1942/07/26	1
M/45352	BURGHARDT	CHARLES	JOE	1940/06/14	
B/143064	BURKE	W	J	1943/12/23	1
B/148981	BURLEY	H	H. R.	1945/03/01	1
M/45129	BURMASTER	ROY	EDWARD	1940/06/11	
B/61049	BURT	S	V	1941/11/25	3
H/102841	BURTON	W	C	1944/10/10	1
B/157009	BUTCHER	H	A	1945/03/25	1
H/64212	BUTCHER	JOHN	D	1943/10/04	1
L/100421	BUTLER	S	C	1943/10/04	1
A/109651	BUTLER	W	G	1945/03/25	1
M/45817	BUTTERWORTH	J	E	1941/06/03	
B/70124	CADE	K	L	1943/07/02	1
M/45082	CAHILL	CLARENCE	PATRICK	1940/06/10	
B/137430	CAIRD	E	R	1943/10/04	1
M/45706	CAIRNS	DONALD		1940/11/22	
M/44812	CALDER	GEORGE	GORDON	1940/06/07	
M/15902	CALKINS	JOHN	WILLETT	1940/06/24	
M/45740	CALLIOU	HENRY	PATRICK	1941/02/19	
B/115810	CAMERON	D	G	1944/10/19	1
M/44787	CAMERON	JAMES	HENRY	1940/06/06	
H/60112	CAMERON	P		1943/07/16	
L/36092	CAMPBELL	B	A	1943/11/19	1
M/44926	CAMPBELL	DUNCAN		1940/06/06	
M/44833	CAMPBELL	GORDON	ALEXANDER	1940/06/06	
L/105366	CAMPBELL	J	A	1945/03/21	1
F/60073	CAMPBELL	J	ELLIOT	1942/06/04	3
M/45132	CAMPBELL	JAMES	RAYMOND	1940/06/11	
M/45409	CAMPBELL	ROY	ALEXANDER	1940/06/14	1
H/99297	CAMPBELL	T	D. W.	1943/10/15	1, 3, 4, 8
M/49007	CANNADY	LYNN	GLENN	1940/06/26	
B/138402	CAREY	E	P	1945/04/12	1
M/45049	CARLSON	JOE	AUGUST	1940/06/11	
L/36212	CARLSON	S		1943/09/24	1
H/10276	CARPENTER	VICTOR	LLOYD	1944/10/08	1, 5
F/52639	CARR	WILLIAM	BORDEN	1944/10/05	1, 5
L/36349	CARRAGHER	JAMES	CHARLIE	1943/09/24	1, 5
M/45191	CARRUTHERS	WILLIAM		1940/06/12	
M/44774	CARSON	PERCY	THOMAS	1940/06/06	
L/54874	CARVELL	G	D	1943/02/12	1
M/44919	CASAVANT	HENRY		1940/06/06	
H/9706	CASE	JAMES	L	1944/09/01	1
M/45099	CASEY	JOHN	JOSEPH	1940/06/13	
M/45727	CASSIDY	TEJUANIS		1940/11/22	
K/51717	CATTAPAN	E	A	1945/04/16	1
B/116815	CHADWICK	F	W	1945/03/24	1
M/45495	CHAMBERS	GEORGE		1940/06/21	
M/45641	CHAMBERS	GIRVEN	LESLIE	1940/06/28	
M/45755	CHANEY	ABB	THOMAS	1941/02/19	
L/102576	CHANEY	VINCENT		1943/09/02	1
L/102745	CHAPLIN	W	S	1943/09/24	1
M/45627	CHAPMAN	ARTHUR	FLEET	1940/06/14	
M/45654	CHAPMAN	PAUL	COREY	1940/06/26	1
M/45670	CHAPMAN	ROY	CECIL	1940/07/16	
M/44832	CHARTRES	JAMES	CLAMPETT	1940/06/06	
L/65326	CHASE	LLOYD	FOSTER	1942/07/26	
M/45134	CHATTERS	GEORGE	LLOYD	1940/06/12	
K/66453	CHENEY	J	D	1943/08/20	1
M/45592	CHERNIWCHAN	WILLIAM		1940/06/25	
M/45580	CHERRINGTON	WILLIAM	THOMAS	1940/06/26	
M/44995	CHESTERMAN	GEORGE		1940/06/10	1, 6
M/45721	CHILDS	VICTOR		1940/11/22	
M/65719	CHIPCHASE	F	C	1943/11/07	
L/108117	CHIPPERFIELD	J	S	1945/03/25	1

NUMBER	LAST NAME	FIRST NAME	MIDDLE NAME	JOIN SAR	NOTES
M/45461	CHISHOLM	ARCHIBALD	ARTHUR	1940/06/21	
M/45344	CHISHOLM	STERLING	ARNOLD	1940/06/17	1
M/45780	CHRISTIAN	HUGH	JAMES	1941/02/19	1
M/44996	CHRISTIE	WILLIAM	DUNCAN	1940/06/10	1
M/44949	CHRISTIENSEN	VILHELM	EMIL	1940/06/08	
M/45568	CITULSKI	NICK		1940/06/27	
M/45361	CLARK	FRED	WATSON	1940/06/19	1, 5
M/44779	CLARK	JOHN	DIXON	1940/06/06	
M/45258	CLARK	ROY	KENNETH	1940/06/14	
K/75476	CLARKE	H		1943/10/04	1
L/22773	CLARKE	H	E	1943/09/24	1
M/44904	CLARKE	HUGH	HARDING	1940/06/07	
D/158812	CLARKE	I	M	1945/04/14	1
B/138803	CLARKE	J	R	1943/10/04	1
M/45599	CLARKIN	JAMES	ANTHONY	1940/06/26	
L/53817	CLAUSEN	E	THOMAS	1943/10/04	1
M/65996	CLAYDON	C	A. G.	1941/08/16	
M/45067	CLEGHORN	WILLIAM		1940/06/12	
D/142275	CLENDENNING	D	R	1944/10/19	1
M/45031	CLIPPERTON	ROBERT	WILTON	1940/06/10	1
M/45763	COATES	ROBERT	McLAREN	1941/02/19	1
M/44997	COFFIN	DELBERT		1940/06/10	
L/106532	COLBRIDGE	D	W	1945/03/30	1
H/18006	COLE	V	A	1944/11/24	1
M/45324	COLLINS	JAMES		1940/06/13	
B/133295	COLLINS	R	F	1943/09/02	
H/95371	COLWELL	DEXTER		1942/07/26	1, 5
M/45562	CONLEY	GORDON		1940/06/24	1
M/43455	CONNAUTON	JAMES	DOUGLAS	1941/02/19	
L/67956	CONNORS	C	E	1945/04/12	1
B/62957	CONWAY	F	J	1944/10/28	1
M/31536	COOK	HAROLD	LAMBERT	1940/11/22	
M/44985	COOPER	HOWARD		1940/06/10	
B/139600	COOPER	JAMES	R	1943/10/04	1
M/45150	COOPER	NORMAN	KINGSTON	1940/06/12	
M/106390	COOPER	R	E	1944/09/16	1
M/44961	COOPER	RICHARD	WILFRED WAYNE	1940/06/08	
M/45653	COPPICK	JAMES	BENJAMIN	1940/06/26	1
M/45256	COREY	THEODORE	EDWARD	1940/06/14	
M/65160	CORMACK	J		1941/08/16	
B/4690	CORMIER	E		1945/03/21	1
D/77099	CORNER	LLOYD	ATKINSON	1944/03/19	1, 5
M/44764	CORRIGAN	JOHN	JOSEPH	1940/06/05	
D/76530	COSGROVE	F	J	1944/03/19	1
M/45613	COTE	LOUIS		1940/06/28	
D/23278	COTE	RAYMOND	RICHARD	1941/11/25	1, 3, 5, 8
B/135714	COTTRELL	E	W. M.	1944/10/31	1
D/121924	COUNTRYMAN	R	H	1944/09/21	1
M/45083	COVERT	ALBERT		1940/06/10	1
B/70096	COWLING	W	W	1943/08/20	
M/45259	COX	BLAIR	HENRY	1940/06/14	
M/45471	COYES	JOHN	JOSEPH	1940/06/17	
M/45576	COYLE	ANDREW		1940/06/24	
M/45364	CRABTREE	TOM		1940/06/19	
M/45201	CRAIG	CECIL	JAMES	1940/06/13	1
L/36288	CRAIG	E	F	1943/09/24	1
B/19746	CRAIG	JOHN	FORREST	1941/11/10	
B/107016	CRAIG	LYLE	LEWIS	1945/02/26	1, 5
D/142356	CRAIG	NORMAN	ROY	1944/09/16	1, 5
M/45287	CRAMER	LOUIS	CLARENCE	1940/06/10	
D/76691	CRAWFORD	ROBERT		1944/03/19	1
M/45202	CRAWFORD	ROBERT	EARL	1940/06/13	2
M/28810	CREAMER	GORDON	S	1941/03/25	1
M/45570	CRERAR	HAROLD		1940/06/24	1
M/45569	CRERAR	PERCY	CAMPBELL	1940/06/24	
B/138554	CRESSWELL	J	W	1943/10/04	1
M/44987	CRICHTON	JOHN	THOMPSON	1940/06/06	1

NUMBER	LAST NAME	FIRST NAME	MIDDLE NAME	JOIN SAR	NOTES	NUMBER	LAST NAME	FIRST NAME	MIDDLE NAME	JOIN SAR	NOTES
M/45424	CRITCHLOW	RALPH		1940/06/20		M/45698	DERVAL	EUGENE	ADELARD	1940/08/26	
D/77831	CROSS	E	J	1944/03/19		D/117541	DERVIN	J	R	1944/10/19	1
M/104849	CROSS	RUDOLPH		1943/03/20	1	L/104221	DESJARDINS	P	E	1943/10/04	1
B/19747	CROTINGER	JOHN	CLIFTON	1941/11/27		A/105460	DEVREKER (MM)	ANTHONY		1943/10/04	1, 5
A/87035	CROUCHER	R	V	1944/05/14	1	M/45285	DEWAR	FRANK		1940/06/12	
B/142036	CROWTHER	A	E	1943/10/04	1	M/45371	DEYOUNG	ERNEST		1940/06/18	1
M/45491	CROY	ARTHUR	JAMES	1940/06/21		M/40849	DeZOUCHE	F	C	1940/07/17	3
M/103162	CROZIER	C	R	1943/10/04		M/45476	DICK	DONALD		1940/06/14	1
M/44935	CRUICKSHANK	NORMAN		1940/06/07		M/45531	DICK	JOHN	SINCLAIR	1940/06/27	
L/84576	CRUSH	G	A	1942/05/30		F/31811	DICKSON	J		1944/05/17	3, 8
M/45164	CUMMINS	WILLIAM	LEENDERT	1940/06/10		M/45571	DICKSON	WILLIAM		1940/06/26	
L/74353	CUMPSTONE	WILLIAM	BRUCE	1942/07/26	1, 6	M/45697	DILWORTH	PERCY	GORDON	1940/08/13	
M/45112	CUNDICT	FREDERICK	CYRIL	1940/06/11		K/2523	DINEEN	G	F	1945/03/25	1
K/50931	CUNLIFFE	D	M	1944/10/19	1	M/45022	DINGLE	ARTHUR	EDWARD	1940/06/07	
M/44990	CUNNAH	THOMAS	ISHMAL	1940/06/06		D/77894	DINOVITZER	N		1944/05/06	1
M/35727	CUNNINGHAM	E	J	1941/08/16	1	M/7212	DIXON	MILTON		1940/06/17	
C/100858	CUNNINGHAM	W	T	1944/11/10	1	M/44983	DIXON	WILLIAM	MELVIN	1940/06/05	
M/45423	CURRIE	ALEXANDER		1940/06/20		B/134745	DOBBS	CLIFFORD	J	1943/10/04	1
M/44780	CURRIE	GEORGE	NEWELL	1940/06/06		M/45116	DOHERTY	WALTER	JOSEPH	1940/06/10	
M/44943	CURRIE	STEVE	WALTER	1940/06/10		M/45718	DOMBROSKY	KLOFIS		1940/11/22	
K/62307	CURRIE	W		1943/07/16		M/45746	DONALD	GUY		1941/02/19	
M/45908	CURRIER	EMILE	JOSEPH	1941/07/14	1	D/76550	DONALD	THOMAS		1944/03/19	1, 5
M/44756	CURRY	MONTAGUE	JOSEPH	1940/06/05		M/44962	DONALDSON	ROBERT	HECTOR	1940/06/08	
M/3807	CUSACK	W	P	1941/03/25	1	M/45612	DONKIN	FREDRICK	IVON	1940/06/27	
M/45796	CYR	MAXIME	RIME	1941/02/19		M/45432	DONNELLY	GEORGE		1940/06/21	
D/106138	CYR	W		1942/05/22	3, 4	M/45639	DONNELLY	LLOYD	McNEIL	1940/06/28	
M/40864	DAHL	A	G	1940/09/09	3	M/45100	DOREY	CHARLES	MATTHIAS	1940/06/13	1
B/156054	DALLAIRE	E	C	1945/03/02	1	H/18195	DORRATT	J	P	1945/03/25	1
M/44751	DALLAMORE	RITCHIE	WILLIAM	1940/06/05		M/45559	DORSCHEID	CHARLES	WILLIAM	1940/06/24	
G/7466	DALY	CARSON	W	1944/05/10	1	M/45560	DORSCHEID	EARL	LEE	1940/06/24	
M/35633	DANIELS	S	J	1941/08/16		M/45458	DOUGHERTY	EVERETT	DAVID	1940/06/17	1
M/44878	DANIELS	WILLIAM	PAUL	1940/06/08		F/56305	DOVE	CLARENCE	W	1943/12/23	1
L/105448	DANIELSON	MELVIN	ALEXANDER	1944/10/19	1, 5	L/84567	DOWNEY	A	R	1942/05/30	1
H/104038	DANROTH	C	A	1944/08/16	1	K/38029	DOYLE	T	W	1944/05/10	1
M/28825	DANYSIUK	W		1941/03/25		M/66038	DRAKE	S	A	1941/08/16	
B/69681	DARNBROUGH	A	C	1944/01/14		D/77349	DREYER	K		1944/03/19	1
M/45388	DASKO	JOHN		1940/06/19		M/45505	DRIVER	HARCOURT	ARNOLD	1940/06/14	
M/44883	DAUBERT	PHILIP		1940/06/08	1, 6	K/37124	DRURY	ALEXANDER	CHARLES	1940/06/10	
D/77188	DAUBNEY	F		1944/03/19		M/45558	DRYER	ARNOLD	JOHN	1940/06/24	1
H/16065	DAVIDSON	A	C	1943/07/02		M/45226	DUBE	ALEXANDER		1940/06/15	1
H/64724	DAVIE	E	G	1944/03/18	3	G/21109	DUBE	L	J	1945/04/12	1
M/45394	DAVIES	ERNEST		1940/06/18	1	B/132548	DUBIE	J	A	1944/12/10	1
M/45468	DAVIES	GEORGE		1940/06/19		H/100080	DUBOIS	ALEXANDER	CHARLES	1942/07/26	1
M/45699	DAVIES	JOHN		1940/09/17	1	M/45016	DUDAR	GEORGE		1940/06/05	
K/73516	DAVIES	L		1941/05/15		M/107039	DUFFY	JACK	CHARLES	1944/10/19	1
M/77	DAVIES	S	L	1940/06		M/45188	DUMAS	EMILE		1940/06/10	
H/100143	DAVIS	DAVID	PERSHING	1942/07/26	1	M/44902	DUNBAR	ARTHUR	NORMAN	1940/06/07	
M/45066	DAVIS	PAUL	ARLINGTON	1940/06/12		M/45622	DUNCAN	EDGAR	JOSEPH	1940/06/18	
M/45213	DAWSON	CHARLES		1940/06/14		M/44927	DUNCAN	JOHN		1940/06/06	1
M/45449	DAWSON	STANLEY	TRAYER	1940/06/17		M/45652	DUNDAS	DOUGLAS	ALBERT	1940/06/26	
M/45518	DEAN	GODFREY		1940/06/21		M/105164	DUNN	D	D	1943/10/04	1
M/45645	DEANS	ANDREW	LAWRENCE	1940/06/28		M/45348	DUNNE	THOMAS	HENRY	1940/06/14	
M/45305	DEARAWAY	CHARLES	BROWNLEE	1940/06/11	1, 6	M/45162	DUNNING	ALBERT	HENRY	1940/06/10	1
F/51209	DEBAY	RODERICK	D	1944/05/10	1	M/45494	DURIE	ROBERT	ALEXANDER	1940/06/14	
M/45509	DEBENHAM	CHARLES	WALTER	1940/06/24	1	G/5391	DURLEY	G	A	1944/12/13	1, 6
M/45766	DEDELS	HOWARD	EDWARD	1941/02/19		M/15828	DUROCHER	SOLOMON		1940/06/24	
M/45198	DELEMONT	ROBERT	PAUL JULES	1940/06/10		M/45257	DUTKA	ADAM		1940/06/14	1, 5
H/64117	DELORME	ALBERT	NOEL JOSEPH	1942/07/26	1	M/45391	DWERNICHUK	STEPHEN		1940/06/19	1
M/45144	DEMARIS	VAN	CLEAVE	1940/06/12		M/31523	DYER	WILLIAM	MELTON	1940/11/22	
A/87232	DEMARS	E		1945/01/18	1	M/44930	DYLER	HARRY	ERNEST	1940/06/06	
H/1661	DEMINICK	A	J	1943/10/04	1	M/45716	DZURMAN	JOSEPH		1940/11/22	
A/86789	DENEAU	T	I	1945/03/02	1	L/20116	EADE	D	L	BY 1944/05	1, 7
M/45389	DENINGTON	CLEMENT	WILLIAM	1940/06/18		P/35386	EARLE	C	R	1944/10/05	1
M/104926	DENNING	ALBERT	W	1944/03/31	1	M/45555	EASTMAN	JAMES	WALTER	1940/06/24	1
M/45493	DEPOLD	JAKE	KARL	1940/06/15	1, 6	M/45667	EASTON	EDGAR	VERNON	1940/07/08	1, 5
B/146422	DeRIVIERE	M	J	1945/02/09	1, 6	M/44948	EASTON	WALTER	RALPH	1940/06/08	
M/45286	DEROCHIE	JOHN	McGRUER	1940/06/10		M/45490	EASTWOOD	THOMAS		1940/06/21	1
M/56992	DEROUIN	LOUIS	GEORGE	1942/07/26		M/44925	EDWARDS	DAVID		1940/06/06	

NUMBER	LAST NAME	FIRST NAME	MIDDLE NAME	JOIN SAR	NOTES
M/45301	EDWARDS	EDWIN	GRANT	1940/06/13	1, 5
M/52075	EDWARDS	W	A	1944/05/14	1
M/44952	EGLEN	SHIRLEY	ALBERT	1940/06/10	
M/45292	EHLERT	ELMER	MAX	1940/06/12	
M/45646	ELLIOTT	WILLIAM		1940/06/28	
M/45499	ELLIOTT	WILLIAM		1940/06/21	
B/137328	ELLIS	C	N	1944/04/07	1
A/116036	ELLIS	W	H. C.	1945/01/30	1
M/44866	ELY	EMERY	ERNEST	1940/06/07	1, 5
B/133249	ENGEL	ALFRED	J	1943/09/24	1
M/45203	ENGLISH	JOSEPH	JAMES	1940/06/13	
M/45457	ENGSTROM	ELIS	ANDREW	1940/06/14	
K/49671	ENNIS	H	E	1945/04/16	1
M/44917	ERVEN	LESLIE	BICKNELL	1940/06/05	1
M/10747	ERWIN	GEORGE		1940/06/12	
B/8446	ESCH	G	J	1944/06/06	1, 4, 8
M/24017	EVANS	ALBERT		1940/07/01	
M/44794	EVANS	ALBERT		1940/06/07	
M/44813	EVANS	GEORGE	DAVIES	1940/06/07	1
A/105434	EVANS	LYLE	ALEXANDER	1944/02/25	1, 5
K/48865	EVANS	W	R	1944/10/19	1
M/45815	EWING	JOHN	McKENZIE	1941/06/03	
M/44896	FADDEN	GORDON	ELMER	1940/06/08	
A/105409	FAHRER	JEROME	W	1943/10/04	1
M/44814	FAIRHURST	ROBERT		1940/06/07	1
M/45145	FAKAS	WILLIAM	BILL	1940/06/12	
M/44881	FARQUHAR	CHARLES		1940/06/08	1
M/45448	FARQUHARSON	JAMES		1940/06/21	1
M/101120	FARRELL	A	M	1943/02/12	1, 3, 4, 8
H/19947	FARRELL	REX	ALBERT	1942/07/26	1
D/76409	FARRELL	V	A	1944/03/19	1
B/136175	FARROW	E	L	1943/10/04	
M/45810	FAST	C	R	1941/05/21	1
M/45455	FAULKNER	ALBERT		1940/06/21	1
A/44112	FEARN	C	B	1944	1
F/87536	FENGLER	GEORGE		1942/07/26	
H/64133	FENGLER	HERBERT	WALTER	1942/07/26	1
M/45690	FERGSTAD	GEORGE	AUGUST	1940/08/12	
M/44851	FERGUSON	JAMES	VERNON	1940/06/08	
M/50737	FERGUSON	N		1941/08/16	
A/87227	FERRIS	G	M	1945/01/18	1
M/45663	FICHT	HERBERT	JOHN	1940/07/08	1
B/8406	FICK	CECIL	H	1941/11/25	1
G/2867	FILIMORE	W	W	1945/04/25	1
D/136972	FINDLAY	J	J. I	1944/03/19	
M/36303	FINKBINER	M	M	1940/10/17	
L/39150	FINNEGAN	D	H	1943/09/24	1
D/3898	FINNERTY	J	J	1944/10/06	1
L/54898	FINNIE	PETER	ALEXANDER	1942/07/26	1
M/52042	FIRTH	J	R	1943/10/04	1
K/65301	FISHER	T	A	1945/05/06	1
M/106324	FITZGERALD	R	J	1944/06/29	1
M/45603	FITZGERALD	THOMAS	MICHAEL	1940/06/26	1
G/1230	FITZPATRICK	MICHAEL	J	1943/10/04	1
D/131456	FITZSIMONS	WILLIAM	J	1943/10/04	1
M/45237	FLATHERS	ABNER	CLARENCE	1940/06/12	
M/45691	FLATHERS	BENJAMIN	WILLFORD	1940/08/12	
M/44755	FLAWS	GRANT	OLIVER	1940/06/05	1
K/49442	FLEMING	R	C	1943/10/04	
M/45819	FLEMING	WILFRED	LAURIER	1941/08/16	
M/45268	FLEMING	WILLIAM	BONAR	1940/06/15	
M/45213	FLETCHER	HARRY	A	1940/06/10	
C/34515	FLIELER	E	J	1942/11/20	1, 3, 4, 8
M/44815	FLOYD	DAVID		1940/06/07	
M/45084	FODEN	GEORGE	LESLIE	1940/06/10	
L/106683	FOLK	JOHN		c. 1944/10	
L/84689	FOLLAND	MELVIN	B	1942/05/30	1
G/4519	FOLLAND	S	E	1943/12/23	1
B/148347	FORBES	C	A	1944/11/04	1
F/45980	FORBES	JAMES	F	1944/05/10	1
M/45354	FORCE	DOUGLAS	CHARLES	1940/06/18	
A/117651	FORD	C	T	1945/04/21	1
M/28822	FORD	R	S. B.	1941/03/25	1
K/553	FORD	W	E	1945/04/16	1
D/76007	FORGET	FERNAND		1944/03/19	1
K/40924	FORLIN	J	A	1945/04/23	1
M/45786	FORREST	GEORGE		1941/02/19	1
M/155	FORSMAN	F	R	1943/04/09	1
D/76983	FORSTER	JAMES	O	1944/03/19	1
M/45130	FORSYTH	BRADWELL	RICHARD	1940/06/11	1
B/116556	FORSYTH	J	A	1944/10/31	1
D/77190	FORTIN	EARL	WINSON	1944/03/19	1, 5
M/35657	FOSTER	ERLE	MILTON	1941/10/04	1, 5
M/45791	FOSTER	JAMES	MARTIN	1941/02/19	1, 5
B/24184	FOSTER	T		1941	3
B/126441	FOURNIER	A	J	1945/03/24	1
D/76054	FOURNIER	J		1944/03/19	1
H/87920	FOX	R	G	1944/03/18	1, 3, 8
M/66028	FRANKLIN	J	C	1941/08/16	
M/66027	FRANKLIN	W	H	1941/08/16	
M/28839	FRANKSON	ERIC	OSCAR	1941/03/25	1, 5
L/2783	FRANKSON	J		1943/02/12	1
G/24213	FRASER	ARTHUR	S	1944/10/19	1
D/76451	FRASER	D	D	1944/11/16	1
M/45050	FRASER	FERGUS	ROSS	1940/06/11	
M/45665	FRASER	HENDRY		1940/06/27	
K/71413	FRASER	J	F	1943/09/10	1
M/45303	FRASER	JOSEPH	CHRIST	1940/06/11	
B/4576	FRASER	R	J	1945/04/12	1
M/45525	FRASER	WILLIAM		1940/06/24	
M/45330	FREDLUND	WILBERT	SEIGFRED	1940/06/17	1
H/37175	FREEMAN	K		1943/08/13	3, 4
M/28840	FREEMAN	LAWRENCE	F	1941/03/25	1
M/44865	FREER	FRANK	ELLSWORTH	1940/06/08	1
M/44870	FREER	HAROLD	LEROY	1940/06/08	1
M/45140	FRENCH	FLOYD		1940/06/13	
M/45331	FRENCH	JACK	ALLEN	1940/06/18	
D/76266	FRENCH	R	W	1944/03/19	1
M/45542	FRICKER	JOHN	FRED	1940/06/25	
M/45770	FRIESEN	GEORGE		1941/02/19	
A/105514	FRIEST	R	A	1943/09/02	1
M/45529	FRIZZELL	GORDON	SAMUEL	1940/06/24	
M/45138	FROMENT	GORDON	LESLIE	1940/06/12	
M/44893	FROST	WILLIAM	MUMFORD	1940/06/07	
B/135376	FULLING	B	C	1944/05/06	1
H/195523	FULTON	HERBERT	J	1944/05/10	1
H/103817	FUNK	W	H	1944/12/28	1
A/107235	FUNNELL	FREDERICK	A	1944/10/08	1
M/44953	GAEBEL	EDWARD	EMIL ELMER	1940/06/10	
M/45350	GAGNON	EVERETT	GORDON	1940/06/13	
M/45674	GALBRAITH	JOHN	REID	1940/07/22	
M/45308	GALIPEAU	JOHN	ALBERT	1940/06/12	1
M/7729	GALLANT	G	M	1944/10/19	1
F/31570	GALLANT	W		1944/09/12	1
G/693	GALLERY	B	L	1944/10/05	1
G/2897	GALLEY	C	R.M.	1945/04/24	1
M/51225	GALLIMORE	G	F	1944/04/30	1
M/50823	GALLIMORE	J	A	1941/09/10	1
M/45422	GANNON	FRANK		1940/06/21	
M/44837	GANNON	GEORGE	PATRICK	1940/06/08	
D/76902	GARAND	HENRI	PAUL	1944/03/19	1
H/18395	GARDINER	JOHN	LEE	1944/12/08	1
F/56130	GARDNER	B	A	1944/04/07	
M/45776	GARDNER	MURRAY	STEWART	1941/02/19	
A/42340	GARDNER	W	J	1944/09/10	1
M/45214	GARGETT	JOHN		1940/06/15	

NUMBER	LAST NAME	FIRST NAME	MIDDLE NAME	JOIN SAR	NOTES
M/45215	GARRY	GERALD		1940/06/15	1
M/45333	GATES	WILFRED	HAZEN	1940/06/17	
F/55779	GAUDET	J	L	1943/10/04	1
H/1819	GAVIN	F	G	1944/03/31	1
M/45522	GEAR	PERCY		1940/06/22	1
L/41462	GEE	ALLAN	JOHN	1944/09/14	1, 5
M/3772	GELDREICH	M	R	1941/03/25	
M/44963	GENDRON	EDWARD	ERNEST	1940/06/08	1, 5
M/44753	GEORGE	SAMUEL	RICHARD	1940/06/05	1
M/45284	GERMAIN	CELO	GRANT	1940/06/14	
B/116622	GERVAIS	G	J	1945/03/25	1
B/149100	GERVAIS	R	J	1944/10/19	1
B/19742	GIBBONS	ARNOLD	MICHAEL	1941/08/25	1
M/45272	GIBBONS	DOLPHIE	LAURENCE	1940/06/19	
M/45659	GIBSON	AUBREY	VERNA	1940/07/08	
M/45340	GIBSON	ERNEST	HENRY JAMES	1940/06/17	
M/45294	GIBSON	FREDERICK	JOHN	1940/06/11	
M/45396	GIBSON	JAMES		1940/06/16	
M/44977	GIESBRECHT	JACK		1940/06/10	
M/44859	GIESEN	JOHN	FRANK	1940/06/08	
M/45689	GILBERT	MAXWELL		1940/08/12	1
M/45085	GILBERT	ROBERT	HOWARD	1940/06/10	
M/51165	GILBOE	A	L	1943/10/04	1
B/77034	GILDNER	E	W. A	1943/10/04	6
M/44932	GILHOOLEY	JOHN		1940/06/06	
M/45196	GILLIES	ROBERT		1940/06/12	
D/76062	GILPIN	ALFRED	R	1944/03/19	1
M/45785	GINGRAS	ARTHUR	AURELIEN	1941/02/19	
M/44909	GIRARD	JOFFRE	JOSEPH	1940/06/17	
L/13457	GIROUX	J	L. G.	1942/11/27	3, 4
D/76534	GLADWIN	F	W	1944/03/19	
M/106150	GLANVILLE	W	E	1943/10/04	
A/86741	GLAUDE	CLIFF		1944/03/19	1
M/45264	GODDARD	WESLEY	HARWOOD	1940/06/15	
M/45553	GOERTZEN	HENRY		1940/06/24	
L/104319	GOKLEY	R	G	1943/12/03	
M/59134	GOLBY	GEORGE	L	1941/03/25	1
M/45620	GOLBY	LEO	JAMES	1940/06/27	5
M/45643	GOLBY	PERCY		1940/06/28	
G/2557	GOLDEN	G	E	1945/03/25	1
M/16689	GOLDRING	EDWARD	DAVID WOODLEY	1940/06/28	
M/44841	GOODALL	JACK	DAL	1940/06/08	
M/44923	GOODWIN	JAMES	THOMAS	1940/06/06	1
D/116325	GOODYER	ROBERT	HENRY	BY 1944/05	1, 5, 7
M/45034	GORDON	EUGENE	RANDOLPH	1940/06/10	
M/45467	GORDON	GEORGE	HENRY	1940/06/17	
L/107298	GORDON	J	C	1945/03/09	1
M/45127	GORMAN	WILLIAM		1940/06/11	
M/45384	GOUDY	JACK	ERNEST	1940/06/18	
A/116091	GOULIN	C	F	1944/12/08	1
M/11084	GOVE	JAMES	KENNETH	1940/06/18	1
K/76106	GOVETT	A	R	1942/12/11	6
B/145038	GOWANS	L	G	1944/10/14	1
B/102689	GRACE	J	P	1945/04/25	1
M/11535	GRACE	R		1941/10/04	1
L/37014	GRAFF	N	H	1943/09/24	1
B/148361	GRAHAM	E	C	1944/10/19	1
M/45173	GRAHAM	GEORGE	LEROY	1940/06/11	
M/45029	GRAHAM	HUGH	WILSON	1940/06/10	
L/51169	GRAHAM	NORMAN	NEWTON	1942/07/26	
M/66025	GRAHN	ARTHUR	L	1941/08/16	1
M/103165	GRAHN	T	R	1945/03/24	1
M/44879	GRANT	IKE		1940/06/08	
M/55654	GRANT	J	P	1941/02/16	
M/44834	GRANT	ROBERT	JOHN FREDERICK	1940/06/07	
B/158908	GRANTON	F	M	1945/03/09	1
D/77531	GRAVEL	M	J	1944/03/19	
M/45454	GRAY	FRANK	GORMAN	1940/06/19	
M/45204	GRAY	ROBERT	CHARLES	1940/06/13	
M/45430	GRAY	ROBERT	MORAN	1940/06/19	
H/1164	GRAY	S		1943/10/04	
M/45252	GRAYDON	JOHN	EDWARD	1940/06/14	
A/105296	GREEN	A	E	1943/10/04	1
K/45107	GREEN	A	E	1943/11/19	1, 3, 4, 8
B/11887	GREEN	JAMES	G	1944/11/24	1
B/145803	GREEN	R	M	1944/10/11	1
M/45787	GREEN	WILLIAM	TRUMAN	1941/02/19	1
M/44880	GREENWOOD	ALBERT	EDWARD	1940/06/08	
M/45588	GREENWOOD	PHILIP	BERTRAM	1940/06/24	
M/44786	GREGORY	JOHN	DENNIS	1940/06/06	
M/44752	GREGORY	PATRICK	BRYAN	1940/06/05	1
D/167112	GRENIER	J	E	1944/05/17	1, 4, 8
M/45683	GREY	CLAUDE	MAURICE	1940/08/09	
M/45634	GREY	HAROLD	JOSEPH	1940/07/08	
M/45282	GRIFFIN	DOUGLAS	ALEXANDER	1940/06/14	1
M/45369	GRIMWOOD	FRANK		1940/06/14	
M/44992	GRINDELL	JAMES	CLARKE	1940/06/07	
—	GROOT	NORMAN		—	
H/63948	GROTH	JOHN		1942/07/26	
M/45262	GROULX	VALMORE		1940/06/14	
M/106354	GROVER	R	M	1943/10/04	1
D/77579	GROVES	A	H	1944/03/19	
H/64092	GUAY	JOHN	JOSEPH MARTIN	1942/07/26	
M/45783	GUDWER	WILLAM	JAMES	1941/02/19	1
L/41557	GULLASON	M	D	1944/11/02	1, 4, 8
M/45631	GULLEY	STEWART	CARLYLE	1940/06/28	
M/49004	GUNDERSON	JOHN	CHARLES	1940/06/26	1
M/37394	GUNN-FOWLIE	JOHN	ALEXANDER	1940/07/01	2
M/65546	GUNTHER	N	J	1944/07/16	1
B/63122	GUZIAK	J	J. S.	1943/07/02	
M/45332	GWILLIAM	KEITH	CALWELL	1940/06/17	
M/45513	HADDOW	ARTHUR		1940/06/24	1
M/65865	HAKES	WILLIAM	HENRY	1941/08/16	1, 6
M/45175	HALKETT	WILLIAM	RALPH	1940/06/11	
L/84636	HALKYARD	A	E	1942/05/30	1
M/10966	HALL	W	A	1945/04/26	1
M/65667	HALL	W	R	1941/08/16	1
M/44885	HALLETT	DONALD	ALLISON	1940/06/08	
M/65359	HALLEY	L	J	1943/10/03	1, 6
M/45205	HALLWORTH	THOMAS		1940/06/12	
H/45935	HALVORSON	F		1943/12/31	1
M/45306	HAMBLING	JAMES		1940/06/12	1
H/18986	HAMILTON	A	J	1945/03/09	1
G/1225	HAMILTON	HOWARD	L	1944/12/10	1
F/31964	HAMM	GERALD	FRANCIS	1944/03/31	1, 5
L/53344	HANLEY	L	C	1943/09/10	
L/36034	HARBIN	JOHN		1943/09/24	1
H/104101	HARDING	M	T	1943/09/02	1
M/45177	HARDING	NORMAN	HEDLEY	1940/06/12	1
B/61759	HARDWICK	R	W	1945/04/18	1
M/45420	HARDY	FRANK		1940/06/19	
M/44772	HARFORD	JAMES	VERNON	1940/06/05	
M/104938	HARKE	A	H	1943/10/04	
D/56911	HARLIG	A		1943/08/20	
B/116229	HARPER	DOUGLAS	EDWARD	1944/11/01	1, 5
D/76959	HARPER	J	G	1944/03/19	
M/45618	HARRINGTON	BERT		1940/06/27	
M/45597	HARRINGTON	JOSEPH		1940/06/24	
M/45510	HARRINGTON	KENNETH		1940/06/22	
M/45438	HARRIS	AUSTIN		1940/06/21	1
M/45816	HARRIS	D		1941/06/03	
U/1926	HARRIS	D	H	1943/08/06	1, 3, 4, 8
M/45051	HARRIS	WALTER	ALTON	1940/06/11	
H/100075	HART	ALVIN	WILLIAM	1942/07/26	

NUMBER	LAST NAME	FIRST NAME	MIDDLE NAME	JOIN SAR	NOTES	NUMBER	LAST NAME	FIRST NAME	MIDDLE NAME	JOIN SAR	NOTES
B/135435	HARTL	W		1943/10/04		M/8691	HORSMAN	W	T	1945/03/25	1
L/27601	HARVEY	D	J	1941/10/04	1	M/45003	HORTON	HERBERT	CHARLES	1940/06/13	
K/66281	HASKELL	MAYNARD		1943/08/20	1	H/204727	HOTEL	G	R	1945/02/22	1
B/160806	HATTON	C	R	1945/03/25	1	M/57052	HOTRA	MICHAEL		1942/07/26	1
B/97197	HAUN	H	A	1943/07/02	1	M/45178	HOUGHTON	JAMES	FERGUSON	1940/06/12	
M/45734	HAWTHORNE	HARVEY	EDMOND	1941/02/19		D/76664	HOULE	A	L	1944/03/19	1
L/64287	HAWTHORNE	J	L	1943/08/17	1	H/195644	HOUSE	S		1943/09/02	1
K/99527	HAWTHORNE	R	L	1943/04/09		M/45481	HOWATT	LORN	DAVID	1940/06/15	
M/51106	HAY	E	S	1944/09/01	1	M/45271	HOWES	FRED	LEONARD	1940/06/13	
D/131334	HAYWOOD	J	C. F.	1943/10/04	1	L/84635	HUBER	W	L	1942/05/30	
D/131023	HAZELL	F	E	1945/03/01	1	H/100065	HUBERT	WALTER	WILLIAM	1942/07/26	
M/28782	HEBERT	E	J	1943/07/02	1	M/65869	HUDEC	A		1941/08/16	
L/84703	HEIMSOTH	T	V. W.	1942/05/30		M/44587	HUDKINS	HUGH	CLIVE	1940/06/24	
M/45684	HELLEKSON	DAVID	ALFRED	1940/08/09		M/44910	HUGHES	BENJAMIN	EVON	1940/06/05	
D/21037	HENDERSON	C	O	1944/03/19		M/44831	HUGHES	FREDERICK	NEWTON	1940/06/06	2
M/44931	HENDERSON	JOHN		1940/06/06		K/53805	HUGHES	G	J	1944/10/19	1
G/28502	HENDERSON	L	E	1944/03/19	1	B/131870	HUMPHREY	J	E	1944/05/17	1
B/102079	HENDERSON	VICTOR	C	1945/03/25	1	M/44950	HUNTER	JOHN		1940/06/10	
M/45401	HENDERSON	WILLIAM		1940/06/20	3	B/147569	HUNTER	S	C	1944/11/09	1
D/128934	HENDRY	ALEXANDER		1942/07/26		B/64063	HUNTLEY	J	M	1943/07/02	
L/84631	HENKE	P		1942/05/30	1	M/44901	HUNTLEY	JOHN	LLOYD	1940/06/07	1
B/136130	HENNING	ROBERT	E	1943/12/31	1	M/44791	HURLEY	CHARLES	OLIVER	1940/06/06	
B/136121	HENNING	S	F	1943/10/04	1	M/31156	HURLEY	M	B	1942/01/01	
M/45707	HENRY	HARRY	EDWIN	1940/11/22		D/76412	HUSSEY	GERALD	JOHN HERBERT	1944/03/19	1, 5
M/45101	HENSEN	MEARL	RAYMOND	1940/06/13		B/89308	HUSSEY	W	G	1944/05/17	3, 8
M/45316	HERTZOG	THOMAS	FREDERICK	1940/06/13		H/64118	HUTCHINSON	JOHN	HUBERT	1942/07/26	1
A/86915	HEYNINCK	L	F	1944/09/16	1	M/45745	HUZAR	ALEX		1941/02/19	
M/44835	HICKS	RICHARD	ALTON	1940/06/07		M/100667	HYATT	EDWARD	THOMAS	1942/07/26	1
M/45230	HIEB	RUBON		1940/06/15		B/148266	HYATT	JAMES	B	1944/10/19	1
D/76748	HIGGS	B	R	1944/03/19	1	M/45304	HYDE	ARMIN	ROY	1940/06/11	
L/54650	HIGGS	H		1944/05/10	1	A/86674	HYTTENBRAUCH	LAWRENCE	W	1944/05/14	1
L/36572	HIGHET	W	A	1943/09/24	1	B/135335	ILTCHUCK	LUKE		1944/10/19	1
M/44758	HILL	ERNEST	FREDERICK	1940/06/05		F/45952	INGRAHAM	F	E	1943/10/04	1
M/45655	HILL	JESSE	JACOB	1940/06/26		L/101842	INMAN	R		1944/10/14	1
B/149417	HILL	L	M	1944/09/16	1	M/45069	IRELAND	LLOYD	OLIVER	1940/06/12	1
L/84501	HILL	W	K	1942/05/30	1	B/94378	IRVING	T	H	1944/08/16	1, 8
M/45456	HINCHBERGER	FRANK		1940/06/13		M/45206	IRWIN	THOMAS	ALFRED	1940/06/13	
M/45068	HINSON	WILLIAM	LESLIE	1940/06/12	1, 5	M/44964	ISAAC	CLIFFORD	JOHN	1940/06/08	
M/10857	HIRST	JESSE		1940/06/27		D/76506	ISAAC	J	W	1944/03/19	1
M/45300	HISLOP	JOHN	KENNETH	1940/06/11		H/64132	ISAAC	ROBERT	DAVIDSON	1942/07/26	1
B/149554	HOAR	JOHN	F	1944/11/08	1	M/45414	ISSARD	JOHN	PERCY	1940/06/21	6
F/44046	HOARE	DENNIS		1944/10/19	1, 5	U/1945	JACK	D	M	1942/12/11	3, 4
M/45151	HOBAL	NICK		1940/06/07		M/45526	JACK	JOB	KITCHENER	1940/06/26	1
K/49155	HODGE	CHARLES	B	1943/12/23	1	M/63305	JACK	N	T	1943/02/12	1
H/22100	HODGES	W	E	1945/03/09	1	M/66033	JACKMAN	C	W	1941/08/16	
B/133592	HODGINS	J	W	1943/09/02	1	L/66483	JACKSON	F	A. M.	1943/10/04	
L/74225	HODGINS	W	R	BY 1944/05	7	M/45413	JACKSON	ROBERT	CHARLES	1940/06/17	
D/77554	HODGSON	D	P	1944/03/19	1	L/36268	JACOBS	D	A	1943/11/19	
B/145641	HOFFMAN	JOHN	M	1944/08/16	1	L/58603	JACOBSEN	STANLEY	E	1944/10/05	1
L/64151	HOLBROOK	HORACE	EDWIN	1942/07/26	1	M/45463	JACOBSEN	THORIE		1940/06/20	1
M/44898	HOLLOWAY	JAMES	EDWARD	1940/06/08		M/45309	JACOBSON	HAROLD	BRANDT	1940/06/12	1, 5
H/64128	HOLM	ALBERT	VICTOR	1942/07/26		B/8569	JAGELEWSKI	GEORGE	J	1941/10/27	3
M/44890	HOLMES	ALLAN	McDOWELL	1940/06/10	1	H/64214	JALKANEN	A		1943/12/23	1
L/84550	HOLMS	R		1942/05/30	1	M/45807	JAMES	ALFRED	T	1941/05/21	1
M/45334	HOLMSTROM	GORDON	EDWARD	1940/06/17	1	D/117289	JAMES	J	H	1944/09/22	1, 4, 8
L/58791	HOLSTEIN	SAMUEL	ALBAN	1942/07/26		M/45797	JAMES	STANLEY		1941/02/19	1
M/45299	HOLT	DWIGHT		1940/06/12	1	M/11435	JAMIESON	J	E	1940/06/18	
H/45765	HOMER	WILFRED	NEWTON	1943/08/20	1, 5	M/45193	JAMIESON	JAMES	HENRY	1940/06/13	
M/45566	HOMMY	GARNETT		1940/06/26	1	M/45052	JANS	HAROLD	GEORGE	1940/06/11	
H/10262	HOOK	E	G	1944/01/09	1	M/45182	JAPP	WALTER	WILLIAM	1940/06/12	
D/76343	HOOLES	J	D	1945/03/01	1	M/45291	JARMAN	STANLEY		1940/06/12	
M/44763	HOPE	HARRY	ROBERT	1940/06/05		M/28815	JAY	J	E	1941/03/25	
M/28823	HORACZEK	T		1941/03/25		M/45446	JEFFERIES	JACK		1940/06/18	1
B/63064	HORNER	S	J	1944/05/10	1	D/125067	JEFFERSON	FRANCIS	F	1944/10/19	1
M/45349	HORNSETH	ALVIN	MARVIN	1940/06/14		M/44762	JELLIS	WALTER	WILLIAM	1940/06/05	1
M/45400	HORNSETH	OLAF		1940/06/19		M/106913	JENKINS	D	J	1944/10/05	1
B/58551	HORRILL	S	M	1943/07/02	1	M/45573	JENKINS	JOHN		1940/06/24	
M/44938	HORSFALL	MAURICE	ALBERT	1940/06/07		L/102573	JENSEN	H	F	1943/10/04	1

NUMBER	LAST NAME	FIRST NAME	MIDDLE NAME	JOIN SAR	NOTES
F/87587	JENSEN	N	J	1944/01/21	3, 4
M/44862	JEVNING	CLIFFORD	JAMES	1940/06/08	
G/802	JIMMO	ALEPH	R	1944/09/01	1
M/45736	JOHANSEN	EGON	CARL	1941/02/19	
M/104611	JOHNSON	E	J	1943/10/04	
M/45135	JOHNSON	ERNEST	LEONARD	1940/06/12	
L/53806	JOHNSON	F	N	1944/02/25	1
M/45039	JOHNSON	GILBERT	GEORGE	1940/06/10	
M/45574	JOHNSON	LEE	GORDON	1940/06/26	
A/42449	JOHNSON	M	E	1945/04/21	1
D/127083	JOHNSON	R		BY 1944/05	7
L/84520	JOHNSON	RAY	A	1942/05/30	1
M/11575	JOHNSON	RODERICK	JOHN	1943/09/10	1
H/64121	JOHNSON	WILLIAM		1942/07/26	1
M/45042	JOHNSTON	HILLES		1940/06/10	
F/32719	JOHNSTON	HUGH	D	1943/10/04	1
K/54890	JOHNSTON	J		1944/10/14	1
A/117011	JOHNSTON	J	R	1943/12/23	1
F/63730	JOHNSTON	MAX	M	1944/02/25	1
A/87238	JOHNSTON	W		1944/10/05	1
M/45724	JOHNSTON	WILLIAM	McKENZIE	1940/11/22	1
D/77608	JOHNSTONE	J	B	1944/03/19	1
B/134647	JONES	F	A	1943/12/23	1
M/45243	JONES	HARRY		1940/06/10	
M/45661	JONES	IVOR	WYNNE	1940/07/08	
M/44886	JONES	JOHN	CYRIL	1940/06/08	
M/44771	JONES	LESLIE	ARTHUR	1940/06/05	1
M/45688	JONES	LESLIE	JAMES	1940/08/12	
B/147511	JONES	R	C	1945/01/18	1
M/45053	JONES	THOMAS	T	1940/06/11	1
D/77416	JONES	W		1944/03/19	1
M/49003	KALOCAK	JOHN		1940/06/26	
M/59339	KALYNUK	H		1941/03/25	
M/45575	KANNENBERG	FREDERICK	ALBERT	1940/06/25	1
M/35301	KANTEN	W	G	1942/05/30	
M/45410	KAPANIUK	WILLIAM		1940/06/14	
M/28831	KATERENCHUK	N		1941/03/25	1
D/125271	KATT	E	T	1945/04/09	1
A/62152	KEACHIE	A	B	1943/02/06	
B/136067	KEAN	A	C. J.	1945/03/07	1
M/56005	KECK	REGINALD		1942/07/26	
D/76622	KEDDY	J	R	1944/03/19	
D/77861	KEEGAN	H		1944/03/19	1
B/9575	KELLAR	D		BY 1944/05	7
K/71178	KELLER	E	L	1944/05/06	1
M/44816	KELLER	OTTO		1940/06/07	
M/8009	KELLY	R	W	1944/11/01	1
K/54782	KENNEDY	I	M	1945/04/07	1
M/100303	KENNEDY	W	A	1943/10/04	1
K/46254	KENYON	E	K	BY 1944/05	1, 7
M/45251	KENYON	WALTER		1940/06/13	1
M/65907	KEREKANICH	J		1941/08/16	
K/69308	KERR	HARRY	C	1943/10/04	1
K/1951	KERR	I	B	1945/03/09	1
M/45323	KERR	ROBERT	JOHN	1940/06/17	1
L/53763	KEW	W	F	1945/03/25	1
C/38299	KIDD	ROBERT	E	1945/02/26	1
M/40848	KILBOURN	H	A	1940/07/17	3
H/64134	KINDZIERSKI	FRANK		1942/07/26	
B/59735	KING	E	L	1944/03/10	1, 3, 8
B/53725	KING	W	F	1943/02/12	3, 4
M/44817	KITCHEN	HENRY	DUDLEY	1940/06/07	
D/77122	KITCHING	E	W. A.	1944/03/19	1
M/45520	KJOSNESS	ALTON		1940/06/22	
H/102851	KLASSEN	D	L	1944/09/16	1
A/108210	KLEPACKI	M		1944/12/23	1
A/86823	KLINGABLE	G	L	1944/10/11	1
L/74579	KLUGHART	GORDON	W	1943/09/24	1

NUMBER	LAST NAME	FIRST NAME	MIDDLE NAME	JOIN SAR	NOTES
M/35537	KNAPP	W	H	1941/08/16	
M/45120	KNOWLES	STANLEY	SAMUEL	1940/06/10	
M/45054	KNOX	JOHN		1940/06/11	1
M/11238	KNOX	WILLIAM	MICHAEL VICTOR	1940/06/26	
L/64319	KONVITSKO	PETER	A	1944/10/11	1
B/105141	KORELL	A		1943/10/04	
L/8490	KOROLUKE	G		1944/02/04	1, 6
L/102926	KOSHNEY	A	A	1943/10/23	
M/45733	KOSHNEY	ALPHONSE	RICHARD	1941/02/19	1
M/45742	KOTUK	KENNETH	PAUL	1941/02/19	
M/45416	KOWAL	WILLIAM	NICHOLAS	1940/06/19	
M/45419	KRALL	EDWARD	LEWIS	1940/06/11	
H/103299	KRENTZ	H		1943/09/02	1
M/10863	KROESING	J	E	1941/10/04	1
M/44941	KROGEL	JOHN		1940/06/10	
D/77857	KROPOLNICK	M		1944/03/19	
M/44770	KRUK	ANTHONY	KASMER	1940/06/05	
M/45514	KUBEC	MIKE		1940/06/24	
M/45115	KUNDER	WILLIAM	EDWARD	1940/06/07	
M/44998	LA CAILLE	HENRY		1940/06/10	
D/76081	LABELLE	B	E	1944/03/19	
D/76908	LACASSE	F	A.J.	1944/03/19	
M/45118	LACEY	FRANK	ENOS	1940/06/10	
B/95320	LADBROOK	W	J	1942/02/12	1, 3, 4, 8
B/148609	LADOUCEUR	R	E. J.	1945/02/07	1
B/63056	LAFLEUR	A	M	1945/03/28	1
M/45651	LAFOY	TIP	ORLANDO	1940/06/26	1, 5
B/118858	LAFRANIER	C	J	1945/04/16	1
M/45158	LAING	ALEXANDER	GEORGE	1940/06/10	2
C/32181	LAING	J	C	1943/10/04	1
M/101852	LAIT	ROBERT	J	1944/10/05	1
K/49590	LAKES	JOHN	R	1943/10/04	1
M/45180	LAMB	JOSEPH	THOMAS	1940/06/12	
M/45004	LAMBERT	EMERY		1940/06/13	
D/77344	LAMBERT	V	T. J.	1944/03/19	1
D/3860	LANCASTER	B		1944/05/06	1
M/44781	LANDELLS	GEORGE	ROBERT	1940/06/06	
B/149158	LANE	H	E	1945/03/09	1
B/115711	LANE	W	G	1945/04/16	1
M/3025	LANGAGER	IVOR		1940/06/05	
M/45392	LANGEN	ADOLPH	JULIUS	1940/06/10	
D/77950	LANGEVIN	C	H	1944/03/19	
M/44836	LANOUETTE	ARTHUR	EMIL	1940/06/08	
A/116350	LAPOINTE	E	G	1945/03/24	1
M/45749	LAPRADE	LLOYD		1941/02/19	1, 5
M/45511	LARDNER	JOHN	CHARLES	1940/06/22	1
H/8712	LARKIN	DANIEL	E	1943/10/04	1
L/36280	LAROCQUE	J		1943/09/24	1
M/44897	LARSON	AUGUST	EDWARD	1940/06/08	
M/45534	LATIMER	CARSON	ROBERT	1940/06/27	1
D/124311	LATREILLE	L	O	1944/10/01	1, 4, 8
H/100118	LAUDINSKY	ADOLPH		1942/07/26	1
L/84518	LAUGHTON	WILFRED		1942/05/30	1, 5
C/27253	LAVERGNE	E	J	1943/10/15	1, 6
B/11826	LAVIGNE	W	L	1944/07/18	1, 6
M/11311	LAVOIE	PETER	ALFRED LEONARD	1940/08/13	1
M/44798	LAVOIE	WILLIAM	JOSEPH	1940/06/06	
M/45711	LAWRENCE	JAMES	RONALD	1940/11/22	1
M/45102	LAWRENCE	WILLIAM	EFFINGHAM E.	1940/06/13	
M/44965	LAWSON	LLOYD	EDWARD	1940/06/08	
M/44818	LAWSON	WALTER	HENRY	1940/06/07	
A/105918	LAYTON	GEORGE	THOMAS	1943/12/23	1
M/45702	LEADER	LOUIS	WILLIAM	1940/11/22	
G/611	LeBLANC	E	J. P.	1944/10/14	1
B/124574	LECKIE	D	T	1944/05/10	1
B/70055	LEDIARD	R	E	1943/06/01	
F/52117	LEDWIDGE	DUNCAN	J	1944/02/25	1

NUMBER	LAST NAME	FIRST NAME	MIDDLE NAME	JOIN SAR	NOTES	NUMBER	LAST NAME	FIRST NAME	MIDDLE NAME	JOIN SAR	NOTES
M/45811	LEE	G	M	1941/05/21		M/44854	MacINTYRE	IAN	JOSEPH	1940/06/08	
M/45270	LEE	GEORGE		1940/06/14		B/116021	MACK	R	C	1944/10/31	1
M/45790	LEE	GLEN	ARTHUR	1941/02/19	1	M/44906	MacKENZIE	ALEXANDER	DAVID	1940/06/07	2
M/61725	LEE	M	D	1941/03/25		M/45778	MacKENZIE	GEORGE	LEES	1941/02/19	
M/45170	LEE	SAMUEL	NEWTON	1940/06/11		M/45017	MACKENZIE	JOHN		1940/06/06	1
H/26049	LEE	W	E	1943/12/10	1, 6	M/16569	MacKENZIE	MAURICE	D. J.	1943/10/04	1
M/45536	LEEKS	FREDERICK	HARRY	1940/06/24		M/45680	MacKENZIE	RICK	HAROLD	1940/07/30	
M/45906	LEGAULT	DAMASSE		1941/06/26		M/45417	MacKENZIE	SIMON		1940/06/21	1
B/149280	LEGROS	E	T	1945/02/06	1	M/44869	MacLACHLAN	GORDON	ROY	1940/06/07	
B/102520	LEISHMAN	R	C	1944/10/10	1	C/123127	MACLENNAN	F	E	1944/12/28	1
D/131293	LEMIEUX	J	O. P. E.	1944/04/07		M/45637	MacLEOD	NEIL	JOHN	1940/06/28	
M/44819	LENNING	HAROLD	DONALD	1940/06/07		M/44784	MacLOCK	FRANKLIN	ROBERT	1940/06/06	
A/117933	LESPERANCE	M	C	1944/11/04	1	D/140644	MacNEIL	L	H	1944/09/01	1
M/45487	LEVERS	LYLE	BURTON	1940/06/14	1	M/60087	MacPHERSON	D		1941/03/25	
M/45486	LEVERS	RALPH	EDWARD	1940/06/14	1	A/107595	MacPHERSON	IAN	S	1944/10/19	1
F/40114	LEWIS	M	E	1943/08/20	1	F/32183	MacRITCHIE	N	J	1943/07/02	1
M/44966	LIEN	JACK	OSCAR	1940/06/08		M/40546	MacTAVISH	ROBERT	JOHN	1940/06/26	1, 6
F/16753	LIGHTIZER	E	J	1944/03/19	6	M/45636	MAGISTAD	JOSEPH	WILLIAM	1940/06/28	
M/45640	LIND	GEORGE	VICTOR	1940/06/28		D/117279	MAHAITS	E	A	1942/09/07	3, 4
M/45235	LINDLAND	LAWRENCE	GEORGE	1940/06/12		M/45696	MAHE	JEAN		1940/08/12	
K/83193	LINTON	R	W	1944/06/01	1, 4, 8	M/107832	MAHONEY	D	J	1944/12/17	1
M/45141	LISCUM	ROY		1940/06/13		M/45801	MAIN	JOSEPH		1941/02/19	1
C/123218	LISK	H		1945/03/21	1	M/45808	MAIR	T	B	1941/05/21	
M/44967	LITTLE	KENNETH	WAYNE	1940/06/08	2	B/94893	MAJOR	G	J	1943/03/07	1, 3, 4, 8
M/45779	LITTLECHILDS	FREDERICK	HENRY	1941/02/19		B/69742	MAKIN	G		1944/08/11	1, 8
M/45701	LOCHHEAD	DAVID	LESLIE	1940/11/22		M/45477	MALONEY	FRANCIS	HARRY	1940/06/14	1
L/84608	LOCKE	E	V	1942/05/30		H/63934	MANAIGRE	ADONAI	MICHAEL	1942/07/26	
D/142246	LOCKHART	J	E. R.	1945/01/30	1	M/106719	MANDRYK	G		1943/12/23	1
M/45673	LOGAN	JOHN		1940/07/20		M/55248	MANNING	J		BY 1944/05	7
L/84599	LOGAN	L	C	1942/05/30		M/45283	MARCOLLI	PHILIP		1940/06/13	1
M/45345	LONG	REGINALD	GEORGE	1940/06/17		M/45096	MARCOTTE	PAUL	AIME	1940/06/12	
M/45357	LONG	WILFRED	RICHARD GEORGE	1940/06/17		H/14702	MARCOUX	O	D	1945/02/26	1
M/45498	LONGMUIR	JOHN		1940/06/26		K/53835	MARKEL	H	L	1941/10/04	1
M/45387	LONTO	FRANCIS	PHILLIP	1940/06/17	1	M/45442	MARSH	WILLIAM	JOHN	1940/06/20	
L/100368	LORENSEN	CLARENCE	WARREN	1943/12/23	1, 5	B/147617	MARSHALL	DAVID	G	1944/09/01	1
M/45554	LOVE	ELLIOTT	ALEXANDER	1940/06/24		M/45238	MARSHALL	WALTER	ROBB	1940/06/12	
M/50588	LOW	DAVID	ALEXANDER	1941/11/02	1, 5	M/44799	MARSHALL	WESLEY		1940/06/06	
L/104836	LOWE	R	J. A.	1944/08/07	1	M/45557	MARTIN	ALBERT		1940/06/24	1
L/84653	LOWES	T	A	1942/05/30		B/137466	MARTIN	ALFRED	E	1944/10/05	1
M/45406	LUCAS	HAROLD	ALFRED	1940/06/19		M/45337	MARTIN	EDWARD	FORSTER	1940/06/17	
M/45298	LUCAS	HOWARD	WESLEY	1940/06/12		D/122977	MARTIN	FREDERICK	ROY	1942/07/26	
M/45399	LUCY	MARCUS	EUGENE	1940/06/18	1	M/45374	MARTIN	MALCOLM	ROBSON	1940/06/14	
H/38966	LUHTALA	G	W	BY 1944/05	1, 7	F/82627	MASON	K		1945/03/05	1
M/45322	LUKE	KENNETH	ALBERT	1940/06/17		M/44783	MASSEY	HAROLD		1940/06/06	
M/45642	LUNDEN	RALPH	HARRY	1940/06/28		M/45789	MATCHETT	SHERRY	JOHN	1941/02/19	
M/45530	LUPASKO	JAMES	MAC	1940/06/24		M/44999	MATHESON	DONALD		1940/06/10	
M/44980	LUTON	EDISON	FRANKLIN	1940/06/10		M/45033	MATHESON	JOHN	MILTON	1940/06/10	
M/45216	LUTON	EDWARD	ALBERT	1940/06/14		M/65174	MATHIASSEN	A	J	1941/08/16	
M/45465	LUTZ	ADAM		1940/06/21		H/94458	MATSON	O		1944/06/19	1, 4, 8
D/131308	LYNCH	C	A	1943/10/04	1	M/45812	MATTHEWS	C	F	1941/05/21	1
M/45737	LYNCH	PATRICK	JOSEPH	1941/02/19	5	F/82478	MATTHEWS	E	H	1945/04/29	1
L/84570	LYNGSTAD	A	M	1942/05/30	1	M/101272	MATTSON	G	A	1944/10/14	1
M/45444	LYONS	WALTER	LESLIE	1940/06/20		M/45500	MAUGHAN	ROBERT		1940/06/21	
M/44842	MacASKILL	ALEXANDER	JOHN	1940/06/08		M/45907	MAVES	REGINALD	MICHAEL	1941/07/02	
B/39866	MACAWBY	V		1943/07/02	3, 4	F/30452	MAXWELL	L	L	1942/05/23	1, 3, 4, 8
B/45349	MacDONALD	C	C	1945/04/12	1	M/45007	MAXWELL	RALPH	KEITH	1940/06/13	
B/17128	MacDONALD	E	D	1944/12/28	1	M/45240	MAY	JAMES	FRANKLIN	1940/06/10	1
M/45427	MacDONALD	GIVIN	WILLARD	1940/06/13		L/58674	MAYER	A	P	1943/07/29	
L/84593	MacDONALD	P		1942/05/30	1	A/87212	MAYNARD	N	C	1944/10/05	1
L/103697	MacDONALD	P		1943/09/02	1	M/65973	MAZETIS	W		1941/08/16	
M/45623	MacDONALD	ROBERT	BRUCE	1940/06/28		M/44924	MAZUR	THOMAS		1940/06/06	
M/45351	MacDONALD	WILLIAM	EDWARD	1940/06/14		M/45550	McARTHUR	HUGH	MUNRO	1940/06/24	
M/45694	MacDONELL	THOMAS	RONALD	1940/08/12		L/36641	McBLAIN	Q		1943/09/24	1
M/45551	MacDONNELL	JOSEPH	AUSTIN	1940/06/26		M/45247	McCAFFREY	GEORGE		1940/06/13	1, 5
M/45433	MacGREGOR	KENNETH	GRANT	1940/06/19	1	M/45070	McCAGHERTY	MITCHELL		1940/06/10	1
F/2870	MacINNIS	JOSEPH	AMBROSE	1944/02/25	1, 5, 6	M/65371	McCAIG	D	B	1941/08/16	1
F/33249	MacINTOSH	M	R	1944/05/10	1	M/8584	McCANN	R	E	1945/04/12	1
						B/156065	MCCARTHY	I	T	1945/03/05	1

NUMBER	LAST NAME	FIRST NAME	MIDDLE NAME	JOIN SAR	NOTES	NUMBER	LAST NAME	FIRST NAME	MIDDLE NAME	JOIN SAR	NOTES
M/45044	McCARTNEY	EDWARD	ARTHUR	1940/06/11	6	M/45648	McKINNON	THOMAS	CAMPBELL	1940/06/26	
M/45321	McCARTY	ARTHUR	STEPHEN	1940/06/13	1	M/45277	McKNIGHT	HARVEY	JOSEPH	1940/06/11	
M/45439	McCLEARY	HUGH		1940/06/21		M/60086	McKNIGHT	JOHN		1941/03/25	1
M/45517	McCLOY	RICHARD	DUNCAN	1940/06/22	1	M/45483	McLACHLAN	ARCHIBALD		1940/06/11	
G/53409	McCLUSKEY	W	C	1944/05/12	1, 3, 8	M/45482	McLACHLAN	JAMES		1940/06/11	
L/84603	McCOMB	R	E	1942/05/30	1	L/36850	McLAREN	I	D	1943/09/24	1
M/51138	McCORMICK	J	E	1943/10/04		M/100496	McLARTY	H	L	1943/09/24	
M/65165	McCORMICK	J	G	1941/08/16		B/115237	McLAUGHLIN	EDWARD	JOSEPH	1945/01/18	1
H/18733	McCOY	W	G	1945/04/17	1	M/44759	McLAUGHLIN	HOWARD	MARK	1940/06/05	
M/45001	McCULLOUGH	WILLIAM	CLARENCE	1940/06/12		L/54728	McLEAN	A	D	1943/10/04	1
M/45143	McCUTCHEON	OSCAR	FLOYD	1940/06/13		M/44839	McLEAN	ALEXANDER		1940/06/08	
M/45626	McDANIEL	KEVIN		1940/06/28	1	A/87254	MCLEAN	J	C	1944/12/07	1
M/45159	McDANIEL	RONALD	FRANCIS	1940/06/11	1	M/52008	McLEAN	KENNETH	E	1944/10/19	1
K/49779	McDANIEL	W	K	1943//11/22	1	M/65604	McLELLAN	A		1941/08/16	1
M/106847	MCDONALD	A	J	1944/11/16	1	M/45632	McLELLAN	ANGUS	NORMAN	1940/06/28	
M/52097	McDONALD	A	M	1944/12/17	1	B/19741	McLELLAN	DANIEL	THEODORE	1941/08/19	
B/136185	McDONALD	C	A	1944/09/16	1	M/45757	McLELLAN	DONALD		1941/02/19	
M/45744	McDONALD	DONALD		1941/02/19		B/136122	McLELLAND	B	W	1943/10/04	
K/69992	McDONALD	DOUGLAS	W	1943/09/02	1	M/45677	McLENAGHAN	ROBERT	BRUCE	1940/07/29	1
M/45005	McDONALD	EDWARD	NAPOLEON	1940/06/13		M/44981	McLEOD	WILLIAM	JOHN	1940/06/10	2
M/12348	McDONALD	GEORGE	ALEXANDER	1941/10/04	1, 5	M/45152	McMAHON	JOHN		1940/06/12	
M/45078	McDONALD	GEORGE	INGLIS	1940/06/08	1	M/44860	McNALLY	ANDREW		1940/06/08	
M/63902	McDONALD	JAMES		1944/05/06	1	M/45197	McNAMARA	ALBERT	MICHAEL	1940/06/13	1
M/45773	McDONALD	ROBERT	SMITH	1941/02/19	1	M/65434	McPHAIL	J	A	1941/08/16	
M/66037	McDONALD	W	J	1941/08/16	1	B/56630	McPHERSON	H	W	1945/02/23	1, 8
L/53251	McDONELL	JOHN	ALEXANDER	1944/09/13	1, 5	M/45441	McPHERSON	NEIL	JOHN	1940/06/20	1
K/15772	McDOUGALL	JOHN	A	1945/03/05	1	M/45006	McPHILLIPS	JAMES		1940/06/13	1
H/102261	McEACHERN	J	C	1944/10/19	1	M/44874	McRAE	DONALD	HUGH	1940/06/07	
A/107461	McEACHERN	N	J	1945/03/04	1	M/45104	McRAE	EDGAR	CALVIN	1940/06/13	
D/76795	McEWING	L	L. A.	1944/03/19	1	M/44838	McRAE	JOHN	GEORGE	1940/06/08	1, 5
M/45567	McFADDEN	HARVEY	DONALD	1940/06/26	5	M/44936	McSHERRY	MATTHEW		1940/06/07	1
M/45231	McGARRY	FRANCES	JACK	1940/06/15	1	M/65177	McWILLIAM	J	A	1941/08/16	
B/138589	McGEE	E	V. J.	1943/10/04	1	L/104529	MEACHER	B	C	1945/04/22	1
M/45071	McGEE	JOHN	PATRICK	1940/06/12		D/201	MEADES	H	A	1943/01/15	1, 3, 4, 8
M/45431	McGILL	JOHN		1940/06/11		M/44908	MEASOR	GORDON		1940/06/05	
M/45460	McGILLIVRAY	ALEXANDER	GORDON	1940/06/21	1	M/44939	MERKLEY	LAWRENCE	EMERSON	1940/06/07	
M/50833	McGILLIVRAY	HAROLD	R	1941/08/16	1	L/36535	MERRILEES	J		1943/09/24	1
B/69830	McGIVERN	KENNETH	SAMUEL	1944/10/28	1	L/36757	MERRITT	KENNETH	FRANKLIN	1943/09/24	1, 5
M/44820	McGLINCHEY	HENRY	PATRICK	1940/06/07		F/35787	MERRITT	S	L	1943/12/23	1
B/137580	McGOVERN	H	N	1943/10/04	1	B/118034	MERTENS	W	R	1945/04/14	1
M/45678	McGRATH	CLAYTON	ERNEST	1940/07/30		M/45281	METCALF	WILLIAM	HENRY	1940/06/14	
M/45185	McGUIRE	HUBERT	THOMAS	1940/06/12		M/45814	METZIG	P		1941/06/03	
M/45103	McHUGH	CHARLES	OSCAR	1940/06/13		M/103975	MEYERS	H		1944/05/17	1
B/139298	McINNES	JAMES	A	1943/10/04	1	M/61781	MICHALOVSKY	E		1945/03/02	1
B/40904	McINTEE	GEORGE	ARTHUR	1941/06/25		M/44821	MIGNEAULT	CLIFFORD	ALEX	1940/06/07	
D/76097	McINTOSH	A	B	1944/03/19		M/45764	MILAN	STANLEY		1941/02/19	5
G/53647	McINTOSH	CLAUDE	L	1944/03/19	1	M/45111	MILES	HARRY	RALPH ARTHUR	1940/06/10	1
D/26765	McINTYRE	DONALD	STEVENSON CAMPBELL	1943/07/02	5	M/45411	MILLAR	ANDREW	LINDEN	1940/06/17	
						D/77409	MILLAR	E		1944/04/07	1
B/148631	McINTYRE	H	P	1945/04/12	1	M/65470	MILLAR	J	H	1941/08/16	1
M/17498	McIVOR	GEORGE		1940/11/23		D/76275	MILLAR	JOHN	C	1944/03/19	1
M/45649	McKAIN	JAMES		1940/06/26		M/65985	MILLER	H	L	1941/08/16	
M/45421	McKAY	JAMES	WILLIAM	1940/06/11		D/77410	MILLER	JAMES		1944/03/19	1
M/45057	McKAY	KENNETH	LLOYD	1940/06/11	1	M/45436	MILLER	JAMES	HARPER	1940/06/13	
L/36329	McKEE	FERNS	ROSS	1943/09/24	1, 5	M/44777	MILLER	JOHN		1940/06/06	
F/13303	McKENNA	L	C	1945/03/24	1	M/44968	MILLER	WILLIAM	JOHN	1940/06/08	
A/86924	MCKENZIE	A	J	1944/10/05	1	M/45253	MILLIGAN	GERALD		1940/06/14	1
M/45772	McKENZIE	ALEXANDER	GORDON	1941/02/19		M/45218	MILLS	JAMES	DOUGLAS	1940/06/14	
M/31414	McKENZIE	E	D	1942/04/01	1	A/87309	MILLS	L	R	1944/10/19	1
M/45174	McKENZIE	JOHN	MATHEW	1940/06/11	1	M/44913	MILLS	THOMAS	ROBERT	1940/06/05	
M/45373	McKENZIE	WILLIAM	ORVILLE	1940/06/13		M/51023	MILNER	THOMAS	E	1944/11/08	1
B/68534	McKEOWN	DOUGLAS	H	1944/05/10	1	L/55262	MILNTHORP	W	D	BY 1944/05	7
M/45307	McKIE	WILLIAM	JOHN	1940/06/12	1	D/76276	MINGE	A	W	1944/03/19	
M/45489	McKINLAY	ALEXANDER		1940/06/20	1	M/45719	MINICH	EMIL		1940/11/22	1
M/44894	McKINLEY	GEORGE	NORMAN	1940/06/07		M/44877	MINTERN	HARRY	ROYEN	1940/06/08	
M/44761	McKINNON	DANIEL	JOHN	1940/06/05		M/45748	MINTKAWETZ	BRUNO	ERIC	1941/02/19	
M/44871	McKINNON	HERRICK	HUGH	1940/06/07	1	M/65987	MITCHELL	M	F	1941/08/16	
M/45671	McKINNON	MALCOLM	JOHN	1940/07/17		L/58773	MITCHELL	RICHARD	ARTHUR	1942/07/26	1

NUMBER	LAST NAME	FIRST NAME	MIDDLE NAME	JOIN SAR	NOTES
M/45353	MOAN	FRANCIS	BERNARD	1940/06/17	1, 5
M/45466	MOFFAT	GEORGE	EINSLEY	1940/06/10	
L/84513	MOFFATT	B	B	1942/05/30	
M/45725	MONILAWS	JOHN	DAVID	1940/11/22	
M/44929	MONILAWS	ROLAND	GREAME	1940/06/06	
M/45167	MONKMAN	LLOYD	EDWARD	1940/06/11	
M/105584	MONTGOMERY	T	R	1943/10/04	1
M/45290	MOORE	ALBERT	EDWARD	1940/06/10	
M/45771	MOORE	GEORGE	ALBERT	1941/02/19	
H/53427	MOORE	JOHN	M	1945/03/25	1
B/61218	MOORE	T	H	1944/01/28	
M/45000	MOORE	WILLIAM	VALENTINE	1940/06/12	
M/44905	MOOREHOUSE	CARL	ERNEST	1940/06/06	
M/45480	MOREAU	HENRY		1940/06/14	5
C/62115	MORENCY	L		1944/11/10	1, 4, 8
M/44907	MORETON	JOHN	PORTER	1940/06/07	2
M/45217	MORETON	LENARD		1940/06/14	
B/142721	MORETTE	B	De C.	1943/12/23	1
M/44928	MORGAN	KEITH	LIONEL	1940/06/06	
C/122087	MORGAN	R	J	1945/03/25	1
M/44946	MORRIS	ALLAN	BERT	1940/06/08	
M/45532	MORRIS	PHILIP		1940/06/27	1
M/45735	MORRIS	WILLIAM	HENRY	1941/02/19	
M/44944	MORRISON	ALEXANDER		1940/06/10	1
M/45055	MORRISON	BILL		1940/06/11	1
M/45650	MORRISON	ROBERT	CAMERON	1940/06/26	
M/45241	MORRISON	SIDNEY	JAMES	1940/06/10	
H/63964	MOTKALUK	KARL		1942/07/26	1
M/44947	MOULD	CHARLES	HENRY	1940/06/10	
M/63655	MOULD	JAMES	DANIEL	1942/07/26	1
M/45018	MUEHLLEHNER	GEORGE		1940/06/06	1
M/44856	MULLAN	FRANK	JOSEPH	1940/06/08	5
C/70531	MULLEN	H	P	1944/03/31	
B/19743	MUNA	DONALD	GEORGE	1941/10/27	
M/44934	MUNFORD	BERTIE	DAVID	1940/06/06	
M/45142	MUNGALL	GEORGE	WILLIAM	1940/06/14	1, 5
M/45712	MUNROE	DONALD		1940/11/22	1
D/131458	MURPHY	D	E	1945/02/07	1
M/45036	MURPHY	JOHN	ARTHUR	1940/06/10	
M/45248	MURRAY	CHARLES	JOHN	1940/06/13	
G/50921	MURRAY	E	H	1944/10/06	1
D/76673	MURRAY	H	T	1944/03/19	
M/49006	MURRAY	KINDER		1940/06/26	
M/45407	MURRAY	SIDNEY		1940/06/20	
M/45346	MURRAY	WILLIAM		1940/06/17	
M/45086	MURTLAND	HARRY		1940/06/10	
M/65981	MUSFELT	H	L	1941/08/16	
M/60263	MYERS	D	J	1941/11/02	
M/45008	MYERS	GEORGE	EDWARD	1940/06/13	
M/44922	MYNOTT	STANLEY		1940/06/06	1
M/45220	NAISMITH	ARCHIBALD		1940/06/15	
A/58048	NEEB	A		BY 1944/05	1, 7
C/121748	NEFF	HOWARD	WILSON	1945/02/26	1, 5
B/135302	NEFF	JOHN	H.M.	1943/10/04	1
M/8944	NEGARD	E	H	1945/03/25	1
H/63943	NEGRYCH	WALTER		1942/07/26	1
M/45368	NELLES	GERALD	KEITH	1940/06/19	1
H/42201	NELSON	A		1944/10/21	1
B/117025	NELSON	D	A	1945/03/09	1
M/28827	NELSON	H	R	1941/03/25	
M/45310	NELSON	JOHN		1940/06/12	
M/45009	NELSON	ROSS	DUNCAN	1940/06/13	
M/65843	NELSON	W	E	1941/08/16	
L/74430	NESSETT	R	M. E.	1942/12/04	1, 3, 4, 8
M/45732	NEUBAUER	WARD	EUGENE	1940/11/20	1
D/77784	NEWMAN	E	L	1944/03/19	
L/37011	NEWSTEAD	L	J	1943/09/24	
M/45335	NEWSTEAD	WILBUR	EDWARD	1940/06/17	1

NUMBER	LAST NAME	FIRST NAME	MIDDLE NAME	JOIN SAR	NOTES
M/45548	NICHOL	RALPH	EARL	1940/06/24	
B/15663	NICHOL	W	L	1943/12/03	6
M/45606	NICHOLS	ERIC	PRICE	1940/06/25	1
H/103955	NICHOLS	J	R	1943/12/23	1
M/45320	NICHOLSON	FREEMAN	JOHN ALFRED	1940/06/15	1
M/31185	NICHOLSON	J	L	1940/11/16	1
M/45221	NICKEL	MICHAEL	JOSEPH	1940/06/15	1, 5
D/77562	NIELD	R		1944/03/19	1
M/45136	NIELSEN	CHRIS		1940/06/12	
M/45219	NIEMAN	ELMER	AMIL	1940/06/14	
M/45608	NIEMAN	EUGENE	JAMES	1940/06/27	
M/45056	NIEMAN	EVULT		1940/06/11	
M/45577	NISSEN	ANGUS		1940/06/25	1
M/45227	NITTEL	JOHN		1940/06/15	
M/45658	NITTELL	WILLIAM	FRED	1940/07/05	
M/45109	NIXON	LAWRENCE		1940/06/11	
M/45582	NOBLE	GEORGE	WILLIAM	1940/06/25	1, 5
M/44822	NOLAN	JOSEPH	HAROLD	1940/06/07	
M/44958	NOLAND	GERALD	LLOYD	1940/06/05	
M/45668	NORBURY	GEORGE		1940/07/16	
M/45579	NORWEST	HENRY	CHARLES	1940/06/26	
M/7823	NOVAK	G		1944/10/19	1
M/45593	NOWISKY	MAURICE		1940/06/24	
H/95340	NYLIN	CLYNORD	BEVERLY	1943/10/04	1
M/45585	O'LAVERY	PETER	JOHN	1940/06/26	
M/45249	O'NEIL	EDWARD	ALBERT	1940/06/13	1
F/65950	O'NEIL	R	L	1944/05/28	8
F/56483	OAKLEY	CHARLES	A	1944/02/25	1
L/36946	OBLEMAN	J	R	1944/10/11	1
M/45453	ODYNUK	MICHEAL		1940/06/20	
M/45037	OLIVER	CHARLES	JAMES	1940/06/10	
M/44888	OLIVER	WILLIAM	EARL	1940/06/10	
M/45207	OLMSTEAD	GUY	EDWARD	1940/06/13	1
M/45693	OLSON	ANCHOR	EDMOND ALBERTINUS	1940/08/12	
M/49008	ORSTEN	CLARENCE	MELVIN	1940/06/26	
M/49009	ORSTEN	JENS	HENRY	1940/06/26	
H/40777	OSBORNE	A	W	1944/09/20	1
M/66039	OSCAR	J	M	1941/08/16	
H/63559	OSHOWAY	L		1943/10/08	1
M/45591	OSTBY	HJALMAR		1940/06/25	
M/44827	OSTER	HAROLD	ALBERT	1940/06/07	1
L/84592	OTTENBREIT	MICHAEL		1942/05/30	1
M/44875	OTTER	WILLIAM	FREDERICK	1940/06/07	
M/105696	OUELLETTE	DENIS		1943/09/02	1, 5
A/57641	OVERBAUGH	R	F	1944/07/16	1
H/102839	OWCZAR	J		1943/09/24	1
M/45380	OWEN	EDWARD		1940/06/20	
B/111305	OWEN	ELDON	MARTIN	1943/07/29	1, 5
M/44989	OWENS	RUSSELL		1940/06/07	
A/108170	OXLEY	A	L	1944/10/19	1
M/44978	OXLEY	WILLIAM	PATRICK	1940/06/10	1
M/45708	OXTON	FLOYD	HEWETT	1940/11/22	
M/44942	PACHAL	WILLIAM	FREDERICK	1940/06/10	1, 5
M/44848	PACKER	ALBERT	HENRY	1940/06/08	1
B/31049	PACKWOOD	R	C	1942/09/25	1, 3, 4, 8
B/94249	PADDON	A	V	1944/06/17	1, 8
B/70013	PADFIELD	A	G	1943/08/20	
M/45179	PAGEE	ARTHUR		1940/06/12	1
K/74390	PAHL	H	W	1943/03/07	3, 4
M/10657	PALFENIER	THEODORE	EMERY	1940/06/18	1, 5
M/45686	PALMER	JOHN	EDMOUR	1940/08/09	
B/137309	PALMER	L	E	1944/05/06	1
M/16169	PALMER	T	H	1941/10/04	
K/83542	PAPPENBERGER	LESLIE	FREDERICK	1942/07/26	1
C/120397	PARCELS	G	A	1944/02/18	
A/107448	PARENT	P	D	1944/10/19	1
C/100542	PARISIEN	J	A	BY 1944/05	7

NUMBER	LAST NAME	FIRST NAME	MIDDLE NAME	JOIN SAR	NOTES	NUMBER	LAST NAME	FIRST NAME	MIDDLE NAME	JOIN SAR	NOTES
M/45607	PARKER	BURTON	MCKENZIE	1940/06/07		M/45079	PODEALUK	HENRY		1940/06/08	
M/50048	PARKER	L	C	1941/10/04	1	M/44823	PODESTA	VICTOR	ALBERT	1940/06/07	
M/50315	PARKER	M	A	1943/03/05		M/45172	POITRAS	NORMAN	WILFRED	1940/06/11	
M/45058	PARNELL	GEORGE		1940/06/11		L/100805	POLISHAK	M		1943/08/20	
M/45260	PARR	STANLEY		1940/06/14	1	L/36691	POLLOCK	G	J	1943/09/24	1
D/131324	PASHKEVITCH	A		1943/10/04		M/44845	POLSKY	ABIE		1940/06/08	1
D/128501	PASHLEY	V	W	1942/04/01	3, 4	L/25706	POMEROY	GORDON	HENRY	1942/07/26	1
B/143383	PASK	R	H	1944/11/02	1	M/45464	POPEY	WILLIAM	JAMES	1940/06/24	
M/45208	PATERSON	ALEXANDER	SCOTT	1940/06/13	1	M/45278	POPOWICH	JULIAN		1940/06/13	
M/44850	PATERSON	JOHN		1940/06/08	2	M/44800	PORTER	JOHN	ALVIN	1940/06/06	1
M/44801	PATERSON	SIDNEY	HERBERT	1940/06/06	1	L/103908	PORTER	JOHN	W	1943/09/02	1
A/86669	PATERSON	T	P	1944/11/16	1	D/117398	POTVIN	M		1944/10/01	1, 4, 8
M/44969	PATERSON	WILLIAM	COPLAND	1940/06/08		M/57059	POULIOUS	ALEXANDER	GREGORY	1942/07/26	1
M/45564	PATON	JAMES	ELWIN	1940/06/27		M/44970	POVEY	GEORGE	STEEL	1940/06/08	1
M/45533	PATRICK	THOMAS	WILLIAM	1940/06/27	1	M/45163	POWELL	JOHN	ANDREW	1940/06/11	
C/94612	PAUL	C	D	1942/07/18	1, 3, 4, 8	M/44782	POWERS	GEORGE	HENRY	1940/06/06	
L/67105	PAULSON	P	V	1943/10/04	1	M/45028	POWLAN	FRANK		1940/06/10	
M/44954	PAWSEY	ARTHUR	SIDNEY	1940/06/10	1	M/45154	PREDIGER	JACOB	JOSEPH	1940/06/12	
M/44956	PAWSEY	EDWARD	ROBERT	1940/06/10		M/45358	PRENEVOST	DOUGLAS	SELVESTER	1940/06/17	1
H/105027	PAXTON	J	F	1944/10/19	1	K/69490	PREST	CLIFFORD		1943/12/23	1
L/36966	PEARSALL	H	R	1945/05/05	1	B/3871	PRICE	ARTHUR	EDWARD	1941/10/12	3
G/14119	PEARSON	W	O	1942/04/01	3	M/45124	PRICE	CLAYTON		1940/06/10	
L/54824	PEARSON	WALLACE	WEBSTER	1942/07/26	1	M/45672	PRICE	LESTER	MELVIN	1940/07/20	
L/2539	PEAT	R	W	1944/10/19	1	D/76347	PRIMEAU	H		1944/03/19	1
L/54843	PEDERSON	C	E	1945/04/16	1	M/31051	PROSSER	R	E	1941/02/07	
D/166662	PELLEY	N	D	1944/02/17	1, 3, 4, 8	B/136008	PROSSER	S	A	1944/10/06	1
D/77017	PELLICCIOTTI	A	V	1944/03/19	1	M/28841	PROSSER	V	D	1941/03/25	
L/106294	PENNER	JOHN	RUFUS	1945/03/28	1	M/45088	PROSSER	WALLACE	PRESTON	1940/06/10	
M/44903	PENNEY	WILLIAM	GEORGE WILFRED	1940/06/06	1	C/120950	PRUNNER	ROBERT	PERCY LAWRENCE	1944/03/31	
B/70039	PENROSE	JOHN		1943/07/02	1	M/44971	PRUSKY	MIKE		1940/06/08	
M/45777	PENTELUK	FRANK		1941/02/19		M/28811	PRYSTUPA	M		1943/12/10	1, 6
M/65333	PERRAULT	R	L. J.	1941/08/16		M/30836TR	PTOSHNUKE	N		1941/05/15	
M/44802	PERRIN	KENNETH	ELIAS	1940/06/06	2	M/45010	PUGH	JAMES		1940/06/13	
L/84613	PERRINS	W		1942/05/30		M/45428	PURDY	MELVILLE	EARL	1940/06/17	
A/11773	PERRY	E	K	1944/10/31	1	M/45131	PURVES	CLIFFORD	LYLE	1940/06/11	1
M/27209	PETERS	G	M	1942/01/02	1	M/45624	QUARTON	JOHN	HENRY	1940/06/28	
M/45347	PETERS	JACK	SYLVESTER	1940/06/17	1	K/69618	QUINN	L	C	1944/05/06	1
M/65818	PETRIE	E		1941/08/16	1	M/45676	QUINN	WILFRED	LYLE	1940/07/29	1
D/77776	PETRIN	EDOUARD		1944/12/12	1	L/54869	QUINNEL	CLARENCE	LEONARD	1943/02/12	1, 5
L/53578	PETTY	P	M	1945/03/07	1	M/103794	RAE	HAROLD	G	1943/07/29	1
M/45381	PEVERELLE	WILLIAM	LOUIS	1940/06/18		K/100039	RAINE	DONALD	FREDERICK	1942/07/26	1
B/116193	PFEIFFER	J	F	1944/11/06	1	B/142218	RALPH	GEORGE	ALBERT FREDERICK	1945/04/15	1
M/65538	PHILBIN	J	L	1941/08/16	1	M/45528	RAMSAY	HUGH	THOMAS	1940/06/24	1
M/45485	PHILLIPS	ARTHUR	WILLIAM	1940/06/17		M/45045	RAMSAY	STANLEY	IRVIN	1940/06/11	
M/65703	PHILLIPS	W	J	1941/08/16		M/28830	RANCH	W	D	1941/03/25	
M/45153	PICKARD	REGINALD	JOHN	1940/06/12	1	M/44768	RANDALL	EDWARD	GEORGE	1940/06/05	
M/45609	PICKEN	JOHN	KENNEDY	1940/06/24		M/44792	RANKINE	DAVID	ALEXANDER	1940/06/06	
G/60657	PICKLE	F	H	BY 1944/05	7	C/120412	RASHOTTE	R	T	1943/12/23	1
M/45087	PIEBINGA	CORNELIUS	ADRIANUS	1940/06/10		M/45365	RASMUSSEN	LEO	JOHN	1940/06/19	
M/44824	PIEPGRASS	LYLE	BOYSON	1940/06/07	2	M/45769	RASMUSSEN	NELS		1941/02/19	1
M/45002	PIERCE	HAROLD	GEORGE	1940/06/10		M/45367	RASMUSSEN	ROBERT	JOSEPH	1940/06/19	1
M/107713	PIERCE	L	W	1945/02/06	1	M/31539	RATHWELL	JOHN		1940/11/22	1
M/45478	PIFFER	WILMER	EARL	1940/06/10		M/44825	RATTRAY	JAMES		1940/06/07	
M/28821	PIGEON	J		1941/03/25	1	H/77452	REDER	AUGUST		1942/07/26	1
M/45107	PILON	EDWARD	JOSEPH	1940/06/11		B/53293	REED	R	W	1943/03/12	3, 4
D/76346	PILOTO	A	E	1944/03/19	1	B/116982	REESON	K	W	1944/11/02	1
M/45644	PINSENT	HERBERT	FREDERICK	1940/06/28	1	M/44991	REID	ALEXANDER		1940/06/05	
M/45072	PIPE	EDWARD	GEORGE VERDUN	1940/06/11	1	M/45222	REID	ERNEST	ALBERT	1940/06/15	
M/65986	PLAHN	FRED	W	1941/08/16	1	L/84660	REID	G	M	1942/05/30	
M/45184	PLANT	HAROLD	CLAYTON	1940/06/12		M/44793	REID	HAROLD	GORDON	1940/06/07	
M/45695	PLANT	RICHARD	WHITMORE	1940/08/13		C/120372	REID	JAMES	C	1943/10/04	1
M/44861	PLANT	VERNON	WHITMORE	1940/06/08		M/45474	REINE	THEODORE	ANDREW	1940/06/10	
M/45750	PLASNIK	MIKE		1941/02/19		M/107269	RELKOV	J	N	1944/10/05	1
M/44957	PLAYNE	RONALD	BLACKWALL	1940/06/10		M/44911	RENN	ADOLPH		1940/06/05	
C/31868	PLOMANDON	J	L	BY 1944/05	7	M/45032	RENN	ARTHUR		1940/06/10	
M/45228	PLOTSKY	LAWRENCE		1940/06/15	1	M/45408	REYNEN	WILFRED		1940/06/20	
B/63219	PLOWMAN	R	C	1943/07/16		M/45360	RHIND	ERNEST	BROCKIE	1940/06/17	

NUMBER	LAST NAME	FIRST NAME	MIDDLE NAME	JOIN SAR	NOTES
M/45472	RHIND	JOHN	ROBERT	1940/06/17	
M/45011	RHODES	JOHN	CHARLES	1940/06/13	
F/66256	RICE	G	H	1943/10/29	1, 3
D/76109	RICE	H		1944/03/19	1
L/53519	RICE	O	A	1945/03/01	1
M/45722	RICE	WALLACE	WILLIAM	1940/11/22	1
M/44921	RICHARDS	FLOYD	ALLEN	1940/06/06	
M/45325	RIEMER	RALPH	PAUL	1940/06/13	1
M/45598	RIGBY	CECIL	STANLEY	1940/06/25	1
M/45341	RILEY	ROBERT	DIGBY	1940/06/17	
M/57036	RILEY	W	F	1945/02/09	1
H/64161	RINTALUHTA	E	V	1943/07/02	1
M/45089	RISDALE	SIDNEY	GEORGE	1940/06/10	1
L/65549	RITCO	NICK		1942/07/26	
B/117190	RIVERS	M	A	1944/12/30	1
M/7783	ROBERTS	I	D	1944/10/31	1
D/96165	ROBERTS	J	G. A.	1943/10/04	6
M/45488	ROBERTS	JOHN	PATRICK	1940/06/20	1
K/22086	ROBERTS	L	F	1941/02/09	
C/94177	ROBERTS	T	A	1945/03/02	1, 8
K/42899	ROBERTSON	ALEXANDER	JAMES	1944/08/16	1, 5
M/44846	ROBERTSON	DARRELL	BOTSFORD	1940/06/06	
M/45126	ROBERTSON	HERBERT		1940/06/11	1
L/36019	ROBIE	E	M	1943/09/24	1
M/44790	ROBINSON	EDEN	WESTBROOK	1940/06/06	1
M/45647	ROBINSON	FREDERICK	CHARLES	1940/06/28	
M/45904	ROBINSON	MICHEAL	LEONARD	1941/06/16	
L/102835	ROBINSON	W	H	1943/09/24	1
A/86639	ROCK	A	C	1944/05/14	1
A/104537	RODD	PHILLIP	H	1944/02/18	1
L/84630	RODGERS	ELWOOD	J. H.	1942/05/30	1
M/44826	RODMAN	ROBERT		1940/06/07	
M/44853	RODNUNSKY	ABRAHAM		1940/06/08	
M/45788	ROGERS	STEPHEN		1941/02/19	
K/66034	ROLKE	R	A	1943/10/04	1, 6
B/28903	ROLLINSON	J	E	1944/02/18	1, 3, 8
M/45245	ROMBOUGH	HOWARD	LeROY	1940/06/12	
M/44873	ROSCOVICH	FRANK		1940/06/07	
M/45060	ROSE	NORMAN	CECIL JOSEPH	1940/06/11	1
M/45059	ROSE	STANLEY	THOMAS	1940/06/11	1
M/45728	ROSENAUER	MARTIN		1940/11/22	
L/84668	ROSENFELT	A		1942/05/30	
M/45703	ROSS	ALLAN	HUGH	1940/11/22	
M/45119	ROSS	GEORGE		1940/06/10	
M/45905	ROSS	GEORGE	HUGH	1941/06/16	
M/45589	ROSS	VERNON	JULIUS	1940/06/26	1
M/44803	ROSS	WALTER	JOHN	1940/06/06	
M/45633	ROTHERY	CLARENCE	GORDON	1940/06/28	
M/45515	ROULSTON	HERBERT		1940/06	1
F/33558	ROUTLEDGE	H	T	1945/04/25	1
M/45090	ROWE	KENDAL		1940/06/10	1, 5
B/143170	ROWE	R	R	1943/12/23	1
M/45233	ROWLAND	ALLAN	EDGAR	1940/06/15	
B/139701	ROY	G	E	1944/10/19	1
M/45775	RUBIN	CLARENCE	MAXWELL	1941/02/19	1
M/101601	RULE	D	R	1945/04/09	1
M/45035	RUMSEY	DAVID	LLOYD	1940/06/10	1
A/116502	RUNNINGS	W	C	1943/08/20	1
B/137416	RUSSELL	R	A	1944/03/19	1
L/13624	RUTTKAY	HENRY		1942/07/26	
D/3003	RYAN	P		1943/07/02	
D/71085	RYDBERG	ASHTON	H	1944/02/18	1
A/118048	RYDER	E	W	1945/03/28	1
M/45717	RYE	DONALD	HARRY	1940/11/22	
M/45155	RYERSE	ROBERT	EDWARD	1940/06/12	
M/44754	RYLEY	CHARLES	RAYMOND	1940/06/05	1
K/50536	SABOK	W		1945/03/29	1
D/77658	SADLER	W	A	1944/03/19	
M/44900	SADY	SAMUEL	SONNY	1940/06/07	
L/54944	SALCHERT	L		1945/02/22	1
M/45194	SALES	WAYNE	KENNETH	1940/06/13	1
D/77442	SALISBURY	J	R	1944/03/19	1
M/44843	SALTZMAN	CASPAR		1940/06/08	
M/45625	SAMPLE	JOHN	ROBINSON	1940/06/28	
M/45601	SAMPSON	CLARE		1940/06/25	1
M/45479	SAMUEL	PHILIP	JENKIN	1940/06/14	1
M/45611	SANDS	ARTHUR	JAMES	1940/06/28	1
M/44892	SAUDER	LLOYD		1940/06/10	
M/45666	SAUNDERS	THOMAS	HAROLD	1940/07/08	
M/37375	SAUNDERS	WILLIAM	FREDERICK	1940/07/01	
C/31028	SAUVE	J		1945/03/09	1, 6
M/50683	SAVILL	D	C	1941/08/16	
B/142584	SAVOLINE	PAUL	J	1944/05/10	1
M/45176	SAWCHUK	MAC	METRO	1940/06/11	1
M/45507	SAWCHUK	WILLIAM		1940/06/24	1
M/45073	SAWYER	DUDLEY		1940/06/11	
L/100050	SAYERS	EDGAR	RALPH	1943/09/24	1
M/44889	SCHAAP	HANK	THEODORE	1940/06/10	
M/45425	SCHAN	NICKLAS		1940/06/11	1
H/63607	SCHAPPERT	RUDOLF		1942/07/26	
M/45063	SCHECTER	JOE		1940/06/11	
K/69421	SCHELL	G	M	1944/01/21	1
M/45105	SCHELL	WILLIAM	ARTHUR	1940/06/13	1
M/45709	SCHEUERMAN	VICTOR		1940/11/22	1
M/45223	SCHLENKER	JACOB		1940/06/14	1
M/45692	SCHLITT	WILLIAM		1940/08/12	
M/44986	SCHMIDT	EDWARD	ALBERT	1940/06/10	
M/65995	SCHMIDT	L	A	1941/08/16	1
M/45774	SCHMIERER	FREDERICK		1941/02/19	
M/45128	SCHMITZ	GRANT		1940/06/11	
H/103919	SCHNEIDER	E	W	1944/09/14	1
M/45146	SCHNEIDER	MELVIN	ALBERT	1940/06/11	
A/117000	SCHRAM	P	S	1943/10/04	
L/36742	SCHULTZ	E		1943/09/24	1
C/20582	SCOBIE	JAMES	C	1943/10/04	1
D/137049	SCOTT	GERALD	ARCHIBALD	1943/10/04	1, 5
B/62388	SCOTT	N	W	1945/03/01	1
L/53911	SCOTT	R	M	1943/08/20	1
M/7926	SCOTT	R	W	1945/03/07	1
M/45097	SCOTT	THOMAS	HAROLD	1940/06/12	
M/45319	SCOTT	WILLIAM		1940/06/17	1
M/45452	SCOTT	WILLIAM		1940/06/18	
M/101011	SCRABIUK	W		1944/10/19	1
M/45429	SCULLY	VINCENT		1940/06/18	
M/45328	SCULTHORPE	ARTHUR	JOHN	1940/06/15	
M/45504	SEAGRAVE	IRVING	GEORGE	1940/06/24	
P/20940	SEAL	CHRISTOPHER		1940/07/11	
M/45903	SEAL	OLIVER		1941/06/16	
B/148559	SEARLE	R	H	1944/11/06	1
M/45359	SECCOMBE	ARTHUR	RAY	1940/06/18	1
M/45106	SECCOMBE	JOHN	RICHARD	1940/06/11	1
M/45484	SEIDLER	JAKE	VALTON	1940/06/15	5
L/51487	SEIFERLING	RAYMOND	K	1943/04/09	1
L/12729	SEMAN	J		1941/10/04	
M/45782	SEMPLE	THOMAS		1941/02/19	1
H/8419	SENEBALD	G	A	1945/01/18	1
A/118008	SEQUIN	O	J	1944/11/04	1
M/45404	SERAFINCHON	JOHN		1940/06/20	
M/45760	SEREDA	ALEXANDER		1941/02/19	
M/44984	SETTLE	ANTHONY		1940/06/10	
M/44857	SEWELL	JOHN	JAMES	1940/06/08	1
B/115380	SEYMOUR	J	L	1945/01/18	1
M/45475	SEYMOUR	VINCENT		1940/06/16	
M/45614	SHABAT	HARRY		1940/06/28	
M/45753	SHANK	EDWARD	CLIFFORD	1941/02/19	
M/45754	SHANK	GEORGE	WILLIAM	1941/02/19	

NUMBER	LAST NAME	FIRST NAME	MIDDLE NAME	JOIN SAR	NOTES	NUMBER	LAST NAME	FIRST NAME	MIDDLE NAME	JOIN SAR	NOTES
M/44766	SHANK	LAWRENCE		1940/06/05		M/45108	SMITH	WILLIAM	HAROLD	1940/06/11	
M/65528	SHANNON	F		1941/08/16		M/45274	SNEDDON	CHARLES	ALEXANDER	1940/06/11	
M/640	SHARDLOW	J	E	1941/10/04		D/77320	SNOW	T	R	1944/03/19	
M/45295	SHARP	ROBERT	WILSON	1940/06/11	1	M/106348	SNOWDON	E	D	1944/12/17	1
M/45061	SHARPE	EDWARD	ALEXANDER	1940/06/11		M/45092	SNYDER	RAY	JOSHWA	1940/06/10	
M/45091	SHEARER	HAROLD		1940/06/10	1	L/101578	SNYDER	V		1943/09/24	
D/228	SHEEHAN	G		1945/02/19	1, 6	B/132439	SOLOMAN	J	D	1943/10/04	1
A/44274	SHELDON	T	B	1944/12/10	1	M/45537	SOLONIUK	ALEX		1940/06/27	
M/45799	SHEPHERD	ROBERT		1941/02/19		L/54842	SOUTH	T	C	1944/06/05	1, 4, 8
M/45802	SHEPHERD	THOMAS		1941/02/19		M/51241	SPACHINSKY	ADOLPH		1944/05/14	1
M/65738	SHEPLAWY	J	S	1942/04/01		M/104878	SPANER	BERNARD		1943/10/04	1
M/104238	SHERET	N	D	1943/09/02	1	M/44940	SPARROW	GEORGE	ALBERT	1940/06/10	
D/77001	SHERIDAN	G	A	1944/03/19		L/11265	SPENCE	CEDRIC	LANCELOT	1944/12/28	1
M/44760	SHERWIN	KENNETH	MORTON	1940/06/05	1	M/45664	SPENCE	JOSEPH	ERNEST	1940/07/08	
M/45225	SHERWOOD	MILTON	HOMER	1940/06/15		M/45402	SPENCE	THOMAS	ALEXANDER	1940/06/20	1
K/46242	SHIELS	H		1944/11/16	1	H/103783	SPENCE	WAYNE	A	1943/09/02	1
M/45437	SHORTRIDGE	HAROLD		1940/06/21		L/36838	SPILLETT	JACK	C	1943/09/24	1
D/77090	SHUTE	FRANK	V	1944/03/19	1	M/45600	ST. ARNAULT	HUBERT		1940/06/26	1
M/52044	SIBLEY	R	B	1944/10/19	1	M/59118	ST. ARNAULT	RAYMOND		1941/02/19	
M/44920	SIGOUIN	JAMES		1940/06/06	1	B/19745	ST. CLAIR	EMILE	SIMON	1941/11/03	
M/45521	SIMONSON	CARL		1940/06/22		M/50384	ST. DENYS	H	J	1941/08/16	
M/45447	SIMPER	JACK	HERBERT	1940/06/20		B/62503	ST. MARIE	R	P	1945/03/25	1
B/136104	SIMPSON	D	W	1943/10/04	1	B/135351	STACKHOUSE	CHARLES	H	1944/02/25	1
M/44955	SIMPSON	JAMES		1940/06/10	1	M/45751	STAPLES	WILLIAM	ROBERT	1941/02/19	
M/45236	SIMPSON	ROBERT		1940/06/12		M/65276	STECK	F		1941/08/16	
M/28836	SIMPSON	W		1941/03/25	1	M/45440	STEELE	LARRY		1940/06/22	
K/98379	SIMPSON	W		1941/04/08		C/70623	STEELE	M	W	1944/02/25	1
K/45320	SIMS	C	W	1944/10/19	1	M/45168	STEER	RALPH	JOHN	1940/06/11	
H/59212	SIMS	F	J	1944/12/28	1	M/65979	STEFANIK	J	S	1941/08/16	
M/65586	SIMS	R	C	1941/08/16		M/45342	STEINBRENNER	FELIX		1940/06/17	
M/45074	SINCLAIR	WILLIAM		1940/06/12	1	M/45660	STENHOUSE	THOMAS	EDWARD	1940/07/08	
M/45547	SINCLAIR	WILLIAM	ROBERT	1940/06/24		M/65147	STEPA	G		1941/08/16	1
M/45075	SKOYEN	JOHN	DONALD	1940/06/10		M/45382	STEPHEN	STANLEY		1940/06/19	
M/45192	SKRYPCHUK	OLIVER		1940/06/13		M/45311	STEPHENS	HARRY	ARTHUR	1940/06/14	
M/45378	SLATER	JOHN	CEDRIC	1940/06/19	1	M/45675	STEPHENSON	GORDON	CHRISTOPHER	1940/07/29	
M/45729	SLEMKO	STEVEN	SAMUEL	1940/11/22	1	A/86667	STEVENS	ELMER		1944/09/14	1
M/45710	SLOAN	CLELL	RUSSELL	1940/11/22		M/45682	STEVENS	FRANK	CLIFFORD	1940/08/08	
M/104551	SMITH	A	M	1944/05/12	1	M/45610	STEVENSON	FRANKLIN	TREVER	1940/06/26	
M/66014	SMITH	C	E	1941/08/16		M/44855	STEVENSON	VAUGHAN	ALLAN	1940/06/08	1
M/45263	SMITH	CHARLES		1940/06/15		M/45043	STEWART	ALLAN		1940/06/10	
M/45581	SMITH	CHARLES	JAMES	1940/06/26	1	B/144213	STEWART	E	D	1944/11/02	1
L/84569	SMITH	D	J	1942/05/30		M/45224	STEWART	FRANK		1940/06/15	
M/45506	SMITH	ERNEST	BIRKS	1940/06/24		M/45181	STEWART	GILBERT	ROBERT	1940/06/12	
D/117172	SMITH	F	J	1942/04/01	3, 4	A/105254	STEWART	JAMES	F	1944/10/14	1
H/1370	SMITH	G	A	1943/10/04	1	M/45019	STEWART	JAMES	HENRY	1940/06/06	
L/36835	SMITH	G	S. F.	1943/09/24		M/45397	STEWART	JOSIAH		1940/06/18	
M/45501	SMITH	GEORGE	JOSEPH	1940/06/26	1	M/45687	STEWART	WILLIAM	ROBERT KENNETH	1940/08/12	
M/45267	SMITH	HAROLD		1940/06/15							
M/45266	SMITH	HAROLD	HAYES	1940/06/10	1	M/45549	STITH	CLARENCE	ARTHUR	1940/06/24	
A/3887	SMITH	J		1943/07/02		M/41761	STONE	JOHN	CHARLES	1941/10/30	1, 5
G/53461	SMITH	J	N	1943/08/13	3, 4	M/45209	STONE	LANGLEY	REID	1940/06/13	
A/87258	SMITH	J	R	1944/09/16	1	M/45026	STONE	RICHARD	SHEA	1940/06/10	1
M/45561	SMITH	JACK		1940/06/26	1	B/32388	STONEY	G	F	BY 1944/05	7
M/31023	SMITH	JAMES		1941/06/08	1	M/105698	STORVIK	VERNON	ELSWORTH	1943/10/04	1, 5
M/45602	SMITH	JAMES		1940/06/24	1	H/14022	STOVER	L	H	1944/10/31	1
M/45502	SMITH	JAMES	CHARLES	1940/06/24	1	M/44972	STRACHAN	JAMES	ALEXANDER	1940/06/08	1
M/45195	SMITH	JOHN	DENIS	1940/06/13		M/45030	STRACHEY	EDWARD	VICTOR	1940/06/10	
M/45390	SMITH	ORVIL	FRANKLIN	1940/06/18		A/105441	STRATHDEE	CLIFFORD		1943/10/04	1
C/16670	SMITH	R	D	1944/02/18	3, 8	M/106262	STRATHERN	J	W	1944/10/05	1
M/45395	SMITH	RALPH	DELMORE MORLEY	1940/06/18		H/9025	STRICKLAND	L	V	1944/11/09	1
M/44895	SMITH	RAY	CLARKE	1940/06/07	2	D/14680	STUART	LESLIE	G	1944/05/28	1, 8
M/44876	SMITH	ROBERT	HENRY	1940/06/07		B/101196	SULLIVAN	S	P		1, 4, 8
L/36707	SMITH	T	L	1943/09/24		B/135447	SULPHUR	J	V	1943/10/04	
A/116516	SMITH	V	L	1944/09/16	1	M/45326	SUNDE	SIVERT	OLOUSE	1940/06/17	
H/104003	SMITH	W		1943/12/23	1	M/45492	SUNDSTROM	FRANK	TYCKO	1940/06/22	
B/143265	SMITH	W	G	1944/09/13	1	M/45679	SUTER	WALTER	PETER	1940/07/30	
H/64006	SMITH	WILFRED	RAYMOND	1942/07/26	1	M/44767	SUTHERLAND	JOHN	CLIFFORD	1940/06/05	
						M/44788	SUTHERLAND	REGINALD	MacGREGOR	1940/06/06	

NUMBER	LAST NAME	FIRST NAME	MIDDLE NAME	JOIN SAR	NOTES
M/45616	SUTLEY	EARL	OLIVER	1940/06/26	1
K/49111	SWAIN	R	T	1944/11/04	1
M/104130	SWANLUND	V	W	1943/08/20	1
M/45186	SWANSON	ALBERT		1940/06/10	
M/45210	SWANSON	WILLIAM	THOMAS	1940/06/13	
B/50053	SWANT	A	L	1945/04/25	1
M/45459	SWEDESKY	WALTER		1940/06/21	
B/69701	SWEENEY	D	L	1943/07/16	
M/45040	SWEET	EARL	RICHARD	1940/06/10	
H/1000	SWEET	J	T	1943/10/04	
C/102715	SWENSON	S	S	1943/12/23	1
L/36320	SYNCO	N		1943/09/24	1
M/65340	SZKOLAR	A		1941/08/16	
L/84693	SZOPKO	F		1942/05/30	
L/84620	TABLER	G		1942/05/30	
M/65589	TAIT	G	G	1941/08/16	
L/84665	TALBOTT	C	T	1942/05/30	1
M/35550	TALSON	T	A	1941/08/16	
M/45546	TANNER	FRANCIS	VICTOR	1940/06/24	1
M/45021	TARR	NORMAN	HARRY	1940/06/07	1
B/145863	TASCH	JOHN	NICHOLAS	1944/12/28	1
M/65373	TATARIN	M		1941/08/16	
D/77100	TAYLOR	EGBERT	J	1944/03/19	1
M/45681	TAYLOR	HARVEY	JOSEPH	1940/07/30	
M/45137	TAYLOR	JAMES	DOUGLAS	1940/06/12	1
M/45356	TAYLOR	JOHN	JAMES	1940/06/17	
M/12378	TAYLOR	NORMAN	HENRY	1941/10/04	
D/76314	TAYLOR	S	V	1944/03/19	
M/45805	TAYLOR	WILFRED	CHARLES	1941/05/21	1
M/45497	TELFER	JACK		1940/06/20	1
A/87260	TELFER	R	J	1945/02/07	1
M/45545	TELFER	THOMAS	WILFRED	1940/06/24	
D/27190	TELFORD	J		1943/07/02	
M/45279	TEMPLER	FREDERICK		1940/06/14	
M/45685	TENNENT	JAMES		1940/08/10	
M/45752	THEROUX	ALCIDE		1941/02/19	1
M/45720	THIBAULT	ANDRE	JULES BERNARD	1940/11/22	6
B/71112	THIBEDEAU	WILLIAM	J	1944/10/28	1
M/44882	THIBERT	ROLAND	ANDRE	1940/06/08	1
H/77367	THOMAS	B	A	1943/04/16	
A/104756	THOMAS	H		1943/08/20	
L/36388	THOMAS	L	R	1943/09/24	
M/45047	THOMAS	LEONARD		1940/06/11	1
M/45363	THOMAS	WALTER	VALE	1940/06/18	
F/5394	THOMPSON	A	C	1944/05/06	1
A/105095	THOMPSON	D	G	1943/10/04	1
M/44804	THOMPSON	HORACE	DIXON	1940/06/06	
B/78670	THOMPSON	J		1943/10/05	
M/28817	THOMPSON	T		1941/03/25	
M/45232	THOMPSON	WILLIAM	BARRETT	1940/06/15	
M/44933	THOMSON	THOMAS	JAMES	1940/07/04	
F/52575	THORBOURNE	H	L	1944/10/11	1
M/15900	THORESEN	R	E	1944/05/12	1
M/45765	THORN	EDWIN	GEOFFREY	1941/02/19	1
A/86936	THORNLEY	W		1944/05/12	
M/45265	THORNTON	SIDNEY	HERBERT	1940/06/15	
M/45629	THORPE	ROBERT	STANLEY	1940/06/24	
M/45261	THRUN	GEORGE	ARTHUR	1940/06/14	1
M/45229	THUESEN	SOREN		1940/06/15	1
M/45275	TILDEN	WILLIAM	BARNES	1940/06/11	
L/106599	TILLSLEY	C	D	1944/10/19	1
M/45445	TOEWS	PETER		1940/06/20	1
F/76417	TOMLINSON	G	A	1943/10/04	1
B/137482	TOMLINSON	J	E	1944/04/07	
L/66565	TOMPKINS	W	R	1943/10/04	
M/63924	TOPOROWSKI	KAZIMER	T	1942/07/26	1
M/45635	TOULAND	JOHN		1940/06/28	

NUMBER	LAST NAME	FIRST NAME	MIDDLE NAME	JOIN SAR	NOTES
M/45239	TOUPIN	ROGER	EDWARD	1940/06/13	1
M/45296	TOUROND	GEORGE	WILLIAM	1940/06/12	1, 5
M/44586	TOWN	LAWRENCE	LESTER	1940/06/26	
B/137489	TRELFORD	EDWARD	P	1943/10/04	1
E/39104	TREMBLAY	E		1943/03/12	3, 4
M/56635	TRIBE	THOMAS	WILLIAM	1942/07/26	
M/45147	TRISKA	JOSEPH		1940/06/12	
B/85244	TROTCHIE	C	J	1945/01/30	1
B/119456	TROTTER	H	L	1945/04/25	1
C/102385	TROTTIER	D	L. J. F.	1944/05/16	1, 6
D/128511	TROWER	A	W	1942/05/11	3, 4
M/45297	TRUITT	JACK	ARTHUR	1940/06/12	
K/49493	TRUTE	W	H	1943/12/23	1
M/44916	TUBBS	ROY		1940/06/05	
A/108547	TUCK	JAMES	BERTRAM	1944/11/04	1
L/101653	TUCKER	S	D	1943/08/20	1
M/45293	TUFF	ALLAN	GEORGE	1940/06/12	1
A/106301	TULETT	S	H	1944/09/16	1
M/45234	TURKO	NICK		1940/06/13	
M/45313	TURNER	HARVEY	WILFORD	1940/06/12	1
M/44805	TURNER	WILLIAM	RICHARD	1940/06/06	1
M/35778	TUSON	R	H	1941/08/16	
M/45552	TWETEN	SAMUEL		1940/06/25	
M/45544	TYLER	FRANK		1940/06/24	
M/45156	UMPHREY	JAMES	NELSON	1940/06/13	
M/44915	UPTON	HARRY		1940/06/05	
K/54516	URQUHART	J	A	1944/11/06	1
L/103119	UTKE	WILFRED	L	1943/09/02	1
A/116237	VACHON	R	M	1944/10/19	1
M/45166	VAELLANCOURT	JOSEPH		1940/06/11	
B/137490	VAILLANCOURT	W	J	1943/10/04	1
M/45657	VAN DER MARK	WALTER		1940/06/26	1
M/45370	VAN HUESEN	EDWARD	VICTOR	1940/06/13	
B/126462	VAN LITH	A	B	1945/04/28	1
M/44809	VAN MEELEN	ANTONIUS	CORNELIUS	1940/06/06	
M/45543	VAN SICKLE	RALPH	DENNIS	1940/06/24	
M/45276	VARGA	STEVE		1940/06/12	
D/131146	VEINOT	G	R	1944/05/06	1
M/44828	VELUX	GENE		1940/06/07	
B/135285	VERNON	FREDERICK		1943/12/23	1
M/45541	VERSAILLES	DAVID	HENRY	1940/06/24	
M/45540	VERSAILLES	JOHN	LOUIS	1940/06/24	
C/102085	VEZINA	G		1943/08/20	
H/100999	VIENNEAU	P	J. F.	1944/10/05	1
D/239	VINCENT	H		1942/04/01	3, 4
M/44914	VIRTUE	RONALD		1940/06/05	1
B/63245	VISCOUNTY	L		1943/07/16	1
M/44829	VITKOVICH	MIRKO	EMRY	1940/06/07	1
L/84516	VORRA	G		1942/05/30	
L/84691	WACK	P	K	1942/05/30	
M/44858	WADE	HAROLD	LORNE	1940/06/08	
M/45012	WAGNER	ADAM	GABRIEL	1940/06/13	
M/31569	WAGNER	G	J	1941/09/11	1
M/44872	WAGNER	JAMES	SHOUP	1940/06/07	1, 5
K/85515	WAIDSON	J	W	1944/02/02	1, 6
L/36564	WAKEFIELD	L	H	1943/11/19	1
M/45025	WALDRON	JOHN	THOMAS	1940/06/10	
M/44847	WALKER	ALEXANDER	WILLIAM	1940/06/08	
H/104017	WALKER	D	A	1943/10/04	1
M/44973	WALKER	EDWARD	BRITTON	1940/06/08	
B/118773	WALKER	ELLWOOD	F	1944/10/11	1
H/104067	WALKER	G	G	1943/09/02	1
A/21379	WALKER	H	E	1942/11/20	3, 4
M/45169	WALKER	HARRY	GEORGE	1940/06/11	5
L/103738	WALKER	J	W	1943/10/04	
M/45013	WALKER	JOHN	LEONARD	1940/06/13	1
K/69485	WALKER	L		1943/09/10	
M/35672	WALKER	R	A	1942/04/15	1

NUMBER	LAST NAME	FIRST NAME	MIDDLE NAME	JOIN SAR	NOTES
M/7160	WALL	JOHN	WILLIAM	1940/06/06	
B/132701	WALLER	F		1943/09/10	1
M/45615	WALMSLEY	JOSEPH		1940/06/24	1
M/107768	WALTERS	D		1944/10/14	1
M/45669	WALTERS	WELDRICH	JOSEPH	1940/07/16	
F/52576	WALTHERR	C	J	1944/10/14	1
F/76425	WALTHERR	R	A	1944/09/13	1
M/57049	WALTON	ALAN	CHARLES	1942/07/26	1
C/38287	WALTON	HARVEY	WILFRED	1943/10/04	1, 5
M/45020	WARD	CHARLES		1940/06/07	
K/73363	WARD	J	B	BY 1944/05	7
M/45594	WARKE	JOHN		1940/06/25	1
C/32336	WARNER	S		1944/10/19	1
C/58365	WARNOCK	P	C	1943/07/02	
M/45246	WARREN	GEORGE	WILLIAM	1940/06/12	
L/53523	WASELICK	JOHN		1943/09/10	1
M/45211	WASHBURN	HAROLD	LAWSON	1940/06/10	
B/139594	WASMANN	JOSEPH		1943/10/04	1
M/45062	WATERS	GEORGE		1940/06/11	
B/69583	WATERS	S	J	1944/10/19	1
M/101742	WATERTON	J	E	1943/08/20	
M/44852	WATKINS	HERBERT		1940/06/08	1
M/44806	WATKINS	JEFFREY	THEODORE	1940/06/06	
M/11415	WATTERS	J	F. G.	1940/07/17	3
M/45093	WEAR	CHARLES	ARTHUR	1940/06/10	1
M/31053	WEAR	ROBERT	DELLATIN	1940/11/06	
—	WEATHERHEAD	LARRY		—	
M/45738	WEBB	GEORGE	WILLIAM	1941/02/19	1
B/139538	WEBB	J	H	1943/10/04	
M/45148	WEBBER	EMERSON	GEORGE	1940/06/12	
M/45496	WEBBER	FRED		1940/06/24	
B/102022	WEBSTER	ARTHUR	V	1944/10/14	1
M/45524	WEDELL	ARVID	RUDOLPH	1940/06/24	
G/28347	WELBON	A	W	1944/11/24	1
L/67454	WELKER	H	G	1943/08/20	
M/45418	WELLS	CHARLES	EDWARD	1940/06/12	1
C/36572	WELLSTOOD	P		1943/03/12	1, 3, 4, 8
M/45813	WELSH	H	J	1941/06/03	
M/45379	WELSH	WILLIAM	WALTER	1940/06/19	
M/44918	WENTLAND	ROY	HAROLD	1940/06/06	
M/65201	WERNER	D	E	1941/08/16	1
B/139716	WESLEY	E	E	1943/10/04	1
H/63757	WESTOVER	ALLAN		1942/07/26	1
M/63572	WHEAT	N	P	1943/08/20	1
H/2569	WHETTELL	C	A	1941/11/25	3
M/45508	WHITE	CHARLES	EWART	1940/06/24	
M/45024	WHITE	CHARLES	HARRY ALEXANDER	1940/06/08	
M/45076	WHITE	CYRIL	CHARLES	1940/06/12	1
M/16923	WHITE	DANIEL	EDWARD	1943/04/09	1
D/76084	WHITE	E	J	1944/03/19	1
M/45157	WHITE	GEORGE	WILLIAM	1940/06/12	1
D/76385	WHITE	J	J	1944/03/19	1
M/45539	WHITE	JOHN	DOUGLAS	1940/06/24	1
M/45595	WHITE	JOHN	TED	1940/06/25	
C/101850	WHITE	R	J	1943/08/20	1
D/77179	WHITE	RUSSEL	J	1944/08/11	1
M/12030	WHITFORD	R	B	1941/11/02	
M/45161	WHITFORD	RALPH		1940/06/11	1
C/121440	WHITNEY	E		1944/12/08	1
M/45572	WHITTEN	NORMAN	EDWIN	1940/06/26	
M/65217	WICHINSKI	C		1941/08/16	
A/105295	WICKE	CARL	J	1943/10/04	1
M/44863	WICKSTROM	KARL	JOHN CLIFFORD	1940/06/08	1, 5
L/105779	WICKSTROM	R	E	1944/11/02	1

NUMBER	LAST NAME	FIRST NAME	MIDDLE NAME	JOIN SAR	NOTES
H/103597	WIEBE	JACOB		1944/09/01	1
M/44830	WIESS	PHILIP	GOTTLIEB	1940/06/07	
D/77250	WIGHT	J	G	1944/03/19	1
B/41822	WILCOX	J	E	1944/10/06	1
M/45094	WILKINSON	WILLIAM	JAMES	1940/06/10	1
F/29903	WILLETT	G	M	1943/08/20	
M/45027	WILLIAMS	DANIEL	DESMOND	1940/06/10	
M/44808	WILLIAMS	FREDERICK	GEORGE	1940/06/06	
M/45470	WILLIAMS	JOHN	STOCKTON	1940/06/19	1
M/44988	WILLIAMS	THOMAS	HAYDN	1940/06/06	
M/40836	WILLIAMS	W	W	1940/07/17	3
A/460	WILLIS	M	G	1945/03/11	1
H/17435	WILSON	D		1944/06/02	1, 4, 8
M/45149	WILSON	IAN		1940/06/12	
K/100163	WILSON	K	E	1942/11/06	1, 3, 4, 8
A/102880	WILSON	LYLE		1943/10/04	1
M/45656	WILSON	ROBERT	WILLIAM	1940/06/26	1
M/45336	WILSON	WALTER	HIBBERT	1940/06/18	1
M/45793	WILTON	DAVID	RUSSELL	1941/02/19	
M/44785	WINQUIST	WILLIAM	WOODROW	1940/06/06	
M/45462	WINTERS	PETER		1940/06/21	1
K/49197	WITHER	D	G	1944/02/25	1
M/45583	WOLDEN	EINER		1940/06/24	
M/59343	WOLFE	L	L	1941/03/25	1
M/36463	WOLFER	A		1940/10/17	
M/45183	WOLGIEN	HERBERT	ALBERT ERIC	1940/06/12	1
M/44807	WONNENBURG	BERNHARDT		1940/06/06	
M/44912	WOOD	BERNARD	ALFRED	1940/06/05	
M/45133	WOOD	CLARENCE	WILSON	1940/06/12	
M/65400	WOOD	E	H	1941/08/16	
M/44951	WOOD	EARLE	ADELBERT	1940/06/10	1
B/95316	WOOD	H		1942/05/14	1, 3, 4, 8
M/45386	WOOD	HAROLD	EDISON	1940/06/19	
F/95763	WOOD	S	E	1944/09/22	1, 4, 8
K/74011	WOOD	W		1944/02/04	1, 3, 8
M/45443	WOOD	WILFRED	CLARENCE	1940/06/20	1
M/35596	WOODLEY	D	E	1941/08/16	
M/45014	WOODRUFF	VERNON	IRVINE	1940/06/13	
H/8567	WOODS	LLOYD	ALFRED	1943/12/23	1, 5
M/49001	WOOLF	GARTH	LEAVITT	1940/06/26	1
M/49002	WOOLF	VICTOR	AMOS	1940/06/26	
M/44974	WOOLFREY	WILLIAM	ARTHUR	1940/06/08	
M/45405	WOOLLAM	JOHN	KENNETH ALFRED	1940/06/19	
L/103751	WORTHINGTON	A	L	1943/10/04	
B/148147	WRIGHT	R	C	1944/09/01	1
L/84615	WUNSCH	E		1942/05/30	
M/65506	WYKA	R		1941/08/16	
M/59137	WYLCHKO	F		1941/03/25	
M/45015	WYLIE	STANLEY	RAYMOND	1940/06/13	
M/45372	WYNNYK	WILLIAM		1940/06/17	
L/39078	YECHTEL	JOHN		1943/09/24	1
H/104013	YEO	R	E	1944/10/05	1
L/36810	YESCHUK	W		1943/09/24	
M/59342	YOUNG	H	J	1941/03/25	1
C/31761	YOUNG	H	T	1944/05/07	1, 3, 4, 8
M/45758	YOUNG	NORMAN	LEWIS	1941/02/19	
M/59138	YOUNG	R	G	1941/03/25	1
M/45415	ZACHARY	STEVE		1940/07/05	1
M/28833	ZIBROWSKI	F		1941/03/25	
L/84727	ZILKOWSKY	A	V	1942/05/30	1
M/55368	ZMARZLY	S		1941/10/04	
B/110992	ZUCK	N		1943/07/16	1
M/45434	ZWICK	HERBERT	ARNOLD	1940/06/15	1
F/51693	ZWICKER	WALTER	St CLAIR	1943/10/04	5

NOTES

ABBREVIATIONS USED IN NOTES
Owing to their great number, highly abbreviated forms of the sources have been utilized in the notes. The full citations will be found in the bibliography.

AHS Army Historical Section
AHQ Army Headquarters
AR Algonquin Regiment
ASH Argyll and Sutherland Highlanders of Canada
CMHQ Canadian Military Headquarters
DEG Donald E. Graves
DHist Directorate of History, DND
HLI Highland Light Infantry
Int(s) Interview(s)
JLS Jack L. Summers
LWR Lincoln and Welland Regiment
MG Manuscript Group
NAC National Archives of Canada, Ottawa
n.d. No date
NNSH North Nova Scotia Highlanders
NPRC Files of the National Personnel Records Centre, Ottawa
NSR North Nova Scotia Highlanders
OL Operations Log
PSN Notes on fatal SAR casualties by Padre Phillip Silcox attached to the November 1946 SAR War Diary
PRO Public Record Office, Kew, Surrey, UK
RG Record Group
SAR South Alberta Regiment
WD War Diary. If no other reference, this is the War Diary of the South Alberta Regiment

PROLOGUE

1. Singer, *History of the 31st*, 448. The exact figures are 981 killed and 2,312 wounded.
2. *Medicine Hat News*, 2 June 1919.
3. *Medicine Hat News*, 2 June 1919.
4. Singer, *History of the 31st*, 445.

1. "WE USED TO PARADE EVERY THURSDAY NIGHT." CANADA: SEPTEMBER 1939-AUGUST 1940

1. "The SAR Song," sung to the tune of "The Stein Song," dates from the mists of time (that is to say the 1930s) and was revived when the Regiment mobilized in 1940; Childs to DEG, 29 Mar 97.
2. *Medicine Hat Daily News*, June-August 1939 and 9 September 1939.
3. *Medicine Hat Daily News*, August 1939.
4. *Canadian Pictorial and Illustrated War News*, 20 June 1885.
5. DHist 11.1.001, "Short History," 5.
6. DHist 11.1.001, "Short History," 2-4.
7. MacDonald, "Summary History"; DHist 11.1001, "Short History," 6-7.
8. DHist 11.1.001, "Short History"; MacDonald, "Summary History"; Hughes, *March Past*, 406.
9. DHist 11.1.001, "Short History," 8.
10. DHist 11.1.001, "Short History," 9; Stacey, *Six War Years*, 13.
11. Horn, *The Dirty Thirties*, 10, 12, 278.
12. Int: D. McLeod, 21 January 1996.

13. Memorandum, "The Defence of Canada," by McNaughton, 28 May 1935, quoted in Stacey, *Arms, Men and Governments*, 3.
14. Stacey, *Arms, Men and Government*, 3.
15. NPRC; Author's conversation with J.L. Summers.
16. Int: A.F. Coffin.
17. Int: A.F. Coffin.
18. Int: G.L. McDougall.
19. Int: N. MacPherson.
20. Int: B. Bean.
21. Int: G.L. McDougall.
22. Foster, *Meeting of Generals*, 78-79.
23. Int: G.L. McDougall.
24. Int: A.F Coffin.
25. Cunniffe, *Scarlet, Riflegreen and Khaki*, 30-31.
26. Stevens, *City Goes To War*, 177.
27. *Medicine Hat Daily News*, 25 May 1939.
28. Stevens, *City Goes To War*, 177.
29. *Medicine Hat Daily News*, 30 August 1939.
30. House of Commons Debates, 8 September 1939, p. 45, quoted in Copp, "Ontario 1939: The Decision for War," 276.
31. Stacey, *Six War Years*, 30-33, 43.
32. Int: D. McLeod, 21 January 1996.
33. Stacey, *Six War Years*, 62.
34. Int: A.G. McGillivray.
35. Int: A.F. Coffin.
36. Ints: A.F. Coffin; Robert Fairhurst; A.G. McGillivray; Harry Quarton; and Herbie Watkins, 7 September 1995. Letter, Herbie Watkins to DEG, 14 January 1995.
37. Stacey, *Six War Years*, 77-79.
38. G.L. McDougall, *Short History*, 17-18. In the *SAR Christmas Magazine*, 1941, it states that this meeting was held on 2 June 1940 and the method of assigning companies was done by drawing slips of paper from a hat.
39. WD, 29 June 1940.
40. Hodder-William, *Princess Patricia's Canadian Light Infantry*, vol. I, 195-196.
41. Int: J. Simpson.
42. *Defence Forces List, November 1939*; McDougall, *Short History*, 17-19; *SAR Christmas Magazine*, December 1941.
43. McDougall, *Short History*, 18-19; *SAR Christmas Magazine 1941*.
44. Recruiting statistics from WD, 29 June 1940. Reasons for enlisting in the SAR based on the following personal memoirs by SAR veterans: Clipperton, "Personal Memories"; Galipeau, "Pee Wees"; and Wood, "The SAR." Other information was contributed by letters from L.O. Ireland to DEG, c. November 1994; Lyle Piepgrass to DEG, February 1995; and Herbie Watkins to DEG, 14 January 1995. The following veterans discussed in personal interviews their reason for joining the SAR in 1940: Gerry Adams, Albert Ball, Robert Barr; Bruce Bean; Adrian Berry; Tom Eastwood; Robert Fairhurst; Jim Gove; J.L. Huntley;

Robert McCloy; A.G. McGillivray; E.V. Nieman; G.E. Olmstead; Harry Quarton; Robert Rasmussen; Jimmy Simpson; Stan Rose; Soren Thuesen; Herbie Watkins; and George White.
45. Clipperton, "Personal Memories."
46. Int: J.L. Huntley.
47. Int: Soren Thuesen.
48. Int: E.V. Nieman.
49. Galipeau, "Pee Wees," 5.
50. Int: E.V. Nieman.
51. Int: Jack Porter.
52. Int: D. McLeod, 21 January 1996.
53. Int: E.V. Nieman.
54. Ints: Robert Fairhurst and Chris Rose; "SAR Pictorial Record."
55. Int: A.F. Coffin.
56. Galipeau, "Pee Wees," 13-14.
57. Int: A.F. Coffin.
58. Galipeau, "Pee Wees," 12; Stacey, *Six Years of War*, 83.
59. Clipperton, "Personal Memories."
60. Galipeau, "Pee Wees," 12.
61. WD, 11 July 1940.
62. Galipeau, "Pee Wees," 8.
63. Wood, "The SAR."
64. Int: D. McLeod, 21 January 1996.
65. Galipeau, "Pee Wees" 16-17.
66. Galipeau, "Pee Wees," 24.
67. Galipeau, "Pee Wees," 24.
68. Wood, "The SAR."
69. WD, 6 August 1940.
70. WD, 2 August 1940.
71. Int: Adam Wagner.

2. "LOOK, ANOTHER DEAD CORPORAL." CANADA: AUGUST 1940-DECEMBER 1941

1. "She Wears Her Pink Pyjamas," SAR Marching Song from the summer of 1940. The words can vary according to the audience.
2. WD, 16 August 1940.
3. Int: Tom Eastwood.
4. WD, August and September 1940, Clipperton, "Personal Memories."
5. Neil MacPherson to DEG, 26 November 1996.
6. Int: J. Galipeau.
7. Int: W. McLeod, 25 August 1995.
8. Wilf Taylor to DEG, c. April 1995.
9. Int: A.F. Coffin.
10. Int: Albert Ball.
11. Lyle Piepgrass to DEG, c. Feb 95.
12. Int: D. McLeod, 21 January 1996.
13. Int: Jim Gove.
14. Int: Jim Gove.
15. WD, August 1940.
16. WD, 23 August 1940.
17. NPRC.
18. WD, 26 August 1940.
19. Int: Bob Rasmussen.
20. Int: Albert Ball.
21. Int: Bob Rasmussen.
22. WD, 28 August 1940.
23. Int: D. McLeod, 21 January 1996; WD 1 October 1940, Transport Instruction, 28 September 1940.
24. Int: Harry Quarton.
25. *SAR Christmas Magazine 1941*.
26. McDougall, *Short History*, 20.

27. Herbie Watkins to DEG, 7 December 1995.
28. Galipeau, "Pee Wees," 33.
29. Int: A.F. Coffin.
30. Galipeau, "Pee Wees," 34.
31. Int: A.F. Coffin, 27 August 1995.
32. Int: A.F. Coffin.
33. Int: Harry Quarton.
34. Int: G.L. McDougall.
35. *Edmonton Journal*, 16 November 1941.
36. Int: Albert Ball.
37. *Army Catering Quantities*, 1.
38. Menus from a "Specimen Weekly Bill of Fare," *Army Catering Quantities*, 8.
39. Int: Adrian Berry.
40. Galipeau, "Pee Wees," 34.
41. Int: E.V. Nieman.
42. Int: G.L. McDougall.
43. Galipeau, "Pee Wees," 34.
44. Nicholson, "1940-1945," 2.
45. Galipeau, "Pee Wees," 35.
46. Childs, "Trumpeter."
47. Int: Adrian Berry.
48. Wood, "The SAR"; Atkinson, "Memoir."
49. WD, 8 January 1941.
50. Int: D. McLeod, 21 January 1996.
51. WD, November 1940-February 1941; Ints: D. McLeod, 21 January 1996 and Albert Ball.
52. Galipeau, "Pee Wees," 7.
53. Int: Chris Rose.
54. Int: Chris Rose.
55 Int: Chris Rose.
56. Atkinson, "Memoir."
57. Clipperton, "Personal Memories."
58. Galipeau, "Pee Wees," 35.
59. Int: Jim Gove.
60. Int: A.F. Coffin; WD, January-March 1941; *SAR Christmas Magazine 1941*.
61. Int: A.F. Coffin.
62. Int: Jay Moreton.
63. Int: G.L. McDougall.
64. Int: G.L. McDougall.
65. NPRC, Brigadier J.B. Stevenson to HQ, Military District 2, 21 July 1941.
66. Int: G.L. McDougall; NPRC.
67. NPRC.
68. Clipperton, "Personal Memories."
69. WD, May 1941.
70. V. Childs to DEG, 29 March 1996; SAR Pictorial Record.
71. *Medicine Hat News*, 19 May 1941.
72. R. Allsopp to DEG, 13 March 1995.
73. SAR Pictorial Record.
74. Int: Adrian Berry.
75. McDougall, *Short History*, 22.
76. *SAR Christmas Magazine 1941*.
77. Int: A.F. Coffin.
78. Int: D. McLeod, 21 January 1996.
79. *SAR Christmas Magazine 1941*.
80. Int: Bob Rasmussen.
81. Childs, "Memories."
82. Atkinson, "Memoirs."
83. Stacey, *Six Years of War*, 447.
84. Int: A.F. Coffin.
85. Gilbert Johnson to DEG, 28 March 1994.
86. Galipeau, "Pee Wees," 25.
87. WD, 12 October 1941.

88. Int: A.F. Coffin.
89. NPRC.
90. WD, September 1941.
91. Int: D. McLeod, 21 January 1996.
92. Stacey, *Six Years of War*, 489.
93. *SAR Christmas Magazine 1941*.
94. Int: D. Mcleod, 21 January 1996.
95. Int: D. McLeod, 21 January 1996.
96. Int: D. McLeod, 21 January 1996.
97. *SAR Christmas Magazine 1941*.
98. Int: D. McLeod, 21 January 1996.
99. Int: D. Mcleod, 21 January 1996.
100. *SAR Christmas Magazine 1941*.
101. *SAR Christmas Magazine 1941*.
102. WD, 19 November 1941.

3. "A LOVELY MAN WHO ENJOYED
THE ARMY." CANADA AND BRITAIN:
DECEMBER 1941–FEBRUARY 1943
1. Glen McDougall, "Operation Order," *SAR Christmas Magazine 1941*, sung to the tune of "Mademoiselle from Armentières."
2. McDougall, *Short History*, 24; SAR Pictorial Record; WD, 5-6 December 1941.
3. McDougall, *Short History*, 24; also WD, 11 December 1941.
4. Nicholson, "1940-1945."
5. WD, 8 February 1942; also WD, January-February 1942.
6. All the units in the Canadian Armoured Corps were numbered sequentially within the corps and this number was used on all official correspondence. Although the South Albertas were now officially the 29th Canadian Armoured Regiment, that does not mean there were twenty-nine such units in the corps as armoured reconnaissance, armoured car and recce regiments were also numbered sequentially. The numbers may have been official but, unofficially, the units continued to call themselves and each other by their older titles.
7. WD, 26 January, 2 February 1942.
8. Worthington, *Worthy*, 1-183.
9. Johnson, *Break-Through*, 127-130; 162-165; 177-178, 243-254.
10. Johnson, *Break-Through*, 243-254, 271; Carver, *Apostles*, 33-53, 47-48; Ogorkiewicz, *Armor*, 16-17, 56-59; Smithers, *Rude Mechanicals*, 1-26; Bidwell and Graham, *Fire-Power*, 176.
11. Graham, *Fire-Power*, 190-191.
12. Corum, *Roots*, 122-123.
13. *Toronto Star*, 23 July 1938.
14. Greenhous, *Dragoon*, 284, 290; Wallace, *Dragons*, 108, 110-113.
15. Worthington, *Worthy*, 153.
16. Brigadier E.J. Schmidlin, *Globe and Mail*, 23 November 1939 quoted in Worthington, *Worthy*, 159.
17. Wallace, *Dragons*, 123-125; DHist 112.1 (D34), Confidential Memo by Worthington, 10 July 1940.
18. DHist 112.1 (D34), Worthington to Stewart, n.d. (received at NDHQ 6 September 1940).
19. DHist 112 (D34): Memorandum by Worthington, n.d. (29 August 1940 from context) and Worthington to Stuart, 10 September 1940; Wallace, *Dragons*, 140.
20. Wallace, *Dragons*, 143-151; DHist, AHS Report No. 38, "Tank Production in Canada."
21. Wallace, *Dragons*, 157-164; Worthy, *Worthington*, 173-177; DHist, AHQ Report No. 43, Training of the 4th and 5th Canadian Armoured Divisions in the United Kingdom, October 1941-July 1944, 2; Stacey, *Six Years of War*, 94-97.
22. Galipeau, "Pee Wees," 67.

23. Nicholson, "1940-1945."
24. Int: G.L. McDougall.
25. WD, 3 February 1942.
26. Int: Jack Porter; also WD for February-May 1942.
27. Int: A.F. Coffin.
28. WD, February-March 1942; also Owen and Watkins, *Royal Armoured Corps*, 17.
29. Int: Isabel Currie, 12 December 1995.
30. WD, February-May 1942.
31. WD, 28 March 1942.
32. WD, 1 April 1942.
33. *Canadian Press News*, 29 August 1942.
34. DHist, Director, Royal Armoured Corps, Monthly Liaison Letter, No. 25.
35. Nicholson, "1940-1945"; also WD, March-June 1942; SAR Pictorial Record.
36. Int: Adam Wagner.
37. WD, 16 April 1942.
38. WD, 17 March 1942; also WD, April-June 1942.
39. Int: Isabel Currie, 12 December 1995.
40. Wood, "The SAR."
41. Galipeau, "Pee Wees," 64.
42. Int: G.L. McDougall.
43. A.F. Coffin to JLS, 15 February 1993.
44. WD, 2 June, 27 July 1942
45. WD, 20-26 June 1942.
46. WD, 16 June 1942.
47. Galipeau, "Pee Wees," 66.
48. Nicholson, "1940-1945."
49. WD, 31 July 1942; also WD, 12 and 21 July 1942.
50. WD, 5 August 1942; SAR Pictorial Record.
51. WD, 22 August 1942; SAR Pictorial Record.
52. Nicholson, "1940-1945."
53. Int: J. Hutchinson.
54. Int: J. Hutchinson.
55. WD, 31 August-1 September 1942.
56. Galipeau, "Pee Wees," 83.
57. Int: R.D. Wear.
58. McDougall, *Short History*, 26.
59. Galipeau, "Pee Wees," 82.
60. Int: Neil Apselet.
61. Smith, *All Tanked Up*, 14.
62. Bob Clipperton to Andy Clipperton, 23 March 1944; DHist, AHS Report No. 59, Food Complaints and Cooks' Training, Canadian Army Overseas, 1939-1943.
63. WD, 15 December 1943; Int: J. Walker.
64. WD, 12 September 1942.
65. WD, 2 November 1942; also WD, October 1942.
66. NPRC.
67. WD, 12 November 1942.
68. WD, November-December 1942.
69. Int: J.H. Redden.
70. WD, 19 November 1942.
71. WD, 25 December 1942.
72. McDougall, *Short History*, 27.
73. Stacey, *Arms, Men and Government*, 399.
74. NAC, RG 24, 10595, File 215.C1 (D 582), McNaughton to GOCs, 4 and 5 Armoured Divisions, 2 December 1942.
75. NAC, RG 24, 10595, File 215.C1 (D582), Worthington to McNaughton, 5 December 1942.
76. WD, 29 December 1942. In fact the Elgins and Sherbrookes were not disbanded, the former becoming an armoured delivery regiment and the latter continuing as a regiment in 2 CAC. Although the South Albertas were now 29 CARR does not mean there were twenty-nine armoured recce regiments in the CAC. There were actually only two such units, the SAR and the Governor General's Horse Guards of 5th Canadian Armoured Division, whose corps number and title was 3 CARR. It is inter-

esting that the only two armoured reconnaissance regiments in the Canadian army were commanded by brothers, Swatty Wotherspoon and Ian Cumberland.
77. WD, 29 December 1942.
78. *Employment of Reconnaissance Units. 1944*, 2.
79. WD, 1 January 1942.
80. WD, 4 CAD, January 1943, Training Bulletin No. 28, 19 January 1943, The Armoured Reconnaissance Regiment.
81. WD, 4 CAD, January 1943, Training Bulletin No. 28, 19 January 1943, The Armoured Reconnaissance Regiment.
82. WD, January and February 1942.
83. McDougall, *Short History*, 27.
84. WD, 14 January 1943.
85. McDougall, *Short History*, 27.
86. WD, 10 October 1942; SAR Pictorial Record.
87. WD, 9, 12, 27 February 1943.

4. "YOU'VE GOT THE SARS, THEY'RE MY
PRIDE AND JOY." BRITAIN: MARCH–
DECEMBER 1943
1. "SAR Song," composed by Corporal Darryl Robertson, Edmonton, 1940.
2. WD, February-March 1943.
3. WD, April 1943.
4. Int: G.L. McDougall.
5. WD, May 1943, Report of Attachment, Sergeant Ernest Hill, 3 May 1943.
6. WD, 8 April 1943.
7. McDougall, *Short History*, 27.
8. Wiley Interview with Wotherspoon, 1986.
9. *RMC Review 1930*, 17.
10. *RMC Review 1930*; Genealogical notes on Wotherspoon family supplied by Richard (Swatty) Wotherspoon of Toronto.
11. Wiley Int: G.D. Wotherspoon, 1986.
12. Wiley Int: G.D. Wotherspoon, 1986.
13. Int: D. McLeod, 21 January 1996.
14. Wiley Int: G.D. Wotherspoon, 1986.
15. Int: R. Allsopp.
16. Int: G. Adams.
17. Int: A.F. Coffin.
18. Int: R. Allsopp.
19. Wiley Int: G.D. Wotherspoon, 1986.
20. WD, 10 May 1943.
21. Int: G. Gallimore.
22. Wiley Int: G.D. Wotherspoon, 1986.
23. Int: D. McLeod, 21 January 1996.
24. Int: G. Adams.
25. Int: L. Caseley.
26. Int: G.L. McDougall.
27. Int: A.F. Coffin.
28. WD, 16 May 1943.
29. WD, May 1942; Ross Munro, "Preparations for Second Front. With Alberta Regiment Training Overseas," *Canadian Press*, 8 May 1943.
30. WD, May 1942.
31. Int: D. McLeod, 21 January 1996.
32. Int: D. McLeod, 21 January 1996.
33. Int: D. McLeod, 21 January 1996.
34. Int: D. McLeod, 21 January 1996.
35. Nicholson, "1940-1945."
36. War Diary, June 1942.
37. WD, 13 June 1943.
38. Int: A.F. Coffin, 18 September 1997.
39. Wiley Int: G.D. Wotherspoon, 1986.
40. WD, June 1942.
41. WD, June 1943, Appendix, Training Instruction No. 2. The Carrier Troop.
42. Wiley Int: G.D. Wotherspoon, 1986.
43. Int: D. McLeod, 21 January 1996.
44. Wiley Int: G.D. Wotherspoon, 1986.
45. Int: E. Campbell.
46. WD, June-July 1943.
47. Wiley Int: G.D. Wotherspoon, 1986.
48. Int: E. Campbell.
49. Wiley Int: G.D. Wotherspoon, 1986.

50. WD, 12 July 1943.
51. Wood, "The SAR."
52. Wiley Int: G.D. Wotherspoon, 1986.
53. Int: R. Allsopp.
54. Don Stewart to Mrs. Stewart, 17 August 1943.
55. Don Stewart to DEG, 10 September 1995.
56. NPRC.
57. Wiley Int: G.D. Wotherspoon, 1986.
58. Taylor and Fry, *Beating Around the Bush*, 59.
59. Taylor and Fry, *Beating Around the Bush*, 60-61.
60. WD, 4 September 1943.
61. McDougall, *Short History*, 29.
62. WD, September 1943.
63. WD, 28 September 1943; also for dates indicated.
64. WD, 1 October 1943.
65. WD, October 1943 and dates indicated.
66. Ian Wotherspoon changed his name to Cumberland, his mother's maiden name, before the war.
67. Int: R. Allsopp; also WD for October 1943, dates indicated.
68. Int: T. Barford.
69. WD, October-November 1943.
70. WD, November 1943, Appendix, Exercise Bridoon, Intelligence Summary No. 1, 29 October 1943.
71. WD, October 1943, dates indicated.
72. Worthington, *Worthy*, 190.
73. WD, November 1943; Worthington, *Worthy*, 191.
74. WD, November 1943.
75. WD, 6 November 1943.
76. WD, 20 December 1943.
77. WD, December 1943.
78. Int: W.E. Boothroyd.
79. Int: R. Allsopp.
80. Int: R. Rasmussen.
81. Int: R. Allsopp.
82. Int: W.E. Boothroyd.
83. Int: H. Watkins.
84. Int: S. Thuesen; also McDougall, *Short History*, 30.
85. Int: C. Daley.
86. Clipperton, "Personal Memories."
87. Bob Clipperton to Andy Clipperton, 25 December 1943.
88. Int: G.L. McDougall.
89. Int: G. Irving.
90. WD, November-December 1943.
91. McDougall, *Short History*, 31.
92. NAC, Canadian Army Newsreel No. 22 (c. December 1943).
93. McDougall, *Short History*, 30.
94. A.F. Coffin to JLS, 15 February 1993.
95. WD, 14 December 1943.
96. WD, 23 December 1943.
97. Bob Clipperton to Andy Clipperton, 30 December 1943.
98. Lakes, "Tomorrow's Rainbow."
99. Lakes, "Tomorrow's Rainbow"; WD for December 1943, dates indicated.

5. "SAY A PRAYER FOR ME."
BRITAIN: JANUARY–JULY 1944
1. SAR Marching Song, quoted in McNair, *Soldiers All*, 165.
2. WD, 22 January 1944.
3. NPRC.
4. NPRC.
5. L.C. Giles, ed., *Liphook, Bramshott and the Canadians*, 22.
6. Wiley Int: G.D. Wotherspoon, 1986; WD for February 1944.
7. WD, 15 January 1944.
8. WD, 7 January 1944.
9. English, *Normandy*, 159-160.
10. English, *Normandy*, 160; Bidwell and Graham, *Fire-Power*, 214.

11. Report of Attachment by Sergeant E. Hill, 3 May 1943, SAR WD, May 43.

12. DHist, Director, Royal Armoured Corps, Monthly Liaison Letter, No. 2.

13. *Notes from Theatres of War. No. 16: North Africa, November 1942-May 1943,* 33.

14. On ranges, see Coox and Marshall, *Survey,* 34.

15. DHist, Director, Royal Armoured Corps Monthly Liaison Letter, No. 1, May 1943.

16. Hogg, *Armour in Conflict,* 112-114; Liddell Hart, *The Tanks,* 307-308; Smithers, *Rude Mechanicals,* 51-74; *War Time Tank Production,* 5-6; John Claydon, "Green Flash", 9-10.

17. House, "Combined Arms," 117.

18. Ogorkiewicz, *Armor,* 196-197; House, "Combined Arms," 117-118.

19. Coox and Marshall, *Survey,* 78.

20. NAC, RG 24, C17, 13111, WD, 2 Cdn Corps, January 1943, Minutes of a Conference held by General Montgomery, 13 January 1944, dated 14 January 1944.

21. *Notes on the Employment of Tanks in Support of Infantry,* no pagination.

22. Wilson, "Tank-Infantry Co-Operation Doctrine," 123.

23. WD 4 CAD, October 43, Training Instruction No. 51, 28 October 1943.

24. WD 4 CAD, November 1943, Training Instruction No. 17, based on 2 Canadian Corps Training Instruction No. 19.

25. WD 4 CAD, November 1943, Training Instruction No. 3, based on 2 Canadian Corps Training Instruction No. 8.

26. DHist, Confidential Report on General F.F. Worthington by Simonds, n.d. but almost certainly early February 1944.

27. Worthington, *Worthy,* 194.

28. Kitching, *Mud and Green Fields,* 195.

29. Galipeau, "Pee Wees," 104-105.

30. Int: G. Kitching.

31. Int: G. Kitching.

32. Kitching, *Mud and Green Fields,* 196-197.

33. Kitching, *Mud and Green Fields,* 197.

34. WD, March-May 1944.

35. DHist, Director, Royal Armoured Corps, Monthly Liaison Letter No. 11.

36. WD, 13 March 1944.

37. Taylor, "Immigrant Boy."

38. Paterson, *Ten Brigade,* 14-15.

39. Int: G. Kitching.

40. WD, April-May 1943; Wilson, "Development of Tank-Infantry Co-Operation Doctrine," 123.

41. Wiley Int: G.D. Wotherspoon, 1986.

42. Wiley Int: G.D. Wotherspoon, 1986.

43. WD, 31 March 1944.

44. Bob Clipperton to Andy Clipperton, 2 May 1944.

45. McNair, *Soldiers All,* 161-162.

46. Int: E. Reardon.

47. Int: D. McLeod, 21 January 1996.

48. WD, 20 May 1944.

49. Int: G. Armstrong.

50. WD, April-May 1944; *Combined Operations. REME. Waterproofing of Vehicles and Equipment. 1944.*

51. WD, May 1944.

52. Int: R.D. Wear.

53. Galipeau, "Pee Wees," 106.

54. Int: G.D. Adams.

55. Don Stewart to Mrs. Stewart, 29 February 1944.

56. Int: R. Allsopp.

57. Int: G.D. Adams.

58. Int: G.D. Adams.

59. Don Stewart to Mrs. Stewart, 16 April 1944.

60. Bob Clipperton to Andy Clipperton, 2 April 1944.

61. Arnold Dryer to his fiancée, 15 June 1944.

62. Int: J. Porter.

63. Bob Clipperton to Andy Clipperton, 2 April 1944.

64. Int: J. Simpson.

65. WD, 6 June 1944.

66. Int: R. Maves.

67. WD, 6 June 1944.

68. Int: J. Moreton.

69. Int: E. Reardon.

70. Lakes, "Tomorrow's Rainbow."

71. WD, 12 June 1944.

72. Int: C. Daley.

73. WD, 4 July 1944.

74. Int: R. Allsopp.

75. Arnold Dryer to his fiancée, 26 June 1944.

76. Bob Clipperton to Andy Clipperton, 2 May 1944. Other sources for preceding paragraph are WD, June-July 1944.

77. WD, 17 July 1944.

78. WD, 18-19 July 1944.

79. Galipeau, "Pee Wees," 107.

80. WD, 19 July 1944.

81. Taylor, "Immigrant Boy."

82. Neff, Diary, 20 July 1944.

83. Taylor, "Immigrant Boy."

84. Nicholson, "1940-1945."

85. WD, 19-20 July 1944.

86. WD, 20 July 1944.

87. Neff, Diary, 21 July 1944.

88. Galipeau, "Pee Wees," 108.

89. Int: J. Bell.

90. J. Galipeau, "Pee Wees," 107.

91. WD, 20-22 July 1944.

92. Int: A. Engel; also WD, 24-25 July 1944; Int: J. Lardner.

6. "EVERYTHING WAS NEW AND WE DIDN'T KNOW WHAT WAS GOING ON." FRANCE: 25 JULY–5 AUGUST 1944

1. One of the many versions of "Lili Marlene," the most popular soldier's song of the Second World War, these words were favoured by the men who fought in northwest Europe in 1944-1945.

2. Unless otherwise stated, my account of the Normandy campaign is based on Graves and Whitby, *The Canadian Summer.*

3. Graves and Whitby, *Canadian Summer,* 126.

4. Int: R. Seccombe.

5. Int: D. Ledwidge. Other source for paragraph is WD, 24-27 July 1944.

6. WD, 29 July 1944.

7. A. Denning to JLS, 30 August 1992.

8. WD, 29 July 1944.

9. Sergeant Leo Gariepy quoted in McKee, *Last Round,* 275.

10. *Tactics of the German Army. Vol. I,* 2.

11. Carell, *Invasion,* 155.

12. *German Infantry in Action (Minor Tactics),* 1.

13. *German Defensive Tactics,* 1-2, 4-17.

14. Memorandum, 1 May 1943, in Lucas, *War on the Eastern Front,* 119.

15. *German Infantry in Action (Minor Tactics),* 23.

16. *Vorläufige Richtlinien,* 21.

17. NAC, RG 24, vol. 10550, file 215 A2 033(D4), The Co-operation of Tanks with Infantry.

18. NAC, RG 24, vol. 10553, file 212A1.083 (D92), Memorandum on British Armour, 21st Army Group, 6 July 1944.

19. Coox and Marshall, *Survey,* 17.

20. Coox and Marshall, *Survey,* 17.

21. NAC, RG 24, G3, vol. 10460, 212C1.1009 (D49), Report by AFV(T), 1st Canadian Army, 2 August 1944.

22. Int: T. Milner.

23. Kitching, *Mud and Green Fields,* 205.

24. DHist 79/705, Operational Research in North West Europe. The Work of No. 2 Operational Research Section with 21 Army Group.

25. NAC, RG 24, vol. 10457, 212C1.1009 (D29), Report No. 14, 1 Canadian Field Research Section, 1 Canadian Army, 14 June 1945.

26. Coox and Marshall, *Survey,* 24.

27. DHist 79/705. Operational Research in North West Europe, The Work of No. 2 Operational Research Section with 21 Army Group.

28. DHist 79/705. Operational Research in North West Europe. The Work of No. 2 Operational Research Section with 21 Army Group.

29. DHist 79/705. Operational Research in North West Europe. The Work of No. 2 Operational Research Section with 21 Army Group.

30. Bidwell and Graham, *Fire-Power,* 190-191.

31. Wiley Int: G.D. Wotherspoon, 1986.

32. Author's conversation with J.L. Summers, 1993.

33. Lakes, "Tomorrow's Rainbow."

34. Int: R. Mitchell.

35. WD, 31 July 1944.

36. Don Stewart to Mrs. Stewart, 7 August 1944.

37. Int: T. Clausen.

38. Int: S. Thuesen.

39. Blackburn, *Guns of Normandy,* 399-400.

40. Int: S. Rose.

41. Arnold Dryer to his fiancée, 1 August 1944.

42. Information on the Sherman V from: Hunnicutt, *Sherman,* 159-171; Fletcher, *Sherman VC, Allied Command, M4A4 (75mm) Sherman V.*

43. D. Marshall to DEG, 30 July 1997.

44. Statistics from Coox and Marshall, *Survey,* 5.

45. Montgomery, Directive, 27 July 1944, quoted in Stacey, *Victory,* 199.

46. Kitching, *Mud and Green Fields,* 208.

47. Kitching, *Mud and Green Fields,* 207.

48. Stacey, *Victory,* 206; WD, 4 CAD, 1 August 1944; WD, 10 Brigade, 1 August 1944; WD, LWR, 1 August 1944; WD, 1 August 1944; Int: H. Watkins.

49. WD, 2 August 1944.

50. DHist 85/240, Analysis of Firepower in Normandy, No. 10; Reynolds, *Steel Inferno,* 200.

51. WD, LWR, 1 August 1944.

52. WD, LWR, 1 August 1944.

53. Lieutenant J.G. Martin in Hayes, *The Lincs,* 27.

54. Int: H. Watkins.

55. Int: J. Galipeau.

56. Int: J. Galipeau.

57. Int: G. Irving.

58. WD, 2 August 1944.

59. WD, LWR, 3 August 1944.

60. Int: R. Bruce.

61. Int: H. Watkins.

62. J. Gove to JLS, 2 September 1992.

63. WD, 3 August 1944.

64. WD, ASH, 5 August 1944.

65. WD, 10 Brigade, 5 August 1944.

66. Spencer, *15 Field,* 92.

67. WD, 10 Brigade, 5 August 1944; also Spencer, *15 Field,* 92-93.

68. WD, ASH, 5 August 1944.

69. Wiley Int: G.D. Wotherspoon, 1986.

70. Int: D. Campbell; also WD, 6 August 1944.

71. WD, ASH, 5 August 1944; also Lehmann and Tiemann, *Leibstandarte,* 178-179; Jackson, *Argyll and Sutherland Highlanders,* 79.

72. Private Anonymous quoted in Fraser, *Black Yesterdays,* 218.

73. Int: S. Thuesen.

74. Int: E. Davies.

75. WD, 6 August 1944; Int: E. Hyatt.

76. English, *Normandy,* 253.

77. Wiley Int: G.D. Wotherspoon, 1986.

78. Private Whit Smelser, in Fraser, *Black Yesterdays,* 217.

79. J. Redden to JLS, n.d. (c. 1992).

80. DHist, 1st Canadian Army Intelligence Summary #43, Operation Order, 1056 Grenadier Regiment, 89th Infantry Division, 4 August 1944.

81. Jackson, *Argyll and Sutherland Highlanders,* 79-80.

82. Int: G. Kitching.

7. "THE GREENEST BLOODY ARMY THAT EVER WENT TO WAR." FRANCE: 6–15 AUGUST 1944

1. Verses from "The LOB Song" sung to the tune of "Lili Marlene" and popular in northwest Europe in 1944-1945. LOB means "left out of battle."

2. Directive by Montgomery, 3 August 1944, quoted in Stacey, *Victory,* 211.

3. DHist, Special Interrogation Report, *Brigadeführer* Kurt Meyer, 29 August 1945.

4. In the spring of 1944 the CAC Operational Training Squadron at Woking experimented with using Ram tanks, with their turrets removed, as APCs. These later evolved into the Kangaroo APC (Int: D. McLeod, 21 January 1996). Before the ill-fated Operation GOOD-WOOD, Major-General Richard O'Connor of the 7th British Armoured Division, ordered that some of the SPGs of his artillery be turned over to his infantry to provide APCs. This order was countermanded, see D'Este, *Decision,* 389.

5. Kitching, *Mud and Green Fields,* 210.

6. Maczek, *Mes Blindés,* 189.

7. Kitching, *Mud and Green Fields,* 210.

8. Kitching to Amy, 14 July 1986, quoted in Amy, "Normandy."

9. Int: H. Watkins.

10. Wood, "The SAR."

11. Neff, Diary, 11 August 1944.

12. WD, 11 August 1944.

13. DHist, Gordon to Nicholson, 1 Feb 1960.

14. Amy, "Normandy."

15. Amy, "Normandy."

16. Amy, "Normandy."

17. Kitching, *Mud and Green Fields,* 213.

18. Stacey, *Victory,* 225; Jamar, *With the Tanks,* 53-64; Maczek, *Mes Blindés,* 182-186.

19. WD, 8 August 1944.

20. Int: R. Seccombe.

21. Int: J. Galipeau.

22. WD, 8 August 1944.

23. Int: G.D. Adams.

24. Jackson, *Argyll and Sutherland Highlanders,* 85.

25. Stacey, *Victory,* 228.

26. Corporal Arthur Haddow, Citation for Military Medal.

27. WD, 9 August 1944.

28. Int: R. Henning.

29. Jackson, *Argyll and Sutherland Highlanders,* 87.

30. WD, 9 August 1944.

31. NPRC; Padre Silcox's Notes.

32. Meyer, *Divisional History*, 176, 179. On 9 August, the 12th SS Panzer Division had twenty MK IV tanks and five Panther tanks. Ten of the Mk IVs were assigned to the neighbouring 85th and 271st Infantry Division. The remainder, along with eight Tigers of 102 SS Heavy Tank Battalion, were in the Quesnay Wood area. Another company of Tigers from the same battalion with seven vehicles was assigned to the 271st Infantry Division.

33. *Foot Guards*, 104.

34. Lieutenant-Colonel Dave Stewart in Fraser, *Black Yesterdays*, 227.

35. Lieutenant-Colonel Dave Stewart, in Fraser, *Black Yesterdays*, 227.

36. Jackson, *Argyll and Sutherland Highlanders*, 89.

37. Hayes, *The Lincs*, 31

38. Duguid, *Canadian Grenadier Guards*, 267-268.

39. WD, 10 August 1944.

40. Int: S. Bayko.

41. NPRC.

42. Int: S. Bayko.

43. MacPherson, "King Dog One."

44. MacPherson, "King Dog One."

45. MacPherson, "King Dog One."

46. WD, 10 August 1944; Rogers, *Lincoln and Welland*, 142-143.

47. DHist 145.2A1 D13(D1), Major G.L. Cassidy, Outline of Events, Aug 9-12, 1944.

48. WD, 10 August 1944.

49. DHist 145.2A1 D13(D1), Major G.L. Cassidy, Outline of Events, August 9-August 12, 1944.

50. *Artillery Training. Vol. I. Tactical Employment. Notes on the Tactical Handling of S.P. Anti-Tank Guns*, 4-7; *History of 5th Anti-Tank*, 29.

51. *History of 5th Canadian Anti-Tank*, 29.

52. Int: J. Moreton.

53. Neff, Diary, 10 August 1944.

54. Corporal C.J. Smith, Citation for Military Medal.

55. Int: J. Moreton.

56. Int: M. Fitzpatrick.

57. Int: C. Daley.

58. NPRC; PSN.

59. *Foot Guards*, 109; Duguid, *Grenadier Guards*, 268.

60. Int: J. Gove.

61. NPRC; PSN.

62. Nicholson, "1940-1945."

63. WD, 12-13 August 1944.

64. Lakes, "Tomorrow's Rainbow."

65. Lakes, "Tomorrow's Rainbow."

66. Directive by Montgomery, 11 August 1944, quoted in Stacey, *Victory*, 234.

67. D'Este, *Decision*, 426-427.

68. English, *Normandy*, 293.

69. WD, 13 August 1944.

70. Wiley Int: G.D. Wotherspoon, 1986.

71. WD, 4 CAD, 13 August 1944.

72. Wiley Int: G.D. Wotherspoon, 1986.

73. DHist, Kitching to Stacey, 17 April 1959.

74. Foster, *Meeting of Generals*, 368.

75. Wiley Int: G.D. Wotherspoon, 1986.

76. Lieutenant-Colonel Bill Cromb in Fraser, *Black Yesterdays*, 234.

77. WD, August 1944, Appendix, Diagram of Formation for Operation TRACTABLE.

78. McDougall, *Short History*, 39.

79. Int: E. Hyatt.

80. WD, 14 August 1944.

81. English, *Normandy*, 296.

82. English, *Normandy*, 296.

83. Kitching, *Mud and Green Fields*, 218-220; Roy, *Canadians*, 240-246.

84. Jackson, *Argyll and Sutherland Highlanders*, 93.

85. Rogers, *Lincoln and Welland*, 153.

86. Clipperton, "Memories."

87. WD, 14 August 1944.

88. DHist, 570.013 (D7A), Air Aspects of Totalize and Tractable.

89. Int: R. Allsopp.

90. Int: J. Simpson.

91. Int: R. Allsopp.

92. NPRC; PSN.

93. Int: H. Watkins.

94. Wiley Int: G.D. Wotherspoon, 1986.

95. WD, 14 August 1944.

96. Neff, Diary, 14 August 1944.

97. Int: G. Irving.

98. Int: D. McLeod, 24 August 1996.

99. WD, 14 August 1944; Meyer, *Divisional History*, 187.

100. WD, 15 August 1944.

101. Int: Bob Rasmussen.

102. NPRC; PSN.

103. Meyer, *Divisional History*, 187.

104. WD, 15 August 1944.

105. Nicholson, "1940-1945".

106. Neff, Diary, 15 August 1944.

107. Nicholson, "1940-1945".

108. NPRC.

109. WD, 15 August 1944.

110. Gallimore, "The Hill at Epancy."

111. Kitching, *Mud and Green Fields*, 220.

112. Kitching, *Mud and Green Fields*, 221.

8. "IT WAS BEGINNING TO LOOK AS IF A BIG SHOW WAS COMING OFF." FRANCE: 16–18 AUGUST 1944

1. "Luger-Luggin' Ludwig," a soldier's song sung to the tune of "Pistol Packin' Mama," dates from the late summer of 1944.

2. McDougall, *Short History*, 51-52.

3. Although the two terms seem to have been used interchangeably by the SAR, there was a difference between a "harbour" and a "laager." A laager was a position in open country in which the armoured regiment "circled the wagons" while it resupplied. A harbour was a defended position near a village or wood.

4. Joly, *Blue Flash*, 57.

5. Keller, "Memoir."

6. Wood, "The SAR."

7. Int: G. Armstrong.

8. Int: Bob Rasmussen.

9. David Marshall to DEG, 12 Aug 1997.

10. Wiley Int: G.D. Wotherspoon, 1986.

11. McDougall, *Short History*, 52.

12. *Operational Feeding. The Use of Field Rations. 1942*, 2-7.

13. Int: T. Barford.

14. Bob Clipperton to Andy Clipperton, 11 August 1944.

15. Int: A. Webster.

16. A. Dryer to fiancée, 24 September 1944.

17. Arnold Dryer to fiancée, 28 July 1944.

18. Wiley Int: G.D. Wotherspoon, 1986.

19. *Canadian Press News*, 26 August 1944.

20. Int: H. Gudwar.

21. Int: S. Arrowsmith.

22. Int: H. Gudwar.

23. WD, November 1945, Appendix containing notes by Padre Silcox on the Regiment's fatal casualties, referred to hereafter as "PSN."

24. Steven, *In This Sign*, 112-113.

25. Int: D. McLeod, 24 August 1996.

26. Galipeau, "Pee Wees," 119.

27. Bob Clipperton to Andy Clipperton, 11 August 1944.

28. According to the records of C Squadron, Elgin Regiment, the armoured delivery unit for 4th Division, the SAR was issued with four Shermans and two Stuarts between 6 and 13 August. These were replacements for tanks totally written off but the Regiment would have suffered other tank casualties that were repaired by the unit.

29. Wiley Int: G.D. Wotherspoon, 1986.

30. Wiley Int: G.D. Wotherspoon, 1986.

31. Kitching *Mud and Green Fields*, 213.

32. Int: G. Kitching.

33. WD, 16 August 1944.

34. Stacey, *Victory*, 245, 249.

35. Stacey, *Victory*, 249-251.

36. WD, 4 CAD, 16 August 1944.

37. WD, 10 Brigade, 16 August 1944.

38. Neff, Diary, 17 August 1944.

39. Int: R. Mitchell.

40. WD, ASH, 16 August 1944.

41. Neff, Diary, 18 August 1944.

42. Cassidy, *Warpath*, 104.

43. Meyer, *Divisional History*, 192.

44. Luton Int: D. Stewart, 1995.

45. NPRC; PSN.

46. Luton Int: D. Stewart, 1995.

47. WD, 16 August 1944; also Cassidy, *Warpath*, 105-106; Kitching, *Mud and Green Fields*, 222-223.

48. Int: D. Cameron.

49. Kitching, *Mud and Green Fields*, 223.

50. Neff, Diary, 18 August 1944.

51. Cassidy, *Warpath*, 107.

52. Cassidy, *Warpath*, 108.

53. Neff, Diary, 18 August 1944.

54. Cassidy, *Warpath*, 108.

55. Neff, Diary, 18 August 1944.

56. Rogers, *Lincoln and Welland*, 156.

57. Rogers, *Lincoln and Welland*, 156.

58. Int: J. Wiebe.

59. Currie, "St. Lambert."

60. Graves and Whitby, *Canadian Summer*, 154.

61. Bernage and McNair, *Le Couloir de la Mort*, 2-4. This would be an opportune time to note that, although the common English spelling is the "Dives River," the correct French spelling is the "Dive" River. Rather than confuse the issue the more familiar English spelling has been retained throughout the text.

62. Currie, "St. Lambert."

63. Citation MBE, Honorary Captain A.P. Silcox.

64. Int: J. Cheney.

65. Int: C. Daley.

66. Int: R. Allsopp.

67. Citation, MBE, Honorary Captain A.P. Silcox.

68. Int: C. Daley.

69. Int: H. Ficht.

70. Maczek, *Mes Blindés*, 196-202; Stacey, *Victory*, 257; Bernage and McNair, *Le Couloir de la Mort*, 26-27.

71. Blumenson, *Break-out*, 505.

72. Stacey, *Victory*, 246-248.

73. Stacey, *Victory*, 254-255.

74. Blumenson, *Break-out*, 521; also Stacey, *Victory*, 254-255.

75. Stacey, *Victory*, 254-255.

76. Wilmot, *Struggle for Europe*, 420.

77. Dufresne, "Normandie;" Meyer, *Divisional History*, 204.

78. Account by 35 Reconnaissance Wing, RAF, quoted in DHist, CMHQ Report No. 169.

79. Account by 35 Reconnaissance Wing, RAF, quoted in DHist, CMHQ Report No. 169.

80. Karl-Ludwig Opitz in Florentin, *Falaise*, 202.

81. DHist, 1st Canadian Army Intelligence Summary No. 66.

82. Luck, *Panzer Commander*, 163. In earlier times the word "truck" meant a two-wheeled cart.

83. Stacey, *Victory*, 252.

84. WD, 4 CAD, 18 August 1944.

85. Kitching, *Mud and Green Fields*, 224.

86. Currie, "St. Lambert."

87. Currie, "St. Lambert."

88. Currie, "St. Lambert."

89. Currie, "St. Lambert."

90. Int: W. Spence.

91. Currie, "St. Lambert."

92. Int: G.D. Adams.

93. Int: J. Cooper.

94. Int: J. Hutchinson.

95. Luton Int: D. Stewart, 1995.

96. Int: J. Eastman.

97. J. Redden to JLS, n.d. (c. 1992).

98. Currie, "St. Lambert."

99. McDougall, *Short History*, 42.

100. WD, 18 August 1944.

9. "THE SITUATION BEGAN TO GET OUT OF HAND." FRANCE: 19–20 AUGUST AM, 1944

1. A verse from the "LOB Song," sung by Canadian soldiers in 1944-1945 to the tune of "Lili Marlene."

2. WD, 19 August 1944.

3. OL, 10 Brigade, 19 August 1944.

4. Int: R. Mitchell.

5. Int: W. Spence.

6. Currie, "St. Lambert."

7. J. Redden to JLS, n.d. (c. 1992).

8. "Smitty" to R. Mitchell, 23 August 1944.

9. Int: S. Thuesen.

10. WD, ASH, 19 August 1944.

11. OL, 10 Brigade, 19 August 1944.

12. Currie, "St. Lambert."

13. WD, 4 CAD, 19 August 1944.

14. Duguid, *Grenadier Guards*, 280.

15. Duguid, *Grenadier Guards*, 280-281; WD, 4 CAD, 19 August 1944.

16. WD, 9 Brigade, 19 August 1944.

17. WD, 19 August 1944.

18. WD, 19 August 1944.

19. Currie, "St. Lambert."

20. Luton Int: D. Stewart.

21. Int: J. Cooper.

22. J. Redden to JLS, n.d. (c. 1992).

23. Int: J. Lardner.

24. J. Redden to JLS, n.d. (c. 1992).

25. Int: J. Lardner.

26. NPRC.

27. J. Redden to JLS, n.d. (c. 1992).

28. J. Redden to JLS, n.d. (c. 1992).

29. WD, 19 August 1944.

30. Taylor, "Immigrant Boy."

31. Gove, "A-1 Troop."

32. Int: H. Watkins.

33. NPRC; PSN; Int: H. Watkins.

34. Int: M. Amyotte.

35. WD, 19 August 1944.

36. Lakes, "Tomorrow's Rainbow."

37. Clipperton, "Memories."

38. Citation, Croix de Guerre with Bronze Star, Sergeant D. Prenevost.

39. NPRC; PSN.

40. Int: B. Rasmussen.

41. Int: E. Reardon.

42. OL, 10 Brigade, 19 August 1944.

43. OL, 10 Brigade, 19 August 1944.

44. OL, 10 Brigade, 19 August 1944.

45. Rogers, *The Lincoln and Welland*, 157; Dunlop, "St. Lambert."

46. OL, 10 Brigade, 19 August 1944.

47. OL, 10 Brigade, 19 August 1944.

48. Rogers, *The Lincoln and Welland*, 158.

49. Int: D. Grant.

50. Int: D. Grant.
51. McDougall, *Short History*, 43.
52. Film shot by Sergeant Jack Stollery, 19 August 1944, Canadian Forces Film Unit.
53. Int: D. Grant.
54. Int: D. Grant.
55. Int: D. Grant.
56. Int: R. Fairhurst.
57. Int: E. Hyatt.
58. BBC Interview with Major David Currie, VC, n.d. (c. early December 1944).
59. Int: T. Barford.
60. Wiley Int: G.D. Wotherspoon, 1986.
61. Report by 35 Reconnaissance Wing, RAF in DHist, CMHQ Report No. 169.
62. Currie, "St. Lambert."
63. Currie, "St. Lambert."
64. Currie, "St. Lambert"; Wiley Int: G.D. Wotherspoon, 1986.
65. Currie, "St. Lambert."
66. Jamar, *With the Tanks*, 141.
67. Jamar, *With the Tanks*, 141.
68. OL, 10 Brigade, 19 August 1944.
69. OL, 10 Brigade, 19 August 1944.
70. OL, 10 Brigade, 19 August 1944; Wiley Int: G.D. Wotherspoon, 1986.
71. Private Art Bridge in Fraser, *Black Yesterdays*, 239.
72. Private Art Bridge in Fraser, *Black Yesterdays*, 240.
73. Hayes, *The Lincs*, 38. Also Dunlop, "St. Lambert"; Jackson, *Argyll and Sutherland Highlanders*, 99.
74. Wiley Int: G.D. Wotherspoon, 1986.
75. OL, 10 Brigade, 19 August 1944.
76. WD, 19 August 1944.
77. OL, 10 Brigade, 19 August 1944.
78. DHist, 1st Canadian Army, Intelligence Summary, No. 51.
79. Dufresne, "Normandie"; Meyer, *Divisional History*, 208.
80. Meyer, *History*, 193-198.
81. Blumenson, *Break-Out*, 537.
82. Lehmann and Tiemann, *Leibstandarte*, 300.
83. Meyer, *Divisional History*, 197; Blumenson, *Break-Out*, 538-540.
84. RG 24, vol. 20522, file 981.50m, Report by *Generalleutnant* Eugen Meindl (hereafter Meindl, Memoir).
85. Meindl, Memoir; Blumenson, *Break-Out*, 538-540; Meyer, *Divisional History*, 198.
86. Lehmann and Tiemann, *Leibstandarte*, 300-301.
87. WD, 20 August 1944.
88. Meindl, Memoir. All subsequent references to Meindl's break-out are from this source.
89. Gove, "A-1 Troop."
90. Galipeau, "Pee Wees," 128.
91. Currie, "St. Lambert."
92. Int: J. Cooper.
93. Nicholson, "1940-1945."
94. Neff, Diary, 20 August 1944.
95. OL, 10 Brigade, 20 August 1944.
96. OL, 10 Brigade, 20 August 1944.
97. OL, 10 Brigade, 20 August 1944.
98. OL, 10 Brigade, 20 August 1944.
99. WD, 20 August 1944.
100. OL, 10 Brigade, 20 August 1944.
101. Florentin, *Falaise*, 240.
102. Luton Int: D. Stewart, 1995.
103. Jackson, *Argyll and Sutherland Highlanders*, 99.
104. NPRC; PSN.
105. Citation, Military Medal, Corporal M. Ottenbreit.
106. Currie, "St. Lambert."
107. Gove, "A-1 Troop."
108. Int: R. Seccombe.

109. WD, 20 August 1944.
110 OL, 10 Brigade, 20 August 1944.
111. WD, 20 August 1944.
112. Galipeau, "Pee Wees," 129.
113. Galipeau, "Pee Wees," 119.
114. WD, 20 August 1944.
115. OL, 10 Brigade, 20 August 1944.
116. Nicholson, *Gunners*, 327.
117. Nicholson, *Gunners*, 327.
118. Spencer, *15 Field*, 119.
119. Nicholson, *Gunners*, 3238.
120. Nicholson, "1940-1945."
121. Neff, Diary, 20 August 1944.
122. Neff, Diary, 20 August 1944.
123. Nicholson, "1940-1945."
124. Author's conversation with J.L. Summers, c. 1983.
125. Neff, Diary, 20 August 1944.
126. Int: S. Rose.
127. OL, 10 Brigade, 20 August 1944.
128. *Fähnrich* Kurt Misch in Meyer, *Divisional History*, 322.
129. *Generalmajor* Heinrich von Lüttwitz in Shulman, *Defeat in the West*, 181.
130. OL, 10 Brigade, 20 August 1944.
131. Meindl, Memoir.
132. Maczek, *Mes Blindés*, 213-217; Blumenson, *Break-Out*, 547-548; Situation Map, 20 August 1944 in *1 Dywizja Pancerna*, 115.
133. OL, 10 Brigade, 20 August 1944.
134. Meindl, Memoir.
135. OL, 10 Brigade, 20 August 1944.
136. WD, 9 Brigade, 20 August 1944.
137. OL, 9 Brigade, 20 August 1944.
138. OL, 9 Brigade, 20 August 1944.
139. WD, 9 Brigade, 20 August 1944; OL, 9 Brigade, 20 August 1944: Intelligence Log, HLI, 20 August 1944.
140. Int: G. Kitching.
141. WD, 9 Brigade, 20 August 1944; OL, 9 Brigade, 20 August 1944; WD, HLI, 20 August 1944; WD, NSH, 20 August 1944; WD, SDG, 20 August 1944.
142. *Foot Guards*, 124.
143. *Foot Guards*, 124.

10. "THE BOYS FROM THE BALD-HEADED PRAIRIE." FRANCE: 20 AUGUST P.M.– 22 AUGUST A.M., 1944

1. Dating back to the early 1930s "The SAR War Dance" was a favourite of the officers of the Regiment and was usually sung in the mess late at night accompanied by a dance which modesty forbids describing.
2. WD, 20 August 1944; Int: B. Rasmussen.
3. DHist 79/705, Operational Research in North West Europe.
4. Bernard "Doc" Spaner, "Memoir."
5. NPRC; PSN.
6. Gove, "A-1 Troop."
7. Luton Int: D. Stewart, 1995.
8. Int: H. Watkins.
9. Neff, Diary, 20 August 1944.
10. Wiley Int: G.D. Wotherspoon, 1986; OL, 10 Brigade, 20 August 1944.
11. Nicholson, "1940-1945."
12. Jack Delong, "City Officer Tells of Fight That Paved Route to Germany," *Edmonton Bulletin*, 19 January 1946; also WD, 20 August 1944.
13. *Generalmajor* Heinrich von Lüttwitz in Shulman, *Defeat* in the West, 181-182.
14. *Oberfeldwebel* Hans Braun in McKee, *Last Round*, 319.
15. *Generalmajor* Heinrich von Lüttwitz in Shulman, *Defeat in the West*, 182.
16. Major David Currie, VC Citation, Statement of Captain R.F. Dickie.
17. Major David Currie, VC Citation, Statement of Captain R.F. Dickie.

18. Major David Currie, VC Citation, Statement of Lance-Sergeant R. Campbell.
19. Int: E. Davies.
20. Int: R. Virtue; also Int: J. Lardner.
21. Wiley Int: G.D. Wotherspoon, 1986.
22. Int: D. McLeod, 21 January 1996.
23. Major David Currie, VC Citation, Statement of Sergeant John Gunderson.
24. Corporal M. Ottenbreit, Military Medal Citation.
25. Int: J. Hutchinson.
26. Currie, "St. Lambert."
27. Wiley Int: G.D. Wotherspoon, 1986.
28. Ints: J. Lardner and J. Eastman.
29. Major David Currie, VC Citation, Statement of Lance-Sergeant R. Campbell.
30. BBC Interview with Major David Currie, VC, c. early December 1944.
31. Report on Actions of J and L Troops attached to WD, 103rd Battery, RCA, August 1944. All statements concerning the actions of this unit on 20 August 1944 are from this source.
32. Int: D. Grant.
33. Currie, "St. Lambert."
34. Currie, "St. Lambert."
35. OL, 10 Brigade, 20 August 1944.
36. Maczek, *Mes Blindés*, 218.
37. Maczek, *Mes Blindés*, 218.
38. WD, 4 CAD, 20 August 1944.
39. Kitching, *Mud and Green Fields*, 226.
40. WD, 4 CAD, 20 August 1944.
41. WD, 10 Brigade, 20 August 1944.
42. WD, 10 Brigade, 20 August 1944.
43. Bird, *No Retreating Footsteps*, 190.
44. Wiley Int: G.D. Wotherspoon, 1986.
45. Bird, *No Retreating Footsteps*, 190; WD, NSH, 20 August 1944.
46. WD, 9 Brigade, 20 August 1944; OL, 9 Brigade, 20 August 1944; WD, HLI, 20 August 1944; Bird, *No Retreating Footsteps*, 195.
47. OL, 10 Brigade, 20 August 1944.
48. Guderian, *Das Letzte Kriegsjahr*, 103.
49. All messages from OL, 10 Brigade, 20 August 1944.
50. Int: G. Stoner.
51. *History of the First Hussars*, 97.
52. OL, 20 August 1944.
53. Currie, "St. Lambert."
54. Wiley Int: G.D. Wotherspoon, 1986.
55. Galipeau, "Pee Wees," 120.
56. Nicholson, "1940-1945."
57. Neff, Diary, 21 August 1944; also Int: G. Olmstead.
58. Int: S. Rose; NPRC; PSN.
59. Nicholson, "1940-1945."
60. Neff, Diary, 21 August 1944.
61. NPRC; PSN.
62. Nicholson, "1940-1945."
63. Nicholson, "1940-1945."
64. Neff, Diary, 21 August 1944.
65. Nicholson, "1940-1945."
66. Int: G. Olmstead.
67. NPRC; PSN.
68. Int: G. Olmstead.
69. Nicholson, "1940-1945."
70. Neff, Diary, 21 August 1944.
71. Currie, "St. Lambert."
72. WD, 10 Brigade, 20 August 1944.
73. OL, 10 Brigade, 21 August 1944.
74. Int: G. Stoner.
75. *History of the First Hussars*, 97.
76. *History of the First Hussars*, 97.
77. OL, 9 Brigade, 21 August 1944.
78. Intelligence Log, HLI, 21 August 1944.
79. Intelligence Log, HLI, 21 August 1944.
80. OL, 9 Brigade, 21 August 1944.
81. OL, 9 Brigade, 21 August 1944.
82. OL, 9 Brigade, 21 August 1944.

83. OL, 10 Brigade, 21 August 1944.
84. OL, 9 Brigade, 21 August 1944.
85. OL, 9 Brigade, 21 August 1944.
86. Intelligence Log, HLI, 21 August 1944.
87. Intelligence Log, HLI, 21 August 1944.
88. OL, 10 Brigade, 21 August 1944.
89. Int: G. Stoner.
90. OL, 9 Brigade, 21 August 1944.
91. Currie, "St. Lambert."
92. WD, 21 August 1944.
93. Int: H. Bergquist.
94. Galipeau, "Pee Wees," 122.
95. Lakes, "Tomorrow's Rainbow."
96. OL, 10 Brigade, 21 August 1944.
97. Charles Debenham to DEG, 2 Sep 97; NPRC; PSN.
98. NPRC; PSN.
99. Currie, "St. Lambert."
100. Int: W. Boothroyd.
101. Int: E. Hyatt.
102. Galipeau, "Pee Wees," 122.
103. Wiley Int: G.D. Wotherspoon, 1986.
104. Guderian, *Das Letzte Kriegsjahr*, 104; Dufresne, "Normandie"; Meindl, Memoir; DHist, 1st Canadian Army, Intelligence Summary No. 293, "Saga of Frundsberg."
105. Duguid, *Grenadier Guards*, 282.
106. A.F. Coffin to DEG, 25 November 1995.
107. Major David Currie, VC Citation, Statement of Sergeant John Gunderson.
108. WD, 21 August 1944.
109. OL, 10 Brigade, 21 August 1944.
110. WD, 21 August 1944.
111. Currie, "St. Lambert."
112. Currie, "St. Lambert."
113. Map showing location of destroyed and abandoned German AFVs and vehicles in DHist 79/705, Operational Research in North-West Europe; analysis of photographs shot at St. Lambert, 19-22 August 1944.
114. Int: C. Daley.
115. Int: T. Warren; also Bernage and McNair, *Le Couloir de la Mort*, 80.
116. Taylor and Fry, *Beating Around the Bush*, 63.
117. DHist 79/705, Operational Research in North West Europe; also Currie, "St. Lambert."
118. DHist 79/705, Operational Research in North West Europe.
119. Dufresne, "Normandie."
120. Maczek, *Mes Blindés*, 219.
121. Kitching, *Mud and Green Fields*, 226-227.
122. Foster, *Meeting of Generals*, 383.
123. The initial locations of the German infantry divisions, their movements and eventual fate are discussed in Blumenson, *Break-Out*, 550-552. All seven formations disengaged with, it appears, little interference from Second British Army.
124. Author's conversation with J.L. Summers, 1994.
125. Clipperton "Memories."
126. Currie, "St. Lambert."
127. Wiley Int: G.D. Wotherspoon, 1986.

11. "WE'RE OFF TO BERLIN!" FRANCE AND BELGIUM: 22 AUGUST–11 SEPTEMBER 1944

1. A verse from "Luger Luggin' Ludwig,", sung to the tune of "Pistol Packin' Mama," dates from the late summer of 1944.
2. WD, 22 August 1944.
3. WD, 23 August 1944.
4. Don Stewart to Mrs. Stewart, 4 August 1944.
5. Galipeau, "Pee Wees," 135.

6. Lakes, "Tomorrow's Rainbow."
7. Int: G. Bird.
8. Int: D. McLeod, 24 August 1996.
9. Bob Clipperton to Andy Clipperton, 23 August 1944.
10. Int: W. Boothroyd.
11. Wilmot, *Struggle*, 462.
12. Wilmot, *Struggle*, 458.
13. Dufresne, "Le Succès Allemand."
14. WD, 25-26 August 1944; also Foster, *Meeting of Generals*, 387-388; Hayes, *Lincs*, 42-43.
15. WD, 27 August 1944.
16. WD, 27 August 1944.
17. Taylor, "Immigrant Boy"; Hayes, *Lincs*, 43; Jackson, *Argyll and Sutherland Highlanders*, 105-106.
18. Foster, *Meeting of Generals*, 388.
19. WD, 31 August 1944.
20. Galipeau, "Pee Wees," 134.
21. Wiley Int: G.D. Wotherspoon, 1986.
22. Wiley Int: G.D. Wotherspoon, 1986.
23. WD, 1-2 September 1944.
24. Wilmot, *Struggle*, 470.
25. Wilmot, *Struggle*, 482-487.
26. WD, 3 September 1944.
27. Wiley Int: G.D. Wotherspoon, 1986.
28. WD, 4 September 1944.
29. WD, September 1944, Appendix.
30. Int: T. Barford.
31. WD, 4 September 1944.
32. Int: I. MacPherson.
33. Marshall, "Me and George," 29,
34. Marshall, "Me and George," 33.
35. Wilmot, *Struggle*, 477-482.
36. Wilmot, *Struggle*, 478, also 477-482.
37. Wilmot, *Struggle*, 480.
38. Wilmot, *Struggle*, 458-471; Moulton, *Antwerp*, 42-43; Whitaker, *Tug of War*, 41-43.
39. DHist, 1st Canadian Army Intelligence Summary, No. 92.
40. De Groot, "Escape of the German Army"; also Wilmot, *Struggle*, 477-482; and Moulton, *Antwerp*, 60-63.
41. Marshall, "Me and George," 35.
42. Marshall, "Me and George," 36.
43. Neff, Diary, 7 September 1944.
44. Galipeau, "Pee Wees," 136.
45. Don Stewart to Mrs. Stewart, n.d. (mid-September 1944).
46. Vlaemynck, *Moerbrugge*, 26-27.
47. Marshall, "Me and George," 38.
48. Neff, Diary, 8 September 1944; NPRC.
49. Foster, *Meeting of Generals*, 403.
50. Major R. Paterson in Fraser, *Black Yesterdays*, 267.
51. Major Pete McKenzie in Fraser, *Black Yesterdays*, 269.
52. Paterson, *10 Brigade*, 34.
53. M.O. Rollefson, *Green Route Up*, 40.
54. Captain J.L. Summers, Citation, Military Cross.
55. M.O. Rollefson, *Green Route Up*, 40; Spencer, *15 Field*, 149-150.
56. Paterson, *10 Brigade*, 35. The author of this book, Major R.A. Paterson, commanded C Company of the Argylls at Moerbrugge.
57. Paterson, *10 Brigade*, 35.
58. Neff, Diary, 9 September 1944.
59. Int: C. Daley.
60. NPRC; PSN.
61. NPRC; PSN.
62. PSN.
63. NPRC.
64. Major R.A. Paterson in Fraser, *Black Yesterdays*, 276.
65. Paterson, *10 Brigade*, 35.
66. Corporal Harry Ruch in Fraser, *Black Yesterdays*, 276.
67. Marshall, "Me and George," 41.

68. Galipeau, "Pee Wees," 139.
69. NPRC; PSN; Corporal Tony Devreker, Citation, Military Medal.
70. Int: G. Irving.
71. Galipeau, "Pee Wees," 140.
72. WD, 11 September 1944; NPRC; PSN; Ints: G. Irving and D. McLeod, 24 August 1996.
73. Galipeau, "Pee Wees," 139.
74. Galipeau, "Pee Wees," 139.
75. Galipeau, "Pee Wees," 140.
76. Int: G. Irving.
77. Int: R. Barr.
78. Int: G. Irving.
79. Marshall, "Me and George," 41; also WD, 10 September 1944.
80. Marshall, "Me and George," 42.
81. Int: E. Davies.
82. Int: T. Glaude.
83. NPRC.
84. Taylor, "Immigrant Boy."
85. NPRC; PSN.
86. NPRC; PSN; Int: G. Irving.
87. Int: G. Irving; NPRC; PSN.
88. WD, 12 September 1944; Int: G. Irving.
89. WD, D Squadron, Elgin Regiment, 9-12 September 1944.
90. Paterson, *10 Brigade*, 37.
91. Foster, *Meeting of Generals*, 403.
92. See Stacey, *Victory*; Moulton, *Battle for Antwerp*; and Whitaker, *Tug of War*.
93. Stacey, *Victory*, 329-330.
94. Stacey, *Victory*, 330-331; Wilmot, *Struggle*, 471-474; Moulton, *Antwerp*, 72-80.
95. Stacey, *Victory*, 331.
96. Stacey, *Victory*, 331.
97. Moulton, *Antwerp*, 49-50.
98. Moulton, *Antwerp*, 95.
99. Moulton, *Antwerp*, 85-100.
100. Galipeau, "Pee Wees," 140.

12. "RECCE AT ITS BEST." BELGIUM AND HOLLAND: 12 SEPTEMBER–21 OCTOBER 1944
1. Verses from the "LOB Song" sung to the tune of "Lili Marlene."
2. Moulton, *Antwerp*, 63.
3. WD, 12 September 1944.
4. Clipperton, "Memories."
5. Author's conversation with Jack Summers.
6. Int: J. Cheney.
7. Clipperton, "Memories."
8. Int: J. Cheney.
9. Int: A. Halkyard.
10. Wiley Int: G.D. Wotherspoon, 1986.
11. Int: D. McLeod, 24 August 1996.
12. Int: D. Mcleod, 24 August 1996.
13. Int: D. McLeod, 24 August 1996.
14. Nicholson, "1940-1945."
15. Neff, Diary, 12 September 1944.
16. Neff, Diary, 12 September 1944: also *Foot Guards*, 144.
17. Neff, Diary, 12 September 1944; Nicholson, "1940-1945."
18. Author's conversation with Bill Luton, December 1996.
19. Wiley Int: G.D. Wotherspoon, 1986.
20. Int: R. Allsopp.
21. Joly, *Take These Men*, 12.
22. Int: Ron Virtue.
23. Lakes, "Tomorrow's Rainbow."
24. Int: G. Irving.
25. Int: G. Irving.
26. Galipeau, "Pee Wees," 172.
27. Int: A. Coffin.
28. Stacey, *Victory*, 361.
29. WD, 10 Brigade, 12 September 1944.
30. Stacey, *Victory*, 362-363.
31. WD, 13 September 1944.
32. DHist, Interrogation Report of *Generalmajor* Sanders, 30 September 1945.
33. Foster, *Meeting of Generals*, 406.

34. DHist, Interrogation Report of *Generalmajor* Sanders, 30 September 1945.
35. Cassidy, *Warpath*, 150.
36. Foster, *Meeting of Generals*, 406.
37. Stacey, *Victory*, 363.
38. Cassidy, *Warpath*, 160; Whitaker, *Tug of War*, 109-110.
39. WD, 13-23 September 1944.
40. Int: E. Reardon.
41. Arnold Dryer to fiancée, 16 September 1944.
42. WD, 16 September 1944.
43. WD, 17 September 1944.
44. Int: A. Halkyard.
45. Int: J. Cheney.
46. Clipperton, "Memories."
47. Int: J. Cheney.
48. WD, 18 September 1944.
49. Int: A. Halkyard.
50. According to information given to the author by Belgian historian George Spittael, this gun was later taken to Eekloo to be used as a promotional device in war bond drives.
51. Int: A. Halkyard.
52. NPRC; PSN.
53. Nicholson, "1940-1945."
54. WD, 18 September 1944.
55. Luton Int: D. Stewart, 1995.
56. Int: J. Hutchinson.
57. NPRC.
58. Int: R. Virtue.
59. Luton Int: D. Stewart, 1995.
60. WD, 19 September 1944.
61. WD, 20 September 1944; NPRC.
62. WD, 21 September 1944.
63. WD, 21 September 1944.
64. Cassidy, *Warpath*, 160.
65. WD, 21 September 1944.
66. WD, 21 September 1944; Cassidy, *Warpath*, 159-160.
67. WD, 24 September 1944.
68. Neff, Diary, 26 September 1944: WD, 24-26 September 1944.
69. WD, 25 September 1944.
70. WD, 25-27 September 1944.
71. Alan Randall, "South Alberta Regiment First Canadian Formation [sic] in Holland," *Canadian Press*, 4 November 1944.
72. Wiley Int: G.D. Wotherspoon.
73. WD, 28 September 1944.
74. WD, 1 October 1944.
75. WD, 7 October 1944.
76. WD, 8 October 1944.
77. Lakes, "Tomorrow's Rainbow"; Neff, Diary, 24 September 1944.
78. Int: D. Stewart.
79. Int: D. McLeod, 24 January 1996.
80. Int: R. Allsopp.
81. Int: R. Rasmussen.
82. Int: G. Gallimore.
83. Int: J. Cheney.
84. Int: G. Gallimore.
85. Int: J. Lakes.
86. Int: D. Stewart.
87. Whitaker, *Tug of War*, 266-267.
88. Stacey, *Victory*, 381-385.
89. Luton Int: D. Stewart, 1995.
90. WD, 9-10 October 1944.
91. WD, 10-19 October 1944.
92. WD, 10-19 October 1944.
93. A.F. Coffin to DEG, 14 August 1997.
94. Galipeau, "Pee Wees," 146.
95. WD, 16 October 1944.
96. Sergeant H.L. Roulston, Citation, Military Medal.
97. WD, 16 October 1944.
98. WD, 12-20 October 1944; Neff, Diary, 17 October 1944.
99. McLeod, "Party."
100. McLeod, "Party."

101. McLeod, "Party."
102. Luton Int: D. Stewart, 1995.
103. WD, October, 1944, Shellreps, 13 October 1944.
104. Bob Clipperton to Andy Clipperton, 13 September 1944.
105. Int: J. Cheney.
106. Int: G. Gallimore.
107. NPRC; PSN.
108. Author's conversation with Jack Summers.
109. Don Stewart to Mrs. Stewart, 14 October 1944.
110. Nicholson, "1940-1945."
111. Int: J. Cheney.
112. Clipperton, "Memories."
113. Moulton, *Antwerp*, 118.
114. Stacey, *Victory*, 387-388; Moulton, *Antwerp*, 118-124.
115. Stacey, *Victory*, 388.
116. Moulton, *Antwerp*, 121.
117. Paterson, *10 Brigade*, 42.
118. Paterson, *10 Brigade*, 43.
119. Captain Jim Swayze in Hayes, *Lincs*, 57-58.
120. Paterson, *10 Brigade*, 43.
121. Paterson, *10 Brigade*, 43.
122. Cassidy, *Warpath*, 177,
123. WD, 20-21 October 1944; Paterson, *10 Brigade*, 43-44.

13. "HELL, BILL, LET'S TAKE THE DAMNED PLACE." BELGIUM AND HOLLAND: 20 OCTOBER–7 NOVEMBER 1944
1. The "Bergen op Zoom" song, written by Lieutenant-Colonel Bill Cromb of the Lincoln and Welland Regiment and sung to the tune of the "Blue Danube," had its first performance at a 10 Brigade officers' dinner held at the Hotel de Draak in Bergen on Halloween Night, October 1944. The words can vary according to the audience.
2. WD, 4 CAD, 15-20 October 1944.
3. NAC, RG 24, Vol. 20523, File 981 SOM (D178), *Oberst* Waring, Battles of LXVIII Inf Corps, 15 Sep-24 Nov 44.
4. NAC, RG 24, Vol. 20523, File 981SOM (D178), *Oberst* Waring, Battles of LXVIII Inf Corps, 15 Sep-24 Nov 44.
5. Paterson, *10 Brigade*, 45.
6. Paterson, *10 Brigade*, 45.
7. Hayes, *The Lincs*, 63.
8. Paterson, *10 Brigade*, 45.
9. WD, 23 October 1944.
10. WD, 24 October 1944.
11. Int: G. Gallimore; NPRC; PSN.
12. WD, 24 October 1944.
13. WD, 24 October 1944.
14. WD, 4 CAD, 24 October 1944.
15. WD, 24 October 1944; McLeod, "Party."
16. Cassidy, *Warpath*, 180.
17. McLeod, "Party."
18. WD, 24-25 October 1944.
19. John Neff to DEG, 21 February 1995.
20. John Neff to DEG, 21 February 1995; also Cassidy, *Warpath*, 179-180 and WD, 25 October 1944.
21. Cassidy, *Warpath*, 180-181.
22]. WD, 25 October 1944.
23. Cassidy, *Warpath*, 180-181; WD, 25 October 1944.
24. WD, 25-26 October 1944.
25. McLeod, "Party."
26. McLeod, "Party."
27. McLeod, "Party."
28. Luton Int: D. Stewart, 1995.
29. McLeod, "Party."
30. WD, 25 October 1944.
31. Luton Int: D. Stewart, 1995; WD, 25 October 1944.
32. McLeod, "Party."

33. NPRC; PSN.
34. McLeod, "Party."
35. WD, 25 October 1944.
36. WD, 4 CAD, 25 October 1944.
37. Foster, *Meeting of Generals*, 413.
38. WD, 4 CAD, 25-26 October 1944.
39. WD, 26 October 1944; WD, 10 Brigade, 26 October 1944; WD, 4 CAD, 26 October 1944; PRO, WO 171, vol. 852, WD 1st Fife and Forfar Yeomanry, 26 October 1944.
40. Luton Int: D. Stewart, 1995.
41. McLeod, "Party."
42. Hayes, *Lincs*, 63-64.
43. McLeod, "Party."
44. Luton Int: D. Stewart, 1995.
45. McLeod, "Party."
46. McLeod, "Party."
47. WD, 26 October 1944.
48. WD, 26 October 1944; WD, 10 Brigade, 26 October 1944; OL, 10 Brigade, 26 October 1944; Nicholson, "1940-1945"; Cassidy, *Warpath*, 181-183.
49. Int: D. Ledwidge.
50. Int: L. Caseley.
51. Cassidy, *Warpath*, 183.
52. Int: C. Fearn.
53. Int: D. Ledwidge.
54. Int: L. Caseley.
55. Spencer, *15 Field*, 177-178.
56. Marshall, "Me and George," 52-53.
57. WD, 26 October 1944; Nicholson, "1940-1945."
58. Nicholson, "1940-1945"; NPRC; PSN.
59. Neff, Diary, 26 October 1944: also Nicholson, "1940-1945"; NPRC; PSN; Int: W. Kenyon.
60. Int: D. Ledwidge.
61. Cassidy, *Warpath*, 182-183; WD, 26 October 1944.
62. Cassidy, *Warpath*, 183.
63. WD, 26 October 1944.
64. *Handbook on German Military Forces*, 486-506.
65. Int: R. Seccombe.
66. Hayes, *Lincs*, 64; PRO, WO 171, vol. 852, WD, Fife and Forfar Yeomanry, 26 October 1944.
67. NPRC; PSN.
68. Int: C.R. Fast.
69. WD, 26 October 1944.
70. Cassidy, *Warpath*, 183.
71. WD, 27 October 1944; WD, 10 Brigade, 27 October 1944; WD, 4 CAD, 27 October 1944; OL, 10 Brigade, 27 October 1944.
72. WD, 27 October 1944; OL, 10 Brigade, 27 October 1944.
73. McLeod, "Party."
74. McLeod, "Party."
75. Int: J. Strathern.
76. McLeod, "Party"; also Holst, "Fallschirm-Jäger-Regiment 6"; and Hoedelmans, "Nabranders," 76-78.
77. Int: J. Strathern.
78. McLeod, "Party."
79. Ralph Allen, "Few hundred cold and tired Canucks pull classic capture of Dutch city," *Globe and Mail*, n.d. (c. early November 1944).
80. Ralph Allen, "Few hundred cold and tired Canucks pull classic capture of Dutch city," *Globe and Mail*, n.d. (c. early November 1944).
81. Int: R. Allsopp.
82. McLeod, "Party."
83. Int: G. Gallimore; Spencer, *15 Field*, 178; Hoedelmans, *Jeeps & klaprosen*, 82-83.
84. Int: G. Irving.
85. Int: G. Irving.
86. Luton Int: D. Stewart, 1995.

87. WD, October 1944, Appendix, Note from Burgomaster, Bergen op Zoom, 28 October 1944.
88. WD, 28 October 1944.
89. WD, 4 CAD, 28 October 1944.
90. Spencer, *15 Field*, 179.
91. Paterson, *10 Brigade*, 47.
92. Neff, Diary, 28 October 1944.
93. Int: D. McLeod, 24 August 1996.
94. McLeod, "Party."
95. Int: D. McLeod, 24 January 1996.
96. Hayes, *Lincs*, 66.
97. Hayes, *Lincs*, 66.
98. Paterson, *10 Brigade*, 47.
99. Paterson, *10 Brigade*, 47.
100. WD, 30 October 1944.
101. Paterson, *10 Brigade*, 47.
102. Marshall, "Me and George," 54-55.
103. Int: E. Aucoin.
104. Marshall, "Me and George," 54.
105. Int: B. Spaner.
106. Neff, Diary, 28 October 1944.
107. Cassidy, *Warpath*, 185.
108. Hoedelmans, *Jeeps & klaprosen*, 86.
109. Int: H. Watkins.
110. Int: C. Farquhar.
111. Lakes, "Tomorrow's Rainbow."
112. Int: G. Gallimore.
113. WD, 6 November 1944.
114. Foster, diary, 6 Nov 1944, in Foster, *Meeting of Generals*, 414.

14. "THE MAJOR WASN'T DRESSED TO VISIT THE KING." HOLLAND: 7 NOVEMBER 1944– 24 JANUARY 1945
1. Poem by Corporal Myrtle "Andy" Clipperton, CWAC, contained in a letter to her husband, Sergeant Bob Clipperton of the SAR, 19 August 1944.
2. Don Stewart to Mrs. Stewart, 5 Nov 1944.
3. WD, 16 November 1944.
4. Galipeau, "Pee Wees," 172.
5. WD, 16-17 November 1944.
6. Marshall, "Me and George," 63.
7. Lakes, "Tomorrow's Rainbow."
8. WD, 25 November 1944.
9. Foster, *Meeting of Generals*, 416.
10. WD, 12 November 1944; Canadian Army Newsreel No. 49, n.d. (c. early December 1944).
11. Major David Currie, BBC Radio Interview, n.d. (c. December 1944).
12. BBC Interview with Major David Currie, n.d. (c. December 1944).
13. Don Stewart to DEG, 21 November 1995.
14. Don Stewart to DEG, 21 November 1995.
15. WD, 27 November 1944.
16. In his book, *Meeting of Generals*, 419, Tony Foster recounts the story of the switch of generals which circulated in higher Canadian army circles in 1944. In October 1944 Lieutenant-General E.L.M. Burns, the commander of 1st Canadian Corps in Italy, was sacked and replaced by Major-General Charles Foulkes, the commander of 2nd Infantry Division. Canadian Military Headquarters in London thereupon sent a telegram to the commander of British Eighth Army (in which 1st Canadian Corps served) stating that Burns's replacement would be the newly-promoted Lieutenant-General C. Foulkes. No one in Eighth Army had ever heard of a Canadian general named "C. Foulkes" but they did know a Canadian general named "C. Vokes" who commanded 1st Infantry Division. Assuming a spelling error in the message, the Brit-

ish informed Chris Vokes that he was now a lieutenant-general and commander of 1st Canadian Corps. When Foulkes arrived in Italy to take over his new command there was terrible embarrassment and, to save face, the senior army staff decided to transfer Vokes laterally out of Italy to northwest Europe and replace him with Harry Foster. This story has never been confirmed but there is a very strong probability that it is true.
17. Vokes, *My Story*, 189.
18. WD, 29 November 1944.
19. Neff, Diary, 29 November 1944.
20. WD, 2 December 1944.
21. Foster, *Meeting of Generals*, 410-411; also Stacey, *Arms, Men and Government*, 440-442.
22. Stacey, *Arms, Men and Government*, 444-459.
23. Stacey, *Arms, Men and Government*, 460-474.
24. Childs, "Zombie Parade."
25. Childs, "Zombie Parade."
26. Verse enclosed in Andy Clipperton to Bob Clipperton, 22 September 1944.
27. Allan Nickleson, "Ceremony is Hasty for V.C.," *Canadian Press News*, 2 December 1944.
28. Int: R. Barr.
29. Source for return home of Major David Currie, VC, is Int: I. Currie, 12 December 1995.
30. BBC Interview, Major David Currie, n.d. (c. December 1944).
31. WD, 4-9 December 1944.
32. NPRC; PSN.
33. NPRC; PSN.
34. NPRC; PSN.
35. Int: R. Rasmussen.
36. Int: G. Irving.
37. WD, 16 December 1944.
38. WD, 20 December 1944.
39. WD, 25 December 1944.
40. Neff, Diary, 25 December 1944.
41. Dryer to fiancée, 25 December 1944.
42. Neff, Diary, 1 January 1945.
43. McDougall, *Short History*, 59; WD, 1 January 1945.
44. Neff, Diary, 1 January 1945.
45. NAC, RG 24, G3, volume 10939, file 245C4.043 (D1), Organization of Recce Units, December 1944.
46. WD, 1 January 1945.
47. Dryer to fiancée, 4 January 1945.
48. Lakes, "Tomorrow's Rainbow."
49. Neff, Diary, 6 January 1944.
50. Int: A. Halkyard.
51. Int: F. Jefferson.
52. Dryer to fiancée, 6 February 1945.
53. WD, 14 January 1945.
54. WD, 15 January 1945.
55. WD, 16 January 1945.
56. WD, January 1945.
57. Cassidy, *Warpath*, 244.
58. WD, 19 January 1945.
59. WD, 22 January 1945.
60. Strathern, Diary, 24 January 1945.
61. WD, 25 January 1945.

15. "IF ONLY WE HAD THE WISDOM OF OUR GENERALS." HOLLAND: 25 JANUARY–21 FEBRUARY 1945
1. "When This Bloody War is Over," a soldier's song from the late war period sung to the tune of "What a friend we have in Jesus."
2. DHist, Interrogation Report of *General* Eugen-Felix Schwalbe.
3. Stacey, *Victory*, 450.
4. Int: A. Engel.

5. Wood, "Elephant," 9.
6. Jamar, *With the Tanks*, 279.
7. Wood, "Elephant," 11.
8. Stacey, *Victory*, 452.
9. Wood, "Elephant," 9.
10. WD, 4 CAD, 14 January 1945.
11. Paterson, *10 Brigade*, 53. The artillery arrangements for Operation ELEPHANT provided for 92,000 rounds of HE and Smoke for calibres ranging from 75 mm tank guns to 5.5 medium guns, see Wood, "Elephant," 10.
12. WD, 10 Brigade, 17 January 1945; Hayes, *Lincs*, 91.
13. Wood, "Elephant," 10.
14. Hayes, *Lincs*, 77-78.
15. Kaufman, *Liberation Album*, 69.
16. Kaufman, *Liberation Album*, 69-70.
17. Hayes, *Lincs*, 91.
18. Hayes, *Lincs*, 78.
19. M.O. Rollefson, *Green Route Up*, 64-65.
20. DHist, Interrogation Report of *Generalleutnant* Hermann Plocher, 13 September 1946.
21. WD, 10 Brigade, 24 January 1945.
22. M.O. Rollefson, *Green Route Up*, 66; also OL, 10 Brigade, 26 January 1945.
23. Hayes, *Lincs*, 79; also OL, 10 Brigade, 26 January 1945.
24. OL, 10 Brigade, 26 January 1945; Hayes, *Lincs*, 82-83.
25. Hayes, *Lincs*, 82-83.
26. Hayes, *Lincs*, 83.
27. Hayes, *Lincs*, 81.
28. Hayes, *Lincs*, 82-83; also OL, 10 Brigade, 26 January 1945.
29. Hayes, *Lincs*, 83.
30. Hayes, *Lincs*, 83-84.
31. Hayes, *Lincs*, 83-84; also, WD, 10 Brigade, 26 January 1945.
32. Int: G. Armstrong.
33. WD, 26 January 1945.
34. WD, 26 January 1945.
35. M.O. Rollefson, *Green Route Up*, 66.
36. WD, February 1945, Appendix, Report of Sergeant V.L. Stevenson.
37. M.O. Rollefson, *Green Route Up*, 66.
38. M.O. Rollefson, *Green Route Up*, 66-67.
39. WD, February 1945, Appendix, Report of Lieutenant Ken Wigg.
40. Int: G. Irving; also OL, 10 Brigade, 26 January 1945; WD, 10 Brigade, 26 January 1945.
41. Spence, *15 Field*, 204.
42. Hayes, *Lincs*, 83-84; Spencer, *15 Field*, 203-204; also WD, 10 Brigade, 26 January 1945; OL, 10 Brigade, 26 January 1945.
43. OL, 10 Brigade, 26 January 1945.
44. M.O. Rollefson, *Green Route Up*, 65.
45. Int: R. Broberg.
46. A. Earp to DEG, n.d. (c. October 1995); also *Green Route Up*, 66.
47. A. Earp to DEG, n.d. (c. October 1995).
48. A. Earp to DEG, n.d. (c. October 1995).
49. WD, 28 January 1945.
50. NPRC; PSN.
51. M.O. Rollefson, *Green Route Up*, 67.
52. WD, 27 January 1945.
53. WD, 28 January 1945; OL, 10 Brigade, 28 January 1945.
54. WD, 28 January 1945.
55. Paterson, *10 Brigade*, 56.
56. WD, ASH, 28 January 1945; OL, 10 Brigade, 28 January 1945; WD, 28 January 1945.
57. Galipeau, "Pee Wees," 59.
58. War Diary, February 1945, Appendix, PW Statement of *Stabsfeldwebel* Heinrich Fischer, 30 January 1945.

59. WD, February 1945, Appendix, PW Statement of *Stabsfeldwebel* Heinrich Fischer, 30 January 1945.
60. Galipeau, "Pee Wees," 159.
61. WD, February 1945, Appendix, PW Statement of *Stabsfeldwebel* Heinrich Fischer, 30 January 1945.
62. NPRC; PSN; also WD, 30 January 1945.
63. WD, 28 January 1945.
64. DHist, Interrogation Report of *General* Eugen-Felix Schwalbe.
65. Wiens, "Intelligence Officer."
66. Wiens, "Intelligence Officer."
67. OL, 10 Brigade, 28 January 1945; WD, ASH, 28 January 1945.
68. WD, 29 January 1945.
69. Int: J. Wiebe.
70. Int: A. Baker.
71. Int: J. Wiebe.
72. Int: E. Hyatt.
73. WD, February 1945, Appendix, Report of Lieutenant Ken Wigg.
74. Int: J. Strathern.
75. Spencer, *15 Field*, 207.
76. WD, 29 January 1945; OL, 10 Brigade, 29-30 January 1945; WD, February 1945, Appendix, Report of Lieutenant K. Wigg.
77. WD, 29 January 1945; WD, 10 Brigade, 29 January 1945; OL, 10 Brigade, 29 January 1945.
78. Int: A.F. Coffin; WD, 29 January 1945.
79. WD, 30 January 1945; OL, 10 Brigade, 30 January 1945; WD, 10 Brigade, 30 January 1945; WD, ASH, 30 January 1945.
80. Int: J. Wiebe.
81. WD, ASH, 30 January 1945.
82. WD, 30 January 1945; OL, 10 Brigade, 30 January 1945.
83. Strathern, "Memoir."
84. WD, 30 January 1945.
85. WD, 30 January 1945.
86. NPRC; PSN.
87. WD, 30 January 1945.
88. Int: C. Allen; also WD, 30 January 1945.
89. WD, 31 January 1945; OL, 31 January 1945.
90. *Toronto Star*, 1 February 1945, in Fraser, *Black Yesterdays*, 351.
91. *Toronto Star*, 1 February 1945, in Fraser, *Black Yesterdays*, 351.
92. Int: J. Wiebe.
93. WD, 31 January 1945.
94. Private Donald Stark in Fraser, *Black Yesterdays*, 352.
95. Paterson, *10 Brigade*, 56.
96. DHist, Interrogation Report of *Generalleutnant* Hermann Plocher.
97. Stacey, *Victory*, 454.
98. WD, 31 January 1945.
99. Hayes, *Lincs*, 93.
100. Hayes, *Lincs*, 93.
101. Hayes, *Lincs*, 93-94.
102. Hayes, *Lincs*, 95.
103. Foster, *Meeting of Generals*, 429.
104. Wiley Int: G.D. Wotherspoon, 1986.
105. Int: G. Irving.
106. Int: J. Wiebe.
107. WD, 31 January 1945.
108. Neff, Diary, 15 January 1945.
109. WD, January-February 1945.
110. Neff, Diary, 17-24 February 1945.
111. Luton, "Seven Days."
112. Int: G.L. McDougall.
113. Luton, "Seven Days."
114. Luton, "Seven Days."
115. Luton, "Seven Days."
116. WD, 18 February 1945.

16. "THROUGH THE MUD AND THE BLOOD." HOLLAND AND GERMANY: 21 FEBRUARY–2 MARCH 1945
1. Words composed by Lieutenant Bill Luton of the SAR while waiting to move forward at the Hochwald on 27 February 1945 to the tune of "Can't think of anything I'd rather do."
2. Stacey, *Victory*, 461-462, 491-492.
3. Stacey, *Victory*, 491-494.
4. WD, 21 February 1945.
5. WD, 23 February 1945.
6. WD, 23 February 1945.
7. Marshall, "Me and George," 77.
8. WD, 23 February 1945.
9. McDougall, *Short History*, 63.
10. WD, 23 February 1945.
11. WD, March 1945, Appendix, Health of the Regiment, March 1945.
12. Int: G.L. McDougall.
13. Canadian Army Newsreel No. 64, n.d. (c. March 1945).
14. Luton, "Seven Days."
15. Luton, "Seven Days"; also WD, 25 February 1944; Cassidy, *Warpath*, 250-252.
16. Int: A. F. Coffin; Cassidy, *Warpath*, 255.
17. DHist, Interrogation Report of *Generalleutnant* Hermann Plocher.
18. Stacey, *Victory*, 509.
19. WD, 23-25 February 1945.
20. Int: E. Thorn.
21. Luton, "Seven Days."
22. WD, 25 February 1945.
23. WD, 25 February 1945.
24. Cassidy, *Warpath*, 252-253.
25. Luton, "Seven Days."
26. Cassidy, *Warpath*, 254.
27. WD, 27 February 1945.
28. Cassidy, *Warpath*, 254.
29. Cassidy, *Warpath*, 255.
30. Int: A.F. Coffin.
31. WD, 27 February 1945.
32. WD, 27 February 1945.
33. Cassidy, *Warpath*, 256.
34. Luton, "Seven Days."
35. WD, 27 February 1945.
36. WD, 27 February 1945.
37. Luton, "Seven Days."
38. Marshall, "Me and George," 82.
39. Allen, *One More River*, 155.
40. Int: F. Freeman.
41. Int: L. Caseley.
42. Luton, "Seven Days."
43. WD, 27 February 1945.
44. Int: G.L. McDougall.
45. Int: G.L. McDougall.
46. *History of the 11th Armoured Division*, 84.
47. Int: E. Thorn.
48. Int: G.L. McDougall.
49. Galipeau, "Pee Wees," 161.
50. Int: G.L. McDougall.
51. Int: E. Thorn.
52. Int: A. Boyer.
53. Int: A. Baker.
54. Int: I. MacPherson.
55. Watkins, "Memoir of Hochwald."
56. NPRC; PSN.
57. Int: J. Bell.
58. Int: G.L. McDougall.
59. Int: J. Bell.
60. Int: G.L. McDougall.
61. Int: G.L. McDougall.
62. Int: R. Seccombe.
63. NPRC.
64. Int: A. Baker.
65. Int: A. Baker.
66. Int: J. Arkles.
67. Int: A. Baker.
68. Int: J. Arkles.
69. Int: J. Arkles.
70. Int: A. Baker.

71. Int: J. Arkles.
72. Int. A. Baker.
73. Int: A. Baker.
74. A. Baker, "Memoir."
75. Int: H. Watkins; H. Watkins, "Memoir."
76. Int: A.F. Coffin.
77. Int: J. Bell; also NPRC; PSN; WD, March 1945.
78. Int: A.F. Coffin.
79. Int: A.F. Coffin.
80. Cassidy, *Warpath*, 260.
81. WD, 27 February 1945.
82. Hunter to Luton, n.d., in Luton "Seven Days."
83. WD, 27 February 1945.
84. WD, 27 February 1945.
85. Luton, "Seven Days"; also WD, 27-28 February 1945.
86. Luton, "Seven Days."
87. DHist, SGR II/201, BLOCKBUSTER draft.
88. Marshall, "Me and George," 85.
89. Luton, "Seven Days."
90. Int: L. Caseley.
91. WD, 28 February 1945.
92. Int: L. Caseley.
93. WD, ASH, 28 February 1945.
94. Marshall, "Me and George," 85.
95. WD, 28 February 1945; Sergeants Fred Freeman and Lawrence Freer, Citations, Military Medal; Int: L. Caseley.
96. Luton, "Seven Days."
97. Marshall, "Me and George," 85.
98. Luton, "Seven Days."
99. WD, 28 February 1945.
100. WD, 28 February 1945.
101. WD, 28 February 1945.
102. Int: R. Rasmussen.
103. Gallimore, Diary, 27-28 February 1945.
104. Paterson, *10 Brigade*, 61.
105. Int: E. Nichols.
106. NPRC; PSN; also WD, November 1945, Appendix; Int: E. Nichol.
107. Luton, "Seven Days."
108. WD, 1 March 1945.
109. Marshall, "Me and George," 86.
110. WD, 1 March 1945.
111. Milner to Luton, n.d, in Luton, "Seven Days."
112. Luton, "Seven Days."
113. Luton, "Seven Days."
114. NPRC; PSN.
115. Luton, "Seven Days."
116. Paterson, *10 Brigade*, 61.

17. "TO THE GREEN FIELDS BEYOND." GERMANY AND HOLLAND: 2 MARCH– 31 MARCH 1945
1. One of the many variants of "Lili Marlene" sung by Allied soldiers in northwest Europe in the last months of the war.
2. WD, 2 March 1945.
3. Wiley Int: G.D. Wotherspoon, 1986.
4. WD, 3 March 1945.
5. DHist, SGR II/201, BLOCKBUSTER Draft.
6. WD, 4 March 1945.
7. WD, 4 March 1945.
8. Marshall, "Me and George," 88.
9. Marshall, "Me and George," 88; and Nicholson, "1940-1945."
10. Denning, "Memoir."
11. Int: J. Cooper.
12. Marshall, "Me and George," 88.
13. Denning, "Memoir."
14. NPRC; PSN; Nicholson, "1940-1945."
15. WD, 5 March 1945.
16. WD, 5 March 1945.
17. Strathern, Diary, 5 March 1945.
18. WD, 10 Brigade, 5 March 1945.
19. Cassidy, *Warpath*, 284.

20. Stacey, *Victory*, 520.
21. WD, 7 March 1945.
22. Cassidy, *Warpath*, 280.
23. Citation, Trooper James Forbes, Military Medal; also WD, 7 March 1945.
24. Int: C. Wicke.
25. WD, 7 March 1945.
26. Cassidy, *Warpath*, 282.
27. Silcox, "Jack Fraser, MC."
28. NPRC; PSN.
29. Galipeau, "Pee Wees," 165.
30. Cassidy, *Warpath*, 280-281.
31. WD, 8 March 1945.
32. Wiens, "Intelligence Officer."
33. WD, 8 March 1945.
34. Silcox, "Jack Fraser, MC."
35. Silcox, "Jack Fraser, MC."
36. Luton, "Seven Days"; also WD, 9 March 1945.
37. The three previous failures had been at the Falaise and the Seine in August and at the Scheldt in September 1944.
38. Galipeau, "Pee Wees," 165-166.
39. WD, 10 March 1945.
40. Silcox, "Jack Fraser, MC."
41. DND to Mary Funnell, 11 March 1945.
42. DND to Mary Funnell, 26 March 1945.
43. Padre Silcox to Mary Funnell, 21 April 1945.
44. DND to Mary Funnell, 9 May 1945.
45. Int: A. Baker.
46. WD, 12 March 1945.
47. Luton, "Seven Days." This is believed to be the first time that an account of Vokes's lecture to his officers, other than the official account, has appeared in print.
48. NAC, RG24, G3 10798, File 225C2.011 (D1), Memorandum of Interview with Lieutenant-General Simonds, 17 December 1946.
49. NAC, RG 24, Volume 10937, File 245C4.016(D5), Op BLOCKBUSTER, Verbal Instrs GOC 4 Cdn Armd Div 22 Feb 45.
50. Wiley Int: G.D. Wotherspoon, 1986.
51. Whitaker, *Rhineland*, 227.
52. Tank losses in Rhineland fighting from NAC, RG 24, G3, volume 10458, File 212C1.1009 (D37), First Canadian Army Tank Casualties, 8 February to 10 March, 1945, dated 14 March 1945. Personnel losses from: Paterson, *10 Brigade*, 163; NPRC; and PSN.
53. DHist 141.4A29C13(D1), 29 Cdn Armd Regt. Record of Op "Blockbuster" as far as it affects 29 Cdn Armd Recce Regt, 26 Feb-2 Mar 1945. The emphasis in all the quotations from this document is the author's.
54. WD, 13 March 1945.
55. WD, 13 March 1945.
56. Marshall, "Me and George," 95.
57. WD, 13 March 1945.
58. WD, 13 March 1945.
59. Neff, Diary, 18 March 1945.
60. Ross Munro, "Alberta Tanks Drive Through to Clear Woods," *Canadian Press*, 27 March 1945.
61. WD, 20 March 1945.
62. Strathern, Diary, 13 March 1945.
63. Wiley Int: G.D. Wotherspoon, 1986.
64. Int: E. Reardon.
65. Int: G. Gallimore.
66. Galipeau, "Pee Wees," 170-171.
67. WD, 17 March 1945.
68. Int: E. Neiman.
69. Wiley Int: G.D. Wotherspoon, 1986.
70. Wiley Int: G.D. Wotherspoon, 1986.
71. WD, 14 March 1945.
72. WD, 14 March 1945.
73. WD, 15 March 1945.

74. WD, 16 March 1945.
75. Galipeau, "Pee Wees," 172; Neff, Diary, 17 March 1945.
76. Luton, "The Rhine."
77. Marshall, "Me and George," 96.
78. Marshall, "Me and George," 97.
79. Marshall, "Me and George," 98.
80. Dollinger, *Decline and Fall*, 93.
81. Luton, "The Rhine."
82. Luton, "The Rhine."
83. Galipeau, "Pee Wees," 172-173.
84. WD, 21-22 March 1945.
85. WD, 23 March 1945.
86. Luton, "The Rhine."
87. Luton, "The Rhine."
88. Luton to fiancée, n.d. in Luton, "Rhine."
89. WD, 28-31 March 1945; Int: J. Galipeau.
90. WD, 28-31 March 1945.
91. Taylor and Fry, *Beating Around the Bush*, 65-66.
92. Luton, "The Rhine."
93. Int: S. Rose; Citation, Corporal Tony Devreker, Military Medal; NPRC.
94. Marshall, "Me and George," 99.
95. Marshall, "Me and George," 99-100.
96. Marshall, "Me and George," 100.
97. Int: S. Rose.
98. Marshall, "Me and George," 100.
99. Marshall, "Me and George," 100.
100. Int: E. Nichol.
101. PSN; NPRC.
102. Marshall, "Me and George," 100-101.
103. WD, 30 March 1945.
104. Int: E. Reardon.
105. WD, March 1945.
106. WD, 31 March 1945; Luton, "The Rhine."

18. "A DING DONG FIGHT IN THE FAILING LIGHT." GERMANY: 1 APRIL–4 MAY 1945

1. "South of the Kusten," a soldier's song dating from April 1945 sung to the tune of "South of the Border."
2. Int: W. Luton, 12 December 1996.
3. WD, 31 March 1945.
4. WD, 1 April 1945.
5. Int: D. McLeod, 24 August 1996.
6. Int: J. Eastman.
7. Luton, "The Rhine."
8. WD, 1 April 1945.
9. WD, 1 April 1945.
10. WD, 2 April 1945.
11. Lakes, "Tomorrow's Rainbow."
12. WD, 2 April 1945; NPRC; PSN.
13. Luton, "The Rhine."
14. WD, 2 April 1945; NPRC; PSN.
15. Marshall, "Me and George," 103.
16. WD, 5 April, 1945; DHist 141.4A29011(1), Memorandum of an Interview Given by LCol G.D. Wotherspoon, "The Final Punch," Operations and Activities of 29 Cdn Armd Recce Regt, April-May 1945 (hereafter Wotherspoon, The Final Punch).
17. WD, 7 April 1945.
18. WD, 7 April 1945.
19. WD, 7 April 1945.
20. Int: A. Engel.
21. Int: D. White.
22. Wood, "The SAR."
23. Marshall, "Me and George," 103.
24. Cassidy, *Warpath*, 301.
25. Luton, "The Rhine."
26. NPRC; PSN.
27. Nicholson, "1940-1945"; Neff, Diary, 3 April 1945.
28. Luton, "The Rhine."
29. Luton, "The Rhine."
30. Luton, "The Rhine."
31. WD, 8-9 April 1945; Watkins, "Rijssen."

32. Int: D. White.
33. Watkins, "Rijssen."
34. Int: H. Watkins; Watkins, "Rijssen"; Wim Porterman to DEG, 15 June 1997.
35. WD, 10 April 1945.
36. Luton, "Armoured Recce."
37. Int: D. McLeod, 24 August 1996.
38. McDougall, *Short History*, 78.
39. WD, 13 April 1945.
40. Wiley Int: G.D. Wotherspoon, 1986.
41. WD, 13 April 1945; Int: McLeod, 21 January 1996.
42. Luton, "Armoured Recce."
43. WD, 13 April 1945.
44. WD, 14 April 1945; Gallimore, Diary, 14 April 1945.
45. Int: G. Gallimore.
46. WD, 14 April 1945; DHist, Wotherspoon, The Final Punch.
47. Marshall, "Me and George," 104.
48. Galipeau, "Pee Wees," 176-177.
49. WD, 15 April 1945.
50. Galipeau, "Pee Wees," 178-179.
51. Int: L. Iltchuck.
52. Nicholson, "1940-1945;" Neff, Diary, 15 April 1945.
53. Int: R. Fairhurst.
54. WD, 15 April 1945; Luton, "Armoured Recce."
55. Int: G. Gallimore.
56. Int: G. Gallimore.
57. Milner, "Action at Varrelbusch."
58. Int: C. Daley.
59. Int: D. McLeod, 24 August 1996.
60. Int: D. McLeod, 24 August 1996.
61. Int: C. Daley.
62. Milner, "Action at Varrelbusch."
63. Int: D. McLeod, 24 August 1996.
64. Int: D. McLeod, 24 August 1996.
65. Luton, "Armoured Recce."
66. Int: D. McLeod, 24 August 1996.
67. Milner, "Action at Varrelbusch."
68. WD, 15 August 1945.
69. Luton, "Armoured Recce."
70. WD, 16 April 1945; Wotherspoon, The Final Punch.
71. NPRC; PSN; WD, April 1945.
72. WD, 16 April 1945.
73. WD, 19 April 1945; Wotherspoon, The Final Punch.
74. Wotherspoon, The Final Punch.
75. Wotherspoon, The Final Punch.
76. Author's conversation with J.L. Summers.
77. Jellis, "Wally's Commandos"; Wotherspoon, The Final Punch.
78. WD, 17 April 1945.
79. Int: M. Amyotte.
80. WD, 17-19 April 1945; Wotherspoon, The Final Punch; Luton, "Armoured Recce."
81. Int: C. Daley.
82. NPRC; PSN.
83. Nicholson, "1940-1945."
84. Luton, "Armoured Recce."
85. Int: G.L. McDougall.
86. Neff, Diary, 20 April 1945.
87. Int: D. McLeod, 24 August 1996.
88. WD, 20-21 April 1945.
89. Luton, "Armoured Recce."
90. Int: J. Wiebe.
91. Luton, "Armoured Recce."
92. Marshall, "Me and George," 116.
93. WD, 23 April 1945.
94. Milner, "DCM Action."
95. Wotherspoon, The Final Punch.
96. WD, 25 April 1945.
97. Luton to fiancée, n.d., in Luton, "Armoured Recce."
98. Ints: D. McLeod, 24 August 1996, C.

Daley.
99. NPRC; PSN.
100. Int: D. McLeod, 24 August 1996.
101. Luton, "Armoured Recce."
102. Int: R. Seccombe.
103. WD, 3 May 1945.
104. Paterson, *10 Brigade*, 68-69.
105. WD, 3 May 1945.
106. Luton, "Armoured Recce."
107. Int: J. Wiebe.
108. Luton, "Armoured Recce."

19. "TRISH HAS A CANADIAN." GERMANY, HOLLAND AND CANADA: MAY 1945–JANUARY 1946

1. "Trees heeft een Canadees" (Trish has a Canadian), a hit song in Holland during the summer of 1945. The translation is mine.
2. WD, 4 May 1945.
3. Clipperton, "Memories."
4. D. Stewart to Mrs. Stewart, 5 May 1945.
5. Wood, "1940-1945."
6. Int: G.L. McDougall.
7. WD, 5 May 1945.
8. Stewart, Diary, 5 May 1945.
9. WD, 5 May 1945.
10. WD, 6 May 1945.
11. Bill Luton to fiancée, 6 May 1945, in Luton, "Armoured Recce."
12. Michael Foss, quoted in Swinson, *A Register*, xiii-xiv.
13. PSN.
14. NPRC; PSN.
15. Int: H. Watkins.
16. WD, D Squadron, Elgin Regiment, July 1944-May 1945.
17. "Royal Canadian Armoured Corps. Roll of Honour. Compiled by E Group, CRU," n.d. (c. 1945-1946).
18. WD, D Squadron, Elgin Regiment, July 1944-May 1945.
19. Douglas Beale in Fraser, *Black Yesterdays*, 440.
20. WD, 8 May 1945.
21. Vokes, *My Story*, 196.
22. WD, 10 May 1945.
23. Int: I. McPherson.
24. Int: J. Wiebe.
25. WD, May 1945; Int: G. Irving.
26. Stewart, Diary, 14 May 1945.
27. WD, 18 May 1945: Int: T. Barford.
28. Int: I. MacPherson.
29. Int: L. Caseley.
30. Int: G.L. McDougall.
31. WD, 26-31 May 1945. The officer party sent to tour the battlefield sites consisted of Major Arnold Lavoie, Captain Jack Summers and Padre Silcox. They took a series of photographs which were reproduced and distributed to the men of the unit.
32. WD, June 1945.
33. WD, July 1945; NPRC.
34. Int: A.F. Coffin, 14 September 1997.
35. Kaufman, *Liberation Album*, 129-131.
36. WD, 16 June 1945.
37. Marshall, "Me and George," 126.
38. Kaufman, *Liberation Album*, 131-133, 137-140, 142.
39. Arnold Dryer to fiancée, 5 July 1945.
40. Arnold Dryer to fiancée, 1 August 1945.
41. WD, June-August 1945; Int: E. Reardon.
42. Wiley Int: G.D. Wotherspoon, 1986.
43. WD, 17 August 1945.
44. Wiley Int: G.D. Wotherspoon, 1986.
45. Int: S. Bayko.
46. NPRC.
47. Int: A. Baker.
48. Material on PW experiences from in-

terviews with A. Baker, J. Arkles and E. Thorn.
49. Int: D. McLeod, 1 October 1996.
50. Int: G. White.
51. Int: C. Allen.
52. WD, September-December 1945.
53. WD, December 1945-January 1946.
54. WD, 14 January 1946.
55. WD, January 1946.
56. Int: G. Armstrong.
57. WD: 18 January 1946.
58. Author's conversation with Richard (Swatty) Wotherspoon, 1995.
59. *Medicine Hat Daily News*, 19 January 1946.
60. *Medicine Hat Daily News*, 19 January 1946.

20. "I WAS OVER AND I CAME BACK." THE REGIMENT IN THE POSTWAR WORLD: 1946–1995

1. "The Armoured 19th," the postwar regimental song of the 19th Alberta Dragoons sung to the tune of "Lili Marlene."
2. *Toronto Star*, 2 April 1985.
3. Int: A. F. Coffin.
4. *Ottawa Citizen*, 28 June 1986; also Int: I. Currie, 12 December 1995.
5. V. Childs to DEG, 12 March 1997.
6. Ints: D. Mcleod, 21 January, 24 August, 1996.
7. Author's conversation with J.L. Summers.
8. Int: R. Broberg.
9. Int: R. Seccombe.
10. Int: J. Walker.
11. Int: J. Bell.
12. Int: L. Angus.
13. Int: R. Virtue.
14. David Marshall, Response to Questionnaire by Agatha Bonga, 13 August 1995.
15. Int: J. Cooper.
16. Int: J.O. White.
17. For obvious reasons, the sources for this quotation and those in the preceding paragraph have been withheld.
18. *Edmonton Journal*, 21 February 1946.
19. Int: H. Quarton.
20. Myrtle (Andy) Clipperton to DEG, n.d. (c. March 1996).
21. Int: A. Halkyard.
22. Int: I. Currie, 12 December 1995.
23. Int: I. Currie, 12 December 1995.
24. Int: D. McLeod, 21 January 1996.
25. Int: D. McLeod, 21 January 1996.
26. Int: D. McLeod, 21 January 1996.
27. Galipeau, "Pee Wees," 194.
28. Author's conversation with Harry Quarton, May 1997.
29. *Globe and Mail*, 2 May 1986.
30. Address by Albert Hartkamp, Chef du Cabinet, Nijverdal, during a ceremony at Holten Cemetery, 8 May 1997.
31. Including a very reluctant historian who was dragged kicking and screaming from a quiet life of detached contemplation of the past and sent willy-nilly into the struggles of the present.
32. Memorandum, Replica Colour, The South Alberta Regiment, by Director of Ceremonial, DND, 13 April 1995.
33. Int: T. Eastwood.

EPILOGUE . "AND NOT TO YIELD." EDMONTON, ALBERTA: 21–24 SEPTEMBER 1995

1. Gordon Towers to Harry Quarton, 12 February 1997.
2. NPRC; PSN.

BIBLIOGRAPHY

UNPUBLISHED SOURCES

NATIONAL ARCHIVES OF CANADA, OTTAWA

Record Group 24
Volume 10458
    File 212C1.1009(D37), First Canadian Army Tank Casualties, 8 February-10 March 1945
Volume 10460
    File 212C1.1009(D29), Report by No. 14. 1st Canadian Army Field Research Section
    File 212C1.1009 (D49), Report by AFV(T), 1st Canadian Army, 2 August 1944
Volume 10550,
    File 215A2 O33 (D2), The Cooperation of Tanks with Infantry,
Volume 10553
    File 212A1.083 (D92), Memorandum on British Armour, 21 July 1944
Volume 10595
    File 215.C1 (D582), Re-Organization of 4th and 5th Armoured Divisions
Volume 10798
    File 225C2.011 (D1), Memorandum of Interview with Lt. Genl. Simonds, 17 December 1946
Volume 10937
    File 245C4.016(D5), Op Blockbuster, Verbal Instructions, GOC, 4 Canadian Armoured Division, 22 February, 1945
Volume 10939
    File 245C4.043(D1), Organization of Recce Units, December 1944
Volume 20522,
    File 981, Memoir by *Generalleutnant* Eugen Meindl
Volume 20523
    File 981 SOM (D178), *Oberst* Elmar Waring, Battles of LXVII Inf Corps Between the Schelde and the Maas, 15 Sep - 25 Nov 44

War Diaries
2nd Canadian Corps, July 1944-May 1945
4th Canadian Armoured Division, September 1942-May 1945
9 Canadian Infantry Brigade, August 1944
10 Canadian Infantry Brigade, January 1944-May 1945
5th Anti-Tank Regiment, August 1944
103rd Anti-Tank Battery, 6th Anti-Tank Regiment, August 1944
The Algonquin Regiment, July 1944-May 1945
The Argyll and Sutherland Highlanders, July 1944-May 1945
The Elgin Regiment, D Squadron, July 1944-May 1945
The Highland Light Infantry of Canada, August 1944
The Lincoln and Welland Regiment, July 1944-May 1945
The North Nova Scotia Highlanders, August 1944
The Stormont, Dundas & Glengarry Highlanders of Canada, August 1944
The South Alberta Regiment, June 1940-January 1946

Operations Logs
4th Canadian Armoured Division, August 1944-May 1945
9 Canadian Infantry Brigade, August 1944
10 Canadian Infantry Brigade, July 1944-May 1945

PUBLIC RECORD OFFICE, KEW, SURREY, UK
WO 171, Vol. 852, War Diary, 1st Fife and Forfar Yeomanry, 26 October 1944

DIRECTORATE OF HISTORY, DEPARTMENT OF NATIONAL DEFENCE, OTTAWA
Army Historical Section Report No. 38, "Tank Production in Canada"
Army Historical Section Report No. 43, "Training of 4th and 5th Canadian Armoured Divisions in the United Kingdom, October 1941-July 1944
Army Historical Section Report No. 59, "Food Complaints and Cooks' Training"
Canadian Military Headquarters Report No. 169
Citations for Awards and Decorations
    Currie, David V., Victoria Cross
    Devreker, Tony, Military Medal
    Forbes, James, Military Medal
    Freeman, Frederick, Military Medal
    Freer, Lawrence, Military Medal
    Haddow, Arthur, Military Medal
    Ottenbreit, Michael, Military Medal
    Prenevost, Douglas, Croix de Guerre with Bronze Star
    Roulston, Herbert, Military Medal
    Silcox, A.P., Member of the British Empire
    Smith, C.J., Miltary Medal
    Summers, J.L. Military Cross
Correspondence Relating to the Official History of the Canadian Army in the Second World War
    M. Gordon to G.W.L. Nicholson, 1 February 1960
    G. Kitching to G.W.L. Nicholson, 17 April 1959
Crerar Files: Correspondence Relating to the Relief of Major-General F.F. Worthington, 1943-1944
DHist 79/705, Operational Research in North-West Europe, The Work of No. 2 Operational Research Section with 21 Army Group
DHist 85/240, Analysis of Firepower in Normandy, No. 10
Director, Royal Armoured Corps, Monthly Liaison Letters, 1943-1945
File 11.1.001, "Short History of the Alberta Mounted Rifles," n.p., c. 1931
File 112.1 (D43), Correspondence concerning the re-organization of 4th and 5th Armoured Divisions
File 141.4A29C13 (D1), Record of Op Blockbuster as far as it affects 29 CARR, 26 Feb-2 Mar 1945
File 141.4A29011(1), Memorandum of an Interview Given by LCol G.D. Wotherspoon, "The Final Punch," Operations and Activities of 29 Cdn Armd Recce Regt, Apr-May 45
File 145.2.A1013 (D1), Account of the Battle Experience of A

Company, Algonquin Regiment; Major G.L. Cassidy, Outline of
Events, August 1944

File 570.013 (D7A), Air Aspects of Normandy

Intelligence Summaries, 1st Canadian Army, 6 June 1944-24 May
1945

Interrogation Reports

Generaloberst Josef "Sepp" Dietrich, 29 August 1945

Brigadeführer Kurt Meyer, 24 August 1945

Generalleutnant Hermann Plocher, 13 September 1946

Generalmajor Sanders, 30 September 1945

General Eugen-Felix Schwalbe, 30 September 1945

General Gustav von Zangen, 30 September 1946

Steiger Collection SGR II/201, Blockbuster Draft

SOUTH ALBERTA REGIMENT HISTORICAL COLLECTION

Correspondence, Wartime

Clipperton, Robert and Myrtle (Andy) Clipperton, 1943-1945.

Dryer, Arnold to his fiancée, 1943-1945.

Funnell, Mary, correspondence with DND, February-May 1945.

Smitty to R. Mitchell, 23 August 1944.

Stewart, Don to Mrs. Stewart, 1943-1945.

Correspondence, Postwar

R. Allsopp to DEG, 13 March 1995; A. Baker to JLS, 29 June 1992; C.
Debenham to DEG, 2 September 1997; V. Childs to DEG, 29 March
1996, 12 March 1997; R. Clipperton to DEG, c. March 1996; A.L.
Coffin to DEG, 15 February 1995, 25 November 1995, 17 August
1997; A. Denning to JLS, 30 August 1992; Director, Ceremonial,
DND, Memorandum, 13 April 1995; A. Earp to DEG, c. October
1995; J. Gove to JLS, 2 September 1992; L.O. Ireland to DEG, c.
November 1994; D. Marshall to DEG, 30 July, 12 August 1997; N.
MacPherson to DEG, 26 November 1996; J. Neff to DEG, 21
February 1995; L. Piepgrass to DEG, February 1995; W. Porterman
to DEG, 15 June 1997; J.H. Redden to JLS, n.d., c. 1992; B. Spaner to
T. Milner, c. autumn 1994; D. Stewart to DEG, 21 November 1995,
10 December 1995; W. Taylor to DEG, c. April 1995; G. Towers to H.
Quarton, 12 February 1997; H. Watkins to DEG, 14 January 1995.

Diaries

Gallimore, George, January-May 1945.

Neff, John, 1 August 1944-May 1945.

Stewart, Don, January-May 1945.

Strathern, Joe, January-May 1945.

Interviews by D.E. Graves

G. Adams, 22 November 1995; C. Allen, 22 August 1995 ; R. Allsopp,
21 September 1995; M. Amyotte, 25 November 1995; L. Angus, 16
August 1996; T. Apselet, 26 August 1996; J. Arkles, 3 December 1995;
G. Armstrong, 14, 18 August 1996; S. Arrowsmith, 13 August 1995;
E. Aucoin; A. Baker, 25 November 1995; A. Ball, 13 August 1996;
C.A. Barford, 13 August 1996; R. Barr, 20 August 1996; S. Bayko, 28
November 1995; B. Bean, 25 November 1995; J. Bell, 26 November
1995; H. Bergquist, 21 August 1996; A. Berry, 21 August 1996; G.
Bird, 23 August 1996; W. Boothroyd, 18 November 1995; A. Boyer,
13 August 1996; R. Broberg, 26 August 1996; R. Bruce, 21 August
1996; D. Cameron, 3 December 1995; E. Campbell, 29 November
1995; L. Caseley, 13 November 1995; J. Cheney, 25 November 1995;
T. Clausen, 28 August 1996; A.F. Coffin, 27 August 1995; J. Cooper,
19 August 1996; I. Currie, 12 December 1995; C. Daley, 12 August
1996; E. Davies, 21 August 1996; J. Eastman, 30 August 1996; T.
Eastwood, 14 August 1996; A. Engel, 19 September 1996; R.
Fairhurst, 19 August 1996; C. Farquhar, 19 September 1996; C.R.

Fast, 14 August 1996; C.B. Fearn, 3 January 1996; H. Ficht, 12
October 1995; M. Fitzpatrick, 22 August 1996; F. Freeman, 13
September 1996; J. Galipeau, 24 September 1995; G. Gallimore, 23
September 1995; C. Glaude, 14 August 1996; J. Gove, 15 August
1996; D.I. Grant, 10 December 1995; H. Gudwer, 28 August 1996; A.
Halkyard, 10 November 1995; V. Henderson, 5 December 1995; R.
Henning, 15 August 1996; J.L. Huntley, 19 August 1996; J.
Hutchinson, 22 August 1996; E. Hyatt, 26 August 1996; L. Iltchuck,
21 August 1996; G.E. Irving, 23 September 1995, 3 January 1996; F.
Jefferson, 24 September 1995; W. Kenyon, 30 August 1996; G.
Kitching, 9 November 1995; J. Lardner, 19 September 1995; P.A.
Konvitsko, 6 December 1995; D. Ledwidge, 26 November 1995; W.C.
Luton, 12 December 1996; G.L. McDougall, 19 September 1995; R.
McCloy, 15 August 1996; A.G. McGillivray, 3 September 1996; ; I.
MacPherson, 5 December 1995; N. McPherson, 19 September 1995;
R. Maves, 19 September 1996; ; W.J. "Danny" McLeod, 24 August
1995, 21 January 1996; T. Milner, 26 November 1995; R. Mitchell, 26
August 1996; J.A. Moreton, 25 November 1995; E. Nichols, 19
August 1996; E.V. Nieman, 23 August 1996; G.E. Olmstead, 29
November 1995; J. Porter, 15 August 1996; H. Quarton, 25 Septem-
ber 1995; R. Rasmussen, 21 September 1995; E. Reardon, 22 Septem-
ber 1995; J.H. Redden, 3 January 1996; C. Rose, 28 August 1996; S.
Rose, 28 August 1996; R. Seccombe, 20 August 1995; J. Simpson, 20
August 1996; B. Spaner, 25 September 1995; W. Spence, 19 Septem-
ber 1996; D.E. Stewart, 19 November 1995; G. Stoner, 11 January
1997; J. Strathern, 19 September 1996; J.L. Summers (conversations,
1976-1993); E. Thorn, 16 August 1996; S. Thuesen, 3 December
1995; R. Virtue, 29 November 1995; A. Wagner, 12 August 1996; J.
Walker, 17 August 1996; T. Warren, 12 December 1996; H. Watkins, 7
December 1995; R.D. Wear, 17 August 1996; A. Webster, 19 August
1996; D. White, 21 September 1996; J.O. White, 15 August 1996; G.
White, 21 September 1995 ; C. Wicke, 8 December 1995; J. Wiebe, 24
September 1995; R. Wotherspoon, 24 September 1995.

Interviews by Others

L. Caseley by W.C. Luton, 1995; D.E. Stewart by W.C. Luton, August
1995; G.D. Wotherspoon by Bill Wiley, 1986.

Memoirs, Postwar

Amy, E.A.C., "Normandy. 1 Squadron Canadian Grenadier Guards.
Phase 2: Operation Totalize, 7/8 August 1944," 1993.

Amyotte, Maurice, untitled memoir, c. December 1994.

Atkinson, Margaret, untitled memoir, c. December 1994.

Childs, Vic, "Once an SAR," "Trumpeter, What Are You Sounding
Now," "The Great Zombie Parade."

Clipperton, Robert, "My Personal Memories of the South Alberta
Regiment from 1940 to 1946."

Currie, David Vivian, "St. Lambert-sur-Dives," c. 1963.

Denning, Albert, Memoir.

Dunlop, J. Arkle, "St. Lambert-sur-Dives, Aug 18-19-20-21/44."

Fast, C.R., untitled memoir.

Galipeau, John, "Pee Wees on Parade," c. 1996.

Gallimore, George, "The Hill at Epancy," c. 1995.

Gove, James, "No. 1 Trp, A Sqn at Dives River, 18-22 August 1944."

Jellis, Wally, "Wally's Commandoes," c. 1995.

Keller, E.L., "Stag", untitled memoir, n.d.

Lakes, John, "Tomorrow's Rainbow: Memoirs of John Rutherford
Lakes."

Luton, W.C., "The Seven Days. A Troop Leader's Memories of the
Battle for the Hochwald Gap"; "The Rhine and the Twente"; and
"Armoured Reconnaissance, the Last Days."

McPherson, Neil, "The Lighter Side of Army Life," "King Dog One."

Marshall, David, "Me and George," c. 1993; Response to Questionnaire by Dr. Agatha Bonga, 13 August 1995.

McLeod, Danny, "I Never Made the Party at the Hotel de Draak.
Memories of the Liberation of Bergen op Zoom, October 1944."

Milner, Tom, "Action at Varrelbusch," and "DCM Action," 27
September 1995.

Nicholson, Jim, "1940-1945 with the South Alberta Regiment. A
Personal Recollection by J.L. Nicholson."

Pashkevitch, Addy, "B Squadron, 1944."

Silcox, Arnold Phillips, "Jack Fraser, MC, K/A Veen, Rhineland, 8
March, 1945.'"

Spaner, Bernard, untitled memoir, c. 1994.

Strathern, Joe, "Escape from Civvies, " c. 1996.

Taylor, Egbert, "Immigrant Boy."

Watkins, Herbert, "Report of What Happened at Uedem," "The
Liberation of Rijssen."

Wiens, David, "Intelligence Officer," c. 1992.

Wood, Earle, "The SAR."

Other Material

Graves, Donald E., "Fists of Mail, Walls of Steel, Armoured Warfare,
1914-1945," 1995.

Hartkamp, Albert, Address at Holten Cemetery, 8 May 1997.

Holst, Charles, "6. Fallschirmjaeger Regiment im West, Oktober
1944."

MacDonald, J.A., "Summary History of the South Alberta Light
Horse," n.p., 1976.

"Royal Canadian Armoured Corps, Roll of Honour," Compiled by E
Group, CRU, 1945-1946.

South Alberta Regiment Christmas Magazine 1941.

Wotherspoon Family Genealogical Notes Compiled by Richard
(Swatty) Wotherspoon.

UNPUBLISHED THESES

Claydon, John. "'Green Flash.' Tanks and 4th Canadian Armoured
Division, Normandy, 1944." Unpublished M.A. Thesis, Carleton
University, 1994.

Wilson, David A. "The Development of Tank-Infantry Co-Operation
Doctrine in the Canadian Army for the Normandy Campaign of
1944." Unpublished M.A. Thesis, University of New Brunswick,
1992.

AUDIO-VISUAL SOURCES

BRITISH BROADCASTING CORPORATION
Interview with Major David Currie, VC, n.d., c. December 1944.

CANADIAN FORCES FILM UNIT, OTTAWA
Film shot by Sergeant Jack Stollery at St. Lambert-sur-Dives, 19
August 1944.

NATIONAL ARCHIVES OF CANADA, OTTAWA
Canadian Army Newsreel No. 22, December 1943.
Canadian Army Newsreel No. 49, February 1945.
Canadian Army Newsreel No. 64, March 1945.

SOUTH ALBERTA REGIMENT HISTORICAL COLLECTION
South Alberta Pictorial Record, 1940-1945, c. 1965.
Presentation of Colours to SAR, Edmonton, September 1995.

PUBLISHED SOURCES

NEWSPAPERS
Canadian Pictorial and Illustrated War News, June 1885.
Canadian Press News, August 1942-May 1945.
Edmonton Bulletin, January 1946.
Edmonton Journal, November 1941, February 1946.
Globe and Mail, November 1939, November 1941, November 1944.
Medicine Hat News and *Daily News*, May 1919, May-September
1939, January 1946.
Toronto Daily Star, July 1938, February 1945.

MILITARY MANUALS, PUBLICATIONS
AND TECHNICAL LITERATURE
Anti-Tank Tactics. 1943. London: War Office, July 1943.
Army Catering Quantities (With a Specimen Bill of Fare). 1939.
Ottawa: King's Printer, 1940.
*Artillery Training. Vol I. Anti-Tank Tactics. Notes on the Tactical
Handling of S.P. Anti-Tank Guns.* London: War Office, 1945.
Crew Duty Card. Sherman V. Parade Maintenance. Bovington Camp,
Dorset: A.F.V. Publications Section, 1944.
Data Book. Canadian Manufactured Tank Type Vehicles. Ottawa:
Department of Munitions and Supply, February 1945.
Defence Forces List, November 1939. Ottawa: Department of Milita
and Defence, 1939.
The Employment of Reconnaissance Units. 1944. London: War Office,
February 1944.
German Infantry in Action (Minor Tactics). London: War Office,
February 1941.
*Handbook on the British Army, with Supplement on the Royal Air
Force and Civil Defence Organization. TM 30-410.* Washington:
War Department, 1942.
Handbook on German Military Forces. TM-E 30-451. Washington:
War Department, 1945.
M4A4 (75mm) Sherman. Reprint of 1942 manual by Allied Com-
mand Publications, Ottawa, 1996.
Memorandum on the Use of Smoke. 1942. London: War Office, July
1942.
Message Writing and R/T. 1944. London: War Office, 1944.
Netting Drill for Wireless Set No. 22. 1944. London: War Office, June
1944.
Notes on the Employment of Tanks in Support of Infantry in Battle.
London: 21 Army Group, February 1944.
*Notes from Theatres of War. No. 16: North Africa, November 1942-
May 1943.* London: War Office, October 1943.
Operational Feeding. The Use of Field Rations. 1942. London: War
Office, October, 1942.
*Royal Armoured Corps Training. Volume I – Tactics. Pamphlet No. 1.
The Armoured Regiment. 1946.* London: War Office, February
1946.
Royal Military College Review. 1930. Kingston: RMC, 1930.
*Signal Tactics. Part IV. The Armoured Regiment and the Armoured Car
Regiment – 1946.* London: War Office, 1946.
*The Tactical Employment of Armoured Car and Reconnaissance
Regiments. Part 1. General Principles regarding the Tactical
Employment of Reconnaissance Regiments.* London: War Office,
May 1943.
*The Tactical Handling of the Armoured Division and its Components.
Part 2. The Armoured Regiment. 1943.* London: War Office,
February 1943.
Tactics of the German Army. Vol. 1. Defence and Withdrawal. 1944.
London: War Office, April 1944.

Tank Country. 1943. London: War Office, June, 1943.

The Tank Troop Leader's Manual. Ottawa; Army Headquarters, 1951.

The Use of Wireless in Armoured Formations. 1942. London: War Office, October 1942.

Vehicle Data Book. Canadian Army Overseas. London: Canadian Military Headquarters, 1944.

Vorläufige Richtlinien für den Einsatz von Panzerabwehrwaffe in der Verteidigung. Berlin: Oberkommando des Heeres, May 1944.

War Time Tank Production. Reports by the Select Committee on National Expenditure and the Replies to these Reports by the Government of the Day. London: HMSO, July 1946.

Waterproofing of Vehicles and Equipment. 1944. London: War Office, May 1944.

BOOKS

Allen, Peter. *One More River. The Rhine Crossings of 1945*. New York: Scribner, 1980.

Bernage, George and Ronald McNair. *Le Couloir de la Mort*. Bayeux: Editions Heimdal, 1994.

Bidwell, Shelford and Dominick Graham. *Fire-Power. British Army Weapons and Theories of War 1904-1945*. Boston: Allen and Unwin, 1985.

Bird, Will R. *No Retreating Footsteps; the Story of the North Nova Scotia Highlanders*. Kentville: The Regiment, n.d.

Blackburn, George. *The Guns of Normandy. A Soldier's Eye View, France, 1944*. Toronto: McClelland & Stewart, Toronto, 1995.

Blumenson, Martin. *Breakout and Pursuit*. Washington: Office of the Chief of Military History, 1961.

Carell, Paul. *Invasion, They're Coming*. New York: Bantam, 1964.

Carver, Michael. *The Apostles of Mobility. The Theory and Practice of Armoured Warfare*. London: Weidenfeld and Nicolson, 1979.

Cassidy, G.L. *Warpath. The Story of the Algonquin Regiment, 1939-1945*. Toronto: Ryerson, 1948.

Chamberlain, Peter and Chris Ellis. *British and American Tanks of World War Two*. New York: Arco Publishing Co., 1969.

——#. *Ram and Sexton*. Windsor, Berkshire: Profile Publications, 1970.

Coox, Alvin and L. Van Loan Marshall. *Survey of Allied Tank Casualties in World War II*. Washington: Operations Research Office, John Hopkins University, 1951.

Corum, James. *The Roots of Blitzkrieg. Hans von Seeckt and German Military Reform*. Lawrence, Kansas: University of Kansas, 1992.

Cunniffe, Richard. *Scarlet, Rifle Green and Khaki: The Military in Calgary*. Calgary: Calgary Century Publishing Company, 1975

D'Este, Carlo. *Decision in Normandy. The Unwritten Story of Montgomery and the Allied Campaign*. London: Collins, 1983.

Dollinger, Hans. *The Decline and Fall of Nazi Germany and Imperial Japan*. New York: Gramercy, 1965.

Duguid, A. Fortescue. *History of the Canadian Grenadier Guards. 1760-1964*. Montreal: Gazette, 1965.

English, Jack. *The Canadian Army and the Normandy Campaign. A Study of Failure in High Command*. New York: Praeger, 1991.

Fletcher, David. *Sherman VC. M4A4 Firefly*. Darlington: Darlington Productions, 1997.

Florentin, Eddy. *Battle of the Falaise Gap*. London: Elek Books, 1965.

Foster, Tony. *Meeting of Generals*. Toronto: Methuen, 1986.

Fraser, Robert. *Black Yesterdays. The Argylls' War*. Hamilton: The Regimental Association, 1996.

Fry, Alan and Wilf Taylor. *Beating Around the Bush*. Madeira Park, BC: Harbour Publishing, 1989).

Giles, L.C., ed. *Liphook, Bramshott and the Canadians*. Bramshott and Liphook Preservation Society, 1986.

Gould, Ed. *All Hell for a Basement*. Medicine Hat: City of Medicine Hat, 1981.

Graves, Donald E. and Michael J. Whitby, *Normandy 1944: The Canadian Summer*. Montreal: Art Global, 1994.

Greenhous, Brereton. *Dragoon. The Centennial History of The Royal Canadian Dragoons. 1883-1983*. Ottawa: The Regiment, 1983.

Guderian, Heinz. *Das Letzte Kriegsjahr im Westen. Die Geschichte der 116. Panzer-Division. Windhunddivision. 1944-1945*. St. Augustin: AZ Offsetdruck Verlag, 1994.

Hayes, Geoffrey. *The Lincs: A History of the Lincoln and Welland Regiment at War*. Alma: Maple Leaf Route, 1986.

A History of the First Hussars Regiment. London: The Regiment, 1951.

Hodder-Williams, Ralph. *Princess Patricia's Canadian Light Infantry, 1914-1919*. Toronto: Hodder & Stoughton, 1923.

Hoedelmans, Piet. *Jeeps & Klaprosen. Een relaas van de periode 1944-'45 in Bergen op Zoom en omgeving*. Bergen op Zoom: Boekhandel Quist, 1990.

Hogg, Ian. *Armour in Conflict. The Design and Tactics of Armoured Fighting Vehicles*. London: Jane's, 1980.

Horn, Michiel, ed. *The Dirty Thirties. Canadians in the Great Depression*. Toronto: Copp, Clark, 1972.

House, Jonathan M. *Toward Combined Arms Warfare: A Survey of 20th-Century Tactics, Doctrine and Organization*. Leavenworth: Combat Studies Institute, 1984.

Hughes, G.W. *A Marchpast of the Corps and Regiments of the Canadian Army. Past and Present*. n.p., 1992

Hunnicutt, R.P. *Sherman. A History of the American Medium Tank*. San Rafael: Presidio Press, 1976.

Jackson, H.M., ed. *The Argyll and Sutherland Highlanders of Canada (Princess Louise's). 1928-1953*. St. Catharines: The Regiment, 1953.

Jamar, K. *With the Tanks of the 1st Polish Armoured Division*. Hengelo: H.L. Smit & Son, 1946.

Johnson, Hugh. *Break-Through! Tactics, Technology, and the Search for Victory on the Western Front in World War I*. Novato: Presidio, 1994.

Jolly, Alan. *Blue Flash. The Story of An Armoured Regiment*. London: Author's publication, 1952.

Joly, Cyril. *Take These Men*. Leatherhead: Ashford, Buchan & Enwright, 1955.

Kaufman, David, ed. *A Liberation Album. Canadians in the Netherlands, 1944-1945*. Toronto: McGraw-Hill Ryerson, 1980.

Kitching, George. *Mud and Green Fields*. Vancouver: Battleline Books, 1986.

Lehmann, Rudolg and Ralf Tiemann. *The Leibstandarte IV/1*. Winnipeg: J.J. Fedorowicz, 1993.

Liddell Hart, Basil. *The Tanks. The History of the Royal Tank Regiment. Volume Two. 1939-1945*. London: Cassell, 1959.

Lucas, James. *War on the Eastern Front. The German Soldier in Russia 1941-1945*. London: Greenhill Books, 1991.

Luck, Hans von. *Panzer Commander. The Memoirs of Colonel Han von Luck*. Westport: Praeger, 1986.

McDougall, G.L. *A Short History of the 29 Cdn Armd Recce Regt (South Alberta Regiment)*. Amsterdam: Spin's Publishing Co., 1945.

Maczek, Stanislaw. *Avec mes Blindés*. Paris: Presses de la Cité, 1967.

McKee, Alexander. *Last Round Against Rommel: Battle of the Normandy Beachhead*. New York: Signet, 1964.

McNair, Sherry. *Soldiers All*. North Battleford: Turner-Warwick, 1994.

Meyer, Hubert. *The History of the 12th SS Panzer Division "Hitlerjugend."* Winnipeg: J.J. Fedorowicz, 1992.

Moulton, J.L. *Battle for Antwerp. The Liberation of the City and the Opening of the Scheldt 1944.* New York: Hippocrene, 1978

Nicholson, G.W.L. *The Gunners of Canada. The History of the Royal Regiment of Canadian Artillery. Volume II. 1919-1967.* Toronto: McClelland and Stewart, 1967.

Ogorkiewicz, Richard. *Armor: A History of Mechanized Forces.* New York: Praeger, 1960.

Owen, Frank and H.W. Watkins. *The Royal Armoured Corps.* London: War Office, 1943.

Paterson, R.A. *A History of the 10th Canadian Infantry Brigade.* n.p., 1945.

The Regimental History of the Governor General's Foot Guards. Ottawa: The Regiment, 1948.

Reynolds, Michael. *Steel Inferno: 1 SS Panzer Corps in Normandy.* New York: Sarpedon, 1997.

Rogers, R.L. *The History of the Lincoln and Welland Regiment.* St. Catharines, Ontario: The Regiment, 1954

Rollefson, M.O., ed. *Green Route Up: 4th Canadian Armoured Division.* Holland, n.p., 1945

Roy, Reg. *1944. The Canadians in Normandy.* Ottawa: The Canadian War Museum, 1984.

Savage, J.M. *History of the 5th Canadian Anti-Tank Regiment, 10 September 1941–10 June 1945.* Lochem: The Regiment, 1945.

Shulman, Milton. *Defeat in the West.* London: Coronet Books, 1968.

Singer, H.C. *History of the 31st Canadian Infantry Battalion (1914-1919), C.E.F.* Calgary: The Battalion Association, Calgary, 1939.

Smith, John O. *All Tanked Up. The Canadians in Headley during World War II.* Headley Down: Author's Publication, 1994.

Smithers, A.J. *Rude Mechanicals: An Account of Tank Maturity During the Second War.* London: Leo Cooper, 1987.

Spencer, Robert A. *History of the Fifteenth Canadian Field Regiment.* Amsterdam: Elsevier, 1945.

Stacey, C.P. *Arms, Men and Government. The War Policies of Canada 1939-1945.* Ottawa: Department of National Defence, 1970.

——#. *Official History of the Canadian Army in the Second World War. Volume III. The Victory Campaign. The Operations in North-West Europe. 1944-1945.* Ottawa: Queen's Printer, 1960.

——#. *Official History of the Canadian Army in the Second World War. Volume I. Six War Years. The Army in Canada, Britain and the Pacific.* Ottawa: Queen's Printer, 1955.

Steven, Walter T. *In This Sign.* Toronto: Ryerson, 1948.

Stevens, G.R. *A City Goes To War.* Edmonton, Loyal Edmonton Regiment, 1964.

Swinson, Arthur, ed. *A Register of the Regiments and Corps of the British Army.* London: Archives Press, 1972.

Vlaemmynk, Carlos. *De Slag om Moerbrugge.* Bruges: Brugsch Handelsblad, 1980.

Vokes, Chris. *My Story by Major General Chris Vokes.* Ottawa: Gallery Books, 1985.

Wallace, John F. *Dragons of Steel: Canadian Armour in Two World Wars.* Burnstown: General Store Publishing House, 1995.

White, B.T. *Armoured Cars – Guy, Daimler, Humber, AEC.* Windsor, Berkshire: Profile Publications, 1970.

Whitaker, W. Denis and Shelagh. *Tug of War: The Canadian Victory that Opened Antwerp.* Toronto: Stoddart, 1984.

——#. *Rhineland: The Battle to end the War.* Toronto: Stoddart, 1989.

Wilmot, Chester. *The Struggle for Europe.* London: Collins, 1952.

Worthington, Larry. *Worthy.* Toronto: Macmillan, 1961.

Zbiorowa, Praca. *1 Dywizja Pancerna w Walce.* Brussels: La Colonne, 1947.

ARTICLES

Copp, Terry. "Ontario, 1939: The Decision for War," *Ontario History,* 86 (September 1994), 269-278.

De Groot, S.J. "Escape of the German Army across the Westerscheldt, September 1944," *Canadian Military History,* Volume 6, Number 1 (Spring 1997), 109-117.

Dufresne, Michel. "Normandie Août 1944. Heurs et malheurs d'une fin de campagne. Les decisions des commandements allies et allemands," *Revue Historique des Armées,* No. 168 (September 1987), 97-119.

——#. "Le succés Allemand sur la Seine (Août 1944)," *Revue Historique des Armées,* No. 176 (September 1989), 48-60.

Hoedelmans, Piet. "Nabranders bij de bevrijding van ons gewest," *De Water Schans* 3, 1995, 76-85.

Wood, Hubert F. "Operation ELEPHANT. The Battle for Kapelsche Veer," *Canadian Army Journal* (September 1949), 8-12.

INDEXES

INDEX, PART I:
PERSONAL NAMES IN TEXT

Adams, Lieutenant Gerald C. D., "Smokey," 30, 70-71, 81, 90-91, 113, 138-139
Allen, Trooper Arnold R., 284
Allen, Trooper Cliff E., 261, 335
Allen, Ralph, 229
Allsopp, Captain Robert H., "Bob," 70, 75, 91, 93, 122, 136, 205, 211, 213, 229
Amey, Trooper Harvey H., 277-278
Amy, Lieutenant-Colonel Edward, "Ned," 112, 295
Amyotte, Trooper Maurice W., 145-146, 317
Andrew, Trooper Walter H., 208, 347
Angus, Trooper Len L., 338
Arkles, Trooper Joseph W., "Joe," 277-278, 334
Armour, Lieutenant Gilbert, 142, 150
Armstrong, Trooper George M., 89, 128, 253, 335
Arrowsmith, Sergeant Sidney, "Sid," 31, 41, 48, 89, 130, 215, 308
Aspeslet, Trooper Lawrence, "Larry," 62
Atkinson, Private Albert J., 43-44, 49
Atkinson, Margaret, 43-44, 49
Aucoin, Trooper Earl J., 233
Baker, Trooper Arthur E., "Art," 259, 277-278, 294, 334
Baldwin, SQMS William S., 58
Ball, Private Albert C., 30, 36-37, 41, 43
Bankey, Trooper B.G., 301
Barford, Captain Cuthbert A. L., "Tommy," 77, 91, 129, 149, 190, 245, 329-331
Barnett, Trooper John J., 309
Barr, Trooper Robert, 30, 199, 243
Bartlett, Trooper John F., 283, 347
Bateman, Trooper Arnold E., 146
Bayko, Corporal Steve, 115-116, 334
Beale, Lieutenant Douglas, 329
Bean, Trooper Bruce E., 25
Beaudry, Sergeant Eugene L. J., "Yudge," 43
Bell, Sergeant Alvin, 171, 347
Bell, Trooper John A., 94, 277-278
Bell, Trooper O. James, "Jimmie," 338

Bellamy, Sergeant Arthur J., 80
Belsey, Trooper Frederick C., "Fred," 277-278
Benamou, Dr. Jean-Pierre, 341, 345
Bennett, Lieutenant, "Benny," 242
Bergquist, Trooper Harvey L. R., 170
Bergquist, Trooper Marvin E., 308
Berry, Corporal Adrian D., 30, 41, 48
Besling, Wes, 229
Bird, Trooper Gerry E., 186, 337
Blackstock, Trooper Cecil P., "Blackie," 74
Blaine, SSM Lawrence B., 58
Blake, Toe, 241
Blunden, Trooper Robert S. M., "Bob," 89, 233
Bodley, Lieutenant Orlando A., 258, 260
Bohnert, *Gefreiter* Johann, 155
Booth, Brigadier Leslie, 87, 112-113, 122, 132
Boothroyd, Captain Wilfred E., RCAMC, 79, 91, 130, 144, 171, 186, 283, 336
Bowick, Lieutenant Smith Fremont, "Tiger," MC, MiD, 240, 253, 255, 263, 276
Boyer, Trooper Arnold, 48, 277
Boyes, Trooper Douglas W., 118
Brabant, Trooper Thomas N., "Tom," 125
Bradburn, Lieutenant-Colonel Robert A., "Bob," 27, 30, 52, 74-76, 82, 88, 91, 107, 117, 121, 206, 210, 217, 220-221, 225-226, 269-272, 278-279, 290, 337, 339, 342
Bradley, General Omar N., 97, 105, 109, 133, 137, 150, 175, 186, 190, 299
Bradshaw, Owen, 130
Brady, Major Edward, 251, 253
Braithwaite, Trooper Lloyd S., 284, 308-309
Brewer, Trooper Charles E., "Charlie," 124
Bristowe, Lieutenant-Colonel Wiliam P., 45-46, 48-49, 51-52, 54, 58, 60, 62, 64, 67-68, 70, 335
Broadbent, Trooper Albert G., DCM, 256-259
Broberg, Trooper Robert E., "Bob," 255, 338
Brooks, Major Dudley, 167
Browning, Sergeant Charles B., 219

Bruce, Trooper Robert A., 106
Buchan, Governor-General John, Lord Tweedsmuir, 27
Bullen, CSM Frederick, "Fred," 50, 341
Burger, Lieutenant Peter M., "Pete," 263-264, 279, 285
Burns, Lieutenant Robert C., 160-161
Burton, Captain Richard B.S., "Dick," 51-52
Caesar, Julius, 32
Cameron, Trooper Duncan G., 107, 134
Campbell, Major Clarence, 223, 231
Campbell, Captain Gordon A., "Gordie," 106, 161, 223, 297, 331
Campbell, Armourer Sergeant J. Elliott, 74
Campbell, Sergeant Roy A., 162, 164
Cannady, Private Lynn G., 48
Carpenter, Trooper Victor Lloyd, "Vic," 320-321
Carr, Trooper Wiliam B., "Bill," 315
Carragher, Trooper James C., 171
Carroll, Captain Henry L., "Hank," 58, 76, 131
Carter, Reverend Doctor David, 346
Carvosso, Lieutenant-Colonel James H., MC, 29-30, 32-37, 43-46, 70, 302, 326, 334
Carvosso, Mrs. James H., 34, 43-44
Case, Trooper James L., "Jim," 286
Caseley, Captain S. Leaman, MC, 58, 71, 224-226, 275, 280-281, 302, 307, 325, 331
Cassidy, Major G. L., 117
Chamberlain, Neville, 26, 28-29
Chaney, Trooper Vincent, 283
Cheney, Trooper J.D., "Jack," 203, 208, 213, 216
Childs, Warrant Officer Victor, "Vic," 42, 242, 337
Christian, Trooper Hugh J., 308
Churchill, Prime Minister Winston, 29, 37, 329
Clark, Bill, 30
Clark, Sergeant Frederick W., "Beans," 284, 347
Clarke, Major Hugh H., "Click," 30, 45, 52, 91, 125, 285, 319, 327
Clarke, Captain Kenneth A.C., RCAMC, 30, 34, 80
Clausen, Trooper E. Thomas, "Tom," 103

Claxton, Brooke, 341
Clerkson, Captain Frederick, MC, 149
Clipperton, Corporal Myrtle, "Andy," CWAC, 80, 89, 91, 93, 186, 340
Clipperton, Trooper Robert W., "Bob," 30, 44, 46, 80-81, 89, 91, 93, 122, 129, 131, 176, 186, 203, 208, 217, 324, 340
Clough, Honorary Captain C.F.A., 34
Coffin, Major Albert F., "Bert," DSO, 24, 26, 29-30, 32-33, 36, 40, 45, 49-50, 52, 58, 60, 67, 70-72, 74-75, 81-82, 91, 131, 172, 190, 206, 214, 239-240, 246, 251, 260, 263-264, 266, 268-272, 276, 278, 279, 281-282, 285, 295-299, 302, 317, 327, 329, 331-332, 335, 346
Colwell, Trooper Dexter, 168, 169
Cook, Private Harold L., "Hal," 43
Cooper, Trooper James R., 139, 144, 154, 286, 339
Coppens, Coba, 228
Corner, Trooper Lloyd A., 216
Coté, Armourer Sergeant Raymond R., 245
Craig, Trooper Lyle L., 317, 346
Craig, Trooper Norman R., 215
Cramer, Sergeant Luois C.,"Lou," 80
Crawford, Lieutenant Robert E., "Bobby," 43, 241, 261, 269, 276-278
Crerar, General Harry, CH, CB, DSO, CD, 92, 105, 133, 138, 143, 175, 201-203, 242, 261, 266, 268, 294
Crichton, Captain James H., 30
Crocker, Lieutenant-General John, GCB, KB, DSO, MC, 250, 251
Cromb, Lieutenant-Colonel William, "Bill," DSO, 91, 121, 188, 229, 231, 234, 251, 337
Crosby, Bing, 54
Cumberland, Brigadier Ian, DSO, OBE, ED, 69, 77, 298, 333
Cunningham, Benjamin, 134
Curley, Lieutenant James, "Jim," 75, 106, 146, 211
Currie, Major David V., VC, 24, 58-59, 74-75, 88, 106-108, 133-136, 138-144, 146-147, 149-152, 154-157, 162-165, 167, 169-172, 176, 189, 205, 219-222, 224, 228, 232, 239-240, 242-244, 270, 327, 336, 340-342, 346, 347

Currie, David, (son of), 60, 243-244, 336

Currie, Isabel, 58, 60, 243-244, 336, 340, 346

Daladier, Premier Edouard, 26, 28

Dalpe, Lieutenant Al, 162-163

Daly, Trooper Carson W., 80, 93, 118, 136, 173, 196, 314, 317

Dandy, Major James, 252-253

Danielson, Trooper Melvin A., 225-226

Davies, Trooper Edward, "Ed," 108, 163, 200

Davies, Lieutenant-Colonel Herbert S., 30, 58

Debay, Trooper Roderick, 215

Dempsey, General Miles, KCB, CBE, DSO, MC, 100, 266

Denning, Trooper Albert W., "Bert," 97, 286-287, 334

De Palthe, Baron, 331

Dervin, Trooper J. R., 301

Devreker, Corporal Anthony, "Tony," MM, 194, 196, 215, 238, 301-302

Dickie, Captain R. F., 162, 172

Diefenbaker, Prime Minister John, 336

Diels, Otto, 274

Dietrich, *Generaloberst* Josef, "Sepp," 137

Donald, Sergeant Thomas, 244, 245

Donaldson, Captain Robert H., "Bob," "Bulgy," 45, 232, 239

Donkin, Lieutenant Ivan F., 71, 241, 247-248, 302, 331

Dorsey, Tommy, 22

Douthwaite, Captain C. Rafe R., 30, 54, 58

Dryer, Corporal Arnold J., 91, 93, 103, 129, 207, 246-247, 333

Dunlop, Lieutenant J. Arkle, 150, 155, 162

Dürer, Albrecht, 229

Dutka, Trooper Adam, 201

Earp, Lieutenant Alan, 255, 256, 261

Eastman, Trooper James W., 139, 164, 304

Easton, Trooper E. Vernon, "Vern," 219

Eastwood, Corporal Thomas, "Tom," 30, 31, 35

Edwards, Trooper Grant E., 134

Eisenhower, General Dwight D., 87, 92, 97, 150, 186, 190, 201, 217, 240

Elder, Lieutenant-Colonel Gordon, 27, 29

Elizabeth, H.R.H. Princess, 71

Elizabeth, H.R.H. Queen, 27

Ely, Corporal Emery E., "Buster," 43, 82, 94, 171

Engel, Corporal Alfred J., "Art," 94, 250, 307

Evans, Corporal George D., 168

Evans, Private John, 147

Evans, Trooper Lyle A., 291, 293

Fairhurst, Sergeant Robert, 149, 284, 313

Farmer, Major J.A., 113

Farquhar, Sergeant Charles, "Charlie," 234

Farr, Tommy, 73, 82

Fast, Corporal C. R., "Speedy," 227, 337

Fearn, Corporal Charles B., "Chuck," 47, 225

Feisal, Emir, "Feisel," 81

Fengler, Corporal Walter H., "Walt," 154, 260, 279, 288, 297

Ferguson, James, "Jim," 200

Ficht, Corporal Herbert J., "Herb," 136

Firlotte, Sergeant, 165

Fischer, *Stabsfeldwebel* Heinrich, 257

Fitzpatrick, Trooper Michael J., "Mike," 118

Flowers, Lieutenant J. R., 164, 165

Forbes, Alan, 336

Forbes, Captain Jack, MC, 225

Forbes, Trooper James F., MM, 290

Fortin, Sergeant Earl W., 245

Foster, Trooper Erle M., 196

Foster, Major-General Harry W., CE, DSO, CD, 25, 175, 188-189, 194, 201, 206-207, 217-218, 220, 222-223, 227, 229, 233, 236, 239-241

Foster, Trooper James M., 227

Foulkes, Lieutenant-General Charles, CB, CE, DSO, CD, 143

Frankson, Trooper Eric O., "Rick," 197, 204

Frankson, Trooper Jack, 204

Fraser, Company Sergeant Major, Fergus R., "Fergie," 43

Fraser, Lieutenant Jack, MC, 290, 291, 293

Freeman, Sergeant Lawrence F., "Fred," MM, 274, 275, 281, 283, 286

Freer, Sergeant Frank E., MM, 193, 281, 283, 297, 299

Freer, Trooper Harold L., 216

Frizzell, Private Gordon S., 43

Funnell, Trooper Frederick A., "Fred," 294

Funnell, Mary, 294

Gable, Clark, 63

Galipeau, Sergeant John A., 31, 33, 36, 41, 44, 50, 57, 60, 94, 106, 112, 126, 156, 170, 171, 186, 196-198, 202, 206, 215, 257, 276, 291, 293, 298, 300, 313, 342

Gallimore, Captain Charles W., 30, 168, 169

Gallimore, Corporal George F., 71, 125, 213, 216, 219, 234, 283, 312-314

Gates, Sergeant, 165

Gee, Trooper Allen J., "Big Gee," 287, 346

Gendron, Corporal Edward E., "Duffy," 28, 31, 72, 115-116, 130, 146, 219, 346

George, Trooper Samuel R., 216

George VI, H.M. King, 27, 87, 103, 239, 240, 242-243, 320, 329

Gilbert, Trooper Maxwell, "Maxie," 276-277

Glaude, Trooper Clifford, "Cliff," 200

Goering, *Reichsmarschall* Hermann, 192

Golby, Lance-Corporal Leo J., 82, 347

Goodman, Benny, 264

Goodyer, Corporal Robert H., 232, 346

Gordon, Lieutenant-Colonel M.K., "Mel," DSO, ED, CD, 111, 112

Gove, Sergeant James K., "Jimmie," CinC, 29, 31, 36, 44, 57-58, 106, 118, 144-146, 156, 161, 337

Graham, Alan, 343

Grant, Lieutenant Donald I., "Don," 146-147, 164

Green, Harold, 130

Gregory, Trooper Patrick B., "Pat," 281, 299

Grimmet, Major A. M., MC, 58

Guderian, *General* Heinz, 56

Guderian, *Major* Heinz, 172

Gudwer, Trooper William J., 130

Gunderson, Sergeant John, 163, 172

Guyot, Lieutenant Jean Marc, "Johnny," 216, 221, 224-226

Haddow, Corporal Arthur, MM, 113-114

Halid, Emir, "Geezil," 81

Halkrus, Sergeant Albert E., "Halkie," MM, 115-117, 203, 208, 219, 228-229, 238, 246, 304-306, 312-314, 340

Halpenny, Lieutenant-Colonel, 132

Halpenny, Lieutenant-Colonel, 132

Hambling, Lance-Corporal James, "Jim," 307

Hamilton, Trooper Howard L., "Hammy," 277

Hamilton, H. S., 27

Hamm, Trooper Gerald F., 201

Harkness, Lieutenant-Colonel Douglas, GM, ED, PC, 166

Harmel, *Generalmajor*, 162

Harper, Trooper Douglas E., 290, 293

Hartkamp, Albert, 342

Hausser, *Generalleutnant* Paul, 151-153, 166

Hay, Lieutenant-Colonel Arthur, "Art," 113

Henderson, Trooper Victor C., "Vic," 336, 342

Henning, Trooper Robert E., "Bob," 114

Hicks, Sergeant Richard A., "Dick," 337

Hill, Lieutenant Ernest F., "Ernie," 68, 241, 256-257, 337

Himmler, *Reichsführer* Heinrich, 193

Hinson, Trooper William L., "Bill," 30, 145

Hitler, Adolf, 22, 24-29, 46, 51, 61, 137, 189-190, 192-193, 245, 266, 269, 285, 299, 317, 321

Hoare, Trooper Dennis, 232, 346

Holmes, Sergeant Allan M., "Al," 168, 208-209, 224

Holmstrom, Trooper Gordon E., 216

Homer, Trooper Wilfred N., 210

Howard, Acting Captain Thomas F., "Peachy," 58, 107, 157, 169

Howard, Cammie, 130

Huffman, Captain Albert, 30, 51, 74-75, 326

Hughes, Captain F. Newton, "Newt," Bronze Star, 52, 91, 131, 337, 342

Hughes, Trooper G. J., "Johnny," 264

Hunter, Captain J. Walter, MM, 30, 43, 50

Hunter, Trooper Samuel C., "Sam," 279

Huntley, Lance Corporal John L., "Jack," 31

Hussey, Sergeant Gerald J. H., 200-201

Hutchinson, Trooper John H., 139, 163, 209

Huygens, Gemma, 228

Hyatt, Trooper Edward T., "Ed," 108, 121, 149, 171, 259

Ilse, 318

Iltchuck, Trooper Luke, 313

Ireland, Trooper Lloyd O., 82

Irving, Captain Gordon E., "Gordie," CdG, MiD, 81, 91, 106, 118, 123, 144, 151, 153, 197-199, 201, 205-206, 230, 245, 255, 262, 282, 298, 330

Jacobsen, Sergeant Harold B., "Jake," 277-278

James, Trooper Stanley, "Stan," 168

Jefferson, Trooper Francis F., "Fred," 247, 337

Jefferson, Brigadier James, "Jim," 88, 105-108, 112, 121, 126, 132-133, 138, 143, 146, 149-150, 154, 159, 162, 165-167, 169-170, 172, 193, 217-220, 222-223, 240, 253, 261-262, 269, 271, 286, 289, 298, 328, 339, 346

Jellis, Sergeant Walter W., "Wally," 316-317

Johnson, Bandsman Gilbert G., 49

Johnston, Lieutenant Earle E., 245-255, 258-259

Johnston, Lieutenant George McD., 306, 347

Joyce, William, "Lord Haw-Haw," 63, 82, 92

Keller, Major-General Rod, CBE, 105

Kelly, Captain John K., "King," RCAMC, 80, 118, 144

Kennedy, Lieutenant Wilfred, "Wilf," 255-256, 260-261

Kenyon, Lance-Corporal Walter, 225

King, Prime Minister Mackenzie, 23, 24, 27, 65, 87, 241, 242

Kitching, Major-General George, CBE, DSO, CD, 86-88, 92, 100, 105, 108, 110, 112-113, 120-122, 126, 132-134, 138, 143, 159, 166, 175, 341-343

Kluge, *Feldmarschall* Hans von, 109, 137, 151

Knox, Corporal John, "Johnnie," 263

Konvitsko, Trooper Peter A., 332, 337

Kreewin, Lieutenant Harold, 221-222

Kroesing, Sergeant James F., MM, 117, 196, 221, 225, 283-284

La Foy, Trooper Tip O., 110, 232, 347

Lach, Elmer, 241

Laing, Lieutenant Alexander G., "Alec," 45, 52, 76

Lakes, Trooper John R., 81, 101, 145, 170, 186, 213, 246, 306

Lambert, Major Owen, 252, 253

LaPrade, Trooper Lloyd, 138, 261

Lardner, Sergeant John C., 94, 144, 163-164

Laughton, Trooper Wilfred, "Wilf," 125

Lavoie, Major Arnold J., 27, 30, 45, 52, 60, 62, 74-75, 88, 94, 105-106, 110, 113, 117, 123, 133, 135, 143, 156, 197, 210-211, 215, 221, 226, 228, 230, 263, 270, 289, 291, 302, 309, 312, 317, 320, 324, 327, 331, 337, 342

Lawson, SSM Walter J., 43

Ledwidge, Trooper Duncan J., 97, 224-226

Lindop, Lieutenant Stuart H. W., "Stu," 214-215, 221

Lindsay, Major Robert A., 28

Little, Lieutenant Kenneth W., "Kenny," 254-257

Lorensen, Trooper Clarence W., 306

Louis, Joe, 73

Low, Trooper David A., 245

Lumsden, Lieutenant Richard, "Dick," 49

Luton, Mary, 324

Luton, Lieutenant William C., "Bill," 263-264, 269, 273, 280-285, 294, 296, 299-301, 304, 306, 308-310, 312, 314-315, 318-322, 324, 335-336

Lüttwitz, Generalmajor Heinrich von, 158, 162, 166, 269, 281

Lynch, Trooper Patrick J., 64

Lynn, Vera, 48, 130

MacInnis, Trooper Joseph A., "Pappy Yokum," 114

Mackenzie, Sergeant 197-198

Mackenzie, RSM John, "Jock," CinC, 43, 58, 67, 70, 80, 131, 212-213, 263, 297, 330, 342

MacKenzie, Major Peter, 195

MacPherson, Trooper Ian S., 191, 330, 346

MacTavish, RQSM Robert J., "Bull of the Woods," 40, 43, 74, 282

Maczek, Major-General Stanislaw, 110, 112, 133, 136, 138, 143, 149, 158, 166, 172, 175-176, 250

Mahlmann, Generalmajor, 158

Mahoney, Major Jock, VC, 243

Main, Trooper Joseph, "Joe," 43, 67, 82, 263

Mallet, Lieutenant David J., "Dave," 157

Maloney, Captain Jock H., RCAMC, 268, 283

Marshall, Trooper David G., 191, 193, 196, 199-200, 225, 233, 274, 281, 284, 287, 299, 302, 308, 319-320, 332, 338, 342

Martin, Major Ivan, 138, 141, 162-163

Massey, Vincent, 62

Matthewson, Lieutenant G. A., 60

Maves, Mrs., 50

Maves, Private Reginald M.,"Reg," 50, 92

McAlinden, Sergeant, 117

McAllister, Private Earl, 147

McBain, Captain Harold E., 40, 80

McCaffrey, Trooper George, 210

McCaig, Corporal D. B., 199

McCarty, Corporal Arthur S., 116

McCloy, Trooper Richard D., 30

McDonald, Trooper George A., 168

McDonell, Trooper John A., 232, 347

McDougall, Major Glenholme L., "Glen," 24-26, 29-30, 40, 45-46, 49, 52, 58, 60, 62, 67-68, 71, 80, 81, 263, 268, 276-288, 292, 298, 302, 317, 319, 324, 327, 331-332, 338, 342

McFadden, Corporal Harvey D., 64

McGillivray, Trooper Alexander G., "Alex" 29, 31

McGillivray, Corporal Harold R., "Snookie," 313

McGivern, Corporal Joseph, "Joe," 276-277

McIntyre, Trooper Donald S., 82

McKechnie, Lieutenant W. H., 290

McKee, Trooper Ross F., 209

McKenzie, Captain Alexander D., "Mo," 45, 116, 263, 302

McKenzie, Major R.D., 251

McKie, Sergeant William J., 260

McLean, Lieutenant-Colonel J. Alfred, 30

McLeod, Major William J., "Danny," MC, 23, 28, 31, 36, 43, 48, 51, 71-72, 89, 124, 131, 186, 204, 215, 219-224, 227-229, 232, 302, 304, 310, 314-315, 319-321, 325, 334, 337, 341, 343, 346

McNaughton, General Andrew G. L., CH, PC (Can.), CM, CB, CMG, DSO, CD, 24, 66, 68, 241

McPherson, Corporal Neil J., 24, 35, 115-117

McQueen, Lieutenant-Colonel J.G., 105-106

McRae, Corporal John G., 31, 134, 347

McSherry, Corporal Matthew, 253, 255

Meindl, Generalleutnant Eugen, 151-154, 158, 172, 175

Merritt, Trooper Kenneth F., "Kenny," 118

Meyer, Brigadeführer Kurt, 109, 112, 114, 124

Milan, Private Stanley, 50

Miles, Major Edward A. W., "Ted," 60, 62

Miller, Glen, 48, 324

Milne, Sergeant, 147

Milner, Sergeant Thomas E., "Tom," DCM, 284, 313-315, 320

Milner, Stan, 343

Mitchell, CSM George, 147

Moan, Corporal Francis B., "Frankie," 215-216, 222-223, 346

Model, Feldmarschall Walter, 151, 189, 190-191

Mogie, Captain Harold, 232

Moncel, Brigadier Robert, OBE, DSO, 132, 143, 159, 175, 188, 193

Montgomery, Field-Marshal Bernard L., KG, GCB, DSO, 72, 79, 85, 87, 92, 97, 99, 105, 108-109, 119-120, 133, 138, 150, 171, 174-175, 186, 189-191, 201-202, 217, 222-223, 227, 229, 266, 299, 337

Moreau, Private Henry, 37

Moreton, Captain John P., "Jay," 45, 52, 64, 67, 89, 90, 92, 117-118, 343

Mullan, Private Frank J., 50

Munck, Ad de, 228

Mungall, Trooper George W., 232, 347

Munro, Ross, 71, 296-297

Murchie, Lieutenant-General J. C., CB, CE, CD, 241

Mussolini, Benito, 24, 44

Mustard, Captain William T., RCAMC, 80

Naismith, Private Archibald, "Archie," 43

Nash, Lieutenant-Colonel Thomas B., "Darby," DSO, 30, 52, 60, 74-75, 80, 140, 146, 150, 157, 161-162, 167-169, 194, 196, 208, 211, 219-221, 225-226, 231, 239, 263, 270, 302, 312, 327, 331, 335, 337, 339, 342

Neff, Trooper Howard W., 286-287

Neff, Trooper John H. M., 110, 123, 125, 133-134, 154, 168-169, 196, 204, 211, 221, 226, 232, 234, 241, 246, 263, 298, 308, 313

Nichol, Corporal 260

Nichols, Trooper Eric P., MiD, 283, 302

Nicholson, Sergeant James, "Jim," 42, 54, 57, 61, 118, 125, 154, 157, 162, 167-169, 204, 209, 225, 246, 287, 308, 313, 332

Nickel, Sergeant Michael J., "Mike," 118

Nieman, Lieutenant E.V. "Ev," 31-32, 41, 43, 72, 241, 298, 331

Nieuwburgh, Baron Thierry Peers de, 193

Niven, David, 22

Noble, Trooper George W., 261

Oakley, Trooper Charles A., 209

Olmstead, Trooper Guy E., 30, 168

Orr, Lieutenant James I., "Jimmy," 272, 283, 318

Ottenbreit, Corporal Michael, "Mickey," 155-156, 163

Ouellette, Trooper Denis, 168

Owen, Trooper Eldon M., 315

Pachal, Trooper William F., "Bill," 168-169

Pagee, Corporal Arthur, "Art," 278

Palfenier, Sergeant Theodore E., "Ted," 29, 201

Paterson, Sergeant John, 305-306

Paterson, Major Robert, "Bob," 194, 195, 196

Paterson, CSM Sidney H., 43

Patton, Lieutenant-General George S., 109, 119, 132-133, 137, 175, 189-190

Pedro, Thomas, 301

Penney, Sergeant George W., 261

Perrin, Captain Kenneth E., "Kenny," 43, 45, 52, 240, 246, 276-278, 325, 346

Perry, Trooper E. K., 309

Piepgrass, Lieutenant Lyle B., 36, 231

Pitman, Lieutenant-Colonel E.A., 30

Plocher, Generalleutnant Hermann, 251, 261, 269

Plotsky, Trooper Lawrence, "Sonny," 314

Portal, Air Chief Marshal Sir Charles, 202

Porter, Audrey, 34

Porter, Sergeant John A., "Jack," 32, 34, 58, 91, 307-308

Porter, Trooper John W., 225

Potts, Major-General A.E., 244

Power, Tyrone, 22

Prenevost, Sergeant Douglas Selvester, "Doug," CdG, MiD, 146

Prest, "Ma," 48

Proctor, Lieutenant-Colonel John, OBE, ED, 262

Punchard, Major C.H., 80

Purdy, Major Stanley R., "Stan," 24, 30, 52, 74, 76, 270, 280, 302, 312-313, 319, 327, 338

Quarton, Warrant Officer J. Henry, "Harry," 29-30, 40, 337, 339, 346, 347

Quinnel, Trooper Clarence L., 116, 130

Rae, Trooper Harold G., 216

Ralston, J. L., 241

Ramsay, Admiral Bertram, 217

Randall, Alan, 211

Rasmussen, Corporal Robert J., 37, 48, 124, 128, 146, 213, 245, 282, 337

Rathwell, Trooper John, "Boney," 43, 196, 334

Reardon, Captain Edward H., "Ed," 75, 89, 90, 92, 145-146, 149, 207, 240, 272, 280-281, 302, 333, 342

Redden, Captain John H., "Big John," 64, 108, 138-139, 142, 144

Reed, Lieutenant James I., 170-171

Richard, Maurice, "The Rocket," 241

Risdale, Corporal Sidney G., "Rizzy," 255-256, 276

Ritco, Trooper Nick, 108

Roberts, Lieutenant John M., "Jack," CinC, 58, 108, 142, 144, 193-194, 199-200, 346

Roberts, Major-General Philip B., CB, DSO, MC, 192

Robertson, Trooper Alexander J., 245

Robertson, Corporal Darrell B., 34

Robinson, Sergeant Eden, 157

Robinson, Major Richard, "Dick," CinC, 30, 49-50, 130, 262, 292, 299

Rockingham, Brigadier John, "Rocky," 143, 150, 159, 164, 167, 169-170, 176, 186

Rodd, Trooper Philip H., 216

Rogers, Ginger, 22

Rommel, Feldmarschall Erwin, 46, 51, 61, 65, 109

Rose, Chris, 43

Rose, Corporal Stanley T., "Stan," MiD, 43, 103, 157, 168, 275, 301, 302

Ross, Lieutenant C. S., 76, 78

Roulston, Sergeant Herbert, "Herb," MM, 156, 215, 297-298

Rowe, Trooper Kendal, 244-245

Rundstedt, Feldmarschall Gerd von, 190

Rutherford, Brigadier Thomas J., 214

Samson, Lieutenant-General E. E., 86

Samuels, Corporal Clare, "Sammy," 43, 263

Sanders, *Generalmajor*, 206, 207

Sands, Sergeant George, "Duke," 113, 156, 258-260, 276, 291

Sansom, Lieutenant-General H. N., CB, DSO, CD, 81

Saud, King Ibn, 81

Saul, Major G. M., 30, 58

Sauve, Keith, 346

Schan, Nicky, 82

Scheer, Oral, 130

Schlemm, *Generaloberst* Alfred, 285, 292

Schulz, *Unterscharführer* Alfred, 133-134

Schwalbe, *General* Eugen-Felix, 249

Scobie, Sergeant James C., "Jim," 145-146

Scott, Trooper Gerald A., "Gerry," 123

Scott, Lieutenant Kenneth, "Kenny," 76

Scott, Lieutenant-Colonel M. J., 122, 124, 126, 132

Scrimger, Captain Alexander C., "Scrimmy," 58, 107, 124, 232, 325, 346

Seal, RSM Christopher, 30, 33-34, 36-37, 42, 45-47, 50, 58, 70, 302, 326

Seccombe, Trooper Robert, "Bob," 97, 112, 156, 227, 321, 338

Seidler, Private Jake V., 46

Sewell, Trooper John J., 145

Shank, "Fergie," 43

Shaw, Artie, 22

Shell, Major Gordon L., "Gordie," 30, 52, 128, 316

Shuster, Sergeant Frank, 93

Sigouin, Private James, 48

Silcox, Honorary Captain Albert Phillips, MBE, 80, 91, 93, 101, 118, 130, 136, 145, 171, 186, 212, 223, 248, 261, 283, 292-294, 296, 302, 324-325, 330, 336, 342

Simonds, Lieutenant-General Guy G., CB, CBE, DSO, 86, 97, 105, 108-110, 112-113, 115, 118-123, 126, 132-134, 136, 138, 143, 149, 159, 161, 166, 175-176, 189, 207, 216, 262, 266, 268, 278, 294-296, 298, 308, 330, 341

Simpson, Corporal James, "Jimmie," 30, 91, 123, 306

Slater, Sergeant John C., 138

Smith, Corporal Charles J., 227

Smith, Lieutenant Clive A., 75

Smith, Private James, "Jimmie," 31

Smith, Sergeant James C., "Smitty," CinC, 118, 209

Smith, Lieutenant Ray C., 197, 199, 347

Smythe, Major Conn, 241

Spaner, Trooper Bernard, "Doc," 160, 234

Spence, Trooper Wayne A., 138, 142, 337

Spillet, Trooper Jack C., 253, 335

Sponheimer, *Generalleutnant* Otto, 218

Spry, Major-General Daniel, DC, CBE, DSO, CD, 143

Stark, Private Donald, 261

Stenner, Sergeant, 165

Stevens, Sally, 62, 340

Stevenson, Brigadier J. B., 45

Stevenson, Sergeant Vaughan A., 253, 255

Stewart, Lieutenant-Colonel David, "Dave," DSO, ED, 106-108, 115, 121, 132, 193, 251

Stewart, Captain Donald E., "Don," 75, 90-91, 101, 134, 139, 144, 155, 161, 190, 193, 209-210, 212-214, 216, 221-223, 230-231, 238-240, 263, 302, 324, 330

Stewart, Trooper Elmer D., 261

Stockloser, Major William, 194

Stollery, Sergeant Jack, 147, 164

Stone, Trooper John C., 232, 347

Stoner, Captain Gerald, "Gerry," 167, 169-170

Storvik, Trooper Vernon E., "Vern," 196

Strachan, Lieutenant-Colonel Harcus, "Hew," VC, 30

Strathdee, Lance-Corporal Clifford, "Cliff," 196, 197

Strathern, Trooper Joseph W., "Joe," 228, 248, 260, 262, 288

Student, *General* Kurt, 192, 251

Summers, Captain John Leslie, "Jack," MC, 24, 64, 93, 124, 157, 176, 195, 216, 260, 263, 302, 316, 335-336, 338, 342

Swayze, Major James, 217, 223, 251, 262

Taylor, Trooper Egbert J., 87, 94, 144, 200, 201

Taylor, Trooper Wilfred C., "Wilf," 76, 174, 301

Tennent, Band Sergeant James, "Jimmie," 42, 58

Thomas, Trooper Leonard, "Len," 117

Thompson, Trooper Thomas, "Tommy," 172

Thoresen, Trooper Robert E., "Bob," 337

Thorn, Trooper Edwin G., "Ed," 269, 276-277, 334

Thuesen, Sergeant Soren, "Swede," 31, 80, 103, 108, 142

Tillsley, Trooper C. D., "Slim," 257, 313

Tourond, Corporal George W., 30, 155

Towers, Lieutenant-Governor Gordon, 343, 346

Turner, Don, 22

Utke, Trooper Wilfred L., "Wilf," 284

Vandermark, Corporal Walter, 134, 186, 205, 210

Viennau, Trooper P. J. F., 301

Viner, Harry, 340

Virtue, Corporal Ronald, "Ron," 163, 205, 210, 338

Vitkovich, Trooper M. Emry "Daddy," 80, 215, 299

Vokes, Major-General Christopher, "Chris," CB, CBE, DSO, CD, 240, 244-245, 250-251, 257-258, 262, 271, 289, 291, 294-296, 298, 311, 320, 329-330, 341

Wagner, Lance-Corporal Adam G., 59

Wagner, Sergeant James S., "Jimmie," 124, 346

Wagner, Trooper "Rocky," 43, 67

Walker, Trooper Harry G., 75

Walker, Trooper James W., "Jimmie," 63, 338

Walmsley, Sergeant Joseph, "Joe," 221, 317

Walton, Trooper Harvey W., 168, 346

Warren, Major Trumbull, 174

Waters, Captain Laughlin E., 149

Watkins, Sergeant Herbert, "Herbie," 29, 30, 40, 80, 105-106, 123, 144-145, 161, 191, 276-278, 309-310, 325

Watts, Captain A. F., 51

Wavell, Field Marshal Sir Archibald, 44

Wayne, Sergeant John "Johnny," 93

Wear, Trooper Robert D, "Bob," 62, 90

Webster, Trooper Arthur, "Art," 129, 342

White, Corporal Daniel E., 30, 307, 309

White, Corporal George W., 30, 335

White, J. O., 338

White, Sergeant Jack, 193

White, Trooper John, 225

White, Corporal Russell J., 215

Whitehead, Lieutenant, 162

Whitford, Trooper Ralph, "Chief," 72-73, 264, 298

Wicke, Corporal Carl J., 290

Wickstrom, Trooper Karl J. C., 30, 308, 347

Wiebe, Sergeant Jacob, "Jake," 258-259, 261-262, 319, 329

Wiens, Lieutenant David, 257, 258

Wigg, Lieutenant Kenneth R., "Kenny," 258-261, 285, 309, 314, 318, 322

Wigle, Lieutenant-Colonel Fred, DSO, OBE, 223, 285, 312

Willson, Major R.F., 146

Winfield, Major Gordon, 150

Wolgien, Trooper Herbert A., "Herb," 309

Wood, Major Hubert Fairlie, 250

Wood, Sergeant Earle A., 33, 34, 60, 74, 110, 128, 307-308, 324

Woods, Lieutenant G. Raynor, 58, 123

Woods, Trooper, Lloyd A., 196, 347

Woolf, Sergeant Garth L., "Pete," 160, 195, 329

Worthington, Lieutenant-Colonel Donald, "Don," 113, 115, 132

Worthington, Major-General Frank F., "Worthy," CB, MC, MM, CD, 55-59, 61-63, 65-68, 69, 70, 73, 75-76, 85-86, 338

Wotherspoon, Lieutenant-Colonel Gordon D. de S., "Swatty," 69-71, 73-75, 77-78, 81-82, 88-90, 93, 101, 105-108, 110, 112, 115, 117, 120-121, 123, 128-132, 136, 138, 140-144, 146, 149-150, 153-167, 169-172, 176, 186, 189-190, 203-205, 207-208, 212-215, 217, 219-223, 228-229, 231, 238-241, 246, 248, 251, 262-263, 285, 295, 297-298, 300-302, 304-306, 309-312, 315-317, 319, 322, 326, 327, 329, 331, 333, 335, 337-339, 342, 346

Wotherspoon, Richard, 335

Wright, Lieutenant-Colonel M. Howard, 30, 51, 58, 74-75, 326

Wyman, Brigadier Robert, "Bob," CBE, DSO, ED, 111

Young, Lieutenant Wallace H., "Wally," 91, 188, 190-191, 197, 199, 347

Young, Trooper H. J., 154

Young, Loretta, 22

Zangen, *General* Gustav von, 193, 202, 218

Zgorelski, Major H. 149

Zwicker, Trooper Walter S., 82

INDEX, PART II: OTHER SUBJECTS IN TEXT

Armoured warfare, development and doctrine, 43-44, 55-56, 83-88, 98-100, 328-329, 356-358

Bergen op Zoom, 228-230, 234

Bergen op Zoom, fight to take, 217-236

Canada,
declaration of war, 27
manpower policy, 65-66, 241-242
mobilization, 28-29
prewar defence policy, 23-25
Royal Visit, 1939, 27
wartime record and wartime history, 335

Falaise Gap, battle of, 132-185

Hochwald, battles of, 266-296

Kapelsche Veer, battle of, 249-262

Landing craft, 94

Maginot Line, 28-29

Military Services, Formations and Units

Allied
First Allied Airborne Army, 190
1st Polish Armoured Division, 110, 133, 135, 149, 153, 157-158, 166, 172, 175, 203, 217

Britain,
21st Army Group, 191, 217, 250, 266, 299, 302, 324
Second Army, 105, 119, 133, 135, 149, 153, 157-158, 166, 172, 175, 190, 203, 217
Eighth Army, 79
1st Corps, 217, 250
30th Corps, 149, 204
Guards Armoured Division, 189, 192
9th Armoured Division, 76, 78
11th Armoured Division, 189, 192, 266, 268, 276
43rd Infantry Division, 304-305
49th British Infantry Division, 217, 266
51st Highland Division, 110
Fife and Forfar Yeomanry, 223, 226

Royal Gloucestershire Regiment, 77-78

1st Special Air Service Regiment, 310-320

17/21 Lancers, 68

22nd Dragoons, 223

47 Royal Marine Commando, 250, 261

Royal Air Force, Bomber Command, 202, 266

Royal Armoured Corps Senior Officers School, 69

Royal Military College, Sandhurst, 71, 75

Royal Tank Corps, 55

Canada

Canadian Armoured Corps, 57, 70, 83, 239

Canadian Armoured Corps Reinforcement Units, 80, 214

Canadian Occupation Force, 329

Canadian Pacific Force, 329, 334-335

Canadian Provost Corps, 217, 250

Military District 13, 29

Officer Candidate Training Units, 71-72

Royal Canadian Engineers, 303-304

Canadian Formations and Units

First Canadian Army, 66, 87, 105, 108, 110, 119, 120, 132, 138, 175, 193, 201-203, 236, 266, 269, 302

2nd Canadian Corps, 81, 86, 97, 112, 135, 149, 175, 266

1st Canadian Infantry Division, 28-29, 74, 79, 86, 240

2nd Canadian Infantry Division, 28-29, 61, 88, 110, 113, 133, 138, 143, 159, 214, 217-218, 266, 268, 270, 284, 317

3rd Canadian Infantry Division, 51, 88, 94, 96-97, 105, 118, 133, 138, 143, 159, 176, 193, 214, 266, 270-271, 287, 302

4th Canadian Infantry Division, 51-52, 55, 57-58

4th Canadian Armoured Division, 55, 63, 65-66, 69-70, 73, 75, 77-78, 86-88, 98, 105, 109-118, 119-126, 136, 138, 149, 158, 166, 175-176, 188-189, 193, 201-203, 206-207, 217-218, 220-222, 236, 240, 320

5th Canadian Armoured Division, 51, 57-58, 61, 63, 77-78, 86

1 Canadian Army Tank Brigade, 57, 61

1 Canadian Armoured Brigade, 79, 88, 98

2 Canadian Armoured Brigade, 111, 120, 122, 125

3 Canadian Armoured Brigade, 59, 66

4 Canadian Armoured Brigade, 66, 86-87, 112, 120, 122, 124, 132-134, 138, 149, 159, 166, 168, 175, 176, 188, 217-219, 227, 233,

9 Canadian Infantry Brigade, 143, 153, 155, 159, 167, 169, 172, 176,

10 Canadian Infantry Brigade, 40, 45, 77, 86-88, 109-118, 119-126, 133-134, 149, 159, 166-167, 169, 172, 176, 188, 195, 201, 217-218, 227-228, 250-262, 266-284, 299, 307, 310, 328-329

Alberta Regiment, 23

Algonquin Regiment, 87-88, 113, 115, 117, 121, 123-124, 133, 138, 143, 159, 206-207, 210-211, 214-215, 217, 224, 227, 268-284, 290-292, 307

Argyll and Sutherland Highlanders, 51, 87-88, 106,115, 121, 123-124, 133, 135, 138, 141-159, 160-176, 188, 193-202, 211, 217, 219, 223-226, 231-233, 250-262, 285-287, 289

Battleford Light Infantry, 24

British Columbia Regiment, 131, 134, 233, 250

Calgary Highlanders, 27-29

Calgary Regiment (Tanks), 24, 29-30, 51

Canadian Grenadier Guards, 66, 112, 114-118, 131, 134, 159, 191, 210, 219, 273, 283-284

Dufferin and Haldimand Rifles, 45

Edmonton Fusiliers, 29-30, 51

Elgin Regiment, 59, 66

Fort Garry Horse, 191

Fusiliers Mont Royal, 215

Governor General's Foot Guards, 66, 114-115, 118, 131, 134, 159, 191, 202, 218

Governor General's Horse Guards, 69, 77, 191

Highland Light Infantry, 143, 159, 167, 169, 170, 172, 189

King's Own Rifles, 24

Lake Superior Regiment, 59, 61, 76, 114, 134, 143, 159, 218

Lincoln and Welland Regiment, 88, 105-106, 113, 117, 121, 123-124, 135, 143, 146, 159, 172, 176, 188-189, 195-197, 199, 200, 217, 219, 224, 228, 232-233, 250-262, 306, 316, 320

Lord Strathcona's Horse (Royal Canadians), 25, 27,

Loyal Edmonton Regiment, 28-30, 35, 51, 88, 346

Manitoba Dragoons, 77, 203, 316, 320

New Brunswick Rangers, 134, 176, 195

North Nova Scotia Highlanders, 96, 143, 159, 167, 170, 172

North Shore Regiment, 118

Princess Louise Fusiliers, 79

Princess Patricia's Canadian Light Infantry, 27, 29-30

Queen's Own Rifles, 96, 118

Régiment de Maisonneuve, 317

Rocky Mountain Rangers, 22-23

Royal Montreal Regiment, 87, 201, 216

Royal Rifles of Canada, 51

Saskatchewan Light Horse, 25, 36, 40, 43, 49, 50, 52, 75

Sherbrooke Fusilier Regiment, 66, 96, 111, 126

South Alberta Light Horse, 341, 346-347

South Alberta Regiment (see below)

Stormont, Dundas and Glengarry Highlanders, 143, 159,

Three Rivers Regiment, 80

Westminster Regiment, 36

Winnipeg Grenadiers, 51

1st Hussars, 96, 98, 191

1st Regiment, Alberta Mounted Rifles, 23

3rd Canadian Mounted Rifles, 23

5th Anti-Tank Regiment, RCA, 117-118, 134, 140, 143-144, 166, 211

13th Machine Gun Battalion, 23, 27

15th Alberta Light Horse, 24-25, 29-30, 51

15th Field Regiment, RCA, 106-107, 195, 217, 220-221, 225-226, 231, 250-262

19th Alberta Dragoons, 29-30, 51, 197, 346

21st Alberta Hussars, 22

31st Battalion, CEF, 19, 20, 23

113th Battalion, CEF, 23

175th Battalion, CEF, 23

187th Battalion, CEF, 23

I Squadron, Canadian Mounted Rifles, 22

8 Field Squadron, RCE, 195, 251-262

9 Field Squadron, RCE, 251-262, 310

No. 1 Canadian Army Film and Photographic Unit, 146-148, 164

Mobile Bath and Laundry Units, 118-119, 214

Royal Canadian Air Force, 29, 60, 122

Royal Canadian Navy, 29, 43, 92
31st Minesweeping Flotilla, RCN, 92

United States

12th Army Group, 201

First US Army, 96, 105

Third US Army, 105, 132, 138, 189, 191

Ninth US Army, 245

Eighth Air Force, 105, 110

90th US Infantry Division, 137

104th US Infantry Division, 217

359th US Infantry Regiment, 149

German

Army Group B, 191, 202

First Parachute Army, 192

Fifth Panzer Army, 137, 175

Seventh Army, 137, 175, 189

Fifteenth Army, 192, 202, 218, 234, 261

2nd Parachute Corps, 151

2nd SS Panzer Corps, 150

47th Panzer Corps, 269

67th Infantry Corps, 218

Grossdeutschland Panzer Division, 320

1st SS Panzer Division, 92, 108

2nd Panzer Division, 158

2nd SS Panzer Division, 150

9th SS Panzer Division, 158

10th SS Panzer Division, 150

12th SS Panzer Division, 92, 96, 112-114, 124, 137,

21st Panzer Division, 137

116th Panzer Division, 269, 274, 281

64th Infantry Division, 193, 211

85th Infantry Division, 124

89th Infantry Division, 112, 114

245th Infantry Division, 193, 206, 218

346th Infantry Division, 218

353rd Infantry Division, 158

2nd Parachute Division, 151

6th Parachute Division, 251-262, 269, 307,

Herman Goering Regiment, 219, 221-222, 307

6th Parachute Regiment, 214, 218, 229,

8th Parachute Regiment, 319

17th Parachute Regiment, 251-262

24th Parachute Regiment, 281

61st Parachute Regiment, 320

Parachute Army Assault Battalion, 289, 292

101st SS Heavy Tank Battalion, 133

102nd SS Heavy Tank Battalion, 114

655th Heavy Anti-Tank Battalion, 269

Kampfgruppe Dreyer, 218

Military Operations,
BLOCKBUSTER, 266-284, 285-296
COBRA, 105
CHARNWOOD, 96
ELEPHANT, 250-262
GOODWOOD, 96-97, 101
GRENADE, 266, 285
HORSE, 250
MARKET GARDEN, 130, 201-203
MOUSE, 250
PEPPERPOT, 300-302
PLUNDER, 300-301
SPRING, 97
SUITCASE, 217-233
TOTALIZE, 132
TRACTABLE, 131, 133
VARSITY, 300
VERITABLE, 266, 295

Normandy campaign, 95-185

Scheldt campaign, 196-236

Ships,
USS *Matthew T. Goldsboro*, 94
CPR *Princess Elizabeth*, 47
HMT *Strathmore*, 61-62
RMS *Queen Elizabeth*, 335

South Alberta Regiment
active service, 1940-1946
mobilization and recruiting, 1940, 29-31
at Prince of Wales Armoury, Edmonton, 1940, 31-32
at Dundurn, 1940, 35-40
at Nanaimo, 1940-1941, 40-46
at Niagara, 1941, 46-52
at Debert and conversion to armour, 1941-1942, 54-61
goes overseas, August 1942, 61-62
at Headley/Bordon, 1942-1943, 62-63

at Aldershot, 1943, 67
at Farnham, 1943, 68-72
at Preston Park, 1943, 72-74
at Norfolk, 1943, 75-79
at Maresfield, 1943-1944, 80, 82-93
early days in Normandy, 97-98, 101-102
Tilly-la-Campagne, 1-5 August 1944, 105-108
in Operation TOTALIZE, 7-12 August 1944, 109-118
in Operation TRACTABLE, 14-15 August 1944, 119-126
at Damblainville, 16-17 August 1944, 132-134
at St. Lambert, 18-22 August 1944, 138-176
advance to Seine, August-September 1944, 186-188
at Moerbrugge, September 1944, 193-202
at Moerkerkke, September 1944, 203-211
at Hulst, September-October 1944, 211-213
at Brasschaet and area, October 1944, 214-217
drive on Bergen op Zoom, October 1944, 218-227
at Bergen, October-November 1944, 227-234
winter, November 1944-January 1945, 236-249
at the Kapelsche Veer, January 1945, 249-262
at the Hochwald, February-March 1945, 267-293
at the Rhine "shoot," March 1945, 301-302
crossing the Rhine, April 1945, 303-304
at the Twente Canal, April 1945, 304-310
drive on Oldenburg, April-May 1945, 310-322
at Oldenburg at end of war, May 1945, 324-325, 329-330
in Holland, May-December 1945, 331-335
coming home, December 1945-January 1946, 335
assessment, 324-329
band, 41, 47
boxing, 67, 82-93, 233, 248, 263
casualties, 325-326
Christmas celebrations, 1940-1945, 44, 54, 64-65, 81, 246, 335
combat, reactions to, 131, 298-299
discipline, 70-71, 212-213
echelons and maintenance, 128-130, 282-283, 297, 360
food and drink, 30, 41, 77, 129, 216-217, 234, 298
medical matters, 79-80, 161, 171, 283, 361
officers and leadership, 35-36, 45-46, 51-52, 68-72, 71-72, 74-75, 90-91, 120-121, 132
organization, 58, 65-67, 79, 87, 246, 353

padre, his work, 130-131, 293-294
Pee Wee platoon, 38, 45
prewar unit, 22-29
postwar activities,
    occupations of veterans, 336-338
    reaction to wartime service, 338-339
    reunions, 339-340
    procuring Colour and erecting memorials, 341-342
    Reunion, Edmonton, 1995, 345-347
prisoners of war, 277-278, 333
Recce Troop, work of, 203-204
sports (other than boxing), 36-37, 43, 59-60, 82, 335
training, armoured and armoured recce, 55, 57-61, 66-75, 81-83, 87-88, 298-299
training, infantry, 32-36, 54-55
uniforms, 29, 32-33, 46, 59, 70, 89, 316-317
Wally's Commandos, 316-317
wives and girlfriends, 60-63
Women's Auxiliary, 43-44
Training schemes and exercises,
BRIDOON, 76, 78
COUGAR I, 73
COUGAR II, 73
COUGAR III, 73
GRIZZLY II, 76-78
HAWK III, 60
REPULSE, 60
SCOUT III, 68
SPARTAN, 68
SUBLIME, 68
TAKEX I, 76
TAKEX II, 76
THIRSTY, 68
TRACKER, 68
Weapons,
Armoured Fighting Vehicles, 49, 56-57, 59-60, 64, 66-68, 73-75, 79, 81-82, 84-85, 92-94, 99-104
other, 59, 64, 68, 73, 75, 92-94, 99-104, 238, 262
small arms, 35, 40, 49, 52, 66, 68, 74

**INDEX, PART III:
ILLUSTRATIONS AND
CAPTIONS**

Alexander, Viscount, 339
Allen, Trooper Cliff E., 237, 292-293
Allsopp, Captain Robert H., "Bob," 70, 80, 190, 213, 295
Anderson, Trooper, 191
Anderson, Acting SQMS James, 70
Andrew, Trooper Walter H., 209
Ashmore, Trooper Edward B., 89
Assenede, Belgium, 211
Atkinson, Private Albert J., 44, 48, 337
Atkinson, Margaret, 44, 337
Austen, Trooper W. F., 236
Bakx, Jenette, 233
Ball, Private Alfred C., 38
Barclay, Trooper J., 327
Barford, Captain Cuthbert A. L., "Tommy," 330

Beaudry, Sergeant Eugene L. J., "Yudge," 247, 318
Bedford, Trooper Cyril H., 70
Bergen op Zoom, Netherlands, 231-236
Besson, Sergeant Howard J., 83
Black, Trooper James, 77
Blaine, SSM Lawrence B., 45
Blunden, Trooper Robert S. M., "Bob," 191
Boothroyd, Captain Wilfred E., RCAMC, 190
Bradburn, Lieutenant-Colonel Robert A., "Bob," 31, 178, 340
Bristowe, Lieutenant-Colonel William P., 66
Brown, Sergeant Hugh A., 131
Buchan, Trooper G. E., 327
Caen, France, 98
Campbell, Sergeant Roy A., 70
Carroll, Captain Henry L., "Hank," 190
Cartoons,
    Guard Post, 1941, 51
    Recruits, 1941, 52
    Waterproofing, May 1944, 58
    "Hello, Baker," June 1944, 93
    Amphibious Landing, July 1944, 98
    Liaison officers, October 1944, 216
    Parking lot at Eekloo, October 1944, 219
Carvosso, Lieutenant-Colonel James H., MC, 39
Caseley, Captain S. Leaman, MC, 225-226, 342
Cassidy, Major G.L., 116, 225, 273, 279
Chadwick, Trooper F. W., 334
Clark, Trooper H., 191
Clarke, Horace, 70
Clarke, Sergeant Hugh, 77
Clarke, Captain Kenneth A.C., RCAMC, 340
Clendenning, Trooper D. R., 292-293
Clipperton, Trooper Robert W., "Bob," 327
Coffin, Lieutenant-Colonel Albert F., "Bert," DSO, 31, 87, 295, 323, 342
Colwell, Trooper Dexter, 74
Convoy, 1942, 61
Coté, Armourer Sergeant Raymond R., 245
Craig, Jack, 70
Craig, Trooper Lyle L., 318
Crawford, Lieutenant Robert E.,"Bobby," 59
Crerar, General Harry, CH, CB, DSO, CD, 241
Crichton, Captain James H., 70
Cromb, Lieutenant-Colonel William, "Bill," DSO, 235
Crossroads near Bergen op Zoom, Netherlands, 225-226
Currie, Major David V., VC, 80, 148, 161-162, 179-181, 183, 229, 243,340
Demars, Trooper Ed, 274
Deneau, Trooper T. I., 327
Denning, Trooper Albert W., "Bert," 287
Debert Camp, Nova Scotia, 54

Dobbs, Trooper Clifford J., 78
Donaldson, Captain Robert H., "Bob," "Bulgy," 70
Dundurn Camp, Saskatchewan, 36-38, 39
Dutka, Trooper Adam, 54
Duval, Major Frank, 25
Eisenhower, General Dwight D., 241
Elizabeth, H.R.H Queen, 26, 87
Ely, Corporal Emery E., "Buster," 83
Engel, Corporal Alfred J., "Art," 327
Evans, Private John, 148
Fairhurst, Sergeant Robert, 54, 70
Fast, Corporal C. R., "Speedy," 184
Feisal, Emir, "Feisel," 81
Ficht, Trooper Herbert J., 131
Fitzgerald, Sergeant Thomas M., 108
Fitzgerald, Trooper R. J., 191
Flaws, SQMS Grant O., 340
Folliard, Trooper, 327
Forbes, Trooper Alan, 272
Ford, Trooper, 327
Forster, Corporal James O., 327
Forsyth, Trooper, 327
Foster, Major-General Harry W., CE, DSO, CD, 175
Frankson, Trooper Eric O., "Rick," 65
Frankson, Trooper Jack, 332
Freer, Sergeant Frank E., MM, 236
Gallimore, Corporal George F., 327
Gaudet, Trooper J. L., 113
Gendron, Corporal Edward E., "Duffy," 59, 337
George VI, H.M. King, 26, 87
Gilboe, Trooper A. L., 327
Golden, Trooper G. E., 327
Gove, Sergeant James K., "Jimmie," CinC, 70
Grant, Lieutenant Donald I., "Don," 148, 152
Gregory, Trooper Patrick B., "Pat," 89
Gudwer, Trooper William J., 334
Gunn-Fowlie, Lieutenant John A., 70, 78
Halid, Emir "Geezil," 81
Halkyard, Sergeant Albert E., "Halkie," MM, 208-209, 229, 314, 327
Hancock, Lieutenant Ronald L., 70
Hartkamp, Albert, 347
Haun, Trooper H. A., 327
Hawthorne, Trooper J. L., 108
Henderson, Trooper Victor C., "Vic," 184, 309, 327
Hill, Lieutenant Ernest F., "Ernie," 70, 340
Hill 117, France, 141
Hitler, Adolf, 126
Hochwald, Germany, 265, 270-271, 273, 275-276, 279
Holland, 1995, 343
Holly Bush pub, Britain, 62
Holmes, Sergeant Allan M., "Al," 8
Holmstrom, Trooper Gordon E., 179
Holten Commonwealth War Graves Cemetery, Netherlands, 347
Hotel de Draak, Bergen op Zoom, Netherlands, 235
Howard, A/Captain Thomas F., "Peachy," 290
Huffman, Captain Albert, 31

Hughes, Captain F. Newton, "Newt," Bronze Star, 190, 213
Huijbergsche Baan, Netherlands, 227
Hunter, Captain J. Walter, MM, 66
Hyttenbrauch, Trooper Larry W., 334
Irving, Captain Gordon E., "Gordie," CdG, MiD, 90, 203
Jacobsen, Trooper Stanley E., 236
James, Trooper Stanley, "Stan," 125
Jellis, Sergeant Walter W., "Wally," 70
Johnson, Trooper J., 332
Kapelsche Veer, Netherlands, 237, 249, 254, 258-259
Kennedy, Trooper W. A., 204
Kerr, Trooper Harry C., 191
Kitching, Major-General George, CBE, DSO, CD, 86
Knox, Corporal John, "Johnnie," 70, 263
Kroesing, Sergeant James F., MM, 247
La Fleur, Trooper A. M., 327
La Franier, Trooper C. J., 334
La Pointe, Trooper E. G. "Icky," 334
Laing, Lieutenant Alexander G., "Alec," 70
Lang, Trooper M. E., 295
Lardner, Sergeant John C., 179
Larkin, Trooper Dan E., 191
Lavoie, Major Arnold J., 27, 31, 90, 340
Layton, Trooper George T., 327
Levers, Corporal Lyle B., "Blackie," 292, 293
Little, Lieutenant Kenneth W., "Kenny," 70
Ludshott Common, Britain, 64
MacDonald, Trooper Pat, 334
Mackenzie, Regimental Sergeant Major John, "Jock," CinC, 85, 190
Main, Trooper Joseph, "Joe," 263
Mallet, Lieutenant David J., "Dave," 53
Maresfield Camp, Britain, 83, 92
Marshall, Trooper David G., 320
May, Trooper James F., "Daisy," 327
Maynard, Trooper N. C., 327
McDougall, Major Glenholme L., 31
McEachern, Trooper Joe C., 272
McGee, Trooper E. V. J., 327
McGillivray, Trooper Alexander G., "Alex," 236
McGovern, Trooper H. N., 327
McKee, Trooper Ross F., 210
McKenzie, Trooper, 327
McLeod, Major William J., "Danny," MC, 54, 59, 70, 228-229, 314, 339, 342
McPherson, Corporal Neil J., 46
McSherry, Corporal Matthew, 327
Medicine Hat, Alberta, 39
military units,
  Rocky Mountain Rangers, 23
  South Alberta Regiment,
    band, 39, 47
    C Squadron, 1943, 53
    echelons, 77
    fitters, 108
    maintenance, 74, 75
    No. 4 Platoon, 45

officers, 31, 43
"Pee Wee" platoon, 38, 45, 200
prewar, 25-26
sports day, 72
track team, 45
15th Alberta Light Horse, 21
19th Alberta Dragoons, 31st Battalion, Canadian Expeditionary Force, 19
Miller, Trooper J., 191
Mills, Lieutenant D. W., 327
Milner, Sergeant Thomas E., "Tom," DCM, 339
Mitchell, Company Sergeant Major George, 148
Mitchell, Trooper Richard A., 179
Moerbrugge, Belgium, 195, 198-199
Moerkerkke, Belgium, 206
"Molly," 83
Monilaws, John D., 70
Montage, Private Carl, 262
Montgomery, Field-Marshal Bernard L., KG, GCB, DSO, 339
Moreton, Captain John P., "Jay," 51, 7, 88, 92, 93, 98
Morrison, Sergeant, 83
Muehllehner, Sergeant George, 65
Munck, Ad de, 228
Munro, Ross, 62
Nash, Lieutenant-Colonel Thomas B., "Darby," DSO, 76
Neff, Trooper John H. M., 78, 79, 207, 264, 332
Nelles, Trooper Gerald, 65
Niagara, Ontario, 48-50, 52
Nicholson, Sergeant James, "Jim," 332
Nickel, Sergeant Michael J., "Mike," 54
Nieman, Lieutenant E.V. "Ev," 78
Nieuwburgh, Baron Thierry Peers de, 194
Norfolk, Britain, 78, 79
Oostcamp, Belgium, 194
Operation TRACTABLE, 120, 124
Owczar, Trooper J., 327
Pachal, Trooper William F., "Bill," 89
Paterson, William C., 70
Patton, Lieutenant-General George S., 126
Penney, Sergeant George W., 70, 290
Perrin, Captain Kenneth E., "Kenny," 28, 70, 87, 241
Petrie, Trooper E., 125
Piepgrass, Lieutenant Lyle B., 46, 243, 337
Plahn, Trooper Fred W., 50
Plotsky, Trooper Lawrence, "Sonny," 72, 327
polder land, Belgium, 212
Pollock, Trooper G. J., 131
Porterman, Wim, 347
Povey, Trooper George S., 264
Prenevost, Sergeant Douglas Selvester, "Doug," CdG, MiD, 46, 190, 327
Preston Park, Britain, 73
Prince of Wales Armouries, Edmonton, Alberta, 32, 34
Purdy, Major Stanley R., "Stan," 31

Quarton, Warrant Officer J. Henry "Harry," 340
Quesnay Wood, France, 116
Raalte, Netherlands, 331
Ramsay, Trooper Hugh T., 327
Rauch, Hauptmann, 148
Reid, Trooper J. C., 125
Relkov, Trooper J. N., 327
Reynaert, Maurits, 194
Roberts, Trooper, 327
Roberts, Lieutenant John M., "Jack," CinC, 194
Robertson, Corporal Darrell B., 125
Robinson, Major Richard, "Dick," CinC, 31, 108
Rose, Corporal Stanley T., "Stan," MiD, 320
Ryley, Trooper Charles R., 78
Saint Lambert-sur-Dives, France, 127, 142, 147-148, 151, 161-162, 173-174
Samuels, Corporal Clare, "Sammy," 263, 327
SAR Memorials, Canada and Europe, 344
SAR Reunion, 1995, Edmonton, Alberta, 385
Sarcee Camp, Alberta, 21
Savard, Private F. T. V., 182
Schmidt, Trooper L. A., 312
Scott, Trooper Gerald A., "Gerry," 113
Scott, Sergeant William, 70
Seiferling, Trooper Ray K., 72
Shell, Major Gordon L., "Gordie," 70
Silcox, Honorary Captain Albert Phillips, MBE, 91, 209, 318, 328
Simonds, Lieutenant-General Guy G., CB, CBE, DSO, 86, 119, 120, 139, 241, 273, 274
Simpson, Corporal James, "Jimmie," 327
Sinclair, Sergeant B., 108
Smith, Corporal, 108
Smith, Corporal Charles J., 263
Smith, Trooper, 320
Smith, Trooper H. N., 312
Smith, Sergeant James C., "Smitty," CinC, 210
Smith, Lieutenant Ray C., 39
Sonsbeck, Germany, 288
Spaner, Trooper Bernard, "Doc," 327
Spence, Trooper Wayne A., 92
Stevens, Sally, 62
Stewart, Captain Donald E., "Don," 155, 161, 327
Stewart, Trooper Elmer D., 292-293
Stollery, Sergeant Jack, 148
Summers, Captain John Leslie, "Jack," MC, 77, 342
Sutley, Trooper Earl O., 233
Swanson, Sergeant William T., "Bill," 70
Tennent, Band Sergeant James, "Jimmie," 47
Thuesen, Sergeant Soren, "Swede," 54, 85
Tilly-la-Campagne, France, 105
Toporoski, Trooper Kazimer T., 327
Trun, France, 140
Tuff, Corporal Allan G., 290

Valley of the Dives, France, 135
Vaux, France, 97
Vehicles, weapons and equipment,
  Armoured Fighting Vehicles,
    Crusader AA, 355
    Jagdpanther, 282
    Panther, 176
    Ram II, 78-79, 89, 354
    Ram OP, 235
    Self-Propelled Guns, 163,
    Sherman V, 100, 102, 123, 140, 185, 198-200, 204, 206, 210, 233, 236-237, 274, 288, 291-293, 318, 344, 354
    Sherman Firefly, 274, 292-293, 320, 322, 332, 354
    Stuart, 115, 235, 259, 291, 309, 312, 355
    Tiger I, 114
    Tiger II, 114
  artillery,
    75 mm PAK gun, 101, 138
    88 mm dual-purpose gun, 101
    315 mm railway gun, 209
  other,
    Armoured Command Vehicle, 213, 344
    Armoured Recovery Vehicle, 354
    carriers, 63, 65
    Humber scout car, 355
    jeep ambulance, 95
    Panzerfaust anti-tank weapon, 162
    Spitfire fighter aircraft 122
    Wireless set, No. 19, 164
Viennau, Trooper P. J. F., 236
Vitkovich, Trooper M. Emry "Daddy," 320
Vokes, Major-General Christopher, "Chris," CB, CBE, DSO, CD, 240, 274
Wakesiah Camp, Nanaimo, British Columbia, 41-42
Warner, Trooper S., 233
Washburn, Private Harold L., 54
Watkins, Sergeant Herbert, "Herbie," 70
Watson, Lieutenant H. D., "Hollywood," 70
White, Corporal George W., 140
White, Sergeant Jack, 194
Wiebe, Sergeant Jacob, "Jake," 237
Woolf, Sergeant Garth L., "Pete," 183, 204
Worthington, Major-General Frank F., "Worthy," CB, MC, MM, CD, 55, 85
Wotherspoon, Lieutenant-Colonel Gordon D. de S., "Swatty," 69, 81, 141, 190, 213, 220, 235, 322-323
Wotherspoon, Richard, 208
Wouwsche Plantage woods, Netherlands, 225
Wright, Lieutenant-Colonel M. Howard, 31
"Yorkie," 125
Young, Lieutenant Wallace H., "Wally," 90
Zoom River, Bergen op Zoom, Netherlands, 230
Zwick, Corporal Hebert A., 70

Simplified Organization Chart, 10th Canadian Infantry Brigade, c. September 1944.

The brigade consisted of three battalions of infantry, an armoured regiment, a field artillery regiment, a support company and a squadron of engineers. Normally the South Albertas were approportioned out by individual squadrons to the different infantry battalions. The support company's heavy Vickers .303 machine guns and 4.2 mortars, the field regiment's two dozen 25-pdr. gun/howitzers and the engineers were allotted as required.

Simplified Wireless Diagram, November 1944.

A vastly simplified diagram of the wireless (radio) system used by the Regiment. Wotherspoon commanded from either his scout car or the ACV halftrack, which had wireless connections not only to the RHQ Troop but also to the Recce, AA, Intercommunication Troops and the MO's halftrack. He communicated both to his superiors and to the various squadrons through the ACV.

At the squadron level the commander either commanded from his Sherman or from a scout car, communicating to RHQ through his "rear link" and directly to the four troops. At the troop level, the troop leader communicated to the squadron commander through his "A Net" and to his troop through his "B Net" although given the unreliability of the "B Net", the A Net was often used for this purpose.

Drawings by Chris Johnson

Simplified Organization Chart, 10th Canadian Infantry Brigade
4th Canadian Armoured Division, c. September 1944

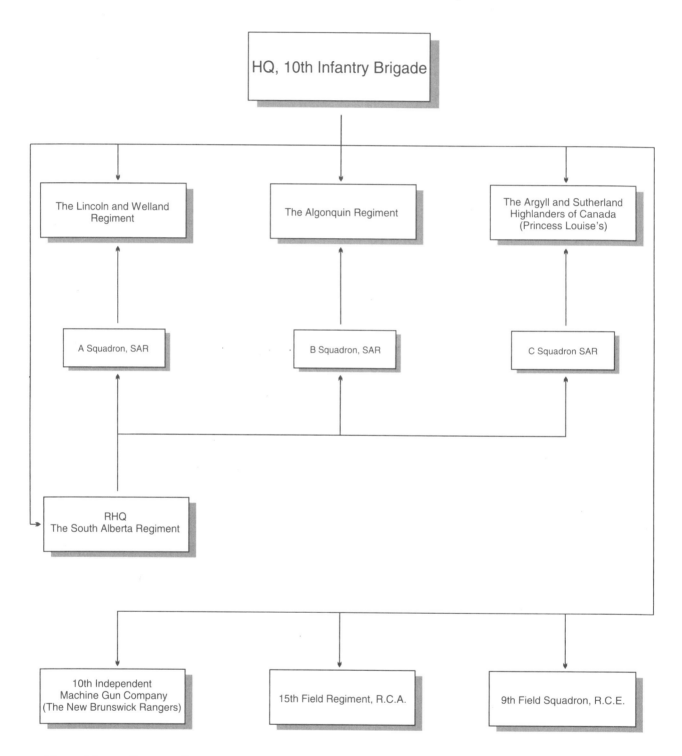

HQ, 10th Infantry Brigade

The Lincoln and Welland Regiment

The Algonquin Regiment

The Argyll and Sutherland Highlanders of Canada (Princess Louise's)

A Squadron, SAR

B Squadron, SAR

C Squadron SAR

RHQ
The South Alberta Regiment

10th Independent Machine Gun Company (The New Brunswick Rangers)

15th Field Regiment, R.C.A.

9th Field Squadron, R.C.E.

Note: Normally one SAR squadron was attached to each of the three infantry battalions.